WORLD OF WARCRAFT®

DUNGEON COMPANION

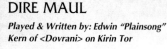

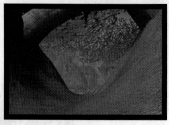

INTRODUCTION TO RAIDING

Almost every *World of Warcraft* player has joined groups during their journey to level 60. Once you reach 60, groups become less common and raids become more common. This guide is for people who are interested in "raiding" but haven't done much of it or may not even be sure what exactly "raiding" means.

Technically, a group becomes a raid when it's converted to a raid group through the Raid tab on the Social window. This allows for up to 40 people, divided into eight teams of five, to join your raid group. When you're a member of a raid, you can't complete most quests that aren't specified as Raid Quests.

Many of the concepts you've learned in groups prior to raiding are used in raid groups. Generally, a good group member can be a great raid member without much trouble.

Getting 40 people to work together is not an easy task for anyone. If you're going to be a raider, you always have to remember that there are 39 other people in the same group with you. Always be respectful, helpful, and attentive. The raid leader is in charge, listen to them and ask questions when you need to.

TYPES OF RAIDS

THE PICKUP

Pickup raids are formed using the Looking for Group channel or by a few different groups of people getting together. Most pickup raids go to Blackrock Spire, the first instance that allows raid groups (of up to 10 people) in it. Sometimes, pickup raids may clear the 20-person instances, Zul'Gurub and Ruins of Ahn'Qiraj, but this is rare because they're quite challenging and require good coordination and planning. Pickup raids are basically just groups that happen to be slightly bigger.

PLANNED RAID

The second type of raid, and the type I am going to focus on, is a well-organized 40-person raid. Most of the time, 40-person raids take place within a guild or in combination with allied guilds. The guild usually has enough members of all the proper classes to fill 40-person raids on at least 2-3 nights per week. These are scheduled, everyone gets together in a big raid group, and they dive into whatever instance is on the plate.

GETTING INTO RAID GROUPS

On each server there is usually at least one group of people that are not in the same guild but organize 40-person raids on a weekly basis. The best way to find groups like this is to check your Realm Forums on the official *World of Warcraft* webpage. There should be a thread that has a list of all raiding groups and guilds with information on joining each of them for most mature servers.

But, for the majority of people, if you want to start raiding, you have to join a raiding guild (or, less commonly, turn your current guild into a raiding guild). Getting into a raiding guild can be challenging. The best advice is to find a guild that raids Molten Core and needs your class. You don't want to go right for guilds clearing Ahn'Qiraj Temple and Blackwing Lair; they're probably full and, since they're well-established, get to pick and choose the people they recruit very carefully. You want a guild that is clearing the 20-person instances and Molten Core. Check the Realm Forums for information on guilds that are recruiting on your server.

YES, OFFICER

You can talk to guilds directly about joining, but you have to do one very important thing: always speak with an officer. Guild officers are there for a reason. They're usually able to help you much more than another member who might not be up to date on what their recruiting policies are.

BEING A GOOD RAIDER

So, you got into a raiding guild/group and you're ready for your first raid. Now what?

PRE-RAID CHECKLIST

1. Stock all spell reagents; bring extras!

2. Refresh your potion supply and get any special potions needed out of the Bank (such as Fire Resistance, Nature Resistance, etc.).

3. Bring any relevant resist gear.

4. Repair everything, including items in your inventory that you aren't wearing.

5. Make sure you have all the special items you may need such as Aqual Quintessence, Gurubashi Mojo Madness, or any special encounter-specific equipment you have.

Always show up to a raid on time and in the designated meeting spot. If your raid does not meet anywhere specific, stay near the instance. Nothing annoys a raid leader more than having someone halfway across the world when they should be at the instance.

Being a good raider really isn't all that difficult. You have to focus on the task at hand and play your class well. Most of the time, anything specific that needs to be done (or needs to be avoided) will be communicated on voice chat or in the Raid channel. Always listen to the raid leaders and do what they tell you to do.

Watch the other members of your class to see what they do. There are probably some very experienced raiders around. If you're totally clueless on what you need to do for a certain boss or pull, ask a fellow member of your class or one of the raid leaders. It's always better to make sure you're doing the right thing instead of guessing and doing the wrong thing. There are some fights where a single person making a mistake can wipe the entire raid.

Paying attention, focusing on the job at hand, and doing your best to play your class well are the most important qualities of a good raider.

There is one last thing to say about being a good raid member: Be willing to listen to criticism and learn from your mistakes or from other more experienced players. Nobody shows up to their first raid knowing everything there is to know about how to play their class in raid groups. Everyone has to relearn their role in 40-person groups. You should always be improving as you gain experience raiding.

COMMON TERMS AND CONCEPTS

Aggro/Threat – This is the amount of hatred a mob has for a certain player. Mobs attack the player at the top of its "Threat List" and continue to attack them until that player becomes incapacitated (by Fear, Stun, any number of mob abilities) or until someone else builds more threat. In general, you want your Warriors (especially your Main Tank) at the top of the Threat List, your DPS classes in the middle, and your healers at the bottom. Warriors are supposed to tank most of the mobs in the game, so they focus on building as much threat as possible. DPS classes can't take the hits of most mobs, so they focus on managing their threat, making sure they do not overtake the Warriors' threat generation.

Cleansing – The removal of curses, diseases, magic effects, and poisons can be summed up as cleansing. Druids can remove curses and poisons. Mages can remove curses. Paladins can remove diseases, magic effects defensively, and poisons. Priests can remove diseases and magic effects both offensively and defensively. Shamans can remove diseases, poisons, and magic effects offensively.

CC – Crowd Control. Any player or mob that does not have control of its actions has been Crowd Controlled (or CC'd). The term CC is used both offensively and defensively. Sometimes, you want to "CC Majordomo's Healers", meaning you want a Mage to Polymorph the Healers. Other times, you will find yourself CC'd by a mob ("This Anubisath is CC'ing me with Fear/Root!").

CTRaid – This is a common and mature mod written by Ts, Cide, and the CTMod team. Most raid leaders require all raid members to have a recent version of CTRaid installed. It provides several features that make raiding much easier.

FF – Focus Fire. This is when everyone who does damage should focus on a single target and kill it as quickly as possible. Usually, you're told what the target is (or given a person to assist to obtain the target). Make sure you have the correct mob targeted and fire away.

FFA – Free for All. Usually used when discussing the raid's loot type; anyone can loot anything.

Healing – Druids, Paladins, Shaman, and Priests. These are the classes that keep you alive during raids. Keeping healers alive and happy is a top priority for any raid group.

Healing Rotation – This is when two or more healers alternate between casting and regenerating mana. The first healer heals until they are low on mana (under 20%), then the second healer takes over as the first regenerates. As soon as the second healer is low on mana, the first healer should be near full mana and ready to heal again. Alliance groups that use Healing Rotations should keep a Paladin's Judgement of Wisdom on the mob being killed so that the healer who is regenerating can attack the mob and regain mana even more quickly.

LOS – Line of Sight. If there are no objects (such as a wall) or terrain obstacles between you and your target, you have LOS to your target. If there is something that blocks your view of your target, making it impossible to cast spells on it, you do not have LOS to your target. If you do not have LOS to your target, it does not have LOS to you either. Do not confuse LOS with range. Range is when something is simply too far away to be affected. LOS is when something can't be affected regardless of distance. LOS is a very important concept that is used in several raiding-level fights. Usually, you want to avoid a mob's LOS so it can't do certain things to you.

It all comes down to knowing when you have LOS and when you don't. Sometimes, for healers, you can position yourself so that you have LOS to heal your target, but are not in LOS of the mob attacking your target. LOS can be very powerful when used (some would say abused) to your advantage. One final thing, if a mob tries to attack a player that it does not have LOS to, one of two things happens: the player is teleported within LOS of the mob, or the mob "evade bugs" and resets its life to 100%. Be careful when hiding in places. You always want to be within LOS of a mob when you have aggro.

MA – Main Assist. The person who everyone should assist for a target. To assist someone, type '/assist <name>' or target the person and press the F key. Every raid has an MA. Make a macro to assist this person and use it!

Melee DPS – Rogues, Paladins, Shaman, and Warriors. Paladins and Shaman usually heal during raids and don't count as Melee DPS, but there are occasional exceptions. Rogues and non-Protection specced Warriors make up the majority of melee DPS.

ML – Master Loot. The loot type where the raid leader assigns the items that drop to specific players in the raid.

MT – Main Tank. The Warrior who is tanking the mob. This is usually predefined by the raid leader before the fight begins.

MT Targets (CTRaid Specific) – CTRaid has a function called MT Targets. These are little windows that show the current target of specific people. To set an MT Target, right-click their name in the CTRaid tab and assign them an MT Target number. MT Targets are shown to everyone with CTRaid in the raid group. You may also set Player Targets (only shown on your screen).

OT – Off Tank, the Warrior(s) who are not necessarily "main" tanking the boss, but they have a very specific job, usually related to any adds the boss has. Off tanks are usually predefined by the raid leader before the fight begins.

Offensive Dispel – Priests and Shaman are able to dispel magic effects offensively. When any mob gains a magic buff (such as Shazzrah's Deaden Magic ability), it should be removed as soon as possible with an offensive dispel. Do not confuse offensively dispelling a magic effect from a hostile target with defensively dispelling a magic effect from a friendly target. Paladins can defensively dispel magic effects, Shamans can offensively dispel magic effects, and Priests can do both.

Positioning – Where you should be and where the mob being fought should be. Some fights require very complicated and precise positioning. Always ask the raid leader if you are unsure of your position in a specific fight.

Pull Aggro – This is what happens when you build too much aggro with a mob and it attacks you. Sometimes, this can be devastating. By pulling aggro, you likely force the mob to change position by running to you. This change in position can cause major problems in fights where the positioning is extremely important. Not only do you mess up the positioning, you probably get yourself killed in the process. Always be mindful of your threat and avoid pulling aggro (unless you're supposed to).

Raid Assistant – Anyone with an (A) next to their name in the Raid Window. Assistants can invite and remove players from the raid, but not much else.

Raid Leader – The person with (L) next to their name in the Raid Window. The raid leader is the only person who can manipulate groups, change the loot type, or promote people to Raid Assistants.

Ranged DPS – Hunters, Mages, and Warlocks. All classes that rely mainly on doing damage from a distance or with damage over time abilities.

Resync (CTRaid Specific) – CTRaid requires that all members of the raid group are "synced" to a specific channel. It uses this channel to communicate things about the raid group that would otherwise be impossible to determine. Every member of the raid should be synced to the same channel. To sync the channel, you must be promoted or the leader. Open the CTRaid General Options and click the Broadcast Channel button.

Tanking – When a mob is attacking a Warrior, it's being tanked. The vast majority of mobs should be tanked by a Warrior. If the mob is not tanked for whatever reason, you should not attack it until a Warrior picks it up.

Threat Reduction/Deaggro – There are several ways to artificially reduce your own threat or have it reduced by a mob. DPS classes that want to cause as little threat as possible should focus on the spells, items, and talents that reduce the amount threat generated. Tanking classes that want to cause as much threat as possible find that many mobs in the game have ways of artificially reducing the threat of the player they are currently attacking. Tanking mobs that have aggro reducing abilities can be very challenging, usually best accomplished by 2 or more Warriors working together.

Tranquilizing Shot – A Hunter ability learned from the Tome of Tranquilizing Shot that drops from Lucifron. This is the only counter to the mob ability Frenzy. When a mob Frenzies, it receives increased attack damage and speed. You do not want mobs to be Frenzied; remove it as quickly as possible with Tranquilizing Shot. Some mobs Frenzy so often that several Hunters in a "Tranquilizing Shot Rotation" are necessary to continually remove Frenzy.

Transition – Many fights start a certain way and change to another way during the encounter. These changes are called transitions. Transitions usually come with predetermined changes in position or strategy. Some specific examples are: Onyxia Phase 2 to Phase 3 transition, Razorgore the Untamed transition after the eggs have been destroyed, and the Twin Emperors transition after a teleport.

Watch Aggro/Threat – Some fights are very hard to tank. The mobs can use all sorts of abilities that make them less likely to attack the Warriors. If you're specifically told to watch your aggro, it means you need to be extra careful with your threat generation.

DISCLAIMER ABOUT ADDONS
Third party AddOns for *World of Warcraft* often affect gameplay and the interface. These are not official and could potentially cause problems down the line. Blizzard has made it perfectly clear that these are "use at your own risk" products and you should treat them as such.

HOW TO USE THE DUNGEON COMPANION

Some direction is required when using a resource of this size. All the dungeons, raids, and outdoor encounters follow the same setup and this section is designed to assist you in deciphering the sections and take full advantage of the information therein.

INTRODUCTION AND DUNGEON INFORMATION

BLACKWING LAIR

Played & Written by: Tyler "Hocken" Morgan of <Pacifist> on Kel'thuzad

Blackwing Lair is the home of Onyxia's brother Nefarian and Brood of the Black Dragonflight. The lair itself was created by the Dark Iron Dwarves and recently conquered by Nefarian and his Dragonkin companions in his quest for power over Azeroth. From Blackwing Lair, Nefarian plots to destroy Ragnaros, something that his father Deathwing failed to do long ago.

①

Until very recently, Blackwing Lair was the hardest dungeon in Azeroth, but Ahn'Qiraj has assumed that mantle. Groups attempting Blackwing should have raiding experience and equipment from Molten Core and Onyxia. You must venture into the lair and fight your way to Nefarian's throne room where he awaits your arrival.

DUNGEON INFORMATION

Name:	Blackrock Mountain
Location:	Contested
Quest	Alliance and Horde
Suggested Levels:	60 (Full 40-person Raid)
Enemy Types:	Dragonkin
Time to Complete:	3 Hours to Several Days

INFORMATION BOX

① This box is an introduction to the dungeon or encounter. It often gives some storyline about the place or target, but won't have actual data or statistics. Also included in this box is the name of the author. With a project of this magnitude, it'd be crazy to think that one person could write everything. We've had a select group of authors pitch in to write the sections and they're listed, with their in-game names, guilds, and servers.

DUNGEON/ENCOUNTER INFORMATION

② These sections provide the location and general information for the area along with an overview of the dungeon and what to expect. If you're not sure whether the dungeon you're planning on entering is going to be too difficult for your 39 Priest, check this table to get an idea.

MAPS

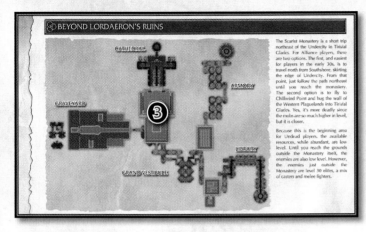

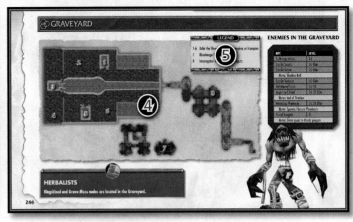

INSTANCE MAP

3 The full instance map is a crucial piece of information for anyone planning on entering an instance. This gives a general layout of the entire zone including branching paths and boss locations.

AREA MAP & LEGEND

4 Quite often, the instance is broken down into smaller sections that require smaller, more detailed maps. These illustrate the exact locations of bosses, pieces of information about that area, areas of interest, and paths to the other areas.

5 The legend is broken down to help you find exactly that for which you're looking. Bosses are often quest targets and some rooms may hold static quest targets like a book or set of plans.

QUEST ENTRIES

QUESTS

ALLIANCE QUESTS

QUEST NAME	QUEST GIVER	QUEST GIVER LOCATION	QUEST RECEIVER	QUEST RECEIVER LOCATION	CHAIN?	MAX EXPERIENCE
Knowledge in the Deeps	Gerrig	Ironforge	Gerrig	Ironforge	No	1,650
REWARD: Sustaining Ring (+1 STA & +4 SPI)						
The Corruption Abroad	Argos Nightwhisper	Stormwind	Gershala Nightwhisper	Auberdine	No	240
Researching the Corruption	Gershala Nightwhisper	Darkshore	Gershala Nightwhisper	Darkshore	Yes	1,450
REWARD: Prelacy Cape (Cloak: 20 Armor & +5 SPI) or Beetle Clasps (Mail Wrists: 83 Armor +2 AGI & +5 STA)						
Seeking the Kor Gem (PALADIN ONLY)	Thundris Windweaver	Darkshore	Thundris Windweaver	Darkshore	Yes	1,750
Twilight Falls	Argent Guard Manados	Darnassus	Argent Guard Manados	Darnassus	No	2,550
REWARD: Heartwood Girdle (Leather Belt: 48 Armor, +4 STA & +4 SPI) or Nimbus Boots (Cloth Feet: 27 Armor, +3 AGI & +5 SPI)						

QUEST TABLE

6 The Quest Table provides a listing of the quests depending on your faction. Some are Alliance-Only, Horde-Only, Shared, or Class-Specific. Make sure to check out the table header to decide which tables apply to your character.

RESEARCHING THE CORRUPTION

Quest Level	18 to Obtain
Location	Darkshore (Auberdine)
Quest Giver	Gershala Nightwhisper
Goal	Collect 8 Corrupted Brain Stems from Naga/Satyrs
Max Experience Gained	1,450
Reward	Prelacy Cape (Cloak: 20 Armor & +5 SPI) or Beetle Clasps (Mail Wrists: 83 Armor +2 AGI & +5 STA)

When in Stormwind City, speak to Argos Nightwhisper; he lets you know that his brother has been seeking help. The real quest begins in Auberdine, where Gershala Nightwhisper is afraid of the twisting power of demonic magic. Knowing that use of evil sorcery twisted the Naga and the Satyrs into what they are, Gershala fears the fate of the Blood Elves. To learn more, he wants you to collect eight Corrupted Brain Stems from the elite Naga and Satyrs in and around Blackfathom Deeps. Lower-level groups can take the time to do this while fighting the outer enemies before the instance, while those doing higher-level quests can accomplish this simultaneously without worrying about farming these monsters. Return to Auberdine and give Gershala the ghastly items for your reward.

THE ORB OF SORAN'RUK

Quest Level	20 to Obtain (WARLOCK ONLY QUEST)
Location	Central Barrens (Doan's Camp)
Quest Giver	Doan Karhan
Goal	Find 3 Soran'ruk Fragments and 1 Large Soran'ruk Fr
Max Experience Gained	2,
Reward	Staff of Soran'ruk (Staff: 16.9 DPS, +6 DMG to Shadow Spells and Effects & +6 DMG to Fire Spells and Effects) or the Orb of Soran'ruk (Off-Hand: +3 DMG to Fire Spells and Effects, +3 DMG to Shadow Spells and Effects, Use: Restores 25 Health every 3 Seconds for 30 Seconds)

This difficult quest takes your Warlock into both Blackfathom Deeps and Shadowfang Keep. For dealing with the Blackfathom section of it, travel into the instance and hunt Twilight Acolytes. These enemies are found later in the instance, by the Moonshrine Ruins. Kill them until you have all three Fragments. For completing the quest, look for the Shadowfang Darksouls (commonly found in Shadowfang Keep and fighting as Level 20-21 Elite monsters). Return to Doan when you are done collecting these items.

THE ESSENCE OF AKU'MAI

Quest Level	17 to Obtain
Location	Ashenvale (Zoram'gar Outpost)
Quest Giver	Je'neu Sancrea
Goal	Collect 20 Sapphires of Aku'Mai
Max Experience Gained	1,800

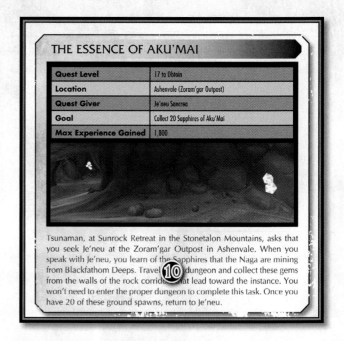

Tsunaman, at Sunrock Retreat in the Stonetalon Mountains, asks that you seek Je'neu at the Zoram'gar Outpost in Ashenvale. When you speak with Je'neu, you learn of the Sapphires that the Naga are mining from Blackfathom Deeps. Travel to the dungeon and collect these gems from the walls of the rock corridors that lead toward the instance. You won't need to enter the proper dungeon to complete this task. Once you have 20 of these ground spawns, return to Je'neu.

QUEST BOXES

These are broken into the appropriate colors for Alliance, Horde, and Shared quests as well. If you're playing Alliance, take a gander at the blue boxes for quests that apply to you. However, don't ignore the Shared Quest (brown) listings. These are quests that apply to both factions with the same quest givers & receivers, targets, and rewards.

7 This is the name of the quest. The quests are usually listed in the order that you'll receive them. For example, prerequisite quests (if they're in the dungeon) are listed before the end quests.

8 This is the hard data for the specific quest including the quest giver, the goal of the quest, the reward for the quest, and more.

9 Take a good look at the associated screenshots. They often give a glimpse of the quest giver, quest target, associated mobs, and related characters.

10 The body of the quest box provides tips and hints on completing the quest and what to do once it's done. If there's a prerequisite quest line necessary, it's often listed here.

ENEMIES

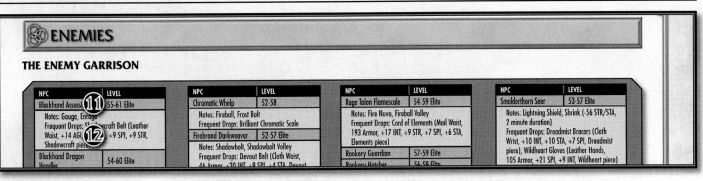

THE ENEMY GARRISON

NPC	LEVEL
Blackhand Assass	55-61 Elite
Notes: Gouge, Enrage Frequent Drops: Shwcraft Belt (Leather Waist, +14 AGI, ?, +9 SPI, +9 STR, Shadowcraft piece)	
Blackhand Dragon Handler	54-60 Elite

NPC	LEVEL
Chromatic Whelp	52-58
Notes: Fireball, Frost Bolt Frequent Drops: Brilliant Chromatic Scale	
Firebrand Darkweaver	52-57 Elite
Notes: Shadowbolt, Shadowbolt Volley Frequent Drops: Devout Belt (Cloth Waist, 46 Armor, +20 INT, +9 SPI, +4 STA, Devout	

NPC	LEVEL
Rage Talon Flamescale	54-59 Elite
Notes: Fire Nova, Fireball Volley Frequent Drops: Cord of Elements (Mail Waist, 193 Armor, +17 INT, +9 STR, +7 SPI, +6 STA, Elements piece)	
Rookery Guardian	57-59 Elite
Rookery Hatcher	56-59 Elite

NPC	LEVEL
Smolderthorn Seer	53-57 Elite
Notes: Lightning Shield, Shrink (-56 STR/STA, 2 minute duration) Frequent Drops: Dreadmist Bracers (Cloth Wrist, +10 INT, +10 STA, +7 SPI, Dreadmist piece), Wildheart Gloves (Leather Hands, 105 Armor, +21 SPI, +9 INT, Wildheart piece)	

GENERAL ENEMY TABLE

(11) These tables list the fodder, those mobs that tend to harass your party while attempting to reach the boss or end of the instance. The names and average levels are indicated as well as whether the mob is elite or not.

(12) Notes and frequent drops from the mobs are listed in this table as well. The notes often indicate some special abilities that the mobs have. Take a look at these before facing a mob for the first time to find out if they're going to have an AoE spell that could wipe the group if you don't spread out, or whether they're melee-oriented and require special attention from your MT.

THE ENEMY LEADERSHIP

NPC	LEVEL	FREQUENT DROP(S)
BANNOK GRIMAXE	**(13)** Rare	Backusarian Gauntlets (Plate Hands, 392 Armor, +9 INT, +15 STA, +9 STR), Chiselbrand Girdle (Mail Waist, 199 Armor, +6 SPI, +6 STA, Passive: +44 Attack Power), Demonfork **(14)** (Main Hand Axe, 38.9 DPS, Chance on Hit: Transfers 10 health every 5 sec.s ? target to the caster for 25 sec.s), Plans: Arcanite Reaper (Requires Blacksmithing (300) & Master Axesmithing)
CRYSTAL FANG	60 Elite	Fullbrush Handgrips (Leather Hands, 107 Armor, +12 INT, +11 SPI, +11 STA, Equip: Increases healing done by spells and effects by up to 20), Fang of the Crystal Spider (One-Hand Dagger, 40.3 DPS, Chance on Hit: Slows target enemy's casting speed, melee attack speed, and range attack speed by 10% for 10 sec.), Sunderseer Mantle (Cloth Shoulder, 65 Armor, +17 INT, +11 SPI, +4 STA, Equip: Increases damage and healing done by magical spells and effects by up to 8)
GENERAL DRAKKISATH	Boss	Beaststalker's Tunic (Mail Chest, 370 Armor, +21 AGI, +13 INT, +6 SPI, +16 STA, +5 STR, Beaststalker Armor piece), Blackblade of Shahram (Two-Hand Sword, 59.4 DPS, Chance on Hit: Summons the infernal spirit of Shahram), Breastplate of Valor (Plate Chest, 657 Armor, +24 STA, +15 STR, +10 AGI, +6 SPI, Battlegear of Valor piece), Brigam Girdle (Plate Waist, 369 Armor, +16 STA, +15 STR, Equip: Improves your chance to hit by 1%), Devout Robe (Cloth Chest, 89 Armor, +24 INT, +15 SPI, +13 STA, Vestments of the Devout piece), Draconian Deflector (Shield, 2153 Armor, 40 Block, +7 STA, +10 Fire Resistance, Passive: Increased Defense +10), Draconian Infused Emblem (Trinket, Use: Increases your spell damage by up to 100 and your healing by up to 190 for 15 sec.), Dreadmist Robe (Cloth Chest, 89 Armor, +21 INT, +13 SPI, +20 STA, Dreadmist Raiment piece), Lightforge Breastplate (Plate Chest, 657 Armor, +21 STA, +16 INT, +13 STR, +8 SPI, Lightforge Armor piece), Magister's Robes (Cloth Chest, 89 Armor, +31 INT, +8 SPI, +9 STA, Magister's Regalia piece), Painweaver Band (Finger, +7 STA, Equip: Improves your chance to get a critical strike by 1%, +16 Attack Power), Pattern: Red Dragonscale Breastplate (Requires: Leatherworking (300) & Dragonscale Leatherworking), Shadow Prowler's Cloak (Back, 45 Armor, +17 AGI, +7 STA), Shadowcraft Tunic (Leather Chest, 176 Armor, +26 AGI, +12 SPI, +13 STA, Shadowcraft Armor piece), Spellweaver's Turban (Cloth Head, 73 Armor, +9 INT, Equip: Increases damage and healing done by magical spells and effects by up to 36, Improves your chance to hit with spells by 1%), Tome of the Lost (Off-Hand, +7 INT, +6 STA, Equip: Increases damage and healing done by magical spells and effects by up to 18), Tooth of Gnarr (Neck, +14 INT, +8 STA, Equip: Restores 2 mana per 5 sec.), Vest of Elements (Mail Chest, 370 Armor, +20 INT, +20 SPI, +13 STA, The Elements piece), Wildheart Vest (Leather Chest, 176 Armor, +20 INT, +20 SPI, +13 STA, Wildheart Raiment piece)
	Notes: Cleave, Conflagrate, Flame ? ?ce Armor, and Rage (+122 damage and +50% attack speed for 15 sec.) **(15)**	
CHOK RACHSHUD	60 Elite	Armswake Cloak (Back, 43 Armor, +15 STA, Equip: +16 Attack Power), Bashguuder (One-Hand Mace, 39.4 DPS, +9 STR, Chance on Hit: Punctures target's armor lowering it by

BOSS TABLE

(13) The names and levels of the bosses in the instance are listed alphabetically for convenience.

(14) The bosses of the instances offer two things: 1) better rewards and 2) a greater challenge. All the data you need to discover what each boss offers as a reward is listed in the "Frequent Drop(s)" column. If you've heard of a specific boss that's said to have incredible drops, check out this column to find the item, the stats of the item, and whether it's applicable to your class.

(15) Bosses in Azeroth have some of the most devastating abilities and spells that you could imagine and they're listed on the boss tables. Peek at them to find out what's in store for your party/raid before each boss battle.

WALKTHROUGH AND STRATEGY

This is the meat of this dungeon companion. The strategies that will take you through each of the world's dungeons and world boss encounters (as of patch 1.10) are the reason you picked up this book. Expert strategy leading you through each of Azeroth's most nefarious dungeons is included in an easy-to-understand format.

The walkthroughs are often broken down by area and include maps and screenshots for reference. If you're having a difficult time in a specific room or with a specific boss, they're easy to find and you can read the strategy for those in particular.

Strategies for each boss and, in the high-end raids, positioning for them give you the best edge when taking them on. Make sure to read up on the encounters to get new ideas about taking down the bosses or how to approach an area.

RUINS OF AHN'QIRAJ

Played & Written by: Chris M. "Phunbaba" Koschik of <Fraternity> on Perenolde

Deep in the deserts of Silithus lies an ancient and powerful race of beings known as the Qiraji. One thousand years ago, the Night Elves and Bronze dragonflight combined their considerable powers to seal the Qiraji behind the Scarab Wall, with the help of the children of some of the Aspects. This is remembered as the War of Shifting Sands.

Recently, it was discovered that some of the Qiraji were finding ways past the wall. Anachronos, the bronze dragon, helped the adventurers of Azeroth open the Scarab Wall to prevent more incursions. The mortal races have now banded together to confront the evil Qiraji in their own land. A champion has opened the gate and the Horde and Alliance have driven the armies of the Qiraji back into ruins in retreat. It now falls to you and your comrades to delve into the lair of the Qiraji and put an end to their masters once and for all.

DUNGEON INFORMATION

Location	Silithus
Territory	Contested
Quests	Shared Alliance and Horde
Suggested Level	60 (20-person raid)
Primary Enemies	Qiraji, Silithids, and Constructs
Time to Complete	3-6 hours. (1-2 days)

GETTING TO THE RUINS OF AHN'QIRAJ

Make your way to Cenarion Hold, in the center of Silithus and begin taking the road west out of town. The path quickly veers south and continues to do so for quite a distance. Eventually you reach a massive wall with a large open portal leading into Ahn'Qiraj.

At this point you have a choice of where to go. Should you go right, you will climb the great stairs to the Temple of Ahn'Qiraj (40-man instance), but should you go straight ahead you will find yourself standing before the portal to the Ruins of Ahn'Qiraj.

THE RUINS

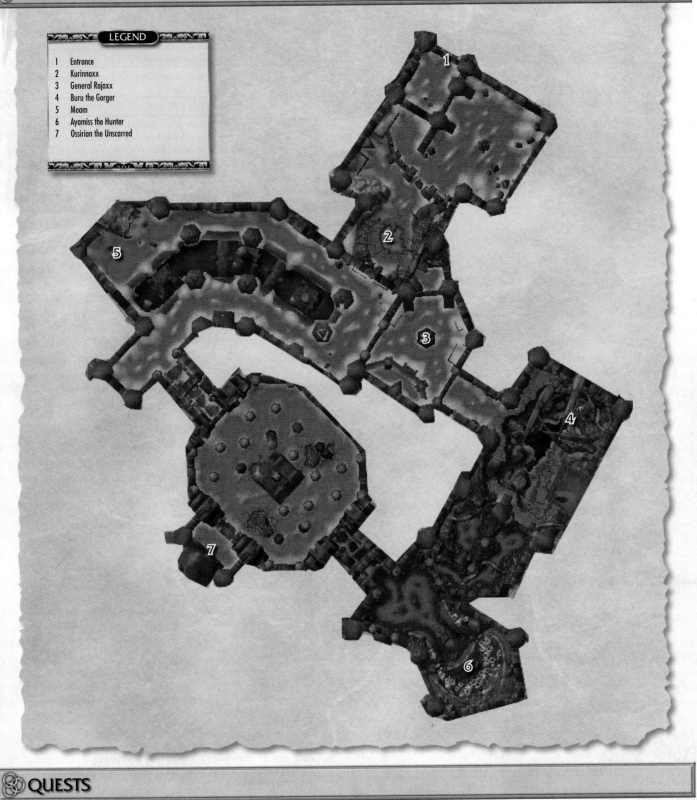

LEGEND

1 Entrance
2 Kurinnaxx
3 General Rajaxx
4 Buru the Gorger
5 Moam
6 Ayamiss the Hunter
7 Ossirian the Unscarred

QUESTS

SHARED ALLIANCE AND HORDE QUESTS

The few quests that are available for the Ruins of Ahn'Qiraj can all be found in Cenarion Hold around the inn. Each NPC offers a set of quests available to each class that requires bringing fairly common drops from the instance.

THE PERFECT POISON

Quest Level	60 to obtain
Location	Cenarion Hold, Silithus
Contact	Dirk Thunderwood
Goal	Bring the Venom Sac of Kurinnaxx and the Venom Sac of Venoxis to Dirk Thunderwood
Experience Gained	4500
Reward	Ravenholdt Slicer (One-handed Sword, 42.7 DPS, 6 STA, Equip: +26 Attack Power) or Shivsprocket's Shiv (Dagger, 41.4 DPS, 13 STA, Equip: Increase healing and damage done by spells and effects by up to 13) or The Thunderwood Poker (Dagger, 42.5 DPS, 13 AGI, 6 STA) or Doomulus Prime (Two-handed Mace, 55.7 DPS, 22 STR, 22 STA, Equip: Improves your chance to hit by 1%) or Fahrad's Reloading Repeater (Crossbow, 33.3 DPS, 4 AGI, Equip: Improves your chance to hit by 1%) or Simone's Cultivating Hammer (One-handed Mace, 41.2 DPS, 6 INT, Equip: Increases healing done by spells and effects by up to 37)

Inside the inn, near the ramp, you will meet a crafty Dwarf from Ravenholdt Keep seeking a new kind of poison. He asks you to enter The Ruins of Ahn'Qiraj and Zul'Gurub to retrieve the venom sacs from two of the bosses there; Kurinnaxx and Venoxis. Once slain, you can loot their venom sacs and return them to Dirk in Cenarion Hold for your choice of reward. Venoxis resides in Zul'Gurub, while Kurinnaxx makes his home in Ahn'Qiraj.

QIRAJI COMMON DROP TABLE

These are drops that can be found on any of the six bosses in the ruins. For boss-specific drops, check out the sections detailing their battles.

Book of Healing Touch XI	Handbook of Backstab IX
Book of Rejuvenation XI	Handbook of Deadly Poison V
Book of Starfire VII	Handbook of Feint V
Codex of Greater Heal V	Libram: Blessing of Might VII
Codex of Prayer of Healing V	Libram: Blessing of Wisdom VI
Codex of Renew X	Libram: Holy Light IX
Formula: Enchant Cloak — Dodge	Manual of Battle Shout VII
Formula: Enchant Cloak — Stealth	Manual of Heroic Strike IX
Formula: Enchant Gloves - Fire Power	Manual of Revenge VI
Formula: Enchant Gloves - Frost Power	Qiraji Ceremonial Ring
Formula: Enchant Gloves - Healing Power	Qiraji Magisterial Ring
Formula: Enchant Gloves - Shadow Power	Qiraji Martial Drape
Formula: Enchant Gloves - Superior Agility	Tablet of Grace of Air Totem III
Grimoire of Corruption VII	Tablet of Healing Wave X
Grimoire of Immolate VIII	Tablet of Strength of Earth Totem V
Grimoire of Shadow Bolt X	Tome of Arcane Missiles VIII
Guide: Aspect of the Hawk VII	Tome of Fireball XII
Guide: Multi-Shot V	Tome of Frostbolt XI
Guide: Serpent Sting IX	

THE FALL OF OSSIRIAN

Quest Level:	60 to obtain
Location	The Ruins of Ahn'Qiraj, Silithus
Contact	Commander Mar'alith
Goal	Return the head of Ossirian the Unscarred to Commander Mar'alith in Cenarion Hold
Experience Gained	5000
Reward	Amulet of the Shifting Sands (Neck, Equip: Increases healing done by spells and effects by up to 46, Equip: Restores 6 mana every 5 seconds) or Pendant of the Shifting Sands (Neck, 14 STR, 21 STA, Equip: +6 Defense) or Charm of the Shifting Sands (Neck, 9 STA, 12 INT, Equip: Increases damage and healing done by spells and effects by up to 25) or Choker of the Shifting Sands (Neck, 16 STA, Equip: +42 Attack Power)

Once you have defeated Ossirian the Unscarred, one player may loot his head and return it to Commander Mar'alith at Cenarion Hold for a choice of one of four rewards.

GET EQUIPPED FOR AHN'QIRAJ

No, not swords, helms, and staves! I speak of much more powerful weapons for your arsenal: programs for your computer, main assists, and Raid Leaders.

Teamspeak or Ventrilo

These are voice programs that allow everyone in the raid to listen and speak over a microphone. The importance of this cannot be stressed enough in the more chaotic battles when the difference between success and failure can be measured in the amount of time it takes to type a sentence or speak it over a microphone. Downloading and utilizing one of these programs will increase your success rate tenfold in all 40 and 20 person raiding. The only stipulation is that all members must be onboard.

CT Raid Assist

This is a third party add-on allowed by Blizzard that makes raiding much easier. It has many options that you can toggle on and off to warn your raid of incoming threats, debuffs, and curses. It also has an option that allows you to see the target of your tank's target. This will serve you in many battles, as you can see who has the aggro of a particular enemy or boss. To utilize this program you must keep informed and updated on all the latest versions of the program. You must also keep your guild informed as well to these updates.

Main Assist

The main assist is a player designated to acquire the most important target first for easy targeting. This role is usually given to a Rogue, as their only responsibility in the raid is to kill things. You can easily create a hotkey to acquire the main assist's target by pressing escape, going into the macro menu, and creating a macro called MA (main assist). The command for setting the main assist is /assist (name of player). Also, in the interface options menu you can toggle on an option that allows you to immediately begin attacking when you press your MA key.

Raid Leader

The raid leader is an extremely important part of your raid. In a nutshell, the raid leader is the player that orders everyone to start attacking or stop attacking. This is needed for tanks to acquire a good amount of aggro before the rest of the raid starts attacking. The MT losing aggro early on can wipe out the raid group, so having a conservative raid leader helps ensure victory.

FOES IN THE SAND

The Ruins of Ahn'Qiraj are full of every manner of insect, pest, and alien thing known to the world of Azeroth. You will square off with mighty beasts and swarms of lesser pests that will test your party's resolve and cunning in a way you have never experienced.

ANUBISATH GUARDIAN — 60 ELITE

These gargantuan statues are the worst enemy you encounter in the zone. They each come with two random abilities that must be handled correctly or it spells doom for your raid.

Meteor: Everyone in a large area takes a total around 12,000 damage. If this flaming rock hits one person, they take the entire damage. However, if everyone is in a nice tight group the damage will be spread out over all players, minimizing death.

Plague: The infected person takes nature damage and causes nature damage to anyone near them. Should you get this ailment, simply run away from the raid until the timer expires, while receiving heals the entire duration. The MT will likely be the first target of the Plague, so the whole raid group must avoid him or her.

Reflect: The Anubisath Guardian reflects two types of spell damage. To discover which he will reflect, simply use the Detect Magic skill.

Thunderclap: Area nature damage. Only the MT should be hit by this. Everyone else can back off and defeat the Guardian with ranged attacks.

Summon Guards: The Anubisath often spawn Anubisath Warriors or Swarmguards to attack the raid. The Warriors can be feared until they disappear, but the Swarmguards should be taken down immediately by Warriors and Rogues so that their cleave does not cause havoc in the raid.

Explode: At 10% the Anubisath's hands burn with fire. If he is not defeated within five seconds, anyone near him takes fatal damage.

CANAL FRENZY — 60 ELITE

This is your basic school of ravenous fish. You only have to engage them if you jump into the water. Handle them as you would any normal enemy.

FLESH HUNTER — 60 ELITE

Although the monstrous blobs known as Flesh Hunters spit acidic bolts if not engaged in melee combat, they're best taken down from range. If anyone is in melee range, they'll consume that player and very rapidly regain health. Stay outside of melee range, prepare to back off if the Flesh Hunter approaches, and take them down.

HIVE'ZARA SOLDIER — 60 ELITE

This insect starts out like any other battle, but as it comes closer to death it begins to retaliate against all melee attacks. When you see the emote stating this, have everyone except the tank back off and finish it with ranged attacks.

HIVE'ZARA SANDSTALKER — 60 ELITE

This bright yellow bug periodically burrows under the ground and appears within the raid group, usually attacking a caster. A quick intercept and taunt by a tank is all you need to counter it.

HIVE'ZARA BUG PACKS — 60 ELITE

You will meet these packs between Buru the Gorger and Ayamiss the Hunter. It's recommended that you double back and skip these completely, but should you wish to cut your way through, you'll be facing a terrible battle indeed.

Allow the Warriors to gain solid aggro prior to doing anything else. If you start to use AoE spells too quickly, the Drones may rush those casters and throw the raid into chaos.

Each pack consists of two Hive'Zara Collectors, two Hive'Zara Drones, and two Hive'Zara Tail Lashers.

Collectors: These have the abilities Web Spray (immobilizes enemies in a frontal cone for 10 sec.), Poison (219-281 Nature damage DoT every 2 sec.), and Deafening Screech (Silences nearby targets for 8 sec.). These are the most dangerous members of the pack and should always be targeted and killed first. Keep them away from casters to prevent Silence and face them away from the raid to avoid the Poison and Web Spray.

Drones: They frequently wipe hate and switch targets, so keep them away from casters if possible.

Tail Lashers: Their two abilities are the same Poison DoT as the Collectors (219-281 Nature damage every 2 sec.) and Tail Lash (AoE melee attack).

HIVE'ZARA WASP PACKS — 60 ELITE

Not a very challenging encounter. Eliminate the white Wasps first, then move onto the Stingers. The Stingers frequently put a debuff called Itch which causes the Stinger to charge them periodically. The tank can chase it down and taunt it back before it can do any real damage.

QIRAJI GLADIATOR — 60 ELITE

These massive Qiraji come in pairs of two, so have two able tanks ready to separate them and hold the agro. Keep in mind they often use a moderate damaging attack called Uppercut, causing knock back. Stuns and massive single target damage make short work of these.

QIRAJI SWARMGUARD — 60 ELITE

These absolutely must be stunned as much as possible and tanked away from the casters. They use Sundering Cleave, and it will tear through cloth wearers if left in camp too long. They also have the Triple Attack ability which adds two instant attacks the next time they attack. Once they are safely out of the camp, use ranged damage to destroy them quickly.

SCARAB PACKS — 60 ELITE

These large squads of insects litter the area surrounding Moam. Massive area damage spells will win this fight quickly and without much trouble. It is more important to heal the casters than the tanks here because they will be taking the brunt of all attacks. Periodically, some of the scarabs charge players knocking them back a long distance. This is more of a nuisance then a threat.

LORDS OF THE RUINS

The Ruins of Ahn'Qiraj are home to six bosses spread out across the entire zone. Each one takes more cunning and strategy than brute force to defeat, so be ready to change tactics from your typical raid encounter.

Kurinnaxx is the first boss you battle in the zone, followed up immediately by General Rajaxx. After Rajaxx falls, you can choose to do any of the remaining four in any order you wish, Buru the Gorger being the easiest, and Ossirian the Unscarred the most difficult.

KURINNAXX

Kurinnaxx is a simple encounter, but it is also a very mobile encounter. You need two or three tanks, all ready to be the MT at anytime. Everyone else should spread out in a circle around Kurinnaxx with ample spacing.

Very often, a bubble pulses up from the sand and explode. The raid must be ready to react to this before it bursts. Should you be near it when it explodes, not only will you take heavy damage, but your chance to hit will be significantly reduced, and you will be silenced. This debuff lasts an extremely long time, so it is incredibly important that everyone is paying attention and ready to shift positions. The MT must continually move around to prevent being hit by Kurinaxx's Sand Trap in addition to all movement by the raid.

The second ability one must be aware of is the debuff that is placed upon the MT. For every stack of Kurinnaxx's Mortal Wound, the player will receive 10% less healing. Should this stack greater than four times, the MT will be in serious trouble. During this time, the other tanks should be building some stable aggro until the MT declares that he or she has four stacks of this debuff. Once it is declared, another tank should taunt Kurinnaxx off the MT and take over as the new MT until they have four stacks of the debuff, at which point, the insect should be taunted off to a new MT and so on.

Kurinnaxx has a Wide Slash ability that acts like a Warrior's Cleave, but in a frontal arc. It adds 500 physical damage on top of his normal melee attack and hits everyone in his frontal cone. At 30% health, Kurinnaxx will Enrage, increasing both his attack speed and damage dramatically. Kurinnaxx does not have much health, so if done correctly, this is a quick battle.

DROPS

ITEM	DESC	STATS
BELT OF THE INQUISITION	Cloth Waist	56 Armor, 15 INT, 14 STA
Equip: Increases healing done by spells and effects by up to 24, Restores 4 mana per 5 seconds		
BELT OF THE SAND REAVER	Plate Waist	494 Armor, 18 STA, 17 STR
Equip: Increased Defense by 5		
QIRAJI REGAL DRAPE	Quest Item	
QIRAJI SACRIFICIAL DAGGER	One-Hand Dagger	48.2 DPS, 15 STA
Equip: 20 Attack Power		
SAND REAVER WRISTGUARDS	Mail Wrist	181 Armor, 16 AGI, 11 STA, 7 INT
TOUGHENED SILITHID HIDE GLOVES	Leather Hands	182 Armor, 18 STA, 15 AGI, 11 STR
VESTMENTS OF THE SHIFTING SANDS	Cloth Chest	102 Armor, 20 STA, 14 INT, 8 SPI
Equip: Increases damage and healing done by magical spells and effects by up to 32, Improves your chance to get a critical strike with spells by 1%		

GENERAL RAJAXX

This is the battle that tests your raid's resolve—and endurance. General Rajaxx is an encounter of not only stamina, but technique. After slaying Kurinnaxx, five NPCs join and they're ready for battle. When you're ready to fight, speak with Lieutenant General Andohov and follow him and his subordinates to the battle field.

General Rajaxx hurls insults and sends wave after wave of his Warriors and Swarmguards into your camp. The first three waves are lead by his captains, the following two have majors at their heads, and the final wave comes to battle behind Rajaxx's colonel. Andohov and his four Kaldorei Elites aid you in this battle, but it's still going to be a brutal encounter.

Lieutenant General Andohov has Aura of Command (heals nearby allies for 200 health every 3 sec. and increases their attack and casting speed by 10%), Bash, and Strike to aid you and his troops. His Kaldorei Elite all have Cleave and Mortal Strike to wear down the enemies.

In addition to leading a wave of Warriors and Swarmguards, all the named mobs have Sunder Armor and Cleave, but each officer also has an ability unique to them as well.

Captain Queez has Intimidating Shout.

Captain Tuubid has the ability to direct all his minions to focus on a single target. Watch for this carefully and make sure to keep that unfortunate player protected. Alliance raids should use Blessing of Protection if necessary.

Captain Drenn casts Lightning Cloud. It deals 653-857 initial Nature damage and the same amount every 3 sec. for 15 sec. if players remain in the affected area.

Major Yeggeth utilizes the Shield of Rajaxx ability, which temporarily makes him immune to all spells for a 5 sec. duration.

Major Pakkon has Sweeping Slam that deals 1750-2250 damage to targets in his frontal cone and knocks those affected targets back.

Colonel Zerran can cast Enlarge, increasing the physical damage of the target by 438-562 for 1 min. This can be Dispelled.

Protect your new allies once the battle's begun in earnest. Assign a healer or two to watch Andohov and his Elites and keep them alive. They take a good portion of the aggro with their massive damage output. Slowly, but surely, take down the Swarmguards first and immediately move on to the Warriors. Tanks should try to pick them up as best as they can, but it can be a very chaotic fight. Have the healers keep an eye on everyone unless they're specifically assigned to the tanks or the NPC allies.

Once the guards are down, turn your attention to the officer be it Captain, Major, or Colonel. Take note of their special abilities and adjust the raid appropriately. As mentioned, protect the single target during Tuubid's wave. Be ready to move during Drenn's wave and call off spells during Yeggeth's. Keep Pakkon faced away from the raid and Zerran tanked at all times and Dispel his massive growth.

After the waves of slaughter, General Rajaxx enters the fray. Hopefully, Andohov and his Elites are still alive and well; it makes taking out Rajaxx much easier. If your Warriors have the gear to become immune to disarm, have them don it before the battle begins. Although General Andohov will likely have aggro during most of the fight, so keep him healed. However, Rajaxx frequently disarms Andohov.

Casters should take note to keep their distance from the Qiraji General. Rajaxx's Thundercrash is an absolutely deadly ability. It's an wider AoE Thunderclap that deals just over 50% of the target's total health to all creatures in the AoE. Since this is based on a percentage (plus a small number), it's only important to keep the tanks at full health; everyone else should be fine with approximately 1000 hit points or so. However, this ability also causes knockback that resets the threat on all affected targets. Tanks must be ready to rotate Taunts when they can to keep Rajaxx from heading to the main body of the raid.

DROPS

ITEM	DESC	STATS
AMBER IDOL	Quest Item	
BOOTS OF THE QIRAJI GENERAL	Mail Feet	285 Armor, 26 AGI, 11 STA
BOOTS OF THE VANGUARD	Leather Feet	138 Armor, 22 AGI, 11 STA, 22 STR
BRACERS OF QIRAJI COMMAND	Cloth Wrist	44 Armor, 13 INT, 12 STA
Equip: Restores 4 mana per 5 seconds		
JASPER IDOL	Quest Item	
LEGPLATES OF THE QIRAJI COMMAND	Plate Legs	644 Armor, 35 STR, 15 STA
MANSLAYER OF THE QIRAJI	Two-Hand Sword	62.5 DPS, 35 STR, 20 STA, 15 AGI
ONYX IDOL	Quest Item	
QIRAJI REGAL DRAPE	Quest Item	
SOUTHWIND'S GRASP	Leather Waist	110 Armor, 13 INT, 11 STA
Equip: Increases damage and healing done by magical spells and effects by up to 16, Improves your chance to get a critical strike with spells by 1%		

BURU THE GORGER

This is one of those battles that requires you to think outside of the box. Immediately upon approaching Buru you should notice the eggs surrounding his pool. The battle begins the instant an egg is struck.

Buru's outer shell is far too hard to damage with spells and swords to be effective, so you must use his own eggs against him. When an egg is destroyed it deals minor damage to any nearby players and an elite silithid will emerge to immediately attack whoever's close. However, if Buru is very close to that egg when it's destroyed two things happen: 1) Buru takes major damage and 2) his speed is reset (to its extremely slow default).

Assign a few people to "bug duty" and have them pick up the silithid that spawn from the eggs. Have the rest of the raid reduce the eggs to low health during the first part of the battle and kill them off whenever Buru gets to be too fast. Use Detect Magic to monitor his movement rate and kill an egg near Buru when he's become a handful. This frees up a few DPS players to attack Buru during this first phase while using the eggs to inflict big damage. This shortens the initial phase considerably.

Buru often "sets his eye" upon a particular player, then proceeds to chase that target down. When this happens, the unfortunate player must lead Buru to one of the weakened eggs. When Buru's in range of the egg, finish it off. One option is to destroy the eggs in a clockwise fashion around the pool so that each player knows what the next egg will be to be destroyed. Again, weakening all the eggs increases both the complexity of the battle and your options when someone's Buru's target, but it speeds up the initial phase by letting the DPS hit Buru as well.

Buru will be hurting badly after a few exploding eggs. Once he reaches the 20% health mark, the real battle begins. Flying into a wild rage, Buru blows his top, exposing his brain to your raid. He then begins to emit a pulse of Nature damage that affects everyone in the raid. This damage increases the longer he stays alive. At this point, your DPS should unload every bit of firepower at their disposal, Priests should be chain casting Prayer of Healing, and everyone else should attack Buru. Warriors, including the MT, should use Recklessness and use Execute every chance they get.

DROPS

ITEM	DESC	STATS
BURU'S SKULL FRAGMENT	Shield	2575 Armor, 47 Block, 20 STA, 11 STR
Equip: Increased Defense by 6		
FETISH OF CHITINOUS SPIKES	Trinket	
Use: Spikes sprout from you causing 25 Nature damage to attackers when hit, Lasts for 30 seconds		
GLOVES OF THE SWARM	Plate Hands	482 Armor, 18 INT, 18 STA, 11 STR, 10 AGI
Equip: Increases damage and healing done by magical spells and effects by up to 12		
QUICKSAND WADERS	Cloth Feet	70 Armor, 14 INT, 14 STA, 11 SPI
Equip: Increases damage and healing done by magical spells and effects by up to 16		
QIRAJI ORNATE HILT	Quest Item	
QIRAJI SPIKED HILT	Quest Item	
SCALED BRACERS OF THE GORGER	Leather Wrist	87 Armor, 15 AGI, 10 STR, 8 STA
SLIME KICKERS	Plate Feet	519 Armor, 18 STR, 12 AGI, 12 STA
Equip: Improves your chance to hit by 1%		
SLIMY SCALED GAUNTLETS	Mail Hands	271 Armor, 18 INT, 18 STA, 6 STR
Equip: Increases damage and healing done by magical spells and effects by up to 12, Improves your chance to get a critical strike with spells by 1%		

MOAM

Moam can either be an incredibly simple fight, or a near impossible one. Raid structure is key here, as abilities and spells that drain mana are the keys to victory.

Moam begins the battle with 0 mana. However, this changes as the battle progresses. When he reaches 100% mana, he casts Arcane Eruption and inflicts massive Arcane damage on anyone within range. It has just over 40 yards in range. If it looks like he's going to reach 100%, have everyone except the MT retreat to the 45-50 yard mark. As Horde, cast PW: Shield on the MT and apply HoTs before retreating. Paladins can cast Divine Shield for the Alliance. Arcane Eruption also shoots anyone affected (the MT is always unlucky) into the air to incur falling damage. Make sure the MT gets healing both during their "flight" and upon landing.

Priests, Warlocks, and Hunters should be draining mana full time. Focus on this. Druids, Paladins, and Shaman should act as the healers since Moam's melee damage is pitiful at best.

If Moam has less than 75% mana, a 90-sec. timer begins counting down towards his "stone form"; otherwise known as Energize. Moam deals no damage in this state, but regenerates 500 mana and health per second during this phase. Continue to burn Moam's health down after he assumes his Energize form. After a short time, Moam will summon three Mana Fiends (approx. 14k health each). They can cast a high-damage Arcane Explosion (800-1000 damage) that can quickly end your raid. Luckily, they're elementals and can be banished by Warlocks. If you have three or more Warlocks, this is simple; Banish the Mana Fiends and stay focused on Moam. Keep him below 100% mana!

Moam does not have much health. Keep pecking away at him while you drain his mana pool and he will soon fall. The key to winning this battle is to keep him under 100% mana and, if possible, Banish the elementals. If you're without the requisite number of Warlocks, Focus Fire on the elementals while you keep the other(s) Banished.

THEORETICALLY...

Since Moam's timer toward his Energize form is only active if he's below 75% mana and he only casts Arcane Eruption at 100% mana, stabilizing him between 76% and 99% mana is an option that will prevent him from: a) Summoning the Mana Fiends, b) regenerating health/mana at 500 per sec., and c) casting his Arcane Eruption.

DROPS

ITEM	DESC	STATS
CHITINOUS SHOULDERGUARDS	Leather Shoulder	151 Armor, 25 AGI, 11 STR, 7 STA
CLOAK OF THE SAVIOR	Back	52 Armor, 11 INT, 10 STA, 10 SPI
Equip: Increases healing done by spells and effects by up to 22		
DUSTWIND TURBAN	Cloth Head	86 Armor, 15 SPI, 29 INT, 18 STA
Equip: Increases healing done by spells and effects by up to 31, Improves your chance to get a critical strike with spells by 1%		
EYE OF MOAM	Trinket	
Use: Increases damage done by magical spells and effects by up to 50, and decreases the magical resistances of your spell targets by 100 for 30 seconds		
GAUNTLETS OF THE IMMOVABLE	Plate Hands	482 Armor, 18 STA, 15 STR
Equip: Increases your chance to parry an attack by 1%, Increased Defense by 5		
GAUNTLETS OF SOUTHWIND	Leather Hands	126 Armor, 13 INT, 11 STA
Equip: Increases damage and healing done by magical spells and effects by up to 25		
LEGPLATES OF THE DESTROYER	Plate Legs	670 Armor, 19 STR, 18 INT, 18 STA, 10 AGI
Equip: Increases damage and healing done by magical spells and effects by up to 12		
MANTLE OF MAZ'NADIR	Cloth Shoulder	78 Armor, 11 STA, 15 INT, 7 SPI
Equip: Increases damage and healing done by magical spells and effects by up to 21		
OBSIDIAN SCALED LEGGINGS	Legs	377 Armor, 16 STR, 18 INT, 18 STA, 10 AGI
Equip: Increases damage and healing done by magical spells and effects by up to 19		
PLANS: BLACK GRASP OF THE DESTROYER		
QIRAJI ORNATE HILT	Quest Item	
QIRAJI SPIKED HILT	Quest Item	
RING OF FURY	Finger	9 STA
Equip: Improves your chance to hit by 1%, 30 Attack Power		
SOUTHWIND HELM	Leather Head	164 Armor, 21 STR, 24 AGI, 14 STA, Equip: Improves your chance to hit by 1%
TALON OF FURIOUS CONCENTRATION	Held In Off-Hand	8 INT, 8 STA
Equip: Increases damage and healing done by magical spells and effects by up to 21, Improves your chance to get a critical strike with spells by 1%		
Thick Silithid Chestguard	Leather Chest	258 Armor, 30 STA, 21 AGI, 15 STR, 5 Fire Resistance, 5 Nature Resistance, 5 Frost Resistance, 5 Shadow Resistance, 5 Arcane Resistance

⊛ AYAMISS THE HUNTER

What could be worse than the endless Wasp pulls you encounter in the Ruins of Ahn'Qiraj? How about a giant Wasp?

The first thing to do is assign a Mage and Warlock to watch the skies for Swarmers. They come in huge droves, swarming their target to death. Their weakness, however, is that they have next to no health. One or two AoEs drops them.

Ayamiss has the ability to sacrifice any person in your raid on her unholy Qiraji altar. This happens approximately every 30 seconds and it's her most dangerous skill. When someone's placed on the altar, a larva rushes forward to the sacrificed person from the base of the altar. There are two spawn points to monitor, so assign a Rogue and Warrior to each.

This larva can't be slowed, snared, or stopped in any way. It must simply be killed before it reaches the top. It's imperative that every single player assigned to watch for the larvae pay attention and move to destroy them immediately. Should the larva reach its target, the player will die instantly, replaced with an elite wasp. If this happens more than once or twice, it will likely spell doom for your party, as the wasps take far too long to defeat to possibly deal with them, the Swarmers, the larvae, and Ayamiss.

Ayamiss begins the encounter by taking to the air, assaulting whoever has aggro with a stackable poison. When she begins to stack poison on a players, that person should cease attacks immediately until the poison wears off, giving someone else a chance to draw her aggro. She lands when she reaches 70% health.

At this point, have everyone not given a previous assignment (Mage/Warlock Swarmer scouts and the Rogue/Warrior Larvae scouts) turn on Ayamiss. When she lands, she clears her hate list, so let the MT get aggro before dumping on the DPS. She gains the Stinger Spray ability when she lands; it deals approximately 800-1000 Nature damage to nearby targets. Ayamiss also has Lash, which knocks her target down for 2 sec. and has a chance to disarm.

Unleash the DPS once the MT has cemented aggro. Should you successfully stop every single larva from reaching their target, the rest of the fight should fall into place.

DROPS

ITEM	DESC	STATS
BOOTS OF THE DESERT PROTECTOR	Plate Feet	519 Armor, 14 STR, 14 INT, 14 STA
Equip: Restores 4 mana per 5 seconds		
BOOTS OF THE FIERY SANDS	Mail Feet	293 Armor, 9 STR, 14 INT, 14 STA
Equip: Restores 4 mana per 5 seconds, Increases damage and healing done by magical spells and effects by up to 12		
BOW OF TAUT SINEW	Bow	38.6 DPS, 8 Nature Resistance
Equip: 22 Attack Power		
GAUNTLETS OF THE IMMOVABLE	Plate Hands	482 Armor, 18 STA, 15 STR
Equip: Increases your chance to parry an attack by 1%, Increases Defense by 5		
HELM OF REGROWTH	Leather Head	162 Armor, 28 INT, 18 STA, 10 SPI
Equip: Increases healing done by spells and effects by up to 22		
QIRAJI ORNATE HILT	Quest Item	
QIRAJI SPIKED HILT	Quest Item	
RING OF THE DESERT WINDS	Finger	9 INT
Equip: Improves your chance to get a critical strike with spells by 1%, Restores 3 mana per 5 sec, Increases damage and healing done by magical spells and effects by up to 9		
SCALED SILITHID GAUNTLETS	Mail Hands	266 Armor, 18 AGI, 18 STA, 8 INT, 7 SPI
STINGER OF AYAMISS	One-handed Mace	41.5 DPS, 7 INT, 9 STA
Equip: Improves your chance to get a critical strike with spells by 1%, Increases damage and healing done by magical spells and effects by up to 36		

OSSIRIAN THE UNSCARRED

While the order you take on the last four bosses is optional, Ossirian the Unscarred is considered to be the final boss of the Ruins of Ahn'Qiraj, and rightfully so. He tests your raid fiercely. This can be a very difficult battle, but once mastered, it is one of the most fun encounters in the game. This is an *extremely* mobile battle.

Ossirian is a might foe. So mighty, in fact, that one swipe from his hands kills almost any player. To counter this, he must be weakened in some way. To begin this battle, everyone should be on his or her mounts, ready to outrun him as best they can. The only way to weaken him is to use one of the crystals when he is within 30 yards of it. When the crystal hits him, he will be debuffed for 1 minute, moving at a normal speed, dealing less damage, and vulnerable to a certain school of magic. *Do not* engage him with your MT until he has been debuffed.

Of course, Ossirian takes longer than 1 minute to defeat, so one crystal debuff won't do. Choose a Druid, using Travel Form, to be your scout during this chaotic battle, looking for the closest crystal to Ossirian. Once the crystal is located, this Druid must ping the map over and over, letting everyone know where the next destination is.

Using two tanks, begin to drag the battle towards the ping on the map before the minute expires. If Ossirian is not dragged to the next crystal in time he will destroy your MT in one or two hits and make even shorter work of the rest of the raid. Using two tanks is necessary since he often uses a spell called Enveloping Winds on the MT, removing him or her from combat for 10 seconds or until they take damage. Once the Enveloping Winds die down on the MT, Ossirian will likely return to the first target.

Ossirian also pounds the ground, War Stomps, dealing moderate physical damage, sending anyone near him flying backwards a great distance. If the MT dragging him has his back towards the next crystal target this knock back actually works to your advantage, advancing the MT even closer to the crystal. Because of this, the MT's back must *always* be to the next crystal being pinged on the map. It is wise for any healers to try and stay a few steps ahead of the MT, anticipating this knock back, ensuring they stay in range at all times.

Ossirian's final ability is called Curse of Tongues. He randomly casts this on raid members throughout the battle increasing the casting time of spells by 75% for 15 seconds. Should this be cast on a healer, that player's spells take far longer to cast than normal, ultimately causing the death of your tanks. This *must* be decursed immediately by anyone that can do so.

One other threat lurks in the sands while you battle Ossirian, and it will cause deaths if not paid attention to closely. A few tornadoes whirl about the area randomly, turning and shifting courses, looking to cause your raid to divide.

These tornadoes must be avoided at all times. Should you see a tornado heading towards the raid, be sure to let everyone know with time to react. If someone becomes caught in this whirlwind, that player immediately takes massive damage, likely causing his or her death.

Keep the DPS on Ossirian at all times, whittling away at his health while you drag him from crystal to crystal. Casters should take note of his current debuff and use that school of magic to damage him, since he will be taking increased damage from whatever school it happens to be for that 30 seconds. It is a long battle, and it forces everyone to give his or her full and undivided attention the entire time. Once it is mastered, it can be a very enjoyable and challenging experience.

Fell Ossirian and bring him to justice!

DROPS

ITEM	DESC	STATS
BRACERS OF BRUTALITY	Plate Wrist	356 ARMOR, 21 STR, 12 AGI, 9 STA
CROSSBOW OF IMMINENT DOOM	Crossbow	41.6 DPS, 7 AGI, 5 STA, 5 STR
Equip: Improves your chance to hit by 1%		
GAUNTLETS OF NEW LIFE	Leather Hands	134 Armor, 20 INT, 19 STA, 11 STR
Equip: Increases healing done by spells and effects by up to 26, Restores 4 mana per 5 seconds		
GLOVES OF DARK WISDOM	Cloth Hands	69 Armor, 20 INT, 19 STA
Equip: Increases healing done by spells and effects by up to 35, Restores 5 mana per 5 seconds		
HEAD OF OSSIRIAN THE UNSCARRED	Quest Item	
HELM OF DOMINATION	Plate Head	661 Armor, 28 STA, 21 STR, 11 AGI
Equip: Increases your chance to parry an attack by 1%, Increased Defense by 7		
LEGGINGS OF THE BLACK BLIZZARD	Cloth Legs	97 Armor, 16 INT, 8 SPI, 14 STA
Equip: Increases damage and healing done by magical spells and effects by up to 41, Improves your chance to get a critical strike with spells by 1%		
MANTLE OF THE HORUSATH	Plate Shoulder	610 Armor, 20 INT, 19 STA, 12 STR
Equip: Increases damage and healing done by magical spells and effects by up to 14		
OSSIRIAN'S BINDING	Mail Waist	258 Armor, 20 AGI, 19 STA, 10 INT
Equip: Improves your chance to get a critical strike by 1%, Improves your chance to hit by 1%		
QIRAJI ORNATE HILT	Quest Item	
QIRAJI SPIKED HILT	Quest Item	
RUNIC STONE SHOULDERS	Mail Shoulder	344 Armor, 20 INT, 19 STA, 12 STR
Equip: Increases damage and healing done by magical spells and effects by up to 14		
SAND POLISHED HAMMER	One-Hand Mace	53.5 DPS, 9 STA
Equip: Improves your chance to get a critical strike by 1%, 20 Attack Power		
SANDSTORM CLOAK	Back	135 Armor, 12 STA, 12 STR
Equip: Increases your chance to dodge an attack by 1%, Increased Defense by 6)		
SHACKLES OF THE UNSCARRED	Cloth Wrist	48 Armor, 12 INT, 9 STA
Equip: Increases damage and healing done by magical spells and effects by up to 21, Decreases the magical resistances of your spell targets by 10		
STAFF OF THE RUINS	Staff	58.4 DPS, 23 INT, 24 STA, 14 SPI
Equip: Increases damage and healing done by magical spells and effects by up to 60, Improves your chance to get a critical strike with spells by 1%, Improves your chance to hit with spells by 1%		

THE TEMPLE OF AHN'QIRAJ

Played & Written by: Chris M. "Phunbaba" Koschik of <Fraternity> on Perenolde

Dark whispers ride on the winds of the Silithus desert. An Old God stirs in his wretched lair and the entire world shall soon be target of his wrath.

After thousands of years of slumber, the Old God, C'thun has awakened and is quickly regenerating his power. Once he has reached full potential nothing will be able to stop him. The dragons that so humbly sacrificed themselves so long ago to imprison C'thun are weakened or enslaved in the temple so the charge of protecting the land falls to you.

You must enter the Temple of Ahn'Qiraj, challenge C'thun's most wicked servants, and slay a God. The road will not be easy and it is wrought with peril at every turn. Will you turn back now, or face C'thun in his mighty lair and put an end to him once and for all?

DUNGEON INFORMATION

Location	Silithus
Territory	Contested
Quests	Shared Alliance and Horde
Suggested Level	60 (40-person raid)
Primary Enemies	Qiraji, Silithids, and Constructs
Time to Complete	6-14 hours. (2-3 days)

GETTING TO THE TEMPLE OF AHN'QIRAJ

The journey to the Temple of Ahn'Qiraj is a short one. Simply fly to Silithus, landing in Cenarion Hold, and take the west road out of town. The roar quickly turns south leading you directly to the Gates of Ahn'Qiraj.

When you enter the gates, you come to a crossroads. Take the right path up the stairs and continue to climb them until you reach a large green portal. This portal takes you to the Temple of Ahn'Qiraj.

THE TEMPLE

LEGEND

1. Entrance
2. The Prophet Skeram
3. Lord Kri
   Princess Yauj
   Vem
4. Battleguard Satura
5. Fankriss the Unyielding
6. Viscidus
7. Princess Huhuran
8. The Twin Emperors
9. Ouro
10. Eye of C'Thun & C'Thun

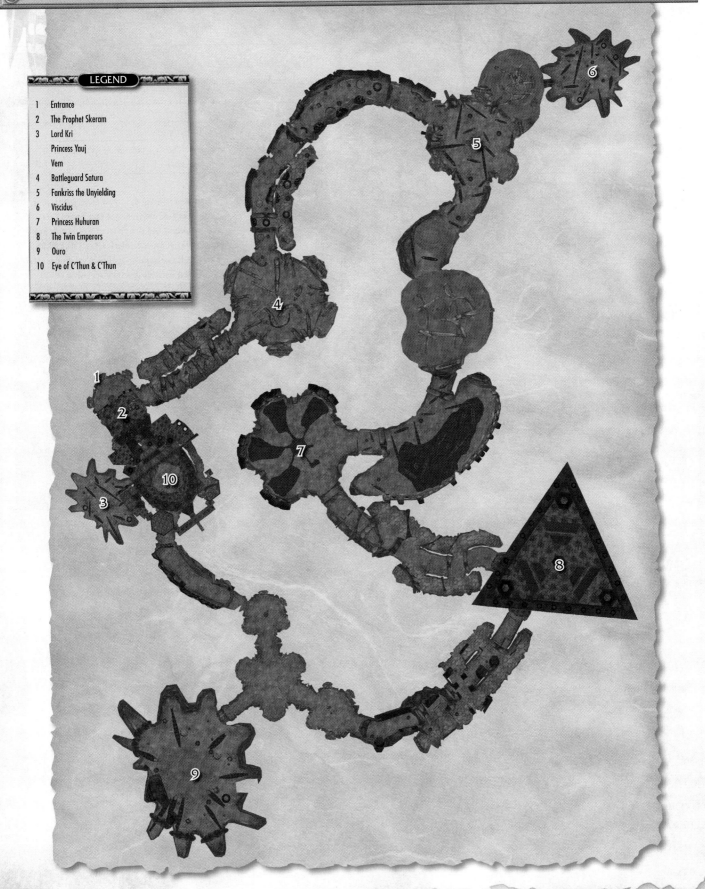

SHARED QUESTS

MORTAL CHAMPIONS

Quest Level	60 to obtain
Location	Ahn'Qiraj
Contact	Kandrostrasz
Goal	Bring a Qiraji Lord's Insignia to Kandrostrasz
Experience Gained	5000
Reward	500 Reputation with the Brood of Nozdormu

Every boss in this instance drops a Qiraji Lord's Insignia for each player. Simply loot it and return it to Kandrostrasz for a quick 500 reputation with the Brood of Nozdormu.

QIRAJI BATTLE GEAR

Quest Level	60 to obtain
Location	Ahn'Qiraj
Contact	Vethsera, Andorgos, Kandrostrasz
Goal	Return the requested items to the correct NPC for powerful rewards
Experience Gained	0
Reward	Varies by class

Once you have slain the first guardian of the Temple of Ahn'Qiraj, the Prophet Skeram, you have access to three quest givers that request specific items dropped from particular bosses and random drops found in coffers and on enemies.

In all, there is a set for each class consisting of five pieces. These sets are incredibly powerful and are worth the effort.

THE SAVIOR OF KALIMDOR

Quest Level	60 to obtain
Location	Ahn'Qiraj
Contact	Caelastrasz, Anachronos
Goal	Speak with Caelastrasz, then return the eye to Anachronos at the Caverns of Time
Experience Gained	0
Reward	Amulet of the Fallen God (Neck, 11 STA, Equip: Increases healing done by spells and effects by up to 57, Equip: Restores 6 mana every 5 seconds), Cloak of the Fallen God (Back, 66 armor, 11 STR, 26 AGI, 15 STA), Ring of the Fallen God (Ring, 5 STA, 6 INT, Equip: Increases damage and healing done by spells and effects by up to 37, Equip: Improves your chance to hit with spells by 1%)

After slaying the Old God, C'thun, one person can loot an epic quest item called the Eye of C'thun. If you bring this eye to Caelastrasz in the next chamber, he praises your name and send you to Anachronos at the Caverns of Time for your reward.

SERVANTS OF THE TEMPLE

The Temple of Ahn'Qiraj is swarming with teams of enemies of which the likes you have never seen before. You will be pitted against endless waves on Silithid insects and lumbering Anubisath giants. Each encounter requires precise reaction and sound strategy.

ANUBISATH SENTINEL   63 ELITE

You face two packs of four Sentinels at the beginning of the instance. You want to have four Warriors ready to pick up the aggro and spread them out. Each Anubisath has a random ability, some more fatal than others, which must be responded to correctly. To find out which ability an Anubisath has in it's arsenal simply cast Detect Magic on each to reveal it. Should a Sentinel fall, each of his brethren gain this ability and a full heal. Thus, you want to eliminate the easiest of the abilities and combinations first, lest you slay the most difficult first, empowering the other three with the most deadly of abilities. The abilities from easiest to hardest are as follows:

Magic Reflection: The Sentinel reflects a particular school of magic to the caster. Simply do not use this school of magic. Should you run out of schools to cast, use your wand, it's better than nothing!

Mending: The Sentinel heals itself for a few hundred damage periodically. Of course, when your raid is dishing out thousands of damage per second, this is not really a problem. Mortal strike also helps in slowing the healing process.

Knock Away: The Anubisath periodically knocks the tank away. It is annoying, but not really a problem.

Mortal Strike: Your tank is struck with a debuff decreasing the value of all heals by 50%. Your Warriors will need a little extra healing here.

Thorns: Each melee attack dealt to the Sentinel returns massive damage to the attacker. It is best to burn this type of Anubisath away with ranged damage, but if your melee feels brave, they can go in and attack with a competent healer backing them up.

Thunderclap: This attack deals heavy area nature damage causing a decrease in attack speed. The only person that should be affected by this is the Warrior whom is tanking it. This enemy should be destroyed from range only. Make sure it is tanked away from the raid as quickly as possible.

Mana Burn: This deadly ability drains massive amounts of mana from any player foolish enough to stray too closely. This type of Anubisath should be tanked away from the raid group at all times.

Shadow Storm: The most deadly of the Anubisath Sentinel's abilities, this attack showers the area around the giant with Shadow Bolts, dealing heavy damage to all players. However, these bolts only strike those at a distance greater than fifteen yards from the Sentinel, so if everyone is at the feet of the Anubisath, nobody takes damage. This enemy should be tanked in the midst of the raid group at all times. The only players that should be taking damage from this storm are the Warriors tanking other Anubisaths away from the raid.

ANUBISATH DEFENDER   63 ELITE

These behemoths are, in a nutshell, more powerful versions of the ones you fight in the Ruins of Ahn'Qiraj. That being said, they should be taken quite a bit more seriously. With double the players, the room for error is also doubled! Each Defender comes with a combination of two different abilities that must be reacted to properly, or it brings doom to the raid.

Meteor: Everyone in a large area takes a total of about 12,000 damage. If this flaming rock hits one person, they take the entire damage. However, if everyone is in a nice tight group the damage is spread out over all players, minimizing any damage.

Plague: The infected person takes nature damage and causes nature damage to anyone near them. Should you get this ailment, simply run away from the raid until the timer expires, while receiving heals the entire duration. The MT will likely be the first target of the Plague, so the whole raid group must avoid him or her.

Reflect: The Anubisath Defender reflects two types of spell damage. To discover which he is reflecting, simply use the Detect Magic skill.

Thunderclap: Area nature damage. Only the MT should be affected by this. Everyone else can back off and defeat the Defender with ranged attacks.

Summon Guards: The Anubisath spawns Anubisath Warriors or Swarmguards to attack the raid. The Warriors can be feared until they disappear, but the Swarmguards should be taken down immediately by Warriors and Rogues so that their cleave does not cause havoc in the raid.

Explode: At 10% the Anubisath's hands burn with fire. If he is not defeated within five seconds, anyone near him takes fatal damage.

Enrage: At 10% the Defender gains an increase to attack speed and power.

ANUBISATH WARDER AND OBSIDIAN NULLIFIERS
63 ELITE

You encounter this deadly combination at the very end of the instance, just before C'thun and Ouro. While it may seem a bit daunting at first, this trio is easily dispatched if handled correctly.

The Nullifiers should be the first to die, and they must be dispatched with the utmost haste. Have anyone in the raid that can drain mana do so, and split them in half. Half of the raid should be mana draining one target, while the other half drains the other. While this is happening, the tanks should be grabbing their aggro as quickly as possible. All damage should be focused on one Nullifier at a time. If the damage is split over both Obsidians you run out of time before they fill their mana bar. If they do fill their mana bar, everyone in the raid is Banished and left with one health point. During this time, you are immune to all damage and cannot attack. When the Banishment wears off the enemies will go on to slaughter everyone in the raid. The goal is to keep their mana suppressed while your DPS burns them down so this does not happen.

The Warder is not an overly powerful foe, but he does come equipped with a few tricks up his sleeve that can make dealing with the Nullifiers more difficult. You must ensure that the Warder is tanked far in front of the raid, so that any abilities the Anubisath has does not affect the raid. His abilities are as follows:

Root: Everyone in the area is rooted for a long duration of time. This is only detrimental to the melee classes if they become rooted out of range of anything they can hit.

Fear: The Warder periodically emits a wave of fear, causing all players to run away for a short duration. Fear Ward and Tremor Totems should be ready at all times for the Warrior tanking the Warder. You obviously do not want your raid to get feared while damaging and draining the Nullifiers since time is of the essence.

Blast Wave: The Anubisath blasts a wave of fire damage, causing heavy damage to anyone in the vicinity.

Dust Cloud: Anyone caught in this attack has their chance to hit reduced by 85%, rendering their attacks near useless. Should this affliction strike the melee while they are attempting to defeat the Nullifiers it spells doom for all.

Once the Nullifiers have been dealt with, the Warder is easy prey. Defeat him as you would any enemy.

OBSIDIAN ERADICATOR
62 ELITE

This is the first enemy you encounter in the Temple of Ahn'Qiraj. They are much like their brethren in the Ruins. Should their mana bar fill up, they emit a pulse of fatal damage to everyone in your raid group.

Defeating this is quite simple. If you can drain mana, do it. All Priest should forgo healing, leaving it up to the Druids, Paladins, and Shamans. All DPS classes should unload as much damage as possible. Drain the Eradicator's mana and burn it's life down as quickly as possible. This battle should take no longer than fifteen seconds.

VEKNISS HIVE CRAWLER
62 ELITE

These giant scorpions come in pairs of two just after you defeat Fankriss the Unyielding. They are not overly difficult to dispatch, just make sure the tanks are kept topped off and the poison cleansing is top notch. They do not have many life points, so they can be defeated quickly.

VEKNISS GUARDIAN
62 ELITE

Vekniss Guardians usually come in large groups of six, so having six tanks is a must. Once each tank has aggro on their particular target, begin to burn then down using main assist, one by one.

Periodically, the Guardian rushes a random player, causing that person to be launched high into the air, and receiving a damage over time debuff. Players need to be thrown a heal while in mid-air or when they land since the fall damage is near fatal. Once they land, they begin to take heavy damage from the Impale debuff. This debuff can be healed over easily.

VEKNISS WARRIOR
62 ELITE

The Vekniss Warriors come at you in groups of three, usually ambushing the raid. They patrol routes along the tunnels quickly so keep an eye open!

At first they seem to be an incredibly easy foe, but the real trick comes when they die. When they fall, they spawn over a dozen smaller elite bugs that can quickly get out of hand if not handled correctly. Keep the Mages and Warlocks healed at all costs while they AoE the bugs down. Make sure your single target damage is only attacking one Vekniss Warrior at a time. You do not want to deal with two or more dead bugs at once, since the amount of smaller bugs will be almost uncontrollable. Simply defeat them one by one, using area spells to defeat the smaller bugs and this battle should be a relatively easy one.

QIRAJI BRAINWASHER — 63 ELITE

The weakest enemy in the entire dungeon, they usually are accompanied by Vekniss Guardians. The Brainwasher almost immediately Mind Controls the Warrior tanking it, so be ready to Sheep or stun the Mind Controlled player. Defeat the Qiraji Brainwasher first when pulled, moving onto the Guardians second. The Brainwasher dies fast.

THE HIVE TUNNEL — 60-62 ELITE

This tunnel span the distance between Battleguard Satura and Fankriss the Unyielding. It is crawling with Vekniss Drones and Soldiers. The entire raid group has to be mobile to make it to the other end unscathed. All casters should use their strongest area spells to defeat the weak Drones while melee attackers burn down the powerful Soldiers. The tunnel's inhabitants respawn quickly, so you must kill on the run. Anyone that falls should release their spirit, zone back into the instance and receive a summon before the next boss when the raid can rest in a safe place.

INSECT PACKS — 60-63 ELITE

You encounter these swarms shortly after Fankriss the Unyielding, but before Princess Huhuran. They usually consist of two Vekniss Wasps, two Vekniss Stingers, and one Qiraji Lasher.

When you pull them, you immediately want the Warrior to secure aggro on the Wasps and Stingers at the front of the raid, and have a Hunter pull the Lasher to the back of the raid. All melee DPS should begin attacking the Stingers first, while ranged DPS burns away at the Lasher.

The Lasher requires two tanks, since she randomly drops aggro and performs cleave in the caster camp, dealing heavy damage and usually killing someone. Keep her stationary as best as possible while the ranged eat away at her health.

The Stingers randomly charge people during the battle. If Catalyst Poison is applied to the target by the Vekniss Wasps, this can prove to be fatal. There's really not too much you can do about the charge, but Catalyst can be dispelled. Your best defense is a good offense here. Take them down hard and fast.

The Vekniss Wasps have a poison, the Catalyst Poison, that multiplies the damage received from a Vekniss Stinger's charge by 10x. 10 seconds before a player gets the poison, they'll receive a warning debuff called "Itch".

QIRAJI CHAMPION PACKS — 61-63 ELITE

You meet these troublesome and annoying groups immediately after you fell the Twin Emperors. They are by far the hardest enemy encounter in the instance, even a little more difficult than some of the bosses!

Each pack consists of one Qiraji Champion and any combination of four Qiraji Slayers and Mindslayers. Have a Hunter pull each pack into the room that you fought the Twin Emperors. Warriors should take care not engage their targets until they have made their way fully down the stairs. Should a tank climb the stairs to grab a target, they will be out of line of sight for heals and end up dead.

The first enemy you want to take out is the Mindslayer. These alien creatures often cast Mindflay on a player, causing heavy shadow damage. Healers should keep and eye on their party for this debuff and heal accordingly. The Qiraji Mindslayer is immune to taunt, so aggro is hard to secure, but a Warrior with enough time should be able to handle it. The Mindslayer also periodically Mind Controls whoever is on the top of their aggro list, causing them to run berserk in the raid. Make sure these players are Sheeped or stunned immediately. When the Mindslayer finally falls it unleashes an area effect causing a slight drain in mana to anyone near and also a fear effect, forcing all nearby players to run around in a panic for a few seconds. This effect can be minimized by pulling the Mindslayer away from the raid before it dies.

Next, you want to eliminate the Slayers. Make sure they are tanked away from the casters at all costs, as they have an area-silencing spell. This also ensures that only the tank is being cleaved. In the mean time, Hunters need to pay special attention to the Qiraji Slayers since they enter a frenzy often, requiring a Tranquilizing Shot. A Hunter should be assigned to each also to watch his or her back and secure secondary aggro. Every fifteen seconds or so the Slayer knocks the tank away, causing the Slayer to attack whomever is second on their aggro list. If this is the Hunter behind the Warrior, the tank can quickly taunt it off and continue tanking it.

The final kill will be the Qiraji Champion. Keep him tanked away from the raid using two Warriors, since he will knock away one tank, only to meet the second. Also, he uses Intimidating Shout quite often, sending anyone near running away in fear. Fear Ward, Tremor Totems, and proper use of Berserker Rage can remedy this easily. The final ability you want to keep an eye out for is when the Champion grows larger. This will cause him to enter an enraged state, gaining an increase to attack power. This can and should be dispelled immediately.

These packs take quite a bit of practice and refinement. If anything, once mastered, they are more of a time sink than anything. Always beware the quadruple Mindslayer packs!

CATCH A RIDE!

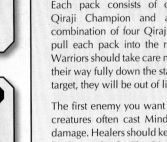

Each enemy has a large chance to drop a Qiraji Resonating Crystal of a certain color. This is an insect mount that can only be used while inside the Temple of Ahn'Qiraj. This is an extremely large instance, and some of the later battles require a long run back if not recoverable. You will come to love your bug.

The Temple of Ahn'Qiraj houses some of the most alien bosses ever seen in the World of Warcraft. Each requires a unique and sound approach. The determination and organization of your raid will be put to the test!

THE PROPHET SKERAM

When you first encounter the Prophet, the battle seems extremely complicated, but nothing could be further from the truth. The Prophet Skeram is, in fact, a simple battle once you know what to do.

Position the raid as shown on the map, making sure that two tanks are ready at each of the designated spots. Your casters should sit atop the upper level, safely away from danger.

The Prophet Skeram does not have much health at all, so DPS notice significant drops in his health.

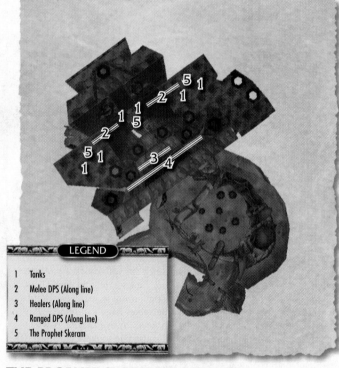

LEGEND

1	Tanks
2	Melee DPS (Along line)
3	Healers (Along line)
4	Ranged DPS (Along line)
5	The Prophet Skeram

THE PROPHET SKERAM'S ABILITIES

Teleport: Every so often the Prophet randomly teleports to one of his three designated spots. The tanks at that point must be ready to taunt him and tank him until he teleports again. *Do not* taunt him again once you have secured his aggro, or he teleports immediately and begins attacking you with his devastating ranged attacks.

Arcane Explosion: Skeram casts an AoE Arcane spell that deals heavy damage to anyone within range. Arcane Explosion can be interrupted with standard interruption abilities (Kick, Shield Bash, and Pummel). The Prophet is also susceptible to Curse of Tongues, making his cast time longer and more easily avoidable.

Earth Shock: If the player that has Skeram's aggro is out of melee range, he chain casts a devastating series of Earth Shocks dealing over 4000 damage per cast. This spells instant death for any player, so making sure that Skeram is always tanked by a Warrior is key!

True Fulfillment: Skeram Mind Controls someone very close to him, forcing him or her to grow far larger in size, deal much more damage, and make all their spells instants. If left unchecked, this player *will* kill others. Mages must be ready to Sheep at a moments notice. Stuns are also acceptable.

Quartile Split: At 75%, 50%, and 25% the Prophet Skeram splits into three copies of himself, each occupying one of his teleport points. Only one is real, so make sure the copies die first. Skeram wipes all debuffs on himself whenever he splits. Keep this in mind and make sure to reapply them if he does so. Each copy has the exact same abilities as the original, but far less health. Be sure to have someone call out which one is fake immediately and begin to destroy it. A worst-case scenario can and will happen when two Skerams teleport onto a single point. This is why you want to have two tanks ready at each point. If one of them is left unchecked for too long, you begin to lose people, if not both tanks at that location. To prevent a quick death in this case, both warriors should use Shield Wall immediately to increase their chances of surviving. Should a tank die when this happens, it is not the end of the world. One of them will usually teleport before the situation gets too out of hand. After you have regained order, be sure to have Druids cast Rebirth on any fallen tanks.

This can be an incredibly chaotic fight, especially if things go wrong, but it should be over shortly if you can react to each of his abilities in a timely manner.

DROPS

ITEM	DESC	STATS
AMULET OF FOUL WARDING	Neck	12 STA, 20 Nature Resistance
Equip: Increased attack power by 24.		
BARRAGE SHOULDERS	Mail Shoulder	348 ARM, 29 AGI, 22 STA
BEETLE SCALED WRISTGUARDS	Leather Wrist	95 ARM, 14 STA, 12 INT, 15 Nature Resistance
Equip: Increased attack power by 18.		
BOOTS OF THE FALLEN PROPHET	Mail Feet	319 ARM, 10 AGI, 15 STR, 15 INT, 15 STA
Equip: Increases damage and healing done by magical spells and effects by up to 20.		
BOOTS OF THE REDEEMED PROPHECY	Plate Feet	567 ARM, 12 AGI, 15 STR, 16 INT, 15 STA
Equip: Increases healing done by spells and effects by up to 33.		
BOOTS OF THE UNWAVERING WILL	Plate Feet	647 ARM, 29 STA, 12 STR, 8 AGI
Equip: Increased Defense by 5.		
BREASTPLATE OF ANNIHILATION	Plate Chest	824 ARM, 37 STR, 13 STA
Equip: Improves the chance to get a critical strike by 1 percent also improves the chance to hit by 1 percent.		
CLOAK OF CONCENTRATED HATRED	Cloth Back	56 ARM, 16 AGI, 11 STR, 15 STA
Equip: Improves the chance to hit by 1 percent.		
HAMMER OF JI'ZHI	Two-Hand Mace	70.7 DPS, 22 INT, 26 STA, 16 STR
Equip: Increases damage and healing done by magical spells and effects by up to 30.		
IMPERIAL QIRAJI ARMAMENTS	Quest Item	
IMPERIAL QIRAJI REGALIA	Quest Item	
LEGGINGS OF IMMERSION	Leather Legs	190 ARM, 22 INT, 15 STA
Equip: Increases damage and healing done by magical spells and effects by up to 39 while restoring 6 mana per 5 seconds.		
PENDANT OF THE QIRAJI GUARDIAN	Neck	17 STA, 12 STR, 11 AGI
Equip: Increased Defense by 6.		
RING OF SWARMING THOUGHT	Finger	
Equip: Increases damage and healing done by magical spells and effects by up to 26 while decreasing the magical resistances of your spell targets by 20.		
STAFF OF THE QIRAJI PROPHETS	Staff	59.1 DPS, 26 INT, 21 STA, 8 SPI, 10 Fire Resistance, 10 Nature Resistance, 10 Frost Resistance, 10 Shadow Resistance, 10 Arcane Resistance
Equip: Gives a chance when your harmful spells land to reduce the magical resistances of your spell targets by 50 for 8 seconds while increasing damage and healing done by magical spells and effects by up to 56.		

LORD KRI, PRINCESS YAUJ, VEM

This is either a simple fight, or an extremely challenging one, depending on how you choose to do it. Each of the three share a loot table, but each has it's own unique loot as well that will *only* come into play if they are defeated *last*. Depending on which you decide to destroy last, the level of challenge increases dramatically.

VEM'S ABILITIES

Knock Away: Vem often knocks a tank away and attacks the person second on his aggro list. The simple solution to this is to have two tanks on him.

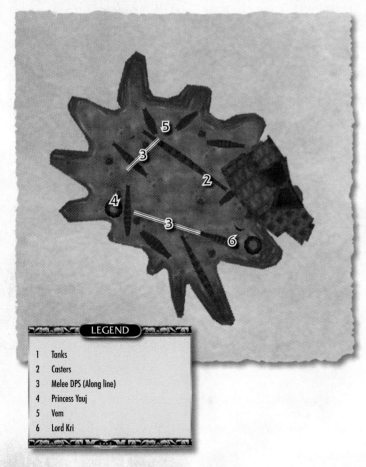

LEGEND

1	Tanks
2	Casters
3	Melee DPS (Along line)
4	Princess Yauj
5	Vem
6	Lord Kri

PRINCESS YAUJ'S ABILITIES

Fear: More often than you'd like, Yauj emits a pulse of fear into the raid causing everyone to run around in a state of panic for 8 seconds. When she does this she usually drops aggro on the player tanking her and rushes at a caster. To save that poor soul and avoid her wrath, have a secondary tank ready to taunt her immediately and take her back to her position until another Fear occurs. The tank that was previously tanking her should switch positions with the new tank and join the casters to prepare.

Greater Heal: With its 2-second casting time, this spell begs to be interrupted and you must do so. Mortal Strike will halve the effects of the 70-80k hit point heal, but it's best to interrupt this.

Ravage: The player tanking her is knocked off their feet for a few seconds and remains unable to act or move.

Vengeance: If Vem is killed and either of the other two bosses (or both) are still alive, they increase their physical damage by 100% and their attack speed by 150%.

Ten Yauj Brood spawn when Princess Yauj is killed. Each Brood has a Headbutt ability that deals 250 damage and interrupts spellcasting. AoE spells and some quick shields and heals on your Mages and Warlocks save the day here.

LORD KRI'S ABILITIES

Cleave: Hits primary target and up to three additional targets in his frontal arc for base damage +189. Keep all other melee combatants behind him to avoid this.

Thrash: Chance to get two additional attacks.

Toxic Cloud: When Lord Kri expires, he leaves behind a cloud of fatal, noxious gas that inflicts 2000 Nature damage per second. Avoid it at all costs.

Toxic Volley: Kri constantly assaults the raid with bolts of poison that deal 500 initial damage and apply a stackable DoT that hits for 150 every 2 sec. per application. *Poison Cleansing is a must!* Things will be made easier if you have access to Greater Nature Protection Potions as well.

Vengeance: See entry under Princess Yauj.

STRATEGY

Vem Last: This is the easiest of all paths to take and recommended to those new to the battle. Position your raid as shown on the map and initiate the pull. Quickly dispatch of Lord Kri and keep away from his Poison Cloud.

Yauj takes a little work to bring down, but with some good tank transitions during the fear, you should be just fine. Use area spells on her spawns and move onto Vem.

When only Vem is last, have your entire raid form around him as close as possible, so that he never runs off towards a far away caster. This also ensures that your Warriors can keep him constantly taunted in place. Burn away at his health and Vem soon falls.

Princess Yauj Last: This scenario might take a little practice, but is not too overly difficult. Start out the fight much as you always would, quickly eliminating Kri, and then move into close position around Vem.

Yauj consumes Kri at this point. Keep two or three tanks on Vem at all times to keep him taunted into submission and have the rest of the tanks keeping the Princess busy. At this point you want to target Vem with ranged attacks while all Rogues pile on Yauj, kicking her when her claws begin to glow golden to interrupt her heal. Keeping her from healing is key at this point. You cannot defeat her or Vem without preventing her from healing. Use Fear Ward and Tremor Totems to ensure that a few Rogues and Warriors can interrupt during a fear. When Vem dies Yauj rushes over to consume him and gains the Vengeance ability.

At this point, the battle becomes a matter of keeping the tanks healed through her damage, transitioning through the fears, and interrupting every one of her heals. Do this successfully and victory is yours.

Lord Kri Last: This is an extremely difficult path to take, but some of the best loot comes from following it. Begin the battle by quickly taking down Princess Yauj while cleansing Kri's Toxic Volley. The key here is speed, as it can be difficult to keep up with the amount of damage Kri inflicts over an area.

Once the Princess falls, have your raid crowd around Vem and dispatch of him as quickly as possible. By this point, you'll be straining to keep up with the Toxic Volley. When Vem dies, Kri sprints over and consumes him, completely dropping aggro on the previous tank and gaining the Vengeance ability.

Have your MT prepare to use Shield Wall, a Rejuvenating Gem, and the Last Stand ability. Once they're down, you'll need to have a tank rotation in place with each tank prepared to do follow the same process. There are other methods for mitigating the physical damage as well. Using the Wail of the Banshee trinket and Lesser Invulnerability Potions is an option. Thunderclap (if your tank isn't using Thunderfury) and Improved Demoralizing Shout also help. Paladins can cast Blessing of Protection if necessary.

Trying to heal through this amount of damage is difficult. Make sure to know the tank rotation and prepare to assist the new tank in any and all ways possible. DPS should be hard at work trying to bring down this beast and should be unleashing their full potential from all fronts. Lord Kri doesn't have much health, so taking him down before you run out of tanks is the way to win. Good luck!

PRINCESS YUAJ'S DROPS

ITEM	DESC	STATS
ANGELISTA'S TOUCH	Finger	17 STA, 11 STR
Equip: Increases the chance to dodge an attack by 1 percent, also increases defense by 6.		
BILE-COVERED GAUNTLETS	Leather Hands	203 ARM, 17 AGI, 21 STA, 10 STR, 20 Nature Resistance
CAPE OF THE TRINITY	Cloth Back	57 ARM, 17 STA, 12 INT
Equip: Increases damage and healing done by magical spells and effects by up to 21.		
GUISE OF THE DEVOURER	Leather Head	250 ARM, 36 STA, 19 AGI, 17 STR
Equip: Increases the chance to dodge an attack by 1 percent.		
IMPERIAL QIRAJI ARMAMENTS	Quest Item	
IMPERIAL QIRAJI REGALIA	Quest Item	
MANTLE OF THE DESERT CRUSADE	Plate Shoulder	642 ARM, 20 INT, 17 STA, 10 STR, 6 AGI
Equip: Increases healing done by spells and effects by up to 44.		
MANTLE OF THE DESERT'S FURY	Mail Shoulder	362 ARM, 20 INT, 17 STA, 6 STR
Equip: Increases damage and healing done by magical spells and effects by up to 28.		
MANTLE OF PHRENIC POWER	Cloth Shoulder	87 ARM, 20 INT, 20 STA
Equip: Increases damage done by Fire spells and effects by up to 33.		
ROBES OF THE TRIUMVIRATE	Cloth Chest	114 ARM, 22 INT, 21 STA, 30 Nature Resistance
Equip: Restores 7 mana per 5 seconds		
TERNARY MANTLE	Cloth Shoulder	86 ARM, 17 INT, 20 SPI, 12 STA
Equip: Increases healing done by spells and effects by up to 44.		
TRIAD GIRDLE	Plate Waist	476 ARM, 26 STR, 19 AGI, 17 STA
UKKO'S RING OF DARKNESS	Finger	13 STA, 20 Shadow Resistance
Equip: Restores 5 health per 5 seconds.		

VEM'S DROPS

ITEM	DESC	STATS
ANGELISTA'S CHARM	Neck	14 INT, 13 STA
Equip: Increases healing done by spells and effects by up to 31 while restoring 6 mana per 5 seconds.		
ANGELISTA'S TOUCH	Finger	17 STA, 11 STR
Equip: Increases the chance to dodge an attack by 1 percent, also increases Defense by 6.		
BOOTS OF THE FALLEN HERO	Plate Feet	581 ARM, 20 STR, 14 AGI, 22 STA
Equip: Improves the chance to hit by 1 percent.		
CAPE OF THE TRINITY	Cloth Back	57 ARM, 17 STA, 12 INT
Equip: Increases damage and healing done by magical spells and effects by up to 21.		
GLOVES OF EBRU	Leather Hands	139 ARM, 15 INT, 15 STA
Equip: Increases damage and healing done by magical spells and effects by up to 27, also improves the chance to get a critical strike with spells by 1 percent.		
GUISE OF THE DEVOURER	Leather Head	250 ARM, 36 STA, 19 AGI, 17 STR
Equip: Increases the chance to dodge an attack by 1 percent.		
IMPERIAL QIRAJI ARMAMENTS	Quest Item	
IMPERIAL QIRAJI REGALIA	Quest Item	
OOZE-RIDDEN GAUNTLETS	Plate Hands	529 ARM, 20 STA, 13 STR, 25 Nature Resistance
ROBES OF THE TRIUMVIRATE	Cloth Chest	114 ARM, 22 INT, 21 STA, 30 Nature Resistance
Equip: Restores 7 mana per 5 seconds		
TERNARY MANTLE	Cloth Shoulder	86 ARM, 17 INT, 20 SPI, 12 STA
Equip: Increases healing done by spells and effects by up to 44.		
TRIAD GIRDLE	Plate Waist	476 ARM, 26 STR, 19 AGI, 17 STA

LORD KRI'S DROPS

ITEM	DESC	STATS
ANGELISTA'S TOUCH	Finger	17 STA, 11 STR
Equip: Increases the chance to dodge an attack by 1 percent, also increases defense by 6.		
CAPE OF THE TRINITY	Cloth Back	57 ARM, 17 STA, 12 INT
Equip: Increases damage and healing done by magical spells and effects by up to 21.		
GUISE OF THE DEVOURER	Leather Head	250 ARM, 36 STA, 19 AGI, 17 STR
Equip: Increases the chance to dodge an attack by 1 percent.		
IMPERIAL QIRAJI REGALIA	Quest Item	
IMPERIAL QIRAJI ARMAMENTS	Quest Item	
PETRIFIED SCARAB	Trinket	
Use: Increases the spell resistances by 100 for 60 seconds. Every time a hostile spell lands on you, this bonus is reduced by 10 resistance.		
RING OF THE DEVOURED	Finger	13 INT, 10 STA
Equip: Increases healing done by spells and effects by up to 15 while restoring 8 mana per 5 seconds.		
ROBES OF THE TRIUMVIRATE	Cloth Chest	114 ARM, 22 INT, 21 STA, 30 Nature Resistance
Equip: Restores 7 mana per 5 seconds.		
TERNARY MANTLE	Cloth Shoulder	86 ARM, 17 INT, 20 SPI, 12 STA
Equip: Increases healing done by spells and effects by up to 44.		
TRIAD GIRDLE	Plate Waist	476 ARM, 26 STR, 19 AGI, 17 STA
VEST OF SWIFT EXECUTION	Leather Chest	229 ARM, 41 AGI, 21 STR, 20 STA
WAND OF QIRAJI NOBILITY	Wand	102.2 DPS, 5 STA
Equip: Increases damage and healing done by magical spells and effects by up to 19.		

◉ BATTLEGUARD SATURA

Battleguard Satura is a battle of control. Every aspect of this fight must be managed and controlled perfectly in order to ensure success.

Position your raid as shown on the map and have a Hunter pull one of her guards to the raid. In the meantime, two other Hunters should do their best to keep the other two guards busy using Scatter Shot and Distracting Shot. These Hunters require heals, so don't forget about them!

The guards randomly send tanks flying away as they try to establish aggro, so it takes more than one Warrior taunting them as they are defeated one by one. The guards also often spin around in a heavily damaging Whirlwind. Make sure they stay away from the casters at all times! When all three guards have been defeated the raid can turn its attention to Satura herself.

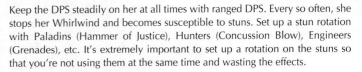

SATURA'S ABILITIES

Berserk: After 10 minutes, regardless of her health, Satura will enter a nearly unstoppable state of damage.

Enrage: Satura gains this ability at 20% health and increases her damage by 124 and her attack speed by 60%.

Sundering Cleave: This is much like a Warrior's Cleave, but it also reduces the target's armor by 1512.

Whirlwind: For most of the encounter, Satura will be in her Whirlwind state, dealing severe area damage to anyone around her. During this time, she ignores all rules of aggro and goes where she pleases. If she decides to charge into the middle of a group of cloth wearers, it's there doom. To avoid this from happening, set up a Taunt rotation with three Warriors coordinating their Taunts to keep her in place as much as possible.

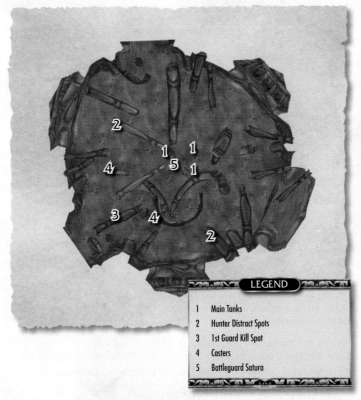

Keep the DPS steadily on her at all times with ranged DPS. Every so often, she stops her Whirlwind and becomes susceptible to stuns. Set up a stun rotation with Paladins (Hammer of Justice), Hunters (Concussion Blow), Engineers (Grenades), etc. It's extremely important to set up a rotation on the stuns so that you're not using them at the same time and wasting the effects.

Have the Rogues run in while she's stunned for the few seconds and deal as much damage as possible. Remember to get out of her range before she begins to use her Whirlwind again! If the battle continues on for more than 10 minutes, Satura deals immense damage while in her Berserk state and this will likely spell doom for your raid.

DROPS

ITEM	DESC	STATS
BADGE OF THE SWARMGUARD	Trinket	
Use: Gives a chance on melee or ranged attack to proc an armor penetration effect on you for 30 seconds, lowering the target's physical armor by 200 to your own attacks. The armor penetration effect can be applied up to 6 times.		
CREEPING VINE HELM	Leather Head	183 ARM, 26 STA, 23 INT, 17 SPI
Equip: Increases healing done by spells and effects by up to 59.		
GAUNTLETS OF STEADFAST DETERMINATION	Plate Hands	535 ARM, 20 STA, 19 STR, 18 AGI
Equip: Increased Defense by 9.		
GLOVES OF ENFORCEMENT	Leather Hands	140 ARM, 20 AGI, 28 ATR, 6 STA
Equip: Improves the chance to hit by 1 percent.		
IMPERIAL QIRAJI ARMAMENTS	Quest Item	
IMPERIAL QIRAJI REGALIA	Quest Item	
LEGGINGS OF THE FESTERING SWARM	Cloth Legs	101 ARM, 23 INT, 17 STA
Equip: Increases damage done by Fire spells and effects by up to 57.		
LEGPLATES OF BLAZING LIGHT	Plate Legs	749 ARM, 9 STR, 23 INT, 17 STA
Equip: Increases healing done by spells and effects by up to 68, also improves the chance to get a critical strike with spells by 1 percent.		
NECKLACE OF PURITY	Necklace	13 INT, 9 STA, 20 Nature Resistance
Equip: Increases damage and healing done by magical spells and effects by up to 8.		
RECOMPOSED BOOTS	Cloth Feet	80 ARM, 21 STA, 13 INT, 20 Nature Resistance
Equip: Increases damage and healing done by magical spells and effects by up to 20.		
ROBES OF THE BATTLEGUARD	Cloth Chest	116 ARM, 23 STA, 17 INT, 8 SPI
Equip: Increases damage and healing done by magical spells and effects by up to 36, also decreases the magical resistances of your spell targets by 20.		
SILITHID CLAW	Main Hand Fist Weapon	57.5 DPS
Equip: Improves the chance to get a critical strike by 1 percent, also increases attack power by 30.		
SATURA'S MIGHT	Held In Hand	6 INT, 6 STA
Equip: Increases healing done by spells and effects by up to 51, also restores 5 mana per 5 seconds.		
SCALED LEGGINGS OF QIRAJI FURY	Legs	422 ARM, 23 INT, 20 STA
Equip: Increases damage and healing done by magical spells and effects by up to 36, also improves the chance to get a critical strike with spells by 1 percent.		
THICK QIRAJIHIDE BELT	Leather Belt	186 ARM, 20 ATA, 17 AGI, 10 STR
Equip: Increases the chance to parry an attack by 1 percent.		

FANKRISS THE UNYIELDING

Fankriss is a chaotic battle to say the least. It requires a combination of superb crowd control, split second reactions, and some incredible DPS. All in all, however, it is not one of the more challenging battles in the Temple of Ahn'Qiraj and can be learned quickly.

Make sure Fankriss is tanked in the middle of the room to avoid drawing aggro from the Drones in the Hive Tunnel. The battle starts off slowly and rapidly evolves into a bath of carnage and slaughter.

First of all, you want to use two tanks on Fankriss. Fankriss applies a debuff on whomever is tanking him reducing all heals by a certain percentage. This debuff can stack up to ten times for a total of 100% rendering all heals useless. Have one Warrior tank him until he has roughly four or five stacks of this debuff and then trade the aggro off to the second tank. Once the second tank has aggro, he becomes the target of the debuffs while the first tank's debuffs fade away. This continues the entire battle, both tanks trading aggro back and forth, until Fankriss is dead.

The rest of the raid should be dealing as much damage to Fankriss as possible during this time. However, there are times that everyone has to react immediately and do something completely different. During the fight, smaller bugs swarm the raid group. Warlocks, Priests, and Warriors should use their fear ability every chance they get to assist in controlling the swarm. Paladins can also use the Consecration ability to draw a bit of the aggro upon themselves, giving the other casters a break from the constant barrage of attacks. Warriors that are not tanking Fankriss should be using two-handed weapons or dual wielding: using Cleave and Whirlwind whenever possible.

The final and deadliest aspect of this encounter is the Spawns of Fankriss. These massive worms come out periodically and attack the raid. *All* DPS must be immediately shifted to these beasts to eliminate them as quickly as possible. Have a couple of your Warriors put away their off-hand weapons and two-handers and switch to tanking mode to deal with the Spawns. Should they survive for longer than 10 seconds, they enter a state of enrage, dealing 11,000 damage plus per hit. It can get ugly real fast.

Keep the damage strong on Fankriss, transition the tanks properly, control the swarm, and eliminate the spawns with haste and the fight will be over in a matter of minutes. Make sure you have a Soulstone, Reincarnation, or Divine Intervention going near the end of the fight, as sometimes the waves of bugs wipe out the raid group after Fankriss dies!

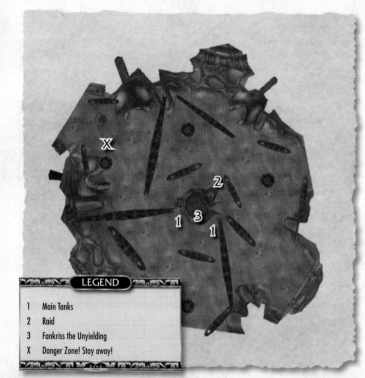

LEGEND

1	Main Tanks
2	Raid
3	Fankriss the Unyielding
X	Danger Zone! Stay away!

DROPS

ITEM	DESC	STATS
ANCIENT QIRAJI RIPPER	One-Hand Sword	58.4 DPS, 11 STA
Equip: Improves the chance to get a critical strike by 1 percent also raises attack power by 20.		
BARB OF THE SAND REAVER	Two-Hand Polearm	76.1 DPS, 41 AGI, 31 STA
BARBED CHOKER	Neck	10 STA
Equip: Improves the chance to get a critical strike by 1 percent also raises attack power by 44.		
CLOAK OF UNTOLD SECRETS	Cloth Back	59 ARM, 21 STA, 20 Shadow Resistance
FETISH OF THE SAND REAVER	Trinket	
Use: Reduces the threat you generate by 70 percent for 20 seconds.		
HIVE TUNNELER'S BOOTS	Leather Feet	216 ARM, 30 STA, 17 AGI, 10 STR
IMPERIAL QIRAJI REGALIA	Quest Item	
IMPERIAL QIRAJI ARMAMENTS	Quest Item	
LIBRAM OF GRACE	Relic	
Equip: Reduces the mana cost of the Cleanse spell by 25.		
MANTLE OF WICKED REVENGE	Leather Shoulder	170 ARM, 30 AGI, 16 STR, 14 STA
PAULDRONS OF THE UNRELENTING	Plate Shoulder	650 ARM, 30 STA, 11 STR
Equip: Increases defense by 9 and the chance to dodge an attack by 1 percent.		
ROBES OF THE GUARDIAN SAINT	Cloth Chest	117 ARM, 20 STA, 22 INT
Equip: Increases healing done by spells and effects by up to 70 while restoring 7 mana per 5 seconds.		
SCALED SAND REAVER LEGGINGS	Mail Legs	427 ARM, 23 STA, 10 INT
Equip: +62 Attack Power, Improves the chance to get a critical strike by 2 percent.		
SILITHID CARAPACE CHESTGUARD	Plate Chest	867 ARM, 23 STA, 17 STR, 14 AGI, 35 Nature Resistance
TOTEM OF LIFE		
Equip: Increases healing done by Lesser Healing Wave by up to 45.		

VISCIDUS

The battle with Viscidus is one of the more creative encounters you will face in the World of Warcraft. The fight is almost completely based around ice attacks, so obviously, the more Mages you have, the better off you are.

Everyone should be wearing a little bit of nature resistance for this encounter. (Carrying a few nature resistance potions wouldn't hurt either!) Circle your raid around Viscidus as shown on the map and unleash as many ice based attacks as you can upon him. Melee can use Frost Oil or Frost-proc weapons to compensate for their lack of spells while other casters use ice damage based wands. Mages should use their Rank 1 Frost Bolt, Frost Nova, and Cone of Cold to freeze Viscidus as quickly as possible. The lower rank Frost Bolt has a shorter recast time. Don't worry about the damage, focus on getting Viscidus into the freeze state.

Anyone that can cleanse poison should be doing it actively as much as possible since Viscidus casts a Poison Volley that can deal heavy nature damage if left uncleansed. Viscidus also has Poison Shock, an instant attack that deals Nature damage to the primary target, and Summon Toxic Slime. This creates long-lasting poison patches that deal 1313-1687 Nature damage every 2 sec. and slows movement to 40%. These should be avoided at all costs. To counter this, have the MT drag Viscidus around and keep him mobile during the entire fight.

The goal here is to freeze him solid. The longer you assault him with ice attacks the slower he attacks and move. When you see the message that he is slowing, you are half way to a frozen state. Keep up the ice attacks!

Eventually he is frozen solid. At this point *everyone*, melee, ranged, and caster, must close in upon him and use melee attacks. This shatters him into an army of smaller blobs. Use main assist and destroy as many as possible while they make their way to the center to reform Viscidus. Depending on how many blobs you slay, a certain percentage is taken away from Viscidus. Spread out and do it again and again!

Eventually he becomes smaller and smaller, spawning less and less blobs when shattered. Keep whittling away at him and turn him into an icy pool of loot!

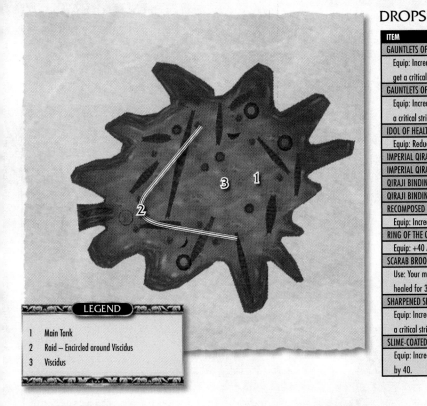

DROPS

ITEM	DESC	STATS
GAUNTLETS OF KALIMDOR	Mail Hands	309 ARM, 14 STR, 13 INT, 10 SPI, 15 STA
Equip: Increases damage and healing done by magical spells and effects by up to 20 while improving the chance to get a critical strike with spells by 1 percent.		
GAUNTLETS OF THE RIGHTEOUS CHAMPION	Plate Hands	549 ARM, 15 STR, 13 INT, 17 STA, 10 SPI
Equip: Increases damage and healing done by magical spells and effects by up to 16, also improves the chance to get a critical strike by 1 percent.		
IDOL OF HEALTH	Relic	
Equip: Reduces the casting time of your Healing Touch spell by 0.15 seconds.		
IMPERIAL QIRAJI ARMAMENTS	Quest Item	
IMPERIAL QIRAJI REGALIA	Quest Item	
QIRAJI BINDINGS OF COMMAND	Quest Item	
QIRAJI BINDINGS OF DOMINANCE	Quest Item	
RECOMPOSED BOOTS	Cloth Feet	80 ARM, 21 STA, 13 INT, 20 Nature Resistance
Equip: Increases damage and healing done by magical spells and effects by up to 20.		
RING OF THE QIRAJI FURY	Finger	12 STA
Equip: +40 Attack Power. Equip: Improves the chance to get a critical strike by 1 percent.		
SCARAB BROOCH	Trinket	
Use: Your magical heals provide the target with a shield that absorbs damage equal to 15 percent of the amount healed for 30 seconds.		
SHARPENED SILITHID FEMUR	Main Hand Sword	41.1 DPS, 7 INT, 14 STA
Equip: Increases damage and healing done by magical spells and effects by up to 72, also improves the chance to get a critical strike with spells by 1 percent.		
SLIME-COATED LEGGINGS	Mail Legs	432 ARM, 28 STA, 16 INT, 28 Nature Resistance
Equip: Increases damage and healing done by magical spells and effects by up to 11, also increases attack power by 40.		

PRINCESS HUHURAN

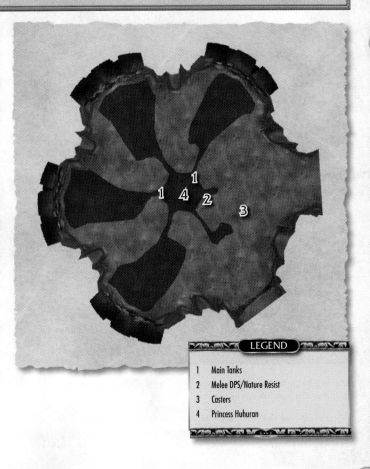

Princess Huhuran is the first real gear dependant boss in the instance. You want to have every Rogue and Warrior in your raid decked out in as much nature resistance armor as possible. Warriors should have over 250 buffed and everyone else should shoot for around 200 buffed. The best nature resistance gear can be found from the four Green Dragons, Maraudon, and Cenarion Circle reputation patterns.

When the battle begins, have two tanks at the front. Keep her turned away from the raid at all times. The 15 players closest to Huhuran should be in their full Nature Resistance gear and take up their positions immediately. Her Poison Bolt Volley is going to constantly hit those 15 players. The casters and remaining players will then move into position behind the Princess.

PRINCESS HUHURAN'S ABILITIES

Frenzy: Huhuran begins to hit harder and attack faster. Hunters with Tranquilizing Shot need to be ready to get rid of this fast.

Poison Bolt Volley: The Princess sends forth a series of poison bolts, dealing medium damage and silencing the target. This damage and effect is *only* be applied to the closest 15 players to Huhuran. The closest 15 should be the ones wearing their Nature Resistance gear.

Wyvern Sting: This hits all players in a small AoE around the target. Make sure to spread out as much as possible from your allies to avoid having groups of your raid become stung. Those affected are put to sleep for the short duration or until hit by physical damage. The MT is going to get hit and reawakened, removing the debuff, so that's not too much of a problem. However, the Wyvern Sting *must* live out its *full* duration on all other players! If it's removed by a raid member, the infected person immediately receives 4000 damage.

Princess Huhuran is a simple fight until she reaches 30%. Keep the DPS steady on her at all times, but do not overdo it. The tanks cannot ever lose aggro. Huhuran applies nature based damage overtime to the main tank that stacks. If this stacks too much that tank dies. In order to avoid this, the main tank should stop building aggro until the secondary tank can pull Huhuran off of him or her. At that point, the secondary tank will hold aggro on the Princess until the first tank's debuff has expired. Once that has happened, the main tank should again begin to build aggro on Huhuran until they are the new target of her aggro. This continues the entire fight.

When she reaches 30%, she panics and begins to unleash a flurry of poison bolts onto the closest fifteen players. Prayer of Healing is a must here, as well as high nature resistance. When she enters this state the battle turns into a game of kill or be killed. Do not hold back on DPS! Bring her down as fast as possible!

DROPS

ITEM	DESC	STATS
CLOAK OF THE GOLDEN HIVE	Cloth Back	59 ARM, 19 STA, 13 STR, 10 AGI
Equip: Increased Defense by 6.		
GLOVES OF THE MESSIAH	Cloth Hands	74 ARM, 17 INT, 13 STA
Equip: Increases healing done by spells and effects by up to 26 while restoring 10 mana per 5 seconds.		
HIVE DEFILER WRISTGUARDS	Plate Wrist	384 ARM, 23 STR, 18 AGI
HUHURAN'S STINGER	Bow	46.3 DPS, 18 AGI
IMPERIAL QIRAJI ARMAMENTS	Quest Item	
IMPERIAL QIRAJI REGALIA	Quest Item	
QIRAJI BINDINGS OF COMMAND	Quest Item	
QIRAJI BINDINGS OF DOMINANCE	Quest Item	
RING OF THE MARTYR	Finger	10 STA
Equip: Increases healing done by spells and effects by up to 51 c 5 mana per 5 seconds.		
WASPHIDE GAUNTLETS	Leather Hands	143 ARM, 16 SPI, 15 INT, 14 STA
Equip: Increases healing done by spells and effects by up to 53.		

THE TWIN EMPERORS

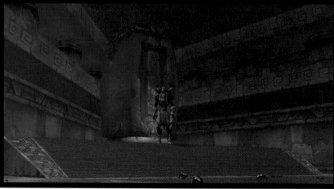

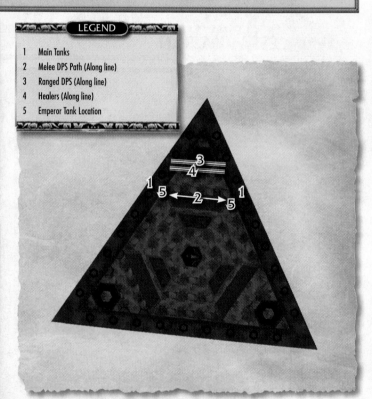

LEGEND

1 Main Tanks
2 Melee DPS Path (Along line)
3 Ranged DPS (Along line)
4 Healers (Along line)
5 Emperor Tank Location

This is a battle that requires flawless execution to win. Discipline will be tested in this encounter like none other.

Pre-position the raid as shown on the map and begin the pull. Use a Hunter to pull Vek'nilash to a waiting Warrior and use a Warlock to secure aggro on Vek'lor. To defeat these enemies you must understand and be able to react to all of their attacks.

EMPEROR VEK'LOR'S ABILITIES

Blizzard: Vek'lor casts this icy spell over a large area. Anyone caught in the storm takes heavy damage that usually turns fatal. Whoever is in the Blizzard area, should exit immediately.

Shadow Bolt: Vek'lor's main attack, this deals heavy shadow damage to a single target. He casts this at whoever is closest to him at the time. This must be the tank! Nobody else can be in range or his aggro becomes chaotic and unpredictable.

Arcane Burst: If Vek'lor has targets close to him, he emits a deadly burst of arcane energy sending anyone in range flying away. This must *never* happen! It not only usually kills the tank near him, but it knocks him or her away causing them to either lose aggro or be out of range of healing spells, only to be finished off by a Shadow Bolt.

Explode Bug: Periodically Emperor Vek'lor forces a nearby insect to explode dealing a high amount of fire damage over a wide area. The bug's legs glow red for a few moments before this happens, so if the tank is near it when this happens he or she should have enough time to avoid it.

Twin Teleport: Vek'lor instantly trades places with his brother.

Twin Heal: If Vek'lor is too close to Vek'nilash both of them begin to heal a large amount of health. If this happens the battle is pretty much over. Keeping them separated the entire time is the key to success.

EMPEROR VEK'NILASH'S ABILITIES

Unbalancing Strike: This attack not only deal extreme damage to the tank, but also reduces his or her defense skill by 100. It is incredibly important that both tanks have over 400 defense skill during this battle. Should they drop below 400, they'll take too much damage to heal through.

Uppercut: Vek'nilash randomly turns and attacks someone in his melee range, dealing damage and knocking them away. When this happens, that player needs to immediately bandage before going back into attack. All melee DPS must be at full health while attacking lest they take another Uppercut, ultimately killing them.

Mutate Bug: Emperor Vek'nilash causes a nearby insect to grow to a gigantic size and attack the raid. Having two tanks in the raid ready to pick up aggro on any of these bugs is crucial. It is the job of all casters to eliminate these bugs as they come.

Twin Teleport: Vek'nilash trades places with his brother.

Twin Heal: If Vek'nilash is too close to Vek'lor both of them begin to heal a large amount of health.

STRATEGY

The first thing that needs to be mentioned is that this is a long fight. Do not rush here. Perfect execution outweighs any sort of speed. The majority of your casters should position themselves on the stairs, healing the main tanks and defeating enraged bugs. If Vek'lor unleashes a Blizzard upon the stairs, you must react fast or you will be killed. It is not a terrible idea to have a Frost Resistance potion active during this battle, but it is not necessary.

There is an aspect of discipline that must be observed during this fight that can be hard for some players to grasp. *There should be NO area attacks used whatsoever.* No Blizzard, no Whirlwind, no Cleave, no hostile totems, no Rain of Fire! Nothing! If an area spell is used, it usually hits one of the small neutral bugs. If this happens, all bugs in that area aggro. Each of their attacks stacks a deadly poison that gets out of control fast. If the neutral bugs should aggro, do not give up hope. Gather them up and use a quick barrage of AoE spells to eliminate them before anymore can aggro.

All damage classes are going to play extremely crucial roles during this battle. There's a setup for each of the Emperors and it needs to be executed perfectly. Each Emperor must be controlled at all times. Every 30 seconds, both Emperors teleport, trading positions. When this happens, anyone close to them becomes the new target of their aggro.

Vek'nilash: Have a Warriors tank him, but make sure they have over 400 defense each. Vek'nilash instantly lowers their defense by 100. Once aggro's solidified on the MT, have the Melee DPS jump in and begin to crush Vek'nilash. Other than that, Emperor Vek'nilash can be tanked as would any boss. Make sure that when tanking him, the Warrior's back is to a wall to prevent them from flying backwards. When the teleport time of 30 seconds is closing in, have a second Warrior head over to the opposite teleport point to pick up the aggro as soon as Vek'nilash appears. Continue this switching off of tanks and spots.

Vek'lor: Vek'lor is immune to physical damage and this is where the Warlocks come into play. Make sure they're Soul-Linked to their Voidwalkers since they're going to be tanking Vek'lor. As soon as Vek'lor appears at the teleport spot, have everyone clear out and have the Warlock assigned to that teleport point begin chain-casting Searing Pain to draw his Shadow Bolt. If anyone's close to Vek'lor, he begins casting Arcane Burst and that'll pretty much wipe anyone out. Shadow Resistance is helpful here, but armor and defense won't do a thing against Vek'lor's Shadow Bolts. Make sure that the tanking Warlock for each point is known and healed throughout the 30-second attack period and don't forget about their pet!

When the Emperors cast Twin Teleport, one tank should already be at the spot to receive Vek'nilash and the other tank should be vacating the other in preparation for the Warlock to begin hitting Vek'lor from range. Allow both the Warrior and Warlock for each side to cement aggro before the rest of the raid begins attacking. Magical, ranged DPS should help out with Vek'lor and all physical DPS should be on Vek'nilash.

The Emperors share life, so if one falls, so does the other. Remember, it's a long battle, but do *not* let it carry on over the 15-minute mark. If they're both alive at that point, they'll use their Berserk abilities and that's almost a guaranteed wipe. You must deal just over 1.7 million damage in under 15 minutes to bring these two down!

EMPEROR VEK'LOR'S DROPS

ITEM	DESC	STATS
BOOTS OF EPIPHANY	Cloth Feet	84 ARM, 19 INT, 18 STA
Equip: Increases damage and healing done by magical spells and effects up to 34.		
IMPERIAL QIRAJI ARMAMENTS	Quest Item	
IMPERIAL QIRAJI REGALIA	Quest Item	
QIRAJI EXECUTION BRACERS	Leather Wrist	103 ARM, 16 AGI, 15 STR, 14 STA
Equip: Improves the chance to hit by 1 percent.		
RING OF EMPEROR VEK'LOR	Finger	100 ARM, 18 STA, 12 AGI
Equip: Increased Defense by 9.		
ROYAL QIRAJI BELT	Plate Waist	512 ARM, 22 STA, 13 STR, 13 AGI
Equip: Increases the chance to parry an attack by 1 percent, also Increases Defense by 8.		
ROYAL SCEPTER OF VEK'LOR	Held In Hand	9 INT, 10 STA
Equip: Improves the chance of a critical strike with spells by 1 percent, also improves the chance to hit with spells by 1 percent while increasing damage and healing done by magical spells and effects up to 20.		
VEK'LOR'S DIADEM	Quest Item	
VEK'LOR'S GLOVES OF DEVASTATION	Mail Hands	320 ARM, 22 AGI, 21 STA, 17 INT
Equip: Improves the chance to get a critical strike by 1 percent.		

EMPEROR VEK'NILASH'S DROPS

ITEM	DESC	STATS
AMULET OF VEK'NILASH	Neck	5 INT, 9 STA
Equip: Increases damage and healing done by magical spells and effects up to 27, also improves the chance to get a critical strike with spells by 1 percent.		
BELT OF THE FALLEN EMPEROR	Plate Waist	512 ARM, 17 STR, 17 STA, 18 INT, 13 AGI
Equip: Increases healing done by spells and effects up to 35.		
BRACELETS OF ROYAL REDEMPTION	Cloth Wrist	54 ARM, 10 INT, 9 SPI, 8 STA
Equip: Increases healing done by spells and effects up to 53.		
GLOVES OF THE HIDDEN TEMPLE	Leather Hands	248 ARM, 22 STA, 21 AGI, 18 STR, 6 Shadow Resistance
GRASP OF THE FALLEN EMPEROR	Mail Waist	288 ARM, 13 STR, 12 AGI, 17 INT, 17 STA
Equip: Increases damage and healing done by magical spells and effects up to 19 while restoring 5 mana per 5 seconds.		
IMPERIAL QIRAJI ARMAMENTS	Quest Item	
IMPERIAL QIRAJI REGALIA	Quest Item	
KALIMDOR'S REVENGE	Two-Hand Sword	81.9 DPS, 24 STR, 18 STA
Chance On Hit: Instantly shocks the target with lightning for 239 to 277 damage.		
REGENERATING BELT OF VEK'NILASH	Leather Waist	133 ARM, 18 INT, 13 SPI, 16 STA
Equip: Increases healing done by spells and effects up to 55.)		
VEK'NILASH'S CIRCLET	Quest Item	

Ouro is one of the most challenging battles in Ahn'Qiraj, so you definitely have your work cut out for you.

Raid positioning is key here, so take note of the map. Reacting to each of his abilities is also important, so make sure you know what to expect!

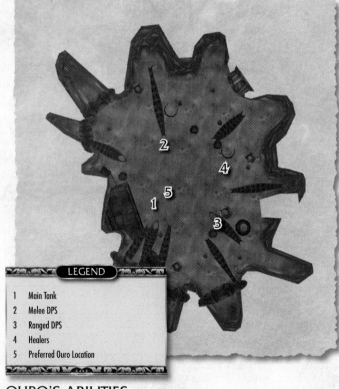

LEGEND

1	Main Tank
2	Melee DPS
3	Ranged DPS
4	Healers
5	Preferred Ouro Location

OURO'S ABILITIES

Sand Blast: This is Ouro's deadliest attack. When cast, anyone in front of him takes over 4,000 Nature damage. Try for a Nature Resistance stat of 325+ to resist this ability. In addition to the damage, the targets are stunned for a short duration. Obviously, your healers should all be wearing Nature Resistance gear and spread out so that they're not all dropped in a single blast. Healers should immediately begin to heal those hit.

Sweep: Ouro unleashes a melee attack dealing medium damage and causing anyone in range to be knocked away. When this happens to the main tank, they must immediately use Intercept to get into melee range again. If Ouro is not engaged by some sort of melee combat for five seconds he burrows under the ground prematurely, causing a great amount of havoc and taking much of the control away from you. If Intercept is on cool down, the main tank must let someone know immediately! Another Warrior or even a Feral Druid can Intercept or Feral Charge to tank him for a few moments, until the main tank is back into range. Once the main tank is back, the temporary tank should return to where he or she needs to be.

Burrow: Every one and a half minutes or three minutes, Ouro retreats underground for thirty seconds. During this time the raid will be avoiding the Dirt Quakes. Make sure the entire raid converges upon the center of the room ten seconds before he re-emerges, so that the point he chooses to burst forth from is predictable and not near a wall. If Ouro comes up by a wall, positioning can be tricky.

Dirt Mound Quake: When Ouro burrows, he sends out a series of quakes that deal a terrible amount of nature damage. Spread out and head for the walls when this happens. Just make sure you head back to the center before he emerges again.

Ground Rupture: When Ouro emerges from a burrow, anyone caught under him takes damage. This damage is rarely fatal, so just take it and get where you need to be.

Scarab Swarm: This is the tricky part. As Ouro emerges from his burrow, he spawns sixteen Scarabs. They can be taunted for a short time. They do not hit too terribly hard, so crowd control is your best bet here. Getting into position trumps everything when Ouro comes up again. Once into position, use fear to control them as best as possible while paying attention to the normal flow of the Ouro encounter. While you can defeat these Scarabs, and should try to take down a few, they actually despawn in about a minute.

Enrage: At 20%, Ouro gains a 150% attack speed increase. If Ouro's primary target pulls back out of melee range, he'll launch boulders at that player dealing roughly 6000 damage.

Remember, you only have one and a half minutes or three minutes to damage Ouro (it is randomly chosen). There is nothing you can do to force him to stay up longer. Keeping this in mind, the ranged DPS need to burn as hard as possible. Ouro will *not* move to engage someone at range, so it is impossible to pull aggro in that sense.

Melee DPS is a bit tricky. They want to avoid the Sweep ability, so they really only have a few moments to DPS Ouro. Even then, the sandworm's aggro is a bit sketchy to anyone in melee and he can easily turn on a player and obliterate them in one or two hits. It is actually best to have the melee use ranged attacks for most of the battle.

When Ouro does burrow, staying alive takes precedence over everything. Do your best to survive the Dirt Mound Quake's, drinking Nature Resistance Potions if need be and run to the middle of the room when a ten second warning is given.

When Ouro does come up, get into position as quickly as possible and do your job as you normally would. Fear the Scarabs as best as possible. If the main tank gets knocked away during Sweep and his or her Intercept is still on cool down, make sure someone is ready to rush in and engage Ouro until the main tank can get back into position.

Within three or four burrows you should have Ouro to 20%. At 20% things get nasty! Ouro *will not* burrow anymore, but he *will* unleash Dirt Mound Quakes, Sand Blasts, and Scarabs the entire time! He also gains an enormous increase to his damage. Keeping the main tank up is paramount here! Healers and ranged DPS should stay in position as best as possible, but do not stand still if a Dirt Mound Quake is heading for you. Melee DPS should now run in and engage Ouro, dealing as much damage as possible. The main tank needs to use Shield Wall while the other Warriors use Recklessness and Execute. Do not hold back here! Ouro has under 2,000,000 health, so 20% is about 400,000 damage that needs to be taken down as quickly as possible. It is not easy, but with some practice, you should be able to kill him before he kills you.

DROPS

ITEM	DESC	STATS
BASE OF ATIESH	Quest Item	
BURROWER BRACERS	Cloth Wrist	54 ARM, 13 INT, 10 STA
Equip: Increases damage and healing done by magical spells and effects by up to 28.		
DON RIGOBERTO'S LOST HAT	Cloth Head	100 ARM, 24 INT, 18 STA
Equip: Increases healing done by spells and effects by up to 64 while restoring 11 mana per 5 seconds.		
IMPERIAL QIRAJI ARMAMENTS	Quest Item	
IMPERIAL QIRAJI REGALIA	Quest Item	
OURO'S INTACT HIDE	Quest Item	
SKIN OF THE GREAT SANDWORM	Quest Item	
WORMSCALE BLOCKER	Shield	3035 ARM, 57 BLO, 13 INT, 10 STA
Equip: Increases healing done by spells and effects by up to 35 while restoring 6 mana per 5 seconds.		

EYE OF C'THUN

You have come to the very end. The Eye of the Old God is before you. His gaze can see far and he knows why you have come. Luckily for you, he is not yet at full power. The time to strike is now!

The Eye of C'thun battle is a dance of raid movement. This phase is actually not terribly difficult. In fact, once mastered, nobody should die except to a freak accident. Executing this phase with near perfection is necessary as well, since you want the majority of your raid group alive when C'thun rises…

Take note of the positioning on the map. This has to be strictly enforced for optimal survival. A simple battle, the Eye of C'thun only has a few options in his arsenal, but each is deadly.

EYE OF C'THUN'S ABILITIES

Eye Beam: If anything kills anyone, it's usually this. C'thun constantly assaults the raid with a green laser beam that deals nature damage. If this hits one person, they almost always survive. However, the trick to this beam is that it chains between players that are too close to each other and increases in damage each time it chains. If two players are near one another, one will take the normal amount of damage, and the next takes even more. Should this hit more than two players it is 100% fatal. The importance of being spaced out during this phase of C'thun cannot be stressed enough. The safety range is measured at fifteen yards.

Dark Glare: Every 45 seconds the Eye turns red, faces a certain direction, and charges up a fatal beam of deadly energy. The moment you see the beam charge up, is time to start moving. If the Eye is facing you when charging you have about 4 seconds to get out of the way. The Eye Beams stop at this point, so spacing is not necessary until the Dark Glare is finished. The Glare slowly make a path around the room in a clockwise or counter clockwise motion. Take note of where you were standing before the Dark Glare. Your group, when the Glare is over, should be in the *opposite* position of the room. After the next Dark Glare, your group should be back in its original position and so forth. This beam is deadly to anyone it touches so always play it safe. A skilled Mage can Blink through it should they so choose.

Spawn Claw Tentacle: C'thun periodically punches a small portion of a tentacle through the ground to attack a player. This initial burst causes a small amount of damage and sends the person flying away. That player *must* get back into position immediately to keep true to the spacing rule, even if they have to get into melee range of the newly spawned claw. All melee DPS in range should immediately shift over and destroy it before it can burrow underground again.

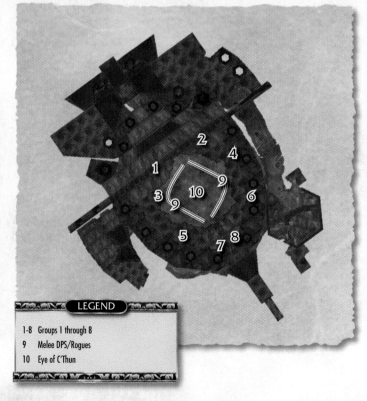

LEGEND	
1-8	Groups 1 through 8
9	Melee DPS/Rogues
10	Eye of C'thun

Spawn Eye Tentacles: Every 45 seconds C'thun summons eight Eye Tentacles that remain stationary around him. These Eyes begin to chain cast Mindflay on players dealing over 800 damage per second. The Warriors and ranged DPS classes positioned around the room should immediately take these out before they cause too much havoc. They can be silenced and interrupted. In an ideal situation, these Eye Tentacles should not stay up for more than 5 seconds. Ranged DPS can assist with these if they're taking too long to destroy. Keep in mind, when an Eye Tentacle spawns, anyone in the immediate vicinity is thrown back, possibly causing a chained Eye Beam, or in a worst case scenario, thrown into a Dark Glare. Just make sure to keep away from that area until they actually spawn.

STRATEGY

The entry is the most important part of this battle. By this time, everyone in your raid should have a Qiraji mount and everyone needs to be mounted. Whichever Warrior is placed in group one or two should be at the front of the raid, ready to go in first. Place a Power Word: Shield on him or her and have them drink a Greater Nature Protection Potion. This player is the sole target of C'thun's Eye Beams while the rest of the raid gets into position. While not completely necessary, it is highly recommended that each player drink a Greater Nature Protection Potion before entry. The entry should be the only time players are not spaced properly, so the potions provide a slight buffer. Still, getting into position fast cannot be stressed enough.

Once in position, the ranged DPS burn away at the Eye of C'thun with maximum DPS. The Eye itself has no aggro properties or way to deal damage other than the Eye Beams and Dark Glare. When Claw Tentacles and Eye Tentacles spawn it is the duty of everyone, but the ranged DPS to deal with them.

When the Dark Glare comes, shift the raid clockwise or counter clockwise accordingly. Make sure you are in position a good 5 seconds before the Glare is over. Once over, the Eye Beams begins again in full force. During the Dark Glare a few Warriors should rush into melee range with the Eye while they move and lay down five Sunder Armors, giving the Rogues a bit more DPS potential.

Repeat these steps until the Eye of C'thun shrivels and dies…you didn't think it would be that easy did you? The Old God reveals himself! C'thun rises!

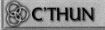
C'THUN

When the Eye of C'thun ceases to exist, the body of C'thun rises. This is an extremely long battle. Victory is determined by how fast the raid can react to the chaos around them.

Several things are similar to the Eye phase, but usually in larger and more powerful quantities. The most important difference, however, is that the spacing rules no longer apply. There is no form of Eye Beam during this phase.

The body of C'thun himself actually has no real abilities to speak of. He just sits there and watches the action from an invulnerable state. However, many things around you demand immediate and proper reaction or things can get out of hand extremely fast.

C'THUN'S ABILITIES

Spawn Giant Claw Tentacle: Once every 40 seconds, an enormous version of the Claw Tentacle spawns, dealing medium knock away damage to anyone caught above it when it surfaces. This must be tanked *immediately*! Whichever Warrior is closest should engage it within 5 seconds. If left above ground with no target for too long, it heals to full and burrows under, only to spawn again shortly, out of turn. Ranged DPS cannot pull aggro on these monstrosities, so they should attack immediately. Rogues and other melee DPS, however, should wait for aggro to be established. Defeat the Giant Claw Tentacle as quickly as possible, but do not ignore the other occurrences happening in the chamber. Claw Tentacles, while important, are actually the lowest priority of things to kill.

Spawn Giant Eye Tentacle: C'thun summons one of these every 40 seconds, but usually separately from the Claw Tentacles. The Giant Eye Tentacle is the second highest priority of killing during this battle since it can chain Eye Beams much like the Eye of C'thun did during phase one. This abomination can be stunned, interrupted, Counterspelled, spell locked, and Scatter Shotted. Do everything in your power to make sure this Eye does not cast! Save all spell control abilities and stuns for these Tentacles! It has extremely low health, so it should die quickly.

Spawn Eye Tentacles: As in phase one, C'thun summons the eight smaller Eye Tentacles around him. However, instead of coming every 45 seconds, they spawn every 30 seconds. Eliminating these are your first priority as they can cause serious havoc in the raid. While most of your DPS will be concentrated in one part of the room, taking down Giant Claws and Giant Eyes, the Mages should spread out around the room and be ready to destroy these Tentacles at a moment's notice. It cannot be stressed enough that while the majority of the raid needs to be taking down the giant adversaries, some of the DPS must be discipline enough to stay put and take these down. If left up for more than 5 seconds, your raid will die.

Consume: C'thun constantly swallows players the entire fight. Once swallowed, that person is teleported to the stomach of C'thun. While in the stomach, there are two Flesh Tentacles that need to be killed in order to make C'thun vulnerable to attacks. Some classes are better at this than others, and some have jobs that need tending to above. In fact, the only classes that should stop to damage the Flesh Tentacles are the ranged DPS classes and Rogues with Evasion available. Healers and melee should apply a DoT and take a whack before immediately stepping on the pad behind the Tentacles to resurface above. While in the stomach, players receive a debuff that deals Nature damage. The longer a player stays in the stomach, the greater the damage. Pay attention to your health and leave before it stacks too greatly. *Do not* take chances! Your raid is *much* better off with you alive! Nobody should die in the stomach, period. If these Flesh Tentacles are not destroyed together, they'll respawn after 1 minute.

As said before, this battle comes down to discipline and reaction. Destroy the Tentacles with the correct priority and things should never get too out of hand.

During this encounter, C'thun is almost completely invulnerable to damage since his Carapace ability reduces damage taken from all attacks by 99%. To weaken him, both Flesh Tentacles must be destroyed. Once eliminated, C'thun ceases to summon anything new for 45 seconds. He also takes full damage from attacks. Every moment of that 45 seconds is best used attacking C'thun.

However, it is not quite that simple. What would happen if you forced C'thun into a vulnerable state when a Giant Claw just spawned or Eye Tentacles came up at the very same time? A large portion of that forty-five seconds would be wasted destroying those Tentacles. If you were to simply ignore these Tentacles while damaging C'thun, you would not only lose a great portion of your raid, but you would be hard pressed to catch up before something new spawned after the vulnerable state was over.

When the final Flesh Tentacle is around 15% health, you want to stop all damage and DoTs. At this moment, you want to time everything perfectly. Someone will usually be in the stomach at any given time, so when the moment is right to strike, an order can be given to finish off the Flesh Tentacle. The right time is just after a Giant Claw has died, a Giant Eye Tentacle is dead or near dead, and the smaller Eye Tentacles were just eliminated. If you can bring C'thun into a weakened state when next to nothing or nothing else is alive you have a full 45 seconds to DPS him. Timing this is invaluable!

When C'thun is weakened he turns purple and an emote in your chat log appears reading, "C'thun is weakened!" If done correctly, you should only require three weakened states to claim victory. Focus on whatever task is at hand, kill Tentacles in the correct priority, and time his weakened state right and the battle is yours.

Congratulate yourself adventurer! You have slain a GOD!

DROPS

ITEM	DESC	STATS
BELT OF NEVER-ENDING AGONY	Leather Waist	142 ARM, 20 STA
Equip: +64 Attack Power, Improves the chance to get a critical strike by 1 percent, also improves the chance to hit by 1 percent.		
CARAPACE OF THE OLD GOD	Quest Item	
CLOAK OF CLARITY	Cloth Back	66 ARM, 12 INT, 7 SPI, 6 STA
Equip: Increases healing done by spells and effects by up to 40, also restores 8 mana per 5 seconds.		
CLOAK OF THE DEVOURED	Cloth Back	66 ARM, 10 INT, 11 STA
Equip: Increases damage and healing done by magical spells and effects by up to 30, also improves the chance to hit with spells by 1 percent.		
DARK EDGE OF INSANITY	Two-Hand Axe	86.6 DPS, 35 STR, 19 AGI, 25 STA
Chance On Hit: Confuses the target, causing it to wander at 40 percent of move speed for up to 3 seconds.		
DARK STORM GAUNTLETS	Cloth Hands	83 ARM, 15 INT, 19 STA
Equip: Increases damage and healing done by magical spells and effects by up to 37, also improves the chance to hit with spells by 1 percent.		
DEATH'S STING	One-Hand Dagger	66.4 DPS, 10 STA
Equip: +38 Attack Power and increases Daggers by 3.		
EYE OF C'THUN	Quest Item	
EYESTALK WAIST CORD	Cloth Waist	75 ARM, 9 INT, 10 STA
Equip: Improves the chance to get a critical strike with spells by 1 percent, also increases damage and healing done by magical spells and effects by up to 41.		
GAUNTLETS OF ANNIHILATION	Plate Hands	615 ARM, 35 STR, 15 STA
Equip: Improves the chance to get a critical strike by 1 percent, also improves the chance to hit by 1 percent.		
GRASP OF THE OLD GOD	Cloth Waist	75 ARM, 19 INT, 15 STA
Equip: Increases healing done by spells and effects by up to 59, also restores 7 mana per 5 seconds.		
HUSK OF THE OLD GOD	Quest Item	
MARK OF C'THUN	Neck	24 STA
Equip: Increased Defense by 10, also increases the chance to dodge an attack by 1 percent and improves the chance to hit by 1 percent.		
RING OF THE GODSLAYER	Finger	27 AGI, 17 STA
SCEPTER OF THE FALSE PROPHET	Main Hand Mace	41.4 DPS, 10 STA, 19 INT
Equip: Increases healing done by spells and effects by up to 187 also restores 3 mana per 5 seconds.		
VANQUISHED TENTACLE OF C'THUN	Trinket	
Use: Summons a Vanquished Tentacle to your aid for 30 seconds.		

BLACKFATHOM DEEPS

Played & Written by: Michael "Kayal" Lummis of <Dovrani> on Kirin Tor

Those who desire to see rare sights, beautiful locations, and fight dire enemies must prepare themselves for the swim into Blackfathom Deeps. These ruins are almost lost to time because of the Naga, Satyrs, and Twilight Hammer cultists who live there. The increase in power of the Twilight Hammer has been linked with this set of ruins. Whether you are Horde or Alliance, these people are your enemies and must be stopped. Look below to find out what can be done and how to destroy the blossoming evil in this former place of Elven beauty.

DUNGEON INFORMATION

Location	Ashenvale
Quests	Alliance and Horde
Region	Contested
Suggested Levels	23-28 (Full Group)
Group Allowed	5 to Quest, 10 for Raids
Primary Enemies	Beasts, Demons, and Humanoids
Time to Complete	2-2.5 Hours

GETTING TO BLACKFATHOM DEEPS

The approach to this dungeon is a simple one, and people of appropriate level can make it to the instance without even breaking a sweat. Search along the Zoram Strand in northwestern Ashenvale. Along the northern end of the beach is a massive set of ruins that are darker than the surrounding pillars littering the beach. Look inside this structure and drop into the water below; there are rocky corridors flowing inward and you won't have to stay wet for too long. Climb back up the other side of the passage and fight your way through elite Naga and Satyrs to reach the instance itself.

WHO TO BRING

Blackfathom Deeps is not as demanding on a group's dynamic as several of the later instances. Success is based more on sticking together, focusing fire, and not biting off too much at any given time. Thus, group leaders are free to invite good players without needing to keep too close of an eye on group configuration. As always, however, a solid tank is a great boon for the front of the group, a dedicated healer makes all instances easier, and it is a nice perk to have someone to cast a spell for water breathing. Try to have at least one character with dependable crowd control skills and experience, especially when planning to run the entire instance.

There are some very large fights in the Deeps, and it won't be rare to have enemy casters involved. In fact, battles with multiple casters (with two healers) happen toward the end of the instance; be prepared to run interference against such forces!

POSSIBLE GROUP MAKEUP

Tank	Warrior, Druid, Paladin
CC	Rogue, Mage
DPS	Rogue, Hunter, Mage, Warlock
Healer	Priest, Shaman, Druid
Free Slot	Anything, Though Support Classes Are Great Here

QUESTS

ALLIANCE QUESTS

QUEST NAME	QUEST GIVER	QUEST GIVER LOCATION	QUEST RECEIVER	QUEST RECEIVER LOCATION	CHAIN?	MAX EXPERIENCE
Knowledge in the Deeps	Gerrig	Ironforge	Gerrig	Ironforge	No	1,650
REWARD: Sustaining Ring (+1 STA & +4 SPI)						
The Corruption Abroad	Argos Nightwhisper	Stormwind	Gershala Nightwhisper	Auberdine	No	240
Researching the Corruption	Gershala Nightwhisper	Darkshore	Gershala Nightwhisper	Darkshore	Yes	1,450
REWARD: Prelacy Cape (Cloak: 20 Armor & +5 SPI) or Beetle Clasps (Mail Wrists: 83 Armor +2 AGI & +5 STA)						
Seeking the Kor Gem (PALADIN ONLY)	Thundris Windweaver	Darkshore	Thundris Windweaver	Darkshore	Yes	1,750
Twilight Falls	Argent Guard Manados	Darnassus	Argent Guard Manados	Darnassus	No	2,550
REWARD: Heartwood Girdle (Leather Belt: 48 Armor, +4 STA & +4 SPI) or Nimbus Boots (Cloth Feet: 27 Armor, +3 AGI & +5 SPI)						

KNOWLEDGE IN THE DEEPS

Quest Level	17 to Obtain
Location	Ironforge (Forlorn Cavern)
Quest Giver	Gerrig Bonegrip
Goal	Find and Return the Lorgalis Manuscript
Max Experience Gained	1,650
Reward	Sustaining Ring (+1 STA & +4 SPI)

This quest takes you into the instance of Blackfathom Deeps. The Manuscript that Gerrig needs is guarded by several foes under the water in the northern part of Ghamoo-ra's room. Swim toward the fully submerged cubby and fight the three Naga there (2 Myrmidons and 1 Sea Witch). The chest they're guarding has the Manuscript; return it to Gerrig for your experience and a magical ring!

THE CORRUPTION ABROAD

Quest Level	18 to Obtain
Location	Stormwind
Quest Giver	Argos Nightwhisper
Goal	Deliver a message to Argos' brother in Auberdine
Max Experience Gained	240

This is a simple primer quest to get you over to Kalimdor in preparation for the instance run. Simply deliver Argos' message to his brother in Auberdine.

RESEARCHING THE CORRUPTION

Quest Level	18 to Obtain
Location	Darkshore (Auberdine)
Quest Giver	Gershala Nightwhisper
Goal	Collect 8 Corrupted Brain Stems from Naga/Satyrs
Max Experience Gained	1,450
Reward	Prelacy Cape (Cloak: 20 Armor & +5 SPI) or Beetle Clasps (Mail Wrists: 83 Armor +2 AGI & +5 STA)

When in Stormwind City, speak to Argos Nightwhisper; he lets you know that his brother has been seeking help. The real quest begins in Auberdine, where Gershala Nightwhisper is afraid of the twisting power of demonic magic. Knowing that use of evil sorcery twisted the Naga and the Satyrs into what they are, Gershala fears the fate of the Blood Elves. To learn more, he wants you to collect eight Corrupted Brain Stems from the elite Naga and Satyrs in and around Blackfathom Deeps. Lower-level groups can take the time to do this while fighting the outer enemies before the instance, while those doing higher-level quests can accomplish this simultaneously without worrying about farming these monsters. Return to Auberdine and give Gershala the ghastly items for your reward.

SEEKING THE KOR GEM

Quest Level	20 to Obtain (PALADIN ONLY QUEST)
Location	Darkshore (Auberdine)
Quest Giver	Thundris Windweaver
Goal	Collect a Corrupted Kor Gem
Max Experience Gained	1,750

To begin this quest, you must first have completed the *Tome of Valor* quest series and have *The Test of Righteousness* in your journal.. Speak with Thundris and learn of the Gem you seek and the Naga who possess it. Travel into Ashenvale and seek Blackfathom Deeps. Blackfathom Oracles, Sea Witches, and Tide Priestesses drop the Kor Gem, and this does not take much time to complete. Return to Auberdine to finish the quest (best done while completing a number of dungeon quests, since the travel time quickly eliminates the value of the experience reward unless you have other things to do in the dungeon).

TWILIGHT FALLS

Quest Level	20 to Obtain
Location	Darnassus (Alchemist's Shop)
Quest Giver	Argent Guard Manados
Goal	Collect 10 Twilight Pendants
Max Experience Gained	2,550
Reward	Heartwood Girdle (Leather Belt: 48 Armor, +4 STA & +4 SPI) or Nimbus Boots (Cloth Feet: 27 Armor, +3 AGI & +5 SPI)

All the cultists in the Twilight Hammer are foul and dangerous, and it is clear that you need to kill them to stop their schemes. Manados understands this and wants you to wage war against the cultists deep inside Blackfathom Deeps. At the Moonshrine Ruins, there are many types of enemies (Acolytes, Reavers, Aquamancers, Loreseekers, Elementalists, and Shadowmages). All of these drop Twilight Pendants; collect ten and return to Manados to prove that you have successfully thwarted your enemy's plans.

HORDE QUESTS

QUEST NAME	QUEST GIVER	QUEST GIVER LOCATION	QUEST RECEIVER	QUEST RECEIVER LOCATION	CHAIN?	MAX EXPERIENCE
Allegiance to the Old Gods	Je'neu Sancrea	Zoram'gar Outpost	Je'neu Sancrea	Zoram'gar Outpost	Yes	3,175
REWARD: Band of the Fist (Ring: +3 STR & +3 AGI) or Chestnut Mantle (Cloth Shoulder: 30 Armor, +2 STA & +6 INT)						
Amongst the Ruins	Je'neu Sancrea	Zoram'gar Outpost	Je'neu Sancrea	Zoram'gar Outpost	Yes	2,750
Trouble in the Deeps	Tsunaman	Stonetalon Mountains (Sunrock Retreat)	Je'neu Sancrea	Ashenvale (Zoram'gar Outpost)	No	45
The Essence of Aku'Mai	Je'neu Sancrea	Zoram'gar Outpost	Je'neu Sancrea	Zoram'gar Outpost	Yes	1,800

ALLEGIANCE TO THE OLD GODS

Quest Level	20 to Obtain
Location	Ashenvale (Zoram'gar Outpost)
Quest Giver	Je'neu Sancrea
Goal	Kill Lorgus Jett
Max Experience Gained	3,175
Reward	Band of the Fist (Ring: +3 STR & +3 AGI) or Chestnut Mantle (Cloth Shoulder: 30 Armor, +2 STA & +6 INT)

This quest starts when you find a Damp Note (dropped with fair frequency by the Tide Priestesses in the pre-instance area). While returning from doing the other pre-instance quests, turn this note in to Je'neu Sancrea at the Zoram'gar Outpost. The second step of this is to kill Lorgus Jett, a follower of the Twilight Hammer cult. Lorgus is hiding out of the way inside a small, northern cubby east of Gelihast's area. Kill him and tell Je'neu of this to receive your earned reward.

TROUBLE IN THE DEEPS

Quest Level	17 to Obtain
Location	Stonetalon Mountains
Quest Giver	Tsunaman
Goal	Speak with Je'neu Sancrea in Ashenvale
Max Experience Gained	240

Get ready for a chain of quests. This is just the first in a series that takes you into the instance. Fly (or run) to the Zoram'gar Outpost on the Zoram Strand in Ashenvale to find Je'neu.

THE ESSENCE OF AKU'MAI

Quest Level	17 to Obtain
Location	Ashenvale (Zoram'gar Outpost)
Quest Giver	Je'neu Sancrea
Goal	Collect 20 Sapphires of Aku'Mai
Max Experience Gained	1,800

Tsunaman, at Sunrock Retreat in the Stonetalon Mountains, asks that you seek Je'neu at the Zoram'gar Outpost in Ashenvale. When you speak with Je'neu, you learn of the Sapphires that the Naga are mining from Blackfathom Deeps. Travel to the dungeon and collect these gems from the walls of the rock corridors that lead toward the instance. You won't need to enter the proper dungeon to complete this task. Once you have 20 of these ground spawns, return to Je'neu.

AMONGST THE RUINS

Quest Level	21 to Obtain
Location	Ashenvale (Zoram'gar Outpost)
Quest Giver	Je'neu Sancrea
Goal	Retrieve the Fathom Core
Max Experience Gained	2,750

Though the quest itself is a simple one, it won't be easy to get to the Fathom Core that Je'neu seeks. This history log of elemental activity in Blackfathom Deeps is in the water underneath the Moonshrine Ruins (fairly deep in the dungeon). Once you enter the cavern with this name, dive into the water and swim underneath the walkways above. The Fathom Core is down there, and there are elite creatures that swim about that should be cleared while heading in. Return to Zoram'gar with the Core when you are done.

There is a second aspect to this quest. Upon opening the Fathom Core, a large Water Elemental (Baron Aquanis) forms and attacks your group. As long as you have cleared the nearly elite creatures, this fight should be quite easy. A globe that is dropped by Baron Aquanis is turned in at Zoram'gar for additional experience and rewards.

SHARED QUESTS

QUEST NAME	QUEST GIVER	QUEST GIVER LOCATION	QUEST RECEIVER	QUEST RECEIVER LOCATION	CHAIN?	MAX EXPERIENCE
Blackfathom Villainy	Argent Guard Thaelrid	Blackfathom Deeps	Varies by Faction	Darnassus (Alliance Alchemy Shop)/ Elder Rise (Thunder Bluff for Horde)	No	2,400
REWARD: Arctic Buckler (Shield: 642 Armor, 13 Block, +3 STA, +8 SPI & +5 Frost Resistance) or Gravestone Scepter (Wand: 29.0 DPS, +1 SPI & +5 Shadow Resistance)						
The Orb of Soran'ruk	Doan Karhan	Barrens	Doan Karhan	Barrens	Yes	2,550
REWARD: Staff of Soran'ruk (Staff: 16.9 DPS, +6 DMG to Shadow Spells and Effects & +6 DMG to Fire Spells and Effects) or the Orb of Soran'ruk (Off-Hand: +3 DMG to Fire Spells and Effects, +3 DMG to Shadow Spells and Effects, Use: Restores 25 Health every 3 Seconds for 30 Seconds)						

BLACKFATHOM VILLAINY

Quest Level	19 to Obtain
Location	Blackfathom Deeps (Inside Instance)
Quest Giver	Argent Guard Thaelrid
Goal	Slay Kelris and Collect His Head
Max Experience Gained	2,400
Reward	Arctic Buckler (Shield: 642 Armor, 13 Block, +3 STA, +8 SPI & +5 Frost Resistance) or Gravestone Scepter (Wand: 29.0 DPS, +1 SPI & +5 Shadow Resistance)

A member of the Argent Dawn is in Blackfathom Deeps. Argent Guard Thaelrid is badly wounded and has hidden himself in a small part of Ghamoo-Ra's room. Swim to the southwestern cubby and up onto the rocks above. Thaelrid is there and asks that you slay Kelris (the local leader of the Twilight's Hammer). Kelris is meditating inside the Moonshrine Sanctum. After killing this powerful foe, bring his head back to Dawnwatcher Selgorm. Selgorm is in northern Darnassus, in the upper part of the Alchemy Shop. Or, if you are a Horde member, take the head to Elder Rise in Thunder Bluff, where it can be turned in for the same rewards.

THE ORB OF SORAN'RUK

Quest Level	20 to Obtain (WARLOCK ONLY QUEST)
Location	Central Barrens (Doan's Camp)
Quest Giver	Doan Karhan
Goal	Find 3 Soran'ruk Fragments and 1 Large Soran'ruk Fragment
Max Experience Gained	2,550
Reward	Staff of Soran'ruk (Staff: 16.9 DPS, +6 DMG to Shadow Spells and Effects & +6 DMG to Fire Spells and Effects) or the Orb of Soran'ruk (Off-Hand: +3 DMG to Fire Spells and Effects, +3 DMG to Shadow Spells and Effects, Use: Restores 25 Health every 3 Seconds for 30 Seconds)

This difficult quest takes your Warlock into both Blackfathom Deeps and Shadowfang Keep. For dealing with the Blackfathom section of it, travel into the instance and hunt Twilight Acolytes. These enemies are found later in the instance, by the Moonshrine Ruins. Kill them until you have all three Fragments. For completing the quest, look for the Shadowfang Darksouls (commonly found in Shadowfang Keep and fighting as Level 20-21 Elite monsters). Return to Doan when you are done collecting these items.

ENEMIES IN THE DEEP

NPC	LEVEL
Aku'mai Fisher	23-24 Elite
Notes: High Armor, Neutral	
Aku'mai Servant	26 Elite
Notes: Elemental Immunities	
Frequent Drops: Elemental Water	
Aku'mai Snapjaw	26-27 Elite
Notes: Aggressive, Very High Armor	
Barbed Crustacean	25-26 Elite
Notes: Aggressive, Fast Moving	
Blackfathom Myrmidon	22-23 Elite
Notes: Social, Warrior Class, Uses Disarm Frequently	
Blackfathom Oracle	21-22 Elite
Notes: Social, Ranged Enemy, Frost Bolts/Nova, Flees	
Blackfathom Sea Witch	23-24 Elite
Notes: Social, Ice Bolt, Blizzard (AoE Frost)	

NPC	LEVEL
Blackfathom Tide Priestess	20-21 Elite
Notes: Social, Heal, Ice Bolt, Flees	
Blindlight Muckdweller	25 Elite
Notes: Social, Flees	
Blindlight Murloc	22-23 Elite
Notes: Social, Flees, Sunder Armor (180)	
Blindlight Oracle	25 Elite
Notes: Social, Flees, Smite	
Deep Pool Threshfin	24-25 Elite
Notes: None	
Fallenroot Hellcaller	24-25 Elite
Notes: Social, Bolts	
Fallenroot Rogue	21-22 Elite
Notes: Social, Stealth	
Fallenroot Satyr	20-21 Elite
Notes: Social	

NPC	LEVEL
Fallenroot Shadowstalker	23-24 Elite
Notes: Social, Stealth	
Murkshallow Snapclaw	22-23 Elite
Notes: High Armor	
Skittering Crustacean	22-24 Elite
Notes: High Armor, Fast Moving, Flees	
Twilight Acolyte	24-25 Elite
Notes: Social, Heal, Flees	
Twilight Aquamancer	25-26 Elite
Notes: Social, Water Elemental Pet, Flees	
Twilight Elementalist	26-27 Elite
Notes: Social, Shock, Flees	
Twilight Loreseeker	24-25 Elite
Notes: Social, Slow, Flees	
Twilight Reaver	25-26 Elite
Notes: Social, Arcing Smash, Flees	
Twilight Shadowmage	25-27 Elite
Notes: Social, Voidwalker Pet, Shadow Bolt, Flees	

LEADERS OF THE DEEPS

NPC	LEVEL	FREQUENT DROP(S)
AKU'MAI	29 Elite	Moss Cinch (Leather Belt: 59 Armor, +5 STA & +11 INT), Leech Pants (Cloth Legs: 42 Armor, +1 STA, +5 INT & +15 SPI), Strike of the Hydra (2H Sword: 25.6 DPS & Chance on Hit: Deal 7 Nature DMG every 3 Sec and add 50 Armor - 30 Sec Duration)
Notes: High Damage, Poison Cloud, Frenzied Rage, Very High Hit Points		
GELIHAST	26 Elite	Algae Fists (Mail Gloves: 133 Armor, +10 STR & +4 STA), Reef Axe (2H Axe: 18.3 DPS, +5 STA & +7 SPI), Murloc Parts, Thick-Shelled Clams
Notes: Social, Dual Wield, Nets (Root)		
GHAMOO-RA	25 Elite	Ghamoo-Ra's Bind (Cloth Belt: 22 Armor, +4 STA & +4 INT), Tortoise Armor (Mail Chest: 311 Armor), Turtle Meat, Thick-Shelled Clams
Notes: Very High Armor, High Hit Points, Trample		
LADY SAREVESS	25 Elite	Darkwater Talwar (MH Sword: 13.4 DPS & On Hit: 25 DMG Shadow Bolt), Naga Battle Gloves (Leather Gloves: 61 Armor, +4 STR, +4 STA & +7 SPI), Naga Headpiercer (Bow: 10.6 DPS), Thick-Shelled Clams
Notes: Social, Lightning Bolts, Frost Nova, Slow		
LORGUS JETT	26 Elite	Silk, Wool
Notes: Lightning Bolt, Lightning Shield, Decent Melee		
OLD SERRA'KIS	26 Elite	Bands of Serra'kis (Leather Bracers: 39 Armor, +4 STR & +2 STA), Glowing Thresher Cape (Cloak: 23 Armor, +3 STR & +8 SPI), Bite of Serra'kis (Dagger: 17.7 DPS & On Hit: Poison for 40 DMG over 20 Sec), Thick-Shelled Clams
Notes: High Hit Points		
TWILIGHT LORD KELRIS	27 Elite	Rod of the Sleepwalker (Staff: 23.7 DPS, +11 INT & +10 SPI), Gaze Dreamer Pants (Cloth Legs: 36 Armor, +7 INT & +6 SPI), Wool, Linen
Notes: Social, Linked Allies, Mind Blast, Sleep, High Hit Points, Strong Melee		

DANK, COLD, AND DANGEROUS: TRAVERSING BLACKFATHOM

LEGEND

1   Entrance to Area From Zoram Strand

2   Instance Portal to Blackfathom Deeps

BLACKFATHOM RUINS

Once you leave Zoram Strand behind and drop into the waters of the outer Blackfathom region, you find that the enemies are now elite. There aren't any soft targets on the way toward the instance, but the levels of the creatures are quite low. People with larger groups that gain little or no experience from fighting these can try to plow through the area quickly (especially when other groups are fighting and keeping the hallways somewhat clear).

Most of the route through this outer dungeon is very simple and leaves you with few choices. The passage turns north early on, taking you into the first monsters of Blackfathom. This outer area has both low level Satyrs and Naga. Alliance players can begin collecting **Corrupted Brain Stems** for the quest: *Researching the Corruption*. The Naga can also drop the **Kor Gem** for the Paladin quest: *Seeking the Kor Gem.*

Along the walls are bright, blue-white gems that can be collected by Horde characters. These **Sapphires of Aku'mai** are needed for the quest: *Essence of Aku'mai*. There are many spawn points for the sapphires, but entire groups working on this quest will take some time to gather enough, so start this one early instead of waiting for a serious run on the instance to complete it.

The first real intersection is at the northern end of the main corridor. The short cubby off to the west has a Giant Clam and a couple of enemies (often a Tide Priestess is in there). However, the route to proceed is to the east (right). Turn in that direction and make another right to start moving south down the next, large passage.

GIANT AND THICK-SHELLED CLAMS

This is the best area for collecting Pearls and Clam Meat! Because there are Giant Clams in many of the areas outside and inside the instance, you're able to collect these goodies even outside of fights. Add the Thick-Shelled Clams dropped by Crabs, Murlocs, Turtles, and Naga, and the entire party should come away with Small Lustrous and Iridescent Pearls too!

Start to organize the group at this stage. Even a higher-level group that is ready for the full instance should get some practice against these lesser monsters, unless you're fully certain that everyone knows what they are doing. Have a puller designate the targets, pull from range, and make sure people have their /assist macros set to the puller. This prevents confusion, consolidates damage, and allows the group to keep aggro on just the right people.

The south passage has more of the Fallenroot. The stealthing Rogues aren't nearly as tough as the similar Satyrs inside the instance, but they give you a good idea of what to expect in the near future. Don't travel too quickly; have higher-level folks in the front for a better chance to spot stealthers *before* they aggro.

The next junction has several tunnels that extend in each direction. The primary choice is to go north then west (into the bluish gateway that begins the instance). Besides a few monsters and more Sapphires to harvest, there is some Bruiseweed in the northern cubby.

THE SUBMERGED RUINS

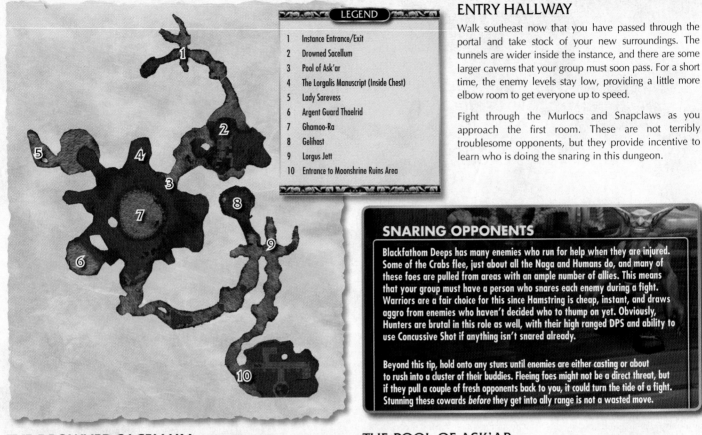

LEGEND

1. Instance Entrance/Exit
2. Drowned Sacellum
3. Pool of Ask'ar
4. The Lorgalis Manuscript (Inside Chest)
5. Lady Sarevess
6. Argent Guard Thaelrid
7. Ghamoo-Ra
8. Gelihast
9. Lorgus Jett
10. Entrance to Moonshrine Ruins Area

ENTRY HALLWAY

Walk southeast now that you have passed through the portal and take stock of your new surroundings. The tunnels are wider inside the instance, and there are some larger caverns that your group must soon pass. For a short time, the enemy levels stay low, providing a little more elbow room to get everyone up to speed.

Fight through the Murlocs and Snapclaws as you approach the first room. These are not terribly troublesome opponents, but they provide incentive to learn who is doing the snaring in this dungeon.

SNARING OPPONENTS

Blackfathom Deeps has many enemies who run for help when they are injured. Some of the Crabs flee, just about all the Naga and Humans do, and many of these foes are pulled from areas with an ample number of allies. This means that your group must have a person who snares each enemy during a fight. Warriors are a fair choice for this since Hamstring is cheap, instant, and draws aggro from enemies who haven't decided who to thump on yet. Obviously, Hunters are brutal in this role as well, with their high ranged DPS and ability to use Concussive Shot if anything isn't snared already.

Beyond this tip, hold onto any stuns until enemies are either casting or about to rush into a cluster of their buddies. Fleeing foes might not be a direct threat, but if they pull a couple of fresh opponents back to you, it could turn the tide of a fight. Stunning these cowards *before* they get into ally range is not a wasted move.

THE DROWNED SACELLUM

The first large chamber is the Drowned Sacellum. There are Murlocs on the ledges around the room and quite a few Crabs and Snapclaws in the water. There's no need to clear the entire room, since the low levels of these foes reduce their aggro range (and the Crabs are neutral anyway). Clear a path toward the south side of the room, where another rock ledge gets your party up onto the broken ruins sticking out of the water. From there, make a series of jumps between the broken walkways to reach the western part of the chamber, where there is solid, and almost dry, ground.

For those with a bit more time (or a wish to be extra thorough), the Sacellum has two Giant Clams on the eastern side of the room (under the water, of course). There is also some Stranglekelp in the water in case any herbalists are interested.

THE POOL OF ASK'AR

The massive chamber at the bottom of the stone ramp is partially submerged. There are a number of important quest targets here (for Alliance folks), and there are also a couple of bosses to fight for those with an interest in challenges and treasure. There's no enforced order for when you wish to take on the different entities in this room, so read the following paragraphs before deciding exactly where your interests lie.

Many groups of Naga are swimming in the water. Your group would be wise to clear these as you go and take on any that are even close to the areas your're approaching. Naga move about enough that you can bump into adds from behind if people are lax in killing them. Beyond that, aquatic combat is frenzied enough when you intentionally pull creatures (having them suddenly attack increases the confusion and makes it more difficult for proper crowd control). Giant Clams are littered throughout the area. There is also more Stranglekelp in here! If there are Warlocks or Shaman in the party with the ability to provide water breathing to everyone, this is the best place to do so.

The room's central island has many neutral Turtles. Among these is a single, aggressive boss named Ghamoo-Ra. This foe has extremely high armor, substantial hit points, and can take a heavy beating. To defeat him, use armor sundering abilities as much as possible and maintain that level during the fight (multiple Sunder Armors from a Warrior not only cement aggro, they ensure that you actually get rage from hitting the beast). To get rage ahead of time, fight one of the neutral turtles from a safe range and don't use any abilities until the boss fight.

The small rock to the north of the island has three Naga (a Myrmidon and two Sea Witches). Try to pull two of these for an easier fight by waiting until the three aren't as close to each other. If you get all of the enemies at once, have a person ready to disrupt the second Sea Witch as often as possible (with interrupts, stuns, Polymorph, etc.). When the Naga are dead, Alliance members can search the chest in the water for the **Lorgalis Manuscript** to complete the quest: *Knowledge in the Deeps*.

The northwestern section of land involves swimming under a stone ceiling and coming up on the other side. More Naga, and possibly even a treasure mob, await. Clear the room from the right to the left, allowing nothing to live behind or beside you. Stay far away from the tunnel beyond until the group has killed the Naga and rested themselves. A simple weapon crate is in the area and can be checked for vendor bait.

There's a Naga with powerful magic in the back area: Lady Sarevess. This caster is Level 25 Elite and calls upon lightning and frost magic. She casts Frost Nova to root people, then pulls back for safe casting. She also casts Slow as a snare, but both of these spells can be dispelled, so have your Priests and Paladins keep an eye out for them. Having your group remain at range while a lone tank advances for the initial root works well (since she's likely to root the tank early and be exposed to the rush from everyone else).

INTERRUPT ORDER

It's best to have a plan ahead of time when facing powerful enemies. Interrupts are vital when beating potent casters, and it's essential that a group doesn't just unload every interrupt they have the first time a caster starts to go.

Have an interrupt order prepared and stick to it during fights with enemies like Lady Sarevess. These cannot be set in stone, since the chaos of combat may put someone out of action when it's their turn to interrupt a foe. The key is to know who tries to interrupt first and have the person next on the list be ready to jump in if said ability fails to disrupt the caster. Doing things this way, groups have many chances to stop both normal, elite, and boss casters from getting as many spells off.

Another place of importance for the Alliance is down by the southwestern cave. Swim under the rocks and into that cave to find the wounded **Argent Guard** who came here looking to slay Twilight Lord Kelris. Though he's wounded, weak, and out of commission, he asks who can take up the quest to slay Kelris. This is the quest: *Blackfathom Villainy*, which is turned in at Darnassus once you have completed the dungeon and slain Kelris. Horde folks can complete the quest as well, but their version is handed in safely in Thunder Bluff instead! Good thing too, as the Darnassus guards have a thing about horde soldiers wandering their streets.

THE SOUTH HALL

Leave the Pool of Ask'ar once you've defeated the two bosses and completed any quests that are pertinent for your group. Clear the Naga from the southern edge of the room and get back onto dry land when the way is clear. A long passage now extends to take you deeper into Blackfathom Deeps. The Satyrs are waiting just a bit ahead; these foes are higher level. Also, there are plenty of patrols in the following section. Slow down, move carefully, and watch for stealthers.

Things get hairy around the eastern bend. Two Fallenroot Shadowstalkers patrol that hallway and a single Twilight Reaver does as well. Combined with the set Blackfathom Myrmidons in that stretch of corridor, you could end up in a huge fight if someone pulls recklessly.

To avoid this, pull at range and fall back to the earlier part of the hall. Fight the small numbers there and repeat the process. Or, for greatest caution, simply wait at the western end of the hallway for the stealthers to come all the way to you and kill them then, when it's safest. This takes a minute or two of waiting, but slightly lower-level groups may prefer the certainly of it. Casters are farther down the hall (Sea Witches in packets of two). As before, pull these back some distance before engaging. This limits the possibility of having a fleeing Naga grab two more casters. Pulling casters at range is difficult if you simply try to shoot and run back to the party. Instead, fire at maximum range and pull all the way *past* your group. This keeps the Naga from getting more than a single spell off and ensures that they come all the way to the party an into melee range. Once your group attacks the Naga, the puller may return to join in the fray.

The dungeon's first Hellcaller is toward the northern bend. These Fallenroot casters are heavy hitters when you don't interrupt them early and keep them on the defensive. Don't let these foes add to fights. Pull them first when looking for targets and engage them before Myrmidons and other lower-priority targets.

The rest of the path north to the next intersection is consistently challenging but not troublesome for groups that maintain patience and order. No bosses wander the halls, and the patrollers who come around have already been dispatched by your group. Advance slowly until you reach the branches.

The small western divot has a couple Naga, but nothing important. Instead, it's the room to the north that has a more interesting battle. Blindlight Murlocs, Muckdwellers, and Oracles control that room. Pull Oracles and kill them back in the hallway then finish off any of the lesser Murlocs who add to the encounters. Kill every foe in the room that isn't standing near the northwestern edge and then wait for the final couple to move far enough away from their large boss. Take them down when you have the shot.

When the room's clear, save for the final Murloc, go after him with fury. Gelihast has nets to root you, but his best trick is to simply dish out damage at an alarming pace. This Murloc dual wields and can trash characters quickly. Give your tank enough time to consolidate aggro and heal/nuke in bursts (that allows characters with Taunt skills to immediately grab aggro back if lost). If no one in the party has Taunt, stay light on damage/healing for the first few rounds to let your tanks consolidate Gelihast's anger.

Don't leave the room after looting Gelihast until everyone has clicked on the Shrine that the Murloc was guarding. This provides everyone with the Blessing of Blackfathom (+15 Frost Damage, +5 INT & +5 SPI) for 60 minutes.

THE EASTERN PASSAGE

Walk to the east to enter the next hallway. There are two more divots to explore here before moving south. The northern cubby has a Hellcaller, a Myrmidon, and **Lorgus Jett** (a Human who is the target for the Horde quest: *Allegiance*

to the Old Gods). Pull the Hellcaller back and deal with him, then wait for the Myrmidon to wander down to kill it. This isolates Lorgus and keeps him from becoming difficult. Still, be ready for your tank to take a lot of damage, since Lorgus has a Lightning Shield and is no slouch in melee.

The eastern tunnel doesn't have any important monsters, but there are several standard enemies (a Shadowstalker hides near a Sea Witch early on, while another stealther stands near the Myrmidon deeper in). The reward for killing these is to loot the chest hidden at the back of the passage.

Travel south while clearing the Sea Witches and Hellcallers first. There are Shadowstalkers here and there, so hold off on pulls for a few moments while everyone tries to spot any unexpected adds. Since the way behind you is clear, long and safe pulls are still the best way to get things done. Also, pull from the left or right side first each time. Pulling from the center bears a slightly higher risk, since you might end up with adds from both sides if the timing turns foul.

Use interrupts wisely, since most of your enemies here have spells. Even the Shadowstalkers are able to debuff people (they use Curse of Weakness). The greatest threat is when Sea Witches add and are able to get Blizzard going. When that happens, pull the entire fight out of the AoE to prevent the group from suffering the full damage.

The Moonshrine Ruins, the final part of this dungeon, are at the bottom of the hallway.

MOONSHRINE RUINS

	LEGEND
1	Instance Entrance/Exit
2	The Fathom Core (Underwater, Beneath Ruins)
3	Old Serra'kis
4	Twilight Lord Kelris
5	Aku'mai
6	Altar of the Deep

TWILIGHT CULTISTS ABOUND

The south hall ends when it empties into an immense, watery chamber. The ruins set above the water are mostly intact and still bear a sense of Elven majesty from lost times. Yet, this place is defiled by the Twilight's Hammer cultists. Make yourself known to them through death and slaughter (a few at a time, at least).

If you want to collect **Twilight Pendants** for the Alliance quest: *Twilight Falls*, this is the area to gather them. The cultists here drop them with fair frequency, so it shouldn't be hard to finish at least a couple people off in a single run. Also, the Acolytes in the outer area can drop **Soran'ruk Fragments** for the Warlock quest: *The Orb of Soran'ruk*.

Horde questers should swim under the ruins. There are some dangerous enemies in the darkness below, including Barbed Crustaceans and Deep Pool Threshfins. Pull these to your group and fight them at the top of the water to avoid drowning. A stone known as the **Fathom Core** is under the ruins; it needs to be examined to complete the goals for the quest: *Amongst the Ruins*. Swim back up to the western ledge when you've completed this. Be extremely careful not to fight near the center of the room until after the enemies on the above walkways are cleared; they can and will aggro if anyone gets too close to them, and that spells a brutal end for your party. It's almost always a wise idea to clear the enemies on the approach to the temple before exploring the water below.

There are Giant Clams and Stranglekelp in the water. Because everything in this area is aggressive, clear all the creatures away. This gives you a safe run at any of these items. For a somewhat hidden boss, swim under the ruins and continue east. There's a section, deep under the building, that bulges somewhat north. Old Serra'kis is back there (a powerful Threshadon). Shoot Old Serra'kis and swim back to a pocket of air for the long fight ahead. This beast drops some interesting items and is safe to defeat as long as your group clears the nearby Crabs first and stays above the waterline.

There are legions of Twilight cult members back on the path into the ruins. Acolytes are the healers, so they're some of your most important targets to tie up in larger fights. The Reavers are trained as Warriors (and have Arcing Smash), so they dish out a solid DPS if you let them fight while close to any non-tanks. Aquamancers have Water Elemental pets, but are actually some of the weaker targets and are relatively easy to control. Finally, Loreseekers have a Slow effect and deal moderate damage.

The best battleplan is to destroy the Acolytes as soon as possible in any fight. After that, bring down Loreseekers and then Aquamancers. Keep Reavers away from soft members of your own party while they hack away at you, then attend to them when the more frustrating foes are dead. When there are double casters incoming, use heavy interrupters to keep them stymied.

After fighting the enemies along the area in front of the walkway, stop and watch the patrollers below. There are a number of Aquamancers and Reavers who wander far and wide. Don't let them make your life miserable. Chat and relax for a few moments while lone patrollers come into position and pull those for easy kills. This pays for itself once you head down the stairs into the lower area. Casters below can dish out the damage. After the wanderers are gone, use long pulls to extract the casters and other cultists from their spots.

There are two non-essential groups of enemies (one to the north just after you descend the steps and another at the end of the eastern walkway). The first group has a chest. It's up to you whether to kill them, but those working on *Twilight Falls* can use them to collect more Pendants.

The southern stairs move the group toward the central shrine. Take these and prepare for several challenging pulls. The enemies are packed very tightly, and even cautious pulls may bring three foes. Stay far enough back to prevent runners from getting more (because if they do, at least a couple more enemies are bound to enter the fight). Be doubly wary of the pillars, since they obscure sight of a few cultists.

Up close, the Aquamancers aren't difficult to control. However, they're a major pain when adding to a fight. Long pulls that bring the Aquamancers all the way to the group without allowing them to have free rein are wise.

MOONSHRINE SANCTUM

There are different cultists that appear in and around the shrine. Elementalists are damage dealers with four spells at their disposal (Shock (direct damage), Frost Shock, Flame Shock, and Earth Shock) and add some decent melee. The Shadowmages bring Voidwalkers with them, and their bolts are damaging. As with the Aquamancers, pet classes do not have elite pets even when the enemies themselves are elite. The Voidwalkers go down fairly quickly once the party targets them.

Use the building entrance as a way to avoid caster bolts when pulling. Attack the Shadowmages and step outside; when you do this, the Warlocks end up running right into your party. Continue with that trick to blow through the cultists near the front of the building; the goal is to deplete as much of the room beyond as possible. Look at the pots along the walls once you slip inside (there are Shadowmages along the walls there, trying to be subtle). Kill them too!

Twilight Lord Kelris is in the center of the room. Kelris is near a couple of casters behind him (though they can be pulled without aggroing him; since he's meditating, they come to his aid when he's pulled). Try to take them down before fighting Kelris, since this caster is the real danger.

When ready, charge the big guy and slap as many DoTs and debuffs onto him as possible. Kelris can cast Sleep and Mind Blast, and he won't be shy about either. As long as you get Kelris without allies around (or with only a single buddy), it won't be too hard to win this fight. If you failed to clear the area and other casters poke their heads out, kill them quickly and return to Kelris (he's a slow target to kill, and removing a fresh caster's DPS is necessary).

The door into Aku'mai's Lair won't open on its own. This is frustrating at first, but notice the incense burners beneath the statue that Kelris was kneeling before. Lighting these should open the way. *Don't light all four burners at the same time* (unless you really want to see an entire group of people panic and earn a beatdown later). This is certain to get everyone killed in a massive onslaught of elite and non-elite monsters.

Light the burners one-at-a-time, waiting until the monsters from each burner are slain before even thinking about lighting the next one. The fights that ensue from lightning these are as follows:

SPAWNS FROM LIGHTING THE BURNERS

4	Barbed Crustaceans
2	Aku'mai Servants
3	Aku'mai Snapjaws
10	Murkshallow Softshells

If done individually, these fights aren't too brutal on a skilled group. The Crustaceans are numerous, but their low level and moderate damage keeps them from being a dire threat. When they appear, rush to one side and fight the first two you see (the others come from the opposite part of the room). This gives you a little extra time to deal damage before the rest arrive.

The two Aku'mai Servants are both high-level Water Elementals. Luckily, you're only facing two enemies. Debuff their damage with things like Demoralizing Shout, focus on one target, and win the fight. It's not terribly hard compared to Kelris.

The Snapjaws come in a group of three. They are slow to kill, but easy to defeat. Have the main tank use Cleave and Challenging Shout early on to grab the aggro and keep the beasts' attention where it should be.

The most exciting fight is against the ten Murkshallow Softshells. Before people realize that these are non-elite enemies, there's often a short burst of fear. Let people know ahead of time that a flood of weaker enemies is on the way. If you group has a ton of AoE potential, use that to bring this cluster of foes down (five appear from each side of the room). Tank-oriented groups often end up dividing the aggro and having to slug things out against a couple at a time. Don't try to have a single person tank all ten foes. This forces the healer to dump mana into them; as a result, the healer will soon be tanking all ten creatures. That isn't good.

When the last enemy from the fourth fight dies, the doors open. You're almost done with Blackfathom Deeps!

AKUMAI'S LAIR

Pull the Snapjaws on the other side of the door. It's fairly simple to defeat them, especially since these can be taken as single fights. In fact, this is a short bit of downtime while people prepare for the final fight. Continue east, fighting Turtles as you go, then look into the last chamber. Aku'mai is there, patrolling the large cavern. He has plenty of heads to keep his eyes out for you; do not approach until you're ready.

Instead, let any Warriors build as much Rage as possible fighting against Turtles while the party prepares. Get some fast healing in after these skirmishes, then rush Aku'mai when he's alone. This won't make things easy, however, since the great Hyrdra is Level 28 Elite and unloads on anything that gets in his way. Expect Poison Cloud damage against close targets, massive melee damage (even more so once Aku'mai Enrages), and a slow fight. Layer on the DoTs and sunder the big guy's armor as early as possible.

Any loss of aggro to the main tanks must be met with Taunt/Challenging Shout/Mocking Blow from Warriors. Paladins should use their ability to heal allies as a way to save casters in danger. Don't even let the casters have a tiny moment of melee fun with Aku'mai, since even mail wearers don't stand up easily to those massive chomps.

Luckily, Aku'mai isn't immune to stuns, so those can be used to mitigate some of his DPS. After pulling the Hydra away from any remaining Turtles, it's even an option to spread out and bounce around his aggro between ranged characters in the event that your tanks are failing and need time for healing potions/healers to be ready again. This is not ideal, but neither is a wipeout.

Once Aku'mai falls, an Alliance-friendly NPC, Morridune, spawns offering a free transport back to Darnassus. Regardless of your faction, touching the Altar of the Deeps teleports you back to the water outside the instance. Make sure you're done with everything Blackfathom Deeps has to offer before accepting either of these teleport options.

Good work! The Twilight's Hammer won't recover from this anytime soon.

BLACKROCK DEPTHS

Played & Written by: Edwin "Plainsong" Kern of <Dovrani> on Kirin Tor

Blackrock Mountain stands on the border overlooking both Searing Gorge and Burning Steppes. Built within this massive mountain is a fortress of evil. Here, the enemy is safe to plot against others in the world. From here they can launch attacks against both the Horde and the Alliance.

It's time to take the fight to them. It's time to show them that, even in their nearly impregnable fortress, they are not safe.

DUNGEON INFORMATION

Location	Between Searing Gorge and Burning Steppes
Quests	Both
Region	Contested
Suggested Levels	52-57
Group Allowed	5
Primary Enemies	Elementals, Humanoids
Time to Complete	3-4 hours

GETTING TO BLACKROCK DEPTHS

Blackrock Depths is located at the bottom of Blackrock Mountain. Follow the chain across the lava and into the mountain until you can't go any further. Horde parties should fly into Kargath (Badlands) and make the trip across Searing Gorge. Alliance groups should fly into Thorium Point (Searing Gorge) to enter through Searing Gorge, or Morgan's Vigil (Burning Steppes).

WHO TO BRING

Having a party with crowd control is essential as many fights involve a large number of enemies. Sap, Polymorph, Mind Control, and Banish are all extremely useful in the chambers under the mountain.

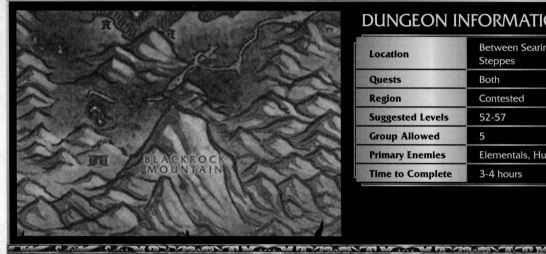

QUESTS FOR BLACKROCK DEPTHS

ALLIANCE QUESTS

QUEST NAME	QUEST GIVER	QUEST GIVER LOCATION	QUEST RECEIVER	QUEST RECEIVER LOCATION	CHAIN?	MAX EXPERIENCE
Marshal Windsor	Marshal Maxwell	Burning Steppes: Morgan Vigil	Marshal Windsor	Blackrock Depths	Yes	5,400
Abandoned Hope	Marshal Windsor	Blackrock Depths	Marshal Maxwell	Burning Steppes: Morgan's Vigil	Yes	5,450
A Crumpled Note	A Crumpled Note	Blackrock Depths	Marshal Windsor	Blackrock Depths	Yes	6,200
A Shred of Hope	Marshal Windsor	Blackrock Depths	Marshal Windsor	Blackrock Depths	Yes	6,200
Jail Break	Marshal Windsor	Blackrock Depths	Marshal Maxwell	Burning Steppes: Morgan's Vigil	Yes	7,750
Hurley Blackbreath	Ragnar Thunderbrew	Dun Morogh: Kharanos	Ragnar Thunderbrew	Dun Morogh: Kharanos	No	7,050
REWARD: Limb Cleaver (2-hand Axe, 42.7 DPS, +21 STR, +6 STA) or Swiftstrike Cudgel (Main-hand Mace, 32.5 DPS, Equip: Improves your chance to hit by 1%) and Dark Dwarven Lager (Use: A potent alcoholic beverage)x10						
The Good Stuff	Oralius	Burning Steppes: Morgan's Vigil	Oralius	Burning Steppes: Morgan's Vigil	No	5,800
REWARD: A Dingy Fanny Pack						
Overmaster Pyron	Jalinda Sprig	Burning Steppes: Morgan's Vigil	Jalinda Sprig	Burning Steppes: Morgan's Vigil	Yes	5,100
Incendius	Jalinda Sprig	Burning Steppes: Morgan's Vigil	Jalinda Sprig	Burning Steppes: Morgan's Vigil	Yes	5,800
REWARD: Stalwart Clutch (Plate Waist, 300 Armor, +12 STA, Equip: Increase Defense +8) or Crypt Demon Bracers (Mail Wrist, 132 Armor, +14 AGI) or Nightfall Gloves (Leather Hands, 91 Armor, +12 STR, +12 AGI) or Sunborne Cape (Back, 36 Armor, +5 Spirit Equip: Increases damage done by Fire spells and effects by up to 12)						
Kharan Mighthammer	King Magni Bronzebeard	Ironforge	Kharan Mighthammer	Blackrock Depths	Yes	6,400
The Bearer of Bad News	Kharan Mighthammer	Blackrock Depths	King Magni Bronzebeard	Ironforge	Yes	6,400
The Fate of the Kingdom	King Magni Bronzebeard	Ironforge	Princess Moira Bronzebeard	Blackrock Depths	Yes	8,050
The Princess' Surprise	Princess Moira Bronzebeard	Blackrock Depths	King Magni Bronzebeard	Ironforge	Yes	9,650
REWARD: Magni's Will (Ring: +6 STR, +7 STA, Improves your chance to get a critical strike by 1%) or Songstone of Ironforge (Ring: +7 INT, +4 SPI, Increases damage and healing done by spells and effects by up to 18)						

MARSHAL WINDSOR

Quest Level	48 to obtain
Location	Burning Steppes (Morgan's Vigil)
Quest Giver	Marshal Maxwell
Goal	Find Marshal Windsor
Max Experience Gained	5,450

After completing *The True Masters* quest chain, Ragged John mentions something about seeing Marshal Windsor being dragged off to prison. Marshal Maxwell doesn't hold Ragged John in high esteem and wants you to verify the information. Find Marshal Windsor to complete this quest.

ABANDONED HOPE

Quest Level	52 to obtain
Location	Blackrock Depths
Quest Giver	Marshal Windsor
Goal	Return to Marshal Maxwell
Max Experience Gained	5,450

Marshal Windsor is alive, but the information he was gathering has been taken. Return to Marshal Maxwell with the bad news.

ONYXIA'S LAIR

Completing first the *Dragonkin Menace* and all *The True Masters* quests opens the *Marshal Windsor* chain. Even after you have completed the quests in Blackrock Depths, the chain has not been completed. It's a long chain with a very important reward: the key to Onyxia's Lair.

A CRUMPLED NOTE

Quest Level	56 to obtain
Location	Blackrock Depths
Quest Giver	A Crumpled Note
Goal	Deliver A Crumpled Note to Marshal Windsor
Max Experience Gained	6,200

A Crumpled Note can be found on the corpse of many of the creatures in Blackrock Depths. A quick examination of the note reveals information Marshal Windsor should be alerted to. Give him the note.

A SHRED OF HOPE

Quest Level	53 to obtain
Location	Blackrock Depths
Quest Giver	Marshal Windsor
Goal	Recover Marshal Windsor's Lost Information
Max Experience Gained	6,200

There's still a chance to get the information Marshal Windsor was collecting. It's being held by two people in Blackrock Depths. Find General Angerforge and Argelmach. They have the information you need and neither will give it over willingly.

JAIL BREAK

Quest Level	56 to obtain
Location	Blackrock Depths
Quest Giver	Marshal Windsor
Goal	Protect Marshal Windsor
Max Experience Gained	7,750

After returning Marshal Windsor's information, the next step is clear: free Marshal Windsor from the prison. He'll need his gear and his friends freed. Protect him until he can make it on his own. Speak to Marshal Maxwell when you have done this.

HURLEY BLACKBREATH

Quest Level	50 to obtain
Location	Dun Morogh
Quest Giver	Ragnar Thunderbrew
Goal	Recover the Lost Thunderbrew Recipe
Max Experience Gained	7,050
Reward	Limb Cleaver (2-hand Axe, 42.7 DPS, +21 STR, +6 STA) or Swiftstrike Cudgel (Main-hand Mace, 32.5 DPS, Equip: Improves your chance to hit by 1%) and Dark Dwarven Lager (Use: A potent alcoholic beverage) x10

The Dark Iron Dwarves have stolen the recipe for Thunderbrew Lager. Destroy any kegs of Thunderbrew Lager and retrieve the Lost Thunderbrew Recipe from Hurley Blackbreath.

THE GOOD STUFF

Quest Level	50 to obtain
Location	Burning Steppes (Morgan's Vigil)
Quest Giver	Oralius
Goal	Gather 20 Dark Iron Fanny Packs
Max Experience Gained	5,800
Reward	A Dingy Fanny Pack

Oralius is jealous of what the Dark Iron Dwarves have. Bring him 20 Dark Iron Fanny Packs to ease this jealousy.

OVERMASTER PYRON

Quest Level	48 to obtain
Location	Burning Steppes (Morgan's Vigil)
Quest Giver	Jalinda Sprig
Goal	Kill Overmaster Pyron
Max Experience Gained	5,100

The mages sent into Blackrock Depths have been meeting untimely and crispy ends. Jalinda wants you to kill the culprit, Overmaster Pyron. Slay him and return.

INCENDIUS

Quest Level	48 to obtain
Location	Burning Steppes (Morgan's Vigil)
Quest Giver	Jalinda Sprig
Goal	Kill Lord Incendius
Max Experience Gained	5,800
Reward	Stalwart Clutch (Plate Waist, 300 Armor, +12 STA, Equip: Increase Defense +8) or Crypt Demon Bracers (Mail Wrist, 132 Armor, +14 AGI) or Nightfall Gloves (Leather Hands, 91 Armor, +12 STR, +12 AGI) or Sunborne Cape (Back, 36 Armor, +5 Spirit, Equip: Increases damage done by Fire spells and effects by up to 12)

When you tell Jalinda about Pyron saying "Incendius" when he died, she becomes very worried. Incendius is much stronger and stands in the way of the expeditions into Blackrock Depths. Kill him.

KHARAN MIGHTHAMMER

Quest Level	50 to obtain
Location	Ironforge
Quest Giver	King Magni Bronzebeard
Goal	Find Kharan Mighthammer
Experience	6,400

The King's men have been unable to find either his daughter or Kharan, who was protecting his daughter. Their only clue is Kharan may be being held in Blackrock Depths. Find him and find what happened to Magni's daughter.

THE BEARER OF BAD NEWS

Quest Level	52 to obtain
Location	Blackrock Depths
Quest Giver	Kharan Mighthammer
Goal	Return to King Magni Bronzebeard
Max Experience Gained	6,400

Kharan has important information that needs to get back to King Magni Bronzebeard.

THE FATE OF THE KINGDOM

Quest Level	52 to obtain
Location	Ironforge
Quest Giver	King Magni Bronzebeard
Goal	Rescue the Princess from Emperor Dagran Thaurissan in Blackrock Depths.
Max Experience Gained	8,050

After completing *The Bearer of Bad News*, King Magni asks you to rescue his daughter from Emperor Dagran Thaurissan at the very end of Blackrock Depths. Remember, she must not be harmed!

THE PRINCESS' SURPRISE

Quest Level	54 to obtain
Location	Blackrock Depths
Quest Giver	Princess Moira Bronzebeard
Goal	Return to King Magni with some surprising news.
Max Experience Gained	9,650
Reward	Magni's Will (Ring: +6 STR, +7 STA, Improves your chance to get a critical strike by 1%) or Songstone of Ironforge (Ring: +7 INT, +4 SPI, Increases damage and healing done by spells and effects by up to 18)

You've rescued the Princess but she doesn't seem very happy about it. To make matters worse, you have some very surprising news to deliver to King Magni and I don't think he's going to take it very well.

HORDE QUESTS

QUEST NAME	QUEST GIVER	QUEST GIVER LOCATION	QUEST RECEIVER	QUEST RECEIVER LOCATION	CHAIN?	MAX EXPERIENCE
Commander Gor'shak	Galamav the Marksman	Badlands: Kargath	Commander Gor'shak	Blackrock Depths	Yes	5,100
What is Going On?	Commander Gor'shak	Blackrock Depths	Commander Gor'shak	Blackrock Depths	Yes	4,350
What is Going On?	Commander Gor'shak	Blackrock Depths	Thrall	Orgrimmar: Valley of Wisdom	Yes	5,450
The Royal Rescue	Thrall	Orgrimmar: Valley of Wisdom	Princess Bronzebeard	Blackrock Depths	Yes	8,050
The Princess Saved?	Princess Bronzebeard	Blackrock Depths	Thrall	Orgrimmar: Valley of Wisdom	Yes	9,950
REWARD: The Eye of Orgrimmar (Ring, +4 SPI, +7 INT, Passive: Increases damage and healing done by magical spells and effects by up to 10) or Thrall's Resolve (Ring, 150 Armor, +7 STA, +4 STR)						
KILL ON SIGHT: Dark Iron Dwarves	Wanted Poster	Badlands: Kargath	Warlord Goretooth	Badlands: Kargath	Yes	5,100
KILL ON SIGHT: High Ranking Dark Iron Officials	Wanted Poster	Badlands: Kargath	Warlord Goretooth	Badlands: Kargath	Yes	5,450
Operation: Death to Angerforge	Warlord Goretooth	Badlands: Kargath	Warlord Goretooth	Badlands: Kargath	Yes	7,750
REWARD: Conqueror's Medallion (Neck, +10 STR, +4 AGI, +11 STA, +5 SPI)						
Lost Thunderbrew Recipe	Shadowmage Vivian Lagrave	Badlands: Kargath	Shadowmage Vivian Lagrave	Badlands: Kargath	No	5,650
REWARD: Limb Cleaver (2-hand Axe, 42.7 DPS, +21 STR, +6 STA) or Swiftstrike Cudgel (Main-hand Mace, 32.5 DPS, Equip: Improves your chance to hit by 1%), and 5 Superior Healing Potions and 5 Greater Mana Potions						
Disharmony of Flame	Thunderheart	Badlands: Kargath	Thunderheart	Badlands: Kargath	Yes	5,100
Disharmony of Fire	Thunderheart	Badlands: Kargath	Thunderheart	Badlands: Kargath	Yes	7,300
REWARD: Stalwart Clutch (Plate Waist, 300 Armor, +12 STA, Equip: Increase Defense +8) or Crypt Demon Bracers (Mail Wrist, 132 Armor, +14 AGI) or Nightfall Gloves (Leather Hands, 91 Armor, +12 STR, +12 AGI) or Sunborne Cape (Back, 36 Armor, +5 Spirit, Equip: Increases damage done by Fire spells and effects by up to 12)						
The Last Element	Shadowmage Vivian Lagrave	Badlands: Kargath	Shadowmage Vivian Lagrave	Badlands: Kargath	Yes	5,450
REWARD: Lagrave's Seal (Ring, +7 STA, +7 INT, +7 Spi)						
The Rise of the Machines	Lotwil Veriatus	Badlands: N.W.	Lotwil Veriatus	Badlands: N.W.	Yes	6,200
REWARD: Azure Moon Amice (Cloth Shoulder, 56 Armor, +8 STA, +15 INT) or Raincaster Drape (Back, 38 Armor, Increases healing done by spells and effects by up to 20) or Basalt Armor (Mail Chest, 313 Armor, +10 STA, +21 SPI) or Lavaplate Gauntlets (Plate Hands, 345 Armor, +17 STR, +5 STA)						

COMMANDER GOR'SHAK

Quest Level	48 to obtain
Location	Badlands (Kargath)
Quest Giver	Galamav the Marksman
Goal	Find Commander Gor'shak
Max Experience Gained	5,100

A message was delivered, rather rudely, to Kargath. It shows an Orc behind bars with the signature of Commander Gor'shak. Galamav is fully aware it's a trap and wants you to rescue the Commander.

WHAT IS GOING ON?

Quest Level	50 to obtain
Location	Blackrock Depths
Quest Giver	Commander Gor'shak
Goal	Defend Commander Gor'shak
Max Experience Gained	4,350

Commander Gor'shak begins telling you about why he allowed himself to be captured when guards arrive. Defend him so he can continue the story.

WHAT IS GOING ON?

Quest Level	50 to obtain
Location	Blackrock Depths
Quest Giver	Commander Gor'shak
Goal	Talk to Kharan Mighthammer, then to Thrall
Max Experience Gained	5,450

Gor'shak has been speaking with Kharan about the kidnapping of Princess Bronzebeard. He wants you to gather all the information Kharan has to offer and take it to Thrall.

THE PRINCESS SAVED?

Quest Level	53 to obtain
Location	Blackrock Depths
Quest Giver	Princess Moira Bronzebeard
Goal	Return to Thrall
Max Experience Gained	9,950
Reward	The Eye of Orgrimmar (Ring, +4 SPI, +7 INT, Passive: Increases damage and healing done by magical spells and effects by up to 10) or Thrall's Resolve (Ring, 150 Armor, +7 STA, +4 STR)

Moira seems to still be partially under Dagran's spell. She curses at you and tells you to return to Thrall. Nothing more can be done. Return to Thrall for your reward.

THE ROYAL RESCUE

Quest Level	51 to obtain
Location	Orgrimmar
Quest Giver	Thrall
Goal	Kill Emperor Dagran Thaurissan
Max Experience Gained	8,050

Thrall wants to save Princess Bronzebeard and return her to Ironforge to help strengthen the ties between the Dwarves and the Orcs. Emperor Dagran Thaurissan has cast a spell on the Princess and needs to be killed before the rescue can happen. Thrall warns you not to harm the Princess.

KILL ON SIGHT: DARK IRON DWARVES

Quest Level	48 to obtain
Location	Badlands (Kargath)
Quest Giver	Wanted Poster
Goal	Kill 15 Anvilrage Guardsman, 5 Anvilrage Footman, and 10 Anvilrage Warden
Max Experience Gained	5,100
Reward	None

The Dark Iron Dwarves have been declared enemies of the Horde and a bounty put on their heads. Slay them in droves and return for your reward.

KILL ON SIGHT: HIGH RANKING DARK IRON OFFICIALS

Quest Level	50 to obtain
Location	Badlands (Kargath)
Quest Giver	Wanted Poster
Goal	Kill 10 Anvilrage Medic, 10 Anvilrage Officer, and 10 Anvilrage Soldier
Max Experience Gained	5,450

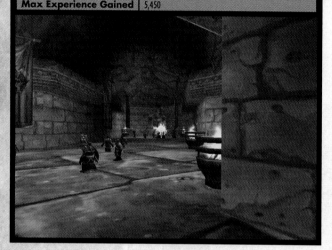

It's not only the low ranks of Dark Iron Dwarves that need to be thinned. Slaughter the enemy and return when your armor is coated in their blood. Speak with Lexlort about finding the man responsible for betraying the Horde after you have completed this quest.

LOST THUNDERBREW RECIPE

Quest Level	50 to obtain
Location	Badlands (Kargath)
Quest Giver	Shadowmage Vivian Lagrave
Goal	Recover the Lost Thunderbrew Recipe
Max Experience Gained	5,650
Reward	Limb Cleaver (2-hand Axe, 42.7 DPS, +21 STR, +6 STA) or Swiftstrike Cudgel (Main-hand Mace, 32.5 DPS, Equip: Improves your chance to hit by 1%) and 5 Superior Healing Potions and 5 Greater Mana Potions

There are rumors that the Dark Iron Dwarves have stolen the recipe for Thunderbrew Lager. Find Hurley Blackbreath and take the Lost Thunderbrew Recipe. You may have to destroy some of the kegs to get him to show.

OPERATION: DEATH TO ANGERFORGE

Quest Level	55 to obtain
Location	Badlands (Kargath)
Quest Giver	Warlord Goretooth
Goal	Kill General Angerforge
Max Experience Gained	7,750
Reward	Conqueror's Medallion (Neck, +10 STR, +4 AGI, +11 STA, +5 SPI)

Once you have brought Grark Lorkrub to justice, Warlord Goretooth entrusts you with an important mission. The leadership of the Dark Iron Dwarves needs to be removed. Kill General Angerforge and return for your reward.

DISHARMONY OF FLAME

Quest Level	48 to obtain
Location	Badlands (Kargath)
Quest Giver	Thunderheart
Goal	Slay Overmaster Pyron
Max Experience Gained	5,100

Something burns in the depths of Blackrock Mountain. The Dark Iron Dwarves have become rather adept at summoning and creating elementals. Find and kill Overmaster Pyron.

DISHARMONY OF FIRE

Quest Level	48 to obtain
Location	Badlands (Kargath)
Quest Giver	Thunderheart
Goal	Recover the Tablet of Kurniya and kill Lord Incendius
Max Experience Gained	7,300
Reward	Stalwart Clutch (Plate Waist, 300 Armor, +12 STA, Equip: Increase Defense +8) or Crypt Demon Bracers (Mail Wrist, 132 Armor, +14 AGI) or Nightfall Gloves (Leather Hands, 91 Armor, +12 STR, +12 AGI) or Sunborne Cape (Back, 36 Armor, +5 Spirit, Equip: Increases damage done by Fire spells and effects by up to 12)

Returning to Kargath after slaying Overmaster Pyron will gain Thunderheart's attention. There is something that controlled Pyron: Incendius. Yet, even Incendius is being controlled. The chain goes too far to intuit without more evidence. Slay Incendius and take the Tablet of Kurniya.

THE LAST ELEMENT

Quest Level	48 to obtain
Location	Badlands (Kargath)
Quest Giver	Shadowmage Vivian Lagrave
Goal	Collect 10 Essence of the Elements
Max Experience Gained	5,450
Reward	Lagrave's Seal (Ring, +7 STA, +7 INT, +7 SPI)

Vivian Lagrave also takes an interest in you when you return with news of Overmaster Pyron's death. The Dark Iron Dwarves have found a way to create terribly powerful golems. Spies report that the power source is an important part of the new design. Vivian asks you to collect 10 Essence of the Elements to study.

THE RISE OF THE MACHINES

Quest Level	53 to obtain
Location	Badlands
Quest Giver	Lotwil Veriatus
Goal	Collect the Head of Argelmach and 10 Intact Elemental Cores
Max Experience Gained	6,200
Reward	Azure Moon Amice (Cloth Shoulder, 56 Armor, +8 STA, +15 INT) or Raincaster Drape (Back, 38 Armor, Increases healing done by spells and effects by up to 20) or Basalt Armor (Mail Chest, 313 Armor, +10 STA, +21 SPI) or Lavaplate Gauntlets (Plate Hands, 345 Armor, +17 STR, +5 STA)

Continuing The Rise of the Machines quest chain brings you to Lotwil Veriatus. He recognizes who is making the machines. He wants you to kill Argelmach and bring his head and 10 Intact Element Cores to him.

SHARED QUESTS

QUEST NAME	QUEST GIVER	QUEST GIVER LOCATION	QUEST RECEIVER	QUEST RECEIVER LOCATION	CHAIN?	MAX EXPERIENCE
Dark Iron Legacy	Franclorn Forgewright	Blackrock Mountain: Molten Span	Shrine of Thaurissan	Blackrock Depths	No	5,100
REWARD: Shadowforge Key						
Ribbly Screwspigot	Yuka Screwspigot	Burning Steppes: Flame Crest	Yuka Screwspigot	Burning Steppes: Flame Crest	No	2,650
REWARD: Penance Spaulders (Leather Shoulder, 104 Armor, +8 AGI, +11 STA, +7 SPI) or Rancor Boots (Cloth Boots, 47 Armor, +12 AGI, +11 INT) or Splintsteel Armor (Mail Chest, 288 Armor, +12 STR, +12 STA, +12 SPI)						
The Love Potion	Mistress Nagmara	Blackrock Depths	Mistress Nagmara	Blackrock Depths	No	5,450
REWARD: Nagmara's Whipping Belt (Leather Waist, 89 Armor, +8 STR, +14 STA, +13 SPI) or Manacle Cuffs (Cloth Wrist, 34 Armor, +6 STA, +15 INT)						
The Heart of the Mountain	Maxwort Uberglint	Burning Steppes: Flame Crest	Maxwort Uberglint	Burning Steppes: Flame Crest	No	5,650
Attunement to the Core	Lothos Riftwaker	Blackrock Mountain: Molten Span	Lothos Riftwaker		No	6,600
REWARD: Teleport to Molten Core						

DARK IRON LEGACY

Quest Level	48 to obtain
Location	Blackrock Mountain (Molten Span)
Quest Giver	Franclorn Forgewright
Goal	Place Ironfel in the Shrine of Thaurissan
Max Experience Gained	5,100
Reward	Shadowforge Key

Franclorn Forgewright is dead. Since only the dead can speak with the dead, this quest can only be obtained while in your spirit form. You are asked to retrieve Ironfel from Fineous Darkvire and place it in the Shrine of Thaurissan.

RIBBLY SCREWSPIGOT

Quest Level	48 to obtain
Location	Searing Gorge
Quest Giver	Yuka Screwspigot
Goal	Collect Ribbly's Head
Max Experience Gained	2,650
Reward	Penance Spaulders (Leather Shoulder, 104 Armor, +8 AGI, +11 STA, +7 SPI) or Rancor Boots (Cloth Boots, 47 Armor, +12 AGI, +11 INT) or Splintsteel Armor (Mail Chest, 288 Armor, +12 STR, +12 STA, +12 SPI)

All family members look out for each other. In the case of the Screwspigots, they've been looking for a way to make money from Ribbly for a while. Now is their chance. There is a bounty on Ribbly's head and Yuka wants it. Collect Ribbly's head and return for your reward.

THE LOVE POTION

Quest Level	50 to obtain
Location	Blackrock Depths
Quest Giver	Mistress Nagmara
Goal	Collect 1 Nagmara's Filled Vial, 10 Giant Silver Veins, and 4 Gromsblood
Max Experience Gained	5,450
Reward	Nagmara's Whipping Belt (Leather Waist, 89 Armor, +8 STR, +14 STA, +13 SPI) or Manacle Cuffs (Cloth Wrist, 34 Armor, +6 STA, +15 INT)

Nagmara is desperately in love with Rocknot, but is having trouble getting him to feel the same way. She asks you to bring her ingredients so she can make a potion to change this. Fill the vial on top of the hill at Golaka Hotsprings in Un'Goro Crater, collect the Giant Silver Veins from the Giants in Azshara, and gather Gromsblood. With all the reagents acquired, return to Nagmara.

THE HEART OF THE MOUNTAIN

Quest Level	50 to obtain
Location	Burning Steppes
Quest Giver	Maxwort Uberglint
Goal	Collect The Heart of the Mountain
Max Experience Gained	5,650

Maxwort is obsessed with a certain gem. The Heart of the Mountain is described as being as big as your hand. The Dark Iron Dwarves have refused to sell it to Maxwort. His only course of action is violence. He's willing to pay you to retrieve the Heart from Watchman Doomgrip. Raiding the relic coffers is the only way to get Doomgrips attention.

ATTUNEMENT TO THE CORE (RAID)

Quest Level	55 to obtain
Location	Blackrock Mountain (Molten Span)
Quest Giver	Lothos Riftwaker
Goal	Retrieve a Core Fragment
Max Experience Gained	6,600
Reward	Teleport to Molten Core

Lothos knows what's behind all the trouble in Blackrock Mountain; it's a being of immense power that isn't even in this world. To reach him, you must travel through Blackrock Depths. Lothos can shorten your future trips if you bring him the Core Fragment from just outside the entrance to Molten Core.

THE ENEMIES OF BLACKROCK DEPTHS

WHAT SURVIVES THE HEAT?

NPC	LEVEL
Anvilrage Captain	55-56 Elite
Anvilrage Footman	51-52 Elite
Notes: Duel-wields, Kick, Strike	
Anvilrage Guardsman	50-51 Elite
Notes: Disarm, Stun, Sunder Armor	
Anvilrage Marshal	54-55 Elite
Notes: Holy Shield, Heal	
Anvilrage Medic	52-53 Elite
Notes: Heal, Mind Blast	
Anvilrage Officer	53-54 Elite
Notes: Shoot (ranged attack)	
Anvilrage Overseer	48-49 Elite
Notes: Strike	
Anvilrage Reservist	49-55
Anvilrage Soldier	52-53 Elite
Anvilrage Warden	49-50 Elite
Notes: Hooked Net (Root)	
Arena Spectator	52-54
Blackbreath Crony	53 Elite
Blazing Fireguard	52-54 Elite
Notes: Fire Shield, Fire Blast, Immolate, Scorch	
Bloodhound	44-50
Notes: Enhanced stealth detection, Rend, Dire Growl (-47 STR/AGI)	
Bloodhound Mastiff	49-55
Notes: Enhanced stealth detection, Rend, Dire Growl (-47 STR/AGI)	
Borer Beetle	49-52

NPC	LEVEL
Burrowing Thundersnout	50-52
Notes: Lightning Bolt, Thunderclap, Dysjunction (Fire, Ice, and Arcane damage taken is increased by 50%, 5 minute duration)	
Cave Creeper	49-52
Dark Guard	53-54 Elite
Dark Screecher	50-52
Notes: Sonic Burst (AoE silence), Aural Shock (Curse, -35% casting speed, 5 minute duration)	
Deep Stinger	45-52
Doomforge Arcanasmith	52-55
Notes: Arcane Missles	
Doomforge Craftsman	49-54
Notes: Throw	
Doomforge Dragoon	54-55 Elite
Notes: Cleave	
Dredge Worm	49-52
Fireguard	50-52 Elite
Notes: Fire Shield	
Fireguard Destroyer	54-56 Elite
Notes: Fire Shield	
Grim Patron	44-52
Guzzling Patron	43-52
Hammered Patron	48-52 Elite
Frequent Drops: Plans: Dark Iron Sunderer (Requires Blacksmithing (275), Requires Weaponsmith)	

NPC	LEVEL
Molten War Golem	55-56 Elite
Quarry Slave	46-48
Notes: Neutral, Strike, Hamstring	
Ragereaver Golem	54-55 Elite
Ribbly's Crony	48-52 Elite
Frequent Drops: Plans: Dark Iron Sunderer (Requires Blacksmithing (275), Requires Weaponsmith)	
Shadowforge Citizen	50-56
Shadowforge Flame Keeper	53-55
Shadowforge Peasant	47-54
Shadowforge Senator	55-56
Twilight Bodyguard	53-54 Elite
Twilight Emissary	52-53 Elite
Twilight's Hammer Ambassador	54-55
Twilight's Hammer Executioner	55-56 Elite
Twilight's Hammer Torturer	50-51 Elite
Voidwalker Minion	57
Warbringer Construct	53-54 Elite
Wrath Hammer Construct	55-56 Elite
Weapon Technician	50-56
Notes: Ranged Attack	

WHAT COMMANDS THE HEAT?

NPC	LEVEL	FREQUENT DROP(S)
AMBASSADOR FLAMELASH	57 Elite	Burst of Knowledge (Trinket, Use: Reduces mana cost of all spells by 100 for 10 sec., Equip: Increases damage and healing done by magical spells and effects by up to 12), Cape of the Fire Salamander (Back, 41 Armor, +6 SPI, +9 STA, +12 Fire Resistance), Circle of Flame (Cloth Head, 74 Armor, +20 STA, +12 Fire Resistance, Use: Channels 75 health into mana every 1 sec for 10 seconds), Flame Wrath (Polearm, 48.2 DPS, Chance on Hit: Envelops the caster with a Fire shield for 15 sec. and shoots a ring of fire dealing 130-170 damage to all nearby enemies), Molten Fists (Mail Hands, 215 Armor, +10 AGI, +11 INT, +11 STA, +10 Fire Resistance)
Notes: Summons several Fire Elementals periodically throughout the fight		
ANGER'REL	55 Elite	
Notes: Strike (like Warrior's Heroic Strike), Shield Block, and Sunder Armor		
ANUB'SHIAH	54 Elite	Carapace of Anub'shiah (Plate Chest, 577 Armor, +11 AGI, +22 STA, +11 STR), Graverot Cape (Back, 36 Armor, +6 SPI, +15 STA), Savage Gladiator Greaves (Mail Feet, 233 Armor, +15 AGI, +13 STA, +10 STR, The Gladiator piece), Shadefiend Boots (Leather Boots, 99 Armor, +4 STR, +9 AGI, +6 STA)
Notes: Enveloping Web (Root), Shadowbolt, Curse of Weakness (Curse, damage dealt is reduced by 41), Immune to Stun, Curse of Tongues		
BAEL'GAR	57 Elite	Force of Magma (Two-Hand Mace, 48.1 DPS, +14 STR, Chance on Hit: Blasts a target for 150 Fire damage), Lavacrest Leggings (Plate Legs, 531 Armor, +12 STA, +28 STR), Rubidium Hammer (Main Hand Mace, 120 Armor, 36.8 DPS, +5 STR), Sash of the Burning Heart (Cloth Waist, 46 Armor, +10 INT, +10 SPI, +10 STA, Equip: Increases damage done by Fire spells and effects by up to 14)
DARK KEEPER BETHEK	55 Elite	Dark Keeper Key
Notes: Amplify Damage (Instant AoE that causes all targets within 30 yards to suffer 100% more damage from all attacks for 10 seconds) and Fireball		
DARK KEEPER OFGUT	55 Elite	Dark Keeper Key
Notes: Anti-Magic Shield (Immune to magic for 10 sec., 2 sec. cast, 10 yd. range) and Arcane Bolt		
DARK KEEPER PELVER	55 Elite	Dark Keeper Key
Notes: Frostbolt		
DARK KEEPER UGGEL	55 Elite	Dark Keeper Key
Notes: Curse of Agony and Shadow Bolt		
DARK KEEPER VORFALK	55 Elite	Dark Keeper Key
Notes: Lightning Bolt and Shock		
DARK KEEPER ZIMREL	55 Elite	Dark Keeper Key
Notes: Holy Smite and Power Word: Shield		
DOOM'REL	57 Elite	
Notes: Summons three Voidwalkers and has the spells Curse of Weakness, Demon Armor, Immolate, and Shadow Bolt Volley		
DOPE'REL	56 Elite	
Notes: Sinister Strike, Gouge, and Backstab		
EMPEROR DAGRAN THAURISSAN	59 Elite	Dreadforge Retaliator (Two-Hand Axe, 50.5 DPS, Equip: Increases your chance to parry an attack by 1%, Improves your chance to get a critical strike by 1%, +30 Attack Power), The Emperor's New Cape (Back, 43 Armor, +7 AGI, +16 STA), Emperor's Seal (Ring, +6 Arcane Resistance, +6 Frost Resistance, +10-11 to two random stats), Force of Will (Trinket, Equip: When struck in combat has a 1% chance of reducing all melee damage done by 25 for 10 seconds, Defense +7), Guiding Staff of Wisdom (Staff, 50.5 DPS, +10 SPI, +11 STA, +10 Frost Resistance, Equip: Increases healing done by spells and effects by up to 53), Hand of Justice (Trinket, Equip: 2% chance on melee hit to gain 1 extra attack, Equip: +20 Attack Power), Imperial Jewel (Neck, +7 STA, Equip: +32 Attack Power), Robes of the Royal Crown (Cloth Chest, 85 Armor, +12 INT, +10 SPI, +19 STA, Equip: Increases damage and healing done by magical spells and effects by up to 18), Ironfoe (Main Hand Mace, 43.5 DPS, Chance on Hit: Grants 2 extra attacks on your next swing), Sash of the Grand Hunt (Mail Waist, 199 Armor, +15 AGI, +6 INT, +14 STA, Equip: Increased Bows/Crossbows/Guns +2), Thaurissan's Royal Scepter (Off-Hand, +5 INT, +10 SPI, +5 STA, Equip: Increases healing done by spells and effects by up to 22), Wristguards of Renown (Leather Wrist, 74 Armor, +10 AGI, +10 STA, +9 STR)
Notes: Avatar of Flame (10 sec. magic immunity and adds 170-230 points of Fire damage to melee attacks), and Hand of Thaurissan (Fire damage and 5 sec. stun)		
EVISCERATOR	54 Elite	Girdle of Beastial Fury (Leather Waist, 89 Armor, +8 STR, +10 STA, Equip: +30 Attack Power), Rubicund Armguards (Mail Wrist, 143 Armor, +8 AGI, +14 STA), Splinthide Shoulders (Leather Shoulders, 138 Armor, +10 INT, +10 STA, +11 STR, Equip: Increases damage and healing done by magical spells and effects by up to 9)
Notes: Anti-Magic Shield, Shadow Bolt Volley, and Vicious Rend (Deals physical damage every 3 sec. for 15 sec.)		
FINEOUS DARKVIRE	54 Elite	Chief Architect's Monocle (Cloth Head, 64 Armor, +27 INT, +3 SPI, +10 STA), Foreman's Head Protector (Plate Head, 469 Armor, +11 INT, +14 STA, +15 STR, Equip: Increases damage and healing done by magical spells and effects by up to 13), Lead Surveyor's Mantle (Mail Shoulder, 246 Armor, +14 INT, +8 SPI, Equip: Increases damage and healing done by magical spells and effects by up to 15), Rubicund Armguards (Mail Wrist, 130 Armor, +6 AGI, +11 STA, Savage Gladiator Grips (Mail Hands, 211 Armor, +9 AGI, +12 INT, +14 STA, +5 STR, The Gladiator Piece), Senior Designer's Pantaloons (Cloth Legs, 69 Armor, +7 INT, +18 SPI, +8 STA, Equip: Increases healing done by spells and effects by up to 40)
Notes: Devotion Aura, Holy Light, Holy Strike, and Kick		
GENERAL ANGERFORGE	57 Elite	Angerforge's Battle Axe (Two-Hand Axe, 48.1 DPS, +11 STA, +27 STR), Force of Will (Trinket, Equip: When struck in combat has a 1% chance of reducing all melee damage taken by 25 for 10 sec., Defense +7), Lord General's Sword (Main-hand Sword, 36.9 DPS, Chance on Hit: Increases attack power by 50 for 30 seconds), Royal Decorated Armor (Mail Chest, 344 Armor, +12 AGI, +26 STA, +8 STR), Warstrife Leggings (Leather Legs, 144 Armor, +6 STR, +6 AGI, +12 STA, Equip: Increases your chance to dodge an attack by 2%)
Notes: Enrage, Flurry, and Sunder Armor; Angerforge calls for help at low health		
GLOOM'REL	56 Elite	
Notes: Cleave, Hamstring, and Mortal Strike		
GOLEM LORD ARGELMACH	58 Elite	Luminary Kilt (Leather Leggings, 147 Armor, +20 INT, +8 SPI, +8 STA, Equip: Increases damage and healing done by magical spells and effects by up to 22), Nagelring (Ring, 50 Armor, +10 STA, Equip: When struck in combat inflicts 3 Arcane damage to the attacker, Increased Defense +5), Omnicast Boots (Cloth Boots, 58 Armor, +9 INT, +6 STA, Equip: Increases damage and healing done by magical spells and effects by up to 22), Second Wind (Trinket, Use: Restores 30 mana every 1 second for 10 seconds, Increases healing done by spells and effects by up to 22)
Notes: Chain Lightning, Lightning Shield, and Shock		
GOROSH THE DERVISH	56 Elite	Bloodclot Band (Finger, +8 INT, +7 SPI, +8 STA, Equip: Increases healing done by spells and effects by up to 15), Flarethorn (One-Hand Dagger, 37.5 DPS, +5 INT, Equip: Increases damage done by Fire spells and effects by up to 17), Leggings of Frenzied Magic (Leather Legs, 142 Armor, +15 INT, +15 STA, Equip: Increases damage and healing done by magical spells and effects by up to 16, Equip: Restores 5 mana per 5 sec.), Savage Gladiator Chain (Mail Chest, 369 Armor, +14 AGI, +13 STA, +13 STR, Equip: Improves your chance to get a critical strike by 2%, The Gladiator piece), Savage Gladiator Helm (Mail Head, 275 Armor, +12 AGI, +28 STA, The Gladiator piece)

NPC	LEVEL	FREQUENT DROP(S)
GRIZZLE	54 Elite	Dregmetal Spaulders (Plate Shoulder, 256 Armor, +6 STR, +5 STA, +15 INT, +10 SPI), Entrenching Boots (Plate Feet, 397 Armor, +5 AGI, +10 INT, +10 STA, +11 STR, Equip: Increases damage and healing done by magical effects by up to 7), Grizzle's Skinner (Main Hand Axe, 36.5 DPS, +6 AGI, +5 STA, +8 STR), Plans: Dark Iron Pulverizer (Requires Blacksmithing (265) & Weaponsmith), Stonewall Girdle (Plate Waist, 484 Armor, +12 STA)
Notes: Cleave and Ground Tremor (2 sec. AoE stun, 5 sec. cooldown)		
HATE'REL	55 Elite	
Notes: Mana Burn, Shadow Bolt, Shadow Shield (deals 27-28 damage to melee attackers, absorbs 550 damage), and Strike (like Warrior's Heroic Strike)		
HEDRUM THE CREEPER	53 Elite	Hookfang Shanker (Dagger, 35.7 DPS, Chance on Hit: Corrosive acid that deals 7 Nature damage every 3 seconds and lowers target's armor by 50 for 30 seconds), Savage Gladiator Helm (Mail Head, 275 Armor, +12 AGI, +28 STA, The Gladiator Piece), Silkweb Gloves (Cloth Hands, 48 Armor, +13 INT, +14 STA, Equip: Restores 3 mana per 5 sec.), Spiderfang Carapace (Plate Chest, 567 Armor, +13 INT, +14 STA, +14 STR, Equip: Increases damage and healing done by magical spells and effects by up to 13)
Notes: Baneful Poison (Heavy instant damage and DoT), Immune to Stun, Paralyzing Poison (8 sec. stun), Web Explosion (AoE root)		
HIGH INTERROGATOR GERSTAHN	52 Elite	Blackveil Cape (Back, 38 Armor, +14 AGI, +6 STR), Enthralled Sphere (Off-Hand, +3 STA, +14 INT, +5 SPI), Greaves of Withering Despair (Mail Feet, 218 Armor, +10 INT, +10 STA, Equip: Increases damage and healing done by magical spells and effects by up to 11, Improves your chance to hit with spells by 1%), Kentic Amice (Cloth Shoulder, 56 Armor, +13 INT, +6 SPI, +5 STA, Equip: Increases damage and healing done by magical spells and effects by up t 14), Spritecaster Cape (Back, 37 Armor, +4 INT, +5 SPI, +4 STA, Equip: Increases damage and healing done by magical spells and effects by up to 14)
Notes: Mana Burn, Psychic Scream (Fear), Shadow Shield, and Shadow Word: Pain		
HIGH PRIESTESS OF THAURISSAN	58 Elite	Ebonsteel Spaulders (Plate Shoulder, 463 Armor, +7 AGI, +16 STA, +6 STR), Hands of the Exalted Herald (Cloth Hands, 52 Armor, +13 INT, +12 SPI, Equip: Increases healing done by spells and effects by up to 33), High Priestess Boots (Cloth Boots, 58 Armor, +20 STA, +7 SPI, +10 Shadow Resistance), Swiftwalker Boots (Leather Boots, 115 Armor, +21 AGI, +7 STA, +4 STR)
Notes: Heal, Renew, Shadow Bolt, and Shadow Word: Pain		
HOUNDMASTER GREBMAR	52 Elite	Blackveil Cape (Back, 38 Armor, +14 AGI, +6 STR), Fleetfoot Greaves (Mail Boots, 218 Armor, +19 AGI, +5 INT, +6 STA), Houndmaster's Bow (Bow, 27.2 DPS, +3 AGI, Equip: Attack Power increased by 24 when fighting beasts), Houndmaster's Rifle (Gun, 27.4 DPS, +3 AGI, Equip: Attack Power increased by 24 when fighting beasts), Spritecaster Cape (Back, 37 Armor, +4 INT, +5 SPI, +5 STA, Equip: Increases damage and healing done by magical spells and effects by up to 14)
Notes: Bloodlust (Increases ally's attack speed by 30% for 30 sec.), Demoralizing Shout, and Pummel		
HURLEY BLACKBREATH	55 Elite	Coal Miner Boots (Leather Feet, 112 Armor, +17 STA, +9 STR, +10 Fire Resistance), Firemoss Boots (Leather Feet, 112 Armor, +18 INT, +8 STA, Equip: Increases healing done by spells and magical effects by up to 20), Hurley's Tankard (Main Hand Mace, 37.6 DPS, +5 AGI, +12 STA), Ragefury Eyepatch (Leather Head, 132 Armor, +6 STR, +9 STA, Equip: Improves your chance to get a critical strike by 2%)
Notes: Drunken Rage and Flame Breath (Frontal cone AoE dealing 550 Fire damage)		
LORD INCENDIUS	56 Elite	Ace of Elementals, Cinderhide Armsplints (Leather Wrist, 71 Armor, +10 Fire Resistance, +9-10 to two random stats), Emberplate Armguards (Plate Wrist, 261 Armor, +10 Fire Resistance, +9-10 to two random stats), Flameweave Cuffs (Cloth Wrist, 35 Armor, +10 Fire Resistance, +9-10 to two random stats), Pyremail Wristguards (Mail Wrists, 148 Armor, +10 Fire Resistance, +9-10 to two random stats)
Notes: Curse of the Firelord (Stacking curse that decreases target's Fire resistance by 100 per application), Fiery Burst (AoE, 500-650 Fire damage, 1.5 sec. cast), Fire Storm (Like Flame Strike, 324-376 initial Fire damage and an additional 185-215 points every 3 sec. for 30 sec.), Immolate, and Mighty Blow (+95 melee damage, knockback)		
LORD ROCCOR	51 Elite	Earthslag Shoulders (Plate Shoulder, 410 Armor, +8 INT, +8 STA, +13 STR, Equip: Increases damage and healing done by magical spells and effects by up to 9), Idol of Ferocity (Unique, Relic, Equip: Reduces the energy cost of Claw and Rake by 3), Mantle of Lost Hope (Cloth Shoulder, 57 Armor, +11 INT, +5 STA, Equip: Increases healing done by spells and effects by up to 26, Restores 3 mana per 5 sec.), Rockshard Pellets (Bullet, 6.0 DPS, 18 damage), Stoneshell Guard (Shield, 1903 Armor, 31 Block, +9 STA, +6 STR)
Notes: Earth Shock, Flame Shock, and Ground Tremor		
MAGMUS	57 Elite	Golem Skull Helm (Plate Head, 477 Armor, +18 STA, +18 STR, Equip: Increased Defense +7), Lavastone Hammer (Two-Hand Mace, 49.7 DPS, +12 INT, +14 STA, +10 STR, Equip: Increases damage and healing done by magical spells and effects by up to 20), Libram of Truth (Unique, Relic, Equip: Increases the armor from your Devotion Aura by 55), Magmus Stone (Off-Hand, +7 STA, +4 SPI, +15 Fire Resistance), Totem of Rage (Unique, Relic, Equip: Increases damage done by Earth Shock, Flame Shock, and Frost Shock by up to 30)
Notes: Fiery Burst and War Stomp		
OK'THOR THE BREAKER	53 Elite	Ban'thok Sash (Cloth Waist, 39 Armor, +10 STA, +11 INT, Equip: Improves your chance to hit with spells by 1%, Increases damage and healing done by magical spells and effects by up to 12), Cyclopean Band (Ring, +7 INT, +4 SPI, +8 STA, +4 STR, Equip: Increases damage and healing done by magical spells and effects by up to 9), Ogreseer Fists (Leather Hands, 97 Armor, +10 INT, +8 SPI, +10 STA, Equip: Increases damage and healing done by magical spells and effects by up to 13), Savage Gladiator Leggings (Mail Legs, 296 Armor, +18 AGI, +19 STA, +12 STR, The Gladiator piece)
Notes: Arcane Bolt, Arcane Explosion, Polymorph, and Slow		
OVERMASTER PYRON	52 Elite	Pattern: Cloak of Fire (Requires Tailoring (275))
Notes: Fire Shield, Fire Blast		
PANZOR THE INVINCIBLE	57 Elite	Rock Golem Bulwark (Shield, 1994 Armor, 36 Block, +10 STA, +10 Arcane Resistance, +10 Nature Resistance), Shalehusk Boots (Plate Feet, 417 Armor, +5 STA, Equip: Increases your chance to dodge an attack by 2%), Soot Encrusted Footwear (Cloth Feet, 55 Armor, +9 INT, +14 SPI, +8 STA, Equip: Increases healing done by spells and effects by up to 20), Stone of the Earth (2-hand Sword, 48.1 DPS, 280 Armor, +12 STA)
PHALANX	55 Elite	Bloodfist (One-Hand Fist Weapon, 36.7 DPS, Chance on Hit: Wounds the target for 20 damage), Fists of Phalanx (Plate Hands, 367 Armor, +20 STR, +9 STA), Golem Fitted Pauldrons (Mail Shoulder, 250 Armor, +13 AGI, +17 STA), Golem Skull Helm (Plate Head, 477 Armor, +18 STR, +18 STA, Equip: Increased Defense +7)
Notes: Fireball Volley, Mighty Blow, and Thunderclap		
PLUGGER SPAZZRING	55 Elite	Barman Shanker (Main Hand Dagger, 36.5 DPS, Chance on Hit: Wounds the target causing them to bleed for 100 damage over 30 seconds), Mixologist's Tunic (Leather Chest, 158 Armor, +11 AGI, +18 STA, +18 STR)
Notes: Vendor; Curse of Tongues, Demon Armor, Immolate, and Shadow Bolt		
PRINCESS MOIRA BRONZEBEARD	58 Elite	Ebonsteel Spaulders (Plate Shoulder, 463 Armor, +7 AGI, +16 STA, +6 STR), Hands of the Exalted Herald (Cloth Hands, 52 Armor, +13 INT, +12 SPI, Equip: Increases healing done by spells and effects by up to 33), High Priestess Boots (Cloth Boots, 58 Armor, +20 STA, +7 SPI, +10 Shadow Resistance), Swiftwalker Boots (Leather Boots, 115 Armor, +21 AGI, +7 STA, +4 STR)
Notes: Heal, Mind Blast, and Renew		
PYROMANCER LOREGRAIN	52 Elite	Flamestrider Robes (Leather Chest, 153 Armor, +5 STA, +6 INT, +16 SPI, +10 Fire Resistance, Equip: Increases damage and healing done by magical spells and effects by up to 20), Kindling Stave (Staff, 45.9 DPS, +12 INT, +13 SPI, +10 STA, +10 Fire Resistance, Equip: Improves your chance to get a critical strike with spells by 1%), Pyric Caduceus (Wand, 52.5 DPS, Equip: Increases damage done by Fire spells and effects by up to 13), Searingscale Leggings (Mail Legs, 277 Armor, +13 AGI, +13 INT, +10 SPI, +13 STA, +10 Fire Resistance)
Notes: Fire Ward, Flame Shock, and Molten Blast		

NPC	LEVEL	FREQUENT DROP(S)
RIBBLY SCREWSPIGOT	53 Elite	Plans: Dark Iron Plate (Requires Blacksmithing (285) & Armorsmith), Ribbly's Bandolier (16-slot ammo bag), Ribbly's Quiver (16-slot quiver), Wayfarer's Knapsack (16-slot bag)
Notes: Gouge and Hamstring		
SEETH'REL	56 Elite	
Notes: Blizzard, Frost Armor, Frost Bolt, Frost Nova, and Frost Ward		
THELDREN	60 Elite	
Notes: Battle Shout, Demoralizing Shout, Disarm, Hamstring, Intercept, Intimidating Shout, and Mortal Strike		
VEREK	55 Elite	Verek's Collar (Neck, +6 STR, +7 STA, Equip: Increases your chance to dodge an attack by 1%), Verek's Leash (Mail Waist, 187 Armor, +8 AGI, +8 INT, +7 SPI, +8 STA, +8 STR, Equip: Increases damage and healing done by magical spells and effects by up to 11)
Notes: Curse of Blood		
VILE'REL	56 Elite	
Notes: Heal, Mind Blast, Power Word: Shield, and Prayer of Healing		
WARDER STILGISS	56 Elite	Arbiter's Blade (Main Hand Sword, 35.2 DPS, +5 INT, +8 STA, Equip: Increases damage and healing done by magical spells and effects by up to 8), Boreal Mantle (Cloth Shoulder, 61 Armor, +8 INT, +5 STA, Equip: Increases damage done by Frost spells and effects by up to 29), Chillsteel Girdle (Mail Waist, 190 Armor, +20 INT, +7 SPI, +10 Frost Resistance), Dark Warder's Pauldrons (Leather Shoulder, 122 Armor, +17 AGI, +7 STA, +11 STR)
Notes: Frost Armor, Frost Bolt, Frost Nova, and Frost Ward		
WATCHMAN DOOMGRIP	55 Elite	
Notes: Sunder Armor, can drink a healing potion in battle		

THE DEPTHS AWAIT

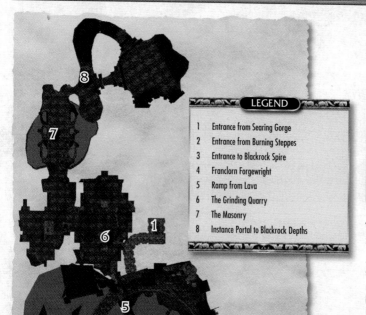

LEGEND

1   Entrance from Searing Gorge
2   Entrance from Burning Steppes
3   Entrance to Blackrock Spire
4   Franclorn Forgewright
5   Ramp from Lava
6   The Grinding Quarry
7   The Masonry
8   Instance Portal to Blackrock Depths

THE MOLTEN SPAN

Walking through the doors brings you to an impressive sight. A large rock structure is suspended over a pool of lava by massive chains. Jump onto the northeast chain and take it to the central structure. If you're traveling in ghost form, now's a good time to pick up the *Dark Iron Legacy* quest from Franclorn Forgewright. Descend through the tomb and across another chain to a landing just above the lava. The Grinding Quarry is just ahead.

WARM FEET?

Should you fall into the lava, all is not lost. There is a ramp on the north wall. Drink a swim speed potion if available and make it to the ramp as quickly as possible. With a healer to support you, survival is possible.

THE GRINDING QUARRY

There are several Anvilrage Wardens and Overseers moving about supervising the many Quarry Slaves. This area is rather easy to move through and can be bypassed altogether by a careful party. However, now is a good time to get a bit of practice against the enemy and help your Warlock stock up on Soul Shards.

Like most jobs, supervising the slaves doesn't totally consume your attention. Watch for pairs of Anvilrage Wardens or Overseers standing around talking. If a fleeing enemy reaches one of these groups, the ensuing fight should be taken seriously.

THE MASONRY

The Quarry Slaves aren't found here. Only pairs of Anvilrage Wardens and Overseers stand along the walkways to the sides and wander in the middle. Fight cautiously as Overmaster Pyron patrols the entire Masonry.

Clear your way to the instance portal and prepare to fight Overmaster Pyron. He has a ranged spell making him difficult to pull. Attack when he is patrolling across the center area. Interrupt his spells when you can and slay him. If the fight takes a turn for the worse, retreat through the instance portal and return to resurrect and regroup.

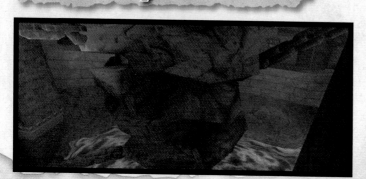

⊛ A CITY WITHOUT SUNLIGHT

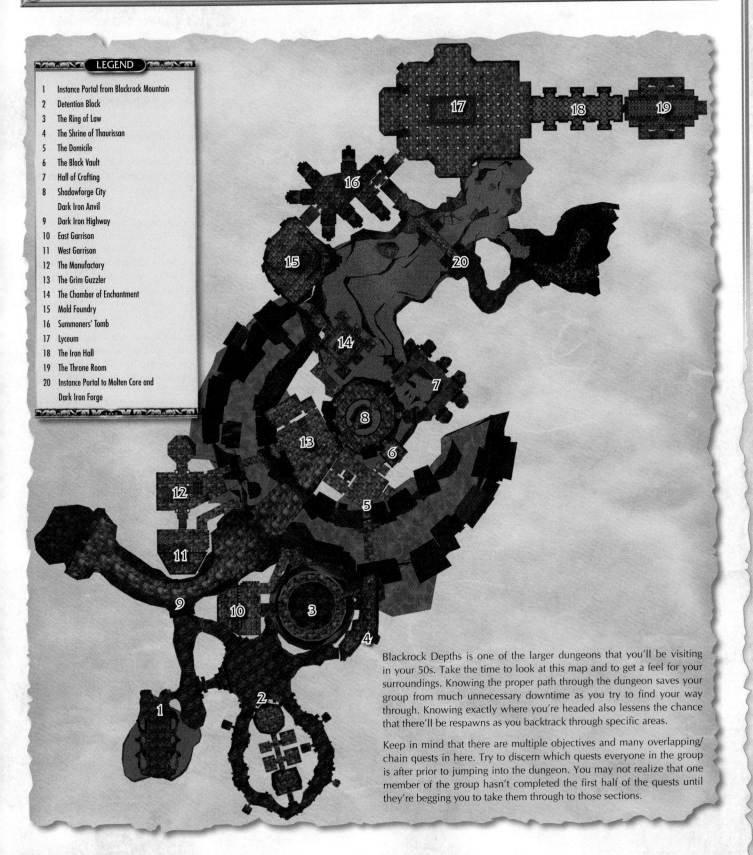

LEGEND

1 Instance Portal from Blackrock Mountain
2 Detention Block
3 The Ring of Law
4 The Shrine of Thaurissan
5 The Domicile
6 The Black Vault
7 Hall of Crafting
8 Shadowforge City
  Dark Iron Anvil
9 Dark Iron Highway
10 East Garrison
11 West Garrison
12 The Manufactory
13 The Grim Guzzler
14 The Chamber of Enchantment
15 Mold Foundry
16 Summoners' Tomb
17 Lyceum
18 The Iron Hall
19 The Throne Room
20 Instance Portal to Molten Core and
   Dark Iron Forge

Blackrock Depths is one of the larger dungeons that you'll be visiting in your 50s. Take the time to look at this map and to get a feel for your surroundings. Knowing the proper path through the dungeon saves your group from much unnecessary downtime as you try to find your way through. Knowing exactly where you're headed also lessens the chance that there'll be respawns as you backtrack through specific areas.

Keep in mind that there are multiple objectives and many overlapping/chain quests in here. Try to discern which quests everyone in the group is after prior to jumping into the dungeon. You may not realize that one member of the group hasn't completed the first half of the quests until they're begging you to take them through to those sections.

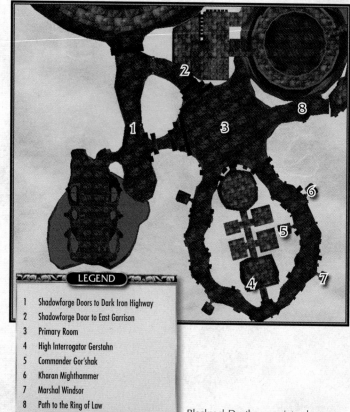

LEGEND

1 Shadowforge Doors to Dark Iron Highway
2 Shadowforge Door to East Garrison
3 Primary Room
4 High Interrogator Gerstahn
5 Commander Gor'shak
6 Kharan Mighthammer
7 Marshal Windsor
8 Path to the Ring of Law

Blackrock Depths opens into a large room with several patrols and many standing enemies. The patrols typically consist of Bloodhounds and Anvilrage Wardens. These are very dangerous as their aggro range is large and the Bloodhounds have the added ability to detect stealth. Pull the patrols as they wander between groups of stationary Anvilrage Dwarves. When the patrols have been thinned, pull the Dwarves. This room should be cleared entirely before continuing.

With the Primary Room clear, begin moving down the southeast passage. Clear the enemies slowly and keep the Dwarves from running for help. There are prison doors along both sides of the passage. These are locked and require the Prison Key or a Rogue with at least 250 lockpicking.

Clear the entire ring before moving to the archway near the High Interrogator. There is a Twilight's Hammer Torturer speaking with Gerstahn. There are also two Bloodhounds and an Anvilrage Warden around the corner to the right. The two groups are linked and it's difficult to pull them separately, but there is another option. Mind Soothe both the Torturer and Gerstahn. Then quickly Mind Control the Torturer near the Anvilrage Warden. The Torturer should draw all the aggro; just make sure that the Torturer dies before the MC breaks.

Gerstahn's Psychic Scream can be quite dangerous for your party and she should be the primary target. All DPS should be focused on Gerstahn while CC should be focused on the Anvilrage Warden or the Torturer. Keep Gerstahn stunned or interrupted to avoid her devastating spells. When Gerstahn falls, killing the Bloodhounds will be fast, and any remaining enemies fall under the "clean up" category.

Remove the **Prison Key** from Gerstahn's Corpse and free your friends. Horde parties need to free Commander Gor'shak. Once you have spoken to him, two parties of Anvilrage Dwarves spawn down either passage. This fight is very difficult as the Dwarves begin the fight enraged and come from both directions. Have your party in one passage when the encounter is started. The enemies in the other passage must be CCed. If you have a healer in addition to a Priest, consider having the Priest Mind Control one to tie them up while the party kills the other three. Once the Dwarves are dead, speak with Gor'shak again.

Alliance groups need to speak with Marshal Windsor. You'll be seeing Windsor a number of times. Once you have spoken with him, he asks you to return to Marshal Maxwell. If your party intends to stay together for a long time, make a return trip to Maxwell now. If your party is only interested in loot, continue. You'll be back soon enough.

Once Marshal Maxwell has been apprised of the situation with Windsor, return to Blackrock Depths. As you kill the Anvilrage Dwarves, watch for a **Crumpled Note** to drop. This needs to be taken to Windsor once you find it.

WINDSOR NEEDS HELP

Once the Crumpled Note is given to Windsor, he asks you to retrieve his information from General Angerforge and Argelmach. Now would be a good time to get this step of the quest as you will be seeing them soon.

You've done all you can do here. Move through the east passage toward the Ring of Law.

THE RING OF LAW AND THE SHRINE OF THAURISSAN

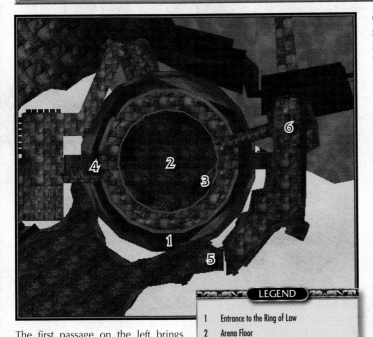

The first passage on the left brings you into the arena. There are two typical options here. Either you fight the "standard" battle by initiating the event with High Justice Grimstone, or trigger "The Challenge" with a Banner of Provocation. Both options are listed below.

LEGEND

1	Entrance to the Ring of Law
2	Arena Floor
3	Ledge
4	Stairs to Second Floor
5	The Shrine of Thaurissan
6	Bridge to The Domicile

THE CHALLENGE

Once one of your party challenges Theldren, a relatively randomized combination of five of NPCs (one of which is always Theldren) will attack during the event. The abilities of each are listed in the following table.

The best tactic is to have either the MT hold Theldren or have an off tank kite him while the rest of the group focuses fire on one caster at a time. Taking out the highest threat first (healers/DPS) is the accepted concept here. Since the bosses are humanoid, they're susceptible to most forms of CC: Blind, Gouge, Polymorph, etc.

Once the casters begin to fall, the threat diminishes greatly. Once Theldren falls, your party will stand victorious as winners of the Challenge.

STANDARD ENCOUNTER

The event triggers once a party member walks onto the center grate. Have your MT move up and begin. High Justice Grimstone will walk over to unlock the east gate and release two groups of enemies. They're inevitably non-elite, so a tank/AoE combo works perfectly (Frost Nova/ AoE is another option). Make sure to keep your ranged DPS and healers in the center of the room and take on the enemies as close to the gate as possible to prevent them from running freely through your party.

Once the two groups of enemies are dead, Grimstone will unlock the west gate. This battle is more difficult, but not anything that should wipe your group. Either a single elite or a pair of elites enters the arena. Definitely have the MT focus on grabbing the aggro initially and take the enemy down with focused fire. However, if you fail to take these enemies down, the gate will still be open and allow you to continue through the rest of the dungeon.

Move through the western gate and up the stairs. There are three pairs of Anvilrage Dwarves (either Footmen or Guardsmen) to the left and four groups to the right. Watch out. A couple Fireguards patrol the room in addition to the standing groups of mobs; aggroing the wrong mob could result in some trouble.

Ignore the enemies for now and take the stairs to the upper arena floor. The Spectators are neutral to you now that you've given them a good show. Move across the area and take the stairs to the Shrine of Thaurissan. There's a large group of Shadowforge Peasants, Twilight Emissaries, or Twilight Bodyguards at the bottom of the stairs.

Wait for the patrolling Fireguard to leave before beginning this battle. The Emissaries and Bodyguards are elite and should be CC'd until the Peasants are killed. Sap, Polymorph, and Mind Control work well in this situation.

With the group eliminated, wait for the Fireguard to return and vanquish him in a cleared area. Clear the passage to the south. There are two more encounters like this at the ramp. The southern passage is a dead end, but you'll be returning later. Take the northern passage when it's clear.

Two Blazing Fireguards prevent access to the bridge. Clear them and move onto the bridge, but don't go too far. Stepping onto the bridge causes an Anvilrage Guardsman to spawn on each side of the on each side of the bridge and, of course, attack! However, if you didn't stray too far onto the bridge, you should only receive the aggro of the one now behind you. Clear the Guardsman and prepare for the other. He occasionally brings the other pair of Fireguards with him when he's pulled, so be wary.

Clear the pair of Blazing Fireguards at the far side of the bridge and enter the Domicile.

ENEMIES IN "THE CHALLENGE"

NPC	RACE	CLASS/DESCRIPTION
THELDREN	Dwarf	Warrior
Notes: Always present during the Challenge; Battle Shout, Demoralizing Shout, Disarm, Hamstring, Intercept, Intimidating Shout, Mortal Strike		
KORV	Tauren	Shaman
Notes: Earthbind Totem, Fire Nova Totem, Frost Shock, Lesser Healing Wave, Purge, War Stomp, and Windfury Totem		
LEFTY	Gnome	Monk
Notes: Dual Wield Fists, Five Fat Finger Exploding Heart Technique (2000 damage if you move), Snap Kick (Spell interrupt and Silence), and Trip (Knockdown)		
MALGEN LONGSPEAR	Centaur	Hunter
Notes: Pet — Gnashjaw, Aimed Shot, Concussive Shot (Chance to stun), Multi-shot, Shoot (8 yard min./30 yard max. bow shot), and Wing Clip		
REZZNIK	Goblin	Engineer
Notes: Arcanite Dragonling, Disorient Grenade (Short Stun), Explosive Sheep, Goblin Dragon Gun, and Recombobulator (Heal and Dispel Polymorph)		
ROTFANG	Gnoll	Rogue
Notes: Crippling Poison, Eviscerate, Gouge, Kick, Kidney Shot, Sinister Strike, and Vanish		
SNOKH BLACKSPINE		
Notes: Blast Wave, Flamestrike, Impact (10% chance of 2 sec. stun to all Fire spells), Polymorph, Pyroblast, and Scorch		
VA'JASHNI	Troll	Priest
Notes: Blackout (Shadow Spells have a 10% chance to stun), Dispel Magic, Flash Heal, Power Word: Shield, Psychic Scream, Renew, and Shadow Word: Pain		
VOLIANA	Undead (Forsaken)	Mage
Notes: Cone of Cold, Frost Bolt (10% bonus slow effect), Frost Nova, Ice Block, and Improved Blizzard		

LEGEND

1 Bridge from the Shrine of Thaurissan
2 The Domicile
3 Entrance to Shadowforge City
4 The Black Vault
5 Entrance to the Hall of Crafting
6 Fineous Darkvire
7 Lord Incendius
  Dark Iron Anvil
8 Bridge to the Dark Iron Highway

With the Bloodhound Mastiffs in the area, stealthing is much more dangerous and Sapping is nearly impossible. Use other forms of CC when the Bloodhounds are nearby. There are four groups in the Domicile's main room. Each group consists of two or three Anvilrage Medics, Footmen, or Soldiers, a Bloodhound Mastiff and a Blazing Fireguard.

Banishing the Fireguard and Polymorphing one of the Dwarves decreases the number of enemies substantially. Your tank should hold the other Dwarves while the party first kills the Bloodhound, then any enemies still on the tank. Kill the CCed enemies as CC breaks and repeat for each of the four groups.

Each of the three smaller rooms has enemies that can be bypassed without adversely affecting anything except the amount of booty you bring back. It's up to you whether you take them out for the goods, or rush through this area to focus on more substantial enemies. Kill the group in the northwest room to clear the way to Shadowforge City.

DARK KEEPER PORTRAIT

There is a clickable portrait on the left in the Black Vault (when facing the vault). When you interact with this portrait, a random Dark Keeper will spawn in one of six locations throughout the instance. After the portrait has been "unlocked", read the nameplate to learn where the Dark Keeper has spawned.

Once you have found and killed the Dark Keeper, he drops a **Dark Keeper Key**. This key is used inside the Black Vault to open the Dark Coffer. Inside the Dark Coffer is a random world drop item and usually, at least one of the following: **Burning Essence, Eye of Kajal, or Black Blood of the Tormented**.

The Burning Essence is used with a Libram of Resilience which adds 20 Fire Resistance to Head or Legs. The Eye of Kajal is used with a Libram of Tenacity which adds 125 Armor to Head or Legs. The Black Blood of the Tormented is used with a Libram of Rumination which adds 150 Mana to Head or Legs. Each of these is an extremely valuable prize.

The enemies in Shadowforge City come in groups of six. Twilight Emissaries, Twilight Bodyguards, and Anvilrage Officers make up the elite portions of the enemies and should be CCed until the Shadowforge Peasants and Doomforge Craftsman are killed. This is a good place for AoEs provided you keep the fight away from the CCed enemies. Kill the first two groups

around the ring. Pull the enemies out of the first room in the Black Vault when you're party is prepared. All six in the room are social and pull at once. With the way clear, attack Warder Stilgiss and Verek. Do not open the coffers when the enemies are dead.

Designate one coffer to be opened last and make sure it's the main tank that does the opening. Open the others with the **Coffer Keys** that have been looted. You need 12 keys to trigger the event. If your party does not have enough, continue and come back to this event when you are fully supplied.

With the opening of the final coffer, Watchman Doomgrip attacks and wakes the four Warbringer Constructs. The Constructs are immune to most forms of CC, but stuns and Freezing Traps work perfectly, so it's a good idea to lay down a Freezing Trap before opening the last coffer.

If possible, have a Paladin open the final coffer and, just before the mobs spawn, cast Divine Shield. This offers the party up to 12 seconds (depending on the Paladin's timing) to kill one of the adds or the boss in relative safety since the Paladin will be "tanking" while invulnerable. Horde groups can use the same tactic with the MT and a Limited Invulnerability Potion. Have the MT work on keeping the attention of the party's target and as many others as possible. Any enemies that run after a ranged ally should be peeled by the off tank or Rogue and returned to the MT. This is the fight in which you should use all your long-timer abilities. The enemies need to be brought down quickly as they hit very hard. Kill the Dwarf first, then the Constructs one at a time. Parties with substantial AoE potential and great faith in themselves can AoE this group, but it's not recommended. With the enemies dead, open the box for a rare item and grab the **Heart of the Mountain** to complete the *Heart of the Mountain* quest.

Return to Shadowforge City and clear the final group. Take the east passage into the Hall of Crafting. The stationary Warbringer Constructs are linked to three Doomforge Craftsmen each. There are several of these groups along the ramp down. There are also two patrols to watch for: a patrolling Warbringer Construct and Fineous Darkvire.

Pull and kill the patrolling Construct when it's away from any groups. With the monstrosity dead, locate Fineous. When Fineous is moving down the ramp or has reached the bottom, engage the first enemy group. The Doomforge Craftsmen throw dynamite rather than entering melee, so CC what you can and kill what you can't. When the last of the Craftsmen are dead, finish off the Construct.

This should be your pattern as you move down the ramp. Kill each group separately and don't engage Fineous until you have the first three groups cleared. This gives you a good spot to kill him without adds. Fineous is fairly powerful, but can't hold his own alone. His attacks can be nullified by a tank with a healer. Hold him away from the party and remind him of the weakness of evil. Loot Ironfel for the *Dark Iron Legacy* quest.

Two Blazing Fireguards defend the doorway to Lord Incendius. Handle these as you have handled all elemental pairs. Banish one and kill the other. Then kill the banished when the spell ends. Incendius patrols on a platform above a lake of lava. The platform is a bad place to engage him as he can knock party members into the lava and out of resurrection range. Have your MT pull Incendius to the entryway. Interrupt Incendius' first spell and drag him back to your party. Once off the walkway, keep Incendius interrupted and the tank's health high. Incendius' Curse of the Firelord should be removed when possible. It reduces Fire Resistance by 100 with each application and it stacks. Killing Incendius completes the second step of *Disharmony of Fire* for Horde parties and *Lord Incendius* for Alliance parties.

Now it's time to do a bit of backtracking. Travel to the Shrine of Thaurissan by way of Shadowforge City and the Domicile. The Shrine sits at the end of the southern passage. Place Ironfel in the statue to complete *Dark Iron Legacy* and receive the Shadowforge Key.

With the key, you can bypass all you have done so far and head straight to the deeper parts of the dungeon on later adventures. Move back to the Detention Block and take the passage to the Dark Iron Highway.

THE DARK IRON HIGHWAY

LEGEND

1 Entrance from the Detention Block
2 Shadowforge Door to East Garrison
3 Bael'Gar
4 Bridge to Lord Incendius

The Dark Iron Highway is not to be taken lightly. Every group you face has a combination of five elites. Of which, one is always a paladin and at least one other is a priest. The groups often change position along the passage and roam. This should be taken slowly and only if you are here for Bael'Gar.

The fight should be started by CCing the Anvilrage Officer and as many of the Anvilrage Medics as possible. Sap should land first if there is a Rogue in your party, followed by Polymorph. Mind Control a Medic if possible. They'll be the first target for the rest of the mobs and still offer healing options if your party gets aggro. Improved Sap is another perfect CC option.

Kill any non-CCed Medics before taking on the Soldiers and Footmen. Footmen should be killed before Soldiers as their damage is higher, but stay on the same target as the rest of the party. The Officer should be killed last as he raises a Divine Shield when low on health.

With the first group dead, pick off the patrolling Blazing Fireguard and the patrolling Dwarf group before continuing. Also watch for the patrolling hounds. Pull them to your party when they are too far to bring friends.

Move along the west passage toward Bael'Gar. Move slowly and keep the area around you cleared. Check for patrollers before starting each fight. There are groups in the north and south edges just before Bael'Gar. Clear these before engaging Bael'Gar.

Shield your tank and charge Bael'Gar. His damage output is devastating, so keep the tank's health high. Turn Bael'Gar around so he is facing away from the party. This makes it easy to see when he changes targets. Should he do so, cease fire. Stop all attacks until the tank has regained Bael'Gar's attention and pulled him back into position. Keep him away from your healer at all times. It's a long fight. Keep hitting him until he doesn't hit back any longer. When he falls, grab the loot and move to the East Garrison Door.

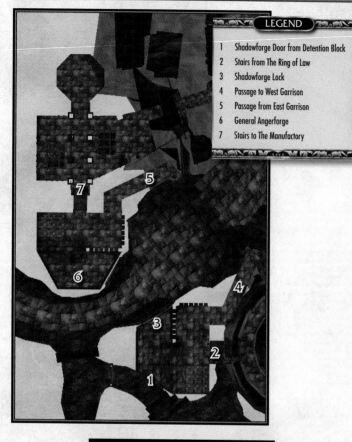

LEGEND

1. Shadowforge Door from Detention Block
2. Stairs from The Ring of Law
3. Shadowforge Lock
4. Passage to West Garrison
5. Passage from East Garrison
6. General Angerforge
7. Stairs to The Manufactory

The enemies in the West Garrison are a bit more powerful than in the East. As before, banish any Fireguard Destroyers and CC the Doomforge Dragoons when possible. The Dragoons have Cleave and can inflict major damage to several party members if left unchecked.

With the top level of the West Garrison cleared, move down the ramp. There's a landing that offers a clear view of the three groups on the lower level. General Angerforge stands in one, but should not be engaged until the other two groups are dealt with.

Take the two Fireguard Destroyers at the end of the ramp first. Banish and focus fire as you have done before. When they are dead, move to the landing and jump down toward the eastern group next.

Put all pets on stay before jumping down. All party members must come down. If someone on the ledge pulls aggro, the enemy will run around the ramp and grab General Angerforge in the process. When everyone, except pets, is down, prepare for the fight.

PETS ARE DANGEROUS

One option is to dismiss your pets, jump down, and resummon them to help in the battle. Jumping down and allowing your pets to find their own path is a recipe for disaster.

A Doomforge Dragoon and two Anvilrage Marshalls wait ahead. This fight is more difficult than the Fireguards as the Dwarves flee when low on health. This cannot be allowed. Kill these and prepare for the fight against Angerforge.

Angerforge is surrounded by four Anvilrage Reservists. They're non-elite, but inflict some serious damage. Have your MT hold aggro while they drag Angerforge back toward the bridge between the two Garrisons, but not all the way to the bridge; several elementals spawn to prevent Angerforge being pulled too far. Any mobs summoned by his call for help appear near his spawn point (up the stairs) and it takes them longer to reach the party if he's pulled away.

Have the MA target Angerforge's allies and begin whipping through them. With the Reservists down, Angerforge is a much easier target. Bring his health down while conserving mana. When Angerforge's health drops substantially, he'll call for help. Hopefully, you'll be away from his spawn point and have time to unleash your party's full DPS to drop Angerforge. It takes a few moments for the cavalry to arrive and you need Angerforge dead before they do.

With Angerforge dead, focus your damage on the enemy healers before engaging the others. When all opposition is down, loot General Angerforge and gain Marshal Windsor's Lost Information for *A Shred of Hope* for Alliance parties. Killing him completes *Operation: Death to Angerforge* for Horde groups. Move down the north stairs to The Manufactory.

The Shadowforge Lock stands in the East Garrison. It's guarded by several groups of Anvilrage Dwarves and Fire Elementals. Clear your way to the lock and use the Shadowforge Key to open the passage to the West Garrison.

With the lock tripped, move up the stairs. Watch out for the patrolling Fireguard. The stairs end at a room you've been in. This time, the enemies need to die.

Three groups of Anvilrage Footman and Guardsman occupy the southern side of the room. Clear them one group at a time and turn your attention to the north side of the room. There are several more groups of Anvilrage Dwarves with Fireguards on the north side of the room. Slowly clear your way to the Bridge to West Garrison.

BE SNEAKY

If you are level 60 and very careful (or a Rogue), you can open the Shadowforge Lock without killing any of the guards around it.

THE MANUFACTORY

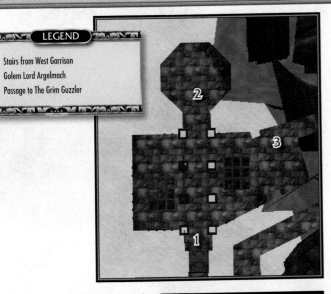

LEGEND

1 Stairs from West Garrison
2 Golem Lord Argelmach
3 Passage to The Grim Guzzler

Pulling is possible if the puller ducks behind one of the many pillars or corners to break line of sight. Doing this forces the enemies to advance around the corner to regain line of sight.

Clear the entire room before resting for Argelmach. Check buffs and be prepared for a frantic fight. The enemies quickly dish out some massive damage. Argelmach and the Golems have several spells that ignore your tank's armor. Bring Argelmach and the Golems into the larger room in case of a total party wipeout.

This is a fight for timed abilities. Golem Lord Argelmach needs to be killed as quickly as possible. Having a secondary tank to peel one of the Golems while a pet takes the aggro of the other, will save the main tank's life and the healer's mana. Argelmach cannot be stunned and casts instant spells. With no way to reduce his damage capability, it comes down to attrition. Make sure he loses the fight by using every damage ability you have. The Golems aren't nearly as dangerous as Argelmach, so don't hold anything back. With Argelmach dead, focus on the golems one at a time and kill them like any other fight.

Killing Argelmach advances the *Rise of the Machines* quest for Horde parties. Alliance parties should loot the **Marshal Windsor's Lost Information** from Argelmach to advance the *A Shred of Hope* quest.

Take the northeast passage to The Grim Guzzler.

The stairs end in a large room with many enemies. All the enemies have ranged attacks and are in large groups. The enemies flee when at low health. These three facts make life difficult for your healer so keep an eye on your healer's health bar.

Take out the single patrolling enemies first. Have AoEs ready when you engage the large groups. The tank should maintain aggro on the Golem while the DPS takes care of all the non-elite enemies.

THE GRIM GUZZLER AND SHADOWFORGE CITY

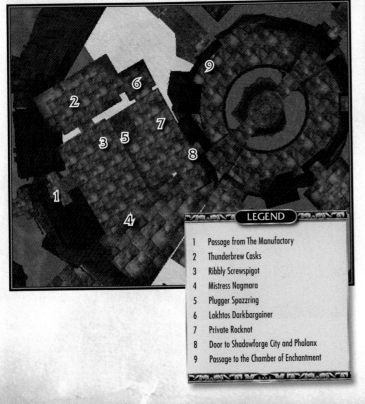

LEGEND

1 Passage from The Manufactory
2 Thunderbrew Casks
3 Ribbly Screwspigot
4 Mistress Nagmara
5 Plugger Spazzring
6 Lokhtos Darkbargainer
7 Private Rocknot
8 Door to Shadowforge City and Phalanx
9 Passage to the Chamber of Enchantment

The passage to The Grim Guzzler is guarded by two groups of three Fireguard Destroyers. These fights are a little more difficult unless you have two Warlocks with you. The strategy is still the same: banish what you can, kill what you can't.

The first thing your party should do when entering The Grim Guzzler is to wait and do nothing. There are a lot of things to do, but if the party runs in different directions, everyone will die. The Patrons are neutral until attacked. When attacked, the entire bar becomes aggressive. Avoid using AoEs if there is any chance a Patron will be caught in them.

Move your party to the room to the left with the Thunderbrew Kegs. From here, send the tank to speak with Ribbly Screwspigot to begin the fight. Once begun, drag him and his Cronies back into the Thunderbrew room before attacking. Keep the fight in here to avoid hitting the Patrons.

Ribbly has a number of friends, but some CC helps that number gets smaller quickly. Take out Ribbly for the *Ribbly Screwspigot* quest, then finish off his Cronies.

Rest up and smash the Thunderbrew Kegs when you're ready. This spawns Hurley Blackbreath and three Blackbreath Cronies at the bar. They take a moment to reach you, so be patient. This fight is much like the fight against Ribbly.

When the enemies are dead, loot them for the *Lost Thunderbrew Recipe* and *Hurley Blackbreath* quests for Horde and Alliance parties.

With the fighting done for now, speak with Mistress Nagmara to begin *The Love Potion* quest. It involves leaving Blackrock Depths, so you won't complete it until your next pass through.

Lokhtos Darkbargainer stands in the alcove on the upper level; he accepts a number of items to increase your reputation with the Thorium Brotherhood. See the table below for a list of what he accepts.

THORIUM BROTHERHOOD REPUTATION

ITEM	NUMBER	REPUTATION
Dark Iron Ore	10	50
Blood of the Mountain	1	200
Core Leather	4	150
Fiery Core	4	200
Lava Core	4	200

Plugger Spazzring walks along the bar and sells rare recipes and drinks. Only one party member should buy the drinks as they are needed to get out of the bar. Have the Rogue Pickpocket Plugger for the Grim Guzzler Key.

Once the talking is done, it's time to deal with Phalanx and leave. Give Private Rocknot drinks until he heads to the kegs. When he starts moving, take your position around Phalanx and prepare for the fight. Remember to avoid using AoEs as there are Patrons nearby. Private Rocknot attacks the kegs causing one to blow the door open. Phalanx becomes aggressive as he moves to guard the now open door. Pull Phalanx to the corner and beat him down.

OPENING THE DOOR

There are two other ways to open the Grim Guzzler Door. One is to complete *The Love Potion* quest. When you give Mistress Nagmara the materials she needs, she takes Private Rocknot through the door and into the alleyway to test the potion.

The other way is to pickpocket the Grim Guzzler Key from Plugger Spazzring. However, this should only be done if: a) you don't want to fight Phalanx and b) you're prepared to aggro him and the rest of the patrons in the bar.

Move through the door and into Shadowforge City. There are three groups around this side of the ring. You need only kill the first two to proceed.

The groups should be taken as before. Sap and/or Polymorph Doomforge Dragoons or Anvilrage Marshals. Banish the Fireguard Destroyer when present. Mind Control a Doomforge Dragoon or Anvilrage Marshal. DPS party members should bring down the non-elites quickly and then take the elites one at a time as CC breaks.

Clear the way to the northwest passage and move to the Chamber of Enchantment.

THE PATH TO THE EMPEROR

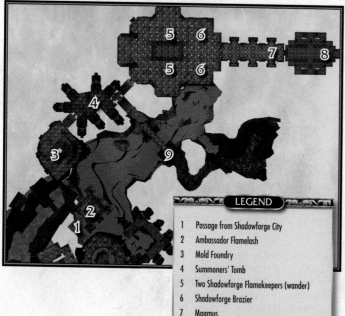

LEGEND

1. Passage from Shadowforge City
2. Ambassador Flamelash
3. Mold Foundry
4. Summoners' Tomb
5. Two Shadowforge Flamekeepers (wander)
6. Shadowforge Brazier
7. Magmus
8. Emperor Dagran Thaurissan
9. Instance Portal to Molten Core

The Chamber of Enchantment seems very clear with only Ambassador Flamelash standing in the center. Once pulled, Flamelash will call for low level fire elementals to come to his aid until he dies. Ignore the elementals. When they reach Flamelash, they self-destruct and provide a small boost to his attack damage. Have your party unleash their full DPS on Flamelash to drop him quickly. As long as your MT retains aggro and their health, this shouldn't be a terribly difficult encounter. Search Flamelash's body for your reward and take the passage to the Mold Foundry.

There are several groups of Molten War Golems and Doomforge Arcanasmiths in this room. There is a patrolling Molten War Golem that should be dealt with before you start attacking the larger groups.

Have your DPS or AoE party members kill the Arcanasmiths while the rest of the party focuses on the Molten War Golem. Take the groups one at a time as you move toward the next room.

There are no enemies, at first glance, in the Summoners' Tomb. There are only a number of ghosts standing in front of their coffins. The path is blocked. You must accept and defeat the challenge issued by Doom'rel to continue.

When the event starts, one of the ghosts becomes hostile and attacks your party. A short while later, the next activates. The chain continues until Doom'rel attacks. The ghosts are on a timer, so if you don't kill one fast enough, another activates so you'll be faced with two simultaneously. The "Seven Dwarves" represent a variety of classes and can be a challenge. Each Dwarf's abilities are listed in the "What Commands the Heat" table earlier in this section. For slower groups, it should be noted that the enemies are, in fact, undead and susceptible to Shackle Undead. If the party is slow in defeating a particular enemy, Shackle the add before continuing.

Work through each Dwarf by focusing on the weakness of the class they represent: Anger'rel (Warrior), Seeth'rel (Caster), Dope'rel (Rogue), Gloom'rel (Warrior), Vile'rel (Priest), and Hate'rel (Caster). Defeat each of the ghosts in succession until Doom'rel (Caster) activates.

When Doom'rel attacks, he brings three Voidwalkers with him. His attacks are not terribly powerful, and as long as your healer has mana, this fight is simple. If your healer is out of mana, fight very aggressively. Kill him first, and then clean up his minions. A chest with two rare items spawns near the now open doors when the fight is finished.

If your party seeks *Attunement to the Core*, take the right path first. There are three elementals guarding the bridge. Warlocks should banish as many as possible while the party kills the elementals one at a time. Their AoE fire attacks are devastating. Keep your party's health at full.

A small catwalk leads into a lavaflow to the left. A lone elemental guards the Dark Iron Forge. Blacksmiths wanting to smelt Dark Iron Ore need this forge, so clear the elemental for them.

Another group of three elementals guards the far side of the bridge. Defeat these as you did the previous group. Standing before you is the large green portal to Molten Core. To the left there's a spike with the necessary Core Fragment. Grab it, recross the bridge, and head north.

The next room is terribly dangerous. It is filled with large groups of non-elite dwarves of all types. The frightening part is the respawn rate. The enemy groups respawn every minute.

The doors on the other side can only be opened when both the Shadowforge Braziers are lit with Shadowforge Torches. The torches drop only from the Shadowforge Flamekeepers. Your party should move east toward the southern brazier. Kill and move quickly to the next fight. AoE is wonderful for the sake of speed. Arcane Explosion and Rain of Fire work wonders. Make sure someone loots the torch from the Flamekeeper on the way

The Shadowforge Torch decays in 5 minutes. Once looted, the person needs to light the brazier as soon as the party engages the Fireguard Destroyer guarding it. With one brazier lit, move to the center of the room for the next Flamekeeper. Get the torch and move to the other brazier to open the doors. Once the doors are open, go through them as quickly as possible.

The next room is occupied by Magmus. There are three statues along each wall. At random intervals during the battle, the statues will throw flame for several seconds. Once the fight is begun, don't stand in front of these. Stand against the wall between them when possible.

Magmus himself is a dangerous foe, but doesn't have anything you haven't fought before. Keep Magmus facing away from the party to make it easier to see when he changes targets. When he pulls away from the tank, all other party members should stop what they are doing until the tank regains Magmus' attention. Stay out of the way of the flame-throwers and bring Magmus down for loot and the way past.

The end is in sight. Standing before his throne is Emperor Dagran Thaurissan with Princess Moira Bronzebeard. All that stands in your way is a roomful of enemies.

Every enemy in the room must die before you engage the Emperor. The Emperor calls for aid as soon as the fight begins. Make sure no one answers.

Many of the enemy groups are one or two elites with several non-elites. Take them as you have been the entire dungeon. When the room is clear rest up and restore buffs. The next fight is a fight to use every item and timed ability you have.

To complete *The Princess Saved?* Quest, you must not kill Moira. This is harder than it sounds for she's under Dagran's influence and will heal him and attack your party freely. Have a Rogue off-tank her and interrupt her heals with Kick while the rest of your party focuses on Dagran. Make sure the MT maintains the highest spot on the threat list for the entirety of the Dagran encounter. Dagran has two abilities that can wreak havoc on ranged DPS members.

Hand of Thaurissian is inflicts Fire damage and a 5 sec. stun to anyone outside of melee range that draws his aggro. Avatar of Flame provides Dagran with a 10 sec. immunity to magic and adds additional Fire damage to his melee attacks. Make sure your casters hold back when he's under the effect of this ability and let loose immediately when it falls.

Use everything you have to bring Dagran down and keep Moira alive. Search his body for your loot and speak with Moira before returning to your people as the conquerors of Blackrock Depths.

BLACKROCK SPIRE

Played & Written by: Edwin "Plainsong" Kern of <Dovrani> on Kirin Tor

The mighty fortress carved within the fiery bowels of Blackrock Mountain was designed by the master dwarf-mason, Franclorn Forgewright. Intended to be the symbol of Dark Iron power, the fortress was held by the sinister dwarves for centuries. However, Nefarian - the cunning son of the dragon, Deathwing - had other plans for the great keep. He and his draconic minions took control of the upper Spire and made war on the dwarves' holdings in the mountain's volcanic depths. Realizing that the dwarves were led by the mighty fire elemental, Ragnaros - Nefarian vowed to crush his enemies and claim the whole of Blackrock mountain for himself.

DUNGEON INFORMATION

Location	Between Searing Gorge and Burning Steppes
Quests	Both
Region	Contested
Suggested Levels	57-60
Group Allowed	5-10
Primary Enemies	Humanoids, Beasts, Dragonkin
Time to Complete	3-5 Hours

GETTING TO BLACKROCK SPIRE

NEFARIAN

Although Lord Victor Nefarius makes an appearance in Blackrock Spire, you don't get to fight him until you brave the depths of Blackwing Lair.

THERE'S ALWAYS TOMORROW

Doing all of Blackrock Spire is a daunting task. The instance is set up in a way to make this an option rather than a necessity. There are several short cuts and bypasses to allow you to complete quests and hunt for loot in shorter, more convenient runs.

Blackrock Mountain stands between Burning Steppes and Searing Gorge. Thus, there are two entrances to Blackrock Mountain.

Horde parties should gather at Kargath (Badlands) and make the trip across Searing Gorge. Alliance groups should fly into Thorium Point (Searing Gorge) to enter through Searing Gorge, or Morgan's Vigil (Burning Steppes).

WHO TO BRING

Every class has a place in Blackrock Spire. Having a well-balanced group is more important than having a specific class. Whether questing in Lower Blackrock Spire (LBRS) or raiding Upper Blackrock Spire (UBRS), you want some of everything.

Warriors fill the role of tank, while Priests, Druids, Paladins, or Shaman can fill the role of healer. That leaves the role of DPS, which can be filled by Rogues, Mages, Hunters, or Warlocks, and the role of crowd control, which can be filled by anyone.

WHAT'S IN IT FOR ME?

While working toward level 60, experience is a great incentive to risk life and limb. Once you hit 60, experience doesn't mean as much. The way to advance your character is now through equipment. Items from many sets can be found in Blackrock Spire. The table on the following page shows which sets drop, what items from those sets, the bonuses for those items, and which creatures can drop them. These should be kept in mind when deciding where to go and what to kill.

SET ITEMS

SET	ITEM	BONUSES	CREATURE
BATTLEGEAR OF VALOR	Bracers of Valor	(Plate Wrist, 261 Armor, +14 STA, +7 STR, +3 AGI, +2 SPI)	Blackhand Iron Guard, Bloodaxe Warmonger, Firebrand Grunt, Firebrand Legionnaire, Quartermaster Zigris, Scarshield Legionnaire, Smolderthorn Axe Thrower
	Breastplate of Valor	(Plate Chest, 657 Armor, +24 STA, +15 STR, +10 AGI, +6 SPI)	General Drakkisath
	Belt of Valor	(Plate Waist, 341 Armor, +14 STR, +8 STA, +7 AGI, +4 SPI)	Highlord Omokk, Quartermaster Zigris
	Spaulders of Valor	(Plate Shoulder, 470 Armor, +17 STA, +11 STR, +9 AGI)	Warchief Rend Blackhand
BEASTSTALKER ARMOR	Beaststalker's Belt	(Mail Waist, 193 Armor, +11 SPI, +10 AGI, +9 INT, +9 STR, +6 STA)	Bloodaxe Raider, Firebrand Grunt, Firebrand Legionnaire, Quartermaster Zigris, Rage Talon Dragon Guard, Scarshield Raider, Smolderthorn Headhunter
	Beaststalker's Tunic	(Mail Chest, 370 Armor, +21 AGI, +16 STA, +13 INT, +6 SPI, +5 STR)	General Drakkisath
	Beaststalker's Mantle	(Mail Shoulder, 266 Armor, +17 STA, +11 AGI, +7 INT, +4 SPI)	Overlord Wyrmthalak
	Beaststalker Gloves	(Mail Hands, 218 Armor, +14 AGI, +10 SPI, +9 STA, +9 INT)	Warmaster Voone
DREADMIST RAIMENT	Dreadmist Bracers	(Cloth Wrist, +10 INT, +10 STA, +7 SPI)	Bloodaxe Summoner, Firebrand Darkweaver, Quartermaster Zigris, Scarshield Warlock, Smolderthorn Seer, Summoned Blackhand Dreadweaver
	Dreadmist Robe	(Cloth Chest, 89 Armor, +21 INT, +20 STA, +13 SPI)	General Drakkisath
LIGHTFORGE ARMOR	Lightforge Breastplate	(Plate Chest, 657 Armor, +21 STA, +16 INT, +13 STR, +8 SPI)	General Drakkisath
	Lightforge Spaulders	(Plate Shoulder, 470 Armor, +15 STA, +11 INT, +9 STR, +5 SPI, +4 AGI)	The Beast
MAGISTER'S REGALIA	Magister's Bindings	(Cloth Wrist, 35 Armor, +15 INT, +5 SPI, +4 STA)	Firebrand Invoker, Quartermaster Zigris, Rage Talon Fire Tongue, Scarshield Spellbinder
	Magister's Robes	(Cloth Chest, 89 Armor, +31 INT, +8 SPI, +9 STA)	General Drakkisath
	Magister's Belt	(Cloth Waist, 46 Armor, +21 INT, +6 SPI, +6 STA)	Quartermaster Zigris, Smolderthorn Mystic
SHADOWCRAFT ARMOR	Shadowcraft Belt	(Leather Waist, +14 AGI, +10 STA, +9 SPI, +9 STR)	Blackhand Assassin, Bloodaxe Warmonger, Firebrand Grunt, Firebrand Legionnaire, Scarshield Legionnaire, Smolderthorn Shadow Hunter
	Shadowcraft Tunic	(Leather Chest, 176 Armor, +26 AGI, +13 STA, +12 SPI)	General Drakkisath
	Shadowcraft Gloves	(Leather Hands, +14 AGI, +10 SPI, +9 STA, +9 STR)	Shadow Hunter Vosh'gajin
	Shadowcraft Bracers	(Leather Wrist, 71 Armor, +15 AGI, +7 STA)	Smolderthorn Shadow Hunter
THE ELEMENTS	Cord of Elements	(Mail Waist, 193 Armor, +17 INT, +9 STR, +7 SPI, +6 STA)	Bloodaxe Evoker, Firebrand Invoker, Firebrand Pyromancer, Quartermaster Zigris, Rage Talon Flamescale, Scarshield Warlock, Smolderthorn Witch Doctor
	Vest of Elements	(Mail Chest, 370 Armor, +20 INT, +20 SPI, +13 STA)	General Drakkisath
	Pauldrons of Elements	(Mail Shoulder, 266 Armor, +15 INT, +14 STA, +6 SPI, +6 STR)	Gyth
	Gauntlets of Elements	(Mail Hands, 218 Armor, +16 INT, +10 SPI, +9 STR, +4 STA)	Pyroguard Emberseer
	Boots of Elements	(Mail Boots, 240 Armor, +17 SPI, +9 AGI)	Urok Doomhowl
VESTMENTS OF THE DEVOUT	Devout Belt	(Cloth Waist, 46 Armor, +20 INT, +9 SPI, +4 STA)	Bloodaxe Summoner, Firebrand Darkweaver, Quartermaster Zigris, Scarshield Spellbinder, Smolderthorn Shadow Priest
	Devout Robe	(Cloth Chest, 89 Armor, +24 INT, +15 SPI, +13 STA)	General Drakkisath
	Devout Mantle	(Cloth Shoulder, 64 Armor, +21 INT, +9 SPI, +4 STA)	Solakar Flamewreath
WILDHEART RAIMENT	Wildheart Gloves	(Leather Gloves, 105 Armor, +21 SPI, +9 INT)	Firebrand Invoker, Firebrand Pyromancer, Scarshield Raider, Smolderthorn Berserker, Smolderthorn Seer
	Wildheart Vest	(Leather Chest, 176 Armor, +20 INT, +20 SPI, +13 STA)	General Drakkisath
	Wildheart Boots	(Leather Boots, 115 Armor, +17 SPI, +10 STA, +9 INT)	Mother Smolderweb
	Wildheart Belt	(Leather Belt, 93 Armor, +17 INT, +10 SPI, +9 STA)	Quartermaster Zigris
	Wildheart Spaulders	(Leather Shoulder, 127 Armor, +18 INT, +9 STA, +8 SPI)	Gizrul the Slavener

QUESTS FOR BLACKROCK SPIRE

There are two types of quests in Blackrock Spire. Dungeon quests can only be completed in a non-raid group while Raid quests can be completed in either a raid or non-raid group. Most quests in Lower Blackrock Spire are Dungeon quests, while those in Upper Blackrock Spire are Raid quests.

ALLIANCE QUESTS

QUEST NAME	QUEST GIVER	QUEST GIVER LOCATION	QUEST RECEIVER	QUEST RECEIVER LOCATION	CHAIN?	MAX EXPERIENCE
Bijou's Belongings	Bijou	Blackrock Spire	Bijou	Blackrock Spire	Yes	6,400
Message to Maxwell	Bijou	Blackrock Spire	Marshal Maxwell	Burning Steppes: Morgan's Vigil	Yes	6,400
Maxwell's Mission	Marshal Maxwell	Burning Steppes: Morgan's Vigil	Marshal Maxwell	Burning Steppes: Morgan's Vigil	Yes	8,550
REWARD: Wyrmthalak's Shackles (Cloth Wrist, 37 Armor, +15 SPI, +9 INT) or Omokk's Girth Restrainer (Plate Waist, 353 Armor, +15 STR, +9 STA, Passive: Improves your chance to get a critical strike by 1%) or Halycon's Muzzle (Leather Shoulder, 127 Armor, +22 INT, +5 SPI, +10 Arcane Resistance) or Vosh'gajin's Strand (Leather Waist, 95 Armor, +9 STR, +6 STA, Passive: Improves your chance to get a critical strike or dodge an attack by 1%) or Voone's Vice Grips (Mail Hands, 221 Armor, +6 STR, +6 AGI, +6 SPI, Passive: Improves your chance to hit by 2%)						
General Drakkisath's Command	Letter	Blackrock Spire: Overlord Wyrmthalak's Corpse	Marshal Maxwell	Burning Steppes: Morgan's Vigil	Yes	6,850
General Drakkisath's Demise (Raid)	Marshal Maxwell	Burning Steppes: Morgan's Vigil	Marshal Maxwell	Burning Steppes: Morgan's Vigil	Yes	10,900
REWARD: Mark of Tyranny (Trinket, 180 Armor, +10 Arcane Resistance, Passive: Increases your chance to dodge an attack by 1%) or Eye of the Beast (Trinket, Passive: Increases your chance to get a critical strike with your spells by 2%) or Blackhand's Breadth (Trinket, Passive: Increases your chance to get a critical strike by 2%)						
Doomriggers Clasp (Raid)	Mayara Brightwing	Burning Steppes: Morgan's Vigil	Mayara Brightwing	Burning Steppes: Morgan's Vigil	Yes	1,650
Delivery to Ridgewell	Mayara Brightwing	Burning Steppes: Morgan's Vigil	Count Remington Ridgewell	Stormwind: Stormwind Keep	Yes	6,600
REWARD: Swiftfoot Treads (Leather Boots, 106 Armor, +18 AGI, +5 STR) or Blinkstrike Armguards (Plate Wrist, 249 Armor, +3 STR, Passive: Improves your chance to get a critical strike by 1%)						
Drakefire Amulet (Raid)	Haleh	Winterspring: Mazthoril	Haleh	Winterspring: Mazthoril	Yes	7,250
REWARD: Drakefire Amulet (Neck, +10 STA, +15 Fire Resistance)						

BIJOU'S BELONGINGS

Quest Level	55 to obtain
Location	Blackrock Spire
Quest Giver	Bijou
Goal	Find Bijou's Belongings
Max Experience Gained	6,400

Bijou is gathering information for the Horde, but has found that the threat in Blackrock is much larger and endangers the Alliance as well. Find her belongings and she'll tell you what she's found.

MESSAGE TO MAXWELL

Quest Level	55 to obtain
Location	Blackrock Spire
Quest Giver	Bijou
Goal	Take Bijou's Information to Marshal Maxwell
Max Experience Gained	6,400

Bijou is true to her word. When you retrieve her belongings she gives you information in which Marshal Maxwell would be interested—the location of Nefarius' subordinates.

MAXWELL'S MISSION

Quest Level	56 to obtain
Location	Burning Steppes (Morgan's Vigil)
Quest Giver	Marshal Maxwell
Goal	Kill War Master Voone, Highlord Omokk, and Overlord Wyrmthalak
Max Experience Gained	8,550
Reward	Wyrmthalak's Shackles (Cloth Wrist, 37 Armor, +15 SPI, +9 INT) or Omokk's Girth Restrainer (Plate Waist, 353 Armor, +15 STR, +9 STA, Passive: Improves your chance to get a critical strike by 1%) or Halycon's Muzzle (Leather Shoulder, 127 Armor, +22 INT, +5 SPI, +10 Arcane Resistance) or Vosh'gajin's Strand (Leather Waist, 95 Armor, +9 STR, +6 STA, Passive: Improves your chance to get a critical strike or dodge an attack by 1%) or Voone's Vice Grips (Mail Hands, 221 Armor, +6 STR, +6 AGI, +6 SPI, Passive: Improves your chance to hit by 2%)

The information Bijou supplied gives Maxwell what he needs to see the big picture. Voone, Omokk, and Wyrmthalak must die for the safety of everyone.

GENERAL DRAKKISATH'S COMMAND

Quest Level	55 to obtain
Location	Blackrock Spire
Quest Giver	Letter drops from Overlord Wyrmthalak
Goal	Take General Drakkisath's Command to Marshal Maxwell
Max Experience Gained	6,850

Searching the body of Overlord Wyrmthalak reveals an envelope from General Drakkisath. Marshal Maxwell will need this information if the assault on Blackrock Spire is to continue.

GENERAL DRAKKISATH'S DEMISE (RAID)

Quest Level	55 to obtain
Location	Burning Steppes (Morgan's Vigil)
Quest Giver	Marshal Maxwell
Goal	Slay General Drakkisath
Max Experience Gained	10,900
Reward	Mark of Tyranny (Trinket, 180 Armor, +10 Arcane Resistance, Passive: Increases your chance to dodge an attack by 1%) or Eye of the Beast (Trinket, Passive: Increases your chance to get a critical strike with your spells by 2%) or Blackhand's Breadth (Trinket, Passive: Increases your chance to get a critical strike by 2%)

The fight has been long and hard. Now it is time to end it. Kill General Drakkisath and return to Marshal Maxwell for a reward as great as the feat you accomplished.

DOOMRIGGERS CLASP (RAID)

Quest Level	57 to obtain
Location	Burning Steppes
Quest Giver	Mayara Brightwing
Goal	Retrieve the Doomriggers Clasp
Max Experience Gained	1,650

After speaking with Count Remington Ridgewell in Stormwind, you are sent to Mayara. She has evidence that one of the Dark Iron Dwarves prized relics has survived the collapse of the room it was hidden in. The Doomriggers Clasp lies buried in Blackrock Spire. Find it and return.

DELIVERY TO RIDGEWELL

Quest Level	58 to obtain
Location	Burning Steppes
Quest Giver	Mayara Brightwing
Goal	Deliver Ridgewell's Crate to Count Remington Ridgewell
Max Experience Gained	6,600
Reward	Swiftfoot Treads (Leather Boots, 106 Armor, +18 AGI, +5 STR) or Blinkstrike Armguards (Plate Wrist, 249 Armor, +3 STR, Passive: Improves your chance to get a critical strike by 1%)

With the Doomrigger Clasp retrieved, there is only one more step. Mayara has packaged the clasp in a crate and needs it safely delivered to Count Ridgewell in Stormwind Keep.

DRAKEFIRE AMULET (RAID)

Quest Level	57 to obtain
Location	Winterspring
Quest Giver	Haleh
Goal	Bring the Blood of the Black Dragon Champion to Haleh
Max Experience Gained	7,250
Reward	Drakefire Amulet (Neck, +10 STA, +15 Fire Resistance)

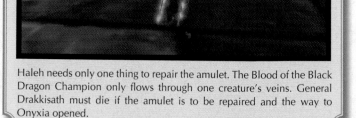

Haleh needs only one thing to repair the amulet. The Blood of the Black Dragon Champion only flows through one creature's veins. General Drakkisath must die if the amulet is to be repaired and the way to Onyxia opened.

HORDE QUESTS

QUEST NAME	QUEST GIVER	QUEST GIVER LOCATION	QUEST RECEIVER	QUEST RECEIVER LOCATION	CHAIN?	MAX EXPERIENCE
Warlord's Command	Warlord Goretooth	Badlands: Kargath	Warlord Goretooth	Badlands: Kargath	Yes	8,550
REWARD: Wyrmthalak's Shackles (Cloth Wrist, 37 Armor, +15 SPI, +9 INT) or Omokk's Girth Restrainer (Plate Waist, 353 Armor, +15 STR, +9 STA, Passive: Improves your chance to get a critical strike by 1%) or Halycon's Muzzle (Leather Shoulder, 127 Armor, +22 INT, +5 SPI, +10 Arcane Resistance) or Vosh'gajin's Strand (Leather Waist, 95 Armor, +9 STR, +6 STA, Passive: Improves your chance to get a critical strike or dodge an attack by 1%) or Voone's Vice Grips (Mail Hands, 221 Armor, +6 STR, +6 AGI, +6 SPI, Passive: Improves your chance to hit by 2%)						
Eitrigg's Wisdom	Warlord Goretooth	Badlands: Kargath	Eitrigg	Orgrimmar: Thrall's Chambers	Yes	6,850
Fore the Horde! (Raid)	Thrall	Orgrimmar: Thrall's Chambers	Thrall	Orgrimmar: Thrall's Chambers	Yes	10,900
REWARD: Mark of Tyranny (Trinket, 180 Armor, +10 Arcane Resistance, Passive: Increases your chance to dodge an attack by 1%) or Eye of the Beast (Trinket, Passive: Increases your chance to get a critical strike with your spells by 2%) or Blackhand's Breadth (Trinket, Passive: Increases your chance to get a critical strike by 2%)						
Blood of the Black Dragon Champion (Raid)	Rexxar	Desolace	Rexxar	Desolace	Yes	10,900
REWARD: Drakefire Amulet (Neck, +10 STA, +15 Fire Resistance)						
Operative Bijou	Lexlort	Badlands: Kargath	Bijou	Blackrock Spire	Yes	6,400
Bijou's Belongings	Bijou	Blackrock Spire	Bijou	Blackrock Spire	Yes	6,400
Bijou's Reconnaissance Report	Bijou	Blackrock Spire	Lexlort	Badlands: Kargath	Yes	6,400
REWARD: Freewind Gloves (Cloth Hands, 48 Armor, +19 SPI) or Seapost Girdle (Mail Waist, 179 Armor, +13 SPI, +8 INT, +8 STA)						
The Darkstone Tablet (Raid)	Shadowmage Vivian Lagrave	Badlands: Kargath	Shadowmage Vivian Lagrave	Badlands: Kargath	No	8,300
REWARD: Swiftboot Threads (Leather Boots, 106 Armor, +18 AGI, +5 STA) or Blinkstrike Armguards (Plate Wrist, 249 Armor, +3 STR, Passive: Improves your chance to get a critical strike by 1%)						

WARLORD'S COMMAND

Quest Level	55 to obtain
Location	Badlands (Kargath)
Quest Giver	Warlord Goretooth
Goal	Kill War Master Voone, Highlord Ommok, Overlord Wyrmthalak and retrieve the Important Blackrock Documents
Max Experience Gained	8,550
Reward	Wyrmthalak's Shackles (Cloth Wrist, 37 Armor, +15 SPI, +9 INT) or Omokk's Girth Restrainer (Plate Waist, 353 Armor, +15 STR, +9 STA, Passive: Improves your chance to get a critical strike by 1%) or Halycon's Muzzle (Leather Shoulder, 127 Armor, +22 INT, +5 SPI, +10 Arcane Resistance) or Vosh'gajin's Strand (Leather Waist, 95 Armor, +9 STR, +6 STA, Passive: Improves your chance to get a critical strike or dodge an attack by 1%) or Voone's Vice Grips (Mail Hands, 221 Armor, +6 STR, +6 AGI, +6 SPI, Passive: Improves your chance to hit by 2%)

Warlord Goretooth gives you a letter when you speak with him. The letter instructs you to take on a mission of grave importance into Blackrock Spire. Voone, Ommok and Wyrmthalak must die and the Documents be collected to return victorious. The Documents can be found near Wyrmthalak. Once looted, they will respawn shortly.

EITRIGG'S WISDOM

Quest Level	55 to obtain
Location	Badlands (Kargath)
Quest Giver	Warlord Goretooth
Goal	Seek the wisdom of Eitrigg
Max Experience Gained	6,850

Warlord Goretooth is not pleased with the information contained in the documents you found. Rend was thought dead long ago, but the documents say he lives. Speak with Eitrigg in Thrall's Chambers in Orgrimmar to learn more.

FOR THE HORDE! (RAID)

Quest Level	55 to obtain
Location	Orgrimmar (Thrall's Chambers)
Quest Giver	Thrall
Goal	Bring Rend's head to Thrall
Max Experience Gained	10,900
Reward	Mark of Tyranny (Trinket, 180 Armor, +10 Arcane Resistance, Passive: Increases your chance to dodge an attack by 1%) or Eye of the Beast (Trinket, Passive: Increases your chance to get a critical strike with your spells by 2%) or Blackhand's Breadth (Trinket, Passive: Increases your chance to get a critical strike by 2%)

The time of Rend has long since passed and it's time for him to die. Remove his head, bring it to Thrall and receive honor as great as your material reward. When you have done this, speak with Thrall again to continue your service.

BLOOD OF THE BLACK DRAGON CHAMPION (RAID)

Quest Level	56 to obtain
Location	Desolace
Quest Giver	Rexxar
Goal	Collect the Blood of the Black Dragon Champion
Max Experience Gained	10,900
Reward	Drakefire Amulet (Neck, +10 STA, +15 Fire Resistance)

After the tangled mission Thrall put you on, Rexxar will ask you to kill General Drakisath and bring back his blood so he can activate the Drakefire Amulet and give you the key you need to enter Onyxia's Lair.

OPERATIVE BIJOU

Quest Level	55 to obtain
Location	Badlands (Kargath)
Quest Giver	Lexlort
Goal	Find Bijou
Max Experience Gained	6,400

Lexlort isn't pleased with what he's found out about one of his operatives. Bijou has been using Horde funds to work for someone else. Find her and bring her back.

BIJOU'S RECONNAISSANCE REPORT

Quest Level	55 to obtain
Location	Blackrock Spire
Quest Giver	Bijou
Goal	Deliver Bijou's Reconnaissance Report to Lexlort
Max Experience Gained	6,400
Reward	Freewind Gloves (Cloth Hands, 48 Armor, +19 SPI) or Seapost Girdle (Mail Waist, 179 Armor, +13 SPI, +8 INT, +8 STA)

Never trust a goblin. With her belongings returned, she gives you the information to deliver to Lexlort. She has no intention of returning to the K.E.F. There is nothing you can do except bring the information to Lexlort.

BIJOU'S BELONGINGS

Quest Level	55 to obtain
Location	Blackrock Spire
Quest Giver	Bijou
Goal	Find Bijou's Belongings
Max Experience Gained	6,400

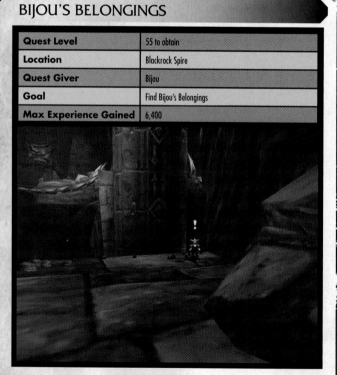

Bijou is willing to return to the K.E.F. peacefully if you find her belongings. She had to stash them when she was nearly discovered and believes the information they hold to be of great value.

THE DARKSTONE TABLET (RAID)

Quest Level	57 to obtain
Location	Searing Gorge (Kargath)
Quest Giver	Shadowmage Vivian Lagrave
Goal	Collect the Darkstone Tablet and return.
Max Experience Gained	8,300
Reward	Swiftboot Threads (Leather Boots, 106 Armor, +18 AGI, +5 STA) or Blinkstrike Armguards (Plate Wrist, 249 Armor, +3 STR, Passive: Improves your chance to get a critical strike by 1%)

An alchemist of great renown recorded his recipes on tablets rather than sharing them with his rivals. Vivian believes one such tablet is hidden within Blackrock Spire. Find it and return for your reward.

SHARED QUESTS

QUEST NAME	QUEST GIVER	QUEST GIVER LOCATION	QUEST RECEIVER	QUEST RECEIVER LOCATION	CHAIN?	MAX EXPERIENCE
Finkly Einhorn, At Your Service	Finkle Einhorn	Blackrock Spire	Malyfous Darkhammer	Winterspring: Everlook	Yes	7,050
Breastplate of Bloodthirst	Malyfous's Catalogue	Winterspring: Everlook	Malyfous Darkhammer	Winterspring: Everlook	No	None
REWARD: Breastplate of Bloodthirst (Leather Chest, 190 Armor, +20 STA, +13 STR, Passive: Improves your chance to get a critical strike by 2% and your chance to dodge an attack by 1%)						
Cap of the Scarlet Savant	Malyfous's Catalogue	Winterspring: Everlook	Malyfous Darkhammer	Winterspring: Everlook	No	None
REWARD: Cap of the Scarlet Savant (Cloth Head, 78 Armor, +20 INT, +17 STA, Passive: Improves your chance to get a critical strike with spells by 2%, Classes: Priest, Warlock, Mage, Druid, Shaman)						
Leggings of Arcana	Malyfous's Catalogue	Winterspring: Everlook	Malyfous Darkhammer	Winterspring: Everlook	No	None
REWARD: Leggings of Arcana (Leather Legs, 166 Armor, +30 SPI, +20 INT, Passive: Increases damage and healing done by magical spells and effects by up to 18)						
Leggings of the Chromatic Defier	Jeziba	Western Plaguelands	Jeziba	Western Plaguelands	Yes	9,950
REWARD: Legguards of the Chromatic Defier (Mail Legs, 349 Armor, +33 AGI, +15 STA, +9 STR, +5 to all Resistances) OR Legplates of the Chromatic Defier (Mail Legs, 349 Armor, +19 INT, +26 SPI, +16 STA, +5 to all Resistances)						
Hot Fiery Death	Human Remains	Blackrock Spire	Malyfous Darkhammer	Winterspring: Everlook	Yes	6,600
Seal of Ascension	Vaelen	Blackrock Spire	Vaelen	Blackrock Spire	Yes	8,300
Seal of Ascension	Vaelen	Blackrock Spire	Vaelan	Blackrock Spire	Yes	10,250
Urok Doomhowl	Warosh	Blackrock Spire	Worosh	Blackrock Spire	No	9,950
REWARD: Prismcharm (Thinket, Use: Increases all resistances by 20 for 30 seconds)						
Egg Freezing (Raid)	Tinkee Steamboil	Burning Steppes: Flame Crest	Tinkee Steamboil	Burning Steppes: Flame Crest	Yes	None
Egg Collection (Raid)	Tinkee Steamboil	Burning Steppes: Flame Crest	Tinkee Steamboil	Burning Steppes: Flame Crest	Yes	9,950
En-Ay-Es-Tee-Why	Kibler	Burning Steppes: Flame Crest	Kibler	Burning Steppes: Flame Crest	No	6,400
REWARD: Smolderweb Carrier (Use: Summons and dismisses your Smolderweb Hatchling)						
Mother's Milk	Ragged John	Burning Steppes: Flame Crest	Ragged John	Burning Steppes: Flame Crest	No	9,950
Put Her Down	Heledis	Burning Steppes: Flame Crest	Helendis	Burning Steppes: Flame Crest	No	6,400
REWARD: Astoria Robes (Cloth Chest, 76 Armor, +20 INT, +10 SPI, +5 STR) or Traphook Jerkin (Leather Chest, 152 Armor, +24 AGI, +5 STR) or Jadescale Breastplate (Mail Chest, 317 Armor, +23 STA, +7 SPI)						
Kibler's Exotic Pets	Kibler	Burning Steppes: Flame Crest	Kibler	Burning Steppes: Flame Crest	No	6,400
REWARD: Worg Carrier (Use: Summons and dismisses your Worg Pup)						
The Demon Forge	Lorax	Winterspring: South	Lorax	Winterspring: South	No	9,550
REWARD: Plans: Demon Forged Breastplate (Requires Blacksmithing (285) and Armorsmithing), 5x Elixer of Demonslaying, and Demon Kissed Sack						
The Final Tablets	Prospector Ironboot	Tanaris: Steamwheedle Port	Prospector Ironboot	Tanaris: Steamwheedle Port	Yes	7,750
Snakestone of the Shadow Huntress	Kilram	Winterspring: Everlook	Kilram	Winterspring: Everlook	No	8,550
REWARD: Plans: Dawn's Edge (Requires Blacksmithing(275) and Master Axesmith), Master Axesmith status						
The Matron Protectorate (Raid)	Awbee	Blackrock Spire	Haleh	Winterspring: Mazorthil	Yes	7,050
Breastplate of the Chromatic Flight	Catalogue of the Wayward	Winterspring	Jeziba	Western Plaguelands: Andorhal	No	None
REWARD: Breastplate of the Chromatic Flight (Plate Chest, 706 Armor, +30 STA, +20 STR, +10 AGI, +15 Fire Resistance)						
Blackhand's Command	Blackhand's Command	Blackrock Spire: Scarshield Quartermaster's Corpse	Orb of Command	Blackrock Spire	No	None
REWARD: Allows teleport from Quatermaster Zigris' room directly to Blackwing Lair						

FINKLE EINHORN, AT YOUR SERVICE

Quest Level	57 to obtain
Location	Blackrock Spire
Quest Giver	Finkle Einhorn
Goal	Deliver the Glowing Chunk of the Beast's Flesh to Malyfous Darkhammer
Max Experience Gained	7,050

Finkle Einhorn will occasionally exit the body of the Beast when you kill it. He was able to survive using a suit crafted for him by Malyfous Darkhammer in Everlook. He asks you to take the sample of the Beast to Malyfous so he can figure out what can be made from the Beast's parts.

BREASTPLATE OF BLOODTHIRST

Quest Level	60 to obtain
Location	Winterspring
Quest Giver	Malyfous's Catalogue
Goal	Collect 1 Pristine Hide of the Beast, 10 Frayed Abomination Stitchings, 5 Arcanite Bars, and 5 Skin of Shadows
Max Experience Gained	None
Reward	Breastplate of Bloodthirst (Leather Chest, 190 Armor, +20 STA, +13 STR, Passive: Improves your chance to get a critical strike by 2% and your chance to dodge an attack by 1%)

Malyfous has crafted many great items in his day. If you bring him what he needs, he'll craft a wondrous piece. One of the items he needs is the Pristine Hide of The Beast. This can only be obtained from the Beast in Upper Blackrock Spire with the help of a skinner of 310 skill.

CAP OF THE SCARLET SAVANT

Quest Level	60 to obtain
Location	Winterspring
Quest Giver	Malyfous's Catalogue
Goal	Collect 1 Pristine Hide of the Beast, 5 Frayed Abomination Stitchings, 8 Arcane Crystals, and 5 Enchanted Scarlet Threads
Max Experience Gained	None
Reward	Cap of the Scarlet Savant (Cloth Head, 78 Armor, +20 INT, +17 STA, Passive: Improves your chance to get a critical strike with spells by 2%, Classes: Priest, Warlock, Mage, Druid, Shaman)

Malyfous has crafted many great items in his day. If you bring him what he needs, he'll craft a magnificent cap. One of the items he needs is the Pristine Hide of The Beast. This can only be obtained from the Beast in Upper Blackrock Spire with the help of a skinner of 310 skill.

LEGGINGS OF ARCANA

Quest Level	60 to obtain
Location	Winterspring
Quest Giver	Malyfous's Catalogue
Goal	Collect 1 Pristine Hide of the Beast, 10 Frayed Abomination Stitchings, 5 Arcanite Bars, and 5 Frostwhisper's Embalming Fluids
Max Experience Gained	None
Reward	Leggings of Arcana (Leather Legs, 166 Armor, +30 SPI, +20 INT, Passive: Increases damage and healing done by magical spells and effects by up to 18)

Malyfous has crafted many great items in his day. If you bring him what he needs, he'll craft leggings for all mail-wearers. One of the items he needs is the Pristine Hide of The Beast. This can only be obtained from the Beast in Upper Blackrock Spire with the help of a skinner of 310 skill.

LEGGINGS OF THE CHROMATIC DEFILER

Quest Level	57 to obtain
Class	Hunter or Shaman
Location	Western Plaguelands
Quest Giver	Jeziba
Goal	Find the pieces necessary for Jeziba to construct the Leggings
Max Experience Gained	9,950
Reward	Legguards of the Chromatic Defiler (Mail Legs, 349 Armor, +33 AGI, +15 STA, +9 STR, +5 to all Resistances) OR Legplates of the Chromatic Defiler (Mail Legs, 349 Armor, +19 INT, +26 SPI, +16 STA, +5 to all Resistances)

You'll need to obtain a few items for this quest, one of which can be found on one of the bosses in Blackrock Spire: the Chromatic Carapace. Only one lord in the spire drops this and it's Gyth in the Hall of Blackhand. The other pieces you'll need to complete the quest are: 10 Brilliant Chromatic Scales, 5 Skins of Shadow, and 10 vials of the Blood of Heroes. Once you've collected all the necessary elements, return to Jeziba.

HOT FIERY DEATH

Quest Level	58 to obtain
Location	Blackrock Spire
Quest Giver	Human Remains
Goal	Bring the Unfired Plate Gauntlets to Malyfous Darkhammer
Max Experience Gained	6,600

Why was someone willing to die to get these? They don't seem that useful. Perhaps Malyfous in Everlook would know more.

SEAL OF ASCENSION

Quest Level	57 to obtain
Location	Blackrock Spire
Quest Giver	Vaelan
Goal	Collect the Gemstones of Spirestone, Smolderthorn, and Bloodaxe as well as the Unadorned Seal of Ascension
Max Experience Gained	8,300

Vaelan is very skilled at hiding and understands a great deal about Blackrock Spire. He knows how you can craft a key to the upper portions. Bring him the gems and the seal and he will tell you.

SEAL OF ASCENSION

Quest Level	60 to obtain
Location	Blackrock Spire
Quest Giver	Vaelan
Goal	Force Emberstrife to forge the Seal of Ascension
Max Experience Gained	10,250

With the Gemstones of Bloodaxe, Smolderthorn, and Spirestone, along with the Unadorned Seal of Ascension, you created the Unforged Seal of Ascension. That's what you need to place before Emberstrife, for only the flames of the Black Dragonflight can forge this into the Forged Seal of Ascension. However, Emberstrife will undoubtedly be unwilling to do this without being coerced. He must be beaten until his will falters; only then can he be forced to do your bidding with the sphere Vaelan gives you.

UROK DOOMHOWL

Quest Level	55 to obtain
Location	Blackrock Spire
Quest Giver	Warosh
Goal	Retrieve Warosh's Mojo
Max Experience Gained	9,950
Reward	Prismcharm (Trinket, Use: Increases all resistances by 20 for 30 seconds)

Warosh doesn't speak very well, so he has written down what he wants you to do. He wants his magic back. It was stolen by Urok Doomhowl. Urok will not face you unless forced. You need to place Omokk's Head on a Roughshod Pike at Urok's Tribute Pile to even gain his attention. Kill him and return Warosh's Mojo to him.

EGG FREEZING (RAID)

Quest Level	60 to obtain
Location	Burning Steppes
Quest Giver	Tinkee Steamboil
Goal	Test the Eggscilloscope Prototype

Tinkee has work for you. She has created a machine that will freeze dragon eggs solid. She needs you to test it for her. There is a room full of dragon eggs in Blackrock Spire.

EGG COLLECTION (RAID)

Quest Level	60 to obtain
Location	Burning Steppes
Quest Giver	Tinkee Steamboil
Goal	Bring 8 Collected Dragon Eggs to Tinkee
Max Experience Gained	9,950

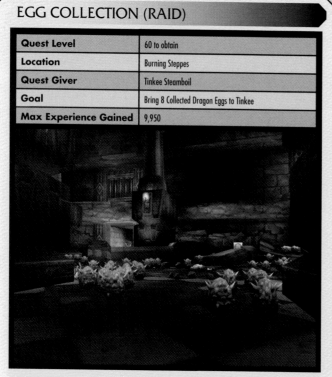

Now that Tinkee knows the Eggscilloscope works, she wants you to collect 8 Dragon Eggs. Each must be frozen before it can be collected.

EN-AY-ES-TEE-WHY

Quest Level	55 to obtain
Location	Burning Steppes
Quest Giver	Kibler
Goal	Collect 15 Spire Spider Eggs
Max Experience Gained	6,400
Reward	Smolderweb Carrier (Use: Summons and dismisses your Smolderweb Hatchling)

Kibler's normal collector is overdue and he wants you to take over. He wants 15 Spider Eggs and he's willing to pay for them.

MOTHER'S MILK

Quest Level	55 to obtain
Location	Burning Steppes
Quest Giver	Ragged John
Goal	Get poisoned and return to John to be 'milked.'
Max Experience Gained	9,950

Mother Smolderweb resides deep in Blackrock Spire. Her poison is one of the most dangerous in the world and Ragged John wants a sample. The only way to get a good sample is to have someone get poisoned, then return to him to be cured.

PUT HER DOWN

Quest Level	60 to obtain
Location	Burning Steppes
Quest Giver	Helendis
Goal	Slay Halycon
Max Experience Gained	6,400
Reward	Astoria Robes (Cloth Chest, 76 Armor, +20 INT, +10 SPI, +5 STR) or Traphook Jerkin (Leather Chest, 152 Armor, +24 AGI, +5 STR) or Jadescale Breastplate (Mail Chest, 317 Armor, +23 STA, +7 SPI)

No matter how many Worgs you kill, there are always more. Somewhere in Blackrock Spire is the cause of this. Find it and kill it.

KIBLER'S EXOTIC PETS

Quest Level	55 to obtain
Location	Burning Steppes
Quest Giver	Kibler
Goal	Bring Kibler a Caged Worg Pup
Max Experience Gained	6,400
Reward	Worg Carrier (Use: Summons and dismisses your Worg Pup)

Kibler deals in exotic pets. The more exotic, the more money he can make. He wants to domesticate Worgs, but needs to get them as pups. The pups are never allowed outside Blackrock Spire, so Kibler's willing to pay you to go inside and get one.

THE DEMON FORGE

Quest Level	58 to obtain
Location	Winterspring
Quest Giver	Lorax
Goal	Return the Soul Stained Pike and the Unforged Rune Covered Breastplate to Lorax
Max Experience Gained	8,550
Reward	Plans: Demon Forged Breastplate (Requires Blacksmithing (285) and Armorsmithing), 5x Elixer of Demonslaying, and Demon Kissed Sack

Goraluk Anvilcrack has made a dangerous enemy. Lorax wants you to kill him and drive the pike into his heart to collect his soul. Bring the pike and the armor Goraluk stole to Lorax and you will be justly rewarded.

THE FINAL TABLETS

Quest Level	56 to obtain
Location	Tanaris (Steamwheedle Port)
Quest Giver	Prospector Ironboot
Goal	Collect the 5th and 6th Mosh'aru Tablets
Max Experience Gained	7,750

While Ironboot studies the 3rd and 4th tablets you brought him, he asks you to collect the others. Voone and Vosh'gajin guard the two tablets and don't like tourists.

SNAKESTONE OF THE SHADOW HUNTRESS

Quest Level	50 to obtain
Location	Everlook (Winterspring)
Quest Giver	Kilram
Goal	Collect Vosh'gajin's Snakestone
Max Experience Gained	8,550
Reward	Plans: Dawn's Edge(Requires Blacksmithing(275) and Master Axesmith), Master Axesmith status

This quest is a Weaponsmithing quest. You need to have Blacksmithing above 270 and be a Weaponsmith to gain access to this quest.

Kilram is willing to teach you how to become a Master Axesmith if you'll help him repay a debt. Vosh'gajin defeated and humiliated Kilram. Kill her, and bring her Snakestone as proof, and you will earn the honor of becoming a Master Axesmith.

THE MATRON PROTECTORATE

Quest Level	57 to obtain
Location	Upper Blackrock Spire
Quest Giver	Awbee
Goal	Deliver Awbee's Scale to Haleh
Max Experience Gained	7,050

Awbee is dying, but doesn't want to die for nothing. Take Awbee's Scale to the caves of Mazthoril in Winterspring and use the cobalt runes to teleport to Haleh. Awbee tells you that Haleh needs only a scale to scry what Awbee saw and felt in Blackrock.

BREASTPLATE OF THE CHROMATIC FLIGHT

Quest Level	57 to obtain
Location	Winterspring
Quest Giver	Catalogue of the Wayward
Goal	Collect 1 Chromatic Carapace, 10 Chromatic Scales, 10 Blood of Heroes, and 5 Frayed Abomination Stitchings
Max Experience Gained	None
Reward	Breastplate of the Chromatic Flight (Plate Chest, 706 Armor, +30 STA, +20 STR, +10 AGI, +15 Fire Resistance)

After running errands for Haleh, you have the opportunity to have Jeziba the Sculptor create a truly magnificent piece of armor for you. Collect the needed materials and speak with Jeziba in the Inn of Andorhal in the Western Plaguelands.

BLACKHAND'S COMMAND

Quest Level	55 to obtain
Location	Blackrock Spire
Quest Giver	Blackhand's Command
Goal	Collect Drakkisath's Brand
Max Experience Gained	None
Reward	Allows teleporting directly to Blackwing Lair

The Scarshield Quartermaster isn't that bright. He holds a letter detailing how you can get to Blackwing Lair quickly. He also has orders to destroy the letter, but he's just a quartermaster. Take the letter and climb to the top of Blackrock Spire and slay General Drakkisath for his brand. Using his brand at the Orb of Command in his chambers opens a much faster way to Blackwing Lair than fighting your way through Blackrock Spire.

ENEMIES

THE ENEMY GARRISON

NPC	LEVEL
Blackhand Assassin	55-61 Elite
Notes: Gouge, Enrage	
Frequent Drops: Shadowcraft Belt (Leather Waist, +14 AGI, +10 STA, +9 SPI, +9 STR, Shadowcraft piece)	
Blackhand Dragon Handler	54-60 Elite
Blackhand Dreadweaver	54-60 Elite
Notes: Shadowbolt	
Blackhand Elite	55-61 Elite
Notes: Backhand (Knockdown)	
Blackhand Incarcerator	57-60
Blackhand Iron Guard	55-61 Elite
Frequent Drops: Bracers of Valor (Plate Wrist, 261 Armor, +14 STA, +7 STR, +3 AGI, +2 SPI, Valor piece)	
Blackhand Summoner	54-61 Elite
Notes: Fireball, Frost Nova	
Blackhand Thug	59-60 Elite
Blackhand Veteran	54-60 Elite
Notes: Shield Charge (Knockdown, knockback)	
Bloodaxe Evoker	55-59 Elite
Notes: Flame Crack (AoE Fire, Knockback), Blast Wave (AoE Fire, Speed debuff)	
Frequent Drops: Cord of Elements (Mail Waist, 193 Armor, +17 INT, +9 STR, +7 SPI, +6 STA, Elements piece)	
Bloodaxe Raider	52-58 Elite
Notes: Cleave	
Frequent Drops: Beaststalker's Belt (Mail Waist, 193 Armor, +11 SPI, +10 AGI, +9 INT, +9 STR, +6 STA, Beaststalker piece)	
Bloodaxe Summoner	53-58 Elite
Notes: Arcane Missles, Summons Allies	
Frequent Drops: Devout Belt (Cloth Waist, 46 Armor, +20 INT, +9 SPI, +4 STA, Devout piece), Dreadmist Bracers (Cloth Wrist, +10 INT, +10 STA, +7 SPI, Dreadmist piece)	
Bloodaxe Veteran	54-59 Elite
Bloodaxe Warmonger	53-58 Elite
Notes: Throw	
Frequent Drops: Bracers of Valor (Plate Wrist, 261 Armor, +14 STA, +7 STR, +3 AGI, +2 SPI, Valor piece), Shadowcraft Belt (Leather Waist, +14 AGI, +10 STA, +9 SPI, +9 STR, Shadowcraft piece)	
Bloodaxe Worg	51-57
Notes: Stealth detection	
Frequent Drops: Red Wolf Meat, Tender Wolf Meat	
Bloodaxe Worg Pup	51-53
Frequent Drops: Red Wolf Meat, Tender Wolf Meat	
Burning Felguard	56-57 Rare
Frequent Drops: Demonskin Gloves (Cloth Hands, 51 Armor, +17 SPI, +9 INT, +9 STA), Phase Blade (Off-Hand Sword, 32.1 DPS, +8 STA, +5 STR)	
Burning Felhound	54-55
Burning Imp	50-55
Chromatic Dragonspawn	54-60 Elite
Frequent Drops: Brilliant Chromatic Scale	
Chromatic Elite Guard	54-60 Elite
Notes: Strike, Mortal Strike, Knockdown	
Frequent Drops: Brilliant Chromatic Scale	

NPC	LEVEL
Chromatic Whelp	52-58
Notes: Fireball, Frost Bolt	
Frequent Drops: Brilliant Chromatic Scale	
Firebrand Darkweaver	52-57 Elite
Notes: Shadowbolt, Shadowbolt Volley	
Frequent Drops: Devout Belt (Cloth Waist, 46 Armor, +20 INT, +9 SPI, +4 STA, Devout piece), Dreadmist Bracers (Cloth Wrist, +10 INT, +10 STA, +7 SPI, Dreadmist piece)	
Firebrand Dreadweaver	57-58 Elite
Notes: Curse of Firebrand (657-843 fire damage every 60 seconds, 5 minute duration)	
Frequent Drops: Devout Belt (Cloth Waist, 46 Armor, +20 INT, +9 SPI, +4 STA, Devout piece), Dreadmist Bracers (Cloth Wrist, +10 INT, +10 STA, +7 SPI, Dreadmist piece)	
Firebrand Grunt	51-57 Elite
Notes: Mark of Flame (+1000 damage from fire, 2 minute duration), Enrage	
Frequent Drops: Beaststalker's Belt (Mail Waist, 193 Armor, +11 SPI, +10 AGI, +9 INT, +9 STR, +6 STA, Beaststalker piece), Bracers of Valor (Plate Wrist, 261 Armor, +14 STA, +7 STR, +3 AGI, +2 SPI, Valor piece), Shadowcraft Belt (Leather Waist, +14 AGI, +10 STA, +9 SPI, +9 STR, Shadowcraft piece)	
Firebrand Invoker	52-57 Elite
Notes: Fire AoE	
Frequent Drops: Magister's Bindings (Cloth Wrist, 35 Armor, +15 INT, +5 SPI, +4 STA, Magister piece), Wildheart Gloves (Leather Gloves, 105 Armor, +21 SPI, +9 INT, Wildheart piece), Cord of Elements (Mail Waist, 193 Armor, +17 INT, +9 STR, +7 SPI, +6 STA, Elements piece)	
Firebrand Legionnaire	57-58 Elite
Frequent Drops: Beaststalker's Belt (Mail Waist, 193 Armor, +11 SPI, +10 AGI, +9 INT, +9 STR, +6 STA, Beaststalker piece), Bracers of Valor (Plate Wrist, 261 Armor, +14 STA, +7 STR, +3 AGI, +2 SPI, Valor piece), Shadowcraft Belt (Leather Waist, +14 AGI, +10 STA, +9 SPI, +9 STR, Shadowcraft piece)	
Firebrand Pyromancer	57-58 Elite
Notes: Plague Cloud (disease, -57 STR/AGI/INT), Immolate	
Frequent Drops: Wildheart Gloves (Leather Gloves, 105 Armor, +21 SPI, +9 INT, Wildheart piece), Cord of Elements (Mail Waist, 193 Armor, +17 INT, +9 STR, +7 SPI, +6 STA, Elements piece)	
Rage Talon Captain	57-62 Elite
Rage Talon Dragon Guard	55-61 Elite
Notes: Cleave, Backhand (Knockdown)	
Frequent Drops: Beaststalker's Belt (Mail Waist, 193 Armor, +11 SPI, +10 AGI, +9 INT, +9 STR, +6 STA, Beaststalker piece)	
Rage Talon Dragonspawn	53-59 Elite
Notes: Enrage	
Rage Talon Fire Tongue	55-61 Elite
Notes: Fireball Volley	
Frequent Drops: Magister's Bindings (Cloth Wrist, 35 Armor, +15 INT, +5 SPI, +4 STA, Magister piece)	

NPC	LEVEL
Rage Talon Flamescale	54-59 Elite
Notes: Fire Nova, Fireball Volley	
Frequent Drops: Cord of Elements (Mail Waist, 193 Armor, +17 INT, +9 STR, +7 SPI, +6 STA, Elements piece)	
Rookery Guardian	57-59 Elite
Rookery Hatcher	56-59 Elite
Notes: Hatches dragon eggs to spawn Rookery Whelps	
Rookery Whelp	51-57
Scarshield Acolyte	50-55 Elite
Notes: Heal	
Scarshield Grunt	48-54 Elite
Notes: Slam (Knockdown)	
Scarshield Legionnaire	50-55 Elite
Notes: Cleave	
Frequent Drops: Bracers of Valor (Plate Wrist, 261 Armor, +14 STA, +7 STR, +3 AGI, +2 SPI, Valor piece), Shadowcraft Belt (Leather Waist, +14 AGI, +10 STA, +9 SPI, +9 STR, Shadowcraft piece)	
Scarshield Quartermaster	50-55 Elite
Frequent Drops: Blackhand's Command	
Scarshield Raider	52-56 Elite
Frequent Drops: Beaststalker's Belt (Mail Waist, 193 Armor, +11 SPI, +10 AGI, +9 INT, +9 STR, +6 STA, Beaststalker piece), Wildheart Gloves (Leather Hands, 105 Armor, +21 SPI, +9 INT, Wildheart piece)	
Scarshield Sentry	48-54 Elite
Scarshield Spellbinder	50-55 Elite
Notes: Arcane Missles	
Frequent Drops: Magister's Bindings (Cloth Wrist, 35 Armor, +15 INT, +5 SPI, +4 STA, Magister piece), Devout Belt (Cloth Waist, 46 Armor, +20 INT, +9 SPI, +4 STA, Devout piece)	
Scarshield Warlock	50-55 Elite
Notes: Opens summoning portal	
Frequent Drops: Cord of Elements (Mail Waist, 193 Armor, +17 INT, +9 STR, +7 SPI, +6 STA, Elements piece), Dreadmist Bracers (Cloth Wrist, +10 INT, +10 STA, +7 SPI, Dreadmist piece)	
Scarshield Worg	49-54 Elite
Frequent Drops: Red Wolf Meat, Tender Wolf Meat	
Smolderthorn Axe Thrower	52-56 Elite
Frequent Drops: Bracers of Valor (Plate Wrist, 261 Armor, +14 STA, +7 STR, +3 AGI, +2 SPI, Valor piece)	
Smolderthorn Berserker	53-57 Elite
Notes: Enrage	
Frequent Drops: Wildheart Gloves (Leather Hands, 105 Armor, +21 SPI, +9 INT, Wildheart piece)	
Smolderthorn Headhunter	53-57 Elite
Notes: Enrage	
Smolderthorn Mystic	51-56 Elite
Notes: Lightning Bolt	
Frequent Drops: Magister's Belt (Cloth Waist, 46 Armor, +21 INT, +6 SPI, +6 STA, Magister piece)	

NPC	LEVEL
Smolderthorn Seer	53-57 Elite
Notes: Lightning Shield, Shrink (-56 STR/STA, 2 minute duration)	
Frequent Drops: Dreadmist Bracers (Cloth Wrist, +10 INT, +10 STA, +7 SPI, Dreadmist piece), Wildheart Gloves (Leather Hands, 105 Armor, +21 SPI, +9 INT, Wildheart piece)	
Smolderthorn Shadow Hunter	51-57 Elite
Frequent Drops: Shadowcraft Belt (Leather Waist, +14 AGI, +10 STA, +9 SPI, +9 STR, Shadowcraft piece), Shadowcraft Bracers (Leather Wrist, 71 Armor, +15 AGI, +7 STA, Shadowcraft piece)	
Smolderthorn Shadow Priest	51-56 Elite
Notes: Frog	
Frequent Drops: Devout Belt (Cloth Waist, 46 Armor, +20 INT, +9 SPI, +4 STA, Devout piece)	
Smolderthorn Witch Doctor	54-57 Elite
Notes: Elemental Protection Totem	
Frequent Drops: Cord of Elements (Mail Waist, 193 Armor, +17 INT, +9 STR, +7 SPI, +6 STA, Elements piece)	
Spire Scarab	57-58
Frequent Drops: Delicate Insect Wing, Husk Fragment	
Spire Scorpid	54-58
Frequent Drops: Mystery Meat	
Spire Spider	53-58 Elite
Frequent Drops: Immature Venom Sac, Ironweb Spider Silk	
Spire Spiderling	50-56
Frequent Drops: Immature Venom Sac, Shadow Silk	
Spirestone Battle Mage	52-58 Elite
Spirestone Enforcer	52-55 Elite
Notes: Strike, Enrage	
Spirestone Mystic	50-56 Elite
Spirestone Ogre Magus	49-55 Elite
Notes: Arcane Missles, Slow (-35% attack speed, -60% movement speed, 8 second duration), Enrage	
Spirestone Reaver	51-56 Elite
Notes: Cleave, Warstomp (AoE stun, 4 second duration), Enrage	
Spirestone Warlord	52-58 Elite
Notes: Enrage	
Summoned Blackhand Dreadweaver	56-60 Elite
Frequent Drops: Dreadmist Bracers (Cloth Wrist, +10 INT, +10 STA, +7 SPI, Dreadmist piece)	
Summoned Blackhand Veteran	57-60 Elite
Urok Enforcer	50-55 Elite
Urok Ogre Magus	52-55 Elite

THE ENEMY LEADERSHIP

NPC	LEVEL	FREQUENT DROP(S)
BANNOK GRIMAXE	59 Rare	Backusarian Gauntlets (Plate Hands, 392 Armor, +9 INT, +15 STA, +9 STR), Chiselbrand Girdle (Mail Waist, 199 Armor, +6 SPI, +6 STA, Passive: +44 Attack Power), Demonfork (Main Hand Axe, 38.9 DPS, Chance on Hit: Transfers 10 health every 5 sec.s from the target to the caster for 25 sec.s), Plans: Arcanite Reaper (Requires Blacksmithing (300) & Master Axesmithing)
CRYSTAL FANG	60 Elite	Fallbrush Handgrips (Leather Hands, 107 Armor, +12 INT, +11 SPI, +11 STA, Equip: Increases healing done by spells and effects by up to 20), Fang of the Crystal Spider (One-Hand Dagger, 40.3 DPS, Chance on Hit: Slows target enemy's casting speed, melee attack speed, and range attack speed by 10% for 10 sec.), Sunderseer Mantle (Cloth Shoulder, 65 Armor, +17 INT, +11 SPI, +4 STA, Equip: Increases damage and healing done by magical spells and effects by up to 8)
GENERAL DRAKKISATH	Boss	Beaststalker's Tunic (Mail Chest, 370 Armor, +21 AGI, +13 INT, +6 SPI, +16 STA, +5 STR, Beaststalker Armor piece), Blackblade of Shahram (Two-Hand Sword, 59.4 DPS, Chance on Hit: Summons the infernal spirit of Shahram), Breastplate of Valor (Plate Chest, 657 Armor, +24 STA, +15 STR, +10 AGI, +6 SPI, Battlegear of Valor piece), Brigam Girdle (Plate Waist, 369 Armor, +16 STA, +15 STR, Equip: Improves your chance to hit by 1%), Devout Robe (Cloth Chest, 89 Armor, +24 INT, +15 SPI, +13 STA, Vestments of the Devout piece), Draconian Deflector (Shield, 2153 Armor, 40 Block, +7 STA, +10 Fire Resistance, Passive: Increased Defense +10), Draconian Infused Emblem (Trinket, Use: Increases your spell damage by up to 100 and your healing by up to 190 for 15 sec.), Dreadmist Robe (Cloth Chest, 89 Armor, +21 INT, +13 SPI, +20 STA, Dreadmist Raiment piece), Lightforge Breastplate (Plate Chest, 657 Armor, +21 INT, +16 INT, +13 STR, +8 SPI, Lightforge Armor piece), Magister's Robes (Cloth Chest, 89 Armor, +31 INT, +8 SPI, +9 STA, Magister's Regalia piece), Painweaver Band (Finger, +7 STA, Equip: Improves your chance to get a critical strike by 1%, +16 Attack Power), Pattern: Red Dragonscale Breastplate (Requires: Leatherworking (300) & Dragonscale Leatherworking), Shadow Prowler's Cloak (Back, 45 Armor, +17 AGI, +7 STA), Shadowcraft Tunic (Leather Chest, 176 Armor, +26 AGI, +12 SPI, +13 STA, Shadowcraft Armor piece), Spellweaver's Turban (Cloth Head, 73 Armor, +9 INT, Equip: Increases damage and healing done by magical spells and effects by up to 36, Improves your chance to hit with spells by 1%), Tome of the Lost (Off-Hand, +7 INT, +6 STA, Equip: Increases damage and healing done by magical spells and effects by up to 18), Tooth of Gnarr (Neck, +14 INT, +8 STA, Equip: Restores 3 mana per 5 sec.), Vest of Elements (Mail Chest, 370 Armor, +20 INT, +20 SPI, +13 STA, The Elements piece), Wildheart Vest (Leather Chest, 176 Armor, +20 INT, +20 SPI, +13 STA, Wildheart Raiment piece)
		Notes: Cleave, Conflagrate, Flame Strike, Pierce Armor, and Rage (+122 damage and +50% attack speed for 15 sec.)
GHOK BASHGUUD	59 Elite	Armswake Cloak (Back, 43 Armor, +15 STA, Equip: +16 Attack Power), Bashguuder (One-Hand Mace, 39.4 DPS, +9 STR, Chance on Hit: Punctures target's armor lowering it by 200. Can be applied up to 3 times.), Hurd Smasher (One-Hand Fist Weapon, 39.4 DPS, Chance on Hit: Knocks target silly for 2 sec.s)
GIZRUL THE SLAVENER	57-60 Elite	Bleak Howler Armguards (Leather Wrist, 75 Armor, +8 INT, +14 SPI, Equip: Increases healing done by spells and effects by up to 15), Rhombeard Protector (Shield, 2089 Armor, 38 Block, +10 SPI, +15 INT), Wildheart Spaulders (Leather Shoulder, 127 Armor, +18 INT, +9 STA, +8 SPI, Wildheart Raiment Piece), Wolfshear Leggings (Cloth Legs, 76 Armor, +25 SPI, +5 STA, +10 Nature Resistance, Equip: Increases healing done by spells and effects by up to 26)
		Notes: Enrage (Increases attack speed up to 60% and damage by 118), Fatal Bite (drains 964 damage from target and grants Gizrul up to 2x that amount), and Infected Bite (Increases damage taken by target and Nature DoT)
GORALUK ANVILCRACK	56-61 Elite	Bottom Half of Advanced Armorsmithing Volume I, Flame Walkers (Mail Feet, 251 Armor, +10 STA, +18 Fire Resistance, Equip: Increases your chance to dodge an attack by 1%), Handcrafted Mastersmith Girdle (Plate Waist, 519 Armor, +10 AGI, +10 STA, +11 STR), Handcrafted Mastersmith Leggings (Plate Legs, 548 Armor, +12 STA, +29 STR), Mastersmith's Hammer (Main Hand Mace, 39.4 DPS, +5 INT, Equip: Increases damage and healing done by magical spells and effects by up to 14), Plans: Arcanite Champion (Requires Blacksmithing (300) & Master Swordsmith), Plans: Invulnerable Mail (Requires Blacksmithing (300) & Armorsmith) Plans: Masterwork Stormhammer (Requires Blacksmithing (300) & Master Hammersmith)
GYTH	Boss	Chromatic Carapace (Quest Item), Dragoneye Coif (Mail Head, 288 Armor, +17 STA, Equip: +38 Attack Power, + Random Stats), Dragonskin Cowl (Cloth Head, 69 Armor, +15 INT, +12 STA, Equip: Increases damage and healing done by magical spells and effects by up to 18, + Random Stats), Gyth's Skull (Plate Head, 509 Armor, +20 STA, Equip: Increased Defense +9, + Random Stats), Pauldrons of Elements (Mail Shoulder, 266 Armor, +15 INT, +14 STA, +6 SPI, +6 STR, The Elements piece), Tribal War Feathers (Leather Head, 137 Armor, +15 INT, +12 STA, Equip: Increases healing done by spells and effect by up to 33, + Random Stats)
		Notes: Corrosive Acid Breath (Nature DoT every 5 sec., 30 sec. duration), Freeze (AoE, Frost damage every 3 sec. for 9 sec.& stun), Flame Breath (1240 Fire damage), and Knock Away
HALYCON	55-59 Elite	Halycon's Spiked Collar (Neck, +7 STA, Equip: +48 Attack Power when fighting Beasts), Ironweave Bracers (Cloth Wrist, 108 Armor, +8 INT, +14 STA, Ironweave Battlesuit piece), Pads of the Dread Wolf (Leather Feet, 116 Armor, +14 STA, Equip: +40 Attack Power), Slashclaw Bracers (Mail Wrist, 155 Armor, +7 AGI, +6 SPI, +7 STA, Equip: Improves your chance to hit by 1%)
		Notes: Rend and Thrash
HIGHLORD OMOKK	Boss	Belt of Valor (Plate Waist, 341 Armor, +7 AGI, +4 SPI, +8 STA, +14 STR, Battlegear of Valor piece), Boots of Elements (Mail Feet, 240 Armor, +9 AGI, +17 SPI, The Elements Piece), Fist of Omokk (Two-Hand Mace, 51.4 DPS, +29 STR, +12 STA), Plate of the Shaman King (Plate Chest, 627 Armor, +15 INT, +15 STA, +12 STR, Equip: Increases damage and healing done by magical spells and effects by up to 18), Skyshroud Leggings (Cloth Legs, 75 Armor, +8 INT, +8 STA, Equip: Increases damage and healing done by magical spells and effects by up to 34), Slamshot Shoulders (Plate Shoulder, 470 Armor, +21 STA, Equip: +20 Attack Power), Tessermane Leggings (Leather Legs, 148 Armor, +14 INT, +15 SPI, +12 STA, Equip: Increases damage and healing done by magical spells and effects by up to 19)
		Notes: Cleave, Enrage, and Knock Away
JED RUNEWATCHER	55-59 Elite	Briarwood Reed (Trinket, Equip: Increases damage and healing done by magical spells and effects by up to 29), Serpentine Skuller (Wand, 54.6 DPS, +10 Shadow Resistance), Starfire Tiara (Cloth Head, 69 Armor, +10 SPI, +28 INT, +10 Fire Resistance)
LORD VALTHALAK	60 Elite	Draconian Aegis of the Legion (Shield, 2153 Armor, 40 Block, +7 STA, Equip: Increases damage and healing done by magical spells and effects by up to 20), Handguards of Savagery (Mail Hands, 231 Armor, +9 INT, +10 STA, Equip: +38 Attack Power), Ironweave Cowl (Cloth Head, 203 Armor, +15 INT, +24 STA, Ironweave Battlesuit piece), Leggings of Torment (Cloth Legs, 78 Armor, +16 INT, +16 STA, Equip: Increases damage done by Shadow spells and effects by up to 34), Lord Valthalak's Staff of Command (Staff, 53.8 DPS, +10 INT, +11 STA, Equip: Increases damage and healing done by magical spells and effects by up to 30, Improves your chance to hit with spells by 1%), Pendant of Celerity (Neck, +15 AGI, Equip: Improves your chance to hit by 1%), Rune Band of Wizardry (Finger, +7 STA, Equip: Improves your chance to hit with spells by 1%, Increases damage and healing done by magical spells and effects by up to 16), Shroud of Domination (Back, 45 Armor, +7 STA, +17 STR)
		Notes: Energy Siphon (1.5 sec cast, mana drain and restores 10k health to Valthalak if successful), Shadow Bolt Volley, Shadow Wrath (500 Shadow initial damage and jumps to nearby targets and increasing damage with each jump), and Summon Spectral Assassin (Summons 2 minions with Defile (10 sec. channeled stun that kills target if not interrupted) and Shadow Shock (700 Shadow damage))

NPC	LEVEL	FREQUENT DROP(S)
MOR GRAYHOOF	60 Elite	Belt of the Trickster (Leather Waist, 97 Armor, +22 AGI, +9 STA), Idol of Rejuvenation (Relic, Equip: Increases healing done by Rejuvenation by up to 50), Ironweave Belt (Cloth Waist, 139 Armor, +11 INT, +17 STA, Ironweave Battlesuit piece), The Jaw Breaker (One-Hand Mace, 40.3 DPS, Equip: Improves your chance to get a critical strike by 1%), Left Piece of Lord Valthalak's Amulet (Quest item), Right Piece of Lord Valthalak's Amulet (Quest Item), Tome of Divine Right (Off-Hand, +5 INT, +4 STA, Equip: Increases healing done by spells and effects by up to 26; Use: Restores 4 mana per 5 sec.)
Notes: Shifts between four forms at various health levels. Caster Form (default): Healing Touch (Heals Mor for 7400-8600, 2 sec. casting time), Hurricane (500 DPS for up to 10 sec., Reduces attack speed by 40%), Moonfire (AoE version of Druid spell, 450 initial Nature damage plus 150 additional per 3 sec. for 12 sec.), and Rejuvination (1000 HP per 3 sec. for 12 sec.) Bear Form (80% health, lasts 10 sec., adds 50% damage absorption from physical attacks): Demoralizing Roar (Reduces attack power by 300), Maul (Damage, Knock Down, and 2 sec. stun), and Swipe Cat Form (60% health, lasts 10 sec., adds 100% melee haste): Ferocious Bite, Rake (DoT), and Shred (Reduces armor of target by 75% and deals damage) Faerie Dragon Form (30% health, lasts until dead, adds 50% magic damage absorption): Arcane Explosion (600 Arcane damage), Chain Lightning, Reflection (Reflects all incoming spells for 5 sec.), Shock (950-1050 Nature damage, 6 sec. cooldown), and Sleep (Random target is put to sleep and stunned, damage wakens target)		
MOTHER SMOLDERWEB	59 Elite	Gilded Gauntlets (Mail Hands, 221 Armor, +15 INT, +14 STA, Equip: Restores 4 mana per 5 sec.), Smolderweb's Eye (Trinket, Use: Poisons target for 20 Nature damage every 2 sec.s for 20 sec.s), Venomspitter (One-Hand Mace, 39.5 DPS, Chance on Hit: Poisons target for 7 Nature damage every 2 sec. for 30 sec.), Wildheart Boots (Leather Boots, 115 Armor, +9 INT, +17 SPI, +10 STA, Wildheart Raiment piece)
Notes: Crystallize (AoE Frontal Cone stun) and Mother's Milk (Potent poison that stuns the target and all nearby allies periodically)		
OVERLORD WYRMTHALAK	Boss	Beaststalker's Mantle (Mail Shoulder, 266 Armor, +17 STA, +11 AGI, +7 INT, +4 SPI, Beaststalker Armor piece), Chillpike (Polearm, 52.3 DPS, Chance on Hit: Blasts target for 160-250 Frost damage), Mark of the Dragon Lord (Finger, Use: A protective mana shield surrounds the caster absorbing 500 damage. While the shield holds, increases mana regeneration by 22 every 5 sec. for 30 min.), Heart of the Scale (Trinket, Use: Increases Fire Resistance by 20 and deals 20 Fire damage to anyone who strikes you with a melee attack for 5 min.), Heart of Wyrmthalak (Trinket, Equip: Chance to bathe your melee target in flames for 120-180 Fire damage), Reiver Claws (Plate Hands, 398 Armor, +15 STA, +9 STR, Equip: Improves your chance to get a critical strike by 1%), Relentless Scythe (Two-Hand Sword, 53.0 DPS, +8 AGI, +8 STA, +20 STR, Equip: Increases your chance to parry an attack by 1%), Trindlehaven Staff (Staff, 52.1 DPS, +25 INT, +12 STA, Equip: Increases damage and healing done by spells and effects by up to 14)
Notes: Cleave, Demoralizing Shout, and Sweeping Slam (Frontal Cone damage and Knockback)		
PYROGUARD EMBERSEER	Boss	Emberfury Talisman (Neck, +8 STA, +5 SPI, +7 Fire Resistance, Equip: Improves your chance to get a critical strike by 1%), Flaming Band (Ring, Equip: Increases damage done by Fire spells and effects by up to 24), Gauntlets of Elements (Mail Hands, 218 Armor, +16 SPI, +10 INT, +9 STR, +4 STA, The Elements piece), Truestrike Shoulders (Leather Shoulders, 129 Armor, Equip: Improves your chance to hit by 2%, +24 Attack Power), Wildfire Cape (Back, 43 Armor, +20 Fire Resistance)
Notes: Fire Nova (PBAoE Fire spell for 1000 damage), Flame Buffet (89-94 Fire damage & debuff causing an additional 91 Fire damage from subsequent Fire attacks; Can stack and lasts 45 sec.)		
QUARTERMASTER ZIGRIS	56-59 Elite	Beaststalker's Belt (Mail Waist, 193 Armor, +11 SPI, +10 AGI, +9 INT, +9 STR, +6 STA, Beaststalker Armor piece), Bracers of Valor (Plate Wrist, 261 Armor, +14 STA, +7 STR, +3 AGI, +2 SPI, Battlegear of Valor piece), Cloudrunner Girdle (Leather Waist, 185 Armor, +15 AGI, +14 STR), Cord of Elements (Mail Waist, 193 Armor, +17 INT, +9 STR, +7 SPI, +6 STA, The Elements piece), Devout Belt (Cloth Waist, 46 Armor, +20 INT, +9 SPI, +4 STA, Vestments of the Devout piece), Dreadmist Bracers (Cloth Wrist, +10 INT, +10 STA, +7 SPI, Dreadmist Raiment piece), Hands of Power (Cloth Hands, 53 Armor, +6 INT, +6 SPI, Equip: Increases damage and healing done by magical spells and effects by up to 26), Magister's Bindings (Cloth Wrist, 35 Armor, +15 INT, +5 SPI, +4 STA, Magister's Regalia piece), Plans: Annihilator (Requires: Blacksmithing (300) & Master Axesmith), Shadowcraft Belt (Leather Waist, 93 Armor, +14 AGI, +9 SPI, +10 STA, +9 STR, Shadowcraft Armor piece), Wildheart Belt (Leather Waist, 93 Armor, +17 INT, +10 SPI, +9 STA, Wildheart Raiment piece)
SHADOW HUNTER VOSH'GAJIN	Boss	Blackcrow (Crossbow, 30.3 DPS, +3 AGI, Equip: Improves your chance to hit by 1%), Demonic Runed Spaulders (Leather Shoulders, 126 Armor, +14 INT, +12 STA, +12 STR), Doomshot (200 Arrows, Adds 20 Damage, 6.7 DPS), Funeral Cuffs (Cloth Wrist, 37 Armor, +14 INT, +5 SPI, +10 Shadow Resistance), Riphook (Bow, 30.2 DPS, +22 Attack Power), Shadowcraft Gloves (Leather Hands, +14 AGI, +10 SPI, +9 STA, Shadowcraft Armor piece), Trueaim Gauntlets (Mail Hands, 218 Armor, Equip: Increased Bows/Guns +8, Improves your chance to hit by 1%)
Notes: Curse of Blood and Hex (AoE Frog, 20 yd. range, 10 sec. duration)		
SOLAKAR FLAMEWREATH	59-60 Elite	Crystallized Girdle (Leather Waist, 97 Armor, +19 INT, +6 SPI, +6 STA, Equip: Increases damage and healing done by magical spells and effects by up to 9), Devout Mantle (Cloth Shoulder, 64 Armor, +21 INT, +9 SPI, +4 STA, Vestments of the Devout piece), Dustfeather Sash (Cloth Waist, 49 Armor, +18 INT, +10 STA, Equip: Increases damage and healing done by magical spells and effects by up to 9), Nightbrace Tunic (Leather Chest, 172 Armor, +5 AGI, +10 STA, +10 Fire Resistance, +10 Shadow Resistance, Equip: +50 Attack Power), Polychromatic Visionwrap (Cloth Chest, 87 Armor, +20 All Resistances)
SPIRESTONE BATTLE LORD	58 Elite	The Nicker (Two-Hand Axe, 49.8 DPS, Chance on Hit: Wounds the target for 50-150 damage and deals an additional 6 damage every 1 sec. for 25 sec.), Swiftdart Battleboots (Mail Boots, 236 Armor, +17 AGI, +10 INT, +9 STA)
SPIRESTONE BUTCHER	57 Rare	Butcher's Apron (Cloak, 41 Armor, +7 STA, +16 SPI), Rivenspike (One-Hand Axe, 38.1 DPS, Chance on Hit: Punctures target's armor lowering it by 200. Can by applied up to 3 times.)
SPIRESTONE LORD MAGUS	58 Rare	Globe of D'sak (Off-Hand, +16 INT, +5 STA, +7 Shadow Resistance), Magus Ring (Ring, +12 INT, +7 SPI, +8 STA), Ogreseer Tower Boots (Cloth Feet, 58 Armor, +13 INT, +13 SPI, +13 STA)
THE BEAST	Boss	Ace of Beasts, Blackmist Armguards (Leather Wrist, 77 Armor, +13 STA, +5 STR, +10 Shadow Resistance, Equip: Improves your chance to hit by 1%), Blademaster Leggings (Leather Legs, 154 Armor, +5 AGI, Equip: Increases your chance to hit by 1%, dodge an attack by 2%, and get a critical strike by 1%), Bloodmoon Cloak (Cloak, 45 Armor, +17 STA, +5 SPI, +7 Arcane Resistance), Finkle's Skinner (Main Hand Dagger, 41.2 DPS, Equip: Skinning +10, +45 Attack Power when fighting Beasts), Frostweaver Cape (Cloak, 45 Armor, +12 INT, +12 SPI, +10 Frost Resistance), Ironweave Boots (Cloth Feet, 150 Armor, +11 INT, +17 STA, Ironweave Battlesuit piece), Lightforge Spaulders (Plate Shoulder, 470 Armor, +15 STA, +11 INT, +9 STR, +5 SPI, +4 AGI, Lightforge Armor piece), Pristine Hide of the Beast (Quest item), Seeping Willow (Two-Hand Mace, 53.9 DPS, Chance on Hit: Lowers all stats by 20 and deals 20 Nature damage every 3 sec. to all enemies within an 8 yard radius of the caster for 30 sec.), Spiritshroud Leggings (Cloth Legs, 78 Armor, +16 INT, +16 SPI, +13 STA, Equip: Increases damage and healing done by magical spells and effects by up to 19), Tristam Legguards (Mail Legs, 324 Armor, +13 STA, Equip: +34 Attack Power, Increases your chance to dodge an attack by 2%)
Notes: Berserker Charge, Immolate, Fire Blast, and Terrifying Roar (5 sec. AoE Fear)		

NPC	LEVEL	FREQUENT DROP(S)
UROK DOOMHOWL	60 Elite	Boots of Elements (Mail Boots, 240 Armor, +17 SPI, +9 AGI, Elements piece), Marksman's Girdle (Mail Waist, 202 Armor, +21 AGI, Equip: Improves your chance to hit by 1%), Ribsteel Footguards (Plate Boots, 438 Armor, +10 STR, +17 STA, +10 AGI), Rosewine Circle (Finger, Equip: Restores 5 mana per 5 sec., Increases healing done by spells and effects by up to 29), Slaghide Gauntlets (Leather Hands, 207 Armor, + Random Stats), Top Half of Advanced Armorsmithing Volume III
Notes: Intimidating Roar, Rend, and Strike		
WAR MASTER VOONE	Boss	Beaststalker Gloves (Mail Hands, 218 Armor, +14 AGI, +10 SPI, +9 STA, +9 INT, Beaststalker Armor piece), Brazecore Armguards (Mail Wrist, 155 Armor, +11 INT, +10 STA, Equip: Restores 3 mana per 5 sec.), Flightblade Throwing Axe (Throwing, 35.5 DPS), Kayser's Boots of Precision (Cloth Feet, 60 Armor, +18 INT, +11 STA, Equip: Improves your chance to hit with spells by up to 1%), Keris of Zul'Serak (One-Hand Dagger, 39.4 DPS, Chance on Hit: Inflicts numbing pain that deals 10 Nature damage every 2 sec. and slows target's attack speed by 10% for 10 sec.), Rosewine Circle (Finger, Equip: Restores 5 mana per 5 sec., Increases healing done by spells and effects by up to 29), Talisman of Evasion (Neck, +13 AGI, Equip: Increases your chance to dodge an attack by 1%)
Notes: Cleave		
WARCHIEF REND BLACKHAND	Boss	Band of Rumination (Ring, Equip: Restores 5 mana per 5 sec. and improves your chance to get a critical strike with spells by 1%), Battleborn Armbraces (Plate Wrist, 287 Armor, Equip: Improves your chance to hit by 1% and your chance to get a critical strike by 1%), Blackhand Doomsaw (Polearm, 54.0 DPS, Chance on Hit: Wounds the target for 324-540 damage), Bonespike Shoulder (Mail Shoulder, 278 Armor, Equip: Deals 60-90 damage when you are the victim of a critical melee strike), Dal'Rend's Sacred Charge (Main-Hand Sword, 41.4 DPS, +4 STR, Equip: Improves your chance to get a critical strike by 1%, Dal'Rend's Arms piece), Dal'Rend's Tribal Guardian (Off-Hand Sword, 100 Armor, 41.4 DPS, Equip: +7 Defense, Dal'Rend's Arms piece), Dragonrider Boots (Cloth Feet, 61 Armor, +16 INT, +5 STA, +10 Fire Resistance, Equip: Increases damage and healing done by magical spells and effects by up to 18), Eye of Rend (Leather Head, 143 Armor, +7 STA, +13 STR, Equip: Improves your chance to get a critical strike by 2%), Faith Healer's Boots (Cloth Feet, 61 Armor, +12 INT, +12 SPI, +10 STA, Equip: Increases healing done by spells and effects by up to 26), Felstriker (One-Hand Dagger, 45.6 DPS, Chance on Hit: All attacks are guaranteed to land and will be critical strikes for the next 3 sec.), Feralsurge Girdle (Mail Waist, 208 Armor, +10 INT, +9 STA, Equip: Restores 8 mana per 5 sec.), Spaulders of Valor (Plate Shoulder, 470 Armor, +17 STA, +11 STR, +9 AGI, Battlegear of Valor piece), Warmaster Leggings (Plate Legs, 575 Armor, +15 STA, +13 STR, Equip: Increases your chance to dodge an attack by 2%)
Notes: Cleave, Enrage, Mortal Strike (300% damage), and Whirlwind (Normal Damage +666 for 2 sec.).		

THE PATH LEADS UP

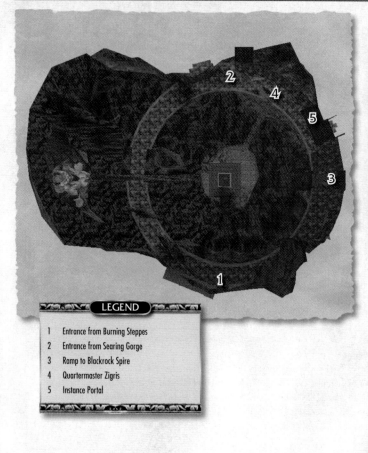

LEGEND

1 Entrance from Burning Steppes
2 Entrance from Searing Gorge
3 Ramp to Blackrock Spire
4 Quartermaster Zigris
5 Instance Portal

THE OUTER GUARDS

The Orcs of Blackrock Mountain have taken the upper portions from the Dwarves. They have guards stationed at the entrance to Blackrock Spire to keep the Dwarves from regaining what once was theirs.

The guards are set in pairs along the path to the instance portal. Crowd Control (CC) isn't needed for these small fights, but now is a good time to prepare for when it is needed.

Further practice can be done in the room to the right of the first pair of guards. There are two groups of three in here. Use these groups as a test of your party's pulling and CC capabilities.

Move up the ramps to the hallway that overlooks the Molten Span. The Chain Shortcut is to the left. He has **Blackhand's Command** in his possession. The entrance to Blackrock Spire is on the right. A quick check will determine whether you need bother with the guards or enter the instance.

LOWER BLACKROCK SPIRE

LEGEND	
1	Instance Portal
2	Shortcut Ledge
3	Vaelan
4	Highlord Omokk
5	Bijou
6	Shadow Hunter Vosh'gajin
7	War Master Voone
8	Mother Smolderweb
9	Quatermaster Zigris
10	Halycon
11	Overlord Wyrmthalak

JUST INSIDE

Once you have more room, pull the patrol when it comes closer. The Orcs in the lower rooms and those on the other side of the larger room are in larger groups and close enough to the portal for a full retreat. Pull a couple to get everyone accustomed to the role they're playing while the portal is close.

The second room on the right side of the lower level leads to the next area. An alternate route would be to take the ramp to the right and jump down.

Move onto the ramp to your right. Wait until the patrol moves away from the larger group then kill the patrol; rest up after. There are four Orcs and two Worgs in the group. Have any Rogues in your group sap the melee Orcs before beginning the fight. The fight should be initiated by the puller (preferably a Hunter or Warrior) or by a Priest Mind Controlling a caster Orc. Once the fight is begun, Druids should sleep the Worg, Mages should Polymorph a melee Orc, and the party should Focus Fire (FF) on a single enemy. The Scarshield Warlocks should be killed first, followed by the Scarshield Spellbinders.

DON'T HIT THE SHEEP!

Keeping party members from disrupting CC and to properly focus fire can be a little clumsy and annoying. Party members should call out which target they are intending to CC when the fight begins. This can be done with shorthand such as "sheeping left caster" or by using a macro to make it even more specific. "Sheeping %t" will show the party the name of your current target. If there are two or more of the same enemy, adding left, right, and center makes it even more specific.

Keeping the party on the same target can be equally challenging. Designating a Main Assist (MA) or target chooser is the first step. Once the MA is chosen, there are two ways to properly assist. Selecting the MA and using the assist hotkey (defaulted to "F") will give you his/her target. Using the "/assist" command in a macro works as well. An assist macro should look like this "/assist Rolf" where "Rolf" is the name of your MA.

This fight offers a good indication of where your party needs to improve before you take on the later fights in Blackrock Spire.

Move through the hallway and into a much larger room. There is a group of four Orcs. Clear this group and move on. Another group of Orcs and Worg waits ahead. Having your puller grab the left-most Worg gets you only the Scarshield Raider and the two Scarshield Worgs. With the group split, it's much more manageable. Wait for Warosh to move away from enemies and get the *Urok Doomhowl* quest.

BUT, I ONLY NEED TO KILL WYRMTHALAK

If Wyrmthalak is all you need, then you can skip a good bit and go straight to the Path to Wyrmthalak. There's a ledge along the wall to your right. Stick along the wall as you drop down into the darkness. Follow the wall until you drop again. Creep along the wall in front of you as you move left. You will emerge from the darkness on a ledge above several Orc groups. Jump down near the lava to avoid inadvertently pulling any. You have now skipped both the Path to Omokk and the Path to Voone.

There's a rocky ramp to your left. Follow it to the top. A Scarshield Infiltrator waits for you to get closer. Approach and Vaelan drops his disguise. From him, you acquire the *Seal of Ascension* quest. Continue clearing Orcs until you have access to the first bridge.

The next few fights should occur on the bridge. Moving onto the platform makes it too easy for running foes to get help. Clear the first few fights before moving onto the platform. Finish clearing the groups of enemies here before moving to the second bridge.

There is a group of four Orcs across the second bridge. Fight this group on the bridge before moving across. The **Roughshod Pikes** needed for *Urok Doomhowl* are along the left wall. Clear the group to your right and the sleeping Orcs ahead before grabbing the pikes.

Clear the Orcs as you move around the platform. Bijou stands below for *Operative Bijou*, but don't jump down. Three Ogres stand guarding the Path to Omokk. There is also a group of Orcs to the right. Kill the Orcs to keep the fighting simple.

VOONE IS MY TARGET

Omokk can be bypassed by moving past the Orc group and straight to the Path to Voone.

THE PATH TO HIGH LORD OMOKK

With the guards down, wait for the patroller to move toward you. Kill him and move down the hallway. There are two Ogres guarding your side of the bridge. Pull them into the hallway as their attacks can knock you off the bridge. Move along the bridges, fighting in the hallways until you get to Mok'Doom (Omokk's Chamber).

Pull the first group across the bridge to make room for you in the chamber. Watch the patroller and pull it when they are alone to keep them from adding to a fight later. Pull the group to the right before killing the group on the rubble.

The rubble group is a difficult fight. Two of the enemies are casters and the melee combatant may be a rare spawn: Spirestone Battle Lord. CC the melee and FF on the casters. Bring the Spirestone Mystic down first as it can inflict great damage to your party if allowed to live. Return to the floor and prepare to dispatch Highlord Omokk.

Highlord Omokk stands alongside two other Ogres. Begin the fight by CCing one of the other Ogres. Your tank should grab Omokk and keep him away from your party. Have your MT place their back against the wall to prevent being thrown away with Omokk's Knock Away ability. The rest of the party should FF on the other Ogre. Kill it and then FF on Omokk until the CC breaks on the first Ogre. FF on the Ogre until it dies and then finish Omokk. Should you have multiple CC classes in your party, CC both the ogres and kill Omokk first.

Omokk hits hard, but he's nothing special without his friends. Killing Highlord Omokk advances your progress in *Warlord's Command* and *Maxwell's Mission*. Loot **Omokk's Head** for *Urok Doomhowl* and the *Gem of Spirestone* for *Seal of Ascension*.

Exit The Ogre area and move to the Path to Voone.

THE PATH TO VOONE

The next room (Tazz'Alaor) is inhabited by many groups of Trolls and has a few patrollers. Pull the Trolls out of the room and onto the ramp to keep the fights clean. Clear the right wall and the table to the left before entering the room in force. Finish clearing the room and camp at the bottom of the ramp leading up to the right.

Only the puller should ascend the ramp for the first couple fights. Pull the enemies down the ramp and around the corner to break line of sight and force enemy casters to come to you.

Pull the enemies from the room until only the three at the back wall remain. Shadow Hunter Vosh'gajin is flanked by two Smolderthorn Shadow Priests. CC one of the Priests to start the fight. The group tank needs to drag Vosh'gajin away from the party to keep her Hex spell (AoE frog) devastating your party. Vosh'gajin also casts Curse of Blood which increases the physical damage taken for 10 min. FF on the other Priest. When the first falls, FF on the second Priest. With both Priests dead, Vosh'gajin is much more manageable. Kill her and take her **Snakestone** to complete the *Snakestone of the Shadow Huntress*.

Move to the large ramp descending into the next chamber. The four Trolls on the center platform need to be removed before you can advance across. Move to the north side of the room and fight your way through the Troll groups. Bijou - for *Operative Bijou* - is on the other side.

Return to the center of the ramps and head down. There are Trolls waiting at the next ledge. Pull them up to you and kill them. Move to where they were and wait for the patrol to come to you. Kill the patrol and prepare to clear the room.

The fights in this room are very dangerous. With so many wandering enemies and no space between groups, unexpected adds are commonplace. You can keep these to a minimum by fighting on the ramps. Only the puller should step onto the floor until he or she gives the word.

First pull the enemies in the southeast corner. The enemies under the ramps should be next. Removing the first few groups in the center of the room should give you a place on the floor to camp while you finish the job. Clear the room and take a look for *Bijou's Belongings*.

With the main room clear, move to the southwest corner. There is a series of rooms with Warmaster Voone inside. The first room has a group of four Trolls while the second room has two Trolls and a berserker. These fights can be handled like any of the other fights you've had, just clean them up and move on. When the party has rested, the fight with Voone can begin.

Your tank should start the fight. Shield the tank if you have a Priest, and allow them several seconds to build aggro before the rest of the party joins the fight. Warmaster Voone hits very hard and can drop a lightly armored party member (Rogue, Druid, Priest, Warlock, or Mage) in a few hits. Keep Voone's back toward the party to make it easier to see when he switches targets. Cease fire and wait for the tank to regain Voone's attention and pull him back into position if this occurs. The reward for killing him is part of *Warlord's Command* and *Maxwell's Mission*, along with the **Gem of Smolderthorn** for *Seal of Ascension*.

Warmaster Voone's chamber holds another battle for those faced with the task of summoning and defeating Mor Grayhoof. Use the Brazier of Beckoning to call upon this boss and get ready for battle. Mor has four forms that he'll switch through during the course of the battle. Use the "Enemy Leadership" table in this section to see his exact abilities.

Have the MT rush in to grab aggro and keep the casters out of range of his Hurricane and AoE Moonfire spells. They're brutal and could add up to serious damage for the softer party members. When he's in his caster form, be sure to interrupt his Healing Touch spell to keep the battle short. Also, have a Mage in your group cast Detect Magic. This will alert you to when Mor casts Rejuvination on himself and allow a Priest to Dispel it.

At 80% health, he switches to bear form; pour on the magic DPS. More DoTs! He's resistant to physical damage in this form and the MT should simply retain aggro while the casters let fly. If you can't drop him to 60% health within 10 sec. of his bear form change, he'll revert back to his caster form.

At 60%, he switches to cat form allowing for a 100% increase in his physical attacks. Again, he'll only retain this form for 10 sec. Without a resistance to either magic or physical damage, this is the perfect opportunity for all members of the group to increase their DPS.

However, once he hits 30% health, he'll switch to his Faerie Dragon form and absorb 50% magic damage and gain another ability that hampers the casters: Reflection. He'll also sleep random targets during the battle and cast Arcane Explosion, so keep the casters outside of the range of this spell. Spread out as much as possible to prevent the Chain Lightning from jumping between targets and drop him as quickly as possible.

Once you've cleared the room, take a quick look around the chamber for *Bijou's Belongings* before moving back to the larger room. Take a quick look around for *Bijou's Belongings* before moving back to the larger room.

THE PATH TO WYRMTHALAK

Move out of the large room and into the hallway filled with Orcs. They are in small groups that can be pulled separately and safely to your location. Kill them as you move down the hallway and turn the corner near the lava.

THE JUMPING ENDS HERE

If you took the shortcut to bypass both Voone and Omokk, this is where you have landed.

This passage is more dangerous. There are groups of enemies on both sides and many of them are casters. Use the corner to break line of sight and force the casters to come to you. This also keeps runners from getting very far. Have a snare effect on them at all times to keep them from getting friends.

The Firebrand Invokers should be killed quickly. Under no circumstances should they be allowed to get near your party's casters, as their AoE fire attacks are quite brutal. Have an off-tank or Rogue ready to intercept them during the pull.

The passage bends left at the end; this is a very dangerous area. The group of Orcs guarding the cart to the left is the least of your worries. There are a couple of sleeping Orcs directly ahead and they're with a group of a few more under a nearby tent. With no corner to break line of sight, the puller will need to run out of range and drag the enemies to the party.

The enemies need to be pulled away from the tent as there are more enemies on the other side. CC the melee targets and kill the casters.

Pull the group near the cart to the left next. This fight is much easier and clears the path ahead. Pull the last couple wandering in the center of the room, then proceed around the corner. Ignore the ramp to the spiders for a moment and focus on the room of Orcs to the right.

There are Firebrand Pyromancers in the room. They have a higher chance to have some of the better loot than the regular Orcs you've fought so far. There are two groups in the room that can be pulled separately. Pull them around the corner to force the casters to come to you.

The Spire Spiders and Spiderlings attack in groups of six. There will be two of the larger Spire Spiders and four of the Spiderlings in each group. If a Druid accompanies you, he/she should keep one of the Spire Spiders slept while your tank should hold the attention of the other; the rest of the party should kill the Spire Spiderlings. When all the Spiderlings are dead, choose one of the spiders and bring it down. When it dies, four more Spiderlings appear and need to be killed before the last spider is attacked. The final spider will also spawn four Spiderlings when it dies. Keep this tactic in mind as you clear your way through the webs.

Spider Eggs litter the ground as you move up the ramp. Make sure your party only opens one at a time as Spire Spiderlings can hatch during the collection process. Grab the eggs to complete *En-Ay-Es-Tee-Why*. Mother Smolderweb waits at the top of the ramp. She can be attacked without drawing another group of spiders onto the party. During the fight, Mother Smolderweb can infect party members with **Mother's Milk**. This is needed to complete the *Mother's Milk* quest. This poison stuns the primary target and anyone unfortunate enough to be close to them. Melee attackers, except for the MT, should remain behind her when possible. Crystallize is an AoE frontal cone stun and it's best to avoid it when possible. If your party intends to turn in *Mother's Milk*, port out with the party poisoned and make your way to Ragged John. If you intend to go after Wyrmthalak, use the venom sacs that have been looted from the spiders to cure yourself and move on.

There are several more groups of spiders as you continue upwards. Clear each one as you have previously until you stand before the Ogres.

Pull and kill the Ogres one at a time or in pairs. They hit hard, but the fights are simple and can be controlled well. When the ledge is clear of Ogres, approach the Tribute Pile with the Roughshod Pike and Omokk's head. Keep your party near the wall to avoid a treacherous fall. Have the MT gain as much aggro from the room as possible before releasing the MA to do their job. During the battle, you can click on the completed pole with Omokk's head to damage all ogres that join the fray. Defeat Urok Doomhowl and collect Warosh's Mojo to complete *Urok Doomhowl*.

The path ahead looks clear, but don't move forward yet! The holes in the right wall hold numerous Spire Scorpids and Scarabs. They attack anyone who tries to move past. Have your tank move first to draw the attention of the bugs. Shield your AoE casters and have them stand on the tank before casting. The fight won't last long. When you've recovered, there is one more fight before you're back in Orc territory.

A Bloodaxe Raider patrols the area along with two Bloodaxe Worgs. Kill them when they move into range. Have your puller move up the ramp and wait until the other patrol comes in sight. Pull it down to the party and take it out.

The path forks here; take the left passage up the ramps. Pull and kill the Bloodaxe as you have before. CC the melee Orcs and kill the casters. FF on the Summoner first as they can bring more enemies to the fight if allowed.

There's a large supply room at the top of the ramps. Quartermaster Zigris wanders amongst the other Bloodaxe. Pull the Orcs in small groups and keep them from running for help. Clear the room methodically to keep the danger out of your fights. Take what you can from Zigris' corpse and move back down the ramps to the fork.

Stay away from the wall to your left and pull the Bloodaxe ahead to the party. Duck around the passage to break line of sight and force the enemy to come to you. The fight is simple as long as the enemy is not allowed the flee into the room on the left.

When the Orcs are dead, rest up and prepare to fight Halycon and her pups. Move into the room on the left; your tank should move first. All party members should use their cage and capture a **Bloodaxe Worg Pup** for *Kibler's Exotic Pets*. This completes the quest and reduces the number of enemies to fight.

Once the party has the pups it needs, kill the others while your tank survives the attention of Halycon. With her pups dead or captured, focus on Halycon to complete *Put Her Down*. Halycon has physical abilities (Rend and Thrash) and she shouldn't be too much trouble. When Halycon falls, casters should immediately start drinking to restore mana and the tank should bandage and move into the hallway. Gizrul the Slavener will be moving down the hallway toward your party. He hits brutally hard and has a few abilities that can cause the tank trouble. Fatal Bite drains health from the target and has the potential to restore twice that amount (nearly 2k health) to Gizrul. Infected Bite increases the damage taken by the target and is a Nature DoT and, when coupled with the attack speed buff Enrage, can be a dangerous combo for the MT. Kill him and search the corpse for unexpected treasure.

Have your party stay at the bottom of the ramp. Only the puller should ascend until he/she gives the word. There are several groups of Orcs in the room. Pull each group down the ramp to the party and CC the Bloodaxe Evokers until the party is ready to kill them. They have an AoE fire and knockback that can be the end of your party if they're allowed near your casters.

Kill the groups one at a time until the entire left wall is clear. Even the sleepers should be pulled before the group comes up the ramp. Pull the first group ahead to clear a new base spot. The next pull is very dangerous.

Pulling the group at the bridge brings four enemies, two of which are casters. CC the melee enemies and FF on the casters. The enemies need to be killed quickly and kept from running. They don't have to go far for friends and a second group attacking you is not what you want. Remember to keep the Evokers away from your casters during this.

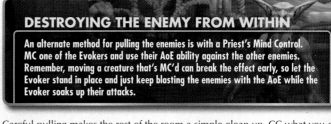

DESTROYING THE ENEMY FROM WITHIN

An alternate method for pulling the enemies is with a Priest's Mind Control. MC one of the Evokers and use their AoE ability against the other enemies. Remember, moving a creature that's MC'd can break the effect early, so let the Evoker stand in place and just keep blasting the enemies with the AoE while the Evoker soaks up their attacks.

Careful pulling makes the rest of the room a simple clean up. CC what you can and FF to end the fights quickly. Move across the bridges and up the ramp when the room is clear.

The ramp ends at a series of bridges. Ogres and Trolls guard the bridges in pairs. CC on and kill them one at a time. Do not fight on the bridge as they can knock you to a lower level if you do. Kill the pairs until you approach Wyrmthalak's chamber.

The first pull from the Chamber of Battle (Wyrmthalak's Chamber) should be pulled across the bridge. Once there's enough space for your party to stand in the room without drawing aggro, move in and look around. There are a couple patrollers and knowing what their routes are keeps the party safe from bringing extra adds.

Move around to the right, killing as you go. The enemies are the same as you've fought before as is the tactic. CC the melee and FF on the casters. However, there's a problem once you reach the first ramp.

SKIPPING IS FUN

The Chamber of Battle (just before Wyrmthalak's room) is just above Highlord Omokk's room. If your group skipped Omokk earlier, they can jump down to him after killing Wyrmthalak. It's a wonderful thing.

The next fight has six enemies. All of them are dangerous and it is unlikely your party will have enough CC for all of them. Have party members declare CC targets before the fight begins. Use Counterspell or LOS pulls to drag the casters back to your party. The tank should also declare his/her first target.

The tank should start the fight to gain early aggro. CC what you can as soon as the tank begins. The tank should keep enemies away from the casters to make it easier to see which enemies are attacking which targets. Anyone who can resurrect themselves should stay away from the enemies' starting point in case of a full party wipe. Rest before you take on Wyrmthalak.

Shield your tank, if you have a Priest, before they engage Wyrmthalak. This gives your tank a few seconds to amass aggro before the healer has to start casting. Keep him facing away from the party and lay into him. Wyrmthalak will call reinforcements when the fight starts turning against him. When he does, party members with CC abilities should run to the ledge and cast down at the adds to CC them as early as possible. Once the adds are CCed, return to Wyrmthalak and bring him down. When Wyrmthalak dies, turn your attention to the adds before looting.

Wyrmthalak is susceptible to Stuns and DoTs are very useful in inflicting damage while helping the tank maintain aggro. When Wyrmthalak gets low on health, he'll call for assistance. Throw everything you have at him and bring him down before his friends arrive.

The death of Wyrmthalak completes *Maxwell's Mission* and *Warlord's Command*. Taking the Gem gives you another piece for the Seal of Ascension.

Evil has been dealt a blow, but something even more sinister awaits deeper in the dungeon. You need more than a standard party of five people to conquer the upper portions of Blackrock Spire. Return to town to turn in quests, restock on potions, food, and poisons, and recruit more friends. You should have a raid group of ten before attempting Upper Blackrock Spire.

UPPER BLACKROCK SPIRE

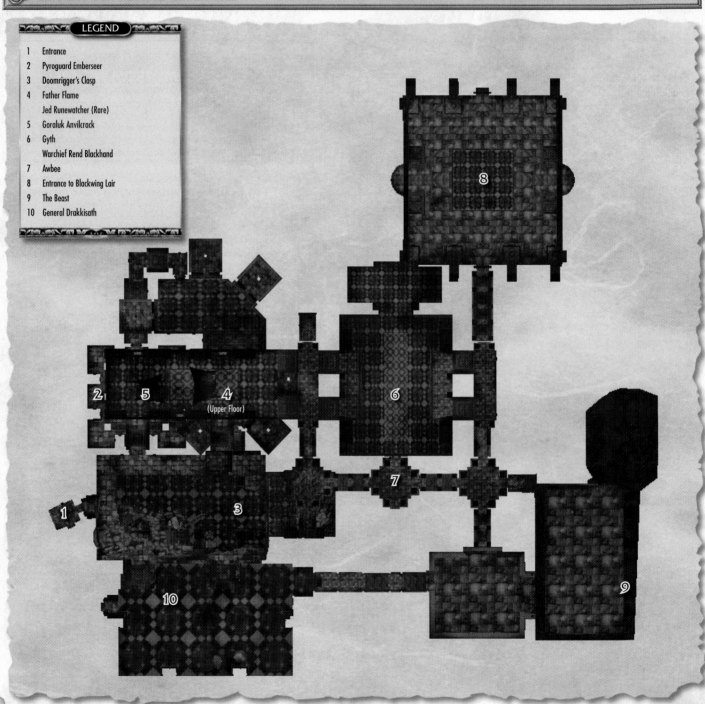

LEGEND

1 Entrance
2 Pyroguard Emberseer
3 Doomrigger's Clasp
4 Father Flame
   Jed Runewatcher (Rare)
5 Goraluk Anvilcrack
6 Gyth
   Warchief Rend Blackhand
7 Awbee
8 Entrance to Blackwing Lair
9 The Beast
10 General Drakkisath

THE GUARDS

The residents of Upper Blackrock Spire don't appreciate visitors and make it very difficult to get through the first few rooms. This should dissuade any casual thieves or adventurers.

Rage Talon Dragonkin patrol the center of the first room. Pull and kill them in pairs. Druids can CC one to keep the fighting simple. Once the dragonkin are clear, it's time to clear the Blackhand Orcs. All enemies in the area must be killed before the passage upward opens.

Each group of Blackhand consists of four Orcs with at least one Summoner and one Dreadweaver. The Summoners should be killed first and the Dreadweavers second. Mop up the rest and prepare for the next fight.

With the death of the final enemy, the door opens to the Hall of Binding. Pyroguard Emberseer is being held atop an altar by seven Blackhand Incarcerators. Move the entire raid into the room before using the dais to your left. The dais interrupts the Incarcerators and they charge you. Since they are not elite, using AoE attacks is the fastest way to finish them.

Once the Incarcerators are dead, prepare for Emberseer. It takes a few moments for him to finish breaking his bonds and the fight only takes a few more moments. Keep the casters back to prevent getting slammed with Fire Nova. The MT is going to suffer under the effects of Flame Buffet, so have your healers stay on their toes. It stacks and could eventually begin inflicting serious damage. Loot his corpse as the door to the Rookery opens.

The door opens to reveal a room full of eggs. These are the eggs you need for *Egg Freezing* and *Egg Collecting*. There are several Rookery Hatchers wandering among the eggs. Pull the Hatchers into Emberseer's chamber. After the Hatchers have been dealt with, start opening the eggs to spawn the Rookery Whelps. Start with the eggs along the left wall.

A ROOM FULL OF EGGS

As your party moves and fights in the Rookery, keep members from stepping on the eggs as they will spawn Rookery Whelps. This isn't a problem when done in a controlled fashion, but having four Whelps jump on a healer tends to make things more difficult.

The Rookery Whelps are not elite and can be fought with AoE abilities. Once the left wall is clear, move you group into the Rookery and to the corner. Clear your way to the Father Flame and use it to start the event. Rookery Hatchers and Guards charge you in pairs. Having a Druid sleep one before they get to you makes the fighting much easier.

After six waves of Rookery Hatchers and Guardians, Solakar Flamewreath attacks. Keep him away from your casters and deal with him as you would any other enemy. Grab your loot and start making your way across the room to the ramp up. Party members that have the *The Darkstone Tablet* should grab it as you move across the room.

The ledge above the Rookery has more Rookery Guardians and Hatchers. Pull them to you in small groups until the ledge is clear. Hold the group in the corner at the top of the ramp. Only the puller should enter the next room until it is clear.

Orcs fill the next room. Blackhand Elite, Veterans, and Dreadweavers make up most of the forces. They are in groups of three to five, but the fights won't be difficult since you have 15. Also Goraluk Anvilcrack and Jed Runewatcher wander the room.

Send the puller through the far entrance to pull the group immediately to his/her left. This group adds to any other group pulled, so it needs to be killed first. Once that group is killed, pull the other groups between the entrance and the left wall. If Anvilcrack joins a fight, back against the wall to keep him from throwing members down onto the eggs of the Rookery. Once the left wall is clear, move the raid group to that position.

Pull the enemy groups along both sides one at a time. There are Dragonkin mixed with the Orcs at the back of the room. If a Rage Talon Flamescale or Fire Tongue joins a fight, kill them first. Their AoE spells are quite damaging.

As you ascend the ramp, there is a passage leading to the right. Bypass this and head to the top of the ramp. Don't let anyone jump down into Blackrock Stadium until everyone is ready to do so. Once the command is given, everyone must jump into the center of the stadium. Stay away from the south gate. Anyone remaining on the ledge will be the doom of the party as they will be attacked and train dozens of mobs onto the raid. Nobody likes to be the obvious cause of a wipe.

Standing on another ledge are Nefarius and Rend. The two call for their underlings to kill you. Several waves of Chromatic Whelps, Chromatic Dragonspawn, and Blackhand Dragon Handlers will attack. Defeat each wave quickly. The next wave enters regardless of whether you're still fighting.

BLACKROCK STADIUM

WAVE	BLACKHAND DRAGON HANDLERS	CHROMATIC DRAGONSPAWN	CHROMATIC WHELPS
1		1	3
2		1	2
3	1	1	2
4	1	1	2
5	1	1	3
6	1	1	3
7	1	2	3

When the final wave of enemies has been defeated, Rend attacks from atop his dragon Gyth. Gyth is a danger unto himself and has a few dangerous abilities. The breath weapons Freeze (stun and Frost damage/DoT), Flame Breath, and Corrosive Acid Breath (Nature DoT) can target and hit multiple players. He also has a knock away ability. Bring Gyth down and force Rend to fight you on foot. Rend deals enough damage to bring down members of your raid, but the chance of a total wipe is fairly slim. His abilities are entirely melee-oriented, but often target multiple players. Don't let a caster get anywhere near him! His Mortal Strike deals 300% damage and could crush one easily. Remain calm and defeat Rend as you would any other enemy.

There is much loot that can drop from the enemies. The **Chromatic Carapace** can drop from Gyth and the **Chromatic Scales** can drop from any of the dragonkin. Both of these are needed to forge *The Breastplate of the Chromatic Flight*.

When Rend falls, the gate raises and you can leave Blackrock Stadium. The room to the south has several groups in it. The first pull will likely get two groups for a total of five enemies. Have CC ready and fight in the Stadium. Clear the final pair of enemies in the room to clear the way to Awbee. Awbee gives you *The Matron Protectorate* quest.

Have Rogues and the puller ascend the ramp to the East. Rogues should sap before the puller pulls the enemies down to the party. The groups are small enough that minimal CC is needed. Once the room is clear, the raid can move in.

The Beast has a Terrifying Roar (5 sec. AoE Fear) that can be the cause of a wipe if a party is too close. If it's relegated to only affecting the melee members, your chance for success increases. Stay alert and at long range if you're a caster and this should go your way.

Finkle Einhorn, At Your Service can be started when the Beast falls and Finkle slips from its corpse. The Beast provides a unique opportunity. Finkle's Skinner can drop from the Beast; it allows 300 level skinners to skin the Beast for the Pristine Hide of the Beast for **Breastplate of Bloodthirst**, **Cap of the Scarlet Savant**, or **Leggings of Arcana**.

Once the Beast is dead, there's another boss that can be summoned to the room for those needing their Dungeon Set 2 items. Lord Valthalak is a brutal adversary and must not be taken lightly. He has three phases during which he always has the potential to wipe your raid.

Use any and all Shadow Protection spells (Priests) and potions (Greater Shadow Protection Potion) for this battle. The MT should definitely be protected at all times.

Phase 1 gives him Shadow powers, minions, and draining/healing abilities. The key here is to force him to fight your game. Allowing Valthalak to cast a successful Energy Siphon is deadly, so interrupting that spell is a must. He'll also cast a chaining spell (Shadow Wrath), so try to remain as spread out throughout the room as possible to limit the number of jumps it can make. Lastly, when he summons his Spectral Assassins, have the MA target them so that they're brought down immediately.

At roughly 40% health, he'll conjure a Shadow Staff and enter Phase 2. This staff grants him extra attacks that deal about 1500 points of Shadow damage. No, this is no small bolt. Stay on him, but try and hold some mana in reserve.

During Phase 3 (approximately 15% health), Valthalak lets loose with Shadow Bolt Volley. Burn him down as quickly as possible using all of your strongest abilities and spells. If you manage to drop him, the rewards are worth it.

Once your challengers are dead, move your party back to the Furnace and prepare for the final stretch leading to General Drakkisath. It's the perfect time to restore food buffs, spell buffs, soulstones, and poisons. All the following pulls will be brought back into this room and your party should be ready. Make sure that everyone knows to remain in place and let the pullers bring the enemies back to the group.

The group guarding the bridge should be pulled as normal. Have a Druid sleep one of the Rage Talons; Rogues or Mages can take care of the Black Hand. Focus Fire on the MT's target and finish the enemies.

While your raid won't have every class at their disposal, everyone has a job to focus on and you've been gearing up for this role for the last 55 levels or so. Here's a short table instructing the positions and jobs of every class.

EVERYONE HAS A JOB

CLASS	POSITION	JOB
Druid	Ledge beside the bridge	Sleep Rage Talon Wyrmkin
Hunter	Moving with puller	Aspect of the Pack and Frost Traps
Mage	Ledge beside the bridge	Polymorph Blackhand Orcs
Paladin	Middle of bridge	Heal puller if needed
Priest	The Furnace	Power Word: Shield as needed
Rogue	Ahead of the puller	Improved Sap
Shaman	The Furnace	Drop Buffing/Healing Totems
Warlock	The Furnace	Fear mobs not otherwise CCed or targeted
Warrior	Moving or The Furnace	Puller or secondary tank

Once each fight begins, everyone should move into the Furnace to avoid being knocked off the bridge. The Rage Talon Fire Tongues should be killed first because of their excessive damage potential and the Rage Talon Dragon Guards should be second because so few classes can keep them CCed. There will be enough time between pulls for everyone to regen mana and health.

GENERAL DRAKKISATH

When all the groups are clear, it's time to take on General Drakkisath—the purpose of this entire journey. The General stands in his nook flanked by his guards. Get ready for battle. The Chromatic Elites with Drakkisath have the abilities Knockdown, Mortal Strike, and Strike (like a Warrior's Heroic Strike). They're not going to be easy targets. Their Mortal Strike specifically is a challenge to deal with and the MT shouldn't be hit with it at all if possible.

Have the MT draw the General to the center of the room and turn him away from the raid. Drakkisath's Conflagrate should hit the MT and an off tank at most. As soon as this battle begins, have the MA begin targeting one guard while the other is CC'd. Take the first down quickly and ensure that the other is controlled while you're working on the first guard. They can cause problems for the entire raid if loose.

Once the first Rage Talon Captain falls, have the MA and everyone except for the MT and their healer(s) target the second guard. Take them down as you did the first. Once they're down, join the MT in taking out Drakkisath.

His melee-oriented abilities aren't the true threat. Conflagrate is another matter. If the MT is Conflagrated, have the OT pick up Drakkisath from the side (keeping him facing away from the raid) until the MT is ready to regain aggro. Make sure to keep Drakkisath facing away from the casters (and away from them in general).

If your party lacks enough CC/tanking power to successfully take out all the adds and Drak himself, there is another, risky option. Have a Hunter shoot Drakkisath or one of the elites while Aspect of the Cheetah is active. Use traps and draw the target into the Beast's room, periodically turning around to fire and retain the aggro. Kiting a large, dangerous mob like this is a dangerous task, but one Hunters are perfectly suited for.

With General Drakkisath dead, Alliance raids have completed *General Drakkisath's Demise*; Horde raids need to loot his body for the *Blood of the Black Dragon Champion*. With an evil like this removed, there is but one last thing to do. Collect **Drakkisath's Brand** and take it to the Orb of Command in Drakkisath's chamber. This completes *Blackhand's Command* and grants you easy access to Blackwing Lair in the future.

It's time for you to return victoriously to your capitol and prepare for another battle. Congratulations on conquering Blackrock Spire!

BLACKWING LAIR

Played & Written by: Tyler "Hocken" Morgan of <Pacifist> on Kel'thuzad

Blackwing Lair is the home of Onyxia's brother Nefarian and Brood of the Black Dragonflight. The lair itself was created by the Dark Iron Dwarves and recently conquered by Nefarian and his Dragonkin companions in his quest for power over Azeroth. From Blackwing Lair, Nefarian plots to do what his father, Deathwing, presumably failed to do: create a Chromatic Dragonflight by capturing members of each of the five flights.

Until very recently, Blackwing Lair was the hardest dungeon in Azeroth, but Ahn'Qiraj has assumed that mantle. Groups attempting Blackwing should have raiding experience and equipment from Molten Core and Onyxia. You must venture into the lair and fight your way to Nefarian's throne room where he awaits your arrival.

DUNGEON INFORMATION

Location	Blackrock Mountain
Region	Contested
Quests	Alliance and Horde
Suggested Levels	60 (Full 40-person Raid)
Enemy Types	Dragonkin
Time to Complete	4 Hours to Several Days

WELCOME TO BLACKWING LAIR

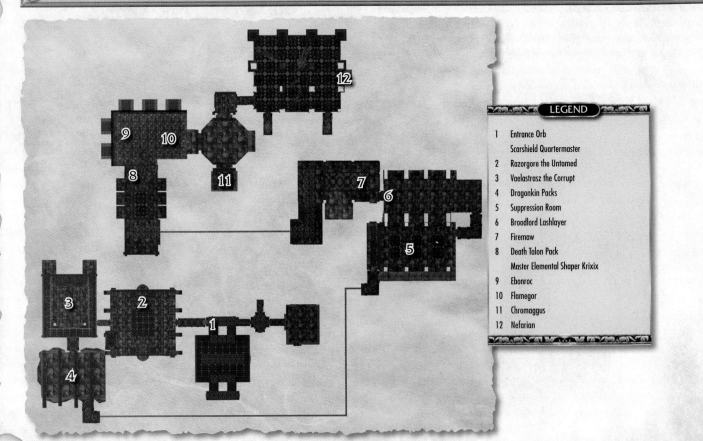

LEGEND

1   Entrance Orb
    Scarshield Quartermaster
2   Razorgore the Untamed
3   Vaelastrasz the Corrupt
4   Dragonkin Packs
5   Suppression Room
6   Broodlord Lashlayer
7   Firemaw
8   Death Talon Pack
    Master Elemental Shaper Krixix
9   Ebonroc
10   Flamegor
11   Chromaggus
12   Nefarian

ONYXIA SCALE CLOAKS

Before venturing into the depths of Blackwing Lair, be sure to acquire an Onyxia Scale Cloak for yourself. To make one, you'll need the assistance of a Tailor and a Leatherworker.

The Tailor needs to create a Cindercloth Cloak by using 5 Bolts of Runecloth, 1 Essence of Fire, and 1 Rune Thread. Of course, they'll need the pattern and it can only be found on Thaurissan Firewalkers in the Burning Steppes.

Once the Cindercloth Cloak's made, the Leatherworker needs to begin plying their trade. A level 300 Leatherworker is fine; Dragonscale Leatherworking is not necessary for this pattern. You'll need the Cindercloth Cloak, 1 Scale of Onyxia, and 1 Rune Thread.

That's it. They're usually for sale on most servers in the auction house, but those prices can be exorbitant. It's really up to you whether you use your gold or guildies. You may be able to get a deal if you provide all the materials.

Regardless, once you have one, you'll be much better off. All three "drake" bosses and Nefarian can ruin a MT that doesn't have one of these equipped. It's best if everyone in the raid has one, but that's just an ideal situation and rarely happens. Just make sure that your MT and their OTs are wearing them and possibly insist that your main healer has donned one as well.

SCARSHIELD SPELLBINDERS

Priests can actually provide a wonderful service to those who may need a bit of extra Fire Resistance for this dungeon. Have a Priest accompany an early group into Blackrock Spire and find some Scarshield Spellbinders.

Mind Control the Spellbinders and use their Fire Resistance buff to receive +82 FR for 60 minutes. This stacks with other FR buffs and is the perfect way to supplement the raid group with addition FR.

ATTUNEMENT

Every player who wishes to enter Blackwing Lair must first complete the attunement quest. This quest is very straightforward and shouldn't take long.

First, you must kill the Scarshield Quartermaster in Blackrock Spire. He's located right next to the orb used to zone into Blackwing. After you kill him, he drops **Blackhand's Command**, which starts a quest.

BLACKROCK'S COMMAND

Quest Level	60
Location	Blackrock Mountain, Upper Blackrock Spire
Starts at	Blackhand's Command, a note dropped by the Scarshield Quartermaster in Blackrock Mountain
Ends at	Orb behind General Drakkisath in Upper Blackrock Spire
Goal	Brand your hand with the Mark of Drakkisath in order to gain access to Blackwing Lair

The note you find on the Quartermaster explains that you must have the Mark of Drakkisath branded on your hand before you can enter Blackwing Lair. Take a group into Upper Blackrock Spire and kill General Drakkisath. The orb is behind Drakkisath; brand your hand to gain access to Blackwing Lair. Click it to complete the quest and gain attunement to Blackwing Lair.

RAZORGORE THE UNTAMED

The first fight in Blackwing Lair is very unique and, once everyone is familiar with their job, not all that difficult to defeat.

Razorgore has been enslaved by the Blackrock Clan to lay eggs for them. He is controlled by the Orb of Command, located on the platform at the south west part of the room. The goal in this fight is to use the Orb, take control of Razorgore, destroy all his eggs, and then kill him.

You can not kill Razorgore before all the eggs are destroyed. If you attempt to kill him before all the eggs are gone, you will be in for a surprise that results in an instant death for everyone in your raidgroup.

ABILITIES

MIND CONTROLLING RAZORGORE

Break Egg: Used to destroy eggs in the room. Has a 3 second casting time and a 7 second cool down.

Cleave: AoE melee damage attack. Has a 6 second cool down. It deals 315 damage on top of the normal melee damage and can hit up to ten targets in front of Razorgore.

Fireball Volley: AoE fireball spell. Does a couple thousand damage to everything nearby. Has about a 25 second cool down.

Calm Dragonkin: Used to put Dragonkin to sleep, similar to Druids' Hibernate; it has about a 25 second cool down.

FIGHTING RAZORGORE

Cleave: AoE melee damage attack.

Conflagrate: Sets the target on fire and disorientates them, doing about 3000 damage over 10 seconds. Additionally, when Conflagrated, you inflict 300 DPS to nearby allies.

War Stomp: AoE 5 second stun attack that does minimal damage.

PREPARATION

EQUIPMENT

The two Warriors who are going to tank Razorgore - once all the eggs are destroyed - need to wear Fire Resistance gear. Everyone else can wear their normal equipment.

GROUP SETUP

The groups are going to be split up into each of the four corners, two groups per corner. Set the groups up with this in mind and follow the legend and map in the *Positioning* section.

Make sure all classes are evenly distributed in each corner. You want to spread the Druids around as much as possible for Hibernate, the Hunters for Freezing Traps, the Warriors for off-tanking, and so on. Just make sure the classes are as well-distributed as possible in each corner.

Once all the eggs have been destroyed, make sure the Warriors tanking Razorgore have a Fire Resistance aura or totem.

HEALING

There's nothing special about healing in this fight.

Before all the eggs are destroyed, heal your corner. After all the eggs are destroyed, heal the two Warriors tanking Razorgore.

POSITIONING

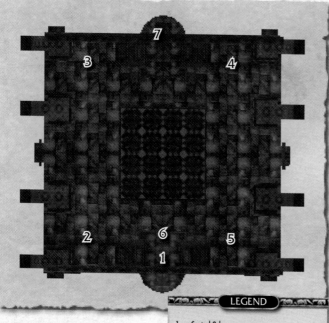

LEGEND

1	Control Orb
2	Groups 1 and 2
3	Groups 3 and 4
4	Groups 5 and 6
5	Groups 7 and 8
6	Grethok the Controller
7	Razorgore

THE FIGHT

CONTROLLING THE ORB

Warriors are the class that's usually selected to control the Orb. The person using the Orb when Razorgore breaks the control is going to get a ton of aggro and Warriors can take a few hits. However, there's a much more detailed strategy for this encounter.

When you click the Orb, a channeled Mind Control type spell takes over Razorgore and your viewpoint switches to that of the dragon. You're able to move him around and utilize his abilities as if they were your own. If you receive damage while controlling the Orb, your hold over Razorgore may break; be ready to gain control at all times. When the channeling wears off, the control will break and you must click the Orb once again to regain control.

The controller of the Orb has a very specific duty: break eggs. Use Razorgore's Break Egg ability efficiently. There's a 3 second cast and a 7 second cooldown on it which gives you ample time to both plan out your route and move to the next target while eating up that cooldown.

Right before the Warrior's control over Razorgore breaks, they should use his Fireball Volley to gain the aggro of nearly every creature in the room. While this is occurring, have another Warrior ready to assume their place at the Orb. This begins a kiting rotation where the Warriors are luring the trained mobs around the room while the rest of the raid and the MC'd Razorgore attack them. The "bait" Warrior must use Piercing Howl and any other movement slowing abilities (Thunder Clap and, in a pinch, Hamstring) to keep the crowd off them.

When control is getting ready to break again, have the initial Warrior make their way toward the Orb to resume control. Just before Razorgore regains control, have the controlling Warrior cast Fireball Volley onto the whole room and make the kiting run as the first Warrior gains control over the Orb. Repeat this process until every egg is destroyed.

Do not use Fireball Volley until either a) the MC is about to break and the Warrior can assume the aggro, or b) there are only two or three eggs left.

So, to recap the Orb controller's job:

- Use Break Egg as quickly and efficiently as possible
- Use Calm Dragonkin to control rampaging dragonkin
- Only use Fireball Volley when the MC is breaking or only a few eggs remain.
- Don't let Razorgore die

STRATEGY

Make sure everyone knows: a) what corner they're supposed to be in, b) who the Orb controllers are, and c) who their assigned main assist is.

Each corner has a different MA. Make sure the corner knows that they're assisting that person. Your goal is to kill things as quickly as possible; assisting and focusing fire on mobs as they spawn is the best method for achieving this goal.

To begin the fight, pull Grethok the Controller and his allies off the platform and away from that area. Grethok has a few awfully nasty spells. Arcane Missiles and Slow are dangerous, but nothing compared to his Mind Control and Greater Polymorph. If either of those spells hits the designated Orb controller while they're attempting to gain control of Razorgore, things could go south quickly. Have a Priest ready to remove the effects from either of his two deadly spells.

The Orcs and Dragonspawn begin spawning shortly after all the groups get to their corners. There's no discernable pattern behind what spawns in each location or how often. Each corner won't get the same amount of mobs at the same rate. Some corners will have it easy while others will be swamped. If a corner's getting overwhelmed by Dragonkin, send a couple members from your corner over to help.

Have the Orb controller use Razorgore to steadily use Break Egg to destroy all the eggs in the room. Once the channeled control gets close to its end, they should use Razorgore's Fireball Volley to draw the attention of every mob in the room and begin the kiting chain. Using the platforms at both ends of the room, it's possible for a Warrior to kite mobs up the stairs and then jump off the ledge forcing the mobs to take the long route back down the stairs. When expertly done, a Warrior can kite a horde of mobs without taking any damage. Have the Warrior use Piercing Howl, the Mages use a Rank 1 Blizzard, and Shaman use Earthbind Totems to slow the enemies.

PRACTICE MAKES PERFECT

The common kiting method is considered the easiest and most accepted strategy for Razorgore. However, some guilds use this dragon as a chance to practice strategies that will serve them well when fighting the harder drakes in the lair.

Focus Fire

Concentrating on and destroying single targets using the MA is crucial to victory in almost any dungeon, but it's vital that those in the raid understand what's going on and what the end result is. Target the casters and the Dragonkin and bring them down quickly.

Control the Boss

This includes positioning, location, turning, and a variety of other concepts, but the overall theme is to keep the raid out of the line of fire while the MT and OTs control Razorgore's facing. This really comes into play once all the eggs are destroyed and Razorgore becomes uncontrollable. His Conflagrate ability is exactly what you'll see in later battles and this is a good warm up.

While the Warriors are using their chained kiting technique and switching between controlling Razorgore and the kiting, keep your corner's focus on the Blackwing Mages and kill them all. The Legionnaires and other Dragonkin should continually be CC'd and kited around the room.

AoE Fear spells and abilities like Psychic Scream and Intimidating Shout can be used in emergencies. Several Priests expertly utilizing a Psychic Scream rotation can keep most of the chamber feared for a considerable amount of time. This is often used when the raid leader chooses to break the raid into two groups instead of four.

As the eggs are broken and the end to this phase nears, have the MT gain control over Razorgore. Once the last egg is broken, all the remaining Orcs and Dragonkin will flee. You won't need to worry about killing/kiting them anymore. Razorgore, on the other hand, becomes uncontrollable and attacks the raid. This is why the MT should be the player to break the final egg. They'll inherit all the aggro piled up by Razorgore during his controlled phase.

Now the game changes. Razorgore's full anger is turned on the raid. Have the MT gain aggro (this shouldn't be difficult if they were the last to control the Orb) and face Razorgore away from the raid. The OT should get onto the opposite side of the dragon and solidify the number 2 spot on the threat list in preparation of Conflagrate.

It doesn't matter where you tank Razorgore as long as two Warriors aren't on top of one another and remain in the top two spots of the threat ladder. The rest of the melee DPS should stay behind the dragon with the OT. Conflagrate is a frontal cone and this is why both tanks should be far enough away from one another to avoid being caught simultaneously within the area of effect of this deadly ability. War Stomp is the worst ability that could hit the melee personnel at his back and it's not really a big deal.

Once the MT is hit by Conflagrate they should run away from all allies and burn in an isolated area; the OT should grab aggro immediately. Razorgore will switch targets to the OT (presuming they're in the second spot on the threat ladder) and the melee DPS should all run to Razorgore's back.

This is going to keep happening and aggro should continually switch back and forth between the tanks. The melee DPS should remain alert and keep an eye for positional changes. Heal the MT while they incur the damage from Conflagrate (3000 over 10 sec.).

The ranged DPS should let loose with the idea that both the Warriors will be under the effects of both Conflagrate and War Stomp continually. Don't max out your DPS if you're in this role as it will only pull Razorgore out of position.

Keep him tanked, keep the tanks alive, and take him down. Thankfully, once all the eggs are destroyed, Razorgore isn't all that difficult.

DROPS

Razorgore will drop two random class set bracers and one additional random item that isn't another class set bracer.

ITEM	DESC	STATS
ARCANE INFUSED GEM	Trinket	
Use: Infuses you with Arcane energy, causing your next Arcane Shot fired within 10 seconds to detonate at the target. The Arcane Detonation will deal 185 to 215 damage to enemies near the target		
Class: Hunter		
BINDINGS OF TRANSCENDENCE	Cloth Wrist	51 Armor, +13 INT, +16 SPI, +9 STA
Equip: Increases healing done by spells and effects by up to 33		
Class: Priest		
BLOODFANG BRACERS	Leather Wrist	98 Armor, +23 AGI, +13 STA
Equip: Improves your chance to hit by 1%		
Class: Rogue		
BRACERS OF TEN STORMS	Mail Wrist	211 Armor, +16 INT, +9 SPI, +13 STA
Equip: Restores 6 mana per 5 sec		
Class: Shaman		
BRACELETS OF WRATH	Plate Wrist	375 Armor, +27 STA, +13 STR
Class: Warrior		
DRAGONSTALKER'S BRACERS	Mail Wrist	211 Armor, +23 AGI, +6 INT, +6 SPI, +13 STA
Class: Hunter		
GLOVES OF RAPID EVOLUTION	Cloth Hands	70 Armor, +12 INT, +32 SPI, +12 STA
JUDGEMENT BINDINGS	Plate Wrist	375 Armor, +9 INT, +8 SPI, +21 STA, +9 STR
Equip: Increases damage and healing done by magical spells and effects by up to 7		
Class: Paladin		
MANTLE OF THE BLACKWING CABAL	Cloth Shoulder	84 Armor, +16 INT, +12 STA
Equip: Increases damage and healing done by magical spells and effects by up to 34		
NEMESIS BRACERS	Cloth Wrist	51 Armor, +11 INT, +6 SPI, +21 STA
Equip: Increases damage and healing done by magical spells and effects by up to 15		
Class: Warlock		
NETHERWIND BRACERS	Cloth Wrist	51 Armor, +15 INT, +8 SPI, +9 STA
Equip: Increases damage and healing done by magical spells and effects by up to 19		
Equip: Restores 4 mana per 5 sec		
Class: Mage		
SPINESHATTER	Main Hand Mace	99-184 Damage, Speed: 2.60, 54.4 damage per second, +16 STA, +9 STR
Equip: Increases Defense +5		
STORMRAGE BRACERS	Leather Wrist	98 Armor, +15 INT, +12 SPI, +11 STA
Equip: Increases healing done by spells and effects by up to 33		
Class: Druid		
THE BLACK BOOK	Trinket	
Use: Empowers your pet, increasing pet damage by 100% and increasing pet armor by 100% for 30 seconds. This spell will only affect an Imp, Succubus, Voidwalker, or Felhunter		
Class: Warlock		
THE UNTAMED BLADE	Two-Hand Sword	192-289 Damage, Speed: 3.40, 70.7 damage per second, +22 AGI, +16 STA
Chance on Hit: Increases Strength by 300 for 8 seconds		

VAELASTRASZ THE CORRUPT

You may recognize Vaelastrasz from one of his other forms: Vaelan (for whom you may have completed the *Seal of Ascension* quest) or Vaelastrasz the Red (during the fight with Rend Blackhand in UBRS). However, this is Vaelastrasz the Corrupt and an entirely new entity.

Vaelastrasz is a powerful red dragon that vowed to hunt Nefarian until he's defeated or death takes him. However, when facing Nefarian in Blackwing Lair, Vaelastrasz was severely wounded and corrupted by the dark blood that flows through his nemesis' veins. In his weakened state, Nefarian places a spell on Vaelastrasz as your raiding party enters the chamber. This forces Vaelastrasz to fight, but Vaelastrasz sees that you may be just what is needed to defeat Nefarian and he casts Essence of the Red on your raid group. Will it give you the necessary power to defeat this deadly adversary and advance?

Vaelastrasz the Corrupt

Vael is arguably the hardest fight in Blackwing Lair. He is capable of killing your entire raid almost instantly. A guild that is new to fighting Vael will probably spend thousands of gold on repairs mastering the encounter. Guilds have broken up over Vael; it's an incredibly challenging, and sometimes awfully frustrating, fight, but when you get it down, it's by far one of the most intense and fulfilling encounters in the game.

NEFARIUS'S CORRUPTION

Anyone working on the *Scepter of the Shifting Sands* quest series can speak with Vaelastrasz and begin the part that involves Blackwing Lair.

Everyone can start the quest by talking to Vael before he is aggressive to the group. Be careful not to click the chat bubble option instead of the quest option! If you can't see the quest he has to offer, you are not far enough on the *Scepter of the Shifting Sands* quest series.

The goal of this quest is to kill Nefarian within 5 hours. If you accomplish this, Nefarian will drop a Red Scepter Shard, completing the quest. Currently he only drops one Shard; only one person can loot it.

ABILITIES

Burning Adrenaline: This is a 20-second debuff that reduces your maximum health by 5% per second for 20 seconds. Essentially, it's a guaranteed death. While under its effects, your damage and attack speed are increased by 100% and all your spells become instant. However, when you die, there's an additional threat; you explode and deal 4376-5624 damage to nearby allies. Vael uses this spell on two entirely separate timers. One timer targets a random mana user and the other timer is on the player who's highest on the threat list (the MT).

Cleave: This is a frontal cone effect that adds 315 points of damage on top of his normal melee attack and can hit up to 10 players.

Essence of the Red: Restores 500 mana, 50 energy, or 20 rage per second for 3 minutes.

Fire Nova: Inflicts 500-700 damage to everyone in the lair every few seconds. This can be reduced with resistance gear, potions, buffs, etc.

Flame Breath: 3500-4500 Fire damage and adds a stacking debuff up to five times dealing an additional 938-1062 damage every 3 seconds.

Tail Sweep: 600-1000 damage and knockback.

PREPARATION

EQUIPMENT

Fire Resistance is the primary concern while solid STA comes in second. Fire Nova chews through anyone that doesn't have over 200 FR. The tanks won't be able to survive the AoE fire or the stacking breath unless they have over 300 buffed FR.

You might have a chance wearing green FR gear, but this is a fight where you really want to invest in the epic, crafted FR gear from the Thorium Brotherhood because it has so much STA on it. Even with good FR, Vael still does solid damage to everyone in the lair, and even more damage to the current tank.

Warriors should use a weapon with a fast attack speed during this fight for improved threat generation. Alcor's Sunrazor or Julie's Dagger are perfect choices. Paladin's often wear only three pieces of the Lawbringer Armor to receive the benefit to their Judgement of Light.

GROUP SETUP

When you're first learning Vael, you will want to bring at least six Warriors (up to eight if you can). The Warriors will be assigned a tanking order; it's best if you organize the tanks based on their average threat generation rate. Use other encounters as a basis for this arrangement. Also, consider keeping the MT back and having them jump in later in the rotation since it'll be easier for them to gain aggro once one of the tanks dies. All Warriors need to know where they are on the tanking order and who is ahead of them.

Arrange groups into damage and support groups. Damage groups should contain Warriors with Battle Shout, Hunters using Trueshot Aura, Shaman for FR, DPS and Stoneskin totems, Paladins for FR auras (one for Judgement of Light and one for Judgement of Wisdom in the melee groups), and Rogues. Warlocks are often placed in these groups for their Imp's Blood Pact as well.

The support groups are the healers and casters. Priests are often included in groups with lower FR to employ their Prayer of Healing if/when necessary.

One good Druid can heal a group of four ranged DPS classes alone. Ranged DPS players take significant damage throughout the fight, but it's over time and can be healed by a single Druid (or even Paladin or Shaman, but you don't want to waste their auras/totems on ranged DPS classes).

HEALING

The Vael battle requires intensive healing. Not only does he inflict insane amounts of damage to the MT, his Fire Nova does significant damage to everyone else.

The MT needs at least five people constantly casting heals on them at all times. The groups should be set up so that most groups have two healers. Assign the Priests in Groups 1-5 to heal the MT and assign any spare healers in Groups 6-8 to be backup MT healers in case a healer in Groups 1-5 dies.

Anyone who's not assigned to the MT should focus all their attention on their own group. Keep the group alive. If you have an MT healer in your group, they are the highest priority. Entire groups should not be dying to Fire Nova. Every group needs a healer dedicated to healing it in addition to the five healers on the MT.

Remember, you have almost unlimited mana during this fight. While Essence of the Red is up, it's difficult to run out of mana. Use it! There should rarely be a time when you're not casting a heal.

POSITIONING

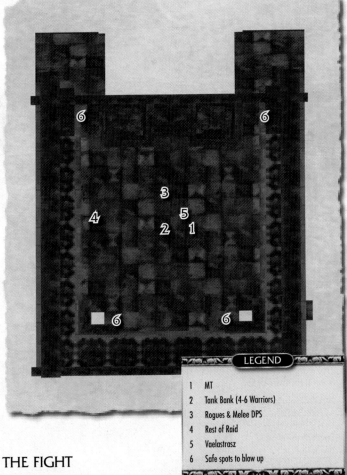

When the current MT gets hit with BA, they're going to die and there's nothing you can do about it. The first thing the MT should do is hit both Shield Wall and Last Stand if they're available. Next, they need to move away from the tank bank and melee DPS so as not to inadvertently blow them up. As the MT shifts position, the Warrior that's currently in the second slot on the threat list needs to assume their previous position and begin Sundering to gain aggro.

If the tank bank has a Paladin using Blessing of Salvation or a Shaman using a Tranquil Air Totem to reduce the threat generation of this group, the new MT must click that off as soon as BA hits the doomed ex-MT. If the state of the second position on the threat ladder is in flux, wait for Vael to face the tank bank and for your raid leader to call out the new target. That Warrior should turn Vael away from everyone else and assume the previous MT's position. As soon as one Warrior has solidified aggro, use Heroic Strike along with Sunder Armor to really hold Vael's attention. As mentioned earlier, almost unlimited rage along with a fast weapon is going to assist in the production of hate.

Horde groups may find it necessary to keep a Priest in each party supplying tanks for the bank - two Warriors max per group. Have the Priest continually use Prayer of Healing to keep the Warriors' health topped off.

Regardless, *keep the tank bank and the melee DPS groups at least 10 yards away from the MT's position.* Getting caught in a Cleave or Flame Breath en masse can be trouble.

A Warrior preemptively pulling aggro is a problem. It's hard to guarantee yourself number 2 on the threat list without going too far. This becomes especially difficult when Vael has under 20% life: Execute range. At 19% have your current MT switch to Battle Stance and announce that they are starting to Execute (the current MT needs to Execute or they will lose aggro). The next MT in line should count 2 seconds and announce that they are Executing. The MT after that should count to 2 and start Executing. Executes must be done in tanking order so that tank transitions go smoothly. You can't avoid Executing all together because it's a huge amount of damage. The Warriors have to know when they are next in line to tank, carefully guarantee themselves number 2 on the threat list without pulling aggro, and communicate with each other to ensure smooth tank transitions.

The healers need to adapt as BA hits random mana users. If BA hits an MT healer, they need to be replaced. If you do not have backup MT healers, get someone who is healing their group to switch to the MT. The group might die, but having the MT die from direct damage is worse. On the other hand, if you find yourself healing a group that is mostly dead to BA, switch to helping the MT. Communication is a key factor in this fight. The raid needs to know if you have BA and are out of the fight so that other people can change who they are healing. If both healers in a group get BA, it should be made known to everyone in the raid that their group needs healing attention. Always keep five healers on the MT and everyone else watching over groups.

DPS classes should go nuts! It's hard to pull aggro from a Warrior with unlimited rage. Personally, I've never seen a ranged DPS class pull aggro. It's the Rogues you have to be worried about. A Rogue chain Backstabbing will probably be able to pull aggro or put themselves at number 2 on the aggro list, both very bad things that will probably wipe the raid. Rogues need to Feint as often as possible, Vanish right after the first MT dies, and be a little careful with their unlimited energy.

When a random mana user gets BA, they just need to run to a safe spot, somewhere that won't hurt anyone when they blow up, and continue healing or doing damage. They are out of the fight when they get BA. As long as people aren't blowing each other up, the random BA isn't much to worry about.

Most groups attempting Vael should spend their time perfecting the tank switches, not worrying so much about doing damage.

LEGEND

1 MT
2 Tank Bank (4-6 Warriors)
3 Rogues & Melee DPS
4 Rest of Raid
5 Vaelastrasz
6 Safe spots to blow up

THE FIGHT
STRATEGY

This fight is all about the ability to quickly alternate between tanks. The Warriors make or break this fight. The healers certainly don't have it easy, but once they know what they're supposed to be doing, the healing isn't so bad.

When you engage Vael, he casts Essence of the Red on everyone in the lair. This is a 3-minute buff that gives you virtually unlimited energy, rage, or mana. Vael is nigh impossible to kill without Essence of the Red; you must kill him within 3 minutes.

The first MT should be the first person to get aggro. Once they have a Sunder Armor up, everyone needs to start attacking. Once Vael has three or four Sunders on him, the second MT should start Sundering, guaranteeing that they are second on the threat list. *It's tremendously important that the Warriors know exactly where they are on the threat list.*

Vael casts his first Burning Adrenaline (BA) 15 seconds after he has been engaged. BA is on two separate timers. The 15-second timer hits a random caster and the 45-second timer hits the MT (assuming they're highest on the threat list). When the MT is hit with BA, a random caster is as well. This continues in the same format thereafter. The player at the top of the threat list and a random caster are hit with each Burning Adrenaline.

Mana users who get BA should simply run away from everyone else (so that they don't blow anyone up when they die) and continue doing whatever they were doing for the next 10-15 seconds. Make good use of BA for the short time you're alive since most of your spells are instant casts while BA is up and it's important to do as much damage (or give as much healing) as possible.

Once you get the tank switches down, start opening up with DPS to see how low you can get him before you run out of tanks. If you're having problems with tank switches, talk to the two tanks involved and see what exactly the problem is. Are they not building enough threat? Are they blowing each other up? Is the next tank in line not getting any healing? Try to isolate the problem before making another run. The fight leaves very little room for error, but, with practice, it becomes something you can do on the first or second try.

DROPS

Vaelastrasz will drop two random class set belts and one additional random item that isn't another class set belt.

ITEM	DESC	STATS
BELT OF TEN STORMS	Mail Waist	271 Armor, +18 INT, +11 SPI, +13 STA, +10 Shadow Resistance
Equip: Improves your chance to get a critical strike with spells by 1%		
Equip: Increases healing done by spells and effects by up to 26		
Class: Shaman		
BELT OF TRANSCENDENCE	Cloth Waist	65 Armor, +26 INT, +9 SPI, +14 STA, +10 Shadow Resistance
Equip: Increases healing done by spells and effects by up to 26		
Class: Priest		
BLOODFANG BELT	Leather Waist	126 Armor, +20 AGI, +15 STA, +13 STR, +10 Shadow Resistance
Equip: Improves your chance to get a critical strike by 1%		
Class: Rogue		
DRAGONFANG BLADE	One-Hand Dagger	69-130 Damage, Speed: 1.80, 55.3 damage per second, +16 AGI, +13 STA
DRAGONSTALKER'S BELT	Mail Waist	271 Armor, +20 AGI, +13 INT, +11 SPI, +15 STA, +10 Shadow Resistance
Equip: Improves your chance to get a critical strike by 1%		
Class: Hunter		
HELM OF ENDLESS RAGE	Plate Head	+26 STR, +26 AGI, +29 STA
JUDGEMENT BELT	Plate Waist	482 Armor, +20 INT, +6 SPI, +14 STA, +8 STR, +10 Shadow Resistance
Equip: Increases damage and healing done by magical spells and effects by up to 23		
Class: Paladin		
MIND QUICKENING GEM	Trinket	
Use: Quickens the mind, increasing the Mage's casting speed by 25% for 20 seconds		
Class: Mage		

ITEM	DESC	STATS
NEMESIS BELT	Cloth Waist	65 Armor, +8 INT, +6 SPI, +18 STA, +10 Shadow Resistance
Equip: Improves your chance to get a critical strike with spells by 1%		
Equip: Increases damage and healing done by magical spells and effects by up to 25		
Class: Warlock		
NETHERWIND BELT	Cloth Waist	65 Armor, +20 INT, +13 SPI, +13 STA, +10 Shadow Resistance
Equip: Increases damage and healing done by magical spells and effects by up to 23		
Class: Mage		
PENDANT OF THE FALLEN DRAGON	Neck	+12 INT, +9 STA
Equip: Restores 9 mana per 5 sec		
RED DRAGONSCALE PROTECTOR	Shield	2787 Armor, 51 Block, +17 INT, +6 SPI, +6 STA
Equip: Increases healing done by spells and effects by up to 37		
RUNE OF METAMORPHOSIS	Trinket	
Use: Decreases the mana cost of all Druid shapeshifting forms by 100% for 20 seconds		
Class: Druid		
STORMRAGE BELT	Leather Waist	126 Armor, +23 INT, +10 SPI, +12 STA, +10 Shadow Resistance
Equip: Increases healing done by spells and effects by up to 26		
Equip: Restores 4 mana per 5 sec		
Class: Druid		
WAISTBAND OF WRATH	Plate Waist	482 Armor, +20 STA, +20 STR, +10 Shadow Resistance
Equip: Increases your chance to block attacks with a shield by 3%		
Equip: Increases Defense +7		
Class: Warrior		

🐲 DRAGONKIN PACKS

There are two groups of Dragonkin in the room immediately after Vaelastrasz. Each group must be pulled separately and killed.

The Dragon Packs are not hard to defeat. Have your Warriors pick which Dragonkin they want to tank, have the Druids pick which Wyrmkin they want to sleep, and do the pull. Follow the usual MA, kill them one at a time, and leave the Wyrmkin for last.

DEATH TALON CAPTAIN — 60-62 ELITE

Aura of Flame: Deals 209 Fire damage to nearby targets.

Cleave: Frontal Cone melee damage attack.

Flame Shock: Damage over time fire spell.

Mark of Detonation: Deals 657-843 to the target and all allies when hit in melee.

DEATH TALON FLAMESCALE — 60-62 ELITE

Berserker Charge: Like Warrior's Charge with knockback and added damage.

Flame Shock: Damage over time fire spell.

DEATH TALON SEETHER — 60-62 ELITE

Charge: Charges random targets and knocks them high into the air.

Flame Buffet: 925-1075 damage and increases Fire damage taken by 1000 for 20 sec.

Frenzy: Increased attack speed.

DEATH TALON WYRMKIN   60-62 ELITE

Wyrmkin can be slept by Druids. The Wyrmkin in each pack should be kept Hibernating until everything else is dead. When you're ready to kill the Wyrmkin, have the Druids keep casting Hibernate on them to minimize the amount of AoE attacks they can do.

Blast Wave: Another AoE fire attack that hits everyone nearby for a few hundred points of damage.

Fireball Volley: AoE fire attack that hits everyone nearby for a few hundred points of damage.

DROPS

Each of the Dragonkin from these packs has a small chance to drop loot.

ITEM	DESC	STATS
CLOAK OF DRACONIC MIGHT	Cloak	54 Armor, +16 AGI, +16 STR, +4 STA
DRACONIC MAUL	Two-Hand Mace	187-282 Damage, Speed: 3.50, 67.0 damage per second, +27 STR, +19 STA
Equip: Improves your chance to get a critical strike by 2%		
BOOTS OF PURE THOUGHT	Cloth Boots	74 Armor, +12 INT, +12 SPI, +8 STA
Equip: Increases healing done by spells and effects by up to 62		

SUPPRESSION ROOM

After killing the packs of Dragonkin, you arrive in a room full of Corrupted Whelps, Death Talon Hatchers, and Blackwing Taskmasters. This room looks very intimidating at first, but you will find that it is rather easy to get through.

The key to getting through this room is to keep moving. The Whelps constantly re-spawn as you progress; there is nothing you can do to stop their re-spawn. The Dragonkin and Orcs re-spawn as well, but on a 10-15 minute timer.

Additionally, there are traps sticking out of the ground called Suppression Devices. When a Suppression Device is activated, it casts a pulsing debuff called Suppression that decreases movement speed, attack speed, and casting speed by 80%. Rogues can disable the devices with Disarm Traps. The devices re-enable themselves randomly, sometimes after just a couple seconds, sometimes after a few minutes.

A group of 3-4 Rogues won't be attacking anything in the Suppression Room. Their sole job is to keep the devices disarmed.

Have one Warrior equip their Fire Resist gear and begin to pull. The MT should completely ignore the Whelps; they need to go after the Dragonkin and Orcs. The Whelps will always be in the way and the classes with AoE spells should be taking care of them.

Pull the Dragonkin and Orcs one at a time and keep moving! Be very careful not to pull more than one Dragonkin or one pack of Orcs. A wipe in the Suppression Room usually means you have to run back and start over; it's very hard to resurrect in there.

Your raid should hug the right wall all the way to Broodlord. Just keep the Whelps under control, keep the Dragonkin and Orcs coming, and keep moving along the right wall until you reach Broodlord Lashlayer.

BROODLORD LASHLAYER

Now that you've cleared the Suppression Room, it's time to fight the Broodlord. He's one of the easiest bosses in BWL and should only take a few tries to defeat. Unfortunately, if you wipe while fighting him, you can't resurrect the raid; you have to run back and do the Suppression Room over again.

It's important that everyone knows what they need to do before you actually reach Lashlayer. You don't want to sit in the Suppression Room for a long time going over strategy; all the mobs continue to re-spawn on a relatively short timer. The last thing you want is a Death Talon Overseer wandering into your boss fight.

WARNING

Broodlord Lashlayer has a very large aggro radius! Do not get too close to him and preemptively start the fight.

ABILITIES

Blast Wave: AoE fire damage and knock back that does a few thousand fire damage to everyone in melee range.

Cleave: AoE melee damage attack.

Knock Away: Knocks the target back and reduces the Broodlord's threat on that target by 50%.

Mortal Strike: Instant melee attack that hits for up to 6000 on Warriors, much higher on non-plate classes.

PREPARATION

EQUIPMENT

Warriors need to focus on hit points and melee damage mitigation. The Broodlord's Mortal Strike can hit for over 6000 damage on a well-equipped Warrior. Sometimes the tank is just going to get killed instantly and there's nothing you can do about it, but the more hit points and the more melee damage mitigation, the better. Although he does have a fire-based attack, the Blast Wave, Fire Resist gear is a low priority for Warriors.

Rogues should equip Fire Resist gear. If they choose to melee (and they should so that the Broodlord dies as quickly as possible) they will be hit by Blast Wave.

Everyone else should wear their normal equipment. They shouldn't get hit by anything.

GROUP SETUP

As mentioned above, it's very important to get your Warriors as much damage mitigation and hit points as possible. Put them in groups with Warlocks and Paladins for Blood Pact and the AC auras respectively. Paladins/Shaman should be grouped with the melee combatants to provide FR aurus/totems when possible.

HEALING

Each Warrior needs a healer assigned to them. That healer does nothing but heal their designated Warrior. These healers need to keep their Warrior topped off so that they aren't killed instantly when they get hit by Mortal Strike.

A group of three to four healers needs to be healing whoever is the Broodlord's current target. This group of healers should be constantly seeing who the Broodlord's target is and casting fast heals on them.

Finally, one Priest needs to be casting Power Word: Shield after every Mortal Strike on the afflicted Warrior. It really helps with those few seconds after a Mortal Strike. Nobody but this Priest should be casting PW:S because you don't want Weakened Soul on a Warrior about to get hit by Mortal Strike.

Set up a healing rotation with the raid's lead healers. This allows them to regenerate mana when needed and allow others to step up to replace them when the need arises.

POSITIONING

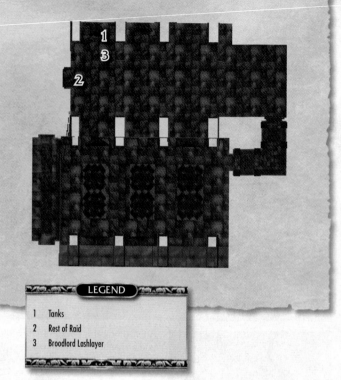

	LEGEND
1	Tanks
2	Rest of Raid
3	Broodlord Lashlayer

THE FIGHT

STRATEGY

The Broodlord is all about aggro management. Everyone but the Warriors needs Blessing of Salvation or a Tranquil Air Totem.

All the Warriors need to fight for aggro on the Broodlord. Knock Back reduces the threat of the current target. The fight can't be tanked by a single person; Lashlayer changes targets after almost every Knock Back, hopefully just between the Warriors. You want to keep all the Warriors as high on the threat list as possible, but eventually they will be hit by Knock Back often enough that the Rogues, Mages, and Warlocks will probably get aggro. Warlocks should place any Soulstones not assigned to the MH or a Druid for combat rez on the Warriors. They're both incredibly important for this battle and the only players likely to die if this encounter's handled correctly.

The fight is pretty simple. Warriors attack the Broodlord and keep themselves high on the threat list while keeping their backs against a wall so they aren't knocked back too far. (Have the Warriors against different walls and spread out so as not to be hit by Cleave when the MT is). Rogues can go up and melee if they have decent Fire Resist and don't mind dying. Ranged DPS dealers should hang back, out of range of the Blast Wave, and burn him down. Healers should focus the vast majority of their healing on the Warriors.

Lashlayer's Mortal Strike occasionally kills a Warrior instantly. It can hit for over 6000 damage on well-geared Warriors. All the Warriors should always be at near full life to reduce the chance of this happening, and there should be a Priest assigned to giving PW:S immediately after someone gets hit with Mortal Strke, but sometimes there's nothing you can do to prevent an instantaneous Warrior death. If a Warrior dies, I suggest getting them battle resurrected and back into the fight, building threat again. You need to keep as many Warriors alive as possible so that the Broodlord is almost always targeting a Warrior.

Eventually, Knock Away reduces the Warriors' threat so much that they lose aggro. At this point, Lashlayer will probably attack a ranged DPS class, someone who is high on the threat list and doesn't have any aggro-reducing abilities. The person who gets aggro needs to immediately run up to where the Warriors are and either lose aggro or die—usually die. There's nothing you can do about it.

The key to ranged DPS "pulling" aggro is that they need to get to the Warriors' location immediately. If they just stand there, the Broodlord will cast a Blast Wave, knocking back all the ranged DPS dealers and possibly the healers. Watch who he's targeting and make sure that person is up by the Warriors to reduce the chance of everyone being hit by Blast Wave.

Ranged DPS classes can't really hold back their damage to prevent pulling aggro. It doesn't work like that. Knock Away is constantly hitting the Warriors, externally reducing their threat with each hit. Eventually, their threat is reduced so much that they simply can't hold aggro regardless of what they try to do. You need to kill the Broodlord before that happens, and you won't be able to kill him that quickly with ranged DPS holding back. It's a fine balance between not trying to pull aggro and killing him quickly enough. Hunters should have no problem clearing their aggro by performing Feign Death as often as possible. It's the Mages and Warlocks that usually get attacked.

Melee DPS, just the Rogues, don't need to worry about threat very much since they have Vanish, Feint, and all sorts of ways to prevent drawing aggro.

Healers won't pull aggro through healing before a ranged DPS class unless something is very wrong. If you have healers getting aggro early in the fight, it's the Warriors' fault for not building threat quickly and efficiently. If they're getting aggro late in the fight, it's the ranged DPS' fault for holding back too much and not killing him quickly enough.

Occasionally, groups of Corrupted Whelps re-spawn on top of you during the fight. When this happens, have the Mages stop attacking the Broodlord and kill them quickly. You should not see Death Talon Overseers re-spawn and attack you during this fight. A couple Overseers might re-spawn during the fight, but none of them should be very close to Lashlayer unless you were too slow in clearing the Suppression Room.

Keep the Warriors alive, keep the Warriors high on the threat list, and make sure ranged DPS knows what to do when they get aggro. Kill him as quickly as possible to move on to the next lord of BWL.

DROPS

Broodlord will drop two random class set boots and one additional random item that isn't another class set boot.

ITEM	DESC	STATS
BLACK BROOD PAULDRONS	Mail Shoulder	357 Armor, +17 AGI, +15 INT, +12 STA
Equip: Restores 9 mana per 5 sec		
BLOODFANG BOOTS	Leather Feet	154 Armor, +25 AGI, +17 STA, +6 STR, +10 Fire Resistance
Equip: Increases your chance to dodge and attack by 1%		
Class: Rogue		
BOOTS OF TRANSCENDENCE	Cloth Feet	80 Armor, +17 INT, +17 SPI, +17 STA, +10 Fire Resistance
Equip: Increases healing done by spells and effects by up to 35		
Class: Priest		
BRACERS OF ARCANE ACCURACY	Cloth Wrist	50 Armor, +12 INT, +9 STA
Equip: Improves your chance to hit with spells by 1%		
Equip: Increases damage and healing done by magical spells and effects by up to 21		
DRAGONSTALKER'S GREAVES	Mail Feet	332 Armor, +30 AGI, +6 INT, +6 SPI, +15 STA, +10 Fire Resistance
Class: Hunter		
GREAVES OF TEN STORMS	Mail Feet	332 Armor, +16 INT, +16 SPI, +17 STA, +10 Fire Resistance
Equip: Increases damage and healing done by magical spells and effects by up to 20		
Class: Shaman		
HEARTSTRIKER	Bow	80-149 Damage, Speed: 2.60, 44.0 damage per second, +9 STA, +24 Attack Power
JUDGEMENT SABATONS	Plate Feet	589 Armor, +14 INT, +8 SPI, +20 STA, +13 STR, +10 Fire Resistance
Equip: Increases damage and healing done by magical spells and effects by up to 18		
Class: Paladin		
LIFEGIVING GEM	Trinket	
Use: Heals yourself for 15% of your maximum health, and increases your maximum health by 15% for 20 sec		
Class: Warrior		
MALADATH, RUNED BLADE OF THE BLACK FLIGHT	One-Hand Sword	86-162 Damage, Speed: 2.20, 56.4 damage per second
Equip: Increases your chance to parry an attack by 1%		
Equip: Increases Swords +4		
NEMESIS BOOTS	Cloth Feet	80 Armor, +17 INT, +6 SPI, +20 STA, +10 Fire Resistance
Equip: Increases damage and healing done by magical spells and effects by up to 23		
Class: Warlock		
NETHERWIND BOOTS	Cloth Feet	80 Armor, +16 INT, +10 SPI, +13 STA, +10 Fire Resistance
Equip: Increases damage and healing done by magical spells and effects by up to 27		
Class: Mage		
SABATONS OF WRATH	Plate Feet	589 Armor, +30 STA, +13 STR, +10 Fire Resistance
Equip: Increases the block value of your shield by 14		
Equip: Increases Defense +7		
Class: Warrior		
STORMRAGE BOOTS	Leather Feet	154 Armor, +17 INT, +11 SPI, +15 STA, +10 Fire Resistance
Equip: Improves your chance to get a critical strike with spells by 1%		
Equip: Increases healing done by spells and effects by up to 26		
Class: Druid		
VENOMOUS TOTEM	Trinket	
Use: Increases the change to apply Rogue poisons to your target by 30% for 20 seconds		
Class: Rogue		

GOBLIN PACKS

The gate opens after Broodlord Lashlayer has been killed. There are a bunch of Goblins and two Blackwing Warlocks behind – what was - his location. You will fight several of these packs as you make your way to the Drakes.

PULL THE PACKS IN NUMERICAL ORDER AS FOLLOWS:

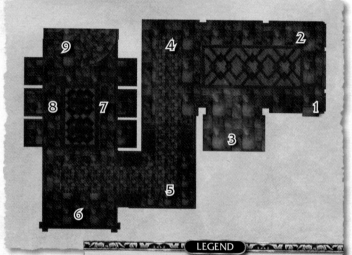

LEGEND

1. 2 Blackwing Warlocks & 8 Blackwing Technicians
2. 1 Death Talon Wyrmguard, 1 Blackwing Spellbinder, 2 Blackwing Warlocks & 8 Blackwing Technicians
3. 1 Death Talon Wyrmguard, 1 Blackwing Spellbinder, 2 Blackwing Warlocks & 8 Blackwing Technicians
4. 3 Death Talon Wyrmguards & 1 Death Talon Overseer
5. 1 Death Talon Wyrmguard, 1 Blackwing Spellbinder, 2 Blackwing Warlocks & 8 Blackwing Technicians
6. 1 Death Talon Wyrmguard, 1 Blackwing Spellbinder, 2 Blackwing Warlocks & 8 Blackwing Technicians
7. 1 Death Talon Wyrmguard, 2 Blackwing Spellbinders, 2 Blackwing Warlocks & 8 Blackwing Technicians
8. 1 Death Talon Wyrmguard, 2 Blackwing Spellbinders, 2 Blackwing Warlocks & 8 Blackwing Technicians
9. 3 Death Talon Overseers & Master Elemental Shaper Krixix

BLACKWING SPELLBINDER — 63 ELITE

These are immune to all magic.

Flamestrike: AoE fire attack.

Greater Polymorph: Polymorphs the closest person every 10 seconds or so.

BLACKWING TECHNICIAN — 60 ELITE

Bottle of Poison: Poison attack that does damage over time and can stack.

Throw Bomb: Direct damage fire attack.

BLACKWING WARLOCK — 63 ELITE

Rain of Fire: AoE fire damage attack.

Shadowbolt: Direct damage shadow attack.

Summon Felguard: Opens a portal that a Felguard will come through about 20 seconds later. The Felguards are Demons and can be banished or feared.

DEATH TALON OVERSEER — 63 ELITE

Cleave: Frontal cone melee attack.

Fire Blast: 1080-1320 Fire damage

DEATH TALON WYRMGUARD — 63 ELITE

The Wyrmguards have a weak to a random magical element.

Cleave: Frontal cone melee damage attack.

War Stomp: AoE stun attack.

STRATEGY

The first Goblin Pack pull only has eight Technicians and two Warlocks, so it is pretty easy to handle. Get the Warlocks tanked, move them away from the Technicians, AoE the Technicians into dust, and kill the Warlocks one at a time.

All the other packs are a little bit trickier because they have more mobs in them.

Assign a Warrior to each Warlock, Spellbinder, and Death Talon Wyrmguard for tanking. Have a Hunter shoot a mob in the pack and run back to the raid. The Warriors should immediately pick up their targets and drag them out of the Technicians. Once the tanked mobs are away from the Technicians, your Ranged DPS (Mages, Warlocks, and Hunters) needs to AoE them to death quickly. As soon as the Technicians are dead, kill the Warlocks one at a time. Finally, after the Warlocks have been killed, all the melee DPS classes should target the Spellbinder and all the ranged DPS classes should target the Wyrmguard.

It should be that simple—in theory. In practice, it can be a little chaotic. The Warlocks have serious damage potential. Make sure everyone stays out of their Rain of Fire and make sure the Felguards they summon get banished, feared, or off-tanked quickly. The Warlocks are by far the most dangerous mobs in the Goblin Packs.

You may have a problem separating and gathering the Technicians from the rest of the pack for AoE. Use LoS to your advantage and make the Warlocks/Spellbinders come to you. It's important that the Technicians are gathered and separated from everything else for quick death to AoE from Mages, Warlocks, and Hunters. They should always be the first targets to die.

It's also possible for an AoE player to hit the Technicians and run in a circle around them. Since they attack with explosives, theoretically the character can avoid damage while CC'ing the mob until the raid's ready to take them down.

The Spellbinders are immune to all magic, but can be stunned and interrupted. Put a Rogue on each Spellbinder to help interrupt their spell casting and keep them stunned.

The Death Talon Wyrmguards are weak to a random magic type. Figure out what they are weak to and exploit it. The Warrior tanking the Wyrmguard should keep in mind they have a Cleave attack; don't tank it near anyone else.

The type of creatures in each pack varies slightly. Read the section on Death Talon Overseers for information about Overseers that is not covered in this section.

DROPS

The mobs in the Goblin Packs have a small chance to drop items.

ITEM	DESC	STATS
BAND OF DARK DOMINION	Ring	+6 INT, +12 STA
Equip: Increases damage done by Shadow spells and effects by up to 33		
DOOM'S EDGE	Axe	One-Hand, 83-154 Damage, Speed: 2.3 seconds, 51.5 damage per second, +16 AGI, +9 STR, +7 STA
ESSENCE GATHERER	Wand	83-156 Damage, Speed: 1.4 seconds, 85.4 damage per second, +7 INT, +5 STA
Equip: Restores 5 mana per 5 seconds		
ELEMENTIUM ORE	Quest item	

FIREMAW

Firemaw is one of the harder fights in Blackwing Lair. Firemaw has an AoE fire attack, enough burst damage to occasionally instantly kill the MT, and is your introduction to what is soon to become your new least-favorite spell: Wing Buffet.

He is definitely the hardest of the three Drakes and some of the strategies learned on him will be used for every Drake. He has an abundance of hit points and takes some practice to kill.

ABILITIES

Wing Buffet: Knock back attack that hits everyone in front of Firemaw, reducing the threat of everyone affected. Some raid leaders instruct their Rogues to run in and intentionally get his with a Wing Buffet to reduce their threat so that they can let loose with the DPS.

Flame Buffet: AoE pulsing fire attack that hits everyone within LoS of Firemaw. It can stack, doing anywhere from a few hundred to a few thousand damage per tick.

Shadow Flame: AoE breath attack that deals 3938-5062 Shadow damage. If anyone affected is not wearing an Onyxia Scale Cloak, the damage is significantly higher as they incur an additional 1750-2250 DPS for approximately 12 seconds. This usually kills the target.

Thrash: Firemaw can gain two extra attacks, giving him the ability to deal significant burst melee damage.

PREPARATION

EQUIPMENT

The MT needs to get over 250 Fire Resistance and over 7000 life (buffed), preferably more like 300 FR and 7500 life. This fight requires a very well-equipped MT.

Warriors other than the MT should wear their Vaelastrasz gear. Stack FR as high as possible.

DPS classes should consider FR, but they have the ability to back out of Flame Buffet when it has stacked really high, so it's not quite as important for them as it is for the Warriors.

Healing classes should take little to no damage from Flame Buffet and should wear their normal equipment.

Lastly, but far from least, make sure everyone in the raid is wearing an Onyxia Scale Cloak so that they don't die instantly to Shadow Flame.

GROUP SETUP

This is another Fire Resistance fight, so spread out your Paladins or Shaman to cover as many Warriors as possible with their auras or totems.

Beyond that, you don't really have to do anything special with groups. Spread out the classes and healing as usual.

HEALING

The MT needs five healers on them, preferably three Priests, a Paladin or Shaman, and a Druid. Firemaw has some extremely high burst DPS and forces an abundance of fast heals. One of the Priests assigned to healing the MT should be casting PW:S before every Shadow Flame.

All the other Warriors need someone assigned to healing them. They inevitably get hit by Shadow Flames and take significant damage while taunting. It's important to keep as many Warriors alive as possible, or the MT will get hit with Wing Buffet.

The vast majority of healing should be on the Warriors. The DPS classes will take damage from Flame Buffet, but they can always move out of LoS when they get low and bandage themselves. Overall, DPS classes should not be taking that much damage. If they're taking serious damage, they are staying in LoS of Flame Buffet for too long.

POSITIONING

LEGEND

1	MT
2	Offtanks
3	Raid
4	Firemaw

THE FIGHT

STRATEGY

Have a Hunter shoot Firemaw and bring him to the MT, who is already in the tanking position. Have the off-tanks close to the MT, but out of Cleave and breath range.

Right off the bat, Firemaw might be out of position. Every time he gets out of position, this is what you need to do and keep in mind:

1. Have one Warrior stand behind Firemaw, Taunt him, and drag him into the correct position.

2. As soon as he's back into position, the MT should Taunt to get him back. The MT should not move at all during a reposition.

3. It is the responsibility of the off-tank Warrior to do the actual repositioning. If the MT moves at all, they will probably go out of LoS from their healers and die.

4. Make sure your off-tanks know how to reposition, it will be necessary almost every time you fight him.

Healers should be able to heal the MT and not take any damage from Flame Buffet. Off-tank healers have a harder time because of how the terrain is set up, but they still should be able to easily back out of Firemaw's LoS if necessary. DPS classes should still be hiding behind the wall, not doing anything, until the first Wing Buffet occurs.

Your first introduction to Shadow Flame hits soon after Firemaw is pulled. *Make sure everyone has their Onyxia Scale Cloaks on.* Shadow Flame only hits people in front of Firemaw, but he's going to be turning around and changing position often. Occasionally, he casts Shadow Flame as he turns and hits a group of people who wouldn't normally expect to be hit by it. This is why everyone, not just the Warriors, needs to equip their Onyxia Scale Cloak.

Shadow Flame itself isn't really a big deal. It hits for around 4000 damage and is resistible. He's going to cast it pretty often, just have a Priest ready to cast PW:S right before it hits and it's pretty much negated.

The problem is that Firemaw likes to gain extra attacks through Thrash immediately after casting Shadow Flame. If he gets lucky with the Thrash attacks, your MT might die instantly. It happens and there's nothing you can do about it. That PW:S before the Shadow Flame greatly reduces the chance of this happening. As long as your five healers on the MT are paying attention and doing their job, the MT will get low after each Shadow Flame but very rarely will they die.

Once you've got Firemaw in position, being tanked, and your healers aren't getting eaten by Flame Buffet, you're in good shape. Nobody else should begin attacking yet. The first Wing Buffet needs to happen so you can time the next one. The first Wing Buffet will probably hit the MT because you can't time it. Have a Warrior ready to reposition him, as explained earlier.

Once the first Wing Buffet has hit, you can time when the next one is coming. Wing Buffet is on a 30-second timer. Every 28 seconds, the Warriors in back need to Taunt, turning Firemaw away from the MT so that Wing Buffet does not hit the MT. Wing Buffet reduces threat, you don't want your MT having their threat reduced because they will lose aggro. However, keep an eye on when Firemaw is getting ready to cast Shadow Flame. Do not reposition him right before a Shadow Flame since this could cause a lot more people to be hit by it than necessary.

Plenty of add-ons exist that warn you when Wing Buffet is 2-3 seconds away. All your off-tanking Warriors in back should have an add-on that tells them when to Taunt. The timing has to be very precise and every Warrior has to be on the ball.

Dealing with Wing Buffet is an important strategy to master. All three Drakes have Wing Buffet so you will be dealing with it in the same way for each of them. It's a simple concept: Point the Drake away from the MT whenever the Drake is about to Wing Buffet. However, it can be complicated by latency, Taunt resists, Warriors not paying attention, dead Warriors, all sorts of things.

No matter how good you get at dealing with Wing Buffet, your MT will occasionally get knocked back. Reposition him and go back into the same routine. If your MT gets hit by Wing Buffet too many times, their threat will have been reduced to the point where they can't hold aggro, and you're probably going to wipe—or, at the very least, switch MTs.

MORE THAN ONE WAY TO DO IT

There are two goals for positioning and tanking.

1. Position Firemaw in such a way that healers can get out of Firemaw's LoS and heal without taking damage from Flame Buffet.

2. Always have Firemaw attacking someone who can take the hits; a well-equipped Warrior in FR/tanking gear.

The way I explain dealing with Wing Buffet involves timing the cast so that Firemaw has someone other than the MT targeted when he casts it. Only one MT is used and they rarely get hit by Wing Buffet.

There are alternate ways of dealing with Wing Buffet by using two MTs. It is the same tanking concept used at Razorgore. When Razorgore uses Conflagrate on the current MT, he switches to number 2 on the threat list (MT2) and continues attacking.

Wing Buffet can be countered the same way; by having two designated Warriors at the top of the aggro list, allowing Firemaw's aggro to bounce between them with each Wing Buffet.

The key part to this strategy is that only one Warrior can be knocked backwards at a time. The two Warriors in front have to stay about 10-15 yards away from each other. Use the width of the closed gate where Firemaw is facing as a reference. If both Warriors are knocked back, Firemaw's position changes a lot, healers start taking damage from Flame Buffet, and constant repositions are required.

As long as the tanking and positioning strategy accomplishes the two goals needed without unnecessary complications, it will work out just fine.

Unfortunately, it only gets worse. Firemaw has another extremely powerful ability: Flame Buffet. Throughout the fight, most of the raid will be getting hit by Flame Buffet. As Flame Buffet gets stacked on players, they need to move out of Firemaw's LoS, wait until it resets, and rush back in. Having all your DPS moving in and out of Flame Buffet severely reduces the amount of damage being done to Firemaw, so be ready for a long fight.

You only really need three Warriors at his back Taunting for the Wing Buffets. Any extra Warriors should hide out of Flame Buffet's LoS, ready to replace a Warrior who has Flame Buffet stacked high and needs to reset it. Once a Warrior behind Firemaw gets to about 15 Flame Buffets, they should swap with another Warrior and go reset it. Sometimes you don't have the Warriors to do this. If that is the case, make sure you have plenty of healing on your off-tanks in the back; they are essential to the fight.

Firemaw has a steep learning curve, but it is essential to get used to the Shadow Flame and Wing Buffet strategies. Just keep Firemaw in position, keep the Warriors alive, prevent Wing Buffet from hitting the MT, and kill him as quickly as possible. The fight does not change from the point Firemaw's at 99% to 1%; make sure everybody knows what they are supposed to be doing and hope everything happens like it should.

Any problems you have fighting Firemaw should have pretty obvious causes. If the MT is losing aggro, they're being hit by Wing Buffet too often and your off-tanks need to figure out what they're doing wrong. If your healers are being killed by Flame Buffet, your positioning has problems. Figure out exactly where the MT and their healers should stand before even pulling Firemaw. If the MT is dying, think about more FR or more HP, depending on what they are lacking, or consider putting more healers on them.

The fight is challenging (and annoying) due to the use of LoS. However, when you finally drop him, be thankful that all the upcoming Drakes are easier.

DROPS

Firemaw will drop two random items.

ITEM	DESC	STATS
BLACK ASH ROBE	Cloth Chest	114 Armor, +22 INT, +17 SPI, +21 STA, +30 Fire Resistance
BLOODFANG GLOVES	Leather Hands	140 Armor, +20 AGI, +20 STA, +19 STR, +10 Shadow Resistance, Immune to Disarm
Class: Rogue		
CLAW OF THE BLACK DRAKE	Main-Hand Fist	102-191 Damage, Speed: 2.60, 56.3 damage per second, +13 STR, +7 STA
Equip: Improves your chance to get a critical strike by 1%		
CLOAK OF FIREMAW	Back	57 Armor, +12 STA, +50 Attack Power
DRAGONSTALKER'S GAUNTLETS	Mail Hands	301 Armor, +20 AGI, +13 INT, +6 SPI, +17 STA, +10 Shadow Resistance
Equip: Improves your chance to get a critical strike by 1%		
Class: Hunter		
DRAKE TALON CLEAVER	Two-Hand Axe	199-300 Damage, Speed: 3.40, 73.4 damage per second, +22 STR, +17 STA
Chance on Hit: Delivers a fatal wound for 240 damage		
DRAKE TALON PAULDRONS	Plate Shoulder	634 Armor, +20 AGI, +20 STR, +17 STA
Equip: Increases your chance to dodge an attack by 1%		
FIREMAW'S CLUTCH	Cloth Waist	64 Armor, +12 INT, +12 STA
Equip: Increases damage and healing done by magical spells and effects by up to 35		
Equip: Restores 5 mana per 5 sec		

ITEM	DESC	STATS
GAUNTLETS OF TEN STORMS	Mail Hands	301 Armor, +17 INT, +13 SPI, +15 STA, +10 Shadow Resistance
Equip: Restores 6 mana per 5 sec		
Equip: Increases damage and healing done by magical spells and effects by up to 8		
Equip: Increases healing done by spells and effects by up to 15		
Class: Shaman		
GAUNTLETS OF WRATH	Plate Hands	535 Armor, +20 STA, +15 STR, +10 Shadow Resistance
Equip: Increases your chance to parry an attack by 1%		
Equip: Increases Defense +7		
Class: Warrior		
HANDGUARDS OF TRANSCENDENCE	Cloth Hands	72 Armor, +20 INT, +13 SPI, +12 STA, +10 Shadow Resistance
Equip: Improves your chance to get a critical strike with spells by 1%		
Equip: Increases healing done by spells and effects by up to 29		
Class: Priest		
JUDGEMENT GAUNTLETS	Plate Hands	535 Armor, +20 INT, +6 SPI, +15 STA, +6 STR, +10 Shadow Resistance
Equip: Restores 6 mana per 5 sec		
Equip: Increases damage and healing done by magical spells and effects by up to 15		
Class: Paladin		
LEGGUARDS OF THE FALLEN CRUSADER	Plate Legs	740 Armor, +28 STR, +22 AGI, +17 INT, +22 STA
NATURAL ALIGNMENT CRYSTAL	Trinket	
Use: Aligns the Shaman with nature, increasing spell damage by 20%, improving heal effects by 20%, and increasing mana cost of spells by 20% for 20 second		
Class: Shaman		
NEMESIS GLOVES	Cloth Hands	72 Armor, +15 INT, +17 STA, +10 Shadow Resistance
Equip: Restores 3 health every 5 sec		
Equip: Increases damage and healing done by magical spells and effects by up to 15		
Equip: Improves your chance to get a critical strike with spells by 1%		
Class: Warlock		
NETHERWIND GLOVES	Cloth Hands	72 Armor, +16 INT, +6 SPI, +16 STA, +10 Shadow Resistance
Equip: Improves your chance to get a critical strike with spells by 1%		
Equip: Increases damage and healing done by magical spells and effects by up to 20		
Class: Mage		
PRIMALIST'S LINKED LEGGUARDS	Mail Legs	417 Armor, +22 INT, +12 SPI, +22 STA
Equip: Improves your chance to get a critical strike with spells by 2%		
Equip: Improves your chance to hit with spells by 1%		
REJUVENATING GEM	Trinket	
Equip: Increases healing done by spells and effects by up to 66		
Equip: Restores 9 mana per 5 sec		
RING OF BLACKROCK	Finger	
Equip: Increases damage and healing done by magical spells and effects by up to 19		
Equip: Restores 9 mana per 5 sec		
SCROLLS OF BLINDING LIGHT	Trinket	
Use: Energizes a Paladin with light, increasing melee attack and spell casting speed by 25% for 20 seconds		
Class: Paladin		
SHADOW WING FOCUS STAFF	Staff	142-237 Damage, Speed: 3.20, 59.2 damage per second, +40 INT, +22 STA, +17 SPI
Equip: Increases damage and healing done by magical spells and effects by up to 56		
STORMRAGE HANDGUARDS	Leather Hands	140 Armor, +19 INT, +15 SPI, +13 STA, +10 Shadow Resistance
Equip: Increases healing done by spells and effects by up to 42		
Class: Druid		
TAUT DRAGONHIDE BELT	Leather Waist	125 Armor, +17 STA, +60 Attack Power
Equip: Increases your chance to dodge an attack by 1%		

DEATH TALON PACKS

There are two groups of three Death Talon Overseers in Blackwing. These are arguably harder than some bosses in the instance, depending on what Brood Afflictions you get.

Each Wyrmguard has random elements to it: a random Brood Affliction attack and a random weakness to a school of magic. Some Brood Afflictions are much more powerful than others.

If your group is new to these pulls, you probably want to send people in to test what Brood Afflictions they have and what their weaknesses are.

The general strategy is to tank them and kill them one at a time. Some types need more than one tank, some types need certain resistance gear, and some are rather trivial.

Make sure you do not fight these too close to the spiral staircase! Ebonroc has a small patrol route that brings him to the bottom of the stairs every now and then. Someone fighting too close and accidently adding Ebonroc is a recipe for disaster.

DEATH TALON WYRMGUARD

Brood Affliction - Black: Direct damage fire attack. You won't see a debuff on the tank, they will just take heavy fire damage. Wear Fire Resistance gear and keep the Warrior alive.

Brood Affliction - Blue: Single-target debuff that reduces attack speed. Only one tank is needed; probably the easiest Brood Affliction.

Brood Affliction - Bronze: When someone gets Bronze they begin spinning and hitting everyone near them for significant damage all the while taking damage themselves. You should not melee Bronze Wyrmguards; burn them down from range.

Brood Affliction - Green: AoE sleep. Green Wyrmguards are by far the most dangerous and can not be tanked easily. Kill them as quickly as possible.

Brood Affliction - Red: Single-target, fire-based DoT that hits for significant damage. Wear Fire Resistance gear and keep the Warrior alive.

War Stomp: All Wyrmguards have an AoE stun attack. Keep them away from the healers.

MASTER ELEMENTAL SHAPER KRIXIX

This Goblin hiding behind the three Death Talon Overseers is the only mob in the game capable of teaching a Miner how to Smelt Elementium. He's as powerful as a regular level 60 Elite, so don't kill him right away.

To teach someone how to Smelt Elementium, Mind Control Krixix; it will be one of his abilities on the Pet Bar. Target the person you want to teach and cast the ability.

He drops no loot and there is nothing else to him.

EBONROC

Ebonroc is the second Drake, both in killing order and difficulty. Overall, he isn't all that hard, but he can be extremely annoying.

As with all the Drakes, he has Wing Buffet and Shadow Flame. You will deal with both attacks the same way you did with Firemaw.

ABILITIES

Shadow of Ebonroc: A debuff cast every 10-15 seconds that causes Ebonroc to heal himself whenever he does damage to someone with the debuff.

Shadow Flame: AoE breath attack that deals 3938-5062 Shadow damage. If anyone affected is not wearing an Onyxia Scale Cloak, the damage is significantly higher as they incur an additional 1750-2250 DPS for approximately 12 seconds. This usually kills the target.

Thrash: Ebonroc has a chance to gain two extra attacks, giving him the potential to inflict high burst melee damage.

Wing Buffet: Knock back attack that hits everyone in front of Ebonroc, reducing the threat of everyone who gets hit by it.

PREPARATION

EQUIPMENT

Everyone is free to wear their normal equipment.

Don't forget those Onyxia Scale Cloaks!

GROUP SETUP

There is nothing special for setting up the groups. Spread out the classes evenly and make sure the Warriors get plenty of healing.

HEALING

Three Priests need to be dedicated to healing whichever Warrior Ebonroc is attacking.

An additional healer needs to be assigned to each of the three Warriors tanking. Shadow Flame hits all the Warriors in front of him; it's important that all Warriors in front have a dedicated healer to keep their life topped off.

Everyone else should focus their attention on keeping the Warriors in back that are taunting for Wing Buffet alive. Warriors are the most important class in this fight.

POSITIONING

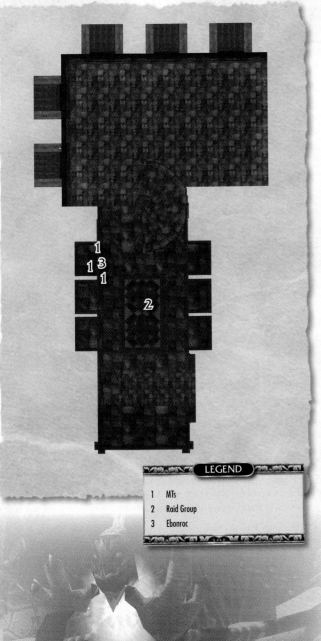

LEGEND	
1	MTs
2	Raid Group
3	Ebonroc

THE FIGHT

STRATEGY

The pull is similar to Firemaw's. Have the MT shoot him and bring Ebonroc into position. The first Shadow Flame will hit, followed by the first Wing Buffet. Position the five MTs around Ebonroc so that only one is hit by Shadow Flame and Wing Buffet at a time. Once the first Wing Buffet occurs, start timing it just like the Firemaw battle.

As soon as Shadows of Ebonroc hits an MT, another should begin taunting immediately and take over the tanking duties. Set up a rotation that allows each tank to recover and be healed while forcing Ebonroc to attack those not afflicted with Shadows of Ebonroc.

Make sure that the new tank has a solid hold on the top position and that it's not lost. Continue this process. Shadow Flame & Wing Buffet are to be endured and Ebonroc should be refaced when he casts his Shadows.

Again, communication is absolutely essential for this fight. If a Taunt is resisted, the next tank in the chain needs to Taunt immediately and reposition Ebonroc to face them. This isn't a horrible situation. Ebonroc's just going to keep turning around in a circle while the tanks trade off as lead. The fight is going to be a bit chaotic due to the amount of times Ebonroc changes targets, but keep your two goals in mind: 1) don't let Ebonroc attack anyone afflicted with Shadows of Ebonroc and 2) don't let a single Warrior get hit by so many Wing Buffets that they unintentionally lose aggro.

As all this is happening, DPS should kill Ebonroc as quickly as possible. He doesn't have an overwhelming amount of life, but he may occasionally heal and that's to be expected, but (with practice) can potentially be avoided altogether. You can minimize any healing that Ebonroc gets by making sure that Mortal Strike and Wound Poison are active at all times.

This fight is almost entirely up to the Warriors' ability to time their Taunts, assess the situation, and react quickly. A raid leader calling out the rotation is helpful. If the Warriors can do their job, the fight should be relatively short and easy. The practice you gained while facing Firemaw's Shadow Flame and Wing Buffet should help immensely.

DROPS

Ebonroc will drop two random items.

ITEM	DESC	STATS
AEGIS OF PRESERVATION	Trinket	
Use: Increases armor by 500 and heals 35 damage every time you take ranged or melee damage for 20 seconds		
Class: Priest		
BAND OF FORCED CONCENTRATION	Ring	+12 INT, +9 STA
Equip: Improves your chance to hit with spells by 1%		
Equip: Increases damage and healing done by magical spells and effects by up to 21		
DRAGONBREATH HAND CANNON	Gun	86-160 Damage, Speed: 2.80, 43.9 damage per second, +14 AGI, +7 STA
DRAKE FANG TALISMAN	Trinket, +56 Attack Power	
Equip: Improves your chance to hit by 2%		
Equip: Increases your chance to dodge an attack by 1%		
DRAKE TALON CLEAVER	Two-Hand Axe	199-300 Damage, Speed: 3.40, 73.4 damage per second, +22 STR, +17 STA
Chance on Hit: Delivers a fatal wound for 240 damage		
DRAKE TALON PAULDRONS	Plate Shoulder	634 Armor, +20 AGI, +20 STR, +17 STA
Equip: Increases your chance to dodge an attack by 1%		
EBONY FLAME GLOVES	Cloth Hands	72 Armor, +12 INT, +17 STA
Equip: Increases damage done by Shadow spells and effects by up to 43		
MALFURION'S BLESSED BULWARK	Leather Chest	392 Armor, +40 STR, +22 STA
REJUVENATING GEM	Trinket	
Equip: Increases healing done by spells and effects by up to 66		
Equip: Restores 9 mana per 5 sec		
RING OF BLACKROCK	Finger	
Equip: Increases damage and healing done by magical spells and effects by up to 19		
Equip: Restores 9 mana per 5 sec		
SHADOW WING FOCUS STAFF	Staff	142-237 Damage, Speed: 3.20, 59.2 damage per second, +40 INT, +22 STA, +17 SPI
Equip: Increases damage and healing done by magical spells and effects by up to 56		
TAUT DRAGONHIDE BELT	Leather Waist	125 Armor, +17 STA, +60 Attack Power
Equip: Increases your chance to dodge an attack by 1%		

CLASS-SPECIFIC GAUNTLETS

The class-specific gauntlets drop off any of the three drakes (Firemaw, Ebonroc, and Flamegor). They're all listed in Firemaw's loot table and in the Item Sets section of this book.

FLAMEGOR

Flamegor is the final and easiest Drake. His only trick can be neutralized with Tranquilizing Shot.

Of course, he has Wing Buffet and Shadow Flame, both of which you should be very familiar with by this point.

ABILITIES

Fire Nova: Only activated when Frenzied; an AoE fire attack that hits everyone for a about 600 damage.

Frenzy: Greatly increases the attack rate of Flamegor.

Shadow Flame: AoE shadow breath attack that hits everyone in front of Flamegor for several thousand damage. A guaranteed death if you are hit by it without wearing your Onyxia Scale Cloak.

Thrash: Ebonroc has a chance to gain two extra attacks, giving him the potential to inflict high burst melee damage.

Wing Buffet: Knock back attack that hits everyone in front of Flamegor, reducing the threat of everyone who gets hit by it.

PREPARATION

EQUIPMENT

No one needs to wear anything special. While he does have a powerful fire attack, Fire Nova, he only uses it while Frenzied, which shouldn't be very often.

As usual, make sure everyone has their Onyxia Scale Cloak on.

GROUP SETUP

Make sure each Hunter has two healers in their group. Hunters are very important for this fight. Beyond that, use the same group setup as Ebonroc.

HEALING

Pretty much all healing will be on the MT. Fire Nova occasionally hits everyone in the raid for a few hundred damage, but it's not that big of a deal.

Keep the Hunters alive at all costs!

POSITIONING

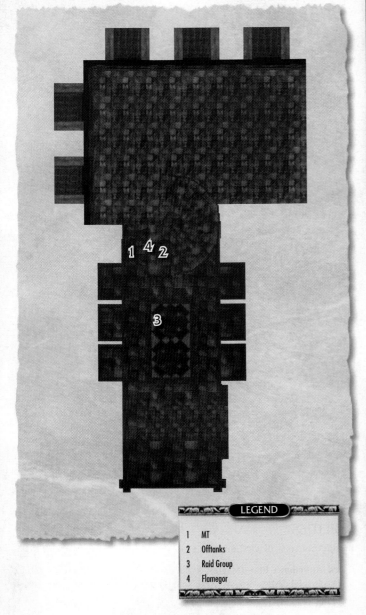

	LEGEND
1	MT
2	Offtanks
3	Raid Group
4	Flamegor

THE FIGHT

STRATEGY

Flamegor's only trick is a Frenzy; when he Frenzies, he begins to rapidly cast Fire Nova. The goal of the fight is to keep hitting him with Tranquilizing Shot, preventing his Frenzy from killing everyone.

The pull is exactly the same as Ebonroc. Get him in position and tanked. As usual, the first Shadow Flame hits, and shortly thereafter the first Wing Buffet hits the MT. Start timing the Wing Buffet and get every other Warrior in back Taunting every 30 seconds. Your Warriors should be near experts at dealing with Wing Buffet by now.

Three Hunters are needed to keep him constantly under the effects of their Tranquilizing Shots (extras are usually welcome). Make sure your Hunters have a Tranquilizing Shot rotation setup and know where they are in the rotation. He's going to use Frenzy about every 5-10 seconds, so your Hunters have to be ready to react. Any extra Hunters not in the Tranquilizing Shot rotation should be emergency backups in case something goes wrong.

Hunters make or break this fight. Flamegor can not be allowed to remain Frenzied for very long or else his Fire Nova will kill the entire raid or, at the very least, waste a ton of the healers' mana.

Keep him Tranquilized, keep the MT alive, deal with Wing Buffet, and you will find that Flamegor is a welcome relief from the previous two Drakes.

THE RAMP

The ramp can be used to break LOS on Flamegor's Fire Nova if necessary using the positions indicated in the previous strategy.

DROPS

Flamegor will drop two random items.

ITEM	DESC	STATS
CIRCLE OF APPLIED FORCE	Ring	+12 STR, +22 AGI, +9 STA
DRAGON'S TOUCH	Wand	107-199 Fire Damage, Speed: 1.60, 95.6 damage per second, +12 INT, +7 STA
Equip: Increases damage and healing done by magical spells and effects by up to 6		
DRAKE TALON CLEAVER	Two-Hand Axe	199-300 Damage, Speed: 3.40, 73.4 damage per second, +22 STR, +17 STA
Chance on Hit: Delivers a fatal wound for 240 damage		
DRAKE TALON PAULDRONS	Plate Shoulder	634 Armor, +20 AGI, +20 STR, +17 STA
Equip: Increases your chance to dodge an attack by 1%		
EMBERWEAVE LEGGINGS	Mail Legs	417 Armor, +22 STA, +17 AGI, +12 INT, +35 Fire Resistance
HERALD OF WOE	Two-Hand Mace	199-300 Damage, Speed: 3.40, 73.4 damage per second, +31 STR, +20 INT, +17 SPI, +22 STA
REJUVENATING GEM	Trinket	
Equip: Increases healing done by spells and effects by up to 66		
Equip: Restores 9 mana per 5 sec		
RING OF BLACKROCK	Finger	
Equip: Increases damage and healing done by magical spells and effects by up to 19		
Equip: Restores 9 mana per 5 sec		
SHADOW WING FOCUS STAFF	Staff	142-237 Damage, Speed: 3.20, 59.2 damage per second, +40 INT, +22 STA, +17 SPI
Equip: Increases damage and healing done by magical spells and effects by up to 56		
SHROUD OF PURE THOUGHT	Back	57 Armor, +11 INT, +10 STA
Equip: Increases healing done by spells and effects by up to 33		
Equip: Restores 6 mana per 5 sec		
STYLEEN'S IMPEDING SCARAB	Trinket	
Equip: Increases your chance to block attacks with a shield by 5%		
Equip: Increases the block value of your shield by 24		
Equip: Increases Defense +13		
TAUT DRAGONHIDE BELT	Leather Waist	125 Armor, +17 STA, +60 Attack Power
Equip: Increases your chance to dodge an attack by 1%		

CLASS-SPECIFIC GAUNTLETS

The class-specific gauntlets drop off any of the three drakes (Firemaw, Ebonroc, and Flamegor). They're all listed in Firemaw's loot table and in the Item Sets section of this book.

CHROMAGGUS

Chromaggus is a very long fight and there's a random element to him. During each instance, he's assigned two different, random breath attacks. Some breaths are more challenging than others.

The fight is made easier by using LoS to avoid getting hit by his breath attacks. Once everyone is familiar with how the fight works, he will take a long time to kill, but isn't all that hard.

ABILITIES

Brood Affliction - Black (Curse): Increases fire damage taken by 100%.

Brood Affliction - Blue (Magic): Reduces your mana by 50 every second, increases spell casting time by 50%, and reduces movement speed to 70%.

Brood Affliction - Bronze: Stuns you for 4 seconds at random intervals.

Brood Affliction - Green (Poison): Deals 250 damage every 5 seconds and reduces healing by 50%.

Brood Affliction - Red (Disease): Deals 50 damage every 3 seconds, and if you die with Red on, you will heal Chromaggus.

Corrosive Acid: Deals 875 to 1125 damage every 3 sec for 15 seconds. Armor reduced by 3938 to 5062 for 15 seconds.

Frenzy: Greatly increases the attack speed of Chromaggus.

Frost Burn: Burns mana and does around 2200 damage. Also reduces attack speed by 80%.

Ignite Flesh: A fire DoT spell that does 657-843 damage every 3 seconds for 60 seconds.

Incinerate: Direct damage fire spell that hits for around 4200.

Shimmering Skin: Causes Chromaggus to become weak to a random magic element.

Time Lapse: Freezes everyone it hits in place for 5 seconds and reduces their life by 50%. Chromaggus will not attack anyone who has Time Lapse. The life reduction will be restored when Time Lapse wears off.

PREPARATION

EQUIPMENT

Depending on what breath Chromaggus has assigned, the MT might want to wear different resist equipment. Even that is debatable; you will probably do fine if everyone wears their normal equipment.

If your Chromaggus has Time Lapse, make sure all the Warriors are wearing their tanking equipment for reasons discussed later.

GROUP SETUP

Nothing special needs to be done with the group setup. Depending on what breath Chromaggus gets, make sure the MT has the proper resistance auras/totems. Don't forget a Hunter for Aspect of the Wild when facing the Corrosive Acid Breath.

HEALING

The Chromaggus encounter is an extremely long fight, so it's smart to put the Priests in a healing rotation for maximum mana. Pair off all the Priests, have the first Priest in each pair heal until they are at about 25% mana, then have the second Priest take over as the first Priest regenerates back to full or until they're up again. Repeat this throughout the fight.

Cleansing is a big deal in this fight. Chromaggus randomly places diseases, poisons, magic effects, and curses on 20 people at a time every 10-20 seconds or so. Designate a few people to cleanse the Brood Afflictions for the entire fight. No one should ever have more than three Brood Afflictions on them at one time.

POSITIONING

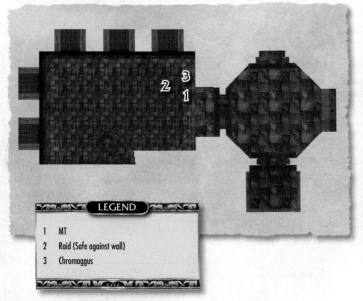

LEGEND

1	MT
2	Raid (Safe against wall)
3	Chromaggus

THE FIGHT

STRATEGY

Chromaggus changes on a weekly basis. The two breaths he uses are randomly set for each instance. Regardless of what breaths he gets, the general strategy remains the same. I will explain some specifics on dealing with each breath type later.

First and foremost, make sure everyone has two or three Hourglass Sands. They are used in this fight to remove Brood Affliction: Bronze. If the raid is short on sands, just give them to the MT, healers, and as many Hunters as possible.

The pull is rather straightforward; he is pretty much standing where he is going to be tanked. Have the MT obtain aggro and back him into position. The MT should barely be within LoS of all the healers along the wall. If the MT retreats too far back, the breath hits everyone along the wall.

Chromaggus goes into a Frenzy about every 30 seconds. Since Tranquilizing Shot is on a 20-second cooldown, the Frenzy should not be a big deal. There should never be a time when he remains Frenzied.

Throughout the fight, Chromaggus becomes weak to random magic elements. He emotes "Chromaggus' skin begins to shimmer" every 20-30 seconds. This means that the school of magic that he was/is weak to has changed. Players should be calling out what he is weak to as often as possible so that his weakness can be exploited. Chromaggus is already a long fight; do as much damage to him as possible by using his magical weaknesses against him.

25 seconds after gaining the initial aggro, everyone except the MT needs to get against the wall in preparation for the first breath which hits 30 seconds after first contact. Nobody should be hit by the breath except the MT.

After the breath hits, everyone should move back into LoS to do damage. The next breath is coming in 30 seconds, so have everyone run back against the wall before the second breath hits.

That is all there is to dealing with Chromaggus' breath. Move everyone out of LoS, against the wall, for every single breath. Nobody should take any damage from the breaths except for the MT (Time Lapse is a little different and it's discussed later). Run up against the wall about 5 seconds before the breath, getting out of LoS, and wait until the breath hits. Once Chromaggus is done, go back in to resume dealing damage. Don't stay in too long because you might get stunned with Brood Affliction: Bronze as you start to run to the wall. Give yourself a few seconds to spare. The healers should never leave their spot against the wall (except after a Time Lapse); they have little to worry about during his breaths.

As discussed in the Healing section, there are curable Brood Afflictions cast throughout the fight. There should be people designated to clearing these debuffs

and no one should ever get over three stacked on them at any given time. If, somehow, someone gets all five Brood Afflictions on them, they turn into a Drakonid and start killing the raid. You should never see this happen, but if it does, kill them immediately.

Keep the MT alive, don't get hit by the breaths, cleanse everyone of Brood Affliction, keep him down using Tranquilizing Shot during his moments of Frenzy, and work him down. He has a lot of life and it is a long fight, but once everyone gets into the routine of what they are supposed to do, you should find it to be a fun, but not exceedingly difficult, encounter.

There are some specific strategies to keep in mind when dealing with certain breath types:

Incinerate: Put some Fire Resistance gear on. Make sure the MT never has Brood Affliction: Black before Incinerate is about to hit or they will probably die.

Ignite Flesh: Again, some Fire Resistance wouldn't hurt. Ignite Flesh is a DoT, so just keep heals on the MT while it is up. Watch out for Brood Affliction: Black.

Corrosive Acid: Make sure there is a Hunter in the MT's group to provide Aspect of the Wild. Beyond that, it's another DoT Breath coupled with an AC debuff, so just keep the heals on the MT.

Frost Burn: By far the most trivial breath. If you get Frost Burn, it's your lucky day.

Time Lapse: This is the breath to watch out for. Sometimes Time Lapse can be awfully challenging to deal with. When Time Lapse hits, the MT becomes stunned and loses aggro. Chromaggus then begins to attack whoever is highest on his aggro list that isn't currently Time Lapsed.

For this reason, the Warriors need to make sure they are very high on the threat list so that they get aggro when the MT loses it. You want Chromaggus to attack a Warrior other than the MT for the few seconds Time Lapse is active. He returns to attacking the MT when Time Lapse is over.

Once he's back on the MT, it's likely that you'll need to reposition Chromaggus. The healers should be prepared for this and move away from the wall. The MT should run forward into Chromaggus' room and then back out until they are back to the proper tanking position. This has to be done rather quickly and the healers must be prepared to move.

Finally, it doesn't matter if everyone but the Warriors and Healers get hit by Time Lapse. DPS classes do not need to get out of LoS before a Time Lapse. It doesn't do any damage and there is no point in running away from it unless you're a Warrior or healer.

DROPS

Chromaggus will drop two random class set shoulders and two to three additional random items that aren't class set shoulders.

ITEM	DESC	STATS
ANGELISTA'S GRASP	Cloth Waist	66 Armor, +20 INT, +13 SPI, +17 STA
Equip: Improves your chance to hit with spells by 2%		
ASHJRE'THUL, CROSSBOW OF SMITING	Crossbow	124-186 Damage, Speed: 3.40, 45.6 damage per second, +7 STA, +36 ranged Attack Power
BLOODFANG SPAULDERS		Leather Shoulders, 169 Armor, +25 AGI, +17 STA, +6 STR, +10 Fire Resistance
Equip: Increases your chance to dodge an attack by 1%		
Class: Rogue		

ITEM	DESC	STATS
CHROMATIC BOOTS	Plate Feet	596 Armor, +20 AGI, +20 STR, +12 STA
Equip: Improves your chance to hit by 1%		
CHROMATICALLY TEMPERED SWORD	One-Hand Sword	106-198 Damage, Speed: 2.60, 58.5 damage per second, +14 AGI, +14 STR, +7 STA
CLAW OF CHROMAGGUS	One-Hand Dagger	37-90 Damage, Speed: 1.50, 42.3 damage per second, +17 INT, +7 STA
Equip: Increases damage and healing done by magical spells and effects by up to 64. Restores 4 mana per 5 sec		
DRAGONSTALKER'S SPAULDERS	Mail Shoulder	362 Armor, +23 AGI, +13 INT, +6 SPI, +15 STA, +10 Fire Resistance
Equip: Improves your chance to hit by 1%		
Class: Hunter		
ELEMENTIUM REINFORCED BULWARK	Shield	2893 Armor, 54 Block, +23 STA
Equip: Increases the block value of your shield by 19		
Equip: Increases Defense +7		
ELEMENTIUM THREADED CLOAK	Back	169 Armor, +13 STA
Equip: Increases your chance to dodge an attack by 2%		
EMPOWERED LEGGINGS	Cloth Legs	103 Armor, +12 INT, +24 SPI, +12 STA
Equip: Increases healing done by spells and effects by up to 77		
Equip: Improves your chance to get a critical strike with spells by 1%		
EPAULETS OF TEN STORMS	Mail Shoulder	362 Armor, +17 INT, +8 SPI, +23 STA, +10 Fire Resistance
Equip: Improves your chance to get a critical strike with spells by 1%		
Class: Shaman		
GIRDLE OF THE FALLEN CRUSADER	Plate Waist	488 Armor, +20 STR, +15 STA, +17 INT, +13 SPI, +10 AGI
JUDGEMENT SPAULDERS	Plate Shoulder	642 Armor, +14 INT, +6 SPI, +20 STA, +13 STR, +10 Fire Resistance
Equip: Restores 5 mana per 5 sec		
Equip: Increases damage and healing done by magical spells and effects by up to 13		
Class: Paladin		
NEMESIS SPAULDERS	Cloth Shoulder	87 Armor, +13 INT, +6 SPI, +20 STA, +10 Fire Resistance
Equip: Restores 3 health every 5 sec		
Equip: Increases damage and healing done by magical spells and effects by up to 23		
Class: Warlock		
NETHERWIND MANTLE	Cloth Shoulder	87 Armor, +13 INT, +12 SPI, +16 STA, +10 Fire Resistance
Equip: Restores 4 mana per 5 sec		
Equip: Increases damage and healing done by magical spells and effects by up to 21		
Class: Mage		
PAULDRONS OF TRANSCENDENCE	Cloth Shoulder	87 Armor, +25 INT, +13 SPI, +12 STA, +10 Fire Resistance
Equip: Increases healing done by spells and effects by up to 26		
Class: Priest		
PAULDRONS OF WRATH	Plate Shoulder	642 Armor, +27 STA, +13 STR, +10 Fire Resistance
Equip: Increases the block value of your shield by 27		
Equip: Increases Defense +7		
Class: Warrior		
PRIMALIST'S LINKED WAISTGUARD	Mail Waist	275 Armor, +16 STR, +16 INT, +15 SPI, +13 STA
Equip: Increases damage and healing done by magical spells and effects by up to 20		
SHIMMERING GETA	Cloth Feet	81 Armor, +17 INT, +13 STA
Equip: Restores 12 mana per 5 sec		
STORMRAGE PAULDRONS	Leather Shoulder	169 Armor, +21 INT, +10 SPI, +14 STA, +10 Fire Resistance
Equip: Increases healing done by spells and effects by up to 29		
Equip: Restores 4 mana per 5 sec		
Class: Druid		
TAUT DRAGONHIDE GLOVES	Leather Hands	142 Armor, +20 INT, +20 STA
Equip: Improves your chance to get a critical strike with spells by 1%		
Equip: Restores 6 mana per 5 sec		
TAUT DRAGONHIDE SHOULDERPADS	Leather Shoulder	170 Armor, +30 STA, +46 Attack Power

NEFARIAN

And so you've reached the final boss of Blackwing Lair. It seems as if Nefarian is both aware of your presence and patiently waiting for you upon his throne. All you have to do is talk to him and to begin the event.

Take a look around the lair; it's a very cool place to be. Prepare yourself for what is probably the most enjoyable fight in the game so far. It's rather complicated, there is a lot to know, but even if it seems overwhelming at first, Nefarian is not harder than some of the previous bosses.

EQUIPMENT

One Warrior on each side needs to wear tanking equipment because they will be tanking Chromatic Drakonids. The MT will be tanking Nefarian and should obviously wear full tanking gear.

Beyond that, make sure everyone has their Onyxia Scale Cloak equipped.

PHASE 1

You won't know what Drakonid types you have until you start the event. For this reason, I suggest having everyone take off their equipment (or log out) and start the event to find out what color Drakonids you have before doing anything else.

Recently, Nefarian was changed to reset 15 minutes after a wipe. If you choose to test the colors before making a real attempt, be prepared to wait at least 15 minutes.

DRAKONID TYPES

Black: Resistant to fire and has a single-target, direct damage fire attack.

Blue: Resistant to ice and has an AoE attack that does minimal damage and burns mana.

Bronze: Has an AoE attack that does damage and slows attack/casting speed.

Chromatic: No abilities, but has an abundance of life.

Green: Has an AoE sleep that only lasts for a second or 2.

Red: Resistant to fire and has a single-target, DoT fire attack.

GROUP SETUP

Spread out the damage as evenly as possible. One side should not have all the Rogues while the other side has all the Hunters; it needs to be evenly distributed. Make sure you don't have, for example, Frost Mages attacking Blue Drakonids; make sure everyone is capable of doing damage to the color on their side.

One Warrior on each side needs to be designated to tank the Chromatic Drakonids. Make sure that Warrior has plenty of healing and a Warlock for Blood Pact.

The MT, the person who will tank Nefarian, should be in a very solid group with a Warlock with Blood Pact up from his Imp, a Hunter with Trueshot Aura, a Paladin/Shaman, and a Priest.

FLASK OF TITANS

Have the Warrior who is going to tank Nefarian drink a Flask of Titans. You need the extra life!

HEALING

For Phase 1, there is nothing particularly noteworthy about the healing. Make sure the Warriors off-tanking Chromatic Drakonids don't die, and heal your side.

POSITIONING

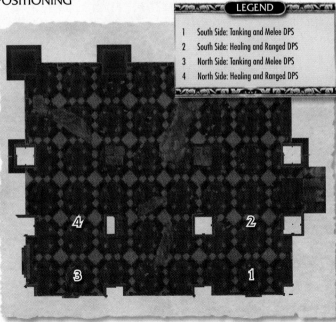

LEGEND	
1	South Side: Tanking and Melee DPS
2	South Side: Healing and Ranged DPS
3	North Side: Tanking and Melee DPS
4	North Side: Healing and Ranged DPS

STRATEGY

The point of Phase 1 is to kill 40 Drakonids; Nefarian lands as soon as 40 have been killed. Designate a person on each side to count how many Drakonids have been killed on their side.

This fight is all about assisting and single target DPS. There will be two MAs per side and two groups assigned to each assist. For example, Groups 1-4 are in the south, Groups 1 and 2 will assist someone (MA1), Groups 3 and 4 will assist someone else (MA2). Try to keep the assists on different targets as often as possible.

All melee classes should be up in the doorway. Do not get spread out. Begin attacking the second something spawns and stay on it until it's dead. Make sure everyone is assisting and attacking the correct Drakonid. Kill them one or two at a time as quickly as possible.

IMPROVED BLIZZARD

In this encounter, and all encounters where Mages are called upon for their AoE capabilities, Improved Blizzard is a huge benefit to the raid.

Nefarian remains in his human form during part of Phase 1 and casts Shadow Bolts and, more importantly, Mind Control while teleporting around the room. Make sure that anyone under the effects of Mind Control is immediately Polymorphed.

Chromatic Drakonids spawn every once in a while. The Warrior assigned to off-tanking them needs to pick them up *immediately*. The MAs should never attack the Chromatics; they should always be on the weaker Drakonids.

Killing Drakonids swiftly enough and keeping the side under control is going to take practice. Keep trying over and over, hopefully killing more and having less deaths with each attempt. Everyone needs to be at the top of their game to kill them fast enough.

With practice, you should reach the point where you have killed 40 Drakonids, have two to three Chromatics being off-tanked per side, and force Nefarian into landing. Phase 2 begins when he lands.

PHASE 2

Bellowing Roar: Nefarian fears everyone within 30 yards of him about every 30 seconds.

Shadow Flame: AoE breath attack that deals 3938-5062 Shadow damage. If anyone affected is not wearing an Onyxia Scale Cloak, the damage is significantly higher as they incur an additional 1750-2250 DPS for approximately 12 seconds. This usually kills the target.

Veil of Shadows: Single target curse that reduces healing effects by 75%.

CLASS CALLS

DRUID: *All Druids will be shifted into Cat Form.* Just make sure the Mages are decursing the MT and this won't be a big deal.

MAGE: *Random targets will be polymorphed.* During a Mage call a Priest needs to constantly cast Dispel Magic on the MT. If the MT gets polymorphed, Nefarian will change targets and possibly Shadow Flame the entire raid. The MT will get polymorphed occasionally, but should not remain polymorphed for more than a second. Beyond that, have everyone who can cleanse magic removing polymorph as they need to.

HUNTER: *Hunters will have their weapons broken when they attack Nefarian.* Use a Field Repair Bot or quickly equip a spare weapon when he calls Hunters.

PALADIN: *Nefarian will gain Blessing of Protection, becoming immune to all melee attacks.* Make sure magic DPS backs off a little bit since the MT can't generate any threat and wait it out.

PRIEST: *Every time a Priest heals they apply a DoT to their target.* Obviously, Priests need to stop healing during a Priest call. Make sure the Druids and Paladins or Shaman keep the MT alive.

ROGUE: *Rogues are teleported and immobilized in front of Nefarian.* When this happens, the MT should run straight through Nefarian, spinning him around so that he faces the opposite direction. That way, the Rogues won't get killed by Shadow Flame.

SHAMAN: *Shamans will begin casting Corrupted Totems that damage the raid or buff Nefarian.* Have the Shaman run across the room so their totems are out of range from Nefarian and the rest of the raid.

WARLOCK: *For each Warlock in the raid 2 Corrupted Infernals will spawn on top of the Warlock.* Kill them quickly.

WARRIOR: *All Warriors will be shifted into Berserker Stance, including the MT.* Make sure lots of healing is on the MT during a Warrior call, they will take thousands of damage very quickly for the entire call. The MT should immediately switch back to Defensive Stance after the call is over. It's also a good time for Warriors to use Last Stand or a Lifegiving Gem for additional hit points.

HEALING

The vast majority of the healing should be on the MT. Keep in mind that Nefarian casts Veil of Shadows on the MT quite often. Make sure it always gets removed as quickly as possible.

Watch for the class calls! Priests need to be ready when they get called or the MT will die (quickly) from Corrupted Healing.

POSITIONING

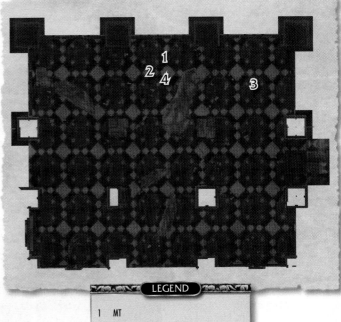

LEGEND

1	MT
2	OTs
3	Raid Group
4	Nefarian

STRATEGY

First and foremost, everyone in the lair will be hit by a Shadow Flame. I can't stress how important it is that everyone is wearing their Onyxia Scale Cloak during this encounter.

The second Nefarian gives his emote that he's landing, the MT needs to run over and meet him. The MT will need two Priests, two Druids, two Paladins or Shaman, and one Mage to go with them for healing and decursing. Nefarian lands with no threat list so the MT should have an easy time getting him tanked and positioned.

As the MT and their healers are getting into position, the rest of the raid should continue assisting and killing Drakonids. There should be a few Chromatics up and possibly a few others roaming; it should only take a minute to clean up the Drakonids. Once all the Drakonids are dead, everyone else should move into position and begin attacking.

Every 30 seconds Nefarian calls out a random class (Class Calls). Deal with each class call appropriately.

Addtionally, he Fears everyone within 30 yards every 30 seconds or so. Healers should never get feared, they can heal from far enough away to avoid it. If you're an Alliance group, use Fear Ward liberally. If you're a Horde group, switch stances and activate Berserker Rage the moment the ground begins to shake.

As long as you handle the Class Calls and Fear adequately, Phase 2 is not horribly difficult. However, Phase 3 is approaching and is triggered when Nefarian reaches 20% life.

PHASE 3

When Nefarian is brought down to 20% life, he resurrects the 40 Drakonids your raid killed in Phase 1. They're now Risen Constructs and it's up to the AoE members of your raid to begin pulling them down. Mages, Warriors, and Warlocks should switch from Nefarian to the Risen Constructs.

Keeping Mages provided with a Soulstoned is a good idea. Of course, keep the Soulstones on the lead healers, but bringing the AoE power of the Mages back to the fray is almost necessary in this battle.

Warriors below the top two on the threat list should be prepared to use Challenging Shout and rotate the use of this ability to bring as much aggro onto themselves as possible, keeping it off the Mages. If the MT is feared or Polymorphed, the second Warrior should jump in to take their place.

Mages under the effect of a Paladin's Blessing of Protection allows them to cast their AoEs more safely. If the Paladins have a moment to take positions prior to bringing Nefarian down to 20%, they can stand near the locations where the Risen Constructs are going to resurrect in groups and hit Divine Shield before AoE'ing the adds as soon as they spawn. If they're shielded before the Constructs appear and cause the initial damage, they should get aggro while invulnerable, allowing them to soak up the initial wave of attacks from the nearby Constructs. The Horde alternative is to use the same method with their Warriors and Lesser Invulnerability Potions.

After all the Risen Constructs are dead (again), finish Nefarian off. Keep dealing with the Class Calls and Fear, maintain maximum DPS, and bring down the beast that made Blackwing Lair his home.

STRATHOLME HOLY WATER

Use Stratholme Holy Water during the Risen Construct rush! They are Undead and you will do thousands of points of damage with a single bottle.

DROPS

Nefarian will drop two random class set chest pieces and two to three additional random items that aren't class set chest pieces.

ITEM	DESC	STATS
ARCHIMTIROS' RING OF RECKONING	Ring	+14 AGI, +28 STA
ASHKANDI, GREATSWORD OF THE BROTHERHOOD	Two-Hand Sword	229-344 Damage, Speed: 3.50, 81.9 damage per second, +33 STA, +86 Attack Power
BLOODFANG CHESTPIECE	Leather Chest	225 Armor, +26 AGI, +17 STA, +12 STR, +10 Fire Resistance, +10 Nature Resistance
Equip: Improves your chance to get a critical strike by 1% Equip: Improves your chance to hit by 2% Class: Rogue		
BOOTS OF THE SHADOW FLAME	Leather Feet	286 Armor, +22 STA, +44 Attack Power
Equip: Improves your chance to hit by 2%		
BREASTPLATE OF TEN STORMS	Mail Chest	482 Armor, +31 INT, +16 SPI, +17 STA, +10 Fire Resistance, +10 Nature Resistance
Equip: Increases damage and healing done by magical spells and effects by up to 23 Class: Shaman		
BREASTPLATE OF WRATH	Plate Chest	857 Armor, +40 STA, +17 STR, +10 Fire Resistance, +10 Nature Resistance
Equip: Increases Defense +11 Class: Warrior		
CLOAK OF THE BROOD LORD	Back	63 Armor, +14 INT, +10 STA
Equip: Increases damage and healing done by magical spells and effects by up to 28		
CRUL'SHORUKH, EDGE OF CHAOS	One-Hand Axe	101-188 Damage, Speed: 2.30, 62.8 damage per second, +13 STA, +36 Attack Power
DRAGONSTALKER'S BREASTPLATE	Mail Chest	482 Armor, +34 AGI, +14 INT, +6 SPI, +17 STA, +10 Fire Resistance, +10 Nature Resistance
Equip: Improves your chance to get a critical strike by 1% Class: Hunter		
HEAD OF NEFARIAN	Starts a quest, discussed below	
JUDGEMENT BREASTPLATE	Plate Chest	857 Armor, +21 INT, +5 SPI, +21 STA, +16 STR, +10 Fire Resistance, +10 Nature Resistance
Equip: Restores 5 mana per 5 sec Equip: Increases damage and healing done by magical spells and effects by up to 25 Class: Paladin		
LOK'AMIR IL ROMATHIS	Main-Hand Mace	47-127 Damage, Speed: 2.10, 41.4 damage per second, +18 INT, +8 SPI, +10 STA
Equip: Increases damage and healing done by magical spells and effects by up to 84		
MISH'UNDARE, CIRCLET OF THE MIND FLAYER	Cloth Head	102 Armor, +24 INT, +9 SPI, +15 STA
Equip: Increases damage and healing done by magical spells and effects by up to 35 Equip: Improves your chance to get a critical strike with spells by 2%		
NELTHARION'S TEAR	Trinket	
Equip: Increases damage and healing done by magical spells and effects by up to 44 Equip: Improves your chance to hit with spells by 2%		
NEMESIS ROBES	Cloth Chest	116 Armor, +16 INT, +8 SPI, +26 STA, +10 Fire Resistance, +10 Nature Resistance
Equip: Improves your chance to get a critical strike with spells by 1% Equip: Increases damage and healing done by magical spells and effects by up to 32 Class: Warlock		
NETHERWIND ROBES	Cloth Chest	116 Armor, +26 INT, +8 SPI, +16 STA, +10 Fire Resistance, +10 Nature Resistance
Equip: Improves your chance to get a critical strike with spells by 1% Equip: Increases damage and healing done by magical spells and effects by up to 32 Class: Mage		
PRESTOR'S TALISMAN OF CONNIVERY	Neck	+30 AGI
Equip: Improves your chance to hit by 1%		
PURE ELEMENTIUM BAND	Ring	+10 INT, +10 SPI, +9 STA
Equip: Increases healing done by spells and effects by up to 53		
ROBES OF TRANSCENDENCE	Cloth Chest	116 Armor, +27 INT, +16 SPI, +17 STA, +10 Fire Resistance, +10 Nature Resistance
Equip: Increases healing done by spells and effects by up to 57 Class: Priest		
STAFF OF THE SHADOW FLAME	Staff	141-247 Damage, Speed: 3.20, 60.6 damage per second, +29 INT, +24 STA, +18 SPI
Equip: Improves your chance to get a critical strike with spells by 2% Equip: Increases damage and healing done by magical spells and effects by up to 84		
STORMRAGE CHESTGUARD	Leather Chest	225 Armor, +25 INT, +17 SPI, +20 STA, +10 Fire Resistance, +10 Nature Resistance
Equip: Improves your chance to get a critical strike with spells by 1% Equip: Increases healing done by spells and effects by up to 42 Class: Druid		
THERAZANE'S LINK	Mail Waist	295 Armor, +12 INT, +12 SPI, +22 STA, +44 Attack Power
Equip: Improves your chance to get a critical strike by 1%		

NEFARIAN'S HEAD

Much like Onyxia, Nefarian always drops a Head of Nefarian in addition to his other loot when he is killed.

The Head is used to start the *The Lord of Blackrock* quest. The quest asks you to bring his head to the throne room of your capital city. The rewards for each side are identical and very desirable:

Again, just like Onyxia, the head will be displayed in the city and everyone nearby will receive the Rallying Cry of the Dragonslayer buff.

ITEM	DESC	STATS
MASTER DRAGONSLAYER'S MEDALLION	Neck	+14 AGI, +24 STA
Equip: Increases Defense +7		
MASTER DRAGONSLAYER'S ORB	Off-Hand	+14 INT, +10 STA
Equip: Increases damage and healing done by magical spells and effects by up to 28		
MASTER DRAGONSLAYER'S RING	Ring	+14 STA, +48 Attack Power
Equip: Improves your chance to hit by 1%		

THE DEADMINES

Played & Written by: Michael "Kayal" Lummis of <Dovrani> on Kirin Tor

For Alliance members who are passing their 20th level and are interested in learning about complex grouping strategies and the greater challenges of World Dungeons, there's a place that provides all that and more: The Deadmines. In the town of Moonbrook, in southwestern Westfall, there's a place of infamy where the Defias Brotherhood launches its foul plans to disrupt Stormwind's fine Kingdom. Its leader is Edwin VanCleef, a former man of esteem and respect who has turned to crime and murder most foul. To make a greater name for yourself, or simply to end his terror, gather four companions and seek the Deadmines!

DUNGEON INFORMATION

Location	Westfall
Quests	Alliance
Region	Alliance
Suggested Levels	18-23 (Full Group)
Group Allowed	5 to Quest, 10 to Raid
Primary Enemies	Humanoids
Time to Complete	2-3 Hours

⊗ GETTING TO THE DEADMINES

It doesn't take much work to reach The Deadmines. Characters are often in Westfall at earlier levels, so it's likely that you already have a fair bit of the map filled out. Even if you don't, the roads take you everywhere you need to go. Sentinel Hill (which is near the inn & flight point) is on the eastern side of the area, just off the road. From there, either take the road south then west until you reach Moonbrook or cut directly southwest from Sentinel Hill.

For Horde characters wishing to venture into Westfall, take the Zeppelin to Grom'Gol in Stranglethorn Vale. If you don't know anyone with higher level characters to help escort your group through the enemies of this area, ask a Shaman to buff your group with Water Walking and run north along the coastal waters, outside the aggro range of the enemies on the shore.

Once in Moonbrook, look for a somewhat small building on the southwestern side of town. There are Defias everywhere, but they're low level and no threat by the time a group is ready to take on this dungeon. Look inside the building in that corner of town and head into its depths. There is a somewhat substantial lead-in piece before you reach the instance itself, so warm up your group by fighting the enemies you aggro on the way in.

This lead-in area has many non-elite miners, a few patrolling elite foes, and at least four good spawns of ore (copper and tin); it's a decent place for folks to harvest material for Blacksmiths and Engineers.

WHO TO BRING

The Deadmines is a very exciting instance, filled with a number of fun events and enjoyable fights. The patrols in the instance are carefully designed to be a bit tricky, especially for newcomers, and it's possible to end up with a couple of enemy groups at the same time. This makes it quite useful to have extra crowd control or tanking abilities when handling the instance. It's always great to have a Mage in here, for Polymorphing duties and added firepower. Rogues are likely to join in the fun as well (because they are useful for Sapping and DPS and because there are a number of solid drops and reward items for them in here).

POSSIBLE GROUP MAKEUP

Tank	Warrior, Druid, Paladin
Crowd Control	Rogue, Mage
DPS	Rogue, Hunter, Mage, Warlock
Healer	Priest, Shaman, Druid
Free Slot	A Secondary Tank or CC Character is Wonderful to Have

QUESTS

There are only Alliance quests for Deadmines and they can be gathered from Stormwind City, Ironforge, and Sentinel Hill in Westfall.

QUEST NAME	QUEST GIVER	QUEST GIVER LOCATION	QUEST RECEIVER	QUEST RECEIVER LOCATION	CHAIN?	MAX EXPERIENCE
Collecting Memories	Wilder Thistlenettle	Stormwind	Wilder Thistlenettle	Stormwind	No	1,350
REWARD: Tunneler's Boots (Mail Feet, 111 Armor, +3 STA, +2 SPI) or Dusty Mining Gloves (Leather Hands, 46 Armor, +3 STR, +2 AGI)						
Oh Brother	Wilder Thistlenettle	Stormwind	Wilder Thistlenettle	Stormwind	No	1,550
REWARD: Miner's Revenge (Two-Hand Axe, 13.0 DPS, +6 SPI)						
Underground Assault	Shoni the Shilent	Stormwind	Shoni the Shilent	Stormwind	No	1,550
REWARD: Polar Gauntlets (Mail Hands, 104 Armor +5 STR) or Sable Wand (Wand, 16.9 DPS)						
Red Silk Bandanas	Scout Riell	Atop Sentinel Hill Tower	Scout Riell	Atop Tower	N	2650
The Defias Brotherhood	Gryan Stoutmantle	Westfall	Gryan Stoutmantle	Westfall	Yes	2,600
REWARD: Chausses of Westfall (Mail Legs, 173 Armor, +11 STR, +5 STA) or Tunic of Westfall (Leather Chest, 92 Armor +11 AGI, +5 STA) or Staff of Westfall (Staff, 20.5 DPS, +5 INT, +11 SPI)						

COLLECTING MEMORIES

Quest Level	14 to Obtain
Location	Stormwind
Contact	Wilder Thistlenettle
Goal	Retrieve 4 Miner's Union Cards
Max Experience Gained	1,350

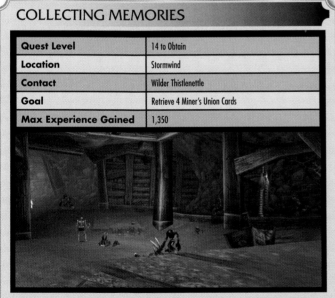

Go to the Dwarven District of Stormwind and walk to the tavern on the eastern side of the quarter (near the Hunter's Guild). Wilder Thistlenettle is in there and he gives two Deadmines quests to people who offer to help him.

This marks one of the easier quests to handle for the Deadmines, and it can be accomplished before you even enter the instance. Travel to the southern section of the mines and search the purple-colored section of the map for the many undead enemies who live there. Kill them and collect the Miner's Union Cards that drop. It should not take too long to get enough for any single member of your group. Do this while fighting back to kill the named mob for the *Oh Brother* quest.

OH BROTHER...

Quest Level	15 to Obtain
Location	Stormwind
Contact	Wilder Thistlenettle
Goal	Find Thistlenettle's Badge
Max Experience Gained	1,550

As with *Collecting Memories*, go to the Dwarven District of Stormwind and walk to the tavern on the eastern side of the quarter (near the Hunter's Guild). Find Wilder Thistlenettle.

Wilder gives you this second quest. While you're collecting the Miner's Union Cards, he wants you to keep an eye out to learn what happened to his brother (who was an explorer). Sadly, his brother came to just as foul an end as the miners, and now walks the very southern part of the outer mine as an undead monster. Look for Foreman Thistlenettle, and give him peace by destroying his undead form. Retrieve Thistlenettle's Badge, and return that to his brother after you leave the mines.

It's far easier to complete *Oh Brother* and *Collecting Memories* than the instance. A group of characters (levels 17-18) that are interested in the quest rewards can fight to the back of the mine and complete these quests.

UNDERGROUND ASSAULT

Quest Level	15 to Obtain
Location	Stormwind
Contact	Shoni the Shilent
Goal	Retrieve the Gnoam Sprecklesprocket
Max Experience Gained	1,550

To begin this quest line, speak with Gnoarn in Ironforge; he's in Tinker Town with the refuge leaders of Gnomeregan. He'll tell you about Shoni, who lives in Stormwind and needs help with an important quest. Shoni is in the Dwarven District, standing a tad north of the Blacksmithing area.

Speak to Shoni and she'll explain what's needed to help the Gnomes keep their interesting machines up to spec. There's a functional Goblin Shredder in the Deadmines, and that means this device has an intact power supply. The Gnomes want it and Shoni wants you to retrieve it by hook or by crook.

The Goblin Shredder is inside the Deadmines instance, found about halfway through (in the Mast Room). As with the greater quest to find and kill Edwin VanCleef, you need to have allies who are experienced and trustworthy to attempt this!

RED SILK BANDANAS

Quest Level	15 to Obtain
Location	Sentinel Hill at the Top of the Tower
Contact	Scout Riell
Goal	Bring 10 Red Silk Bandanas to the scout
Max Experience Gained	2,650

Collecting the red silk bandanas is a simple collection quest that you'll complete just by going through the mines. There are plenty of Defias in the Deadmines both before you enter the instance and within. If you have a full group of five in need of bandanas, consider clearing out as many Defias as possible even before entering the instance to increase your chances that everyone will complete this quest.

THE DEFIAS BROTHERHOOD

Quest Level	14 to Obtain
Location	Westfall
Contact	Gryan Stoutmantle
Goal	Return with VanCleef's Head
Max Experience Gained	2,600

This is available at the end of a Westfall quest chain bearing the same, consistent name (*The Defias Brotherhood*). Talking to Gryan starts it off. First, fly to Lakeshire to speak with Wiley (upstairs in the Lakeshire Inn). Upon returning to Westfall, you're sent to Stormwind to talk with Mathias Shaw of SI:7 (in the Barracks in Old Town, Stormwind). The first difficult quest of the chain is given on your return: find and kill the Defias Messenger to snag an important letter.

This messenger is found between the road out of Moonbrook and the two Defias mines along the coastal cliffs of Westfall. It's a long patrol route, but it often doesn't take too long to find the Messenger (ask for help from others who may be looking and band together if you find such a group, since the drop item is shared by everyone).

The next stage is an escort quest between Sentinel Hill and a building deep in Moonbrook (the secret entrance to the Deadmines). The Defias Traitor stands near the tower on Sentinel Hill. Gather an ally or two and begin the quest. Stay close to the traitor and move along the road until you approach Moonbrook. At this point, get a bit ahead of the former Defias man and kill anything that gets in your way. Be especially quick to bring down the Defias Pillagers (they will kill the Traitor quickly if you cannot get their attention).

With the town cleared, the Traitor should arrive at the entrance to the Deadmines and show you where it is; your quest is complete. Return to tell Gryan and then gather a full force. It'll take everything that you have to enter the Deadmines and kill Edwin VanCleef. He's at the very back of the dungeon, and he's guarded by many elite foes. Imagine a fight with five enemies (all elite, and all between levels 20-22). If that sounds tough but possible, you're ready!

Follow the dungeon walkthrough to make your way back to VanCleef, kill him, and bring proof of the kill back to Gryan for one of the three fine rewards he's offering.

ENEMIES IN THE DEADMINES

GENERAL ENEMIES

NPC	LEVEL
Defias Blackguard	19-20 Elite
Notes: Stealth, Linked with Mr. Smite and Edwin VanCleef	
Defias Conjurer	15-16 Elite
Notes: Mage, Patroller	
Defias Evoker	17-18+
Notes: Mage, Patroller	
Defias Henchman	15-16 Elite
Notes: Patroller	
Defias Magician	16-17 Elite
Notes: Mage, Patroller	
Defias Miner	17-18
Notes: Non-Elite, Set Location, Pierce Armor (50% Armor Debuff, 20 Seconds)	
Defias Overseer	17-18 Elite
Notes: Patroller	

NPC	LEVEL
Defias Pirate	19-20 Elite
Notes: Patrols, Has Pet (Defias Companion Level 15, Self-Enrage)	
Defias Squallshaper	19-20 Elite
Notes: Mage	
Defias Strip Miner	18-19
Notes: Non-Elite, Set Location, Pierce Armor (50% Armor Debuff, 20 Seconds)	
Defias Taskmaster	18-19 Elite
Notes: Patroller	
Defias Watchman	16-17 Elite
Notes: Patroller	
Defias Wizard	18-19 Elite
Notes: Mage, Patroller	
Defias Worker	16-17
Notes: Set Location, Sunder Armor	

NPC	LEVEL
Goblin Engineer	18-19 Elite
Notes: Have Ranged Weapons, Summon Pet (Remote Control Golem Level 18)	
Goblin Shipbuilder	19-20 Elite
Goblin Woodcarver	17-18 Elite
Notes: Can Use Ranged Weapons, Cleave	
Skeletal Miner	17-18 Elite
Notes: Undead, Drops Quest Item for Collecting Memories	
Undead Dynamiter	17-18 Elite
Notes: Undead, Drops Quest Item for Collecting Memories	
Undead Excavator	17-18 Elite
Notes: Undead, Cast "Call of the Grave" (Short Casting Time 1.5, Deals Damage after 60 Seconds), Drops Quest Item for Collecting Memories	

THE MASTERS OF THE DEADMINES

NPC	LEVEL	FREQUENT DROP(S)
Brainwashed Noble	14-18	Girdle of Nobles (Cloth Belt, 18 Armor, +3 INT, +2 STA), Staff of Nobles (Staff, 11.9 DPS, +2 STA, +4 SPI)
Notes: Rare Spawn		
Captain Greenskin	20 Elite	Emberstone Staff (Staff, 19.7 DPS, +5 STA, +8 INT, +5 SPI), Impaling Harpoon (Polearm, 14.4 DPS, +7 AGI), Blackened Defias Belt (Leather Waist, 45 Armor, +5 STR)
Notes: High Hit Points, Linked with Pirate Patrol, Cleave		
Cookie	20 Elite	Cookie's Stirring Rod (Wand, 22.3 DPS), Cookie's Tenderizer (One-hand Mace, 10.5 DPS, +3 STR), Cat Carrier (Siamese)
Notes: Acid Splash		
Edwin VanCleef	22 Elite	Blackened Defias Armor (Leather Chest, 94 Armor, +4 STR, +3 AGI, +11 STA), Cape of the Brotherhood (Cloak, 21 Armor, +6 AGI, +3 STA), Corsair's Overshirt (Cloth Chest, 42 Armor, +5 STA, +11 SPI), Cruel Barb (One-hand Sword, 15.5 DPS, Equip: +12 Attack Power)
Notes: Linked with 2 Blackguards, Spawns 2 More Blackguards at Low Health, Dual-Wield, High Hit Points, Drops 2 Quest Items (The Defias Brotherhood & An Unsent Letter)		
Foreman Thistlenettle	20 Elite	Foreman's Gloves (Leather Hands, 48 Armor, +5 STR), Foreman's Boots (Cloth Feet, 24 Armor, +4 STA, +2 INT), Foreman's Leggings (Mail Legs, 147 Armor, +3 STA, +3 AGI, +3 SPI)
Notes: Undead, Drops Quest Item for Oh Brother		
Gilnid	20 Elite	Lavishly Jeweled Ring (Ring, +2 AGI, +6 INT), Smelting Pants (Leather Legs, 69 Armor, +5 STA, +4 SPI)
Notes: High Hit Points		
Marisa du'Paige	18 Elite	Walking Boots (Cloth Feet, 22 Armor, +3 INT, +2 AGI), Noble's Robe (Cloth Chest, 32 Armor, +1 STR, +3 STA, +3 SPI)
Notes: Rare Spawn		
Miner Johnson	19 Elite	Gold-Plated Buckler (Shield, 471 Armor, 9 Block, +2 AGI, +5 STA), Miner's Cape (Back, 16 Armor, +3 STA)
Mr. Smite	21 Elite	Smite's Mighty Hammer (Two-hand Mace, 19.7 DPS +11 STR, +4 AGI), Smite's Reaver (One-hand Axe, 11.1 DPS, +2 STR, +1 STA, +1 SPI), Thief's Blade (One-hand Sword, 11.2 DPS, +3 AGI)
Notes: Linked with 2 Blackguards, Uses Multiple AoE War Stomps to Stun Group, Changes Weapons, High Hit Points, Can Stun w/ 2H Hammer		
Rhahk'Zor	20 Elite	Rhahk'Zor's Hammer (Two-hand Mace, 11.9 DPS), Rockslicer (Two-hand Axe, 13.8 DPS, +7 STR)
Notes: High Hit Points		
Sneed	21 Elite	Taskmaster Axe (Two-hand Axe, 19.6 DPS, +8 STA, +8 SPI), Gold-flecked Gloves (Cloth Gloves, 22 Armor, +4 STR, +3 INT)
Notes: Spawns when Sneed's Shredder dies		
Sneed's Shredder	20 Elite	Buzz Saw (One-hand Sword, 10.4 DPS, +2 STR, +2 AGI)
Notes: Patrols, Drops Quest Item for Underground Assault, Distracting Pain, Terrify		

THE OUTER MINES

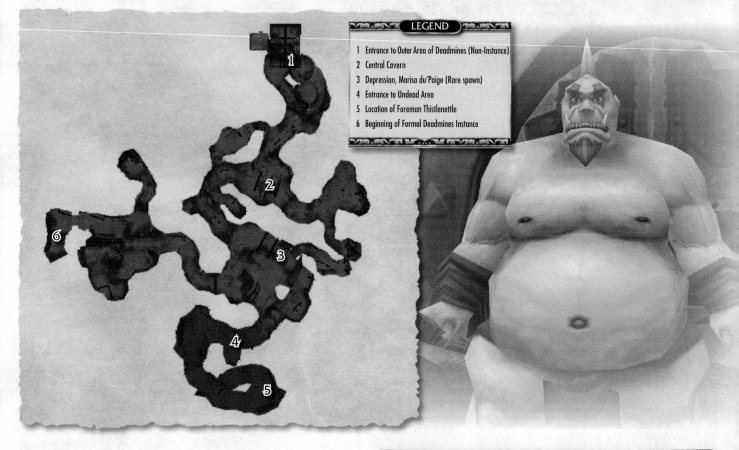

The initial area that leads into the Deadmines is not an instance at all. First, you have to pass a number of miners (not elite), and a number of patrollers who are far more powerful but very low level compared to future challenges.

Miners in the area are always close to the walls and busy at work. Though it's a given that you are going to aggro many of them, these weaker enemies can be brought down quickly. The only time they pose a threat is when they join during fights against the patrolling, elite enemies in the region. Once the Miners (and future non-elite workers) in the mines join, they try to debuff people's armor, and that can be quite painful if there is already an elite Henchmen whacking you.

Try to clear Miners quickly and efficiently so that Henchmen who are wandering back and forth can be taken down when they're alone or only near a single Miner. At this point, a group that's serious about doing the entire Instance and all Deadmines quests shouldn't have any trouble killing several Miners and a Henchmen at the same time (future fights will be against much higher-level opponents). If your group is having problems, it's best to shoot for getting the *Collecting Memories* and *Oh Brother* quests done this time and wait a few levels before coming back.

MINING IN THE DEADMINES

There is tin and copper all over the place in this region, so feel free to take a whack at things here and there after your group has dispatched the enemies in the various caverns.

Make sure to ask the group leader if they're comfortable with that before rushing off to grab those nodes, however, since some people aren't interested in sparing the time for such things. Go with the will of the group, since it's far more important to keep everyone happy than to cause dissent before even reaching the instance.

The approach to the central cavern doesn't take very long. Patrollers have long paths, the fights are short, and there aren't special enemies with which to contend. Clear the Miners and take a look around the large cavern that soon looms ahead. The eastern path is a longer one that isn't necessary. It's the western path (to your right) that doesn't take long to reach either the branch for the instance or the tunnel into the undead area.

It's at this time that you start to see a tad more variety in the enemies. Defias Conjurers patrol along with the Henchmen here. That provides more potential for a couple elites in the same fight and the problem of ranged opponents. Practice group dynamics here to minimize pulls and keep the fights in areas where you can see enemies approaching.

RANGED PULLING

It's always easier to pull enemies at range. This limits the problem of grabbing extra targets due to proximity aggro. Instead, only the creatures that link with the attacked target will head over to fight you (since they are covering the distance, you even have time to react if anything unexpected joins).

Though young Mages may be eager to pull at long range with their potent bolts, it's better to have someone tough use a simple, ranged attack to get a foe's attention. This way, it is easier for the group to assign aggro to the tanks instead of fighting to peel enemies off of a caster right from the start.

When a caster engages your group unexpectedly (perhaps by wandering down the tunnel when everyone is already engaged), consider having the person being attacked pull back and continue retreating until the Mage comes into the group attack range. This way, nobody has to run ahead and aggro extra Miners while trying to stop the caster. As long as the way behind you is clear, this tactic is very sound.

THE GREAT DEPRESSION

The second large cavern is dominated by a giant depression. This cavern has two Defias Magicians at the bottom of the depression and a woman named Marisa du'Paige (a rare spawn). Bring down the casters first if you wish to kill Marisa, then turn to her once the lower area is clear of these higher-DPS targets.

Another good rule that should be put into practice now, even though it isn't as important until later, is to wait each time you enter a large room and watch the enemies who are moving around. Because of the longer patrol ranges that enemies have in and around instances, a room may only have a fraction of its total defenders when you first enter it. Do these checks from time to time before advancing; once you're inside the instance, it's critical to take down patrollers before engaging in some of the larger fights, and waiting for them to come to you is the key.

UNDEAD MINERS: CHEAP LABOR!

If you're doing *Oh Brother* and *Collecting Memories*, avoid the next split to the right from the depression room (this is the tunnel that leads to the instance). Instead, take the passage on the far side of the room the leads south into the purple part of the map.

The fights are a tad more challenging in the undead area, and this makes it a bit bitter for ramping up your group (these battles are closer to what you'll see early in the proper instance). Try to interrupt the Undead Excavators when they try to cast their damage curses (or have a Druid/Mage remove the curse), and advance slowly to prevent fights from escalating in size. Pulls of two or three enemies should be quite manageable, and ranged attacks ensure that those numbers don't blossom.

Deeper into the southern part of the caverns are more concentrated undead. If there's anyone of slightly lower-level in the group, make sure they don't stay near the front of the party and accidentally aggro enemies in the tunnels.

While killing the undead, look for the Miner's Badges. They drop about one time for every four kills. If your entire groups needs to do this quest, it may take some time to complete everything, which is why a number of people come here to do that quest before even considering going after VanCleef.

At the back corner of the undead section is a small, open area with Foreman Thistlenettle. It's pretty easy to grab him with only a single add. Killing this poor creature and looting it completes your requirements for *Oh Brother*.

TO THE INSTANCE!

There are Watchmen and Magicians patrolling the passage that heads west toward the instance. Take this route from the depression chamber and look down (to the right) when you come to a small bridge. The glowing, blue portal below is the gateway into the instance. Enemies can't follow you through that from either side, so it's perfectly side to drop down and rush through if you want to avoid a couple encounters. Otherwise, slay the Defias Workers as you come to them and keep an eye out for the wandering casters.

⟳ THE INNER MINES

LEGEND

1 Entry Room
2 Open Chamber
3 Rhahk'Zor's Room
4 Miner Johnson
5 Mast Room
6 Goblin Foundry
7 Defias Gunpowder
8 Doors to Hidden Harbor

Patrols are more frequent, complex, and dangerous from this point forward. The higher-level elite and generic enemies inside the instance make it important to pay close attention to what's nearby. Add to this that there are specific points where patrols spawn behind you, and it's clear that your group needs to be serious from this point forward.

There are many Defias Miners in the entry. These are higher in level than the workers you fought previously, and their more powerful armor debuff adds immense pain to attacks if your lead tank is affected. Pull warily to create pockets of open area for safe fighting against patrols, then wait for the Overseers to come to you. Try to make even more room before going after Evokers, since they bring range and even more DPS to a fight.

The good news is that the way forward is linear, so you won't have to worry about taking the wrong path or making mistakes in that sense. Clear the first room, move on to the open chamber beyond, and repeat the process. Critters (rats to be specific) skitter around the floor, and can be used for rage or similar such benefits when between fights. The open chamber has three patrollers (two Overseers and an Evoker).

HE CERTAINLY ROCKS

The small, red room at the end of the long tunnel has a powerful Ogre living there. Rhahk'Zor is Level 19+ and has enough hit points to last for quite some time against similarly-leveled opponents, or even those who have substantially outleveled him. Notice that there are two Syndicate Watchmen here as well; they're linked to Rhahk'Zor (any pull will bring all three of these foes).

Bring down the Watchmen with concentrated attacks as soon as your tank has secured aggro, and make sure to eliminate their DPS from the battle quickly. Rhahk takes more time, and in this case that means he's better saved for last. Still, see that he's properly debuffed the whole way through (Demoralizing Shouts, a Thunder Clap, Curses, and any class stuns).

Rhahk'Zor may be tough, but he can't stand up forever once his allies are gone and he's isolated. Stack on as many DoTs as possible, since the fight is long and they provide efficient damage, then keep mitigating as much damage as possible. If your healers tap out of mana, shift aggro onto decent secondary tanks or even the poor leather wearers to keep from having your main tank go down (this person can always run off until aggro is changed). Once Rhahk dies, the door into the eastern hallway opens.

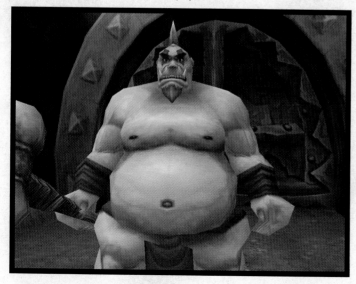

WATCH FOR PATROLS

This is a good time to wait for the patrol that's soon to come from behind while you gather your strength. The patrols often come just as you're heading into a new area after opening a door.

TOWARD THE MAST ROOM

There isn't much new material to worry about while you take the winding tunnel down to the Mast Room in the south. Yet, the small route on the left (halfway down) has a loot mob that is worth fighting. Look town this thick tunnel of Defias Miners and kill Miner Johnson, who is 19+. The Evokers and Overseers in the area aren't terribly powerful compared to the fights ahead.

MOVEMENT DEBUFFS WORK!

The enemies are packed closer together in this hallway, and that raises the chance for a running opponent to find allies. Because of this, it's wise to debuff their run speed early and often. This doesn't take much rage or mana, and even a single case where it prevents an unwanted battle pays for the entire practice.

Down in the south, the hallway ends at a door than can simply be right-clicked to open the way. This reveals the first part of the Mast Room, a place of intense combat. Goblins are busy in here at all times, working on the many projects needed to keep VanCleef's ship in good repair. These Goblins have throwing axes and have learned to support each other well. Expect to fight multiple enemies simultaneously. Combine that with their ability to Cleave and your group suddenly is taking more damage than before; watch out!

Even the first fight in the room is tough because it's almost certainly though you are going to get three Goblin Woodcarvers. Have people in lighter-armor stand back to avoid being the Cleave targets, and (if at all possible) have the main tank hold aggro fiercely to prevent those guys from peeling onto your healers. If said tank is a Warrior, use AoEs early to grab aggro and build fast rage from the many incoming attacks (Demoralizing Shout, a single Thunder Clap, then move into Defensive Stance and immediately Taunt anyone who peels). For tanks with healing (Paladins, Druids, and very explorative Shamans), the use of healing to restore health and get back aggro is effective.

East in the room is the patrolling Shredder that people need to destroy for the Underground Assault quest. Sneed's Shredder is well-constructed, at Level 20+, and can debuff casters with Distracting Pain for a 35% Casting Speed decrease.

Pull the Shredder when it's away from other Goblins (or pull the Goblins and entirely clear the room while the Shredder is away) then fight it in a cleared area. When the machine is destroyed, Sneed himself will pop out of it and attack your group. Easily killed, the Goblin may drop goodies. His Shredder has the Power Core that you seek. During the fight, use armor-reducing attacks heavily to improve melee damage against the Shredder, since it has both high hit points and armor. The far doors out of the Mast Room open after Sneed is killed.

THE GOBLIN FOUNDRY

Before reaching the large Goblin Foundry ahead, there are a few more Human patrols to eliminate. Heed this warning: there is a large patrol in front of you with Taskmasters and an Evoker. Yet, there is also a patrol with Overseers and an Evoker that spawns back before the Mast Room and comes down the tunnel behind you. Clear the early part of these passages and ambush the patrols (don't get caught fighting extra Strip Miners and let multiple wanderers hit you from both sides).

There's much more potential for ranged attacks in the enemies here, since there are Taskmasters, a few Goblin Woodcarvers, and some casters. That makes it all the more important to clear space and have tons of room before major battles. Debuff and ravage all fleeing opponents, as before.

The next door opens into the Foundry. The Goblin Craftsmen on the ramp down don't seem too tough when they aren't using Melt Ore on you, but that AoE hurts (140 damage over time and a 30% movement debuff). Get a strong feel for these rascals as you move down the ramp, and resist any urge to simply jump down to the feel before. Fight all targets methodically and be patient. The Foundry seems simple, but the room is just waiting to have things go wrong for you.

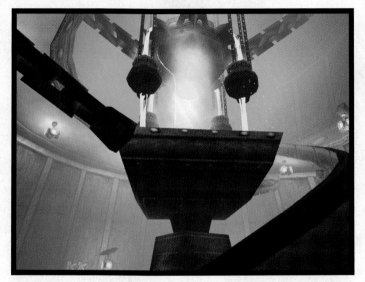

Toward the floor, you start seeing the Goblin Engineers; those guys are pet users, and they bring Level 18 Remote Control Golems into the fray. Engineers also have guns to attack from range (and all of your enemies run when badly wounded). You're probably starting to see how things can go poorly in this room, since the enemies have AoE, range, go for help, and have plenty of backup. Take out the Engineers before even worrying about their pets! They'll just bring another pet to bear if you destroy their first one.

ENGINEERING SUPPLY CRATES

There are a couple spawn points for Engineering Parts boxes in the Foundry. Look for these while heading through for some free items!

Take out foes near the wall and up on the inner circle of the room and pull them back near the ramp each time (giving you more space to react when they flee). Use interrupts to prevent as many Melt Ore attacks as possible, and make your way around to the north end of the chamber.

JUST IN CASE

You probably don't need it, but there is a fully-functional anvil in the Goblin Foundry. If anyone in the group needs a bit of extra equipment, ammunition, or whatever else made, this is the right time and place to deal with it. It also provides a perfect chance for ore collectors to open up a little space in their inventory if they're holding multiple stacks of the same type of ore.

Before the next set of doors is Gilnid the Smelter; this large Goblin brings whatever allies are close to him when pulled, but that won't be too bad as long as you cleared the area well beforehand. The fight itself isn't too bad because it's all about the situation. Gilnid isn't very powerful at all, but his ally potential means a great deal. Without the room cleared, your group would end up in a swarm that has AoE potential and debuffs! Not good, and not safe in the least.

ALMOST TO VANCLEEF'S HIDEOUT

Taskmasters and Strip Miners guard the last stretch of the formal mines. Pull the Taskmasters into cleared areas by having a single, tough character shoot and retreat past the group (as you practiced earlier in the dungeon). This prevents the Taskmasters from bringing a bunch of extra Strip Miners to each fight.

An especially deadly patrol with a Defias Wizard and two Defias Taskmasters is out there, so stay at high health and mana while drawing them forward. These three patrol the entire corridor; once you have a clear section, wait for them to come over to you. A single Overseer is also patrolling and should be stomped any time he is clear of major reinforcements.

WATCH YOUR BACK

With larger patrols being around, it's better than ever to watch your back. This section of narrow corridor makes it impossible to avoid a wandering group that wants to pass through, and you certainly don't want them doing that when you are fully engaged. With the front part of this corridor cleared, wait and ambush all those patrollers before advancing.

The last set of doors is at the end of the tunnel. Though a Rogue can pick the locks there, it's more fun to use the cannon nearby. Search the northern cubby that is just a short run back from the door; there's a barrel of Defias Gunpowder there. Take the powder and have the person who steals it load the cannon at the end of the tunnel. The process is fun to watch and gets the door open in a serious fashion.

Two Defias Pirates rush to see what all the commotion is about when you open the doors, and this is a great time to see how they fight. The Pirates have Level 15 Companions that fight alongside their masters. These pets can Enrage and deal some damage, so it's not like they are a total joke (though the sounds they make are hilarious during the battles).

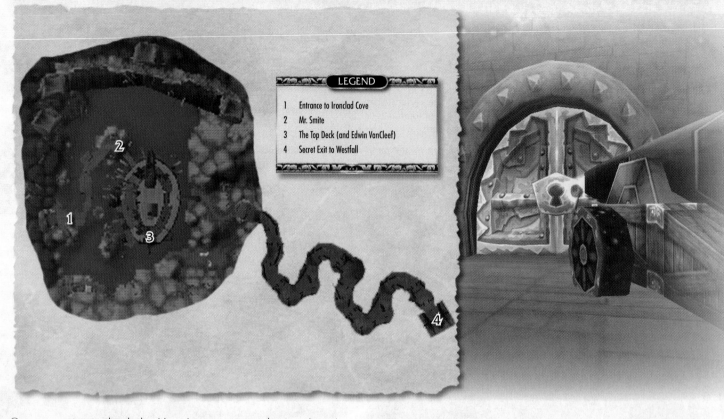

LEGEND

1 Entrance to Ironclad Cove
2 Mr. Smite
3 The Top Deck (and Edwin VanCleef)
4 Secret Exit to Westfall

Once you get onto the docks, it's quite easy to see where you're going. That said, there are a few enemies of interest to the sides if you desire to kill everything that moves in this dungeon. Up on the rocks are Goblin Shipbuilders (they are often Level 19+ and aren't nearly as vicious as some of the other elites in the area).

Patrolling the piers are Pirates (with more birds), and Squallshapers (Mages with Frost Armor, Fire Blast, Frost Nova, and adequate hit points for casters). Stick with ranged pulling and move toward the end of the docks. There is a ramp onto the scaffolding around the ship. Don't walk directly up to this yet. There are two stealthy Defias Blackguards standing by the base of this, and they are fully linked with the Tauren Warrior named Mr. Smite who stands at the top. Buff, restore all hit points and mana, and get any bombs or other goodies onto your quickbars before triggering this intense fight. Mr. Smite doesn't pull any punches.

SHORTCUT TO MR. SMITE

If you want to avoid the pier, simply drop in the water and swim as deep as possible and head to Smite's location. There's a piece of land that allows you to get back on the pier without having to deal with the Pirates and their annoying little birds. Having a Warlock in the party casting Demon Breath is a great chance to avoid a bunch of battles if you're in a hurry.

MR. SMITE

Here's what to expect from the dark-furred Tauren when you begin to fight. Mr. Smite rushes down once the Blackguards are engaged, so hit those lower two with everything you have as quickly as possible. Try to kill the Blackguards without any delay, and let your main tank grab Mr. Smite and the second Blackguard as soon as possible. Don't even try to deal damage to the big guy until the others are down, because he loves to use War Stomp and Stun hapless parties once he starts getting hurt.

With the Blackguards dead, stack DoTs, armor debuffs, and any other goodies onto Mr. Smite. He'll do his first AoE Stun and grab better weaponry after he's taken about one-third of his health. At this stage of the fight, unleash any extra Stuns, Bombs, and other items to make sure that Mr. Smite has fewer options. Then, when the Tauren is down to about one-third of his life, he'll Stun everyone again and grab his two-handed hammer. Now he can do cruel things. Do whatever it takes to finish off Mr. Smite without letting your healer go down. Trade aggro, use healing potions, and keep your fingers crossed.

There are still a few tough fights ahead, but only VanCleef himself can rival the battle you just survived. Rest and cheer your group onward, because it's likely that everyone will succeed at this point.

Climb the scaffolding and fight the remaining Pirates and Squallshapers. There are wandering Shipbuilders as well, but none of this is too bad as long as you look carefully before climbing each level of the scaffolds.

At the top level, parallel to the deck of VanCleef's ship, there's another fight with these general Defias troops. Try not to approach the ship itself while fighting, since Captain Greenskin wanders up there with two buddies. Stay away from that cluster while clearing the scaffolding, then wait for full rest before attacking Captain Greenskin.

The Captain has a Pirate and a Squallshaper with him. Attack the Squallshaper first, for the faster kill, then kill Greenskin second. He has tons of hit points and a Cleave that just isn't fun to see land. Stay away from the small structure on your right while fighting, since Edwin himself is in there, and the worst thing of all would be to draw him out prematurely (though there's enough room that it's unlikely to occur).

EDWIN VANCLEEF

VanCleef is tough. Do not underestimate him or the damage he can withstand; this is a foe who can dish it out and take it as well. Beyond that, there are two Defias Blackguards at his side at all times; later on in the coming fight, two more will arrive, so there are considerable numbers to face here.

The battle itself is not as intricate as the skirmish against Mr. Smite, but there are ultimately five, elite enemies involved and VanCleef does enough damage to make this a battle of attrition. Make sure all potion cooldowns are completed and that your tanks are ready to do everything in their power to survive, hold aggro, and keep as little pressure on the casters as possible early in the fight.

Have secondary healers do the restorative work early in the battle unless things get dire while the tanks build momentum. Kill those two Blackguards first, since it's going to be a long haul and their damage will add up. Those who have damage-efficient DoTs and such should slap them on both Blackguards, and even VanCleef as well (so long as the main tank has solid aggro). This leads to a faster kill of the peripheral fiends.

After the Blackguards drop, turn all firepower onto VanCleef. This is a dead run to kill the guy now, and even when he summons two more Blackguards (at one-third health or thereabout) it's worth sticking on him. Start with any good Stun effects early on, when there are all three targets, and use any additional Bombs/Abilities once the new Blackguards join the fight. When VanCleef finally falls, turn to his second pair of defenders and kill them.

IT'S NOT PRETTY

In a worst-case scenario (where the group isn't going to be able to survive against VanCleef and all four defenders), slay VanCleef first and have everyone grab his head immediately to ensure that the quest is complete. That isn't a pretty way to get things done, and it's almost a certain way to end up with the wrong person getting a superior item drop, but an under-leveled group might have to make such a sacrifice if they feel like the battle is going to turn against them.

Search VanCleef's body to take the Unsent Letter (involved with a Stockades quest chain for the future) and the head of this foul villain. This proves that your group was able to defeat VanCleef and end his traitorous reign.

On the eastern side of the ship, the docks lead to the far side of the cavern. Few enemies are there, but one of the more amusing fights is against a Murloc (Cookie), who drops a very high-DPS wand or mace (you just have to equip the mace). Though the fight is often short against this gurgling monster, his Acid Splash does more than enough damage to give people some pain if the entire group stands close enough to be affected by the AoE.

Once off of the docks, there is a small camp on the rocks below. More importantly, a tunnel leads east and back out of the instance. This dumps the group into a cave that is west from Moonbrook. You won't be able to return to the Instance once you leave the mines, so only take this way out if you are truly interested in leaving.

You won't be able to return to the Instance through this exit, but that shouldn't be a problem because at this point you and your party have defeated VanCleef and ended the Defias threat in Westfall. Thanks to you, the kingdom of Stormwind will sleep a little softer tonight. All hail!

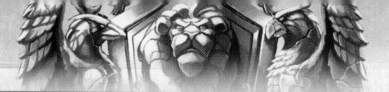

DIRE MAUL

Played & Written by: Edwin "Plainsong" Kern of <Dovrani> on Kirin Tor

Deep in the forests of Feralas lies the Elven fortress of Dire Maul. The fortress is now host to a wide range of residents from Ogres to Ancient Guardians. While it's rumored that some Highborne still reside in the Athenaeum, the mystery surrounding Dire Maul draws adventurers from all over the world. What else lies within the decaying walls?

DUNGEON INFORMATION

Location	Feralas
Quests	Both
Region	Contested
Suggested Levels	55-60
Group Allowed	5
Primary Enemies	Undead, Elementals, Humanoids
Time to Complete	3-5 hours

GETTING TO DIRE MAUL

Horde parties can fly into Camp Mojache and travel west along the road while Alliance parties fly into Thalanar and travel west along the road. In the center of the High Wilderness a path branches north from the road. Take this to the gates of Dire Maul.

WHO TO BRING

With a group limit of 5 people, each character is given the opportunity to shine. Every class has its place in Dire Maul. The thing to keep in mind when forming a group is variety. Having a group of the same class is very challenging.

Several abilities will make your trip easier. Crowd control (Warlock, Mage, Rogue, Priest, Hunter), tanking (Warrior, Paladin), and healing (Priest, Druid, Paladin, Shaman) should be your first choices. Once these are filled, select characters that can bring a healthy does of DPS to round out your party. Another consideration to take into account is that Dire Maul is divided into three distinct wings: East, North and West. Each wing has its own selection of creatures and challenges, so you may want to create a group specifically tailored to an individual wing over trying to compile one with a more well-rounded structure.

A number of the doors in Dire Maul are locked. Killing until you find the key is one option, but there are others. Rogues can pick locks, Blacksmiths can make skeleton keys and Engineers can make explosives.

QUESTS FOR DIRE MAUL

All quests in Dire Maul are Dungeon quests. You don't have to worry about whether or not you are in a Raid group as only 5-man groups can enter the ruins.

ALLIANCE QUESTS

QUEST NAME	QUEST GIVER	QUEST GIVER LOCATION	QUEST RECEIVER	QUEST RECEIVER LOCATION	CHAIN?	MAX EXPERIENCE
The Light and How to Swing It	The Light and How to Swing It	Dire Maul	Lorekeeper Mykos	Dire Maul: Athenaeum	No	7,050
REWARD: Royal Seal of Eldre'Thalas (Trinket, Class: Paladin, +10 Fire Resistance, Passive: +150 Armor, Increases healing done by spells and effects by up to 22)						
Elven Legends	Scholar Runethorn	Feralas: Feathermoon Stronghold	Scholar Runethorn	Feralas: Feathermoon Stronghold	No	8,550
Lethtendris' Web	Latronicus Moonspear	Feralas: Feathermoon Stronghold	Latronicus Moonspear	Feralas: Feathermoon Stronghold	No	7,550
REWARD: Lorespinner (Main-hand Dagger, 37.7 DPS, +5 SPR, +6 INT, +5 STA, Passive: Restores 3 mana every 5 seconds)						
Ancient Equine Spirit	Lord Grayson Shadowbreaker	Stormwind City	Lord Grayson Shadowbreaker	Stormwind City	Yes	4,950

THE LIGHT AND HOW TO SWING IT

Quest Level	60 to obtain
Class	Paladin
Location	Random
Quest Giver	The Light and How to Swing It
Goal	Return the book to Lorekeeper Mykos
Max Experience Gained	7,050
Reward	Royal Seal of Eldre'Thalas (Trinket, Class Paladin, +10 Fire Resistance, Passive: +150 Armor, Increases healing done by spells and effects by up to 22)

The Light and How to Swing It book can be found on the corpses of many of the high level enemies in Dire Maul. Returning the book to Lorekeeper Mykos in the Athenaeum in Dire Maul will earn you both the Royal Seal and his gratitude.

LETHTENDRIS'S WEB

Quest Level	54 to obtain
Class	All
Location	Feralas (Feathermoon Stronghold)
Quest Giver	Latronicus Moonspear
Goal	Retrieve Lethtendris's Web
Max Experience Gained	7,550
Reward	Lorespinner (Main-hand Dagger, 37.7 DPS, +5 SPR, +6 INT, +5 STA, Passive: Restores 3 mana every 5 seconds)

Lethtendris has created a magic web that can drain the energy from entire areas. With all the magic in Dire Maul snared, Lethtendris would be quite dangerous indeed. Kill her and bring the web back to Latronicus so its power can be released back into the world.

ELVEN LEGENDS

Quest Level	54 to obtain
Class	All
Location	Feralas (Feathermoon Stronghold)
Quest Giver	Scholar Runethorn
Goal	Find Kariel Winthalus
Max Experience Gained	8,550

Kariel took great knowledge with him when he fled the destruction of his land. Rumor has it he ran to Dire Maul. Kariel must be found and the knowledge recovered.

Kariel can be found in the Dire Maul Library next to Lorekeeper Mykos.

You must complete this quest prior to attempting any of the Libram quests.

ANCIENT EQUINE SPIRIT

Quest Level	60 to obtain
Class	Paladin
Location	Stormwind City
Quest Giver	Lord Grayson Shadowbreaker
Goal	Gather the Manna-Enriched Horse Feed and Kill Tendris Warpwood
Max Experience Gained	4,950

This is a two part quest. First, you must gather the feed required for a spectral horse and only Merideth Carlson in Southshore has the knowledge you need to get it.

Once you've obtained the Manna-Enriched Horse Feed from Merideth, you must travel to Dire Maul and slay Tendris Warpwood to release the Ancient Equine Spirit. Feeding the spirit the horse feed is all you must do to finish this quest and enchant the barding.

HORDE QUESTS

QUEST NAME	QUEST GIVER	QUEST GIVER LOCATION	QUEST RECEIVER	QUEST RECEIVER LOCATION	CHAIN?	MAX EXPERIENCE
Frost Shock and You	Frost Shock and You	Dire Maul	Lorekeeper Javon	Dire Maul: Athenaeum	No	7,050
REWARD: Royal Seal of Eldre'Thalas (Trinket, Class: Shaman, +10 Fire Resistance, Passive: Increases damage and healing done by spells and effects by up to 23)						
Elven Legends	Sage Gorolusk	Feralas: Camp Mojache	Sage Gorolusk	Feralas: Camp Mojache	No	8,550
Lethtendris' Web	Talo Thornhoof	Feralas: Camp Mojache	Talo Thornhoof	Feralas: Camp Mojache	No	7,550
REWARD: Lorespinner (Main-Hand Dagger, 37.7 DPS, +5 SPR, +6 INT, +5 STA, Passive: Restores 3 mana every 5 seconds)						

FROST SHOCK AND YOU

Quest Level	60 to obtain
Class	Shaman
Location	Random
Quest Giver	Frost Shock and You
Goal	Return the book to Lorekeeper Javon
Max Experience Gained	7,050
Reward	Royal Seal of Eldre'Thalas (Trinket, Class Shaman, +10 Fire Resistance, Passive: Increases damage and healing done by spells and effects by up to 23)

The *Frost Shock and You* book can be found on the corpses of many of the high level enemies in Dire Maul. Returning the book to Lorekeeper Javon in the Athenaeum in Dire Maul will earn you both the Royal Seal and his gratitude.

ELVEN LEGENDS

Quest Level	54 to obtain
Class	All
Location	Feralas (Camp Mojache)
Quest Giver	Sage Gorolusk
Goal	Find Kariel Winthalus
Max Experience Gained	8,550

Kariel took great knowledge with him when he fled the destruction of his land. Rumor has it he ran to Dire Maul. Kariel must be found and the knowledge recovered.

Kariel can be found in the Dire Maul Library next to Lorekeeper Mykos.

You must complete this quest prior to attempting any of the Libram quests.

LETHTENDRIS'S WEB

Quest Level	54 to obtain
Class	All
Location	Feralas (Camp Mojache)
Quest Giver	Talo Thornhoof
Goal	Retrieve Lethtendris's Web
Max Experience Gained	7,550
Reward	Lorespinner (Main-hand Dagger, 37.7 DPS, +5 SPR, +6 INT, +5 STA, Passive: Restores 3 mana every 5 seconds)

Lethtendris has created a magic web that can drain the energy from entire areas. With all the magic in Dire Maul snared, Lethtendris would be quite dangerous indeed. Kill her and bring the web back to Talo so its power can be released back into the world.

SHARED QUESTS

QUEST NAME	QUEST GIVER	QUEST GIVER LOCATION	QUEST RECEIVER	QUEST RECEIVER LOCATION	CHAIN?	MAX EXPERIENCE
Arcane Refreshment	Lorekeeper Lydros	Dire Maul: Athenaeum	Lorekeeper Lydros	Dire Maul: Athenaeum	No	6,600
Codex of Defense	Codex of Defense	Dire Maul	Lorekeeper Kildrath	Dire Maul: Athenaeum	No	
REWARD: Royal Seal of Eldre'Thalas (Trinket, Class: Warrior, +10 Fire Resistance, Passive: +200 Armor)						
Foror's Compendium	Foror's Compendium of Dragon Slaying	Dire Maul	Lorekeeper Lydros	Dire Maul: Athenaeum	Yes	9,950
The Forging of Quel'Serrar	Lorekeeper Lydros	Dire Maul: Athenaeum	Lorekeeper Lydros	Dire Maul: Athenaeum	Yes	None
The Forging of Quel'Serrar	Lorekeeper Lydros	Dire Maul: Athenaeum	Lorekeeper Lydros	Dire Maul: Athenaeum	Yes	None
REWARD: Quel'Serrar (Main-Hand Sword, Class: Warrior, Paladin, 52.5 DPS, +12 STA, Chance on Hit: Grants the wielder 20 Defense and 200 Armor for 10 seconds)						
Dreadsteed of Xoroth	Mor'zul Bloodbringer	Burning Steppes: Altar of Storms	Mor'zul Bloodbringer	Burning Steppes: Altar of Storms	Yes	7,050
Garona: A Study on Stealth and Treachery	Garona: A Study on Stealth and Treachery	Dire Maul	Lorekeeper Kildrath	Dire Maul: Athenaeum	No	7,050
REWARD: Royal Seal of Eldre'Thalas (Trinket, Class: Rogue, +10 Fire Resistance, Passive: Improves your chance to hit by 2%)						
Harnessing the Shadows	Harnessing the Shadows	Dire Maul	Lorekeeper Mykos	Dire Maul: Athenaeum	No	7,050
REWARD: Royal Seal of Eldre'Thalas (Trinket, Class: Warlock, +10 Fire Resistance, Passive: Increases damage and healing done by magical spells and effects by up to 23)						
Holy Bologna: What the Light Won't Tell You	Holy Bologna: What the Light Won't Tell You	Dire Maul	Lorekeeper Javon	Dire Maul: Athenaeum	No	7,050
REWARD: Royal Seal of Eldre'Thalas (Trinket, Class: Priest, +10 Fire Resistance, Passive: Increases healing done by spells and effects by up to 33, Restores 4 mana every 5 seconds)						
The Arcanist's Cookbook	The Arcanist's Cookbook	Dire Maul	Lorekeeper Kildrath	Dire Maul: Athenaeum	No	7,050
REWARD: Royal Seal of Eldre'Thalas (Trinket, Class: Mage, +10 Fire Resistance, Passive: Restores 8 mana every 5 seconds)						
The Emerald Dream…	The Emerald Dream: Fact or Carefully Planned Out Farce Perpetuated by My Brother	Dire Maul	Lorekeeper Javon	Dire Maul: Athenaeum	No	7,050
REWARD: Royal Seal of Eldre'Thalas (Trinket, Class: Druid, +10 Fire Resistance, Passive: Increases healing done by spells and effects by up to 44)						
The Greatest Race of Hunters	The Greatest Race of Hunters	Dire Maul	Lorekeeper Mykos	Dire Maul: Athenaeum	No	7,050
REWARD: Royal Seal of Eldre'Thalas (Trinket, Class: Hunter, +10 Fire Resistance, Passive: +48 Ranged Attack Power)						
Libram of Focus	Libram of Focus	Dire Maul	Lorekeeper Lydros	Dire Maul: Athenaeum	No	None
REWARD: Arcanum of Focus (Use: Permanently adds +8 to your healing and damage from spells to a leg or head slot item. Does not stack with other enchantments for the selected equipment slot)						
Libram of Protection	Libram of Protection	Dire Maul	Lorekeeper Lydros	Dire Maul: Athenaeum	No	None
REWARD: Arcanum of Protection (Use: Permanently adds 1% Dodge to a leg or head slot item. Does not stack with other enchantments for the selected equipment slot)						
Libram of Rapidity	Libram of Rapidity	Dire Maul	Lorekeeper Lydros	Dire Maul: Athenaeum	No	None
REWARD: Arcanum of Rapidity (Use: Permanently adds 1% Attack Speed to a leg or head slot item. Does not stack with other enchantments for the selected equipment slot)						
The Gordok Ogre Suit	Knot Thimblejack	Dire Maul	Knot Thimblejack	Dire Maul	No	6,600
REWARD: Gordok Ogre Suit (Unique, Use: Disguise yourself as one of the Gordok Ogres, and maybe even fool a particular captain in the process! The suit will only hold together for 10 minutes)						
Pusillin and the Elder Azj'Tordin	Azj'Tordin	Feralas: Lariss Pavilion	Azj'Tordin	Feralas: Lariss Pavilion	No	7,750
REWARD: Spry Boots (Leather Feet, 102 Armor, +12 AGI, Passive: Increases your chance to dodge an attack by 1%) or Sprinter's Sword (Two-Hand Sword, 44.3 DPS, Chance on Hit: Increases run speed by 30% for 10 seconds)						
The Madness Within	Shen'dralar Ancient	Dire Maul	Shen'dralar Ancient	Dire Maul	Yes	10,250
The Treasure of the Shen'dralar	Shen'dralar Ancient	Dire Maul	The Treasure of the Shen'dralar	Dire Maul: Athenaeum	Yes	675
REWARD: Blackwood Helm (Mail Head, 301 Armor, +21 AGI, +9 INT, +9 SPI, +13 STR, Passive: Improves your chance to get a critical strike by 1%) or Bonecrusher (Two-Hand Mace, 53.8 DPS, +30 STR, Passive: Improves your chance to get a critical strike by 1%) or Sedge Boots (Leather Feet, 121 Armor, +18 STA, +11 INT, +5 Nature Resistance, +5 Shadow Resistance)						
Unfinished Gordok Business	Captain Kromcrush	Dire Maul	Captain Kromcrush	Dire Maul	No	8,300
Shards of the Felvine	Rabine Saturna	Moonglade	Rabine Saturna	Moonglade	No	8,300
REWARD: Milli's Lexicon (Held-in-Hand, +7 INT, +6 STA, Passive: Restores 6 mana every 5 seconds) or Milli's Shield (Shield, 2106 Armor, 37 Block, +7 SPI, +7 STA, Passive: Restores 3 health every 5 seconds)						

ARCANE REFRESHMENT

Quest Level	60 to obtain
Class	Mage
Location	Dire Maul (North Wing)
Quest Giver	Lorekeeper Lydros
Goal	Retrieve the Hydrospawn Essence
Max Experience Gained	6,600
Reward	Learn Spell: Conjure Water

Lorekeeper Lydros needs a sample from the Hydrospawn in the Warpwood Quarter of Dire Maul. He's willing to teach you to conjure level 60 water as payment.

CODEX OF DEFENSE

Quest Level	60 to obtain
Class	Warrior
Location	Random
Quest Giver	Codex of Defense
Goal	Return the Codex of Defense to Lorekeeper Kildrath
Max Experience Gained	7,050
Reward	Royal Seal of Eldre'Thalas (Trinket, Class Warrior, +10 Fire Resistance, Passive: +200 Armor)

The *Codex of Defense* can be found on the corpses of many of the high level enemies in Dire Maul. Returning the book to Lorekeeper Kildrath in the Athenaeum in Dire Maul will earn you both the Royal Seal and his gratitude.

FOROR'S COMPENDIUM

Quest Level	60 to obtain
Class	Warrior, Paladin
Location	Random
Quest Giver	Foror's Compendium of Dragon Slaying
Goal	Return Foror's Compendium of Dragon Slaying to Lorekeeper Lydros
Max Experience Gained	9,950
Reward	The Dull and Flat Elven Blade

Foror's Compendium of Dragon Slaying is different from the other books found in Dire Maul. The seal has been broken and the book is incomplete. Return the book to Lydros and undertake a quest you won't regret.

THE FORGING OF QUEL'SERRAR

Quest Level	60 to obtain
Class	Warrior, Paladin
Location	Dire Maul
Quest Giver	Lorekeeper Lydros
Goal	Return to Lorekeeper Lydros with the Treated Ancient Blade
Max Experience Gained	7,050
Reward	Quel'Serrar (Main-Hand Sword, Class: Warrior, Paladin, 52.5 DPS, +12 STA, Chance On Hit: Grants the wielder 20 Defense and 200 Armor for 10 seconds)

The end is in sight. Take the Unfired Ancient Blade to Onyxia's Lair. Plant it in the ground in front of her before she breathes fire, kill her quickly, and drive the sword into her corpse to get the Treated Ancient Blade. Return to Lydros for your reward.

THE FORGING OF QUEL'SERRAR

Quest Level	60 to obtain
Class	Warrior, Paladin
Location	Dire Maul
Quest Giver	Lorekeeper Lydros
Goal	Give Lorekeeper Lydros the Dull and Flat Elven Blade
Max Experience Gained	7,050
Reward	Unfired Ancient Blade

Lydros has a difficult quest for you. Give him the Dull and Flat Elven Blade to show him you are interested.

DREADSTEED OF XOROTH

Quest Level	60 to obtain
Class	Warlock
Location	Burning Steppes (Altar of Storms)
Quest Giver	Mor'zul Bloodbringer
Goal	Summon and Capture a Dreadsteed of Xoroth
Max Experience Gained	7,050
Reward	Learn Spell: Summon Dreadsteed

After doing Mor'zul's bidding in Scholomance, he gives you a scroll detailing what you need to accomplish to summon and capture a Dreadsteed of Xoroth.

After doing Mor'zul's bidding in Scholomance, he gives youf a scroll detailing what you need to accomplish to summon and capture a Dreadsteed of Xoroth. The Goblin nearby has many of the items you'll need for the quest. The rest must be done in Dire Maul.

Make the journey to Dire Maul and destroy the mana pylons as if you were only going to kill Immol'thar. You spell must be cast in Immol'thar's Prison and it's doubtful he'll share the space.

GARONA: A STUDY ON STEALTH AND TREACHERY

Quest Level	60 to obtain
Class	Rogue
Location	Random
Quest Giver	Garona: A Study of Stealth and Treachery
Goal	Return Garona: A Study of Stealth and Treachery to Lorekeeper Kildrath
Max Experience Gained	7,050
Reward	Royal Seal of Eldre'Thalas (Trinket, Class: Rogue, +10 Fire Resistance, Passive: Improves your chance to hit by 2%)

Garona: A Study on Stealth and Treachery can be found on the corpses of many of the high level enemies in Dire Maul. Returning the book to Lorekeeper Kildrath in the Athenaeum in Dire Maul will earn you both the Royal Seal and his gratitude.

HARNESSING SHADOWS

Quest Level	60 to obtain
Class	Warlock
Location	Random
Quest Giver	Harnessing Shadows
Goal	Return Harnessing Shadows to Lorekeeper Mykos
Max Experience Gained	7,050
Reward	Royal Seal of Eldre'Thalas (Trinket, Class Warlock, +10 Fire Resistance, Passive: Increases damage and healing done by magical spells and effects by up to 23)

Harnessing Shadows can be found on the corpses of many of the high level enemies in Dire Maul. Returning the book to Lorekeeper Mykos in the Athenaeum in Dire Maul will earn you both the Royal Seal and his gratitude.

HOLY BOLOGNA: WHAT THE LIGHT WON'T TELL YOU

Quest Level	60 to obtain
Class	Priest
Location	Random
Quest Giver	Holy Bologna: What the Light Won't Tell You
Goal	Return Holy Bologna: What the Light Won't Tell You to Lorekeeper Javon
Max Experience Gained	7,050
Reward	Royal Seal of Eldre'Thalas (Trinket, Class: Priest, +10 Fire Resistance, Passive: Increases healing done by spells and effects by up to 33, Restores 4 Mana every 5 seconds)

Holy Bologna: What the Light Won't Tell You can be found on the corpses of many of the high level enemies in Dire Maul. Returning the book to Lorekeeper Javon in the Athenaeum in Dire Maul will earn you both the Royal Seal and his gratitude.

THE ARCANIST'S COOKBOOK

Quest Level	60 to obtain
Class	Mage
Location	Random
Quest Giver	The Arcanist's Cookbook
Goal	Return The Arcanist's Cookbook to Lorekeeper Kildrath
Max Experience Gained	7,050
Reward	Royal Seal of Eldre'Thalas (Trinket, Class: Mage, +10 Fire Resistance, Passive: Restores 8 Mana every 5 seconds)

The Arcanist's Cookbook can be found on the corpses of many of the high level enemies in Dire Maul. Returning the book to Lorekeeper Kildrath in the Athenaeum in Dire Maul will earn you both the Royal Seal and his gratitude.

THE EMERALD DREAM...

Quest Level	60 to obtain
Class	Druid
Location	Random
Quest Giver	The Emerald Dream: Fact or Carefully Planned Out Farce Perpetuated by My Brother
Goal	Return The Emerald Dream: Fact or Carefully Planned Out Farce Perpetuated by My Brother to Lorekeeper Javon
Max Experience Gained	7,050
Reward	Royal Seal of Eldre'Thalas (Trinket, Class: Druid, +10 Fire Resistance, Passive: Increases healing done by spells and effects by up to 44)

The Emerald Dream: Fact or Carefully Planned Out Farce Perpetuated by My Brother can be found on the corpses of many of the high level enemies in Dire Maul. Returning the book to Lorekeeper Javon in the Athenaeum in Dire Maul will earn you both the Royal Seal and his gratitude.

THE GREATEST RACE OF HUNTERS

Quest Level	60 to obtain
Class	Hunter
Location	Random
Quest Giver	The Greatest Race of Hunters
Goal	Return The Greatest Race of Hunters to Lorekeeper Mykos
Max Experience Gained	7,050
Reward	Royal Seal of Eldre'Thalas (Trinket, Class: Hunter, +10 Fire Resistance, Passive: +48 Ranged Attack Power)

The Greatest Race of Hunters can be found on the corpses of many of the high level enemies in Dire Maul. Returning the book to Lorekeeper Mykos in the Athenaeum in Dire Maul will earn you both the Royal Seal and his gratitude.

LIBRAM OF FOCUS

Quest Level	58 to obtain
Class	All
Location	Random
Quest Giver	Lorekeeper Lydros
Goal	Bring 1 Libram of Focus, 1 Pristine Black Diamond, 4 Large Brilliant Shards, and 2 Skin of Shadow to Lorekeeper Lydros
Reward	Arcanum of Focus (Use: Permanently adds +8 to your Healing and Damage from spells to a leg or head slot item. Does not stack with other enchantments for the selected equipment slot)

Lorekeeper Lydros can make you an item to enchant either a leg or head slot item if you bring him the necessary ingredients. This is quite a feat as improving leg and head slot items is fairly rare.

LIBRAM OF PROTECTION

Quest Level	58 to obtain
Class	All
Location	Random
Quest Giver	Lorekeeper Lydros
Goal	Bring 1 Libram of Protection, 1 Pristine Black Diamond, 2 Large Brilliant Shards, and 1 Frayed Abomination Stitching to Lorekeeper Lydros
Reward	Arcanum of Protection (Use: Permanently adds 1% Dodge to a leg or head slot item. Does not stack with other enchantments for the selected equipment slot)

Lorekeeper Lydros can make you an item to enchant either a leg or head slot item if you bring him the necessary ingredients. This is quite a feat as improving leg and head slot items is fairly rare.

LIBRAM OF RAPIDITY

Quest Level	58 to obtain
Class	All
Location	Random
Quest Giver	Lorekeeper Lydros
Goal	Bring 1 Libram of Rapidity, 1 Pristine Black Diamond, 2 Large Brilliant Shards, and 2 Blood of Heroes to Lorekeeper Lydros
Reward	Arcanum of Rapidity (Use: Permanently adds 1% Attack Speed to a leg or head slot item. Does not stack with other enchantments for the selected equipment slot)

Lorekeeper Lydros can make you an item to enchant either a leg or head slot item if you bring him the necessary ingredients. This is quite a feat as improving leg and head slot items is fairly rare.

THE GORDOK OGRE SUIT

Quest Level	56 to obtain
Class	All
Location	Dire Maul
Quest Giver	Knot Thimblejack
Goal	Bring 4 Bolts of Runecloth, 6 Rugged Leathers, 2 Rune Threads, and 1 Ogre Tannin to Knot Thimblejack
Max Experience Gained	6,600
Reward	Gordok Ogre Suit (Unique, Use: Disguise yourself as one of the Gordok Ogres, and maybe even fool a particular captain in the process! The suit will only hold together for 10 minutes)

If you bring Knot the materials, he will fashion a disguise for you. This is used to sneak in, kill and replace the King, and then get tribute from the other ogres. It's good to be the King.

PUSILLIN AND THE ELDER AZJ'TORDIN

Quest Level	54 to obtain
Class	All
Location	Feralas (Lariss Pavilion)
Quest Giver	Azj'Tordin
Goal	Retrieve the Book of Incantations
Max Experience Gained	7,750
Reward	Spry Boots (Leather Feet, 102 Armor, +12 AGI, Passive: Increases you chance to dodge an attack by 1%) or Sprinter's Sword (Two-hand Sword, 44.3 DPS, Chance on Hit: Increases run speed by 30% for 10 seconds)

Azj'Tordin has given up immortality, but he wants his *Book of Incantations* back. An imp by the name of Pusillin stole it from him and is hiding in Dire Maul. Find Pusillin and retrieve the book.

THE MADNESS WITHIN

Quest Level	56 to obtain
Class	All
Location	Dire Maul
Quest Giver	Shen'dralar Ancient
Goal	Kill Immol'thar and Prince Tortheldin
Max Experience Gained	10,250

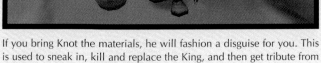

The age of the immortals has passed. Now it is time for the immortals to pass as well. Destroy the five Pylons to bring down the shield around Immol'thar. Kill Immol'thar then confront the Prince.

THE TREASURE OF THE SHEN'DRALAR

Quest Level	56 to obtain
Class	All
Location	Dire Maul
Quest Giver	Shen'dralar Ancient
Goal	Collect the Treasure of the Shen'dralar
Max Experience Gained	675
Reward	Blackwood Helm (Mail Head, 301 Armor, +21 AGI, +9 INT, +9 SPI, +13 STA, Passive: Improves your chance to get a critical strike by 1%), Bonecrusher (Two-hand Mace, 53.8 DPS, +30 STR, Passive: Improves your chance to get a critical strike by 1%), and Sedge Boots (Leather Boots, 121 Armor, +18 STA, +11 INT, +5 Nature Resistance, +5 Shadow Resistance)

The Shen'dralar Ancient knows of only one way to thank you for slaying Immol'thar and Prince Tortheldin. In the Athenaeum is The Treasure of the Shen'dralar. It is yours now.

UNFINISHED GORDOK BUSINESS

Quest Level	56 to obtain
Class	All
Location	Dire Maul
Quest Giver	Captain Kromcrush
Goal	Retrieve the Gauntlet of Gordok Might
Max Experience Gained	8,300

Once you have killed King Gordok and become the new king, the remaining Ogres are friendly to you. Captain Kromcrush will tell you about a gauntlet that Prince Tortheldin stole. He asks you to retrieve it. Prince Tortheldin cannot be attacked until Immol'thar is killed. See the Madness Within to kill Immol'thar.

SHARDS OF THE FELVINE

Quest Level	56 to obtain
Class	All
Location	Moonglade
Quest Giver	Rabine Saturna
Goal	Use the Reliquary of Purity to collect the Felvine Shard
Max Experience Gained	8,300
Reward	Milli's Lexicon (Held In Hand, +7 INT, +6 STA, Passive: Restores 6 mana every 5 seconds) or Milli's Shield (Shield, 2106 Armor, 37 Block, +7 SPI, +7 STA, Passive: Restores 3 health every 5 seconds)

After retrieving the Reliquary of Purity for Rabine, it's time to put it to use. Deep in Dire Maul there are extremely potent Felvines. Find a shard and use the Reliquary to contain it during the trip back to Rabine.

THE INHABITANTS OF A SHATTERED ELVEN STRONGHOLD

ENEMIES OF THE MAUL

NPC	LEVEL
Alzzin's Minion	51-56
Ancient Equine Spirit	60
Arcane Aberration	54-60 Elite
Notes: Arcane Volley	
Arcane Feedback	54-60
Notes: Lightning Shield	
Arcane Torrent	54-60 Elite
Notes: Lightning Storm (AoE)	
Cadaverous Worm	57-60
Frequent Drops: Hero's Belt (Mail Waist, 179 Armor, +13 SPI, +13 STA)	
Carrion Swarmer	52-58
Death Lash	53-58 Elite
Doomguard Minion	54-60
Dread Guard	56-60
Eldreth Apparition	53-58 Elite
Notes: Frost Armor, Cone of Cold (AoE)	
Eldreth Darter	55-59 Elite
Eldreth Phantasm	54-59 Elite
Notes: Shrink (Curse, -58 STR, -58 STA, 2 minute duration), Call of the Grave (2030 Shadow damage after 60 seconds)	
Eldreth Seether	55-59 Elite

NPC	LEVEL
Eldreth Sorcerer	55-59 Elite
Notes: Lightning Bolt	
Eldreth Spectre	53-59 Elite
Notes: Stealth	
Eldreth Spirit	53-58 Elite
Notes: Ribbon of Souls (AoE), Silence	
Eye of Immol'thar	59-61
Fel Lash	48-56 Elite
Gordok Brute	52-60 Elite
Gordok Bushwacker	55-59 Elite
Gordok Captain	57-60 Elite
Notes: Fear	
Gordok Enforcer	47-54 Elite
Gordok Hyena	47-54
Notes: Stealth detection	
Gordok Mage-Lord	52-58 Elite
Notes: Fireball	
Gordok Mastiff	52-59
Notes: Stealth detection	
Gordok Mauler	47-54 Elite
Gordok Ogre-Mage	46-53 Elite
Notes: Fireball	
Gordok Reaver	53-61 Elite
Notes: Cleave	

NPC	LEVEL
Gordok Spirit	60 Elite
Gordok Warlock	54-60 Elite
Highborne Summoner	55 Elite
Hydroling	52-57
Ironbark Protector	53-59 Elite
Mana Burst	54-60
Mana Remnant	52-59 Elite
Notes: Chain Lightning, Blink	
Netherwalker	55-60 Elite
Notes: Detect Stealth	
Old Ironbark	58 Elite
Petrified Guardian	55-59 Elite
Petrified Treant	55-59 Elite
Phase Lasher	46-55 Elite
Notes: Shadowbolt Volley, Fireball Volley	
Residual Monstrosity	54-60 Elite
Rotting Highborne	55-59 Elite
Shen'dralar Spirit	56-58 Elite
Shen'dralar Zealot	59 Elite
Skeletal Highborne	54-58
Wandering Eye of Kilrogg	55-60
Notes: Stealth detection, Summons two Netherwalkers	

NPC	LEVEL
Warpwood Crusher	53-56 Elite
Notes: Crush Armor	
Warpwood Guardian	53-58 Elite
Warpwood Stomper	52-58 Elite
Warpwood Tangler	52-56 Elite
Notes: Entangling Roots, Lightning Bolt	
Warpwood Treant	51-55 Elite
Whip Lasher	49-54
Wildspawn Betrayer	47-56 Elite
Wildspawn Felsworn	47-56 Elite
Wildspawn Hellcaller	51-57 Elite
Wildspawn Imp	51-56
Wildspawn Rogue	51-57 Elite
Wildspawn Satyr	47-56 Elite
Wildspawn Shadowstalker	51-56 Elite
Notes: Stealth, Stealth detection, Slowing Poison (Poison, -20 % attack speed, -34% movement speed, 24 second duration)	
Wildspawn Trickster	55-57 Elite
Xorothian Imp	56-60

THE COMMANDERS OF A SHATTERED ELVEN STRONGHOLD

NPC	LEVEL	FREQUENT DROP(S)
ALZZIN THE WILDSHAPER	56-58 Elite	Energetic Rod (Main-hand Mace, 38.7 DPS, +5 INT, Passive: Increases damage and healing done by magical spells and effects by up to 14), Energized Chestplate (Plate Chest, 617 Armor, +13 STR, +20 STA, +12 INT, Passive: Restores 5 Mana every 5 seconds), Fiendish Machete (One-hand Sword, 38.8 DPS, +5 AGI, Passive: +36 Attack Power when fighting Elementals), Gloves of Restoration (Leather Hands, 105 Armor, +10 STA, +9 INT, Passive: Increases healing done by spells and effects by up to 37), Merciful Greaves (Mail Feet, 240 Armor, +14 INT, +14 STA, Passive: Increases healing done by spells and effects by up to 20), Razor Gauntlets (Plate Hands, 386 Armor, +8 STR, Passive: When struck in combat, inflicts 3 Arcane damage to the attacker), Ring of Demonic Guile (Ring, +10 INT, Passive: Restores 6 Mana every 5 seconds), Ring of Demonic Potency (Ring, +10 STA, Passive: Restores 4 Health every 5 seconds), Shadewood Cloak (Back, 42 Armor, +13 STR, +7 STA, +7 Nature Resistance), Whipvine Cord (Cloth Waist, 47 Armor, +9 INT, Passive: Restores 6 Mana every 5 seconds and Increases healing done by spells and effects by up to 31), Class Books
CAPTAIN KROMCRUSH	56-61 Elite	Boots of the Full Moon (Cloth Feet, 60 Armor, +12 INT, +9 SPI, +12 STA, Passive: Increases healing done by spells and effects by up to 26), Kromcrush's Chestplate (Plate Chest, 777 Armor, +16 STR, +16 STA, +10 Defense), Monstrous Glaive (Polearm, 53.1 DPS, +23 STA, +7 Defense, Passive: Increases your chance to parry an attack by 1%), Mugger's Belt (Leather Waist, +16 STA, +5 Daggers, Passive: Increases your chance to get a critical strike by 1%), Class Books
CHO'RUSH THE OBSERVER	56-60 Elite	Cho'Rush's Blade (One-hand Sword, 40 DPS, +28 Attack Power), Insightful Hood (Leather Head, +15 INT, +9 SPI, +12 STA, Passive: Increases your chance to get a critical strike with spells by 1% and increases healing done by spells and effects by up to 33), Mana Channeling Wand (Wand, 60.9 DPS, Passive: Restores 4 Mana every 5 seconds), Observer's Shield (Shield, 2089 Armor, 38 Block, +14 INT, +5 SPI, +9 STA), Class Books
FERRA	58-60 Elite	Grizzled Mane
GUARD FENGUS	54-59 Elite	Gordok Nose Ring (Ring, +9 STA, +5 STR), Hyena Hide Belt (Leather Waist, +13 STA, +28 Attack Power), Jagged Bone Fist (Main-hand Fist Weapon, 35.8 DPS, +8 STR, +7 STA), Modest Armguards (Mail Wrist, 141 Armor, +10 INT, Passive: Increases healing done by spells and effects by up to 12), Ogre Pocket Knife (One-hand Sword, 35.8 DPS, +7 STA, +16 Attack Power), Unsophisticated Hand Cannon (Gun, 27.8 DPS, +8 STR), Robe of Combustion (Cloth Chest, 77 Armor, +17 INT, Passive: Increases damage done by Fire spells and effects by up to 26), Gallant's Wristguards (Plate Wrist, 249 Armor, +14 INT, Passive: Increases healing done by spells and effects by up to 29), Class Books
GUARD MOL'DAR	54-59 Elite	Gordok Nose Ring (Ring, +9 STA, +5 STR), Hyena Hide Belt (Leather Waist, +13 STA, +28 Attack Power), Jagged Bone Fist (Main-hand Fist Weapon, 35.8 DPS, +8 STR, +7 STA), Modest Armguards (Mail Wrist, 141 Armor, +10 INT, Passive: Increases healing done by spells and effects by up to 12), Ogre Pocket Knife (One-hand Sword, 35.8 DPS, +7 STA, +16 Attack Power), Unsophisticated Hand Cannon (Gun, 27.8 DPS, +8 STR), Robe of Combustion (Cloth Chest, 77 Armor, +17 INT, Passive: Increases damage done by Fire spells and effects by up to 26), Gallant's Wristguards (Plate Wrist, 249 Armor, +14 INT, Passive: Increases healing done by spells and effects by up to 29), Class Books
GUARD SLIP'KIK	55-59 Elite	Gordok Nose Ring (Ring, +9 STA, +5 STR), Hyena Hide Belt (Leather Waist, +13 STA, +28 Attack Power), Jagged Bone Fist (Main-hand Fist Weapon, 35.8 DPS, +8 STR, +7 STA), Modest Armguards (Mail Wrist, 141 Armor, +10 INT, Passive: Increases healing done by spells and effects by up to 12), Ogre Pocket Knife (One-hand Sword, 35.8 DPS, +7 STA, +16 Attack Power), Unsophisticated Hand Cannon (Gun, 27.8 DPS, +8 STR), Robe of Combustion (Cloth Chest, 77 Armor, +17 INT, Passive: Increases damage done by Fire spells and effects by up to 26), Gallant's Wristguards (Plate Wrist, 249 Armor, +14 INT, Passive: Increases healing done by spells and effects by up to 29), Class Books
HYDROSPAWN	52-57 Elite	Tempest Talisman (Neck, +7 INT, +6 SPI, Passive: Improves your chance to get a critical strike with spells by 1%), Waterspout Boots (Leather Feet, 114 Armor, +6 INT, +6 SPI, Passive: Increases damage and healing done by magical spells and effects by up to 25), Class Books, Ace of Elementals
ILLYANNA RAVENOAK	58-60 Elite	Force Imbued Gauntlets (Plate Hands, 538 Armor, +14 STA, +7 Defense), Padre's Trousers (Cloth Legs, 76 Armor, +20 INT, Passive: Restores 6 Mana every 5 seconds and increases healing done by spells and effects by up to 42), Gauntlets of Accuracy (Mail Hands, 204 Armor, +15 AGI, Passive: Improves your chance to hit by 1%), Well Balanced Axe (One-Hand Axe, 36.3 DPS, +11 AGI), Class Books
Notes: Concussion Shot, Multi-Shot, Root		

NPC	LEVEL	FREQUENT DROP(S)
IMMOL'THAR	58-61 Elite	Bile-etched Spaulders (Plate Shoulder, 485 Armor, +17 STR, +6 STA, +6 INT, +7 Defense), Cloak of the Cosmos (Back, 44 Armor, +11 INT, +7 STA, Passive: Increases healing done by spells and effects by up to 26), Demon Howl Wristguards (Mail Wrist, 160 Armor, +17 STA, +14 Attack Power), Evil Eye Pendant (Neck, +15 AGI, +7 Defense), Eyestalk Cord (Leather Waist, 98 Armor, +15 INT, +9 STA, Passive: Increases healing done by spells and effects by up to 35), Odious Greaves (Mail Feet, 251 Armor, +18 STA, +9 INT, +22 Attack Power), Quickdraw Gloves (Leather Hands, 109 Armor, +8 AGI, +7 STR, +7 STA, Passive: Increases your chance to dodge an attack by 1%), Robe of Everlasting Night (Cloth Chest, 88 Armor, +13 INT, +11 STA, +5 SPI, Passive: Increases damage and healing done by magical spells and effects by up to 27), Vigilance Charm (Trinket, Passive: Increases your chance to dodge an attack by 2%), Blade of the New Moon (One-hand Dagger, 40.7 DPS, +5 STA, Passive: Increases damage done by Shadow spells and effects by up to 19), Class Books
KING GORDOK	58-62 Elite	Band of the Ogre King (Ring, +14 STR, +13 STA), Barbarous Blade (Two-hand Sword, 53.9 DPS, +60 Attack Power, Passive: Increases your chance to get a critical strike by 1%), Bracers of Prosperity (Leather Wrist, 77 Armor, +10 INT, +8 STA, +5 SPI, Passive: Increases healing done by spells and effects by up to 22), Brightly Glowing Stone (Held in Hand, +7 STA, Passive: Increases healing done by spells and effects by up to 37), Crown of the Ogre King (Cloth Head, 73 Armor, +18 INT, +11 SPI, +16 STA, Passive: Improves your chance to get a critical strike with spells by 1%), Grimy Metal Boots (Plate Feet, 552 Armor, +17 STR, Passive: Improves your chance to dodge an attack by 1%), Harmonious Gauntlets (Mail Hands, 231 Armor, +5 INT, +5 SPI, +5 STA, Passive: Increases healing done by spells and effects by up to 51), Leggings of Destruction (Mail Legs, 324 Armor, +14 AGI, +13 INT, +20 STA, Passive: Improves your chance to get a critical strike by 1%), Class Books
LETHTENDRIS	52-57 Elite	Felhide Cap (Leather Head, 134 Armor, +21 AGI, +14 STA, +8 Fire Resistance, +8 Shadow Resistance), Quel'dorai Channeling Rod (Staff, 49.6 DPS, +18 INT, +8 STA, +8 SPI, Passive: Restores 8 Mana every 5 seconds), Band of Vigor (Ring, +8 STR, +7 STA, +7 AGI), Lethtendris's Wand (Wand, 50.9 DPS, Passive: Increases damage and healing done by magical spells and effects by up to 9), Class Books
LORD HEL'NURATH	61-62 Elite	Diabolic Mantle (Cloth Shoulder, 66 Armor, +16 STA, Passive: Restores 8 Mana every 5 seconds), Dreadguard's Protector (Shield, 2121 Armor, 39 Block, +18 STR, +5 STA), Fel Hardened Bracers (Plate Wrist, 283 Armor, +12 STR, +12 STA, +3 Defense), Xorothian Firestick (Gun, 31.7 DPS, +6 STA, +4 AGI, +6 Shadow Resistance)
MAGISTER KALENDRIS	56-60 Elite	Elder Magus Pendant (Neck, +10 INT, +7 SPI, +6 STA, +10 Fire Resistance), Flamescarred Shoulders (Leather Shoulder, 131 Armor, +12 AGI, +12 STR, +11 STA, +10 Fire Resistance), Mindtap Talisman (Trinket, Passive: Restores 11 Mana every 5 seconds), Amplifying Cloak (Back, 39 Armor, Passive: Increases damage and healing done by spells and effects by up to 18), Magically Seal Bracers (Plate Wrist, 383 Armor, +3 Defense), Class Books
MUSHGOG	60 Elite	Random Rare Items
PIMGIB	54-56 Elite	Pimgib's Collar (Trinket, Class Warlock, Passive: Increases the damage of your Imp's Firebolt spell by 8), Runecloth
PRINCE TORTHELDRIN	59-61 Elite	Bracers of the Eclipse (Leather Wrist, 76 Armor, +10 AGI, +9 STA, +24 Attack Power), Chestplate of Tranquility (Leather Chest, 174 Armor, +20 INT, +6 SPI, +10 STA, Passive: Increases damage and healing done by magical spells and effects by up to 23), Distracting Dagger (Off-hand Dagger, 40.8 DPS, +6 Daggers), Eldritch Reinforced Legplates (Plate Legs, 566 Armor, +15 STR, +20 STA, +9 AGI, Passive: Increases your chance to get a critical strike by 1%), Emerald Flame Ring (Ring, +12 INT, +8 SPI, +7 STA, Passive: Increases healing done by spells and effects by up to 15), Fluctuating Cloak (Back, 44 Armor, +15 to a random Resistance, Passive: Restores 3 Health every 4 seconds), Mind Carver (Main-hand Sword, 40.8 DPS, +8 INT, Passive: Increases damage and healing done by magical spells and effects by up to 12), Silvermoon Leggings (Mail Legs, 320 Armor, +16 INT, +10 SPI, +16 STA, +6 AGI, Passive: Increases damage and healing done by magical spells and effects by up to 18), Stone Shatter (Crossbow, 31.7 DPS, +4 Crossbows), Timeworn Mace (One-hand Mace, 40.7 DPS, +7 STR, +11 STA)
PUSILLIN	56-57 Elite	Recipe: Runn Tum Tuber Surprise (Requires Cooking (275)), Crescent Key
SKARR THE UNBREAKABLE	55-58 Elite	Random Rare Items
STOMPER KREEG	54-59 Elite	Class Books
Notes: Vendor NPC		
TENDRIS WARPWOOD	55-60 Elite	Tanglemoss Leggings (Leather Legs, 150 Armor, +20 INT, +13 SPI, +12 STA, Passive: Improves your chance to get a critical strike with spells by 1%), Warpwood Binding (Mail Waist, 202 Armor, +14 AGI, +9 INT, +6 STA, Passive: Improves your chance to get a critical strike by 1%), Petrified Bark Shield (Shield, 1861 Armor, 58 Block), Stoneflower Staff (Staff, 47.3 DPS, +24 INT, Passive: Improves your chance to get a critical strike with spells by 1%), Class Books
THE RAZZA	56-60 Elite	Random Rare Items
TSU'ZEE	55-59 Elite	Brightspark Gloves (Cloth Hands, 53 Armor, +15 INT, +9 STA, Passive: Improves your chance to get a critical strike with spells by 1%), Murmuring Ring (Ring, +10 INT, Passive: Increases your resistance to silence by 5%), Threadbare Trousers (Cloth Legs, 68 Armor, +13 STA, Passive: Increases damage done to Undead by magical spells and effects by up to 35)
Notes: Rare Spawn		
XOROTHIAN DREADSTEED	61-62 Elite	Felcloth
ZEVRIM THORNHOOF	52-57 Elite	Fervent Helm (Mail Head, 279 Armor, +14 STA, +15 to random Resistance, Passive: Restores 5 Health every 5 seconds), Helm of Awareness (Plate Head, 493 Armor, +17 STA, Passive: Increases your chance to dodge an attack by 2%), Satyr's Bow (Bow, 29.8 DPS, +7 AGI, Passive: Improves your chance to hit by 1%), Clever Hat (Leather Head, 122 Armor, +11 INT, +10 STA, Passive: Restores 7 Mana every 5 seconds), Gloves of Shadowy Mist (Cloth Hands, 47 Armor, +12 STA, Passive: Increases damage done by shadow spells and effects by up to 19)

AN ANCIENT CITY

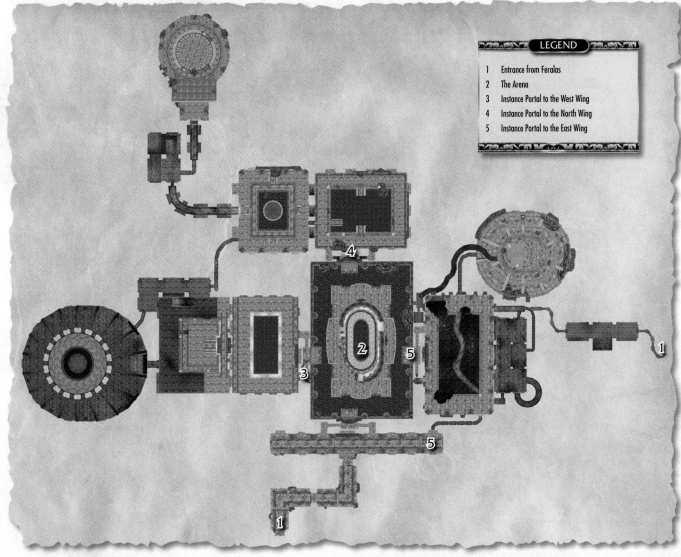

LEGEND

1   Entrance from Feralas
2   The Arena
3   Instance Portal to the West Wing
4   Instance Portal to the North Wing
5   Instance Portal to the East Wing

THE ARENA

The Ogres guarding the entrance from Feralas are much lower than the enemies inside and pose no threat to you. Parties of higher level can bypass these Ogres by moving around them carefully. Keep an eye out for the patrols. They aren't powerful enough to bring your party down, but they can slow you down or add to an existing fight.

There are three monstrous enemies that call the Arena their home: The Razza, Mushgog, and Skarr the Unbreakable. They are rather tough, but the rewards for defeating them are impressive.

THE RAZZA

The two abilities to fear are Poison Bolt and Chain Lightning. The Razza's Chain Lightning deals increasing damage to each consecutive target, so make sure to spread out when tackling this beast. The Poison Bolt inflicts minor initial damage but has a DoT effect as well.

MUSHGOG

Mushgog has three spells: Spore Cloud, Entangling Roots, and Thorn Volley. Entangling Roots is an AoE, damage-inflicting root effect that may last up to 15 seconds. Mushgog's Thorn Volley is an AoE damage and stun spell.

SKARR THE UNBREAKABLE

This mob has three beastly abilities that can crush those within melee range. Keep the casters well back from Skarr. His Mortal Strike deals 300% weapon damage and reduces the healing received by the target. Skarr's Knockdown is a single-target damage ability with a 2 second stun. Cleave can crush a soft target near the tank, so stay back.

An added danger to participating in the Arena battles is that it automatically flags you for PvP regardless of the server type. Roaming groups of enemy factions in Dire Maul can easily spoil your victory. Take time to carefully look around prior to entering into battle within the Arena.

There are several entrances to Dire Maul. Take the one which will best serve your parties goals. Many parties decide this ahead of time and only do one wing at a time.

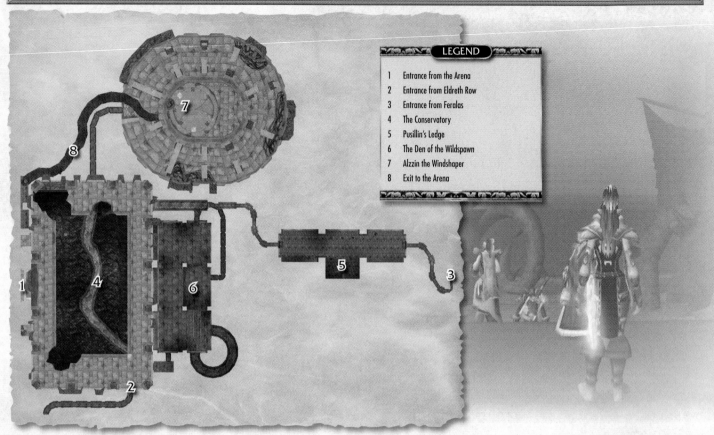

LEGEND

1 Entrance from the Arena
2 Entrance from Eldreth Row
3 Entrance from Feralas
4 The Conservatory
5 Pusillin's Ledge
6 The Den of the Wildspawn
7 Alzzin the Windshaper
8 Exit to the Arena

THE CONSERVATORY

Upon entering, Pusillin stands immediately to your left. It will be quite some time before you can corner him, but confronting him now will send him on his way and keep you from needing to come back.

Speaking with Pusillin triggers the quest for the Crescent Key. Your party has to chase him through half the instance before confronting him after the pursuit. Once you engage, and eventually defeat, Pusillin, you can loot the **Crescent Key** that's used to open many of the doors throughout Dire Maul.

The path ahead is lined with Warpwood Crushers, Phase Lashers, and patrolled by Warpwood Treants and Tanglers. Clearing the enemies slowly and carefully is the key to success.

Warpwood Treants and Tanglers are linked and cannot be separated. Having a Hunter in the party to Freeze Trap one is quite helpful. In the event that you have no CC available, keep the party focused on one enemy at a time.

Warpwood Crushers and Phase Lashers are not linked, but need to be pulled carefully to avoid adds. Crushers have high armor and do high damage, but keeping a Warrior standing in front will keep the party safe. The Phase Lashers have a number of AoE spells and should be killed quickly.

Groups of Whip Lashers are scattered along the path. Pull these and have party members with AoE attacks bring them down all at once.

WHAT DID I JUST STEP IN?

Warpwood Pods grow throughout Dire Maul. Stepping on these, or even stepping too close, can release a variety of effects. Poisons, Entangling Roots, or even mobs of enemies can spew from these innocent looking pods.

However, the pods aren't completely useless. There are two drops that are much sought after: Thornling Seeds and Runn Tum Tubers.

The Thornling Seeds act like Target Dummies with a few differences. Since they're "living," they can be healed (and even shielded). They also cast an AoE taunt that damages nearby foes. The Runn Tum Tubers are used by Cooks to make Runn Tum Tuber surprise.

Move around the room in a counter-clockwise fashion. Confront Pusillin when you get to him and keep him moving. Ignore the passage leading south as it leads to Eldreth Row. Move to the northeast corner to proceed.

CHASING PUSILLIN

Many of the enemies you will fight are now Wildspawn Satyrs. Have your highest level party member move slightly ahead of the party as you move down the eastern passage. Wildspawn Shadowstalkers move around these passages stealthed. When they are spotted, consolidate the party to avoid fighting several enemies at once.

Make sure your healers are ready to take care of the softer members of your party and lay in with the AoE goodness.

The passage opens into a large room with several groups of Wildspawn and roaming Lashers. Pull each group back to the entrance until the path to Pusillin is clear. Confront him and he'll run up a ramp on the south side of the room.

Clear your way to the ramp and ascend. Pusillin is all alone with no where to run. Don't fall for his trick. He's standing beside a Warpwood Pod. Clear the pod and, if you have a Hunter in the party, turn his trick against him before confronting Pusillin. Put down a Freezing Trap to grab one of his friends when they spawn. Now that you have him cornered, Pusillin won't run from you. He calls for help and attacks instead.

Once you've caught up with Pusillin and the Wildspawn Imps that he's called to his side, have your MT grab aggro and AoE the group into dust. The Wildspawn Imps have a nasty Fire Blast spell, but should fall quickly.

Keep someone that can interrupt spells on Pusillin. He has a few spells (Fireball, Fire Blast, and Blast Wave) that can hurt the softer targets in the group. Interrupt his Fireball when possible. A Rogue having a Rank 5 Kick ability can prevent any spells from that line for 5 seconds. The chase may have been annoying, but the reward is great. Pusillin can drop several Crescent Keys. With these, you can move about Dire Maul without needing a Rogue to pick the locks. He also drops the **Book of Incantations** for *Pusillin and the Elder Azj'Tordin*.

Finish clearing the room and take the tunnel east. This tunnel exits Dire Maul under the Lariss Pavilion. Take a moment to complete *Pusillin and the Elder Azj'Tordin* before re-entering Dire Maul.

THE DEN OF THE WILDSPAWN

Move back to the passage exiting the Conservatory. This time, take the southern passage. This room looks very familiar. There are groups of Wildspawn and Lashers scattered throughout the room.

Clear your way south along the east wall. Pull carefully and avoid charging forward. In the southeast corner are both a ramp up and a passage down. Take the ramp up first.

Lethtendris and her assistant, Pimgib, are pacing around a table. Lethtendris has quite an array of spells, but the Void Bolt has a 4 second cast and is interruptible. Shadow Bolt Volley is an AoE shadow damage spell; Curse of Tongues increases the casting time of spells; Curse of Thorns gives a chance that the target will take extra damage on attack. However, keep in mind that all these spells can be shut down with a solid interrupt.

Pimgib has a spell selection exactly like Pusillin: Fireball, Fire Blast, and Blast Wave. Interrupt the Fireball (longest casting time) to prevent her assistant from causing massive damage to the group.

Have an interrupt order for Lethtendris to keep her from bringing her full force against your party. If possible, have the off-tank assigned to Pimgib be a Rogue to offer interrupt abilities against the assistant as well. Lethtendris has nearly 3x as many hit points as Pimgib, so take out the assistant before focusing on his master.

Once they're dead, make sure to collect **Lethtendris' Web**.

Take the circling passage down. This room also has several groups of Wildspawn and Lashers moving about. As before, pull the groups to you and clear the room slowly. In a pool in the center of the room stands Hydrospawn.

Hydrospawn is not as dangerous as the Hydrolings that spawn. Have AoE attacks ready to take out the Hydrolings before they attack your healer. Hydrospawn has the spells Riptide, Massive Geyser, and Submersion (a stacking Stamina debuff that decreases a player's STA by 10 per application).

Kill Hydrospawn and loot the **Hydrospawn Essence** for *Arcane Refreshment*.

With Hydrospawn defeated, move to the passage in the northeast corner. Follow the passage up to find Zevrim Thornhoof. Clear the enemies to the right before you engage Zevrim.

Zevrim is a dangerous opponent. He periodically throws a party member onto the ritual slab and Sacrifices them. This leaches 300 health per second and stuns the target – ready the healers! His other spell, brutal in its own right, is Intense Pain. It's an AoE version of Shadow Word: Pain that deals 200 damage every 3 seconds for 15 seconds. Keep the casters out of range if possible.

A solid tactic is to have a Warlock Enslave either the Wildspawn Shadowstalker or Wildspawn Hellcaller and use them to attack Zevrim. This deals significant damage to Zevrim while maintaining high levels of mana for everyone else in the party. Once the enslaved demon falls, gang rush Zevrim and drop everything you can on him to bring him down in a flash. With Zevrim dead, Old Ironbark can now assist you in the Conservatory. Move down the passage and across the room to the southwest corner. This passage leads to the lower level of the Conservatory.

THE CONSERVATORY (LOWER)

The lower floor of the Conservatory is very dangerous. Death Lashes and groups of Whip Lashers stand guard along both sides of the path forward. Large groups of Warpwood Guardians and Stompers patrol quickly across the path.

Do not run forward. Do not attempt to avoid the patrols. Take your time getting across the room. Pull each group to your party. When fighting the elite enemies, CC and focused fire will keep your party from taking too much damage. AoE attacks will make short work of the non-elite enemies.

Speak with Ironbark the Redeemed and ask him to help you open the door forward. Continue clearing to the north side of the room. Take the passage north.

ALZZIN'S LAIR

The passage opens into a large circular room. Both paths lead down along the edge of the circle. There are Warpwood Crushers guarding along the paths and patrolling. They are always alone, so the fights aren't difficult.

Clear the Crushers until you reach the bottom of the circle. In the center stand Alzzin the Windshaper and several groups of Death Lashes and Whip Lashers. Pull the Lashers to you and clear the room until Alzzin stands alone.

Alzzin the Wildshaper doesn't look tough. In fact, when you begin the encounter, you're lead to believe that illusion. However, the true danger lies in Alzzin's ability to shapeshift.

In his initial form, Alzzin has the spells Thorns, Enervate, and Wither. Thorns reflects damage back to the attacker on a successful melee attack, Enervate drains 200 mana per second from the target (and is considered a Poison effect), and Wither is a damage spell with a Disease effect that decreases the target's strength by 100. Enervate and Wither are interruptible, so take advantage of that when possible.

When he shifts into Tree Form, his armor is increased significantly. Unload everything you have on him when he's in this form. He gains the Wild Regeneration spell while in Tree Form. DoTs and attacks that ignore armor are your most effective weapons against Alzzin's Tree Form. Casting armor reducing spells and using Sunder Armor will help your melee members.

Alzzin can also shapeshift into Dire Wolf Form and gains the Mangle ability; it's a damage DoT with a 20 second snare. This form is extremely dangerous as it increases his damage substantially. When he shifts in the Dire Wolf Form, have all the members refrain from attacking for a moment to give the Warrior (or other MT) enough time to establish the top spot on the threat list. If Alzzin attacks a soft member of the party while in the Dire Wolf Form, it could mean a quick wipe.

When Alzzin is brought down to 35% health, he summons several Lashers to his aid. Use AoE attacks to bring these down quickly. Once Alzzin is defeated, grab the **Felvine Shards** from his hut for *Shards of the Felvine*.

The path behind his hut leads out to the Arena. It's only a short trip home from there. There are typically two to three Rich Thorium Veins in the tunnel leading out of the instance. Make sure your Miners take advantage of these veins.

THE NORTH WING

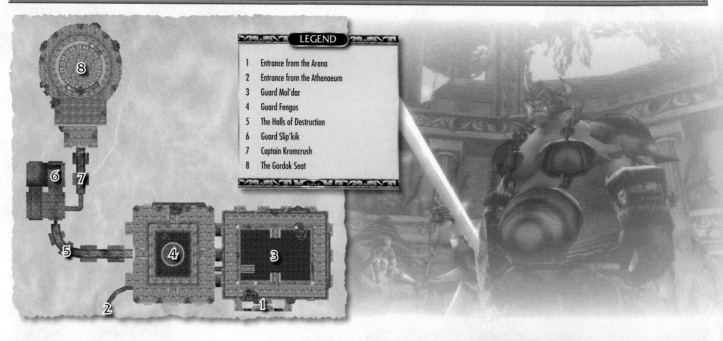

LEGEND	
1	Entrance from the Arena
2	Entrance from the Athenaeum
3	Guard Mol'dar
4	Guard Fengus
5	The Halls of Destruction
6	Guard Slip'kik
7	Captain Kromcrush
8	The Gordok Seat

OGRES

Take a moment to survey the area before moving in. On the upper edge, Gordok Brutes and Mage-Lords stand in small groups with Gordok Mage-Lords and Mastiffs patrolling. On the lower edge, Gordok Brutes and Mage-Lords stand in groups on the left and Gordok Mastiffs stand in groups on the right.

TRIBUTE RUN

If you're in the North Wing for a Tribute Run, the route and actions you take will be slightly different. These will be noted. The most important difference is the named enemies. Avoid them.

Move along the east wall, then the north walls for the next two rooms. Your enemies will be Gordok and Carrion Swarmers. The Swarmers are non-elite and should be killed with AoE attacks.

As the Gordok are humanoid, they're much easier to CC. When fighting them, CC the melee Gordok and kill the caster quickly. Kill the Gordok near the entrance and proceed down the right side of the ramp. Clear the Gordok Mastiffs one group at a time to make room for the fight with Guard Mol'dar. When your party's prepared, pull Mol'dar.

He has melee-focused abilities, so keep your casters back a bit, but keep them close enough not to draw new aggro from other threats in the area. Along with Strike, Shield Bash, and Knock Away, Mol'dar has Shield Charge. Basically, it's like Charge, but has a knockback effect. Get your MT in there and wipe the floor with him.

TRIBUTE RUN

Do not kill Guard Mol'dar. Avoid him as you move along the north wall.

With Mol'dar dead, ascend the northern ramp and clear your way west. Stomper Kreeg is dancing in the northwest corner of the room. Clear the ogres around him and then focus on Stomper Kreeg. He has the abilities War Stomp, Whirlwind, and Booze Spit. Booze Spit intoxicates players and decreases their chances to hit by 75%. After demolishing Kreeg, proceed west into the courtyard.

TRIBUTE RUN

Do not kill Stomper Kreeg. Wait for him to go to sleep before sneaking your group past and into the courtyard.

GORDOK COURTYARD

Clear the Gordok Brutes, Mage-Lords, and Mastiffs on your way to the ramp just south of you. Take the ramp up and survey the area. There are two patrols of to be watchful: 1) Guard Fengus and 2) a Gordok Mage-Lord with three Gordok Mastiffs. Clear a spot and wait for the patrols to come by before engaging them.

Guard Fengus has the same ability set as Guard Mol'dar. Just as you did then, keep the melee fighters on Fengus and the softer targets out of melee range. The **Gordok Shackle Key is** one of the random drops that can be found on any of the creatures in the North Wing**.** If you find one, you can free Knot Thimblejack. Speak with him to begin the quest. After freeing him, a crate containing crafting items and, usually, a rare recipe is your reward. With the area clear, grab the **Gordok Inner Door Key** from Fengus' Chest and move down the west ramp. Open the door and move into the Halls of Destruction.

TRIBUTE RUN

Do not kill Guard Fengus. Move your party along the north wall to the ramp. If you have a Rogue or Druid in your party, have him or her stealth to the chest when the patrols are away, grab the key and stealth back.

If you are without a Rogue or Druid, pull the enemies to the left and right to the ramp, one group at a time, when the patrollers are away. When the patrols are away, have your fastest moving member (Hunters using Aspect of the Cheetah are good for this) go grab the key before the patrols return.

Clear your way to the northwest corner and watch for Guard Fengus. He patrols all the way up to the corner. When he is away, pull the Gordok Brutes and Mage-Lords around the corner. Watch again for the patrols before moving to the door to the Halls of Destruction.

THE HALLS OF DESTRUCTION

Watch for the Wandering Eye of Kilrogg. Once it notices you, you have to kill it quickly or it will summon two Netherwalkers. Gordok Reavers and Gordok Warlocks stand in groups with the Warlock's pet. CC the Gordok and kill the pet first. Then kill the Warlock, then Reaver. This will allow your party to kill the softer enemies before the CC wears off on the tougher opponents.

Continue down the hall until it opens into a room. Pull the enemies in the first section until you have a good amount of room. Wait for Guard Slip'kik to move away before pulling the Gordok near the fire. You must pull them all the way back; have interrupts ready for enemy casters. With the main group dead, engage Slip'kik when he returns. Again, like Guards Mol'dar and Fengus, keep the casters out of melee range and take him out.

TRIBUTE RUN

Don't kill Guard Slip'kik. Use a Thorium Widget and Frost Oil to repair the broken trap on the ground. Guard Slip'kik will walk into it and be frozen. Don't speak with Knot Thimblejack yet. Move past him and continue.

There are several Gordok in the northwest corner on this level. These can be killed or bypassed as your group decides. Move up the ramp to a group of Gordok guarding a basket. Kill them and rest up. When you open the basket to get the **Ogre Tannin** needed for *The Ogre Suit* a Gordok Bushwacker attacks you. Kill him and continue.

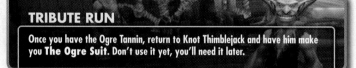

TRIBUTE RUN

Once you have the Ogre Tannin, return to Knot Thimblejack and have him make you **The Ogre Suit**. Don't use it yet, you'll need it later.

At the top of the ramp, several Gordok guard the Gordok Inner Door. Clear the Gordok one group at a time and open the door with the key from Fengus' chest. This lock can not be picked.

This hall has a group of Gordok near a fire in the center and Captain Kromcrush guarding the doorway farther in. Pull and kill the Gordok group as normal and rest up before dealing with Kromcrush. He's got brutal abilities to deal with, but they're mostly melee-oriented. However, he calls for help when brought down to roughly 25% of his health, so make sure that you're out of range of any other Gordok enemies.

Kromcrush has Mortal Cleave, Intimidating Shout, and Retaliation. Mortal Cleave is a combination of Mortal Strike (150% weapon damage and healing reduction on target) and Cleave. Again, keep the casters back.

TRIBUTE RUN

Don't kill Captain Kromcrush. Put on the Ogre Suit to become an Ogre and speak with him. Convince him that you captured the rest of your party and Guard Fengus called him a Gnoll-lover. He'll head off to give Guard Fengus a piece of his mind; the path is now clear.

GORDOK'S SEAT

Gordok Captains stand in groups on both sides of the room and Gordok Mastiffs patrol the center. Pull the Captains back into the Halls of Destruction to kill them. They can Fear party members and having people running into additional enemy groups won't help. CC one and focus fire on the other. Keeping the combat target stunned helps a great deal when trying to avoid Fear.

When both sides are clear, pull the Gordok Mastiffs. Kill them as you would any other enemy and move up the ramp. Rest up and prepare for the fight with the King.

King Gordok is not alone. Cho'Rush the Observer stands by, ready to heal at the first sign of danger. Cho'Rush the Observer has the spells Heal, Mind Blast, Power Word: Shield, and Psychic Scream. Both Heal and Mind Blast have prolonged casting times and are interruptible.

King Gordok has the following melee abilities: Berserker Charge, Sunder Armor, Mortal Strike, and War Stomp. His Berserker Charge is nasty. It's a Charge that inflicts 300 damage and has a Knockback effect.

There are two viable options when attempting this encounter.

Option 1: Kill Cho'Rush while having the MT hold onto King Gordok. This is a solid plan, but the healer(s) must be aware that the MT will be incurring solid damage throughout this fight. Use any interrupts that you can while depleting Cho'Rush's health. Once Cho'Rush falls, have everyone jump on King Gordok

and begin using any/all of the highest damage abilities available. Your MT should have had more than enough time to generate threat and won't need to manage aggro much more than that.

Option 2: If you're on a Tribute Run, Cho'Rush must live. Send a Rogue (and possibly a tanking pet) over to Cho'Rush to interrupt his heals and to keep him off of the party. Everyone else should focus on taking King Gordok down. Use armor-reducing abilities and any spells that ignore armor. This option forces the MT to generate threat quickly and efficiently so as not to let the King dash over to the rest of the party. Having multiple healers using weaker Heals allows them to split the threat produced. Just keep Cho'Rush occupied until the King falls.

Once both King Gordok is dead, Mizzle the Crafty comes forward and puts a chest on the ground. The chest has treasure your party will be interested in. Speak with Mizzle and he will declare you the new king. This makes all remaining Ogres friendly to you.

TRIBUTE RUN

With King Gordok dead (make sure not to kill Cho'Rush) and you the new king, it's time to collect on your investment. Captain Kromcrush is standing in the courtyard with Guard Fengus and is involved in the *Unfinished Gordok Business* quest. Guard Slip'kik, Guard Fengus, and Guard Mol'dar give you two hour buffs that are quite useful. Stomper Kreeg will give or sell you alcohol.

THE WEST WING

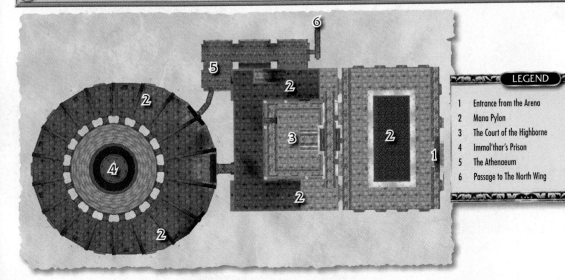

THE PYLONS

The first thing to be aware of upon entering is the patrolling treants. Pull them into the entrance hallway since another patrol will come by before you are done with the first enemy. The Eldreth Spirits are invisible, not stealthed. This is the perfect time to take full advantage of a Warlock's Detect Invisibility spell.

Once the patrols are clear, move to the center of the room. A mana pylon stands guarded by Arcane Aberrations and Mana Remnants. To the north and the south of the pylon are groups of Petrified Treants and Petrified Guardians, but they are not required for the completion of this wing. Kill them if you like, ignore them if you don't.

The first pull from the mana pylon will likely get you three enemies. All pulls after will be only two enemies. If you have a Warlock in your party, banish the strongest of the enemies and take the smaller enemies one at a time. If you don't have a Warlock, focus fire on the largest enemy first. Continue pulling and killing the Elementals until the mana pylon is clear. The elementals are immune to all arcane spells, so it's a waste for your Mages to blast them with anything from this line. The Arcane Aberrations have an unbelievably nasty effect when they die; they cast a melee-ranged AoE mana burn upon death. Any class that's mana-dependent should stay away from them as they near their demise.

THE COURT OF THE HIGHBORNE

Take the center doorway down into the Court of the Highborne. Tendris Warpwood awaits, but don't attack him yet! Make sure that you've cleared all the remaining ancients from the rest of the area. Tendris will summon any remaining to his aid.

Tendris Warpwood has an AoE melee ability (Trample), a point-blank knockdown and immobilizing ability (Grasping Vines), Uppercut, and Entangle which is similar to Entangling Roots.

Refrain from going through the door when Tendris falls. Head back and take the northern doorway. Keep your party in the northeast corner of the room. Your tank should move forward alone until he or she is attacked by an Eldreth Spectre as it unstealths and attacks. Drag the enemy back to the party to dispatch it. Repeat this a couple more times to try and lure the wandering stealthers before your group starts the real fights. The Eldreth Spirits are invisible, not stealthed. This is the perfect time to take full advantage of a Warlock's Detect Invisibility spell.

Continue camping in the corner while the tank begins pulling from the room. The path to the ramp needs to be clear, so pull from the right side of the room. Focus fire on Eldreth Spirits first as their Ribbon of Souls can damage multiple party members and their Silence can make casters much less effective. Watch your party members for Call of the Grave and Shrink. These should be cured as soon as possible.

When the path to the ramp is clear, move your party across the room and begin to move up the ramp. Make sure you're rested up! Have the MT move up the ramp and look for Eldreth Spectres. When the area's clear, find Magister Kalendris; he can be found upstairs and should be pulled to the ramp. He has a variety of priestly spells: Mind Blast (the only interruptible one), Mind Flay, Shadow Word: Pain, and Mind Control. Interrupt him as often as possible and take him down. With him down, move around the room in a clockwise fashion, taking the northeast section first.

Clear the Elves and Darters one group at a time until the way to the mana pylon is clear. Defeat the Elementals here as you did before. When the mana pylon is clear, continue moving clockwise. Guarding the way forward are Skeletal and Rotting Highborne. These enemies are non-elite and numerous. Make sure your healers are ready to take care of the softer members of your party and lay in with the AoE goodness.

The Shendralar Ancient stands here and asks for your help. She asks you to kill Prince Tortheldrin. Accept *The Madness Within* and continue. Skeletal and Rotting Highborne also guard this side of the bridge. Use your AoE attacks to defeat them as you did before. This clears the way to the next mana pylon.

The Elementals guarding this pylon are no different than the ones before. Defeat them and prepare your party. Wandering along the upper floor of the Court of the Highborne are Illyanna Ravenoak and her pet Ferra. These two pose a serious threat and are a true challenge if handled incorrectly. Like Hunters, the majority of Illyanna's abilities require a minimum range to be effective. Her three strongest abilities, Multi-Shot, Concussive Shot, and Volley can all be negated by sticking close to her. The only ability that you have to worry about after that is her Immolation Trap.

Illyanna's pet, Ferra, has both Charge and Maul. However, your party should focus on taking out the master before taking on the pet. Just have a non-caster off-tank the pet and take her out once Illyanna's dead.

With both mana pylons on this floor destroyed, jump down to the center of the Court of the Highborne. Your party needs a Crescent Key or a Rogue with sufficient Lock Picking skill to continue.

The hallway leading to Immol'thar's Prison hides a recent addition to the halls of Dire Maul. Revanchion, active during the Scourge Invasion events, now resides there waiting to lay waste to any parties foolish enough to enter.

IMMOL'THAR'S PRISON

Open the door and move down the hallway clearing Eldreth Spectres and Phantasms as you go. The hallway opens into a much larger room with a lot of enemies moving about. Take a moment to get used to the enemies movements. The Arcane Torrents and Arcane Feedbacks move in groups of five and patrol from the inner shield to the outer wall. The Residual Monstrosities patrol the edge of the shield.

Warlocks really pay for themselves here. If you have one in your party, have him or her Banish the Arcane Torrent while the party kills the Arcane Feedbacks. If your party is without a Warlock, the Warrior should keep the Torrent facing away from the party while they kill the Feedbacks, then the Torrent. Both the Arcane Torrents and Arcane Feedbacks are immune to all arcane spells and effects.

Move south along the wall to the mana pylon. Clear the Elementals around it as you have before. Move back to the doorway and this time move north. There will be another group of an Arcane Torrent and Arcane Feedbacks. Kill it like before and deal with the Elementals guarding the final mana pylon.

With all the mana pylons deactivated, the shield drops. Once the shield drops, you'll notice some Elves attacking Immol'thar. As long as you have solid health and mana levels, have the MT jump in and gain Immol'thar's aggro. If done correctly, the elves will contribute significant damage during the fight and help you in your battle.

In addition to the abilities listed below, Immol'thar has Infected Bite (a nature DoT that increases physical damage dealt to those infected).

During the fight, Immol'thar will summon Eyes to assist. Designate someone before the fight to kill the Eyes. The fight is straight-forward, but still dangerous. Immol'thar will trample all melee attackers near him. He will enrage at 50% health, so have your healer prepared. Immol'thar randomly teleports your party members to the center of the lair. If this happens to your tank, give them a moment to regain aggro before jumping in to resume the attack. Having a Mage or Healer remain on top of the threat list is a horrible situation for this battle.

Immol'thar's massive size can make it difficult to see who is being attacked. Keep Immol'thar facing away from the group so it's very apparent when the tank loses aggro. Rogues and other melee party members who aren't the main tank should retreat from battle and bandage if they are wounded. This keeps your healer's mana high and threat low.

If your party contains a Warlock with *The Dreadsteed of Xoroth* quest, there is still much to do here. Rest to full hitpoints and mana and rebuff. The fight ahead is long and dangerous.

Activate the items to start the event. Three totems will appear around the circle. Each does something different, but all are important to keep functional. Xorothian Imps spawn in large numbers are charge your party. With the totems active, the Imps only do 1 point of damage each attack and are more a nuisance than a danger.

AoE the Imps, but keep them off the Warlock. The Warlock needs to use soul shards to recharge the totems whenever they fall to the ground. The Imps hitting the Warlock will slow the recharging.

After several minutes and many Imps, Dreadguards begin to spawn. These are elite and more dangerous then the Imps. The tank should have plenty of rage from killing the Imps and needs to land hits early on to build aggro. Killing the Dreadguards quickly is very important.

Even killing with maximum efficiency, you won't have the Dreadguard killed before the next spawns. Enslave an add and use it to fight against the Imps or other Dreadguards. If you are still getting overwhelmed, Banish a Dreadguard. This knocks them out of the fight long enough for you to regain your footing.

Hunter pets are great for pulling Dreadguards off the healers. Your AoE damage dealer will be the one that will probably end up pulling Imps off the healer. Continue this mad frenzy of a fight for several more minutes.

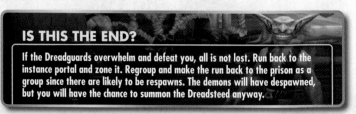

IS THIS THE END?

If the Dreadguards overwhelm and defeat you, all is not lost. Run back to the instance portal and zone it. Regroup and make the run back to the prison as a group since there are likely to be respawns. The demons will have despawned, but you will have the chance to summon the Dreadsteed anyway.

The demons will eventually be pulled back to their realm. Rest and rebuff when this happens as you're safe until you activate the next portion of the event. When your party is ready, summon the Dreadsteed.

The Dreadsteed has many hitpoints and the Berserk Charge ability. It charges anyone beyond minimum distance and throws them into the air. The charge itself does damage as does the landing. If your health is low, stop and bandage before re-engaging.

Fairly early in the fight, the Lord Hel'nurath will spawn as well. Put a Hunter or Warlock pet on him and concentrate your fire on the Dreadsteed. You need to kill one of them quickly and the Dreadsteed is already wounded.

Keep your tank at full health to avoid a lucky critical from depriving your party of victory. Bring the Dreadsteed down and change targets to Hel'nurath. He's a very straightforward enemy and won't give you any surprises if you've made it this far.

When both are dead, loot the bodies and speak with the Spirit of the Dreadsteed. It will teach Warlocks the Summon Dreadsteed spell.

With Immol'thar dead, Prince Tortheldrin will now be attackable by your party. Watch the Residual Monstrosities as your party exits the prison and moves to the door to the northeast.

THE ATHENAEUM

Following the hallway brings you to the Athenaeum. The Shen'dralar Provisioner in the southeast corner can repair your equipment, buy excess treasure, and sell drinks for casters. Restock before challenging Tortheldrin.

Prince Tortheldrin stands in the southwest corner of the lower level. His melee attacks are extremely powerful and he can cause trouble if you grant him too much mobility. His abilities are melee-oriented and can crush a caster, so keep them back. Whirlwind strikes all surrounding enemies while Thrash grants him two immediate extra attacks. Counterspell and Arcane Blast are also at his disposal. Make sure to have another healer pick up the slack if your main healer is Counterspelled. Arcane Blast deals approximately 875 to 1125 arcane damage and knocks the target back.

To limit his mobility, fight Tortheldrin in the southwest corner. Lower his attack power as soon as possible and keep any/all debuffs on him constantly. Healers should focus on keeping everyone's health topped-off since the prince has amazing burst damage potential. Since he's the final enemy in this wing (and probably the instance for those who made a full run), use your timed abilities to inflict optimal damage quickly or minimize his damage.

Killing Prince Tortheldrin completes *The Madness Within* and *Unfinished Gordok Business*. Now it's time to return to the Shen'dralar Ancient in the Court of the Highborne. She tells you of the chest under the ramp in the Athenaeum, inside which is your reward for *The Treasure of the Shen'dralar*.

There are many quests that end in the Athenaeum. Be sure to look around to see if anyone has any books to return before you leave.

The other exit from the Athenaeum leads near the entrance to the North Wing. Your party can make a run to the entrance or take the walk back through the West Wing.

GNOMEREGAN

Played & Written by: Michael "Kayal" Lummis of <Dovrani> on Kirin Tor

Gnomeregan is the technologic and political capital of the Gnomish people, yet it's been abandoned by their finest (and healthiest) minds. While preparing a potent weapon against the Troggs, the Gnomes made a few mistakes and ended up poisoning the entire capital. Now, only damaged machines, diseased creatures, and other horrors wander through the once learned halls. Yet, the Gnomes are not content to sit by and ignore this problem; many of them yearn to restore Gnomeregan to its glory, and maintain their level of technologic expertise. It's likely that you'll be called upon to aid in this task. Steady yourself and seek Gnomeregan when the time is right!

DUNGEON INFORMATION

Location	Dun Morogh
Quests	Alliance and Horde
Region	Alliance
Suggested Levels	30-36
Group Allowed	5 to Quest, 10 to Raid
Primary Enemies	Humanoids & Machines
Time to Complete	3-4 Hours

GETTING TO GNOMEREGAN

Gnomeregan is located in the northwestern section of Dun Morogh. For Alliance folks, it's easy to reach the instance (and you may have seen the area around it quite some time ago if you leveled in Dun Morogh as a young adventurer). Travel to the area of the map labeled as Gnomeregan and look for the diseased Gnomes. An even greater indicator that the city is close comes when you start to see green mist coming out of tunnels in the ground. Yup, that's Gnomeregan. The central entrance is out by the mountains, father northwest from the outer village areas. Though lowly level 9-10 Gnomes are on the outside of the tunnel, the fights quickly turn into ones against non-elite Gnomes in their mid-20s once you enter.

Horde players can't fly into Dun Morogh, but it is possible for them to make it out to Gnomeregan without legging it across half of the continent! Go to the Engineering Shop in Orgrimmar (where you get Rig Wars, the quest from Nogg). Sovlik there gives you a quest to talk to Scooty in Booty Bay. Accept that quest. Then, take a ship from Ratchet to Booty Bay. Talk to a Goblin there named Scooty in the port; he's near the lower floor of the inn, outside and to the northeast of the building. He has a teleporter that takes people all the way into Gnomeregan. For the trip back at a later point, have everyone use their Hearthstones or return to the teleporter; fast and simple on both counts.

WHO TO BRING

Gnomeregan is an instance with major fighting against large groups of machines, Troggs, and diseased Gnomes. This makes the inclusion of a secondary tank an extremely sound investment for a group, especially when that person has the ability to switch into backup healing when needed. Group organization and morale is hugely important in these battles, which can get kind of crazy if the main tank lets things unravel.

POSSIBLE GROUP MAKEUP

Tank	Warrior, Druid, Paladin
Secondary Tank	Druid, Paladin
CC	Rogue, Mage
DPS	Rogue, Hunter, Mage, Shadow Priest, Warlock
Healer	Priest, Shaman, Druid

QUESTS FOR GNOMEREGAN

ALLIANCE QUESTS

QUEST	QUEST GIVER	QUEST GIVER LOCATION	QUEST RECEIVER	QUEST RECEIVER LOCATION	CHAIN?	MAX EXPERIENCE
Data Rescue	Master Mechanic Castpipe	Ironforge	Master Mechanic Castpipe	Ironforge	No	3,650
REWARD: Repairman's Cape (Cloak 21 Armor, +1 INT, +6 SPI) or Mechanic's Pipehammer (2H Mace 20.4 DPS, +10 STA, +3 INT)						
Essential Artificials	Klockmort Spannerspan	Ironforge	Klockmort Spannerspan	Ironforge	No	3,050
Gnogain and The Only Cure is More Green Glow	Ozzie Togglevolt	Dun Morogh	Ozzie Togglevolt	Dun Morogh	Yes	2,450
Gyrodrillmatic Excavationators	Shoni the Shilent	Stormwind City	Shoni the Shilent	Stormwind City	No	2,450
REWARD: Shilly Mitts (Cloth Hands 27 Armor +6 INT/+6 SPI) or Shoni's Disarming Tool (OH Axe 16.1 DPS, Chance on Hit: Disarm for 5 Sec)						
Save Techbot's Brain!	Tinkmaster Overspark	Ironforge	Tinkmaster Overspark	Ironforge	No	2,700
The Grand Betrayal	High Tinker Mekkatorque	Ironforge	High Tinker Mekkatorque	Ironforge	No	2,750
REWARD: Dual Reinforced Leggings (Mail Legs 391 Armor +7 Defense) or Triprunner Dungarees (Leather Legs 101 Armor +3 STR/+18 AGI/+6 STA) or Civinad Robes (Cloth Chest 54 Armor +7 STA/+18 SPI)						

DATA RESCUE

Quest Level	25 to Obtain
Location	Ironforge (Tinker Town)
Contact	Master Mechanic Castpipe
Goal	Bring a Prismatic Punch Card Back from Gnomeregan
Max Experience Gained	3,650

Mechanic Castpipe needs a group to head into Gnomeregan and bring back a very high level security card. This can only be done by getting a common drop (a White Punch Card), and use that card on a series of terminals, in order. Using the card on Punchographs A, B, C, then D transforms the item into a Prismatic Punch Card, which can then be taken back for the experience and item rewards. Also note that each punch card can be viewed and translated from binary into amusing jokes. There are two Engineering plans that are sometimes found while changing the cards over; this certainly adds extra appeal for crafters doing the quest.

Take the White Punch Card to the Matrix Punchograph 3005-A. This reader is very close to the beginning of the outer dungeon, not far from the lift down into the city or the teleporter from Booty Bay. Look to the north of these and use the White Punch Card there to turn it into the Yellow Punch Card.

Next, look for the Matrix Punchograph 3005-B in the lower level, by the Dormitories. Use that reader to earn the Blue Punch Card.

Search the Launch Bay platform for the Matrix Punchograph 3005-C terminal (look out for the Electrocutioner 6000 there). That one gives you the Red Punch Card.

Take the Red Punch Card to the Matrix Punchograph 3005-D that is located at the base of the Engineering Labs. Use that final terminal to complete the run.

ESSENTIAL ARTIFICIALS

Quest Level	24 to Obtain
Location	Ironforge (Tinker Town)
Contact	Klockmort Spannerspan
Goal	Collect 12 Essential Artificials
Max Experience Gained	3,050

Klockmort is trying to find a fair supply of a nearly-universal machine component that the Gnomes used heavily in Gnomeregan: Essential Artificials. There are many containers deep inside the ruined capital that have the substance. Klockmort wants you to open some Artificial Extrapolators and return with 12 Units of Artificial Essentials. There are spawn points for this all over the main instance, so it isn't hard for large groups to get many of these in a single run.

GNOGAIN AND THE ONLY CURE IS MORE GREEN GLOW

Quest Level	27 to Obtain
Location	Dun Morogh (Kharanos)
Contact	Ozzie Togglevolt
Goal	Retrieve High Potency Radioactive Fallout
Max Experience Gained	2,450

There are two quests that Ozzie Togglevolt gives to groups that are heading into Gnomeregan. First, talk to Gnoarn in Ironforge, a Gnome who has lost his hair in the radiation leak of Gnomeregan. He tells you to seek Ozzie in Kharanos. Go there and talk to Ozzie; his first quest is to use a collection phial on Irradiated Pillagers or Invaders inside Gnomeregan. This must be done while the enemies are still alive. Use Sap or other CC types for an easy completion, or have other characters distract a target while you complete the quest (and return the favor for them).

Take the Full Leaden Collection Phial back to Ozzie and start the next step of the quest (The Only Cure is More Green Glow). In this step, you need High Potency Radioactive Fallout; take it from Irradiated Slimes, Lurkers, or Horrors. As before, use the rest of the group to distract the enemy while you do this, then return the favor. Take the item back to Ozzie as soon as the group is done.

GYRODRILLMATIC EXCAVATIONATORS

Quest Level	20 to Obtain
Location	Stormwind City (Dwarven District)
Contact	Shoni the Shilent
Goal	Collect 24 Robo-Mechanical Guts
Max Experience Gained	2,450

Shoni is working to collect spare parts for assembling a fleet of Gyrodrillmatic Excavationators. The problem is that she needs so many that only Gnomeregan has enough machines to cannibalize. Travel there and start destroying the machines that wander about the city. There are many mobs that drop this Quest Item as you fight into Gnomeregan, so this quest is very easy to do while working on other chores at the instance. Return to Shoni when you have all 24 of these for a decent reward! Note that even some of the Humanoid mobs carry and drop these parts, so getting all 24 isn't too hard.

SAVE TECHBOT'S BRAIN!

Quest Level	20 to Obtain
Location	Ironforge (Tinker Town)
Contact	Tinkmaster Overspark
Goal	Retrieve Techbot's Memory Core
Max Experience Gained	2,700

Tinkmaster Overspark once had a machine of great knowledge and utility called Techbot. Something damaged Techbot during the fall of Gnomeregan and now this device has become dangerous. Tinkmaster Overspark is distressed by this, but he hasn't given up hope for his beloved machine. Indeed, he asks that you search through the tunnels of the city and find Techbot. When you finally discover Techbot's current location, fight and disable the machine, then loot its Memory Core and take it to Ironforge. Luckily, Techbot isn't vary far into Gnomeregan, so groups that want to do this one at lower levels are free to get the quest out of the way (Techbot is outside the instance, in a Loading Room north of the Train Station).

THE GRAND BETRAYAL

Quest Level	25 to Obtain
Location	Ironforge (Tinker Town)
Contact	High Tinker Mekkatorque
Goal	Slay Mekgineer Thermaplugg
Max Experience Gained	2,750

The High Tinker was betrayed by Mekgineer Thermaplugg, who now sits over the rulership of Gnomeregan. Though Thermaplugg rules over only the diseased, irradiated, and destroyed, the High Tinker sees the death of this Mekgineer as an important step in recovering the capital. As such, you're charged with slaying the betrayer! Thermaplugg is very deep inside Gnomeregan, and the battle against him won't be easy (many dangerous machines protect him). Once Thermaplugg is dead, return to the High Tinker and receive a choice of some extremely high-end rewards.

Note that this is the most difficult quest to complete in the entire dungeon. If you have a Workshop Key, you can bypass a good chunk of the dungeon. The other method for skipping a bunch of the instance is to walk straight ahead from the main entrance and jump down to the gear nearest the group in the courtyard below. From this point, head west into the Launch Bay. If you need the Workshop Key, kill Executioner 6000. Jump down to the ring above the floor and walk around to the south side of the room before jumping to the ground level. You now have the option to either sneak or fight your way down the corridor to Thermaplugg. A party of level 33-35 players is recommended.

SHARED QUESTS

QUEST NAME	QUEST GIVER	QUEST GIVER LOCATION	QUEST RECEIVER	QUEST RECEIVER LOCATION	CHAIN?	MAX EXPERIENCE
A Fine Mess	Kernobee	Gnomeregan	Scooty	Booty Bay	No	2,450
REWARD: Fire-Welded Bracers (Mail Wrist 87 Armor, +1 STA, +6 AGI), Fairywing Mantle (Cloth Shoulder 32 Armor, +1 STA, +8 INT)						
Grime-Encrusted Ring	Grime-Encrusted Ring	Gnomeregan Drop	Sparklematic 5200	Gnomeregan	Yes	2,700
REWARD: Inscribed Gold Ring (+4 STA/+4 SPI)						
Return of the Ring	Sparklematic 5200	Gnomeregan	Varies by Faction	Varies by Faction	Yes	2,700
The Sparklematic 5200!	Sparklematic 5200	Gnomeregan	Sparklematic 5200	Gnomeregan	No	None
REWARD: Varies						

A FINE MESS

Quest Level	22 to Obtain
Location	Gnomeregan
Contact	Kernobee
Goal	Escort Kernobee to the Clockwerk Run Exit
Max Experience Gained	2,450

Just past the Clean Zone, is a set of rooms east of the punchcard reader. Kernobee was knocked out by a punch of nasty Dark Iron Dwarves and dumped in there for the Troggs. He wants the group to escort him to the Clockwerk Run exit; he also says that people can report to Scooty later (in Booty Bay) for a bit of a reward. Help the little guy out. The escort itself is quite easy. Be careful not to leave the instance early though; wait until the quest gives everyone credit before heading out, even if you are done with the instance.

GRIME-ENCRUSTED RING

Quest Level	28 to Obtain
Location	Gnomeregan
Contact	Drop Item from Dark Iron Agent
Goal	Take Ring to be Cleaned
Max Experience Gained	2,700

The Dark Iron Agents are able to drop a Grime-Encrusted Ring that you use to begin this quest. These rings are so dirty that they need cleaning before anyone can use them. Luckily, there are cleaning machines inside Gnomeregan, and they are still in working order. At least one of them is. Take the Grime-Encrusted Ring to the area with the Alliance-Friendly Gnome Holdouts. There's a Sparklematic 5200 that continues to operate normally (and a few that are just not functioning). Try out these machines until you find the working one and out pops your perfectly shiny, new ring! This chains into the next step of the quest (*Return of the Ring*).

RETURN OF THE RING

Quest Level	28 to Obtain
Location	Gnomeregan
Contact	Sparklematic 5200
Goal	Take the Ring to its Inscriber
Max Experience Gained	2,700

After cleaning the Grime-Encrusted Ring in the Sparklematic 5200, you have the option of keeping it or returning it to the person who inscribed it. In the long run, this quest leads to a final step where you receive the ring again, but get to keep it as a +5 STA/+5 SPI ring, which is certainly quite nice for its level. The person who inscribed the ring on the Alliance side is Talvash del Kissel. Alliance players should seek Talvash in the Mystic Ward of Ironforge. Horde players need to find Nogg (who gives a Horde-only quest into Gnomeregan anyway). Nogg waits in Orgrimmar, in Nogg's Machine Shop (Valley of Honor).

The final stage of the chain is to bring the inscriber 30 Silver, a Moss Agate, and a Silver Bar. This is what upgrades the ring to +5/+5 and gets you another burst of experience.

THE SPARKLEMATIC 5200!

Quest Level	25 to Obtain
Location	Gnomeregan
Contact	Sparklematic 5200
Goal	Clean Grime-Encrusted Objects
Max Experience Gained	None

The Sparklematic 5200 machine is good for cleaning the Grime-Encrusted Ring, but it also cleans the far more common Grime-Encrusted Objects that you find. For three silver coins, the machine takes the object and spits out something more useful. These items vary, but include such things as Rough, Coarse, and Heavy Stones, Tin, and various gems! This can be repeated as often as you like, so long as people in the group have Grime-Encrusted Objects.

HORDE QUESTS

QUEST NAME	QUEST GIVER	QUEST GIVER LOCATION	QUEST RECEIVER	QUEST RECEIVER LOCATION	CHAIN?	MAX EXPERIENCE
Rig Wars	Nogg	Orgrimmar	Nogg	Orgrimmar	No	2,750
REWARD: Dual Reinforced Leggings (Mail Legs 391 Armor +7 Defense) or Triprunner Dungarees (Leather Legs 101 Armor +3 STR/+18 AGI/+6 STA) or Civinad Robes (Cloth Chest 54 Armor +7 STA/+18 SPI)						

RIG WARS

Quest Level	25 to Obtain
Location	Orgrimmar (Valley of Honor)
Contact	Nogg
Goal	Return with Rig Blueprints and Thermaplugg's Safe Combination
Max Experience Gained	2,750

Nogg has grown to realize the power and danger of Gnomish technology. Because of this, you're charged with finding the Blueprints for a Gnomish Rig that surpasses even those of Goblin construction. Kill Mekgineer Thermaplugg, at the very end of Gnomeregan, and take the Safe Combination from him; the Blueprints you need are inside the nearby safe! Look on the northern side of the chamber, up on the slightly higher ledge that surrounds the room. The safe is there, and the key opens it to reveal the Blueprints your group needs. Bring those to Nogg for a fine selection of rewards.

ENEMIES

NPC	LEVEL
Addled Leper	24-25
Notes: Battle Stance, Hamstring, Heroic Strike	
Frequent Drops: Silk, Wool, White Punch Card (Quest Item)	
Alarm-a-Bomb 2600	20
Notes: Summons Enemies When Groups Are Detected	
Arcane Nullifier X-21	32-33 Elite
Notes: Dispels Debuffs	
Frequent Drops: Robo-Mechanical Guts (Quest Item), Heavy Blasting Powder, Fused Wiring, Coarse Blasting Powder, Delta Access Card, Copper Modulator, Bronze Tube, Bronze Framework	
Caverndeep Ambusher	25-27
Notes: Fast Movement, Patrols, Flees	
Frequent Drops: Silk, Grim-Encrusted Object (Quest Item), Robo-Mechanical Guts (Quest Item), Wool	
Caverndeep Burrower	25-27 Elite
Notes: Defensive Stance, Sunder Armor (-180 Armor), Flees	
Frequent Drops: Silk, Grime-Encrusted Object (Quest Item), Wool, Robo-Mechanical Guts (Quest Item)	
Caverndeep Invader	25-26 Elite
Notes: Radiation Bolt, Radiation Aura (Light Damage), Flees	
Frequent Drops: Silk, Grime-Encrusted Object (Quest Item), Wool, White Punch Card (Quest Item), Robo-Mechanical Guts (Quest Item)	
Caverndeep Looter	26 Elite
Notes: Flees	
Frequent Drops: Grime-Encrusted Object (Quest Item), Silk, Wool	
Caverndeep Pillager	24-25 Elite
Notes: Gouge (As Rogue Ability), Enrage (When Health is Low), Flees	
Frequent Drops: Silk, Grime-Encrusted Object (Quest Item), Wool, White Punch Card (Quest Item)	

NPC	LEVEL
Caverndeep Reaver	27-28 Elite
Notes: Arcing Smash (Cleave Effect), Flees	
Frequent Drops: Silk, Grime-Encrusted Object (Quest Item), Robo-Mechanical Guts (Quest Item), Wool	
Corrosive Lurker	28-29 Elite
Notes: Slimes	
Frequent Drops: Robo-Mechanical Guts (Quest Item)	
Dark Iron Agent	32-33 Elite
Notes: Flees	
Frequent Drops: Silk, Grime-Encrusted Object (Quest Item), Grim-Encrusted Ring (Quest Item), Wool, Robo-Mechanical Guts (Quest Item)	
Gnomeregan Evacuee	24-25
Notes: Alliance Friendly	
Frequent Drops: Silk, Wool, Battered Junkbox	
Holdout Medic	29-30 Elite
Notes: Alliance Friendly	
Frequent Drops: Silk, Grime-Encrusted Object (Quest Item), Wool, Heavy Stone, Tin, Battered Junkbox, Coarse Stone	
Holdout Technician	29-30 Elite
Notes: Alliance Friendly	
Frequent Drops: Silk, Wool, Grime-Encrusted Object (Quest Item)	
Holdout Warrior	29-30 Elite
Notes: Alliance Friendly, Strike	
Frequent Drops: Silk, Grime-Encrusted Object (Quest Item), Wool	
Irradiated Horror	28-29 Elite
Notes: Elemental Immunities	
Frequent Drops: Bubbling Water, Robo-Mechanical Guts (Quest Item), Elemental Water	
Irradiated Invader	24-26 Elite
Notes: Radiation Aura, Poisoned Blood (Spreads Radiation to Nearby Troggs upon Death)	
Frequent Drops: Silk, Grime-Encrusted Object (Quest Item), Wool, Robo-Mechanical Guts (Quest Item), White Punch Card (Quest Item)	

NPC	LEVEL
Irradiated Pillager	25-26 Elite
Notes: Radiation Bolt, Radiation Aura, Poisoned Blood (Spreads Radiation to Nearby Troggs Upon Death)	
Frequent Drops: Silk, Grime-Encrusted Object (Quest Item), Wool, Robo-Mechanical Guts (Quest Item)	
Irradiated Slime	27-28 Elite
Notes: Radiation Cloud	
Frequent Drops: Robo-Mechanical Guts (Quest Item)	
Leper Gnomes	9-10
Notes: Poor Diseased Guys Have No Chance	
Frequent Drops: Linen	
Leprous Assistant	28-29
Notes: Very Social, Ranged, Low Hit Points	
Frequent Drops: Silk, Wool, Robo-Mechanical Guts (Quest Item)	
Leprous Defender	28-29 Elite
Notes: Very Social	
Frequent Drops: Silk, Grime-Encrusted Object (Quest Item), Wool, Robo-Mechanical Guts (Quest Item)	
Leprous Machinesmith	29-30
Notes: Very Social, Ranged Weapons (Wrench), Machine Channeling	
Frequent Drops: Silk, Grime-Encrusted Object (Quest Item), Wool, Robo-Mechanical Guts (Quest Item)	
Leprous Technician	29-30
Notes: Very Social, Ranged Weapons (Wrench), Machine Channeling, Low Hit Points	
Frequent Drops: Silk, Grime-Encrusted Object (Quest Item), Wool, Robo-Mechanical Guts (Quest Item)	
Mechanized Guardian	31-32 Elite
Notes: Mechanical Immunities, Electrified Net (Root)	
Frequent Drops: Silk, Wool, Robo-Mechanical Guts (Quest Item), Heavy Blasting Powder, Fused Wiring, Coarse Blasting Powder, Copper Modulator	

NPC	LEVEL
Mechanized Sentry	28-29 Elite
Notes: Mechanical Immunities, High Hit Points	
Frequent Drops: Silk, Robo-Mechanical Guts (Quest Item), Wool, Heavy Blasting Powder, Coarse Blasting Powder	
Mechano-Flamewalker	30-31 Elite
Notes: Flamespray (Cone Effect Fire Attack), Fire Nova (Point Blank, Instant AoE), Mechanical Immunities	
Frequent Drops: Silk, Wool, Robo-Mechanical Guts (Quest Item), Heavy Blasting Powder, Fused Wiring, Coarse Blasting Powder	
Mechano-Frostwalker	31-32 Elite
Notes: Ice Shield, Hailstorm (AoE that Damages Over Time), Ice Blast (Instant, Point-Blank AoE), Mechanical Immunities	
Frequent Drops: Silk, Wool, Robo-Mechanical Guts (Quest Item), Fused Wiring, Heavy Blasting Powder, Copper Modulator	
Mechano-Tank	29-30 Elite
Notes: High Hit Points, High Armor, Mechanical Immunities	
Frequent Drops: Silk, Wool, Robo-Mechanical Parts (Quest Item), Heavy Blasting Powder, Copper Modulator, Coarse Blasting Powder	
Peacekeeper Security Suit	30-31 Elite
Notes: Pacify (Stun), High Hit Points, Mechanical Immunities	
Frequent Drops: Robo-Mechanical Guts (Quest Item), Fused Wiring, Heavy Blasting Powder, Bronze Tube, Coarse Blasting Powder, Bronze Framework, Copper Modulator	

GNOMEREGAN'S LEADERS

NPC	LEVEL	FREQUENT DROP(S)
CROWD PUMMELER 9-60	32 Elite	Robo-Mechanical Guts (Quest Item), Gnomebot Operating Boots (Leather Boots 68 Armor +8 STA/+3 SPI), Manual Crowd Pummeler (2H Mace 29.0 DPS +16 STR/+5 AGI, Use: +50% Attack Speed for 30 Seconds), Heavy Blasting Powder, Bronze Tube
Notes: Arcing Smash (Cleave), Trample		
DARK IRON AMBASSADOR	33 Elite	Glass Shooter (Gun 17.9 DPS), Wool, Emissary Cuffs (Leather Bracers 47 Armor +5 Arcane Resistance, Additional Stats Chosen at Random), Grime-Encrusted Object (Quest Item)
Notes: Rare Spawn, Flees		
ELECTROCUTIONER 6000	32 Elite	Workshop Key, Robo-Mechanical Guts (Quest Item), Spidertank Oilrag (Cloth Bracer 20 Armor +7 AGI), Electrocutioner Lagnut (Ring +4 STA/+9 SPI) Silk, Electrocutioner Leg (MH Sword 22.1 DPS Chance on Hit: Deal 10-20 Nature DMG), Wool, Heavy Blasting Powder, Fused Wiring
Notes: Chain Bolt, Megavolt, Shock		
GRUBBIS	32 Elite	Silk, Grime-Encrusted Object (Quest Item), Grubbis Paws (Mail Gloves 144 Armor +6 STR/+5 AGI/+9 SPI), Wool
Notes: Has Pet (Chomper, 30 Elite)		
MEKGINEER THERMAPLUGG	34 Elite	Robo-Mechanical Guts (Quest Item), Thermaplugg's Central Core (Shield 795 Armor 18 Block +3 SPI, 5% Chance to Inflict 35-65 Nature Dmg When Hit), Thermaplugg's Safe Combination (Quest Item), Thermaplugg's Left Arm (2H Axe 32.6 DPS +18 STR/+7 STA), Electromagnetic Gigaflux Reactivator (Cloth Helm 44 Armor +15 INT/+12 SPI Use: Bolt that deals 147-167 Nature Dmg to all Enemies in front, 10 Second Barrier Forms), Charged Gear (Ring +5 Arcane Res/+5 Nature Res, Additional Random Stats), Copper Modulator, Fused Wiring
Notes: Knock Away, Activity Remote Bombs, High Hit Points, Mechanical Immunities, High Damage		
TECHBOT	26 Elite	Techbot's Memory Core (Quest Item), Techbot CPU Shell (Shield 475 Armor 9 Block), Robo-Mechanical Guts (Quest Item), Heavy Blasting Powder, Bronze Tube, Coarse Blasting Powder
Notes: Lag, Battle Net (AoE Root), Mechanical Immunities, Summon Dupe Bug (Minor Pet), Patch (Kill pet to heal Techbot)		
VISCOUS FALLOUT	30 Elite	Bubbling Water, Acidic Walkers (Cloth Boots 34 Armor +4 AGI/+8 INT/+7 SPI/+5 Nature Res), Toxic Revenger (1H Dagger 20.5 DPS Chance on Hit: Deal 5 DMG Every 5 Seconds to any Enemy in 8 Yard Area for 15 Seconds), Hydrocane (Staff 21.6 DPS, +15 Frost Resist, Equip: Grants Underwater Breathing), Elemental Water
Notes: Elemental Immunities		

⚙ RETAKING THE GNOMISH CAPITOL

LEGEND

1. Entrance via Dun Morogh Elevator
2. Goblin-Controlled Teleporter to Booty Bay (Horde)
3. Train Depot
4. Loading Room (Techbot)
5. Workshop Entrance (Requires Key/High Lockpicking)
6. Standard Instance Entrance

OUTER REACHES OF GNOMEREGAN

STARTING POINTS

Alliance players must begin outside Gnomeregan, but Horde players get to start inside (due to the teleporter).

The tunnel leading into Gnomeregan is filled with non-elite Gnomes. At first, you face the Leper Gnomes (Level 9ish), who cannot begin to harm anyone in your party. Push these aside and battle down toward the elevator at the base of the tunnel. There are Addled Lepers when you start to get down a ways, but these are also very low-level and non-elite. Gather them into clumps and dispatch them en masse for a faster set of fights. You may notice some Evacuees in the tunnel, especially around the elevator; these are friendly to Alliance characters and are civilians (Dishonorable Kills) for the Horde. Let the Evacuees pass and get onto the elevator. This takes groups down to the outside part of Gnomeregan (before the instance itself).

Fight the group of Addled Lepers in the first room, at the bottom. Again, fight them in clusters to make things go as quickly as possible. This gives you an idea for the future as well. Gnomeregan is about fighting groups far more often than dealing with single enemies. In fact, pulling just a lone target is so rare in Gnomeregan that the few fights of that nature stand out! Get used to having a solid tank gather aggro and guide your group carefully, even though these fights are quite easy. This practice is essential, because later fights take you against Level 30 Elite enemies in groups of four to six targets.

AGGRO DUTIES

There are two sides to the aggro wars in a group. Warriors, Druids, and Paladins are often the classes on one side of the equation. Their duties involve gathering targets onto themselves, keeping those targets locked in battle, and reducing damage to the party in various ways.

Other members of the group are just as important for keeping aggro on your Main Tank. Have the MT focus on using Sunder Armor, Revenge, and (if you must) Taunt to establish a solid spot on the threat list. Doing too much damage on any single target peels that enemy onto a person as well. Make sure that every person in the group understands what they should be attacking. Designate a group member (Main Assist) and put all /assist macros onto them. This ensures that people don't start grabbing the wrong targets in heavy melee situations.

If you're chosen as a group leader for targeting enemies, be very careful about switching targets during a fight. You must not divvy up the group's damage (this makes aggro harder to maintain and slows the kill rate of your group). If you hit Tab or right-click and accidentally get a target that you weren't planning for, consider that it might be better to accept the mistake, kill that foe, and move on from there. Otherwise, half of your group may end up on one target (and half on the other).

It's very easy to find **White Punch Cards** from the creatures you fight in this area. These security cards are a running gag throughout the dungeon; they are also involved in an Alliance quest (Data Rescue). Take these and read them; they contain merely a long string of 0s and 1s. These actually are messages written in binary. There are programs online designed to translate these if you don't want to do the codework yourself. Though the messages won't assist you in completing Gnomeregan, you might certainly enjoy the humor in their content.

THE TELEPORTER AREA

The tunnel out of the initial area heads west before turning north. A room ahead has several points of exit, and there are elite enemies to fight there; Caverndeep Pillagers are tougher than the weak Gnomes you've been facing. These Troggs have been damaged by radiation. Irradiated Invaders (there's one nearby) have an Aura of Radiation. This infects other Troggs when the radiated ones are slain.

Kill the elite enemies in small groups, but don't worry too much, as they are low-level for this area and cannot threaten a persistent group. When the room is clear, look at the various exits. The rooms to the south of this area have the Teleporter to Booty Bay (Note: This is where Horde characters enter the pre-instance). To the west is a tunnel of enemies that terminates in the standard instance entrance. Or, to the north is the hallway toward the Train Depot (and Techbot). A backdoor to the deep part of the instance is up there as well, though it requires a Workshop Key or a very high-level Lockpicker.

PVP SERVER SKIRMISHES

Horde and Alliance characters mix a fair bit in the pre-instance area. This is especially poignant by the Teleporter area. Be prepared to face your factional enemies as well as the Troggs and Gnomes. Stay with the group, be alert for bodies and other signs that your foes may be near, and hurry off to the instance zone if you think your group is outgunned.

Gnomeregan is an Alliance controlled area, meaning that Alliance can attack Horde whenever they want, but the Horde must wait until Alliance takes the first swing in order to attack.

NORTHERN HALL TO THE TRAIN DEPOT

Walk up the northern hallway into the Train Depot and fight down the tiny, western corridor of the room for a somewhat safe trip to the bottom. The lower section of the Depot has several places of importance; the western room there has **Techbot**, a quest target for the Alliance. There are also card readers at the northern lip of the room, by another passage. These **Matrix Punchograph 3005-As** turn White Punch Cards into Yellow ones.

The Addled Lepers in the lower area continue to hone your party in slightly larger pulls because they are well-linked (even ranged pulls do little to curb the size of the fights, though it prevents future adds).

One piece of good news is that Techbot is off on his own. Charging into the Loading Room keeps you from having to worry about the Gnomes joining in to help the damaged machine. Sunder Techbot's armor and bring him down. Have a single, high-DPS character take care of all the adds as they spawn. It prevents Techbot from putting any additional damage against the group and also keeps him from destroying them to heal himself.

The northern corridor is useless the first time you enter the dungeon, unless you have someone who have Pick Locks with over a 180 skill. The door there is locked via the Workshop Key (found deep inside the instance, on the Electrocutioner 6000).

WESTERN HALLWAY INTO THE INSTANCE

Troggs cover the western route into the instance. There are Pillagers and Invaders throughout the hallway. Pulling at range avoids the wandering mobs, and leads to small and simple encounters. If you retreat slightly during the battles (while still fighting), it provides more than enough room to dispatch any foes before patrollers get close enough to add.

Then, at the end of the west hall, is the portal into the proper instance. Take this when you wish and get ready for the real challenges. Gnomeregan is a very tough instance for its level, and it tests a group's ability to cooperate. At this point, if you have developed serious doubts about a pick-up-group's ability to function as a team, perhaps suggest that everyone refocus their efforts (because the fights aren't going to get easier).

INTO THE GNOMISH CAPITOL

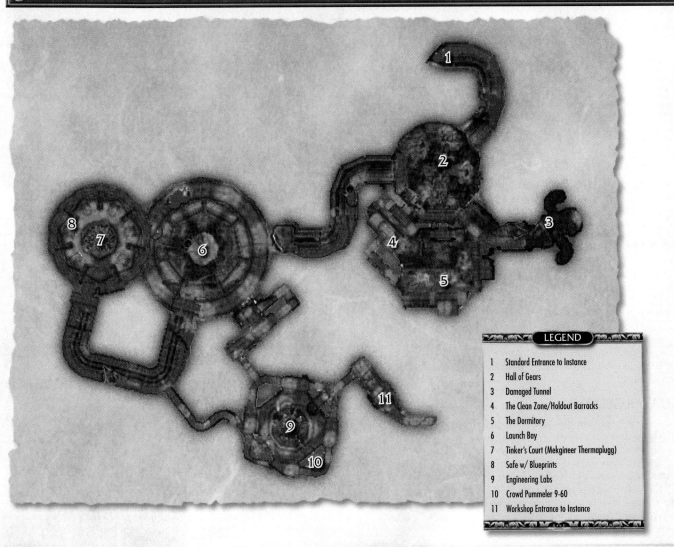

	LEGEND
1	Standard Entrance to Instance
2	Hall of Gears
3	Damaged Tunnel
4	The Clean Zone/Holdout Barracks
5	The Dormitory
6	Launch Bay
7	Tinker's Court (Mekgineer Thermaplugg)
8	Safe w/ Blueprints
9	Engineering Labs
10	Crowd Pummeler 9-60
11	Workshop Entrance to Instance

THE CLOCKWERK RUN AND THE HALLS OF GEARS

Enemy levels jump slightly as soon as you enter the instance. The Caverndeep Burrowers in the first hall are in their high 20s, so they take a bit more damage before falling. Be sure to use movement debuffing to limit the Troggs' ability to run off and cause further trouble during encounters.

You should see some of the Caverndeep Ambushers as you move into the huge chamber at the end of the Clockwerk Run. These seem laughably weak at first, being lower in level and non-elite. Don't underestimate what the Ambushers can cause; these fast Troggs are small and obnoxious. They patrol over decent areas and love to wander into your group during existing battles. Kill these wanderers quickly and don't allow them to engage you when there are other Troggs to link.

FAST RESPAWNS IN GNOMEREGAN

This instance is not slow to respawn its defenders. Groups cannot retreat over large distances and still expect to find the way clear. Because of this, it's wise to choose your paths ahead of time, decide which quests are being worked on, and get the job done. Trying to clear the same, large rooms multiple times can lead to runs that take 4 full hours. That is some serious time to spend in one instance and some groups lose of bit of cohesion by the end of that period.

The Hall of Gears is so massive that it takes up two tiers. Don't try to jump down onto the lower floor (you can reach it easily enough later on). Clear the pathway around the top ledge of the room and pause, as needed, to content with the patrollers. Luckily, Troggs don't link nearly as well as the Gnomes, so there is more tolerance for mistakes up here.

The Pillagers use Radiation Bolts at range, so they make better targets when you go against groups of Troggs up on the ledges. These Troggs are also slightly faster to bring down compared to their somewhat beefier companions.

The Pillagers are the mobs that you must collect radiation from if you're working on the *Gnogain* and *The Only Cure is More Green Glow* quests.

If you're trying to get all the treasure that Gnomeregan has to offer, clear the entire ledge and use the bridge on the west end to reach the center part of the room; there is a locked, Large Iron Chest there and a Box of Assorted Parts for Engineering goodies.

There are two safe exits from the upper Hall of Gears. For heavy fighting and a way down to the lower level, take the southwestern passage (this takes you to either the Dormitory or Clean Zone). Or, for a single treasure-fight, use the southeastern hallway into the ruined part of Gnomeregan. Either of these options have their place, but to keep things simple we'll deal with the shorter option first.

THE DAMAGED TUNNEL

The southeastern path from the upper Hall of Gears has seen better times. This area was almost destroyed, and future cave-ins seem almost certain. Fortunately, there aren't too many enemies as you first approach the end of the area. Instead, there is a stranded Alliance worker named Blastmaster Emi Shortfuse; you know that this person is in bad shape because she's perfectly willing to accept Alliance *or* Horde assistance. Her goal is to do some blasting and stop the new flow of Troggs from entering Gnomeregan; this won't get you an experience award, but the fighting is fine (and there is a guaranteed treasure drop at the end).

WATCH OUT ABOVE!

Don't stand too close to the explosives and falling rocks! You may wind up hurting yourself.

To help Emi, talk to her and get her started on her blasting route. She walks west a short ways, back where you came, and looks at the south wall. After a moment, Troggs start to break out of the wall and boil into the corridor. While Emi sets charges to seal this gap, fight off the waves of non-elite Troggs. Tanks: Don't worry about losing individual targets aggro-wise. Instead, be sure to use multi-target abilities like Cleave and Whirlwind. Also, don't hesitate to use Challenging Shout to draw an entire group onto you.

Emi seals the southern breach before long, but the northern wall doesn't look so great either. Sure enough, here come the Troggs! This batch contains a few elite members, though their arrival is spaced out enough for your group to eliminate them in turn. At the end of the rush, two interesting characters join the fray. Grubbis (a tougher, Elite Trogg) and his Crocalisk "Chomper" attack. This isn't too taxing a fight, and you are certain to get some treasure from Grubbis when he falls! That done, Emi is able to rest a bit easier. Return to the Hall of Gears and continue your greater quests.

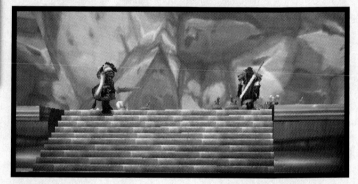

THE CLEAN ZONE

The southwest passage from the upper Hall of Gears has quite a number of the same Troggs you've been facing. More Burrowers and Pillagers are there, and you're forced to choose whether to travel north or south. North leads down some stairs into the Alliance-Friendly Clean Zone. The Gnomes there only attack Horde characters. Or, to the south is one of the entrances into the Dormitory (where legions of Troggs roam).

Most of the time, people are going to take the northern route, into the Clean Zone (there isn't too much of interest in the Dormitory unless people are use the card reader there). Even Horde characters need to enter the Clean Zone at some point; this is where characters find the **Sparklematic 5200**. Grime-Encrusted Objects and Rings are brought here to be cleaned.

If you're in a Horde group, stay on the stairs and pull various Gnomes back to you until the room is clear enough to safely enter. Alliance players can wander in without a care in the world, but the machines there operate just as well for either faction. Only one of the Sparklematics is still in full, operational order, so don't fret if you grimy loot doesn't do anything in the first machine you try.

The bottom exit from the Clean Room takes a group into the Dormitory from its lower area. Another shared quest is nearby; Kernobee was wounded and captured, and a number of Troggs guard his location just north from the Clean Room. Escorting him out of the dungeon is a quest (*A Fine Mess*). Look inside the small rooms outside of the Clean Zone and take Kernobee up

to the top of the Clockwerk Run when you find him. Don't leave the instance prematurely (or at all); make sure that the quest completes properly.

THE DORMITORY

There are Troggs all over the place inside the Dormitory. The sheer numbers are enough to make any group wary, but the smaller link area for Troggs keep these fights from becoming pure nightmares. Have the MT pull the Troggs from range and then duck behind the corner to the rest of the party. Line of Sight (LOS) pulls are a favorite tactic in most instances and this is no exception. You gain the advantage of eliminating the ranged abilities of most mobs as they'll chase your MT around the corner and into melee range of the whole party. Be calm and methodic. Don't try to scout around with stealth (this area has many ways to bounce a person out of stealth, and being aggroed by a couple groups of Troggs without group support leads to a sticky demise).

There are **Matrix Punchograph 3005-B** readers on the lower part of the Dormitory. These convert Yellow cards into Blue ones.

The first substantial concentration of Reavers is found here. These Warrior Troggs have the Cleave ability, and they take a bit longer to bring down. Keep your non-melee members at range and have the MT turn the Trogg around so that the other melee members of the party can stay behind it. This erases any advantage that Cleave may have given the Trogg. Other than that, make sure to crush the softer enemies while your MT grabs the aggro of any melee-oriented Troggs.

Your goal while fighting through this area is to reach the northern area (the lower tier of the Hall of Gears). Irradiated Slimes are there. Though more powerful than the Troggs, the enemies there are quite isolated. Use single, ranged pulls for fast and easy fights. Clear the way to the northern section of the Hall, and practice your techniques against the poisoned Water Elementals in that part of the room. The generic ones of these are called Irradiated Horrors. As with all Elementals, they scoff at a number of class abilities (such as Rend and a number of additional DoTs). Use physical damage and non-nature attacks to kill these.

When the group has its feet wet with the Elementals, pull the more powerful Viscous Fallout from the northeast. This Elemental is high on hit points and deals substantial damage. Though troublesome and slow to defeat, this enemy is certain to drop one of several good items when it dies, so groups should stop to kill when they go through (unless they are bypassing the eastern part of the dungeon).

WEST, INTO THE LAUNCH BAY

The western passage from the lower Hall of Gears leads into the deeper areas of Gnomeregan. Again, the fights increase in difficulty, and groups soon face the tougher machines and larger pulls that characterize this instance. This western corridor has two tiers (the upper one has more fighting and somewhat less room to do it). For an easier push, take the lower path and stay on the right edge of it while advancing.

There are both non-elite and elite Gnomes in this area and they could cause problems for an unprepared group. There are two options when taking out these groups.

Option 1 – No AoE: Groups without any AoE abilities should have the tank rush forward to grab the aggro of the elite Gnome while the Main Assist (MA) begins picking off the non-elites with the rest of the party. You can bring the regular Gnomes down relatively quickly while the MT absorbs the attacks of the dangerous elite.

Option 2 – AoE: Taking out these groups is much easier when you have at least one party member with AoE abilities. Have the MT grab the aggro of the elite and then lay into the rest with AoE spells. (Frost Nova/Arcane Explosion is a favorite among Mages.) This is a standard attack procedure in later dungeons (Uldaman's scorpions and Stratholme's skeletons come to mind) and it's a

good idea to practice it to perfection from this point on. Stay and watch some of the Sentries and Gnomes at range to get a feel for the patrols of this area. There's quite a bit of danger for getting involved in a fight that is too large for your group to handle. Longer pulls at range help, but there is danger even then.

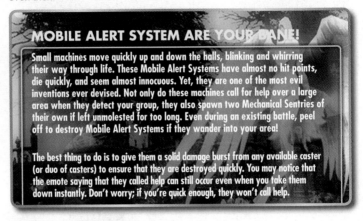

MOBILE ALERT SYSTEM ARE YOUR BANE!

Small machines move quickly up and down the halls, blinking and whirring their way through life. These Mobile Alert Systems have almost no hit points, die quickly, and seem almost innocuous. Yet, they are one of the most evil inventions ever devised. Not only do these machines call for help over a large area when they detect your group, they also spawn two Mechanical Sentries of their own if left unmolested for too long. Even during an existing battle, peel off to destroy Mobile Alert Systems if they wander into your area!

The best thing to do is to give them a solid damage burst from any available caster (or duo of casters) to ensure that they are destroyed quickly. You may notice that the emote saying that they called help can still occur even when you take them down instantly. Don't worry; if you're quick enough, they won't call help.

THE LAUNCH BAY

The Launch Bay is another room with immense dimensions. Again, this place has two tiers and dozens of foes (much like a meaner version of the Hall of Gears). Your group first enters the upper tier of the room. West from your location is a central ledge with the Electrocutioner 6000, but it takes some fighting to reach the necessary walkway.

Before going anywhere, look at the size of the Gnomes/Machine clusters around the tier. Fights with groups of four or five enemies are now going to be normal. Linking is such in the Launch Bay that you cannot avoid getting a swarm if you touch anyone who's remotely close to their allies. As always, wait for patrollers to come all the way to you to keep them from adding during the already intense fights.

Many of the weaker Gnomes have ranged attacks (Technicians and, later, Mechanesmiths). It's best to rush in and eliminate their ranged advantage or use a LOS pull to bring the entire group to your party in a cluster.

This is where you start to see the Peacekeeper Security Suits as well as the Peacekeeper Sentries and Mechanized Sentries. All of these are quite powerful and have limited crowd control, so the fights against them are slow. Continue to target Gnomes first to eliminate soft targets at high speed, then go after the Mechs when the Gnomes aren't there to support or repair them.

The bridge to the central area is only lightly guarded compared to the rest of the room, but the reasoning for that is soon revealed; the Electrocutioner 6000 is more than capable of defending itself. When fully healed, rested, and buffed, attack this machine with full force. Use armor and damage debuffing as early as possible, and make use of the wide battle space on the ledge to spread out your group. Have the main tank on one side of the Mech, other melee allies on the opposite side, and keep ranged buddies away from the fight entirely. This gives the MT considerable time to regain aggro if it is lost. Executioner 6000 has three special abilities, but one could be devastating to your party if you don't manage it correctly. Both Megavolt and Shock are single-target abilities and your MT will likely absorb these spells. However, Chain Bolt is much like Chain Lightning and your party should spread out to reduce the potential dangers of this spell.

Loot the Electrocutioner 6000 for the Workshop Key (this lets you use the secondary instance entrance and bypass many of the early fights if you ever wish to return to Gnomeregan). Also on the center ledge is a **Matrix Punchograph 3005-C** to turn your Blue Punch Cards into Red ones.

The southern ramp, on the upper ledge, leads down to a lower tier of the area. Fighting cools down slightly while you are on the ramp itself, though there are still Sentries and Leprous Defenders. The easier part is that these are smaller and simpler fights.

You're given a choice at the hallway below. Either take the hallway northwest and move back into the Launch Bay (this is the direction for heading toward Mekgineer Thermaplugg) or, push farther down the hall to the west and make for the Engineering Labs. Either way, it's important to be wary of the patrollers in the hall. There are Peacekeepers and Mobile Alert Systems. Stay on guard, and keep your fights out of the way (back on the ramp even), until there is enough room to safely fight.

LAUNCH BAY - LOWER TIER

The lower floor of the Launch Bay has similar Gnomes, but they're supported by Mechano-Tanks! These machines are very sturdy, and there are enough Gnomes around that it can be challenging to attack them when they aren't going to have them around. Look for smaller pockets and use these for safer clearing of the room. Fighting west around the circle is the faster way to get where you want. This way soon opens into a descending hall.

The southern hall is guarded by a different enemy; there are many Dark Iron Agents out there. They have a chance to drop the **Grime-Encrusted Ring** for both Horde and Alliance characters. This offers a short quest chain for either faction, so it's certainly nice to find! Another nifty thing about the Dark Iron

Dwarves is that they aren't as well linked as the Gnomes, so the fights are tough but not as hectic. The Agents try to set Mines during the battles, but these take ten seconds to arm (so you can pull the battles back and away from them in time to avoid trouble). Also, characters can peel from battle to destroy them, if that is your wish instead.

Another interesting development is the introduction of Arcane Nullifiers to the fight. These machines are capable of dispelling negative effects, so it's hard to land and keep debuffs going when they're in the battles. However, their most dangerous trait is their ability to reflect all spells (including abilities like Hammer of Justice). The reflection ability does have a visible particle effect when activated, but it's wiser to avoid using spells against this mob completely. Though the Arcane Nullifiers aren't fast kills, nothing in this hallway is super fast to bring down, so going after the machines before the Dwarves may be useful for some groups (especially those that count on DoTs and other non-nuke magic during battle).

There are several parts to the hallway. A thin ledge that offers little space for the battles is on the left side. Its advantages are that it meets an adjoining hall that connects to another Engineering Lab passage. You can also continue down the upper part of the ramp until it reaches the bottom. The lower route on the same ramp is wide enough to give groups greater space while fighting. Yet, the action is a tad thicker there. There's another upper ledge above to the right, but it can only be reached from the bottom of the ramp.

Look around while fighting for a rare Dwarf to be here; the Dark Iron Ambassador drops some interesting equipment if you are lucky enough to spot him and bring the foul creature down. Not all instance spawns are going to have the Ambassador, so it's really a matter of timing and sheer luck.

When the trip to the bottom is done, rebuff your allies and prepare for the final couple of battles to end Mekgineer Thermaplugg's rule over this wounded city.

TINKER'S COURT

This is the door into Tinker's Court, though it doesn't take any effort to open the way. Beyond it is a final line of defense before the Gnome traitor himself faces you. The fight, which you must take en masse, is against five non-elite Gnomes (Machinesmiths), an Arcane Nullifier, and a Mechanized Guardian. Since none of these can be pulled away from the others, it's better to charge forward and begin the fight on your terms.

Kill the Machinesmiths with all due haste to remove their support for the machines and low damage. Once isolated, the Nullifier and the Guardian won't be able to do nearly as much to your group. Take down the Nullifier next, then finish with the Guardian (a slug-fest by that point). Rest and rearm yourself once that battle is done, because an even greater challenge awaits!

Mekgineer Thermaplugg stands at the center of the large chamber (or sits, as the case may be). He is positioned inside a large battlemech. This device adds a heavy serving of armor and hit points to the Gnome, and that isn't all that he has going for him in Tinker's Court. The six statues around the room aren't for decoration; they are machines that spit forth deadly bombs once the battle begins. Thermaplugg engages these in a random sequence, and the bombs head in toward the party without much delay.

Before worrying about how to defeat Thermaplugg (who is actually the lesser challenge here), you must develop a plan to keep the bombs from ravaging your group. If you have a decently high-level person with keen ranged power, it is possible to have them intercept the bombs en route. This gets very challenging later in the battle, when there are almost always two of them incoming in a short span.

The more dependable tactic is to disarm the machines as they come online. Take two members of the group (not healers), and have them focus on each side of the room. One takes the left, one takes the right. Stay fairly close to the center machine (this way, no matter what activates it won't be a long run), and push the red, candy-like buttons that are found on the lower parts of the devices. This stops the bombs. Thermaplugg's activation sequence reveals which statue is coming online next; look for the lightning charge that he sends to do this for a hint at where to run!

A few are going to pop out anyway, as the first bomb is very fast to engage, but the runners can quickly shoot/hit the bombs to steal their attention and keep them from trashing the rest of the group. As long as your runners each have a Healing Potion ready, they shouldn't even need healing from the main group (no single bomb does enough damage to be too vicious when hitting a single target).

As for the central battle, Thermaplugg isn't so tough when the bombs aren't blasting the party to shreds. Keep your lead DPS player, tank, and healer on the big battle, and have them use their proper long-term abilities. Have the tank in front, the other two behind the Mech, and make sure to let your tank hold that aggro solidly.

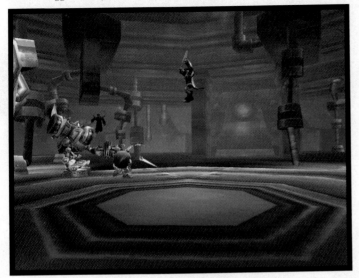

Eventually, it'll all be over. With a sound strategy, this is a very doable fight (though if the group loses cohesion everything kind of melts). Loot the foul Gnome and pat yourselves on the back. For Horde characters, the safe that you seek is on the northern side of the room (inside are the **Blueprints** that Nogg requested). You are done!

Yet, there is one section of Gnomeregan that we haven't gone over. Rewind a bit and deal with the Engineering Labs. The reason these are saved for the end of the walkthrough is because they are most often seen by groups returning for a second run through the instance. These labs connect the Launch Bay, the ramp by Tinker's Court, and the backdoor of the instance (the Workshop Door). The Labs are important because they allow groups to bypass quite a large number of the early fights. Characters of higher level can skip straight to battles that are worth more experience to them and offer greater rewards!

THE ENGINEERING LABS

First off, look on the map and see the three entrances to the Engineering Labs. You can approach from the west (via the small passage on the ramp to Tinker's Court). You can come from the north (by taking the hallway southwest from the Launch Bay). Or, you can come into the instance using the **Workshop Key** and fight your way west into the Labs.

No matter which way you choose, there are many fights, but these are challenges that you have mostly dealt with before. The distinct aspect of the Engineering Labs is that they have two Mechs that aren't found elsewhere in the dungeon. Mecho-Flamewalkers and Mechano-Frostwalkers are found in this area.

These elemental machines have cone attacks and point-blank AoEs. Keep ranged characters back to avoid the excess damage, while even non-tank melee combatants should stay on behind of the machines to avoid the cone sprays. Fights in and around the labs are somewhat dangerous, but they are more resource intensive than anything else.

There are several items of interest inside the actual labs. The elevator that connects the upper and lower tiers of the room is on the northeast side. The **Matrix Punchograph 3005-D** is in the room (this is the final Punch Card upgrader, and gives you a Prismatic Punch Card). Finally, the upper tier has a loot boss that you can fight without engaging other enemies. This enemy is the Crowd Pummeler 9-60. Though a melee boss, this machine deals damage to groups at high speed, using its version of Cleave and Trample with high frequency. Keep everyone except for the MT behind the Pummeler to avoid incurring major damage among all party members.

While clearing the way around the upper tier, be wary and note the Mobile Alert Systems and other patrollers that litter the ledge. Even experienced groups should stay organized and avoid getting involved with a large fight while patrollers are incoming.

With that boss defeated, your group has seen all that Gnomeregan has to offer. With the Workshop Key and your experience in the dungeon, it should take substantially less time to clear important parts of the dungeon in the future (you can hit the bosses in the western part of Gnomeregan without spending 2 1/2 hours setting everything up). Not only is that useful for you if you wish to farm loot; taking allies in to kill Thermaplugg is great if they still have a quest to do that but aren't interested in doing everything that the dungeon has to offer.

So, keep that Workshop Key in your bank for at least a few levels while leaving the option open to return whenever you like.

MARAUDON

Played & Written by: Ken "Birk" Schmidt of <Blame the Mage> on Perenolde

From the demon-infested Mannoroc Coven, to the Kodo Graveyard, Desolace is a barren land; yet it's the original home to all centaurs of Kalimdor. Maraudon is considered the holiest of ground to these centaurs, and their fiercest warriors guard its secrets. The measures taken by the centaurs, plus the appearance of demons in Maraudon's depths, have piqued curiosities all over the continent, and there are many people willing to reward an adventurous group's foray into the depths—so long as the group doesn't return empty-handed.

VALLEY OF SPEARS

MARAUDON

SHADOWPREY VILLAGE

DUNGEON INFORMATION

Name	Maraudon
Location	Desolace
Quests	Alliance & Horde
Suggested Levels	45-52 (Full Group)
Enemy Types	Elemental, Demon, Giant, Humanoid, Beast, Plant
Time to Complete	5-6 Hours

GETTING TO MARAUDON

Tucked away in the Valley of Spears in Desolace, Maraudon has every type of centaur guarding it: scouts, wranglers, windchasers, and even the spirits of fallen warriors. The Valley of Spears is west of the Kodo Graveyard and north of Shadowprey Village; the entrance to Maraudon is in the deepest part of the valley, marked by immense stone doors. The centaurs on either side of the doors shouldn't pose any problem to a group ready to face the perils of Maraudon. A solid group makeup for this dungeon run would be a Warrior, Priest, Rogue, Paladin/Shaman and any respectable DPS class to round it out.

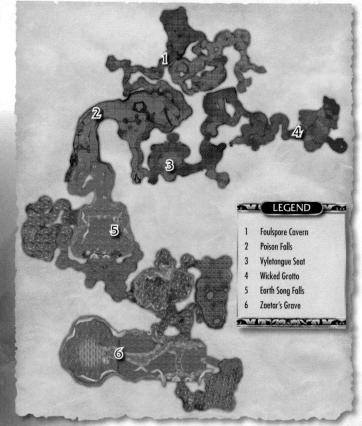

LEGEND

1	Foulspore Cavern
2	Poison Falls
3	Vyletongue Seat
4	Wicked Grotto
5	Earth Song Falls
6	Zaetar's Grave

QUESTS

QUEST NAME	QUEST GIVER	QUEST GIVER LOCATION	QUEST RECEIVER	QUEST RECEIVER LOCATION	CHAIN?	MAX EXPERIENCE
Shadowshard Fragments	Archmage Tervosh	Dustwallow Marsh	Archmage Tervosh	Dustwallow Marsh	No	3,450
REWARD: Prodigious Shadowshard Pendant (Neck, +10 INT) or Zealous Shadowshard Pendant (Neck, +20 Attack Power)						
Shadowshard Fragments	Uthel'Nay	Orgrimmar	Uthel'Nay	Orgrimmar	No	3,450
REWARD: Prodigious Shadowshard Pendant (Neck, +10 INT) or Zealous Shadowshard Pendant (Neck, +20 Attack Power)						
The Pariah's Instructions	Centaur Pariah	Desolace	Centaur Pariah	Desolace	No	5,450
REWARD: Mark of the Chosen (Trinket, When struck in combat, 2% change of all stats increasing by 25)						
Seed of Life	Zaetar's Spirit	Maraudon	Remulos	Moonglade	No	6,100
Vyletongue Corruption	Talendira	Desolace	Talendira	Desolace	No	5,250
REWARD: Branchclaw Gauntlets (Plate Hands, 284 Armor, +12 STR) or Sagebrush Girdle (Leather Waist, 71 Armor, +15 Agility) or Woodseed Hoop (Ring, +5 STA/+9 INT),						
Vyletongue Corruption	Vark Battlescar	Desolace	Vark Battlescar	Desolace	No	5,250
REWARD: Branchclaw Gauntlets (Plate Hands, 284 Armor, +12 STR) or Sagebrush Girdle (Leather Waist, 71 Armor, +15 Agility) or Woodseed Hoop (Ring, +5 STA/+9 INT)						
Twisted Evils	Willow	Desolace	Willow	Desolace	No	5,250
REWARD: Hulkstone Pauldrons (Plate Shoulder, 341 Armor, +5 STR/+13 STA) or Relentless Chain (Mail Chest, 258 Armor, +10 STA/+10 INT, Equip: +20 Attack Power) or Sprightring Helm (Leather Head, 103 Armor, +15 AGI/+10 STA) or Acumen Robes (Cloth Chest, 61 Armor, +20 INT)						
Legends of Maraudon	Cavindra	Maraudon	Celebras	Maraudon	No	3,400
REWARD: Scepter of Celebras						
Corruption of Earth and Seed	Keeper Marandis	Desolace	Keeper Marandis	Desolace	No	6,100
REWARD: Verdant Keeper's Aim (Bow, 28.2 DPS, +1 -4 Nature Damage) or Resurgence Rod (Staff, 45.8 DPS, Restores 8 mana/2 health every 5 seconds) or Thrash Blade (1H Sword, 35.2 DPS, Chance on hit: grants 2 attacks on next swing)						
Corruption of Earth and Seed	Selendra	Desolace	Selendra	Desolace	No	6,100
REWARD: Verdant Keeper's Aim (Bow, 28.2 DPS, +1 -4 Nature Damage) or Resurgence Rod (Staff, 45.8 DPS, Restores 8 mana/2 health every 5 seconds) or Thrash Blade (1H Sword, 35.2 DPS, Chance on hit: grants 2 attacks on next swing)						

SHARED QUESTS

SHADOWSHARD FRAGMENTS

Quest Level	Obtained at level 39
Location	Dustwallow Marsh (Alliance) / Orgrimmar (Horde)
Quest Giver	Archmage Tervosh (Alliance) / Uthel'nay (Horde)
Goal	Collect 10 Shadowshard Fragments
Experience Gained:	350-3450
Reward	Prodigious Shadowshard Pendant (Neck, +10 INT) or Zealous Shadowshard Pendant (Neck, +20 Attack Power)

Inside the Shadowshard side of Maraudon are Shadowhard Smashers and Rumblers. These are the enemies that drop Shadowshard Fragments. They appear only outside of the instanced area of Maraudon.

THE PARIAH'S INSTRUCTIONS

Quest Level	Obtained at level 39
Location	Desolace
Quest Giver	Centaur Pariah
Goal	Obtain the Amulet of Union
Experience Gained	550-5450
Reward	Mark of the Chosen (Trinket, When struck in combat, 2% chance of all stats increasing by 25)

The Centaur Pariah is found in the southernmost part of Mannoroc Coven. After obtaining the quest, head inside Maraudon and take on the Nameless Prophet, found near the stone door entrance. He drops The Amulet of Spirits, which is needed to pick a fight with the spirits of the khans.

The five khans roam the rocky paths of Maraudon in different locations. Three of the khans are outside the instanced portion of Maraudon. One of the khans patrols the Wicked Grotto in the Shadowshard side of the instanced area, about halfway to Vyletongue's Seat. The final khan is not far inside the instance entrance of the Ambershard side.

SEED OF LIFE

Quest Level	Obtained at level 40
Location	Maraudon
Quest Giver	Zaetar's Spirit
Goal	Seek out Remulos in Moonglade and give him the Seed of Life
Experience Gained	1200-6100
Reward	Money only

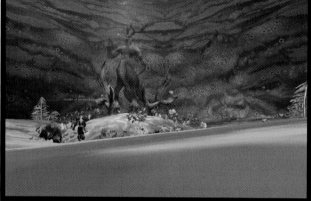

After defeating Princess Theradras, Zaetar's Spirit appears and offers this quest. Druids should have an easier time completing this quest than others who have yet to visit Moonglade.

VYLETONGUE CORRUPTION

Quest Level	Obtained at level 41
Location	Desolace
Quest Giver	Talendira (Alliance) / Vark Battlescar (Horde)
Goal	Heal 8 plants
Experience Gained	525-5250
Reward	Branchclaw Gauntlets (Plate Hands, 284 Armor, +12 STR) or Sagebrush Girdle (Leather Waist, 71 Armor, +15 Agility) or Woodseed Hoop (Ring, +5 STA/+9 INT)

The orange crystal pool needed to fill the Coated Cerulean Vial is just past Cavindra. Once it's full, enter the Ambershard side of the instance and look for small, green plants with an orange-red color at the base of their leaves. When you use the Filled Cerulean Vial near one of these plants, one Noxxious Essence and a few Noxxious Scions spawn. Killing the Essence cleanses the plant.

TWISTED EVILS

Quest Level	Obtained at level 41
Location	Desolace
Quest Giver	Willow
Goal	Collect 25 Theradric Crystal Carvings
Experience Gained:	525-5250
Reward	Hulkstone Pauldrons (Plate Shoulder, 341 Armor, +5 STR/+13 STA) or Relentless Chain (Mail Chest, 258 Armor, +10 STA/+10 INT, Equip: +20 Attack Power) or Sprightring Helm (Leather Head, 103 Armor, +15 AGI/+10 STA) or Acumen Robes (Cloth Chest, 61 Armor, +20 INT)

The Theradric Crystal Carvings drop from elite enemies inside Maraudon. With 25 to collect for each person in the group, expect this quest to take most of the run for everyone to complete.

LEGENDS OF MARAUDON

Quest Level	Obtained at level 41
Location	Maraudon
Quest Giver	Cavindra
Goal	Obtain the Celebrian Rod and Celebrian Diamond, and find a way to speak with Celebras.
Experience Gained	340-3400
Reward	Scepter of Celebras

Look for Cavindra in the Ambershard side of Maraudon. Obtain the Celebrian Rod by defeating Noxxion in the Ambershard side of the instanced portion of Maraudon. Lord Vyletongue in the Shadowshard side holds the Celebrian Diamond.

After obtaining these two parts, you must find and defeat Celebras the Cursed in the Poison Falls area. His spirit appears afterward and provides further instructions about combining the Rod and Diamond.

CORRUPTION OF EARTH AND SEED

Quest Level	Obtained at level 45
Location	Desolace
Quest Giver	Keeper Marandis (Alliance) / Selendra (Horde)
Goal	Slay Princess Theradras
Experience Gained	1200-6100
Reward	Verdant Keeper's Aim (Bow, 28.2 DPS, +1 -4 Nature Damage) or Resurgence Rod (Staff, 45.8 DPS, Restores 8 mana/2 health every 5 seconds) or Thrash Blade (One-handed Sword, 35.2 DPS, Chance on hit: grants 2 attacks on next swing)

Princess Theradras is deep inside Maraudon, in Zaetar's Grave. The encounter against Princess Theradras is covered in greater detail in the "Zaeter's Grave" section of the this text.

WITHIN THE DEPTHS

ENEMIES OUTSIDE THE INSTANCE

NPC	LEVEL
Ambereye Basilisk	40 - 41 Elite
Notes: Petrify	
Ambereye Reaver	41 - 42 Elite
Notes: Petrify, Cleave	
Ambershard Crusher	41 -42 Elite
Notes: Crush Armor	
Ambershard Destroyer	42 - 43 Elite
Notes: Earth Shock	
Rock Borer	40 - 41 Elite
Notes: Tunneler Acid	
Rock Worm	41 - 42 Elite
Notes: Acid Spit	
Shadowshard Rumbler	40 - 41 Elite
Notes: Trample	
Shadowshard Smasher	41 - 42 Elite
Notes: Knockdown, Knock Away	

ENEMIES INSIDE THE INSTANCE

NPC	LEVEL
Barbed Lasher	44 - 45 Elite
Notes: Thorn Volley, Thrash, Entangling Roots	
Cavern Lurker	45 - 46 Eilte
Notes: Knockdown	
Cavern Shambler	46 - 47 Elite
Notes: Wild Regeneration, Knockdown	
Celebrian Dryad	45 - 46 Elite
Notes: Throw, Slowing Poison, Dispel Magic	
Corruptor	43
Notes: Noxious Catalyst, Corruption	
Constrictor Vine	45 - 46 Elite
Notes: Entangling Roots	
Creeping Sludge	45 - 46 Elite
Notes: Poison Shock	
Deep Borer	46 - 48
Notes: appears in linked groups	
Deeproot Stomper	43 - 44 Elite
Notes: War Stomp	
Deeproot Tangler	44 - 45 Elite
Notes: Entangling Roots	

NPC	LEVEL
Noxxious Scion	42
Notes: spawns during Viletongue Corruption quest, Noxious Catalyst, Corruption	
Noxxious Slime	46 - 47 Elite
Notes: Emits noxious cloud when killed	
Poison Sprite	42 - 43
Notes: Poison Bolt	
Pimordial Behemoth	48 - 49 Elite
Notes: Trample, Boulder	
Putridus Satyr	43 - 44 Elite
Notes: Gouge, Sinister Strike, Putrid Breath	
Putridus Shadowstalker	43 - 44 Elite
Notes: Stealth, Evasion, Hamstring, Putrid Breath	
Putridus Trickster	44 - 45 Elite
Notes: Thrash, Poison, Putrid Breath	
Sister of Celebrian	46 - 47 Elite
Notes: Throw, Strike	
Vile Larva	45 - 47
Notes: Larva Goo, appears in linked groups	

NPC	LEVEL
Noxxious Essence	42 Elite
Notes: spawns during Viletongue Corruption quest, Noxious Catalyst, Corruption	
Spewed Larva	46 Elite
Notes: Catalyst	
Stolid Snapjaw	46 - 47
Corrupt Force of Nature	44
Notes: linked to Celebras	
Subterannean Diemetradon	46 - 48 Elite
Notes: Sonic Burst	
Theradrim Guardian	47 - 48 Elite
Notes: Knockdown, divides into Theradrim Shardlings when killed	
Theradrim Shardlings	46
Notes: Strike	
Thessala Hydra	46 - 47 Elite
Notes: Water Jet, Thrash	

LEADERS OF MARAUDON

NPC	LEVEL	FREQUENT DROP(S)
CELEBRAS THE CURSED	49 Elite	Claw of Celebras (Off Hand Fist, 34.4 DPS, Chance on hit: Poisons target for 9 Nature damage every 2 seconds), Grovekeeper's Drape (Cloak, 37 Armor, +12 STA/+10 Nature Resistance), Soothsayer's Headpiece (Leather Head, +7 STA/+25 INT/ +8 SPI)
Notes: Curse of Celebras, spawns additional Corrupt Forces of Nature		
LANDSLIDE	50 Elite	Helm of the Mountain (Plate Head, 683 Armor, +10 Nature Resistance, Equip: Defense +10), Cloud Stone (Off Hand, +10 INT/+10 SPI/+10 Arcane Resistance), Rockgrip Gauntlets (Mail Hands, +10 STA/+10 INT, Equip: +28 Attack Power), Fist of Stone (MH Mace, 35.3 DPS, +11 STA/+5 SPI, Chance on hit: restores 50 mana)
Notes: Trample, Knock Away, spawns Theradrim Shardlings		
LORD VYLETONGUE	49 Elite	Infernal Trickster Leggings (Mail Legs, 263 Armor, +20 AGI/+9 INT, Equip: Bows +4), Satyr's Lash (Dagger, 33.2 DPS, Chance on hit: Shadow Bolt for 55 to 85 Shadow Damage), Satyrmane Sash (Cloth Waist, 40 Armor, +10 STA/+15 INT/+10 Shadow Resist)
Notes: Shot, Multishot, Smoke Bomb, Blink		
MESHLOK THE HARVESTER	48 Elite	Bloomsprout Headpiece (Mail Head, 249 Armor, +18 STA/+10 Nature Resistance, Equip: +36 Attack Power), Fungus Shroud Armor (Leather Chest, 148 Armor, +25 AGI/+10 STA), Nature's Embrace (Cloth Chest, 73 Armor, Increase Holy spell effects by up to 22, Restores 8 mana every 5 seconds)
Notes: Rare spawn, War Stomp, Earth Shock, Harvester Strike		
NAMELESS PROPHET	41 Elite	Amulet of Spirits
Notes: Curse of Blood, Earth Shock		
NOXXION	48 Elite	Noxxion's Shackles (Plate Wrist, 235 Armor, +5 STA/+15 Nature Resistance), Heart of Noxxion (Trinket, +10 Nature Resistance, Use: Remove 1 poison effect), Noxious Shooter (Wand, 50.0 DPS, +7 STA/+5 Nature Resistance)
Notes: Toxic Volley, Uppercut, spawns smaller versions of self		
PRINCESS THERADRAS	51 Elite	Bracers of the Stone Princess (Mail Wrist, 141 Armor, +6 STA/+5 INT, Equip: +30 Attack Power), Blackstone Ring (Ring, +6 STA, Equip: +20 Attack Power, Improves your chance to hit by 1%), Princess Theradras' Scepter (2H Mace, 46.5 DPS, Chance on hit: Wounds target for 160, lowers their armor by 100), Elemental Rock Leggings (Plate Legs, 496 Armor, +20 STR/+18 STA/+10 Nature Resistance), Gemshard Heart (Neck, +10 STA/+10 INT/+6 SPI), Eye of Theradras (Cloth Head, 63 Armor, +13 STA/+20 INT/+11 SPI), Charstone Dirk (Dagger, 35.9 DPS, +11 INT, Equip: restores 2 mana every 5 seconds)
Notes: Dust Field, Repulsive Gaze, Boulder (silences)		
RAZORLASH	48 Elite	Chloromesh Girdle (Cloth Waist, 37 Armor, +20 Nature Resistance), Brusselhide Leggings (Leather Legs, 118 Armor, +11 STA/+15 INT/+10 Nature Resistance), Phytoskin Spaulders (Leather Shoulder, 111 Armor, +16 AGI/+10 STA/+10 Nature Resistance), Vinerot Sandals (Cloth Feet, 50 Armor, +12 INT/+12 SPI/+12 Nature Resistance)
Notes: Cleave, Puncture		
ROTGRIP	50 Elite	Rotgrip Mantle (Cloth Shoulder, 57 Armor, +17 INT/+11 SPI), Albino Crocscale Boots (Leather Feet, 105 Armor, +20 AGI/+5 STA, +5 Nature Resistance), Gatorbite Axe (2H Axe, 45.8 DPS, Chance on Hit: wounds target for 230 damage over 30 seconds)
Notes: Puncture, Fatal Bite		
TINKERER GIZLOCK	50 Elite	Gizlock's Hypertech Buckler (Shield, 1835 Armor, 32 Block, +5 STA/+10 INT, Equip: restores 4 mana every 5 seconds), Inventor's Focal Sword (1H Sword, 35.2 DPS, +6 INT, Equip: improves chance to get critical strike with spells by 1%), Megashot Rifle (Gun, 27.4 DPS, +5 Arcane Resistance, Equip: +19 Ranged Attack power)
Notes: Dragon Goblin Gun, Shoot, Bomb		

BEYOND THE STONE DOORS

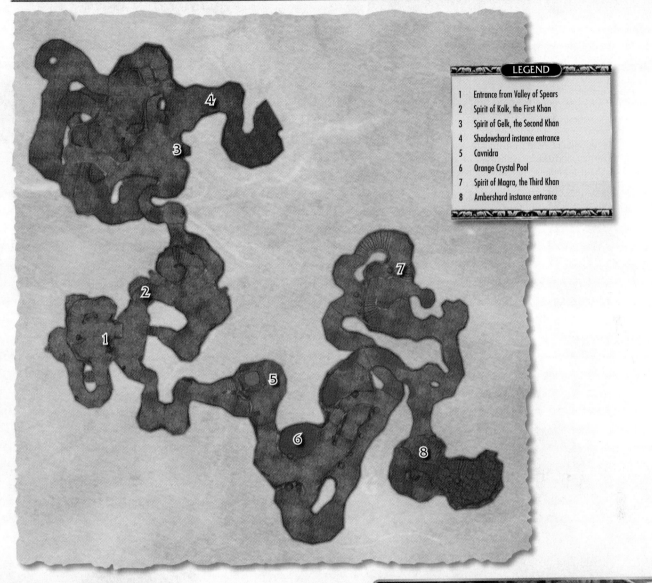

LEGEND

1 Entrance from Valley of Spears
2 Spirit of Kolk, the First Khan
3 Spirit of Gelk, the Second Khan
4 Shadowshard instance entrance
5 Cavnidra
6 Orange Crystal Pool
7 Spirit of Magra, the Third Khan
8 Ambershard instance entrance

INTO THE CAVERNS

The path to follow beyond the stone doors through the initial area is fairly straightforward. The single noteworthy encounter here is with the Nameless Prophet, who has Curse of Blood and Earth Shock at his disposal. There are a few shortcuts available (usually by jumping off staircases instead of following them down), but all paths lead to a pair of centaur statues.

RESOURCES FOR GATHERERS

The resources found inside Maraudon are sparse. While Ghost Mushrooms are common, few other herbs appear. Look for some Blindweed in Earth Song Falls, Stranglekelp in Zaetar's Grave; and some of the plant-like enemies drop herb odds and ends. There are a handful of Mithril nodes punctuated by the rare Truesilver spawn. Skinners should stay busy in the Ambershard area outside the instance and again when venturing deep inside Maraudon, but there's a large gap between these two areas.

INVENTORY AND QUEST SPACE NEEDED!

With multiple collection quests, and a few quests to pick up after entering Maraudon, don't start a run until after you've created room in your inventory and quest log. Expect a long run with no spot to sell off vendor trash cluttering your inventory.

The path that runs between the statues ends at the stationary Spirit of Kolk, the first Khan. While the five khans equip different weapons, none of the encounters are particularly challenging or radically different. The small room behind Kolk becomes functional with a **Scepter of Celebras** (obtained after completing the *Legends of Maraudon* quest) as a shortcut to Earth Song Falls. Going north from the centaur statues leads to the Shadowshard area, while south leads to the Ambershard side.

SHADOWSHARD SIDE

The Shadowshard area is essentially a deep pit with a spiral path that winds through a handful of caves. The Spirit of Gelk, the Second Khan, is about halfway down the path, almost directly underneath where your group first overlooks the pit.

The Shadowshard Rumblers and Smashers needed to complete the *Shadowshard Fragments* quest are found throughout this area, mixed in with two types of giant worms. Both worm types have a ranged attack: Acid Spit inflicts nature damage, while Tunneler Acid reduces armor and stacks with itself in a manner similar to Sunder Armor. Shadowshard Rumblers are the least threatening of the elite

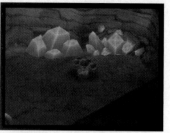

enemies since their only special skill is Trample. Shadowshard Smashers are far more dangerous with both Knockdown and Knock Away. Knockdown is mostly an annoyance (until a big heal is interrupted), but Knock Away is extremely dangerous. It throws characters a good distance, so work to keep your back to a wall while fighting these rocky foes.

AMBERSHARD SIDE

The enemies waiting to greet you amongst the orange crystals include Ambereye Basilisks and Reavers, both with the Petrify ability. Reavers also employ Cleave, so keep your healer behind the enemy to avoid being tagged by a dangerous skill.

There are two pools of note in this area. The first holds Cavindra, who offers the quest *Legends of Maraudon*. The second pool is used to fill the vial for the *Vyletongue Corruption* quest.

The entrance into the Ambershard side of the instance is buried in the back of the area. On the way to the entry, you encounter the Spirit of Magra, the Third Khan, near a small alcove filled with orange crystals.

INSIDE THE INSTANCE: SHADOWSHARD

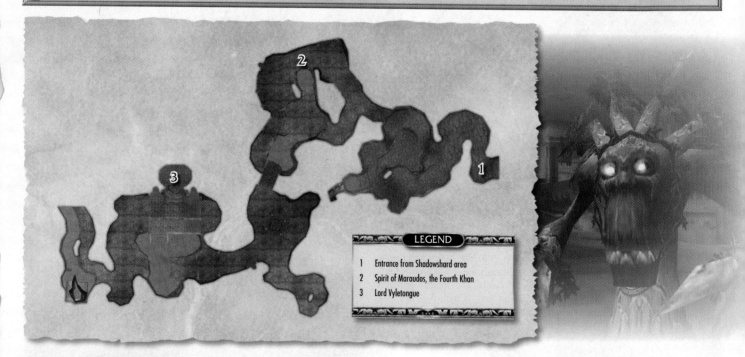

LEGEND

1   Entrance from Shadowshard area
2   Spirit of Maraudos, the Fourth Khan
3   Lord Vyletongue

THE WICKED GROTTO

The Wicked Grotto is the initial area inside the Shadowshard instance area and is filled with multiple types of demons. The smallest are not elite and are typically found in small groups. These Corruptors and Poison Sprites stay back and attack with ranged abilities that inflict status effects.

The Putridus Satyrs and Tricksters mingle with these groups, while the Putridus Shadowstalkers patrol the area, often stealthed, looking to surprise unprepared groups. Rogue abilities are divided between these three Putridus species, but they share the Putridus Breath attack.

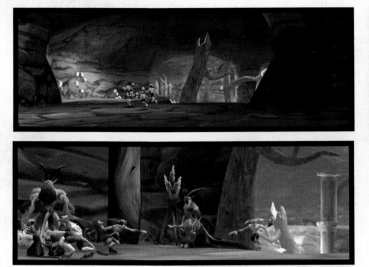

The elementals that roam the area are Deeproot Stompers and Deeproot Tanglers. The enemy's name gives you a clue about the attack you should expect from them. Deeproot Stompers use War Stomp, similar to the Tauren racial ability. Deeproot Tanglers emulate the Druid ability, Entangling Roots.

Drop, or fight, down to the bowl-shaped area, then follow the path that leads out of the bowl, and away from the waterfall. The Spirit of Maraudos, the Fourth Khan, makes a slow circuit of this area

VYLETONGUE'S SEAT

Multiple Putridus Shadowstalkers patrol this area, so never rush ahead without first checking for their stealthy presence. The deeper your group moves into the area, the larger the number of elites per pull. The best way to handle these more difficult encounters is to focus on the non-elite enemies with the higher DPS classes while your designated tank keeps the elites occupied. Once the non-elites and their ranged skills are eliminated, move the pile back toward the area already cleared by your group. This reduces the chance of a stealthed roamer entering the battle at an inopportune time.

Lord Vyletongue appears to be alone, but don't believe what you see; there are two sets of stealthed guards. The first two guards are just inside the hallway and can be pulled individually with a careful ranged attack. The second pair of guards is linked with Lord Vyletongue, so you have a messy boss battle ahead.

Lord Lord Vyletongue has two abilities that can be eliminated by staying close to him and engaging him in melee combat: Shoot and Multi-shot. They have a minimum range of 5 yards, so stay in melee range when possible. He does tend to blink away to set up his ranged attacks again, but a quick group can get close to him to prevent him from using his more powerful attacks. He should be the primary target since he's the most mobile enemy, and has an AoE ranged attack. Once he's down, take out his guards, then restore mana and health. The fun is just about to start!

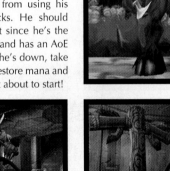

If your next destination is Foulspore Cavern—which is only necessary to complete quests or farm Razorlash and Noxxion—you have the option of pushing ahead to the Poison Falls or exiting the instance through the portal in the Shadowshard area, then reentering the instance through the portal in the Ambershard side. (Unlike Scarlet Monastery, Maraudon is one contiguous instance with multiple entry points.) Either choice leads to the same general area, so the difference maker (assuming you must complete quests) is likely to be how much your group wants avoid fighting more demons, or how eager they are to face giant plants.

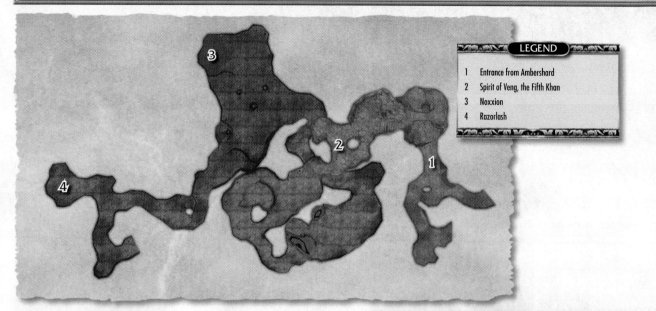

LEGEND

1 Entrance from Ambershard
2 Spirit of Veng, the Fifth Khan
3 Noxxion
4 Razorlash

FOULSPORE CAVERN

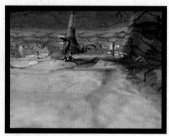

Tests of patience and group coordination await your team in Foulspore Cavern. Expect to face up to four elite plants in a single encounter, with a Hunter's Freezing Trap being the only means to keep an enemy out of commission for an appreciable amount of time. Constrictor Vines are the smaller enemies, and they use Entangling Roots to hold one target in place while they dash off to attack someone else. Barbed Lashers are the greater threat with Entangling Roots, Thrash (grants an extra attack), and a sweeping attack called Thorn Volley, which both damages and knocks down the target.

The only break you can expect from the plant fights in the early portion of Foulspore Cavern is the widely wandering Spirit of Veng, The Fifth Khan.

Beyond the Constrictor Vines and Barbed Lashers, linked groups of non-elite Vile Larva blanket the cavern's floor. Pull a group at a time and use AoE skills to

efficiently clear the way. Look for the Larva Spewer and any Spewed Larva that emerge from it. The larger larva are elite enemies and cover ground quickly. Use the Larva Spewer (you should get the bronze gear pointer on a mouseover) to shut down its production.

Noxxion patiently awaits your party in the back of a pool, beyond the Vile Larva. Noxxion is a necessary battle when you're trying to complete the Legends of Maraudon quest. Noxxion has a sweeping attack with Toxic Volley, and a knock away skill called Uppercut. At certain points in the fight, Noxxion temporarily splits into smaller versions of himself. While it's not necessary to pull Noxxion out of his pool, it will make finding these smaller spawns easier. When these smaller versions are defeated, Noxxion reforms and the fight continues until his health is depleted.

A single named enemy is left in Foulspore Cavern, the stationary Razorlash. Razorlash isn't part of any quest, so skipping the fight is an option. However, considering his loot table, you should prepare to deal with a possible mutiny from the cloth and leather wearing contingent of your group should someone suggest avoiding him.

Razorlash has a nasty bag of tricks, including a brutal DoT called Puncture. Keep the casters well away from the action since Razorlash's Cleave has monstrous range. Fortunately, he appears alone and backed into a cave, so there's essentially no chance for additional enemies to wander into this fight.

After dealing with Razorlash, there are a few more encounters to clean up before reaching Poison Falls. However, the closer your group comes to Poison Falls, the greater the chance that a roaming duo of Celebrian Dryads and/or Sister of Celebrian blunders in your fight.

FINALLY! HUMANOIDS AND BEASTS

While the enemies aren't any easier from this point forward, the appearance of the more familiar humanoids and beasts opens up many more crowd control methods.

THE FALLS

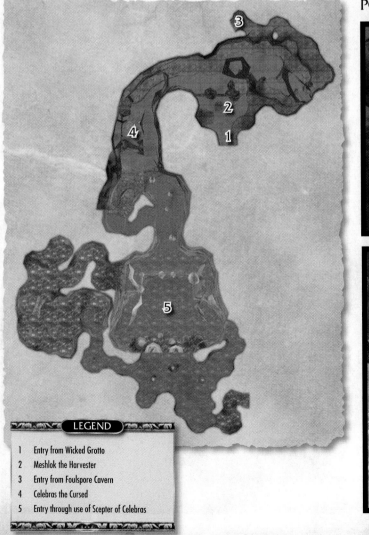

POISON FALLS

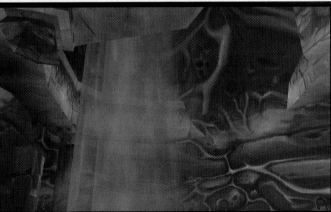

LEGEND

1 Entry from Wicked Grotto
2 Meshlok the Harvester
3 Entry from Foulspore Cavern
4 Celebras the Cursed
5 Entry through use of Scepter of Celebras

The enemies previously encountered in Foulspore Cavern and the Wicked Grotto appear in small pockets near the entry points to their respective areas. Near the Wicked Grotto entry point, Creeping Sludges mindlessly discharge Poison Shock, so stay wide of them if you're trying to stealth through to scout ahead. These enemies are brutal in close quarters, but they move at the proverbial snail's pace. Pull them from maximum range, then pour it on as they crawl to your position. By the time they reach your location, they should be close to dead. The Noxious Slimes that appear closer to the Foulspore Cavern side are linked and emit a poisonous cloud when they're killed.

You can skip some of the enemies though the Poison Falls running through the water or by sticking to land. The elemental Cavern Lurkers and Shamblers that appear in the water are easier to deal with than the slimes and centaurs that appear on dry land. Lurkers have a single-target knockdown, while Shamblers do them one better with an AoE knockdown and Wild Regeneration to restore lost health.

MESHLOK THE HARVESTER

Wandering the fouled water of the Poison Falls is the rarely spawning Meshlok the Harvester. There's little to distinguish him from the Cavern Lurkers and Shamblers that appear here, so check the names of each enemy that appears before continuing.

Celebras the Cursed is on the edge of the Poison Falls and is flanked by three Corrupted Forces of Nature. Fortunately, these guardians are not elite, but they continually spawn while Celebras is alive. Celebras has four spells: Wrath, Force of Nature, Entangling Roots, and Twisted Tranquility.

Wrath is the one that Celebras casts most often and that's a blessing in disguise since it's interruptible. Using Kick to interrupt this spell prevents Celebras from bringing his full force against the party. Force of Nature summons a new guardian should one of his fall, Entangling Roots is just like the Druid spell of the same name, and Twisted Tranquility slows both attack rate (by 75%) and movement speed (by 70%) and has a damaging DoT that deals 194 points of damage/tick for 10 seconds.

Target Celebras and make sure to set up an interrupt order. Bring him down as quickly as possible before focusing on the clean up of any remaining Corrupted Forces of Nature.

After defeating Celebras, his redeemed spirit appears and shows the members of your group with the quest how to create the Scepter of Celebras. This is an extremely significant event as you're able to use the Scepter outside the instance to open a portal into the next section of Maraudon, Earth Song Falls, and bypass the demons and plants in future runs.

SCEPTER-LESS?

Did you misplace your Scepter of Celebras? The redeemed spirit of Celebras offers another one if you ask him.

EARTH SONG FALLS

Beyond Celebras the Redeemed is Earth Song Falls, and there are two ways to reach the bottom. The first way involves taking the long path down and fighting the linked, non-elite Deep Borers. There's also the smart way, which consists of running to the edge of the waterfall and jumping into the giant pool of water below.

Whichever path you choose to take, your next destination is the same. Head south through the pool to the point marked by the large, yellow-flowered plants. The Thessala Hydra that appear here use Thrash to gain an extra attack, and they also have Water Jet to blast away opponents and interrupt spells and skills. The greatest danger is being thrown into another of the wandering beasts and suddenly finding a tougher fight than expected.

A soon-to-be-familiar sight greets you just past the yellow flowers: Subterannean Diemetradons come in two colors, and encounters with them must be handled carefully. Every group encountered is linked, so don't waste any time trying to pull them singly. Casters should stand well back from the action to avoid the AoE silence skill these beasts possess.

While advancing through this area and taking on the dinosaurs, keep a close eye on the patrolling rock Elementals. The large ones are Theradrim Guardians, which split into the smaller Theradrim Shardlings when killed. Some patrols are a mix of both types, and all patrols cover a large area. These enemies have a bad habit of reappearing just as you're sure they aren't coming back.

LANDSLIDE AND ZAETAR'S GRAVE

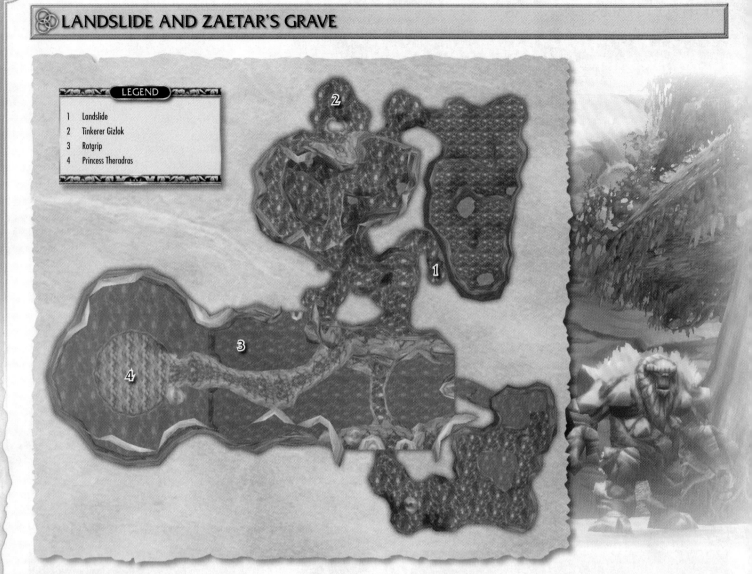

LEGEND

1 Landslide
2 Tinkerer Gizlok
3 Rotgrip
4 Princess Theradras

ZAETAR'S GRAVE

After a few uphill Diemetradon and rock patrol encounters, you reach a flat area, at which point, you face a choice. Taking an easterly course leads down to an encounter with the deranged goblin, Tinkerer Gizlock. Heading west continues the upward climb to encounters with the giants, Landslide, and Princess Theradras.

To avoid excess backtracking, first head west and upward to Landslide's location. The Primordial Behemoths are large, but so long as they're pulled solo (rock patrols persist here!) and kept away from the soft, cloth-wearing casters, they aren't an insurmountable obstacle. Communication is key here as these giants don't always move location to switch targets, opting instead to use Boulder, and when you're fighting up close, your view may be limited to ankles and kneecaps. Casters, if you're being hit, say something! Don't assume the tank is immediately able to tell that he's lost aggro.

Up in the highest point of the area is the named giant, Landslide. His skills are similar to the Primordial Behemoths already encountered, but he has an additional pair of tricks. Knock Away shouldn't be difficult to deal with since he appears in an enclosed area; just keep the fight deep in his alcove. The nastier skill is Summon Theradrim Shardlings, which stuns anyone too close. These Shardlings despawn once Landslide is defeated.

A causeway guarded by Primordial Behemoths is all that remains between your group and Princess Theradras. Once they're cleared, take a few minutes to organize and position your group, because this is not an encounter to rush into blindly.

Before engaging the Princess, move the group to the back of the cavern. Princess Theradras has multiple attacks that drive away anyone engaged with her, so fighting her near the narrow causeway and waterfall is asking for trouble. The aptly named Repulsive Gaze is a Fear that scatters people in all directions. Having a Dwarf Priest (Fear Ward) is a great help, as are the Warrior abilities Recklessness (although risky due to the increased damage taken) and Berserker Rage (which cancels a Fear effect when activated). Horde parties should have their Shaman drop Tremor Totems for this battle.

Dust Field is her other skill, which pushes away the pesky gnats who dare engage her. It also damages, so if you're at all able to deal ranged damage, stay out of Dust Field's area of effect! Since Princess Theradras has two skills that move the pile of battle, you should take a moment to assess any new location before continuing the fight. There are a handful of turtles in the water who will contentedly watch the battle, but if they're hit with an attack or AoE skill, they're coming after you. The Princess is tough enough; she doesn't need the help.

Once Princess Theradras is defeated and you've checked in with the Spirit of Zaetar, look over the edge of the waterfall for a slow-moving, large, white island and a few Hydras. That island is actually the giant crocolisk, Rotgrip, your next foe, making a slow circuit of the entire pool at the base of Zaetar's Grave.

Drop into the water away from the Hydras and engage Rotgrip in an area where you're safe from adds in the middle of the fight. Rotgrip has powerful attacks that match its incredible size. Puncture goes through health as quickly as an overeager Mage does mana, and it's a DoT. Most importantly, don't let anyone's health get too low as a single Fatal Bite could reduce your group's number by one before anyone realizes it.

There's one more named enemy left standing in Maraudon, but he's not the most stable of individuals. To reach Tinkerer Gizlock after defeating Rotgrip, exit the pool (there's only one way out), and follow the path back up to the lower bridge that spans Rotgrip's pool. This eventually brings you back to the flat area described previously, where you could go east or west. This time, take the downward path heading east.

The path to Gizlock leads through clusters of non-elite worms and one final Elemental patrol. Do not start the fight against the Tinkerer until this patrol has been dispatched! Gizlock's abilities are range-dependent. If you rush up into melee range, he won't be able to take advantage of his three abilities: Shoot (single-target) and Bomb (AoE). He can still use his  Goblin Dragon Gun, so it's wise to have the MT face him away from the rest of the group. With everyone else behind him, they'll be safe from the effects of his gun.

With all of Maraudon explored and its artifacts in your possession, it's time to travel and claim your rewards. There are multiple stops for members of the Horde and Alliance to make, and for many adventurers, their first trip to Moonglade lies ahead. However, a lingering question remains: Is all the interest in Maraudon strictly for knowledge of the past, or is there something sinister darkening the future?

THE MOLTEN CORE

Played & Written by: Chris M. "Phunbaba" Koschik of <Fraternity> on Perenolde

Over 300 years ago, the emperor of the Dark Iron Dwarves, Emperor Thaurissian, sought to utterly destroy his enemies during the War of Three Hammers. However, in his misguided attempt to find the means to do so, he accidentally summoned a being much more powerful, and uncontrollable, then even he could have forseen: Ragnaros the Firelord.

Instead of summoning a potentially willing slave, the emperor opened the gate to the Elemental Plane through which Ragnaros erupted. This summoning was so devastating that it created entire Azerothian regions that are now known as some of the most dangerous areas on the eastern continent: the Searing Gorge, the Burning Steppes, and, of course, Blackrock Mountain.

Now, some three centuries later, Ragnaros slumbers at the core of the mountain—regaining his strength. His powerful elementals command the Dark Iron Dwarves with an iron fist, enslaving them to create a formidable enemy born of earth and fire.

It's your duty to enter the bowels of Blackrock Mountain, into the Molten Core itself, to slay the agents of Ragnaros and, ultimately, summon The Fire Lord whom you must send back to the Elemental Plane from whence he came.

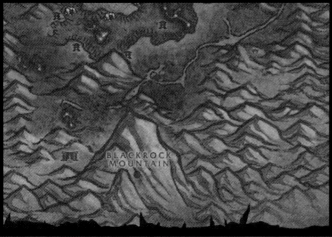

DUNGEON INFORMATION

Location	Searing Gorge, Blackrock Mountain
Territory	Contested
Quests	Shared Alliance and Horde
Suggested Level	60 (40-person raid)
Primary Enemies	Giants, Elementals
Time to Complete	4-12 hours (1-3 days)

GETTING TO THE MOLTEN CORE

Getting to the Molten Core is easily accomplished, but a bit tricky. Alliance parties should gather at Thorium Point to begin the trek south, while Horde parties often gather at Kargath to begin their adventure. Blackrock Mountain is the destination, but you'll need to reach the entrance to Molten Core within the mountain.

When you arrive at the gates to the mountain, you wind through a short hallway, eventually reaching the hallowed interior of the volcano. Immediately turn left and traverse the chain to the stone spiral in the middle of the lava. Work your way down the spiral as if you were heading to the Blackrock Depths instance and you will come face to face with a High-Elf named Lothos Riftwaker. The attunement crystal is to the left of him. Laying your hand on the crystal immediately teleports you into the Molten Core if you're attuned.

If you're not attuned, there's a quest that must be completed prior to being allowed access: **Attunement to the Core.**

THE MAP

LEGEND

1   Entrance
2   Lucifron
3   Magmadar
4   Gehennas
5   Garr
6   Baron Geddon
7   Shazzrah
8   Golemagg the Incinerator
9   Sulfuron Harbinger
10   Majordomo Executus
11   Ragnaros

SHARED ALLIANCE AND HORDE QUESTS

ATTUNEMENT TO THE CORE

Level	55 to obtain
Location	Blackrock Mountain
Contact	Lothos Riftwaker
Goal	Retrieve a core fragment from outside the Molten Core instance portal in Blackrock Depths
Max Experience Gained	6600

After speaking with Lothos, you must descend into the Blackrock Depths instance with a group of your closest comrades and secure a core fragment.

Make your way into Blackrock Depths, as you would with any group, and advance all the way to the room of the seven dwarfish ghosts. The hallway to the Lyceum will be opened after you clear the room. However, instead of going to the Lyceum, exit the room and turn right instead of continuing straight ahead. There's a bridge guarded by a number of Fireguard Destroyers. Defeat the Fireguards and make your way to the large, green, swirling portal. This is the portal to the Molten Core. Instead of going into the portal, look to the left of it. You will see a large stone that allows interaction. Clicking on this stone yields the core fragment you need to complete the quest.

Now, whenever you need to meet your raid group for the Molten Core, you will not have to clear Blackrock Depths every time. You need simply to click the stone next to Lothos Riftwaker.

POISONED WATER

Quest Level	55 to obtain
Location	Azshara
Contact	Duke Hydraxis
Goal	Return 12 Discordant Bracers to Duke Hydraxis
Max Experience Gained	4350

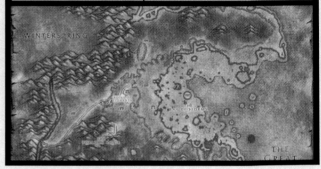

Duke Hydraxis is your main contact for most of the quests relating to the Molten Core. He's on a small island off the southeastern coast in Azshara, as pictured and marked in the map. In order to receive the quests for the Molten Core, you must first perform a few less glorious tasks for him.

This quest takes you to the Eastern Plaguelands. To complete the quest, seek out the lake in the southeastern area of the Plaguelands and find a spawn of water elementals that have been corrupted by the scourging of Lordaeron. Simply use the Aspect of Neptulos you acquired from Duke Hydraxis on the elementals and they will transform into Discordant Surges – the enemy that you need to defeat to retrieve the bracers. Repeat this process 12 times to complete the quest.

STORMERS AND RUMBLERS

Quest Level	55 to obtain
Location	Azshara
Contact	Duke Hydraxis
Goal	Defeat 15 Desert Rumblers and 15 Dust Stormers
Max Experience Gained	6000

Make your way to Silithus in the southwestern corner of Kalimdor. Upon landing in the Cenarion Hold, head northwest to the far corner of the region. Once you discover the location of the ravaged twilight camp, you'll notice that it's patrolled by the very Desert Rumblers you need to slay. Defeat 15 Rumblers and make your way south of the camp.

It won't be long before you see the Dust Stormers mulling about the sands. These enemies can be dangerous for several reasons: a) their melee attacks completely ignore armor and b) they have a lighting cloud spell that blankets an area in front of them with nature damage every few seconds. To avoid this spell, simply back away from the shadow of the cloud, the Stormer will soon follow. Defeat 15 of these and return to Duke Hydraxis.

EYE OF THE EMBERSEER

Quest Level	56 to obtain
Location	Azshara
Contact	Duke Hydraxis
Goal	Defeat the Pyroguard Emberseer and return his eye to Duke Hydraxis
Max Experience Gained	7500

Things get a little more complicated now. You must venture into Upper Blackrock Spire and defeat the Emberseer. Upper Blackrock Spire is a 10-person raid zone, so finding a good group for it can be a little tricky, but once you do, your goal is not too terribly far in.

The key to Upper Blackrock Spire is known as the "Seal of Ascension" and it's a good idea to make sure that someone in the party has one before trying to get inside. Once inside, clear the rune rooms filled with Orcs to open the door to Emberseer's prison. Interrupt the spell that the Orcs are casting on Emberseer by touching the altar, then begin to slay them all.

A few moments after the Orcs die, the Emberseer will break free and attack your party. The Pyroguard Emberseer is not an awfully difficult fight, so your group should make short work of him. Loot the eye and complete the quest.

AGENT OF HYDRAXIS

Quest Level	60 to obtain
Location	Azshara
Contact	Duke Hydraxis
Goal	Become Honored with the Hydraxxian Waterlords
Max Experience Gained	6500

Are you ready for the long haul? Nobody ever said this was going to be easy! Out of all the tasks Duke Hydraxis has asked and will ask you to perform, this requires the most patience.

The premise is simple. Attain an honored faction with the Hydraxxian Waterlords. However, achieving that reputation is another story altogether.

Do not fret! There's a method that makes this madness a bit easier. By now, you may have gone to the Molten Core a few times, or your guild is gearing up to run it. This could not have come at a better time. Every enemy and boss in the core yields a high number of reputation points pushing you closer and closer to the desired status.

Another way to gain faction is by defeating the lesser enemies of the Hydraxxians. Remember the Desert Rumblers and Dust Stormers you defeated in an earlier quest? Each one of these yields reputation until you are halfway through the friendly reputation bar. After that, you will only receive reputation gain from Molten Core kills, but it gives you a head start on a future quest.

THE MOLTEN CORE

Quest Level	60 to obtain
Location	Azshara
Contact	Duke Hydraxis
Goal	Defeat one Molten Giant, one Firelord, one Ancient Core Hound, and one Lava Surger
Max Experience Gained	9950

This quest is pretty self-explanatory. Enter the Molten core with your raiding group and eliminate each one of the listed creatures before returning to Duke Hydraxis. A detailed description on how to kill each type is listed in this walkthrough.

HANDS OF THE ENEMY

Quest Level	60 to obtain
Location	Azshara
Contact	Duke Hydraxis
Goal	Return the hands of Lucifron, Gehennas, Shazzrah, and Sulfuron Harbinger to Duke Hydraxis
Max Experience Gained	9950
Reward	Ocean's Breeze (Ring: +4 STR, +4 STA, +7 AGI, +15 FIRE RES) or Tidal Loop (Ring: +4 STA, +4 SPI, +7 INT, +15 FIRE RES)

Lethe
<Shadows of Alterac>

Phunbaba
<Shadows of Alter

This is the final quest the Duke of the waterlords has you perform. To complete this quest, slay all four captains of the Molten Core and return their hands to Duke Hydraxis. If you have the quest, the hands appear as drops on the bosses' corpses. The number of hands that can be looted is unlimited, meaning everyone that has the quest may loot a hand.

The reward may, at first, look a bit too small for all the work you have done, but its usefulness quickly becomes apparent when you seek to do battle with Ragnaros himself. That being said, make sure you save the ring.

From this point on, you can secure a flask of Aqual Quintessence anytime you wish. This flask is used to douse the runes in the Molten Core, calling forth Majordomo Executus from his lair. It's wise to have seven or more complete the quests up to this point or you'll never be able to summon Ragnaros. There are seven runes in the Molten Core.

SCRYING GOGGLES? NO PROBLEM!

Quest Level	60
Location	Silverpine Forest
Quest Giver	Inconspicuous Crate
Goal	Obtain Narain's Scrying Goggles
Reward	3 Major Rejuvenation Potions

After completing *Stewvul, Ex-B.F.F.*, this quest leads you to the Molten Core to get the goggles off of one of the mobs. Once you've obtained the goggles, head to Tanaris to turn them in to Narain.

THUNDERAAN THE WINDSEEKER

Quest Level	60 to obtain
Location	Silithus
Contact	Highlord Demitrian
Goal	Bring both halves of the Bindings of the Windseeker, the Essence of the Firelord, and ten Elementium Bars to Highlord Demitrian
Max Experience Gained	None
Reward	Thunderfury, Blessed Blade of the Windseeker (Legendary Sword: Main Hand 53.9 DPS +16-30 Nature Damage, +5 AGI, +8 STA, +8 FIRE RES, +9 NAT RES, Chance on Hit: Blasts your enemy with lightning, dealing 300 nature damage and then jumping to additional nearby enemies. Each jump reduces that victim's nature resistance by 25. Affects 5 targets. Your target is also consumed in a cyclone, slowing its attack speed by 20% for 12 seconds.)

This is an incredibly difficult quest to complete, perhaps the hardest in the entire game. However, the reward is worth it. To begin this quest, you need a lot of luck. Baron Geddon and Garr both have a 4% chance to drop the Bindings of the Windseeker and you need both halves.

Should you get lucky enough to come into possession of one of these halves, take it to the far northwestern corner of Silithus and speak to Highlord Demitrian. He then gives you the quest to summon Thunderaan, his lord and master. From this point on, you will be seeking three more items to complete your quest.

The first, of course, is the other half of the bindings. This is based purely on luck. It could drop for you next week or it could take six months. Be prepared to be patient – it's worth the wait!

The second required item is the Essence of the Firelord. This is a 100% drop from killing Ragnaros if you have the quest.

The third item is a little tricky. Elementium bars are legendary items smelted only by truly seasoned miners. To even think about smelting ten of these bars you must first delve deep into Blackwing Lair, until you meet a Goblin named Krixix. A Priest must use Mind Control on him and force him to use his special ability on a miner in your raid. The ability is called Teach Smelt Elementium. After that is done, you must combine ten Arcanite Bars (created by Alchemists), three Elemental Flux (bought from Blacksmithing vendors), one Fiery Core (random drop from mobs in the Molten Core), and one Elementium Ore (random drop from the Goblin Technicians in Blackwing Lair). Sound expensive? Well it is!

Once you have acquired all these items, bring them to Highlord Demitrian and wait for him to summon Thunderaan to destroy you. Rest assured though. As difficult as collecting the items to summon him were, he is not a difficult challenge for a 40-person raid and, indeed, even a 20-person raid can handle him. Your reward is the blade. This sword has the ability to slow any player's, any enemy's, any boss's melee attack speed in the game by 20%. That alone makes this blade invaluable to any guild. Good luck.

GET EQUIPPED FOR THE MOLTEN CORE

No, not swords, helms, and staves! I speak of much more powerful weapons for your arsenal: Programs for your computer, main assists, and raid leaders.

Teamspeak or Ventrilo

These are voice programs that allow everyone in the raid to listen and speak over a microphone. The importance of this cannot be stressed enough in the more chaotic battles when the difference between success and failure can be measured in the amount of time it takes to type a sentence or speak it over a microphone. Downloading and utilizing one of these programs will increase your success rate tenfold in all 40-person raids. The only stipulation is that all 40 members must be onboard.

CT Raid Assist

This is a third party add-on allowed by Blizzard that makes raiding much easier. It has many options that you can toggle on and off to warn your raid of incoming threats, debuffs, and curses. It also has an option that allows you to see who your tank's target is targeting. This serves you well in many battles, as you can see who has the aggro of a particular enemy or boss. To utilize this program, you must stay informed and updated on all the latest versions. You must also keep your guild informed to these updates as well.

Decursive

This addon helps classes with debuff removal abilities. You can bind a hotkey to automatically remove a debuff from the target if you have a spell or ability that will do so. This is a fantastic mod for many of the bosses in MC specifically.

Main Assist

The main assist is a player designated to acquire the most important target first for easy targeting. This role is usually given to a Rogue or a Hunter, as their only responsibility in the raid is to target and kill things. You can easily create a hotkey to acquire the main assist's target by pressing escape, going into the macro menu, and creating a macro called MA (main assist). The command for setting the main assist is /assist <name of player>. Also, you can toggle on an option that allows you to immediately begin attacking when you press your MA key; it's in the interface options menu.

Raid Leader

The raid leader is an extremely important part of your raid. In a nutshell, the raid leader is the player that orders everyone to start attacking or stop attacking. This is needed for tanks to acquire a good amount of aggro before the rest of the raid starts attacking. Having the MT lose aggro early on can wipe the raid group, so having a conservative raid leader helps to ensure victory.

CREATURES OF THE CORE

Molten Core is filled with many types of creatures that pose a formidable challenge to any raid group. As time progresses, you will learn to deal with these monsters in more efficient ways, cutting down the time it takes you to clear the path.

MOLTEN GIANT — 62 ELITE

Molten Giants always come in pairs of two at the beginning of the instance.

Attributes: High Armor, High Health

Knock Down: This ability is used on your MT every 15 seconds or so. If your tank is knocked back, there's a chance he/she may lose aggro, causing the giant to run rampant through your raid.

FIRELORD — 61 ELITE

Attributes: High Damage, Debuffs

Incinerate: The most frequently used ability by the Firelord is directed toward your MT. This debuff causes the player to take extra fire damage and, since all the Firelord's attacks are fire-based, the longer your MT tanks the Firelord, the more harmful its attacks become. This debuff also stacks upon itself, so your MT may want to wait for it to fade away before tanking another enemy with fire-based attacks. Another solution to this is to have another tank pick up the next Firelord.

Soul Burn: The Firelord randomly targets nearby players and casts Soul Burn on them. While this debuff is active, the player can't cast spells and takes a fair amount of fire damage over time. It's a Magic effect and can be removed by Priests or Paladins.

Lava Spawn: The Firelord periodically creates a smaller version of itself called a Lava Spawn. This spawn is not a huge threat alone, but must be dealt with immediately. If the spawn survives too long, it divides into two and - given enough time - those two split into four. Needless to say, this can quickly wipe the raid. The best way to deal with this threat is to have all the Mages blanket the area around the Firelord with Blizzard. Next, have a competent Rogue or Hunter become your MA, immediately acquiring the spawn as a target so the rest of the melee players can switch targets to eliminate the spawn hastily.

LAVA ANNIHILATOR — 61 ELITE

Attributes: High Armor

Drop Aggro: This isn't really a visible ability, but it needs to be mentioned. Every five seconds or so the Lava Annihilator will simply ignore who had aggro last and acquire a new target to attack. To control this lack of aggro, a tank rotation can be set into effect. With four tanks chain taunting him he will be locked into place for easy killing. Even if he does run loose for a few seconds, the Lava Annihilator is not an especially dangerous foe.

BANISH THEM!

The Lava Annihilators and Surgers are easy prey for a Warlock's Banish. Keep them out of the fight until your raid can take them down at its convenience.

LAVA SURGER — 61 ELITE

The Lava Surger has a fast respawn timer and you always have to watch your back for them. The respawn time is approximately 20 minutes until Garr has been defeated, which eliminates the respawn time.

Attributes: High Armor and Damage

Patrol: The Lava Surger's a patrolling mob. It patrols back and forth along a preset route, never stopping.

Surge: As you may guess from the name, the Lava Surger has the ability to Surge through your party causing all spellcasting to be interrupted and felling everyone for a few seconds. The Surger targets the farthest possible target within a 40 yard range. It's possible to force the Surger to target one person, but it'll still deal damage to the nearby melee attackers when it begins its Surge. Keep the majority of your raid on one side of the Surger and relatively close to it (20-25 yard range for casters and ranged DPS); place the "target" on the opposite side at about 35 yards. This prevents the spell interruptions, but opens the raid up to potential mistimed pulls with the odd positioning.

ANCIENT CORE HOUND — 62 ELITE

The Ancient Core Hound has a short (~20 min) respawn timer until Magmadar has been defeated, which eliminates all Ancient Core Hound respawns. Watch your back when you're in an area with these hounds.

Attributes: High Damage, Large Aggro Radius, Detect Stealth

Patrol: The Ancient Core Hound patrols a set path. However, they move so slowly that you can easily see them coming. Every hound does this.

Flame Breath: Every hound often breathes forth a massive cone shaped blast of fire. Have your MT face the Ancient Core Hound away from your raid group so only he/she is damaged by it.

Every Ancient Core Hound only has one of the following abilities attributed to it. Which ability that is, however, is completely random.

Withering Heat: This debuff reduces your maximum health by 35%. Needless to say, the less maximum health your MT has, the harder they are to keep alive. It must be removed from them first and foremost. This is a magic debuff.

Ancient Despair: This forces all players in the immediate area to wander around in a confused state for five seconds. To counter this, keep your MT's health topped off since it will likely be a few moments before they can receive a heal. Also, give your MT a little extra time on aggro since they will be confused the first five seconds of the battle.

Ancient Dread: It reduces your casting and attack speed by 50%. Clearly, this needs to be removed off of the healers first and the DPS second. This is a magic debuff.

Ground Stomp: An AoE stun that lasts for five seconds. Treat this exactly like the Ancient Despair debuff and keep the MT's health topped off with a little extra aggro time.

Ancient Hysteria: Probably the worst of all the Ancient Core Hound's abilities, this debuff reduces all players' INT and SPI by 50%. This ability is a curse, so the Mages and Druids need to remove this from the healers and casters as quickly as possible.

MOLTEN DESTROYER — 63 ELITE

The farther you go into the Core, the more likely Molten Giants will be replaced with Molten Destroyers.

Attributes: High Health, High Damage, High Armor

Ground Pound: The Molten Destroyer uses this attack quite often. Ground Pound knocks all players in the immediate area down, causing them to be stunned for three seconds. Make sure your MT grabs the Molten Destroyer as far from the casters as possible and away from any other battles going on. All melee players attacking the Destroyer take high damage, so the healers need to work extra hard.

FLAME IMP — 61 ELITE

The Flame Imp has an incredibly fast respawn timer. They respawn in approximately 7 minutes, so you need to move fast.

Attributes: Social

Note: The Flame Imps are extremely social and have the Fire Nova spell (like a Mage's Blast Wave without the debuff component). There are a few acceptable strategies for taking them down. First, Mages can Frost Nova the Imps in place and then AoE them. Second, have a single Warrior charge in using Challenging Shout and Whirlwind to get their aggro while Mages nuke them. Lastly, have a Paladin "Shield Pull" them and get their initial aggro while Mages AoE them.

CORE HOUND PACK — 61 ELITE

The tricky part about Core Hound Packs is how to kill them. Every Core Hound must die within ten seconds of the first one or they begin to resurrect each other to full health and you must start over again. Have your Warriors pre-select targets and drag them back to the group. After all the warriors have acquired aggro on their hounds, your raid leader should call out a barrage of AOE attacks such as Blizzard and Rain Of Fire, all the while your main assist is choosing the target with the highest health for your melee DPS to attack, ensuring that all of the Core Hounds are at generally even health and dying at the same time—or close to it.

Attributes: Social

Serrated Bite: This is a DoT inflicted by the Core Hound every few seconds. The damage starts out to be minimal, but over time it begins to stack upon itself and becomes quite a bother. Good healing is really the only remedy for this affliction.

LAVA PACK — 61-63 ELITE

Attributes: Social

There are four types of enemies you encounter in a Lava Pack, so they are broken down and listed below. The Lava Packs are the single most difficult non-boss battle in the Molten Core.

FIREWALKER — 61 ELITE

This should be your primary target in the pack.

Flame Buffet: This is a small AOE pulse that lowers the fire resistance of all targets. The counter for this is wearing as much fire resistant gear as possible.

Fire Blossom: This is a high-damage string of fireballs directed at a single target; the Firewalker performs this often. The damage is so high that sometimes it completely annihilates a player without even giving them a chance to heal. Again, the counter for this is high fire resistance.

FLAMEGUARD — 62 ELITE

This is the second target in the priority list and should be taken out as soon as the Firewalker is dead.

Melt Armor: This is a large AOE pulse that the Flameguard emits. Every pulse lowers the armor of the target by 1000.

Flame Cone: This is the main attack of the Fireguard. It spews forth a cone-shaped inferno, dealing high damage to anyone in the path of it. To alleviate this problem, simply have your tank face him into a corner or wall, forcing him to only damage the tank.

LAVA ELEMENTAL — 62 ELITE

Pyroblast Barrage: This is a directional-based attack that stuns all the targets in its path and applies a heavy DoT. When pulled, this mob should be immediately Banished by the Warlocks until the Flameguard and Firewalker are destroyed. When you're ready to tackle this foe, make sure your MT turns him away from the raid.

Note: Each pack features either two Lava Elementals or one Lava Reaver. This is the final foe of the pack that should be destroyed.

LAVA REAVER — 63 ELITE

Cleave: The Lava Reaver often uses a heavy damaging frontal attack called cleave. Anyone that is not a tank will likely die from it, so make sure your MT has him faced away from the raid when you attack.

Note: Being the least lethal, this is the last monster you will want to defeat.

BANISH THEM!

The Lava Elementals and Reavers can be Banished by a Warlock for easy crowd control. Take them out of the fight to destroy the other members of the pack if you must.

SET PIECES

Every class in the game will find an epic set in the Molten Core. Bosses drop most of these items, but two pieces of each set are randomly dropped by the enemies that roam the halls of the core. Every mob you meet has a small chance to drop one or more of the following items.

DRUID

ITEM	DESC	STATS
CENARION BELT	Leather Belt	113 Armor, 22 INT, 10 SPI, 10 STA, 7 FIRE RES
Equip: Restores 4 mana every 5 seconds		
Equip: Increases damage and healing done by spells and effects by up to 9		
CENARION BRACERS	Leather Wrists	88 Armor, 14 INT, 13 SPI, 13 STA
Equip: Increases all damage and healing done by spells and effects by 6		

HUNTER

ITEM	DESC	STATS
GIANTSTALKER'S BELT	Mail Belt	237 Armor, 18 AGI, 9 INT, 4 SPI, 16 STA, 7 FIRE RES
Equip: Improves your chance to get a critical strike by 1%		
GIANTSTALKER'S BRACERS	Mail Wrists	185 Armor, 20 AGI, 6 INT, 5 SPI, 11 STA

MAGE

ITEM	DESC	STATS
ARCANIST BELT	Cloth Belt	57 Armor, 26 INT, 10 SPI, 10 STAM, 7 FIRE RES
Equip: Increases damage and healing done by spells and magical effects by up to 9		
ARCANIST BINDINGS	Cloth Wrists	44 Armor, 20 INT, 8 SPI, 6 STA
Equip: Increases damage and healing done my spells and effects by up to 6		
Equip: Restores 2 mana every 5 seconds		

PALADIN

ITEM	DESC	STATS
LAWBRINGER BELT	Plate Belt	421 Armor, 20 INT, 8 SPI, 15 STA, 13 STR, 7 FIRE RES
Equip: Increases healing done by spells and effects by up to 18		
LAWBRINGER BRACERS	Plate Wrists	328 Armor, 8 INT, 11 SPI, 11 STA, 10 STR
Equip: Restores 4 mana every 5 seconds		

PRIEST

ITEM	DESC	STATS
GIRDLE OF PROPHECY	Cloth Belt	57 Armor, 22 INT, 10 SPI, 10 STA, 7 FIRE RES
Equip: Restores 4 mana every 5 seconds		
Equip: Increases damage and healing done by spells and magical effects by up to 9		
VAMBRACES OF PROPHECY	Cloth Wrists	44 Armor, 12 INT, 7 SPI, 8 STA
Equip: Restores 2 mana every 5 seconds		
Equip: Increases healing done by spells and effects by up to 20		

ROGUE

ITEM	DESC	STATS
NIGHTSLAYER BELT	Leather Belt	113 Armor, 17 AGI, 18 STA, 9 STR, 7 FIRE RES
Equip: Improves your chance to get a critical strike by 1%		
NIGHTSLAYER BRACELETS	Leather Wrists	88 Armor, 20 AGI, 15 STA

SHAMAN

ITEM	DESC	STATS
EARTHFURY BELT	Mail Belt	237 Armor, 21 INT, 7 SPI, 12 STA, 7 FIRE RES
Equip: Restores 4 mana every 5 seconds		
Equip: Increases healing done by spells and effects by up to 18		
EARTHFURY BRACERS	Mail Wrists	185 Armor, 17 INT, 11 SPI, 10 STA
Equip: Increases damage and healing done by spells and effects by up to 6		

WARLOCK

ITEM	DESC	STATS
FELHEART BELT	Cloth Belt	57 Armor, 14 INT, 13 SPI, 14 STA, 7 FIRE RES
Equip: Restores 4 health every 5 seconds		
Equip: Increases damage done by Shadow spells and effects by up to 11		
FELHEART BRACERS	Cloth Wrists	44 Armor, 11 INT, 8 SPI, 18 STA
Equip: Restores 2 health every 5 seconds		
Equip: Increases damage done by Shadow spells and effects by up to 7		

WARRIOR

ITEM	DESC	STATS
BELT OF MIGHT	Plate Belt	421 Armor, 21 STR, 15 STA, 7 FIRE RES
Equip: +5 Defense		
Equip: Increase your chance to dodge an attack by 1%		
BRACERS OF MIGHT	Plate Wrists	321 Armor, 23 STA, 11 STR

MISCELLANEOUS

ITEM	NOTES
LAVA CORE AND FIERY CORE	Used in trade skills

THE IMMORTAL RAID

Even the best raid group faces the bitter taste of defeat once in a while; starting over from scratch can demoralize your party faster than anything, but all hope is not lost!

Should your raid be defeated in a somewhat safe and clear spot, a Warlock Soulstone can be just the ticket you need to a quick recovery.

Keeping a Soulstone on a Shaman, Paladin, or Priest ensures that no nasty surprises end your raid. That being said, make sure you have one ready for EVERY boss fight. You never know when things will go sour.

TRADE ITEMS

The following list of items shows you what can possibly drop off bosses in the way of formulae, patterns, plans, recipes & schematics. They are *not* boss-specific.

TRADE ITEMS

ITEM	REQUIREMENTS
FORMULA: ENCHANT WEAPON HEALING POWER	300 Enchanting
Teaches you how to permanently enchant a weapon to add up to 55 healing to spells	
FORMULA: ENCHANT WEAPON SPELL POWER	300 Enchanting
Teaches you how to permanently enchant a weapon to add up to 30 damage to spells	
PATTERN: CORE ARMOR KIT	300 Leatherworking
Teaches you how to craft a Core Armor Kit	
PATTERN: FLARECORE WRAPS	Requires: 300 Tailoring
Teaches you how to sew Flarecore Wraps	
PLANS: ELEMENTAL SHARPENING STONE	300 Blacksmithing
Teaches you how to make an Elemental Sharpening Stone	
RECIPE: MAJOR REJUVENATION POTION	300 Alchemy
Teaches you how to make a Major Rejuvenation Potion	
SCHEMATIC: BIZNICKS 247x128 ACCURASCOPE	300 Engineering
Teaches you how to make a Biznicks 247x128 Accurascope	
SCHEMATIC: CORE MARKSMAN RIFLE	300 Engineering
Teaches you how to make a Core Marksman Rifle	
SCHEMATIC: FORCE REACTIVE DISK	300 Engineering
Teaches you how to make a Force Reactive Disk	

MASTERS OF THE CORE

In the Molten Core, you will face a grand total of ten bosses. Lucifron, Magmadar, Gehennas, Garr, Baron Geddon, Shazzrah, Golemagg the Incinerator, and Sulfuron Harbinger are the initial eight. Majordomo Executus is the final barrier before reaching the lord of the core: Ragnaros. Each requires teamwork, skill, and strategy. Are you up to the challenge?

LUCIFRON

Lucifron is the first boss in the Molten Core. The weakest of the four captains, but still requiring technical prowess, he is the first real test of your raid's organization and skill.

After clearing the first two Core Hound Packs in his room, your raid group should buff up and prepare for the pull. Lucifron comes with two guards that should be dispatched in the back of the room while being tanked by two capable tanks. The positioning of your raid for the battle should be as the following map shows.

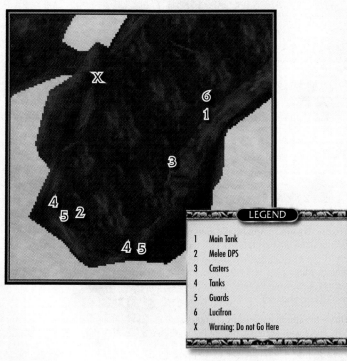

LEGEND

1	Main Tank
2	Melee DPS
3	Casters
4	Tanks
5	Guards
6	Lucifron
X	Warning: Do not Go Here

It cannot be stressed enough that you remind your raid to stay away from the hallway marked on the map. If a member of the raid strays too close to this cave, you will aggro the quick-spawning Flame Imps and Lava Surgers. In essence, you'll be utterly wiping your raid.

The guards are your first priority. Before launching into the fray, make sure every Warrior in the raid prepares to use Intimidating Shout on the first available target. This way, it'll still be on cooldown if Lucifron Mind Controls a Warrior during the battle.

While the MT pulls Lucifron to his spot, a pair of hunters should be ready to peel the Flamewalkers from Lucifron to a pair of tanks ready to taunt them off the hunters, pull them to the back of the room. It must be noted that these guards have a very dangerous Mind Control attack and they use it often. *Priests must be quick to dispel this!* If the MT becomes Mind Controlled during the pull, don't panic. A well-timed Dispel is all it takes to get him/her back into the

fray. If your raid is low on Priests, have Mages ready to Polymorph the MC'd target. They'll even replenish some of their health while sheeped. After the MT successfully has Lucifron placed, begin draining his mana with your Warlocks and Hunters. Leaving Lucifron with no mana forces him to rely on pure melee damage—your MT's specialty.

Use the MA to eliminate the guards, then shift your attention to Lucifron himself. Hopefully, the healers in your raid have kept the MT up and healthy this whole time so he/she will have secure aggro; this allows your raid to use strong DPS right from the start. Lucifron has two abilities that must be mentioned before going any further.

LUCIFRON'S ABILITIES

Curse of Lucifron: This is a truly nasty curse. It forces everyone in range to use twice the amount of mana, energy, or rage spent for any spell or attack. Your first priority of removal should be the healers and then the ranged DPS. The MT should be your next target and finally the melee DPS last.

Impending Doom: This is what will kill your MT. Ten seconds after inflicting this debuff to a target, Lucifron's ability slams them with 2000 shadow damage. This kind of burst damage can be quite deadly to your MT, so make sure it's cleansed immediately.

If your druids and mages were skilled in removing the *Curse of Lucifron* up until this point, your raid should have plenty of mana to finish off Lucifron. Lucifron has relatively low health compared to some of the other bosses in the core (approximately 350k) and it shouldn't take a solid raid group too long to bring him down.

LUCIFRON'S LOOT TABLE

DRUID

ITEM	DESC	STATS
CENARION BOOTS	Leather Boots	138 Armor, 16 STA, 13 INT, 15 SPI, 7 SHAD RES
Equip: Restores 3 mana every 5 seconds		
Equip: Increases healing done by spells and effects by up to 18		

MAGE

ITEM	DESC	STATS
ARCANIST BOOTS	Cloth Boots	70 Armor, 13 STA, 15 INT, 14 SPI, 10 SHAD RES
Equip: Increases your chance to get a critical strike with spells by 1%		
Equip: Increases damage done by Frost spells and effects by up to 11		

PALADIN

ITEM	DESC	STATS
LAWBRINGER BOOTS	Plate Boots	515 Armor, 7 STR, 20 STA, 13 INT, 10 SPI, 7 SHAD RES
Equip: Restores 2 mana every 5 seconds		
Equip: Increases healing done by spells and effects by up to 18		

SHAMAN

ITEM	DESC	STATS
EARTHFURY BOOTS	Mail Boots	290 Armor, 15 STA, 10 INT, 22 SPI, 7 SHAD RES
Equip: Increases healing done by spells and effects by up to 18		

WARLOCK

ITEM	DESC	STATS
FELHEART GLOVES	Cloth Gloves	63 Armor, 18 STA, 15 INT, 8 SPI, 7 FIRE RES
Equip: Increases your chance to get a critical strike with spells by 1%		
Equip: Increases damage done by Shadow spells and effects by 9		

WARRIOR

ITEM	DESC	STATS
GAUNTLETS OF MIGHT	Plate Gloves	468 Armor, 22 STR, 17 STA, 7 FIRE RES
Equip: Improves your chance to hit by 1%		
Equip: +5 Defense		

MISCELLANEOUS ITEMS

ITEM	DESC	STATS
CHOKER OF ENLIGHTENMENT	Necklace	9 STA, 10 INT, SPI
Equip: Increases damage and healing done by spells and effects by up to 18		
CRIMSON SHOCKER	Wand	73.2 DPS, 10 INT, 10 FIRE RES
FLAMEWAKER LEGPLATES	Plate Legs	748 Armor, 12 STR, 22 STA, 11 FIRE RES, 11 SHAD RES
Equip: Increases your chance to dodge an attack by 1%		
HEAVY DARK IRON RING	Ring	110 Armor, 20 STA
Equip: +5 Defense		
HELM OF THE LIFEGIVER	Mail Helmet	324 Armor, 14 STA, 30 INT, 9 SPI
Equip: Increases healing done by spells and effects by up to 42		
MANASTORM LEGGINGS	Cloth Legs	85 Armor, 19 STA, 14 INT
Equip: Restores 14 mana every 5 seconds		
RING OF SPELL POWER	Ring	
Equip: Increases damage and healing done by spells and effects by up to 33		
ROBE OF VOLATILE POWER	Cloth Chest	102 Armor, 10 STA, 15 INT, 10 SPI
Equip: Improves your chance to get a critical strike with spells by 2%		
Equip: Increases damage and healing done by spells and effects by up to 23		
SALAMANDER SCALE PANTS	Leather Legs	171 Armor, 14 STA, 14 INT, 10 FIRE RES
Equip: Increases healing done by spells and effects by up to 51		
Equip: Restores 9 mana every 5 seconds		
SORCEROUS DAGGER	Main Hand Dagger	42.1 DPS, 8 STA, 17 INT
Equip: Increases damage and healing done by spells and effects by up to 20		
WRISTGUARDS OF STABILITY	Leather Wrists	86 Armor, 24 STR, 8 STA

CLASS TOMES

ITEM	DESC	CLASS
TOME OF TRANQUILIZING SHOT	Hunter	
Teaches you how to use the skill Tranquilizing Shot		

MAGMADAR

This beast of a hound is usually the second boss you face in the Molten Core. When your raid is set, pull him and position your raid as is indicated on the map.

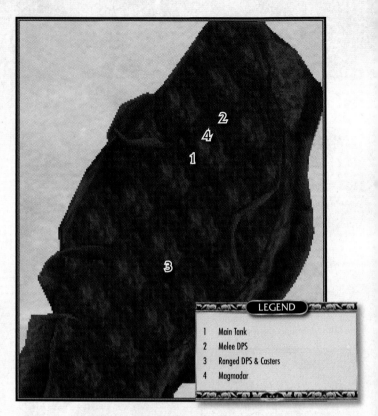

LEGEND

1   Main Tank
2   Melee DPS
3   Ranged DPS & Casters
4   Magmadar

MAGMADAR'S ABILITIES

Frenzy: Magmadar often enters a state of pure rage, almost doubling his damage output. The only remedy is to set up a rotation of Hunters to use their newly-acquired Tranquilizing Shot (learned from Lucifron) on Magmadar. There are two ways for you to know that Magmadar is entering a Frenzy. The first is a message in your chat log saying, "Magmadar goes into a killing frenzy!" and the second is a more visual representation—Magmadar grows in size. The Hunters must be quick to use the shot or your MT will end up taking far more burst damage than he/she can withstand.

Panic: Every 30 seconds, Magmadar emits a large AoE fear. Fear Ward and Tremor Totems can help alleviate this danger for your MT. However, if you do not have either, your MT will have to time his/her Berserker Rage to be in effect right before the fear hits to become immune to fear. If the MT does get feared, Magmadar will run rampant through your raid until the fear runs its course. Keep your casters at max healing range so there is never a break in the healing on your MT.

Flame Breath: Magmadar frequently breathes a cone-shaped stream of fire at the MT. Have your MT keep his/her back to the wall so only they are affected.

Lava Bomb: These appear as burning globs of fire on the ground around Magmadar. Make sure you move away if one lands on you. If you stand in it too long, it deals 3200 points of Fire damage over 8 seconds.

Once Magmadar is in position, give your MT a little extra time to coordinate his/her Berserker Rage with Magmadar's Panic. Once aggro is established, have your melee DPS close in behind Magmadar while the rest of the raid assumes a position out of range of his Panic. Assign a few secondary healers to the melee DPS group.

Keeping the MT from being feared and using quick Tranquilizing shots ensure a smooth battle against Magmadar. After he dies, Ancient Core Hounds no longer respawn in the Molten Core; that's a wonderful feeling.

MAGMADAR'S LOOT TABLE

DRUID

ITEM	DESC	STATS
CENARION LEGGINGS	Leather Legs	175 Armor, 18 STA, 19 INT, 20 SPI, 10 SHAD RES
Equip: Improves your chance to get a critical strike with spells by 1%		
Equip: Restores 4 mana every 5 seconds		
Equip: Increases healing done by spells and effects by up to 22		

HUNTER

ITEM	DESC	STATS
GIANTSTALKER'S LEGGINGS	Mail Legs	369 Armor, 32 AGI, 15 STA, 6 INT, 8 SPI, 10 SHAD RES
Equip: Improves your chance to get a critical strike by 1%		

MAGE

ITEM	DESC	STATS
ARCANIST LEGGINGS	Cloth Legs	89 Armor, 23 STA, 24 INT, 13 SPI, 10 SHAD RES
Equip: Increases your chance to get a critical strike with spells by 1%		
Equip: Increases damage done by Frost spells and effects by up to 14		

PALADIN

ITEM	DESC	STATS
LAWBRINGER LEGPLATES	Plate Legs	655 Armor, 7 STR, 24 STA, 18 INT, 18 SPI, 10 SHAD RES
Equip: Restores 3 mana every 5 seconds		
Equip: Increases healing done by spells and effects by up to 22		

PRIEST

ITEM	DESC	STATS
PANTS OF PROPHECY	Cloth Legs	89 Armor, 18 STA, 24 INT, 20 SPI, 10 SHAD RES
Equip: Restores 6 mana every 5 seconds		
Equip: Increases healing done by spells and effects by up to 22		

ROGUE

ITEM	DESC	STATS
NIGHTSLAYER PANTS	Leather Legs	175 Armor, 10 STR, 33 AGI, 15 STA, 10 SHAD RES
Equip: Improves your chance to get a critical strike by 1%		

SHAMAN

ITEM	DESC	STATS
EARTHFURY LEG GUARDS	Mail Legs	369 Armor, 18 STA, 19 INT, 21 SPI, 10 SHAD RES
Equip: Restores 6 mana every 5 seconds		
Equip: Increases damage and healing done by spells and effects by up to 12		

WARLOCK

ITEM	DESC	STATS
FELHEART PANTS	Cloth Legs	89 Armor, 20 STA, 19 INT, 19 SPI, 10 SHAD RES
Equip: Restores 5 health every 5 seconds		
Equip: Increases damage done by Shadow spells and effects by up to 12		

WARRIOR

ITEM	DESC	STATS
LEGPLATES OF MIGHT	Plate Legs	655 Armor, 24 STR, 23 STA, 10 SHAD RES
Equip: Increases your chance to parry by 1%		
Equip: +7 Defense		

MISCELLANEOUS ITEMS

ITEM	DESC	STATS
AGED CORE LEATHER GLOVES	Leather Gloves	130 Armor, 15 STR, 15 STA, 8 FIRE RES, 5 SHAD RES
Equip: Improves your chance to get a critical strike by 1%		
Equip: Increased daggers +5		
DEEP EARTH SPAULDERS	Mail Shoulders	399 Armor, 11 STA, 12 INT, 7 SPI
Equip: Increases damage done by Nature spells and effects by up to 40		
EARTHSHAKER	Two-Handed Mace	62.6 DPS
Chance on hit: Knocks down all nearby enemies for 3 seconds		
Equip: +22 Attack Power		
ESKHANDAR'S RIGHT CLAW	Main-hand Fist	48.0 DPS, 4 AGI
Chance on hit: Increases your attack speed by 30% for 5 seconds		
FIRE RUNED GRIMOIRE	Off-hand	12 STA, 21 INT
Equip: Increases damage and healing done by spells and effects by up to 11		
FLAMEGUARD GAUNTLETS	Plate Gloves	488 Armor, 13 STA
Equip: Improves your chance to get a critical strike by 1%		
Equip: +54 Attack Power		
FLAMEWAKER LEGPLATES	Plate Legs	748 Armor, 12 STR, 22 STA, 11 FIRE RES, 11 SHAD RES
Equip: Increases your chance to dodge an attack by 1%		
MAGMA TEMPERED BOOTS	Plate Boots	544 Armor, 19 STA, 18 INT, 12 SPI, 8 FIRE RES
Equip: Increases healing done by spells and effects by up to 18		
MANA IGNITING CORD	Cloth Belt	61 Armor, 12 STA, 16 INT
Equip: Increases damage and healing done by spells and effects by up to 25		
Equip: Improves your chance to get a critical strike with spells by 1%		
MEDALLION OF STEADFAST MIGHT	Necklace	9 STR, 13 STA
Equip: Increases your chance to dodge by 1%		
Equip: 8 Defense		
OBSIDIAN EDGED BLADE	Two-Handed Sword	64.7 DPS, 42 STR
Equip: Increased Two-Handed Swords +8		
QUICKSTRIKE RING	Ring	5 STR, 8 STA
Equip: Improves your chance to get a critical strike by 1%		
Equip: +30 Attack Power		
SABATONS OF THE FLAMEWALKER	Mail Boots	298 Armor, 27 STA, 11 INT
Equip: +30 Attack Power		
STRIKER'S MARK	Bow	39.6 DPS
Equip: +22 Attack Power		
Equip: Improves your chance to hit by 1%		
TALISMAN OF EPHEMERAL	Trinket	
Use: Increases damage healing done by spells and effects by up to 175 for 15 seconds		

GEHENNAS

Typically the third boss you face in the raid, Gehennas is like Lucifron in many ways, but a bit trickier. Like Lucifron, he comes with two guards that must be destroyed first. The map shows the positioning for your raid.

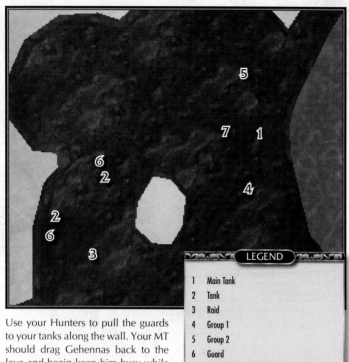

Use your Hunters to pull the guards to your tanks along the wall. Your MT should drag Gehennas back to the lava and begin keep him busy while the guards die.

The MT has two groups Healing and Decursing everyone in their party during this time. The guard tanks must be given extra time for aggro, as these guards have a large AoE stun. Make sure all your casters remain at a safe distance from the guards or their spells will be interrupted by the stun. Having all the tanks (MT and off tanks) use Free Action Potions before charging in is a fantastic way to avoid the stun effect (Fist of Ragnaros) from Gehnnas' adds. Fist of Ragnaros lasts for 4 seconds and occurs in a frontal arc. Non-tank melee DPS can avoid it by staying behind the target.

Once the guards are dead, have the entire raid move to Gehennas and begin attacking him. Make sure you know what Gehennas can do before you take him on; his abilities can be brutal.

GEHENNAS'S ABILITIES

Curse of Gehennas: This is a very dangerous curse. It effectively reduces the effects of all heals by 75%. Your Mages and Druids must be quick to remove this or your MT will face a quick death.

Rain of Fire: A large AoE spell that Gehennas often casts to inflict heavy damage. Your raid must pay attention to this at *all* times. Regardless of where he casts this, you must move out of the affected area no matter what. *The only exception is the MT.* With the amount of healing on the MT that should be coming in, the rain won't affect him/her much. Also, keep your raid spread out over a wide area. This ensures that his Rain does not affect many people at once.

Shadow Bolt: Gehennas has a nasty Shadow Bolt that inflicts 2250 to 2750 points of shadow damage with a 3-6 second cooldown. However, this spell is actually on two separate timers. The first timer targets the player highest on his threat list (MT). The second targets a random player in the raid. That damage is enough to kill a caster, so make sure your Priests cast Shadow Protection before the raid begins. Try to keep everyone's health topped off to prevent one-shot kills.

Besides a few healers and decursers on the MT, the rest of the raid should focus on the guards away from Gehennas. This keeps the raid out of Gehennas' range and his curse is exactly what you want to avoid. Once the guards fall, have the ranged DPS immediately switch targets to Gehennas. If you've got sufficient healing/decursing, have the melee DPS groups rush Gehennas as well, but you may want to hold them back and let the MT and ranged DPS handle him. If your raid's targeted with Rain of Fire, move immediately to avoid incurring serious damage.

Once your raid begins to pound away at Gehennas, he should drop without too much concern. Like Lucifron, he has approximately 350k health, but makes up for it with some insane damage output. Stay out of the Rain of Fire, keep people Decursed, and ensure that the MT stays alive. Victory will soon be yours!

GEHENNAS'S LOOT TABLE

HUNTER

ITEM	DESC	STATS
GIANTSTALKER'S BOOTS	Mail Boots	290 Armor, 28 AGI, 14 STA, 6 SPI, 7 SHAD RES

ROGUE

ITEM	DESC	STATS
NIGHTSLAYER GLOVES	Leather Gloves	125 Armor, 12 STR, 18 AGI, 17 STA, 7 FIRE RES
Equip: Improves your chance to hit by 1%		

PALADIN

ITEM	DESC	STATS
LAWBRINGER GAUNTLETS	Plate Gloves	468 Armor, 10 STR, 15 STA, 15 INT, 14 SPI, 7 FIRE RES
Equip: Increases healing done by spells and effects by up to 18		

PRIEST

ITEM	DESC	STATS
GLOVES OF PROPHECY	Cloth Gloves	63 Armor, 10 STA, 15 INT, 15 SPI, 7 FIRE RES
Equip: Restores 6 mana every 5 seconds		
Equip: Increases healing done by spells and effects by up to 18		

SHAMAN

ITEM	DESC	STATS
EARTHFURY GAUNTLETS	Mail Gloves	264 Armor, 14 STA, 13 INT, 15 SPI, 7 FIRE RES
Equip: Improves your chance to get a critical strike with spells by 1%		
Equip: Increases damage and healing done by spells and effects by up to 9		

WARRIOR

ITEM	DESC	STATS
SABATONS OF MIGHT	Plate Boots	515 Armor, 15 STR, 26 STA, 7 SHAD RES
Equip: +5 Defense		

MISCELLANEOUS ITEMS

ITEM	DESC	STATS
CRIMSON SHOCKER	Wand	73.2 DPS, 10 INT, 10 FIRE RES
FLAMEWAKER LEGPLATES	Plate Legs	748 Armor, 12 STR, 22 STA, 11 FIRE RES, 11 SHAD RES
Equip: Increases your chance to dodge an attack by 1%		
HEAVY DARK IRON RING	Ring	110 Armor, 20 STA
Equip: +5 Defense		
HELM OF THE LIFEGIVER	Mail Helmet	324 Armor, 14 STA, 30 INT, 9 SPI
Equip: Increases healing done by spells and effects by up to 42		
MANASTORM LEGGINGS	Cloth Legs	85 Armor, 19 STA, 14 INT
Equip: Restores 14 mana every 5 seconds		
RING OF SPELL POWER	Ring	
Equip: Increases damage and healing done by spells and effects by up to 33		

ITEM	DESC	STATS
ROBE OF VOLATILE POWER	Cloth Chest	102 Armor, 10 STA, 15 INT, 10 SPI
Equip: Improves your chance to get a critical strike with spells by 2%		
Equip: Increases damage and healing done by spells and effects by up to 23		
SALAMANDER SCALE PANTS	Leather Legs	171 Armor, 14 STA, 14 INT, 10 FIRE RES
Equip: Increases healing done by spells and effects by up to 51		
Equip: Restores 9 mana every 5 seconds		
SORCEROUS DAGGER	Main Hand Dagger	42.1 DPS, 8 STA, 17 INT
Equip: Increases damage and healing done by spells and effects by up to 20		

GARR

Garr is usually the fourth boss you take on in the Molten Core. With eight guards, Garr can seem very intimidating; but, if you handle him correctly, he's actually quite simple.

The first thing that must be mastered in this battle is target calling. Knowing which of his guards to tank and which of his guards to Banish is very important and helps alleviate some of the chaos at the beginning of the fight. As a general rule, you will want to Banish four of his guards and tank four right off the bat.

In order to call targets, have your Hunters mark four different Firesworn and have a tank assist each for their targets. Next, have a Priest in each of the Warlock's groups cast Mind Vision on a different guard until all four guards have Mind Vision on them, then have the Warlock assist the Priest in his or her group. When you're ready, position your raid as shown in the map shortly after pulling.

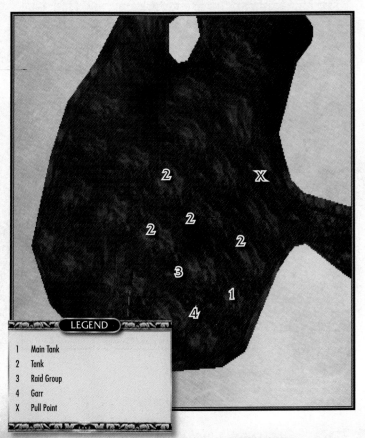

LEGEND

1	Main Tank
2	Tank
3	Raid Group
4	Garr
X	Pull Point

You will want to destroy the four guards being tanked by the Warriors first. When Garr's guards are pulled too far away from him, they gain "Separation Anxiety" which dramatically increases their damage output. Have your MA choose a target and begin dropping its health. At about 30% health, have your tank pull the guard back to the pull point only dealing ranged DPS to it. At this point, your MA should choose a new guard to destroy. When the previous guard reaches 0% health, he explodes dealing area damage. That's the reason for pulling him away from the raid and only dealing ranged DPS from 30% until death. Deal with all four Firesworn in the same way.

After this is done, have your MA select one of the Warlock's targets to attack and wait for it to become Unbanished. As soon as Banish breaks, one of the free tanks must pick up its aggro and deal with it exactly like the previous four. You should now have three Firesworn left. Leave them banished for the rest of the battle and shift your attention to Garr.

You will want to destroy the four guards being tanked by the Warriors first. Have your MA choose a target and begin dropping its health. At about 30% health, have your tank pull the guard back to the pull point only dealing ranged DPS to it. At this point, your MA should choose a new guard to destroy. When the previous guard reaches 0% health, he explodes dealing area damage.

That's the reason for pulling him away from the raid and only dealing ranged DPS from 30% until death. Deal with all four Firesworn in the same way.

After this is done, have your MA select one of the Warlock's targets to attack and wait for it to become Unbanished. As soon as Banish breaks, one of the free tanks must pick up its aggro and deal with it exactly like the previous four. You should now have three Firesworn left. Leave them banished for the rest of the battle and shift your attention to Garr.

GARR'S ABILITIES

Antimagic Pulse: Garr emits a pulse that purges all targets of buffs. For this reason, buffing before battling Garr is not even necessary.

Magma Shackles: This effectively lowers all the targets' movement speed to 40% of normal in a small area for 15 seconds.

Erupt Firesworn: As Garr's life continually lowers, he will attempt to force one of his Firesworn to explode. If the Firesworn are kept Banished, however, his call will be in vain.

Before engaging Garr, you must keep two important things in mind. Garr's attack speed increases with every Firesworn slain. At the beginning of the battle Garr is very slow and weak. However, after slaying five of his kin, his attack speed increases greatly. Make sure one of the free tanks keeps Thunderclap on him. The second thing to keep in mind is rare but can happen. If for some reason, he is successful in forcing all of his Firesworn to explode, a swarm of miniature "Garrs" begin to pour into the room, exploding shortly thereafter. If this happens, it is not the end of your battle, but it does make it much more difficult. Make sure your Warlocks are quick with the Banishes.

Garr has a lot of health, so it takes a few minutes to bring him down. However, he's not extremely dangerous without his minions to assist him. After Garr falls, you must then defeat the remaining three guards exactly the way you did the first. You may now rest assured that no more Lava Surgers will be respawning anytime soon!

GARR'S LOOT TABLE

DRUID

ITEM	DESC	STATS
CENARION HELM	Leather Helmet	163 Armor, 26 STA, 28 INT, 13 SPI, 10 FIRE RES
Equip: Increases damage and healing by spells and effects by up to 12		

HUNTER

ITEM	DESC	STATS
GIANTSTALKER'S HELMET	Mail Helmet	343 Armor, 23 AGI, 23 STA, 15 INT, 8 SPI, 10 FIRE RES
Equip: Improves your chance to get a critical strike by 1%		

MAGE

ITEM	DESC	STATS
ARCANIST CROWN	Cloth Helmet	83 Armor, 14 STA, 35 INT, 8 SPI, 10 FIRE RES
Equip: Increases damage and healing done my spells and effects by up to 15		

PALADIN

ITEM	DESC	STATS
LAWBRINGER HELM	Plate Helmet	608 Armor, 9 STR, 20 STA, 24 INT, 10 SPI, 10 FIRE RES
Equip: Restores 4 mana ever 5 seconds		
Equip: Increases healing done by spells and effects by up to 22		

PRIEST

ITEM	DESC	STATS
CIRCLET OF PROPHECY	Cloth Helmet	83 Armor, 17 STA, 27 INT, 20 SPI, 10 FIRE RES
Equip: Increases damage and healing done by spells and effects by up to 12		

ROGUE

ITEM	DESC	STATS
NIGHTSLAYER COVER	Leather Helmet	163 Armor, 6 STR, 20 AGI, 19 STA, 10 FIRE RES
Equip: Improves your chance to get a critical strike by 2%		

SHAMAN

ITEM	DESC	STATS
EARTHFURY HELMET	Mail Helmet	333 Armor, 24 STA, 23 INT, 13 SPI, 10 FIRE RES
Equip: Restores 6 mana every 5 seconds		
Equip: Increases healing done by spells and effects by up to 22		

WARLOCK

ITEM	DESC	STATS
FELHEART HORNS	Cloth Helmet	83 Armor, 27 STA, 20 INT, 12 SPI, 10 FIRE RES
Equip: Restores 3 health every 5 seconds		
Equip: Increases damage done by Shadow spells and effects by up to 14		

WARRIOR

ITEM	DESC	STATS
HELM OF MIGHT	Plate Helmet	608 Armor, 15 STR, 36 STA, 10 FIRE RES
Equip: Increases your chance to dodge an attack by 1%		
Equip: +7 Defense		

MISCELLANEOUS ITEMS

ITEM	DESC	STATS
AGED CORE LEATHER GLOVES	Leather Gloves	130 Armor, 15 STR, 15 STA, 8 FIRE RES, 5 SHAD RES
Equip: Improves your chance to get a critical strike by 1%		
Equip: Increased daggers +5		
AURASTONE HAMMER	One-Handed Mace	44.6 DPS, 10 STA, 10 INT
Equip: Restores 5 mana every 5 seconds		
Equip: Increases damage and healing done by spells and effects by up to 25		
BINDINGS OF THE WINDSEEKER	The right half of Thunderaan's eternal prison	
BRUTALITY BLADE	One-Handed Sword	51.6 DPS, 9 STR, 9 AGI
Equip: Improves your chance to get a critical strike by 1%		
DEEP EARTH SPAULDERS	Mail Shoulders	399 Armor, 11 STA, 12 INT, 7 SPI
Equip: Increases damage done by Nature spells and effects by up to 40		
DRILLBORER DISK	Shield	2539 Armor, 46 Block, 10 STA
Equip: When struck in combat, inflicts 3 arcane damage to the attacker		
Equip: Increases your chance to block attacks with a shield by 2%		
Equip: Increases the block value of your shield by 23		
FIRE RUNED GRIMOIRE	Off-hand	12 STA, 21 INT
Equip: Increases damage and healing done by spells and effects by up to 11		
FLAMEGUARD GAUNTLETS	Plate Gloves	488 Armor, 13 STA
Equip: Improves your chance to get a critical strike by 1%		
Equip: +54 Attack Power		
FLAMEWAKER LEGPLATES	Plate Legs	748 Armor, 12 STR, 22 STA, 11 FIRE RES, 11 SHAD RES
Equip: Increases your chance to dodge an attack by 1%		
GUTGORE RIPPER	One-Handed Dagger	50.6 DPS
Chance on hit: Sends a shadowy bolt at the enemy causing 75 shadow damage and lowering all stats by 25 for 30 seconds		
MAGMA TEMPERED BOOTS	Plate Boots	544 Armor, 19 STA, 18 INT, 12 SPI, 8 FIRE RES
Equip: Increases healing done by spells and effects by up to 18		
MANA IGNITING CORD	Cloth Belt	61 Armor, 12 STA, 16 INT
Equip: Increases damage and healing done by spells and effects by up to 25		
Equip: Improves your chance to get a critical strike with spells by 1%		
OBSIDIAN EDGED BLADE	Two-Handed Sword	64.7 DPS, 42 STR
Equip: Increased Two-Handed Swords +8		
QUICKSTRIKE RING	Ring	5 STR, 8 STA
Equip: Improves your chance to get a critical strike by 1%		
Equip: +30 Attack Power		
SABATONS OF THE FLAMEWALKER	Mail Boots	298 Armor, 27 STA, 11 INT
Equip: +30 Attack Power		
TALISMAN OF EPHEMERAL	Trinket	
Use: Increases damage healing done by spells and effects by up to 175 for 15 seconds		

BARON GEDDON

Baron Geddon is probably the most amusing fight the Molten Core has to offer. Position your raid in Garr's room as shown on the map.

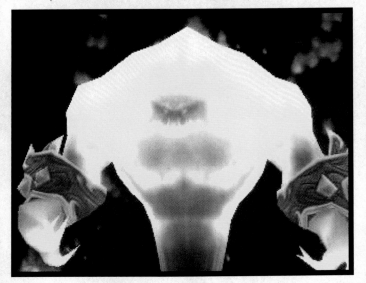

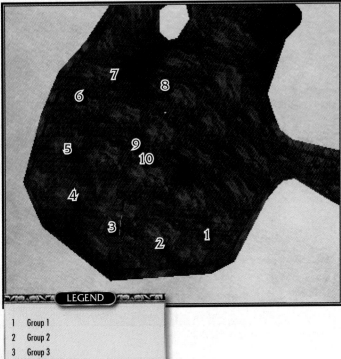

BARON GEDDON'S ABILITIES

Ignite Mana: This is a nasty debuff that burns away 400 mana every 3 seconds converting it into damage. Clearly, this needs to be Dispelled as quickly as possible. There is no need to remove this from Rogues and Warriors, as they suffer nothing from it.

Inferno: Often referred to as "Hellfire" by players since it resembles a Warlock's spell of that name, Inferno is a common occurrence during the Baron Geddon fight. He emits several pulses of fire that deal progressively greater damage the longer a player stays within range. The damage is dealt in waves; take advantage of that and use it as a warning to get out of range. The first "tick" deals 375 base Fire damage and the final one deals 5000!

Living Bomb: This is where the fun begins. Every 15 seconds or so, Baron Geddon places a Living Bomb on a random member of the raid. After 8 seconds, the target explodes dealing heavy damage to anyone around him or her. CTRA has an option to warn the raid of this debuff and it is highly suggested you make use of it. Make sure your raid leader is on the ball in letting raid members know over your voice server if someone is "The Bomb". If you're the target of this debuff and you realize it in time, you must run to the wall behind your group. A well-timed Priest shield can save a life if it's cast before they explode. If the melee DPS is the target, the must run to the tunnel east of Garr's room to ensure they do not explode near the MT. Should the MT receive the Living Bomb, he/she should hold fast and stand their ground. Have the remaining melee DPS move back to their respective groups. If the MT receives the Living Bomb during a Flame Pulse, he/she should run to an open space while the raid leader informs nearby healers to be ready.

There is something about Living Bomb that requires a special note. While it can't be dispelled, it can be removed with Ice Block or Divine Shield.

As long as your raid members are quick to realize Living Bomb targets and take the necessary steps not to blow their groups up, Baron Geddon is a relative walk in the park. With roughly 580k health, he's not even close to one of the toughest bosses in the core.

If your raid is having trouble with the eight 5-man party setup due to a lack of casters with Dispel, try switching to four 10-man groups.

BARON GEDDON'S LOOT TABLE

DRUID

ITEM	DESC	STATS
CENARION SPAULDERS	Leather Shoulders	150 Armor, 13 STA, 20 INT, 10 SPI, 7 SHAD RES
Equip: Restores 4 mana every 5 seconds		
Equip: Increases healing done by spells and effects by up to 18		

MAGE

ITEM	DESC	STATS
ARCANIST MANTLE	Cloth Shoulders	76 Armor, 10 STA, 24 INT, 5 SPI, 7 SHAD RES
Equip: Restores 4 mana every 5 seconds		
Equip: Increases damage done by Frost spells and effects by up to 11		

PALADIN

ITEM	DESC	STATS
LAWBRINGER SPAULDERS	Plate Shoulders	562 Armor, 10 STR, 22 STA, 15 INT, 8 SPI, 7 SHAD RES
Equip: Increases healing done by spells and effects by up to 18		

SHAMAN

ITEM	DESC	STATS
EARTHFURY EPAULETS	Mail Shoulders	317 Armor, 17 STA, 18 INT, 10 SPI, 7 SHAD RES
Equip: Restores 4 mana every 5 seconds		
Equip: Increases healing done by spells and effects by up to 18		

WARLOCK

ITEM	DESC	STATS
FELHEART SHOULDER PADS	Cloth Shoulders	76 Armor, 25 STA, 17 INT, 7 SPI, 7 SHAD RES
Equip: Increases damage done by Shadow spells and effects by up to 9		

MISCELLANEOUS ITEMS

ITEM	DESC	STATS
AGED CORE LEATHER GLOVES	Leather Gloves	130 Armor, 15 STR, 15 STA, 8 FIRE RES, 5 SHAD RES
Equip: Improves your chance to get a critical strike by 1% Equip: Increased daggers +5		
BINDINGS OF WINDSEEKER	The left half of Thunderaan's eternal prison	
DEEP EARTH SPAULDERS	Mail Shoulders	399 Armor, 11 STA, 12 INT, 7 SPI
Equip: Increases damage done by Nature spells and effects by up to 40		
FIRE RUNED GRIMOIRE	Off-hand	12 STA, 21 INT
Equip: Increases damage and healing done by spells and effects by up to 11		
FLAMEGUARD GAUNTLETS	Plate Gloves	488 Armor, 13 STA
Equip: Improves your chance to get a critical strike by 1% Equip: +54 Attack Power		
FLAMEWAKER LEGPLATES	Plate Legs	748 Armor, 12 STR, 22 STA, 11 FIRE RES, 11 SHAD RES
Equip: Increases your chance to dodge an attack by 1%		
MAGMA TEMPERED BOOTS	Plate Boots	544 Armor, 19 STA, 18 INT, 12 SPI, 8 FIRE RES
Equip: Increases healing done by spells and effects by up to 18		
MANA IGNITING CORD	Cloth Belt	61 Armor, 12 STA, 16 INT
Equip: Increases damage and healing done by spells and effects by up to 25 Equip: Improves your chance to get a critical strike with spells by 1%		
OBSIDIAN EDGED BLADE	Two-Handed Sword	64.7 DPS, 42 STR
Equip: Increased Two-Handed Swords +8		
QUICKSTRIKE RING	Ring	5 STR, 8 STA
Equip: Improves your chance to get a critical strike by 1% Equip: +30 Attack Power		
SABATONS OF THE FLAMEWALKER	Mail Boots	298 Armor, 27 STA, 11 INT
Equip: +30 Attack Power		
SEAL OF THE ARCHMAGUS	Ring	11 STA, 11 INT, 11 SPI, 6 ARC RES, 6 FIRE RES, 6 NAT RES, 6 FRS RES, 6 SHAD RES
Equip: Restores 3 mana every 5 seconds		
TALISMAN OF EPHEMERAL	Trinket	

SHAZZRAH

Shazzrah is one of the most difficult encounters in Molten Core. Your raid must be spread out in Garr's room in three separate groups as show in the map. Make sure each of the three groups has a warrior in it! Some raids may call for a two- or four-group setup. It's up to the raid leader to make that decision.

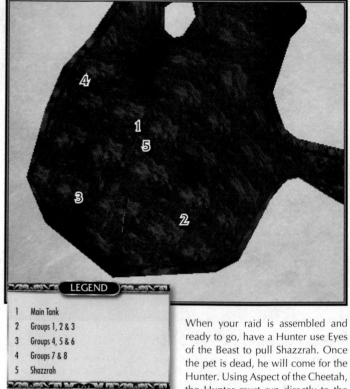

LEGEND

1	Main Tank
2	Groups 1, 2 & 3
3	Groups 4, 5 & 6
4	Groups 7 & 8
5	Shazzrah

When your raid is assembled and ready to go, have a Hunter use Eyes of the Beast to pull Shazzrah. Once the pet is dead, he will come for the Hunter. Using Aspect of the Cheetah, the Hunter must run directly to the MT until Shazzrah is in the middle of the room and being tanked by the MT. Now the fun part begins!

SHAZZRAH'S ABILITIES

Blink: Every 40-45 seconds Shazzrah drops all aggro on the MT, Blinks to a random raid member and begins casting.

Arcane Explosion: Shazzrah often casts a large AoE that deals 925 to 1075 points of arcane damage.

Curse of Shazzrah: This curse doubles all magical damage done to the target. This must be Decursed immediately in groups. Those that have the curse on when he Blinks into their group will take double damage from his Arcane Explosion if the curse is not removed. Needless to say, this must always be removed from the MT as quickly as possible.

Deaden Magic: This is a self-buff cast by Shazzrah on himself every few seconds. It effectively reduces all magic damage on him by 50%. The only way to see this buff is to assign a Mage to cast Detect Magic on him and assign a Priest to Dispel it. This must be done or the battle will last too long, incurring too many casualties.

When your raid is assembled and ready to go, have a Hunter use Eyes of the Beast to pull Shazzrah. Once the pet is dead, he will come for the Hunter. Using Aspect of the Cheetah, the Hunter must run directly to the MT until Shazzrah is in the middle of the room and being tanked by the MT. Now the fun part begins!

After Shazzrah is pulled, he almost always Blinks away to another group. Aggro control is *extremely* important in this fight, so make sure nobody attacks until the call is given. The reason for having a tank in each group is to ensure Shazzrah gets dragged out of the group as quickly as possible. Make sure he's dragged to the middle where the MT will pick up his aggro again.

As soon as Shazzrah is back in the middle of the room and being tanked, you have a short window to deal damage. The moment he is secure, have a Mage cast Detect Magic on him, and a Priest cast Dispel to remove his buff. Give the order to attack as soon as possible; you won't have much time before the next Blink. Remember to remind your raid not to use DoT spells. These last through the Blink, generating aggro on the caster, making it more difficult to secure aggro for the MT.

45 short seconds later, you'll be faced with another Blink. Repeat the previous strategy to win this battle. You may have to practice many times to get it just right, but fear not—practice makes perfect.

SHAZZRAH'S LOOT TABLE

DRUID

ITEM	DESC	STATS
CENARION GLOVES	Leather Gloves	125 Armor, 17 STA, 18 INT, 15 SPI, 7 FIRE RES
Equip: Increases healing done by spells and effects by up to 18		

HUNTER

ITEM	DESC	STATS
GIANTSTALKER'S GLOVES	Mail Gloves	264 Armor, 18 AGI, 12 STA, 7 FIRE RES
Equip: Improves your chance to hit by 2%		

MAGE

ITEM	DESC	STATS
ARCANIST GLOVES	Cloth Gloves	63 Armor, 17 STA, 18 INT, 10 SPI, 7 SHAD RES
Equip: Restores 4 mana every 5 seconds		

PRIEST

ITEM	DESC	STATS
BOOTS OF PROPHECY	Cloth Boots	70 Armor, 17 STA, 18 INT, 15 SPI, 7 SHAD RES
Equip: Increases healing done by spells and effects by up to 18		

ROGUE

ITEM	DESC	STATS
NIGHTSLAYER BOOTS	Leather Boots	138 Armor, 26 AGI, 18 STA, 7 SHAD RES

WARLOCK

ITEM	DESC	STATS
FELHEART SLIPPERS	Cloth Boots	70 Armor, 27 STA, 10 INT, 8 SPI, 7 FIRE RES
Equip: Increases damage done by Shadow spells and effects by up to 11		

MISCELLANEOUS ITEMS

ITEM	DESC	STATS
CRIMSON SHOCKER	Wand	73.2 DPS, 10 INT, 10 FIRE RES
FLAMEWAKER LEGPLATES	Plate Legs	748 Armor, 12 STR, 22 STA, 11 FIRE RES, 11 SHAD RES
Equip: Increases your chance to dodge an attack by 1%		

ITEM	DESC	STATS
HEAVY DARK IRON RING	Ring	110 Armor, 20 STA
Equip: +5 Defense		
HELM OF THE LIFEGIVER	Mail Helmet	324 Armor, 14 STA, 30 INT, 9 SPI
Equip: Increases healing done by spells and effects by up to 42		
MANASTORM LEGGINGS	Cloth Legs	85 Armor, 19 STA, 14 INT
Equip: Restores 14 mana every 5 seconds		
RING OF SPELL POWER	Ring	
Equip: Increases damage and healing done by spells and effects by up to 33		
ROBE OF VOLATILE POWER	Cloth Chest	102 Armor, 10 STA, 15 INT, 10 SPI
Equip: Improves your chance to get a critical strike with spells by 2%		
Equip: Increases damage and healing done by spells and effects by up to 23		
SALAMANDER SCALE PANTS	Leather Legs	171 Armor, 14 STA, 14 INT, 10 FIRE RES
Equip: Increases healing done by spells and effects by up to 51		
Equip: Restores 9 mana every 5 seconds		
SORCEROUS DAGGER	Main Hand Dagger	42.1 DPS, 8 STA, 17 INT
Equip: Increases damage and healing done by spells and effects by up to 20		
WRISTGUARDS OF STABILITY	Leather Wrists	86 Armor, 24 STR, 8 STA

GOLEMAGG THE INCINERATOR

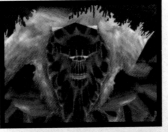

Golemagg is an incredibly simple fight that will be mastered in the first one or two tries. Two hounds called "Core Ragers" guard him. Use the map to position your raid shortly after pulling.

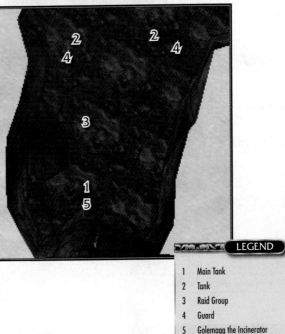

LEGEND	
1	Main Tank
2	Tank
3	Raid Group
4	Guard
5	Golemagg the Incinerator

Make sure that Golemagg and the Core Ragers are a safe distance from each other. If the Ragers are too close to Golemagg, they receive an attack power and speed bonus that can be the death of your off tanks.

The first thing to note is that Golemagg the Incinerator has no real abilities to mention. He casts Pyroblast now and then that inflicts an initial 1388 to 1612 Fire damage and an additional 200 every 3 seconds for 12 seconds, but it's nothing that your healers can't remedy. The second aspect of this battle that should be noted is that *the Core Ragers are invincible.* If their health is brought to 50% or less, they will refuse to die and completely heal themselves. The two Warriors that tank the Core Ragers are basically there to keep them as far away from Golemagg as possible and to keep them busy until their master dies. Golemagg does have a chance to proc Magma Splash when struck with melee attacks. It's a Fire-based DoT with a stacking debuff effect. Each separate effect deals 50 damage every 3 seconds and reduces the target's armor by 250.

Once your MT has secured aggro on Golemagg, your raid should immediately begin to inflict heavy DPS as hard as they can. This giant has more than 800k health, so he takes quite some time to defeat, but nothing he does proves to be terribly lethal.

At 10% health, Golemagg's damage increases dramatically and he gains the Earthquake effect. It deals approximately 1500 AoE melee damage when he strikes. Heals need to be taken up a notch from here on out until the giant is slain. When Golemagg falls, his Core Ragers follow suit within moments of him hitting the ground.

GOLEMAGG THE INCINERATOR'S LOOT TABLE

DRUID

ITEM	DESC	STATS
CENARION VESTMENTS	Leather Chest	200 Armor, 23 STA, 24 INT, 16 SPI, 10 FIRE RES
Equip: Restores 3 mana every 5 seconds		
Equip: Increases healing done by spells and effects by up to 22		

HUNTER

ITEM	DESC	STATS
GIANTSTALKER'S BREASTPLATE	Mail Chest	422 Armor, 26 AGI, 23 STA, 11 INT, 10 FIRE RES
Equip: Improves your chance to get a critical strike by 1%		

MAGE

ITEM	DESC	STATS
ARCANIST ROBES	Cloth Chest	102 Armor, 19 STA, 33 INT, 14 SPI, 10 FIRE RES
Equip: Increases damage and healing done my spells and effects by up to 16		

PALADIN

ITEM	DESC	STATS
LAWBRINGER CHESTGUARD	Plate Chest	749 Armor, 8 STR, 26 STA, 21 INT, 13 SPI, 10 FIRE RES
Equip: Increases healing done by spells and effects by up to 22		

PRIEST

ITEM	DESC	STATS
ROBES OF PROPHECY	Cloth Chest	102 Armor, 20 STA, 27 INT, 17 SPI, 10 FIRE RES
Equip: Increases healing done by spells and effects by up to 22		

ROGUE

ITEM	DESC	STATS
NIGHTSLAYER CHESTPIECE	Leather Chest	200 Armor, 10 STR, 29 AGI, 20 STA, 10 FIRE RES
Equip: Improves your chance to get a critical strike by 1%		

SHAMAN

ITEM	DESC	STATS
EARTHFURY VESTMENTS	Mail Chest	422 Armor, 17 STA, 27 INT, 13 SPI, 10 FIRE RES
Equip: Improves your chance to get a critical strike with spells by 1%		
Equip: Increases healing done by spells and effects by up to 22		

WARLOCK

ITEM	DESC	STATS
FELHEART ROBES	Cloth Chest	102 Armor, 31 STAM, 20 INT, 10 SPI, 10 FIRE RES
Equip: Increases damage done by Shadow spells and effects by up to 12		

WARRIOR

ITEM	DESC	STATS
BREASTPLATE OF MIGHT	Plate Chest	749 Armor, 20 STR, 28 STA, 10 FIRE RES
Equip: Improves your chance to block with a shield by 3%		
Equip: +7 Defense		

MISCELLANEOUS ITEMS

ITEM	DESC	STATS
AGED CORE LEATHER GLOVES	Leather Gloves	130 Armor, 15 STR, 15 STA, 8 FIRE RES, 5 SHAD RES
Equip: Improves your chance to get a critical strike by 1%		
Equip: Increased daggers +5		
AZURESONG MAGEBLADE	Main-hand Sword	42.5 DPS, 7 STA, 12 INT
Equip: Improves our chance to get a critical strike with spells by 1%		
Equip: Increases damage and healing done by magical spells and effects by up to 40		
BLASTERSHOT LAUNCHER	Gun	40.2 DPS, 6 STA
Equip: Improves your chance to get a critical strike by 1%		
DEEP EARTH SPAULDERS	Mail Shoulders	399 Armor, 11 STA, 12 INT, 7 SPI
Equip: Increases damage done by Nature spells and effects by up to 40		
FIRE RUNED GRIMOIRE	Off-hand	12 STA, 21 INT
Equip: Increases damage and healing done by spells and effects by up to 11		
FLAMEGUARD GAUNTLETS	Plate Gloves	488 Armor, 13 STA
Equip: Improves your chance to get a critical strike by 1%		
Equip: +54 Attack Power		
FLAMEWAKER LEGPLATES	Plate Legs	748 Armor, 12 STR, 22 STA, 11 FIRE RES, 11 SHAD RES
Equip: Increases your chance to dodge an attack by 1%		
MAGMA TEMPERED BOOTS	Plate Boots	544 Armor, 19 STA, 18 INT, 12 SPI, 8 FIRE RES
Equip: Increases healing done by spells and effects by up to 18		
MANA IGNITING CORD	Cloth Belt	61 Armor, 12 STA, 16 INT
Equip: Increases damage and healing done by spells and effects by up to 25		
Equip: Improves your chance to get a critical strike with spells by 1%		
OBSIDIAN EDGED BLADE	Two-Handed Sword	64.7 DPS, 42 STR
Equip: Increased Two-Handed Swords +8		
QUICKSTRIKE RING	Ring	5 STR, 8 STA
Equip: Improves your chance to get a critical strike by 1%		
Equip: +30 Attack Power		
SABATONS OF THE FLAMEWALKER	Mail Boots	298 Armor, 27 STA, 11 INT
Equip: +30 Attack Power		

ITEM	DESC	STATS
STAFF OF DOMINANCE	Staff	57.1 DPS, 16 STA, 37 INT, 14 SPI
Equip: Improves our chance to get a critical strike with spells by 1%		
Equip: Increases damage and healing done by magical spells and effects by up to 40		
TALISMAN OF EPHEMERAL POWER	Trinket	
Use: Increases damage healing done by spells and effects by up to 175 for 15 seconds		

TRADE ITEMS

ITEM	DESC
SULFURON INGOT	Used in the creation of the Sulfuron Hammer

SULFURON HARBINGER

At first, this boss looks quite intimidating. Flanked by four healers, who wouldn't be a little scared to face off against it? Luckily for you, this fight is not nearly as difficult as it looks. Pull him much like any boss and position your raid as shown on the map.

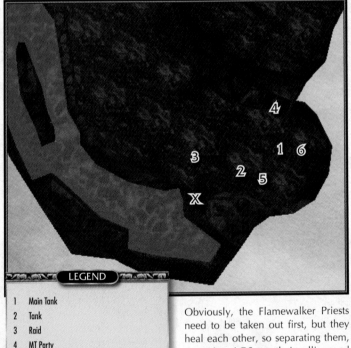

LEGEND

1	Main Tank
2	Tank
3	Raid
4	MT Party
5	Guard
6	Sulfuron Harbinger
X	Kill Spot

Obviously, the Flamewalker Priests need to be taken out first, but they heal each other, so separating them, removing LOS to their allies and eliminating them individually is the only way to defeat them. Have three of your tanks pull the guards along the bottom wall while the MT tanks Sulfuron Harbinger at his spot. Your fourth tank will drag their target north, out of range of the other healers, and begin to tank the him. Rogues must kick the target to interrupt any spell casting. The healers will also cast a series of DoT spells on your tanks that need to be Dispelled immediately. One by one, drag the healers north and destroy them. Within a few short minutes, your raid can then focus their attention on Sulfuron.

SULFURON HARBINGER'S ABILITIES

Fist of Ragnaros: This is a short duration AoE stun that he often casts. During the stun, he attempts to move out of melee range of the MT and begin throwing spears. Simply move to him and re-engage him in melee combat.

Demoralizing Shout: An AoE shout that lowers all melee and ranged attack power by 300. There is no counter to this.

Flame Spear: This is a ranged attack with a 45 yard range and a 2 second cooldown dealing 850 to 1150 damage to the primary target and some carryover splash damage to others close to that player.

Inspire: Now this is a nasty buff that increases physical damage by 25% while also boosting his attack speed by 100% for 10 seconds.

Sulfuron has a lot of armor so he takes some time to take down. However, he is not as lethal as the previous captains, so it's only a matter of time until he falls. Keep the heals up, the damage pumping, and the corpse of Sulfuron Harbinger shall soon lie at your feet.

FLAMEWALKER PRIEST ABILITIES

Dark Mending: This powerful healing spell restores 27,750 to 32,250 HP to the target. It has a 2 second casting time and a 60 yard range. That casting time allows for interruptions and should be the focus of an interrupt order.

Shadow Word: Pain: It's like the Priest spell, but deals 440 Shadow damage every 3 seconds for 18 secs.

Dark Strike: Adds 570 to 630 melee damage to the next successful melee attack. All damage dealt is considered Shadow damage.

Immolate: This is an instant cast DoT that deals 760 to 840 Fire damage and 380 to 420 damage every 3 seconds for 21 secs.

SULFURON HARBINGER'S LOOT TABLE

HUNTER

ITEM	DESC	STATS
GIANTSTALKER'S EPAULETS	Mail Shoulders	317 Armor, 24 AGI, 14 STA, 5 INT, 9 SPI, 7 SHAD RES
Equip: Improves your chance to hit by 1%		

PRIEST

ITEM	DESC	STATS
MANTLE OF PROPHECY	Cloth Shoulders	76 Armor, 13 STA, 23 INT, 10 SPI, 7 SHAD RES
Equip: Increases damage and healing done by spells and effects by up to 9)		

ROGUE

ITEM	DESC	STATS
NIGHTSLAYER SHOULDER PADS	Leather Shoulders	150 Armor, 3 STR, 26 AGI, 12 STA, 7 SHAD RES
Equip: Improves your chance to hit by 1%		

WARRIOR

ITEM	DESC	STATS
PAULDRONS OF MIGHT	Plate Shoulders	562 Armor, 15 STR, 22 STA, 7 SHAD RES
Equip: Improves your chance to block with a shield by 2%		
Equip: +5 Defense		

MISCELLANEOUS ITEMS

ITEM	DESC	STATS
CRIMSON SHOCKER	Wand	73.2 DPS, 10 INT, 10 FIRE RES
FLAMEWAKER LEGPLATES	Plate Legs	748 Armor, 12 STR, 22 STA, 11 FIRE RES, 11 SHAD RES
Equip: Increases your chance to dodge an attack by 1%		
HEAVY DARK IRON RING	Ring	110 Armor, 20 STA
Equip: +5 Defense		
HELM OF THE LIFEGIVER	Mail Helmet	324 Armor, 14 STA, 30 INT, 9 SPI
Equip: Increases healing done by spells and effects by up to 42		
MANASTORM LEGGINGS	Cloth Legs	85 Armor, 19 STA, 14 INT
Equip: Restores 14 mana every 5 seconds		
RING OF SPELL POWER	Ring	
Equip: Increases damage and healing done by spells and effects by up to 33		

ITEM	DESC	STATS
ROBE OF VOLATILE POWER	Cloth Chest	102 Armor, 10 STA, 15 INT, 10 SPI
Equip: Improves your chance to get a critical strike with spells by 2%		
Equip: Increases damage and healing done by spells and effects by up to 23		
SALAMANDER SCALE PANTS	Leather Legs	171 Armor, 14 STA, 14 INT, 10 FIRE RES
Equip: Increases healing done by spells and effects by up to 51, Equip: Restores 9 mana every 5 seconds		
SORCEROUS DAGGER	Main Hand Dagger	42.1 DPS, 8 STA, 17 INT
Equip: Increases damage and healing done by spells and effects by up to 20		
SHADOWSTRIKE	Pole-arm	59.4 DPS
Chance on hit: Steals 100-180 life from target enemy		
Use: Transform Shadowstrike into Thunderstrike		
WRISTGUARDS OF STABILITY	Leather Wrists	86 Armor, 24 STR, 8 STA

LORDS OF THE CORE

MAJORDOMO EXECUTUS

This is - by far - the most technical fight the Molten Core has to offer. Majordomo Executus is bolstered on all sides by eight guards of two varieties. However, before Majordomo even shows his face, *all* seven runes of the Firelord must be doused. Once they are, Executus yells, announcing his arrival into the Molten Core.

The pull is like any boss, except that you are taking care of eight guards instead of two or four. Immediately sheep all four healers at the beginning of the battle and line up the Flamewalker Elites along the east wall as shown in the map.

Majordomo *must* be kept busy this entire fight by either two Warriors, one Warrior and a Hunter, a Warrior and a Shaman/Paladin, or one Warrior and a Druid in Bear Form. The reasoning behind this is the fact that every 25-30 seconds, Executus simply drops aggro on the MT and goes on a killing spree. Having a Warrior and another player constantly fighting for his attention keeps him off the rest of the raid. Rage can be a problem as long as his shield is up, but you must do the best you can. Your MT will make good use of Bloodrage in this battle for certain.

MAJORDOMO EXECUTUS'S ABILITIES

Aegis of Ragnaros: This is an instant spell that heals Majordomo to full health if he's damaged. In essence, it makes him unkillable.

Damage Shield: This buff gives all of Majordomo's allies a shield that reflects 100 Arcane damage when his minions are struck with a melee attack. Majordomo alternates between using this and his Magic Reflection buff.

Magic Reflection: Watch for this spell, it's a buff that grants all of Majordomo's allies a 50% chance to reflect harmful spells for 10 seconds. Majordomo alternates between using this and his Damage Shield buff.

Teleport: Majordomo periodically teleports a random player to a fire pit near his spawn point. It has a 25-30 second cooldown and appears to completely wipe the Majordomo's threat list.

Teleport (2): Executus occasionally teleports his primary target to the fire pit. Again, this has a 25-30 second cooldown and completely wipes his threat list.

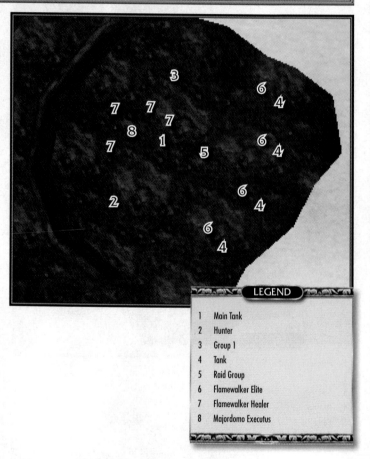

LEGEND	
1	Main Tank
2	Hunter
3	Group 1
4	Tank
5	Raid Group
6	Flamewalker Elite
7	Flamewalker Healer
8	Majordomo Executus

FLAMEWALKER ELITE ABILITIES

Blast Wave: Again, similar to the Mage spell, it hits nearby targets for 763 to 887 Fire damage and reduces their movement speed to 50% for 8 seconds.

Fire Blast: Instantly hits a single target for 1188 to 1452 points of Fire damage.

Fireball: This is similar to the Mage spell of the same name and hits a single target for 1275 to 1725 Fire damage.

FLAMEWALKER HEALER ABILITIES

Shadow Bolt: This is similar to the Warlock spell and deals 1350 to 1650 Shadow damage.

Shadow Shock: An instant attack that deals approximately 800 points of Shadow damage to nearby targets.

After four of Majordomo's guards (either Elites or Healers) have been slain, Flamewalker Healers become immune to Polymorph.

As soon as the fight begins, the DPS must defeat the first Flamewalker Elite that is being tanked. Remember to space these guards far enough apart that their AoE flame bursts won't overlap on tanks. As soon as the guard is down, the free tank should begin to break the sheeped targets one by one, tanking them, until all four are defeated. Have your raid leader ready to speak over your voice when the healers bring their shield up. They have two types of shields that must be taken seriously if you hope to survive. The first reflects 100 Arcane damage back to the attacker from a melee strike for a few seconds. While this shield is up, your melee DPS *must not* attack. The second shield returns all magic damage back to the owner(s) for a few seconds. As with the melee shield, your casters *must not* attack during this time.

Once all four healers are defeated, have your raid finish off the remaining three Flamewalker Elites being tanked along the wall. When there's only one of Majordomo's allies standing, he'll heal them completely and buff them to increase their damage output. When all eight guards are defeated, Majordomo Executus reveals his true colors and surrenders. He then leaves for you a chest of spoils and asks you to meet him in the center of the Molten Core—the lair of Ragnaros the Firelord! If the entire raid leaves, you have 30 minutes before Majordomo despawns from the soft reset. However, as long as you leave one player inside, Majordomo won't. Regardless, step on it!

CACHE OF THE FIRELORD LOOT TABLE

ITEM	DESC	STATS
ANCIENT PETRIFIED LEAF	This item begins a quest	Hunter, A very large petrified leaf
CAUTERIZING BAND	Ring	9 STA, 12 INT
Equip: Increases healing done by spells and effects by up to 46		
CORE FORGED GREAVES	Plate Boots	634 Armor, 28 STA, 12 FIRE RES, 8 SHAD RES
Equip: +4 Defense		
CORE HOUND TOOTH	One-Handed Dagger	51.2 DPS, 9 STA
Equip: Improves your chance to get a critical strike by 1%		
Equip: +20 Attack Power		
EYE OF DIVINITY	Trinket	Quest Item
FINKLE'S LAVA DREDGER	Two-Handed Mace	67.1 DPS, 25 STA, 24 INT, 15 FIRE RES
Equip: Restores 9 mana every 5 seconds		
FIREGUARD SHOULDERS	Leather Shoulders	159 Armor, 28 STA, 22 FIRE RES
FIREPROOF CLOAK	Back	54 Armor, 12 STA, 9 INT, 8 SPI, 18 FIRE RES
GLOVES OF THE HYPNOTIC FLAME	Cloth Gloves	67 Armor, 18 STA, 19 INT, 8 SPI
Equip: Increases damage done by Fire spells and effects by up to 23		
Equip: Increased damage and healing done by spells and effects by up to 9		
SASH OF WHISPERED SECRETS	Cloth Belt	61 Armor, 17 STA
Equip: Increases damage done by Shadow spells and effects by up to 33		
Equip: Restores 4 health every 5 seconds		
WILD GROWTH SPAULDERS	Leather Shoulders	159 Armor, 11 STA, 12 INT, 10 SPI
Equip: Increases healing done by spells and effects by up to 62		
WRISTGUARDS OF TRUE FLIGHT	Mail Wrist	198 Armor, 19 AGI, 11 STA, 6 INT
Equip: Improves your chance to hit by 1%		

RAGNAROS THE FIRELORD

So you've beaten every boss in the Molten Core and now you stand in the lair of Ragnaros ready to summon him forth, thinking you're hot stuff. Well Ragnaros has news for you! He was hot stuff long before you were ever a twinkle in your mother's eye! This battle commands every resource your raid group can muster—and then some.

The first thing to work on is your fire resistance. Nearly every attack Ragnaros throws at you is fire-based (melee is still melee). Your Warriors should try to aim for 315 buffed fire resistance; a daunting task, yes, but very necessary. Everyone else in your raid should shoot for 200 buffed fire resistance to stand a chance against the Firelord himself. There are many ways to attain these resistance levels. The most effective is via Thorium Brotherhood faction. These able dwarves hold many plans to suits of armor with a great amount of fire resistance to them. The second path is via random drops and the Auction House. Items such as rings of fire resistance become incredibly useful in this fight, as is your previous reward from Duke Hydraxis at the end of his quest line.

The second item you will want to procure is the Greater Fire Protection Potion. Skilled alchemists can make these using a simple list of ingredients. You should have as many of these as possible to make the battle run smoothly. Drinking two or three of these per Ragnaros battle extends the life of your raid by a great amount.

When you think you're ready to take on Ragnaros, speak with Majordomo Executus and watch in awe as he summons forth the Firelord. You now have exactly two hours to kill Ragnaros before he despawns. Quickly move your raid into the positions shown on the map, making sure your casters are spread out widely to avoid his Might of Ragnaros.

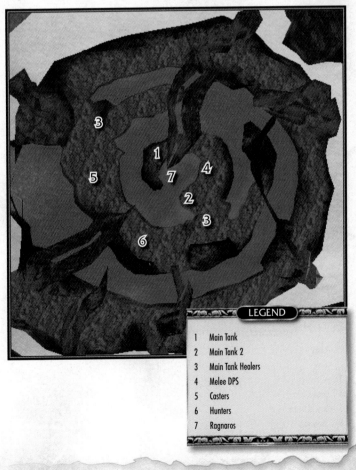

	LEGEND
1	Main Tank
2	Main Tank 2
3	Main Tank Healers
4	Melee DPS
5	Casters
6	Hunters
7	Ragnaros

RAGNAROS'S ABILITIES

Elemental Fire: This is a fire-based DoT proc that deals 4800 damage over 8 seconds.

Melt Weapon: Every time you strike Ragnaros with a melee weapon there is a chance its durability will be decreased. Bring a spare or a repair bot just in case.

Wrath of Ragnaros: Every 30 seconds Ragnaros attempts to deal damage to and knock back all players in melee range—your MT is the one to receive this the most often. 315 fire resistance makes your MT almost immune to this attack, but if your MT does get sent flying, your secondary MT should be there to pick up the aggro until your MT can return. Players often use CT Raid Assist to time his Wrath, so all melee attackers (except the MT) can back away in time to avoid it safely. Regardless, anyone that gets knocked back takes extreme fall damage, so the healers must make sure that their health gets topped-off in mid-air.

Magma Blast: This is a ranged spell that deals 6000 base Fire damage. Ragnaros only reverts to casting this spell if there's nobody engaged in melee combat with him. This is why it's important to have your secondary tank grab aggro in the event that your MT is sent flying from Wrath of Ragnaros. Some guilds simply have two tanks take the hit from Wrath of Ragnaros to ensure that at least one resists it.

Might of Ragnaros: Quite often, Ragnaros fires off a large ball of flame at a random person in the raid dealing heavy fire damage and sending this player - and anyone around them - flying away. This often knocks a raid member into the lava. As long as they have a nearby healer and a Greater Fire Protection Potion, they should be able to survive this attack.

This fight is totally different from anything you've experienced before. It's impossible for the ranged DPS to pull aggro because of Ragnaros's rooted nature. He cannot leave his spot to go attack someone else. The MT should be the only target of his melee attacks. So, the second the MT starts to attack Ragnaros, the ranged DPS can begin attacking at full strength. It's important that they inflict as much DPS as possible. Ragnaros must be at 50% or less after the first 3 minutes or you may not survive the ordeal.

After a few seconds, the melee DPS can join in the battle and add their damage to the fight. After about 2 minutes and 45 seconds, the entire raid needs to reform to the positions shown on this map.

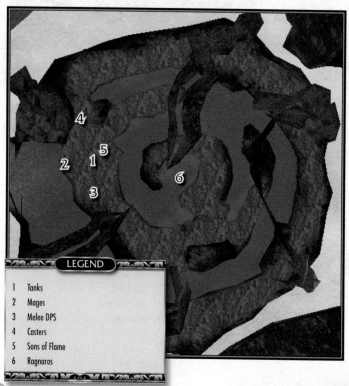

LEGEND

1 Tanks
2 Mages
3 Melee DPS
4 Casters
5 Sons of Flame
6 Ragnaros

After 3 minutes, Ragnaros submerges into the lava becoming completely immune to attack. He summons forth the Sons of Flame. These creatures are lesser firelords that deal pure melee fire damage, so your tanks should drink a Greater Fire Protection Potion at the beginning of this phase. They have an AoE mana drain, so keeping them out of the casters is extremely important in this phase. Have a warrior use Challenging Shout to round them all up, using your other tanks to grab the stragglers and prepare to have your mages use Blizzard like they've never done before. Your mages must alternate Frost Novas to keep them in place while your warriors try to keep them on them as much as possible. Once all of them are rounded up and rooted, your mages must begin to cast Blizzard. If you have five or more mages, this phase is incredibly easy, but if you have less it might just be a challenge. If you take longer than 1 minute, Ragnaros re-emerges and resumes the battle.

Sons of Flame are vulnerable to a variety of CC methods including: Banish, Fear, and Freezing Trap. Use these to buy the tanks time to get them into the correct positions. Some guilds prefer to have one tank use Challenging Shout to gather the Sons, but many guilds also assign a single tank to every Son that's not CC'd. It's up to your raid leader to define the parameters of this battle. Have your MA lead the Rogues through the swarm of Sons of Flame bringing them down one by one while the Blizzard is being cast. However, before you defeat the final Son of Flame, have your raid return to their original phase 1 positions. When the last Son dies, Ragnaros shows himself again. Repeat this phase just as you did the first 50% of his health. With a little luck - and a lot of DPS - you might just drop him before the next 3 minutes is up. If you don't, however, prepare to crush another wave of Sons of Flames.

Do your best and practice plenty. Ragnaros has over 1 million HP and taking him down is as challenging as it is rewarding. You've gotten this far; it's only a matter of time until you stand victorious. With a bit of teamwork combined with determination and skill, the orange hammer of Ragnaros will soon be resting in that pool of lava, just begging to be looted.

Congratulations on completing the Molten Core! Now enjoy the spoils!

RAGNAROS'S LOOT TABLE

DRUID

ITEM	DESC	STATS
STORMRAGE LEG GUARDS	Leather Legs	197 Armor, 17 STA, 26 INT, 23 SPI, 10 ARC RES, 10 FIRE RES
Equip: Increases healing done by spells and effects by up to 48		

HUNTER

ITEM	DESC	STATS
DRAGONSTALKER'S LEG GUARDS	Mail Legs	422 Armor, 31 AGI, 17 STA, 10 INT, 11 SPI, 10 ARC RES, 10 FIRE RES
Equip: Improves your chance to hit by 2%		

MAGE

ITEM	DESC	STATS
NETHERWIND PANTS	Cloth Pants	101 Armor, 16 STA, 27 INT, 17 SPI, 10 ARC RES, 10 FIRE RES
Equip: Increases damage and healing done by spells and effects by up to 30		

PALADIN

ITEM	DESC	STATS
JUDGMENT LEGPLATES	Plate Legs	749 Armor, 26 STA, 27 INT, 17 SPI, 10 ARC RES, 10 FIRE RES
Equip: Increases healing done by spells and effects by up to 35		

PRIEST

ITEM	DESC	STATS
LEGGINGS OF TRANSCENDENCE	Cloth Legs	101 Armor, 16 STA, 21 INT, 21 SPI, 10 ARC RES, 10 SHAD RES
Equip: Increases healing done by spells and effects by up to 46		

ROGUE

ITEM	DESC	STATS
BLOODFANG PANTS	Leather Legs	197 Armor, 11 STR, 37 AGI, 17 STA, 10 ARC RES, 10 FIRE RES
Equip: Improves your chance to get a critical strike by 1%		

SHAMAN

ITEM	DESC	STATS
LEGPLATE OF TEN STORMS	Mail Legs	422 Armor, 16 STA, 18 INT, 20 SPI, 10 ARC RES, 10 FIRE RES
Equip: Improve your chance to get a critical strike with spells by 1%		
Equip: Increases damage and healing done by spells and effects by up to 29		

WARLOCK

ITEM	DESC	STATS
NEMESIS LEGGINGS	Cloth Legs	101 Armor, 27 STA, 17 INT, 16 SPI, 10 ARC RES, 10 FIRE RES
Equip: Increases damage and healing done by spells and effects by up to 30		

WARRIOR

ITEM	DESC	STATS
LEGPLATES OF WRATH	Plate Legs	749 Armor, 19 STR, 27 STA, 10 ARC RES, 10 FIRE RES
Equip: Increases your chance to dodge by 2%		
Equip: +11 Defense		

MISCELLANEOUS ITEMS

ITEM	DESC	STATS
BAND OF ACCURIA	Ring	16 AGI, 10 STA
Equip: Improves your chance to hit by 2%		
BAND OF SULFURAS	Ring	13 STA, 23 INT, 10 SPI
BONEREAVER'S EDGE	Two-Handed Sword	75.9 DPS, Chance on hit Reduces target's armor by 300 for 10 seconds
Equip: Improves your chance to get a critical strike by 1%		
CHOKER OF THE FIRELORD	Necklace	7 STA, 7 INT
Equip: Increases damage and healing done by spells and effects by up to 34		
CLOAK OF THE SHROUDED MISTS	Back	57 Armor, 22 AGI, 12 STA, 6 FIRE RES, 6 NAT RES
CROWN OF DESTRUCTION	Mail Helmet	392 Armor, 23 STA, 9 INT, 9 SPI, 10 FIRE RES
Equip: Improves your chance to get a critical strike by 2%		
Equip: +44 Attack power		
DRAGON'S BLOOD CAPE	Back	116 Armor, 22 STA, 9 STR, 5 ARC RES, 5 FIRE RES, 5 SHAD RES
ESSENCE OF PURE FLAME	Trinket	Equip When struck in combat inflicts 13 fire damage to the attacker
EYE OF SULFURAS	Use	The Eye of Sulfuras can be combined with the Sulfuron Hammer to create Sulfuras, the legendary Hammer of Ragnaros
MALISTER'S DEFENDER	Shield	2822 Armor, 52 Block, 9 STA, 12 INT
Equip: Restores 9 mana every 5 seconds		
ONSLAUGHT GIRDLE	Plate Belt	494 Armor, 31 STR, 11 STA
Equip: Improves your chance to get a critical strike by 1%		
Equip: Improves your chance to hit by 1%		
PERDITION'S BLADE	One-Handed Dagger	58.3 DPS, Chance on hit Blasts a target for 40-56 fire damage
SHARD OF THE FLAME	Trinket	Equip Restores 14 health every 5 seconds
SPINAL REAPER	Two-Handed Axe	74.7 DPS
Equip: Restores 150 mana or 20 rage when you kill a target that gives experience		
This effect cannot occur more than once every 10 seconds		
Equip: +34 Attack Power		

ONYXIA'S LAIR

Played & Written by: Tyler "Hocken" Morgan of <Pacifist> on Kel'thuzad

Onyxia, daughter of the Black Dragonflight leader Deathwing, has made her lair deep in the swamps of Dustwallow Marsh. Players looking to kill Onyxia must perform an elaborate series of quests to obtain the Drakefire Amulet—the key to her lair. Only the most seasoned and prepared players should attempt to slay Onyxia. If you succeed, you will be rewarded with powerful items and hailed as a champion in your capital city.

DUNGEON INFORMATION

Location	Dustwallow Marsh
Territory	Contested
Quests	Alliance and Horde
Suggested Levels	60 (Full Raid)
Primary Enemies	Dragonkin
Time to Complete	20 Minutes to Several Hours

DRAKEFIRE AMULET

Everyone who wants to fight Onyxia must perform a long series of quests to obtain a Drakefire Amulet. Not only is it a decent fire resist necklace, it's the key to Onyxia's Lair. You do not need to equip the amulet to enter her lair; it just has to be in your inventory. The quests for Alliance and Horde are different and equally challenging.

ALLIANCE QUEST SERIES

DRAGONKIN MENACE

Quest Level	48 to obtain
Location	Burning Steppes
Starts at	Helendis Riverhorn
Ends at	Helendis Riverhorn
Goal	Kill 15 Black Broodlings, 10 Black Dragonspawn, 4 Black Wyrmkin, and 1 Black Drake
Max Experience Gained	5450

Do your part in helping the Dragonkin problem around Burning Steppes. These dragons can be found in several camps along the eastern and western sides of Burning Steppes. Bring some friends for the elite ones.

THE TRUE MASTERS

Quest Level	48 to obtain
Location	Burning Steppes (Morgan's Vigil), Red Ridge Mountains (Lakeshire)
Starts at	Helendis Riverhorn
Ends at	Magistrate Solomon
Goal	Deliver a message to Magistrate Solomon in Lakeshire
Max Experience Gained	4100

Helendis is making a plea to Lakeshire for troops to help with the Dragonkin. He wants you to take his plea to Magistrate Solomon in Red Ridge Mountains at the town of Lakeshire. Mount up and head south to the town.

THE TRUE MASTERS (CONTINUED)

Quest Level	48 to obtain
Location	Red Ridge Mountains (Lakeshire), Stormwind City (Stormwind Keep)
Starts at	Magistrate Solomon
Ends at	Highlord Bolvar Fordragon
Goal	Take the letter to Highlord Bolvar Fordragon in Stormwind Keep
Max Experience Gained	550

News of the Black Dragonflight in Burning Steppes concerns Magistrate Solomon; he Fears that Lakeshire would not be able to defend against both the Blackrock Orcs and the Dragonkin. You must take this letter to High Bolvar Fordragon, located at next to the King at the throne of Stormwind Keep in Stormwind City, in hopes of getting help.

THE TRUE MASTERS (CONTINUED)

Quest Level	49 to obtain
Location	Stormwind City (Stormwind Keep), Red Ridge Mountains (Lakeshire)
Starts at	Highlord Bolvar Fordragon
Ends at	Magistrate Solomon
Goal	Return to Magistrate Solomon with Bolvar's Decree
Max Experience Gained	5450

Bolvar has decided to make you an acting deputy of Stormwind and has given you the task of returning to him as soon as you have proof of the Black Dragonflight working with the Blackrock Orcs. Take this information back to Magistrate Solomon.

THE TRUE MASTERS (CONTINUED)

Quest Level	48 to obtain
Location	Stormwind City (Stormwind Keep)
Starts at	Highlord Bolvar Fordragon
Ends at	Highlord Bolvar Fordragon
Goal	Learn about Dragonkin and the Black Dragonflight from Lady Katrana Prestor
Max Experience Gained	550

Bolvar is willing to consider the request for help, but needs proof of the problem before he can commit. He urges you to learn about Dragonkin from the wise Lady Katrana Prestor, and return to him after.

THE TRUE MASTERS (CONTINUED)

Quest Level	49 to obtain
Location	Red Ridge Mountains (Lakeshire), Burning Steppes (Morgan's Vigil)
Starts at	Magistrate Solomon
Ends at	Marshal Maxwell
Goal	Report for duty to Marshall Maxwel in Burning Steppes
Max Experience Gained	550

Magistrate Solomon sends you back to Burning Steppes to report for duty to Marshal Maxwell.

tormwind Royal Guard

Stormwind Royal Gua

THE TRUE MASTERS (CONTINUED)

Quest Level	49 to obtain
Location	Burning Steppes
Starts at	Marshall Maxwell
Ends at	Ragged John
Goal	Learn about the fate of Marshal Windsor from Ragged John
Max Experience Gained	550

Maxwell has already been gathering information on the Blackrock Orcs and the Black Dragonflight, but the information was with Marshal Windsor who has gone missing. Without Windsor, Maxwell has no evidence. You must find Ragged John at the camp along the north edge of Burning Steppes, just above the Ruins of Thaurissan. He may have information on the fate of Windsor.

MARSHAL WINDSOR

Quest Level	49 to obtain
Location	Burning Steppes, Blackrock Depths
Starts at	Ragged John
Ends at	Marshal Windsor
Goal	Travel into Blackrock Depths to locate Windsor or proof of his death
Max Experience Gained	5450

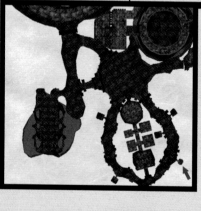

Ragged John tells the story of how Windsor was attacked by the Blackrock Orcs and taken to a prison inside Blackrock Depths. Bring a full group and head into the dungeon, enter the large circular room directly in front of you as you zone in. Windsor is down the third hallway from the right, in the second cell on the left.

ABANDONED HOPE

Quest Level	51 to obtain
Location	Blackrock Depths, Burning Steppes (Morgan's Vigil)
Starts at	Marshal Windsor
Ends at	Marshal Maxwell
Goal	Give Marshal Maxwell the news from Windsor.
Max Experience Gained	5450

Windsor claims that his information is gone and that Bolvar's proof of the Black Dragonflight stands right next to him at the throne. He orders you to return to Maxwell with the bad news.

After returning to Maxwell he does not offer a new quest. The next part of the series comes from a random drop off humanoids in any part of Blackrock Depths. You must speak to Maxwell before the note drops for you and you have to be at least level 56. It should drop quickly, within 5-20 kills.

A CRUMPLED UP NOTE

Quest Level	56 to obtain
Location	Blackrock Depths
Starts at	Randomly dropped note from humanoids in Blackrock Depths
Ends at	Marshal Windsor
Goal	Deliver the note you have found to Windsor
Max Experience Gained	6200

Windsor thinks all his information has been lost, but you have found a note that may have been written by him. Maybe there is hope to regain the proof!

A SHRED OF HOPE

Quest Level	56 to obtain
Location	Blackrock Depths
Starts at	Marshal Windsor
Ends at	Marshal Windsor
Goal	Kill General Angerforge and Golem Lord Argelmach in Blackrock Depths
Max Experience Gained	6200

Windsor reads from the note you found that General Angerforge and Golem Lord Argelmach are holding his lost information. Kill them both and bring the information back to Windsor. Argelmach is a particularly hard fight and a full group of level 58+ members with two tanks, two healers, and a damage dealing class is recommended.

Make sure anyone else doing the Jail Break! quest in your party has turned in A Shred of Hope and is ready to accept the Jail Break! quest before starting it.

JAIL BREAK!

Quest Level	56 to obtain
Location	Blackrock Depths
Starts at	Marshal Windsor
Ends at	Marshal Maxwell
Goal	Escort Windsor out of jail
Max Experience Gained	7750

Windsor is breaking out of jail and wants you to help him. Of course, he has some things to take care of on the way out and ends up traveling all over the caverns. Before even starting this quest you have to clear all of the hallways that have cells and the large circular room in the middle. Open all the doors and cells that you can as you kill monsters. As he travels cell to cell, killing or freeing prisoners, new monsters spawn on top of you. Stay ahead of Windsor and have the monsters attack you instead of him. You can't heal him; if he dies, you fail the quest. This can be a frustrating escort and it may take a few attempts.

STORMWIND RENDEZVOUS

Quest Level	56 to obtain
Location	Burning Steppes (Morgan's Vigil), Stormwind City
Starts at	Marshal Maxwell
Ends at	Reginald Windsor
Goal	Meet Windsor at the gates of Stormwind
Max Experience Gained	700

Windsor must deliver news to Stormwind that will "shake the very foundation of the kingdom!" Fly to Stormwind and head to the gates; Windsor spawns and rides up. Speak with him when he arrives.

Make sure your party members have turned in Stormwind Rendezvous and are ready to accept The Great Masquerade before continuing!

THE GREAT MASQUERADE

Quest Level	56 to obtain
Location	Stormwind City
Starts at	Reginald Windsor
Ends at	Highlord Bolvar Fordragon
Goal	Escort Windsor to face Lady Katrana Prestor
Max Experience Gained	10550

Follow Windsor as he confronts General Marcus Johnathan at the gates, and is allowed to pass to the Keep. Once he arrives at the throne of Stormwind, you need to hide down the stairs a little ways. Windsor unmasks Lady Prestor for who she really is, and Dragonkin quickly attack the throne room. Bolvar is quite the fighter, able to fend off the entire attack by himself. As long as the dragons attack him instead of you, there's nothing to worry about. If the dragons attack you, you will almost certainly die and fail the quest.

THE DRAGON'S EYE

Quest Level	56 to obtain
Location	Stormwind City, Winterspring (Mazthoril)
Starts at	Highlord Bolvar Fordragon
Ends at	Haleh
Goal	Seek out someone who is able to restore power to the Fragment of the Dragon's Eye
Max Experience Gained	7250

The medallion key to Onyxia's lair has been destroyed in the battle; all that remains is a powerless fragment. You must search the world for someone of dragon blood who can restore power to the key.

Haleh, protector of the Blue Dragon's lair, Mazthoril in Winterspring, is the only person who can help you. She's not easy to reach. Fly to Everlook and head southwest to the cave of Mazthoril. Fight or corpse-hop through the cave until you reach the final room; there's a blue rune on the floor. Step on the rune to teleport to Haleh.

An alternate way to complete this quest is to assemble a strong 20+ person raid group and help Bolvar fight the Dragonkin. But you don't have to do this; you can complete this quest without any help if you choose.

DRAKEFIRE AMULET

Quest Level	56 to obtain
Location	Winterspring (Mazthoril), Upper Blackrock Spire
Starts at	Haleh
Ends at	Haleh
Goal	Bring the Blood of the Black Dragon Champion to Haleh so she may restore power to the amulet
Max Experience Gained	9050

Haleh can restore power to the amulet, but she needs the Blood of the Black Dragon Champion to do it. Get a 10-person group together and go kill General Drakkisath in Upper Blackrock Spire.

Return to Haleh and turn in the quest to receive the Drakefire Amulet, key to Onyxia's lair.

HORDE QUEST SERIES

WARLORD'S COMMAND

Quest Level	55 to obtain
Location	Badlands (Kargath), Lower Blackrock Spire
Starts at	Warlord Goretooth
Ends at	Warlord Goretooth
Goal	Travel to LBRS and kill Highlord Omokk, War Master Voone, and Overlord Wyrmthalak.
Max Experience Gained	8550

Speak with Warlord Goretooth in the town of Kargath. Listen to his story and, after you have spoken with him, he offers a quest to kill several bosses in Lower Blackrock Spire. Take a strong group; Omokk is a pretty hard fight. You must also find the Important Blackrock Documents, which are a random spawn on the ground at any of the three bosses you must kill.

EITRIGG'S WISDOM

Quest Level	55 to obtain
Location	Badlands (Kargath), Orgrimmar
Starts at	Warlock Goretooth
Ends at	Thrall
Goal	Speak with Eitrigg in Orgrimmar and then report to Thrall

Goretooth is alarmed that Rend is still alive and urges you to inform Eitrigg in Thrall's Hall. Talk to Thrall after speaking with Eitrigg.

FOR THE HORDE!

Quest Level	55 to obtain
Location	Orgrimmar, Upper Blackrock Spire
Starts at	Thrall
Ends at	Thrall
Goal	Kill Warchief Rend Blackhand in UBRS
Max Experience Gained	10900

Thrall orders you to travel to Upper Blackrock Spire and kill the Warchief Rend Blackhand. Take another strong group into UBRS and complete the arena event to kill Rend. This quest can be completed in a raid group. When you have his head, return to Thrall.

THE CHAMPION OF THE HORDE

Quest Level	56 to obtain
Location	Orgrimmar, Desolace
Starts at	Thrall
Ends at	Rexxar
Goal	Find Rexxar who wanders Desolace
Max Experience Gained	5450

A horde champion named Rexxar may know of a way into Onyxia's lair. Travel to Desolace and find him. He wanders along the north/south path throughout the entire zone.

WHAT THE WIND CARRIES

Quest Level	56 to obtain
Location	Orgrimmar
Starts at	Thrall
Ends at	Thrall
Goal	Listen to Thrall's news
Max Experienced Gained	725

Thrall has received news from Eastern Kingdoms, listen to it. Speak to him again afterwards.

THE TESTAMENT OF REXXAR

Quest Level	56 to obtain
Location	Desolace, Western Plaguelands (Sorrow Hill)
Starts at	Rexxar
Ends at	Myranda the Hag
Goal	Speak with Myranda the Hag in Western Plaguelands
Max Experience Gained	5450

Rexxar knows only one person who can help you get into Onyxia's lair. The illusionist Myranda the Hag, who sits on a log at the Sorrow Hill graveyard in Western Plaguelands, might be able to help deceive the dragons.

OCULUS ILLUSIONS

Quest Level	56 to obtain
Location	Western Plaguelands (Sorrow Hill), Upper Blackrock Spire
Starts at	Myranda the Hag
Ends at	Myranda the Hag
Goal	Collect 20 Black Dragonspawn Eyes from Upper Blackrock Spire Dragonkin
Max Experience Gained	7250

Myranda can provide the illusion you need, but she requires 20 Black Dragonspawn Eyes to do it. The eyes drop from the Dragonkin in Upper Blackrock Spire. Take a group (or a raid, it is a Raid quest) to UBRS and collect the eyes, they are pretty common drops when you have the quest. Return to Myranda when you have the required components.

THE TEST OF SKULLS, SCRYER

Quest Level	56 to obtain
Location	Dustwallow Marsh (Wyrmbog), Winterspring (Mazthoril)
Starts at	Emberstrife
Ends at	Emberstrife
Goal	Travel to Winterspring and kill Scryer
Max Experience Gained	7250

Your first task is to slay the Blue Dragonflight Champion Scryer. He's found near the caves of Mazthoril, southwest of Everlook in Winterspring. Bring a few friends, kill him, and bring his skull back to Emberstrife.

EMBERSTRIFE

Quest Level	56 to obtain
Location	Western Plaguelands (Sorrow Hill), Dustwallow Marsh (Wyrmbog)
Starts at	Myranda the Hag
Ends at	Emberstrife
Goal	Travel to Desolace and wear the Amulet of Draconic Subversion to trick Emberstrife into talking to you
Max Experience Gained	5450

Emberstrife is an old, powerful dragon that has the job of testing new Dragonkin who wish to serve in Onyxia's elite guard. You must wear the Amulet of Draconic Subversion that Myranda has given you to trick him into thinking you are a Dragonkin, and accept whatever tests he gives. Don the amulet and speak with him.

THE TEST OF SKULLS, SOMNUS

Quest Level	56 to obtain
Location	Dustwallow Marsh (Wyrmbog), Swamp of Sorrows
Starts at	Emberstrife
Ends at	Emberstrife
Goal	Travel to the Swamp of Sorrows and kill Somnus
Max Experience Gained	7250

Next up is Somnus, Champion of the Green Dragonflight. He wanders the swamp to the east of the Sunken Temple. Gather some help, kill him, and bring his skull back to Emberstrife.

THE TEST OF SKULLS, CHRONALIS

Quest Level	56 to obtain
Location	Dustwallow Marsh (Wyrmbog), Tanaris
Starts at	Emberstrife
Ends at	Emberstrife
Goal	Travel to Tanaris and kill Chronalis
Max Experience Gained	7250

Emberstrife wants you to kill Chronalis, who guards the Caverns of Time in a mountain along the eastern edge of Tanaris. Return his skull to Emberstrife once you and your mates have killed him.

ASCENSION...

Quest Level	56 to obtain
Location	Dustwallow Marsh (Wyrmbog), Desolace
Starts at	Emberstrife
Ends at	Rexxar
Goal	Return to Rexxar
Max Experience Gained	5450

Emberstrife has rewarded you with a Dulled Drakefire Amulet and instructs you to take it to General Drakkisath in Upper Blackrock Spire for its final enchantment, but the illusion Myranda created for you won't work within Blackrock Spire. Seek out Rexxar and explain your problem, hopefully he knows what to do.

THE TEST OF SKULLS, AXTROZ

Quest Level	56 to obtain
Location	Dustwallow Marsh (Wyrmbog), Wetlands (Grim Batol)
Starts at	Emberstrife
Ends at	Emberstrife
Goal	Travel to Grim Batol and kill Axtroz
Max Experience Gained	7250

Head over to Grim Batol in the northeastern part of Wetlands and kill the Red Dragonflight Champion Aztroz. Return to Emberstrife when you have his skull.

BLOOD OF THE BLACK DRAGON CHAMPION

Quest Level	56 to obtain
Location	Desolace, Upper Blackrock Spire
Starts at	Rexxar
Ends at	Rexxar
Goal	Journey to Upper Blackrock Spire and kill General Drakkisath, bring his blood back to Rexxar.
Max Experience Gained	10900

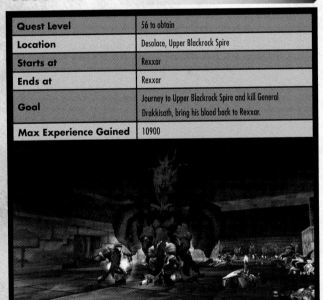

You're pleased to hear that only the Blood of the Black Dragon Champion from General Drakkisath in Upper Blackrock Spire is needed to finalize the amulet. Bring a strong group and slay Drakkisath.

Return to Rexxar when you have the blood. He gives you the Drakefire Amulet, key to Onyxia's lair.

PLAYERS

A group learning how to kill Onyxia should bring a full level 60 raid group—40 people. Every raider needs to have their Drakefire Amulet in their inventory before zoning in.

The classes you have at your raid should be pretty evenly distributed. There are eight classes and raids can hold 40 people, so most raid encounters are balanced for a raid group consisting of five people from each class. This is true for Onyxia. It's important to have good healing and solid ranged damage dealers. Melee damage classes have limited usefulness during Phase 2 of the fight, but are important for Onyxian Whelps and the times when she's on the ground.

People often ask if the talents your character has are going to make or break a PvE raid encounter. Yes and no. Experienced raid groups/guilds often plan out their raid by having people spec certain ways. There is typically a "preferred" spec for each class and, in fact, there may be a need for different specs for the same class.

Most high-end encounters are planned out ahead of time and require certain specs to work properly. This is especially important before you get your higher-end equipment from the dungeons that you're raiding. You can benefit greatly from those items and that's when your spec becomes less important. A totally geared up, Tier 2 Warrior may be able to handle some raids without a full Protection spec, but it's unlikely that they'll do that.

It all depends on the demands of the group that you're planning on raiding with and whether they can assimilate your current spec into their plans. To be invited to a raid group, simply ask what type of spec they require or would like and get into the raid. Don't try to force your way in as your own spec unless you've been raiding for a while and have tested that spec.

EQUIPMENT

The main tank (MT) is the most important person as far as equipment goes. They should have over 150 fire resist (FR) and over 7500 life (buffed). Dark Iron armor from the Thorium Brotherhood is good at providing hit points and FR. Without decent FR and hit points, your healers won't be able to keep the MT alive while Onyxia is on the ground attacking.

Everyone else in the raid should be equipped in at least level 55+ superior quality items from UBRS, LBRS, Stratholme, Scholomance, and Dire Maul. You don't need epic quality gear to kill Onyxia, but you probably won't survive in greens.

OTHER ITEMS

Greater Fire Resist Potions are always a good idea if you can get the materials. They absorb a solid amount of fire damage, making Phase 2 and Phase 3 easier.

Lung Juice Cocktail from the repeatable quest in Blasted Lands is easy to obtain and gives 25 stamina, nice for your MT. The Flask of Titans, made by alchemists, is much harder to make but is nice to have for an additional 1200 hit points.

All PVP reward class trinkets that remove Fear and the Glimmering Mithril Insignia (from the Blacksmithing quests) are useful for Phase 3 when Onyxia is using this ability.

GROUP SETUP

The raid is going to be split in half—even-numbered groups and odd-numbered groups. Evenly distribute the classes for each side.

The MT should have a Priest, a Warlock (for Blood Pact), and a Shaman or Paladin (for fire resist) in their group.

Mages should have Priests because they will need to AoE Onyxian Whelps at some point.

GETTING TO ONYXIA

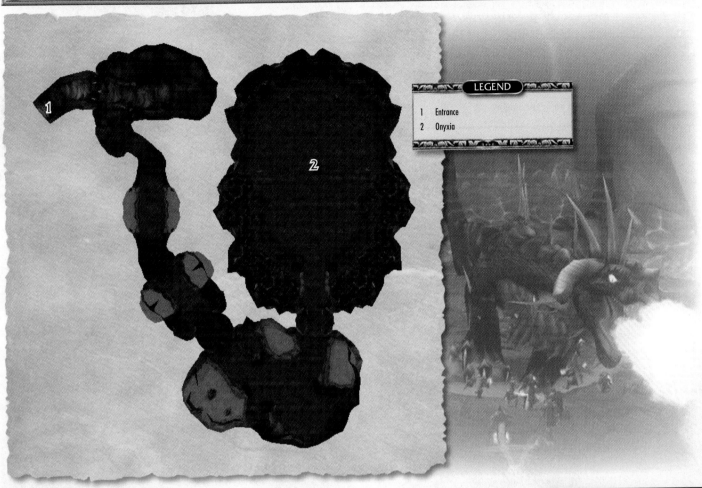

LEGEND

1 Entrance
2 Onyxia

ONYXIAN WARDERS

Onyxia's Lair is a small instance and only has four Onyxian Warders blocking the way to her. The warders have a very powerful AoE (Fire Nova) that hits everyone within 20 yards. In addition, they have Cleave, Flame Lash (112-120 Fire damage and reduces Fire resistance by 68 for 45 sec.), and Pierce Armor (reduces target's armor by 75% for 20 sec.).

Flame Lash can be dispelled and the other two abilities are melee-oriented. Only the MT should be in range of their AoE attack while everyone else should be attacking from range.

Wait for each warder to walk as close as possible before you pull. They have long patrol routes and you don't want to fight more than one at a time.

Your raid is formed, everyone is there, the warders are dead; all that remains is a large sleeping dragon to kill. It's time to wake her up and see if you have what it takes to bring her down.

Get fully buffed up before rushing in. Make sure everybody knows where they are supposed to be. Double check everyone is ready and run in.

PHASE 1
SPECIAL ATTACKS

Fire Breath: Cone shaped fire breath attack that hits everything in front of her for 3063-3937 damage. It is resistible.

Solution: Always keep her pointed north, away from the groups on the sides. Only the MT should be hit by her breath.

Wing Buffet: A knock back attack (563-937 damage) that hits everyone in front of her, tossing them a fair distance.

Solution: Correctly position yourselves at her sides as far away as possible while still being in melee range. Keep your back away from the eggs.

Tail Whip: Another knock back attack (600-1000 damage) that hits everyone behind her, near the tail. Tail Whip throws players much further than Wing Buffet, likely well into the eggs if their back is to them.

Solution: Never stand behind an angry dragon.

Cleave: Deals melee damage +315 to the primary target and up to ten other targets in front of Onyxia.

Solution: Remain in your assigned positions and let the MT adjust who will be hit by this attack.

POSITIONING

LEGEND

1	Odd-numbered groups area
2	Main Tank (MT) position
3	Even-numbered groups area

Onyxia should always be facing north and attacking the MT. The MT needs to be 10-15 yards away from the wall; being against the wall causes you to bounce to either side when she knocks you back with Wing Buffet. You want to bounce off the north wall and Onyxia shouldn't turn much when she knocks you back.

The rest of the raid splits in half, odd-numbered groups on the left, even-numbered groups on the right. Everyone should be at least 10 yards north of the egg caves, nobody should ever go near them or near Onyxia's tail during Phase 1, because you'll be tail whipped into the eggs. Try to keep your back facing east or west (depending on which side you're on) in case you do get knocked back; you won't end up in the eggs.

STRATEGY

MT should rush in a good 20-30 yards ahead of everyone to make sure they get initial aggro.

There should be no whelp spawns whatsoever during this Phase unless someone gets knocked into the eggs. If there are whelps, have a couple mages use Frost Nova and AoEs to wipe them out. Keep Priests/Warriors ready to help if things turn sour. You should be able to handle any amount of whelps that come, but any more than about 15 may significantly damage the raid's long term survivability. Don't get anywhere near the whelps and you'll be fine.

> The eggs do not require you to stand on top of them before they spawn like the UBRS Rookery room; their spawn distance is much larger.

Have the MT slowly move into position at the north center of the lair. The MT's exact position is very important due to the knock back. They need to be 10-15 yards away from the north wall. When positioned correctly, the knock back from Wing Buffet should bounce the MT against the north wall and have them land very close to their original position.

Again, Onyxia should always be facing north.

Once the MT has built 30+ seconds of threat, everyone can attack. Mind your DPS. Hunters: use Feign Death as often as you can. Rogues: Feint when it's up. Mages: don't over do the nukes. Priests: use Fade only if you draw aggro. If the MT loses aggro, Onyxia will turn to one of the sides and probably kill everyone with a Fire Breath. Remember, she's immune to Taunt and Mocking Blow.

With an inexperienced raid group and, especially an MT, Rogues should stick to using their default attacks (no combos/finishing moves) and casters should wait a few seconds between each spell. It's best to survive the run slowly than continue to pull aggro from the MT and likely wipe the raid. Kill her slowly and steadily by keeping her on the MT and in position.

When she's reached 70% life, take a good 30-second break on attacking to let the MT rebuild aggro; better safe than sorry. During that break is a good time to drink a fire absorption potion in preparation for Phase 2.

At 65%, Onyxia walks from the north to the south and takes flight. Phase 2 begins.

> Aggro management and MT positioning are the keys to this Phase. This Phase is remarkably easy compared to the next two due to its straightforward "MT tank her in the middle, healers keep MT alive, everyone else DPS slowly" strategy. There should be no deaths and no whelps alive when Phase 2 starts. There shouldn't be any need to drink any potions (except maybe a fire protection) or use anything with a noticeable cooldown during this Phase.

PHASE 2
SPECIAL ATTACKS

Fireball: Onyxia spits fire at random people. The fire hits for approximately 1700-2300 damage ato anyone in the AoE.

Solution: Stay spread out to avoid the fire hitting people near you. Use bandages to heal yourself so your healers don't use all their mana.

Deep Breath: When you see the emote: "Onyxia begins to take a deep breath," approximately 5 seconds pass before a huge column of fire erupts along the floor from her spot. It's more than likely that it can instantly kill everyone it hits. This attack completely destroys the run if it's not dealt with properly.

Solution: Deep Breath simply can't be avoided, so you'll have to dodge it to the best of your ability. Every time Onyxia is going to move, there's a 30% chance that she'll decide to advance forward, a 35% chance that she'll move left, and a 35% chance that she'll move right. If she chooses to move forward, she'll use Deep Breath. There's a relatively intuitive method to avoid her flame. Imagine that her lair is a giant clock. If she's facing 6:00 (south), you will be out of range as long as you are three clock positions away (3:00 or 9:00). Otherwise, you'll be caught in the blast.

POSITIONING

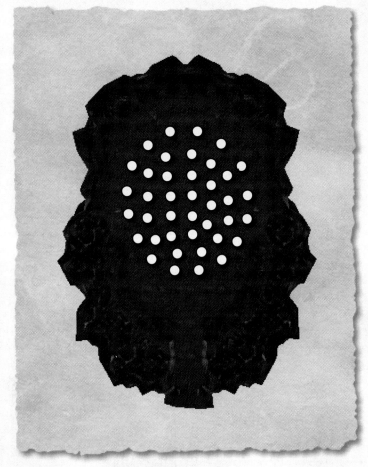

As you can see from the map, you need to be spread out all around the lair. This setup is important for two reasons: avoiding a Deep Breath attack, and minimizing the damage done by Engulfing Flames. Keep moving around until there is nobody within about 5-10 yards of you. Ranged damage dealers will have to change positions as she flies around to stay within attack range.

The most common place people get clustered up at is near the eggs because whelps are now spawning during Phase 2. Melee classes attacking whelps need to make sure they aren't on top of each other.

Stay within range of your healer and generally on your group's side of the lair. You don't want to be on the wrong side when she's about to land.

An alternate strategy used by some guilds is to follow Onyxia throughout the fight while remaining as spread out as possible as opposed to remaining stationary and reacting to her facing. To make this strategy work, everyone in the raid must be acutely aware of her location at all times. Have the raid leader use a macro to identify her position or a voice program to call her position out.

Do not go too far south. There is an Onyxian Warder at the mouth of her lair; *don't aggro it.*

STRATEGY

As soon as Onyxia leaps in the air, the first wave of 15-20 whelps appears, and everyone needs to help with them immediately. After the first wave is dead, melee classes should be focused on keep the whelps under control. The occasional Mage AoEing is useful as well. If they get out of control, everyone needs to help deal with them and go right back to attacking Onyxia once they're dead. Throughout this Phase, whelps are almost constantly spawning; make sure to keep them from killing healers.

Have everyone move into position and spread out. Melee classes should kill whelps since they aren't impressive with ranged DPS. Healers should keep whelp killers and Engulfing Flames victims alive. Focus everyone else on ranged damage DPS.

Ranged damage is the most important factor. The goal is to get her back on the ground as quickly as possible. Cast every DoT, curse, and damage spell you have. Zap wands. Remember, this Phase is long and you need to recast curses and DoTs as they wear off.

Stop casting all DoTs when she reaches 42%. You do not want to build any threat with Onyxia through damage spells once she lands.

At around 45%, have the MT start building rage on whelps to pull Onyxia back onto him when she lands. At this point, ranged DPS should be unloading, the whelps should be under control, and the MT should have rage.

Once Onyxia's health reaches 40%, she's going to land any second. Move the MT to the center of the lair where Onyxia is going to land and have them ready to draw aggro. Everyone else should stop attacking the second she hits on the ground. Phase 3 begins.

Seconds before she lands, everyone needs to move away from the egg entrances to avoid being Feared into them. Everyone needs to go back to their Phase 1 positions against the wall.

CEASE FIRE!

It's absolutely crucial that everyone stop attacking when she lands. The MT is going to have a hard time getting Onyxia focused on them and anyone attacking during this transition could wipe the entire raid.

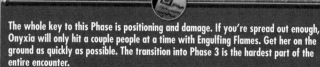
PHASE 3

SPECIAL ATTACKS

Everything from Phase 1.

Bellowing Roar: The ground shakes and Onyxia Fears everyone in the lair. Simultaneously, the lava fissures explode with lava causing even more havok. The Fear is resistible.

Solution: Alliance players should bring a Dwarf Priest along for Fear Ward because it negates the MT getting Feared. Fear Ward is on a 30 second cool down, so bring two Dwarf Priests to be safe. Horde MTs have to rely on changing to Berserker stance, activating Berserker Rage, and quickly changing back to Defensive stance. An experienced Horde Warrior will be able to do this very quickly. Shamans should also be placing tremor totems, which occasionally remove Fear on party members. It's very bad for the MT to be Feared because Onyxia will then turn and face the MT as they run around, possibly blasting a Fire Breath attack while facing a side of players.

Eruption: The floor shoots lava every time Onyxia Fears the raid. You will see the ground shake, the Fear hit, and the lava fissures explode, damaging players within range for about 1500 life.

Solution: If you can get rid of the Fear and control where your character is standing, stay away from cracks in the floor; the explosions have limited range. If you do get Feared, and you usually will, there isn't much you can do about it. Bandage yourself as often as you can.

POSITIONING

Similar to Phase 1. The only difference is that you're going to have a new element to keep in mind—Lava Fissures. Find as safe a spot as possible and stand their to avoid damage during the eruption of the lava fissures.

STRATEGY

Once Onyxia lands, the MT should be waiting under her with near-full rage to Sunder Armor and do everything possible to climb the threat ladder. Nobody else should attack until the MT has aggro.

Regaining aggro in Phase 3 is tricky. There seems to be no clear reasoning behind which player she targets as she lands. She may clear her threat list completely, nobody really knows. The MT just needs time to build enough threat and get back to number one on the threat list. Anyone who has aggro needs to move to the MT's location so that Onyxia is not facing a side. You always want her facing north to avoid the Fire Breath attack.

As soon as the MT gains aggro, have them move to the Phase 1 position, now mindful of cracks in the floor.

It's likely that the MT will get Feared and lose aggro before they're position. Assuming the MT has enough threat, she will chase them around while they are Feared. If she doesn't, the second person on her aggro list is probably going to die. If she uses Fire Breath on a bunched up side while the MT doesn't have aggro, it's almost certainly a wipe.

Beyond the floor exploding with lava, being Feared into the lava, the MT losing aggro or changing positioning often - and everyone being low on life and mana - this is exactly like Phase 1. Mind your DPS and position. Deal with the whelps if any come. Let the MT tank and keep them alive at all costs. If the MT dies when she's at even 5% life, the run is likely over.

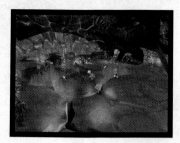

Anyone that can do damage should be focused on balancing DPS and threat while surviving. Anyone that can heal should be healing the MT. If your Priests say the MT is under control, backup healers should be keeping people hit by the exploding lava alive.

Just keep the MT alive, keep yourself alive, and do as much damage as possible. Kill her before she kills all of you.

VICTORY

Congratulations, you've defeated a powerful raid boss and a treacherous villain of both the Alliance and Horde. It's not an easy task to get 40 people working together and the experience you gain from defeating Onyxia is invaluable in future raid encounters.

ONYXIA'S HEAD

Aside from her normal drops, Onyxia always drops a Head of Onyxia.

This item is used to start a quest called *Victory for the Alliance/Horde*. Each quest asks you to return to Stormwind or Orgimmar and present the head at the city's throne. The rewards are identical for both factions and very impressive:

In addition, when you turn in the quest, Onyxia's head is displayed in the city and everyone nearby gets a powerful 2-hour buff. This buff, the Rallying Call of the Dragonslayer, has a cooldown and won't affect those in the city if it's recently been triggered.

You can only complete the Head of Onyxia quest once per character.

Dragonslayer's Signet	Ring	+12 INT, +6 SPI, +12 STA, +10 Fire Resist
Equip: Improves your chance to get a critical strike with spells by 1%		
Onyxia Tooth Pendant	Necklace	+12 AGI, +9 STA, +10 Fire Resist
Equip: Improves your chance to hit by 1%		
Equip: Improves your chance to get a critical strike by 1%		
Onyxia Blood Talisman	Trinket	+15 Fire Resist
Equip: Increases your chance to parry an attack by 1%		
Equip: Increased Defense +8		
Equip: Restores 5 health every 5 seconds		

THE DRAGON'S HOARD

ITEM	DESC	STATS
ANCIENT CORNERSTONE GRIMOIRE	Off-Hand	+15 INT, +11 SPI, +10 STA, Use: Summons a Skeleton that will protect you for 60 sec.
BLOODFANG HOOD	Leather Head	183 Armor, +27 AGI, +25 STA, +19 STR, +10 Frost Resist, +10 Shadow Resist, Equip: Improves your chance to get a critical strike by 1% (Bloodfang Armor)
DEATHBRINGER	One-Hand Axe	56.4 DPS, Chance on Hit: Sends a shadowy bolt at the enemy causing 110 to 140 Shadow damage
DRACONIC FOR DUMMIES	Quest Item	
DRAGONSTALKER'S HELM	Mail Head	392 Armor, +27 AGI, +16 INT, +8 SPI, +26 STA, +10 Frost Resist, +10 Shadow Resist, Equip: Improves your chance to get a critical strike by 1% (Dragonstalker Armor)
ESKHANDAR'S COLLAR	Neck	+17 STA, Equip: Increases your chance to dodge an attack by 1%, Improves your chance to get a critical strike by 1%
HALO OF TRANSCENDENCE	Cloth Head	94 Armor, +27 INT, +22 SPI, +17 STA, +10 Fire Resist, +10 Frost Resist, Equip: Increases healing done by spells and effects by up to 48 (Vestments of Transcendence)
HEAD OF ONYXIA	Quest Item	
HEATED ANCIENT BLADE	Quest Item	Use: Drive into the heart of the brood mother to temper the heated blade
HELM OF WRATH	Plate Head	696 Armor, +40 STA, +17 STR, +10 Frost Resist, +10 Shadow Resist, Equip: Increased Defense +6 (Battlegear of Wrath)
HELMET OF TEN STORMS	Mail Head	392 Armor, +24 INT, +12 SPI, +20 STA, +10 Frost Resist, +10 Shadow Resist, Equip: Increases your chance to get a critical strike with spells by 1%, Increases damage and healing done by magical spells and effects by up to 9, Increases healing done by spells and effects by up to 18 (The Ten Storms)
JUDGEMENT CROWN	Plate Head	696 Armor, +23 INT, +6 SPI, +18 STA, +17 STR, +10 Frost Resist, +10 Shadow Resist, Equip: Increases damage and healing done by magical spells and effects by up to 32 (Judgement Armor)
LEGPLATES OF MIGHT	Plate Legs	655 Armor, +23 STA, +24 STR, +10 Shadow Resist, Equip: Increases your chance to parry an attack by 1%, Increased Defense +7 (Battlegear of Might)
MATURE BLACK DRAGON SINEW	Quest Item	
NEMESIS SKULLCAP	Cloth Head	94 Armor, +16 INT, +6 SPI, +26 STA, +10 Frost Resist, +10 Shadow Resist, Equip: Restores 4 health per 5 sec., Increases damage and healing done by magical spells and effects by up to 32 (Nemesis Raiment)
NETHERWIND CROWN	Cloth Head	94 Armor, +26 INT, +7 SPI, +17 STA, +10 Frost Resist, +10 Shadow Resist, Equip: Restores 4 mana per 5 sec., Increases damage and healing done by magical spells and effects by up to 32 (Netherwind Regalia)
NEXUS CRYSTAL	Trade	
ONYXIA HIDE BACKPACK	Container	18 Slot Bag
RING OF BINDING	Ring	60 Armor, +10 to All Resistances, Equip: Increased Defense +4
SAPPHIRON DRAPE	Back	55 Armor, +17 INT, +10 STA, +6 Arcane Resise, +6 Frost Resist, Equip: Increases damage and healing done by magical spells and effects by up to 14
SCALE OF ONYXIA	Trade	
SHARD OF THE SCALE	Trinket	Equip: Restores 16 mana per 5 sec. (Shard of the Gods)
STORMRAGE COVER	Leather Head	183 Armor, +31 INT, +12 SPI, +20 STA, +10 Frost Resist, +10 Shadow Resist, Equip: Restores 6 mana per 5 sec., Increases healing done by magical spells and effects by up to 29 (Stormrage Raiment)
VIS'KAG THE BLOODLETTER	One-Hand Sword	55.2 DPS, Chance on Hit: Delivers a fatal wound for 240 damage

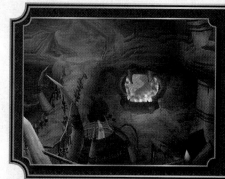

RAGEFIRE CHASM

Played & Written by: Daniel "Sachant" Vanderlip of <UDL> on Archimonde
Updated by: Edwin "Plainsong" Kern of <Dovrani> on Kirin Tor

Orgrimmar is a shining beacon to the Orcs and Trolls of the Horde. At last there is a place where one can be safe and raise children. Is Orgrimmar really safe? Enemies have burrowed up from beneath the streets of Orgrimmar. They have avoided all the guards on the walls and landed in the center of this bastion of hope. Find who they are and show them the error of their ways.

DUNGEON INFORMATION

Location	Orgrimmar (Cleft of Shadow)
Quests	Horde
Region	Horde
Suggested Levels	13-18
Group Allowed	5 to Quest, 10 for Raids
Primary Enemies	Elemental, Beast, and Humanoid
Time to Complete	1-1.5 Hours

GETTING TO RAGEFIRE CHASM

At level 13, Horde characters are still fairly scattered amongst the starting areas. Orcs and Trolls likely already have made the trek to Orgrimmar as they begin their lives in Durotar. Tauren need to make the journey across the Barrens and through Durotar. Undead characters take the Zeppelin on the lower platform from just outside Undercity.

Alliance parties should not attempt to get to Ragefire Chasm. It is deep in the heart of the Horde capital. At this level you will be unable to get to the portal without several deaths.

WHO TO BRING

It's fairly important to have a good variety in classes as there is little overlap with abilities at this level. Having a tank is always important. A Warrior is the best choice, but a Shaman or Druid (in bear form) can be used also. Druids, Priests, and Shamans all have the ability to act as a healer, but don't ask a Druid or Shaman to be both healer and tank. Mages are very useful for their Polymorph spell's ability to control combat.

After the more difficult jobs are filled, it's time to add some damage to your group. Every class can add damage. Extra Warriors can serve as backup for the main tank while they cut through the enemies. Additional Priests can serve as backup healers while they blast the enemies with the power of shadows.

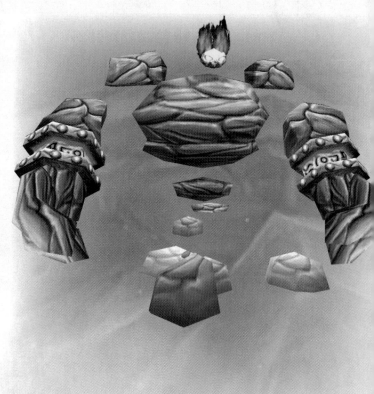

QUESTS FOR RAGEFIRE CHASM

All quests involving Ragefire Chasm are Dungeon quests. These can not be completed in Raid groups. Raid groups should be avoided unless treasure is your only goal.

QUEST NAME	QUEST GIVER	QUEST GIVER LOCATION	QUEST RECEIVER	QUEST RECEIVER LOCATION	CHAIN?	MAX EXPERIENCE
Testing an Enemy's Strength	Rahauro	Thunder Bluff: Elder Rise	Rahauro	Thunder Bluff: Elder Rise	Yes	None
REWARD: 7s						
Hidden Enemies	Thrall	Orgrimmar: Valley of Wisdom	Thrall	Orgrimmar: Valley of Wisdom	Yes	1150
REWARD: 8s						
Hidden Enemies	Thrall	Orgrimmar: Valley of Wisdom	Neeru Fireblade	Orgrimmar: Cleft of Shadow	Yes	110
Hidden Enemies	Neeru Fireblade	Orgrimmar: Cleft of Shadow	Thrall	Orgrimmar: Valley of Wisdom	Yes	1450
REWARD: Kris of Orgrimmar (One-Hand Dagger, 9.0 DPS, +1 STA, +1 SPI) or Hammer of Orgrimmar (Main-Hand Mace, 9.1 DPS, +1 STR, +1 STA) or Axe of Orgrimmar (Two-Hand Axe, 11.8 DPS, +3 STA, +3 STR) or Staff of Orgrimmar (Staff, 11.8 DPS, +2 SPI, +4 INT)						
The Power to Destroy	Varimathras	Undercity: Royal Quarter	Varimathras	Undercity: Royal Quarter	No	None
REWARD: Ghastly Trousers (Cloth Legs, 28 Armor, +2 STA, +4 INT), Dredgemire Leggings (Leather Legs, 65 Armor, +2 AGI, +2 STA, +2 SPI), Gargoyle Leggings (Mail Legs, 141 Armor, +2 STR, +2 AGI, +2 STA)						
Searching for the Lost Satchel	Rahauro	Thunder Bluff: Elder Rise	Maur Grimtotem's Corpse	Ragefire Chasm	Yes	875
Returning the Lost Satchel	Maur Grimtotem's Corpse	Ragefire Chasm	Rahauro	Thunderbluff: Elder Rise	Yes	1450
REWARD: Featherbead Bracers (Cloth Wrist, 14AR, +3INT), Savannah Bracers (Leather Wrist, 33AR, +3STA)						
Slaying the Beast	Neeru Fireblade	Orgrimmar: Cleft of Shadow	Neeru Fireblade	Orgrimmar: Cleft of Shadow	No	1150
REWARD: 8s						

TESTING AN ENEMY'S STRENGTH

Quest Level	12 to Obtain
Location	Thunder Bluff (Elder Rise)
Person	Rahauro
Goal	Kill 8 Ragefire Shaman, Kill 8 Ragefire Troggs
Max Experience Gained	950

Rahauro is located in Elder Rise in Thunder Bluff. He's in the main tent. Killing enough of the needed Troggs and Shaman is simple and straightforward.

HIDDEN ENEMIES

Quest Level	9 to Obtain
Location	Orgrimmar (Valley of Wisdom)
Person	Thrall
Goal	Kill Jergosh the Invoker, Kill Bazzalan
Max Experience Gained	1400

This quest takes you all the way to the end of the instance. Bazzalan is a little tricky to find unless you pay close attention to a path that climbs the back of the cave above Jergosh the Invoker. Both of the target mobs are near each other.

THE POWER TO DESTROY

Quest Level	10 to Obtain
Location	Undercity (Royal Quarter)
Person	Varimathras
Goal	Obtain the Spells of Shadow and the Incantations from the Nether and return them to Varimathras
Max Experience Gained	1250
Reward	Ghastly Trousers (Cloth Legs, 28 Armor, +2 STA, +4 INT) or Dredgemire Leggings (Leather Legs, 65 Armor, +2 AGI, +2 STA, +2 SPI) or Gargoyle Leggings (Mail Legs, 141 Armor, +2 STR, +2 AGI, +2 STA)

Varimathras is located in the Royal Quarter of Undercity. It's a secluded area off of the Apothecarium. The books for the quest can drop off of any of the Searing Blade Cultists toward the back of the instance. It's a random drop, but isn't extremely rare and when it drops, it drops for everyone.

SEARCHING FOR THE LOST SATCHEL

Quest Level	12 to Obtain
Location	Thunderbluff (Elder Rise)
Person	Rahauro
Goal	Find Maur Grimtotem's Corpse and return anything that may be found on it.
Max Experience Gained	875

Maur Grimtotem's Corpse is in a small room up a ramp and is guarded by some Ragefire Troggs and Oggleflint the Ragefire Chieftain. Once they're dead, loot Maur Grimtotem's corpse.

RETURNING THE LOST SATCHEL

Quest Level	12 to Obtain
Location	Ragefire Chasm
Person	Maur Grimtotem's Corpse
Goal	Return Maur Grimtotem's satchel to Rahauro
Max Experience Gained	1250
Reward	Featherbead Bracers (Cloth Wrist, 14 Armor, +3 INT), Savannah Bracers (Leather Wrist, 33 Armor, +3STA)

After retrieving the satchel from Maur Grimtotem's corpse, return it to Rahauro in the Elder Rise in Thunder Bluff.

SLAYING THE BEAST

Quest Level	9 to Obtain
Location	Orgrimmar (Cleft of Shadow)
Person	Neeru Fireblade
Goal	Kill Taragaman the Hungerer and get his heart
Max Experience Gained	1250

Taragaman the Hungerer is located at the center of the lava pools toward the end of the instance. Kill him and collect his heart.

THE FORCES OF RAGEFIRE

ENEMIES

NPC	LEVEL
Earthborer	13-14 Elite
Notes: Poison and Armor reduction	
Frequent Drops: Slimy Ichor, Gelatinous Goo	
Molten Elemental	13-15 Elite
Frequent Drops: Coarse Stone, Rock Chip, Lifeless Stone	
Ragefire Trogg	13-15 Elite
Notes: Social, Flees	
Frequent Drops: Linen Cloth	
Ragefire Shaman	14-15 Elite
Notes: Social, Flees, Lightning Bolt, Heal	
Frequent Drops: Linen Cloth	
Searing Blade Cultist	14-15 Elite
Notes: Curse of Agony	
Frequent Drops: Linen Cloth	
Searing Blade Enforcer	13-14 Elite
Notes: Strike, Shield Slam (Knockdown)	
Frequent Drops: Linen Cloth	
Searing Blade Warlock	13-15 Elite
Notes: Voidwalker Minion, Shadowbolt	
Frequent Drops: Linen Cloth	
Voidwalker Minion	13-15 Elite

THE LEADERS OF RAGEFIRE

NPC	LEVEL	FREQUENT DROP(S)
BAZZALAN	16 Elite	
Notes: Sinister Strike, Poison		
JERGOSH THE INVOKER	16 Elite	Robe of Evocation (Cloth Chest, 32 Armor, +4 INT, +3 STA), Cavedweller Bracers (Mail Wrist, 71 Armor, +1 STR, +2 STA), Chanting Blade (One-Hand Dagger, 9.0 Dps, +1 AGI, +1 STA)
Notes: Curse of Weakness, Immolate		
OGGLEFLINT, RAGEFIRE CHIEFTAIN	16 Elite	
Notes: Cleave		
TARAGAMAN THE HUNGERER	16 Elite	Crystalline Cuffs (Cloth Wrist, 14 Armor, +2 SPI, +1 INT), Subterranean Cape (Cloak, 16 Armor, +2 AGI, +2 STR), Cursed Felblade (Main-Hand Sword, 9.0 Dps, Chance on Hit: Reduces target enemy's Attack Power by 15 for 30 seconds)
Notes: Uppercut, Fire Nova		

BENEATH ORGRIMMAR

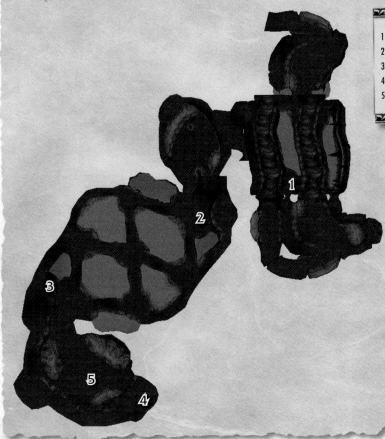

LEGEND

1. Maur Grimtotem's Corpse
2. Taragaman the Hungerer
3. Ramp up to Bazzalan
4. Bazzalan
5. Jergosh the Invoker

Just inside the instance are several Earthborers and Molten Elementals. These can be pulled singly and dispatched. If you have a Warlock in your party, now is a good time for her to stock up on Soul Shards. While these fights are easy, use the time to practice your roles. For some, this will be the first time in a full group.

Tanks should practice holding aggro. Healers should practice healing without pulling aggro off the tank. DPS classes should practice dealing damage without pulling aggro off the tank. There are several of the smaller fights, so your party has time to work out any kinks that show up.

The path leads down to a large intersection that is filled with Ragefire Troggs and Shaman. Now it's time for more practice, except the stakes are a good bit higher. There are two groups and a wanderer. When the wanderer is between the two groups, the tank should pull with a ranged attack. This will be a small pull, but it makes the next two pulls much easier.

If you have a Mage in your group, you'll be using crowd control (CC) from now on. After the tank pulls the Troggs, the Mage Polymorphs (sheeps) the Shaman. It's important that the tank hits first. If the Mage sheeps before the tank pulls, the Troggs will run straight for the Mage. This makes the Mage's job reactionary and more difficult. To make it easier, the Mage can target before the pull and let the party know who she intends to sheep.

DON'T HIT THE SHEEP!

The Mage can turn an enemy into a harmless sheep for a very long time...unless someone hits it. Hitting a sheep will instantly cancel the spell and give you another enemy to worry about. Declare who you're going to sheep before the pull (unless you're sheeping an add). Watch your targeting. Don't attack until you've found a non-sheeped target.

If you do not have a Mage in your group, the ranged damage party members need to kill the Shaman quickly. The tank will hold the melee enemies while the damage classes kill the enemy healer. Be careful about healing your ranged damage classes unless they are risking death. Healing them can pull one of the Troggs off the tank onto the healer.

Ranged damage classes need to wait until the tank engages an enemy before opening fire. A careful eye or keystroke will make sure you're fighting the same enemy the tank is. If you don't see which enemy the tank shot, select the tank and use the Friendly Target button. This is defaulted to 'f' and gives you the tanks target. Making a macro can also serve this function. "/assist Rolf" where Rolf is the name of your tank will give you Rolf's target every time you push it.

With the intersection clear, take the first path to the right. If you have a Hunter in your party, he should be using Track Humanoids to watch for roamers. Warning the party before a pull about an incoming roamer can save everyone the walk from the graveyard.

The stationary enemies stand mostly in pairs along this path. Pull and CC. This keeps the fights small and easy. If you are without a Hunter, be ready for patrolling Troggs to add to a fight. Should this happen, stop healing (unless someone is going to die) until the tank has a chance to hit the new target a couple times. If you only have one enemy when a patroller adds, the Mage can sheep it instead.

There is a small tunnel ahead with a larger group of enemies just on the other side. There are two Ragefire Troggs and a Ragefire Shaman. You won't be able to see all the enemies, so be ready to sheep or kill the Shaman as soon as he comes into view.

HEALERS MAKE ME INVINCIBLE!

While it's true that having an entire party makes encounters much easier and allow you to take opponents that are much tougher, you have to be careful. Watch the Health and Mana bars of your party members. If anyone is low on health or mana, do not start the next fight until they are replenished. Casters will often have to sit and drink water to replenish mana faster. Do not get impatient and run off. Stay with the casters until they have what they need to help the party.

At the top of the path is a small cave. Keep all except your tank down on the ramp. Pull the two Troggs standing guard down the ramp to the party. With them dispatched, once again only the tank should approach the cave. Inside are two Troggs, Oggleflint, and Maur Grimtotem's Corpse. Pull the two Troggs and run back to the party. This is a standard fight and will pose no trouble to your party.

Rest up and prepare to fight Oggleflint. Bring the entire party up to the cave entrance. The tank should charge in to start the fight. Give the tank a few moments to establish aggro before healing and dealing damage. Oggleflint is higher level and hits harder than anything you've encountered so far, so it's important that the tank take the beating. If Oggleflint attacks any other party member, cease attacks and heals (unless someone is in peril of death) until the tank can regain Oggleflint's attention. Once this is done, continue the fight.

Killing Oggleflint gets you access to Maur Grimtotem. Unfortunately Maur was dead long before you got here as Rahauro suspected. Collect his satchel to finish *Searching for the Lost Sachel* and start *Returning the Lost Satchel*.

THE MEANING OF DEATH

Death inside an instance is much like death outside with a few differences. You respawn as a ghost at the nearest graveyard, but you don't resurrect at your corpse. Instead, you run into the instance portal. This resurrects you just inside the instance and you run back to where you died. Make sure the entire group has entered the instance before making the trek back to the site of your demise.

Take care to avoid getting near the ledge when you exit the cave. There are Ragefire Troggs and Shamans along a path below you. If they see you, they will run around the path to get to you. This wouldn't be a problem if they didn't get the help of every other enemy as they went. Make your way back to the intersection and take the next path to the right. It climbs well above where you just were and leads deeper into the dungeon.

Wandering along the ramp are the same Earthborers and Molten Elementals you've fought before. Pull them to you singly or in small groups and defeat them. Stay focused and avoid the temptation of charging in. It's effective now, but will get you into trouble later.

At the top of the ramp is a large area with several Molten Elementals moving about. Watch their movements and pull each one when it is away from all others. Clearing this area is slow, but trying to clear it quickly will kill your party just as quickly. Follow the path as it descends again. Ahead are pools of lava and the Searing Blade.

LAVA IS HOT

Do not walk on the lava here. It will most definitely kill you.

There is a lot of lava in this section and stone bridges that converge to a central high point. Taragaman the Hungerer is located there but to get to him you will need to do a bit of fighting.

Hunters should watch the patrolling Searing Blade Enforcers. Let the tank know when it is safe to pull. If your party is without a Hunter, wait for a patrol to pass before pulling. The enemies are in large groups of Searing Blade Enforcers, Cultists, and Warlocks.

The Warlocks have Voidwalker Minions which makes these fights against a minimum of four enemies. Pull as you have before. Have your Mage sheep the Warlock or kill it first. If you have a Warlock or Hunter in your party, have their pet attack the Voidwalker Minion when it gets close. The tank needs to grab and hold the two melee attackers while the DPS members kill them one at a time. Once the melee attackers are dead, kill the Voidwalker Minion before attacking the Warlock.

After each fight, pull back a bit and watch for the patrollers. Have people watching both directions to make sure you don't get any surprises. If a patroller comes behind your during a fight, a melee party member should grab it and drag it to the main tank. The main tank can then taunt it without dragging all the enemies all over.

It takes two fights to clear the first landing. There are now two bridges to choose from. At this point, the decision is moot as both lead you to your target…Taragaman the Hungerer. Choose a direction and have your tank move onto the bridge. The party should stay on the landing or just on the bridge, but not in sight of the next landing.

A BIT OF LIGHT READING

As you kill the Searing Blade Cultists, watch for the *Spells of Shadow* and the *Incantations from the Nether*. These books are needed for *The Power to Destroy* quest and can be dropped by any of the Cultists. The Cultists are pretty nice about carrying around extra copies though. If you find one, you'll find enough for your entire party.

The next landing has as many Searing Blade members as the previous. Locate the patrollers and wait for them to leave or come to you. If a patroller is approaching the party, return to the first landing and let them attack you without their friends. Kill them and find the next patroller. When all the patrols are clear, the tank should head to the top of the bridge.

Pull the enemy closest to you and run over the bridge and back to the party. The bridges are quite solid and the enemies can't see through them. This means that any enemy casters have to come to the top of the bridge to see your party and attack. When they crest the top of the bridge, begin the fight. Sheep the Warlock or kill it first. Send a pet to off-tank the Voidwalker Minion. Tank the two melee enemies. Kill the melee enemies one at a time. Kill the Voidwalker Minion. Kill the Searing Blade Warlock. This pattern will serve you well for the remainder of the instance.

Pull the rest of the landing in the same fashion. When the landing is entirely clear of enemies, move your party forward. Over the next ramp is Taragaman. If you haven't cleared all the patrols already, now is the time to wait for them. Taragaman is going to be a handful without any help. Rest to full before engaging. Take the fight to him.

This gives your Warriors a chance to charge and start the fight with rage. It also gives your Priest a chance to shield the tank before the fight starts. This lets the tank establish aggro without taking much damage. Give the tank a moment or two to get Taragaman's full attention before the rest of the party joins. Taragaman has a Fire Nova attack that hits all party members near him. Melee party members who aren't the tank, should use Healthstones (if you have a Warlock) or potions to heal the damage. This keeps the healer focusing on the tank and Taragaman from noticing the healer.

Ranged characters should stay at range. Start the fight by stacking every DoT you have on him. This starts the damage while giving the tank more time to really anger Taragaman. Once all the DoTs are stacked on him, start the simple blasting. It's not elegant, but it gets the job done. As with Oggleflint, if your tank loses aggro, stop attacking or casting until the tank regains aggro and pulls Taragaman back into position.

Once Taragaman finally dies, loot his heart to complete *Slaying the Beast*. No wonder Taragaman was so hearty…he had five hearts!

There are two paths from Taragaman's landing. Take the bridge to the right. Once again there are two large groups of enemies. Pull across the bridge to break line of sight and defeat them as you have before. When the landing is entirely clear, move your party across.

Again, you have a choice of paths. An ascending path lays hidden in the shadows against the cavern wall, while a bridge leads to another landing and out of the lava pools. The hidden path will be useful later, so remember where it is. First, you need to head across the bridge. On the other side is another landing filled with Searing Blade enemies.

Pull them across the bridge as you have before. These fights are the same as you have done so stay focused and use the same tactics. Sheep or kill the Warlock. Send a pet against the Voidwalker Minion. Tank the two melee enemies. Kill the melee enemies one at a time. Kill the Voidwalker Minion. Kill the Warlock.

As you ascend the ramp, there are three Searing Blade Enforcers guarding the way forward. Pull the left and run back to your party. This will give you two enemies to fight. Kill the Enforcers and then kill the final guard. In this area, there are two small groups and Jergosh the Invoker.

Keep your party on the ramp and pull each group back. Defeat the enemies until Jergosh stands alone. Rest to full health and mana before engaging. If you have a Warlock, now is a good time to hand out new Healthstones.

If you were uncomfortable pulling all the enemies, Jergosh will have an ally or two. This is not the end of the world and can be dealt with quickly. Start the fight by shielding your tank and charging Jergosh. Your tank needs to hold him while your party deals with his allies. Sheep and kill until Jergosh stands alone.

Now that Jergosh is alone, bring all your might against him. Interrupt his Shadowbolts when possible and stack DoTs on him. Use Healthstones and potions to keep the healer's mana high and aggro on the tank. When Jergosh falls, you are one step closer to completing *Hidden Enemies*.

Return to the ascending path hidden in shadows. This leads you up the cavern wall and to Bazzalan. The way up is guarded by pairs of Searing Blade. With nothing to use to break line of sight, the casters will be more difficult. If you have a Mage, sheep the caster as soon as the tank pulls. If you don't, have someone else pull. The puller needs to use a ranged weapon to hit the Searing Blade Warlock, then run. Run past the party and keep running until the Warlock gets to the party and the tank engages. As soon as the tank has the Warlock, return.

This keeps the enemies coming to you and keeps them from running for help. Slowly clear your way up the ramp. Rest to full after every fight as it's very easy for a fight against two to become a fight against four. If you get four enemies, kill the Warlock quickly and sheep one of the melee enemies. Use Warlock and Hunter pets to hold aggro from some of the enemies as your tank won't survive the attention of so many. With the fight more controlled, focus fire on one enemy at a time until all are dead.

There are two Searing Blade standing in front of Bazzalan on the top ledge. These can be pulled without effecting Bazzalan. Pull and kill them to leave Bazzalan standing alone. Shield your tank and charge to start the fight. Give your tank a moment to gain Bazzalan's undivided attention before joining the fight.

Bazzalan is a Rogue with Sinister Strike. This allows him to do incredible damage in a very short period of time. The tank should keep Bazzalan as far away from the softer members of the party at all times. Keep your party's health at full to keep Bazzalan from cutting a teammate down before you can react.

With his most dangerous ability mitigated, kill Bazzalan. Stack the DoTs on him before using your most damaging attacks. Keep blasting away until there is nothing but a burn mark on the rocky floor. Bazzalan is now dead and you have completed *Hidden Enemies*.

At this point you should have all of the quests complete and ready to turn in. Check to make sure everyone has their quests completed. If you still have not found the books for The Power to Destroy, head back to the lava pools and clear the remaining landings. It's time to decide how to get home. You can use your Hearthstone or walk out. Don't let the party separate. If you choose to walk out, there are likely to be respawns and you'll need everyone there to kill them again.

Once out, you have a little running to do. Thrall has a couple more things for you to do for Hidden Enemies, but they don't even require you to leave Orgrimmar. You can do them now or at your convience. Rest assured that you have done much good this day.

RAZORFEN DOWNS

Played & Written by: Edwin "Plainsong" Kern of <Dovrani> on Kirin Tor

A bastion of power for the Quilboar sits in southern Barrens. Or is it? Skeletons and spirits wander the passages alongside the Quilboar. Have they been infected with the Plague? Have they learned necromancy? Either option is a danger to all in Kalimdor.

Leave daylight behind and find what has happened to the Quilboar and stop it—if you can.

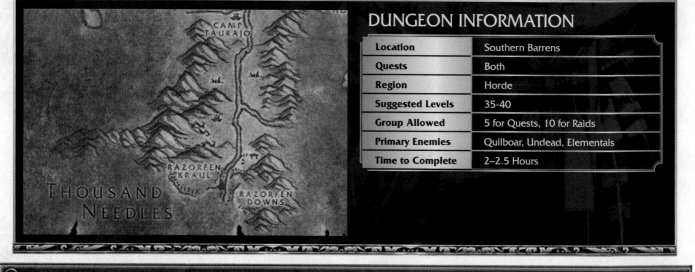

DUNGEON INFORMATION

Location	Southern Barrens
Quests	Both
Region	Horde
Suggested Levels	35-40
Group Allowed	5 for Quests, 10 for Raids
Primary Enemies	Quilboar, Undead, Elementals
Time to Complete	2–2.5 Hours

GETTING TO RAZORFEN DOWNS

The western entrance to Razorfen Downs is northeast of The Great Lift in Southern Barrens. It's directly across the road from Razorfen Kraul.

The southern entrance can be found through the Grimtotem camps on Darkcloud Pinnacle in the Thousand Needles. The southern entrance is closer to both Horde and Alliance flight points (Freewind Post and Thalanaar respectively) and bypasses The Great Lift. The time saved by using this entrance makes it ideal.

LEGEND	
1	Freewind Post
2	Thalanaar
3	Ramp to Grimtotem Compound
4	Southern Entrance to Razorfen Downs

WHO TO BRING

While forming your party, consider bringing someone who can cure diseases (Paladin, Priest, or Shaman). The Quilboar have forged an alliance with the Scourge. You'll be afflicted with many diseases as you travel through Razorfen Downs and having the ability to cure them makes this assault easier, even possible to some groups.

A number of fights have several enemies. Having strong AoE potential in the party can make these fights much easier. Mages and Warlocks are ideal for this with Hunters being a reasonable backup.

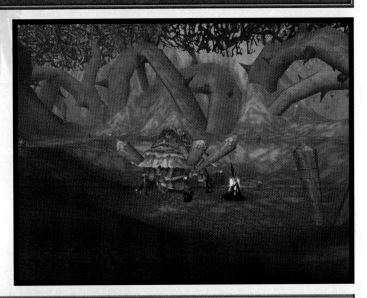

QUESTS FOR RAZORFEN DOWNS

ALLIANCE QUEST

QUEST NAME	QUEST GIVER	QUEST GIVER LOCATION	QUEST RECEIVER	QUEST RECEIVER LOCATION	CHAIN?	MAX EXPERIENCE
Bring the Light	Archbishop Bendictus	Stormwind: Cathedral District	Archbishop Bendictus	Stormwind: Cathedral District	No	4,300
REWARD: Vanquisher's Sword (One-Hand Sword, 26.6 DPS, +16 Attack Power) or Amberglow Talisman (Neck, +1 AGI, +10 SPR)						

BRING THE LIGHT

Quest Level	39 to obtain
Location	Stormwind (Cathedral District)
Person	Archbishop Bendictus
Goal	Kill Amnennar the Coldbringer
Max Experience Gained	4,300
Reward	Vanquisher's Sword (1H Sword, 26.6 DPS, +16 Attack Power) or Amberglow Talisman (Neck, +1 AGI, +10 SPR)

The Scourge have found allies in the Barrens. The Quilboar of Razorfen Downs have joined forces with the Scourge. A Lich by the name of Amnennar the Coldbringer is leading the Quilboar and building an army. The Scourge must be stamped out whatever the cost, wherever the threat. Kill Amnennar for the sake of Azeroth.

HORDE QUESTS

QUEST NAME	QUEST GIVER	QUEST GIVER LOCATION	QUEST RECEIVER	QUEST RECEIVER LOCATION	CHAIN?	MAX EXPERIENCE
Bring the End	Andrew Brownell	Undercity: Magic Quarter	Andrew Brownell	Undercity: Magic Quarter	No	4,300
REWARD: Vanquisher's Sword (One-Hand Sword, 26.6 DPS, +16 Attack Power) or Amberglow Talisman (Neck, +1 AGI, +10 SPI)						
An Unholy Alliance	Varimathras	Undercity: Royal Quarter	Varimathras	Undercity: Royal Quarter	Yes	3,500
REWARD: Zealot's Robe (Cloth Chest, 48 Armor, +12 STA, +4 INT, +3 SPI) or Nail Spitter (Gun, 14.7 DPS) or Skull Breaker (Mainhand Mace, 18.7 DPS, +3 STA, +5 INT)						

BRING THE END

Quest Level	43 to obtain
Location	Undercity (Magic Quarter)
Person	Andrew Brownell
Goal	Collect the Skull of the Coldbringer
Max Experience Gained	4,300
Reward	Vanquisher's Sword (1H Sword, 26.6 DPS, +16 Attack Power) or Amberglow Talisman (Neck, +1 AGI, +10 SPI)

The initial scouting of Razorfen Downs did not worry the Horde. With undead showing up, a new assessment was made. The Quilboar of Razorfen Downs have formed an alliance with The Scourge. This cannot be allowed to continue. The Scourge should have no foothold this close to the people of the Horde. Amnennar the Coldbringer is The Scourge's link to Razorfen Downs. Bring the Skull of the Coldbringer to Andrew Brownell as proof the link is no longer.

AN UNHOLY ALLIANCE

Quest Level	32 to obtain
Location	Undercity (Royal Quarter)
Person	Varimathras
Goal	Collect Ambassador Malcin's Head
Max Experience Gained	3,500
Reward	Zealot's Robe (Cloth Chest, 48 Armor, +12 STA, +4 INT, +3 SPI) or Nail Spitter (Gun, 14.7 DPS) or Skull Breaker (Mainhand Mace, 18.7 DPS, +3 STA, +5 INT)

The Scourge is working to solidify their power in Razorfen Downs. They have sent Ambassador Malcin to see to this. Bring his head to Varimathras and send a message to The Scourge to collect your reward.

SHARED QUESTS

QUEST NAME	QUEST GIVER	QUEST GIVER LOCATION	QUEST RECEIVER	QUEST RECEIVER LOCATION	CHAIN?	MAX EXPERIENCE
A Host of Evil	Myriam Moonsinger	Barrens: Razorfen Downs	Myriam Moonsinger	Barrens: Razorfen Downs	No	3,450
REWARD: 70 s						
Scourge of the Downs	Belnistrasz	Razorfen Downs	Belnistrasz	Razorfen Downs	Yes	30
Extinguishing the Idol	Belnistrasz	Razorfen Downs	Brazier	Razorfen Downs	Yes	4,250
REWARD: Dragonclaw Ring (Ring, +4 SPI, +10 STA)						

A HOST OF EVIL

Quest Level	28 to obtain
Location	Southern Barrens (Razorfen Downs Entrance)
Person	Myriam Moonsinger
Goal	Kill 8 Death's Head Cultists, Razorfen Thornweavers, and Razorfen Battleguards
Max Experience Gained	3,450
Reward	70s

Myriam Moonsinger has been observing the Quilboar. Problems are stirring quickly and help may not arrive in time. You are asked to slow the Quilboar by slaying a number of them. Return to Myriam when you have slain the appropriate enemies.

SCOURGE OF THE DOWNS

Quest Level	32 to obtain
Location	Razorfen Downs
Person	Belnistrasz
Goal	Give Belnistrasz an Oathstone
Max Experience Gained	30
Reward	None

During his imprisonment, Belistrasz has had time to see how the Quilboar are attaining their new power and needs your help to put a stop to it. Return his oathstone to him to open Extinguishing the Idol.

EXTINGUISHING THE IDOL

Quest Level	32 to obtain
Location	Razorfen Downs
Person	Belnistrasz
Goal	Escort and defend Belnistrasz
Max Experience Gained	4,250
Reward	Dragonclaw Ring (Ring, +4 SPI, +10 STA)

Belnistrasz can stop the Quilboar from getting any more power from the idol, but he needs you to cut a path through the enemy to the idol and defend him while he works. When he is done, examine the brazier he leaves behind to collect your ring. Plaguemaw the Rotting spawns when the quest is finished.

RAZORFEN LEGIONS

NPC	LEVEL
Battle Boar Horror	34-37
Frequent Drops:	
Boar Ribs	
Boneflayer Ghoul	38-39 Elite
Notes: Cleave, Ghoul Rot (Disease, Chance to hit reduced by 10%, 10 minute duration)	
Death's Head Cultist	33-34 Elite
Notes: Shadow Bolt, Death and Decay (AoE, Curse of Blood effect), Curse of Blood (Damage taken increased by 36)	
Death's Head Geomancer	35-36 Elite
Notes: Flame Spike (AoE, Fire), Slow, Fireball	
Death's Head Necromancer	36-37 Elite
Notes: Shadow Bolt, Cripple, Withered Touch (Disease, 60 Shadow damage and 60 Mana leeched every 10 seconds, 5 minute duration)	
Freezing Spirit	38-40 Elite
Notes: Frost Nova, Chilling Touch	

NPC	LEVEL
Frozen Soul	37-38 Elite
Notes: Silence	
Razorfen Battleguard	32-34 Elite
Notes: Slam (Knockdown)	
Razorfen Thornweaver	32-34 Elite
Notes: Thorns, Entangling Roots	
Skeletal Frostweaver	37-38 Elite
Notes: Frost Bolt	
Skeletal Shadowcaster	35-36
Notes: Shadowbolt	
Skeletal Summoner	39-40 Elite
Notes: Curse of Weakness, Lightning Bolt, Summon Skeletons	
Splinterbone Captain	39-40 Elite
Notes: Backhand (Knockdown)	
Splinterbone Centurion	36-39
Notes: Thunderclap	
Splinterbone Skeleton	34-35
Splinterbone Warrior	36-38
Frequent Drops: Silk	

NPC	LEVEL
Thorn Eater Ghoul	37-38 Elite
Notes: Ravenous Claw, Ghoul Rot (Disease, Chance to hit reduced by 10%, 10 minute duration), Sunder Armor (-296 Armor, 6 Second duration)	
Tomb Fiend	34-35
Tomb Reaver	37 Elite
Withered Battle Boar	34
Frequent Drops: Boar Ribs	
Withered Quilguard	35-36 Elite
Notes: Withered Touch (Disease, 100 Shadow damage every 10 seconds, 100 Mana leeched every 10 seconds, 3 minute duration)	
Withered Reaver	35-36 Elite
Notes: Cleave	
Withered Spearhide	34-35 Elite
Notes: Disease Shot (Disease, -27 Str and −27 AGI, 5 minute duration), Ranged Attacks, Enrages at 25% HP, Infected Spine (Damage taken is increased by 8)	
Withered Warrior	34-35 Elite
Notes: Enrages at 25% HP	

MASTERS OF RAZORFEN

NAME	LEVEL	FREQUENT DROP(S)
AMBASSADOR MALCIN	36 Elite	Ambassador Malcin's Head
Notes: Curse of Blood, Shadow Bolt, Thorns Aura		
AMMENNAR THE COLDBRINGER	36 Boss	Coldrage Dagger (Dagger, 29.7 DPS, Chance on Hit: deals 20 – 30 frost damage and slows enemy movement by 50% for 5 seconds), Deathchill Armor (Mail Chest, 270 Armor, +20 SPI, +9 INT, +3 STA), Icemetal Barbute (Plate Head, 383 Armor, +15 STR, +7 SPI, +10 STA, +10 FR), Robes of the Lich (Cloth Chest, 64 Armor, +10 INT, +20 STA), Bone Fingers (Leather Hands, 73 Armor, +9 STA, +9 INT)
Notes: Frost Nova, Frost Bolt, Ice Armor, Summons 4 Frost Spectres at 66% HP and again at 33% HP, Amnennar's Wrath (Knockback)		
GLUTTON	40 Elite	Glutton's Cleaver (1H Axe, 23 DPS, Chance on Hit: Wounds target causing 50 damage over 30 seconds), Fleshhide Shoulders (Leather Shoulders, 95 Armor, +5 STR, +6 AGI, +15 STA)
Notes: Disease Cloud, Enrages at 10% HP		
MORDRESH FIRE EYE	35 Boss	Deathmage Sash (Cloth Waist, 33 Armor, +6 STA, +15 Int), Glowing Eye of Mordresh (Neck, +5 INT, +11 SPI), Mordresh's Lifeless Skull (Held in Off-Hand, +5 STA, +11 SPI)
Notes: Fireball, Fire Nova		
PLAGUEMAW THE ROTTING	40 Elite	Plaguerot Sprig (Wand, 37.2 DPS, +7 Shadow Resistance, Mage Only), Swine Fists (Leather Hands, 68 Armor, +8 AGI, +8 STR)
Notes: Triggered by the *Extinguishing the Idol* quest. Putrid Stench (Silence, -50 STR & AGI for 10 sec.), Withered Touch (Disease: 68-69 shadow damage and drains 68-69 mana every 10 sec. for 3 min.)		
RAGGLESNOUT	37 Boss	Boar Champion's Belt (Mail Waist, 147 Armor, +15 STR, +6 STA), Savage Boar's Guard (Shield, 1287 Armor, 22 Block, +11 STR, +6 STA), X'caliboar (2H Sword, 37.3 DPS, +20 STR, +8 STA)
Notes: Rare spawn, Shadowbolt, Shadow Word: Pain, Heal		
TUTEN'KASH	36 Boss	Silky Spider Cape (Back, 30 Armor, +11 STA, +5 SPI), Arachnid Gloves of. . . (Leather Hands, 79 Armor, +10 Nature Resist, Various other stat bonuses based on suffix), Carapace of Tuten'Kash (Plate Chest, 373 Armor, +10 STR, +8 AGI, +15 STA)
Notes: Virulent Poison, Curse of Tuten'Kash (Curse, reduces attack and casting speed by 15%, 15 minute duration), Web Spray		

INTO THE TANGLE

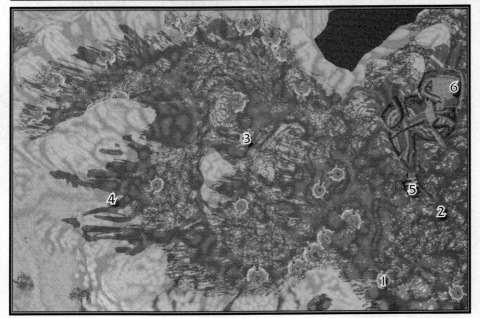

LEGEND

1	South Entrance
2	Myriam Moonsinger
3	Ambassador Malcin
4	West Entrance
5	The Boar's Mouth
6	Instance Portal

THE THICKET

After crossing the bridge from the Grimtotem on Darkcloud Pinnacle, there is a ledge to the right that leads to our quarry.

The enemies are spread out and can be pulled singly or in small groups relatively easily. The Death's Head Cultists have an AoE attack that can disease your entire party, so be sure not to stand in it.

Move northeast past the first camp. As you come to the large boar-head construct, turn southeast and move up the hill. Perched above is Myriam Moonsinger, who will give you *A Host of Evil*.

Standing beside the hut to the south is Ambassador Malcin and a small party of Quilboar. Killing the Death's Head Cultist and Ambassador Malcin quickly ensures that your party remains at high health. The Cultist and Malcin are both casters. Their most potent attacks can be nullified with well-timed interrupts. Their lack of hitpoints ensures a fast fight. Finish the Razorfen Thornweaver and Battleguard. Horde parties should grab **Ambassador Malcin's Head** to complete *An Unholy Alliance*.

Kill your way toward the West entrance to finish *A Host of Evil*. These targets are easy enough that your party will use few resources, but high enough level that any Warlocks have the chance to fill up on Soul Shards before heading in. With this accomplished, return to Myriam Moonsinger then move north into The Boar's Mouth.

THE BOAR'S MOUTH

There is a distinct change in the Quilboar as you move deeper. The Withered Spearhides and Withered Warriors are a definite sign that something isn't right. The Quilboar are still spread out and can be fought in small groups.

The withered Quilboar won't back down from a fight and actually become more dangerous near death. Have your damage dealers ready to bring the enemy down when they Enrage at 25% health.

The Death's Head Geomancers are far more dangerous than the Cultists. They have an AoE fire attack that can cause massive damage to your party. Have your interrupts ready and kill them as quickly as possible.

Fight your way through the Quilboar to the Instance Portal. The path is short and direct.

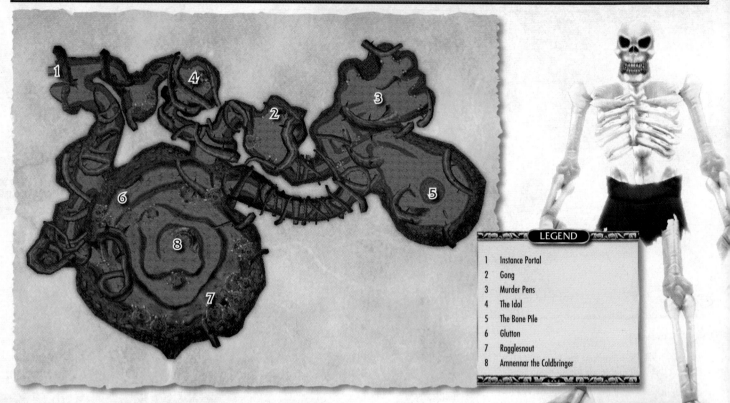

LEGEND

1	Instance Portal
2	Gong
3	Murder Pens
4	The Idol
5	The Bone Pile
6	Glutton
7	Ragglesnout
8	Amnennar the Coldbringer

THE PROBLEM PRESENTS ITSELF

A glance down the southern passage will prove beyond any doubt that something is very wrong. There are undead in Razorfen Downs. A Skeletal Frostweaver, two Frozen Souls, and two Thorn Eater Ghouls guard the south passage. This is a fight should be left until later when your party is fully warmed up and working well together. Less dangerous targets can be found by taking the east passage. This gives your party time to figure out the best way to work together and helps fill your bags.

A couple single Withered Spearhides with wandering Death's Head Geomancers and Withered Warriors block the east passage. Attack the Withered Spearhides when the wanderers are away from them and will not come to help. With the Spearhides dead, ambush the wanderers when they come back toward you. At the end of the passage are a Withered Spearhide and four Withered Battle Boars. Kill the Boars first as they are softer and make your tank's life difficult if left alive. With the Boars dead, the Spearhide will not pose a threat.

WATCHING THE PATROLS

If you have a Hunter in your party, he should use Track Beast to monitor the wandering boars. Later he will need to use Track Undead to monitor the patrols.

At the back of the room are a Withered Spearhide, a Withered Warrior and a Death's Head Geomancer. This formation (ranged attacker, melee attacker, and caster) is common in the Downs. Your party should start practicing your battle plan. Casters should be brought down first due to their lower HP and higher damage output. Ranged attackers should be kept in close range, by snares or roots, to keep them from using their more powerful attacks.

In the next passage are a Death's Head Geomancer and a Withered Warrior. A Battle Boar Horror runs up and down this passage. Its patrol speed is quick enough to come upon you in the middle of a fight. Keep an eye out for it as you clear the Quilboar and attack it away from the others. A Withered Spearhide and four Withered Battleboars guard the entrance to the next room. Dispatch them as you did before.

The room has an altar on the left side, and two groups of enemies on the far side. Each group consists of a Death's Head Geomancer, Withered Warrior, and Withered Spearhide. The groups are very difficult to pull separately. It's better to assume they will pull together. Start the fight by CCing the Withered Spearhides. They do high damage, but aren't your first targets. The Death's Head Geomancers need to be interrupted until they are dead. One party member should focus on keeping a Geomancer interrupted, while the rest of the party kills the other. This will keep you from suffering double AoEs. If the Spearhides are still CCed, kill the Warriors first.

The next room is heavily guarded. Two groups, consisting of a Death's Head Necromancer, Skeletal Servant, Withered Quilguard, and Withered Reaver, guard the two entrances to the room and another group of a Death's Head Necromancer, two Withered Quilguards, and a Withered Reaver guards the ledge to the right. Pull one group at a time into the hallway. Hiding around the tunnel walls will even force the casters to come to you.

FOR WHOM THE GONG TOLLS

A large Gong stands on the north side of the next room. Many groups of Quilboar guard the room and must be cleared before the Gong is used. Each group is made up of a Death's Head Necromancer, Skeletal Servant, Withered Reaver, and two Withered Quilguards. Pull them into the passage one at a time to keep the fighting controlled.

When the room is entirely clear, it's time for the Gong. Have your party stay to one side of the room. The Gong ringer should run back to the party immediately after ringing. The first hit brings three groups of five Tomb Fiends. This fight is fairly easy and your AoE members will enjoy it. All must be killed before you can ring the gong again. The second ring brings two groups of two Tomb Reavers. You can fight these groups separate from each other and they shouldn't pose a threat to your group. The third ring brings Tuten'Kash. Your tank should grab Tuten'Kash's attention and keep him away from the more fragile party members. Keep him facing away from the party so it's easy to see when aggro is lost. Should Tuten'Kash attack anyone but the tank, cease fire. Hold attacks until the tank has regained aggro. If the tank is webbed, whoever has Tuten'Kash's attention needs to drag him back to the tank. Kill him and find the wonders he was carrying.

THE MURDER PENS

Kill the Withered Quilguards, Death's Head Necromancer, Withered Reavers and wandering Battle Boar Horrors on your way to the next room. The passage forward is clear while a Death's Head Necromancer, Skeletal Servant, Withered Reaver, and Withered Quilguard guard the ramp on the left. Clear the ramp as you ascend.

Another group - similar to the first - guards the second ramp. They are hiding on the right side to ambush any who come. Eliminate the group to gain access to the pens. In the left of the west pens stands Henry Stern. He can teach you the recipe for Goldthorn Tea if you have sufficient cooking skill. Goldthorn Tea can be extremely useful to casters as it restores 1344 Mana over 27 seconds and is made with Goldthorn and Refreshing Spring Water (one of each provides four Goldthorn Tea). In the north pen is Belnistrasz, who is involved with both the *Scourge of the Downs* and *Extinguishing the Idol* quests.

The way is clear for the escort part of *Extinguishing the Idol*. Simply follow Belnistrasz back to the altar. Guarding him is quite difficult. Multiple waves of enemies spawn without leaving you time to rest between waves. Each wave has a Death's Head Geomancer, Withered Quilguard, and two Withered Battle Boars. Any group without strong AoE potential should avoid this fight as killing the enemies one at a time isn't fast enough and you will get overwhelmed. Close to the end of the battle, Plaguemaw the Rotting will spawn to complicate matters. Send a tank in to keep him busy and continue to guard Belnistrasz. Should you guard Belnistrasz for the full 5 minutes, he leaves a bowl on the ground in which you can find your reward for *Extinguishing the Idol*.

THE END OF THE LIVING

There is little left alive in Razorfen Downs. Return to the Murder Pens and take the bridge to the Bone Pile. Another AoE opportunity presents itself. Dozens of Splinterbone Skeletons are gathered around a pile of bone on which stands Mordresh Fire Eye. Taking the fight to Mordresh will keep him from being able to cast on your party from afar. Warriors should be shielded by a Priest so they can charge and use Retaliation to make sure all the Splinterbone Skeletons are wounded and in one spot so they can be killed by the party's AoE members quickly. Keep Mordresh interrupted and claim your treasure when he falls.

BACKTRACK

After you kill Mordresh, make a 180 and work your way back to the entrance to take the "left" path toward Amnennar. This is the more difficult path, so it's best that you save it for last.

The eastern passage is filled with patrols. Thorn Eater Ghouls are paired with Skeletal Frostweavers or Frozen Souls. A pair of Splinterbone Skeletons runs along the passage. Clear each patrol when it is alone.

As the passage widens, groups of undead stand guard at regular intervals. The standard enemy formation is a Thorn Eater Ghoul, a Skeletal Frostweaver, and two Splinterbone Warriors. There is little deviation from this pattern. The Frostweaver should be kept interrupted while the DPS members of the party bring down the Splinterbones. The Frostweaver and Ghoul should follow.

A LUMBERING DANGER

Glutton wanders this section of the passage. Keep a careful watch for him. If he begins moving toward a fight your party is engaged in, your party needs to move quickly. Kill the enemies and run or drag the enemies away from Glutton. His attacks, armor, and HP are immense and will make a dangerous fight alone and spell your party's destruction if he joins a fight in progress.

Move with the passage as it curls south and begins to spiral in on itself. Fight each guard group as you have and watch for patrollers as you make your way around the spiral. Ragglesnout can sometimes be found along the southwest wall. He is a rare-spawn loot mob and a skeleton may be standing by the hut instead.

Take the spiral slowly and carefully. You are very near your goal and eagerness may become carelessness. At the top of the ramp stand the final guards. A Skeletal Summoner, Splinterbone Captain, and four Splinterbone Centurions are your opponents. The fight will be hard on both your tank and healer as there will be a lot of damage coming in. Kill the Skeletal Summoner before it can bring more enemies, then move to the Centurions. A party with strong AoE potential should kill the Centurions all at once.

Amnennar the Coldbringer stands in a hut at the top of the spiral. When your party is rested, bring the end to Amnennar. Keep Amnennar interrupted to significantly reduce the damage your party takes. When Amnennar reaches 66% HP, and again at 33% HP, he summons four Frost Spectres. These creatures will dissipate when Amnennar dies. If your party is dealing damage quickly, ignore the ghosts and bring down the boss. If your party is dealing damage slowly (or has strong AoE potential) kill the ghosts quickly to avoid taking unnecessary damage.

EVEN THE UNDEAD FEAR GRAVITY

If your party is being overwhelmed by the ghosts Amnennar summons, there is still hope. One party member should gain the aggro of the ghosts without gaining Amnennar's attention. This can be done with a low damage AoE attack (Frost Nova, Thunderclap, etc.). Once aggro is gained, the party member should drop off the ledge. The ghosts will take the spiral around to get to the party member and leave Amnennar to deal with the other four party members alone. This tactic should be used in the direst emergencies as the member who pulls the ghosts away may soon become one.

Since Amnennar is a casting enemy, it's even more important for the tank to keep him facing away from the party. This makes it much easier to notice when Amnennar has changed targets. Any party member, aside from the tank, who comes under attack by the Lich should cease fire. Any damage or healing done will make it harder for the tank to pull the Lich off the party member. Amnennar's demise will complete *Bring the Light* for Alliance parties while his skull will complete *Bring the End* for Horde parties. Head home knowing that the Scourge has one fewer bastions of power in Kalimdor.

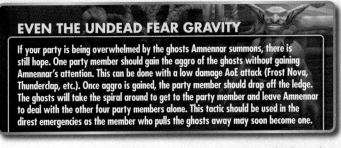

RAZORFEN KRAUL

Played & Written by: Edwin "Plainsong" Kern of <Dovrani> on Kirin Tor

Little is known of this stronghold of the Quilboar. All who enter are killed. Those who escape do so in such a state, that they never make it far before death catches up with them. Why do the Quilboar fight so fervently? What is Charlga Razorflank so adamant about defending? Steel yourself and prepare for the hardships that wait.

DUNGEON INFORMATION

Location	Southern Barrens
Quests	Both
Region	Horde
Suggested Levels	25-30
Groups Allowed	5 for Quests, 10 for Raiding
Primary Enemies	Quilboar
Time to Complete	2.5 – 3 hours

GETTING TO RAZORFEN KRAUL

Razorfen Kraul sits northwest of the Great Lift to Thousand Needles. Horde parties can form at either Camp Taurajo or The Great Lift before entering. Alliance parties will have a more difficult time approaching the entrance as it's deep within Horde territory. Gather your group at Theramore and make the run through Dustwallow Marsh to the Barrens. Hugging the mountains along the east side of Barrens keeps you out of eyesight of many of the Horde while you make your way to Razorfen Kraul.

THE GREAT LIFT

Alliance parties face a problem. One of the quests for Razorfen Kraul and a closer flight point are in Thousand Needles. The only way to Thousand Needles (The Great Lift) is guarded by two high-level Tauren. Watch the elevators a moment to understand the timing. As one elevator descends, run along the ramp to the other elevator. If you time it correctly, your entire party can get on the elevator without taking significant damage. If any party member becomes dazed or takes significant damage, they should jump off the cliff. It guarantees death, but the graveyard is very close and there aren't any enemies at the bottom.

WHO TO BRING

Because the multitude of Quilboars use magic and ranged attacks, having a party member who is familiar with the dungeon can make the assault easier. If the entire party is new to Razorfen Kraul, take it slow and have someone who is familiar with pulling casters and ranged attackers lead. Using terrain to pull enemies into melee range will keep the Quilboar from feasting on your corpses.

Characters with ranged interrupts make this easier. Mages with Counterspell and Shamans with Earth Shock can force enemy casters to come to you.

QUESTS FOR RAZORFEN KRAUL

All quests for Razorfen Kraul are Dungeon quests. These can not be completed in a Raid group.

ALLIANCE QUESTS

QUEST NAME	QUEST GIVER	QUEST GIVER LOCATION	QUEST RECEIVER	QUEST RECEIVER LOCATION	CHAIN?	MAX EXPERIENCE
Fire Hardened Mail	Furen Longbeard	Stormwind: Dwarven District	Furen Longbeard	Stormwind: Dwarven District	Yes	2,300
REWARD: Fire Hardened Hauberk (Mail Chest, 218 Armor, +5 STR, +14 STA, Use: Increases Rage by 30, Warrior Only)						
Mortality Wanes	Heralath Fallowbrook	Razorfen Kraul	Treshala Fallowbrook	Darnassus: Tradesman's Terrace	No	3,050
REWARD: Mourning Shawl (Cloak, 21 Armor, -3 SPI, +7 STA) or Lancer Boots (Leather Boots, 64 Armor, +5 STA, +6 Agi)						
The Crone of the Kraul	Falfindel Waywarder	Thousand Needles: Thalanaar	Falfindel Waywarder	Thousand Needles: Thalanaar	No	3,350
REWARD: "Mage-Eye" Blunderbuss (Gun, 12.5 DPS) and Berylline Pads (Cloth Shoulders, 39 Armor, +6 SPI, +5 STA, +10 INT) or Stonefist Girdle (Mail Waist, 234 Armor, +6 STR, +5 STA) or Marbled Buckler (Shield, 775 Armor, 17 Block, +5 AGI, +5 STR, +5 SPI, +5 STA)						

FIRE HARDENED MAIL (WARRIOR ONLY)

Quest Level	20 to obtain
Location	Stormwind (Dwarven District)
Contact	Furen Longbeard
Goal	Collect Vial of Phlogiston
Max Experience Gained	2,300
Reward	Fire Hardened Hauberk (Mail Chest, 218 Armor, +5 STR, +14 STA, Use: Increases Rage by 30, Warrior Only)

This quest is Warrior only and can only be obtained after you have completed *The Shieldsmith*. One of the pieces Furen needs for your Warrior's Fire Hardened Hauberk is the Vial of Phlogiston. Only one person in the world can make the Phlogiston: Roogug in Razorfen Kraul. Kill him and take the Vial of Phlogiston and the other materials needed to Furen to claim your armor.

MORTALITY WANES

Quest Level	26 to obtain
Location	Razorfen Kraul
Contact	Heralath Fallowbrook
Goal	Find Treshala's Pendant and take it to Treshala Fallowbrook
Max Experience Gained	3,050
Reward	Mourning Shawl (Cloak, 21 Armor, -3 SPI, +7 STA) or Lancer Boots (Leather Boots, 64 Armor, +5 STA, +6 AGI)

Finding a wounded ally is usually a sign of good fortune for them, but this is not the case when you find Heralath. With his last breaths, he asks you to retrieve the pendant his wife gave him when they were married. One of the Quilboars has taken it. His last wish was that Treshala receives the pendant and news of his death. Find Treshala's Pendant by killing the Quilboars en masse. Once you have it, return it to Treshala in the Tradesman's Terrace in Darnassus. She's on the second floor across from the weapon shop.

THE CRONE OF THE KRAUL

Quest Level	29 to obtain
Location	Thousand Needles (Thalanaar)
Contact	Falfindel Waywarder
Goal	Bring Razorflank's Medallion to Falfindel
Max Experience Gained	3,350
Reward	"Mage-Eye" Blunderbuss (Gun, 12.5 DPS) and Berylline Pads (Cloth Shoulders, 39 Armor, +6 SPI, +5 STA, +10 INT) or Stonefist Girdle (Mail Waist, 234 Armor, +6 STR, +5 STA) or Marbled Buckler (Shield, 775 Armor, 17 Block, +5 AGI, +5 STR, +5 SPI, +5 STA)

Upon delivering Lonebrow's Journal (found in his dead hand on a hill near the bottom of the Great Lift in Thousand Needles) to Falfindel, you are asked to kill Charlga Razorflank. She is building an army in Razorfel Kraul and must be stopped. Tear the medallion from her corpse and return it to Falfindel as proof of your actions.

QUEST NAME	QUEST GIVER	QUEST GIVER LOCATION	QUEST RECEIVER	QUEST RECEIVER LOCATION	CHAIN?	MAX EXPERIENCE
Brutal Armor	Thun'grim Firegaze	Barrens: Thorn Hill	Thun'grim Firegaze	Barrens: Thorn Hill	Yes	3,650
REWARD: Brutal Hauberk (Mail Chest, 203 Armor, +5 STR, +14 STA, Use: Increases Rage by 30, Warrior Only)						
Going, Going, Guano!	Master Apothecary Faranell	Undercity: Apothecarium	Master Apothecary Faranell	Undercity: Apothecarium	No	3,300
A Vengeful Fate	Auld Stonespire	Thunderbluff: Center Rise	Auld Stonespire	Thunderbluff: Center Rise	No	8,100
REWARD: Berylline Pads (Cloth Shoulders, 39 Armor, +6 SPI, +5 STA, +10 INT) or Stonefist Girdle (Mail Waist, 234 Armor, +6 STR, +5 STA) or Marbled Buckler (Shield, 775 Armor, 17 Block, +5 AGI, +5 STR, +5 SPI, +5 STA)						
An Unholy Alliance	Small Scroll	Razorfen Kraul	Varimathras	Undercity: Royal Quarter	No	2,100

BRUTAL ARMOR (WARRIOR ONLY)

Quest Level	20 to obtain
Location	Barrens (Atop Thorn Hill)
Contact	Thun'grim Firegaze
Goal	Collect Vial of Phlogiston
Max Experience Gained	3,650
Reward	Brutal Hauberk (Mail Chest, 203 Armor, +5 STR, +14 STA, Use: Increases Rage by 30, Warrior Only)

This quest is Warrior only and can only be obtained after you have completed *The Trial at the Field of Giants*. One of the pieces Thun'grim needs for your Warrior's Brutal Hauberk is the Vial of Phlogiston. Only one person in the world can make the Phlogiston: Roogug in Razorfen Kraul. Kill him and take the Vial of Phlogiston and the other materials needed to Thun'grim to claim your armor.

GOING, GOING, GUANO!

Quest Level	30 to obtain
Location	Undercity (Apothecarium)
Contact	Master Apothecary Faranell
Goal	Collect the Kraul Guano
Max Experience Gained	3,300

Master Apothecary Faranell needs help with an experiment. He needs some Kraul Guano, but is too busy overseeing the Apothecarium to get it himself. The Kraul Guano can be obtained by killing the Kraul Bats and Greater Kraul Bats at the back of Razorfen Kraul. Bring the Kraul Guano to him to open the Hearts of Zeal quest.

A VENGEFUL FATE

Quest Level	29 to obtain
Location	Thunderbluff (Center Rise)
Contact	Auld Stonespire
Goal	Remove Razorflank's Heart
Max Experience Gained	8,100
Reward	Berylline Pads (Cloth Shoulders, 39 Armor, +6 SPI, +5 STA, +10 Int) or Stonefist Girdle (Mail Waist, 234 Armor, +6 STR, +5 STA) or Marbled Buckler (Shield, 775 Armor, 17 Block, +5 AGI, +5 STR, +5 SPI, +5 STA)

Not everyone leaves the past behind. Auld can't get over the conflicts of old. Only one thing will allow him to die in peace…the heart of his enemy. Tear Razorflank's Heart out and bring it to him.

AN UNHOLY ALLIANCE

Quest Level	28 to obtain
Location	Razorfen Kraul
Contact	Small Scroll
Goal	Take the Small Scroll to Varimathras in Undercity
Max Experience Gained	2,100

After killing Charlga Razorflank, take the Small Scroll from her body and read it. It seems there is more happening here than first presented itself. Take the scroll to Varimathras in Undercity. He should be alerted at once.

SHARED QUESTS

QUEST NAME	QUEST GIVER	QUEST GIVER LOCATION	QUEST RECEIVER	QUEST RECEIVER LOCATION	CHAIN?	MAX EXPERIENCE
Blueleaf Tubers	Mebok Mizzyrix	Barrens: Ratchet	Mebok Mizzyrix	Barrens: Ratchet	No	420
REWARD: A Small Container of Gems						
Willix the Importer	Willix the Importer	Razorfen Kraul	Willix the Importer	Razorfen Kraul	No	3,050
REWARD: Monkey Ring (Ring, +6 AGI), or Snake Hoop (Ring, +6 INT), or Tiger Band (Ring, +6 STR)						

BLUELEAF TUBERS

Quest Level	20 to obtain
Location	Barrens (Ratchet)
Contact	Mebok Mizzyrix
Goal	Collect 6 Blueleaf Tubers
Max Experience Gained	420
Reward	A Small Container of Gems

Mebok is always on the lookout for some fast coin. He's willing to pay you handsomely if you help him with his latest scheme. He needs you to collect 6 Blueleaf Tubers from Razorfen Kraul. It sounds much easier than it really is. Before you head off to the Kraul, be sure to pick up the Crate with Holes, Snufflenose Owner's Manual, and the Snufflenose Command Stick that are beside Mebok. Take this time to familiarize yourself with how you are to harvest the Blueleaf Tubers. When you're ready, head to Razorfen Kraul and collect your tubers.

WILLIX THE IMPORTER

Quest Level	24 to obtain
Location	Razorfen Kraul
Contact	Willix the Importer
Goal	Escort Willix out of Razorfen Kraul
Max Experience Gained	3,050
Reward	Monkey Ring (Ring, +6 AGI), or Snake Hoop (Ring, +6 INT), or Tiger Band (Ring, +6 STR)

Willix is a shrewd fellow. Rather than coming up with his own idea, he listened to Mebok and tried to beat him to the tubers. He underestimated the danger of such an undertaking. Escort him out of Razorfen Kraul, and he'll make it worth your while.

THE DENIZENS OF RAZORFEN KRAUL

ENEMIES IN THE KRAUL

NPC	LEVEL
Agam'Ar	24-25 Elite
Blood of Agamaggan	27 Elite
Notes: Curse of Blood (Physical damage taken is increased by 14. 10 minute duration)	
Boar Spirit	18-20 Elite
Notes: Summoned by Aggem Thorncurse	
Death's Head Acolyte	28-29 Elite
Death's Head Adept	27-28 Elite
Notes: Chains of Ice (Root), Frostbolt	
Death's Head Priest	26-27 Elite
Notes: Shadow Bolt, Heal	
Death's Head Sage	29 Elite
Notes: Healing Ward V (Healing totem), Elemental Protection Totem	
Death's Head Seer	28-29 Elite
Notes: Healing Ward V, Lava Spout Totem	
Death's Head Ward Keeper	15
Notes: Maintains the ward holding Agathelos the Raging.	

NPC	LEVEL
Greater Kraul Bat	32 Elite
Notes: Sonic Burst (AoE Silence. 6 second duration)	
Frequent Drops: Kraul Guano	
Heralath Fallowbrook	25
Notes: Alliance Quest NPC	
Kraul Bat	30-31 Elite
Frequent Drops: Kraul Guano	
Quilguard Champion	30-31 Elite
Notes: Defensive Stance (-10% damage taken), Devotion Aura (AoE armor increase), Sunder Armor (reduces armor by 180 each)	
Raging Agam'ar	25-26 Elite
Notes: Enrage	
Razorfen Beast Trainer	28-29 Elite
Notes: Frost Shot (Reduces movement speed. 8 second duration), Ranged attack, accompanied by Tamed Boar or Hyena	
Razorfen Beastmaster	30-31 Elite
Notes: Ranged attack, accompanied by Tamed Boar or Hyena	

NPC	LEVEL
Razorfen Defender	27-28 Elite
Notes: Improved Blocking, Defensive Stance	
Razorfen Dustweaver	28-29 Elite
Notes: Accompanied by Wind Howler	
Razorfen Earthbreaker	30-31 Elite
Notes: Mind Tremor (reduces casting speed by 20%. 10 minute duration)	
Razorfen Geomancer	25 Elite
Notes: Lightning Bolt	
Razorfen Groundshaker	27-28 Elite
Notes: Ground Tremor (AoE knockdown)	
Razorfen Handler	25-26 Elite
Notes: Accompanied by Tamed Boar or Hyena	
Razorfen Quilguard	25-26 Elite
Notes: Thunderclap	
Razorfen Servitor	23-24 Elite
Razorfen Spearhide	29-30 Elite
Notes: Whirling Rage (AoE)	
Frequent Drops: Armor Piercer (Polearm, 19.8 DPS, +11 AGI)	

NPC	LEVEL
Razorfen Stalker	28-29 Elite
Notes: Stealth	
Razorfen Totemic	29 Elite
Notes: Healing Ward V, Earthgrab Totem	
Razorfen Warden	25-26 Elite
Razorfen Warrior	24-25 Elite
Rotting Agam'Ar	28 Elite
Notes: Cursed Blood (reduces INT by 15. 10 minute duration)	
Stone Rumbler	21 Elite
Notes: Elemental Pet	
Tamed Battle Boar	22-23 Elite
Notes: Pet	
Tamed Hyena	27 Elite
Notes: Pet	
Ward Guardian	31 Elite
Notes: Heal	
Wind Howler	25 Elite
Notes: Immune to DoT, Elemental Pet	

LEADERS OF RAZORFEN

NAME	LEVEL	FREQUENT DROP(S)
AGATHELOS THE RAGING	33 Elite	Ferine Leggings (Leather Legs, 87 Armor, +9 STR, +8 AGI), Swinetusk Shank (Dagger, 23 DPS, +6 STA, +4 SPI)
Notes: Enrage and Rampage		
AGGEM THORNCURSE	30 Elite	Thornspike (Dagger, 15.6 DPS)
Notes: Battle Shout, Chain Heal, Summons Boar Spirit		
BLIND HUNTER	32 Elite	Batwing Mantle (Cloth Shoulders, 37 Armor, +3 AGI, +10 INT, +5 SPI), Nightstalker Bow (Bow, 16.2 DPS, +3 AGI), Stygian Bone Amulet (Neck, +4 STA, +8 SPI)
Notes: Very rare spawn		
CHARLGA RAZORFLANK	33-34 Elite	Small Scroll (An Unholy Alliance quest for Horde parties), Razorflank's Heart, Agamaggan's Clutch (Ring, +5 STA, +9 SPI), Heart of Agamaggan (Shield, 776 Armor, 17 Block, +7 STA, +8 SPI), Pronged Cleaver (Axe 1H, 24 DPS, +6 STR, +5 SPI), Razorflank's Medallion
Notes: Chain Bolt, Mana Spike (Full mana restore), Purity (2-second invulnerability), Renew (HoT)		
DEATH SPEAKER JARGBA	30 Elite	Death Speaker Mantle (Cloth Shoulder, 32 Armor, +7 INT, +3 SPI), Death Speak Robes (Cloth Chest, 44 Armor, +3 STA, +8 INT, +6 SPI), Death Speaker Scepter (Mace Mainhand, 17.1 DPS, +1 SPI, Equip: Increases healing spells and effects by up to 10, Equip: Increases shadow damage by up to 5)
Notes: Shadow Bolt		
EARTHCALLER HALMGAR	32 Elite	Whisperwind Headdress (Leather Head, 79 Armor, +3 STA, +7 INT, +7 SPI), Wind Spirit Staff (Staff, 26.7 DPS, +3 STA, +5 INT, +15 SPI)
Notes: Lightning Bolt, Earthbind Totem		
OVERLORD RAMTUSK	32 Elite	Tusken Helm (Mail Head, 168 Armor, +9 STR, +8 AGI), Corpsemaker (Axe 2H, 28.9 DPS, +15 STR, +8 STA)
Notes: Thunderclap, Battle Shout		
ROOGUG	28 Elite	Vial of Phlogiston
Notes: Warrior Quest target, Lightning Bolt		

THE VINES ENCROACH

LEGEND

1 First Fork
2 Path to Roogug
3 Roogug
4 The Trenches
5 The Prison
6 Path to Razorflank
7 Aggem Thorncurse
8 Death Speaker Jargba
9 Overlord Ramtusk
10 Earthcaller Halmgar
11 Bat Cavern
12 Agathelos the Raging's Ward
13 Charlga Razorflank

THE FIRST FORK

Fighting past the Razorfen Servitors to get to the entrance of Razorfen Kraul is quick and easy. Pull them one at a time or run past them and enter the instance.

There is a wandering Razorfen Geomancer and Stone Rumbler before the first intersection. Eliminate them when they wander away from the two Quilguards; once they're finished, take the Quilguards.

Parties have a decision to make here. If there are any Warriors in the party with the *Brutal Armor* or *Fire Hardened Mail* quests, then move west. Else, move east.

THE PATH TO ROOGUG

The route to Roogug is fairly short. Follow the tunnel west. There are roaming Razorfen Handlers with pets and a Razorfen Quilguard. Pull them one at a time to keep the fights simple. The real work is yet to come.

LINE OF SIGHT

The tunnel walls can hinder the enemy as much as they hinder you. They can be of great help when used correctly. When pulling casters or ranged attackers, pull around a tunnel corner. The enemy will rush around the corner to restore line of sight. This gives your party an opportunity to kill the enemy without having to charge into a room.

When the tunnel is clear, proceed across the large vine to Roogug's area. There are many enemies here. Death's Head Adepts, Death's Head Seers and Razorfen Quilguards fill the landing. Pull them in small groups and slowly clear the room.

Roogug, a Stone Rumbler, a Razorfen Defender, and a Death's Head Adept should be all that remain. These cannot be separated by anything short of death. The Adept's Chains of Ice will make the fight much more difficult by rooting your melee characters. Your tank should charge in and pull the Stone Rumbler and Defender away from the party while all DPS focuses on the Adept. Crowd Control Roogug to keep him form terrorizing your party. With the Adept down, focus fire on the Defender, then the Stone Rumbler. Keep Roogug CC'd though this process as well. When Roogug is alone, heal your party and engage him. Use stuns to keep him from being fully effective and bring everything you have left at him. Loot Roogug for the **Vial of Phlogiston**.

DOWN IN THE TRENCHES

Return to the First Fork and take the east passage. There is a pair of Razorfen Defenders patrolling the next room. Wait for the Defenders to move way from the Death's Head Adepts and the Groundshaker(s) before pulling them. With the melee enemies dead, charge and eliminate the casters in the room. Move west into The Trenches.

The Trenches are filled with roaming Blood of Agamaggan, Rotting Agam'ar, Agam'ar, and Raging Agam'ar. Having someone who can remove curses makes this much easier, but it's not required. Fight the enemies individually as you move through The Trenches.

As you move, now is a good time to release your Snufflenoses to look for Blueleaf Tubers. Each party member needs 6 to complete the *Blueleaf Tubers* quest. Use the box to release your gopher, use the command stick to tell it to look for tubers, then defend it while it looks. The enemies love the taste of gopher apparently.

At the end of The Trenches is a ramp guarded by Quilboar. Pull the two Razorfen Warden's then kill the Death's Head Priests one at a time. Make your way to the hut at the top of the ramp. Remove the two Wardens at the hut to gain entrance. Alliance parties should speak with Heralath Fallowbrook first to receive the *Mortality Wanes* quest. Both factions can escort *Willix the Importer* to the entrance.

THE PATH TO RAZORFLANK

Once Willix has been escorted out safely, return to the entrance to The Trenches. Move north instead of west this time to find the leader of this dungeon.

The next room is more difficult as there are higher ledges on both sides. Keep your party moving down the middle to avoid drawing the attention of casters and ranged attacks above. Should you be spotted from above, retreat out of the instance to regroup. A whole wave of enemies will be coming for you and you don't want to be inside when they do. Move down this room slowly. Kill the enemies in small groups to avoid being overwhelmed. At the end of the room is a ramp that leads in three directions. Pull as many of the enemies near the ramp down to you before ascending.

Move onto the southern ledge. There are two small huts with a Razorfen Groundshaker in each. These should be pulled separately as their Ground Tremor complicates fights enough. You don't need two of them knocking you down.

Moving up the ledge is more dangerous. There are many casters and no corners to pull them around. Rest up before engaging the adds are likely. When your team is fully prepared, rush the first enemy. If a second adds, kill the first and immediately attack the second. When there are no adds, be sure to rest before starting the next fight. Keep your position in mind if things start going sour. When more enemies than your party can handle join the attack, jump off the ledge and make a run to the entrance.

At the top of the ledge is a small pen. Two Razorfen Beast Trainers with pets and Aggem Thorncurse guard the pen. Pull the Beast Trainers and their pets before attacking Aggem. When the area is clear, Aggem's time in this area is coming to an end. He will summon Boar Spirits to aid him in the fight. Kill these as quickly as possible. He can summon more than one at a time and can increase their attack power with his Battle Shout. If the Boar Spirits are ignored, you may find your party fighting an army. Designating one person to kill the boar spirits allows the rest of your party to focus on Aggem.

With Aggem dead and the southern ledge clear, return to the ramp and look towards the northern ledge. Clearing your way to the top is quick as many of the enemies can be pulled singly. Be aware of the Razorfen Totemic and keep it's totems down.

At the top, two Razorfen Groundshakers are waiting with two Death's Head Acolytes and Death Speaker Jargba. Pull the closer Groundshaker and Acolyte around the corner and kill them to thin the room a bit. Once the room is down to only three enemies, begin the attack. Send your tank against Jargba, but the Groundshaker should be your first target. Its Ground Tremor will make the fight much longer and more dangerous if allowed to live. With the Groundshaker dead, keep Jargba's Shadow Bolts interrupted while you kill the Acolyte. Continue to interrupt Jargba's spells while your party unleashes its fury. With no allies, Jargba will fall quickly.

Moving back to the ramp, there is a room to the west with an upper ledge and a lower passage. Kill the two Quilguard Champions before entering the room. Pull the Death's Head Sages around the corner one at a time to clear your way to the upper ledge.

Overlord Ramtusk is flanked by two Razorfen Spearhides. This will be a difficult fight. All three have powerful melee attacks. Ramtusk is dual wielding fast weapons while the Spearhides have AoE attacks. Keep your casters well away from the fight. All enemies should be snared to slow any enemies who charge your casters. These few precious seconds can give the melee party members a chance to gain aggro again. Keeping the enemy's attack power decreased can save your melee members and your healer. Your main tank (if a Warrior) should use Defensive Stance and hold Ramtusk's attention while the party kills the Spearhides. Once the Spearhides are dead, focus on Ramtusk.

The key to surviving the fight is to bring the Spearhides down quickly. Don't try to AoE them as it will mean the death of your party. Instead focus all your attacks on one to ensure a quick kill. Your tank won't survive long against all three and your healer will be the next target if the tank goes down. Once the Spearhides are down, the tank's life becomes much easier. By this time there is little that will pull Ramtusk off your tank, so blast him down without hesitation.

THE PATH IS LONG

Once Ramtusk is dead, follow the lower passage west. There are many enemies in this room. Clearing them all slowly will keep from having unexpected adds. Pull back around the corner and force ranged and casting enemies to fight on your terms. With the Quilguard Champions always pairing and the Beast Masters having pets, you can bet on having at least two enemies each fight.

When all the cubbies are clear, take the two Quilguard Champions guarding the large vine. Move across the vine slowly. There is a lot of aggro on the next landing. A Razorfen Stalker, a Razorfen Totemic, a Razorfen Beast Tamer and it's Tamed Battleboar guard Earthcaller Halmgar. There is no way to split the group, so prepare for a large fight (restore health, mana, and buffs).

The Razorfen Totemic's low HP and ability to drop totems make it an ideal first target. Kill it quickly and move to Earthcaller Halmgar. Halmgar can also drop a rooting totem. These must be destroyed immediately. They will immobilize your group and allow Halmgar to run to casting range where you don't want him. After Halmgar falls, it's simply a matter of cleaning up. Keep your party healed and bring down the Beast Tamer, Battleboar and Stalker.

Keep your casters here while having your tank move to the next landing. There are two Quilguard Champions on the right that are hidden from view. When you tank proximity aggros them, pull back to the center of the bridge and fight there.

Also on the landing are a Razorfen Earthbreaker, Death's Head Sage, and a Razorfen Stalker. Wait until the patrol pair of Quilguard Champions moves away, then charge the Earthbreaker. It has a 10 minute casting speed debuff that should be avoided if possible. Kill it before it can make your healer's life difficult. Bring down the Sage and it's totems next, then move on to the Stalker. Rest back on the bridge as the patrol should be nearing your position again.

Quilguard Champion

When you are rested begin moving across the bridges. There are several pairs of Quilguard Champions along the bridges. These should be easier fights as there are only two with no casters. Kill them and cross the bridges to the Bat Cavern.

WHAT LIES AHEAD?

The ever present Quilboar are not to be seen in much of the Bat Cavern. Kraul Bats and Greater Kraul Bats wander aimlessly through this area. Pull the bats one at a time. Keep them away from your casters as the bats have an AoE silence that lasts 8 seconds. Horde parties collect the Kraul Guano for the *Going, Going, Guano!* quest. Each bat only drops one guano, but there are plenty of bats.

Clear the area and follow the southern wall. Quilboar guard a shimmering wall of energy that blocks off part of the cave. Is there something even the Quilboar fear in there?

A Death's Head Seer and two Ward Guardians stand guard while two Death's Head Ward Keepers maintain the barrier. Focus on the three guards as the Ward Keepers are not aggressive. The Seer's Lava Spout Totem is something to be avoided. The best way to avoid it is to kill the Seer quickly. Once down, split your party to deal with the two Guardians. Both have high armor, high HP, and the ability to heal themselves or others. Have one party member keep a Guardian interrupted while the rest of the party kills the other. When only one stands, the fight can be finished.

Killing the two Ward Keepers brings the shimmering barrier down. Rest before entering the tunnel. At the back is Agathelos the Raging. Keep your casters back so they aren't hit by his Rampage (AoE knockdown). With good teamwork, he should fall easily. Have stuns ready when he reaches 25% HP. He will become Enraged and much more dangerous.

Keep your tank on one side of Agathelos while you party stays on the other. This makes it very easy to see if the tank loses aggro. In the event that Agathelos attacks another party member, cease fire. All attacks should stop until the tank regains aggro and pulls Agathelos back into position. The tank should signal the party when to attack once again.

Return to the Bat Cavern and continue making your way to Charlga Razorflank. As you clear the bats, keep an eye out for the Blind Hunter. He is a rare enemy that carries some rare equipment.

At the northwest edge of the Bat Cavern is a ramp guarded by more Quilboar. The first guards are a Quilguard Champion and a Razorfen Stalker. Pull the Champion to get the two to come to you. Pull the roaming Quilguard Champion next and kill the Razorfen Totemic and Earthbreaker last.

Move through the tunnel onto a landing with a stairs leading to a single hut. Within the hut is Charlga Razorflank, so now would be a good time to restore buffs and rest.

Charlga is content to stay in her hut, so your casters will need to move to the middle of the landing to have line of sight once the fight begins. A party member with an interrupt should start the fight. Get her attention and when she starts to cast, interrupt her and bring her down onto the landing. Her Chain Bolt puts a lot of pressure on your healer if it's not interrupted. Have an interrupt order to nullify her casting. When she gets low on health, she will cast Renew to slowly restore it. Putting DoTs such as Rend, Deadly Poison, Shadow Word: Pain, and Curse of Agony on her will slow this process and even turn it around. She will cast Mana Spike to instantly restore her entire mana pool when she gets low on mana. Her Purity spell grants her a 2-second invulnerability. Keep her interrupted and bring her down.

Remove Razorflank's Medallion or Heart depending on which faction you follow and return home with the knowledge that much good has been done this day.

SCARLET MONASTERY

Played & Written by: Ken "Birk" Schmidt of <Blame the Mage> on Perenolde

The Scarlet Monastery, home to the Scarlet Crusade, is a prime location for those players who have reached mid-30s in level and are looking for a good challenge with spectacular rewards. The Scarlet Crusade was once dedicated to wiping the Scourge from its foothold on Northern Azeroth, but it has since become corrupted. Their focus has shifted from the Scourge itself to sending all who oppose them into the twisting nether. Located northeast of the Ruins of Lordaeron, the known center of Undead power, the Scarlet Monastery is home to this fanatical group of soldiers, crusaders, monks, and practitioners of magic.

DUNGEON INFORMATION

Location	Tirisfal Glades
Territory	Horde
Quests	Alliance / Horde
Suggested Levels	33-40
Primary Enemy Type	Humanoid
Time to Complete	3-4 hours

BEYOND LORDAERON'S RUINS

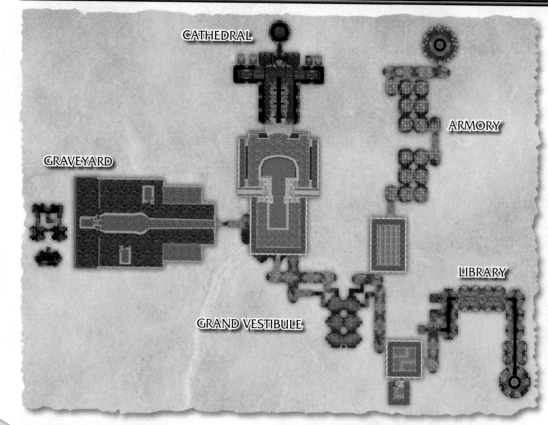

The Scarlet Monastery is a short trip northeast of the Undercity in Tirisfal Glades. For Alliance players, there are two options. The first, and easiest for players in the early 30s, is to travel north from Southshore, skirting the edge of Undercity. From that point, just follow the path northeast until you reach the monastery. The second option is to fly to Chillwind Point and hug the wall of the Western Plaguelands into Tirisfal Glades. Yes, it's more deadly since the mobs are so much higher in level, but it is closer.

Because this is the beginning area for Undead players, the available resources, while abundant, are low level. Until you reach the grounds outside the Monastery itself, the enemies are also low level. However, the enemies just outside the Monastery are level 30 elites, a mix of casters and melee fighters.

WHO TO BRING

While you can tailor your group based on the destination within the monastery (Graveyard, Library, Armory, or Cathedral), a good general group is possible. A solid tank (Paladins and Feral Druids work fine in lieu of a Warrior) helps during the bigger pulls and most boss encounters. A Priest is indispensable for the Shackle Undead, Dispel and Mind Control options in addition to the obvious healing advantage. Mages are fantastic for Polymorph and AoE options while Warlocks can take advantage of their DoT madness and Curse of Recklessness to prevent runners. Shaman are a perfect fit since they're so versatile and can fill in the blanks for most SM groups. Lastly, DPS is a necessity in most encounters; Rogues and Hunters have this in spades. They also offer a few CC options that should help in many encounters. As mentioned previously, Paladins and Druids can fit in as a tank, but they're also great as backup healers and off-tanks.

QUESTS

ALLIANCE QUESTS

QUEST NAME	QUEST GIVER	QUEST GIVER LOCATION	QUEST RECEIVER	QUEST RECEIVER LOCATION	CHAIN?	MAX EXPERIENCE
Mythology of the Titans	Mae Paledust	Ironforge	Mae Paledust	Ironforge	No	3550
REWARD: Explorer's League Commendation (Neck, +6 STA/+6 SPI)						
In the Name of the Light	Raleigh the Devout	Hillsbrad Foothills	Raleigh the Devout	Hillsbrad Foothills	Yes	4700
REWARD: Sword of Serenity (One-Hand Sword, 30.0 DPS, +9 STA/+4 SPI) or Orb of Lorica (Off-Hand, +6 INT/+11 SPI) or Black Menace (Dagger, 29.7 DPS, Chance on Hit: Sends shadowy bolt at the enemy, causing 30 Shadow damage) or Bonebiter (2H Axe, 38.8 DPS, +20 STR/+10 STA)						

MYTHOLOGY OF THE TITANS

Quest Level	28 to Obtain
Location	Ironforge
Quest Giver	Mae Paledust
Goal	Retrieve *Mythology of the Titans*
Max Experience Gained	3550
Reward	Explorers' League Commendation (Neck: +6 STA/+6 SPI)

Pay a visit to the Explorers' League inside Ironforge. One of its members is Mae Paledust who seeks the knowledge contained inside a book named *Mythology of the Titans*. In order to obtain this book, you must search the Library inside the Scarlet Monastery.

The book spawns near the end of the Library section of the instance, close to the encounter with Arcanist Doan. The book vanishes after each member in the group picks it up, so some patience is required when everyone needs to complete this quest.

IN THE NAME OF THE LIGHT

Quest Level	34 to Obtain
Location	Hillsbrad Foothills
Quest Giver	Raleigh the Devout
Goal	Kill High Inquisitor Whitemane; Scarlet Commander Mograine; Herod, the Scarlet Champion; and Houndmaster Loksey
Max Experience Gained	4700
Reward	Sword of Serenity (1H Sword, 30.0 DPS, +9 STA/+4 SPI) or Orb of Lorica (Off-Hand, +6 INT/+11 SPI) or Black Menace (Dagger, 29.7 DPS, Chance on hit: Sends a shadowy bolt at the enemy causing 30 Shadow damage.) or Bonebiter (Two-Handed Axe, 38.8 DPS, +20 STR/+10 STA)

In order to obtain this quest, you must first complete a quest entitled Down the Scarlet Path, which begins at Cathedral Square in Stormwind, and culminates at Nijel's Point in Desolace. Once these early steps are complete, travel to Southshore and speak with Raleigh the Devout.

The four targets of this quest are scattered around the instanced areas of Scarlet Monastery. Houndmaster Loksey and the three Tracking Hounds that serve as his guardians are at the Huntsman's Cloister, found inside the Library wing. Herod, the Scarlet Champion, awaits you at the end of the Armory. The greatest test comes at the hands of High Inquisitor Whitemane and Scarlet Commander Mograine, found together inside the Cathedral.

MAGE QUEST

QUEST NAME	QUEST GIVER	QUEST GIVER LOCATION	QUEST RECEIVER	QUEST RECEIVER LOCATION	CHAIN?	MAX EXPERIENCE
Rituals of Power	Tabetha	Dustwallow Marsh	Tabetha	Dustwallow Marsh	Yes	3150

RITUALS OF POWER (MAGE ONLY)

Quest Level	30 to Obtain
Location	Faction-Specific Mage Trainer
Quest Giver	Tabetha
Goal	Retrieve *Rituals of Power*
Max Experience Gained	3150

Once a mage reaches level 30, the mage trainer sends you to Dustwallow Marsh in order to speak with Tabetha. She asks you to retrieve a book entitled *Rituals of Power*. First, you are directed to Shimmering Flats to speak with Magus Tirth.
Unfortunately, Magus Tirth has fallen on hard times and lacks a copy. However, he sends you to the Scarlet Monastery to obtain the book. It's in the same area as *Mythology of the Titans*, inside the Library near Arcanist Doan.

HORDE QUESTS

QUEST NAME	QUEST GIVER	QUEST GIVER LOCATION	QUEST RECEIVER	QUEST RECEIVER LOCATION	CHAIN?	MAX EXPERIENCE
Compendium of the Fallen	Sage Truthseeker	Thunder Bluff	Sage Truthseeker	Thunder Bluff	No	
REWARD: Vile Protector (Shield, 1051 Armor, +4 STR, Equip: when struck in combat has a 1% chance of inflicting 105 to 175 Shadow damage to the attacker) or Forcestone Buckler (Shield, 1051 Armor, +3 STA/+8 SPI) or Omega Orb (Increases damage and healing done by magical spells and effects by up to 11)						
Hearts of Zeal	Master Apothecary Faranell	Undercity	Master Apothecary Faranell	Undercity	Yes	3300
Into the Scarlet Monastery	Varimathras	Undercity	Varimathras	Undercity	No	5150
REWARD: Dragon's Blood Necklace (Neck, +12 STA/+5 SPI) or Prophetic Cane (Off-hand, +5 STA/+12 INT) or Sword of Omen (1H Sword, 29.7 DPS, +9 STR/+3 AGI/+4 STA)						
Test of Lore	Parqual Fintallas	Undercity	Parqual Fintallas	Undercity	Yes	2100

INTO THE SCARLET MONASTERY

Quest Level	33 to Obtain
Location	Undercity
Quest Giver	Varimathras
Goal	Kill High Inquisitor Whitemane; Scarlet Commander Mograine; Herod, the Scarlet Champion; and Houndmaster Loksey
Max Experience Gained	5150
Reward	Dragon's Blood Necklace (Neck, +12 STA/+5 SPI) or Prophetic Cane (Off-Hand, +5 STA/+12 INT) or Sword of Omen (One-Hand Sword, 29.7 DPS, +9 STR/+3 AGI/+4 STA)

The Scarlet Crusade's continued existence so close to the Undead's stronghold is cause for concern. Varimathras wishes to eliminate this threat by destroying its leadership.

The four targets of this quest are scattered around the instanced areas of Scarlet Monastery. Houndmaster Loksey and the three Tracking Hounds that serve as his guardians are at the Huntsman's Cloister, found inside the Library wing. Herod, the Scarlet Champion, awaits you at the end of the Armory. The greatest test comes at the hands of High Inquisitor Whitemane and Scarlet Commander Mograine, found together inside the Cathedral.

HEARTS OF ZEAL

Quest Level	33 to Obtain
Location	Undercity
Quest Giver	Master Apothecary Faranell
Goal	Collect 20 Hearts of Zeal
Max Experience Gained	3300

After completing a quest named Going, Going, Guano! For Master Apothecary Faranell, he requests a second component for his chemical experimentation.

Because Hearts of Zeal drop from any of the elite enemies of the Scarlet Crusade, it's not necessary to enter any of the instances to complete this task. However, it's more efficient to collect these Hearts while fulfilling the obligations to other quests inside the instanced areas.

TEST OF LORE

Quest Level	33 to Obtain
Location	Undercity
Quest Giver	Parqual Fintallas
Goal	Retrieve Beginnings of the Undead Threat
Max Experience Gained	2100

This quest is part of the series started by Braug Dimspirit in Stonetalon Mountains. The Beginnings of the Undead Threat book is in one of the first side rooms on the left side of the Library. The book lies open on a desk.

COMPENDIUM OF THE FALLEN

Quest Level	28 to Obtain
Location	Thunder Bluff
Quest Giver	Sage Truthseeker
Goal	Retrieve Compendium of the Fallen
Max Experience Gained	3550
Reward	Vile Protector (Shield, 1051 Armor, +4 STR, When struck in combat has a 1% chance of inflicting 105 to 175 Shadow damage to the attacker.) or Forcestone Buckler (Shield, 1051 Armor, +3 STA/+8 SPI) or Omega Orb (Off-Hand, Increases damage and healing done by magical spells and effects by up to 11)

This quest is not available to Undead characters, in keeping with the storyline. The Compendium of the Fallen book is on a bookshelf in the hallway just before you reach Arcanist Doan's chamber.

THE GRAND VESTIBULE

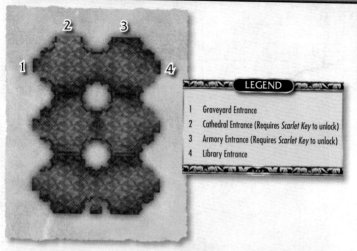

ENEMIES IN THE GRAND VESTIBULE

NPC	LEVEL
Scarlet Augur	30-31 Elite
Notes: Shadow Bolt	
Scarlet Disciple	30-31 Elite
Notes: Holy Smite	
Scarlet Sentry	30-31 Elite

The Grand Vestibule is remarkable only for holding the entries to the four instances: Graveyard, Library, Armory, and Cathedral. Unless you're trying to collect **Hearts of Zeal**, the best idea for your group is to hurry to the instance of choice as quickly as possible.

Scattered amongst the columns, side-rooms, and statues are stationary guards and a handful of roaming enemies. If your level is high enough to have acquired any of the quests for this location, these guards pose little threat when taken in small numbers.

Of the four entry points, two are initially locked. In order to access the Armory and Cathedral, you must first venture though the Library, defeat Arcanist Doan, and claim the Scarlet Key from his strongbox. The two open portals are for the Graveyard (western-most entrance) and Library (eastern-most entrance). The locked door on the eastern half of the Grand Vestibule leads to the Armory. Beyond the other locked door is the Cathedral.

PVP IN THE MONASTERY

Are you on a PVP server? Scarlet Monastery is located in a Horde controlled zone, making it possible to choose your PVP battles. If you're Horde, you can choose to attack Alliance players at any time. If you're Alliance, you can't attack the Horde unless they take the first swing or are already flagged for PvP. Pick your fights carefully; you never know when that high-level Rogue is going to unstealth and kill everyone who is flagged for PVP combat!

LOCKPICKING

A Rogue with a Lockpicking skill of at least 175 can pick the locked doors for you if you don't have the Scarlet Key.

GRAVEYARD

ENEMIES IN THE GRAVEYARD

NPC	LEVEL
Suffering Victim	25
Scarlet Sentry	30 Elite
Scarlet Scryer	30 Elite
Notes: Shadow Bolt	
Scarlet Torturer	30 Elite
Unfettered Spirit	32-33
Anguished Dead	32-33 Elite
Notes: Veil of Shadow	
Haunting Phantasm	32-33 Elite
Notes: Spawns Illusory Phantasm	
Vorrel Sengutz	8
Notes: Gives quest to Horde players	

HERBALISTS

Kingsblood and Grave Moss nodes are located in the Graveyard.

LEADERS OF THE GRAVEYARD

NPC	LEVEL	FREQUENT DROP(S)
AZSHIR THE SLEEPLESS	33 Elite	Necrotic Wand (Wand, 33.2 DPS), Ghostshard Talisman (+9 STA/+4 SPI), Blighted Leggings (Cloth Legs, 45 Armor, +17 SPI, Increase Shadow damage up to 7.)
Notes: Rare Spawn , Call of the Grave (60 sec. "bomb" that inflicts 330 damage if not dispelled), Soul Siphon (12 sec. health drain), Terrify (4-second, single-target Fear)		
FALLEN CHAMPION	33 Elite	Embalmed Shroud (Cloth Head, 42 Armor, +7 STA/+11 INT/+12 SPI), Ebon Vise (Leather Hands, 70 Armor, +4 STR/+6 AGI, +8 STA), Morbid Dawn (Two-Handed Sword, 30.2 DPS, +10 STR/+15 STA)
Notes: Rare Spawn, Cleave, Execute		
INTERROGATOR VISHAS	32 Elite	Bloody Brass Knuckles (Fist Weapon, 16.6 DPS), Rare Drop: Torturing Poker (Dagger, 21.2 DPS, +5 Fire Damage)
Notes: Immolate and Shadow Word: Pain		
IRONSPINE	33 Elite	Ironspine's Ribcage (Mail Chest, 235 Armor, +6 STR/+3 AGI/+17 STA), Ironspine's Eye (Ring, +4 STR/+9 AGI), Ironspine's Fist (One-Hand Mace, 22.9 DPS, +7 STR)
Notes: Rare spawn, Curse of Weakness, Poison Cloud		
BLOODMAGE THALNOS	34 Elite	Bloodmage Mantle (Cloth Shoulder, 35 Armor, +8 INT/+4 SPI), Orb of the Forgotten Seer (Off-Hand, Increase magic effects by up to 7)
Notes: Shadow Bolt, Flame Spike (AoE), Fire Nova (AoE), Flame Shock		

CHAMBER OF ATONEMENT

The path to the Graveyard winds through a short hallway with two guards, then ends at the Chamber of Atonement. There are two points of interest inside this room. One is Interrogator Vishas, who stands over Vorrel Sengutz, around the corner from the entryway. Before you meet him, clear out the guards from the doorway, then take the roaming caster. With those nuisances out of the way, it's time to face Vishas and the Scarlet Scryer who stand at the table. Vishas is a tough nut to crack but does not possess any noteworthy tricks.

The other point of interest is the chest that appears almost directly across from the entryway, very close to four members of the Scarlet Crusaders torturing a nameless Undead. If your group has minimal levels for the quests for the Scarlet Monastery, taking on four enemies simultaneously promises to be a tough fight, but the items found inside chests in world dungeons are generally worth the effort.

VORREL'S REVENGE

If you're playing Horde and you're at least level 25, Interrogator Vishas' victim has a quest to share with you.

FORLORN CLOISTER

Follow the short hallway and flight of stairs beyond the Chamber of Atonement to the Forlorn Cloister. This is the true graveyard, and it has been overrun by wandering spirits and reanimated, rotting carcasses.

The good news is that the whitish Unfettered Spirits wandering the graveyard are not elites. The bad news is that they are plentiful and often roam in groups of three. The black Haunting Phantasms are elite and should be eliminated individually. They have a nasty trick where they summon Illusory Phantasms to harass the group. These Illusory Phantasms despawn after a single hit, so assign one person in the group to eliminate any as they appear.

HONOR'S TOMB

Beyond the courtyard is an underground tomb that holds an encounter with a powerful bloodmage. The steps leading down are guarded by the same undead types that roam the courtyard. The key to surviving encounters in confined spaces with many enemies is patience. Never pull more enemies than your group can reasonably handle. Always pull toward your group with a spell or ranged attack. Never charge into a cluster of enemies when you can't see what's around the corner.

Bloodmage Thalnos awaits you in the lowest level of Honor's Tomb. Keep the casters clear of his immediate area, as he makes liberal use of both of his Area of Effect spells: Fire Nova, Flame Shock, and Flame Spike. Assign a main tank (preferably one with no significant ranged ability) to keep Thalnos' attention, then hammer away at him outside the range of his spells while keeping the tank alive and kicking. Savor this victory, but don't get cocky. Greater challenges await you deeper inside the Scarlet Monastery!

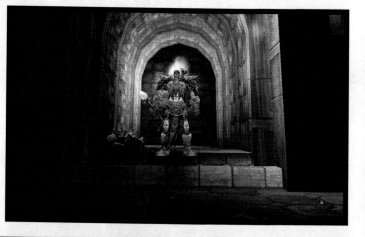

IMMUNITIES ABOUND

A common theme in many encounters with named enemies is that main debuff skills have no effect. A handful do work, but you're better off focusing on inflicting damage and healing as necessary.

⚙ LIBRARY

LEGEND

1 Houndmaster Loksey
2 Beginnings of the Undead Threat
3 Compendium of the Fallen
  Mythology of the Titans
  Rituals of Power
4 Arcanist Doan

ENEMIES IN THE LIBRARY

NPC	LEVEL
Scarlet Adept	33-34 Elite
Notes: Holy Smite, Heal	
Scarlet Gallant	33-34 Elite
Notes: Crusader Strike, Hammer of Justice	
Scarlet Beastmaster	34-35 Elite
Notes: Linked to Scarlet Tracking Hounds, Ranged attacks, Exploding Shot	
Scarlet Chaplain	34-35 Elite
Notes: Renew	
Scarlet Diviner	34-35 Elite
Notes: Fireball	
Scarlet Monk	34-35 Elite
Notes: Unarmed, fast attacks; Uses Kick to stop skills/spells	
Scarlet Tracking Hound	34-35 Elite
Notes: Linked to Scarlet Beastmaster	

HERBALISTS

Fadeleaf and Liferoot nodes are located in the Library.

LEADERS OF THE LIBRARY

NPC	LEVEL	FREQUENT DROP(S)
HOUNDMASTER LOKSEY	34 Elite	Dog Training Gloves (Leather Hands, 62 Armor, +30 Attack Power vs. Beasts), Dog Whistle (Summons Tracking Hound guardian) Rare Drop: Loksey's Training Stick (Staff, 31.3 DPS, +60 Attack Power vs. Beasts)
Notes: Guarded by three Scarlet Tracking Hounds, Battle Shout, Bloodlust (+30% attack speed for 30 sec.)		
ARCANIST DOAN	34-35 Elite	Illusionary Rod (Staff, 34.7 DPS, +7 STA/+15 INT/+10 SPI), Mantle of Doan (Cloth Shoulder, 38 Armor, +8 INT/ +7 SPI), Hypnotic Blade (Dagger, 26.8 DPS, +8 INT/+3 SPI), Robe of Doan (Cloth Chest, 50 Armor, +4 STA/+13 SPI)
Notes: Silence, Arcane Bubble (shield), Arcane Explosion (AoE), Sheep, Detonation (AoE).		

HUNTSMAN'S CLOISTER

There are multiple groups of two and three Scarlet Adepts and Gallants that line the first hallway inside the Library, and there's enough space that careful pulls should bring only a manageable number of enemies at the same time. The danger lies in a pair of patrols that move through the hallway. Quickly dispatch the first pair of guards just inside the hallway; then wait for the patrols to move close, and eliminate them before advancing down the hallway.

If any member of the group is even slightly under level here, it's a better idea to pull individual enemies into the hallway after clearing it out. Scarlet Beastmasters and Tracking Hounds roam the interior courtyard, and the stone path around it is packed with Scarlet Gallants. One wrong step, or one fleeing enemy, could result in suddenly overwhelming odds against your group.

Tucked away in an alcove off the Huntsman's Cloister is Houndmaster Loksey and three Scarlet Tracking Hounds. Loskey is the most dangerous of the quartet, and he should be the first target for the group. To start the fight, put as many of the Hounds out of commission as your group has available skills. Use Sheep (Mage) and Hibernate or Root (Druid) to keep the Hounds from entering the fray until after Loksey is eliminated. Loksey doesn't have many tricks, but he does have an impressive number of hit points and sometimes uses Bloodlust to add some punch to his attacks.

The books actually work to disguise dangerous pockets of Scarlet Crusaders, hidden in small alcoves off the main, carpeted path through the library. Do everything in your power to prevent any enemies fleeing battle from reaching one of these spots, or your group could suddenly be outnumbered.

FURTHER READING AVAILABLE

Scattered among the bookshelves, tables, and benches are a handful of books from which you can read selected chapters. Mouse over any book that catches your eye, and wait for the magnifying glass pointer to appear.

Keep fights contained in as small an area as possible. Stick to the red carpet, or clear out a room, and continue to pull enemies into it to reduce the number of ways they can escape and bring reinforcements.

GALLERY OF TREASURES

Another short hallway with scattered groups of Scarlet Gallants and Adepts leads from the Huntsman's Cloister to the Gallery of Treasures, which marks the true beginning of the Scarlet Monastery's collection of books. If you have any of the quests that require retrieving a book, the end of that quest is at hand.

ATHENAEUM

This is the final part of the Library. There are two rooms filled with books on both sides of the carpeted walkway. Scarlet Monks are the most common enemies waiting for your group. It is vital to keep the group's healers clear of the Monks. They lash out with a Kick attack identical to the ones known by rogues. Having the group's healing spells unavailable for any amount of time could turn the tide of any battle.

When you reach the circular room at the end of the Athenaeum, do not cross the threshold into it until all enemies outside have been eliminated! Arcanist Doan is a difficult fight and you don't want to provide him with any assistance. Once the room outside of Doan's chambers is cleared, take the time to heal, restore mana and buffs, and prepare to tackle a powerful Mage.

Before you leave Doan's study, look for the lockbox near the back of the room and loot the **Scarlet Key** from inside. Everyone in the group can pick it up and should do so. This key grants access to the Armory and the Cathedral.

Because both Arcane Explosion and Detonation are area of effect spells, keep the group's cloth wearers in the doorway and Doan far enough away from it that they aren't caught inside their range. Expect Doan to sheep whichever group member catches his attention for a while. When this happens, keep the fight close to that sheeped group member, and wait for another AoE to break the spell. Doan's final trick is a shield called Arcane Bubble. Once he deploys this and you manage to crack it, the fight is essentially over.

⟳ ARMORY

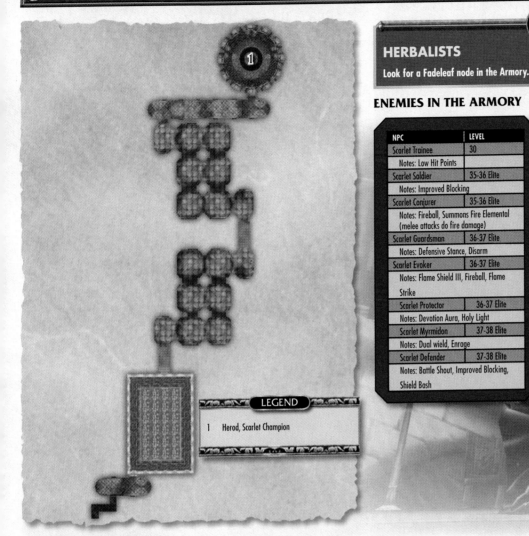

LEGEND

1	Herod, Scarlet Champion

HERBALISTS

Look for a Fadeleaf node in the Armory.

ENEMIES IN THE ARMORY

NPC	LEVEL
Scarlet Trainee	30
Notes: Low Hit Points	
Scarlet Soldier	35-36 Elite
Notes: Improved Blocking	
Scarlet Conjurer	35-36 Elite
Notes: Fireball, Summons Fire Elemental (melee attacks do fire damage)	
Scarlet Guardsman	36-37 Elite
Notes: Defensive Stance, Disarm	
Scarlet Evoker	36-37 Elite
Notes: Flame Shield III, Fireball, Flame Strike	
Scarlet Protector	36-37 Elite
Notes: Devotion Aura, Holy Light	
Scarlet Myrmidon	37-38 Elite
Notes: Dual wield, Enrage	
Scarlet Defender	37-38 Elite
Notes: Battle Shout, Improved Blocking, Shield Bash	

LEADER OF THE ARMORY

NPC	LEVEL	FREQUENT DROP(S)
HEROD	40 Elite	Raging Berserker's Helm (Mail Head, 213 Armor, +13 STR/+8 STA, Improves crit chance 1%), Herod's Shoulder (Mail Shoulder, 196 Armor, +6 STR/+15 STA), Scarlet Leggings (Mail Legs, 233 Armor, +20 STR/+10 STA), Ravager (2H Axe, 37.3 DPS, Chance on Hit: You attack all nearby enemies for 9 seconds causing weapon damage plus an additional 5 every 3 sec.)
Notes: Cleave, Rushing Charge (like Warrior's Charge), Whirlwind (Stops his movement and deals damage to nearby targets)		

TRAINING GROUNDS

The initial hallway inside the Armory is sparsely guarded, which may seem comforting at first, but don't let that quiet lull you into any sense of security. Beyond this first hallway, the enemy groups are numerous and packed densely.

After eliminating the two guards at the end of the hallway, set your group inside, but keep them out of the direct line of sight of the Training Grounds. The first order of business is to eliminate the roaming unit that patrols the walkway around the Training Ground's Courtyards. Pull the roamer first, eliminate it, and continue the pattern for the stationary enemies closest to the doorway. When targeting an enemy from the stone walkway, check the interior courtyard for any potential adds to the pull.

When the area is secured except for the final sets of enemies near the stairs leading to the next area, watch for a second roamer that paths to the bottom of the stairs. Before advancing up the stairway, dispatch the roamer, and set up to fight either on the stairwell or just below.

FOOTMAN'S ARMORY

Just like the Training Grounds, pull the enemies closest to the stairwell into areas that you've already cleared. A single runner could pull up to three new elite enemies into battle. Unless your group is of an extremely high level or possesses many ways to hold enemies out of combat (such as Sheep), this typically results in a trip to the local graveyard and a run back into the instance to reclaim your bodies.

When you draw closer to the exit to the next area, watch for yet another roamer that walks between the Footman's Armory and the Crusader's Armory. Allow this Scarlet Crusader to reach the end of his path before engaging him. If you fight too close to the hallway leading to the next area, you may draw the enemies just inside the hallway into the fray.

CRUSADER'S ARMORY

The hallway past the stairs is packed with various types of Scarlet Crusaders, so pull the first two groups down into the stairway to limit the danger of runners. Continue to work methodically through the clumps of Scarlet Crusaders, and watch for the two roaming enemies.

There is at least one other point of interest in this area, and that is the barrels of Red Rockets. These are flashy fireworks, not a ranged weapon, but they are free and fun! Clear the final hallway past the Crusader's Armory, then take some time to restore health and mana and set up the group's buffs for an encounter with an opponent with powerful melee attacks.

HALL OF CHAMPIONS

This hall dedicated to fallen heroes is the stage for the final battle inside the Armory against the Scarlet Champion, Herod. For this battle, keep anyone with ranged attacks on either side of the staircase, but move close enough to maintain line of sight on your target: Herod for damage, others in the group for healing.

Herod possesses enormous strength, a powerful Two-Handed Axe, a large health pool, and one other trick, Cleave. The good news for you is that Herod announces his intention to initiate Cleave by shouting a plea to the Light.

Have the melee attackers back off when Herod signals that he's going to use his Whirlwind; it's deadly to anyone within melee range, but offers the perfect chance for casters to bandage and regain a bit of mana. Herod is immune to magic while using his Whirlwind. There are no other tricks to watch for while Herod lives, so focus on keeping Herod off the cloth- and leather-wearing types. Once Herod falls, everyone should drop down to the floor and bunch together as tightly as possible. A large contingent of non-elite Scarlet Trainees fills the room and swarms over the group. Fortunately, these trainees have little health, but their strength lies in numbers.

There's a good chance any mages and warlocks in the party have been itching to unleash area of effect spells that would've drawn too much attention in the hallways packed with elites, so consider this encounter a reward for their patience. Let loose with everything that hits multiple targets, and tear through the Trainees as quickly as possible.

⊛ CATHEDRAL

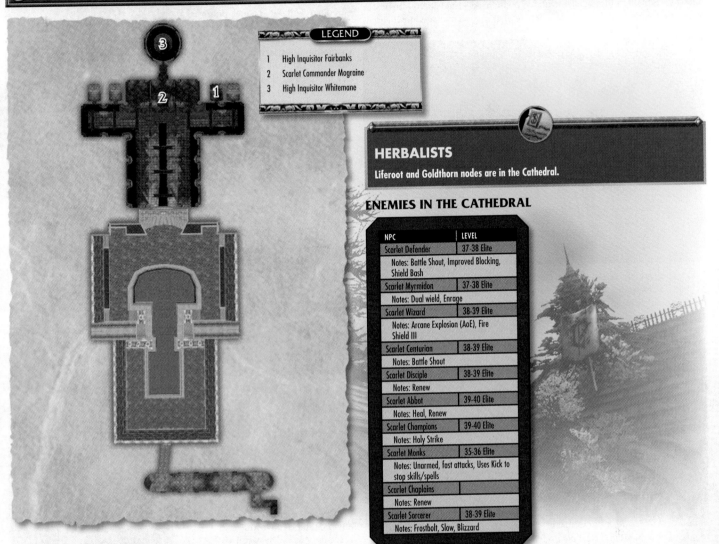

LEGEND

1 High Inquisitor Fairbanks
2 Scarlet Commander Mograine
3 High Inquisitor Whitemane

HERBALISTS

Liferoot and Goldthorn nodes are in the Cathedral.

ENEMIES IN THE CATHEDRAL

NPC	LEVEL
Scarlet Defender	37-38 Elite
Notes: Battle Shout, Improved Blocking, Shield Bash	
Scarlet Myrmidon	37-38 Elite
Notes: Dual wield, Enrage	
Scarlet Wizard	38-39 Elite
Notes: Arcane Explosion (AoE), Fire Shield III	
Scarlet Centurion	38-39 Elite
Notes: Battle Shout	
Scarlet Disciple	38-39 Elite
Notes: Renew	
Scarlet Abbot	39-40 Elite
Notes: Heal, Renew	
Scarlet Champions	39-40 Elite
Notes: Holy Strike	
Scarlet Monks	35-36 Elite
Notes: Unarmed, fast attacks, Uses Kick to stop skills/spells	
Scarlet Chaplains	
Notes: Renew	
Scarlet Sorcerer	38-39 Elite
Notes: Frostbolt, Slow, Blizzard	

LEADERS OF THE CATHEDRAL

NPC	LEVEL	FREQUENT DROP(S)
HIGH INQUISITOR FAIRBANKS	40 Elite	Branded Leather Bracers (Leather wrist, 49 Armor, +4 STA, +14 Attack Power), Dusty Mail Boots (Mail Feet, 221 Armor, +9 STA), Inquisitor's Shawl (Cloth Shoulder, +8 INT, Increases damage and healing done by magical spells and effects by up to 9)
Notes: Fear, Sleep, Curse of Blood, Dispel Magic, Heal, Power Word: Shield		
SCARLET COMMANDER MOGRAINE	42 Elite	Aegis of the Scarlet Commander (Shield, 1548 Armor, +7 STR/+8 STA/+7 SPI), Mograine's Might (Two-Handed Mace, 38.9 DPS, +17 STA, +16 SPI), Gauntlets of Divinity (Mail Hands, 168 Armor, +7 STA, +32 Attack Power), Scarlet Leggings (Mail Legs, 233 Armor, +20 STR/+10 STA)
Notes: Hammer of Justice, Retribution Aura, Divine Shield, Crusader Strike		
HIGH INQUISITOR WHITEMANE	42 Elite	Whitemane's Chapeau (Cloth Head, 52 Armor, +9 STA/+14 INT/+14 SPI), Triune Amulet (Neck, +7 STA/+7 INT/+7 SPI), Hand of Righteousness (1H Mace, 29.8 DPS, +8 SPI, up to +14 to spell effects)
Notes: Holy Smite, Deep Sleep, Scarlet Resurrection, Mind Control		

CHAPEL GARDENS

Hushed whispers and ominous music assault the senses upon entering the first hallway. Light filters through the windows on both sides, and guards are posted at several points. This first hallway is somewhat easy to manage, however, as most enemies are singles.

Two guards are at the end of the hallway. Slay them, and the hallway is yours to use as a safe pull location. There are some roaming defenders just outside the doorway leading into the garden; they're able to cause severe chain aggro if they're not pulled into the recently cleared hallway. Go slow and pull carefully. It's a good idea to bring them into the hallway away from the opening. This does two things: 1) It limits additional incoming enemy aggro. 2) It forces those nasty casters into the hallway as they have direct line of sight rules. It's definitely not a good thing to have a caster standing by the fountain sending ice bolts at your party!

After securing the area around the archway, continue pulling enemies that patrol around the fountains. Several groups are to the immediate left and right of the archway; they'll definitely aggro low-level party members. Not all enemies need be killed though, as the far left and right should ignore your party. When it looks safe, lead your party out to the fountains and climb in. If you cleared all of the roamers around the fountains from your safe spot in the hallway, then there should be no problem running through the fountain to the waterfall. If you left a few roamers, take your time and pull them into the fountains. Your goal is to reach the waterfall safely.

There are stairs leading up to the higher level of the garden to the left and right of the far end of the fountain and, coincidentally, the main chapel itself. Both sets of stairs lead to the same general area, but for each instance, a chest can randomly spawn at the top of either set of stairs. Look for the chest upon reaching the top of the stairs. If it isn't there, turn around and look across the courtyard. You can climb into the fountain to cross the courtyard without acquiring aggro. Clear to the chest, and the goodies inside are yours!

The entire courtyard is visible from the fountain. Watch the movements of the roaming enemies, and pull them at the most opportune time. Several are casters; Wizards are point blank area of effect casters and charge the party. Sorcerers are long-range casters, so different strategies are required. Having a mage Counterspell the sorcerers usually brings them to you. Or you can have your puller run far enough back to bring the caster to the group.

Like the lower level, you can generally leave the far left and right sides alone. However, kneeling between the fountain and the chapel doors is a "hidden" enemy. Many a time he has surprised a group by standing up and aggroing unexpectedly. It's a good idea to kill him before continuing to the chapel doors. The chapel is guarded by two sets of enemies, each independent from one another. Dispose of them before continuing to the chapel. The doors themselves require either the Scarlet Key or a skilled rogue to open.

CRUSADER'S CHAPEL

Thundering beats fill the air as you step inside the chapel. The war-like music sets the scene for combat, and all around are enemies kneeling in respect and prayer for their cause. Commander Mograine is at the far end of the chapel standing near the decrepit and stained altar. Tread cautiously here, as one wrong move can cause the death of the entire party.

One of the best strategies is to position your group at the base of the stairs to the chapel doors and have one puller run just inside the chapel to pull. Generally, you get a minimum of two mobs per pull. Clear up the right side of the chapel, bringing mobs down to your waiting group below. Remember to pull the kneeling enemies along the right set of pillars as well, as these will aggro as you walk past them. Your goal is to clear the entire right side to the far end, leaving Mograine alone.

At this point it's safe to bring your group inside. A group of three enemies is at the far end, around the corner and to the right. Charge these, keeping the fight down at the end and as far away from Mograine as possible. After killing them, proceed into the small room nearby. A monk kneels before a small table of candles. Dispose of him and rest up. The room may not look like anything out of the ordinary, but take a second look. The torch is the key to a hidden side room with a named enemy inside!

High Inquisitor Fairbanks awaits you and your party. He's a fun fight and anything can happen. His arsenal of skills consists of: 1) A nasty Curse that can be removed by a mage or druid, 2) A mean Fear spell that can cause the best of groups to flounder in disarray and chaos, 3) Power Word: Shield that gives him a nice damage absorb, 4) Heal, which can be quite frustrating if not interrupted, 5) Dispel Magic, which strips buffs in a short time, 6) Sleep, a spell that renders you useless for the duration of the battle unless you take damage or are cleansed by a Priest or Paladin.

Initially, Fairbanks lies on the ground and does not aggro until you start the encounter. If you survive the wrath of Fairbanks, expect a few nice pieces of equipment. Congratulations! Once again, you can use this area to rest up, cure any curses, and rebuff yourselves before continuing.

Head back out into the main chapel area, and over to the chapel doors where you first entered. Once there, work the left side in a fashion similar to how you cleared the right side. Your group should be safe to stay inside the chapel for this side as long as everyone stays far back from the enemies. After the left side is clear, lead the group around to the left side of the far-back section of the chapel (opposite Fairbanks). Three mobs stand outside two rooms, with each room containing mobs as well. Stand near the corner just before turning left down the side hall, and pull the first room to your group. If you don't, they may aggro as you walk past. Afterwards, pull the closest enemy to you in the main left hall; two of them are separate from the third and farthest mob. Proceed to kill these, then pull the third mob. All that should be left is the final room. Clear this room as well.

After clearing the left hall, every mob in the chapel should be dead except for Scarlet Commander Mograine and the presently out-of-sight High Inquisitor Whitemane. Rest up, rebuff, and prepare yourselves for a very fun, scripted fight.

KILL EVERYTHING

Make sure you kill every single mob in the chapel before engaging Scarlet Commander Mograine! If anyone is left alive in the chapel, they will immediately assist their Commander, making the fight much more difficult.

Aggroing him starts the script. Mograine has a few tricks up his sleeves. He's considered a Paladin; however, he does not heal himself. He uses the Hammer of Justice skill, which is a lovely little stun, and Retribution Aura, a damage shield based off of Holy damage. At some point during the fight, depending on how long it takes to kill him, he uses Divine Shield, which gives him invulnerability from attacks for the duration. After you kill him, don't bother trying to loot his body.

The second he dies, the doors open nearby and Inquisitor Whitemane makes her first appearance. Charge her, as she is a priest and stands back while casting Holy Smite on the first person she sees. She is immune to stun and frequently uses Holy Smite and Retribution Aura. After she's dropped down to half health, she casts an irresistible and unstoppable AoE sleep spell. This is where it gets tricky, and your party needs to be on its toes.

Whitemane proceeds to run to the fallen Mograine and bring him back to life. She heals both Mograine and herself to full health. At this point, your sleep spell should wear off, and the fight resumes. It's a good tactic to have your tank hold the aggro of both Mograine and Whitemane, but have your group focus on Whitemane. Slay her first before moving on to Mograine. Be on the lookout for spell graphics dark in nature. This isn't a shadow bolt coming your way, but instead, Whitemane is attempting to take over the mind of one party member! If this happens, do not kill your party member! Your party member becomes attackable by your group, and also attacks someone in your group. When Whitemane uses her Mind Control ability, the target then becomes susceptible to the same forms of crowd control used against humanoid mobs – like Polymorph and Blind. Polymorph has the added benefit of allowing the party member to regenerate health while they're "Sheeped". Try to hold out until the mind control breaks, or, with a priest available, dispel it. Killing Whitemane also breaks the mind control.

After Whitemane is dead, work on killing Mograine, again. He uses the same skills, but if he already used Divine Shield, he won't use it again. This time, when Mograine dies, you can loot his body.

When you report back with the successful completion of so many tasks, expect relieved faces to greet the news. The deaths of the High Inquisitor and Commander have struck a blow to the upper levels of the Scarlet Crusade. With the loss of their Champion, Herod, the morale of the rank and file of the Crusade should be at an all-time low. In addition, the tomes rescued from the library all provide knowledge to aid you should the Crusade rise from the ashes of this devastating defeat.

SCHOLOMANCE

Played & Written by: Edwin "Plainsong" Kern of <Dovrani> on Kirin Tor

The ancient ruins at Caer Darrow remind us about what once was there: an Elven Runestone that was sacred to the High Elves of Quel'Thalas. However, the Runestone was later hacked to pieces and used to create the Altars of Storms.

Much later, the Barov family restored the fortress and, through dealings with Kel'Thuzad, transformed it into a school of necromancy: Scholomance. Now, Scholomance is home to spirits and old denizens of the town who seek to gain some measure of vengeance for wrongs committed against them in the past.

It's up to Azeroth's adventurers to brave the depths of the fortress and restore peace to Caer Darrow.

DUNGEON INFORMATION

Location	Western Plaguelands
Quests	Both
Region	Contested
Suggested Levels	55-60
Group Allowed	5
Primary Enemies	Humanoids, Undead
Time to Complete	3-4 hours

GETTING TO SCHOLOMANCE

Scholomance is in the southern portion of the Western Plaguelands. Horde parties can gather at Undercity and travel from Light's Hope Chapel or Tarren Mill, while Alliance parties can group at Stormwind and begin their treks from Aerie Peak (via the semi-secluded path), Chillwind Point, or Light's Hope Chapel.

WHO TO BRING

Having a party with crowd control is essential as many fights involve a large number of enemies. Sap, Polymorph, Mind Control, and Shackle Undead are all extremely useful in this school of magic. AoEs are also extremely helpful as there are many fights with large numbers of non-elite enemies.

WHAT'S IN IT FOR ME?

While working toward level 60, experience is a great incentive to risk life and limb. Once you hit 60, experience doesn't mean as much. The way to advance your character is now through equipment. Items from many sets can be found in Scholomance as well as entire sets. These should be kept in mind when deciding where to go and what to kill.

SET ITEMS FOUND IN SCHOLOMANCE

SET	ITEM	BONUSES	CREATURE
BATTLEGEAR OF VALOR	Boots of Valor	Plate Feet, 424 Armor, +20 STA, +8 STR, +4 AGI, +3 SPI	Kirtonos the Herald
	Helm of Valor	Plate Head, 526 Armor, +23 STA, +15 STR, +9 AGI, +8 SPI	Darkmaster Gandling
BEASTSTALKER ARMOR	Beaststalker's Cap	Mail Helm, 297 Armor, +20 AGI, +20 STA, +10 INT, +6 SPI	Darkmaster Gandling
BLOODMAIL REGALIA	Bloodmail Belt	Mail Waist, 202 Armor, +12 AGI, +9 INT, +11 STA, +12 STR	Doctor Theolen Krastinov, Instructor Malicia, Lady Illucia Barov, Lord Alexei Barov, Lorekeeper Polkelt, The Ravenian
	Bloodmail Boots	Mail Feet, 247 Armor, +9 AGI, +10 INT, +10 STA, +9 STR	Doctor Theolen Krastinov, Instructor Malicia, Lady Illucia Barov, Lord Alexei Barov, Lorekeeper Polkelt, The Ravenian
	Bloodmail Gauntlets	Mail Hands, 225 Armor, +10 INT, +10 STA, +9 STR, Passive: Improves your chance to get a critical strike by 1%	Doctor Theolen Krastinov, Instructor Malicia, Lady Illucia Barov, Lord Alexei Barov, Lorekeeper Polkelt, The Ravenian
	Bloodmail Hauberk	Mail Chest, 360 Armor, +15 INT, +10 SPI, +15 STA, +10 STR, Passive: Increases your chance to dodge an attack by 1%	Doctor Theolen Krastinov, Instructor Malicia, Lady Illucia Barov, Lord Alexei Barov, Lorekeeper Polkelt, The Ravenian
	Bloodmail Leggaurds	Mail Legs, 315 Armor, +12 AGI, +15 INT, +16 STA, +15 STR	Doctor Theolen Krastinov, Instructor Malicia, Lady Illucia Barov, Lord Alexei Barov, Lorekeeper Polkelt, The Ravenian
CADAVEROUS GARB	Cadaverous Armor	Leather Chest, 172 Armor, +8 STR, +8 AGI, Passive: +60 Attack Power	Doctor Theolen Krastinov, Instructor Malicia, Lady Illucia Barov, Lord Alexei Barov, Lorekeeper Polkelt, The Ravenian
	Cadaverous Belt	Leather Waist, 97 Armor, +12 STA, +40 Attack Power	Doctor Theolen Krastinov, Instructor Malicia, Lady Illucia Barov, Lord Alexei Barov, Lorekeeper Polkelt, The Ravenian
	Cadaverous Gloves	Leather Hands, 107 Armor, +9 STA, +44 Attack Power	Doctor Theolen Krastinov, Instructor Malicia, Lady Illucia Barov, Lord Alexei Barov, Lorekeeper Polkelt, The Ravenian
	Cadaverous Leggings	Leather Legs, 150 Armor, +18 STA, +52 Attack Power	Doctor Theolen Krastinov, Instructor Malicia, Lady Illucia Barov, Lord Alexei Barov, Lorekeeper Polkelt, The Ravenian
	Cadaverous Walkers	Leather Feet, 118 Armor, +20 STA, +24 Attack Power	Doctor Theolen Krastinov, Instructor Malicia, Lady Illucia Barov, Lord Alexei Barov, Lorekeeper Polkelt, The Ravenian
DEATHBONE GUARDIAN	Deathbone Chestplate	Plate Chest, 637 Armor, +12 STA, Passive: Increased Defense +17, Passive: Restores 5 mana every 5 sec.	Doctor Theolen Krastinov, Instructor Malicia, Lady Illucia Barov, Lord Alexei Barov, Lorekeeper Polkelt, The Ravenian
	Deathbone Gauntlets	Plate Hands, 398 Armor, +14 STA, Passive: Increased Defense +10, Passive: Restores 4 mana every 5 sec.	Doctor Theolen Krastinov, Instructor Malicia, Lady Illucia Barov, Lord Alexei Barov, Lorekeeper Polkelt, The Ravenian
	Deathbone Girdle	Plate Waist, 358 Armor, +15 STA, Passive: Increased Defense +9, Passive: Restores 4 mana every 5 sec.	Doctor Theolen Krastinov, Instructor Malicia, Lady Illucia Barov, Lord Alexei Barov, Lorekeeper Polkelt, The Ravenian
	Deathbone Legguards	Plate Legs, 557 Armor, +20 STA, Passive: Increased Defense +13, Passive: Restores 5 mana every 5 sec.	Doctor Theolen Krastinov, Instructor Malicia, Lady Illucia Barov, Lord Alexei Barov, Lorekeeper Polkelt, The Ravenian
	Deathbone Sabatons	Plate Feet, 438 Armor, +9 STA, Passive: Increased Defense +10, Passive: Restores 6 mana every 5 sec.	Doctor Theolen Krastinov, Instructor Malicia, Lady Illucia Barov, Lord Alexei Barov, Lorekeeper Polkelt, The Ravenian
DREADMIST RAIMENT	Dreadmist Mantle	Cloth Shoulders, 64 Armor, +15 INT, +14 STA, +9 SPI	Jandice Barov
	Dreadmist Mask	Cloth Head, 71 Armor, +23 INT, +15 STA, +12 SPI	Darkmaster Gandling
	Dreadmist Wraps	Cloth Hands, 52 Armor, +14 SPI, +9 INT, +13 STA	Lorekeeper Polkelt, Scholomance Necromancer
LIGHTFORGE ARMOR	Lightforge Bracers	Plate Wrists, 261 Armor, +10 STA, +8 SPI, +7 STR, +4 AGI	Lord Alexei Barov, Risen Protector, Risen Warrior
	Lightforge Helm	Plate Head, 526 Armor, +20 STA, +13 STR, +14 INT, +10 SPI, +6 AGI	Darkmaster Gandling
MAGISTER'S REGALIA	Magister's Crown	Cloth Head, 71 Armor, +30 INT, +5 SPI, +11 STA	Darkmaster Gandling
	Magister's Gloves	Cloth Hands, 52 Armor, +14 SPI, +14 INT, +9 STA	Doctor Theolen Krastinov, Scholomance Adept
	Magister's Mantle	Cloth Shoulders, 64 Armor, +22 INT, +6 SPI, +6 STA	Ras Frostwhisper
NECROPILE RAIMENT	Necropile Boots	Cloth Feet, 60 Armor, +10 INT, +9 SPI, +15 STA, Passive: Increases damage and healing done by magical spells and effects by up to 11	Doctor Theolen Krastinov, Instructor Malicia, Lady Illucia Barov, Lord Alexei Barov, Lorekeeper Polkelt, The Ravenian
	Necropile Cuffs	Cloth Wrists, 38 Armor, +11 INT, +7 SPI, +12 STA	Doctor Theolen Krastinov, Instructor Malicia, Lady Illucia Barov, Lord Alexei Barov, Lorekeeper Polkelt, The Ravenian
	Necropile Leggings	Cloth Legs, 76 Armor, +18 INT, +12 SPI, +21 STA	Doctor Theolen Krastinov, Instructor Malicia, Lady Illucia Barov, Lord Alexei Barov, Lorekeeper Polkelt, The Ravenian
	Necropile Mantle	Cloth Shoulders, 65 Armor, +11 INT, +9 SPI, +17 STA	Doctor Theolen Krastinov, Instructor Malicia, Lady Illucia Barov, Lord Alexei Barov, Lorekeeper Polkelt, The Ravenian
	Necropile Robe	Cloth Chest, 87 Armor, +12 INT, +12 SPI, +22 STA, Passive: Increases damage and healing done by magical spalls and effects by up to 8	Doctor Theolen Krastinov, Instructor Malicia, Lady Illucia Barov, Lord Alexei Barov, Lorekeeper Polkelt, The Ravenian
SHADOWCRAFT ARMOR	Shadowcraft Boots	Leather Feet, 115 Armor, +21 AGI, +9 STA	Rattlegore
	Shadowcraft Bracers	Leather Wrists, 71 Armor, +15 AGI, +7 STA	Dark Shade, Instructor Malicia, Risen Construct, Scholomance Occultist
	Shadowcraft Cap	Leather Head, 141 Armor, +20 AGI, +18 STA, +13 STR, +5 SPI	Darkmaster Gandling
THE ELEMENTS	Coif of Elements	Mail Head, 297 Armor, +23 INT, +13 STA, +12 SPI, +7 STR	Darkmaster Gandling
VESTMENTS OF THE DEVOUT	Devout Crown	Cloth Head, 71 Armor, +24 INT, +15 SPI, +13 STA	Darkmaster Gandling
WILDHEART RAIMENT	Wildheart Belt	Leather Waist, 93 Armor, +17 INT, +10 SPI, +9 STA	Scholomance Handler, Spectral Teacher, The Ravenian
	Wildheart Cowl	Leather Head, 141 Armor, +20 INT, +20 SPI, +10 STA, +6 STR	Darkmaster Gandling

The leaders of the forces in Scholomance are the only enemies that can drop the Scholomance specific sets. There are only 5 pieces in each set and the set bonuses are listed below.

BONUSES OF SCHOLOMANCE SPECIFIC EQUIPMENT SETS

SET	2 PIECES	3 PIECES	4 PIECES	5 PIECES
Necropile Raiment	Increased Defense +3	+5 INT	+15 All Resistances	Increases damage and healing done by magical spells and effects by up to 23
Cadaverous Garb	Increased Defense +3	+10 Attack Power	+15 All Resistances	Improves your chance to hit by 2%
Bloodmail Regalia	Increased Defense +3	+10 Attack Power	+15 All Resistances	Increases your chance to parry an attack by 1%
Deathbone Guardian	Increased Defense +3	+50 Armor	+15 All Resistances	Increases your chance to parry an attack by 1%

QUESTS FOR SCHOLOMANCE

ALLIANCE QUESTS

QUEST NAME	QUEST GIVER	QUEST GIVER LOCATION	QUEST RECEIVER	QUEST RECEIVER LOCATION	CHAIN?	MAX EXPERIENCE
Barov Family Fortune	Weldon Barov	Alterac Mountains: Chillwind Point	Weldon Barov	Alterac Mountains: Chillwind Point	Yes	6,600
Judgment and Redemption	Lord Grayson Shadowbreaker	Stormwind: Cathedral Square	Lord Grayson Shadowbreaker	Stormwind: Cathedral Square	Yes	None
Scholomance	Commander Ashlam Valorfist	Alterac Mountains: Chillwind Point	Alchemist Arbington	Alterac Mountains: Chillwind Point	Yes	825
Skeletal Fragments	Alchemist Arbington	Alterac Mountains: Chillwind Point	Alchemist Arbington	Alterac Mountains: Chillwind Point	Yes	4,500
Mold Rhymes with…	Alchemist Arbington	Alterac Mountains: Chillwind Point	Krinkle Goodsteel	Tanaris: Gadgetzan	Yes	600
Fire Plume Forged	Krinkle Goodsteel	Tanaris: Gadgetzan	Alchemist Arbington	Alterac Mountains: Chillwind Point	Yes	4,500
Araj's Scarab	Alchemist Arbington	Alterac Mountains: Chillwind Point	Alchemist Arbington	Alterac Mountains: Chillwind Point	Yes	6,600
REWARD: Key to Scholomance						

BAROV FAMILY FORTUNE

Quest Level	52 to obtain
Location	Alterac Mountains (Chillwind Point)
Quest Giver	Weldon Barov
Goal	Collect: The Deed to Brill, The Deed to Caer Darrow, The Deed to Southshore, and The Deed to Tarren Mill
Max Experience Gained	6,600

There are only two heirs to the Barov Family fortune. Weldon and Alexi are both searching for the deeds to areas owned by their family. The deeds are somewhere in Scholomance and both are willing to pay handsomely to get the deeds.

JUDGMENT AND REDEMPTION

Class	Paladin
Quest Level	60
Location	Stormwind City (Cathedral Square)
Quest Giver	Lord Grayson Shadowbreaker
Goal	Give the Charger's Redeemed Soul and the Blessed Arcanite Barding to Darkreaver's Fallen Charger
Max Experience Gained	9,950

When you have finished *The Divination Scryer*, Lord Grayson Shadowbreaker gives you a satchel with everything you need in it. Travel to Scholomance and use the Divination Scryer in the heart of the Great Ossuary's basement to summon the spirits that you must judge. Death Knight Darkreaver attacks when you're finished judging the spirits. You must defeat him to reclaim the lost soul of the fallen charger and continue the quest for your own charger.

SKELETAL FRAGMENTS

Quest Level	55 to obtain
Location	Alterac Mountains (Chillwind Point)
Quest Giver	Alchemist Arbington
Goal	Collect 15 Skeletal Fragments
Max Experience Gained	4,500

Creating a key to Scholomance is a delicate and difficult process. Many reagents will be needed. The first reagent is a bunch of 15 Skeletal Fragments from the skeletons in Andorhal. Smash skeletons and retrieve fragments until you have enough to return to Arbington.

SCHOLOMANCE

Quest Level	55 to obtain
Location	Alterac Mountains (Chillwind Point)
Quest Giver	Commander Ashlam Valorfist
Goal	Speak with Alchemist Arbington at Chillwind Point
Max Experience Gained	825

By completing *All Along the Watchtowers* you have proven yourself a valued warrior of the Alliance. Scholomance is on the island of Caer Darrow. Alchemist Arbington knows better how to make a key to gain entrance into the school of magic.

MOLD RHYMES WITH...

Quest Level	55 to obtain
Location	Alterac Mountains (Chillwind Point)
Quest Giver	Alchemist Arbington
Goal	Deliver the Imbued Skeletal Fragments and 15 Gold to Krinkle Goodsteel in Gadgetzan
Max Experience Gained	600

With the skeletal fragments imbued, now you need a mold for the key. The only person qualified to make the mold is Krinkle Goodsteel in Gadgetzan. Unfortunately, his work isn't cheap and Alchemist Arbington doesn't have the money, so you'll have to pay the 15 Gold.

FIRE PLUME FORGED

Quest Level	56 to obtain
Location	Tanaris (Gadgetzan)
Quest Giver	Krinkle Goodsteel
Goal	Use 2 Thorium Bars and the Skeleton Key Mold at Fire Plume Ridge in Un'Goro Crater to create the Unfinished Skeleton Key
Max Experience Gained	4,500

With the mold created, you now need to create the stem of the key. It needs to be made of Thorium, so you need to acquire two bars. Take the mold and the bars to the lava lake at the top of Fire Plume Ridge in Un'Goro. Dip the mold into the lava and wait for the volcano do to the rest. Take the Unfinished Skeleton Key to Alchemist Arbington at Chillwind Point.

ARAJ'S SCARAB

Quest Level	55 to obtain
Location	Alterac Mountains (Chillwind Point)
Quest Giver	Alchemist Arbington
Goal	Collect Araj's Scarab
Max Experience Gained	6,600

The key is nearly complete. All that is needed is the scarab of Araj the Summoner. Araj used to be the leader of Scholomance before he took over Andorhal. Destroy the four summoning crystals in the Andorhal towers to force him to fight you. Defeat him and take his scarab from his phylactery.

HORDE QUESTS

QUEST NAME	QUEST GIVER	QUEST GIVER LOCATION	QUEST RECEIVER	QUEST RECEIVER LOCATION	CHAIN?	MAX EXPERIENCE
Barov Family Fortune	Alexi Barov	Tirisfal Glades: The Bulwark	Alexi Barov	Tirisfal Glades: The Bulwark	Yes	6,600
Scholomance	High Executor Derrington	Tirisfal Glades: The Bulwark	Alchemist Dithers	Tirisfal Glades: The Bulwark	Yes	825
Skeletal Fragments	Alchemist Dithers	Tirisfal Glades: The Bulwark	Alchemist Dithers	Tirisfal Glades: The Bulwark	Yes	4,500
Mold Rhymes with...	Alchemist Dithers	Tirisfal Glades: The Bulwark	Krinkle Goodsteel	Tanaris: Gadgetzan	Yes	600
Fire Plume Forged	Krinkle Goodsteel	Tanaris: Gadgetzan	Alchemist Dithers	Tirisfal Glades: The Bulwark	Yes	4,500
Araj's Scarab	Alchemist Dithers	Tirisfal Glades: The Bulwark	Alchemist Dithers	Tirisfal Glades: The Bulwark	Yes	6,600
REWARD: Key to Scholomance						
The Darkreaver Menace	Sagorne Creststrider	Orgrimmar: Valley of Wisdom	Sagorne Creststrider	Orgrimmar: Valley of Wisdom	Yes	None
REWARD: Skyfury Helm (Mail Head, 324 Armor, +14 STA, +13 STR, +12 SPI, Passive: Improves your chance to get a critical strike with spells by 2%, Improves you chance to get a critical strike by 1%)						
NOTE: Shaman only						

260

BAROV FAMILY FORTUNE

Quest Level	52 to obtain
Location	Tirisfal Glades (The Bulwark)
Quest Giver	Alexi Barov
Goal	Collect: The Deed to Brill, The Deed to Caer Darrow, The Deed to Southshore, and The Deed to Tarren Mill
Max Experience Gained	6,600

There are only two heirs to the Barov Family fortune. Weldon and Alexi are both searching for the deeds to areas owned by their family. The deeds are somewhere in Scholomance and both are willing to pay handsomely to get the deeds.

SCHOLOMANCE

Quest Level	55 to obtain
Location	Tirisfal Glades (The Bulwark)
Quest Giver	High Executor Derrington
Goal	Speak with Alchemist Dithers at The Bulwark
Max Experience Gained	825

After finishing *All Along the Watchtowers*, you have proven yourself be a valiant warrior for the Horde. Scholomance sits on the island of Caer Darrow. Alchemist Dithers knows better how to make a key to gain entrance into the school of magic.

SKELETAL FRAGMENTS

Quest Level	55 to obtain
Location	Tirisfal Glades (The Bulwark)
Quest Giver	Alchemist Dithers
Goal	Collect 15 Skeletal Fragments
Max Experience Gained	4,500

Creating a key to Scholomance is a delicate and difficult process. Many reagents are needed and the first is a collection of 15 skeletal fragments from the skeletons in Andorhal. Smash skeletons and retrieve fragments until you have enough to return to Dithers.

MOLD RHYMES WITH...

Quest Level	55 to obtain
Location	Tirisfal Glades (The Bulwark)
Quest Giver	Alchemist Dithers
Goal	Deliver the Imbued Skeletal Fragments and 15 Gold to Krinkle Goodsteel in Gadgetzan
Max Experience Gained	600

With the skeletal fragments imbued, you now need a mold for the key. The only person qualified to make the mold is Krinkle Goodsteel in Gadgetzan. Unfortunately, his work isn't cheap and Alchemist Dithers doesn't have the money, so you'll have to pay the 15 Gold.

ARAJ'S SCARAB

Quest Level	55 to obtain
Location	Tirisfal Glades (The Bulwark)
Quest Giver	Alchemist Dithers
Goal	Collect Araj's Scarab
Max Experience Gained	6,600

The key is nearly complete. All that is needed is the scarab of Araj the Summoner. Araj used to be the leader of Scholomance before he took over Andorhal. Destroy the four summoning crystals in the Andorhal towers to force him to fight you. Defeat him and take his scarab from his phylactery.

FIRE PLUME FORGED

Quest Level	56 to obtain
Location	Tanaris (Gadgetzan)
Quest Giver	Krinkle Goodsteel
Goal	Use 2 Thorium Bars and the Skeleton Key Mold at Fire Plume Ridge in Un'Goro Crater to create the Unfinished Skeleton Key
Max Experience Gained	4,500

With the mold created, you need to create the stem of the key. It needs to be made of Thorium, so you need to acquire two bars. Take the mold and the bars to the lava lake at the top of Fire Plume Ridge in Un'Goro. Dip the mold into the lava and wait for the volcano do to the rest. Take the Unfinished Skeleton Key to Alchemist Dithers at The Bulwark.

THE DARKREAVER MENACE

Class	Shaman
Quest Level	58 to obtain
Location	Orgrimmar (Valley of Wisdom)
Quest Giver	Sagorne Creststrider
Goal	Collect Death Knight Darkreaver's head
Max Experience Gained	None
Reward	Skyfury Helm (Mail Head, 324 Armor, +14 STA, +13 STR, +12 SPI, Passive: Improves your chance to get a critical strike with spells by 2%, Improves you chance to get a critical strike by 1%)

Once you have finished Material Assistance, it is time to end Darkreaver's meddling. Travel to Scholomance and use the Divination Scryer in the heart of the Great Ossuary's basement. Defeat the spirits until Death Knight Darkreaver approaches. Slay him and return with his head.

SHARED QUESTS

QUEST NAME	QUEST GIVER	QUEST GIVER LOCATION	QUEST RECEIVER	QUEST RECEIVER LOCATION	CHAIN?	MAX EXPERIENCE
Plagued Hatchlings	Betina Bigglezink	Eastern Plaguelands: Light's Hope Chapel	Betina Bigglezink	Eastern Plaguelands: Light's Hope Chapel	Yes	6,200
Healthy Dragon Scale	Healthy Dragon Scale	Scholomance	Betina Bigglezink	Eastern Plaguelands: Light's Hope Chapel	Yes	None
REWARD: Increases your reputation with the Argent Dawn						
Doctor Theolen Krastinov, the Butcher	Eva Sarkhoff	Western Plaguelands: Caer Darrow	Eva Sarkhoff	Western Plaguelands: Caer Darrow	Yes	6,600
Krastinov's Bag of Horrors	Eva Sarkhoff	Western Plaguelands: Caer Darrow	Eva Sarkhoff	Western Plaguelands: Caer Darrow	Yes	6,600
Kirtonos the Herald	Eva Sarkhoff	Western Plaguelands: Caer Darrow	Eva Sarkhoff	Western Plaguelands: Caer Darrow	Yes	8,300
REWARD: Mirah's Song (One-hand Sword, 40 DPS, +9 AGI, +9 STR) or Penelope's Rose (Held in Hand, +11 INT, +11 SPI, +10 STA) and Spectral Essence (Trinket, Equip: Allows communication with the deceased of Caer Darrow)						
The Lich, Ras Frostwhisper	Magistrate Marduke	Western Plaguelands: Caer Darrow	Magistrate Marduke	Western Plaguelands: Caer Darrow	Yes	10,900
REWARD: Darrowshire Strongguard (Shield, 2153 Armor, 40 Block, +8 SPI, +8 STA, +10 Nature Resistance, +10 Frost Resistance) or Warblade of Caer Darrow (Two-hand Sword, 57.4 DPS) or Crown of Caer Darrow (Cloth Head, 73 Armor, +20 INT, +20 SPI, +8 STA, +15 Frost Resistance) or Darrowspike (One-hand Dagger, 41.3 DPS)						

PLAGUED HATCHLINGS

Quest Level	55 to obtain
Location	Eastern Plaguelands (Light's Hope Chapel)
Quest Giver	Betina Bigglezink
Goal	Kill 20 Plagued Hatchlings
Max Experience Gained	6,200

The necromancers in Scholomance are raising their own plagued dragonflight. If the hatchlings are allowed to grow fully, this will certainly turn the tide against both the Horde and the Alliance. Travel to Scholomance and kill the hatchlings before they grow large enough to become a real threat.

HEALTHY DRAGON SCALE

Quest Level	58 to obtain
Location	Scholomance
Quest Giver	Healthy Dragon Scale
Goal	Deliver the Healthy Dragon Scale to Betina Bigglezink
Max Experience Gained	None
Reward	Increases your reputation with the Argent Dawn

To begin this quest, you must first complete *Plagued Hatchlings* and return to Scholomance. This scale isn't like the many others covering the Plagued Hatchlings. While the others show signs of disease, this one is entirely healthy. Bring the scale to Betina in Light's Hope Chapel. Bring any and all you find.

DOCTOR THEOLEN KRASTINOV, THE BUTCHER

Quest Level	55 to obtain
Location	Western Plaguelands (Caer Darrow)
Quest Giver	Eva Sarkhoff
Goal	Kill Doctor Theolen Krastinov and burn the Remains of Eva Sarkhoff and the Remains of Lucian Sarkhoff
Max Experience Gained	6,600

The Sarkhoffs are unable to rest peacefully as their remains have been desecrated by Doctor Theolen Krastinov. He's killed thousands and deserves to die. Eva asks you to burn the remains of herself and her husband once you kill Krastinov.

KRASTINOV'S BAG OF HORRORS

Quest Level	55 to obtain
Location	Western Plaguelands (Caer Darrow)
Quest Giver	Eva Sarkhoff
Goal	Kill Jandice Barov and bring Krastinov's Bag of Horrors to Eva Sarkhoff
Max Experience Gained	6,600

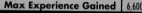

Krastinov is dead, but there is more work to be done. He had a master by the name of Kirtonos. Before you can defeat Kirtonos, you must first learn how to summon him. Jandice Barov was a go between for Krastinov and Kirtonos. Kill her and look for clues. Return to Eva with the new information.

I CAN'T FIND MAGISTRATE MARDUKE

Magistrate Marduke is a ghost in Caer Darrow. To see and interact with him, you need to have the Spectral Essence equipped. The Spectral Essence is a quest reward from the quest chain beginning with *Doctor Theolen Krastinov, the Butcher*.

KIRTONOS THE HERALD

Quest Level	56 to obtain
Location	Western Plaguelands (Caer Darrow)
Quest Giver	Eva Sarkhoff
Goal	Kill Kirtonos the Herald
Max Experience Gained	8,300
Reward	Mirah's Song (One-hand Sword, 40 DPS, +9 AGI, +9 STR) or Penelope's Rose (Held in Hand, +11 INT, +11 SPI, +10 STA) and Spectral Essence (Trinket, Equip: Allows communication with the deceased of Caer Darrow)

With the Blood of Innocents you found in *Krastinov's Bag of Horrors*, you have the chance to slay Kirtonos the Herald. Travel into Scholomance and find the porch. Place the Blood of Innocents in the brazier to summon Kirtonos. When he comes, slay him to avenge the innocent lives taken. Return to Eva for your reward and sleep better at night.

THE LICH, RAS FROSTWHISPER

Quest Level	60 to obtain
Location	Western Plaguelands (Caer Darrow)
Quest Giver	Magistrate Marduke
Goal	Collect the Human Head of Ras Frostwhisper
Max Experience Gained	10,900
Reward	Darrowshire Strongguard (Shield, 2153 Armor, 40 Block, +8 SPI, +8 STA, +10 Nature Resistance, +10 Frost Resistance) or Warblade of Caer Darrow (Two-hand Sword, 57.4 DPS) or Crown of Caer Darrow (Cloth Head, 73 Armor, +20 INT, +20 SPI, +8 STA, +15 Frost Resistance) or Darrowspike (One-hand Dagger, 41.3 DPS)

You have everything you need to bring an end to Ras Frostwhisper. Find him in Scholomance and use the Soulbound Keepsake on the lich. He reverts to his mortal self and it is in that instant that you must strike him down for all the evils he has committed.

CLASS-SPECIFIC QUESTS

QUEST NAME	QUEST GIVER	QUEST GIVER LOCATION	QUEST RECEIVER	QUEST RECEIVER LOCATION	CHAIN?	MAX EXPERIENCE
Imp Delivery	Gorzeeki Wildeyes	Burning Steppes: Altar of Storms	Gorzeeki Wildeyes	Burning Steppes: Altar of Storms	Yes	7,050

IMP DELIVERY

Class	Warlock
Quest Level	60 to obtain
Location	Burning Steppes
Quest Giver	Gorzeeki Wildeyes
Goal	Take the Imp in a Jar to the alchemy lab in Scholomance, and then return it to Gorzeeki Wildeyes
Max Experience Gained	7,050

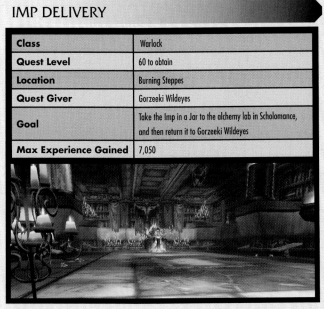

To finish making Mor'zul's parchment, you need paper infused with Xorothian. Gorzeeki doesn't have the equipment to make it, but the alchemy lab in Scholomance does. He can't journey there himself, but he gives you a very clever Imp who can work the equipment. Take the Imp to the alchemy lab and let him loose. When you have the parchment, return the Imp in a Jar to Gorzeeki.

ENEMIES

A School Dedicated to Magic. What Could Go Wrong?

NPC	LEVEL
Aspect of Banality	60 Elite
Frequent Drops: Tome of Arcane Brilliance	
Aspect of Corruption	60 Elite
Aspect of Malice	60 Elite
Frequent Drops: Book: Gift of the Wild II, Tome of Arcane Brilliance	
Aspect of Shadow	60 Elite
Banal Spirit	57-60
Corrupted Spirit	57-60 Elite
Dark Shade	54-59 Elite
Notes: Immune to physical damage and taunt Frequent Drops: Shadowcraft Bracers (Leather Wrist, 71 Armor, +15 AGI, +7 STA), Book: Gift of the Wild II, Codex: Prayer of Fortitude II, Tome of Arcane Brilliance	
Diseased Ghoul	53-59 Elite
Malicious Spirit	57-60 Elite
Necrofiend	53-60 Elite
Notes: Web Explosion (AoE Root) Frequent Drops: Shadow Silk, Thick Spider's Silk	
Plagued Hatchling	52-59
Notes: Poison Spit	

NPC	LEVEL
Ragged Ghoul	55-59 Elite
Reanimated Corpse	53-59
Risen Aberration	52-58
Risen Bonewarder	53-59 Elite
Risen Construct	53-61 Elite
Frequent Drops: Shadowcraft Bracers (Leather Wrists, 71 Armor, +15 AGI, +7 STA)	
Risen Guard	52-59 Elite
Risen Guardian	54-61
Notes: Sunder Armor	
Risen Lackey	55-56
Notes: Summoned by Scholomance Dark Summoner	
Risen Protector	53-60 Elite
Frequent Drops: Lightforge Bracers (Plate Wrists, 261 Armor, +10 STA, +8 SPI, +7 STR, +4 AGI)	
Risen Warrior	54-61 Elite
Frequent Drops: Lightforge Bracers (Plate Wrists, 261 Armor, +10 STA, +8 SPI, +7 STR, +4 AGI)	

NPC	LEVEL
Scholomance Acolyte	52-58 Elite
Notes: Mind Flay, Shadow Word: Pain	
Scholomance Adept	53-59 Elite
Notes: Frost Bolt Frequent Drops: Magister's Gloves (Cloth Hands, 52 Armor, +14 SPI, +14 INT, +9 STA)	
Scholomance Dark Summoner	53-59 Elite
Notes: Summons Risen Lackey	
Scholomance Handler	54-60 Elite
Frequent Drops: Wildheart Belt (Leather Waist, 93 Armor, +17 INT, +10 SPI, +9 STA)	
Scholomance Necrolyte	52-58 Elite
Scholomance Necromancer	57-59 Elite
Notes: Call of the Grave (curse, massive damage after 60 seconds) Frequent Drops: Dreadmist Wraps (Cloth Hands, 52 Armor, +14 SPI, +9 INT, +13 STA)	
Scholomance Neophyte	52-58 Elite
Notes: Shadowbolt	

NPC	LEVEL
Scholomance Occultist	53-59 Elite
Notes: Changes into Dark Shade when low on health Frequent Drops: Shadowcraft Bracers (Leather Wrists, 71 Armor, +15 AGI, +7 STA)	
Scholomance Student	54-59 Elite
Shadowed Spirit	59-60 Elite
Skulking Corpse	57-59
Spectral Projection	53-60
Spectral Researcher	53-60 Elite
Notes: Knockback	
Spectral Teacher	55-61 Elite
Frequent Drops: Wildheart Belt (Leather Waist, 93 Armor, +17 INT, +10 SPI, +9 STA)	
Spectral Tutor	53-60 Elite
Notes: Splits into several Spectral Projections and reforms	
Splintered Skeleton	54-60 Elite
Frequent Drops: Runecloth	
Unstable Corpse	53-59

DEATH IS NO EXCUSE FOR TARDINESS

NPC	LEVEL	FREQUENT DROP(S)
BLOOD STEWARD OF KIRTONOS	57 Elite	Doombringer (Two-Hand Sword, 51.4 DPS, Chance on Hit: Sends a shadow bolt at the enemy causing 125 to 275 Shadow damage), Serathil (One-Hand Axe, 40.0 DPS, +9 STR), Five of Elementals
Notes: Curse of Impotence (decreases spell damage by 91 for 2 min), Curse of Weakness, Paralyzing Poison (stun target for 8 sec)		
DARKMASTER GANDLING	61 Elite	Pattern: Robe of the Void (Requires Tailoring(300)), Headmaster's Charge (Two-hand Staff, 58.4 DPS, +30 STA, +20 SPI, Use: Increases target's INT by 30), Detention Strap (Mail Waist, 205 Armor, +17 INT, +11 SPI, +10 STA), Witchblade (One-hand Dagger, 40.6 DPS, +8 INT, Passive: Increases damage done by Arcane and Shadow spells and effects by up to 14), Boots of the Shrieker (Leather Feet, 120 Armor, +10 INT, +10 SPI, +10 STR, +10 STA, +10 Shadow Resistance), Vigorsteel Vambraces (Plate Wrist, 283 Armor, +17 STA, +7 AGI), Bonecreeper Stylus (Wand, 62.6 DPS, +4 INT, Passive: Increases damage and healing done by magical spells and effects by up to 11), Silent Fang (Main-hand Sword, 40.6 DPS, Chance on Hit: Silences an enemy, preventing it from casting spells for 6 seconds), Tombstone Breastplate (Leather Chest, 174 Armor, +4 STR, +10 STA, +6 SPI, Passive: Increases your chance to get a critical strike by 2%), Devout Crown (Cloth Head, 71 Armor, +24 INT, +15 SPI, +13 STA), Dreadmist Mask (Cloth Head, 71 Armor, +23 INT, +15 STA, +12 SPI), Wildheart Cowl (Leather Head, 141 Armor, +20 INT, +20 SPI, +10 STA, +6 STR), Beaststalker's Cap (Mail Head, 297 Armor, +20 AGI, +20 STA, +10 INT, +6 SPI), Helm of Valor (Plate Head, 526 Armor, +23 STA, +15 STR, +9 AGI, +8 SPI), Magister's Crown (Cloth Head, 71 Armor, +30 INT, +5 SPI, +11 STA), Shadowcraft Cap (Leather Head, 141 Armor, +20 AGI, +18 STA, +13 STR, +5 SPI), Lightforge Helm (Plate Head, 526 Armor, +20 STA, +13 STR, +14 INT, +10 SPI, +6 AGI), Coif of Elements (Mail Head, 297 Armor, +23 INT, +13 STA, +12 SPI, +7 STR), Ace of Portals
Notes: Arcane Missiles, Curse of Darkmaster (-50 STA/STR for 1 min.), Shadow Portal (Periodically teleports a player into an adjacent room), Shadow Shield (Absorbs 610 damage and deals 30-31 damage to melee attackers)		
DEATH KNIGHT DARKREAVER	62 Elite	Necromantic Band (Ring, Unique, Passive: Restores 5 health every 5 seconds), Spectre's Blade (One-hand Dagger, 40.8 DPS, Passive: +45 Attack Power when fighting Undead), Malicious Axe (Two-hand Axe, 52.9 DPS, +30 STA, Passive: +26 Attack Power), Oblivion's Torch (Wand, 62.5 DPS, +11 INT), Charger's Lost Soul
Notes: Blood Leech (AoE HP drain, heals caster for 3x amount drained), Cleave, Mind Control, Shadow Bolt		
DOCTOR THEOLEN KRASTINOV	60 Elite	Magister's Gloves (Cloth Hands, 52 Armor, +14 SPI, +14 INT, +9 STA), Scholomance Set Items (See Set Items)
Notes: Knock Away, Rend, Increases attack speed at 50% health		
INSTRUCTOR MALICIA	60 Elite	Shadowcraft Bracers (Leather Wrists, 71 Armor, +15 AGI, +7 STA), Scholomance Set Items (See Set Items)
Notes: Call of the Grave (Curse "Bomb" for 2100 damage after 60 sec.), Corruption, Heal, Renew, Slow (-35% attack speed & -60% movement speed)		
JANDICE BAROV	61 Elite	Royal Cap Shoulders (Mail Shoulders, 274 Armor, +13 SPI, +9 INT, +8 STA, Passive: Increases healing done by spells and effects by up to 26), Ghostloom Leggings (Leather Legs, 152 Armor, +18 INT, +13 SPI, +10 STA, Passive: Restores 6 mana every 5 seconds), Darkshade Gloves (Cloth Hands, 55 Armor, +7 INT, +6 STA, +6 SPI, +10 Shadow Resistance, +15 Arcane Resistance), Dreadmist Mantle (Cloth Shoulders, 64 Armor, +15 INT, +14 STA, +9 SPI), Barovian Family Sword (Two-hand Sword, 52.1 DPS, Chance on hit: Deals 30 Shadow damage every 3 seconds for 16 seconds. All damage done is transferred to the caster), Krastinov's Bag of Horrors , Staff of Metanoia (Staff, 53.1 DPS, +15 INT, +13 SPI, +15 STA, Passive: Increases healing done by spells and effects by up to 35.)
Notes: Summons several Illusions of Jandice Barov, Banish, Curse of Blood (increases physical damage received)		
KIRTONOS THE HERALD	60 Elite	Loomguard Armbraces (Mail Wrists, 157 Armor, +7 INT, +6 STA, Passive: Increases healing done by spells and effects by up to 33), Heart of the Fiend (Necklace, +15 SPI, +5 INT, +5 STA), Clutch of Andros (Cloth Waist, 49 Armor, +22 INT, +3 STA, +8 SPI), Stoneform Shoulders (Plate Shoulders, 688 Armor, Passive: Increased Defense +7), Frightalon (One-hand Dagger, 40 DPS, Chance on hit: Lowers all attributes of the target by 10 for 60 seconds), Windreaver Greaves (Mail Feet, 247 Armor, +20 AGI, +7 SPI, +7 STR), Gargoyle Slashers (Leather Hands, 107 Armor, +5 AGI, +10 STR, +12 STA, Passive: Improves your chance to get a critical strike by 1%), Gravestone War Axe (Two-hand Axe, 53.1 DPS, Chance on hit: Diseases target enemy for 55 Nature damage every 12 seconds for 60 seconds), Boots of Valor (Plate Feet, 424 Armor, +20 STA, +8 STR, +4 AGI, +3 SPI)
Notes: Curse of Tongues, Disarm, Pierce Armor (-50% armor for 20 sec.), Shadow Bolt Volley, Swoop (Frontal Cone Damage), Wing Flap (Frontal Cone Knockback), Casts in human form and focuses on melee in gargoyle form		
LADY ILLUCIA BAROV	60 Elite	Scholomance Set Items (See Set Items)
Notes: Curse of Agony (AoE), Dominate Mind (Like Priest Mind Control), Fear, Silence (AoE), Shadow Shock		
LORD ALEXEI BAROV	60 Elite	Lightforge Bracers (Plate Wrists, 261 Armor, +10 STA, +8 SPI, +7 STR, +4 AGI), Scholomance Set Items (See Set Items)
Notes: Immolate, Unholy Aura (AoE 150 Shadow damage per sec.), Veil of Shadow (Curse, reduces effect of healing spells by 75%)		
LOREKEEPER POLKELT	60 Elite	Dreadmist Wraps (Cloth Hands, 52 Armor, +14 SPI, +9 INT, +13 STA), Scholomance Set Items (See Set Items)
Notes: Corrosive Acid (AoE -960 armor), Noxious Catalyst (-88 Nature resist for 2 min.), Volatile Infection (Target deals 540 Nature damage to all nearby allies every 15 sec.)		
MARDUK BLACKPOOL	58 Elite	Ebon Hilt of Marduk (Main-hand Sword, 38.9 DPS, Chance on hit: Corrupts the target, causing 210 damage over 3 seconds), Death Knight Sabatons (Plate Feet, 424 Armor, +11 STR, +11 STA, +11 INT, +9 SPI)
Notes: Cleave, Defiling Aura (decreases Shadow resist by 100), Shadow Shield (absorbs 580 damage and returns damage to attackers), Shadow Bolt Volley		
RAS FROSTWHISPER	62 Elite	Death's Clutch (Leather Shoulders, 131 Armor, +12 INT, +11 SPI, +11 STR, +12 STA), Shadowy Mail Greaves (Mail Feet, 251 Armor, +22 STA, +10 Shadow Resistance), Maelstrom Leggings (Mail Legs, 320 Armor, +6 AGI, +20 SPI, +20 INT, +10 STR), Boneclenched Gauntlets (Plate Hands, 624 Armor, +10 Frost Resistance), Freezing Lich Robes (Cloth Chest, 88 Armor, +15 Frost Resistance, Passive: Increases damage done by Frost spells and effects by up to 43), Frostbite Girdle (Cloth Waist, 98 Armor, +5 STR, +15 AGI, +15 STA, +10 Frost Resistance), Bonechill Hammer (One-hand Mace, 40.6 DPS, Chance on hit: Blasts target for 90 Frost damage), Magister's Mantle (Cloth Shoulders, 64 Armor, +22 INT, +6 SPI, +6 STA), Intricately Runed Shield (Shield, 2121 Armor, 39 Block, +8 STA, Passive: Increases the block value of your shield by 24)
Notes: Chill Nova (AoE, ~675 Frost damage, knockback, 10 sec. movement reduction), Frost Armor, Fear, Freeze (Stun and 149 Frost damage every 3 sec. for 15 sec.), Frost Bolt Volley (AoE)		
RATTLEGORE	61 Elite	Deadwalker Mantle (Cloth Shoulders, 66 Armor, +19 STA, +9 INT, Passive: Increases damage done by Shadow spells and effects by up to 13), Bone Ring Helm (Leather Head, 141 Armor, +6 STR, +30 STA, +6 SPI, +6 INT, +5 AGI), Corpselight Greaves (Plate Feet, 445 Armor, +22 STA, +10 Shadow Resistance), Shadowcraft Boots (Leather Feet, 115 Armor, +21 AGI, +9 STA), Frightskull Shaft (Two-hand Mace, 50.4 DPS, Chance on hit: Deals 8 Shadow damage every 2 seconds for 30 seconds and lowers their STR for the duration of the disease), Rattlecage Buckler (Shield, 2121 Armor, 39 Block, +7 SPI, +12 INT, +7 STA, +7 Shadow Resistance), Bone Golem Shoulders (Mail Shoulders, 274 Armor, +19 AGI, +9 INT, +9 STA), Top Half of Advanced Armorsmithing: Volume II, Viewing Room Key
Notes: Knock Away, Strike, War Stomp		
THE RAVENIAN	60 Elite	Wildheart Belt (Leather Waist, 93 Armor, +17 INT, +10 SPI, +9 STA), Scholomance Set Items (See Set Items)
Notes: Cleave, Knock Away, Sundering Cleave (Frontal Cone version of Sunder Armor), Trample (AoE melee damage)		
VECTUS	60 Elite	Skullsmoke Pants (Cloth Legs, 76 Armor, +20 INT, +20 STA, +10 Fire Resistance, +5 Shadow Resistance), Dark Advisor's Pendant (Necklace, +8 STA, +7 INT, Passive: Increases damage done by Shadow spells and effects by up to 20)
Notes: Blast Wave, Flame Strike		

BEHIND CLOSED DOORS

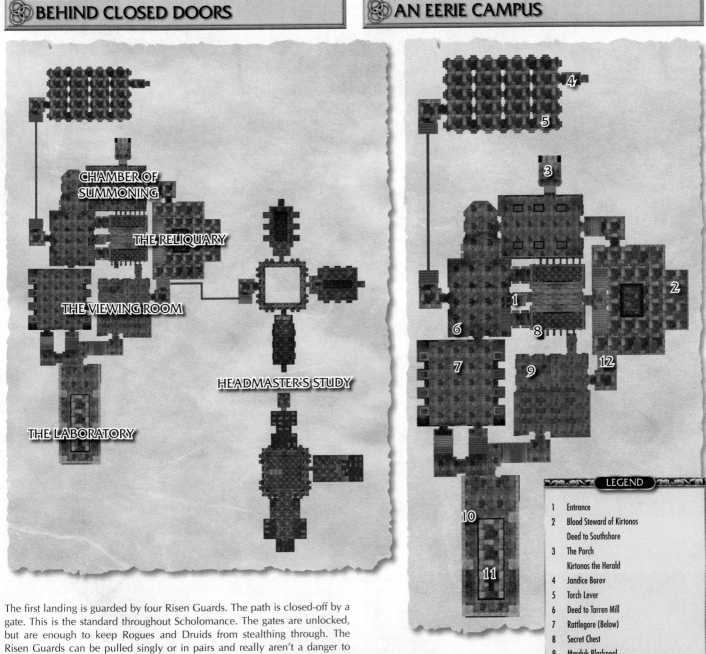

CHAMBER OF SUMMONING

THE RELIQUARY

THE VIEWING ROOM

HEADMASTER'S STUDY

THE LABORATORY

AN EERIE CAMPUS

The first landing is guarded by four Risen Guards. The path is closed-off by a gate. This is the standard throughout Scholomance. The gates are unlocked, but are enough to keep Rogues and Druids from stealthing through. The Risen Guards can be pulled singly or in pairs and really aren't a danger to your party.

GETTING IN

There are three ways to enter Scholomance. A party member with a key, a Rogue with 280 or higher lockpicking, or someone already past the door using the torch can open the door for your party.

The next room gives you an idea of what you'll be facing. Groups of necromancers and spirits litter the room in small groups. The casters have ranged attacks and the spirits can knock you across the room, so it's safer if you pull the enemies up the stairs and back onto the landing. This forces the casters to come around the corner to restore line of sight and keeps the spirits from knocking your party into other groups of enemies. Party members should call out who they are CCing before the fight starts to avoid accidental breaks.

Pull each group up to the landing until the Reliquary is clear. A deed for *Barov Family Fortune* is on a table in the northeast corner. The Blood Steward of Kirtonos is in another corner. This enemy drops the **Blood of Innocents** you need later for *Kirtonos the Herald* (The **Blood of Innocents** can also be dropped by Doctor Theolen Krastinov and Jandice Barov.) The steward has a couple curses and the Paralyzing Poison special attack that is an 8 sec. stun. Have Mages ready to remove the curses and take the steward down.

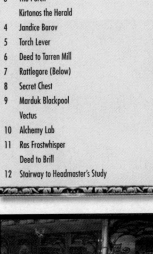

There are two exits to this room. The northern passage reveals a balcony with the Brazier of the Herald. Placing the Blood of Innocents in the brazier summons Kirtonos the Herald and allows you to complete *Kirtonos the Herald*.

Kirtonos the Herald has two forms and each requires a different strategy. Regardless, have your MT gain aggro and place his/her back against the wall. This keeps Kirtonos faced away from the party and prevents the MT from being knocked back. While in human form, Kirtonos uses his caster abilities. This isn't a horrible threat, just make sure to have a Mage or Druid clear Curse of Tongues if it's on a healer.

Kirtonos periodically shapeshifts into his gargoyle form at which point his attacks become melee-oriented. If you keep you MT highest on the threat list, this becomes a non-issue since he'll be focusing on the best target for this type of ability.

The doorway west leads to a large room of enemies. Pull the Risen Guards and Necrofiends patrolling before setting foot in the room. With the patrols dead, clear the right side and move into the room.

The room can be cleared as normal. Pull each group and CC the casters. Be wary of the Spectral Tutors. They split into several non-elite enemies and later reform several times. These need to be killed with AoEs as soon as they split or your healer will end up with unwanted attention.

The east passage takes you to the Viewing Room. The way is closed and you need a key to continue on, so head north instead. The Chamber of Summoning lies through the gate and around a corner; there are several groups of enemy casters and spirits waiting as well. Pull the patrolling enemies as they move away from the stationary groups. When all the patrollers have been dispatched, begin pulling the groups. Have your puller duck around a corner to force enemy casters to come to you. This keeps your melee members from running into the room and potentially pulling more enemies.

With the room clear, you now have three choices on how to proceed. Take the passage west first; it descends into the catacombs. Follow the stairs until you come to a large room. There are several groups of undead milling around inside. Casters and ranged party members should be on the stairs while melee fight on the bottom landing. Pull one group of enemies at a time.

NOT DEAD YET!

Death didn't stop the enemies before, and this time is no different. Watch out for Reanimated Corpses. They rise approximately 10 sec. after they were killed. Risen Aberrations are immune to non-Holy magic. Plagued Ghouls spew a visible poison cloud when they die that deals ~350 Nature damage per sec. Evacuate the area immediately since the fog can weaken the entire party and lasts for several seconds.

Have your party follow along the right wall once it's clear. Take out the enemies in front of the door on the east side before using the torch on the south wall. This opens the way to Jandice Barov.

Jandice has several tricks up her sleeve, the deadliest of which allows her to create multiple copies of herself to aggravate the party. They must be targeted and attacked individually (AoEs won't work) and a Rogue or Fury-specced Warrior is perfect for this task. However, the other option is to simply focus fire on Jandice and ignore the spectres. Her other two spells are Banish and Curse of Blood. When she falls, search her corpse for **Krastinov's Bag of Horrors**. Before leaving the area, find a torch in the southwest corner of Jandice's room. It opens a gate barring access to a treasure chest near the Viewing Room. Ascend the ramp back to where you were and continue.

Before you take the passage to the south, grab the deed in the southwestern corner for *Barov's Family Fortune*. It opens into The Great Ossuary and is filled with Plagued Hatchlings and casters. Pull small groups of the hatchlings into the previous room and around the corner so they have to come to you. If you have any party members who aren't level 60, you'll need to clear the entire room instead of only the left side. Parties with a Priest have a second option. Mind Control the Scholomance Handlers and use their AoE spells to kill off the Plagued Hatchlings.

THE FAST WAY DOWN

There are several openings along the walls. Stay away from them. They lead into the next room and will land you on top of several enemies. Also, be very careful about targeting when near the holes as a stray arrow down one can bring dozens of enemies onto your party.

Continue down the twisting passage to the next room. Your party needs to remain on the steps while the puller brings enemies to you one at a time. The enemies have AoE attacks, so the tank should stay at the bottom of the stairs while the rest of the party remains on the first landing.

Pull Rattlegore when the Risen Constructs are clear. Rattlegore hits very hard. Rattlegore has melee-oriented abilities, so keep your casters well back from the fray; he can nearly kill a cloth-wearer in a single shot. Have the MT face Rattlegore away from the main party and bring him down by reducing his armor for melee and using solid damage from casters. When Rattlegore falls, search his body for the **Viewing Room Key**.

Paladins and Shamans have class specific quests to act on once the room's clear. Place the Divination Scryer in the center of the room and retreat to the southeast corner. The Spirits spawn in waves. Paladins can Judge Seals to affect each wave most effectively. Using the correct Judgment on the mob stuns it and reduces its health by roughly 10%. If there are other mobs nearby, the Judgment will hit them as well, so focus on tightly-knit groups of mobs. Each wave of spirits is followed by an "Aspect." They're slightly tougher versions of the spirits themselves, with frequently better drops.

WAVE	SEAL TO BE JUDGED
1	Seal of Wisdom
2	Seal of Justice
3	Seal of Righteousness
4	Seal of Light

The first wave is comprised of many non-elite ghosts that spawn on top of you. AoE these and have your casters start drinking as soon as the last one is dead. The ghosts in the second wave are elite melee attackers. Pull and shackle to keep from getting overwhelmed.

The third wave is the most difficult as many of the groups are linked. Pull the ghosts from the northeast corner to get the fewest. The fourth wave consists of elite casters. Have your priest give everyone shadow resistance and defeat the enemies.

Death Knight Darkreaver spawns when the final wave is killed. This knight can be the death of a party caught unawares. Darkreaver can Mind Control a member of your party, so be ready to have a Priest dispel it or Polymorph that player. However, it's Blood Leech that you need to be fearful of. It's an AoE life drain that heals Darkreaver for three times the amount drained. That can prolong the battle considerably and everyone should except the MT should stay well back to prevent this from affecting the entire group. When he dies, Paladins use the Charger's Lost Soul at the Divination Scryer to get the **Charger's Redeemed Soul** and complete *Judgment and Redemption*. Shamans need only loot his head for *The Darkreaver Menace*.

Move back to the large room and take the eastern passage. This leads you into a room directly beneath the entrance walkway. Pull the patrolling Necrofiends and Risen Warriors before pulling the stationary groups. With the room clear, move to the south wall and open the Viewing Room Door.

HAVE TO GO TO WORK?

If a party member has left or disconnected, now is a good time to get a replacement. The person needs only enter Scholomance and jump off the landing to join the party. Having a Warlock eliminates the need for this, of course.

The Viewing Room is full of non-aggressive students. Speaking to any of them will bring the entire room upon your party. Move quickly through the room to the south wall and through the passage. Marduk and Vectus are standing on the raised platform. To clear the way to Marduk and Vectus, pull the students one group at a time into an adjacent room. Once cleared, Vectus and Marduk can be handled separately. Vectus is a soft target with Fire-based spells. Set an interrupt order to negate his strength and bring him down quickly. Marduk has a passive effect (Defiling Aura) that affects anyone within range and his Shadow Shield damages all those that attack in melee. Have the MT keep him locked in place and burn him down from range.

The passage leads to Ras Frostwhisper. Clear the room by pulling the groups into the hallway one at a time. Duck around the corner to break line of sight (LoS) and force the enemies to come to you. When Ras is alone, rest to full and charge in. Give the tank a few seconds to gather aggro before joining the fight.

Frostwhisper has a tome of spells at his disposal. The big threats are his Fear, Freeze, Chill Nova, and Frost Bolt Volley; Frost Armor isn't too dangerous. He can deal serious damage quickly. Designate an interrupt order to decrease the damage and have the MT keep him facing away from the main party. When you see him begin to cast a spell, interrupt him with anything available: Kick, Pummel, Silence, Counterspell, etc.

In order to complete the quest *The Lich, Ras Frostwhisper*, you must first use the book provided by the quest giver to turn him into his human form. Designate one person to do this and start his transformation as soon as the fight begins; it takes a while to cast. If you get interrupted, try again. You won't be able to complete this quest if you kill Ras while he's in his Lich form.

After killing Frostwhisper, there are a few things to do. Druids should grab the Embalming Fluid and Warlocks should set loose their Imp in a Jar. The Alchemy Lab in the room is a wonderful place for Alchemists (obviously). This is where they'll create Flasks. With these objectives completed, move back through the Viewing Room and take the east passage to the Headmaster's Study.

THE HEADMASTER'S STUDY

BALCONY & 2ND FLOOR

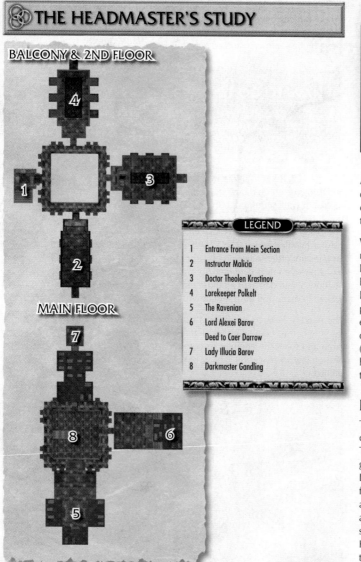

MAIN FLOOR

LEGEND

1	Entrance from Main Section
2	Instructor Malicia
3	Doctor Theolen Krastinov
4	Lorekeeper Polkelt
5	The Ravenian
6	Lord Alexei Barov
	Deed to Caer Darrow
7	Lady Illucia Barov
8	Darkmaster Gandling

With so much of the student body destroyed, it's time to take the fight to the administration of this unholy school. The Headmaster's Study consists of six rooms on two floors with a large room connecting them in the center. The order in which you clear each room is not important. The important part is that each room must be cleansed before the Headmaster will show himself.

LOREKEEPER POLKELT

Lorekeeper Polkelt resides in the northern room on the upper level. He's guarded by several Unstable Corpses and Diseased Ghouls. The puller should shoot each group and then jump over the railing into the center room. This forces the enemies to shamble slowly over to the stairs before they can descend after the puller. This time can be used to CC or kill the enemies.

Avoid clumping the enemies and killing them with AoE attacks unless you can do it from range. The Diseased Ghouls emit a poison gas cloud on death that can kill even the stoutest warrior in several seconds. If multiple ghouls die at the same time, party members in the cloud are doomed.

When the room is clear and your party rested to full, pull Polkelt. As with the minions, have the puller jump off the railing. Instead of attacking Polkelt as he runs around the stairs, let him get to the lower level and have your warrior hold him there. This way, your party can open fire from the safety of the upper ledge. If Polkelt breaks away from the warrior and runs up the stairs to your party, jump down to the warrior. This keeps Polkelt, who is a melee-based enemy, out of range of anyone but your tank and nullifies nearly all of his damage potential. Polkelt's spells are all short-ranged—even Corrosive Acid (AoE). Volatile Infection can ruin a clumped party and using this tactic keeps him in tight with your MT. Anyone infected should separate from the rest of the party to keep the damage to a minimum.

DOCTOR THEOLEN KRASTINOV

The eastern room on the upper floor is called the Hall of the Damned. Doctor Theolen Krastinov conducts his gruesome experiments in this room. Let your tank engage Krastinov for a few seconds before joining the fight and back up against a wall. Keeping aggro on your tank makes this a simple and straightforward fight until Krastinov reaches 50% health. Once  this occurs, his attack speed increases dramatically and your MT will incur some serious damage. Keep up the heals and this won't be too much trouble. Keep Krastinov facing away from your party to make the tanks job easier. When the Doctor has been vanquished, search the room for the **Remains of Eva Sarkhoff** and **Lucian Sarkhoff**. Burn these to complete *Doctor Theolen Krastinov, The Butcher.*

INSTRUCTOR MALICIA

The Coven is a greater threat. The Scholomance Occultists of the southern room on the upper floor are commanded by Instructor Malicia. Pull the Occultists into the main room in small groups. CC all but one and focus fire on a single target at a time. When the Occultists are gravely wounded, they change forms into Dark Shades. Dark Shades are immune to all physical damage and taunt. When an Occultist changes to a Dark Shade, all magic users in the party (including healers) need to bring it down quickly.

Once all the students are dead, engage Malicia. She has a variety of spells at her disposal: Slow, Heal, Renew, Corruption, and the deadly Call of the Grave. Make sure to interrupt all of her Heals using an interrupt order and have Mages or Druids remove Call of the Grave on everyone cursed. As before, allow your tank a few seconds to gain aggro before joining in the fight. Keep your party members' health high and keep her facing away from the party. She has few tricks up her sleeves and won't be a genuine threat to your party if you're careful.

LADY ILLUCIA BAROV

Risen Bonewarders stand guard in the Shadow Vault. The northern room on the lower floor is home to Lady Illucia Barov. Pull the Bonewarders into the center room one at a time and destroy them. When the way to Illucia is clear, shield your tank and send him in. Give him a few seconds to turn Illucia away from the party and establish aggro. Lady Illucia can Mind Control a party member. Make sure to Polymorph them or dispel the Dominate Mind spell as soon as possible. With two AoEs (Curse of Agony and Silence), she can be a danger. Destroying Illucia quickly is the key to winning this fight.

ALEXEI BAROV

The Barov Family Vault, eastern room on the lower floor, holds one of the more difficult fights. Pull the first pair of skeletons and dispose of them to clear the way to Lord Alexei Barov and his bodyguards. The green liquid on the lower section of the room is poisonous and foolish to fight in. Pull Alexei and his guards to the upper portion for the fight.

Both of the skeletons hit very hard and are not as dangerous as Alexei. CC them using either shackle, or a secondary tank. Hunter and Warlock pets work very well as secondary tanks. They can survive long enough for your party to focus fire on one of the skeletons and kill it. Paladins should feel free to use Turn Undead on the minions to CC them almost indefinitely and Hunters can use Freezing Traps before the battle to take one Skeleton out of the battle for a bit if necessary. If you don't have enough CC, then have your main tank pull Alexei away from the party and hold him while the party kills the skeletons one at a time. This increases the aggro on the tank instead of endangering the healer early. The dangerous spell from Barov is Veil of Shadow: a curse that decreases the effect of healing spells by 75%. Unholy Aura is an AoE that inflicts a Shadow damage DoT to all within range. When Alexei is dead, take the last deed for *Barov Family Fortune* from the lower area.

THE RAVENIAN

The southern room on the lower level is home to The Ravenian. Splintered Skeletons wander the room as well, but they can be pulled and disposed of without trouble. Allow your tank to engage The Ravenian for several seconds before the rest of the party joins. He hits extremely hard and fast, but is a close-range enemy. Although he's generally melee-oriented, The Ravenian has an AoE damage ability (Trample) and a armor reducing cone ability (Sundering Cleave). Keep him facing away from the party and retain aggro on the tank. Should The Ravenian charge another party member, cease fire until the tank regains aggro and has pulled The Ravenian back into position.

SCHOOL IS IN SESSION

Before you kill the final of the six bosses, make sure all your party is in the same room and not in the center room. When the final boss dies, Darkmaster Gandling spawns in the center room. Rest up before engaging him.

DARKMASTER GANDLING

When the fight begins, your tank should hold Gandling on the lower floor while the ranged members of your party make their way up the stairs. This keeps them out of quick range of Gandling, but within healing and blasting range themselves. Gandling has a ton of hit points and won't go down easily.

To make matters worse, he periodically casts Shadow Portal and teleports a party member into one of the six rooms. The party member will be locked in the room until they can defeat the enemies that spawn or Gandling is killed. Determining who will take over essential duties (tanking and healing) if the wrong person is teleported away can prevent a lot of panic during the fight. If you've cleared the Study quickly enough, none of the bosses should repop. Quickly kill the enemies that have spawned in the room into which you've been teleported and rejoin the battle against Gandling.

Have an interrupt order in place to mitigate some of his damage if he begins casting Arcane Missiles. It's channeled and is easy to interrupt. He will also weaken your melee players with Curse of the Darkmaster and Shadow Shield. Have a Mage or Druid remove the Curse of the Darkmaster immediately! If your party has multiple healers, they should use smaller heals more frequently to spread the aggro between them and help the tank keep Gandling's attention. Bring justice to the head of Scholomance and collect your winnings.

SHADOWFANG KEEP

Played & Written by: Ken "Birk" Schmidt of <Blame the Mage> on Perenolde

Horde players approaching level 20 have likely discovered Silverpine Forest and undertaken many quests revolving around a renegade Archmage of the Kirin Tor named Arugal. His stronghold, known as Shadowfang Keep, is located south of The Sepulcher. This Archmage has populated the keep with Worgen and Worg, while the keep's once-human guards and servants have been cursed to roam the grounds as spirits, maintaining it for a new master.

DUNGEON INFORMATION

Name	Shadowfang Keep
Location	Silverpine Forest
Territory	Horde
Quests	Horde, two Class-specific quests
Suggested Levels	20-26
Primary Enemy Type	Humanoid/Undead
Time to Complete	2-3 hours

OF WORGEN AND WANDERING SPIRITS

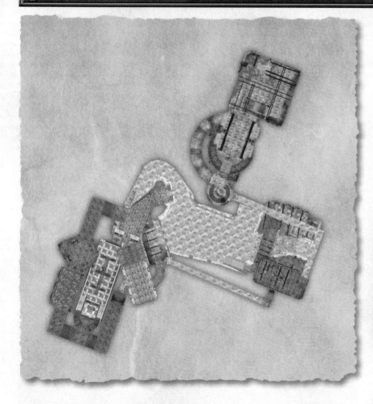

Shadowfang Keep overlooks the Great Sea in the southern part of Silverpine Forest, near Pyrewood Village. Once a human outpost, it has been occupied by the host of Arugal, a blend of Worgen and human spirits.

The entrance to the keep is at the end of a path that diverges from the entrance to Pyrewood Village, then runs above it. Alliance characters have little to fear from the residents of Pyrewood; in fact, there are a few vendors inside the village's smithy. Members of the Horde need only stay outside of the village for a relatively safe trip inside the Keep.

BRING A SKINNER AND DEBUFF REMOVAL SKILLS

Don't expect to find any mining or herb nodes inside Shadowfang Keep, but there's an abundance of skinnable enemies. Don't let this treasure trove of leather go to waste!

You can also expect to face a host of debuffs, including Curses, Magic and Diseases. If you want to make your trip through this world dungeon more manageable, bring classes that can remove these maladies.

QUESTS

QUEST NAME	QUEST GIVER	QUEST GIVER LOCATION	QUEST RECEIVER	QUEST RECEIVER LOCATION	CHAIN?	MAX EXPERIENCE
Deathstalkers in Shadowfang	High Executor Hadrec	The Sepulcher	High Executor Hadrec	The Sepulcher	No	2000
REWARD: Ghostly Mantle (Cloth Shoulder, 31 Armor, +5 INT/+5 SPI)						
The Book of Ur	Keeper Bel'dugur	The Undercity	Keeper Bel'dugur	The Undercity	No	2000
REWARD: Grizzled Boots (Leather Feet, 63 Armor, +2 STR/+7 STA) or Steel-clasped Bracers (Mail Wrist, 85 Armor, +6 STA/+1 SPI)						
Arugal Must Die	Dalar Dreamweaver	The Sepulcher	Dalar Dreamweaver	The Sepulcher	No	3300
REWARD: Seal of Sylvanas (Ring, +3 STR/+8 STA)						

DEATHSTALKERS IN SHADOWFANG

Quest Level	Obtained at level 18
Location	The Sepulcher
Quest Giver	High Executor Hadrec
Goal	Locate two Deathstalkers
Max Experience Gained	2000 XP
Reward	Ghostly Mantle (Cloth Shoulder, 31 Armor, +5 INT/+5 SPI)

The first Deathstalker is found inside a cell under the guard of Rethilgore, the Cell Keeper. Speak with Deathstalker Adamant and he unlocks the door to the courtyard. The second Deathstalker, Vincent, is in the courtyard, near the portcullis. Speak with him to complete the quest.

THE BOOK OF UR

Quest Level	Obtained at level 16
Location	Undercity
Quest Giver	Keeper Bel'dugur
Goal	Retrieve The Book of Ur
Max Experience Gained	2000 XP
Reward	Grizzled Boots (Leather Feet, 63 Armor, +2 STR/+7 STA) or Steel-clasped Bracers (Mail Wrist, 85 Armor, +6 STA/+1 SPI)

After defeating Fenrus the Devourer, search the shelves in the same room for this book.

ARUGAL MUST DIE

Quest Level	Obtained at level 18
Location	Silverpine Forest
Quest Giver	Dalar Dawnweaver
Goal	Kill Archmage Arugal
Max Experience Gained	3300 XP
Reward	Seal of Sylvanas (Ring, +3 STR/+8 STA)

Arugal spins his plans deep inside Shadowfang Keep, guarded by a host of Worgen, spirits, and a nasty Worg named Fenrus the Devourer. Your task is to battle through these guards and kill Arugal; however, this Archmage has a few tricks at his disposal.

CLASS-SPECIFIC QUESTS

QUEST NAME	QUEST GIVER	QUEST GIVER LOCATION	QUEST RECEIVER	QUEST RECEIVER LOCATION	CHAIN?	MAX EXPERIENCE
The Test of Righteousness	Jordan Stillwell	Ironforge	Jordan Stillwell	Ironforge	Yes *	
*NOTE: This is only one part of the Paladin Quest.						
The Orb of Soran'ruk	Doan Karhan	The Barrens	Doan Karhan	The Barrens	Yes*	
*NOTE: This is only one part of the Warlock Quest.						

THE TEST OF RIGHTEOUSNESS (PALADIN ONLY)

Quest Level	Obtained at level 20
Location	Ironforge
Quest Giver	Jordan Stilwell
Goal	Retrieve Jordan's Smithing Hammer
Reward	Jordan's Smithing Hammer

Only one of the four components required to complete this stage of *The Test of Righteousness* is found inside Shadowfang Keep. After Sorcerer Ashcrombe opens the door to the Keep's courtyard, look for the stables directly across from the doorway. Jordan's Smithing Hammer rests on a crate just inside the door.

THE ORB OF SORAN'RUK (WARLOCK ONLY)

Quest Level	Obtained at level 20
Location	The Barrens
Quest Giver	Doan Karhan
Goal	Retrieve a Soran'ruk Fragment
Reward	Large Soran'ruk Fragment

A visit to Shadowfang Keep fulfills only half of this quest. In order to complete this quest, you must also visit Blackfathom Deeps. To collect the Large Soran'ruk Fragment, locate Shadowfang Darksouls inside Shadowfang Keep and eliminate them until one drops a Fragment.

⊛ ENEMIES IN SHADOWFANG KEEP

ENEMIES IN THE KEEP

NPC	LEVEL
Arugal's Voidwalker	24/25
Notes: Dark Offering	
Bleak Worg	18 Elite
Notes: Beast, Wavering Will	
Fel Steed	20 Elite
Notes: Undead, Fel Stomp	
Haunted Servitor	20 Elite
Notes: Undead, Haunting Spirits	
Lupine Horror	24 Elite
Notes: Undead, Spawns Lupine Delusions	
Slavering Worg	18 Elite
Notes: Beast	
Shadow Charger	20 Elite
Notes: Undead	
Shadowfang Darksoul	21 Elite
Notes: Humanoid, Befuddlement, immune to Shadow effects	
Shadowfang Glutton	21 Elite
Notes: Humanoid, Blood Tap	

NPC	LEVEL
Shadowfang Moonwalker	20 Elite
Notes: Humanoid, Anti-magic Shield	
Shadowfang Ragetooth	24 Elite
Notes: Humanoid, Wild Rage	
Shadowfang Whitescalp	18/19 Elite
Notes: Humanoid, Frost Armor, immune to Frost/Ice effects	
Shadowfang Wolfguard	20 Elite
Notes: Humanoid, Patrols with Wolfguard Worg	
Son of Arugal	24/25 Elite
Notes: Humanoid, Arugal's Gift	
Tormented Officer	24 Elite
Notes: Undead, Forsaken Skills	
Wailing Guardsman	21/22 Elite
Notes: Undead, Screams from the Past	

WARDENS OF SHADOWFANG

LEADERS OF SHADOWFANG KEEP

NPC	LEVEL	FREQUENT DROP(S)
ARCHMAGE ARUGAL	26 Elite	Belt of Arugal (Cloth Waist, 26 Armor, +2 AGI/+10 INT/+3 SPI), Robes of Arugal (Cloth Chest, 46 Armor, +3 AGI/+5 STA/+9 INT/+10 SPI), Meteor Shard (Dagger, 18.3 DPS, Chance on Hit: Blasts a target for 35 Fire damage)
Notes: Void Bolt, Thundershock, Shadow Port		
BARON SILVERLAINE	24 Elite	Baron's Scepter (Main-Hand Mace, 12.7 DPS, +4 STR), Silverlaine's Family Seal (Ring, +7STR/+3 STA)
Notes: Veil of Shadow		
COMMANDER SPRINGVALE	24 Elite	Arced War Axe (Two-Handed Axe, 17.6 DPS, +6 STR/+6 STA), Commander's Crest (Shield, 623 Armor, 13 Block, +6 STR/+3 STA/+3 SPI)
Notes: Hammer of Justice, Divine Shield, Holy Light		
DEATHSWORN CAPTAIN	25 Elite	Haunting Blade (Two-Handed Sword, 17.5 DPS, +9 SPI), Phantom Armor (Mail Chest, 201 Armor, +3 STR/+11 STA/+5 SPI)
Notes: Rare Spawn, Cleave, Hamstring		
FENRUS THE DEVOURER	25 Elite	Fenrus' Hide (Cloak, 20 Armor, +4 AGI/+2 STA), Black Wolf Bracers (Leather Wrist, 38 Armor, +5 STA)
Notes: Toxic Saliva		
ODO THE BLINDWATCHER	24 Elite	Girdle of the Blindwatcher (Leather Waist, 49 Armor, +3 STA/+5 INT), Odo's Ley Staff (Staff, 21.7 DPS, +5 STA/+12 SPI)
Notes: Linked with Vile Bat and Blood Seeker, Howling Rage		
RAZORCLAW THE BUTCHER	22 Elite	Bloody Apron (Cloth Chest, 37 armor, +8 STA), Butcher's Slicer (One-Hand Sword, 11.6 DPS, +2 STR/+2 STA), Butcher's Cleaver (One-Hand Axe, 16.2 DPS, +5 STR/+2 AGI)
Notes: Butcher Drain		
RETHILGORE	20 Elite	Rugged Spaulders (Leather Shoulder, 55 Armor)
Notes: Soul Drain		
SEVER	25 Elite	Abomination Skin Leggings (Cloth Legs, 37 Armor, +8 INT, +7 STA, Equip: Increases damage and healing done by magical spells and effects by up to 9), The Axe of Severing (Two-Hand Axe, 21.0 DPS, +14 STR)
Notes: Intimidating Roar and Diseased Spit		
WOLF MASTER NANDOS	25 Elite	Feline Mantle (Cloth Shoulder, 34 Armor, +2 AGI/+10 INT/+3 SPI), Wolfmaster Cape (Cloak, 20 Armor, +4 AGI/+2 STA)
Notes: Summons Worg		

SUPERNATURAL ENCOUNTERS

RUN AHEAD QUICKLY!

After appearing in the Keep's interior, run quickly ahead to catch Arugal taunting the downed Deathstalker, Vincent.

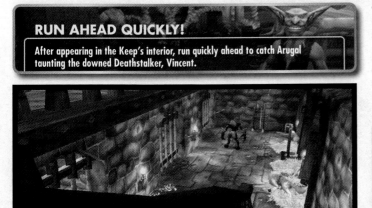

A portcullis blocks access to the courtyard, leaving a doorway to the right as the only direction in which to travel. A Bleak Worg and a Shadowfang Whitescalp are just inside the doorway, and more of each wait beyond them. The Whitescalps use Frost Armor, which works the same as the Mage spell of the same name. Wavering Will slows down any character afflicted with it. It impacts casting speed, attack speed and movement.

After a few encounters with Whitescalps and Bleak Worgs, look for a descending staircase leading to a small dungeon, and the first encounter against a named enemy. However, before you rush in to take him on, try to pull the single Worgen under stairs. It may not be visible initially, but it's there and you don't

want to tackle it, the named, and the Worgs waiting nearby at the same time. Rethilgore's Soul Drain is a nasty stun, so be prepared to remove it the moment anyone's hit by it.

If you want to continue your trek into Shadowfang Keep, you must take out Rethilgore and free one of his charges behind the cell doors. If you're with the Horde, free Deathstalker Adamant, then speak with him in his cell. Sorcerer Ashcrombe, in another cell, opens the door for any Alliance groups in Shadowfang Keep.

COURTYARD

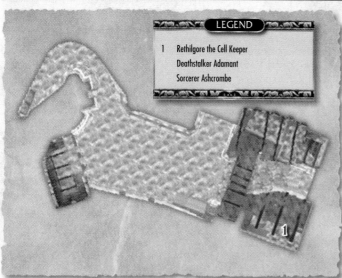

LEGEND

1   Rethilgore the Cell Keeper

     Deathstalker Adamant

     Sorcerer Ashcrombe

When enough of the courtyard is cleared, and you have the proper quest, speak with the second Deathstalker, Vincent. He's on the ground near the portcullis. Stabled horses, known as Fel Steeds and Shadow Chargers, are on the opposite side of courtyard from Vincent. For questing Paladins, the hammer sought rests on a crate just inside the doorway.

A host of new enemies appears in the courtyard beyond the portcullis. Shadowfang Moonwalkers, Slavering Worg and the first undead encountered, Haunted Servitors, patrol the area. Watch for a green glow from the Moonwalkers' hands; this signifies the appearance of their Anti-Magic Shield. When these Worgen are surrounded by a green glow, don't bother using any magic against them. Anyone afflicted by the Haunting Spirits curse used by Haunted Servitors should expect random spirits to appear and attack. The good news is that a single hit dispels these spirits. The bad news is that the curse tends to go off at inopportune times, such as when stealthed or in the midst of a battle.

KITCHEN AND DINING AREA

LEGEND

1   Razorclaw the Butcher

2   Baron Silverlaine

3   Commander Springvale

4   Odo the Blindwatcher

5   Deathsworn Captain

With the courtyard cleared, look for a doorway leading down into a kitchen area. Eliminate the Haunted Servitors outside the prep area, then prepare for another encounter with a named Worgen. Pull Razorclaw the Butcher into the now-empty room to make the battle easier.

THE HIGH ROAD

If you skip the door down to the dining area, you take the floor above the dining area and miss out on at least two good drops. It's worth your time to fight through the dining area!

The dining room is occupied by Shadowfang Gluttons, Haunted Servitors and Baron Silverlaine. Baron Silverlaine's ability, Veil of Shadow, reduces healing effects by 75%, so don't let it linger on any member of the group.

Take the stairs behind the Baron up and then to the left. Turning right at the top of the stairs takes you to a room filled with undead and, eventually, back to the ramp leading back down to the courtyard.

WATCH COMMANDER

Shadowfang Darksouls appear for the first time in the short hallway above the dining area. These are the enemies that drop the Large Soran'ruk Fragment needed by Warlocks. The other new enemies to watch for are the Shadowfang Wolfguards who have long patrols through this area with their companion Wolfguard Worgen. Do not hurry ahead into the next area until after dealing with the patrolling Wolfguard and accompanying Worgen.

A room filled with more Undead is at the end of the hallway and up a short flight of stairs. The Haunted Servitors are no different from the ones faced previously, but the Wailing Guardsmen must be dealt with carefully. Their special skill, Screams from the Past, is an Area of Effect Silence. Keep spellcasters well back, and don't take on too many of

these guards at once. They have a knack for timing Screams from the Past to keep parties silenced for long periods if you face more than one at a time. If there's a Priest in the group, keep them back and have them Dispel the Screams while remaining out of range.

Commander Springvale, the named enemy in the room, stands behind a table just to left as you enter. The Commander was a Paladin during his life, and retains many of those skills. He uses Hammer of Justice during the battle, and resorts to Divine Shield as his health meter is diminished.

BATTLEMENTS

After clearing the remaining enemies from the room with Commander Springvale, take the stairs that lead up to the battlements. The first stretch of the battlements means more encounters with Wailing Guards and the, likely hated by now, Screams of the Past skill.

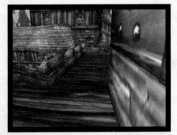

OVER THE EDGE

If you jump over the wall of the battlements away from the courtyard (which is visible while high on the wall) you land outside of the keep, and zone out of the instanced portion of this World Dungeon. It's a big enough drop that you should expect to take some damage from the fall.

At the end of the battlements, take the wooden staircase up and around to a bat aviary, and its trio of guards. Don't be fooled if one of the three sits alone in a corner. All three enemies, including the Worgen named Odo the Blindwatcher, are linked. Disturb one of them, and all three react. The Vile Bat uses a powerful dive attack, and the Blood Seeker drains life, but the greatest danger from this encounter is facing three elites at once. Use Sheep, or Hibernate (if a druid is along) to make this fight manageable.

Beyond Odo and his bats is another run atop one of the keep's walls, and a new type of Undead known as Tormented Officers. They use a powerful curse called Forsaken Skills to reduce any afflicted party member's skill with random (and incredibly specific) weapons and spells. The overall curse lasts five minutes, but the curses it spawns all last one minute. Multiple curses can appear on the same character if you don't remove the main curse. The other noteworthy appearance in this area is the rarely-spawning Deathsworn Captain, who often drops an excellent breastplate.

WORGEN NESTING AREA

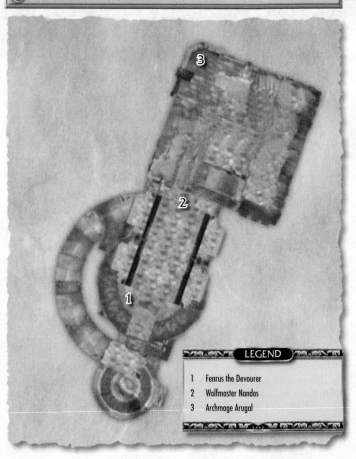

LEGEND

1	Fenrus the Devourer
2	Wolfmaster Nandos
3	Archmage Arugal

Three new lupine enemies make their first appearance in this tower. When their health gets low, Shadowfang Ragetooth use Wild Rage to increase the amount of damage they inflict. The ghostly Lupine Horrors summon Lupine Delusions in the midst of battle. When one of these Delusions appears, attack it quickly as a single hit is enough to dispel it. The hulking Sons of Arugal enjoy sharing the Gift of Arugal, a Curse that inflicts an enormous amount of Shadow damage over time.

Navigating through this area is a bit tricky as the path seems to double back on itself. Keep following the stairs though this area and you should make it through with relative ease.

The next spiral staircase is lightly defended, but the fight waiting at the end makes up for it. Fenrus the Devourer has a nasty bite and a large pool of health. After you manage to defeat him, Arugal appears and spawns Voidwalkers that use an ability called Dark Offering to heal each other.

Victory in these two battles opens the gate that Fenrus was guarding. Follow the stairs up, then go through the spot where Arugal appeared after the defeat of Fenrus. One final spiral stairway leads to Wolf Master Nandos and his pack of one Bleak Worg, Wolfguard Worg, Slavering Worg and Lupine Horror. The four Worg are linked, but Wolf Master Nandos won't join the fray until disturbed, or all four Worg are killed. You must work quickly to eliminate Nandos. If given enough time, he begins to summon a new pack of Worg. Killing Nandos opens the doors to Arugal's chambers.

FINAL CHAMBER

Between you and the final battle with Arugal are three Sons of Arugal. There's a broken ledge that rings the interior walls of this final chamber. It's narrow (a few hops are required to make it around the room). It's tempting to run up a gravelly ramp to reach Arugal and bypass the Sons of Arugal. This is a trap of sorts.

Arugal has a few skills, including Shadow Port. He may start the battle on the side of the room where he first appears, but during the battle he teleports across the room to the landing where your group entered. If you skipped the Sons of Arugal before engaging the Archmage, they are now between your party and your most dangerous foe. Arugal's Void Bolts are deadly from a distance, and likely outdamage anything you can throw back at him.

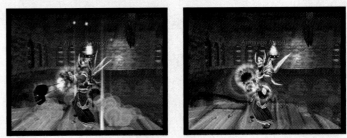

Pull the Sons of Arugal individually up the stairs before facing Arugal. Two at a time shouldn't be a problem for a group that's survived to this point, but there's no need to take chances this close to the end. After dealing with all three, take the time to position your group for the battle against Arugal. Leave spellcasters on the ground so they don't need to move as much when Arugal teleports between platforms. You have the option to leave one group member near the door where you entered the room to cut down on the amount of time Arugal is free to fire away with spells (the time required for the melee members of the party to run between platforms). The previously mentioned Void Bolts are complemented by a short range skill, Thundershock, but a well-prepared, and informed, group should be able to eliminate Arugal in short order.

After crushing Arugal and his supernatural followers, report back to the Sepulcher with the news. With Arugal's threat removed, the Undercity's Deathstalkers are free to scout elsewhere, and continue the search for other, possibly more dangerous incursions into their home soil. As always, the danger of the Scourge lurks, and all must be wary.

THE STOCKADES

Played & Written by: Michael "Kayal" Lummis of <Dovrani> on Kirin Tor

There's corruption in the heart of Stormwind. Those loyal to the people and the crown have tried to lock it away in the darkness beneath the city, but evil festers and grows in such places. One of the city jails, called simply "The Stockade", has been overrun by its prisoners. Primarily those loyal to the Defias, these evil folks have murdered some of the guards and chased out the others. They're in full control now, and it's all that the Warden can do to keep them from spilling into the city. You and other good adventurers are needed to quell this rebellion and stop the Defias by any means possible.

DUNGEON INFORMATION

Location	Stormwind City
Quests	Alliance
Region	Alliance
Suggested Levels	24-29
Group Allowed	5 to Quest, 10 to Raid
Primary Enemies	Humanoids Only
Time to Complete	1-1.5 Hours

GETTING TO THE STOCKADE

Finding the Stockade is easy. Travel to Stormwind City and bind at an inn. Following that, gather a group and form at the large building between the Park and the Mage's Quarter. There is certainly time to collect the local quests from the city, which as discussed later, but more distant quests should be gathered ahead of time (there are additional Stockade quests in the Wetlands, Redridge Mountains, and Duskwood). Going into the blue portal at the bottom of the fortified building zones your group into the formal instance, and that's where the fun begins.

WHO TO BRING

The Stockade is quite small allowing a quick run through; it's also forgiving about the type of group entering the area. It's possible to try non-traditional groups and still be successful without much adaptation. Thus, tank groups, DPS parties, and so forth are perfectly fine. The humanoid base of the area makes Sap a very successful CC type, and any Rogues in the group are certainly able to add a great deal to a fight. Of course, Mages have their fun as well. CCing in this dungeon is easier than usual, and the massive prevalence of melee targets ensures that pulls are fairly predictable.

POSSIBLE GROUP MAKEUP

Tank	Warrior, Druid, Paladin
CC	Rogue, Mage
DPS	Rogue, Hunter, Mage, Warlock
Healer	Priest, Shaman, Druid, Paladin
Free Slot	Anything at all

QUESTS FOR STOCKADES

ALLIANCE QUESTS

QUEST	QUEST GIVER	QUEST GIVER LOCATION	QUEST RECEIVER	QUEST RECEIVER LOCATION	CHAIN?	MAX EXPERIENCE
Crime and Punishment	Councilman Millstipe	Darkshire	Councilman Millstipe	Darkshire	No	2,100
REWARD: Darkshire Mail Leggings (Mail Legs 163 Armor +6 STR/+6 SPI) or Ambassador's Boots (Leather Boots 59 Armor +4 AGI/+4 STA)						
Quell the Uprising	Warden Thelwater	Stormwind Stockade	Warden Thelwater	Stormwind Stockade	No	2,650
The Color of Blood	Nikova Raskol	Stormwind Old Town	Nikova Raskol	Stormwind Old Town	No	2,650
The Fury Runs Deep	Motley Garmason	Dun Modr, Wetlands	Motley Garmason	Dun Modr, Wetlands	Yes	2,750
REWARD: Belt of Vindication (Leather Belt 50 Armor +4 AGI/+2 STA) or Headbasher (Two-Handed Mace 17.6 DPS +8 STR/+3 STA)						
The Stockade Riots	Warden Thelwater	Stormwind Stockade	Warden Thelwater	Stormwind Stockade	Yes	2,350
What Comes Around	Guard Berton	Lakeshire, Redridge	Guard Berton	Lakeshire, Redridge	No	2,000
REWARD: Hardened Root Staff (Staff 16.8 DPS +1 STR/+8 SPI) or Lucine Longsword (Main-Hand Sword 12.8 DPS +4 STA)						

CRIME AND PUNISHMENT

Quest Level	22 to Obtain
Location	Duskwood (Darkshire)
Contact	Councilman Millstipe
Goal	Bring Back the Hand of Dextren Ward
Max Experience Gained	2,100

The honorable representative of Duskwood, Councilman Millstipe, asks that justice be done in the name of Darkshire. Dextren Ward was caught stealing bodies for the most foul of purposes, but Stormwind City whisked him away for imprisonment there instead of allowing him to be executed in Darkshire (as the people there requested). Travel to the Stockade and bring justice to this foul man and return with his hand as proof of the deed.

QUELL THE UPRISING

Quest Level	22 to Obtain
Location	Stormwind City (Outside the Stockade)
Contact	Warden Thelwater
Goal	Slay 8 Defias Insurgents, 8 Defias Convicts, and 10 Defias Prisoners
Max Experience Gained	2,650

The Warden is not the most competent man in Stormwind, and it seems that much has turned against him of late. He is trying to keep word of the uprising as quiet as possible, but that won't stand for long if things continue. To silence the Defias, he asks that you hurry into the prison and kill a fair number of the rioting Defias. With a full group, this won't be a lengthy task; he believes it will serve to end the uprising and return the Stockade to Stormwind control. Return to the Warden when the requisite numbers of Defias are slain.

THE COLOR OF BLOOD

Quest Level	22 to Obtain
Location	Stormwind City (Old Town)
Contact	Nikova Raskol
Goal	Collect 10 Red Wool Bandanas
Max Experience Gained	2,650

Nikova Raskol wanders the streets of Old Town, a grim look found often on her aged face. She bears the weight of her grandson's death; the young lad was killed in the Stockade when he reprimanded the Defias members for showing gang colors. Nikova wants vengeance, and she isn't shy about asking for it. Slay enough Defias inside the prison to collect ten Red Wool Bandanas and take those to her. This is all that she asks. All of the Defias in the prison are able to drop these with a moderate chance, so even a full group can finish the quest without much more than a single run through the instance.

THE FURY RUNS DEEP

Quest Level	25 to Obtain
Location	Wetlands (Near Dun Modr)
Contact	Motley Garmason
Goal	Return With Kam Deepfury, Minus His Body
Max Experience Gained	2,750

To get this quest, you must first complete *The Dark Iron War* for Motley (a Level 25 Kill Quest in Dun Modr). That quest also requires that you kill elite enemies, so taking a group up there is essential for success. After those vicious Dwarves are slain, Motley gives you the task of killing Kam Deepfury for his part in the attack on Thandol Span. Travel to the Stockade and search the eastern wing for Kam. After killing him and retrieving his head, return with it to Motley for your reward.

THE STOCKADE RIOTS

Quest Level	16 to Obtain
Location	Stormwind City (Outside The Stockade)
Contact	Warden Thelwater
Goal	Return with the Head of Bazil Thredd
Max Experience Gained	2,350

This is yet another step in a very long chain of quests. The whole thing starts when you kill Edwin VanCleef (the final boss of the Deadmines instance). He drops a Strange Letter that implies worse things for the future of Stormwind. That letter must be taken to Baros Alexston (a city architect for Stormwind in City Hall—Cathedral District).

Baros sends you on to the Stockade where you should talk to Warden Thelwater there; he'll give you permission to speak with Bazil. The rub is that the uprising has blocked access to all prisoners. You must go into the prison and get your information by force, then kill Bazil and bring back his head as proof of your loyalty to Stormwind.

From there, the quest continues for some time as you gather more information about VanCleef, his allies, and the corruption that is prevalent in certain areas of Stormwind.

WHAT COMES AROUND

Quest Level	22 to Obtain
Location	Redridge Mountains (Lakeshire)
Contact	Guard Berton
Goal	Return With the Head of Targorr the Dread
Max Experience Gained	2,000

Targorr the Dread is an Orc with a dark reputation in Redridge Mountains. The things that he did to the defenders there while serving under Gath'Ilzogg have to be answered for, yet a noble in Stormwind has placed a hold on the execution of this fiend. Guard Berton of Lakeshire smells treachery, and he pleads for you to find Targorr and enact justice before this honorless Orc has a chance to escape punishment. Return to Berton with the head of Targorr to receive your reward.

HOST OF THE REBELLION

INMATES

NPC	LEVEL
Defias Captive	23-24 Elite
Notes: Backstab, Infected Wound (+5 to Physical Damage Taken for 5 Minutes)	
Defias Convict	24-25 Elite
Notes: Backhand (Knockdown + Stun), Infected Wound (Increased Physical Damage Taken), Rend	
Defias Inmate	24-25 Elite
Notes: Rend	
Defias Insurgent	25-26 Elite
Notes: Demoralizing Shout, Battle Shout	
Defias Prisoner	23-24 Elite
Notes: Disarm	

INSTIGATORS

NPC	LEVEL	FREQUENT DROP(S)
BAZIL THREDD	29 Elite	
Notes: Dual Wields Swords, Smoke Bomb, Battle Shout		
BRUEGAL IRONKNUCKLE	26 Elite	Jimmied Handcuffs (Mail Bracer 89 Armor +3 STR/+7 STA), Iron Knuckles (Fist Weapon 16.5 DPS On Hit: Chance to Pummel for 4 DMG + Interrupt), Prison Shank (1H Dagger 16.7 DPS +5 AGI/+2 STA), Silk
Notes: Extremely Rare Spawn		
DEXTREN WARD	26 Elite	
Notes: Intimidating Shout, Strike (like Heroic Strike)		
HAMHOCK	28 Elite	
Notes: Chain Lightning, Bloodlust		
KAM DEEPFURY	27 Elite	
Notes: Shield Slam, Shield Wall		
TARGORR THE DREAD	24 Elite	
Notes: Dual Wield Swords, Thrash		

SEIZING THE PRISON

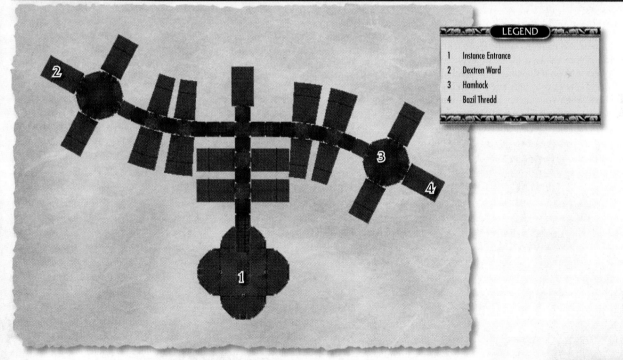

LEGEND
1 Instance Entrance
2 Dextren Ward
3 Hamhock
4 Bazil Thredd

THE MAIN HALL

There isn't any fighting until you enter the instance, but there are certainly enemies waiting for you just a short run after the zone edge. The main hall of the prison is at the base of the ramp; there are three halls in total, so this isn't a very large area to explore.

Don't rush ahead. Each hallway has both static guards and patrollers. Combine this with 3-4 foes inside every room along the sides and there is a huge potential for a simple pull to go sour. Linking can bring people who are close to the doorways inside a room, and fleeing Defias are likely to run into clusters of their buddies. As with earlier instances, ranged pulling by tanks is highly suggested. Warriors unskilled in ranged weapons still serve well here. As long as they get the aggro of the target, they've served their purpose. Or, a Druid who pulls at range and switches to Bear form can accomplish the same thing. Rogues trained in Sap and Stealth can start the fights with a Sap pull and serve admirably as scouts throughout the dungeon.

Determine who's pulling, who everyone is following target-wise (set your assist macros now), and divvy out debuff work. Movement debuffs are an instance staple, and it's no different here. Running Defias are your bane. Many of these fights are entirely simple unless a fleeing target escapes the group. Snare early and often.

The main hallway has five rooms (a set of two across from each other, a second such set, and a final room at the end of the passage). There are also about half a dozen Defias waiting in the hall. Pull the ones at the bottom of the ramp first, when the patrollers aren't close enough to link. Wait for the wanderers and do the same to them before targeting enemies in either room. Then, use more ranged pulling to bring targets from one room out and back to the ramp. Deal with them there to keep adds from either the hall or the back of the room from attacking.

MULTIPLE LOCATIONS

Some of the targets in the Stockade are not set; they may be found in any number of rooms. Targorr the Dread and Kam Deepfury are like this. One of them may appear as early as the first room on the right, or they may be deep in the wings of the prison. It's wise to clear all rooms as you go, since that allows for a wide combat area without fear of adds. Doing this keeps the group safer while allowing for a thorough search.

Clear the rooms as you pass, attempting to do them in two pulls each. The Defias in the cell areas don't come all the way out of the rooms, but they do wander inside their areas. Be cautious while approaching the archways for the rooms, especially if your puller is lower in level (if that is the case, consider a higher-level person even if they aren't an ideal class). The reason for this concern is the possibility of proximity aggro from both rooms if there are Defias close to the door when you approach. That is another reason why Rogue scouting and pulls are very useful in this instance.

CHESTS AND LOOT

There are a couple of chests that spawn in the dungeon. The position for these moves around, just like some of the quest NPCs. Having a person with Blacksmith Keys or a Rogue to pick the locks is nice for scoring a bit of extra treasure.

This is doubly important for a dungeon that's otherwise sparse on treasure. The only NPC who drops consistently fine loot is very rare, and often won't be found in the instance. Though elite enemies drop decent treasure with higher frequency, goodies in the Stockade are somewhat dearth.

The split at the end of the hallway divides the prison into its side wings. To the left is the western wing (with Dextren Ward at its terminus), and to the right is the eastern wing (where Bazil Thredd waits). If you're clearing the entire instance, it doesn't matter which hallway you choose first.

WESTERN WING

Two Defias Inmates block entry to the western side. Pull these back, kill them, then start to clear the rooms ahead. These rooms are quite full, with some having four Defias. There are Prisoners, Inmates, and Captives here. The add range for linking is high enough that solo pulls are nearly impossible at this point. With a full group and proper debuffs, that won't be much of a problem.

Continue along the hallway, methodically clearing the rooms. Cloth drops extremely well in the Stockade, so people with First Aid are free to compliment their group's healing with any drops. This reduces downtime and allows the healers to keep the group moving.

The large room at the end of the hallway has several foes, but won't take too long to clear. There are three more cells off this chamber. Four standard Defias wait in the left room (kill them first). The right chamber is an uglier prospect, possessing five enemies! Wait for one to approach the doorway and pull (better a fight with two or three than to end up with all five).

Finally, Dextren Ward is in the center room with five more opponents (two Inmates, two Captives, and a Prisoner). Though it would sure be nice to have Dextren come on his own, even a patient pull is going to bring several foes. The best bet is to shoot the Defias closest to the front and let Dextren add.

Ward is a mysterious foe, and his abilities are not what you would expect to look at him (he has Warrior abilities, with Intimidating Shout and Strike). Because of this, Dextren adds quite a bit to his allies. Eliminate the side targets early in the fight, then focus on Dextren (he isn't a higher-damage boss, so this is a fair tactic).

Once Dextren is dead, people can collect their proof of the dead and return to the central corridor. If there's a chest in Ward's room, be sure to open that for some well-deserved loot as well.

EASTERN WING

A lone Insurgent patrols the early part of the eastern wing; he can wander quite a way up the ramp toward the main hallway. Pull him, then wade into the Convicts below. The rooms down this hall aren't quite as populated as the ones in the other side of the prison, but most of them still have three targets. Kam Deepfury is likely to be in one of these rooms, if you haven't already encountered him. That Dwarf can take quite a bit of damage, so debuff his armor early, lay on the DoTs, and be sure to clear side targets before cutting into him.

The real fighting comes in the larger room at the end of the hall. As with the western wing, this is an open room with three cells adjoining it. In the center is Hamhock, an Ogre with magical powers. Pull Hamhock directly and use the doorframe for cover as he approaches. Have everyone jump onto Hamhock when he attacks (the main tank should ensure that the two Insurgent adds who link don't go after any allies, but otherwise all damage should go toward Ham). The Ogre casts Chain Lightning and uses Bloodlust to deal fair melee damage as well. Luckily, his hit points are low. As long as your group unloads quickly, Hamhock won't be so fierce.

Once the open room is clear, clean the two side cells. There are four Defias in each (and one of their wanderers practically enters the room from time to time). Shoot for pulls of two enemies per fight. It won't be long until you're ready for the central cell. Rest fully, restore buffs ahead of time, and look inside. Luckily, Bazil Thredd has fewer allies than Dextren Ward. There are only three people in the room (Bazil, an Inmate, and a lone Insurgent).

Wait for a short time and watch the closer enemy (the Inmate). He'll wander enough for a solo range pull if you are patient and very fast to fire once the poor bloke gets into the right position. This means that Bazil is practically alone when you go after him (charge full in at that point, since it's a full fight either way).

Debuff Bazil's damage as much as possible, since he cuts into people fairly well. Being a dual-wielder, Bazil is especially affected by anything that reduces damage per hit (good thing for him Shamans don't often enter the Stockade). In any event, Bazil is tough, but he can't pull down an entire group without having several buddies. Trade aggro if your tank is about to go down, and that should provide enough time for the group to slay Bazil.

That's it for the Stockade. Though there are a full six quests in this small instance, it doesn't take very long to get everything done. The people of Stormwind shall hold you in high regard for keeping the peace. Because of the finite treasure in these runs, it's very useful to get all of the quests ahead of time and handle the instance in a single, fiery sweep. This isn't one of the better places to return to for consistent farming (unless you are interested in raking in a great deal of cloth without heading anywhere far away).

STRATHOLME

Played & Written by: Edwin "Plainsong" Kern of <Dovrani> on Kirin Tor

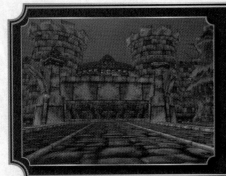

Standing on the northern border of the Eastern Plaguelands, little is known about Stratholme. Rumors say that some of the town's residents were able to survive the horror that devastated the lands outside. How could people survive with the cauldrons contaminating the air around them?

How much power does the Lich King have here? Journey past the shambling hordes of undead and into the stronghold to learn the truth.

DUNGEON INFORMATION

Location	Northern border of Eastern Plaguelands
Quests	Both
Region	Contested
Suggested Levels	55-60
Group Allowed	5
Primary Enemies	Undead, Humanoids
Time to Complete	3-5 Hours

GETTING TO STRATHOLME

Little has survived the plague that retains some element of sanity. The Scarlet Crusade will attack any non-crusader to protect themselves from the Scourge. Only the small Argent Dawn outpost of Light's Hope Chapel stands. Here both Horde and Alliance can land and prepare for the trials ahead. With the plague attacking both sides, there isn't time for petty bickering between factions. There are larger problems.

To complete Stratholme and all the quests in a single session, you will need to port out of the dungeon twice.

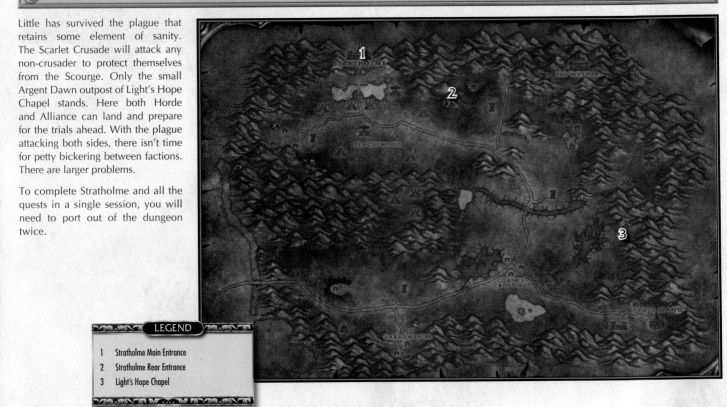

LEGEND

1	Stratholme Main Entrance
2	Stratholme Rear Entrance
3	Light's Hope Chapel

WHO TO BRING

ABILITY	CLASS
Tank	Warrior, Paladin, Druid
Primary Healer	Priest, Druid
Secondary Healer	Priest, Druid, Shaman, Paladin
Humanoid CC	Mage, Rogue, Hunter
Undead CC	Priest, Hunter, Warlock
Damage	Mage, Rogue, Hunter
AoE Damage	Mage, Warlock
Resurrection	Priest, Shaman, Paladin
Wipe Recovery	Shaman, Warlock, Paladin
Doors	Rogue

There are several abilities you'll want in your group. Each class can fill several of these roles and it's important to fill as many as possible without over-burdening one player.

WHAT'S IN IT FOR ME?

There are many pieces of armor class sets and spellbooks within the walls of Stratholme. The table following lists them by set and item and which enemy can drop them. Spellbooks drop from any enemy inside Stratholme.

SPELLBOOKS

Codex: Prayer of Fortitude II

Codex: Prayer of Shadow Protection

Tome of Arcane Brilliance

Book: Gift of the Wild

CLASS SET PIECES

BEASTSTALKER	Beaststalker's Bindings	Crimson Defender, Fleshflayer Ghoul, Ghoul Ravener
	Beaststalker's Boots	Nerub'enkan
	Beaststalker's Pants	Baron Rivendare
DEVOUT	Devout Bracers	Crimson Conjuror, Crimson Initiate, Crimson Priest, Thuzadin Necromancer, Thuzadin Shadowcaster
	Devout Gloves	Archivist Galford
	Devout Skirt	Baron Rivendare
DREADMIST	Dreadmist Belt	Crimson Sorcerer, Thuzadin Necromancer, Thuzadin Shadowcaster
	Dreadmist Sandals	Baroness Anastari, Maleki the Pallid
	Dreadmist Leggings	Baron Rivendare
ELEMENTS	Bindings of Elements	Crimson Monk, Crypt Beast, Crypt Crawler
	Kilt of Elements	Baron Rivendare
LIGHTFORGE	Lightforge Belt	Crimson Gallant, Crimson Guardsman, Rockwing Gargoyle
	Lightforge Boots	Balnazzar
	Lightforge Gauntletss	Timmy the Cruel
	Lightforge Legplates	Baron Rivendare
MAGISTER'S	Magister's Belt	Crimson Battle Mage, Crimson Conjuror, Crimson Sorcerer, Thuzadin Necromancer, Thuzadin Shadowcaster
	Magister's Boots	Hearthsinger Forresten
	Magister's Leggings	Baron Rivendare
POSTMASTER'S	The Postmaster's Band	Postmaster Malown
	The Postmaster's Seal	Postmaster Malown
	The Postmaster's Treads	Postmaster Malown
	The Postmaster's Trousers	Postmaster Malown
	The Postmaster's Tunic	Postmaster Malown
SHADOWCRAFT	Shadowcraft Bracers	Plague Ghoul
	Shadowcraft Pants	Baron Rivendare
	Shadowcraft Spaulders	Cannon Master Willey
VALOR	Belt of Valor	Bile Spewer, Venom Belcher
	Gauntlets of Valor	Ramstein the Gorger
	Legplates of Valor	Baron Rivendare
WILDHEART	Wildheart Belt	Bile Spewer, Venom Belcher
	Wildheart Bracers	Crimson Inquisitor, Shrieking Banshee, Wailing Banshee
	Wildheart Kilt	Baron Rivendare

STRATHOLME

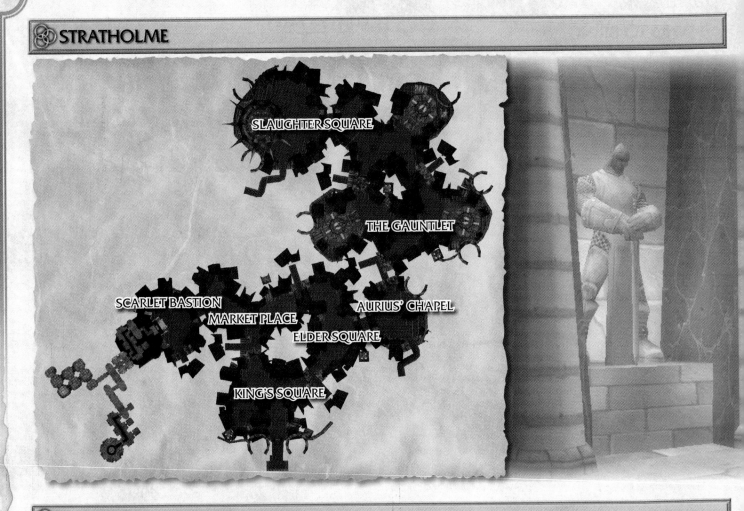

SLAUGHTER SQUARE

THE GAUNTLET

SCARLET BASTION

AURIUS' CHAPEL

MARKET PLACE

ELDER SQUARE

KING'S SQUARE

QUESTS FOR STRATHOLME

SHARED QUESTS

QUEST NAME	QUEST GIVER	QUEST GIVER LOCATION	QUEST RECEIVER	QUEST RECEIVER LOCATION	CHAIN?	MAX EXPERIENCE
Menethil's Gift	Leonid Barthalomew the Revered	Eastern Plaguelands: Light's Hope Chapel	Menethil's Gift	Stratholme: Baron's Chamber	Yes	7,050
Menethil's Gift	Menethil's Gift	Stratholme: Baron's Chamber	Leonid Barthalomew the Revered	Eastern Plaguelands: Light's Hope Chapel	Yes	8,800
Of Love and Family	Artist Renfray	Western Plaguelands: Caer Darrow)	Tirion Fordring	Eastern Plaguelands	Yes	6,600
The Flesh Does Not Lie	Betina Bigglezink	Eastern Plaguelands: Light's Hope Chapel	Betina Bigglezink	Eastern Plaguelands: Light's Hope Chapel	Yes	6,850
The Active Agent	Betina Bigglezink	Eastern Plaguelands: Light's Hope Chapel	Betina Bigglezink	Eastern Plaguelands: Light's Hope Chapel	Yes	6,850
REWARD: Seal of the Dawn (Trinket, +81 Attack Power when fighting Undead)						
The Archivist	Duke Nicholas Zverenhoff	Eastern Plaguelands: Light's Hope Chapel	Duke Nicholas Zverenhoff	Eastern Plaguelands: Light's Hope Chapel	Yes	8,550
The Truth Comes Crashing Down	Head of Balnazzar	Stratholme	Duke Nicholas Zverenhoff	Eastern Plaguelands: Light's Hope Chapel	Yes	8,800
Above and Beyond	Duke Nicholas Zverenhoff	Eastern Plaguelands: Light's Hope Chapel	Duke Nicholas Zverenhoff	Eastern Plaguelands: Light's Hope Chapel	Yes	8,800
REWARD: Argent Avenger (One-hand Sword, 40.7 DPS, Chance on Hit: Increases attack power against undead by 200 for 10 seconds) or Argent Defender (Shield, 2121 Armor, 39 Block, Passive: Has a 1% chance when struck in combat of increasing chance to block by 50% for 10 seconds) or Argent Crusader (Staff, 53 DPS, +30 INT, +6 STA, +10 SPI)						
Medallion of Faith	Aurius	Stratholme	Aurius	Stratholme	No	None
Corruption	Seril Scourgebane	Winterspring: Everlook	Seril Scourgebane	Winterspring: Everlook	No	8,550
REWARD: Plans: Blazing Rapier (Requires Blacksmithing (280), Requires Master Swordsmith)						
Cap of the Scarlet Savant	Malyfous's Catalogue	Winterspring: Everlook	Malyfous Darkhammer	Winterspring: Everlook	No	None
REWARD: Cap of the Scarlet Savant (Cloth Head, 78 Armor, +20 INT, +17 STA, Passive: Improves your chance to get a critical strike with spells by 2%, Classes: Priest, Warlock, Mage, Druid, Shaman)						
Breastplate of Bloodthirst	Malyfous's Catalogue	Winterspring: Everlook	Malyfous Darkhammer	Winterspring: Everlook	No	None
REWARD: Breastplate of Bloodthirst (Leather Chest, 190 Armor, +20 STA, +13 STR, Passive: Improves your chance to get a critical strike by 2% and your chance to dodge an attack by 1%)						
Leggings of Arcana	Malyfous's Catalogue	Winterspring: Everlook	Malyfous Darkhammer	Winterspring: Everlook	No	None
REWARD: Leggings of Arcana (Mail Legs, 166 Armor, +30 SPI, +20 INT, Passive: Increases damage and healing done by magical spells and effects by up to 18)						
Breastplate of the Chromatic Flight	Catalogue of the Wayward	Winterspring	Jeziba	Western Plaguelands: Andorhal	No	None
REWARD: Breastplate of the Chromatic Flight (Plate Chest, 706 Armor, +30 STA, +20 STR, +10 AGI, +15 Fire Resistance)						

MENETHIL'S GIFT (PART I)

Quest Level	60 to obtain
Location	Eastern Plaguelands (Light's Hope Chapel)
Quest Giver	Leonid Barthalomew the Revered
Goal	Take the Keepsake of Remembrance to Stratholme
Max Experience Gained	7,050

This chain of quests begins with *Doctor Theolen Krastinov, the Butcher.* Leonid was there when the Lich King transformed Ras Frostwhisper. It happened over a pentagram drawn on the floor of Baron Rivendare's chamber. That's where you must take the Keepsake of Remembrance.

OF LOVE AND FAMILY

Quest Level	53 to obtain
Location	Western Plaguelands (Caer Darrow)
Quest Giver	Artist Renfray
Goal	Recover of Love and Family
Max Experience Gained	6,600

This quest chain starts with the quest *Carrion Grubbage.* The painting *Of Love and Family Deep* is in Stratholme. It was painted over to protect it. Find the painting of the *Twin Moons* and chip away at the paint to reveal the true painting. Take it to Tirion Fordring.

MENETHIL'S GIFT (PART II)

Quest Level	60 to obtain
Location	Stratholme (Baron's Chamber)
Quest Giver	Menethil's Gift
Goal	Return to Leonid Barthalomew the Revered with the Soulbound Keepsake
Max Experience Gained	8,800

The Keepsake of Remembrance transforms into the Soulbound Keepsake when placed on the pentagram. Return to Leonid with it for your next assignment.

THE FLESH DOES NOT LIE

Quest Level	55 to obtain
Location	Eastern Plaguelands (Light's Hope Chapel)
Quest Giver	Betina Bigglezink
Goal	Collect 20 Plagued Flesh Samples
Max Experience Gained	6,850

After helping Betina with Blackrock Spire, she has more work for you. She has been studying the plague closely. Her original data showed the plague was getting weaker, but upon traveling to the Eastern Plaguelands she has revised that opinion. The plague seems to be growing stronger. She wants samples so she can test her theory.

THE ACTIVE AGENT

Quest Level	58 to obtain
Location	Eastern Plaguelands (Light's Hope Chapel)
Quest Giver	Betina Bigglezink
Goal	Collect the Scourge Data
Max Experience Gained	6,850
Reward	Seal of the Dawn (Trinket, +81 Attack Power when fighting Undead)

The samples you brought have spurred another request for data. Search the ziggurats in Stratholme for the Scourge Data and return to Betina for your reward.

THE ARCHIVIST

Quest Level	55 to obtain
Location	Eastern Plaguelands (Light's Hope Chapel)
Quest Giver	Duke Nicholas Zverenhoff
Goal	Kill the Archivist and burn the Archives
Max Experience Gained	8,550

The Scarlet Crusade has killed countless innocents in their campaign against the Scourge. Duke Nicholas wants you to venture into Stratholme and kill Archivist Galford and burn his Archives. This must be completed to open *The Truth Comes Crashing Down*.

THE TRUTH COMES CRASHING DOWN

Quest Level	58 to obtain
Location	Stratholme
Quest Giver	Head of Balnazzar
Goal	Deliver the Head of Balnazzar to Duke Nicholas Zverenhoff
Max Experience Gained	8,800

After you have completed *The Archivist* and battle the Grand Crusader of the Scarlet Crusade, an interesting event occurs. Balnazzar shows himself. A demon has been leading the Scarlet Crusade. Duke Nicholas must be told of this. Take Balnazzar's head as proof.

ABOVE AND BEYOND

Quest Level	57 to obtain
Location	Eastern Plaguelands (Light's Hope Chapel)
Quest Giver	Duke Nicholas Zverenhoff
Goal	Collect Baron Rivendare's Head
Max Experience Gained	8,800
Reward	Argent Avenger (One-hand Sword, 40.7 DPS, Chance on Hit: Increases attack power against undead by 200 for 10 seconds) or Argent Defender (Shield, 2121 Armor, 39 Block, Passive: Has a 1% chance when struck in combat of increasing chance to block by 50% for 10 seconds) or Argent Crusader (Staff, 53 DPS, +30 INT, +6 STA, +10 SPI)

Duke Nicholas is pleased with your work. He now wants you to set your mark higher. Kill Baron Rivendare and return with his head. After speaking with Duke Nicholas, then Lord Maxwell Tyrosus, you have the opportunity to select a reward from the Argent Hold.

THE MEDALLION OF FAITH

Quest Level	60 to obtain
Location	Stratholme
Quest Giver	Aurius
Goal	Return the Medallion of Faith to Aurius
Max Experience Gained	None
Reward	Will of the Martyr (Neck, +10 STA, +30 Attack Power) or Blood of the Martyr (Ring, +15 STA, +10 INT)

Aurius has been able to resist the taint of the Scourge, but at a terrible price. He has been unable to leave the chapel and has only been able to watch as his friends fell to the taint. Recover the Medallion of Faith from the Scarlet area of Stratholme and return it to him. With the new protection, he can pay Baron Rivendare back for all the wrongs done.

After giving him the Medallion of Faith, Aurius will aid you when you fight Baron Rivendare. After the fight, speak with Aurius for your reward.

CORRUPTION

Quest Level	54 to obtain
Location	Winterspring (Everlook)
Quest Giver	Seril Scourgebane
Goal	Collect the Insignia of the Black Guard
Max Experience Gained	8,550
Reward	Plans: Blazing Rapier (Requires Blacksmithing (280), Requires Master Swordsmith)

The plans for one of the more powerful swords were stolen by the Scourge. Seril wants you to make your way into Stratholme and find them. They are guarded by the Black Guard, an elite unit of Baron Rivendare's, so it won't be easy. Bringing back proof of your success will warrant your elevation to Master Swordsmith and grant you your first set of plans.

CAP OF THE SCARLET SAVANT (CLOTH)

Quest Level	60 to obtain
Location	Winterspring
Quest Giver	Malyfous's Catalogue
Goal	Collect 1 Pristine Hide of the Beast, 5 Frayed Abomination Stitchings, 8 Arcane Crystals, and 5 Enchanted Scarlet Threads
Max Experience Gained	None
Reward	Cap of the Scarlet Savant (Cloth Head, 78 Armor, +20 INT, +17 STA, Passive: Improves your chance to get a critical strike with spells by 2%, Classes: Priest, Warlock, Mage, Druid, Shaman)

Malyfous has crafted many great items in his day. If you bring him what he needs, he'll craft a beautiful headpiece. One of the items he needs is the Pristine Hide of The Beast. This can only be obtained from the Beast in Upper Blackrock Spire with the help of a skinner of 310 skill.

BREASTPLATE OF BLOODTHIRST (LEATHER)

Quest Level	60 to obtain
Location	Winterspring
Quest Giver	Malyfous's Catalogue
Goal	Collect 1 Pristine Hide of the Beast, 10 Frayed Abomination Stitchings, 5 Arcanite Bars, and 5 Skins of Shadows
Max Experience Gained	None
Reward	Breastplate of Bloodthirst (Leather Chest, 190 Armor, +20 STA, +13 STR, Passive: Improves your chance to get a critical strike by 2% and your chance to dodge an attack by 1%)

Malyfous has crafted many great items in his day. If you bring him what he needs, he'll craft an incredible piece. One of the items he needs is the Pristine Hide of The Beast. This can only be obtained from the Beast in Upper Blackrock Spire with the help of a skinner of 310 skill.

LEGGINGS OF ARCANA (LEATHER)

Quest Level	60 to obtain
Location	Winterspring
Quest Giver	Malyfous's Catalogue
Goal	Collect 1 Pristine Hide of the Beast, 10 Frayed Abomination Stitchings, 5 Arcanite Bars, and 5 Frostwhisper's Enbalming Fluids
Max Experience Gained	None
Reward	Leggings of Arcana (Mail Legs, 166 Armor, +30 SPI, +20 INT, Passive: Increases damage and healing done by magical spells and effects by up to 18)

Malyfous has crafted many great items in his day. If you bring him what he needs, he'll craft a gorgeous set of leggings. One of the items he needs is the Pristine Hide of The Beast. This can only be obtained from the Beast in Upper Blackrock Spire with the help of a skinner of 310 skill.

BREASTPLATE OF THE CHROMATIC FLIGHT (PLATE)

Quest Level	57 to obtain
Location	Winterspring
Quest Giver	Catalogue of the Wayward
Goal	Collect 1 Chromatic Carapace, 10 Chromatic Scales, 10 Blood of Heroes, and 5 Frayed Abomination Stitchings
Max Experience Gained	None
Reward	Breastplate of the Chromatic Flight (Plate Chest, 706 Armor, +30 STA, +20 STR, +10 AGI, +15 Fire Resistance)

After running errands for Haleh, you have the opportunity to have Jeziba the Sculptor create a truly magnificent piece of armor for you. Collect the needed materials and speak with Jeziba in the Inn of Andorhal in the Western Plaguelands.

PICKING STITCHINGS AND THREADS

The quests on this page are chains, all of which begin in other areas (most of them require freeing Finkle in Blackrock Spire). However, they require Frayed Abomination Stitches or Enchanted Scarlet Threads to complete, which drop only in Stratholme.

ENEMIES

WHAT STILL LIVES?

NPC	LEVEL
Bile Slime	54-60
Bile Spewer	54-60 Elite
Notes: Summons Bile Slimes	
Frequent Drops: Belt of Valor (Plate Waist, 341 Armor, +14 STR, +8 STA, +7 AGI, +4 SPI) Wildheart Belt (Leather Waist, 93 Armor, +17 INT, +10 SPI, +9 STA), Frayed Abomination Stitching	
Black Guard Sentry	53-59 Elite
Broken Cadaver	50-56
Cannibal Ghoul	52-55
Crimson Battle Mage	55-60 Elite
Notes: Immolate, Blast Wave, Arcane Explosion	
Frequent Drops: Magister's Belt (Cloth Waist, 46 Armor, +21 INT, +6 SPI, +6 STA)	
Crimson Conjuror	52-58 Elite
Notes: Frost Nova, Scorch, Frost Bolt, Summons Water Elementals	
Frequent Drops: Devout Bracers (Cloth Wrist, 35 Armor, +10 INT, +10 SPI, +7 STA), Dreadmist Belt (Cloth Waist, 46 Armor, +17 INT, +10 STA, +9 SPI), Magister's Belt (Cloth Waist, 46 Armor, +21 INT, +6 SPI, +6 STA)	
Crimson Defender	54-59 Elite
Notes: Devotion Aura, Hammer of Justice, Divine Shield, Holy Light	
Frequent Drops: Beaststalker's Bindings (Mail Wrist, 148 Armor, +15 AGI, +7 STA)	
Crimson Gallant	54-60 Elite
Notes: Holy Strike, Crusader Strike, Retribution Aura	
Frequent Drops: Lightforge Belt (Plate Waist, 341 Armor, +15 INT, +6 SPI, +9 STA, +10 STR)	

NPC	LEVEL
Crimson Guardsman	52-58 Elite
Frequent Drops: Lightforge Belt (Plate Waist, 341 Armor, +15 INT, +6 SPI, +9 STA, +10 STR)	
Crimson Initiate	52-58 Elite
Notes: Mind Blast, Flash Heal, Renew	
Frequent Drops: Devout Bracers (Cloth Wrist, 35 Armor, +10 INT, +10 SPI, +7 STA)	
Crimson Inquisitor	54-60 Elite
Notes: Shadow Word: Pain, Mind Flay, Mana Burn, Shadow Barrier	
Frequent Drops: Wildheart Bracers (Leather Wrist, 71 Armor, +15 INT, +7 STR)	
Crimson Monk	53-60 Elite
Frequent Drops: Bindings of Elements (Mail Wrist, 148 Armor, +10 INT, +10 SPI, +7 STA)	
Crimson Priest	54-59 Elite
Notes: Power Word: Shield, Heal, Smite, Holy Fire	
Frequent Drops: Devout Bracers (Cloth Wrist, +10 INT, +10 SPI, +7 STA)	
Crimson Rifleman	58-60 Elite
Crimson Sorcerer	53-59 Elite
Notes: Fire Blast, Arcane Bolt, Polymorph, Frost Armor	
Frequent Drops: Magister's Belt (Cloth Waist, 46 Armor, +21 INT, +6 SPI, +6 STA)	
Crypt Beast	54-60 Elite
Frequent Drops: Bindings of Elements (Mail Wrist, 148 Armor, +10 INT, +10 SPI, +7 STA)	
Crypt Crawler	53-59 Elite
Frequent Drops: Bindings of Elements (Mail Wrist, 148 Armor, +10 INT, +10 SPI, +7 STA)	

NPC	LEVEL
Eye of Naxxramas	50-63
Notes: Stealth, Stealth Detection	
Fleshflayer Ghoul	54-60 Elite
Frequent Drops: Beaststalker's Bindings (Mail Wrist, 148 Armor, +15 AGI, +7 STA)	
Ghostly Citizen	51-57 Elite
Ghoul Ravener	53-59 Elite
Frequent Drops: Beaststalker's Bindings (Mail Wrist, 148 Armor, +15 AGI, +7 STA)	
Mangled Cadaver	50-56 Elite
Notes: Can spawn a Broken Cadaver on death.	
Mindless Skeleton	56-60
Mindless Undead	51-57
Patchwork Horror	52-58 Elite
Frequent Drops: Frayed Abomination Stitching	
Plague Ghoul	52-58 Elite
Frequent Drops: Shadowcraft Bracers (Leather Wrist, 71 Armor, +15 AGI, +7 STA)	
Plagued Rat	50-55
Notes: Stealth Detection	
Ravaged Cadaver	51-57 Elite
Notes: Can spawn a Broken Cadaver on death.	
Rockwing Gargoyle	52-58 Elite
Frequent Drops: Lightforge Belt (Plate Waist, 341 Armor, +15 INT, +6 SPI, +9 STA, +10 STR)	
Rockwing Screecher	53-59 Elite
Notes: Silence	
Frequent Drops: Lightforge Belt (Plate Waist, 341 Armor, +15 INT, +6 SPI, +9 STA, +10 STR)	
Shrieking Banshee	52-58 Elite
Notes: Silence	
Frequent Drops: Wildheart Bracers (Leather Wrist, 71 Armor, +15 INT, +7 STR)	

NPC	LEVEL
Skeletal Berserker	51-57
Skeletal Guardian	50-56
Spectral Citizen	50-56 Elite
Stitched Horror	52-58 Elite
Thuzadin Acolyte	54-60
Thuzadin Necromancer	55-61 Elite
Notes: Summon Skeletal Servant, Bone Armor, Soul Tap	
Frequent Drops: Dreadmist Belt (Cloth Waist, 46 Armor, +17 INT, +10 STA, +9 SPI), Magister's Belt (Cloth Waist, 46 Armor, +21 INT, +6 SPI, +6 STA), Devout Bracers (Cloth Wrist, 35 Armor, +10 INT, +10 SPI, +7 STA)	
Thuzadin Shadowcaster	53-59 Elite
Notes: Shadowbolt, Cripple, Piercing Shadow	
Frequent Drops: Dreadmist Belt (Cloth Waist, 46 Armor, +17 INT, +10 STA, +9 SPI), Magister's Belt (Cloth Waist, 46 Armor, +21 INT, +6 SPI, +6 STA), Devout Bracers (Cloth Wrist, 35 Armor, +10 INT, +10 SPI, +7 STA)	
Undead Postman	53-58 Elite
Frequent Drops: Letter from the Front, Municipal Proclamation, Town Meeting Notice, Fras Siabi's Advertisement	
Undead Scarab	52-57
Notes: Stealth Detection	
Venom Belcher	55-61 Elite
Notes: AoE Poison	
Frequent Drops: Belt of Valor (Plate Waist, 341 Armor, +14 STR, +8 STA, +7 AGI, +4 SPI)	
Wailing Banshee	54-59 Elite
Frequent Drops: Wildheart Bracers (Leather Wrist, 71 Armor, +15 INT, +7 STR)	

THERE'S STILL A CHAIN OF COMMAND?

NPC	LEVEL	FREQUENT DROP(S)
ARCHIVIST GALFORD	60 Elite	Devout Gloves (Cloth Hands, 52 Armor, +4 AGI, +7 STA, +10 INT, +17 SPI), Tomb of Knowledge (Off-hand, +8 STR, +8 AGI, +8 STA, +8 INT, +8 SPI), Foresight Girdle (Mail Waist, 202 Armor, +13-14 to two stats, Restores 3 health every 5 seconds), Archivist Cape (Back, 43 Armor, +9-10 to two stats, Restores 4 mana every 5 seconds), Ash Covered Boots (Leather Feet, 118 Armor, +13 AGI, +13 STA, Increases your chance to dodge an attack by 1%)
Notes: Pyroblast, Fire Nova, Burning Winds		
BALNAZZAR	62 Elite Boss	Book of the Dead (Off-hand, +10 SPI, +15 INT, +8 STA, Use: Summons a Skeleton that will protect you for 60 seconds.), Pattern Truefaith Vestments (Requires Tailoring (300)), Crown of Tyranny (Mail Head, 301 Armor, +20 STA, -10 SPI, +40 Attack Power, Improves your chance to get a critical strike by 1%), Demonshear (Two-hand Sword, 53.9 DPS, Chance on hit: Sends a shadowy bolt at the enemy causing 150 Shadow damage and dealing 8 damage every 2 seconds for 30 seconds), Fire Striders (Cloth Feet, 61 Armor, +5 SPI, +15 Fire Resistance, Increases damage done by Fire spells and effects by up to 29), Gift of the Elven Magi (Dagger, 41.3 DPS, +5 STA, +10 INT, +6 SPI), Star of Mystaria (Neck, +8 SPI, +9 INT, +9 STA, Equip: Improves your chance to hit with spells by 1%.), Wyrmtongue Shoulders (Leather Shoulders, 132 Armor, +23 AGI, +10 STA), Lightforge Boots (Plate Feet, 424 Armor, +18 STA, +9 SPI, +8 STR), Hammer of the Grand Crusader (Two-hand Mace, 53.9 DPS, +26 INT, +10 STA, +9 SPI, Increases healing done by spells and effects by up to 22), Grand Crusader's Helm (Plate Head, 584 Armor, +16 STR, +16 STA, +12 SPI, +15 Shadow Resistance)
Notes: Mind Blast, Shadow Shock, Sleep, Domination, Pyschic Scream		
BARON RIVENDARE	62 Elite Boss	Runeblade of Baron Rivendare (Two-hand Sword, 59.4 DPS, Equip: Increases movement speed and life regeneration rate.), Dracorian Gauntlets (Mail Hands, 231 Armor, +10 STA, +11 INT, +18 SPI), Robes of the Exalted (Cloth Chest, 89 Armor, +5 INT, +11 SPI, Equip: Increases healing done by spells and effects by up to 68), Scepter of the Unholy (Main-hand Mace, 41.2 DPS, +5 STA, Equip: Increases damage done by Shadow spells and effects by up to 24), Seal of Rivendare (Ring, +17 INT, +7 SPI), Tunic of the Crescent Moon (Leather Chest, 176 Armor, +14 STA, +12 INT, +11 SPI, Equip: Increases damage and healing done by magical spells and effects by up to 15. Improves your chance to get a critical strike with spells by 1%.), Thuzadin Mantle (Cloth Shoulder, 67 Armor, +11 STA, +18 INT, Equip: Increases damage and healing done by magical spells and effects by up to 12.), Ritssyn's Wand of Bad Mojo (Wand, 63.8 DPS, +4 STA, Equip: Increases damage and healing done by magical spells and effects by up to 11.), Garrett Family Crest (Shield, 2121 Armor, 39 Block, +5 AGI, +4 INT, +17 SPI), Gauntlets of Deftness (Mail Hands, 311 Armor, +23 AGI, +10 STA), Cape of the Black Baron (Cloak, 45 Armor, +15 AGI, Equip: +20 Attack Power.), Skullforge Reaver (One-hand Sword, 41.4 DPS, Chance on hit: Drains target for 2 Shadow damage every 1 sec and transfers it to the caster. Lasts for 30 sec.), Helm of the Executioner (Plate Head, 534 Armor, +14 STR, +20 STA, Equip: Improves your chance to hit by 2%.), Bonescraper (Dagger, 40.7 DPS, Equip: +30 Attack Power), Beaststalker's Pants (Mail Legs, 315 Armor, +6 STR, +26 AGI, +6 STA, +12 SPI), Devout Skirt (Cloth Legs, 76 Armor, +12 STA, +15 INT, +23 SPI), Dreadmist Leggings (Cloth Legs, +21 SPI, +15 STA, +14 INT), Kilt of Elements (Mail Legs, 315 Armor, +12 STR, +6 AGI, +7 STA, +15 INT, +20 SPI), Legplates of Valor (Plate Legs, 557 Armor, +23 STR, +11 AGI, +15 STA, +4 SPI), Lightforge Legplates (Plate Legs, 557 Armor, +20 STR, +8 AGI, +14 STA, +12 INT, +9 SPI), Magister's Leggings (Cloth Legs, 76 Armor, +12 STA, +20 INT, +21 SPI), Shadowcraft Pants (Leather Legs, +12 STR, +25 AGI, +12 STA), Wildheart Kilt (Leather Legs, 150 Armor, +13 STR, +12 AGI, +14 STA, +14 INT, +14 SPI)
Notes: Summons Skeletons from the Bone Piles periodically, Cleave, Mortal Strike, Shadow Bolt, Dark Pact, Unholy Aura		
BARONESS ANASTARI	59 Elite Boss	Anastari Heirloom (Neck, +15 STA, Equip: Increases damage done by Shadow spells and effects by up to 13.), Dreadmist Sandals (Cloth Feet, 58 Armor, +17 STA, +10 SPI, +9 INT), Banshee Finger (Wand, 59.7 DPS, +10 Frost Resistance), Screeching Bow (Bow, 30.7 DPS, +3 STA, +10 Shadow Resistance), Shadowy Laced Handwraps (Cloth Hands, 53 Armor, +15 INT, +12 Shadow Resistance, Equip: Restores 5 mana every 5 seconds), Coldtouch Phantom Wraps (Cloth Chest, 77 Armor, +20 Frost Resistance, +13 Arcance Resistance), Chillhide Bracers (Leather Wrist, 67 Armor, +15 Frost Resistance), Windshrieker Pauldrons (Mail Shoulder, 242 Armor, +20 Arcane Resistance), Banshee's Touch (Plate Hands, 356 Armor, +13 Frost Resistance, +13 Arcane Resistance), Wail of the Banshee (Use: Reduces and enemy's chance to hit by 10% for 12 Seconds.)
Notes: Banshee Curse, Banshee Wail, Possesses characters periodically		
BLACK GUARD SWORDSMITH	57-62 Elite	Bottom Half of Advanced Armorsmithing: Volume III, Book: Gift of the Wild II, Tome of Arcane Brilliance, Codex: Prayer of Fortitude II
CANNON MASTER WILLEY	55-60 Elite	Plans: Heartseeker (Requires Blacksmithing (300)), Master Cannoneer Boots (Plate Feet, 438 Armor, +10 STR, +21 STA), Cannonball Runner (Trinket, Use: Summons a cannon that will fire at enemies in front of it that are attacking you), Willey's Portable Howitzer (Gun, 31.2 DPS, +9 STA, Equip: +8 Attack Power.), Shadowcraft Spaulders (Leather Shoulders, 127 Armor, +22 AGI, +9 STA), Barrage Girdle (Mail Waist, 202 Armor, +6 INT, +6 SPI, +6 STA, Equip: Increases damage and healing done by magical spells and effects by up to 23), Redemption (Staff, 52.1 DPS, +12 SPI, Equip: Increases healing done by spells and effects by up to 66.), Willey's Back Scratcher (Main hand Fist Weapon, 40.2 DPS, +12 STA, Equip: +10 Attack Power.), Mantle of the Scarlet Crusade (Cloth Shoulder, 65 Armor, +11 STA, +11 INT, +12 SPI, Equip: Increases healing done by spells and effects by up to 20.), Diana's Pearl Necklace (Neck, +8 STA, +8 INT, Equip: Improves your chance to hit with spells by 1%. Increases damage and healing done with spells and effects by up to 9.)
Notes: Summons Crimson Riflemen, Shoot, Knock Away, Pummel		
CRIMSON HAMMERSMITH	59-60 Elite	Bottom Half of Advanced Armorsmithing: Volume II
FRAS SIABI	58-61 Elite	Siabi's Premium Tobacco
GRAND CRUSADER DATHROHAN	57-62 ELITE BOSS	
Notes: Changes into Balnazzar, Crusader Strike, Holy Strike, Crusader's Hammer, Mind Blast		
HEARTHSINGER FORRESTEN	52-57 Rare	Magister's Boots (Cloth Feet, 58 Armor, +14 SPI, +14 INT, +9 STA), Woolies of the Prancing Minstrel (Mail Legs, 301 Armor, +10 STA, +12 SPI, Equip: Restores 10 mana per 5 sec.), Songbird Blouse (Leather Chest, 165 Armor, +13 AGI, +13 SPI, +13 STR, +13 INT, +13 STA), Rainbow Girdle (Plate Waist, 341 Armor, +10 STR, +10 STA, +9 SPI, +10 INT, +9 AGI), Piccolo of the Flaming Fire (Trinket, Use: Causes nearby players to dance)
Notes: Enchanting Lullaby, Demoralizing Shout, Shoot, Multi-Shot		
JARIEN	60 Elite	
Notes: Cleave, Cripple, Mortal Strike, and Shadow Shock		
MAGISTRATE BARTHILAS	53-58 Elite	Key to the City, Peacemaker (Two-hand Polearm, 50.4 DPS, Equip: Improves your chance to get a critical strike by 1%, +56 Attack Power), Death Grips (Plate Hands, 404 Armor, +22 STR, Immune to Disarm), Magistrate's Cuffs (Leather Wrist, 73 Armor, +15 STA, Equip: Restores 4 mana every 5 seconds), Royal Tribunal Cloak (Back, 42 Armor, +16 INT, +7 STA), Crimson Felt Hat (Cloth Head, 68 Armor, +8 INT, +8 SPI, +8 STA, increases damage and healing done by magical spells and effects by up to 30)
Notes: Knockback, AoE Stun		
MALEKI THE PALLID	56-61 Elite	Skull of Burning Shadows (Off-hand, +15 Fire Resistance, +10 Shadow Resistance), Devout Sandals (Cloth Feet, 58 Armor, +17 SPI, +10 INT, +9 STA), Maleki's Footwraps (Cloth Feet, 60 Armor, +9 STA, +9 INT, Equip: Increases damage done by Shadow spells and effects by up to 27), Bone Slicing Hatchet (One-hand Axe, 40.6 DPS, +13 AGI, +5 STA), Plate Moon Cloak (Cloak, 44 Armor, +8 STR, +12 STA, +10 Shadow Resistance), Flamescarred Girdle (Leather Waist, 89 Armor, +20 Fire Resistance), Darkbind Fingers (Cloth Hands, 50 Armor, +20 Shadow Resistance), Lavawalker Greaves (Plate Feet, 404 Armor, +20 Fire Resistance), Twilight Void Bracers (Mail Wrist, 145 Armor, +15 Shadow Resistance), Clutch of Foresight (Use: Counters the enemy's Spellcast, preventing any spell from that school of magic from being cast for 10 sec. Generates a high amount of threat.)
Notes: Drain Life, Drain Mana, Frost Bolt, Icy Tomb		

NPC	LEVEL	FREQUENT DROP(S)
MALOR THE ZEALOUS	55-60 Elite	
Notes: Holy Light, Lay on Hands, Head Crack, Ground Smash		
NERUB'ENKAN	55-60 Elite Boss	Beaststalker's Boots (Mail Feet, 240 Armor, +21 AGI, +9 STA), Husk of Nerub'enkan (Shield, 2089 Armor, 38 Block, +10 STA, +15 Nature Resistance), Carapace Spine Crossbow (Crossbow, 31.2 DPS, +9 STA, +4 AGI), Thuzadin Sash (Cloth Waist, 49 Armor, +12 INT, +11 STA, +11 SPI, Equip: Increases damage and healing done by magical spells and effects by up to 11), Chitinous Plate Leggings (Plate Legs, 557 Armor, +20 INT, +20 STA, Equip: Restores 5 mana every 5 seconds), Crypt Stalker Leggings (Leather Legs, 136 Armor, +18 Nature Resistance, +18 Shadow Resistance), Darkspinner Claws (Mail Hands, 204 Armor, +13 Nature Resistance, +13 Shadow Resistance), Fangdrip Runners (Cloth Feet, 54 Armor, +20 Nature Resistance), Acid-etched Pauldrons (Plate Shoulder, 434 Armor, +20 Nature Resistance), Eye of Arachnida (Use: Summons an Eye of Kilrogg and binds your vision to it. The eye is stealthy and quick, but very fragile.)
Notes: Encasing Webs, Pierce Armor, Crypt Scarabs		
POSTMASTER MALOWN	57-60 Elite Boss	The Postmaster's Seal (Ring, +17 SPI, +3 AGI, +6 INT), Malown's Slam (Two-hand Mace, 52.1 DPS, Chance on Hit: Knocks target silly for 2 seconds and increases Strength by 50 for 30 seconds), The Postmaster's Trousers (Cloth Legs, 76 Armor, +12 AGI, +20 SPI, +20 INT), The Postmaster's Tunic (Cloth Chest, 87 Armor, +10 SPI, +13 STA, +20 INT, Equip: Increases damage and healing done by magical spells and effects by up to 15.), The Postmaster's Treads (Cloth Feet, 60 Armor, +15 INT, +14 STA, +6 SPI, Equip: Increases damage and healing done by magical spells and effects by up to 7.), The Postmaster's Band (Cloth Head, 70 Armor, +25 INT, +10 STA, +10 SPI, Equip: Increases damage and healing done by magical spells and effects by up to 14.)
Notes: Backhand, Fear, Curse of Weakness, appears with three Undead Postmen when summoned.		
RAMSTEIN THE GORGER	55-61 Elite Boss	Gauntlets of Valor (Plate Hands, 386 Armor, +17 STR, +10 STA, +8 SPI, +3 AGI), Crest of Retribution (Shield, 2057 Armor, 38 Block, Equip: Deals 5 to 35 damage every time you block), Soulstealer Mantle (Cloth Shoulder, 64 Armor, +9 SPI, +22 INT), Slavedriver's Cane (Staff, 51.3 DPS, +29 STR, +12 STA), Ramstein's Lightning Bolts (Trinket, Use: Harness the power of lightning to strike down all enemies around you for 200 Nature damage), Band of Flesh (Ring, Unique, +16 STA, +6 STR, +3 AGI), Animated Chain Necklace (Neck, +7 STA, +6 SPI, Equip: Increases healing done by spells and effects by up to 33), Frayed Abomination Stitching
Notes: Trample, Knockout		
SKUL	57-58 Rare	Skul's Fingerbone Claws (Leather Hands, 105 Armor, +10 STA, Equip: +40 Attack Power), Skul's Cold Embrace (Plate Chest, 617 Armor, +20 STA, +19 STR, +10 Frost Resistance, Equip: Increased Defense +6), Skul's Ghastly Touch (Wand, 55.8 DPS, Equip: Increases damage done by Shadow spells and effects by up to 14)
Notes: Rare Spawn, Frost Bolt, Frost Shock, Frost Armor		
SOTHOS	60 Elite	
Notes: Fear, Shadow Bolt Volley, Shield Block, Shield Charge, and Shield Slam		
STONESPINE	55-60 Rare	Verdant Footpads (Leather Feet, 118 Armor, Equip: Increases healing done by spells and effects by up to 37. Increases damage done by Nature spells and effects by up to 24.), Gargoyle Shredder Talons (Off-hand Fist Weapon, 38.9 DPS, Chance on Hit: Wounds the target causing them to bleed for 110 damage over 30 seconds), Stoneskin Gargoyle Cape (Back, 43 Armor, +8 AGI, +7 STR, +14 STA)
Notes: Rare Spawn, Viscious Rend		
THE UNFORGIVEN	54-57 Elite	Wailing Nightbane Pauldrons (Plate Shoulders, 448 Armor, +14 STA, +14 STR, +10 Shadow Resistance, Equip: Increased Defense +3), Mask of the Unforgiven (Leather Head, 132 Armor, +12 STA, Equip: Improves your chance to hit by 2%, Improves your chance to get a critical strike by 1%), Soul Breaker (Main-hand Axe, 37.5 DPS, Chance on Hit: Target enemy loses 12 health and mana every 3 seconds for 30 seconds), Tearfall Bracers (Cloth Wrist, 35 Armor, +9 - 10 to two stats)
Notes: Rare Spawn, Frost Nova, spawns additional enemies		
TIMMY THE CRUEL	54-58 Elite	Lightforge Gauntlets (Plate Hands, 386 Armor, +14 SPI, +14 STR, +9 STA), Timmy's Galoshes (Mail Feet, 240 Armor, +17 AGI, +11 INT, +11 STA), Grimgore Noose (Cloth Waist, 47 Armor, +10 SPI, +9 STA, +17 INT), Vambraces of the Sadist (Plate Wrist, 270 Armor, +7 STA, +6 STR, Equip: Improves your chance to get a critical strike by 1%), The Cruel Hand of Timmy (One-hand Mace, 40 DPS, Chance on Hit: Lowers all attributes of target by 15 for 60 seconds)
Notes: Ravenous Claw		

LEGEND

1 Entrance
2 Skul
  Stratholme Courier
  Fras Siabi
3 Hearthsinger Forresten
4 The Unforgiven
5 Timmy the Cruel
6 Archivist Galford
7 Balnazzar
8 Cannon Master Willey
  Grand Crusader Dathrohan
9 Back Entrance
10 Aurius

KING'S SQUARE AND MARKET ROW

The gates slam shut behind your party. Take the time to cast buffs, apply poisons, soulstone rezzers, and discuss any special battle plans.

The enemies you face in King's Square are of two general types: stationary and patrolling. Patrolling enemies can be pulled and killed alone while stationary targets attack in large groups.

Wait for the Patchwork Horror to wander away from the stationary enemies. Pull it alone and kill it. Repeat this for any other wanderers. They have a faster respawn timer, but having them add in the middle of a fight can be devastating.

THE EYES. GO FOR THE EYES!

The Eyes of Naxxramas wander around while stealthed. Watch your chat log while moving or fighting. Should you see the Eyes yell "The living are here!" look around. The Eyes take several seconds before they can summon allies and are quite fragile. This gives you time to find and slay them before they bring friends.

With the patrollers dead again, resume pulling the stationary groups. The groups have a couple different patterns. Some have only a few Mangled Cadavers and are relatively easy to fight. The groups made up of Mangled Cadavers and skeletons are more difficult.

The tank should pull with a ranged weapon if possible. If you have a Priest, shackle one of the elites before it gets to your party. Hunters should put their pets on any elites that aren't shackled or engaged by the tank. This keeps the elites off you for now. AoE the Skeletal Berserkers and Guardians. With the non-elites dead, turn to the elites and bring them down one at a time.

NO EXPIRATION DATE?

Supply crates are scattered throughout Stratholme. The crates sometimes hold Stratholme Holy Water and sometimes hold swarms of stealth detecting vermin. Keep your party together when searching the crates. The dwarf racial ability "Find Treasure" can be used to uncover crates that hold treasure.

There are a few things to be aware of when fighting the Mangled Cadavers. Once you defeat them, they may not be dead. Broken Cadavers can rip themselves from the bodies and attack you. These are non-elite, but can be dangerous if ignored. The Cadavers, as well as the Horrors, can drop the **Plagued Flesh Samples** for *The Flesh Does Not Lie*.

Look for the Stratholme Courier near Fras Siabi's shop. He drops three random keys when killed. Use the keys to open the appropriate mailboxes to summon Postmaster Malown.

POSTMASTER MALOWN

Fighting Malown is a dangerous goal. His curses can cripple your tank if left alone. Keep him as far from the party as possible and facing away. This gives the tank maximum time to regain aggro if she loses it. Dispel the curses as fast as Malown casts them. Most are instant cast, but some can be interrupted. Have an interrupt order to capitalize on this. Keep your tank's health high and wear him down.

STRATHOLME POST

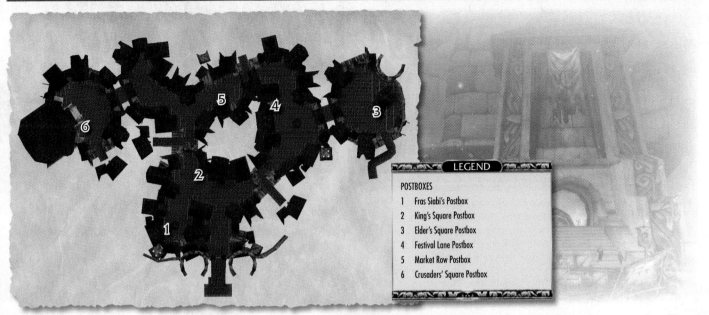

Move northwest through King's Square to Market Row. It's much the same as King's Square. There are Plague Ghouls wandering in addition to the Eyes of Naxxmaras and Patchwork Horrors. Clear the enemies in the same fashion as you move west toward Scarlet Bastion.

THE SCARLET BASTION

As you exit Market Row to the west, the enemies change dramatically. The Scarlet Crusade has managed to survive all this time inside Stratholme. With such a change in enemies, there is also a change in tactics your party should employ.

Pulls should be started by Rogues sapping (if your party has them). The Scarlet Conjurors need to be CCed and the Scarlet Guardsmen pulled to the party. Avoid getting behind the Guardsmen since their charge also knocks you back. Getting knocked back into another group is dangerous.

When the melee opponents are dead, take the casters one at a time. Have a ranged interrupt (Shaman: Earth Shock or Mage: Counterspell) ready to force them to come to you. The Conjurers can summon elementals if given time.

Clear the Scarlet Crusade groups one at a time. There are a few fights between the Crusade and undead. Join these fights with caution as both sides will attack you if given the chance. Timmy the Cruel spawns when the last enemies are cleared from the courtyard.

Timmy has a skill that restores HP and hits like a falling dragon. Your tank needs to engage him as far from the party as possible and keep him facing away. If Timmy changes targets, the party needs to cease fire until the tank regains Timmy's attention and moves him back into position. Keep your tank's health high and you won't have any trouble with Timmy.

With Timmy down, the way into the Scarlet Bastion is clear. The Scarlet Crusade won't give up without a fight. The enemy is almost always in groups of four. Crowd control the casters and kill the melee enemies first. Watch for patrols.

After you clear a hallway of enemies in the Scarlet Bastion, either two Scarlet Gallants spawn at the end of the hallway near the door to the next room or a small group of undead spawn in the previous room and wander into the group. Take the time to get your group into good condition before taking on the final pull of each hallway.

Move down the hall and prepare for the fight against Malor the Zealous. Malor inflicts high damage, has an AoE knockdown and can heal himself. Keep your ranged damage near their maximum range to avoid the knockdown, and interrupt (Kick and Shield Bash) his heals and the fight should go smoothly. When Malor is brought down, search his strongbox for **The Medallion of Faith**.

Continue killing the Scarlet Crusade until you reach the next long hallway. Take the western door. The enemies are much the same in ability and formation until you get the Cannon Master Willey.

HEARTHSTONING?

If your party will be using hearthstones to port out, take the southern path first, then return to this one. This gives your hearthstones a chance to cool down before you need them again.

Designate someone in your group for cannon duty. When the fight begins, move your entire party behind the cannons. The member on cannon duty should stop at one of cannonball stacks and grab a cannonball before joining the fight. As the fight continues, reinforcements arrive and stand at the end of the hallway to use ranged attacks. Use the cannon to blow down the new enemies. As soon as the person on cannon duty uses their cannonball, they need to get another immediately. They should have their attention divided between the hallway and Cannon Master Willey. Whenever there are reinforcements in the hallway, use the cannons.

Cannon Master Willey isn't terribly dangerous on his own. Since your party's in cramped corners, it'll be more difficult to keep him off your softer party members. The difficulty lies in Knock Away being a threat wipe. If the main tank is hit with this skill, Cannon Master Willey changes targets to the next person on the threat list. If this happens, give the main tank some time to regain his attention before the group starts up with its attacks. With Cannon Master Willey down, return to the long hallway and take the southern door.

The southern door leads into another hallway. Watch the wandering Crimson Monk and Battle Mage as you enter. Wait for them to come to you and away from the others before you pull. With the wanderers clear, pull one group of enemies at a time. Pull the final group back and well away from the two doorways. If the enemy knocks one of your party members through either, it could spell defeat for the entire group.

Clear the room to the left before moving right into the next hallway. Clear this room entirely and prepare to fight the Archivist. Pull the Archivist out of his room and down the hall before fully engaging him. Allow the tank to accumulate aggro for several seconds before the party jumps in. Keep the Archivist interrupted or stunned and the fight is much easier.

HEY! YOU INTERRUPTED MY INTERRUPT!

Establish an interrupt order before any fight that will require several. This keeps the party from using all its interrupts at the same time and having them on cooldown when the enemy casts next.

Having everyone jam on their Pummel/Kick/Shield Bash/Counterspell keys at the same time is a recipe for disaster. Assign an order so that everyone knows when their turns up.

There is much to do in this room once the Archivist is dead. A picture of *Two Moons* is to the right. Examine it closer to reveal *Of Love and Family*. Be sure to burn the archives to complete *The Archivist*.

TO THE CHAPEL

With the Archivist dead, his archives burned, and the plagued flesh samples collected, it's time for a quick run to Light's Hope Chapel. Horde parties with a mage should take a portal to Undercity. All other parties should use their hearthstone and fly to Light's Hope Chapel. Turn in *The Archivist* and *The Flesh Does Not Lie* and pick up *Active Agent*.

RETURN TO STRATHOLME

Make the run back to Stratholme. You should be ahead of most of the respawns. Keep your party together and don't delay. Kill any patrollers you come across as you make your way back to the Archivist's room. With *The Archivist* completed and turned in, you will be able to collect Balnazzar's head and begin *The Truth Comes Crashing Down*.

Rebuff and rest to full before engaging Grand Crusader Dathrohan. Shield your tank before starting the encounter. Wait several seconds to allow the tank to build aggro before the rest of the party starts attacking. Dathrohan's attacks aren't terribly damaging at this point, but don't give him the chance to engage any of your softer members. Pull him to the back wall, facing away from the party. Keep the party's ranged damage 10 to 15 yards away to avoid his stun. Around 40% health, Dathrohan sheds his disguise and becomes Balnazzar, a demon. Balnazzar retains all threat from the battle, so don't worry about the tank re-establishing aggro. While your enemy has changed, your tactics shouldn't. Keep him away from your casters and wear him down. Most of his skills are considered Magic and can be removed by a Priest. When he is defeated, undead spawn outside the room, which is the reason for fighting near the throne. Move away from the doorway (if you were feared in that direction) before finishing the battle. Collect his head for *The Truth Comes Crashing Down*.

Jarien and Sothos must be summoned in this room after defeating Balnazzar for the Mage and Priest Dungeon Set 2 upgrade quest: *The Right Piece of Lord Valthalak's Amulet*. They're two former members of the Scarlet Crusade who were executed.

When one is finally killed and no longer undead, they'll rise as a spirit to assist you in defeating their still-undead sibling. However, the undead one regains all their health and gains more power as a result of the "death" of the other.

Jarien has four abilities. Cleave (damage +207 to up to four targets in front of her) and Mortal Strike (200% weapon damage and 50% reduced healing for 5 sec.) are mainly going to hit your tank. Cripple reduces movement, attack speed, and strength by 50%. Her Shadow Shock deals roughly 800 Shadow damage to a single target.

Her brother, Sothos, is a true danger with his Shadow Bolt Volley that deals 650 Shadow damage to all nearby targets and his single-target, 6-second Fear. However, his other abilities are all melee oriented: Shield Block, Shield Charge (Charge and weapon damage +150), and Shield Slam (140 damage and 2-sec. stun).

Make a quick run back to Light's Hope Chapel to turn in quests. You can also hearthstone or portal and then fly to Light's Hope Chapel. Speed isn't important this time as you will be dealing with East Stratholme when you return.

EAST STRATHOLME

LEGEND

1 Entrance
2 Skul
3 Back Entrance
4 Aurius
5 Stonespine
6 Baroness Anastari
7 Nerub'enkan
8 Maleki the Pallid
9 Magistrate Barthilas
10 Abomination Gate
11 Ramstein the Gorger
12 Baron Rivendare

ELDER'S SQUARE

There are two ways to enter Elder Square. The back entrance to Stratholme (use the key dropped by Magistrate Barthilas to get past the gate) and going northeast through King's Square both get you there. Large groups of skeletons and ghouls await you. As in the west side, CC the elite ghouls and AoE the non-elite skeletons. With the skeletons dead, your entire party can focus on the ghouls.

Kill your way to the chapel. Inside is Aurius. He will ask you to give him the **Medallion of Faith.** As you collected it when you were going through West Stratholme, give it to him. He agrees to spend his last breaths aiding you against the Baron. Clear the way to the Baron and Aurius appear to help you. Move north through the gate to the Gauntlet.

SNEAKING THROUGH THE BACK ALLEY

If you came in the back entrance and you don't need to speak with Aurius, you can skip several enemies by sneaking behind the Chapel. Pull the enemies just before the gate all the way back into the alley before killing them. This clears the way for a sneak through the gates.

THE GAUNTLET

The Gauntlet has the same groups of enemies with a few exceptions. The first and most important are the patrollers. There are Crypt Crawlers patrolling slowly and Gargoyles patrolling quickly. Stay at the gates and pull each patroller as it moves away from the static groups. Don't move forward until all the patrols are dead.

When the patrollers are cleared, head northeast. Clear the path to Baroness Anastari's ziggurat. On the south side of the ziggurat are some Blacksmithing Plans. the Blackguard Swordsmith attacks when you loot them. Defeat him to collect the plans for Corruption and the Insignia of the Blackguard for **Corruption**.

MULTIPLE CASTER ENCOUNTERS

There are groups of Thuzadin casters with skeletal pets in a few spots around the ziggaruts. Thuzadin Necromancers engage the party at close range and present fewer problems than Thuzadin Shadowcasters.

To start each encounter, select an intial CC target and find a way to bring the Shadowcasters toward your group. Earthshock, Counterspell, and Silence are all effective skills to accomplish this task. Tear down the casters one at a time, then focus on the non-elite enemies.

When the area is clear, have your tank shoot Anastari and run back to the gates. She has ranged attacks, so the tank must run through the party in order to draw her within range. Anastari fights like any other enemy until she possesses a party member. Anastari vanishes and takes control of one party member while she heals.

Attack the person with everything you have *except* DoTs. When the person drops to 25% health, Anastari jumps out. Your healer should be ready to use a large heal on the player as soon as Anastari jumps out. It's very important that you don't use DoTs on the afflicted party member. These remain after Anastari leaves the person and can kill your friend.

The Baroness does this several times during the fight, but with consistent firepower, your party will prevail. Have your tank run through the ziggaraut and gather the enemies and bring them to your AoE. With the enemies dead, enter the ziggurat to collect the Scourge Data for **The Active Agent**.

With Baroness Anastari's ziggurat down, return to the gate and move west to Nerub'enkan's ziggurat. There are several groups at the base of Nerub'enkan's ziggurat. Nerub'enkan moves around a great deal when you fight him, so you need to clear all other enemies first. Pull each group back and destroy them.

Pull Nerub'enkan well off his perch and back toward the gate. He summons eight short-duration pets that attack for ten seconds before they die. If he roots your tank and changes targets, whoever has aggro should drag him back to the tank. Keep your party's health high and bring him down. When he falls, the doors to the ziggurat open. Have your tank run through and bring the Thuzadin Acolytes out together.

There's only one more ziggarat to clear. Move north toward Maleki the Pallid's ziggurat. Clear the enemies as normal on the way.

Maleki's ziggarut is no different from the other two. Clear mobs from both sides before pulling the group on the stairs. The group on the stairs can be pulled without pulling Maleki. When all his possible allies are destroyed, charge Maleki and make him pay for his evil ways.

His attacks are fairly light. If your party was able to beat the Baroness, Maleki only poses a problem if you relax. Keep with the tactics you've used in the past. The tank should turn Maleki away from the party. Cease fire if Maleki changes targets until the tank has regained his attention and has him back in place.

When Maleki falls have your tank run through the building and bring the enemies back to the party. With the final ziggurat breached, the way to Slaughter Square is open. There is only one final task.

Clear the enemies as you move west. Magistrate Barthilas stands to the north of the gates to Slaughter Square. Rest to full before engaging him.

Give your tank a few seconds to build aggro before joining the fight. Barthilas hits very hard and has a good number of hitpoints, so it's important to keep him beating on the tank. He also has a knockback that clears aggro. Anytime you see the tank get thrown into the air, cease firing. The tank will need a few seconds to get aggro back and continuing to attack Barthilas only makes it more difficult. Keep aggro on your tank and keep everyone's health high, since Barthilas does so much damage each swing, and the fight will end in your favor. Loot Barthilas and rest before entering the gates.

SLAUGHTER SQUARE

There are legions of Bile Spewers and Venom Belchers guarding the square. Keep your party between the two gates and pull one of the abominations. The Bile Spewers can release Bile Slimes throughout the fight and when they die. These are non-elite enemies and should be killed with AoE attacks before they congregate around your healer. The Venom Belchers have an AoE poison attack that does significant damage.

EVERYBODY IN

Everyone in the group must be through the back gate before anyone pulls the first abomination. As soon as you pull, the gate drops to prevent you from fleeing. However, without a Warlock in the group, your party members will end up staying on the other side of the barrier and probably end the run.

Once the first is pulled, a timer is started. More wander to the gates one at a time in intervals. This means you must have your target dead before the next arrives. There are several longer intervals where resting can occur. When the party chooses to rest, have the tank stand at the forward gates and hold any enemy that comes until the rest of the party is ready.

Casters shouldn't wait for the long intervals and should drink every chance they get. This consumes supplies quickly, but it's important to keep your mana as high as possible at this stage.

When the final abomination is dead, the doors to the Slaughter House open long enough for Ramstein the Gorger to step out. The abomination walks slowly to the gates, so your party has plenty of time to regenerate health and mana.

Keep your softer party members spread out and well away from Ramstein. His damage is extremely high and he can demolish a cloth wearer in a few hits. Your tank should slowly pull Ramstein to the gates if you engaged him in the courtyard and keep him facing away from the rest of the party. As soon as Ramstein falls, all party members need to retreat to the gate with all haste and start recovering mana and health.

Ramstein's defeat causes the west gate to open and release dozens of non-elite zombies and skeletons to charge your party. You have a few moments before they reach your group, so make them count. Use every AoE damage skill available to the party (including spare Stratholme Holy Water) and the undead should drop in short order.

Moments after the last of the enemies are dead, the doors to the Slaughter House release more guards. Five Black Guard Sentries advance on your party. Your tank will not be able to withstand the pounding of all five enemies. Hunters, Paladins, and Priests need to CC as many of the Sentries as possible. Do not allow more than three enemies to engage your tank at a time. Back up tanks should pull aggro from one target each and then focus fire with the rest of the party if you don't have any other CC.

Bring the enemies down one at a time. When the last falls, the doors to the Slaughter House open permanently and Baron Rivendare awaits. Rest to full before entering the building.

Move into the room and hug the wall on the left. The Baron has an Unholy Aura that deals Shadow damage each second you are exposed to it. Several bone piles are stacked against the walls. Skeletons spawn from these bone piles during the fight.

When your party is prepared, shield the tank and have them charge the Baron. Give them a few seconds to build aggro before the party jumps in. Keep the Baron on the opposite side of the room as your party and keep him facing away from them. If the Baron changes targets, cease fire until aggro is reestablished. During the fight (assuming you turned in the Medallion of Faith earlier), Aurius joins you and fights against Rivendare. With the help of Aurius and the small skeletons being taken care of (have Mages or Warlocks AoE, or use Stratholme Holy Water) before Baron Rivendare uses Dark Pact to restore his health from them, the Baron becomes a long, but simple fight. Keep your tank alive, keep aggro on your tank, and bring the Baron down. When Baron Rivendare finally falls, so does Aurius.

Speak with Aurius while breath is still with him (if he falls to 0 HP before you eliminate Baron Rivendare, the quest is considered failed). Use the rune in the center of the floor to complete *Menethil's Gift*. Your task is complete. Return to Light's Hope Chapel victorious.

THE TEMPLE OF ATAL'HAKKAR

Played & Written by: Edwin "Plainsong" Kern of <Dovrani> on Kirin Tor

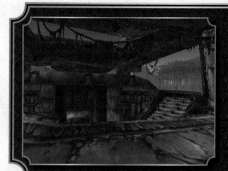

Deep in the Swamp of Sorrows, half submerged, stands the Temple of Atal'Hakkar. Long have the followers kept outsiders from entering. Now sages from distant lands feel a disturbance. Something is moving within the temple. What has changed in recent times? What or who is causing such a shift?

The best defense is a good offense. Find what stirs within the ruins and put an end to any threat it my pose to your people.

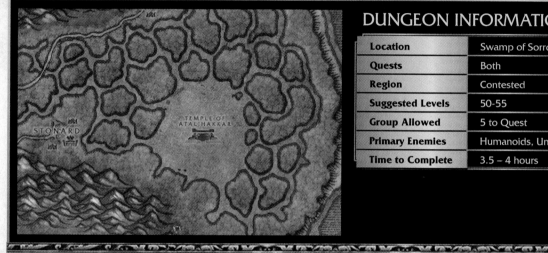

DUNGEON INFORMATION

Location	Swamp of Sorrows
Quests	Both
Region	Contested
Suggested Levels	50-55
Group Allowed	5 to Quest
Primary Enemies	Humanoids, Undead, Dragonkin
Time to Complete	3.5 – 4 hours

GETTING TO THE TEMPLE OF ATAL'HAKKAR

In the center of Swamp of Sorrows is a large lake with the Temple of Atal'Hakkar showing. Swim across to the south facing and climb the stairs to enter.

The trip is rather quick from the nearby flight points. Horde parties can gather in Stonard while Alliance parties gather at Nethergarde Keep.

WHO TO BRING

Having a group that can deal with a variety of situations will make the passage through the temple much easier. There are many foes inside and each should be dealt with and reacted to differently. Several of the fights will be against a few elite enemies and several non-elite enemies making characters with AoE attacks (Mage, Warlock) important. Some fights are against several elite enemies, making characters with crowd control abilities (Priest, Druid, Mage) useful.

A TEMPLE BY ANY OTHER NAME...

Ruins as old as the Temple of Atal'Hakkar are often known by many names. Many people in the World of Warcraft have come to know it as the Sunken Temple and few even know its full name.

Whether you call it Sunken Temple or the Temple of Atal'Hakkar, the danger is still the same.

QUESTS

ALLIANCE QUESTS

QUEST NAME	QUEST GIVER	QUEST GIVER LOCATION	QUEST RECEIVER	QUEST RECEIVER LOCATION	CHAIN?	MAX EXPERIENCE
Into the Temple of Atal'Hakkar	Brohann Caskbelly	Stormwind: Dwarven District	Brohann Caskbelly	Stormwind: Dwarven District	No	7,100
REWARD: Guardian Talisman (Trinket: Equip: Have a 2% chance when struck in combat of increasing armor by 350 for 15 seconds)						
Haze of Evil	Gregan Brewspewer	Feralas: Twin Colossals	Gregan Brewspewer	Feralas: Twin Colossals	Yes	5,100

INTO THE TEMPLE OF ATAL'HAKKAR

Quest Level	42 to obtain
Location	Stormwind (Dwarven District)
Quest Giver	Brohann Caskbelly
Goal	Collect 10 Atal'ai Tablets
Max Experience Gained	7,100
Reward	Guardian Talisman (Trinket: Equip: Have a 2% chance when struck in combat of increasing armor by 350 for 15 seconds)

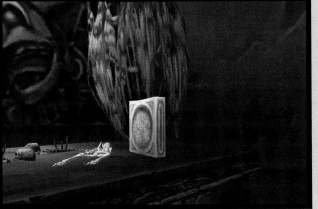

The Temple of Atal'Hakkar is a wealth of lost history. Being guarded by fanatical worshippers makes artifacts even more valuable. Brohann is willing to reward you greatly for braving the dangers of the Sunken Temple.

HAZE OF EVIL

Quest Level	47 to obtain
Location	Feralas (Twin Colossals)
Quest Giver	Gregan Brewspewer
Goal	Collect 5 Atal'ai Haze
Max Experience Gained	5,100

After talking with Muigin in Un'Goro regarding his plant problem, you are sent to Gregan in Feralas. Gregan knows how to help, but can't collect the necessary items himself. He needs 5 Atal'ai Haze. Atal'ai Haze can be found on any of the slimes or worms in the lower portions of the Temple of Atal'Hakkar.

HORDE QUESTS

QUEST NAME	QUEST GIVER	QUEST GIVER LOCATION	QUEST RECEIVER	QUEST RECEIVER LOCATION	CHAIN?	MAX EXPERIENCE
Pool of Tears	Fel'zerul	Swamp of Sorrows: Stonard	Fel'zerul	Swamp of Sorrows: Stonard	Yes	4,450
The Temple of Atal'Hakkar	Fel'zerul	Swamp of Sorrows: Stonard	Fel'zerul	Swamp of Sorrows: Stonard	Yes	5,900
REWARD: Guardian Talisman (Trinket: Equip: Have a 2% chance when struck in combat of increasing armor by 350 for 15 seconds)						
Zapper Fuel	Liv Rizzlefix	The Barrens: Ratchet	Larion	Un'Goro Crater: Marshal's Refuge	Yes	5,100

POOL OF TEARS

Quest Level	38 to obtain
Location	Swamp of Sorrows (Stonard)
Quest Giver	Fel'zerul
Goal	Collect 10 Atal'ai Artifacts
Max Experience Gained	4,450

There have been strange occurrences in the Temple of Atal'Hakkar. First, the temple has been sunk. Second, green dragons are guarding the site. Fel'zerul needs you to collect 10 Atal'ai Artifacts to aid him in the investigation. The artifacts can be found on the ground around and inside the lake. After Fel'zerul examines the artifacts he will ask you to bring them to an exile in the Hinterlands.

THE TEMPLE OF ATAL'HAKKAR

Quest Level	38 to obtain
Location	Swamp of Sorrows (Stonard)
Quest Giver	Fel'zerul
Goal	Collect 20 Fetish of Hakkar
Max Experience Gained	5,900
Reward	Guardian Talisman (Trinket: Equip: Have a 2% chance when struck in combat of increasing armor by 350 for 15 seconds)

The information from the Hinterlands alarms Fel'zerul greatly. He asks you to collect 20 Fetishes to further his investigation. These can be taken from many of the Trolls inside the Temple of Atal'Hakkar.

ZAPPER FUEL

Quest Level	48 to obtain
Location	The Barrens (Ratchet)
Quest Giver	Liv Rizzlefix
Goal	Collect 5 Atal'ai Haze
Max Experience Gained	5,100

After Larion asks you for help in Un'Goro, you are sent to Rizzlefix in Ratchet. She is willing to give you a prototype of her bug zapper, but you need to collect the fuel for it. Atal'ai Haze can be found on the slimes and worms in the lower portion of the Temple of Atal'Hakkar. Bring the Zapper and Haze to Larion in Un'Goro for your reward.

SHARED QUESTS

QUEST NAME	QUEST GIVER	QUEST GIVER LOCATION	QUEST RECEIVER	QUEST RECEIVER LOCATION	CHAIN?	MAX EXPERIENCE
Into the Depths	Marvon Rivetseeker	Tanaris: Broken Pillar	Altar of Hakkar	Temple of Atal'Hakkar	No	4,900
Secret of the Circle	Marvon Rivetseeker	Tanaris: Broken Pillar	Altar of Hakkar	Temple of Atal'Hakkar	Yes	6,100
REWARD: Hikkari Urn						
Jammal'an the Prophet	Atal'ai Exile	Hinterlands: Shadra Alor	Atal'ai Exile	Hinterlands: Shadra Alor	No	6,550
REWARD: Helm of the Exile (Mail Head: 266 Armor, +11 AGI, +18 INT, +18 SPI) or Rainstrider Leggings (Cloth Legs, 69 Armor, +8 AGI, +7 STA, +27 SPI)						
The Essence of Eranikus	Essence of Eranikus	Temple of Atal'Hakkar	Essence Font	Temple of Atal'Hakkar	No	2,800
REWARD: Chained Essence of Eranikus (Trinket: Use: Summons a cloud of poison that deals 50 nature damage every 5 seconds to any enemy in an 8 yard radius around the caster for 45 seconds)						
The God Hakkar	Yeh'kinya	Tanaris: Steamwheedle Port	Yeh'kinya	Tanaris: Steamwheedle Port	Yes	7,900
REWARD: Avenguard Helm (Plate Head: 461 Armor, +10 SPI, +5 AGI, +25 STA) or Lifeforce Dirk (One-Hand Dagger: 35.9 DPS, +11 STA) or Gemburst Circlet (Cloth Head: 63 Armor, +5 AGI, +17 INT, +18 SPI, +9 STA)						

INTO THE DEPTHS

Quest Level	46 to obtain
Location	Tanaris (Broken Pillar)
Quest Giver	Marvon Rivetseeker
Goal	Find the Altar of Hakkar
Max Experience Gained	4,900

After retrieving his Stone Circle from his shop in Ratchet, Marvon tells of his investigation in the Temple of Atal'Hakkar. While inside, he noticed an altar at the bottom of the temple. He believes the stone circle is a key to unlock the altar.

COLORING OUTSIDE THE LINES

Manipulating the statues out of order will bring misery to not only you. It will affect anyone close to you. The statues cause an AoE curse that reduces STR by 50% when used out of order.

SECRET OF THE CIRCLE

Quest Level	46 to obtain
Location	Tanaris (Broken Pillar)
Quest Giver	Marvon Rivetseeker
Goal	Discover the secret hidden in the statues
Max Experience Gained	6,100
Reward	Hikkari Urn

When inside the Temple, Marvon was able to activate a set of lights. These must be guarding a treasure of immense importance. Activating the Altar of Hakkar at the bottom of the lowest level will start the light sequence. Green light will show on the balconies above in a specific order. This shows you which order to manipulate the statues.

The sequence is south, north, southwest, southeast, northwest, northeast. When the statues are manipulated in the proper order, a statue and Atal'alarion spawn in the water at the bottom. The statue holds the Hikkari Urn. Open the Urn to find your reward.

JAMMAL'AN THE PROPHET

Quest Level	38 to obtain
Location	Hinterlands (Shadra Alor)
Quest Giver	Atal'ai Exile
Goal	Collect the Head of Jammal'an
Max Experience Gained	6,550
Reward	Helm of the Exile (Mail Head: 266 Armor, +11 AGI, +18 INT, +18 SPI) or Rainstrider Leggings (Cloth Legs: 69 Armor, +8 AGI, +7 STA, +27 SPI)

The Atal'ai Exile isn't happy that he was exiled for questioning Jammal'an. He will reward you if you carry out his vengeance and remove Jammal'an's head.

THE ESSENCE OF ERANIKUS

Quest Level	48 to obtain
Location	The Temple of Atal'Hakkar
Quest Giver	Corpse of the Shade of Eranikus
Goal	Place the Essence of Eranikus in the Essence Font
Max Experience Gained	2,800
Reward	Chained Essence of Eranikus (Trinket: Use: Summons a cloud of poison that deals 50 nature damage every 5 seconds to any enemy in an 8 yard radius around the caster for 45 seconds)

When the Shade of Eranikus falls, its Essence can be removed. Placing the Essence in the Essence Font will chain it to your will. You will be able to use it as equipment thereafter.

THE GOD HAKKAR

Quest Level	44 to obtain
Location	Tanaris (Steamweedle Port)
Quest Giver	Yeh'kinya
Goal	Collect the Filled Egg of Hakkar
Experience:	7,900
Reward	Avenguard Helm (Plate Head: 461 Armor, +10 SPI, +5 AGI, +25 STA) or Lifeforce Dirk (One-Hand Dagger: 35.9 DPS, +11 STA) or Gemburst Circlet (Cloth Head: 63 Armor, +5 AGI, +17 INT, +18 SPI, +9 STA)

Once you bring Yeh'kinja the Ancient Egg he asked for, he asks you to fill it with part of the god Hakkar. The way to do this is the summon an Avatar of Hakkar in the Sunken Temple and defeat it. You must remove the Hikkar'i Blood from the Hikkar'i Bloodkeepers and extinguish the four braziers in the room to engage the Avatar.

CLASS QUESTS

All class quests listed here are the end of a chain of quests that begin with a class trainer.

QUEST NAME	QUEST GIVER	QUEST GIVER LOCATION	QUEST RECEIVER	QUEST RECEIVER LOCATION	CHAIN?	MAX EXPERIENCE
(Druid) A Better Ingredient	Torwa Pathfinder	Un'Goro Crater	Torwa Pathfinder	Un'Goro Crater	Yes	2,550
REWARD: Forest's Embrace (Leather Chest, 151 Armor, +8 INT, +7 SPI, Equip: Increases healing done by spells and effects by up to 55.) or Grizzled Pelt (Leather Chest, 151 Armor, +17 STR, +16 AGI, +11 STA) or Moonshadow Stave (Staff, 45.0 DPS, Equip: Increases damage and healing done by magical spells and effects by up to 19. Restores 7 mana every 5 sec. Improves your chance to get a critical strike with spells by 1%.)						
(Hunter) The Green Drake	Ogtinc	Azshara	Ogtinc	Azshara	Yes	2,550
REWARD: Devilsaur Eye (Trinket, Use: Increases your attack power by 150 and your chance to hit by 2%. Effect lasts for 20 seconds.) or Devilsaur Tooth (Trinket, Use: Your pet's next attack is guaranteed to critically strike if that attack is capable of striking critically.) or Hunting Spear (Polearm, 45.0 DPS, +17 STA, Equip: Improves your chance to get a critical strike by 1%. Restores 5 mana per 5 sec.)						
(Mage) Destroy Morphaz	Archmage Xylem	Azshara	Archmage Xylem	Azshara	Yes	2,550
REWARD: Arcane Crystal Pendant (Neck, +6 INT, Equip: Increases damage and healing done by magical spells and effects by up to 16.) or Fire Ruby (Trinket, Use: Restores 1 to 500 mana and increases the damage of your next Fire spell by up to 100. Effect lasts for 1 min.) or Glacial Spike (Dagger, 34.6 DPS, +4 INT, Equip: Your Frostbolt spells have a 6% chance to restore 50 mana when cast.)						
(Paladin) Forging the Mightstone	Ashlam Valorfist	Western Plaguelands	Ashlam Valorfist	Western Plaguelands	Yes	2,550
REWARD: Chivalrous Signet (Ring, +7 STR, +7 STA, +7 INT, Equip: Increases healing done by spells and effects by up to 15.) or Lightforged Blade (Two-hand Sword, 44.8 DPS, +9 STR, +9 STA, +10 Fire Resistance, +10 Frost Resistance, +10 Shadow Resistance., Equip: Increases damage done by Holy spells and effects by up to 16.) or Sanctified Orb (Trinket, Use: Increases your critial strike chance with spells and melee attacks by 3%. Lasts 25 sec.)						
(Priest) Blood of Morphaz	Ogtinc	Azshara	Greta Mosshoof	Felwood	Yes	2,550
REWARD: Blessed Prayer Beads (Trinket, Use: Increases healing done by spells and effects by up to 190 for sec.) or Circle of Hope (Ring, +6 Shadow Resistance, Equip: Increases the critical effect chance of your Holy spells by 1%.) or Woestave (Wand, 51.3 DPS, +3 STA, Equip: Increases damage done by Shadow spells and effects by up to 11.)						
(Rogue) The Azure Key	Archmage Xylem	Azshara	Lord Jorach Ravenholdt	Hillsbrad Foothills	Yes	2,550
REWARD: Duskbat Drape (Cloak, 37 Armor, +14 AGI, Equip: Reduces damage from falling.) or Ebon Mask (Leather Head, 122 Armor, +11 Stam, Equip: Improves your chance to get a critical strike by 1%. +36 Attack Power.) or Whisperwalk Boots (Leather Feet, 104 Armor, +18 AGI, +4 STA, Equip: Increases your effective stealth level by 1.)						
(Shaman) Da Voodoo	Bath'rah the Windwatcher	Alterac Mountains	Bath'rah the Windwatcher	Alterac Mountains	Yes	2,550
REWARD: Azurite Fists (Mail Hands, 195 Armor, +6 AGI, +7 STA, +7 INT, +6 SPI, Equip: Improves you chance to get a critical strike with spells by 1%.) or Enamored Water Spirit (Trinket, Use: Summons a Mana Spring Totem with 5 health at the feet of the caster for 24 sec that restores 27 mana every 2 seconds to group members within 20 yards.) or Wildstaff (Staff, 45.0 DPS, +10 STR, +10 STA, +9 INT, Equip: Improves your chance to hit by 1%. Improves you chance to get a critical strike by 1%.)						
(Warlock) Trolls of a Feather	Impsy	Felwood	Impsy	Felwood	Yes	2,550
REWARD: Abyss Shard (Trinket, Use: Casts your Summon Voidwalker spell with no mana or Soul Shard requirements.) or Robes of Servitude (Cloth Chest, 75 Armor, +15 STA, +10 INT, Equip: Increases damage done by Fire spells and effects by up to 23. Increases damage done by Shadow spells and effects by up to 23.) or Soul Harvester (Staff, 44.8 DPS, +16 STA, Equip: Improves your chance to hit with spells by 1%. Increases damage done by Shadow spells and effects by up to 24.)						
(Warrior) Voodoo Feathers	Fallen Hero of the Horde	Swamp of Sorrows	Fallen Hero of the Horde	Swamp of Sorrows	Yes	2,550
REWARD: Diamond Flask (Trinket, Use: Restores 9 health every 5 sec and increases your Strength by 75. Lasts 1 min.) or Fury Visor (Plate Head, 445 Armor, +18 STR, Equip: Improves your chance to get a critical strike by 1%. Improves your chance to hit by 1%.) or Razorsteel Shoulders (Plate Shoulder, 410 Armor, +10 STR, +10 AGI, +9 STA, Equip: Improves your chance to hit by 1%.)						

A BETTER INGREDIENT

Quest Level	50 to obtain
Location	Un'Goro Crater
Quest Giver	Torwa Pathfinder
Goal	Retrieve a Putrid Vine
Max Experience Gained	2,550
Reward	Forest's Embrace (Leather Chest, 151 Armor, +8 INT, +7 SPI, Equip: Increases healing done by spells and effects by up to 55.) or Grizzled Pelt (Leather Chest, 151 Armor, +17 STR, +16 AGI, +11 STA) or Moonshadow Stave (Staff, 45.0 DPS, Equip: Increases damage and healing done by magical spells and effects by up to 19. Restores 7 mana every 5 sec. Improves your chance to get a critical strike with spells by 1%.)

Follow the directions provided in the quest *Secret of the Circle* to summon Atal'alarion. Dispatch him, loot the Putrid Vine and return to Un'Goro Crater to claim your prize.

THE GREEN DRAKE

Quest Level	50 to obtain
Location	Azshara
Quest Giver	Ogtinc
Goal	Retrive the Tooth of Morphaz
Max Experience Gained	2,550
Reward	Devilsaur Eye (Trinket, Use: Increases your attack power by 150 and your chance to hit by 2%. Effect lasts for 20 seconds.) or Devilsaur Tooth (Trinket, Use: Your pet's next attack is guaranteed to critically strike if that attack is capable of striking critically.) or Hunting Spear (Polearm, 45.0 DPS, +17 STA, Equip: Improves your chance to get a critical strike by 1%. Restores 5 mana per 5 sec.)

Morphaz is one of the green drakes guarding the way to Eranikus. Kill him, then return to Ogtinc with his Tooth in your possession.

DESTROY MORPHAZ

Quest Level	50 to obtain
Location	Azshara
Quest Giver	Archmage Xylem
Goal	Retrieve the Arcane Shard
Max Experience Gained	2,550
Reward	Arcane Crystal Pendant (Neck, +6 INT, Equip: Increases damage and healing done by magical spells and effects by up to 16.) or Fire Ruby (Trinket, Use: Restores 1 to 500 mana and increases the damage of your next Fire spell by up to 100. Effect lasts for 1 min.) or Glacial Spike (Dagger, 34.6 DPS, +4 INT, Equp: Your Frostbolt spells have a 6% chance to restore 50 mana when cast.)

Morphaz is one of the green drakes guarding the way to Eranikus. Kill him, then return to Archmage Xylem with the Arcane Shard in your possession.

BLOOD OF MORPHAZ

Quest Level	50 to obtain
Location	Azshara
Quest Giver	Ogtinc
Goal	Retrieve the Blood of Morphaz
Max Experience Gained	2,550
Reward	Blessed Prayer Beads (Trinket, Use: Increases healing done by spells and effects by up to 190 for sec.) or Circle of Hope (Ring, +6 Shadow Resistance, Equip: Increases the critical effect chance of your Holy spells by 1%.) or Woestave (Wand, 51.3 DPS, +3 STA, Equip: Increases damage done by Shadow spells and effects by up to 11.)

Morphaz is one of the green drakes guarding the way to Eranikus. Kill him, then find Greta Mosshoof in Felwood to exchange the Blood of Morphaz for the reward of your choice.

FORGING THE MIGHTSTONE

Quest Level	50 to obtain
Location	Western Plagelands
Quest Giver	Ashlam Valorfist
Goal	Retrieve the voodoo feathers
Max Experience Gained	2,550
Reward	Chivalrous Signet (Ring, +7 STR, +7 STA, +7 INT, Equip: Increases healing done by spells and effects by up to 15.) or Lightforged Blade (Two-hand Sword, 44.8 DPS, +9 STR, +9 STA, +10 Fire Resistance, +10 Frost Resistance, +10 Shadow Resistance., Equip: Increases damage done by Holy spells and effects by up to 16.) or Sanctified Orb (Trinket, Use: Increases your critial strike chance with spells and melee attacks by 3%. Lasts 25 sec.)

There are six trolls in the Temple of Atal'Hakkar assigned to guard the shield that protects Jammal'an. Each of these trolls holds one of the feathers you need to complete this quest.

THE AZURE KEY

Quest Level	50 to obtain
Location	Azshara
Quest Giver	Archmage Xylem
Goal	Return the Azure Key
Max Experience Gained	2,550
Reward	Duskbat Drape (Cloak, 37 Armor, +14 AGI, Equip: Reduces damage from falling.) or Ebon Mask (Leather Head, 122 Armor, +11 Stam, Equip: Improves your chance to get a critical strike by 1%. +36 Attack Power.) or Whisperwalk Boots (Leather Feet, 104 Armor, +18 AGI, +4 STA, Equip: Increases your effective stealth level by 1.)

Morphaz is one of the green drakes guarding the way to Eranikus. Kill him, then take the Azure Key to Lord Jorach Ravenholdt in Hillsbrad Foothills.

DA VOODOO

Quest Level	50 to obtain
Location	Alterac Mountains
Quest Giver	Bath'rah the Windwatcher
Goal	Retrieve the voodoo feathers
Max Experience Gained	2,550
Reward	Azurite Fists (Mail Hands, 195 Armor, +6 AGI, +7 STA, +7 INT, +6 SPI, Equip: Improves you chance to get a critical strike with spells by 1%.) or Enamored Water Spirit (Trinket, Use: Summons a Mana Spring Totem with 5 health at the feet of the caster for 24 sec that restores 27 mana every 2 seconds to group members within 20 yards.) or Wildstaff (Staff, 45.0 DPS, +10 STR, +10 STA, +9 INT, Equip: Improves your chance to hit by 1%. Improves you chance to get a critical strike by 1%.)

There are six trolls in the Temple of Atal'Hakkar assigned to guard the shield that protects Jammal'an. Each of these trolls holds one of the feathers necessary to complete this quest.

TROLLS OF A FEATHER

Quest Level	50 to obtain
Location	Felwood
Quest Giver	Impsy
Goal	Retrieve the voodoo feathers
Max Experience Gained	2,550
Reward	Abyss Shard (Trinket, Use: Casts your Summon Voidwalker spell with no mana or Soul Shard requirements.) or Robes of Servitude (Cloth Chest, 75 Armor, +15 STA, +10 INT, Equip: Increases damage done by Fire spells and effects by up to 23. Increases damage done by Shadow spells and effects by up to 23.) or Soul Harvester (Staff, 44.8 DPS, +16 STA, Equip: Improves your chance to hit with spells by 1%. Increases damage done by Shadow spells and effects by up to 24.)

There are six trolls in the Temple of Atal'Hakkar assigned to guard the shield that protects Jammal'an. Each of these trolls holds one of the feathers necessary to complete this quest.

VOODOO FEATHERS

Quest Level	50 to obtain
Location	Swamp of Sorrows
Quest Giver	Fallen Hero of the Horde
Goal	Retrieve the voodoo feathers
Max Experience Gained	2,550
Reward	Diamond Flask (Trinket, Use: Restores 9 health every 5 sec and increases your Strength by 75. Lasts 1 min.) or Fury Visor (Plate Head, 445 Armor, +18 STR, Equip: Improves your chance to get a critical strike by 1%. Improves your chance to hit by 1%.) or Razorsteel Shoulders (Plate Shoulder, 410 Armor, +10 STR, +10 AGI, +9 STA, Equip: Improves your chance to hit by 1%.)

There are six trolls in the Temple of Atal'Hakkar assigned to guard the shield that protects Jammal'an. Each of these trolls holds one of the feathers necessary to complete this quest.

WORSHIPPERS OF THE LOST

ENEMIES

NPC	LEVEL
Atal'ai Corpse Eater	49-50 Elite
Atal'ai Deathwalker	49-51 Elite
Notes: Fear, Shadow Word: Pain	
Atal'ai Deathwalker's Spirit	50-51 Elite
Notes: Spawns from Atal'ai Deathwalker on death, moves slowly, immune to all types of damage	
Atal'ai High Priest	49-51 Elite
Notes: Summons Atal'ai Skeletons	
Atal'ai Priest	46-47 Elite
Notes: Heal	
Atal'ai Skeleton	46-47
Notes: Summoned by Atal'ai High Priests	

NPC	LEVEL
Atal'ai Slave	44-47
Atal'ai Warrior	48-49 Elite
Notes: Rend, Warrior Strike (melee attack)	
Atal'ai Witch Doctor	49-50 Elite
Notes: Heal, Shadowbolt	
Cursed Atal'ai	45-46 Elite
Notes: Call of the Grave (Curse, 900 Shadow damage after 60 seconds)	
Deep Lurker	47-49 Elite
Notes: Trample (AoE physical damage)	
Enthralled Atal'ai	45-46 Elite
Notes: Fixate	
Fungal Ooze	41-46 Elite
Notes: Plague Cloud (Disease, -11 AGI, STR, STA)	
Hakkar'i Bloodkeeper	49 Elite
Notes: Shadowbolt	

NPC	LEVEL
Hakkar'i Frostwing	49-50 Elite
Notes: Frostwing Swoop (knockdown), Frostbolt Volley	
Hakkar'i Sapper	49-50 Elite
Notes: Wing Flap (knockback), Shadow Bolt	
Mummified Atal'ai	46-47 Elite
Notes: Fevered Plague (High damage initial hit and 19 nature damage every 5 seconds, 3 minute duration)	
Murk Slitherer	45-46 Elite
Murk Spitter	46-47 Elite
Notes: Venom Spit	
Murk Worm	47-48 Elite
Notes: Slowing Poison (-20% attack speed, 42% movement speed)	

NPC	LEVEL
Nightmare Scalebane	50-51 Elite
Notes: Shield Spike	
Nightmare Suppressor	49-50 Elite
Nightmare Wanderer	49-50 Elite
Nightmare Whelp	44-50
Nightmare Wyrmkin	50-51 Elite
Notes: Sleep, Acid Spit	
Oozlings	40
Notes: Fast Wanderers	
Saturated Ooze	47 Elite
Notes: Summons Oozlings	
Slime Maggot	45-46
Notes: Linked	
Unliving Atal'ai	48-49 Elite
Notes: Wandering Plague, Enrage	

THE LEADERS OF THE LOST

NPC	LEVEL	FREQUENT DROP(S)
ATAL'ALARION	50 Elite	Atal'alarion's Tusk Ring (Plate Waist: 302 Armor, +18 STR, +8 STA), Headspike (Polearm: 44.2 DPS, +15 STR, +18 STA), Darkwater Bracers (Leather Wrist, 66 Armor, +7 Shadow Resistance, +9-10 for 2 random stats)
Notes: AoE knockdown, Sweeping Slam (AoE knockback, massive damage)		
AVATAR OF HAKKAR	50 Elite	Bloodshot Greaves (Mail Feet, 221 Armor, +5 STR, +6 AGI, +20 STA), Featherskin Cape (Back, 39 Armor, +4 STA, +4 INT, +15 SPI), Windscale Sarong (Leather Legs, 136 Armor, +7 AGI, +10 STA, +10 INT, +20 SPI), Warrior's Embrace (Plate Chest, 567 Armor, +4 AGI, +11 STA), Might of Hakkar (Main-hand Mace, 35.8 Dps, +11 STA, +5 SPI), Spire of Hakkar (Staff, 46.5 Dps, +16 STA, +16 SPI, Equip: Increases damage and healing done by magical spells and effects by up to 10), Embrace of the Windserpent (Cloth Chest, 86 Armor, +30 SPI, +17 INT, +9 STA, +12 Nature Resistance)
Notes: Mind Control		
DREAMSCYTHE	53 Elite	Smoldering Claw (Polearm: 46.6 DPS, +10 Fire Resistance, Chance on Hit: Hurls a fiery ball that causes 135 fire damage and an additional 15 over 6 seconds), Firebreather (One-Hand Sword: 35.2 DPS, Chance on Hit: Hurls a fiery ball that causes 70 fire damage and an additional 9 over 6 seconds), Drakefang Butcher (Two-Hand Sword: 45.9 DPS, +15 STR, Chance on Hit: Wounds the target causing them to bleed for 150 damage over 30 seconds), Drakestone of the Owl (Held in Off-Hand: +9-10 INT, +9-10 SPI, Equip: Increases damage and healing done by magical spells and effects by up to 4), Drakeclaw Band (Ring: +9-10 to 2 random stats) Nightfall Drape (Back: +14 STA, +8 SPI), Bloodfire Talons (Leather Hands: 96 Armor, +5 INT, +9 SPI, +10 Fire Resistance, Equip: Increases damage and healing done by magical spells and effects by up to 10), Dawnspire Cord (Cloth Waist: 43 Armor, +19 INT, +8 SPI)
Notes: Acid Breath (36 nature damage every 5 seconds), Wing Flap (knockback)		
GASHER	50-51 Elite	Atal'ai Boots (Mail Feet: 185 Armor, +11-12 to 2 random stats), Atal'ai Gloves (Cloth Hands: 47 Armor, +12-13 to 2 random stats), Atal'ai Breastplate (Mail Chest: 311 Armor, +16-17 to 2 random stats), Atal'ai Girdle (Plate Waist: 280 Armor, +11-12 to 2 random stats), Atal'ai Spaulders (Leather Shoulders: 193 Armor, +12-13 to 2 random stats), Atal'ai Leggings (Leather Legs: 120 Armor, +14-15 to 2 random stats)
Notes: Dual-wield		
HAZZAS	53 Elite	Same as Dreamscythe
Notes: Acid Breath (36 nature damage every 5 seconds), Wing Flap (knockback)		
HUKKU	52 Elite	Same as Gasher
Notes: Shadow Bolt, Summons Voidwalker, Imp and Succubus		
JAMMAL'AN THE PROPHET	54 Elite	Gloves of the Atal'ai Prophet (Cloth Hands: 49 Armor, +5 STR, +6 STA, +20 SPI), Kilt of the Atal'ai Prophet (Cloth Legs: 69 Armor, +4 STR, +9 STA, +18 INT, +18 SPI), Vestments of the Atal'ai Prophet (Cloth Chest: 78 Armor, +11 INT, +27 SPI)
Notes: Linked with Ogom the Wretched, Hex of Jammal'An, Healing Wave, Flamestrike		
KAZKAZ THE UNHOLY	48 Elite	Mageweave, Troll Sweat
LORO	51 Elite	Same as Gasher
Notes: Shield Spike		
MIJAN	52 Elite	Same as Gasher
Notes: Greater Healing Ward		

NPC	LEVEL	FREQUENT DROP(S)
MORPHAZ	52 Elite	Same as Dreamscythe
Notes: Acid Breath (36 nature damage every 5 seconds), Wing Flap (knockback)		
OGOM THE WRETCHED	53 Elite	Eater of the Dead (Main-Hand Axe: 32 DPS, Equip: +30 Attack Power when fighting undead), Blade of the Wretched (Main-Hand Sword: 32.1 DPS, Chance of Hit: Corrupts the target, causing 90 damage over 3 seconds), Fist of the Damned (One-Hand Mace: 32.1 DPS, Chance on Hit: Steals 30 life from the target)
Notes: Shadow Bolt, Shadow Word: Pain , Curse of Weakness		
SHADE OF ERANIKUS	54-55 Elite	Rod of Corrosion (Wand, 55 Dps, +10 Nature Resistance), Tooth of Eranikus (Main-hand Axe, 37.1 Dps, +6 STR, Equip: Increases your chance to hit by 1%), Horns of Eranikus (Mail Head, 271 Armor, +27 INT, +11 SPI), Dire Nail (One-hand Dagger, 36.7 Dps, +5 Shadow Resistance, 1 random bonus), Crest of Supremacy (Shield, 1930 Armor, 35 Block, +6 STR, +6 AGI, +7 STA, +7 INT, +7 SPI), Dragon's Eye (Neck, +6 STA, +15 SPI), Dragon's Call (One-hand Sword, 41.4 DPS, Chance on Hit: Calls forth an Emerald Dragon Whelp to protect you in battle for a short period of time.)
Notes: Warstomp (AoE knockback and stun), Deep Slumber, Thrash, Acid Breath		
SPAWN OF HAKKAR	51 Elite	Slitherscale Boots (Leather Feet: 104 Armor, +5 STR, +12 STA, +15 SPI), Wingveil Cloak (Back: 34 Armor, +12 SPI)
VEYZHAK THE CANNIBAL	48 Elite	Random level 42-45 Uncommon equipment, Mageweave, Troll Sweat
WEAVER	51 Elite	Same as Dreamscythe
Notes: Acid Breath (36 nature damage every 5 seconds), Wing Flap (knockback)		
ZEKKIS	48 Elite	Random level 42-45 Uncommon equipment, Mageweave, Troll Sweat
ZOLO	51 Elite	Same as Gasher
Notes: Chain Lightning, Skeleton Summoning Totem		
ZUL'LOR	52 Elite	Same as Gasher
Notes: Frailty (Curse, AoE, -10 all stats, 1 minute duration)		

WHAT LIES BENEATH?

LEGEND

1 Entrance from Swamp of Sorrows
2 Hall of Masks
3 Chamber of Blood
4 The Butchery
5 Den of the Caller
6 Hall of Ritual
7 Hall of Bones
8 Instance Portal

THE WAY IN

Getting to the Hall of Masks is relatively easy. The Murk Slitherers and Fungal Oozes can be pulled singly and are good practice targets for your group. Once through, take the right hallway down the stairs to the Chamber of Blood.

The stairs bring you to the lower level of the Chamber of Blood. There are a number of Atal'ai Priests, Cursed Atal'ai, and Enthralled Atal'ai. This area will give you party practice in dealing with fleeing enemies and some of the special attacks you will encounter later in the dungeon. This is also a good place to start gathering Fetishes of Hakkar and Atal'ai Tablets.

Once the room is clear, ascend the stairs and take the left corridor from the Hall of Masks. There's a room to the left at the bottom of the first steps. The Butchery has relatively few enemies, but Veyzhak the Cannibal is a rare-spawn in this room. Should he be present, prepare for a straightforward fight.

Give the tank a couple seconds to establish aggro before laying into Veyzhak. High DPS parties can bring him down before he has the chance to do significant damage. Parties with less DPS need to be ready to heal the tank. Drop DoTs on him and prepare for the long haul.

Taking the hallway as it curls to the right brings you to the Den of the Caller. This room should be approached cautiously. There are two pair of Atal'ai Priests and another Atal'ai Priest wandering solo. With that much healing power, the fight could be very difficult should you gain the entire rooms attention. Pull the groups one at a time around the corner until the room is clear before proceeding.

Take the stairs to the south to the upper ledge of the Chamber of Blood. Kazkaz the Unholy can often be found here and is a quick fight. Once Kazkaz is no longer, return to the Den of the Caller and move down the eastern hallway.

The Hall of Ritual is another dangerous room. There are several groups without much space between them. Pull the groups one at a time around the corner and deal with them. Keep the enemy from running as a fleeing opponent here can spell doom for your party. Moving down the stairs brings you to the Hall of Bones.

There are two ways to get to the Instance Portal. You can jump to the middle level (not recommended unless you've been here before), or take the stairs on the right to the middle level. Fight your way to the northwest side on the middle level to gain access to the Instance Portal.

FALLING ISN'T THE END

Should you attempt the jump to the middle level and miss, you will find yourself on the lower level and under attack. All is not lost. Your party should aid you however they can from their vantage point until the party is not under attack. Then form on the lower level and take the stairs on the south side to the middle level.

THE PUZZLE

LEGEND

1 Hall of Serpents
2 Altar of Hakkar
3 Pit of Refuse

UNLOCKING THE MYSTERY

The Pit of Refuse is populated by a variety of aggressive enemies and a number of neutral Slime Maggots. Do not let this fool you. When you engage any of the aggressive enemies, the Slime Maggots will come to their aid.

Clear around the Altar of Hakkar and the pool beneath before examining the altar to complete *Into the Depths*. When the altar is activated, green light will shine on the balconies overhead one at a time. The order is important as it is the key to the mystery. Having a piece of paper handy to mark the sequence makes it much easier to remember.

With the order noted, move back to the Instance Portal and take the forward right passage. Take the stairs down from the first landing to the Hall of Serpents.

The enemies in the Hall of Serpents are very similar to the enemies in the Pit of Refuse with a few exceptions. There are slow wandering Elite enemies and fast wandering non-Elite enemies to watch for. The Spawn of Hakkar also wanders the Hall.

Move around the Hall of Serpents clearing all opposition. The enemy tends to guard in groups with a Deep Lurker, several Murk Worms, or a Saturated Ooze accompanied by many Slime Maggots.

THE PENALTY FOR ERROR

Do not activate the statues out of order. Doing so will cause and AoE -50% STR curse to be cast on your party. Leave the statues until you can activate them in the order the lights showed

With the Hall of Serpents clear, activate the statues to complete *Secret of the Circle*. The Idol of Hakkar and Atal'alarion will spawn in the Pit of Refuse. Jump down to the level below, but don't jump into the water. Rest up at the steps in preparation for the fight.

Atal'alarion has a lot of hit points and does tremendous damage. If that weren't enough, he has an aggro clearing ability. He can knock party members high into the air. The party members take falling damage when they finally land, and Atal'arion attacks other members.

Start the fight by having the tank drag Atal'alarion against a wall. Keep your healers and ranged damage dealers away from Atal'alarion, but move everyone into the water. This way when he throws the melee party members, he'll have a long walk to get to anyone soft and the water prevents falling damage from the knockup attack.

Layer Atal'alarion with DoTs to keep the damage going even if you must kite him around while the melee members are in flight. Have heals ready when party members land.

The constant damage will wear Atal'alarion down and leave you free to pillage the Idol of Hakkar. Inside you find the Hakkari Urn. It holds a number of items to reward you for your trouble.

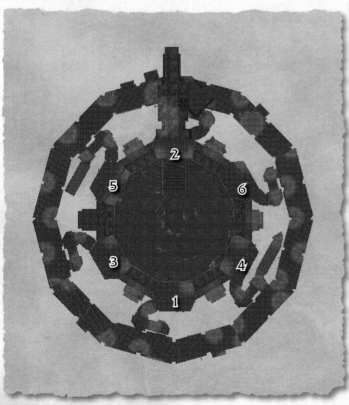

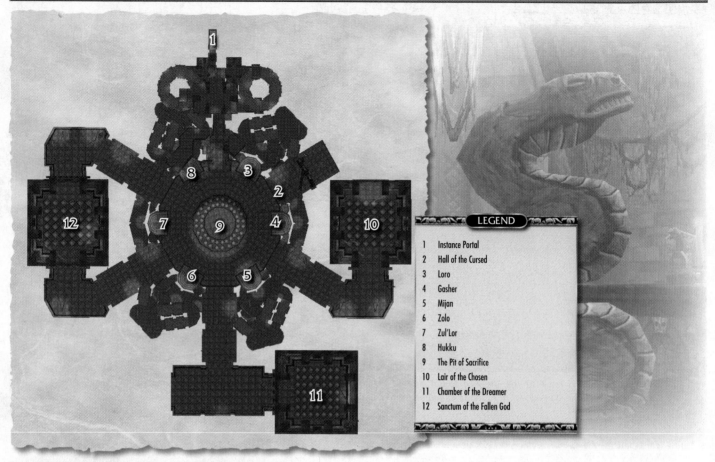

LEGEND

1. Instance Portal
2. Hall of the Cursed
3. Loro
4. Gasher
5. Mijan
6. Zolo
7. Zul'Lor
8. Hukku
9. The Pit of Sacrifice
10. Lair of the Chosen
11. Chamber of the Dreamer
12. Sanctum of the Fallen God

BREECHING JAMMAL'AN'S SHIELD

There are many barricades and safeguards between you and your objectives. Taking them out in the proper order is the only way to leave the Temple of Atal'Hakkar victorious.

There are four passageways leading from the instance portal: one on your left, one on the right, and two in front of you. Take the passage that's second from the left. There are many groups consisting of both living and unliving Atal'ai. The Unliving Atal'ai are immune to much of the crowd control your party has. (A Priest's Shackle Undead is a great root). Use your CC on the Atal'ai Witchdoctors and kill the others first. As you ascend the stairs, you will also encounter Atal'ai Slaves in the groups. These can be dealt with at your convenience and pose no immediate threat to your party.

At the first large landing, there is a passage toward the center of the Temple and stairs continuing up. The passage leads to a ledge overlooking the Pit of Sacrifice. More importantly, it is guarded by Loro. Loro and his companions use their power to hold a shield protecting Jammal'an. You must kill all six of the shielders before Jammal'an is vulnerable to attack. Begin by killing Loro. Continue up the stairs.

The stairs end at the Hall of the Cursed. This hall runs around the edge of the Pit of Sacrifice. There are several passages leading off the circle. These lead to the other balconies above the Pit of Sacrifice.

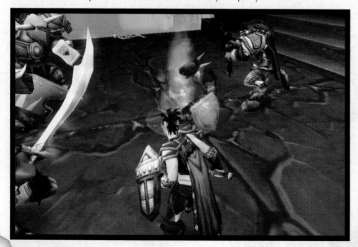

There are wandering Atal'ai Warriors that should be watched for. At several points around the circle there are groups of Atal'ai guarding. These groups usually consist of at least one Atal'ai Witchdoctor, one melee enemy (either Unliving Atal'ai, Atal'ai Corpse Eater, or Atal'ai Warrior) and another melee enemy or a group of Atal'ai Slaves. The Witchdoctors, Corpse Eaters, and Warriors can be CCed to keep the find from getting out of hand. Clear the groups while watching your back for wanderers.

Move around the Hall of the Cursed in a clock-wise direction, killing Gasher, Mijan, Zolo, Zul'Lor, and Hukku. There are stairs on the inside of the circle leading directly to the ledges of Gasher and Zul'Lor, while there are stairs on the outside of the circle leading to platforms with passages to the ledges of the other four.

With the six guardians dead, the shield guarding Jammal'an falls. You objective is one step closer. Return to the Instance Portal and take the stairs to your left.

MOVING ON JAMMAL'AN

Your enemies have changed, but the tactics are very similar. The Nightmare Wyrmkin can cast Sleep (dispellable by Priests and Paladins) and have a ranged poison attack and should be considered extremely dangerous. The wrong party member sleeping can spell doom for your group. Once the Wyrmkin is dead, focus on the Nightmare Wanderers and Nightmare Scalebane. When the last of the Elite enemies has fallen, clean up the Nightmare Whelps.

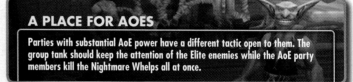

A PLACE FOR AOES

Parties with substantial AoE power have a different tactic open to them. The group tank should keep the attention of the Elite enemies while the AoE party members kill the Nightmare Whelps all at once.

Move into the Pit of Sacrifice. There are many groups of Dragonkin. Allof these must be dealt with before you confront Jammal'an. Move around the room, avoiding the hole in the center, and systematically exterminate the Dragonkin.

DRAGONKIN PULLS

If you have a hard time handling multiple elite dragonkin at the same time, use a Hunter's Freezing Trap or the Druid ability Hibernate to put enemies temporarily out of action.

Proceed down the east passage to the Lair of the Chosen. This room is one of the most dangerous in the dungeon. Melee enemies are mixed with casters. Pull the enemies back around the corner. This is very important as leaving the Atal'ai High Priests at range will make your life much more difficult. The High Priests should be killed first and quickly. They can summon Atal'ai Skeletons to their aid if left alive.

With the High Priests dead, turn your attention to the Atal'ai Deathwalkers. They can cast Fear and should not be engaged near the room. One party member being feared into the Lair of the Chosen means a total party wipeout. On death, the Deathwalkers spawn Atal'ai Deathwalker's Spirit. These are immune to all damage while still inflicting damage. They are also very slow and dissipate after a few seconds. Anytime a party member becomes engaged by a Deathwalker's Spirit, they need to kite it (move around to keep the enemy out of attack range) until it dissipates. The character assigned to tank Jammal'an should burn up all his or her long cooldown abilities during these fights.

Once the room is clear of smaller targets, it's time for Jammal'an the Prophet and his assistant Ogom the Wretched. Ogom has much less health and should be pulled away from Jammal'an, then killed quickly. Jammal'an is very dangerous. Hex of Jammal'an transforms its target into an Atal'ai Berserker under the Prophet's control. This only lasts a short while, but the controlled character attacks other party members with every special ability available. While under control, the character moves more slowly, but hits hard. Spread out your party as much as possible. Party members under attack should keep out of range until the spell wears off. Use DoTs and nukes to whittle away at his health until he falls to his knees for the last time.

Collecting the Head of Jammal'an will complete the *Jammal'an the Prophet* quest. The primary objective is complete, but there is still treasure to be had.

CLEARING THE WAY TO ERANIKUS

With the death of Jammal'an, the drakes Weaver and Dreamscythe have appeared in the Pit of Sacrifice. It's possible to pull each singly if you wait for one to pass around the circle, then shoot the one that's trailing behind, provided they have enough distance between them. These fights are fairly straightforward, if a bit difficult. The tank should keep the drakes facing away from the party to minimize the damage caused by their breath weapons. If both drakes come at the same time, select a second tank to occupy one of them while its health is drained. Another option is to use a Hunter to kite the drake around while the rest of the party drops the other target. Bring them down one at a time and continue to the southern passage.

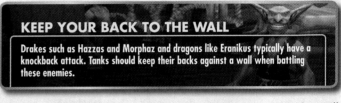

KEEP YOUR BACK TO THE WALL

Drakes such as Hazzas and Morphaz and dragons like Eranikus typically have a knockback attack. Tanks should keep their backs against a wall when battling these enemies.

Here, there are two more drakes by the names of Hazzas and Morphaz. Kill them as you killed the others and prepare for the fight against the Shade of Eranikus who resides in the Chamber of the Dreamer.

The Shade of Eranikus summons all Dragonkin left alive to aid him. A quick survey to make sure all the Dragonkin are dead may be in order if your party is unsure. The winged serpents in the western section won't answer his summons.

Eranikus has a number of abilities that make him very dangerous. Warstomp is an AoE stun that centers on him. Keep as much of your party out of this as possible. The more party members at range, the better.

If a single party member is being too effective against him, Eranikus will cast Deep Slumber. This single target spell puts one of your members to sleep for a long time. If your tank is slept, a secondary tank (Druid in bear form, a Paladin, or a Rogue with Evasion available) should grab and hold Eranikus until the main tank can be woken.

With Eranikus under control, let your DPS fly. This is a long fight with a lot of pounding before the Shade falls so be careful about pulling aggro off the tank. DPS classes should use skills such as Feign Death and Feint to reduce the amount of threat generated by their attacks.

Remove the **Essence of Eranikus** from the corpse and begin the *Essence of Eranikus* quest. The Essence Font is in the same room and placing the Essence in the Font completes the quest.

THE GOD HAKKAR

The passages on the west side of the Pit of Sacrifice lead to the Sanctum of the Fallen God. The Hakkar'i Sappers and Frostwings can be fought individually and pose little threat to your party. Eliminate them and have you entire party move into the chamber before proceeding.

Use the Ancient Egg to begin the fight. The enemies spawn endlessly. Kill them until the Hakkar'i Bloodkeeper spawns. Slay the Hakkar'i Bloodkeeper, grab the Hakkar'i Blood from the corpse and extinguish the braziers quickly. Only one brazier can be extinguished per blood, but it won't take long until another arrives.

MAKING IT EASIER

Select a person to extinguish the braziers and set looting to Free-for-All so he can loot any of the bodies. This makes extinguishing them much faster and easier. Remember to set looting back once the Avatar of Hakkar spawns.

When the Avatar of Hakkar first shows, he doesn't attack provided no one in the group is near the center of the chamber. Before extinguishing the final brazier, have everyone move close to a wall and take this time to clear any left over spawns in the room. Having spawns in the room when the Avatar attacks is a recipe for disaster. Should this occur, the tank needs to hold Hakkar while the party finishes clean up before engaging the Avatar.

Once the room is clear of everything save the Avatar of Hakkar, take a few moments to rest and restore mana. If your tank gets in trouble while your healers are out of mana, have a secondary tank pull Hakkar off the main tank. Druids in bear form, a Paladin, or a Rogue (with Evasion) can pull Hakkar off and hold him long enough for the main tank to bandage. Once the casters have mana again (use Mana Tide Totems or Judgement of Wisdom to help restore mana) it's time to end the fight. Unload all your damage and keep the tank healed. With the resources of your party restored, don't hold back anything.

With the Avatar of Hakkar fallen, collect the essence for **The God Hakkar**.

With friends still alive, and bags full, it's time to head home.

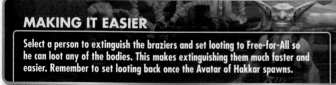

ULDAMAN

Played & Written by: Edwin "Plainsong" Kern of <Dovrani> on Kirin Tor

Digging deep beneath the surface of the Badlands, the Dwarves of Ironforge discovered ruins more ancient than anything previously unearthed. Shortly after the discovery, Troggs invaded the dig sites with terrible ruthlessness. Now Shadowforge Dwarves are seeking to control the ruins. What lies buried that has so many warring so fervently? Descending into the darkness of the caves and tunnels is the only way to claim the treasures for yourself.

DUNGEON INFORMATION

Location	Badlands
Quests	Both
Region	Contested
Suggested Levels	40–45
Group Allowed	5 for Quests, 10 for Raiding
Primary Enemies	Humanoids, Golems
Time to Complete	2.5–3 Hours

GETTING TO ULDAMAN

The primary entrance into Uldaman is just south of the Loch Modan border in Badlands. It's easy to spot by the multitude of Shadowforge Dwarves roaming around the dig site. Fight past these into the tunnels.

Alliance groups should fly into Thelsamar in Loch Modan and head south into Badlands. Horde parties have a longer run if they've never been there before. Fly to Hammerfall in Arathi Highlands and head south through Wetlands and Loch Modan into Badlands. Before you start your run into Uldaman, make the trek west to Kargath to get the Flightpoint.

BACK ENTRANCE

If you have been to Uldaman before, the back door is through a tunnel east of Hammertoe's Digsite.

WHO TO BRING

Having a party member with high armor and high HP is crucial for surviving this dungeon. Chain-wearing classes can handle the Shadowforge Dwarves and the Troggs, but when you reach the Golems, you'll need someone in plate. The Golems hit extremely hard and have very high health. Another necessity for Uldaman is including classes that have snare abilities. Many enemies flee when at low health and there are always more enemies close by.

QUESTS FOR ULDAMAN

All the quests for Uldaman are Dungeon quests. These cannot be completed in a Raid group. Avoid Raid groups unless your are going in for the treasure alone.

ALLIANCE QUESTS

QUEST NAME	QUEST GIVER	QUEST GIVER LOCATION	QUEST RECEIVER	QUEST RECEIVER LOCATION	CHAIN?	MAX EXPERIENCE
A Sign of Hope	Prospector Ryedol	Badlands: Hammertoe's Dig Site	Hammertoe Grez	Uldaman	Yes	2,750
Amulet of Secrets	Hammertoe Grez	Uldaman	Hammertoe Grez	Uldaman	Yes	3,150
Prospect of Faith	Hammertoe Grez	Uldaman	Prospector Ryedol	Badlands: Hammertoe's Dig Site	Yes	2,350
Prospect of Faith	Prospector Ryedol	Badlands: Hammertoe's Dig Site	Historian Karnik	Ironforge: Hall of Explorers	Yes	3,150
The Lost Tablets of Will	Advisor Belgrum	Ironforge: Hall of Explorers	Advisor Belgrum	Ironforge: Hall of Explorers	Yes	5,850
REWARD: Medal of Courage (Neck, +9 STA, +3 SPI)						
Agmond's Fate	Prospector Ironband	Loch Modan: Ironband's Excavation Site	Prospector Ironband	Loch Modan: Ironband's Excavation Site	No	2,850
REWARD: Prospector Gloves (Leather Hands, 65 Armor, +8 AGI, +7 INT)						
The Lost Dwarves	Prospector Stormpike	Ironforge: Hall of Explorers	Baelog	Uldaman	Yes	341
The Hidden Chamber	Baelog	Uldaman	Baelog	Uldaman	Yes	3,900
The Shattered Necklace	Shattered Necklace	Uldaman: Random Drop	Talvash del Kissel	Ironforge: Mystic Ward	Yes	3,300
Lore for a Price	Talvash del Kissel	Ironforge: Mystic Ward	Talvash del Kissel	Ironforge: Mystic Ward	Yes	3,900
Back to Uldaman	Talvash del Kissel	Ironforge: Mystic Ward	Remains of a Paladin	Uldaman	Yes	2,550
Find the Gems	Remains of a Paladin	Uldaman	Talvash del Kissel	Phial of Scrying	Yes	3,600
Restoring the Necklace	Talvash del Kissel	Phial of Scrying	Talvash del Kissel	Ironforge: Mystic Ward	Yes	925
REWARD: Talvash's Enhancing Necklace (Neck, +10 STA, +1 INT, +10 SPI)						
Uldaman Reagent Run	Ghak Healtouch	Loch Modan: Thelsamar	Ghak Healtouch	Loch Modan: Thelsamar	Yes	3,450
REWARD: 5 Restorative Elixirs (Removes all negative effects)						
Reclaimed Treasures	Krom Stoutarm	Ironforge: Hall of Explorers	Krom Stoutarm	Ironforge: Hall of Explorers	No	3,600
The Platinum Discs	The Platinum Discs	Uldaman	The Platinum Discs	Uldaman	Yes	5,250
The Platinum Discs	The Platinum Discs	Uldaman	High Explorer Magellas	Ironforge: Hall of Explorers	Yes	5,250

A SIGN OF HOPE

Quest Level	35 to obtain
Location	Badlands (Hammertoe's Dig site)
Contact	Prospector Ryedol
Goal	Find Hammertoe Grez
Max Experience Gained	2,750

This quest begins when you find a Crumpled Map in Hammertoe's Dig Site. Take the map to Prospector Ryedol. He explains that Hammertoe has been kidnapped by the Shadowforge Dwarves. Hammertoe is hiding in a small dead-end tunnel just east of the instance portal. Find Hammertoe and he offers you the *Amulet of Secrets* quest.

AMULET OF SECRETS

Quest Level	36 to obtain
Location	Uldaman
Contact	Hammertoe Grez
Goal	Find and return Hammertoe's Amulet
Max Experience Gained	3,150

The Shadowforge Dwarves have already had their way with Hammertoe, and Magregan Deepshadow has Hammertoe's Amulet. This is a problem as it leads them to some highly sensitive scrolls. With these scrolls, the Shadowforge Dwarves plan on creating even more deadly Golems. Your mission is clear: find and slay Magregan, and return the amulet to Hammertoe. Magregan can be found in the southeast section of the tunnels outside the instance. Completing this quest leads to the *Prospect of Faith* quest.

PROSPECT OF FAITH

Quest Level	36 to obtain
Location	Uldaman
Contact	Hammertoe Grez
Goal	Take Hammertoe's Amulet to Prospector Ryedol
Max Experience Gained	2,350

The amulet is out of Magregan's hands, but the scrolls are still in danger. Hammertoe asks you to take his amulet to Prospector Ryedol. He's familiar with Hammertoe's work and can best determine the next course of action. Bringing Hammertoe's Amulet to Prospector Ryedol opens the next step of this quest chain.

PROSPECT OF FAITH

Quest Level	36 to obtain
Location	Uldaman
Contact	Prospector Ryedol
Goal	Deliver Hammertoe's Amulet to Historian Karnik
Max Experience Gained	3,150

It appears Ryedol wasn't as in touch with Hammertoe's work as was believed, but all is not lost. Hammertoe was working closely with Historian Karnik in Ironforge. Surely he'll know what should be done next. Speaking with Karnik unlocks the *Passing Word of a Threat* and *An Ambassador of Evil* quests in the Badlands.

THE LOST TABLETS OF WILL

Quest Level	38 to obtain
Location	Ironforge
Contact	Advisor Belgrum
Goal	Find the Tablet of Will
Max Experience Gained	5,850
Reward	Medal of Courage (Neck, +9 STA, +3 SPI)

If you have completed the *Passing Word of a Threat* and *An Ambassador of Evil* quests (which stemmed from the *Prospect of Faith* quest), Advisor Belgrum has more work for you. The Shadowforge clan has been weakened by your efforts, but the Tablet of Will still resides in Uldaman. You need to get it before they do. The Tablet of Will can be found deep within Uldaman in the northwestern area.

AGMOND'S FATE

Quest Level	31 to obtain
Location	Loch Modan (Ironband's Excavation Site)
Contact	Prospector Ironband
Goal	Collect 4 Carved Stone Urns
Max Experience Gained	2,850
Reward	Prospector Gloves (Leather Gloves, 65 Armor, +8 AGI, +7 INT)

With the news of Agmond's death, Prospector Ironband is worried. He believes the Carved Stone Urns found at the dig site incited the Troggs. To test this, he'll need some. The urns can be found in the tunnels or taken from the monsters.

THE LOST DWARVES

Quest Level	35 to obtain
Location	Ironforge
Contact	Prospector Stormpike
Goal	Find Baelog
Max Experience Gained	341

The invasion of the Troggs was very quick. Stormpike believes that an expedition lead by his friend (which left for the deeper part of the ruins the day before the invasion) may still be alive and cut off from aid. He charges you with finding them. Baelog and his expedition are indeed alive, and can be found through a whole in the south wall just inside the instance.

THE SHATTERED NECKLACE

Quest Level	37 to obtain
Location	Uldaman
Contact	Item begins quest
Goal	Return the Shattered Necklace to Talvash del Kissel
Max Experience Gained	3,300

The Shattered Necklace from the dwarves outside the instance. A close inspection finds the initials TdK engraved on it. Talvash del Kissel can be found in the Mystic Ward in Ironforge and may want his necklace back. Returning the Shattered Necklace opens the *Lore for a Price* quest.

THE HIDDEN CHAMBER

Quest Level	39 to obtain
Location	Uldaman
Contact	Baelog
Goal	Explore the Hidden Chamber
Max Experience Gained	3,900

Baelog and his expedition are alive. They were cut off by Troggs before they could open a special room nearby. Baelog would like you to continue his work and explore the Hidden Chamber. His journal, which is on the table beside him, details how to open the door in the Map Room. You need the Gni'kiv Medallion and the Shaft of Tsol to open the door. The Gni'kiv Medallion is in Baelog's Chest on the table. The Shaft of Tsol is in the hands of Revelosh (he's in a room to the northwest). Combining the two items and inserting them into the building in the center of the Map Room opens the door to the Hidden Chamber. Defeat its guardian, explore the chamber and return to Baelog for your reward.

LORE FOR A PRICE

Quest Level	37 to obtain
Location	Ironforge (Mystic Ward)
Contact	Talvash del Kissel
Goal	Collect 5 Silver Bars
Max Experience Gained	2,450

Talvash has fallen on hard times. He'll tell you about the necklace if you help him complete an order. He needs five Silver Bars to finish. The bars can be obtained from a Miner or the Auction House. Giving him the bars opens the *Back to Uldaman* quest.

BACK TO ULDAMAN

Quest Level	37 to obtain
Location	Ironforge (Mystic Ward)
Contact	Talvash del Kissel
Goal	Find the previous owner
Max Experience Gained	2,550

Talvash's current business luck is directly tied to the necklace you found. His competitor has spread rumors that the necklace cursed the Paladin who bought it. Talvash wants his name cleared and asks for your help. If he could reconstruct the necklace, he could prove that it isn't cursed. The Paladin who bought the necklace probably knows what happened to it.

Finding the Paladin is fairly easy, though not terribly cheerful. The Remains of a Paladin can be found just inside the instance in the second northern hallway. There's nothing you can do for the Paladin, but you can still help Talvash. Examining the Paladin's journal leads to the *Find the Gems* quest.

FIND THE GEMS

Quest Level	37 to obtain
Location	Uldaman
Contact	Remains of a Paladin
Goal	Find the Shattered Necklace Ruby, Sapphire, and Topaz
Max Experience Gained	3,600

The Paladin did one final deed that makes your (and Talvash's) life easier. He jotted down information on the gems.

1. The Shattered Necklace Topaz is hidden in an Urn near Baelog.

2. The Shattered Necklace Ruby is stashed in the northern area of the dungeon.

3. The Shattered Necklace Sapphire is held by Grimlok, who can be found in the northern area of the dungeon.

When all the gems are found, contact Talvash using the Phial of Scrying he gave you. Contacting Talvash grants the Restoring the Necklace quest.

RESTORING THE NECKLACE

Quest Level	38 to obtain
Location	Uldaman
Contact	Talvash del Kissel (via Phial of Scrying)
Goal	Find the Shattered Necklace Power Source
Max Experience Gained	925
Reward	Talvash's Enhancing Necklace (Neck, +10 STA, +1 INT, +10 SPI)

Even with the gems collected, Talvash needs something to power the necklace. He suggests that you take the power source from the largest Construct you can find. The largest Construct is at the end of the dungeon. With as much power as it brings against you, it'll surely make a wonderful necklace.

ULDAMAN REAGENT RUN

Quest Level	38 to obtain
Location	Loch Modan (Thelsamar)
Contact	Ghak Healtouch
Goal	Collect 12 Magenta Fungus Caps
Max Experience Gained	3,450
Reward	5 Restorative Elixirs (Removes all negative effects)

If you have completed the *Badlands Reagent Run*, Ghak has more work for you. Magenta Fungus Caps grow deep in the Uldaman site and Ghak wants a dozen for alchemical research. The fungus can be found on the ground or taken from the many denizens of Uldaman.

RECLAIMED TREASURES

Quest Level	33 to obtain
Location	Ironforge
Contact	Krom Stoutarm
Goal	Retrieve Krom's priced possession
Max Experience Gained	3,600

Krom's story is fairly sad. He was a digger in Uldaman when the Troggs invaded. To escape with his life, he abandoned his most treasured possession. He had it locked in a chest that the Troggs won't be able to open, but he can't get past the Troggs. You can. The chest is in the North Common Hall. It can be found in the southern area before the instance portal.

THE PLATINUM DISCS

Quest Level	40 to obtain
Location	Uldaman (Final Room)
Contact	The Platinum Discs
Goal	Take the Miniature Platinum Discs home
Max Experience Gained	5,250

After examining the discs again, you will find the Miniature Platinum Discs in your bags. It's time to tell your people what you have learned. Return the discs to High Explorer Magellas in Ironforge.

THE PLATINUM DISCS

Quest Level	40 to obtain
Location	Uldaman (Final Room)
Contact	The Platinum Discs
Goal	Learn more
Max Experience Gained	5250

The Platinum Discs are found in the final room of Uldaman. After examining them, the stone watcher appears nearby. Speak with the stone watcher to learn more about the dungeon. After speaking with the watcher and learning everything you can, return to the discs to open the The Platinum Discs quest.

HORDE QUESTS

QUEST NAME	QUEST GIVER	QUEST GIVER LOCATION	QUEST RECEIVER	QUEST RECEIVER LOCATION	CHAIN?	MAX EXPERIENCE
Necklace Recovery	Dran Doffers	Orgrimmar: The Drag	Dran Doffers	Orgrimmar: The Drag	Yes	2,450
Necklace Recovery, Take 2	Dran Doffers	Orgrimmar: The Drag	Remains of a Paladin	Uldaman	Yes	2,450
Translating the Journal	Remains of a Paladin	Uldaman	Jarkal Mossmeld	Badlands: Kargath	Yes	3,450
Translating the Journal	Jarkal Mossmeld	Badlands: Kargath	Jarkal Mossmeld	Badlands: Kargath	Yes	350
Find the Gems and Power Source	Jarkal Mossmeld	Badlands: Kargath	Jarkal Mossmeld	Badlands: Kargath	Yes	3,750
Uldaman Reagent Run	Jarkal Mossmeld	Badlands: Kargath	Jarkal Mossmeld	Badlands: Kargath	Yes	3,450
REWARD: 5 Restorative Elixirs (Removes all negative effects)						
Reclaimed Treasures	Patrick Garrett	Undercity: Bat Handler	Patrick Garrett	Undercity: Bat Handler	No	4,250
The Platinum Discs	The Platinum Discs	Uldaman	The Platinum Discs	Uldaman	Yes	5,250
The Platinum Discs	The Platinum Discs	Uldaman	Sage Truthseeker	Thunderbluff: Center Rise	Yes	5,250

NECKLACE RECOVERY

Quest Level	37 to obtain
Location	Orgrimmar (The Drag)
Contact	Dran Doffers
Goal	Recover the Shattered Necklace
Max Experience Gained	2,450

Rumors have reached Orgrimmar about a Paladin who died in Uldaman. This isn't uncommon and wouldn't be worthy of interest if he hadn't been wearing a rather expensive jeweled necklace. Dran, not willing to let an opportunity pass him by, would like you to retrieve the necklace for him. The Shattered Necklace can be found on one of the enemies in the entrance to Uldaman or in Uldaman itself. Recovering the Shattered Necklace opens the *Necklace Recovery, Take 2* quest.

NECKLACE RECOVERY, TAKE 2

Quest Level	37 to obtain
Location	Orgrimmar (The Drag)
Contact	Dran Doffers
Goal	Find the Remains of a Paladin
Max Experience Gained	2,450

The necklace was what held the jewels and it's the jewels that Dran wants. He decides there is a good chance the jewels are still inside Uldaman. The first place to look would be on the Remains of a Paladin. This can be found shortly after entering the Uldaman instance. Finding the Remains of a Paladin will unlock the *Translating the Journal* quest.

TRANSLATING THE JOURNAL

Quest Level	37 to obtain
Location	Uldaman
Contact	Remains of a Paladin
Goal	Translate the Journal
Max Experience Gained	3,450

On the body of the Paladin is a journal. The only problem is that you can't read it. Before you can find the jewels, you need first get the journal translated. Kargath post is likely a good place to start. Bringing the journal Jarkal Mossmeld in Kargath opens the next part in the *Translating the Journal* quest.

TRANSLATING THE JOURNAL

Quest Level	39 to obtain
Location	Badlands (Kargath)
Contact	Jarkal Mossmeld
Goal	Allow Jarkal to borrow the Shattered Necklace
Max Experience Gained	350

Jarkal is willing to translate the journal for you, for a price. He wants to study the necklace to learn how to make it. If you let him borrow the Shattered Necklace, he'll translate the journal for you so you can find the jewels. After studying the necklace, Jarkal will offer the *Find the Gems and Power Source* quest.

FIND THE GEMS AND POWER SOURCE

Quest Level	39 to obtain
Location	Badlands (Kargath)
Contact	Jarkal Mossmeld
Goal	Collect the Shattered Necklace Ruby, Topaz, Sapphire and the Shattered Necklace Power Source
Max Experience Gained	3,750

Jarkal has studied the necklace and can repair it if you bring him the parts. He needs the gems that were taken from the necklace and a power source. The journal mentions that the gems can be found in Uldaman.

1. The Shattered Necklace Topaz is hidden in an Urn near Baelog in a southern tunnel near the entrance.

2. The Shattered Necklace Ruby is stashed in the northern area of the dungeon.

3. The Shattered Necklace Sapphire is held by Grimlok, who can be found in the northern area of the dungeon.

For a power source, Jarkal suggests you find the largest construct in Uldaman and destroy it. This will be in the final room of the dungeon.

ULDAMAN REAGENT RUN

Quest Level	36 to obtain
Location	Badlands (Kargath)
Contact	Jarkal Mossmeld
Goal	Collect 12 Magenta Fungus Caps
Max Experience Gained	3,450
Reward	5x Restorative Elixir (Removes all negative effects on you)

If you have completed the *Badlands Reagent Run*, Jarkal has more work for you. Magenta Fungus Caps grow deep in the Uldaman site and Jarkal wants a dozen for alchemical research. The fungus can be found on the ground or taken from the many denizens of Uldaman.

RECLAIMED TREASURES

Quest Level	33 to obtain
Location	Undercity (Near Bat Handler)
Contact	Patrick Garrett
Goal	Recover the Garrett Family Treasure
Max Experience Gained	4,250

Patrick Garrett is tired of his lot in life. He tells of a time when his family worked as diggers in Uldaman. He also tells of a rather secure chest that has the Garrett Family Treasure in it. He's willing to give you what little he has made if you help him reclaim his birthright. The Garrett Family Treasure can be found in a chest in the North Common Hall in Uldaman. It's a large room on the southern side before the instance portal.

THE PLATINUM DISCS

Quest Level	40 to obtain
Location	Uldaman (Final Room)
Contact	The Platinum Discs
Goal	Learn more
Max Experience Gained	5250

The Platinum Discs are found in the final room of Uldaman. After examining them, the stone watcher appears nearby. Speak with the stone watcher to learn more about the dungeon. After speaking with the watcher and learning everything you can, return to the discs to open the *The Platinum Discs* quest.

THE PLATINUM DISCS

Quest Level	40 to obtain
Location	Uldaman (Final Room)
Contact	The Platinum Discs
Goal	Take the Miniature Platinum Discs home
Max Experience Gained	5,250

After examining the discs again, you will find the Miniature Platinum Discs in your bags. It's time to tell your people what you have learned. Return the discs to Sage Truthseeker in Thunder Bluff.

SHARED QUESTS

QUEST NAME	QUEST GIVER	QUEST GIVER LOCATION	QUEST RECEIVER	QUEST RECEIVER LOCATION	CHAIN?	MAX EXPERIENCE
Indurium	Martek the Exiled	Badlands: Valley of Fangs	Martek the Exiled	Badlands: Valley of Fangs	Yes	2,750
Power Stones	Rigglefuzz	Badlands: Valley of Fangs	Rigglefuzz	Badlands: Valley of Fangs	No	3,500
REWARD: Duracin Bracers (Mail Wrists, 95 Armor, +7 AGI, +3 STA) or Energized Stone Circle (Shield, 678 Armor, 14 Block, +2 STA, +7 SPI) or Everlast Boots (Cloth Feet, 33 Armor, +11 SPI)						
Solution to Doom	Theldurin the Lost	Badlands: Agmonds End	Theldurin the Lost	Badlands: Agmonds End	No	3,150
REWARD: Doomsayer's Robe (Cloth Chest, 53 Armor, -10 STA, +20 SPI)						

INDURIUM

Quest Level	31 to obtain
Location	Badlands (Valley of Fangs)
Contact	Martek the Exiled
Goal	Collect 10 Indurium Flakes
Max Experience Gained	2,750

If you have done the *Martek the Exiled* quest from Shimmering Flats, Martek will ask you to help him fill the order. He needs 10 Indurium Flakes to create the pistons for Fizzle's car. These can be mined in Uldaman or taken from the Stonevault Troggs in Uldaman or in Badlands.

POWER STONES

Quest Level	30 to obtain
Location	Badlands (Valley of Fangs)
Contact	Rigglefuzz
Goal	Collect 8 Dentrium Power Stones and 8 An'Alleum Power Stones
Max Experience Gained	3,500
Reward	Duracin Bracers (Mail Bracer, 95 Armor, +7 AGI, +3 STA) or Energized Stone Circle (Shield, 678 Armor, 14 Block, +2 STA, +7 SPI) or Everlast Boots (Cloth Boots, 33 Armor, +11 SPI)

Rigglefuzz was kidnapped and taken to Angor Fortress to examine some stones found in Uldaman. He's been released and wants another opportunity to work with the stones. If you bring him some, he'll make you an item. The stones can be taken from Shadowforge Dwarves throughout Uldaman.

SOLUTION TO DOOM

Quest Level	30 to obtain
Location	Badlands (Agmonds End)
Contact	Theldurin the Lost
Goal	Find the Tablet of Ryun'eh
Max Experience Gained	3,150
Reward	Doomsayer's Robe (Cloth Chest, 53 Armor, -10 STA, +20 SPI)

Theldurin has foreseen a doom coming. He wants you to get the Tablet of Ryun'eh for him. It can be found in the center of the Sealed Hall in the southern area before the instance portal.

CLASS QUEST

QUEST NAME	QUEST GIVER	QUEST GIVER LOCATION	QUEST RECEIVER	QUEST RECEIVER LOCATION	CHAIN?	MAX EXPERIENCE
Power in Uldaman	Tabetha	Dustwallow Marsh	Tabetha	Dustwallow Marsh	Yes	3,900

POWER IN ULDAMAN (MAGE ONLY QUEST)

Quest Level	35 to obtain
Location	Dustwallow Marsh
Contact	Tabetha
Goal	Retrieve an Obsidian Power Source
Max Experience Gained	3900

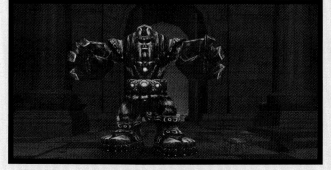

At level 35, your respective Mage trainer sends you to visit Tabetha in Dustwallow Marsh. After a trip to Desolace, the next destination is the back entrance to Uldaman and a battle with an Obsidian Sentinal. Defeat the Obsidian Sentinel and loot the Obsidian Power Source and return to Tabetha to continue the chain of quests.

THE OTHER DIGGERS

NPC	LEVEL
Cleft Scorpid	34-35
Notes: Social, Poison, Skinnable. Frequent Drops: Long Redwood Bow (Bow, 14.3 DPS), Mystery Meat	
Deadly Cleft Scorpid	41-43
Notes: Social, Skinnable	
Earthen Custodian	43-45
Notes: Social, Fire Ball, Healing	
Earthen Guardian	43-45
Notes: Social, Melee	
Earthen Hallshaper	44-45
Notes: Social, Fire Ball, Healing	
Earthen Rocksmasher	37-43
Notes: Social, Warrior, Strike (Enhanced melee attack)	
Earthen Sculptor	38-43
Notes: Social, Flame Shield IV, Flame Buffet (+42 damage from fire spells)	
Earthen Stonebreaker	41-45
Notes: Social, Melee	
Earthen Stonecarver	43-45
Notes: Social, Melee	
Jadespine Basilisk	39-40 Elite
Notes: Crystalline Slumber (Sleep), Skinnable	

NPC	LEVEL
Obsidian Golem	38 Elite
Notes: Construct, High HP, High Armor	
Obsidian Sentinel	42 Elite
Notes: Construct, High HP, High Armor, Spawns 2 Obsidian Shards at 66% HP and again at 33% HP.	
Obsidian Shard	35
Notes: Construct, Spawned by the Obsidian Sentinel	
Shadowforge Ambusher	43-44 Elite
Notes: Social, Backstab	
Shadowforge Archaeologist	43-44 Elite
Notes: Social, Defensive Stance, Disarm	
Shadowforge Darkcaster	43-44 Elite
Notes: Social, Spell Bomb (does 300 damage each cast, 10 second duration), Shadow Bolt, Shadow Bolt Volley	
Shadowforge Digger	35 Elite
Notes: Social, Sunder Armor (-270 Armor), Defensive Stance	
Shadowforge Geologist	40-41 Elite
Notes: Social, Fireball, Flame Spike (AoE)	
Shadowforge Relic Hunter	39-40 Elite
Notes: Social, Heal Spell	

NPC	LEVEL
Shadowforge Ruffian	36-37 Elite
Notes: Social, Gouge	
Shadowforge Sharpshooter	42-44 Elite
Notes: Social, Ranged attacks	
Shadowforge Surveyor	34-36 Elite
Notes: Social, Frost Shield, Fire Ball	
Shrike Bat	38 Elite
Notes: Skinnable, Sonic Burst (AoE Silence)	
Starving Buzzard	35-37
Stone Keeper	46 Elite
Notes: Construct, Minor Tremor (AoE Stun), Self Destruct (AoE damage on death), High Armor	
Stone Steward	44 Elite
Notes: Social, Construct, Self Destruct, Ground Tremor (AoE Knockdown)	
Stonevault Ambusher	33-35
Notes: Social, Fast moving, Wanders, Backstab, Flees	
Stonevault Basher	39-40 Elite
Notes: Social, Flees	
Stonevault Brawler	43-44 Elite
Notes: Social, Enrage, Flees	
Stonevault Cave Hunter	36-37 Elite
Notes: Ranged attacks, Net, Flees	

NPC	LEVEL
Stonevault Cave Lurker	37-39 Elite
Notes: Social, Stealth, Deadly Poison, Flees	
Stonevault Flameweaver	44-45 Elite
Notes: Social, Fireball, Flame Shield, Flame Spike (AoE), Flees	
Stonevault Geomancer	43-44 Elite
Notes: Social, Fireball, Flame Buffet (+43 damage taken from fire), Flees	
Stonevault Mauler	44-45 Elite
Notes: Social, Very Large, Enrage	
Stonevault Oracle	37-38 Elite
Notes: Social, Healing Ward (Healing Totem), Lava Spout Totem (AoE Fire Totem), Healing Wave, Lightning Shield, Flees	
Stonevault Rockchewer	36-37 Elite
Notes: Enrage	
Stonevault Seer	39-40 Elite
Notes: Social, Fire Ball, Flees	
Vault Warder	45 Elite
Notes: Construct	
Venomlash Scorpid	39-40 Elite
Notes: Skinnable, Poison (On hit)	

NPC	LEVEL	FREQUENT DROP(S)
ANCIENT STONE KEEPER	44 Elite	Cragfists (Plate Gloves, 300 Armor, +7 Defense, Random Enchantment)
Notes: Construct, Harsh Winds (AoE Silence and slow), High Armor		
ARCHAEDAS	Boss	Archaedic Stone (Ring, Random Enchantment), Stoneslayer (Two-Handed Sword, 42.7 DPS, Chance on Hit: Increases damage by 10 per hit for 8 seconds), The Rockpounder (Two-Handed Mace, 42.7 DPS, +5 STR, +2% Critical Chance)
Notes: High HP, High Armor, High Damage		
BAELOG	41 Elite	Nordic Longshank (One-Hand Sword, 29.3 DPS, +8 AGI, +5 STA)
Notes: Social, Ranged Attack, Alliance Quest Giver		
DIGMASTER SHOVELPHLANGE	38 Elite	Expert Goldminer's Helmet (Leather Helm, 95 Armor, +5 AGI, +6 STA, +7 Axe Skill), Shovelphlange's Mining Axe (One-Hand Axe, 25.7 DPS, +6 STR, +10 Attack Power), Tromping Miner's Boots (Leather Boots, 73 Armor, +8 STR, +7 STA)
Notes: Rare spawn, Sunder Armor		
ERIC "THE SWIFT"	40 Elite	Horned Viking Helmet (Plate Helm, 303 Armor, +10 AGI, +15 STA, Use: Charge an enemy knocking it silly for 30 seconds. Also knocks you down, stunning you for a short period of time. Any damage will revive the target), Worn Running Boots (Leather Boots, 72 Armor, +11 AGI, +3 STA)
Notes: Social, Increased movement speed, Intercept		
GALGANN FIREHAMMER	Boss	Galgann's Firehammer (One-Hand Mace, 27.5 DPS, Chance on Hit: Blasts target for 80-112 fire damage), Flameseer Mantle (Cloth Shoulders, 51 Armor, +10 SPI, Increases damage done by fire spells by up to 10), Galgann's Fireblaster (Gun, 25.4 DPS, +1-3 Fire Damage), Emberscale Cape (Cloak, 30 Armor, +12 STA, +3 SPI)
Notes: Social, Flame Shock (DoT, Instant cast), Amplify Flames (+100 damage from fire spells), Flamelash (-26 Fire resistance), Fire Nova (AoE, Instant cast)		
GRIMLOK	54 Elite	Grimlok's Charge (Two-Handed Polearm, 40.9 DPS, +10 STR, +15 AGI, +15 STA), Grimlok's Tribal Vestments (Cloth Chest, 68 Armor, +10 STA, +5 INT, +20 SPI)
Notes: Social, AoE Shrink (-32 STR, -32 STA, 3 minute duration), Lightning Bolt, Chain Bolt, Flees, Bloodlust (+30% attack speed for 30 seconds)		
IRONAYA	Boss	Ironshod Bludgeon (Staff, 37.2 DPS, +8 STR, +20 STA), Stoneweaver Leggings (Cloth Legs, 51 Armor, +9 STA, +8 INT, +15 SPI), Ironaya's Bracers of (Mail Wrist, 165 Armor, Random Enchantment)
Notes: Construct, Arcing Smash, War Stomp, Knock Away		
OLAF	40 Elite	Olaf's All Purpose Shield (Shield, 1287 Armor, 22 Block, +11 STA, Use: reduces fall speed for 10 seconds), Oil of Olaf (+50 Armor for 1 hour)
Notes: Social, Shield Slam (Knockdown)		
REVELOSH	40 Elite	Revelosh's Spaulders (Leather Shoulders, 84 Armor, Random Enchantment), Revelosh's Gloves, (Cloth Gloves, 33 Armor, Random Enchantment), Revelosh's Boots (Plate Boots, 206 Armor, Random Enchantment), Revelosh's Armguards (Mail Bracers, 101 Armor, Random Enchantment)
Notes: Social, Chain Lightning, Lightning Bolt		

INTO THE RUINS

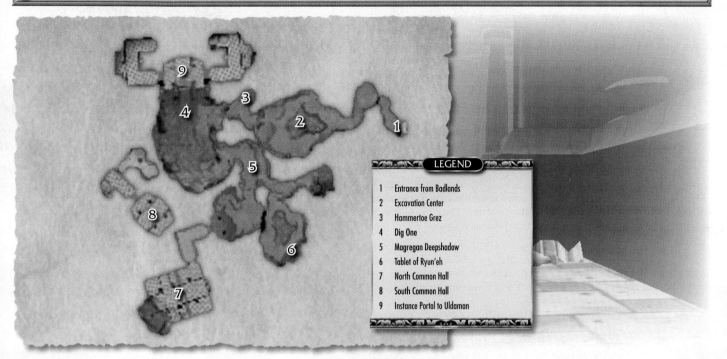

LEGEND

1. Entrance from Badlands
2. Excavation Center
3. Hammertoe Grez
4. Dig One
5. Magregan Deepshadow
6. Tablet of Ryun'eh
7. North Common Hall
8. South Common Hall
9. Instance Portal to Uldaman

EXCAVATION CENTER

As the tunnel walls close around you, the escape routes narrow. The creatures on the way to the instance portal are not much more difficult than the ones outside. The big difference is the tunnels themselves. They provide the enemy with a quick route to friends while providing you few escape options. Now is a good time to practice the skills your group needs to make it through Uldaman. Pull from cleared areas, organize aggro, and prevent the wounded enemies from fleeing.

LINE OF SIGHT

The tunnel walls can hinder the enemy as much as they hinder you. They can be of great help when used correctly. When pulling a group with a caster (or a caster only), pull around a tunnel corner. The caster will rush around the corner to restore line of sight. This gives your party an opportunity to kill the caster without having to fight an entire room.

The way forward is blocked by groups of Shadowforge Dwarves. They're very social and difficult to pull separately. Be sure to keep the Ruffians in front of you as they have backstab. The Surveyors should be killed fairly quickly. The Diggers should be killed last.

There is little of importance in this room. Clear the upper ledge to avoid a messy fight before you head through the tunnel on the lower level.

A small cave along the right wall reveals a Dwarf sitting by a fire. He's alone, wounded, and obviously not a Shadowforge. Alliance parties will recognize him as Hammertoe Getz who they were asked to find in *A Sign of Hope*.

SNARING OPPONENTS

Few of the enemies in Uldaman don't fear death. When low on health, many make a run for help. Nearly all the Stonevault Troggs and Shadowforge Dwarves do this. It's important to make sure they don't get the chance to bring reinforcements. Having someone in your party who can keep each enemy snared makes the fights much easier. Warriors with Hamstring or Rogues with Crippling Poison are often good choices, with Hamstring being the more consistent of the two.

Characters' instant damage abilities, such as Arcane Shot or Moonfire, should be ready to bring down a fleeing foe if it escapes snaring.

DIG ONE

Following the tunnel brings you to an upper ledge of Dig One and reveals the Instance Portal. Don't make a run for the portal. There's still much to do.

Move east and continue clearing the groups of Shadowforge Dwarves. The Diggers along the left wall come in pairs when pulled at range and should be easy fights. Watch for the Surveyors that wander along the tunnels. Clear the room when the Surveyor is away, then attack the Surveyor when it returns.

Magregan Deepshadow also wanders the tunnels. When your party is prepared, deal with Magregan and Alliance parties can finish *Amulet of Secrets*. Magregan is a vicious opponent if he closes with your party. His Whirlwind attack hits multiple people and can devastate any party members in light armor. Be sure to keep him away from your casters.

There's a room with more Shadowforge Dwarves and an Obsidian Golem to the southeast. Pull the Dwarves back to the intersection to keep them from running back to friends. Once the Dwarves are clear, engage the Golem. It has high HP, high armor, and is immune to DoTs. Warriors make such fights much easier as they can lower the enemy's armor (Sunder Armor)  while boosting the party's attack power (Battle Shout). Once the Golem is down, the **Tablet of Ryun'eh** can be taken for *Solution to Doom*.

Move back to the where you felled Magregan and take the southwest tunnel. The Stonevault Troggs have taken this area. Pull enemies around the corner to force the Cave Hunters, who have ranged attacks, to come to you. Keeping the fights small is important. The Cave Hunters have nets and an immobilized party may quickly find itself in trouble.

NORTH COMMON HALL

The rough stone gives way to smooth tiles. Stonevault Rockchewers and Cave Hunters line the hallway. As before, pull the Cave Hunters around a corner to force them to come close to your party. The hallway should be quick work.

The North Common Hall has a number of Cave Hunters and would be quite a fight if your party charged in. Play it safe and pull them one at a time. Once the room is clear, Alliance Parties can get **Krom Stoutarm's Treasure** for *Reclaimed Treasures*. Backtrack a bit to Dig One and head west.

SOUTH COMMON HALL

After clearing the room in front of the instance portal, take the tunnel in the west wall. This tunnel is also infested with Stonevault Rockchewers and Cave Hunters. The tunnel is narrow and very twisted. This will make pulling the Cave Hunters to you easier. Clear the tunnel and move under the purple sculpture into the South Common Hall.

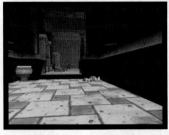

There are 6 Stonevault Cave Hunters scattered about the room. They are far enough apart that they can be pulling one at a time and dealt with. Grab the chest on the ledge for *Reclaimed Treasures* if your character owes allegiance to the Horde. All that is left is Uldaman itself.

A LONG DEAD CIVILIZATION

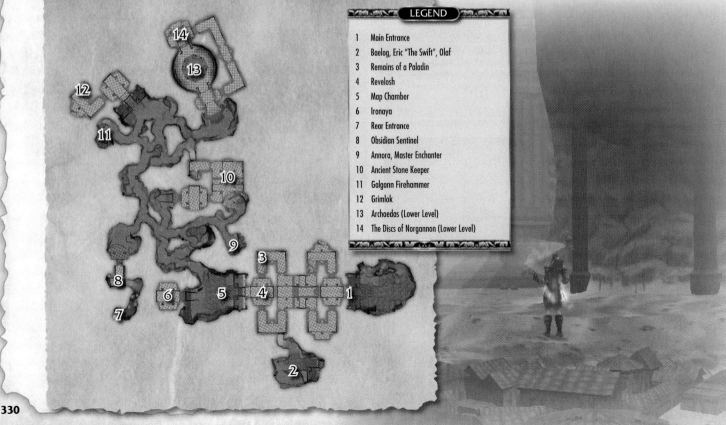

	LEGEND
1	Main Entrance
2	Baelog, Eric "The Swift", Olaf
3	Remains of a Paladin
4	Revelosh
5	Map Chamber
6	Ironaya
7	Rear Entrance
8	Obsidian Sentinel
9	Annora, Master Enchanter
10	Ancient Stone Keeper
11	Galgann Firehammer
12	Grimlok
13	Archaedas (Lower Level)
14	The Discs of Norgannon (Lower Level)

HALL OF THE KEEPERS

There are passages to the north and the south. Failure to clear both can lead to unexpected adds later on. Head north first. The hall is short and only has a handful of Stonevault Oracles and Rockchewers. The Oracles can cast healing spells and use totems. Those totems can make the fights much longer if not brought down quickly. The Rockchewers can become enraged. Stun them to reduce the damage they can inflict. The hall ends with some debris blocking the way to a large room. You can backtrack to the southern hallway or jump over the debris.

HOW LONG IS THE LEASH?

Jumping over the debris can be dangerous to the party if a Warlock or Hunter is with you. The pet will not jump over the debris with you. It will instead run through the southern hall and through the room to get to you. It brings a great number of enemies with it.

To avoid this, Warlocks and Hunters should unsummon or dismiss their pets until the debris is traversed. Going around is another option.

The southern hallway is almost a mirror of the northern. Clear it and make your way to the large room. Clearing the east side of this room is much like the hallways. Watch for the Stonevault Ambushers that patrol before trying to clear the west side of the room. The Ambushers are not elite, but move quickly and call for help immediately when engaged. If one adds to a fight, things can go very poorly.

After clearing the room, clear the southern hallway of the Stonevault Rockchewers and Oracles. Keep watch behind you as there may be more Stonevault Ambushers patrolling. There is a tunnel broken in the wall. Your tank should move slowly toward the tunnel after the hallway is clear. There are Stonevault Cave Lurkers in the tunnel stealthed. Pull them one at a time and proceed through the tunnel.

Inside Dig Two there are Stonevault Oracles and Cave Lurkers on the lower level and Baelog, Olaf, and Eric "The Swift" on the upper ledge. Clear the Troggs before approaching the Dwarves. Alliance parties can stroll up to the Dwarves and speak to them for *The Lost Dwarves*. Horde parties need to fight the Dwarves for loot and access to the chest on the table.

Eric can charge and intercept. This makes him a very dangerous opponent as he can keep multiple party members stunned by running into them constantly. Unleash all your party's burst DPS into Eric and bring him a swift end.

With Eric dispatched, tank Olaf while crowd controlling Baelog. Olaf won't last long under the combined might of your party, but don't switch to Baelog until Olaf is dead. Should someone break the crowd control on Baelog before Olaf is dead, they should immediately stop attacking so Baelog can be re-CCed.

There's a chest with the Gni'kiv Medallion on the table which is needed later. The urn nearby is the home of **The Shattered Necklace Topaz** for the Alliance quest *Find the Gems* and the Horde quest *Finding the Gems and Power Source*.

Taking the northern hallway reveals the **Remains of a Paladin**. *Necklace Recovery, Take 2* and *Back to Uldaman* for the Horde and the Alliance, respectively, are completed here. Revelosh and some Stonevault Rockchewers are in the new room. This group is linked and cannot be broken up. With that in mind, use the element of surprise and bring Revelosh down quickly.

Shield your tank, if you have a Priest, and charge in. CC the Rockchewers, with Polymorph, Frost Nova, or pets, and move all your damage to Revelosh. His Chain Lightning can be very damaging to multiple party members, so keep him interrupted. Once Revelosh is down, cease fire until the tank chooses the next target. Allowing the tank to break the CC keeps attention on someone in heavier armor.

With the enemies dead, search for loot. The Shaft of Tsol should be picked up or given to the person in possession of the Gni'kiv Medallion. The two become the Staff of Prehistoria when joined.

THE MAP CHAMBER

At the entrance to this chamber are two Stonevault Cave Lurkers. Pull these into the Hall of the Keepers to kill them. At the bottom of the stairs lay a trap. There are three Stonevault Ambushers on each side of the stairs for six total. You can pull them up the stairs or fight them at the bottom. Be sure to keep them snared as their run speed is high and their friends close.

The room has many groups of Stonevault Oracles and Cave Lurkers. These must be pulled slowly and carefully to avoid large fights. Once the room's clear, rest and place the Staff of Prehistoria in the model building. This opens the door to The Hidden Chamber and releases Ironaya.

Ironaya is quite a handful. She has high armor, high HP and is immune to DoTs. Keep her facing the tank and away from the party to minimize the effect of her Cleave and make it very apparent when she changes targets. Keep the tank healed and pour on the damage. Should Ironaya change targets, cease fire and don't run. She may be large, but you can't outrun Ironaya and running makes it more difficult for your tank to regain her attention. Stay put and use any threat reduction abilities you have. Disengage and Feint are prime examples of threat reduction abilities and Fade is a temporary hate wipe. These make your tank's life easier during heavy battles of this sort. Bring Ironaya down and collect your prize. Alliance parties should enter the room she came out of to complete *The Hidden Chamber*.

THE TUNNELS

The tunnels are more dangerous than anything you've found yet. The uneven walls and floor make it very difficult to see enemies lying in wait. The room north of the Map Chamber is an excellent example. There are eight Cleft Scorpids in a pit just to the right of the entrance. Entering the room will draw them to you, so leave any party members with low HP in the Map Chamber

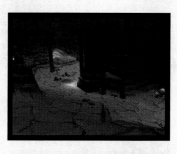

and pull the Scorpids back. If you have faith in your parties AoE capabilities, destroy the Scorpids all at once. Shield your tank and have him use attacks and/or taunts that affect multiple creatures to keep the healer from getting swarmed.

Once the Scorpids are dealt with, clear the room by pulling the Jadespine Basilisk and the Shrike Bats one at a time. Interrupt the Basilisk's cast to avoid have a party member sleeping on the job. The Shrike Bat's Sonic Burst is something for casters to avoid if possible.

FIGHTING AT YOUR BEST

A number of the enemies in the deeper area of Uldaman have status ailments. Sleep, Silence, and others can keep your party from functioning at full power. Any time a character is afflicted with one of these during battle, they should let the party know so its counter can be cast or tactics changed.

If a party member is still under the effect after the fight has ended, cure it or wait until it wears off. Continuing to pull when a party member isn't at full health/mana is a quick way to start a long corpse run.

Move north and clear the Shrike Bat and Basilisk from the room. This will be your base for a short while. The room immediately east contains another group of Cleft Scorpids, a Jadespine Basilisk and a wandering Shrike Bat. Clear the Bat, then the Basilisk before engaging the Scorpids to avoid a massive battle that puts your party in peril.

Farther east, the tunnel splits north and south. Clear the Venomlash Scorpids and the patrolling Shrike Bat and move along the southern tunnel. The room has only eight Cleft Scorpids in it at first look. After clearing the Scorpids, Annora makes herself apparent. High level Enchanters become well acquainted with Annora as she is the only Enchanter Trainer that can train artisans.

Ignore the northern tunnel split for now and head back to your camp. The tunnel west soon splits to the north and south. Beyond the southern tunnel is another bastion of the Shadowforge Dwarves and the rear entrance/exit to the Badlands.

The Shadowforge Relic Hunters and Geologists can be pulled in small groups. Pull around a corner to bring the Geologists into melee range and bring them down quickly. The Geologists can cast Flame Spike (an AoE fire spell) and should be interrupted at all costs. After the Geologist is down, your party should make short work of the Relic Hunter.

FEET IN THE FIRE?

A few of the enemies can cast AoE spells that hit more than once. If an enemy manages to land this (the ground bursts into fire and continues burning), move! These spells hit several times over the course of several seconds and do substantial damage to anyone in the area. Standing in an AoE spell instead of moving out of the area makes your healer very unhappy.

The Shadowforge Dwarves can be killed without angering the Obsidian Sentinel at the back of the room. At first the steps seem to provide an obstacle to any warrior wishing to begin the fight by charging. Move to the side to find an avenue of attack. The Obsidian Sentinel has the high HP, high armor, and DoT immunity common to the constructs of Uldaman. At 66% health, and again at 33%, the Obsidian Sentinel will spawn 2 Obsidian Shards. These are non elite, but make the healer's life much more difficult. Change targets and bring the Shards down before returning to the Sentinel.

Once the Sentinel is dead, the Back Door is clear. Keeping in mind where it connects to Badlands can make returning at a later time (for enchanting training or quest completion) easier than going through the front.

The northern split of the tunnel leads into a room of ledges with Shrike Bats on them. Careful pulling can keep your party from fighting more than one at a time. This is important as the multiple silences keep casters from doing anything and make the fights much harder.

There's another room farther to the north with a pit of Scorpids in it. This fight is more difficult than previous Scorpid pits. The Deadly Cleft Scorpids are higher level and can poison party members. There are also ten in this pit. Shield your tank have have him wade into the room and begin the fight. Secondary tanks should be extra watchful about casters getting aggro. The main tank will have his/her hands full and won't be able to peel. The main tank should keep the Scorpids in front of him/her whenever possible to make better use of Block and Parry.

Dig Three, through the west tunnel, is guarded by two Shadowforge Sharpshooters. Pull them around the corner toward the room with ledges you already cleared. Once you have them in melee range, they fall quickly. Keep fights along the west wall at all costs. The Troggs in the northern room are very social. Move into the tunnel where the Sharpshooters were and survey the room. Multiple groups of Shadowforge Darkcasters and Archaeologists populate the room. Pull them back to the ledge room one group at a time.

SOMEONE SET US UP THE BOMB

The Shadowforge Darkcasters cast Spell Bomb. This is a 10 second effect that will inflict 300 damage to the target any time they cast a spell. If any of your casters, especially your healer, are affected with this, they must stop casting or risk death.

Once the Archaeologists and Darkcasters are cleared, take a rest and restore buffs. The next fight is brutal. Galgann Firehammer and two Shadowforge Geologists are waiting against the west wall. Combine the Flame Spike of the Geologists and the Fire Nova of Firehammer, there's huge AoE potential your party must get through. The tank should start the fight to gain early aggro and keep Firehammer away from the rest of the party (Fire Nova is a PBAoE). Bring the Geologists down first. CC one and have everyone concentrate fire and level the other. Firehammer is immune to CC and it will take the blood and sweat of your tank to keep him busy. He also has a number of debuffs that increase damage taken from fire. Dispel these from the tank as quickly as possible. Once the Geologists are dead, heal the tank and kill Galgann.

The Shattered Necklace Ruby for *Find the Gems and Finding the Gems and Power Source* is hidden in a box along the northern wall and *The Lost Tablets of Will* are laying against the western wall.

Head back to the camp room, several rooms back, and head north. There are strange, semi-dwarf looking creatures called the Earthen in this room. The Earthen are not elite, but these fights are always big. The Earthen Sculptors and Rocksmashers are linked. Each fight will bring several enemies. Wait for the Stone Steward to wander into the other room before you pull the Earthen.

PROGRAMMED?

The Earthen react in groups of five or six. There are always at least four melee and one caster in each group. This near perfect grouping across distances is eerie and very efficient. Having such patterns can be used against them. Bring down casters (the paler of the two types) as there are few of them and move to the melees.

Once you have the room clear of Earthen, fight the Stone Steward. It has the typical high HP, high armor and DoT immunity, but it also has Ground Tremor. This is a PBAoE knockdown that makes fighting them much more dangerous. They can also Self Destruct, when low on health, causing damage to all party members near them.

The room to the east (Temple Hall) has another group of Earthen. Pull them around the corner and eliminate them as you have all other who have opposed you.

Further east is a much larger room with many Earthen, two Stone Stewards wandering amongst the rooms, and an Ancient Stone Keeper against the north wall. Pull the Earthen on the hill and beside the Ancient (you can pull them without it adding) when the Stewards are away. When the Earthen are clear, pull the stewards one at a time. Keep away from the ledge the Ancient is on as it moves forward occasionally.

The Ancient Stone Keeper fights much like the Stone Stewards. It's only bigger and a bit meaner. Bring it down with much the same strategy.

Move through the tunnel to the west. Stick close to the southern wall as you make your way back to the room where you killed the Deadly Cleft Scorpids. The Troggs have lived long enough.

The room to the north, The Stone Vault, has many Stonevault Brawlers and Geomancers. Pull them around the wall to bring the Geomancers to you. Fighting in The Stone Vault before significant clearing is folly. Slowly clear the way to the north wall. Once clear, move to the platform and clear the room to the north.

Pull the Stonevault Brawlers and Geomancers from the hallway to the east back to the room. You can hide behind the doorway to bring the casters to you. Clearing the hall sets the stage for a fight with Grimlock. He stands at the end of the hall with a Jadespine Basilisk, Stonevault Brawler, and a Stonevault Geomancer.

Grimlock has many abilities and spells that could spell the doom for your party. Charge in and bring all your DPS against him. Keep his casting interrupted as his spells are quite devastating. Killing him before he can use his AoE Shrink spell or his Chain Bolt is an accomplishment and makes the remainder of the fight much easier. After he falls, the Geomancer should be your next target, then the remaining two. Pry **The Shattered Necklace Sapphire** from his dead hands to advance the *Find the Gems* and *Finding the Gems and Power Source* for Alliance and Horde groups, respectively.

Moving through The Stone Vault east is dangerous as the tunnel is filled with Stonevault Flameweavers and Maulers. These have the potential to inflict serious damage to your party. Pull and kill them away from adds. Bringing the Flameweavers down before they can cast their AoE fire spell will do wonders for your party's health.

Clear the room and head north into the Hall of the Crafters. Camp in the small room and pull the Earthen from the larger room. They will attack in groups of four Stone Breakers, one Stone Carver, and one Stone Steward. The Steward is the only Elite in the group. Bring the others down, then focus on the Steward. There are three groups in the room.

Once the Earthen are cleared, rest and restore buffs. There is an altar surrounded by four statues in the center and a locked door to the north. At least four party members must activate the altar to move forward. One of the Stone Keepers will awake and attack the party. Its AoE knockdown and sheer level makes it a difficult fight. Move back to the smaller room as you fight. Keep lower HP characters away from it when it nears death. When near death, the Stone Keeper can Self Destruct and do significant damage to all party members nearby. When it dies, the next awakens and attack the party. Use the few seconds it takes for the enemy to travel to restore health and mana. Once you have the second down, the third awakens and again for the fourth.

With the death of the final Stone Keeper, the doors to the north open. The way forward is blocked by several groups of Earthen with support from Stone Stewards. Pull them as you have been. These fights are enough to keep you from relaxing and prepare you for the final engagement.

Entering the Final Room reveals a huge statue in the center of the room, a circle of six smaller statues, many statues ringing the walls and two large statues on the sides of the room with an altar in the center. Again, you will need most of your party to activate the altar to begin the fight. Rest and restore buffs first.

When the altar is activated, Archaedas will awaken and attack the party. His high HP, high armor and high damage ensure a long fight. He's not willing to fight you alone, however. Periodically through the fight, he awakens one of the Earthen Hallshapers along the walls. The burst DPS of the party should bring these non-elites down quickly. If one person can't bring them down before Archaedas awakens another, everyone except the tank and healer should break off Archaedas and kill the Earthen.

When Archaedas drops to 66% health, he awakens the six Earthen Guardians around him all at once. The tank needs to grab aggro quickly so the softer party members don't go down. Kill the Guardians and resume the previous tactic.

A WARRIOR'S PLAYGROUND

The waking of the Earthen Guardians provides a moment where the warrior can truly shine. Battle Stance warriors should use Challenging Shout, then Retalliation to grab and maintain agro while the party slaughters the enemies. Defensive Stance warriors should use Challenging Shout and Demoralizing Shout to grab aggro.

Archaedas isn't out of tricks. At 33% health, he awakens the two Stone Keepers against the walls. These head straight for the character with the most threat, which is all too often a healer. The tanks must grab aggro quickly. Once aggro is drawn, concentrate all party fire on Archaedas. The Keepers deactivate once he falls.

Congratulations. Your party has accomplished a mighty feat. Remove The **Shattered Necklace Power Source** from Archaedas. It's needed in the *Restoring the Necklace* quest for Alliance parties and **Finding the Gems and Power Source** quest for Horde groups.

With Archaedas dead, the door at the back of the room opens to reveal a treasure vault. In the center of the room stand **The Platinum Discs** and a coffer sits to one side. The coffer holds a wealth of equipment and the Discs hold a wealth of knowledge. Learn what you can and access the Discs again to get your own copy.

The people of your homeland will want to see these for sure!

WAILING CAVERNS

Played & Written by: Daniel "Sachant" Vanderlip of <UDL> on Archimonde
Updated by: Edwin "Plainsong" Kern of <Dovrani> on Kirin Tor

The Wailing Caverns are a right of passage for Horde adventurers that have been spending much of their time in the Barrens. For many, it's their first instanced dungeon experience (especially if they have passed on Ragefire Chasm in Orgrimmar). There are many quests that take players through this dungeon and it's a good way to learn more about group dynamics and the roles of group members in precision pull areas.

The storyline tied with this dungeon is one of a Druid known as Naralex who sought to enter into the Emerald Dream in order to heal the land and return it to the lush environment it once was. Instead, things went wrong and his dream became a nightmare unleashing many creatures and dangers. Nearly all of the quests in this dungeon intertwine and even when you think you have returned to the beginning and ended your time here, you will find there is one last thing to do, awaken Naralex himself if you have slain all of the Druids that have bound him in his sleep.

DUNGEON INFORMATION

Location	The Barrens (SW of Crossroads)
Quests	Both
Region	Horde
Suggested Levels	18-25
Group Allowed	5 to Quest, 10 for Raids
Primary Enemies	Beast and Humanoid
Time to Complete	2 Hours

GETTING TO WAILING CAVERNS

Reaching Wailing Caverns is a stroll in the park for most Horde adventurers. Trolls, Orcs, and Tauren have likely already been through Crossroads and can fly there to form the party. Most Undead will also have the flightpoint, but there might be someone who needs to run from Orgrimmar.

Alliance groups wishing to enter Wailing Caverns have a much harder journey. There are several ways to get to Barrens, but the safest for parties at this level will be running from Astranaar in Ashenvale. There is a breach in the wall to the left as you approach the border to Barrens. This keeps you out of sight of the NPC guards, but players will still be a problem. Follow the western zone wall south (don't enter Stonetalon Mountains). This will keep you out of sight of Crossroads. As you cross the road to Stonetalon, start moving S.E. toward Wailing Caverns.

WHO TO BRING

Most of the enemies in Wailing Caverns are elite and hit fairly hard. You need a tank that can survive these hits and someone to heal them. With these two components found, look for a player with an interrupt or stun ability (Warrior - Shield Bash, Rogue - Kick, Shaman - Earthshock, Druid - Bash, Paladin - Hammer of Justice). There are several enemy casters that can make your life much more difficult if not kept in check.

Some of the casters can sleep party members. This can be detrimental if your healer gets put to sleep early in the fight as the sleep lasts a very long time. Having someone to wake party members is good. Having two people to wake party members is better. Only a couple classes have abilities that wake others: Shaman - Tremor Totem, Paladin - Clense, and Priest - Dispel Magic. If you have fewer than two in your party, make sure to have a second person with an interrupt ability.

SKINNERS REJOICE!

To get the most out of Wailing Caverns, bring a skinner and some empty bag space. Many of the enemies are skinnable and the added revenue can add up quickly. Skinning in Wailing Caverns has the added benefit of garnering Deviate Scales and Perfect Deviate Scales.

QUESTS

All quests involving the Wailing Caverns are Dungeon quests. This means they can not by completed in a Raid group. Avoid Raid groups unless treasure is your only goal.

THE QUESTS ARE IN THE EYE!

Getting to a couple of the quest givers at the Wailing Caverns location can be a bit tricky. They're located in a cave above the entrance and must be accessed by climbing the mountain just to the north. Once up the hill, carefully drop down to the ledge on the right (facing south) and then drop once more (carefully) to another ledge. It may take you a couple of times to hit it just right and the entrance itself even once you make the second ledge is a bit evasive at first, but is a V-shaped cave opening with a few NPCs inside (two crafters and two quest givers).

HORDE QUESTS

QUEST	QUEST GIVER	QUEST GIVER LOCATION	QUEST RECEIVER	QUEST RECEIVER LOCATION	CHAIN?	MAX EXPERIENCE
Leaders of the Fang	Nara Wildmane	Thunderbluff: Elder Rise	Nara Wildmane	Thunderbluff: Elder Rise	Yes	2200
REWARD: Crescent Staff (Staff, 20.3 DPS, +7 STA, +7 SPI, +7 INT) or Wingblade (Main-Hand Sword, 15.7 DPS, +5 AGI, +2 STA)						
Serpentbloom	Apothecary Zamah	Thunderbluff: Pools of Vision	Apothecary Zamah	Thunderbluff: Pools of Vision	No	1050
REWARD: Apothecary Gloves (Cloth Hands, 20 Armor, +3 INT, +2 SPI)						

LEADERS OF THE FANG

Quest Level	18 to Obtain
Location	Thunderbluff (Elder Rise)
Quest Giver	Nara Wildmane
Goal	Collect Collect the Gem of Cobrahn, the Gem of Serpentis, the Gem of Pythas and the Gem of Lady Anacondra.
Max Experience Gained	2200
Reward	Crescent Staff (Staff, 20.3 DPS, +7 STA, +7 SPI, +7 INT) or Wingblade (Main-Hand Sword, 15.7 DPS, +5 AGI, +2 STA)

A prerequisite for this quest is the *Altered Beings* quest. You must also speak with Hamuul Runetotem before you can speak with Nara Wildmane to get this quest.

Each of the Gems will be collected off one of the named Druids (Lady Anacondra, Lord Cobrahn, Lord Pythas & Lord Serpentis) in the various sections of the Wailing Caverns. Each Druid is progressively harder than the previous, but with a good group it can be accomplished. By killing all of the Druids, you'll also be able to speak with the Disciple of Naralex at the start of the instance to start an escort quest and face the final boss mob. Once completed, return to Nara Wildmane.

SERPENTBLOOM

Quest Level	14 to Obtain
Location	Thunderbluff (Pools of Vision)
Quest Giver	Apothecary Zamah
Goal	Collect 10 Serpentbloom
Max Experience Gained	1050
Reward	Apothecary Gloves (Cloth Hands, 20 Armor, +3 INT, +2 SPI)

This quest can be completed without ever entering the instance, though it takes time and patience to both handle the outer spawn and wait on the Serpentbloom if others are also collecting. For Herbalists, this can be made easier by activating the Find Herbs skill and using the mini-map to locate them. No special skill is needed to gather the serpentbloom however. Return to Apothecary Zamah to turn it in.

QUEST	QUEST GIVER	QUEST GIVER LOCATION	QUEST RECEIVER	QUEST RECEIVER LOCATION	CHAIN?	MAX EXPERIENCE
Trouble at the Docks	Crane Operator Bigglefuzz	Barrens: Ratchet	Crane Operator Bigglefuzz	Barrens: Ratchet	No	1350
Smart Drinks	Mebok Mizzyrix	Barrens: Ratchet	Mebok Mizzyrix	Barrens: Ratchet	Yes	1350
Deviate Hides	Nalpak	Barrens: Wailing Caverns	Nalpak	Barrens: Wailing Caverns	No	950
REWARD: Deviate Hide Pack (10-Slot Bag) or Slick Deviate Leggings (Leather Legs, 65 Armor, +4 AGI, +4 STA)						
Deviate Erradication	Ebru	Barrens: Wailing Caverns	Ebru	Barrens: Wailing Caverns	No	1250
REWARD: Sizzle Stick (Wand, 17.6 DPS) or Dagmire Gauntlets (Mail Hands, 107 Armor, +5 STR, +2 AGI)						
The Glowing Shard	The Glowing Shard	Wailing Caverns: Mutanus the Devourer	Falla Sagewind	Barrens: Wailing Caverns	Yes	2650
In Nightmares	Falla Sagewind	Barrens: Wailing Caverns	Hamuul Runetotem	Thunderbluff: Elder Rise	Yes	2000
REWARD: Talbar Mantle (Cloth Shoulder, 30 Armor, +3 STA, +6 INT) or Quagmire Galoshes (Mail Feet, 126 Armor, +6 STA)						

TROUBLE AT THE DOCKS

Quest Level	18 to Obtain
Location	Ratchet
Quest Giver	Crane Operator Bigglefuzz
Goal	Retrieve the 99-Year-Old Port
Max Experience Gained	1350
Reward	10 silver pieces

Crane Operator Bigglefuzz is located near the shoreline in Ratchet closest to the bank. This quest is easily accomplished without ever entering the Wailing Caverns themselves. Mad Magglish is located in three spots within the outer caves fairly close to the front entrance. He's a stealthed level 18 Elite Goblin.

His first possible location is the easiest to reach. It's just to the right of the entrance to the cave in a small nook. If he's not there, he'll be in one of the two other spots east or west of the pool of water just a little farther in. The most difficult part of this quest is carefully controlling the mobs in the area since there are stealthed Deviate Stalkers roaming among the visible mobs. Once complete, return to Crane Operator Bigglefuzz to turn it in.

SMART DRINKS

Quest Level	13 to Obtain
Location	Ratchet
Quest Giver	Mebok Mizzyrix
Goal	Collect 6 Wailing Essence
Max Experience Gained	1350
Reward	10 Silver Pieces

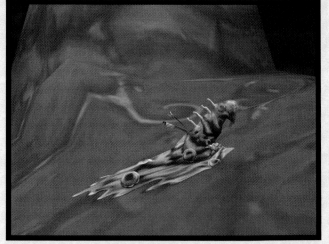

In order to obtain this quest, you must have previously completed *Raptor Horns*. Mebok Mizzyrix is located just outside the bank in Ratchet. This quest can be completed without ever entering the Wailing Caverns. Kill the Ectoplasms and collect the essence. You will most likely have to kill quite a few of them in order to get the required amount.

It's easiest to do this quest at the same time you do the quests within the instances, since you can kill on your way in and there are many wandering Ectoplasms within the instance itself. Once completed, return to Mebok Mizzyrix and turn it in.

DEVIATE HIDES

Quest Level	14 to Obtain
Location	Wailing Caverns
Quest Giver	Nalpak
Goal	Collect 20 Deviate Hides
Max Experience Gained	950
Reward	Deviate Hide Pack (10-Slot Bag) or Slick Deviate Leggings (Leather Legs, 65 Armor, +4 AGI, +4 STA)

Deviate Hides can come from many of the mobs within the Wailing Caverns. This is a quest that you could do without ever entering the instance. However, it goes more quickly for the entire party within the instance itself. Return to Nalpak when you have all the scales.

DEVIATE ERRADICATION

Quest Level	15 to Obtain
Location	Wailing Caverns
Quest Giver	Ebru
Goal	Kill 7 Deviate Dreadfangs, 7 Deviate Shamblers, 7 Deviate Vipers and 7 Deviate Ravagers
Max Experience Gained	1250
Reward	Pattern Deviate Scale Belt (Requires Leatherworking) or Sizzle Stick (Wand, 17.6 DPS) or Dagmire Gauntlets (Mail Hands, 107 Armor, +5 STR, +2 AGI)

Enter the Wailing Caverns instance to kill all the Deviates required. As you progress through the different areas of the Wailing Caverns, you'll easily be able to accomplish this. If, for some reason, you miss some Vipers before doing the Boss Mob at the end, you'll have a chance while escorting the Disciple of Naralex since a few more will spawn on the way. Return to Ebru when you're done.

THE GLOWING SHARD

Quest Level	15 to Obtain
Location	Wailing Caverns: Mutanus the Devourer
Quest Giver	The Glowing Shard
Goal	Speak first with Sputtervalve in Ratchet, then Falla Sagewind above Wailing Caverns
Max Experience Gained	2650
Reward	None

This is a two part quest. You'll obtain the Glowing Shard from Mutanus the Devourer (the last boss mob in the Wailing Caverns). To get to the boss, kill all four named Druids in a single run and speak to the Disciple of Naralex at the start of the instance again. He asks you to escort him to the Dreamer's Rock to awaken Naralex at last. Many fun and interesting mobs try to kill you until a very large and nightmare-inducing albino Murloc comes out of the water to try to finish you. Once you have killed him, loot the glowing shard and right-click it to start the quest.

For the first part, you'll need to seek out Sputtervalve in Ratchet. He won't give you a reward at this time, but instead he'll point you to yet another person with whom you must speak.

Falla Sagewind is on top of the mountain above the Wailing Caverns on the east side in a small hut. She'll take a look at the shard and send you to Thunderbluff to speak to Hamuul Runetotem.

IN NIGHTMARES

Quest Level	16 to Obtain
Location	Barrens
Quest Giver	Falla Sagewind
Goal	See Hamuul Runetotem in Thunder Bluff (Elder Rise) or Mathrengyl Bearwalker in Darnassus
Max Experience Gained	2000
Reward	Talbar Mantle (Cloth Shoulder, 30 Armor, +3 STA, +6 INT) or Quagmire Galoshes (Mail Feet, 126 Armor, +6 STA)

Falla Sagewind sends you on your way depending on your faction. For the Alliance, you're off to meet Mathrengyl Bearwalker in Darnassus; for the Horde, Hamuul Runetotem in Thunder Bluff is your next point of contact. This is the end of this series of quests.

THE CORRUPTED

NPC	LEVEL
Deviate Adder	18-19 Elite
Deviate Coiler	15-16 Elite
Frequent Drops: Light Feather, Light Leather, Deviate Hide	
Deviate Creeper	15-16 Elite
Frequent Drops: Light Leather, Deviate Hide	
Deviate Crocolisk	18-19
Frequent Drops: Crocolisk Meat, Light Leather, Deviate Hide	
Deviate Dreadfang	20-21 Elite
Notes: Fear	
Frequent Drops: Light Feather	
Deviate Guardian	18-19 Elite
Frequent Drops: Light Leather	

NPC	LEVEL
Deviate Lasher	19-20
Notes: Cleave	
Frequent Drops: Forest Mushroom Cap, Red-speckled Mushroom, Spongy Morel	
Deviate Lurker	17 Elite
Notes: Aquatic	
Frequent Drops: Small Barnacled Clam, Deviate Hide	
Deviate Mocassin	20-21 Elite
Deviate Python	18-19
Frequent Drops: Light Leather, Deviate Hide	
Deviate Ravager	18-19 Elite
Frequent Drops: Light Leather	
Deviate Shambler	19-20 Elite
Notes: Regen	

NPC	LEVEL
Deviate Slayer	16-17 Elite
Frequent Drops: Light Leather, Deviate Hide	
Deviate Stalker	
Notes: Stealth	
Frequent Drops: Light Leather, Deviate Hide	
Deviate Stinglash	16-17 Elite
Frequent Drops: Light Feather, Light Leather, Deviate Hide	
Deviate Venomwing	20-21 Elite
Notes: Poison Spit (Ranged Nature attack) Frequent Drops: Light Feather	
Deviate Viper	20 Elite

NPC	LEVEL
Devouring Ectoplasm	16-17 Elite
Notes: Spawns a Cloned Ectoplasm when low on health Frequent Drops: Wailing Essence	
Druid of the Fang	19-21 Elite
Notes: Lightning Bolt, Heal, Sleep Frequent Drops: Gloves of the Fang (Leather Hands, 47 Armor, +3 AGI, +2 STR), Wool Cloth, Linen Cloth	
Evolving Ectoplasm	17-18 Elite
Notes: Spawns a Cloned Ectoplasm when low on health Frequent Drops: Wailing Essence	
Nightmare Ectoplasm	20-21
Frequent Drops: Wailing Essence	

THE LEADERS

NAME	LEVEL	FREQUENT DROP(S)
BOAHN	20 Elite	Boahn's Fang (Two-Handed Axe, 17.6 DPS, +9 STR, +4 SPI), Brambleweed Leggings (Leather Legs, 68 Armor, +4 AGI, +4 SPI), Wool Cloth, Linen Cloth
Notes: Rare Spawn		
DEVIATE FAERIE DRAGON	20 Elite	Firebelcher (Wand, 20.3 DPS), Feyscale Cloak (Cloak, 17 Armor, +3 STA, +2 SPI)
Notes: Rare Spawn		
KRESH	20 Elite	Kresh's Back (Shield, 471 Armor, 9 Block, Passive: Increased Defense +4), Worn Turtle Shell Shield (412 Armor, 6 Block), Small Barnacled Clam, Deviate Hide
LADY ANACONDRA	21 Elite	Belt of the Fang (Leather Waist, 45 Armor, +3 STA, +2 AGI), Serpent's Shoulders (Leather Shoulder, 59 Armor), Wool Cloth
Notes: Lightning Bolt, Sleep, Healing Touch, Thorns Aura		
LORD COBRAHN	21 Elite	Cobrahn's Grasp (Mail Waist, 111 Armor, +8 STR, +3 AGI), Leggings of the Fang (Leather Legs, 79 Armor, +5 STR, +4 STA, +9 AGI), Robe of the Moccasin (Cloth Chest, 36 Armor, +2 STR, +2 STA, +6 SPI), Wool Cloth
Notes: Lightning Bolt, Sleep, Healing Touch, Serpent Form at Low health (damage increased by 50, attack speed -30%)		
LORD PYTHAS	22 Elite	Stinging Viper (One-Hand Mace, 15.5 DPS, Chance on Hit: Poisons target for 7 Nature damage every 3 seconds for 15 seconds), Armor of the Fang (Leather Chest, 82 Armor, +2 STR, +7 SPI), Wool Cloth
Notes: Lightning Bolt, Sleep, Healing Touch, Thunderclap		
LORD SERPENTIS	22 Elite	Venomstrike (Bow, 11.5 DPS, +3-6 Nature Damage), Savage Trodders (Mail Feet, 122 Armor, +6 STA), Serpent Gloves (Cloth Hands, 23 Armor, +5 AGI, +4 INT), Footpads of the Fang (Leather Feet, 57 Armor, +4 STA, +4 AGI), Wool Cloth
Notes: Lightning Bolt, Sleep, Healing Touch		
MAD MAGGLISH	18 Elite	Wool Cloth
Notes: Stealth		
MUTANUS THE DEVOURER	24 Elite	Slime-encrusted Pads (Cloth Shoulder, 34 Armor, Passive: Restores 3 health every 4 seconds), Deep Fathom Ring (Ring, Unique, +6 SPI, +3 STA, +3 INT), Mutant Scale Breastplate (Mail Chest, 211 Armor, +13 STR, +5 STA), Glowing Shard, Murloc Eye, Murloc Fin, Thick-shelled Clam, Shiny Fish Scales, Slimy Murloc Scale
Notes: Summoned by escorting the Disciple of Naralex, Thundercrack, Terrify		
SKUM	21 Elite	Glowing Lizardscale Cloak (Cloak, 20 Armor, +6 AGI, +2 SPI), Tail Spike (One-Hand Dagger, 11.1 DPS, +2 AGI, +2 STR), Thunder Lizard Tail
Notes: Chained Bolt		
TRIGORE THE LASHER	19 Elite	Serpent's Kiss (One-Hand Axe, 13.4 DPS, Chance on Hit: Poisons target for 7 Nature damage every 3 seconds for 15 seconds), Runescale Girdle (Mail Waist, 94 Armor, +5 STR), Small Barnacled Clam
Notes: Rare Spawn		
VERDAN THE EVERLIVING	22 Elite	Seedcloud Buckler (Shield, 566 Armor, 11 Block, +3 SPI, +6 INT), Living Root (Staff, 21.2 DPS, +12 SPI, +2 STA, +5 Nature Resistance), Sporid Cape (Cloak, 18 Armor, +3 STA, +2 SPI)
Notes: Grasping Vines		

⚙ ENTRANCE TO WAILING CAVERNS

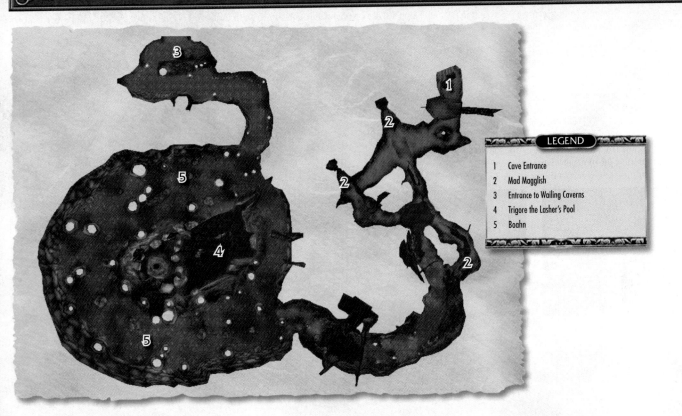

LEGEND

1	Cave Entrance
2	Mad Magglish
3	Entrance to Wailing Caverns
4	Trigore the Lasher's Pool
5	Boahn

HAVING A PLAN

You'll need a pulling strategy in this instance (and just about every instance). You should choose one puller and keep the rest of the party away from danger. The party should be back twice the distance of aggro range. So, if it takes 10 yards to aggro, the party should remain 20 yards from the mobs. Just the puller advances and pulls; no one goes with him. If he makes a bad pull (e.g. he pulls five mobs when he was hoping to get two), the group can let him die. Always pull with a ranged weapon or spell.

Another great pull is to have a Warrior or Hunter using a gun or ranged weapon. Warriors can take the damage. Should you be using a Hunter instead, their pet can serve as a great tank and a Hunter's ranged and stunning abilities can help in a cleaner pull. This works perfectly in conjunction with a Mage who can sheep an add.

Every party should have a healer(s) who can resurrect. It's easier for the puller to take the death and be resurrected than causing the whole party to die and run back to the instance. There are two types of mobs that need to be pulled past the party: Druids and Flyers. To do this, the puller needs to draw aggro and run past the party (and continue going) until the mob reaches the main force.

These mobs attack using ranged attacks. The idea is to make them chase you until they reach the party and not stand there and trade shots with you.

1. Druids: They cast Lightning.
2. Flyers: There are many of them and they have ranged attacks.

From the entrance to the Wailing Caverns you'll need to clear your way. These mobs are a precursor to what you'll face. Before going too far, take a moment to check the first nook to the right for Mad Magglish. He's a stealthed mob and isn't always easy to see since he's a level 18 elite mob. If he's not there, continue a little deeper into the opening caverns. There are three possible spawn points (as noted on the map) for this mob.

Head northeast until you reach the first intersection on your left. Take that left and enter the shallow pool area. There are three choices at this intersection. North leads to the instance. East and west are the two additional spawn points for Mad Magglish who has the brandy from the *Trouble at the Docks* quest in Ratchet. Don't forget to start gathering **Serpentbloom** as you go through as well.

Have your interrupts ready as you fight the ectoplasms. At low health, they summon a Cloned Ectoplasm. Anytime it begins to clone itself, hit it with an interrupt.

Continue north until you get to the next pool. This pool is much deeper and Deviate Lurkers wait beneath the surface of the water. The Deviate Lurkers are purely aquatic enemies and will not follow you onto land. For this reason, you can simply swim across the pond and ignore the Lurkers. Before doing this, gaze into the pool. Trigore the Lasher is a rare spawn that is not purely aquatic. If he's in the pool, pull him onto land where the Lurkers can't help him and dispatch him. Once safely across the pond, enter to Cavern of Mists.

Taking the right path is the shortest way to the instance portal. Make sure you don't fall in the hole on the right side of the path. Even experienced players often fall through the hole if they don't pay attention. Falling forces you to swim through a few extra mobs to get to the Instance. If any party members fall, everyone should also. It's important to keep the group together no matter what. Splitting up will spell the end of your group.

Boahn is a rare spawn enemy who resides along the left path. Take this path if the fighting is simple and to check for Boahn. He has a very long respawn timer and is often absent.

THE INSTANCE

The Disciple of Naralex is just inside the Instance. Speak to him to receive his Mark of the Wild. If you have a Druid in your party, this isn't important, but the buff will help you greatly for as long as it lasts if you're without one. A Deviate Guardian is the first mob you'll see. Pull it toward you as many of the raptors scream for help when low on health.

LEGEND

1	Entrance to WC and Disciple Of Naralex
2	Lady Anacondra
3	Naralex (The Sleeper)
4	Lord Cobrahn
5	Skum
6	Lord Serpentis and Verdan the Everling
7	Lord Pythas
8	Deviate Faerie Dragon
9	Leap of Faith

The roaming Ectoplasm is next. Wait until it gets out of range of the two Deviates and pull it solo. It follows quite a distance, so don't pull it too soon, or you'll find yourselves fighting a trio. The two Deviates are next. The guardian is a screamer that calls adds if they're within range, so pull them back as far as they'll come. Sheep, Hibernate or stun the add if you can.

As soon as you make the right into the main cavern, there are a few more mobs. They're not linked, but remain in a relatively tight group and a couple may come. Just pull them and take them out. Drag them back to the main group and wipe them out. These few end the first section of the caverns. It only gets harder from this point on.

SCREAMING GULLY

At first look, there are only a couple raptors here, but looks are deceiving. A Druid of the Fang and an Ectoplasm patrol across this area. Watch the patrols and pull the raptors into the previous room when the patrollers are away. Their screams can bring the Druid if you don't pull them far enough back.

Once the raptors are dead, pull the patrollers one at a time. Once the Druid starts casting at you, run around the corner back into the previous room. Once you break line of sight, the Druid is forced to come to you. Don't attack it until it's in the room with you. The Ectoplasm is an easy fight. Be sure to interrupt it before it can clone itself.

If you don't have a Mage, have one party member with interrupt abilities keep the Druid occupied while the party kills the other. Using a pet to hold the Deviate during this time is ideal. If you are without pets, the tank will need to hold both it and a Druid.

Lady Anacondra has several spawn points. Clear these upper ledges until you've found and killed her. If you killed Lady Anacondra, drop into the water. Have your puller pull across that little bridge where you just killed the Druids and Deviate. The main party should wait before the bridge and have the puller pull the mobs to them. Watch those Deviates; timing it right gives you a good pull.

CONTROLLING AGGRO

If the main group crosses the little bridge, whatever is pulled should aggro Lady Anacondra. If that happens, there could be a group of four attacking your group. Don't panic! It's just a challenge that you must overcome. Sheep Lady Anacondra and kill the Druid first. Have the tank cover the two Deviates. It's a bit crazy, but possible. Having Hunter or Warlock pets hold the Deviates makes the tank's job easier.

If you manage to kill the two Deviates without bringing Lady Anacondra, the fight should go much more smoothly. Pull and run across the bridge. The Druids should start casting and, if you run away and force the Druid to chase you, you won't aggro the spawns behind them. However, if you charge in, the spawns in back will join in. Cast and run! If there's a Mage in the group, Sheep the Lady as soon as she's in range.

DRUIDS

Druids cast Sleep and Lightning. Sleep's deadly since it completely removes you from the fight. This is where your interrupts pay for themselves. Lightning is actually the least of your worries. Hold your interrupts for when either white or green energy glows around their hands. This means they are casting Sleep or Heal.

Should the Druids be successful in sleeping one of your party members, the Paladin, Priest or Shaman needs to wake them quickly. Paladins can Cleanse, or Priests can cast Dispel Magic on the party member, while Shamans drop a Tremor Totem. The Tremor Totem can even be dropped before the spell completes and will still wake the sleeping party member.

Take the path to the left. It ascends to a small group of enemies. There are three mobs: a Deviate raptor, a Druid and either another Druid or Lady Anacondra. The one Druid roams, the other doesn't. Wait until the roaming Druid gets to the end of his roaming path farthest away from you. If you time it right, you can pull that Deviate solo. It's hard and has a high fail rate, but it's worth a try. If you get everything, sheep one of the Druids and focus fire on the other.

Once Lady Anacondra's dead, and you've gotten her gem for *The Leaders of the Fang,* jump into the water and head west. The Crocolisks are not elites and you can chew through them quickly. Kresh roams through the waterway. He's neutral and won't attack, but has a chance to drop a great shield for your tank. Continue west into the Pit of Fangs killing all the Crocolisks. They drop **Deviate Hides** for the *Deviate Hides* quest, so they're worth it. They also drop the occasional green item. (At the very least your Enchanter will get new materials.)

PIT OF FANGS

Stop at the bottom of the next ramp! This is the first "wipe spot," as in "there's a great chance your group will get wiped out." There are wandering Deviates and Druids up there. Your best bet is to use a Rogue to scout the ramp. Make sure nothing is roaming close when pulling. If this isn't an option, use the highest level character with ranged attacks to pull.

The first thing you'll see is a wandering Ectoplasm. If you don't see it, wait until you do. When it approaches the bottom of the ramp, kill it. Now for the fun part. You should have a good head start on the *Deviate Eradication* quest and, if you don't have all of your **Deviate Hides** yet, there are plenty of chances to get them all as you pass through this next area.

The first mobs you see are Deviate Adders and Vipers. However, there's also a wandering Druid. Wait until you see the Druid head back up the ramp. There are so many columns to hide the Druid that you must be sure that he's gone before provoking another attack. Pull the Viper to the left and hug the wall as you return to the group. Two mobs may come and that's fine. Keep the group at the bottom of the ramp and pull to them. Don't let them follow you up until you're sure that it's clear. If you don't grab the second Deviate, go back and pull it (watching for the Druid).

DEVIATE VIPERS HAVE BITE

Deviate Vipers have a Localized Toxin that does a good amount of poison damage over time. Having a Shaman, Priest, or Paladin (or someone with First Aid) to cure this in your group is a boon.

Bring your group to the top of the ramp and take out the Druid. Hit him and run to the bottom of the ramp to bring the Druid into your party. Don't charge the Druid since there's a bunch of mobs near him. Take out any other stragglers at the top of the ramp and move the group up a bit more.

There are three mobs in the corner. This is a common sight since they're often protecting a chest. The chests in the dungeons have good loot, so don't pass up the chance to snag it.

Head north by northwest. Druids and mobs are often on this path and they're surrounded by snakes. The pulls are easy in this area if you pay attention. AoEs are great against the snakes since they aren't elites. A wandering Druid and Deviate Viper could cause a bit of trouble, so keep your eyes open.

Keep clearing out the mobs to reach the next trio. Wait for the Druid to get close and pull it; there's a good chance to pull the Druid solo. The Druid casting the green spell won't come on the first pull. Wipe out the trio and grab the chest if it's there. Continue south, but watch out. The mobs can easily chain and that could cause problems. Remain at max pulling range and keep your main force behind at all times. Study the area for a few seconds before pulling. Those seconds could save your group.

Lord Cobrahn, the next boss, is in the very next group. Try to pull any mobs that you think may come solo (the ones to the left) and then pull the snake and run! Lord Cobrahn hits like a truck. Tackle him by dumping as much damage and armor debuffs onto him as possible. He can heal and cast Lightning, but if you overload him on the damage, he'll be too busy focusing on surviving to dish out some reciprocity. The Warriors and Rogues should interrupt anything that the boss begins casting. With the tank and interrupts on Cobrahn, have your DPS members kill the snakes before joining the fight against Cobrahn. If left unattended, the snakes will find their way to your healer and complicate the fight greatly.

Once Cobrahn joins Anacondra in death, loot the gem from him for Leaders of the Fang. Move to the edge of the cliff to the north. There is are outcroppings that can be used to get back to the Screaming Gully without take the long way.

Drop down and keep dropping until you reach the bottom. Do it as a group or send the warrior to aggro any stray mobs. Head east back into the Screaming Gully. If you did that entire run quickly enough, it should be clear of mobs. Pass up the entrance and continue east. Continue killing all the Crocolisks, but beware of the wandering Ectoplasms. Keep in mind that all wanderers respawn about every 15 minutes. Head east and south until you reach the Crag of Everliving. You can ignore some of the Crocolisks in this area, but if members still need Deviate Hides for the quest, kill them all.

CRAG OF EVERLIVING

You'll reach a section where you spy your first Shambler. This is where it starts to get hard again. Shamblers tend to cast Wild Regeneration on themselves once you get them down to about half their life, so be quick in killing them or disrupt the Wild Regeneration with Kick, Shield Bash, or Earth Shock.

There are two wanderers: a Shambler and Ectoplasm. Make sure they're not around when you pull the first group. The first Shambler and Druid are linked. Pull the Shambler and keep going until the Druid reaches the group. You know that routine by now. Wait for the wandering Ectoplasm and Shambler and kill them before snagging the next group.

Right next to them are two Druids and another Shambler that are linked. Another one of your standard groups of three. Sheep or Sap a Druid, if possible, and kill the other Druid first. The Shamblers hit hard, so let a Warrior tank them. Make sure when you finally attack the Shambler that the whole group attacks them. They cast a decent Regeneration spell, that can outdo the damage of one or two people. Drop a damage dump on the Shamblers to take them out quickly. Head north.

You'll come across a Druid and a Shambler, take them out. Smoke the next trio while ignoring the one casting the green spell. Run back to the group and there's a chance that you'll only pull the Shambler and the Druid. Continue north until you run into the Lashers. These annoying little plants that are easily crushed with a single AoE. They're not elite and die quickly, but they do hit multiple party members for decent damage so take them seriously. Their biggest threat is their ability to disrupt the healers and casters. Keep them away from the bulk of your party at all costs.

DEVIATE LASHERS

Deviate Lashers are always in groups of three or four and are linked. If one comes your way expect them all.

Keep going and kill the batches of Lashers and the Druids. Once you reach the Shamblers and Druids, take them out. You're pretty much on auto pilot until you reach the Winding Chasm.

THE WINDING CHASM

The Winding Chasm is aptly named. It has a ton of twists and turns. Kill the Shambler and head northeast into the water. While in the water, wait for the wandering mobs (Ectoplasm and Shambler) before taking on the Shamblers and Druid at the end of the water. After you Sheep/Sap kill the Druid and Shamblers, slow down! You've reached another wipe spot. This happens to be one of the most dangerous areas in the instance. If you get past this, you're golden. Lord Pythas is waiting here and he's not easy.

(Use the pictures below to see how "right" and "left" are used in the strategy.) There are mobs all around. Everything needs to be cleared before attempting to take Pythas on. Pull the Lashers and the Druid and remember to run the Druid into the group. There's another tunnel to the left with two Shamblers and a few Lashers. The tunnel to the right has a wandering Ectoplasm, a couple Druids and a few Lashers. There's nothing to really worry about if you take your time and stay sharp.

If you pull a Lasher the Druids should follow, so pull everything into your main force. Kill everything in site and then take out the two Shamblers to the north. They won't link with Pythas, so make sure to take both of them out before tackling the third boss.

A Druid is by Pythas and it's a difficult trick to bring him solo, so just grab the two mobs and Sheep or Sap Pythas and take the Druid out of the picture. Drop that damage dump on Pythas. He fights like Cobrahn, but hits harder. He uses Lightning, Sleep, a Thunderclap and can heal himself. Interrupt anything that looks like a cast and pile on the damage. Keep him away from your tank and wake your tank if you need. If Pythas gets to your healer, your party is in terrible danger. Keep him interrupted and pile on the stuns. He won't live long, but the trick is to make sure you live longer. Loot the gem from Pythas to advance *The Leaders of the Fang*.

Head south in the tunnel to the right. Mop up any mobs and snag any chests that may be around. Continue south until you notice the first Deviate Dreadfang. The Dreadfangs are needed for *Deviate Eradication* and should be killed on sight, but they should be pulled far from other enemies. The Dreadfangs can fear your party members and having a teammate run into another enemy group spells doom for you all.

It should be in a room with Druids and a bunch of candles. There are more mobs (Shambler, Druids, etc.) in the room, so make sure the roaming Druid is out of site before pulling anything. Clear the room and continue southeast. (Take the extra room if you'd like; it leads back to the main area.)

Send a Rogue to scout ahead to see if there's a chest in the room worth fighting for or just move on.

Pull the Venomwing and Druid out and kill them. Move your group up and take out anything that's in your way. Stay close to the wall and away from any mobs in the room (if you skipped it) or just start grabbing the Lashers and Druid.

Take out Skum's bodyguards before engaging him. Sheep or otherwise CC one Druid and have the tank keep the other interrupted as he pulls it back to the party. Kill the Druids one at a time and rest up for Skum. Skum's restricted to his pen for good reason. He hits hard and has a mountain of hitpoints. Give the tank a few moments to establish aggro before stacking DoTs on Skum. Don't use  any of your large attacks until every DoT you have is on him. This gives your tank even more time to establish aggro. Keep Skum's attention on your tank and this fight is won. You tank's health shouldn't be allowed to drop below half as Skum's critical attacks can be monstrous.

Continue west and clear out the next room. Be careful, there are two groups and they'll aggro. Continue through the rooms and head south (to the *left* not right) killing any mobs that pop up.

The next room is full of Venomwings and Druids, but you should be able to pull them in twos if you're careful. Once you're through clearing the room, you'll be back in the Crag of Everliving at the Leap of Faith. This jump is very important to make. If you fail, you will fall to your death and out of resurrection range. Use the walk button (defaulted to "/") and approach the ledge slowly. Find where the shortest distance is before backing up again. Make sure you are out of walk mode before making a running jump off the ledge. If one party member fails the jump, all may not be lost if there is a Warlock in your party. As long as the Warlock and two others make it to the other side, the Warlock can summon the person as soon as they run back to the instance.

BACK IN THE CRAG OF EVERLIVING

Clear the enemies as you ascend the ramp. You've been in here enough to know what to expect. Move slowly and clear as you go. Lord Serpentis is in the next room. He wanders, so wait until he gets far away from the Venomwing before pulling it. Wait for the wandering Ectoplasm before even thinking about taking on Lord Serpentis. When he stands alone, it's time to end it.

Shield your tank before charging in. Serpentis hits very hard and your tank will need a few moments to establish aggro. If you have a second person with interrupts, this person should keep Serpentis from casting. Your tank's entire attention should be on keeping aggro. Serpentis will level a softer party member in only a few swings.

Make sure your party fights near Serpentis. Having a member wander too close to Verdan the Everliving will doom your party, while having a party member get knocked off the cliff isn't good either.

Drop your DoTs on him before blasting him down. As the final member of The Leaders of the Fang falls, the Disciple of Naralex screams "At last! Naralex can be awakened! Come aid me, brave adventurers!" While the cause is just, there's one problem. There are only two ways down: jumping to your death or through Verdan the Everliving.

Verdan isn't a part of any quest, but he has a proper name and that can only mean one thing…loot! He has a mountain of hitpoints and a lot of armor. Shield your tank before charging in. Your tank won't live long without heals, but you need to give him a couple seconds to establish aggro before jumping in. Stack every DoT you have on him before blasting away. Verdan is huge, so keep your party members at maximum range so you can see what's going on. Melee members who aren't the tank should try to remain behind Verdan.

This fight won't be fast. Keep Verdan snared and on the tank. If the healer is falling behind, a secondary tank should try to grab aggro long enough for the tank to bandage. Use potions, healthstones, and timed abilities for this fight. Don't hold anything in reserve as Verdan certainly won't. Once he finally falls, loot his body for your reward.

Now it's time to head to the entrance. There is a hold in the floor at the north edge of Verdan's cave. Jump in. You fall a very long ways, but you land safely in water. Follow the water back to the Screaming Gully.

BACK IN SCREAMING GULLY

Head west and start clearing everything again; you're not done yet. You've been in the dungeon a long time now and chances are everything's respawned up near the entrance. You need to head up the ramp to the entrance and this is a bad place now. Roaming Druids and Ectoplasms cause havok, so make sure they're cleared before taking on the Deviates (or just keep an eye out for them). Pull the Guardians as far away as possible and try to reach the area where you took out Lady Anacondra. Clear the whole bridge again and the area past the bridge.

Clear all the mobs past Lady Anacondra's spawn location. Continue on and clear the next room. Return to the beginning of the instance and speak with the Disciple of Naralex. He's going to walk you to the area you just cleared and you've already cleaned it up a bit. However, as you reach the camp, more mobs will spawn. This is a good time to get any of the last of the Deviate Adders you may have missed for the *Deviate Eradication* quest.

The Disciple of Naralex is taking you to the Dreamer's Rock to the sleeper and casts a spell to wake him.

DREAMER'S ROCK: THE SLEEPER AWAKENS

Mobs will spawn at this point to remove your presence. First are the Deviate Mocassins and Nightmare Ectoplasms. They'll seem to come from all directions and, truth be told, they do. It's easy for an entire group to get crushed if you don't stay focused. Call targets and focus your fire. You'll need to work quickly to minimize the damage they inflict.

You may be fighting up to five at a time and they're not that difficult, but there are a bunch of them. Consolidate aggro on your tank and AoE them down. A timely shield on your AoEer will make sure she survives the encounter. When the last falls, eat and drink immediately. You don't have much time and will need as much health and mana as possible.

Mutanus the Devourer is a 24 elite mob and if you haven't had nightmares about Murlocs yet, you will. He's a large albino Murloc on steroids. He's much like the last two bosses in that he hits hard and has a ton of hit points. Shield your tank and charge in. Hold Mutanus well away from ranged party members.

Much like Verdan, it's very important to keep aggro on your tank. Use DoTs to start the fight and be ready to cease fire. Should the tank lose aggro, stop casting or fighting. Everyone should stop what they are doing except the tank. The tank now has to regain Mutanus' attention and continued casting makes his job much harder. Once the tank regains aggro, pull Mutanus back into position before continuing the attack.

Keep him snared to slow his progress toward other party members and keep the DoTs on him. Recast them as soon as they fall. If you have a secondary healer, this is when they will pay for themselves. Be ready to take over healing if the primary healer runs out of mana. If the primary healer runs out of mana, he should stop casting. This sounds obvious, but you don't regenerate mana for 5 seconds after casting a spell, that means he will stop regenerating mana as soon as he starts casting again. The primary healer should stop casting and use non-magical attacks until he has full mana or the backup healer is out of mana. Rotating healers is a useful skill and will aid you in later instances.

Mutanus may be huge and ugly, but he's mortal. He will eventually fall. Check his body for the **Glowing Shard**. There is much to do now. Sputtervalve in Ratchet can direct you to someone who knows more about the Glowing Shard, and your bags are full. Walk out of the instance or hearthstone out. Make sure the entire party does one or the other. Keeping the party together until you are all in the safety of town is important.

ZUL'FARRAK

Played & Written by: Michael "Kayal" Lummis of <Dovrani> on Kirin Tor

Zul'Farrak is a place of ancient worship, where the Trolls of Tanaris fiercely guard the approach to their leaders and sacred beasts. Rumors have it that a Hydra of immense power dwells there, and that the dead are brought back to life through ancient rituals. West across the vast sands of Tanaris, past Gadgetzan and any vestige of civilization, this fortress of Trolls stands against both the Horde and the Alliance.

DUNGEON INFORMATION

Location	Tanaris (NW Side)
Quests	Horde and Alliance
Region	Contested
Suggested Levels	43-48
Group Allowed	5 to Quest, 10 to Raid
Primary Enemies	Trolls, Basilisks (And More Trolls)
Time to Complete	2 Hours

GETTING TO ZUL'FARRAK

Getting the Tanaris Flight Point in Gadgetzan is the only issue here. Have everyone fly down to Gadgetzan and move out to the west from there. Zul'Farrak is in the far northwest of Tanaris, and the instance portal is practically out in the open (it's just inside a small set of ruins). Low-level Elite Trolls are found in the areas nearby, and are good to hunt while preparing for a Zul'Farrak run.

WHO TO BRING

Zul'Farrak is a short instance area, but the fights make up for that in terms of size and ferocity. Large Troll/Basilisk patrols, a noticeable respawn rate, and the impressive set encounters all keep Zul'Farrak from being a cakewalk. Appropriately leveled groups should consider a secondary tank or healer to reduce the dangers of some of the larger (and longer) fights. Crowd control is necessary in almost every encounter, and combinations of such abilities are successful here as well; using Sap to begin encounters while Mages Polymorph additional threats is a sound tactic. Priest Mind Control, used to disrupt larger enemy groups and reduce pull size, is risky. Yet, the risk is sometimes quite acceptable. Fights with five or six elite Trolls demand serious methods!

POSSIBLE GROUP MAKEUP

Tank	Warrior, Druid, Paladin
CC	Rogue, Mage, Priest
DPS	Rogue, Hunter, Mage, Warlock
Healer	Priest, Shaman, Druid, Paladin
Support Slot	Secondary Tank or Healer is Suggested

QUESTS

ALLIANCE QUESTS

QUEST NAME	QUEST GIVER	QUEST GIVER LOCATION	QUEST RECEIVER	QUEST RECEIVER LOCATION	CHAIN?	MAX EXPERIENCE
Nekrum's Medallion	Thadius Grimshade	Blasted Lands	Thadius Grimshade	Blasted Lands	Yes	5,250

NEKRUM'S MEDALLION

Quest Level	40 to Obtain
Location	NE Blasted Lands (Nethergarde Keep)
Contact	Thadius Grimshade
Goal	Slay Nekrum Gutchewer and Loot His Medallion
Max Experience Gained	5,250

This quest is part of a chain that starts with *Witherbark Cages* in the Hinterlands. Though killing Nekrum is easy, getting to him can be quite difficult. This Troll won't spawn unless you release the prisoners from the Troll pyramid, at the northern end of Zul'Farrak. This starts a very long fight against dozens of Elite and Non-Elite Trolls, and Nekrum is one of the two final spawns during that encounter. This requires a full group and fairly high level for this instance, since the battle is quite long and brutal.

SHARED QUESTS

QUEST NAME	QUEST GIVER	QUEST GIVER LOCATION	QUEST RECEIVER	QUEST RECEIVER LOCATION	CHAIN?	MAX EXPERIENCE
Divino-matic Rod	Chief Engineer Bilgewhizzle	Gadgetzan	Chief Engineer Bilgewhizzle	Gadgetzan	No	6,300
REWARD: Masons Fraternity Ring (Ring +13 AGI/+5 STA) or Engineer's Guild Headpiece (Leather Helm 113 Armor +23 INT/+9 SPI)						
Gahz'rilla	Wizzle Brassbolts	Mirage Raceway	Wizzle Brassbolts	Mirage Raceway	No	7,100
REWARD: Speedy Racer Googles (Cloth Helm 53 Armor +14 AGI/+14 INT) or Carrot on a Stick (Trinket +3% Mount Speed)						
Scarab Shells	Tran'rek	Gadgetzan	Tran'rek	Gadgetzan	No	3,900
Tiara of the Deep	Tabetha	Dustwallow Marsh	Tabetha	Dustwallow Marsh	No	6,050
REWARD: Gemshale Pauldrons (Plate Shoulders 334 Armor +10 STR/+9 STA) or Spellshifter Rod (Staff 35.7 DPS +6 STA/+16 INT)						
The Prophecy of Mosh'aru	Yeh'Kinya	Steamwheedle Port	Yeh'Kinya	Steamwheedle Port	Yes	5,250
Troll Temper	Trenton Lighthammer	Gadgetzan	Trenton	Lighthammer	No	3,900

DIVINO-MATIC ROD

Quest Level	40 to Obtain
Location	Tanaris (Gadgetzan)
Contact	Chief Engineer Bilgewhizzle
Goal	Retrieve the Divino-matic Rod
Max Experience Gained	6,300

The Chief Engineer needs the Divino-matic Rod back from the traitorous Sergeant Bly, who is in Zul'Farrak currently. Bly is a captive of the Trolls, but he is quite a cantankerous and dangerous fellow nonetheless. On top of the pyramid in the northern end of Zul'Farrak, Bly and the other prisoners are kept in cages. Kill the Troll Executioner that guards these people and the nearby Basilisks, then release the group. A very long fight ensues as the captives make their way to the bottom of the pyramid. Once this is done, talk to the Goblin to have him open the way to the Troll's king, then talk to Bly and demand the Rod (Bly attacks your group, but he cannot survive this assault). Take the Rod when Bly is dead and return it to Gadgetzan.

GAHZ'RILLA

Quest Level	40 to Obtain
Location	Thousand Needles (Mirage Raceway)
Contact	Wizzle Brassbolts
Goal	Slay Gahz'rilla and Collect His Electrified Scale
Max Experience Gained	7,100

 This is not the easiest quest for Zul'Farrak, and it takes more than a few minutes of setup time. Travel out to the Shimmering Flats and talk to Wizzle Brassbolts in the raceway. Wizzle wants Gahz'rilla's Scale to add extra power to his car. This involves summoning the great Hydra, and a random group wandering through Zul'Farrak isn't going to encounter this legendary beast.

Instead, you must travel to the Hinterlands and climb the Altar of Zul. Kill the Elite Trolls up there to receive the Sacred Mallet (take a group even for this, since the fight contains multiple Elite, Troll Casters). Next, travel to the southeastern edge of the Hinterlands and climb through the levels of Trolls to the top of the area, where the Sacred Mallet can be charged (use the Mallet on the Altar on top of city).

With the Mallet properly charged, return to Zul'Farrak and use this item on the Gong by the pool inside the Instance. This is on the western side of the area. Fully clear the room before activating the encounter, and read the battle strategy farther down in the walkthrough. Collect Gahz'rilla's Electrified Scale from the body when the creature falls, and return to the Mirage Raceway for your reward. Note: Only one party member needs to have the Mallet for Gahz'rilla to be summoned.

SCARAB SHELLS

Quest Level	40 to Obtain
Location	Tanaris (Gadgetzan)
Contact	Tran'rek
Goal	Collect 9 Uncracked Scarab Shells
Max Experience Gained	3,900

There are non-elite/neutral Scarabs all over Zul'Farrak. These creatures have a fairly high chance on death to drop their Shells for people on this quest. Hunting the eastern side of Zul'Farrak is best for quickly polishing off Scarab Shells, since there is a room there with many of the beetles.

TIARA OF THE DEEP

Quest Level	40 to Obtain
Location	Central Dustwallow Marsh
Contact	Tabetha
Goal	Slay Hydromancer Velratha and Collect the Tiara of the Deep
Max Experience Gained	6,050

The first part of this quest is simply to find Tabetha. She lives in the middle of Dustwallow Marsh, so it isn't terrible easy to get to her. She is found east and a bit south of the Barrens entrance to the zone. Speak to her and receive the quest, then look in the western end of Zul'Farrak from Hydromancer Velratha (she is the only Hydromancer in the area by the pool). Slay this lone caster and take the Tiara from her.

THE PROPHECY OF MOSH'ARU

Quest Level	40 to Obtain
Location	Tanaris (Steamwheedle Port)
Contact	Yeh'kinya
Goal	Collect the 2 Mosh'aru Tablets
Max Experience Gained	5,250

This quest is the second step in a chain of good errands. The first step takes you into Feralas, where you collect Screecher Spirits! In this step, you enter Zul'Farrak and need to kill two enemies (one on the east side, and one of the west). To the east is Theka the Martyr, a Troll who goes immune to all physical damage when low on health. Stack as many DoTs as possible on him before he reaches 1/3 health, use finishing moves at the last moment, then have the casters of your group go to town on him (loot his tablet afterward). To the west is Hydromancer Velratha; she is needed for the Tiara of the Deep quest anyway, so slay her and collect her tablet and the Tiara.

TROLL TEMPER

Quest Level	40 to Obtain
Location	Tanaris (Gadgetzan)
Contact	Trenton Lighthammer
Goal	Collect 20 Troll Tempers
Max Experience Gained	3,900

Trenton Lighthammer is a member of the Mithril Order, but he gives this quest to anyone who is willing to fight the Trolls of Zul'Farrak. All of the Trolls inside the World Dungeon drop these with a high frequency. For characters of low level, this quest can be quite safely but very slowly by also fighting the Trolls that guard the towers outside of Zul'Farrak. The drop rate is terrible for the Trolls outside, but they are low level and can be fought one-at-a-time.

HORDE QUESTS

QUEST NAME	QUEST GIVER	QUEST GIVER LOCATION	QUEST RECEIVER	QUEST RECEIVER LOCATION	CHAIN?	MAX EXPERIENCE
The Spider God	Master Gadrin	Durotar	Master Gadrin	Durotar	Yes	4,850

THE SPIDER GOD

Quest Level	42 to Obtain
Location	Durotar (Sen'jin Village)
Contact	Master Gadrin
Goal	Read the Tablet on Theka in Zul'Farrak
Max Experience Gained	4,850

This Horde quest starts in Sen'jin village as part of a long chain. The chain starts in the Hinterlands, with the Venom Bottles quest, and eventually leads all the way down to Sen'jin, where Master Gadrin asks you to seek Zul'Farrak. The goal is to read the tablet near Theka the Maryyr (on the eastern side of Zul'Farrak). It isn't hard to find the tablet, in the area where Theka patrols. Your group can either wait and slip by Theka, to get the quest done without extra fighting, or take down the troublesome Troll, as needed. After reading the tablet to find out the name of the Spider God, return to Gadrin. The next step in the chain is to actually summon the creature, up in the Hinterlands.

TROLLS, AND BASILISKS, AND SCARABS (OH MY)

ENEMIES IN THE SAND

NPC	LEVEL
Sandfury Blood Drinker	44-45 Elite
Notes: Leech Life (Steal Hit Points, AoE)	
Sandfury Cretin	43-45 Elite
Sandfury Executioner	46 Elite
Notes: Uses Cleave	
Sandfury Guardian	45-46 Elite
Notes: Tamable by Hunters, Very Social	
Sandfury Shadowcaster	43-44 Elite
Notes: Shadow Bolts	
Sandfury Shadowhunter	45-46 Elite
Notes: Hex (Frog Polymorph), Ranged	
Sandfury Soul Eater	45-46 Elite
Notes: Soul Bite, Low Hit Points, High DPS	
Sandfury Witch Doctor	44-45 Elite
Notes: Heal, Healing Totem, AoE Fire Totem	

NPC	LEVEL
Scarab	44-46
Notes: Plague Cloud (Disease, -11 STR/AGI/INT), Neutral	
Sul'lithuz Abomination	47 Elite
Notes: Petrify (Long-Duration Stun)	
Sul'lithuz Broodling	40 Elite
Sul'lithuz Sandcrawler	45-47 Elite
Notes: Petrify	
Zul'Farrak Dead Hero	45-46 Elite
Notes: Undead Immunities	
Zul'Farrak Zombie	43-44 Elite
Notes: Undead Immunities	

LEADERS OF ZUL'FARRAK

NPC	LEVEL	FREQUENT DROP(S)
ANTU'SUL	48 Elite	Lifeblood Amulet (Necklace +13 STA/+5 SPI), The Hand of Antu'sul (Main-Hand Mace 32.2 DPS Chance on Hit: Thunderclap for 7 Nature Damage and 10% Attack Speed Debuff), Vice Grips (Plate Hands 318 Armor +14 Attack Power/Variable Bonuses), Sang'thraze the Deflector(One-hand Sword, 29.1 DPS, Equip: Increases your chance to parry an attack by 1%.)
Notes: Summons Basilisks, Flash Heal, Earthgrab Totem, Fire Nova Totem, Healing Ward, Earth Shock, Chain Lightning		
CHIEF UKORZ SANDSCALP	48 Elite	Ripsaw (Main-Hand Axe 33.3 DPS Chance on Hit: Wounds for 75 DMG), The Chief's Enforcer (Staff 43.5 DPS Chance on Hit: Stun Target for 3 Seconds), Big Bad Pauldrons (Plate Shoulders 396 Armor +12 STR/+12 STA/+8 SPI), Embrace of the Lycan (Leather Head 118 Armor +8 STR/+16 STA/+5 SPI/+32 Attack Power), Jang'thraze the Protector (Main-hand Sword, 33.4 DPS, Use: Combines Jang'thraze and Sang'thraze to form the mighty sword, Sul'thraze. Chance on hit: Shields the wielder from physical damage, absorbing 55 to 85 damage. Lasts 20 seconds.) Mageweave, Silk, Troll Temper (Quest Item), Flask of Mojo
Notes: Wide Slash (Whirlwind Attack), Cleave, Enrage (temporary increase to damage dealt)		
GAHZ'RILLA	46 Elite	Gahz'rilla Scale Armor (Mail Chest 290 Armor +10 STA/+23 SPI), Gahz'rilla's Fang (Dagger 28.1 DPS Chance on Hit: 10 DMG Nature Shield for 15 Seconds)
Notes: AoE Throw (Massive Falling Damage), Icicle, Freeze Solid (Magic)		
HYDROMANCER VELRATHA	46 Elite	Tiara of the Deep (Quest Item), Second Mosh'aru Tablet (Quest Item), Mageweave, Silk, Flask of Mojo
Notes: Moderate Hit Points, Wanders Alone, Shadow Bolt, Healing Wave, Wrath of Zum'rah Totem		
NEKRUM GUTCHEWER	45-46 Elite	Nekrum's Medallion (Quest Item), Mageweave, Silk, Troll Temper (Quest Item), Flask of Mojo
Notes: Appears After Pyramid Battle, Fevered Plague (Disease)		
RUUZLU	46 Elite	Mageweave, Silk, Troll Temper (Quest Item), Flask of Mojo
Notes: High Hit Points, Assists Chief Sandscalp, Cleave, Execute		
SHADOWPRIEST SEZZ-ZIZ	47 Elite	Jinxed Hoodoo Skin (Leather Chest 144 Armor +8 STR/+10 STA/+20 SPI), Diabolic Skiver (Polearm 42.8 DPS Chance on Hit: Deal 160-180 Extra DMG), Jinxed Hoodoo Kilt (Leather Legs 126 Armor +10 INT/+24 SPI), Bad Mojo Mask (Cloth Head 54 Armor +24 INT Adds up to 10 to Shadow Spells and Effects), Mageweave, Silk, Troll Temper (Quest Item), Flask of Mojo
Notes: Appears After Pyramid Battle, Shadow Bolt, Psychic Scream, Renew, Heal		
THEKA THE MARTYR	45-46 Elite	First Mosh'aru Tablet (Quest Item), Mageweave, Silk, Troll Temper (Quest Item), Flask of Mojo
Notes: Goes Immune to Melee and Shadow Damage at 1/3 Health, Fevered Plague (Disease)		
WITCH DOCTOR ZUM'RAH	46 Elite	Jumanza Grips (Cloth Hands, 42 Armor, +11 INT, +10 SPI, +10 STA), Zum'rah's Vexing Cane (Staff, 40.9 DPS, +10 INT, +10 STA, Equip: Increases damage and healing done by magical spells and effects by up to 21.), Mageweave, Silk, Troll Temper (Quest Item), Flask of Mojo
Notes: Neutral Until Approached, Low Hit Points, Calls Undead Allies, Healing Wave, Shadow Bolt		
ZERILLIS	45 Elite	Sandstalker Ankleguards (Leather Boots 95 Armor +6 STR/+17 AGI/+3 SPI), Mageweave, Silk, Troll Temper (Quest Item), Flask of Mojo
Notes: Rare Spawn		

WAR AGAINST THE TROLLS

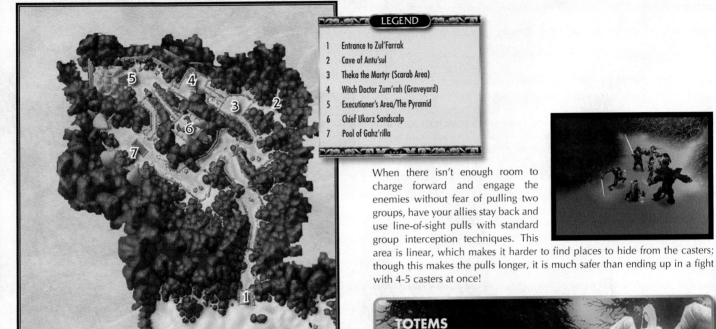

LEGEND

1 Entrance to Zul'Farrak
2 Cave of Antu'sul
3 Theka the Martyr (Scarab Area)
4 Witch Doctor Zum'rah (Graveyard)
5 Executioner's Area/The Pyramid
6 Chief Ukorz Sandscalp
7 Pool of Gahz'rilla

When there isn't enough room to charge forward and engage the enemies without fear of pulling two groups, have your allies stay back and use line-of-sight pulls with standard group interception techniques. This area is linear, which makes it harder to find places to hide from the casters; though this makes the pulls longer, it is much safer than ending up in a fight with 4-5 casters at once!

TOTEMS

The Witch Doctors love their Healing and Fire Totems. Destroy these with one of your group's faster attackers. The AoE damage from the Fire Totems is substantial over time, and it is very hard to pull the Trolls away from the area without ending us getting the melee but not the casters. Rogues are splendid at trashing Totems, though any fast attacker is suitable for this task.

The first open area to the north has no side passages. This place is merely an obstacle. The neutral scarabs you see wandering around drop their shells for the Scarab Shell quest. Pull them ahead of time to avoid agroing them with AoE spells during fights. Nothing shares a social faction with the scarabs, so there you will not get other creatures by pulling them. Cure the Plague Cloud disease that the scarabs inflict on people, since it lowers STR/AGI/INT by 11!

By making longer pulls, your group avoids the dilemma of having the wounded Trolls run into other parties when seeking help. Yet, the patrolling Trolls of Zul'Farrak are common sights, and it's always wise to snare Trolls before they run, just in case patrollers come near. Have a Warrior Hamstring targets or keep a Rogue up front with their Crippling Poison to slow enemies down. Hunters too are simply cruel against running foes, and are great to have around.

At the end of the path into the main junction there are Shadowhunters. These Trolls are extremely troublesome at times; they have a Hex ability that is even worse to face than Polymorph. The Trolls change you into a Frog and effectively control you without the issue of their spell breaking when you take damage. Unless your group can dispel magic (or has access to Grounding Totems), this ability is an unpleasant fact of life when fighting the Shadowhunters.

ENTERING THE SOUTH SIDE

Though there is no danger of attack at the portal itself, there isn't much lead in before the Trolls start to defend Zul'Farrak. From the beginning, your group can spot clusters of Trolls milling about. This linear route into the main junction of Zul'Farrak passes through about ten or so fight of these Trolls, so it's great to get your strategy honed here and now.

The majority of the fights at this stage of the Instance are against three Trolls. These come in a somewhat random mix of Blood Drinkers (melee Warriors with a Life Stealing ability), Shadowcasters (that love their Shadow Bolts), and Witch Doctors (who Heal and drop damaging totems).

MIND OVER MONSTERS

Using Mind Control (first available to Priests at level 30) to open fights with large groups of enemies becomes more common in higher level instances where the number of enemies are greater than what your group can handle safely. The first step for a Mind Control pull should be to Soothe (Mind on Humanoids, and Animal on Beasts) enemies around the designated target to avoid a premature start to the battle.

Mind Control generates an enormous amount of threat, so if the spell breaks before the target is killed, you must quickly pull the Priest's fat from the fire or you may be down a healer for the rest of the fight.

During most encounters, focus on the Witch Doctors first to remove their support from the enemy group. Use Mind Control pulls or Stuns to interrupt these foes, since it's tough to say during a casting whether they are using a Totem or a Heal (and the Totems can't be interrupted with normal abilities). Tear through these foes while using your tougher group members to peel and use their interrupts on the Shadowcasters instead. After the Witch Doctors, bring down the remaining casters, then focus on the Blood Drinkers last.

The central junction allows parties to travel either east or west into Zul'Farrak. The eastern path is somewhat easier, so it makes a better choice if you are doing all of the quests. Either way, the route to the right has Theka the Martyr, many Scarabs, Antu'sul (Treasure Mob), and leads around to the northern area with slightly less fighting than the western route. Alternatively, the western route has Hydromancer Velratha and the gong to summon Gahz'rilla. For now, we'll face the eastern wing.

EASTERN WING

The first room down the eastern path has many more Trolls but no bosses or items of consequence. Clear a path to the northern side of the area and continue from there. The group quickly arrives at a massive pen of Scarabs; this infestation is better to ignore unless characters are working on *Scarab Shells*. If that is the case, stay here and collect these items quickly and efficiently. The only hostile Troll in the area is Theka the Martyr.

Theka is easily dealt with once a party knows his gameplan. This Troll does light damage, but he goes immune to all melee damage at 1/3 health (he also is fully resistant to Shadow Magic at this point). To counter this, stack as many DoTs on the Troll when he reaches half health or so. These continue to deal damage after the immunity hits. Also, have casters hold back a bit on their damage early in the fight, then fully unload once Theka tries to save himself. It's a simple fight when handled in this fashion. Theka drops one of the two **Mosh'aru Tablets**. Also in the area is Theka's Tablet that reveals the name of the **Spider God**, as part of a Horde-only quest. Be sure to read that if appropriate.

Though the passages lead northwest from the Scarab Chamber, there is a hard-to-see path that leads east instead. This trickles over toward a cave where Antu'sul and a number of Basilisks and Trolls live. Do not approach the cave at first. Instead, use ranged attack to pull all of the Basilisks and Trolls outside. Kill everything you can, then fully buff and prepare for an ugly fight.

Antu'sul is a treasure mob, so he isn't needed for any quests. Low-level groups should avoid him entirely, but those with experience and skill need not worry. Here is what to expect: Antu'sul summons seven non-elite Basilisks once he detects enemies coming toward his cave. Have everyone stay close to the main tank so that your defender can quickly steal the attention of these incoming Basilisks. Immediately lay into these Basilisks for fast kills. Mage and Warlock AoEs work wonders here if done under the veil of a Warrior's Challenging Shout, and all characters in the group must focus on dealing high DPS early on. Also, having the entire region cleared means that Fear can be used without the specter of adds clouding the action. The first elite Basilisk appears when Antu'sul is around 75% health, and two more are summoned when his health hits 25%.

Antu'sul has quite a selection of spells and totems from which to choose. His totems - Earthgrab Totem, Fire Nova Totems, and Healing Ward - are dangerous, but it's a problem easily solved. Assign a Rogue or Hunter to focus on them as soon as they spawn. He also has Chain Lightning and Earth Shock. His last spell, Flash Heal, should be interrupted immediately.

THROWN ABOUT

The knockback that sometimes occurs during the battle with Antu'sul is actually an in-game mechanism preventing you from training him too far away from his spawn point. He's intended to be fought with his basilisk minions and that's the way to approach this encounter[md]you're taking them all on.

The reason for immediacy during the Antu'sul fight comes from the Basilisks. Those enemies have a very good stun. This takes your main tank out of the fight from time to time; clearing a number of the Basilisks early makes it easier for the tank to reengage and snag aggro again after such an event. With high group DPS, the non-elite Basilisks die quickly. Then, it's only the three elites and Antu'sul himself. Clear them with standard aggro management and combat techniques.

The way into the northern area, back from the Scarab Room, is filled with side rooms. Each of these contains similar Trolls to the ones you have already been facing. There are more Shadowhunters than before in this region, however, and the Soul Eaters are there as well (these casters can be brought down quickly, and are good early targets for this reason).

If your group is high enough in level, it is possible to avoid these rooms and their encounters by going down the middle of the hall. However, characters of lower level for Zul'Farrak should clear everything, to avoid drawing foes from the rooms during any existing fights.

NORTHERN STRUCTURES

The next open area is a graveyard where the Trolls leave their fallen to become Zombies. All of these graves can be looted, though it is common for one or two Zombies to spawn during each such event. Don't allow characters to loot multiple graves at the same time, of course, and select a single person to loot if this is being done. There aren't many good items in these graves, but this is a good way to get more cloth and some money. Also, the Zombies and occasional Dead Heroes that spawn drop **Troll Tempers**, so this allows groups to complete the *Troll Temper* quest very easily.

Inside the small shrine by the graveyard is Witch Doctor Zum'rah. Though he appears neutral, Zum'rah just wants to wait until characters come near before he attacks. For the easiest possible fight, clear all of the graves before attacking Zum'rah, but this is hardly necessary (Zum'rah summons the dead to aid him, yet the fight is not a difficult one). For a fast kill, have everyone rush in and use their better melee attacks to slice Zum'rah down (you can Kick him out of spells), then turn to face his allies when their leader is dead. Your main tank shouldn't have problems taking aggro from each of the adds when they arrive.

Note that any free-standing Undead in the area come to Zum'rah's aid when he is attacked. If someone is already looting the graves when Zum'rah aggros, this can be quite bad! Also, there are Troll patrols from the north that come through the graveyard, so fight inside the shrine even if you are a caster (better than accidentally getting attacked from behind by a couple Soul Eaters). Loot Zum'rah and his chest before leaving.

The open plaza in the north is a buffet of Trolls. There are set groups of enemies, patrols (with Basilisks), and a leader to kill at the top of the far-standing pyramid. Kill every group that is close to the base of the pyramid, then wait for the patrols to come by and take them out as well. For the trouble ahead, it's very wise to have everything cleared out.

At the top of the pyramid is the Sandfury Executioner; he is flanked by two Sul'lithuz Sandcrawlers (and their nasty Petrify Stuns). The great news is that the Executioner can be pulled and won't bring the Basilisks with him! Kill this easy boss and eliminate the Basilisks afterward. The Executioner drops the key to the prisoner's cages. The proper way to deal with these folks is to release them, (which is useful for Divino-matic Rod and is always needed for the Alliance quest: *Nekrum's Medallion*).

The actual fight that triggers after the prisoners begin to escape is complex. Enemies spawn at the base of the pyramid and come up to your position. There are multiple goals while staying alive in this encounter; try to bring down elite Trolls first, because the non-elites are quite weak, protect the prisoners, and keep your hit points/mana as high as possible by using efficient abilities. Shadowpriest Sezz'ziz has four spells: Heal, Psychic Scream, Renew, and Shadow Bolt. Psychic Scream and Renew can't be interrupted, but focus on her Heal spell. Remove the Renew effect when she casts it. Nekrum Gutchewer has the Fevered Plague spell, which is a weaker version of the one Theka the Martyr uses.

Stay at the top of the pyramid and don't get onto the stairs until Bly says to start descending. Getting onto the stairs puts the fight into a constant mode that precludes the short periods of downtime that otherwise occur. Use downtime for bandages first, since a few seconds are sometimes all that you get. Then, use food and water if a long rest window opens.

Your main tank is needed to grab the elites and casters off of the prisoners. Challenging Shout is great for this when Warriors are filling said role. Have someone else in the group call targets and let the other members assist that person with bringing down elites, then casters, then the rest of the Trolls that add into the fighting.

GOBLINS BEFORE HUMANS

Don't talk to Bly before speaking with the Goblin! The Goblin must blow up the door that leads to the Chief before you speak with Bly and fight him. If you kill Bly before speaking with the Goblin, you won't be able to kill the end boss.

Once at the bottom, your group faces two named Elites (Sezz'ziz and Nekrum Gutchewer). Go after Shadowpriest Sezz'ziz first, then finish off Nekrum (who drops the **Medallion** for the Alliance Quest). Rest with all the enemies dead, but keep a watch out for respawning patrollers. Then, ask the Goblin to blow up the door that blocks your way toward the Chief! Before leaving, speak with Bly and demand the Divino-matic Rod; Bly gets very angry and attacks your party. Kill the ingrate and take the **Divino-matic Rod** to complete the Gadgetzan quest.

SIEGING THE THRONE ROOM

Walk up the path toward the Throne Room of the Chief very carefully. There are two Basilisks (Sul'lithuz Abominations), and four Sandfury Guardians there. These can be pulled in two fights without drawing the Chief and Ruuzlu, his ally, away from their areas. Have a sturdy character approach the room and shoot the Abominations if they don't automatically aggro, then repeat this later to kill the serpentine Sandfury Guardians.

Chief Ukorz Sandscalp and Ruuzlu are at the back of the room. When all is clear, race forward to attack Ruuzlu and focus all damage on him for the fast kill. If your group has a strong secondary tank, have that person pull the Chief away during this short stage of the fight and tank him while the other members slay Ruuzlu; the Chief's Wide Slash and Cleave give him the ability to harm many targets in front of him (have as many attack him from behind as possible), which is why it's useful to draw him away. Groups that only have one or two melee members can disregard this, of course.

All told, the fight against these two isn't as hard as the brawl by the pyramid or a couple of the other boss fights in Zul'Farrak. The rewards are wonderful as well, as the Chief has a number of useful drops! Decide who needs what, loot happily, and move on to the western side of the region.

WESTERN EDGE, HOME OF GAHZ'RILLA

There isn't much to do on the western side; there is only one large room (the smaller southern area has nothing of importance or value, save for more Troll fighting). The room by the pool is where all the action comes together.

The first and most important action in Gahz'rilla's area is to clear everything. Kill all Trolls, and make sure the patrols are down and out. This takes quite some time, but it's very risky to take on the following challenges without having a ton of room. For the early fights, when the room is choked with Trolls and add-potential, have a puller attack from range and draw everything back to the hallway where your group waits.

Look for Hydromancer Valratha on the eastern side of the pool. Her main spell is the ability to create a totem called "Wrath of Zum'rah" that summons skeletal adds. She also has Healing Wave and Shadow Bolt. Attack her when the patrols are not in the area. She drops the **Second Mosh'aru Tablet** and the **Tiara of the Deep** when you defeat her.

The worst of the smaller encounters is in the northeast part of the room; there are five Trolls near each other who do not wander. It takes quite a bit of work to clear this fight safely. If your group is too low level to survive that much aggro at once, clear all of the other fights first, then use Fear and other risky CC abilities to make the attack manageable without the danger of adds. If Mind Control is an option, this is the type of fight to risk it! Getting one of those Trolls killed off while wounding another is a fine solution; the group can most certainly defeat four Trolls, especially with one of them injured!

At last, your group has done it! Gahz'rilla is the final challenge of Zul'Farrak. Those who took the time and energy to find the **Sacred Mallet** and charge it atop the altar in southeastern Hinterlands can unlock the encounter by hitting the Gong on the southern side of the pool. Gahz'rilla steps out along the north side of the water and waits for your party there (this is one of the reasons it's great to clear everything ahead of time).

Charge Gahz'rilla in his pool and have the melee characters keep the beast's attention. Attacking in the pool prevents the falling damage from his Slam ability (which knocks players into the air). If you attempt to fight Gahz'rilla on land, be prepared to heal those knocked into the air. Don't have the casters get anywhere near the beast. Gahz'rilla also has the Icicle (like Frost Bolt) and Freeze Solid spells. Freeze Solid is a DoT and stun, but since it's considered a magic debuff, it can be dispelled. Even melee-capable classes, like Shaman and Druids, should hang back and let the Warriors and Rogues handle the melee DPS for this battle.

Done without adds and by a party that anticipates Gahz'rilla's throws, the fight is quite fair and exciting! Use attack-reducing abilities (Demoralizing Shout), DoTs, Sundering, and keep someone on the lookout for any unexpected adds as they cast. If any patrols weren't cleared or respawn, be sure to drag the fight away before the threat of adds become a reality.

Gahz'rilla drops the **Electrified Scale** upon death, and that is used for a fine turnin up in the Shimmering Flats.

Congratulations everyone; this is another instance under your belt, and you are well on your way into the most fierce level of dungeons in the game.

ZUL'GURUB

Played & Written by: Chris M. "Phunbaba" Koschik of <Fraternity> on Perenolde

Ages ago, Zul'Gurub served as the capital city for a powerful Troll tribe called the Gurubashi. This would not last for long, however, as it was soon destroyed by civil war and corruption from within.

Now, centuries later, Atal'ai Priests and Priestesses use the once great city for their evil deeds, attempting to summon the Blood God, Hakkar the Soulflayer, who has vowed to consume the world whole.

In response to the Atal'ai's treachery, the remaining Troll tribe sent its five champions to seal away Hakkar for all eternity. However, instead of a great victory over the Blood God, they found utter defeat, as Hakkar himself corrupted them, forcing them to make him even stronger.

It now falls to you to enter the ruins of Zul'Gurub, slay the five aspects of Hakkar, battle the Blood God himself, and return peace to Stranglethorn Vale!

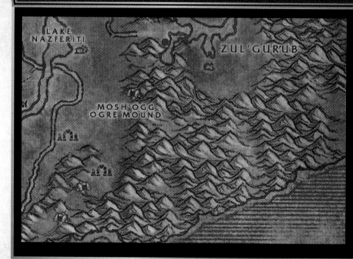

DUNGEON INFORMATION

Location	Stranglethorn Vale
Territory	Contested
Quests	Shared Alliance and Horde
Suggested Level	60 (20-person raid)
Primary Enemies	Trolls, Beasts
Time to Complete	3-7 hours (1-2 days)

GETTING TO ZUL'GURUB

Getting to Zul'Gurub is easy. Simply enter Stranglethorn Vale either via Booty Bay or Duskwood and head due east of Lake Nazferiti.

A few elite trolls guard the entrance, but they can be handled by small groups, unlike their brethren inside the instance. At the top of the stairs you'll find an unlocked door guarding the instance portal.

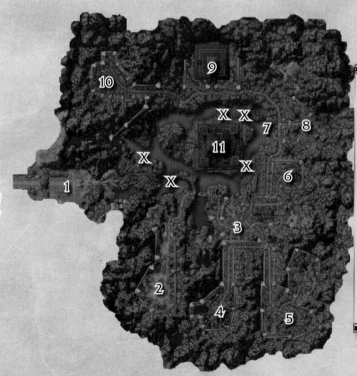

LEGEND

1   Entrance
2   High Priestess Jeklik (Bat Aspect)
3   High Priest Venoxis (Snake Aspect)
4   High Priestess Mar'li (Spider Aspect)
5   Bloodlord Mandokir
6   EDGE OF MADNESS
    Gri'lek of the Iron Blood
    Hazza'rah the Dreamweaver
    Renataki of the Thousand Blades
    Wushoolay the Storm Witch
7   Gahz'ranka
8   High Priest Thekal (Tiger Aspect)
9   High Priestess Arlokk (Panther Aspect)
10   Jin'do the Hexxer
11   Hakkar
X   Muddy Churning Waters (for Gahz'ranka)

QUESTS FOR ZUL'GURUB

SHARED QUESTS

All Zul'Gurub quests can be found on Yojamba Island. To reach this island, head directly west from Lake Nazferiti, or northwest of the Grom'gol Base camp, past the Vile Reef.

QUEST NAME	QUEST GIVER	QUEST GIVER LOCATION	QUEST RECEIVER	QUEST RECEIVER LOCATION	CHAIN?	MAX EXPERIENCE
Paragons of Power	Al'tabim the All-Seeing, Jin'rokh the Breaker, Maywiki of Zulzadar, Falthir the Sightless	Yojamba Island	Al'tabim the All-Seeing, Jin'rokh the Breaker, Maywiki of Zulzadar, Falthir the Sightless	Yojamba Island	Yes	2500
Gurubashi, Vilebranch, and Witherbark Coins	Vinchaxa	Yojamba Island	Vinchaxa	Yojamba Island	No	0
REWARD: Zandalar Honor Token (Use: Permanently increase your reputation with the Zandalar Tribe.)						
Zulian, Razzashi, and Hakkari Coins	Vinchaxa	Yojamba Island	Yojamba Island	Vinchaxa	No	0
REWARD: Zandalar Honor Token (Use: Permanently increase your reputation with the Zandalar Tribe.)						
Sandfury, Skullsplitter, and Bloodscalp Coins	Vinchaxa	Yojamba Island	Vinchaxa	Yojamba Island	No	0
REWARD: Zandalar Honor Token (Use: Permanently increase your reputation with the Zandalar Tribe.)						
Nat's Measuring Tape	Item Drop	Zul'Gurub	Nat Pagle	Duskwood (Tidefury Cove)	No	0
The Heart of Hakkar	Molthor	Yojamba Island	Molthor	Yojamba Island	No	9300
REWARD: Zandalar Hero Badge (Use: Increase to Armor and DEF), Zandalar Hero Charm (Use: Increase to Healing and Spell Damage), Zandalar Hero Medallion (Use: Increase to Melee and Ranged DAM)						
Essence of Mangoes	Rin'wosho the Trader	Yojamba Island	Rin'wosho the Trader	Yojamba Island	No	0
REWARD: Essence Mango						
A Collection of Heads	Exzhal	Yojamba Island	Exzhal	Yojamba Island	No	0
REWARD: Belt of Shrunken Heads (Cloth, Leather, Mail or Plate depending on your class. Stats vary by type.)						
Zanza's Potent Potables	Rin'wosho the Trader	Yojamba Island	Rin'wosho the Trader	Yojamba Island	No	0
The Perfect Poison	Dirk Thunderwood	Silithis (Cenarion Hold)	Dirk Thunderwood	Silithis (Cenarion Hold)	No	6600

PARAGONS OF POWER

Quest Level	60 to obtain
Location	Yojamba Island, Stranglethorn Vale
Contact	Al'tabim the All-seeing, Jin'rokh the Breaker, Maywiki of Zulzadar, Falthir the Sightless
Goal	Return all the items necessary to create your class armor
Max Experience Gained	2500
Reward	Varies by Class

Three quests exist for each class to obtain small sets of armor from Yojamba Island by returning a number of drops from Zul'Gurub. Each piece of the armor requires a different level of reputation with the Zandalar Tribe. Speak with these quest givers to find out what they have in store for you. They require drops from the enemies and the bosses in Zul'Gurub.

GURUBASHI, VILEBRANCH, AND WITHERBARK COINS

SANDFURY, SKULLSPLITTER, AND BLOODSCALP COINS

ZULIAN, RAZZASHI, AND HAKKARI COINS

Quest Level	60 to obtain
Location	Yojamba Island, Stranglethorn Vale
Contact	Vinchaxa
Goal	Give Vinchaxa one of each coin
Max Experience Gained	0
Reward	Zandalar Honor Token (Use: Permanently increase your reputation with the Zandalar Tribe)

Vinchaxa offers three different quests to turn in a certain combination of coins. Simply return one of each requested coin to this Troll and he shall reward you with a Zandalar Honor Token. You can use this token to gain a permanent reputation boost with the Zandalar Tribe.

NAT'S MEASURING TAPE

Quest Level	60 to obtain
Location	Zul'Gurub
Contact	Nat Pagle
Goal	Return Nat's Measuring Tape to Nat Pagle in Dustwallow Marsh
Max Experience Gained	650

This quest allows you to summon an optional boss named Gahz'ranka from the murky depths of the river that runs through Zul'Gurub. In order to learn how to fish this beast up, you must first return Nat's Measuring Tape to a fellow named Nat Pagle in Dustwallow Marsh.

To locate the Measuring Tape, look for a tackle box near some Crocodiles by the river, just south of the Tiger section. Once you have secured the Measuring Tape, take a quick trip to Theramore Island in Dustwallow Marsh and head south into the water. Nat Pagle is on a small island just off the coast. After listening to his story, he teaches you all you need to know to fish out Gahz'ranka. Buy a few Mudskunk Lures off of him and head back to Zul'Gurub when the time is right.

Go to Pagle's Point in Zul'Gurub and look for the Muddy Churning Waters to drop your pole into. When you have enough of them, load them up into your new lure and start fishing! It won't be long before Gahz'ranka comes in for a snack!

THE HEART OF HAKKAR

Quest Level	60 to obtain
Location	Yojamba Island, Stranglethorn Vale
Contact	Molthor
Goal	Return the Heart of Hakkar to Molthor
Max Experience Gained	9300
Reward	Zandalar Hero Badge (Trinket: Use: Increases your armor by 2000 and your defense by 30 for 20 seconds. Every time you take melee or ranged damage, the bonus is reduced by 200 Armor and 3 DEF) or Zandalar Hero Charm (Trinket: Use: Increases your spell damage by up to 280 and your healing by up to 560 for 20 seconds. Every time you cast a spell, the bonus is reduced by 35 spell damage and 70 healing) or Zandalar Hero Medallion (Trinket: Use: Increases your melee and ranged damage by 40 for 20 seconds. Every time you attack, the bonus is reduced by 2 damage)

After slaying Hakkar, the Blood God drops a single Heart of Hakkar that can be looted by your raid group. The person that wins this item must take it back to Molthor on Yojamba Island and choose one of the three trinket rewards.

After completing the quest, Molthor has the heart destroyed by his priests on the adjacent island. Should your raid choose to stay in close proximity to the ceremony, they receive a 2-hour buff that lasts through death called *The Spirit of Zandalar*. This buff increases your movement speed by 10%, dodge chance by 5% and all stats by 15%.

ESSENCE MANGOES

Quest Level	60 to obtain
Location	Yojamba Island, Stranglethorn Vale
Contact	Rin'wosho the Trader
Goal	Give Rin'wosho the Trader three Zandalar Honor Token
Max Experience Gained	0
Reward	Essence Mango (Food)

A simple turn-in quest that allows you to forgo using your Zandalar Honor Tokens for reputation and, in turn, you receive a very powerful food that replenishes your health and mana at a rapid rate when eating. This quest requires that you hold a Revered faction with the Zandalar Tribe.

A COLLECTION OF HEADS

Quest Level	60 to obtain
Location	Yojamba Island, Stranglethorn Vale
Contact	Exzhal
Goal	String 5 Channeler's Heads onto the Sacred Cord, then return the Collection of Troll Heads to Exzhal on Zandalar Isle.
Max Experience Gained	9950
Reward	Belt of Shrunken Heads (Plate Belt: 408 Armor, 23 STR, 11 STA, 7 AGI) or Belt of Shrunken Heads (Cloth Belt: 55 Armor, 17 INT, 13 STA, Passive: Restores 7 mana every 5 seconds) or Belt of Shrunken Heads (Leather Belt: 108 Armor, 15 AGI, 14 STR, 11 STA, Passive: Improves your chance to hit by 1%) or Belt of Shrunken Heads (Mail Belt: 7 SPI, 18 STA, 11 INT, 11 AGI)

Exzhal gives you a Sacred Cord to string the heads on. Anytime you defeat a High Priest or Priestess in Zul'Gurub you can loot a head. Once you have five in your inventory, simply use the cord to create a Head Collection to return on Yojamba Island.

ZANZA'S POTENT POTABLES

Quest Level	60 to obtain
Location	Yojamba Island, Stranglethorn Vale
Contact	Rin'wosho the Trader
Goal	Give Rin'wosho the Trader one Zandalar Honor Token
Max Experience Gained	0

Bring Rin'wosho one Zandalar Honor Token to receive your choice of a few very powerful potions. Not only do they have unique effects, but the effects transcend death and won't be removed when you die. The "Zanza Flasks" can be stacked with the Flasks from Alchemists.

THE PERFECT POISON

Quest Level	60 to obtain
Location	Silithis (Cenarion Hold)
Contact	Dirk Thunderwood
Goal	Return Venoxis' Venom Sac and Kurinnaxx's Venom Sac to Dirk
Max Experience Gained	6600
Reward	Varies by Class

Half of this quest must be completed in Ahn'Qiraj, but the other half occurs in Zul'Gurub. Loot Venoxis' Venom Sac after defeating him to obtain an important part of the quest resolution.

NAVIGATING ZUL'GURUB

Zul'Gurub is basically one big circle. A river runs around the center of the ruins where Hakkar resides. The five High Priests and Priestesses are at five different points around the map; they must be destroyed in order to defeat Hakkar. There are also several side areas that house optional bosses used for quest items or unique loot. It's up to you whether or not you want to do the minimum to defeat Hakkar or bring vengeance upon the entire zone.

ZANZA THE RESTLESS

As you near the Edge of Madness area in Zul'Gurub, you should notice a temple with a long set of stairs leading up to it. Upon further investigation, you find an undead Troll named Zanza the Restless.

Speaking with this fellow is completely optional, but he allows you to turn in some rare items from around the world for a very powerful enchant that can be used on your legs, head, or shoulders. The leg and head enchants require a Friendly reputation, while the shoulder enchant requires that you attain an Exalted status. Speak to Zanza to see what he requires from you.

Each enchant requires a class-specific Punctured Voodoo doll attained from the Hoodoo Piles spread across the zone and a Paragon of Power dropped by bosses.

This is not an easy task he sets before you and only the most dedicated of players ever see one of these enchants.

GET EQUIPPED FOR ZUL'GURUB

No, not swords, helms, and staves! I speak of much more powerful weapons for your arsenal: Programs for your computer, main assists, and raid leaders.

Teamspeak or Ventrilo

These are voice programs that allow everyone in the raid to listen and speak over a microphone. The importance of this cannot be stressed enough in the more chaotic battles when the difference between success and failure can be measured in the amount of time it takes to type a sentence or speak it over a microphone. Downloading and utilizing one of these programs increases your success rate tenfold in all 40- and 20-person raids. The only stipulation is that all members must be onboard.

CT Raid Assist

This is a third party add-on allowed by Blizzard that makes raiding so much easier. It has many options that you can toggle on and off to warn your raid of incoming threats, debuffs, and curses. It also has an option that allows you to see the target of your tank's target. This serves you in many battles, as you can see who has the aggro of a particular enemy or boss. To utilize this program, you must keep informed and updated on all the latest versions of this program. You must also keep your guild informed about these updates.

Main Assist

The main assist (MA) is a player designated to acquire the most important target first for easy targeting. This role is usually given to a Rogue, as their only responsibility in the raid is to kill things. You can easily create a hotkey to acquire the MA's target by pressing escape, going into the macro menu, and creating a macro called MA. The command for setting the main assist is /assist (name of player). (For example: /assist Phobos) Also, in the interface options menu, there's an option that allows you to immediately begin attacking when you press your MA key.

Raid Leader

The raid leader is an extremely important part of your raid. In a nutshell, the raid leader is the player that orders everyone to start attacking or stop attacking. This is needed for tanks to acquire a good amount of aggro before the rest of the raid starts attacking. Having an MT lose the aggro early on can wipe out the raid group, so having a conservative raid leader helps to ensure victory.

ENEMIES IN THE RUINS

An army of Trolls, beasts, and other monstrosities, all loyal to Hakkar the Soulflayer, populates Zul'Gurub. While few of them are particularly strong alone, you will find that when they come, they come in great numbers, making this one of the most lethal zones in the game. Do not underestimate anything.

ATAL'AI MISTRESS — 60 ELITE

These undead ladies always come in packs of four or five. The tanks should be quick to pick them up and pull them together for an AoE pounding. They have Pummel (like Warrior ability), Snap Kick (Deals about 875-1125 damage and stuns target for 2 sec.), and Thrash (chance to get two extra attacks). Should you require crowd control, Priests can shackle the Mistresses.

BLOODSEEKER BAT — 60 NON-ELITE

Easy prey. They usually accompany a stronger enemy when pulled. Simply use your AoE attacks to obliterate them completely.

GURUBASHI AXE THROWER — 60 ELITE

The Axe Throwers always come in pairs along with whatever they are being pulled with. If no one is in melee range, they start to throw high-damage axes at the casters. These must either be Sheeped or tanked immediately. Every so often they begin a devastating attack called Whirling Trip. This forces the Gurubashi Axe thrower into a whirlwind of blades, causing heavy damage to all within range. Sheep the whirling axe thrower to stop the madness.

GURUBASHI BAT RIDER — 61 ELITE

At first, the Bat Riders seem like a simple enemy. They will, however, be the death of a careless raid group. Your tanks must separate the Bat Riders from all other members of the raid group as quickly as possible. Use ranged damage to take their health down to 40% and prepare for an explosion. Rather than fighting until the end, the Gurubashi Bat Riders choose to explode, causing deadly damage to all in the vicinity. When a Bat Rider gets a "crazed look in his eyes" (check your text box) he roots himself for about 3 seconds, giving your tank just enough time to run away, before exploding. If your Warrior is at full health when the Bat Rider explodes, there is a good chance that he or she may survive, but it's better to be safe than sorry. The other, safer, option is to assist the MA and take down the Bat Riders before they can explode. Of course, this requires more coordination, but it's the preferred method.

GURUBASHI BERSERKER — 62 ELITE

The bane of all raid groups, these hulking Trolls patrol many areas of Zul'Gurub, so you must continually be on the lookout for them. Once pulled, the casters must stand as far away as possible to avoid the AoE fear that the Berserker frequently uses. Have your tank drag him back to the wall to avoid the imminent knock-back. When your tank is knocked back or feared, the Berserker typically heads straight for a caster; having a tank ready to pick up his aggro in advance is a good idea. Make sure you bring him down in a spot far away from any other pulls, or you risk being feared into another group of enemies.

GURUBASHI BLOOD-DRINKER — 60 ELITE

This is a deceptively powerful foe. Just when you think you have this Troll beat, he surprises you by healing entirely back to full health. When pulled, these should be the first to be Sheeped and the last to be killed. Make sure they are tanked away from your raid group so that their AoE health drain affects as few members as possible. When it's time to defeat them, save your stuns for the final seconds of the battle. When the health of the Blood-Drinker is around 30%, you want to chain as many stuns as possible on him to keep him from healing back to full again.

GURUBASHI CHAMPION — 60 ELITE

Not a terribly difficult enemy to dispatch, the Champions do single-target damage to your tanks and randomly charge members of your raid, sending them flying through the air, before returning to the tank.

GURUBASHI HEADHUNTER — 60 ELITE

If they're not being tanked, they shoot their bows at members of your raid. Make sure they are tanked or Sheeped immediately.

HAKKARI BLOODPRIEST — 60 ELITE

Treat these much like the Gurubashi Blood-Drinker except for one major difference. Rather than having a close range health drain, the Bloodpriest drains life from those farthest away from them. Make sure everyone is at close range. Stun lock at 40%.

HAKKARI PRIEST — 60 ELITE

Whenever these are in a group of enemies that you pull, make sure that they're the first to die. Stuns and Counterspells ensure they never even get a chance to heal or AoE fear your raid. Hakkari Priests frequently become immune to magic. This means that most forms of CC won't affect them. Pull them as far back as possible to prevent a group-mate being feared into more mobs and drawing adds to the group.

HAKKARI SHADOWHUNTER — 60 ELITE

Combat these much as you would combat the Gurubashi Headhunters, using tanks and Polymorph. Every few seconds the Shadowhunter casts Hex on a member of your raid, effectively turning them into a frog for a short duration. Nearly all their abilities are used from range (Multi-shot, Volley, etc.), so get in melee range to nullify their strength.

HAKKARI SHADOWPRIEST — 60 ELITE

Use Sheep on these immediately while you defeat any enemies that come with them. When it's time to bring them down, have your tanks face the Shadowpriest away to avoid the directional Shadow Bolt they cast on everyone in front of them.

HAKKARI WITCHDOCTOR — 60 ELITE

Not a terribly challenging foe to take down. Assist and destroy the totems as they pop up while you bring him down.

HOOKTOOTH FRENZY — 60 ELITE

You only have to deal with these should you choose to take a swim. They have light damage and low health—easy prey.

HAKKARI WITCHDOCTOR — 60 ELITE

Not a terribly challenging foe to deal with. Assist and destroy the totems as they pop up while you bring him down.

MAD SERVANT · 60 ELITE

These large Imps can really be a pain to take down for an unprepared raid group. They come in packs of three and should be taken down with care. Your Warlocks really shine here as they can use Enslave Demon to make one their pet as they banish another. Destroy the third and wait for the portal to open and spit out two Mad Voidwalkers. After defeating the Voidwalkers, destroy the next Mad Servant and so on until all three are dead.

RAZZASHI ADDER · 60 ELITE

This deadly serpent can be Polymorphed or Slept for crowd control purposes. When engaged, the tank should face the Adder away from the raid to ensure its directional poison volley does as little damage to the group as possible.

RAZZASHI SERPENT · 60 ELITE

Like the other snakes in this zone, this enemy can be Slept or Sheeped. When pulled, you usually want to defeat these first, as they randomly cast Sleep on members of your raid.

RAZZASHI RAPTOR · 60 ELITE

These always come in large packs of four or more. Take the Raptors down quickly and efficiently by assisting the MA. Bring them down one at a time and move on.

RAZZASHI BROODWIDOW · 60 ELITE

These are the largest of the spiders you encounter; this beast of an arachnid should be taken down with single target DPS from Hunters and Rogues. Leave this enemy for last. Upon death, they spawn several Razzashi Venombrood spiders that can overwhelm the softer members of your group if they gang up and spawn during a prolonged battle. The Broodwidows have a stun ability: Web Spin.

RAZZASHI VENOMBROOD · 60 ELITE

Yet another large spider that must be taken down with single target DPS. This spider poisons you with an Intoxicating Venom that causes you to occasionally fall down or drop your weapon. It also gets you drunk!

RAZZASHI SKITTERER · 60 ELITE

The Skitterer is a small spider that causes no serious threat alone; however, they almost always come in large groups. Use AoE spells to make short work of them. Your AoE casters should require extra heals during this onslaught.

SACRIFICED TROLLS · 55-60 ELITE

These are the Trolls in the "skeleton pit" during the Jin'do the Hexxer encounter. They're weak mobs.

SON OF HAKKAR · 60 ELITE

These winged serpents patrol the stairs leading to Hakkar the Blood God. They can, and should, be Slept for crowd control. When killed, they emit a cloud of poison that poisons your blood. They have a very fast respawn time.

SOULFLAYER · 61 ELITE

The Soulflayer usually accompanies Sons of Hakkar patrols. This monster can be CC'd with Hibernate, but it really should be the first you defeat in any group. It is not terribly deadly, but it can knock down members of your raid, interrupting spells, if not taken down quickly. The worst thing about the Soulflayers is the randomization of their abilities. Sometimes they Fear, sometimes they knock players down. They frequently use a spell that deals significant damage to a single player while rendering that player unable to cast spells or use abilities. When this begins to happen, the Soulflayer needs to be reigned in and stunned as quickly as possible.

VOODOO SLAVE · 60 ELITE

These dangerous little Gnomes are located near Jin'do the Hexxer. They tend to break polymorph very quickly, so killing them as soon as possible is a great idea. They're Warlocks who summon Infernals, use Rain of Fire, and have a powerful Shadowbolt. Don't underestimate them!

WITHERED MISTRESS · 60 ELITE

Much like the Atal'ai Mistresses, these undead Trolls always come in groups of four or five. Use Shackle Undead for crowd control and AoE to finish them off. They have a brutal curse (Curse of Blood) that increases the damage to the target by 500 for 10 minutes. Have Mages remove this asap since it can bring down the MT. They also have Dispel Magic, Unholy Frenzy (increases ally attack speed by 50%, but also deals 200 Nature damage every 2 sec.), and Veil of Shadow (decreases healing effects on target by 75% for 10 sec.).

ZULIAN CROCOLISK · 60 ELITE

These deadly reptiles are only found on the shores of the river that runs throughout Zul'Gurub. Simply pull them together and AoE them into dust.

ZULIAN CUB · 60 NON-ELITE

Easily defeated. Snare them when they reach low health or they will flee to seek assistance from stronger tigers.

ZULIAN PANTHER · 60 ELITE

These felines usually patrol a set route, attacking anything that comes too close. AoE and single target MA damage makes quick work of them.

ZULIAN STALKER · 60 ELITE

The Stalker is a massive cloaked panther that attacks out of nowhere. The tanks must pick it up quickly before it kills a caster or two. Once the aggro is acquired, it's defeated easily.

ZULIAN TIGER · 60 ELITE

These tigers almost always come in large packs along with various types of Trolls. Use crowd control on the Trolls and AoE the tigers into oblivion first.

THE IMMORTAL RAID

Even the best raid group faces the bitter taste of defeat once in a while. Starting over from scratch can demoralize your party faster than anything, but all hope is not lost! Should your raid be defeated in a somewhat safe and clear spot, a Warlock Soulstone can be just the ticket you need for a quick recovery.

Keeping a Soulstone on a Shaman, Paladin, or Priest ensures that no nasty surprises end your raid. That being said, make sure you have one ready for *every* boss fight. You never know when things will go sour.

THE HIGH PRIESTS OF ZUL'GURUB

Zul'Gurub houses five High Priest bosses that must be defeated before Hakkar, and a number of optional bosses that are required for quest items—or loot. Either way, the journey through Zul'Gurub is fraught with peril and dangers at every turn. Each boss fight requires you to use a different and unique strategy.

PRIMAL HAKKARI PIECES

All High Priests and Priestesses, Bloodlord Mandokir, and Jindo the Hexxer have the potential of dropping one of the Primal Hakkari Pieces. Each of these is used for specific Class enchants and quests. Use the table below to identify which pieces are the most important to you.

PRIMAL HAKKARI PIECE	CLASS ENCHANT	CLASS QUESTS
PRIMAL HAKKARI AEGIS	Warrior	Hunter Shoulders
		Priest Shoulders
		Rogue Chest
PRIMAL HAKKARI ARMSPLINT	Warlock	Rogue Wrists
		Shaman Wrists
		Warrior Wrists
PRIMAL HAKKARI BINDINGS	Druid	Hunter Wrists
		Mage Wrists
		Paladin Wrists
PRIMAL HAKKARI GIRDLE	Mage	Rogue Belt
		Shaman Belt
		Warrior Belt
PRIMAL HAKKARI KOSSACK	Rogue	Mage Chest
		Warlock Chest
		Warrior Chest

PRIMAL HAKKARI PIECE	CLASS ENCHANT	CLASS QUESTS
PRIMAL HAKKARI SASH	Shaman	Druid Belt
		Priest Belt
		Warlock Shoulders
PRIMAL HAKKARI SHAWL	Paladin	Hunter Belt
		Mage Shoulders
		Paladin Belt
PRIMAL HAKKARI STANCHION	Hunter	Druid Wrists
		Priest Wrists
		Warlock Wrists
PRIMAL HAKKARI TABARD	Priest	Druid Chest
		Paladin Chest
		Shaman Chest

HIGH PRIESTESS JEKLIK

High Priestess Jeklik holds the title of the Bat Aspect in Zul'Gurub. After clearing the Trolls and Bat Riders around her area, you will see her standing atop a wall performing some vile ceremony.

Before the pull, split your raid in two. Have the casters and healers form a tight group a safe distance away from the MT so that when she summons bats, the AoE will reach maximum efficiency; it also keeps the casters out of range of her AoE silence. When you're ready to pull, have your MT use a ranged attack to get her attention.

She immediately transforms into a large bat and attacks your MT. Be sure to give the MT plenty of time for aggro so that you can unload maximum DPS when the time is right. Several times during this phase she calls forth bat minions to attack. They usually head straight for your healers, so make certain your Mages and Warlocks are ready to AoE them as quickly as possible. It's wise to have a Warrior ready to use Challenging Shout to draw all the bat adds to the casters. Casters should maintain a safe distance throughout this entire phase as she occasionally emits a sonic burst, silencing all in the vicinity.

At 50% health, she transforms back into her humanoid self and begins to heal. Watch her hands for the casting animation; this warns you of an incoming heal. Set up an interrupt rotation with your Warriors and Rogues. Continue going down the chain until the heal is interrupted and maintain this strategy each time she attempts to heal.

While you take out her remaining health, the raid group must spread out around her area and remain mindful of the Bat Riders flying overhead and dropping vials of burning liquid. Standing in this fire causes you to take heavy damage; make sure everyone pays attention. If a bat drops the fire on top of your MT, they must shift positions to a safe spot.

Interrupt her heals, stay out of the fire, keep the damage constantly onher, and she will eventually die, thanking you for setting her free fromHakkar's control.

HIGH PRIESTESS JEKLIK'S LOOT TABLE

ITEM	DESC	STATS
ANIMIST'S SPAULDERS	Leather Shoulders	201 Armor, 18 INT, 12 SPI, 11 STA
Passive: Increases healing done by spells and effects by up to 37		
JEKLIK'S CRUSHER	Two-Handed Mace	56.5 DPS
Chance on Hit: Wounds the target for 200 to 220 damage		
JEKLIK'S OPALINE TALISMAN	Necklace	
Passive: Increases damage and healing done by magical spells and effects by up to 22		
Passive: Restores 3 mana per 5 second		
PEACEKEEPER BOOTS	Plate Boots	486 Armor, 12 INT, 10 STA
Passive: Restores 6 mana per 5 seconds		
Passive: Increases healing done by spells and effects by up to 22		
PRIMALIST'S BAND	Ring	10 INT, 8 STA
Passive: Restores 6 mana per 5 second		
SEAFURY BOOTS	Mail Boots	274 Armor, 15 INT, 10 STA
Passive: Increases damage and healing done by magical spells and effects by up to 12		
Passive: Restores 5 mana per 5 seconds		
ZULIAN DEFENDER	Off-Hand Shield	2312 Armor, 43 Block, 15 STA, 9 INT, 8 SPI

HIGH PRIEST DROPS

The five High Priests in Zul'Gurub have a chance to drop some common items. Here's a list containing some of the more sought-after pieces.

ITEM	DESCRIPTION	STATS
Band of Servitude	Ring	+9 INT, +8 STA
Equip: Increases damage and healing done by magical spells and effects by up to 23		
Belt of Untapped Power	Cloth Waist	54 Armor, +7 INT, +6 STA
Equip: Increases damage and healing done by magical spells and effects by 29		
Blooddrenched Mask	Leather Head	153 Armor, +22 AGI, +17 STA
Equip: Improves your chance to hit by 2%		
Cloak of the Hakkari Worshipers	Back	48 Armor, +6 INT, +6 STA
Equip: Increases damage and healing done by magical spells and effects by 23		
Gloves of the Tormented	Mail Hands	249 Armor, +19 AGI, +9 STA
Equip: Improves your chance to get a critical strike by 1%		

ITEM	DESCRIPTION	STATS
Might of the Tribe	Back	48 Armor, +18 STA
Equip: +28 Attack Power		
Sacrificial Gauntlets	Plate Hands	441 Armor, +19 STR
Equip: Improves your chance to get a critical strike by 1%, Equip: Improves your chance to hit by 1%		
Seal of the Gurubashi Berserker	Ring	+13 STA
Equip: +40 Attack Power		
Zulian Headdress	Cloth Head	78 Armor, +15 INT, +14 SPI, +13 STA
Equip: Increases healing done by spells and effects by up to 55		
Zulian Scepter of Rites	One-Hand Mace	41.0 DPS, +8 INT, +9 STA
Equip: Increases healing done by spells and effects by up to 26, Equip: Restores 4 mana per 5 sec.		

HIGH PRIEST VENOXIS

Venoxis, the Snake Aspect, is tucked away in an alcove teaming with all sorts of vipers. After clearing the exceptionally large pull of snakes in his room, he'll be standing atop a stairway with four serpentine guards.

Assign Poly and Hibernate targets for the snakes so that you can take them out one by one before engaging Venoxis. When the pull is executed, have your MT drag Venoxis far away from your raid group, near the fire, and have the MA begin targeting the snakes for elimination. It's important that your raid group stays near the doorway in this phase, keeping a healthy distance from Venoxis the entire time.

When the time to battle Venoxis is at hand, keep your casters at maximum distance and the melee players as close to him as possible. If any of your casters stray too near to Venoxis or one of your melee players strays too far, it will probably be the cause of a wipe your entire raid group.

Venoxis often casts Holy Wrath which is similar to a Shaman's Chain Lightning. However, instead of dealing less damage with each successive target, it deals *more*! Anyone in the middle zone between your melee group and the casters is going to get fried and potentially allow the jump to reach the casters. The safest way to negate this is to spread out as much as possible. Some groups learning the instance and encounter for the first time may decide to keep some of their melee group (Warriors & Rogues) at range with the casters. Venoxis will still cast the spell, but with the MT being the only player in range of the spell, and without a potential "jump" target, the danger of the spell is negated.

At 50% health, Venoxis transforms into a giant snake. At this time, your melee DPS must back away for a few moments until the MT has control of the situation. During this phase, Venoxis occasionally emits a putrid cloud of poison that inflicts heavy damage to anyone caught in it. To avoid having this happen to your MT, the Warrior must drag Venoxis in circles around the fire, making sure he's never standing in one place for too long, leaving the clouds of poison behind him.

While your MT drags the High Priest in circles around the fire, the melee DPS should be running hit and run attacks, steering clear of the poison while the ranged DPS unloads maximum damage.

Also, assign a Rogue or a Hunter to eliminate the Parasitic Serpents that try to make their way to the casters during this phase of the fight. If they make their way into a player's body, that player will receive a deadly DoT debuff that could cause them to die.

Keep Venoxis mobile, destroy the Parasitic Serpents, avoid the poison, and victory over the High Priest will soon be yours as you set him free from Hakkar's evil grasp.

HIGH PRIEST VENOXIS'S LOOT TABLE

ITEM	DESC	STATS
BLOODDRENCHED FOOTPADS	Leather Boots	129 Armor, 21 AGI, 10 STA
Passive: Improves your chance to hit by 1%		
FANG OF VENOXIS	Main Hand Dagger	41.2 DPS, 8 INT, 6 SPI
Passive: Increases damage and healing done by magical spells and effects by up to 24 Passive: Restores 6 mana per 5 second		
RUNED BLOODSTAINED HAUBERK	Mail Chest	416 Armor, 15 INT, 19 STA
Passive: Increases Attack Power by 58 Passive: Improves your chance to get a critical strike by 1%		
ZANZIL'S BAND	Ring	13 INT
Passive: Improves your chance to hit with spells by 1% Passive: Restores 4 mana per 5 second		
ZULIAN STONE AXE	Two-Handed Axe	58.6 DPS, 22 INT
Passive: Increases Attack Power by 44 Passive: Improves your chance to get a critical strike by 1%		
ZULIAN TIGERHIDE CLOAK	Cloth Cloak	48 Armor, 13 AGI, 10 STA
Passive: Improves your chance to hit by 1%		

HIGH PRIESTESS MAR'LI

High Priestess Mar'li is the wretched Spider Aspect and she proves to be a formidable opponent. After clearing the swarms of spiders in her area, prepare your raid for battle. Group your casters closely together and make sure a Warrior is on standby within that group.

When the pull is executed, make short work of the speaker in front of her and begin the assault. Keep ranged DPS and healers at max range while Mar'li's in her Troll form to avoid her Poison Bolt Volley attack. Have those in the raid that are able ready to heal and cleanse after the volley. Serpent Sting and Mana Drain are particularly useful here, as they can prevent her Life Drain spell from ever being cast. If she does begin to cast it on your MT, however, use Kick, Shield Bash, and Pummel to interrupt it as quickly as possible. During this phase, she also summons spiders, the Spawns of Mar'li, to attack your caster camp. These spiders start out to be rather small and harmless, but as time progresses, they become larger and deadlier. Use AoE and single target DPS to destroy the spawns as quickly as possible.

She soon transforms into a huge spider, snaring the MT and all players in the vicinity with an immobilizing web. During this time, she tries to run rampant through your casters, easily dispatching them while your MT stands helpless in the web. This is where the standby Warrior comes into play. The moment she snares the MT and runs into the caster camp, this Warrior must be ready to taunt her out of the casters and bring her back to the MT and allow them to reacquire the High Priestess's aggro. The standby warrior should then head back to the caster camp, ready to do it again. While she's in her Spider form, she won't attack anyone that's webbed. A Paladin's Blessing of Freedom makes you immune to the web effect; cast it on the MT right before, or after, the web has been spread.

Once the MT has reacquired aggro, unleash your full DPS upon her until she transforms back into her humanoid form. She continues to alter between forms throughout the duration of the battle. Execute the same strategy for each phase in the exact same way and she'll soon be thanking you for ending her servitude to Hakkar.

HIGH PRIESTESS MAR'LI'S LOOT TABLE

ITEM	DESC	STATS
BAND OF JIN	Ring	14 AGI, 8 STA
Passive: Improves your chance to hit by 1%		
BLOODSTAINED GREAVES	Plate Boots	274 Armor, 21 AGI, 10 INT, 10 STA
Passive: Increased Defense by 5		
FLOWING RITUAL ROBES	Cloth Robe	100 Armor, 24 SPI, 23 INT, 15 STA
Passive: Increases damage and healing done by magical spells and effects by up to 22		
MAR'LI'S EYE	Trinket	
Use: Restores 60 mana every 5 sec for 30 seconds		
MAR'LI'S TOUCH	Wand	76.8 DPS, 11 INT, 6 SPI, 5 STA
TALISMAN OF PROTECTION	Necklace	8 STA
Passive: Increased Defense by 9 Passive: Increases your chance to dodge an attack by 1%		

HIGH PRIEST THEKAL

The feral High Priest Thekal is known as the Tiger Aspect. He's one of the tougher battles you face in Zul'Gurub, but the encounter is not impossible to learn quickly. The first thing you should notice about this encounter is that two Zealots, both bosses in and of themselves, flank him.

Your first priority is to kill the two tigers that accompany the zealots and Thekal. Taking out the tigers is a simple, but necessary, step. Once they're down, have three Warriors pick up the aggro of the two zealots and Thekal. Immediately get a Rogue on Lor'Khan and an OT on Zath (both attacking from behind their targets).

Zealot Lor'Khan is a healer and, therefore, a threat. With the spells Dispel Magic, Greater Heal (this should be interrupted at all times), and Lightning Shield, she should be the primary target for the MA. She also has the Disarm ability and this could lead to the tank assigned to her losing threat quickly.

Zealot Zath has the Rogue abilities Kick, Gouge, Sweeping Strikes, and Sinister Strike. This is why it's important to keep a second tank behind her. Once she hits the Warrior who was assigned to be her tank with Gouge, the second Warrior should Taunt her and keep her in place. This also negates any chance for catching both tanks in Sweeping Strikes.

In his human form, High Priest Thekal has Bloodlust (+75% attack speed for an ally for 30 sec.), Mortal Cleave (Mortal Strike and Cleave), and Silence (single-target, 10 sec.). Keep any non-MT melee attackers at his back to avoid that

Mortal Cleave. Once Thekal assumes his Tiger form, he has the abilities Charge, Force Punch (AoE Knockback and damage), and Speed Slash.

At low health, Thekal enrages and increases his damage output to crazy levels.

However, even though everything sounds easy to this point, there is one little snag: the three bosses must die within 7 seconds of one another or they'll begin resurrecting each other with full life and mana. There are two options.

OPTION 1

Assign a Warrior to both Zealots and the High Priest. After the pulls been made, have the Warriors spread out as much as possible; send one Warrior north, one south and leave the third at the spawn point. This prevents Zealot Lor'Khan from healing the other two.

Target one Troll at a time, bringing them to about 5-9% life, but refrain from killing any of them. As soon as you have all three Trolls under 10%, kill them quickly.

OPTION 2

Again, assign a Warrior to each target and bring them together at the spawn point. Have your MA select a target and instruct everyone to begin using single target DPS until the selected target's at about 20%. Your MA's going to be switching targets, so make sure everyone's on board with the transitions. Once you have each of the bosses under 20% health, begin using AoE to finish them off. If one has more health than the others, have a couple Rogues and Hunters switch over to that boss to bring them down within range of the other two.

Once down, High Priest Thekal enters a rage and transforms into a massive tiger. Pull him into the hallway before his podium and tank him with your back to the wall. The rest of the raid should be on the opposite wall healing the MT. It is also a smart idea to actually use two tanks during this fight, as aggro can be a bit sketchy because of his knock back and high damage. Every 15 seconds or so, Thekal sends out a directional knock back that sends the tanks flying a huge distance. This can be countered, however, if your tanks have their backs to the wall. At this point, Thekal turns on the casters and begins to unleash his deadly claws. Priests should immediately shield whoever he targets. This will save a life while your tanks run over to pick up his aggro again. Once in position, begin to crush him with DPS until the next knock back, then repeat the steps listed above. During this phase, tigers spawn and begin to attack your raid group. Use Hunters and Rogues to single target DPS them until they are defeated, then turn their attention back to Thekal.

High Priest Thekal does not have a ton of health, so take him down as quickly as possible to prevent dragging the battle out and opening the door for errors. A few minutes later, he will lie defeated and ready to be looted, free of the Blood God's control.

HIGH PRIEST THEKAL'S LOOT TABLE

ITEM	DESC	STATS
BETRAYER'S BOOTS	Cloth Boots	69 Armor, 12 SPI, 12 INT, 8 STA
Passive: Increases damage and healing done by magical spells and effects by up to 30		
PEACEKEEPER LEGGINGS	Plate Legs	618 Armor, 18 INT, 14 STA
Passive: Increases healing done by spells and effects by up to 37 Passive: Restores 7 mana per 5 seconds		
RITUALISTIC LEGGUARDS	Cloth Legs	84 Armor, 20 SPI, 14 INT, 13 STA
Passive: Increases healing done by spells and effects by up to 37		
SEAFURY LEGGINGS	Mail Legs	348 Armor, 15 STR, 15 STA, 15 INT, 14 SPI
Passive: Increases damage and healing done by magical spells and effects by up to 16		
SEAL OF JIN	Ring	8 STA
Passive: Improves your chance to get a critical strike by 1% Passive: Increases Attack Power by 20		
SWIFT ZULIAN TIGER	Mount	Use: Summons and dismisses a rideable Tiger. This is a very fast mount
THEKAL'S GRASP	Main Hand Fist Weapon	47.0 DPS, 13 STA
Passive: Improves your chance to get a critical strike by 1%		
ZULIAN SLICER	One-Hand Sword	44.8 DPS
Chance on Hit: Slices the enemy for 72 to 96 Nature damage Passive: Increases Attack Power by 12 Passive: Skinning Increased by 10		

HIGH PRIESTESS ARLOKK

High Priestess Arlokk, the Panther Aspect, is one of the more interesting battles you face in Zul'Gurub. There is no other fight like it in the game, so be prepared to think outside of the box.

To begin the encounter, you must ring the gong in the back of her room. When that's done, she appears out of nowhere and begins to attack. Your MT must be quick to pick up her aggro, or your raid will suffer casualties; her damage is quite high. After the MT begins to tank her, your DPS must begin to unleash maximum damage on her before she vanishes.

After a few moments of battle, High Priestess Arlokk calls forth an army of non-elite panthers into the room. She then places a debuff on a random player, making that player the sole target of the panthers. The debuff is the Mark of Arlokk. This target changes several times during the encounter, so be prepared to adjust to those changes. The Mark of Arlokk target must do everything in their power to keep them busy, running them in circles around the room, with Mages using Frost Nova once they are away from any players. When Arlokk vanishes, take the opportunity to kill off the panthers. Focus fire on the individual panthers to bring them down one at a time.

Several times during the fight, Arlokk simply vanishes, leaving your raid to survive the panthers for a minute or so. Do your best to keep everyone alive and the panthers busy until she reappears. When she does, have the MT pick up her aggro as quickly as possible and your DPS lay into her. You only have a short window of opportunity to damage her between vanishes, so make every second count. Arlokk also has the Rogue abilities Gouge and Backslash at her disposal, along with the Priest ability Shadow Word: Pain.

While she assumes her panther form, Arlokk has a few new abilities that are all melee-oriented. She has Whirlwind (attack everyone in melee range) and Thrash (chance for two extra attacks) along with Ravage (+500 damage and stun on next attack).

Her health isn't phenomenal, so done right, this encounter should go quickly. She will soon be singing your praises for setting her free from the hold of Hakkar.

SCAREDY CATS

While Arlokk is still engaged in the battle, you may choose to set up a Fear rotation with your Priests (Psychic Scream) and Warriors (Intimidating Shout) to keep the panthers occupied until she vanishes. When she disappears, use movement impairing effects (Piercing Howl, Improved Blizzard, and Earthbind Totems) to slow them down. Use AoE to kill the panthers while you can.

There's a cap of 40 panthers that can be in the chamber at one time.

HIGH PRIESTESS ARLOKK'S LOOT TABLE

ITEM	DESC	STATS
ARLOKK'S GRASP	Off-Hand Fist Weapon	41.7 DPS
Chance on Hit: Sends a shadowy bolt at the enemy causing 55 to 85 Shadow damage		
ARLOKK'S HOODOO STICK	Held In Hand	8 STA
Passive: Improves your chance to get a critical strike with spells by 1% Passive: Increases healing done by spells and effects by up to 22		
BLOODSOAKED GREAVES	Plate Boots	486 Armor, 25 STA, 8 AGI
Passive: Increased Defense by 5		
OVERLORD'S ONYX BAND	Ring	11 STA
Passive: Increases your chance to block attacks with a shield by 2% Passive: Increases your chance to dodge an attack by 1%		
WILL OF ARLOKK	Two-Handed Staff	55.5 DPS, 35 SPI, 19 INT, 15 STA
Passive: Increases healing done by spells and effects by up to 46		

WARLORDS OF ZUL'GURUB

Zul'Gurub's "big" bosses have some fantastic loot. It's possible to kill Hakkar and leave both Bloodlord Mandokir and Jin'do the Hexxer alone, but most raids drool at the chance to get some of the drops offered by those two.

HAKKAR, THE SOULFLAYER

After carefully clearing the top level of the altar upon which Hakkar stands, gather your raid at the top of the stairs directly in front of him. The raid leader should take a moment to explain how this encounter is going to work.

The Sons of Hakkar patrol along each side of the area surrounding Hakkar. These two Sons are on 45 second respawn timers. That's an important piece of information as you'll soon learn.

Have *at least* two Warriors jump in to tank Hakkar. He will periodically Mind Control whoever's highest on the threat list (the MT) and the next tank(s) need to be ready to grab aggro immediately so Hakkar doesn't run into the raid. Polymorph the MC'd Warrior as soon as possible.

Hakkar has one ability, above all others, to which you must pay particularly close attention: Poisonous Blood Siphon. This powerful attack hits everyone in the raid, sucking their blood and regenerating vast amounts of health for Hakkar.

The key to countering this is a green mist left behind by the Sons of Hakkar when they're killed. If a player should be caught within this mist, they're infected with Poisonous Blood. It's absolutely essential that every person step into the green mist and receives the debuff *before* Hakkar uses his Poisonous Blood Siphon attack. *Do not cleanse this poison!* Yes, Poisonous Blood has negative effects, but it's a necessary element to the battle that everyone be poisoned. A single person missing the debuff can significantly damage the group's chances of defeating this boss. Make sure that absolutely everyone (it can't be stressed enough) is ready to enter the green mist when a Son of Hakkar falls.

When Hakkar uses his Poisonous Blood Siphon on a raid group that's been poisoned by the green mist, your blood actually damages Hakkar instead of healing him! If you're not poisoned, you'll take damage instead and Hakkar will heal.

One person needs to be assigned to pulling the Sons of Hakkar well before a Poisonous Blood Siphon occurs. Leave time to kill the Son and get everyone poisoned. However, Hakkar's self-poisoning won't be enough to take him down alone. You'll need to get ranged DPS to focus on Hakkar whenever they can to reduce his health. At the 10 minute mark, he will Enrage and increase both his attack speed and power, reducing your raid's chances for success.

BUG FIXED

You can no longer pull Hakkar into a position that keeps the majority of the raid out of LOS of his abilities. If you try to do this, he will reset.

Hakkar's other note-worthy ability is Corrupted Blood. He randomly targets a raid member and hits them with 1000 points of Nature damage which splashes over to anyone close to them. In addition, it applies a DoT to the primary target.

As long as everyone is familiar with the tactics for this battle and what their role is concerning Poisonous Blood Siphon and Poison Blood, the fight itself won't be horribly difficult. Use at least two Warriors to tank him and bring him down with a combination of DPS from the raid and his self-inflicted damage via the Siphon. Make sure that everyone is poisoned from the green mist when the Sons of Hakkar die.

HAKKAR'S LOOT TABLE

ITEM	DESC	STATS
AEGIS OF THE BLOOD GOD	Off-Hand Shield	2575 Armor, 47 Block
Passive: Increases the block value of your shield by 30 Passive: Increased Defense by 7 Passive: Increases your chance to block attacks with a shield by 2%		
ANCIENT HAKKARI MANSLAYER	One-Hand Axe	49.8 DPS
Chance on Hit: Steals 48 to 54 life from target enemy		
BLOODCALLER	Main Hand Sword	41.2 DPS, 15 INT, 12 STA
Passive: Increases damage and healing done by magical spells and effects by up to 33		
BLOODSOAKED LEGPLATES	Plate Legs	674 Armor, 36 STR, 21 STA
Passive: Increased Defense by 10		
CLOAK OF CONSUMPTION	Cloth Cloak	52 Armor, 10 INT
Passive: Increases damage and healing done by magical spells and effects by up to 23 Passive: Improves your chance to hit with spells by 1%		
FANG OF THE FACELESS	One-Hand Dagger	49.7 DPS
Passive: Improves your chance to get a critical strike by 1% Passive: 28 Attack Power		
GURUBASHI DWARF DESTROYER	Gun	38.9 DPS
Passive: Increases Attack Power by 30		
HEART OF HAKKAR		
PEACEKEEPER GAUNTLETS	Plate Gloves	482 Armor, 12 INT, 7 STA
Passive: Increases healing done by spells and effects by up to 59 Passive: Restores 4 mana per 5 seconds		
SEAFURY GAUNTLETS	Mail Gloves	271 Armor, 10 STR, 9 INT, 9 STA
Passive: Improves your chance to get a critical strike by 1% Passive: Improves your chance to get a critical strike with spells by 1% Passive: Restores 7 mana per 5 second		
SOUL CORRUPTER'S NECKLACE	Necklace	16 INT, 8 SPI, 10 STA
Passive: Improves your chance to hit with spells by 1%		
TOUCH OF CHAOS	Wand	82.0 DPS
Passive: Increases damage and healing done by magical spells and effects by up to 18		
WARBLADE OF THE HAKKARI	Main Hand Sword	49.7 DPS
Passive: Increases Attack Power by 28 Passive: Improves your chance to get a critical strike by 1%		
ZIN'ROKH, DESTROYER OF WORLDS	Two-Handed Sword	64.6 DPS, 28 STA
Passive: Increases Attack Power by 72		

BLOODLORD MANDOKIR

Bloodlord Mandokir is mounted and that's the quickest distinction between him and other bosses. You will, in fact, have to fight his mount as well as the Bloodlord. Luckily, his mount is a much bigger push over than he is.

When you pull Mandokir, he dismounts and charges straight for the raid. Have your MT pick up Mandokir and another tank grab the aggro of the Raptor. Pull the Bloodlord away from the raid, as he has a Whirlwind attack, and begin using single target DPS to defeat his mount. When the mount, Oghan, dies, he enters a state of rage and does considerably more damage for a full minute and a half. It increases his attack damage by 50 and his attack speed by 65%. Some raids find it to be a safer tactic to just kill him first and off-tank Oghan during the fight. That's up to your raid leader. Oghan has the Thrash (chance for two extra attacks) and Sunder Armor abilities. To be safe, only use ranged DPS for this minute.

There are a couple things to keep in mind while fighting Mandokir. The first is the presence of ghosts floating around the area. Should you die, a ghost sacrifices itself to resurrect you. Obviously, once the ghosts are depleted, you receive no more free resurrections.

The other important note is that every time a member of your raid falls, Bloodlord Mandokir gains experience and ultimately "levels up." Should he gain enough levels, he will begin to hit so hard that it's almost impossible to keep your MT alive. He also grows in size with each level. A comedic interlude occurs if Jindo the Hexxar is alive at this point. The Bloodlord yells, "Ding!" and Jindo replies, "Grats mon!" Hopefully, you never have to see this amusing exchange take place!

The final, and most important, part of this encounter is the Bloodlord's watch ability. Every few seconds Mandokir calls out a name that he is *watching*. It's absolutely imperative that the person called stops doing whatever it is they're doing. The player being "watched" will have a debuff called "Threatening Gaze." If that player continues to attack and generates too much threat, Mandokir will use his Guillotine ability. This is even nastier than it sounds. It inflicts weapons damage *+10,000!* This would even take out even the mightiest of tanks. This in turn causes the MT to chase the Bloodlord down while he goes on a rampage of killing in your raid.

Bloodlord Mandokir has a few other abilities to bring against the raid: Charge, Mortal Strike, and Overpower. They're all based off the Warrior abilities.

This battle is really about endurance, paying attention, and keeping people alive. Should you have all these things under your belt, Bloodlord Mandokir won't present too much of a challenge for you.

BLOODLORD MANDOKIR'S LOOT TABLE

ITEM	DESC	STATS
ANIMIST'S LEGGINGS	Leather Legs	240 Armor, 18 SPI, 18 INT, 15 STA
Passive: Increases healing done by spells and effects up by to 35		
BLOOD SCYTHE	Herbalist	Use: Allows an Herbalist to collect Bloodvine from Zul'Gurub Flora when carried
BLOODDRENCHED GRIPS	Leather Gloves	122 Armor, 16 STA
Passive: 34 Attack Power, Improves your chance to get a critical strike by 1%		
BLOODLORD'S DEFENDER	Main Hand Sword	48.2 DPS, 80 Armor, 15 STA
Passive: Increased Defense 4		
BLOODSOAKED PAULDRONS	Plate Shoulder	552 Armor, 16 STA, 16 STR, 11 AGI
Passive: Increased Defense by 3		
BLOODTINGED KILT	Cloth Legs	87 Armor, 20 INT, 20 STA
Passive: Increases damage and healing done by magical spells and effects by up to 28		
HAKKARI LOA CLOAK	Cloth Cape	50 Armor, 8 SPI, 6 INT, 6 STA
Passive: Increases healing done by spells and effects up by to 33		
HALBERD OF SMITING	Polearm	62.6 DPS
Passive: Chance to decapitate the target on a melee swing, causing 452 to 676 damage		
MANDOKIR'S STING	Bow	37.5 DPS
Equip: 11 AGI, 8 STA		
OVERLORD'S CRIMSON BAND	Ring	9 STR, 10 STA, 8 AGI
Passive: Increased Defense 7		
PRIMALIST'S SEAL	Ring	12 INT, 8 SPI
Passive: Increases healing done by spells and effects up by to 29		
SWIFT RAZZASHI RAPTOR	Mount	Use: Summons and dismisses a rideable Raptor. This is a very fast mount
WARBLADE OF THE HAKKARI	Off-Hand Sword	47.9 DPS
Passive: 40 Attack Power		
ZANZIL'S SEAL	Ring	10 INT, 10 STA
Passive: Improves your chance to hit with spells by 1% Passive: Increases damage and healing done by magical spells and effects by up to 11		

Jin'do the Hexxer is the single most difficult battle in Zul'Gurub. This battle forces every single member of your raid to pay perfect and accurate attention to everything that is going on throughout the entire encounter.

Make sure you use two tanks for this fight, as one of them will be Mind Controlled from time to time. After assigning the tanks, make sure you have a Mage by the skeleton pit, ready to AoE them into dust any time a member of your raid gets teleported into them. This happens quite often, so this Mage will be doing this almost full-time.

Once pulled, notice Jin'do often places a curse upon a member of your raid. Do *not* remove this curse from your raid. This curse allows a person to see the Shades of Jin'do that populate the area. These invisible beings run unchallenged throughout your raid, doing potentially high damage to your casters and slowing their casting time. Should anyone but the tanks receive this curse, they must drop whatever it is they are doing and do single target damage to the Shades as long as they have the curse. If too many shades are left alive, your casters will suffer greatly at their hands and your raid may eventually fall prematurely. Once the curse is gone, Jindo casts it upon another member of the raid, and the previous victim should go right back to whatever they were doing prior to receiving the curse.

Jin'do is a Shaman. Therefore, he uses powerful totems to aid him in his battle against you. There are two types of totems to deal with. The first is a Mind Control Totem. He casts this totem almost constantly during the entire fight. This totem randomly enslaves a member of your raid for as long as it is left up. Make sure that every single Warrior in your raid uses his or her Intimidating Shout as soon as they can, as this fear can have devastating results if used against your raid. To deal with this totem, everyone must assist your MA immediately whenever one pops up. Anyone that's doing damage to the Hexxer must stop whatever it is they are doing and assist the MA to destroy the totem as quickly as possible.

The second type of totem is not so deadly; however, when left standing long enough, it can cause problems. Every 30 seconds or so Jindo drops a Healing Totem. This totem has extremely low health and can usually be taken down with two or three hits. If left around for more than 3 seconds, this totem heals Jin'do for tens of thousands of health. You obviously don't want this happening, as it forces the battle to last much longer. Jin'do also has the infamous Hex spell and will "frog" players randomly. This effect can be dispelled.

To defeat this challenge, kill the Shades when cursed, use high damage on Jin'do when you can, and assist the MA to drop totems as quickly as possible. This battle is a struggle and requires some practice, but the rewards are well worth it.

JINDO THE HEXXER'S LOOT TABLE

ITEM	DESC	STATS
ANIMIST'S BOOTS	Leather Boots	184 Armor, 14 SPI, 14 INT, 9 STA
Passive: Increases healing done by spells and effects up to 29		
BLOODDRENCHED LEGGINGS	Leather Legs	170 Armor, 35 AGI, 15 STA
BLOODSOAKED GAUNTLETS	Plate Gloves	460 Armor, 17 STR, 14 STA
Passive: Increased Defense by 5		
Passive: Increases your chance to dodge an attack by 1%		
BLOODSTAINED COIF	Mail Helm	337 Armor, 14 INT, 14 STA
Passive: Improves your chance to get a critical strike by 2%		
Passive: Increases Attack Power by 28		
BLOODSTAINED LEGPLATES	Mail Leggings	363 Armor, 24 AGI, 15 STA, 11 INT
Passive: Improves your chance to get a critical strike by 1%		
BLOODTINGED GLOVES	Cloth Gloves	62 Armor, 10 SPI, 10 INT, 10 STA
Passive: Increases damage and healing done by magical spells and effects by up to 19		
Passive: Improves your chance to hit with spells by 1%		
JIN'DO'S BAG OF WHAMMIES	Held In Hand	11 INT, 8 STA
Passive: Increases damage and healing done by magical spells and effects by up to 18		
Passive: Improves your chance to hit with spells by 1%		
JIN'DO'S EVIL EYE	Necklace	11 INT, 6 SPI, 5 STA
Passive: Increases healing done by spells and effects by up to 44		
JIN'DO'S HEXXER	Main Hand Mace	41.2 DPS, 9 INT, 6 STA
Passive: Increases healing done by spells and effects by up to 51		
Passive: Improves your chance to get a critical strike with spells by 1%		
JIN'DO'S JUDGMENT	Staff	55.9 DPS, 10 INT, 10 STA
Passive: Improves your chance to hit with spells by 2%		
Passive: Restores 14 mana per 5 seconds		
Passive: Increases damage and healing done by magical spells and effects by up to 27		
OVERLORD'S EMBRACE	Cloth Cloak	140 Armor, 10 STA
Passive: Increased Defense by 7		
Passive: Increases your chance to block attacks with a shield by 1%		
THE HEXXER'S COVER	Cloth Helm	81 Armor, 10 INT, 10 STA
Passive: Increases damage and healing done by magical spells and effects by up to 41		

FUN WITH WARLOCKS

A popular tactic for those experienced with Zul'Gurub is to have the Warlocks in the raid enslave the demons from the Edge of Madness. They can be very effective against the Shades.

OPTIONAL BOSSES OF ZUL'GURUB

While not required for defeating Hakkar, these bosses can reveal hidden rewards. Gahz'ranka has some unique loot, but it's mostly meant for fun. The other four bosses can be found inside the Edge of Madness area. Only one can be summoned per instance and which one you get changes almost every week. Each one drops an item that can be combined with a Punctured Voodoo Doll to create a powerful class trinket.

GAHZ'RANKA

This beast of a hydra is fished out of the river using the Mudskunk Lures received from Nat Pagle. This is actually quite a simple boss to overcome and should be defeated on your first or second try.

Gahz'ranka should be fought in the water to avoid falling damage from his attack that sends everyone into the air. Of course, this means that there's a high likelihood that you'll get adds, but it's much better than incurring constant, heavy damage.

To defeat Gahz'ranka, simply have a tank on either side of him fighting for aggro. When one tank is sent flying back, the other tank is ready to pick up his aggro. Occasionally, Gahz'ranka uses an attack that sends anyone near him flying into the air, forcing him or her to take falling damage when they land—it's not lethal. Simply make sure a Priest is ready to shield the tanks when they hit the ground.

GAHZ'RANKA'S LOOT TABLE

ITEM	DESC	STATS
FOROR'S EYEPATCH	Leather Helm	160 Armor, 19 STA
Passive: Improves your chance to get a critical strike by 2% Passive: Increases Attack Power by 44		
NAT PAGLE'S BROKEN REEL	Trinket	
Use: Increases the chance to hit with spells by 10% for 15 seconds		
NAT PAGLE'S FISH TERMINATOR	Staff	61.4 DPS, 41 STR, 19 STA
TIGULE'S HARPOON	Polearm	58.5 DPS, 20 STA
Passive: Improves your chance to hit by 2% Passive: Increases Attack Power by 60 when fighting Beasts		

GRI'LEK

Gri'lek is a really big troll with a really big temper. He is also, however, a really big pushover.

Once engaged, he simply attacks your MT for a few moments, doing light damage. Make sure you're using this time to damage him, as his true ability is about to be revealed. Every so often he grows in size by an enormous amount. During this phase he attempts to root members of your raid in place, forcing them to stand and take his attacks. Make sure this root is dispelled immediately. When you do see him grow, have your MT run away from him until he shrinks down to normal size. During this time his movement speed is incredibly slow, so it's easy to avoid him, and you will want to do so with great effort. If he hits someone while he's enlarged, they will take fatal damage.

Just keep your distance from him while he's in his massive state and this battle is a breeze.

GRI'LEK'S LOOT TABLE

ITEM	DESC	STATS
GRI'LEK'S BLOOD		
GRI'LEK'S CARVER	Two-Handed Axe	58.5 DPS
Passive: Increases Attack Power by 117 when fighting Dragonkin		
GRI'LEK'S GRINDER	One-Hand Mace	44.8 DPS
Passive: Increases Attack Power by 48 when fighting Dragonkin		

HAZZA'RAH

This boss can be a real pain for an unprepared raid group, so make sure you're in position and ready for the fight right when you see it is Hazza'rah that is summoned.

The first thing to do is spread your casters out. He has a Mana Drain that chains from one person to anyone standing near and so on, so if everyone is standing closely together you can kiss that mana goodbye for everyone.

The next thing to do is have all of your Rogues and Warriors pile on him immediately. They are the main source of DPS on this boss since your casters will be busy taking care of the spawns he sets forth.

These spawns have the ability to kill almost anyone in your raid with one swipe. The good news is, however, that they can be taken down with one or two attacks and they move incredibly slowly. AoE and a Hunter's Multishot come in handy like never before against these spawns.

The final attack he unleashes is an AoE Sleep spell. This has a short duration – luckily - so your MT should be able to pick his aggro up again almost immediately without too much trouble. Hazza'rah also has the Earth Shock spell; spellcasters should take note of this.

If everyone pays attention to their role, defeats the spawns immediately as they arrive, and keeps the DPS constant on Hazza'rah, this fight should be over sooner than later.

HAZZA'RAH'S LOOT TABLE

ITEM	DESC	STATS
FIERY RETRIBUTER	Main Hand Sword	60 Armor, 44.7 DPS, 7 STR
Passive: Increased Defense by 5 Passive: Adds 2 fire damage to your melee attacks		
HAZZA'RAH'S DREAM THREAD		
THOUGHTBLIGHTER	Wand	71.7 DPS
Passive: Restores 5 mana per 5 second		

RENATAKI

Renataki is a Rogue boss, so naturally you can expect some trickery and sneaky attacks from this scoundrel.

The MT does a lot of chasing during this encounter. First of all, Renataki has an AoE gouge, leaving everyone in melee distance disoriented for a few seconds while Renataki heads straight for the casters. Whoever he attacks should head straight for the MT, so he or she can taunt him off as soon as possible.

Renataki really only has one other trick up his sleeve. He randomly Vanishes for a few moments, appearing soon after to deal a heavy Ambush to someone in the raid. Once again, whomever he is on should run immediately to the MT before they die. The Ambush can be fatal at times to cloth users, so be ready for anything! Power Word: Shield can go a long way here.

Arguably the "coolest" of Renataki's abilities, Thousand Blades is Renataki's chance to whip several daggers at nearby targets in rapid succession.

RENATAKI'S LOOT TABLE

ITEM	DESC	STATS
PITCHFORK OF MADNESS	Polearm	58.4 DPS
Passive: Increases Attack Power by 117 when fighting Demons		
RENATAKI'S SOUL CONDUIT	Main Hand Sword	40.7 DPS
Passive: Increases damage and healing done by magical spells and effects by up to 16		
Passive: Restores 6 mana per 5 seconds		
RENATAKI'S TOOTH	Quest Item	

WUSHOOLAY

Wushoolay is the most difficult boss in the Edge of Madness, but still not that terrible of a boss for a prepared raid group.

The first, and most important, thing to do is to have the MT face Wushoolay away from everyone. Wushoolay often performs a frontal lightning attack, dealing heavy damage to anyone in its cone of effect.

The second ability Wushoolay uses against you is a poison cloud that applies medium damage to anyone standing inside of it. Your MT must move Wushoolay out of the cloud when this happens, while the melee DPS moves out as well.

The third and final attack is a Druid spell called Lightning Cloud. This attack deals heavy AoE nature damage to anyone inside the perimeter. To avoid this attack, your MT must move Wushoolay out from under the cloud at all costs. If anyone stands in it too long, they usually die. A little nature resist gear can really go a long way here too for the Warrior tanking Wushoolay.

Wushoolay has a Chain Lightning spell that work a bit differently than the Shaman spell of the same name. Instead of continually decreasing the amount of damage from target to target, it increases causing much more damage to the last target than the first. To avoid the full effect of this spell, spread out and try to prevent the "jump" from happening. The spell stops if there's not a valid target to jump to.

The MT will inevitably be moving quite a bit for this entire fight. The raid must be ready to move with him or her, mainly to avoid ever being caught in front of Wushoolay or in an AoE. With a little practice, this battle should run quite smoothly once you get a feel for the rhythm of it.

WUSHOOLAY'S LOOT TABLE

ITEM	DESC	STATS
HOODOO HUNTING BOW	Bow	35.0 DPS, 10 AGI, 4 STA
WUSHOOLAY'S MANE	Quest Item	
WUSHOOLAY'S POKER	Main Hand Dagger	40.6 DPS
Passive: Increases healing done by spells and effects by up to 31		
Passive: Restores 6 mana per 5 seconds		

FACTION!

Zul'Gurub is one of the first instances where faction plays a significant role. Gaining reputation with the Zandalar Tribe has many different benefits and is required for most quests available from the Trolls on Yojamba Island.

GAINING FACTION

The easiest way to gain faction with Zandalar Tribe is by simply killing monsters inside of Zul'Gurub. Almost everything you kill within the instance grants a small amount of faction; the bosses give a significant amount as well. Any player can go from Neutral to Exalted solely by killing things inside the instance.

However, there are other ways to gain faction:

QUESTS: Just about every single quest you do for the Zandalar Tribe gives you faction. This includes all class specific armor quests, completing an enchant, turning in the Heart of Hakkar, the Collection of Heads quest, and many others on Yojamba Island.

BIJOUS: You have the option of turning in different colored Bijous that drop inside of the instance to receive faction and a Zandalar Honor Token.

COINS: Simular to the Bijou turn in quests, you can also provide the Trolls with the various Coins that drop inside of Zul'Gurub for a faction bonus and a Zandalar Honor Token.

ZANDALAR HONOR TOKENS: If you complete the Bijou or Coin turn in quests, you receive these tokens as a reward. They can be used for other quests or they can be "destroyed" for further reputation gains. When they say "destroy" the token, don't take it literally and destroy it from your inventory. Bring it to the altar on Yojamba Island and right click it to destroy the token properly.

REPUTATION REWARDS

1 BIJOU	+75 Reputation, 1 Honor Token
3 COINS	+25 Reputation, 1 Honor Token
ZANDALAR HONOR TOKEN	+50 Reputation

FACTION REWARDS

FRIENDLY	Superior Class Armor Quest Reward
	Class-Specific Necklace (Uncommon)
	Access to Zul'Gurub Specific Head and Leg Enchants
HONORED	Superior Class Armor Quest Reward
	Class-Specific Necklace Upgrade (Superior)
REVERED	Epic Class Armor Quest Reward
	Class-Specific Necklace Upgrade (Superior)
	Access to "Zanzil Flasks" Quests (Zanza's Potent Potables)
EXALTED	Class-Specific Necklace Upgrade (Epic)
	Access to Class Specific Shoulder Enchants

In addition to these standard rewards for every class, masters of different professions have many unique recipes available for sale at Yojamba Island from Rin'wosho the Trader. There are some very desirable recipes for most professions at every faction level.

VICTORY!

While Zul'Gurub may be a 20-person raid zone, do not ever underestimate it. It was created much harder than intended and even Blizzard Entertainment has stated it plans on changing several things in the instance to bring it to the level they intended it to be. All the enemies in this guide will always exist in Zul'Gurub, but their quantities may change. Either way, once you have defeated every boss in the zone, congratulate yourself. You have truly conquered one of the great challenges in *World or Warcraft* to date.

AZUREGOS

Played & Written by: Edwin "Plainsong" Kern of <Dovrani> on Kirin Tor

Azshara was once a beautiful bastion of the High Elves. Their magic was nearly unsurpassed in Azeroth before their fall. Now Naga and Blood Elves have returned to scour the ruins. Are they trying to reclaim a lost heritage? What lies hidden in Azshara?

To find out, you must deal with more than merely Naga. One of the Blue Dragonflight has made it his duty to protect the magic of Azshara. Azuregos won't allow anyone to possess these items of power. Defeating him will be difficult, but the rewards could be wonderous.

ENCOUNTER INFORMATION

Location	Southeast Azshara
Quests	Hunter
Region	Contested
Suggested Level	60
Group Allowed	Raid of 40
Enemy Type	Dragon
Time to Complete	20-30 Minutes

GETTING TO AZUREGOS

Azuregos wanders throughout southeast Azshara. Horde raids should fly into Valormok and head to the gathering point. Alliance raids have a farther walk as they need to fly into Talrendis Point and run from the entrance of Azshara.

WHO TO BRING

With a raid of 40 people, it's likely you have the abilities you need to defeat Azuregos. You need a main tank (MT) and a an off tank (OT) to take over should the main fall. You need healers to keep the raid members alive and you need sustainable DPS to kill Azuregos.

Warlocks are useful in getting the raid in position by summoning and their DPS isn't something to sniff at. There are several enemies in the area that need to be cleared and can be sharded. Once the raid is started, everyone should head to the gathering point. Warlocks can summon the stragglers with the help of two others.

WHAT TO BRING

Frost Resistance is important when fighting Azuregos. Being a member of the Blue Dragonflight, most of his attacks are cold based. Grab trinkets and rings that increase your resistance to Frost.

The main and off tanks have the most difficult decision of anyone in the raid. They should balance additional Armor and Defense with Frost Resistance and Stamina.

QUESTS FOR AZUREGOS

Hunters often seek Azuregos while questing for the **Ancient Sinew Wrapped Lamina.** Others seek him for the *Scepter of the Shifting Sands* quest chain.

HUNTER QUESTS

QUEST NAME	QUEST GIVER	QUEST GIVER LOCATION	QUEST RECEIVER	QUEST RECEIVER LOCATION	CHAIN?	MAX EXPERIENCE
The Ancient Leaf	Ancient Petrified Leaf	Cache of the Firelord: Molten Core	Hastat the Ancient	Felwood: Irontree Woods	Yes	None
Ancient Sinew Wrapped Lamina Raid	Hastat the Ancient	Felwood: Irontree Woods	Hastat the Ancient	Felwood: Irontree Woods	Yes	None
REWARD: Ancient Sinew Wrapped Lamina 18 Slot Quiver, Class: Hunter, Passive: Increases ranged attack speed by 15%						

THE ANCIENT LEAF

Quest Level	60 to obtain
Class	Hunter
Location	Molten Core
Quest Giver	Ancient Petrified Leaf
Goal	Find the owner
Max Experience Gained	None
Reward	None

After forcing Majordomo to concede in Molten Core, you're given a chance to open the Cache of the Firelord. An Ancient Petrified Leaf may be inside. Should it be, the Hunters of the raid should decide (through debate or rolling) who gets the Leaf. Only one Hunter can get it each time and it's not always in the cache.

Once you have the Leaf, journey to Felwood. An island stands in the corrupted lake in Irontree Woods. Climb to the highest point on the island for the spirits to reveal themselves. Each has a quest that leads you somewhere in the world. Hastat the Ancient rewards you with a quiver should you complete his quest.

ANCIENT SINEW WRAPPED LAMINA RAID

Quest Level	60 to obtain
Class	Hunter
Location	Felwood: Irontree Woods
Quest Giver	Hastat the Ancient
Goal	Collect the Mature Blue Dragon Sinew
Max Experience Gained	None
Reward	Ancient Sinew Wrapped Lamina 18 Slot Quiver, Class: Hunter, Passive: Increases ranged attack speed by 15%

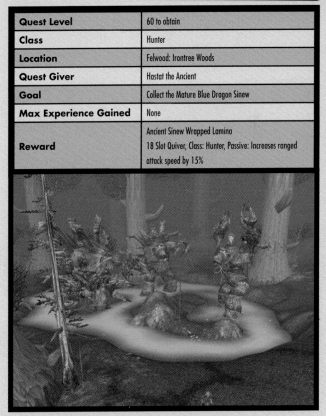

For the quiver, Hastat asks for Mature Blue Dragon Sinew. This can be obtained by killing the blue dragonkin in Winterspring, but it takes a very long time. A better way to get it may be to kill a much older blue dragon. Azuregos can be found in Azshara and is the largest living blue dragon to be seen.

AZUREGOS'S MAGICAL LEDGER

If you are working on the Scepter of the Shifting Sands, then you must collect Azuregos's Magical Ledger from Azuregos while trying to obtain the Blue Scepter Shard. He'll give it to those that need it.

WHAT IS HE PROTECTING?

ITEM	TYPE	STATS
COLD SNAP	Wand	85.3 DPS, +7 INT
PASSIVE: INCREASES DAMAGE DONE BY FROST SPELLS AND EFFECTS BY UP TO 20		
CRYSTAL ADORNED CROWN	Cloth Head	85 Armor, +14 INT, +13 SPI
PASSIVE: INCREASES HEALING DONE WITH SPELLS AND EFFECTS BY UP TO 92		
DRAPE OF BENEDICTION	Cloak	52 Armor, +13 INT, +11 STA, +8 SPI
PASSIVE: INCREASES HEALING DONE BY SPELL AND EFFECTS BY UP TO 31		
ESKHANDER'S LEFT CLAW	Off-Hand Fist-Weapon	48 DPS, +4 AGI
CHANCE ON HIT: Slows enemy's movements to 40% of normal speed and causes them to bleed for 150 damage over 30 seconds		
FANG OF THE MYSTICS	Dagger	51.7 DPS, +10 INT
PASSIVE: Improves your chance to get a critical strike with spells by 1%		
PASSIVE: Restores 4 mana every 5 seconds		
LEGGINGS OF ARCANE SUPREMACY	Cloth Legs	93 Armor, +24 INT, +14 SPI, +14 STA, +10 Frost Resistance, +10 Arcane Resistance
PASSIVE: Increases damage done by Arcane spells and effects by up to 36		
MATURE BLUE DRAGON SINEW	Quest Item	
PUISSANT CAPE	Cloak	54 Armor, +12 STA
PASSIVE: +40 ATTACK POWER		
PASSIVE: Improves your chance to hit by 1%		
SNOWBLIND SHOES	Cloth Feet	73 Armor, +10 INT, +10 STA
PASSIVE: Increases damage and healing done by magical spells and effects by up to 32		
PASSIVE: Restores 5 mana every 5 seconds		
TYPHOON	Two-Hand Sword	64.7 DPS, +14 STR, +20 AGI, +10 STA
PASSIVE: Increases your chance to parry an attack by 1%		
UNMELTING ICE GIRDLE	Plate Waist	452 Armor, +14 AGI, +14 STR, +14 STA, +16 Frost Resistance
PASSIVE: Increased Defense +8		

DEFEATING AZUREGOS

SETTING UP

GATHERING POINT

Refer to the map in the "Encounter Information" to see the best gathering point for Azuregos. Azuregos patrols nearby and there are only a few mobs that will interfere with your battle. Once people start arriving, begin killing the mobs in the area. This gives you more room and supplies soul shards to your Warlocks for summoning.

Most of the enemies are nothing more than annoyances. The Hippogryphs can be soloed and the Deer are neutral until attacked. The Cliff Walkers are another story. They're aggressive and elite. They can be dealt with by only a couple raid members, but are dangerous to solo. Clear the area of all monsters and prepare for Azuregos to patrol toward you.

Azuregos makes your life a bit easier by being neutral. His only duty is to protect the legacy of the High Elves and keep dangerous magic out of the hands of mortals. It's a pity you're here for that magic.

Organize the groups as you would a normal raid. The MT's group should contain the MH, a Warlock with an imp pet (for Blood Pact), a Hunter using Trueshot Aura since it translates from more damage to more threat, and a Paladin/Shaman for auras/totems. The other groups should be relatively balanced between damage and healers since there's only a minimal need for

CC during a fight like this. Once all groups have been finalized, begin the buffing process. Priests, Mages, and Druids have a good bit of work here, but it makes a tremendous difference and shouldn't be considered pointless.

Any abilities that increase Frost Resistance, specifically Shaman totems, should be used frequently.

ADAPTING TO AN AGELESS PROTECTOR

Azuregos possesses many abilities. He's far too powerful for characters to counter any of these, so adapting to them is your key to victory. With the mountain of hitpoints this ancient protector has, a long and steady fight should be your goal.

FORWARD AOES

Azuregos' claws are massive and he can catch several people in a single swipe. He also has a cone of frost breath that hits everything in front of him. For these reasons, any melee member who isn't the tank should stay behind Azuregos whenever possible.

For many fights in your career, the MT has always turned the enemy away from the party. This is not feasible when the opponent is Azuregos. The MT will have their hands full keeping Azuregos from eating the entire raid, so if you're in front of the blue dragon and you aren't the tank - *move*!

Having at least one Paladin or Shaman assigned to keeping the tank's Frost Resistance high also lowers the need for healing.

TELEPORTING

Many times during the fight, Azuregos summons all nearby raid members and teleports them with him to a nearby location. It's important that all raid members are close enough to be teleported. When he teleports, he reduces the threat of all members teleported with him to 0. This means that anyone who was not teleported will have aggro and must run to the tank quickly.

Once teleported, Azuregos stands atop your entire raid. Run to his sides as quickly as possible. Don't run outside of his teleporting range. Hunters' minimum range is a good measuring tool. That puts them far enough away to avoid many of the AoEs but close enough to be teleported. If you are unsure if you're too far away, find a Hunter to stand near.

Do not attack Azuregos for a few seconds after getting out from under him. Your main tank has had her aggro cleared and needs time to rebuild it. After a few seconds, re-engage.

SPELL REFLECTING

When Azuregos' claws glow with blue energy, he has activated his spell shield. Any spells cast at him during this time are reflected back on the caster. Casters should use wands while his shield is up.

Raid leaders should consider making macros to alert the raid to the raising and lowering of Azuregos' spell shield. This keeps members with their graphic settings turned down from being killed by their own spells.

MARK OF FROST

With the close proximity of the graveyard, the thought of running back to re-engage after dying is very appealing. Don't do this. Azuregos has lived longer than your entire raid combined and understands the power of a graveyard.

When you die, you're afflicted with Mark of Frost. This makes you more vulnerable to Azuregos if you resurrect during the next 15 minutes. Once afflicted with Azuregos' Mark of Frost, you become susceptible to his Aura of Frost. It freezes players that are simply near him. It's a good idea to wait for the Mark of Frost to fall before resurrecting unless there's an immediate need for your type of healing. If you do resurrect, do everything you can to stay away from Azuregos and just heal/attack from the fringes of the battle.

Should many of the members of the raid begin to fall, there is still hope. Keep the MT alive until raid members can resurrect without Mark of Frost. This draws out the battle considerably, but gives you another chance for victory.

THE ENGAGEMENT

Knowing what Azuregos does is the first step to defeating him. Knowing what you need to do and not do is just as important. Below is a list of recommendations that everyone needs to understand followed by a list organized by class.

GENERAL

What to Do

- Get Teleported
- Move out of combat for mana and health regeneration
- Stay alive

What not to Do

- Ressurect before Mark of Frost falls
- Run from Azuregos if you have aggro

DRUID

Druids can serve a variety of roles depending on need. Typically, you'll be filling either the role of tank or healer.

What to Do

- Move between forms as needed
- Assume the role of healing and know your primary target(s)
- Use HoTs

What not to Do

- Cast from long range
- Spam Moonfire

HUNTER

Hunters have a difficult role and the tools to accomplish it. They're attention is split between Azuregos and the surrounding area. No matter how your character is specialized, a Hunter can benefit the raid.

What to Do

- Stay mobile and attack when possible
- Send your pet to attack any mobs that add during the fight
- Feign Death to escape combat and eat/drink as necessary

What not to Do

- Have your pet Growl at Azuregos
- Fire from maximum range
- Use Feign Death against Azuregos

MAGE

Azuregos' mountain of hit points makes a Mage's life difficult. Running out of mana is unavoidable. Knowing how to manage your mana will keep you in the battle longer and help you be more effective.

What to Do

- Cast in bursts and use your wand while you regenerate mana
- Run out of range after Azuregos teleports and drink to get mana back
- Keep Frost Ward up

What not to Do

- Cast while Azuregos' spell shield is up
- Use Frost spells against a member of the Blue Dragonflight

PALADIN

It's unlikely that a Paladin will be able to hold Azuregos' attention well enough to be MT. However, having two Paladins on Azuregos to maintain both Judgment of Light and Wisdom is a great idea. Other Paladins should focus on healing, cleansing, and maintaining their Frost Resistance Aura.

What to Do

- Be ready to heal the MT and other healers
- Keep Blessing of Sacrifice on the tanks and Wisdom on the healers
- Stay in melee with Azuregos and keep Frost Resistance Aura up

What not to Do

- Try to tank Azuregos
- Allow the main tank to die
- Use Diving Intervention unless it's a raid-saving emergency

PRIEST

In a raid with an abundance of Priests, a Shadow Priest could actually perform moderately well as a secondary healer. Shadow Priests are also great for Shadow Weaving as a combo with the Warlocks of the raid. However, the normal rules of wanting a true healing Priest on the raid applies.

What to Do

- Focus healing on the MT, but keep your raid members alive
- Keep an eye on other healers' health
- Shield the tank when needed

What not to Do

- Use Mind Blast
- Stand too far away from Azuregos
- Run out of combat to regen mana without telling your backup

ROGUE

Rogues are pretty simple and straightforward. Many of your tricks in combat won't work against Azuregos. He's seen it all before.

What to Do

- Inflict max DPS
- Use Vanish to escape combat to regenerate health
- Use Instant Poison

What not to Do

- Try to stun Azuregos
- Stand in front of Azuregos
- Hit Azuregos after a teleport until the tank has

WARLOCK

Warlocks have some of the same duties as Hunters, but with a twist. Against enemies like Azuregos, the Warlock's ability to DoT or debuff really shines. While DPS is the Warlock's main function, be careful on timing. Casting Curse of Doom immediately before an Azuregos teleport could land you on top of the threat ladder.

What to Do

- Stack high-damage curses and DoTs on Azuregos
- Keep a phase-shifted imp out with Blood Pact for your party
- Focus on DPS and DoT adds when necessary

What not to Do

- Cast while Azuregos has his spell shield up
- Send your pet against Azuregos
- Stand too far from Azuregos

SHAMAN

Shaman have a lot on their plate. As a healer, damage dealer, or buffer, you won't be short of duties.

What to Do

- Heal when necessary
- Drop totems near casters and melee
- Cast in bursts to conserve mana

What not to Do

- Use Earth Shock
- Use Rock Biter
- Use your Ankh while Mark of Frost is active

WARRIOR

Warriors are likely to be in one of two positions. Either tank or melee DPS. While melee damage is simple, tanking Azuregos is not.

What to Do

- Use Sunder Armor
- Reestablish threat immediately after a teleport using any means necessary
- Use a shield

What not to Do

- Taunt adds
- Leave Defensive Stance for more than a brief time
- Waste rage on non-threat-generating abilities

DEFEATING THE OPPOSING FACTION

There is still something to be aware of. As Azuregos is an outdoor raid boss, the other faction can interfere with your assault force. Generally, common courtesy makes this a non-issue. Do not interfere with their fight and they shouldn't interfere with yours. However, the golden rule doesn't always have a place in Azeroth.

Should the other faction be unwilling to grant you a fair chance against Azuregos (or you fear they won't), remember all the other warriors of your side in the capital cities. Send word to them and ask for their assistance.

It's important that you do as little as possible to get yourself killed. On normal rule-set servers, this means do *not* put your PvP flag up. Should it be up, do not join the fight against Azuregos until it's down.

On PvP servers, having groups to defend your raid is often a necessity.

DRAGONS OF NIGHTMARE

Played & Written by: Tyler "Hocken" Morgan of <Pacifist> on Kel'thuzad

Emeriss, Lethon, Taerar, and Ysondre, once trusted servants of Ysera in the Emerald Dream, have been corrupted by the nightmare that's spread throughout the dream.

In their madness they've left the dream and entered Azeroth through portals scattered throughout the land, set on bringing destruction to the mortal realm.

YSERA AND THE GREEN DRAGONFLIGHT

Ysera, the great Dreaming dragon Aspect rules over the enigmatic green dragonflight. Her domain is the fantastic, mystical realm of the Emerald Dream - and it is said that from there she guides the evolutionary path of the world itself. She is the protector of nature and imagination, and it is the charge of her flight to guard all of the Great Trees across the world, which only druids use to enter the Dream itself.

In recent times, Ysera's most trusted lieutenants have been warped by a dark new power within the Emerald Dream. Now these wayward sentinels have passed through the Great Trees into Azeroth, intending to spread madness and terror throughout the mortal kingdoms. Even the mightiest of adventurers would be well advised to give the dragons a wide berth, or suffer the consequences of their misguided wrath.

LOCATIONS

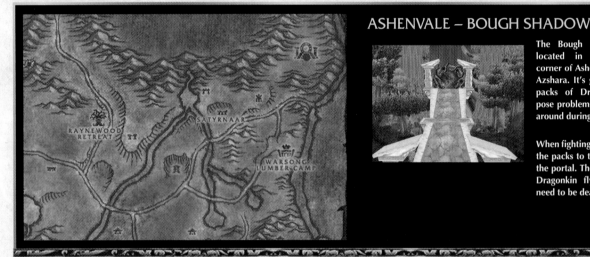

ASHENVALE – BOUGH SHADOW

The Bough Shadow portal is located in the northeastern corner of Ashenvale, just west of Azshara. It's guarded by several packs of Dragonkin that can pose problems if you leave them around during the battle.

When fighting in Ashenvale, clear the packs to the left and right of the portal. There is also a named Dragonkin flying around; he'll need to be dealt with as well.

DUSKWOOD – THE TWILIGHT GROVE

The portal in the Twilight Grove is the only portal without Dragonkin guarding it. It's located within the ring of mountians in the middle of Duskwood.

FERALAS – DREAM BOUGH

The Dream Bough is in the north of Feralas, just south of the Desolace border. It's on an island populated by Dragonkin.

When fighting in Feralas, clear the pack to the right of the portal. Clearing the pack on the left doesn't hurt, but isn't absolutely necessary. There's also a named Dragonkin flying around in front of the portal that needs to be killed.

HINTERLANDS – SERADANE

Seradane is in the northeastern area of the Hinterlands. It's patrolled by Dragonkin who guard the portal in packs.

When fighting in the Hinterlands, the only pack you need to clear is on the path in front of the portal. There's also a named Dragonkin flying around - Rothos - on a large patrol route. Make sure to kill him to prevent him from wandering into your raid during the battle.

SPAWNS

The four dragons spawn simultaneously at their separate shrines. However, there's not a set shrine allocated to each dragon and they often switch their spawn positions. They typically spawn within 3-5 days of a server restart.

It's difficult to predict exactly when they'll spawn, but since they all spawn at the same time, the entire server will know when they're up.

This can be challenging on a PvP server since the raid can easily be hampered by a roaming group of enemy players. It's best to get some guildies to post up near the edges of the battle to alert the raid of incoming fighters.

The best advice I can give is to make alts and park them at each of the spawn points. Check them frequently throughout the week to see if anything has spawned.

PERFECT TIMING

Did your raid group just finish an Onyxia, MC, or BWL run? Check the Dragon spawn points before everyone takes off! The time immediately after completing a raid is a great time to go after world spawns.

SHARED TRAITS

All Ysera's underlings in the green dragonflight are similar in a few ways. They have special abilities that are universal and it's good to know what generalities you can assume prior to taking them on.

MARK OF NATURE

You receive Mark of Nature whenever any of the four dragons causes your death. This is a 15-minute debuff that immediately puts you to sleep if you approach an Emerald Dragon who's engaged in combat. Azuregos casts a similar debuff, Mark of Frost, that prevents people from engaging him while they have it.

Mark of Nature exists so that you can't "graveyard zerg" the dragons. If someone dies during a fight with any Emerald Dragon, they're out of the fight for 15 minutes. However, there is one exception with Lethon which is discussed later. Anyone with the Mark of Nature should immediately release and run back, but their usefulness is extremely limited when they return.

INTERVAL SPECIALS

Each of the dragons has a special ability that they use three times during their battles. The ability's cast when they reach *roughly* 75%, 50%, and 25% of their health: +/- a couple percent. The variance to the interval was a recent inclusion to offer more challenge to the battles. However, the attack/ability is the same at each interval and if you make it past the first wave successfully, your raid should be in good shape to finish the dragon off.

The special attack is specific to each dragon as is covered later in this section. It bears repeating that the interval specials *do not* occur at *exactly* 25% intervals. The strategies listed have taken that variance into account, but each encounter changes depending on exactly when those interval specials are triggered. Whether a dragon's ability is triggered at 77% or 73% could be the difference between success or defeat.

DREAM FOG

All the dragons spread clouds of green gas that put everyone nearby to sleep for 5 seconds. There are two clouds that randomly roam around that will cause people to sleep.

The clouds are easy to spot. They move quickly and their sleep range is slightly bigger than the cloud itself. Being put to sleep by these dragons won't do any damage; it just incapacitates the unlucky individual caught in its spell. This effect can't be dispelled.

The easiest way to deal with the clouds is to avoid them, but there are times when they sneak up on you. Overall, they're more of an annoyance than anything else. It doesn't really matter if DPS classes get slept; it's the healers that need to be careful.

The MT occasionally gets put to sleep by the cloud. This usually isn't a big deal as long as you have an off tank ready to snag Azuregos' aggro. It's a fine line trying to keep an off tank in the second spot on the threat list, but it's a tactic that could save the raid from having to deal with a few high-DPS players going down quickly.

NOXIOUS BREATH

What's a dragon without a breath attack? Every member of Ysera's dragonflight has a nature-damage breath attack that hits everyone in front of them.

Two things happen when you're hit with Noxious Breath: 1) you lose a significant amount of life throughout the duration of the breath to a DoT effect and 2) your ability/spell cool downs are increased by 10 seconds per stack.

The breath stacks up to six times. This means that someone who has Noxious Breath stacked on them six times will be taking thousands of nature damage per second, as well as having their abilities take an additional 60 seconds to cool down.

Ideally, only the MT should be the only one ever hit by the breath. The dragons should never be facing the raid in such a way that Noxious Breath hits everyone. A solid raid group can usually withstand a few erroneous breaths on large amounts of people, but absorbing too many wastes too much mana keeping everyone alive.

It's important that everyone understands the MT has up to 60-second cool downs on their threat generating skills. DPS classes have to be extremely careful not to pull aggro off the MT since they're not generating nearly as much threat as they can on most other bosses.

These aren't quick, "DPS the boss down as quickly as possible" fights. They're slow, controlled fights. If you try to rush anything, especially damage, you'll find yourself wiping.

TAIL SWEEP

Each dragon will knock back anyone behind them and inflict 600-1000 points of damage. This is a typical dragon attack and can be easily avoided by never standing behind them.

☼ THE HOARD

The four dragons have the chance to drop the same equipment. It's well worth trying to coax it out of them; rather, it's well worth the time it takes to slay the dragons. Treasure is always a strong impetus in the search for (and subsequent felling of) Azeroth's strongest bosses. These dragons are no exception.

DROPS

ITEM	LEVEL	DESCRIPTION/STATS	DRAGON (IF DRAGON-SPECIFIC)
ACID INSCRIBED GREAVES	Plate Feet	559 Armor, +19 STA, +8 STR, +25 Nature Resistance	
Passive: Increased Defense +6			
ACID INSCRIBED PAULDRONS	Plate Shoulder	610 Armor, +16 STA, +12 STR, +25 Nature Resistance	YSONDRE ONLY
Passive: Increased Defense +6			
ANCIENT CORRODED LEGGINGS	Mail Legs	401 Armor, +33 AGI, +16 INT, +11 SPI, +21 STA	
BELT OF THE DARK BOG	Cloth Waist	61 Armor, +16 STA, +8 INT, +25 Nature Resistance	LETHON ONLY
Passive: Increases damage and healing done by magical spells and effects by up to 14			
BLACK BARK WRISTBANDS	Cloth Wrist	48 Armor, +15 STA, +4 INT, +4 SPI	LETHON ONLY
Passive: Increases damage and healing done by magical spells and effects by up to 25			
BOOTS OF THE ENDLESS MOOR	Mail Feet	311 Armor, +16 STA, +12 INT, +25 Nature Resistance	EMERISS ONLY
Passive: Restores 3 mana per 5 sec.			
BOOTS OF FRIGHT	Leather Feet	148 Armor, +12 INT, +10 SPI, +11 STA	TAERAR ONLY
Passive: Increases damage and healing done by magical spells and effects by up to 34			
CIRCLET OF RESTLESS DREAMS	Leather Head	175 Armor, +21 AGI, +38 STA	EMERISS ONLY
Passive: Increased Daggers +6			
DARK HEART PANTS	Leather Legs	296 Armor, +20 STA, +48 Attack Power	LETHON ONLY
Passive: Improves your chance to get a critical strike by 2%			

ITEM	LEVEL	DESCRIPTION/STATS	DRAGON (IF DRAGON-SPECIFIC)
DEVIATE GROWTH CAP	Leather Head	175 Armor, +16 STA, +14 INT	LETHON ONLY
Passive: Increases healing done by spells and effects by up to 64			
Passive: Restores 8 mana per 5 sec.			
Passive: Improves your chance to get a critical strike with spells by 1%			
DRAGONBONE WRISTGUARDS	Plate Wrist	351 Armor, +13 STA, +9 STR	
Passive: Increases your chance to parry an attack by 1%.			
DRAGONHEART NECKLACE	Neck	+21 STA, +6 INT, +6 SPI, +24 Attack Power	EMERISS ONLY
DRAGONSPUR WRAPS	Leather Wrist	93 Armor, +17 STA, +4 Fire Resistance, +4 Nature Resistance, +4 Frost Resistance, +4 Shadow Resistance, +4 Arcane Resistance, +32 Attack Power	
EMERALD DRAGONFANG	One-Hand Dagger	66-123 Damage, Speed: 1.80, 52.5 DPS, +12 AGI	YSONDRE ONLY
Chance on Hit: Blasts the enemy with acid for 87 to 105 Nature damage			
GAUNTLETS OF THE SHINING LIGHT	Plate Hands	509 Armor, +15 STR, +12 AGI, +16 INT, +10 SPI, +15 STA	LETHON ONLY
Passive: Increases healing done by spells and effects by up to 22			
GLOVES OF DELUSIONAL POWER	Cloth Hands	69 Armor, +14 STA, +16 INT	
Passive: Restores 5 mana per 5 sec.			
Passive: Increases damage and healing done by magical spells and effects by up to 27			
GREEN DRAGONSKIN CLOAK	Back	54 Armor, +12 STA, +20 Nature Resistance	
Passive: Restores 3 health every 5 sec.			
HAMMER OF BESTIAL FURY	Main-Hand Mace	69-130 Damage, Speed: 1.90, 52.4 DPS, 90 Armor, +13 STR, +12 STA, +154 Attack Power (Cat, Bear, and Dire Bear forms only)	
HIBERNATION CRYSTAL	Trinket		YSONDRE ONLY
Use: Increases healing done by magical spells and effects by up to 350 for 15 seconds			
JADE INLAID VESTMENTS	Cloth Chest	109 Armor, +18 INT, +16 STA, +8 SPI	YSONDRE ONLY
Passive: Increases damage and healing done by magical spells and effects by up to 44			
LEGGINGS OF THE DEMENTED MIND	Mail Legs	401 Armor, +26 INT, +25 STA, +16 SPI, +8 STR	YSONDRE ONLY
Passive: Increases healing done by spells and effects by up to 40			
MALIGNANT FOOTGUARDS	Mail Feet	315 Armor, +10 STR, +14 INT, +12 STA, +11 SPI	LETHON ONLY
Passive: Increases damage and healing done by magical spells and effects by up to 27			
MENDICANT'S SLIPPERS	Cloth Feet	75 Armor, +23 INT, +12 STA, TAERAR ONLY	TAERAR ONLY
Equip: Restores 10 mana per 5 sec.			
MINDTEAR BAND	Finger	+6 INT, +8 STA	TAERAR ONLY
Passive: Increases damage and healing done by magical spells and effects by up to 22			
Passive: Improves your chance to get a critical strike with spells by 1%			
NIGHTMARE BLADE	One-Hand Sword	99-185 Damage, Speed: 2.70, 52.6 DPS, 70 Armor, +9 STA, +32 Attack Power	TAERAR ONLY
NIGHTMARE ENGULFED OBJECT	Starts Quest		
POLISHED IRONWOOD CROSSBOW	Crossbow	101-153 Damage, Speed: 3.10, 41.0 DPS, +5 STA, +7 Nature Resistance, +24 Attack Power	EMERISS ONLY
RING OF THE UNLIVING	Finger	+21 AGI, +16 STA	EMERISS ONLY
STAFF OF RAMPANT GROWTH	Staff	113-184 Damage, Speed: 2.60, 57.1 DPS, +16 INT, +12 STA, +20 Nature Resistance	
Passive: Increases healing done by spells and effects by up to 84			
Passive: Restores 11 mana per 5 sec.			
STAFF OF RAMPANT GROWTH	Staff	113-184 Damage, Speed: 2.60, 57.1 DPS, +16 INT, +12 STA, +20 Nature Resistance	
Passive: Increases healing done by spells and effects by up to 84			
Passive: Restores 11 mana per 5 sec			
STRANGELY GLYPHED LEGPLATES	Plate Legs	712 Armor, +20 STR, +12 AGI, +21 INT, +16 SPI, +20 STA	YSONDRE ONLY
Passive: Increases healing done by spells and effects by up to 29			
TRANCE STONE	Off-Hand	+9 STA, +8 INT, +8 SPI	
Passive: Increases damage and healing done by magical spells and effects by up to 25			
UNNATURAL LEATHER SPAULDERS	Leather Shoulder	161 Armor, +19 STA, +8 SPI, +25 Nature Resistance, +18 Attack Power	TAERAR ONLY

EMERISS

A mysterious dark power within the Emerald Dream has transformed the once-majestic Emeriss into a rotting, diseased monstrosity. Reports from the few who have survived encounters with the dragon have told horrifying tales of putrid mushrooms erupting from the corpses of their dead companions. Emeriss is truly the most gruesome and appalling of Ysera's estranged green dragons.

The Emeriss encounter can be incredibly challenging to learn and sometimes near impossible to overcome on a PvP server, but if you can get an experienced raid and no opposition, he isn't all that bad.

ABILITIES

Spore Cloud

Whenever someone dies to Emeriss, they turn into a mushroom. Anyone who gets near a mushroom will be stunned and take thousands of damage from Spore Cloud. Only level 60 players create mushrooms when they die.

Solution

Ideally, don't die and there won't be any mushrooms. Realistically, avoid the mushrooms at all costs. Move Emeriss around as needed if there are mushrooms near the MT or healers.

Volatile Infection

Emeriss randomly casts Volatile Infection on nearby players. The player hit and people near them will take around 1000 nature damage every 2 seconds.

Solution

Thankfully, Volatile Infection is a curable disease. Make sure someone who can cure diseases is constantly watching for it and cleansing it immediately.

SPECIAL - Corruption of the Earth

Emeriss' interval special can be devastating to a raid if not handled correctly. Everyone afflicted with this spell receives a debuff that reduces their life by 20% every 2 seconds for 10 seconds. Essentially, it's death unless you receive healing during those 10 seconds.

Solution

The detailed strategy is listed within "The Fight" section, but the concept is to have most of your raid avoid being hit (by fleeing) and ride back in to save the poor souls that risked their lives to keep Emeriss at bay for those 10 seconds.

PREPARATION

The MT should have as much Nature Resist gear as possible and there should be a Hunter in their group giving Aspect of the Wild.

Groups 1-3 need to be well-balanced with plenty of healing and ranged DPS. These three groups will be remaining at Emeriss' location for the interval special attack. Everyone else will be running away.

THE FIGHT

Clear the necessary Dragonkin packs and named Dragonkin flying around before doing anything else; you don't want adds during the fight. Pulling Emeriss is easy; have the MT walk up to the portal, shoot him, and run down into tanking position.

The tanking location doesn't really matter as long as Emeriss is pointed away from the rest of the raid. Only the MT should be hit by the Noxious Breath attack.

Once he's in a good position and being tanked, give the MT time to build aggro. Remember, the cool downs of the MT's abilities are increased by 10 seconds with every stack of Noxious Breath. Give them time to build enough threat.

Shortly after Emeriss is engaged, the two sleep clouds appear and begin chasing after your healers. Avoid them as needed.

As soon as the MT has built 30-45 seconds of aggro, DPS classes can engage. Take it slow, there is no need to rush the fight and you don't want to pull aggro off the MT.

Keep DPS steady until 79% life. At 79% life everyone needs to stop attacking (except the MT, of course). This can't be stressed enough. *Everyone has to stop attacking at 79%!* You do not want to preemptively cause his interval special.

At roughly 80% life, everyone except groups 1-3 needs to run away until they are out of combat. Being out of combat guarantees that you won't be hit by Corruption of the Earth.

Once Groups 4-8 have run away and are out of combat, the remaining three groups should bring him down and trigger his special. Be careful not to be put to sleep by the clouds; you need to be able to heal your group immediately after he casts his special attack.

At roughly 75% Emeriss casts his special: Corruption of the Earth. Everyone near Emeriss gets a debuff that reduces their life by 20% every 2 seconds for 10 seconds. This is a guaranteed death unless you get a heal during these 10 seconds.

Emeriss yells throughout the zone when he casts Corruption of the Earth. The second he yells, everyone who ran away should start running back in (preferably on their mounts). They need to get back to the fight and help heal everyone who was hit by Corruption of the Earth.

Priests should immediately cast Prayer of Healing on their group as the Druids and Paladins/Shaman keep the MT alive. Everyone has to get a heal or they'll die and turn into a mushroom.

Ideally, nobody should die during the initial Corruption of the Earth. Only groups 1-3 should be hit by it and everyone else should arrive shortly after to help heal.

If anyone has died and been turned into a mushroom, avoid it at all costs. Move the tanking position and the entire raid if necessary. Getting stuck next to a mushroom is usually a death sentence. The mushrooms have a snowball effect; as soon as one person dies and turns into a mushroom, someone else near them will die and turn into another mushroom that hits even more people. The mushrooms are extremely dangerous unless they're isolated and made easy to avoid.

If you made it through the first special without much trouble, you're well on your way to defeating Emeriss. DPS classes should start attacking again and bring him down to 54%.

At 54%, just repeat exactly what you did last time. Since this will be the second Corruption of the Earth, you may want to have one or two extra healers stay in, depending on the mana of group 1-3's healers. It usually isn't necessary for the second interval, but can be crucial during the final special.

That's all there is to it! Have most of the raid run away before the interval specials, don't let anyone die, and avoid the mushrooms if there are any. It's a slow, controlled fight. Don't rush it.

⊛ LETHON

Lethon's exposure to the aberration within the Emerald Dream not only darkened the hue of the mighty dragon's scales, but also empowered him with the ability to extract malevolent shades from his enemies. Once joined with their master, the shades imbue the dragon with healing energies. It should come as no surprise, then, that Lethon is considered to be among the most formidable of Ysera's wayward lieutenants.

Lethon is by far the hardest Emerald Dragon. Only experienced raid groups should even attempt him.

ABILITIES

Shadow Bolt Whirl

This is a rather complicated AoE Shadow Bolt attack that hits everyone for 800-1200 or so damage every 2 seconds.

Shadow Bolt Whirl only hits people on one side of Lethon at a time. Every time Lethon's feet glow black, he has cast Shadow Bolt Whirl. After four casts, the side that he's casting Shadow Bolts out of will change.

Solution

The main goal is to keep the side Shadow Bolt Whirl is being cast from pointed away from the raid by turning Lethon 180 degrees after every set of four casts. Sometimes, this is easier said than done.

One person has to be dedicated to calling out the turns. They need to watch Lethon's feet closely. Every time his feet glow black, it indicates that he's just cast Shadow Bolt Whirl. After every four casts, the caller must tell the MT to turn Lethon around. It's hard for the MT to see Lethon's feet since they're up close holding aggro. It's best to have a ranged DPS class take care of the calls.

Getting the count started can be difficult because the side that Shadow Bolt Whirl is being cast out of is random when he's initially engaged. If your entire raid is getting hit immediately after the pull, turn Lethon around right away. In the beginning, your raid may get hit by a few Shadow Bolts as the count is begun.

Once you have the count managed correctly, the caller must pay close attention to his feet, announcing turns consistently and accurately. This is a key part of the fight and there's little room for error.

A few times during the fight, the MT will be put to sleep by the green cloud when it's time to turn Lethon. The raid may get hit by a Shadow Bolt or two and the MT should turn Lethon as quickly as possible as soon as they are awake.

SPECIAL – Draw Spirit

Draw Spirit's two effects – stun and summoning shades – don't seem too horrible. That is, until you realize that the stun is a group stun and the shades Lethon summons each heal him for a reasonable amount should they reach him. One shade is summoned for every player near Lethon at the time of the casting.

Solution

Target the shades individually since they're immune to AoE effects and bring down as many as possible before they reach Lethon. It's to be expected that Lethon will be healed for roughly 10-40% at each interval and this should be taken into account regarding the length of the battle.

PREPARATION

Nothing special needs to be done with the group setup beyond having an MT with Nature Resist gear equipped and a Hunter in their group for Aspect of the Wild.

Make sure the Priests cast Shadow Protection on everyone before engaging. Many guilds quaff Greater Shadow Protection Potions for this battle and it's sound enough advice to be mentioned here.

THE FIGHT

Clear the needed packs around the portal before engaging. Track down any named Dragonkin flying around that need to be killed.

The pull should be straightforward. Have the MT walk up, shoot Lethon, and run down into the tanking position.

It's important that the raid is only on one side of Lethon. You can't surround him because people on the wrong side of him will be hit by Shadow Bolt Whirl.

Chances are that a few Shadow Bolts will hit everyone while the MT is moving into position. Turn Lethon 180 degrees if he's in position and the Shadow Bolts are still hitting people. Get the count started. Getting the Shadow Bolts counted correctly may take a minute in the beginning of the fight.

As soon as you have the Shadow Bolts under control, keep calling out those turns after his feet glow for the fourth time. Dealing with Shadow Bolt Whirl takes a lot of practice.

The sleep cloud should be making its way around, looking for people to put to sleep. Avoid it as necessary. If the MT gets put to sleep, keep counting the Shadow Bolts and turn him as soon as possible when needed.

Slowly take him down to 79%. Keep in mind the MT's abilities have up to an additional 60 seconds on cool downs and they won't be able to build nearly as much threat as they usually can. Make sure that the MT has not used their Mortal Strike ability up to this point. Immediately before the interval special ability is triggered, have the MT slam Lethon with Mortal Strike to reduce the potential healing from the upcoming shades in half. Do not pull aggro.

At roughly 75%, Lethon casts his special spell: Draw Spirit.

Draw Spirit has two effects: 1) group stun and 2) a summoning of shades that heal Lethon when they get close to him.

The stun is not a big deal. Lethon loses his current target and does not attack the MT while everyone is stunned. Also, the stun itself does not do any damage, making it easier for the raid to recover from the ability.

However, the shades can be rather annoying. A shade is summoned for every person near Lethon when he casts Draw Spirit. The shade runs directly to Lethon, ignoring the raid group and not attacking anyone. If the shade reaches Lethon, it heals him for a fair amount. To counter the effectiveness of the healing that the Shades offer, have your Warriors hit Lethon with Mortal Strike before (or immediately after) he casts Draw Spirit.

You should try to kill as many shades as possible. They're immune to AoE spells, so they must be targeted individually. It's almost impossible to kill all of them; expect Lethon to regain approximately 15-40% of his life every time he casts Draw Spirit.

Shadow Bolt Whirl is still being cast throughout the Draw Spirit stun. The player counting the casts and calling the turns should continue doing so.

Since Lethon heals himself three times throughout the fight with each cast of Draw Spirit, this can be a long battle. Conserve your mana, run away and drink if you must. Make sure there is always plenty of healing available for the MT.

Keep counting those turns and you'll be well on your way to providing Azeroth with a dead Lethon.

⊛ TAERAR

Taerar was perhaps the most affected of Ysera's rogue lieutenants. His interaction with the dark force within the Emerald Dream shattered Taerar's sanity as well as his corporeal form. The dragon now exists as a specter with the ability to split into multiple entities, each of which possesses destructive magical powers. Taerar is a cunning and relentless foe who is intent on turning the madness of his existence into reality for the inhabitants of Azeroth.

As long as you have good Warriors, Taerar isn't very hard to kill. He's probably the second easiest of the Dragons.

ABILITIES

Arcane Blast

Single-target random knock back attack that inflicts 1050 to 1350 points of Arcane damage.

Solution

This usually isn't a big deal. Make sure nobody gets knocked into a Dragonkin pack and brings adds.

Bellowing Roar

Taerar Fears everyone within 30 yards about every 30 seconds.

Solution

Alliance: Use Fear Ward on the MT.
Horde: Use Tremor Totems and Berserker Rage.

SPECIAL – Shades of Taerar

Taerar summons three Shades of Taerar into the battle while banishing himself. The three Shades have two abilities: 1) a breath effect similar to, but weaker than, Taerar's, and 2) a poisonous cloud that swirls beneath their feet.

Solution

Have the off tanks quickly grab the aggro of all three Shades. Then, with the help of the MA, begin taking down the Shades one by one.

PREPARATION

The MT should be wearing as much Nature Resist gear as possible and have a Hunter in their group for Aspect of the Wild.

Three off-tanks (OTs) are needed during the fight. Make sure the Warriors who are off-tanking have strong healing in their group.

Beyond that, evenly distribute classes as usual.

THE FIGHT

Clear any Dragonkin packs around the portal and any named Dragonkin flying around. You don't want them adding halfway through the fight.

Have the MT pull Taerar into position. Once he's properly situated, give the MT 30 seconds or so to build threat. After the MT has built a decent amount of threat up, DPS classes can begin attacking. DPS classes need to keep in mind that the MT has up to 60 seconds added to the cool downs of their threat generating abilities and won't be able to build nearly as much threat as they can against most bosses.

Be careful with your damage output and don't pull aggro off the MT! Slowly take him down to trigger the first interval special. At roughly 75% Taerar banishes himself and splits into three Shades of Taerar. Get the three Shades tanked immediately. They can't be allowed to run around killing healers. The OTs should pick them up right away.

Each Shade has two abilities: 1) a breath attack similar to but not nearly as powerful as Noxious Breath, and 2) the ability to summon green clouds of poison under them. Make sure the Shades are pointed away from the raid so that the breath attack does not hit anyone but the Warrior tanking it, and make sure you move the Shade out of the poison cloud when it appears.

Assist and kill the Shades one at a time. Taerar remains banished until either the last Shade falls or time "runs out" and Taerar rejoins the fight sensing that his Shades were not killed in a timely manner. Before the last Shade dies, make sure the MT is in position, ready to go back to tanking Taerar.

As soon as all the Shades are dead, Taerar removes the Banish on himself and begins attacking again. If you can get through the first split without much trouble, the second split shouldn't be too hard either. Be ready to pick up the Shades for tanking at the remaining two intervals.

Burn him down slowly, get the Shades tanked right as they spawn, kill the Shades one at a time, and you'll have a dead Taerar!

⊛ YSONDRE

Once one of Ysera's most trusted lieutenants, Ysondre has now gone rogue, sewing terror and chaos across the land of Azeroth. Her formerly beneficent healing powers have given way to dark magics, enabling her to cast smoldering lightning waves and summon the aid of fiendish druids. Ysondre and her kin also possess the ability to induce sleep, sending her unfortunate mortal foes to the realm of their most terrifying nightmares.

Ysondre is an extremely easy fight and a great green dragonflight choice to start with.

ABILITIES

Lightning Wave

This is a multi-target spell that increases in power through the "chain" of nearby targets. The primary target receives 525 base Nature damage and each of the successive nine targets (ten total) receives successively greater damage. The last player hit suffers approximately 2500 points of Nature damage.

Solution

Spread out during the battle to prevent the wave from jumping to another target. If there's not a new target within range of the current one, the spell ends. This isn't a horribly powerful spell and general healing should be able to handle the damage inflicted. However, keep in mind that should a caster be the final link in the chain, someone could fall.

SPECIAL – Demented Druid Spirits

Ysondre summons a Demented Druid Spirit for every member of the raid. The Druid Spirits have various spells that are addressed in "The Fight" section.

Solution

Focus on the Demented Druid Spirits and let the MT tank Ysondre. Her summoned allies fall quickly from AoE and the raid should wipe them out before resuming their attack on Ysondre.

PREPARATION

Nothing special is needed for Ysondre other than having an MT wearing Nature Resist gear and a Hunter in their group for Aspect of the Wild.

THE FIGHT

Clear out the packs around the portal and kill the named Dragonkin flying around so that they don't add during the fight.

The pull should be pretty straightforward. Have the MT run up, shoot Ysondre, and run down to the tanking position.

Once Ysondre's in position, let the MT build about 30 seconds of threat before engaging. After 30 seconds, DPS classes can begin attacking. Keep in mind that the MT's threat generating abilities have up to 60 seconds added to their cool downs and the MT won't be able to generate nearly as much threat as they usually can. Be careful with your damage output; do not pull aggro from the MT.

Slowly bring Ysondre's health down to trigger her first interval special. At roughly 75%, Ysondre summons a Demented Druid Spirit for every member of the raid group. The Druid Spirits have three spells at their disposal: Moonfire, Silence, and Curse of Thorns which causes the target to suffer 158 to 202 damage 50% of the time that they inflict a melee attack. Curse of Thorns lasts for 3 minutes or until it's dispelled.

The Demented Druid Spirits are susceptible to AoE spells and aren't the toughest enemies. Have the raid focus on killing the spirits while the MT holds Ysondre's attention. Once the final spirit falls, resume the assault on the green dragon.

That's all there is to this fight. Trigger each of her second and third intervals carefully and deal with the Demented Druid Spirits in the same manner as you did the first time. She'll soon fall and you'll be the victors!

NIGHTMARE ENGULFED OBJECT

Every Emerald Dragon always drops a **Nightmare Engulfed Object**. This is used to start a quest.

SHROUDED IN NIGHTMARE

Quest Level	60
Location	Moonglade
Starts at	Nightmare Engulfed Object
Ends at	Keeper Remulos
Goal	Bring the object to Keeper Remulos, maybe it provides a clue as to why the Emerald Dragons are leaving the dream.
Reward	Malfurion's Signet Ring (+17 STA, +20 Nature Resistance)

The Nightmare Englufed Object may have something to do with the Emerald Dragons' presence on Azeroth. Seek out Keeper Remulos in Moonglade and present the object to him.

The quest can only be completed once per character.

LORD KAZZAK

Played & Written by: Edwin "Plainsong" Kern of <Dovrani> on Kirin Tor

The Blasted Lands will never be safe again. The wildlife has been forever tainted by the demonic energies issuing froth from the Dark Portal. Demons of incredible power have made the Tainted Scar their home.

A demon lord has made himself known. Lord Kazzak resides with his minions in the Tainted Scar. What evil is he plotting from inside the dying valley? A pre-emptive strike will keep his plots from coming to fruition.

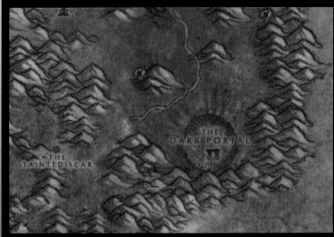

ENCOUNTER INFORMATION

Location	Blasted Lands (Tainted Scar)
Quests	Priest
Region	Contested
Suggested Level	60
Group Allowed	Raid of 40
Enemy Type	Demon
Time to Complete	3 Minutes of fighting, 10-15 minutes of travel

GETTING TO LORD KAZZAK

Lord Kazzak resides deep in the Tainted Scar of the Blasted Lands. Alliance raids should fly into Nethergarde keep while Horde raids have to come from Stonard in the Swamp of Sorrows.

WHO TO BRING

With 40 people, you're likely to have most of what you need to defeat the demon lord. Mages and Druids are important as they can cast Remove Curse. Priests and Paladins with Dispel Magic are equally important. Beyond a main (MT) and off (OT) tank, fill your raid with DPS classes. The fight against Lord Kazzak has to be fast.

WHAT TO BRING

The fight against Lord Kazzak is fast and frantic. Items that regenerate health and mana over time are not as useful as items that provide additional STA or INT. Elixirs of Demonslaying are the perfect choice for this battle and should be quaffed by all DPS-focused classes taking on Lord Kazzak.

Potions that increase damage, provide protection from Shadow damage, or restore health or mana are also important. Mana users need to trust the healers of the raid and use the mana potions, while non-mana users should bring the health potions.

QUESTS FOR LORD KAZZAK

Only Priests have a quest that involves Lord Kazzak. All other raid members are here for the items this monster plans to use to bring the downfall of both the Alliance and the Horde

PRIEST QUESTS

QUEST NAME	QUEST GIVER	QUEST GIVER LOCATION	QUEST RECEIVER	QUEST RECEIVER LOCATION	CHAIN?	MAX EXPERIENCE
Balance of Light and Shadow	Drop: Eye of Divinity	Cache of the Firelord	Molten Core		Yes	
Balance of Light and Shadow	Eris Havenfire	Eastern Plaguelands	Eris Havenfire	Eastern Plaguelands	Yes	
REWARD: Splinter of Nordrassil						
Balance of Light and Shadow	Eris Havenfire	Eastern Plaguelands			Yes	
REWARD: Benediction (Staff, 59.3 DPS, +31 INT, +10 STA, +12 SPI, +20 Shadow Resistance, Use: Calls forth Anathema, Passive: Increases the critical effect chance of your healing spells by 2%, Increases healing done by spells and effects by up to 106, Priest Only)						
REWARD: Anathema (Staff, 59.3 DPS, +31 INT, +22 STA, +20 Shadow Resistance, Use: Calls forth Benediction, Passive: Restores 7 mana every 5 seconds, Increases damage done by Shadow spells and effects by up to 69, Priest Only)						

BALANCE OF LIGHT AND SHADOW (RAID)

Quest Level	60 to obtain
Class	Priest
Location	Molten Core
Quest Giver	Eye of Divinity
Goal	Use the Splinter of Nordrassil to combine the Eye of Divinity and the Eye of Shadow
Max Experience Gained	None
Reward	None

After forcing Majordomo to concede in Molten Core, you're given a chance to open the Cache of the Firelord. An Eye of Divinity may be inside. Should it be, the Priests of the raid should decide (through debate or rolling) who will get the Eye. Only one Priest can get it each time and it's not always in the cache.

Once you have the Eye, journey to Eastern Plaguelands. Eris Havenfire waits inside a cave near Stratholme. She can only be seen with the Eye of Divinity equipped. This means the quest she gives must be completed alone.

BALANCE OF LIGHT AND SHADOW

Quest Level	60 to obtain
Class	Priest
Location	Eastern Plaguelands
Quest Giver	Eris Havenfire
Goal	Save 50 Peasants before 15 die
Max Experience Gained	None
Reward	Splinter of Nordrassil

Speaking with Eris begins the event immediately, so come prepared. Groups of peasants are fleeing Stratholme. You must escort them to the light while keeping them alive. They're being attacked by both melee and ranged skeletons.

You can't do anything about the ranged skeletons, but the melee skeletons go down quickly using Oil of Immolation and Stratholme Holy Water. Keep the melee skeletons down and use Renew and low-level heals to keep the ranged skeletons from claiming any peasants.

Many of the peasants glow green or purple with poison or disease. They need to be cured quickly. Keep a watch on your charge as they can become poisoned or diseased again.

Escort the peasants in groups of 10-15 from Stratholme to the light. When you have saved 50 before 15 die, return to Eris.

BALANCE OF LIGHT AND SHADOW (RAID)

Quest Level	60 to obtain
Class	Priest
Location	Eastern Plaguelands
Quest Giver	Eris Havenfire
Goal	Use the Splinter of Nordrassil to combine the Eye of Divinity and the Eye of Shadow
Max Experience Gained	None
Reward	Benediction (Staff, 59.3 DPS, +31 INT, +10 STA, +12 SPI, +20 Shadow Resistance, Use: Calls forth Anathema, Passive: Increases the critical effect chance of your healing spells by 2%, Increases healing done by spells and effects by up to 106, Priest Only)
Reward	Anathema (Staff, 59.3 DPS, +31 INT, +22 STA, +20 Shadow Resistance, Use: Calls forth Benediction, Passive: Restores 7 mana every 5 seconds, Increases damage done by Shadow spells and effects by up to 69, Priest Only)

A difficult task is still ahead. You have secured the Eye of Divinity and the Splinter of Nordrassil. Now you must find the Eye of Shadow.

Lord Kazzak guards this and will not let it go without a fight. Gather your forces and take the fight to this lord of demons. The quest reward for this is a Priest-specific staff. Benediction and Anathema are two sides of the same coin. "Using" the staff switches it between its healing version and its damage version.

AN ARMORY OF MAGIC INTENDED TO CONQUER AZEROTH

ITEM	TYPE	STATS
AMBERSEER KEEPER	Staff	56.4 DPS, +20 INT, +5 Fire/Nature/Frost/Shadow/Arcane Resistance
PASSIVE: Restores 12 mana per 5 seconds PASSIVE: Increases damage and healing done by magical spells and effects by up to 44		
BLACKLIGHT BRACER	Cloth Wrist	44 Armor, +13 INT, +8 SPI, +11 STA
PASSIVE: Improves your chance to get a critical strike with spells by 1%		
BLAZEFURY MEDALLION	Neck	+13 AGI, +14 STA, +12 Fire Resistance
PASSIVE: Adds 2 Fire damage to your melee attacks		
DOOMHIDE GAUNTLETS	Leather Hands	133 Armor, +13 AGI, +14 STA, +8 Fire/Shadow Resistance
PASSIVE: +42 Attack Power		
EMPYREAN DEMOLISHER	Main-Hand Mace	48 DPS
CHANCE ON HIT: Increases your attack speed by 20% for 10 seconds		

ITEM	TYPE	STATS
ESKANDAR'S PELT	Cloak	51 Armor, +20 STA
PASSIVE: Improves your chance to get a critical strike by 1%		
EYE OF SHADOW	Quest Item	
FEL INFUSED LEGGINGS	Cloth Legs	95 Armor, +21 STA
PASSIVE: Increases damage done by Shadow spells and effects by up to 64		
FLAYED DOOMGUARD BELT	Leather Waist	115 Armor, +18 INT, +18 STA
PASSIVE: Improves your chance to get a critical strike with spells by 1%		
PASSIVE: Increases damage and healing done by magical spells and effects by up to 14		
INFERNAL HEADCAGE	Mail Head	358 Armor, +25 INT, +13 SPI, +24 STA, +10 Fire/Shadow Resistance
PASSIVE: Increases damage and healing done by magical spells and effects by up to 16		
RING OF ENTROPY	Ring	+13 INT, +11 STA, +8 SPI
PASSIVE: Improves your chance to get a critical strike with spells by 1%		

⊗ DEFEATING LORD KAZZAK

SETTING UP

GATHERING POINT

First, begin to gather at the entrance to the Tainted Scar. There are roaming enemies throughout this area, so don't rush in solo.

Once you have at least 10 members of your raid together, begin clearing your way southeast. Climb the incline to see Lork Kazzak patrolling around a crater. When he's on the north side of the crater, move around the southern side of the crater. There should still be enemies in your way, but don't stop to fight them until you have arrived at the Gathering Point.

With a Warlock and friends, the rest of the raid has an easy way to reach you.

No enemies will come within aggro range of your raid. Begin summoning and organizing groups. Each group should have a Mage or Druid for removing curses and a Priest or Paladin for dispelling magic. If you don't have enough decursers/dispellers in the raid to supply one of each to each party, there are other options. Pulling the health bars for other parties so you can see the debuffs is one option. There are also user mods (Decursive) that assist in debuff removal for the entire raid. Take advantage of whatever situation/alternative presents itself and be ready for a lot of action.

Take the time to fully buff your raid. The actually fight is very short and you'll need every buff you have. Mark of the Wild, Power Word: Fortitude, Arcane Intellect and Shadow Resistance are very helpful. Also take this time to dismiss all pets.

A FRANTIC FIGHT

Lord Kazzak has little patience for the interference of mortals. Once the fight begins, you have 3 minutes to destroy the massive demon before he increases the rate at which he throws Shadow Bolt Volley. Essentially, this could wipe a raid, so use that 3 minute point as a benchmark time.

There is little time for directions and orders, so knowing what he'll throw at you and how to react can save your raid.

Capture Soul: Should any member of your raid die, Kazzak regains a great deal of health. For this reason, do not let any member die for any reason.

Cleave: While Kazzak's normal melee attacks are not devastating, his Cleave hits multiple people in his front melee arc for reasonable damage. Should Kazzak decide to Cleave several times in a short period, your frontal melee members are likely to be looking the worse for wear. Make sure to keep your non-tank, melee DPS players behind Kazzak to avoid the Cleave.

Void Bolt: Being a demon lord, Kazzak's magical attacks are extremely dangerous. Should he tire of your MT's existence, he can blast them for incredible damage. The good news is that it's Shadow damage and any Shadow Resist gear/buffs will keep the tank from dying instantly.

Keep your MT at high health to keep Kazzak from presenting a terrible surprise—your MT's dead body on the field of battle.

Shadow Bolt Volley: One of Lord Kazzak's most damaging spells is his Shadow Bolt Volley. It hits every member in your raid for substantial Shadow damage. This attack ignores line of sight. Heal people lowest on health first in case Kazzak decides to cast a second.

If you're low on health, use a potion. Death is unacceptable. Should your fight last longer than 3 minutes, Kazzak will declare himself supreme and cast this spell every second to the demise of your raid.

Twisted Reflection: Kazzak can magically debuff a random person in your raid. This debuff restores a great amount of health to Kazzak any time the debuffed target takes damage. Priests and Paladins need to be on top of their game and keep this dispelled. Raid members affected by this should declare so in party or raid chat to speed dispelling.

Mark of Kazzak: The most common cause of early wipes against Lord Kazzak is this curse. It has two parts.

Part 1: It's a simple mana drain. The concern is how quickly your mana drains.

Part 2: When any raid member reaches zero mana, Kazzak causes them to explode and kill - or nearly kill - everyone around them. With Kazzak gaining health each time someone dies, this is a major concern.

Mages and Druids should remove this curse immediately. Members should report in party or raid chat any time they are afflicted. To give the Mages and Druids time to remove the curse, do not let your mana drop below 1,000. This gives them roughly 4 seconds to remove the curse before you explode.

THE ENGAGEMENT

With only 3 minutes to defeat Lord Kazzak, there isn't much room for error or time to perfect the techniques needed to bring him down. The incredibly long walk from the graveyard makes failure even more dismal.

GENERAL

What to Do

- Give the tank several seconds to establish aggro before engaging
- Use timed abilities to maximize damage output
- Stay alive at all costs

What not to Do

- Fall below 1,000 mana
- Allow yourself to be curse or debuffed without saying something

DRUID

Lord Kazzak's Mark of Kazzak and Shadow Bolt Volley are devastating. Druids should put their weapons away and stand with the healers where they are needed most.

What to Do

- Remove Mark of Kazzak as soon as possible
- Heal when needed
- Use HoTs on everyone not at full health

What not to Do

- Drop below 1,000 mana
- Spam Moonfire and unleash DPS capabilities

HUNTER

Without their pets, Hunters may feel a bit naked. This feeling quickly passes as their role is realized. Hunters are going to be relied on to do damage. The more the better.

What to Do

- Let loose on the DPS
- Use Rapid Fire to increase damage
- Use Trueshot Aura to help the DPS of your party

What not to Do

- Get within melee range
- Drop below 1,000 mana

MAGE

Mages have a finite amount of mana and so much to do. They are part of the damage backbone of your raid and they have to keep the raid uncursed. Do damage as long as you have mana, but be ready to turn off the DPS machine to keep your friends alive.

What to Do

- Dispel Mark of Kazzak as soon as possible
- Damage when you have mana
- Ice Block to avoid death

What not to Do

- Drop below 1,000 mana

PALADIN

Paladins serve extremely well as backup healers and off tanks when facing Azeroth's biggest bosses. Typically, two Paladins maintain constant Judgments of Light and Wisdom on the boss. The remaining Paladins should remain at range as healers using Blessing of Light and Flash of Light to heal the raid.

What to Do

- Cleanse Twisted Reflection as soon as possible
- Heal and Bless as time permits
- Stay at range unless the situation calls for some additional DPS

What not to Do

- Try to serve as MT
- Drop below 1,000 mana

PRIEST

Regardless of specialization, Priests are going to bear the brunt of the healing duties. Stay out of melee range, watch your mana and the health of everyone within range.

What to Do

- Keep your raid members alive
- Dispel Twisted Reflection as soon as possible
- Shield the tank when needed

What not to Do

- Use Shadow magic
- Drop below 1,000 mana

ROGUE

Rogues are pretty simple and straightforward. Many of your tricks in combat won't work against Kazzak. He's seen it all before, but damage is still damage.

What to Do

- Unload with your full DPS
- Bandage if low on health
- Use timed abilities to increase damage

What not to Do

- Try to stun Lord Kazzak
- Stand in front of Lord Kazzak

SHAMAN

Shaman have plenty to do. They fill the roles of support and secondary healer quite well.

What to Do

- Provide DPS enhancing and mana-regenerating totems depending on your location/role
- Heal when mana allows
- Engage Kazzak in melee if the situation allows

What not to Do

- Use Shocks since you're generally conserving mana for healing
- Drop below 1,000 mana

WARLOCK

Warlocks have some of the same duties as Hunters and they should focus on casting their heavy DoTs on Kazzak whenever they drop.

What to Do

- Stack curses and DoTs on Kazzak and maintain them throughout the battle
- Unlock the DPS potential allowed to your class
- Summon a phase-shifted imp with Blood Pact for the STA benefit

What not to Do

- Drop below 1,000 mana
- Use DPS or tanking pets

WARRIOR

Warriors are likely to be in one of two positions: MT or melee damage. While melee damage is simple, tanking Lord Kazzak is not.

What to Do

- Use Sunder Armor
- Unleash your full DPS and debuff potential by using any/all timed abilities
- Set up a process by which another tank can replace the MT if their health becomes an issue

What not to Do

- Allow Kazzak to run around
- Try to stun Lord Kazzak

ITEM SETS

The universally desired item sets are what drive adventurers into the deepest pits in Azeroth. The most incredible challenges offer the most amazing rewards. This section details what each set piece is, what bonuses the sets offer, and gives you an idea about what they'll look like on your character, provided it's a set that you can use.

SET LIST

Each class has a list of sets designed specifically to enhance their roles and augment their abilities. Granted, Dungeon Set 1 pieces are applicable to anyone that can wear that type of armor (Warriors and Paladins can wear every dungeon set), but it's assumed that even those are designed for a specific class. Here's the list so that you'll have an idea what to look for in the tables that follow this introduction.

Keep in mind that there are many additional sets and not all of them are armor. Some sets include trinkets, rings, and weapons in addition to or in lieu of the armor.

DRUID

Dungeon Set 1	Wildheart Raiment
Dungeon Set 2	Feralheart Raiment
Tier 1 Raid Set	Cenarion Raiment
Tier 2 Raid Set	Stormrage Raiment
Tier 3 Raid Set	Dreamwalker Raiment

HUNTER

Dungeon Set 1	Beaststalker Armor
Dungeon Set 2	Beastmaster Armor
Tier 1 Raid Set	Giantstalker Armor
Tier 2 Raid Set	Dragonstalker Armor
Tier 3 Raid Set	Cryptstalker Armor

MAGE

Dungeon Set 1	Magister's Regalia
Dungeon Set 2	Sorcerer's Regalia
Tier 1 Raid Set	Arcanist Regalia
Tier 2 Raid Set	Netherwind Regalia
Tier 3 Raid Set	Frostfire Regalia

PALADIN

Dungeon Set 1	Lightforge Armor
Dungeon Set 2	Soulforge Armor
Tier 1 Raid Set	Lawbringer Armor
Tier 2 Raid Set	Judgment Armor
Tier 3 Raid Set	Redemption Armor

PRIEST

Dungeon Set 1	Vestements of the Devout
Dungeon Set 2	Vestements of the Virtuous
Tier 1 Raid Set	Vestements of Prophecy
Tier 2 Raid Set	Vestements of Transcendence
Tier 3 Raid Set	Vestements of Faith

ROGUE

Dungeon Set 1	Shadowcraft Armor
Dungeon Set 2	Darkmantle Armor
Tier 1 Raid Set	Nightslayer Armor
Tier 2 Raid Set	Bloodfang Armor
Tier 3 Raid Set	Bonescythe Armor

SHAMAN

Dungeon Set 1	The Elements
Dungeon Set 2	The Five Thunders
Tier 1 Raid Set	The Earthfury Raiment
Tier 2 Raid Set	The Ten Storms Raiment
Tier 3 Raid Set	The Earthshatterer

WARLOCK

Dungeon Set 1	Dreadmist Raiment
Dungeon Set 2	Deathmist Raiment
Tier 1 Raid Set	Felheart Raiment
Tier 2 Raid Set	Nemesis Raiment
Tier 3 Raid Set	Plagueheart Raiment

WARRIOR

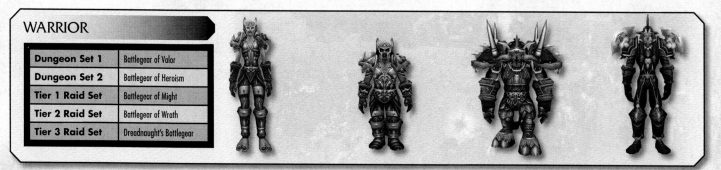

Dungeon Set 1	Battlegear of Valor
Dungeon Set 2	Battlegear of Heroism
Tier 1 Raid Set	Battlegear of Might
Tier 2 Raid Set	Battlegear of Wrath
Tier 3 Raid Set	Dreadnaught's Battlegear

ARCANIST REGALIA

3 Pcs: Increases damage and healing done by magical spells and effects by up to 18
5 Pcs: Decreases the magical resistances of your spell targets by 10
8 Pcs: Decreases the threat generated by your spells by 15%

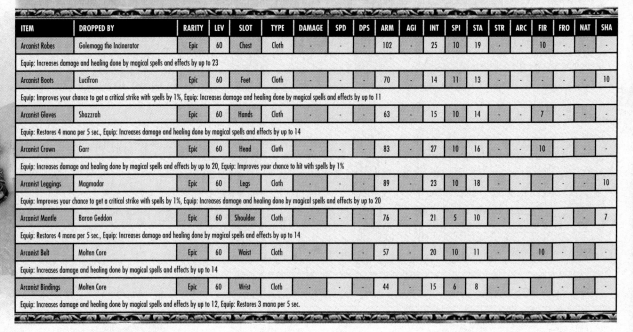

MAGE

ITEM	DROPPED BY	RARITY	LEV	SLOT	TYPE	DAMAGE	SPD	DPS	ARM	AGI	INT	SPI	STA	STR	ARC	FIR	FRO	NAT	SHA
Arcanist Robes	Golemagg the Incinerator	Epic	60	Chest	Cloth	-	-	-	102	-	25	10	19	-	-	10	-	-	-
Equip: Increases damage and healing done by magical spells and effects by up to 23																			
Arcanist Boots	Lucifron	Epic	60	Feet	Cloth	-	-	-	70	-	14	11	13	-	-	-	-	-	10
Equip: Improves your chance to get a critical strike with spells by 1%, Equip: Increases damage and healing done by magical spells and effects by up to 11																			
Arcanist Gloves	Shazzrah	Epic	60	Hands	Cloth	-	-	-	63	-	15	10	14	-	-	7	-	-	-
Equip: Restores 4 mana per 5 sec., Equip: Increases damage and healing done by magical spells and effects by up to 14																			
Arcanist Crown	Garr	Epic	60	Head	Cloth	-	-	-	83	-	27	10	16	-	-	10	-	-	-
Equip: Increases damage and healing done by magical spells and effects by up to 20, Equip: Improves your chance to hit with spells by 1%																			
Arcanist Leggings	Magmadar	Epic	60	Legs	Cloth	-	-	-	89	-	23	10	18	-	-	-	-	-	10
Equip: Improves your chance to get a critical strike with spells by 1%, Equip: Increases damage and healing done by magical spells and effects by up to 20																			
Arcanist Mantle	Baron Geddon	Epic	60	Shoulder	Cloth	-	-	-	76	-	21	5	10	-	-	-	-	-	7
Equip: Restores 4 mana per 5 sec., Equip: Increases damage and healing done by magical spells and effects by up to 14																			
Arcanist Belt	Molten Core	Epic	60	Waist	Cloth	-	-	-	57	-	20	10	11	-	-	10	-	-	-
Equip: Increases damage and healing done by magical spells and effects by up to 14																			
Arcanist Bindings	Molten Core	Epic	60	Wrist	Cloth	-	-	-	44	-	15	6	8	-	-	-	-	-	-
Equip: Increases damage and healing done by magical spells and effects by up to 12, Equip: Restores 3 mana per 5 sec.																			

AUGUR'S REGALIA

2 Pcs: Restores 4 mana per 5 sec.
3 Pcs: Improves the duration of your Frost Shock spell by 1 sec.
5 Pcs: Increase the range of your Lightning Bolt spell by 5 yds.

SHAMAN

ITEM	DROPPED BY	RARITY	LEV	SLOT	TYPE	DAMAGE	SPD	DPS	ARM	AGI	INT	SPI	STA	STR	ARC	FIR	FRO	NAT	SHA
Zandalar Augur's Hauberk	Quest: Paragons of Power: The Augur's Hauberk (Zul'Gurub)	Epic	60	Chest	Mail	-	-	-	416	-	15	-	19	-	-	-	-	-	-
Equip: Increases damage and healing done by magical spells and effects by up to 34, Equip: Improves your chance to get a critical strike with spells by 1%																			
Unmarred Vision of Voodress	Quest: The Unmarred Vision of Voodress (Zul'Gurub)	Epic	60	Neck	Misc	-	-	-	-	-	10	9	10	6	-	-	-	-	-
Equip: Decreases the mana cost of your Healing Stream and Mana Spring totems by 20																			
Wushoolay's Charm of Spirits	Punctured Voodoo Doll (Zul'Gurub)	Epic	60	Trinket	Misc	-	-	-	-	-	-	-	-	-	-	-	-	-	-
Use: Increases the damage dealt by your Lightning Shield spell by 100% for 20 sec.																			
Zandalar Augur's Belt	Quest: Paragons of Power: The Augur's Belt (Zul'Gurub)	Epic	60	Waist	Mail	-	-	-	221	-	21	-	10	-	-	-	-	-	-
Equip: Increases damage and healing done by magical spells and effects by up to 12, Equip: Restores 4 mana per 5 sec.																			
Zandalar Augur's Bracers	Quest: Paragons of Power: The Augur's Bracers (Zul'Gurub)	Epic	60	Wrist	Mail	-	-	-	172	-	11	-	12	-	-	-	-	-	-
Equip: Increases damage and healing done by magical spells and effects by up to 13, Equip: Restores 4 mana per 5 sec.																			

AVENGER'S BATTLEGEAR

3 Pcs: Increases the duration of your Judgements by 20%
5 Pcs: Increases damage and healing done by magical spells and effects by up to 71

PALADIN

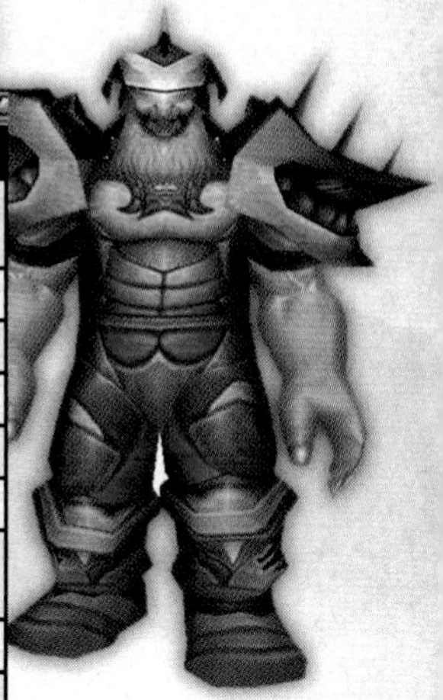

ITEM	DROPPED BY	RARITY	LEV	SLOT	TYPE	DAMAGE	SPD	DPS	ARM	AGI	INT	SPI	STA	STR	ARC	FIR	FRO	NAT	SHA
Avenger's Breastplate	Quest: Avenger's Breastplate (Ahn'Qiraj)	Epic	60	Chest	Plate	-	-	-	985	12	24	11	24	23	-	-	-	-	-
Equip: Increases damage and healing done by magical spells and effects by up to 18, Equip: Improves your chance to get a critical strike with spells by 1%, Equip: Improves your chance to get a critical strike by 1%																			
Avenger's Greaves	Quest: Avenger's Greaves (Ahn'Qiraj)	Epic	60	Feet	Plate	-	-	-	604	13	14	6	18	18	-	-	-	-	-
Equip: Increases damage and healing done by magical spells and effects by up to 14, Equip: Restores 4 mana per 5 sec.																			
Avenger's Crown	Quest: Avenger's Crown (Ahn'Qiraj)	Epic	60	Head	Plate	-	-	-	739	12	22	12	22	20	-	-	-	-	-
Equip: Increases damage and healing done by magical spells and effects by up to 23, Equip: Improves your chance to get a critical strike by 1%																			
Avenger's Legguards	Quest: Avenger's Legguards (Ahn'Qiraj)	Epic	60	Legs	Plate	-	-	-	796	12	22	9	22	21	-	-	-	-	-
Equip: Increases damage and healing done by magical spells and effects by up to 16, Equip: Improves your chance to get a critical strike by 1%, Equip: Restores 4 mana per 5 sec.																			
Avenger's Pauldrons	Quest: Avenger's Pauldrons (Ahn'Qiraj)	Epic	60	Shoulder	Plate	-	-	-	659	14	13	6	15	18	-	-	-	-	-
Equip: Increases damage and healing done by magical spells and effects by up to 14, Equip: Restores 3 mana per 5 sec.																			

BATTLEGEAR OF ETERNAL JUSTICE

3 Pcs: 20% chance to regain 100 mana when you cast a Judgement

PALADIN

ITEM	DROPPED BY	RARITY	LEV	SLOT	TYPE	DAMAGE	SPD	DPS	ARM	AGI	INT	SPI	STA	STR	ARC	FIR	FRO	NAT	SHA
Cape of Eternal Justice	Quest: Cape of Eternal Justice (Ahn'Qiraj)	Epic	60	Back	Cloth	-	-	-	52	-	12	-	13	11	-	-	-	-	-
Equip: Restores 5 mana per 5 sec.																			
Ring of Eternal Justice	Quest: Ring of Eternal Justice (Ahn'Qiraj)	Epic	60	Finger	Misc	-	-	-	-	-	12	-	11	12	-	-	-	-	-
Equip: Increases damage and healing done by magical spells and effects by up to 13																			
Blade of Eternal Justice	Quest: Blade of Eternal Justice (Ahn'Qiraj)	Epic	60	Main Hand	Sword	83-154	2.30	51.5	-	-	7	-	11	9	-	-	-	-	-
Equip: Restores 4 mana per 5 sec.																			

BATTLEGEAR OF HEROISM

2 Pcs: +8 All Resistances
4 Pcs: Chance on melee attack to heal you for 88 to 132
6 Pcs: +40 Attack Power
8 Pcs: +200 Armor

ITEM	DROPPED BY	RARITY	LEV	SLOT	TYPE	DAMAGE	SPD	DPS	ARM	AGI	INT	SPI	STA	STR	ARC	FIR	FRO	NAT	SHA
Breastplate of Heroism	Quest: Saving the Best for Last (Ironforge/Orgrimmar)	Epic	60	Chest	Plate	-	-	-	684	13	-	-	26	21	-	-	-	-	-
Equip: Improves your chance to hit by 1%																				
Boots of Heroism	Quest: Anthion's Parting Words (Ironforge/Orgrimmar)	Epic	60	Feet	Plate	-	-	-	470	-	-	-	20	20	-	-	-	-	-
Equip: Improves your chance to hit by 1%																				
Gauntlets of Heroism	Quest: Just Compensation (Ironforge/Orgrimmar)	Epic	60	Hands	Plate	-	-	-	393	-	-	-	12	18	-	-	-	-	-
Equip: Improves your chance to get a critical strike by 1%																				
Helm of Heroism	Quest: Saving the Best for Last (Ironforge/Orgrimmar)	Epic	60	Head	Plate	-	-	-	556	-	-	-	32	18	-	-	-	-	-
Equip: Improves your chance to get a critical strike by 1%																				
Legplates of Heroism	Quest: Anthion's Parting Words (Ironforge/Orgrimmar)	Superior	60	Legs	Plate	-	-	-	601	11	-	-	16	25	-	-	-	-	-
Equip: Increased Defense +5																				
Spaulders of Heroism	Quest: Anthion's Parting Words (Ironforge/Orgrimmar)	Superior	60	Shoulder	Plate	-	-	-	507	12	-	-	18	12	-	-	-	-	-
Belt of Heroism	Quest: Just Compensation (Ironforge/Orgrimmar)	Superior	60	Waist	Plate	-	-	-	380	9	-	-	12	15	-	-	-	-	-
Equip: Increased Defense +7																				
Bracers of Heroism	Quest: An Earnest Proposition (Ironforge/Orgrimmar)	Superior	60	Wrist	Plate	-	-	-	296	5	-	-	14	9	-	-	-	-	-
Equip: Increased Defense +3																				

BATTLEGEAR OF MIGHT

3 Pcs: Increases the block value of your shield by 30
5 Pcs: Gives you a 20% chance to generate an additional Rage point whenever damage is dealt to you
8 Pcs: Increases the threat generated by Sunder Armor by 15%

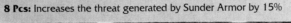

ITEM	DROPPED BY	RARITY	LEV	SLOT	TYPE	DAMAGE	SPD	DPS	ARM	AGI	INT	SPI	STA	STR	ARC	FIR	FRO	NAT	SHA
Breastplate of Might	Golemagg the Incinerator	Epic	60	Chest	Plate	-	-	-	749	-	-	-	28	20	-	10	-	-	-
Equip: Increases your chance to block attacks with a shield by 3%, Equip: Increased Defense +7																				
Sabatons of Might	Gehennas	Epic	60	Feet	Plate	-	-	-	515	-	-	-	26	15	-	-	-	-	7
Equip: Increased Defense +5																				
Gauntlets of Might	Lucifron	Epic	60	Hands	Plate	-	-	-	468	-	-	-	17	22	-	7	-	-	-
Equip: Improves your chance to hit by 1%, Equip: Increased Defense +5																				
Helm of Might	Garr	Epic	60	Head	Plate	-	-	-	608	-	-	-	35	15	-	10	-	-	-
Equip: Increases your chance to dodge an attack by 1%, Equip: Increased Defense +7																				
Legplates of Might	Magmadar	Epic	60	Legs	Plate	-	-	-	655	-	-	-	23	24	-	-	-	-	10
Equip: Increases your chance to parry an attack by 1%, Equip: Increased Defense +7																				
Pauldrons of Might	Sulfuron Harbinger	Epic	60	Shoulder	Plate	-	-	-	562	-	-	-	22	15	-	-	-	-	7
Equip: Increases your chance to block attacks with a shield by 2%, Equip: Increased Defense +5																				
Belt of Might	Molten Core	Epic	60	Waist	Plate	-	-	-	421	-	-	-	15	21	-	7	-	-	-
Equip: Increases your chance to dodge an attack by 1%, Equip: Increased Defense +5																				
Bracers of Might	Molten Core	Epic	60	Wrist	Plate	-	-	-	328	-	-	-	23	11	-	-	-	-	-

BATTLEGEAR OF UNYIELDING STRENGTH

3 Pcs: -2 rage cost to Intercept

WARRIOR

ITEM	DROPPED BY	RARITY	LEV	SLOT	TYPE	DAMAGE	SPD	DPS	ARM	AGI	INT	SPI	STA	STR	ARC	FIR	FRO	NAT	SHA
Drape of Unyielding Strength	Quest: Drape of Unyielding Strength (Ahn'Qiraj)	Epic	60	Back	Cloth	-	-	-	52	9	-	-	9	15	-	-	-	-	-
Equip: Improves your chance to hit by 1%																			
Signet of Unyielding Strength	Quest: Signet of Unyielding Strength (Ahn'Qiraj)	Epic	60	Finger	Misc	-	-	-	-	-	-	-	14	11	-	-	-	-	-
Equip: Improves your chance to get a critical strike by 1%																			
Sickle of Unyielding Strength	Quest: Sickle of Unyielding Strength (Ahn'Qiraj)	Epic	60	One-Hand	Axe	75-141	2.10	51.4	-	6	-	-	9	15	-	-	-	-	-
Equip: Increased Defense +4																			

BATTLEGEAR OF VALOR

2 Pcs: +200 Armor

4 Pcs: +40 Attack Power

6 Pcs: Chance on melee attack to heal you for 88 to 132

8 Pcs: +8 All Resistances

WARRIOR

ITEM	DROPPED BY	RARITY	LEV	SLOT	TYPE	DAMAGE	SPD	DPS	ARM	AGI	INT	SPI	STA	STR	ARC	FIR	FRO	NAT	SHA
Breastplate of Valor	General Drakkisath	Superior	58	Chest	Plate	-	-	-	657	10	-	6	24	15	-	-	-	-	-
Boots of Valor	Kirtonos the Herald	Superior	54	Feet	Plate	-	-	-	424	4	-	3	20	8	-	-	-	-	-
Gauntlets of Valor	Ramstein the Gorger	Superior	54	Hands	Plate	-	-	-	386	3	-	8	10	17	-	-	-	-	-
Helm of Valor	Darkmaster Gandling	Superior	57	Head	Plate	-	-	-	526	9	-	8	23	15	-	-	-	-	-
Legplates of Valor	Baron Rivendare	Superior	56	Legs	Plate	-	-	-	557	11	-	4	15	23	-	-	-	-	-
Spaulders of Valor	Warchief Rend Blackhand	Superior	55	Shoulder	Plate	-	-	-	470	9	-	-	17	11	-	-	-	-	-
Belt of Valor	Bile Spewer, Patchwork Horror, Smolderthorn Berserker, Venom Belcher	Superior	53	Waist	Plate	-	-	-	341	7	-	4	8	14	-	-	-	-	-
Bracers of Valor	Blackrock Depths	Superior	52	Wrist	Plate	-	-	-	261	3	-	2	14	7	-	-	-	-	-

BATTLEGEAR OF WRATH

3 Pcs: Increases the attack power granted by Battle Shout by 30

5 Pcs: 20% chance after using an offensive ability requiring rage that your next offensive ability requires 0 less rage to use

8 Pcs: 4% chance to parry the next attack after a block

ITEM	DROPPED BY	RARITY	LEV	SLOT	TYPE	DAMAGE	SPD	DPS	ARM	AGI	INT	SPI	STA	STR	ARC	FIR	FRO	NAT	SHA
Breastplate of Wrath	Nefarian	Epic	60	Chest	Plate	-	-	-	857	-	-	-	40	17	-	10	-	10	-
Equip: Increased Defense +11																			
Sabatons of Wrath	Broodlord Lashlayer	Epic	60	Feet	Plate	-	-	-	589	-	-	-	30	13	-	10	-	-	-
Equip: Increases the block value of your shield by 14, Equip: Increased Defense +7																			
Gauntlets of Wrath	Ebonroc, Firemaw, Flamegor	Epic	60	Hands	Plate	-	-	-	535	-	-	-	20	15	-	-	-	-	10
Equip: Increases your chance to parry an attack by 1%, Equip: Increased Defense +7																			
Helm of Wrath	Onyxia	Epic	60	Head	Plate	-	-	-	696	-	-	-	40	17	-	10	-	10	-
Equip: Increased Defense +11																			
Legplates of Wrath	Ragnaros	Epic	60	Legs	Plate	-	-	-	749	-	-	-	27	19	10	10	-	-	-
Equip: Increases your chance to dodge an attack by 2%, Equip: Increased Defense +11																			
Pauldrons of Wrath	Chromaggus	Epic	60	Shoulder	Plate	-	-	-	642	-	-	-	27	13	-	10	-	-	-
Equip: Increases the block value of your shield by 27, Equip: Increased Defense +7																			
Waistband of Wrath	Vaelastrasz the Corrupt	Epic	60	Waist	Plate	-	-	-	482	-	-	-	20	20	-	-	-	-	10
Equip: Increases your chance to block attacks with a shield by 3%, Equip: Increased Defense +7																			
Bracelets of Wrath	Razorgore the Untamed	Epic	60	Wrist	Plate	-	-	-	375	-	-	-	27	13	-	-	-	-	-

BEASTMASTER ARMOR

2 Pcs: +8 All Resistances

4 Pcs: Your normal ranged attacks have a 4% chance of restoring 200 mana

6 Pcs: +40 Attack Power

8 Pcs: +200 Armor

ITEM	DROPPED BY	RARITY	LEV	SLOT	TYPE	DAMAGE	SPD	DPS	ARM	AGI	INT	SPI	STA	STR	ARC	FIR	FRO	NAT	SHA
Beastmaster's Tunic	Quest: Saving the Best for Last (Ironforge/Orgrimmar)	Epic	60	Chest	Mail	-	-	-	387	25	13	-	16	-	-	-	-	-	-
Equip: Increases your pet's armor by 10%, Equip: Improves your chance to get a critical strike by 1%																			
Beastmaster's Boots	Quest: Anthion's Parting Words (Ironforge/Orgrimmar)	Epic	60	Feet	Mail	-	-	-	266	24	-	-	9	-	-	-	-	-	-
Equip: Increases damage dealt by your pet by 3%																			
Beastmaster's Gloves	Quest: Just Compensation (Ironforge/Orgrimmar)	Epic	60	Hands	Mail	-	-	-	223	14	10	-	12	-	-	-	-	-	-
Equip: Increases your pet's critical strike chance by 2%																			
Beastmaster's Cap	Quest: Saving the Best for Last (Ironforge/Orgrimmar)	Epic	60	Head	Mail	-	-	-	314	22	12	-	21	-	-	-	-	-	-
Equip: Improves your chance to hit by 1%, Equip: Increases your pet's maximum health by 3%																			
Beastmaster's Pants	Quest: Anthion's Parting Words (Ironforge/Orgrimmar)	Superior	60	Legs	Mail	-	-	-	339	28	9	-	14	-	-	-	-	-	-
Beastmaster's Mantle	Quest: Anthion's Parting Words (Ironforge/Orgrimmar)	Superior	60	Shoulder	Mail	-	-	-	286	12	10	-	18	-	-	-	-	-	-
Beastmaster's Belt	Quest: Just Compensation (Ironforge/Orgrimmar)	Superior	60	Waist	Mail	-	-	-	214	16	10	-	16	-	-	-	-	-	-
Beastmaster's Bindings	Quest: An Earnest Proposition (Ironforge/Orgrimmar)	Superior	60	Wrist	Mail	-	-	-	167	16	5	-	7	-	-	-	-	-	-

BEASTSTALKER ARMOR

2 Pcs: +200 Armor
4 Pcs: +40 Attack Power
6 Pcs: Your normal ranged attacks have a 4% chance of restoring 200 mana
8 Pcs: +8 All Resistances

HUNTER

ITEM	DROPPED BY	RARITY	LEV	SLOT	TYPE	DAMAGE	SPD	DPS	ARM	AGI	INT	SPI	STA	STR	ARC	FIR	FRO	NAT	SHA
Beaststalker's Tunic	General Drakkisath	Superior	58	Chest	Mail	-	-	-	370	21	13	6	16	5	-	-	-	-	-
Beaststalker's Boots	Nerub'enkan	Superior	54	Feet	Mail	-	-	-	240	21	-	-	9	-	-	-	-	-	-
Beaststalker's Gloves	War Master Voone	Superior	54	Hands	Mail	-	-	-	218	14	9	10	9	-	-	-	-	-	-
Beaststalker's Cap	Darkmaster Gandling	Superior	57	Head	Mail	-	-	-	297	20	10	6	20	-	-	-	-	-	-
Beaststalker's Pants	Baron Rivendare	Superior	56	Legs	Mail	-	-	-	315	26	-	12	6	6	-	-	-	-	-
Beaststalker's Mantle	Overlord Wyrmthalak	Superior	55	Shoulder	Mail	-	-	-	266	11	7	4	17	-	-	-	-	-	-
Beaststalker's Belt	Blackrock Depths	Superior	53	Waist	Mail	-	-	-	193	10	9	11	6	9	-	-	-	-	-
Beaststalker's Bindings	Crimson Defender, Fleshflayer Ghoul, Ghoul Ravener, Rage Talon Dragonspawn	Superior	52	Wrist	Mail	-	-	-	148	15	-	-	7	-	-	-	-	-	-

BLOODFANG ARMOR

3 Pcs: Increases the chance to apply poisons to your target by 5%
5 Pcs: Improves the threat reduction of Feint by 25%

ROGUE

ITEM	DROPPED BY	RARITY	LEV	SLOT	TYPE	DAMAGE	SPD	DPS	ARM	AGI	INT	SPI	STA	STR	ARC	FIR	FRO	NAT	SHA
Bloodfang Chestpiece	Nefarian	Epic	60	Chest	Leather	-	-	-	225	26	-	-	17	12	-	10	-	10	-
Equip: Improves your chance to get a critical strike by 1%, Equip: Improves your chance to hit by 2%																			
Bloodfang Boots	Broodlord Lashlayer	Epic	60	Feet	Leather	-	-	-	154	25	-	-	17	6	-	10	-	-	-
Equip: Increases your chance to dodge an attack by 1%																			
Bloodfang Gloves	Ebonroc, Firemaw, Flamegor	Epic	60	Hands	Leather	-	-	-	140	20	-	-	20	19	-	-	-	-	10
Equip: Immune to Disarm																			
Bloodfang Hood	Onyxia	Epic	60	Head	Leather	-	-	-	183	27	-	-	25	19	-	10	-	10
Equip: Improves your chance to get a critical strike by 1%																			
Bloodfang Pants	Ragnaros	Epic	60	Legs	Leather	-	-	-	197	37	-	-	17	11	10	10	-	-
Equip: Improves your chance to get a critical strike by 1%																			
Bloodfang Spaulders	Chromaggus	Epic	60	Shoulder	Leather	-	-	-	169	25	-	-	17	6	-	10	-	-
Equip: Increases your chance to dodge an attack by 1%																			
Bloodfang Belt	Vaelastrasz the Corrupt	Epic	60	Waist	Leather	-	-	-	126	20	-	-	15	13	-	-	-	10
Equip: Improves your chance to get a critical strike by 1%																			
Bloodfang Bracers	Razorgore the Untamed	Epic	60	Wrist	Leather	-	-	-	98	23	-	-	13	-	-	-	-	-
Equip: Improves your chance to hit by 1%																			

BLOODMAIL REGALIA

2 Pcs: Increased Defense +3

3 Pcs: +10 Attack Power

4 Pcs: +15 All Resistances

5 Pcs: Increases your chance to parry an attack by 1%

ITEM	DROPPED BY	RARITY	LEV	SLOT	TYPE	DAMAGE	SPD	DPS	ARM	AGI	INT	SPI	STA	STR	ARC	FIR	FRO	NAT	SHA
Bloodmail Hauberk	Scholomance Bosses	Superior	56	Chest	Mail	-	-	-	360	-	15	10	15	10	-	-	-	-	-
Equip: Increases your chance to dodge an attack by 1%																			
Bloodmail Boots	Scholomance Bosses	Superior	56	Feet	Mail	-	-	-	247	9	10	-	10	9	-	-	-	-	-
Equip: Improves your chance to hit by 1%																			
Bloodmail Gauntlets	Scholomance Bosses	Superior	56	Hands	Mail	-	-	-	225	-	10	-	10	9	-	-	-	-	-
Equip: Improves your chance to get a critical strike by 1%																			
Bloodmail Legguards	Scholomance Bosses	Superior	56	Legs	Mail	-	-	-	315	12	15	-	16	15	-	-	-	-	-
Bloodmail Belt	Scholomance Bosses	Superior	56	Waist	Mail	-	-	-	202	12	9	-	11	12	-	-	-	-	-

CADAVEROUS GARB

2 Pcs: Increased Defense +3

3 Pcs: +10 Attack Power

4 Pcs: +15 All Resistances

5 Pcs: Improves your chance to hit by 2%

ITEM	DROPPED BY	RARITY	LEV	SLOT	TYPE	DAMAGE	SPD	DPS	ARM	AGI	INT	SPI	STA	STR	ARC	FIR	FRO	NAT	SHA
Cadaverous Armor	Scholomance Bosses	Superior	56	Chest	Leather	-	-	-	172	8	-	-	-	8	-	-	-	-	-
Equip: +60 Attack Power																			
Cadaverous Walkers	Scholomance Bosses	Superior	56	Feet	Leather	-	-	-	118	-	-	-	20	-	-	-	-	-	-
Equip: +24 Attack Power																			
Cadaverous Gloves	Scholomance Bosses	Superior	56	Hands	Leather	-	-	-	107	-	-	-	9	-	-	-	-	-	-
Equip: +44 Attack Power																			
Cadaverous Leggings	Scholomance Bosses	Superior	56	Legs	Leather	-	-	-	150	-	-	-	18	-	-	-	-	-	-
Equip: +52 Attack Power																			
Cadaverous Belt	Scholomance Bosses	Superior	56	Waist	Leather	-	-	-	97	-	-	-	12	-	-	-	-	-	-
Equip: +40 Attack Power																			

CENARION RAIMENT

DRUID

3 Pcs: Damage dealt by Thorns increased by 4 and duration increased by 50%

5 Pcs: Improves your chance to get a critical strike with spells by 2%

8 Pcs: Reduces the cooldown of your Tranquility and Hurricane spells by 50%

ITEM	DROPPED BY	RARITY	LEV	SLOT	TYPE	DAMAGE	SPD	DPS	ARM	AGI	INT	SPI	STA	STR	ARC	FIR	FRO	NAT	SHA
Cenarion Vestments	Golemagg the Incinerator	Epic	60	Chest	Leather	-	-	-	200	-	24	16	23	-	-	10	-	-	-
Equip: Restores 3 mana per 5 sec., Equip: Increases healing done by spells and effects by up to 22																			
Cenarion Boots	Lucifron	Epic	60	Feet	Leather	-	-	-	138	-	13	15	16	-	-	-	-	-	7
Equip: Restores 3 mana per 5 sec., Equip: Increases healing done by spells and effects by up to 18																			
Cenarion Gloves	Shazzrah	Epic	60	Hands	Leather	-	-	-	125	-	18	15	17	-	-	7	-	-	-
Equip: Increases healing done by spells and effects by up to 18																			
Cenarion Helm	Garr	Epic	60	Head	Leather	-	-	-	163	-	28	13	26	-	-	10	-	-	-
Equip: Increases damage and healing done by magical spells and effects by up to 12																			
Cenarion Leggings	Magmadar	Epic	60	Legs	Leather	-	-	-	175	-	19	20	18	-	-	-	-	-	10
Equip: Improves your chance to get a critical strike with spells by 1%, Equip: Restores 4 mana per 5 sec., Equip: Increases healing done by spells and effects by up to 22																			
Cenarion Spaulders	Baron Geddon	Epic	60	Shoulder	Leather	-	-	-	150	-	20	10	13	-	-	-	-	-	7
Equip: Restores 4 mana per 5 sec., Equip: Increases healing done by spells and effects by up to 18																			
Cenarion Belt	Molten Core	Epic	60	Waist	Leather	-	-	-	113	-	22	10	10	-	-	7	-	-	-
Equip: Restores 4 mana per 5 sec., Equip: Increases damage and healing done by magical spells and effects by up to 9																			
Cenarion Bracers	Molten Core	Epic	60	Wrist	Leather	-	-	-	88	-	14	13	13	-	-	-	-	-	-
Equip: Increases damage and healing done by magical spells and effects by up to 6																			

CHAIN OF THE SCARLET CRUSADE

2 Pcs: +10 Armor

3 Pcs: Increased Defense +1

4 Pcs: +5 Shadow Resistance

5 Pcs: +15 Attack Power when fighting Undead

6 Pcs: Improves your chance to hit by 1%

ITEM	DROPPED BY	RARITY	LEV	SLOT	TYPE	DAMAGE	SPD	DPS	ARM	AGI	INT	SPI	STA	STR	ARC	FIR	FRO	NAT	SHA
Scarlet Chestpiece	Scarlet Champion	Superior	34	Chest	Mail	-	-	-	250	-	-	-	19	8	-	-	-	-	-
Scarlet Boots	Scarlet Monastery	Superior	30	Feet	Mail	-	-	-	161	5	-	-	12	-	-	-	-	-	-
Scarlet Gauntlets	Scarlet Centurion	Uncommon	33	Hands	Mail	-	-	-	139	7	-	-	-	8	-	-	-	-	-
Scarlet Leggings	Herod, Scarlet Commander Mograine	Superior	38	Legs	Mail	-	-	-	233	-	-	-	10	20	-	-	-	-	-
Scarlet Belt	Scarlet Defender, Scarlet Myrmidon	Uncommon	32	Waist	Mail	-	-	-	123	-	-	-	7	8	-	-	-	-	-
Scarlet Wristguards	Scarlet Guardsman, Scarlet Protector	Uncommon	31	Wrist	Mail	-	-	-	95	-	-	-	8	-	-	-	-	-	-

CONFESSOR'S RAIMENT

2 Pcs: Increases healing done by spells and effects by up to 22
3 Pcs: Increase the range of your Smite and Holy Fire spells by 5 yds.
5 Pcs: Reduces the casting time of your Mind Control spell by 0.5 sec.

ITEM	DROPPED BY	RARITY	LEV	SLOT	TYPE	DAMAGE	SPD	DPS	ARM	AGI	INT	SPI	STA	STR	ARC	FIR	FRO	NAT	SHA
The All-Seeing Eye of Zuldazar	Quest: The All-Seeing Eye of Zuldazar (Zul'Gurub)	Epic	60	Neck	Misc	-	-	-	-	-	8	13	8	-	-	-	-	-	-
Equip: Increases healing done by spells and effects by up to 18, Equip: Increases the amount of damage absorbed by Power Word: Shield by 35																			
Zandalar Confessor's Mantle	Quest: Paragons of Power: The Confessor's Mantle (Zul'Gurub)	Epic	60	Shoulder	Cloth	-	-	-	78	-	24	15	11	-	-	-	-	-	-
Equip: Increases healing done by spells and effects by up to 22																			
Hazza'rah's Charm of Healing	Punctured Voodoo Doll (Zul'Gurub)	Epic	60	Trinket	Misc	-	-	-	-	-	-	-	-	-	-	-	-	-	-
Use: Reduces the casting time of your Greater Heal spells by 40%, and reduces the mana cost of your healing spells by 5% for 15 sec.																			
Zandalar Confessor's Bindings	Quest: Paragons of Power: The Confessor's Bindings (Zul'Gurub)	Epic	60	Waist	Cloth	-	-	-	78	-	24	15	11	-	-	-	-	-	-
Equip: Increases healing done by spells and effects by up to 22																			
Zandalar Confessor's Wraps	Quest: Paragons of Power: The Confessor's Wraps (Zul'Gurub)	Epic	60	Wrist	Cloth	-	-	-	41	-	11	12	10	-	-	-	-	-	-
Equip: Increases healing done by spells and effects by up to 24																			

CONQUEROR'S BATTLEGEAR

3 Pcs: Decreases the rage cost of all Warrior shouts by 35%
5 Pcs: Increase the Slow effect and damage of Thunder Clap by 50%

ITEM	DROPPED BY	RARITY	LEV	SLOT	TYPE	DAMAGE	SPD	DPS	ARM	AGI	INT	SPI	STA	STR	ARC	FIR	FRO	NAT	SHA
Conqueror's Breastplate	Quest: Conqueror's Breastplate (Ahn'Qiraj)	Epic	60	Chest	Plate	-	-	-	985	24	-	-	38	34	-	-	-	-	-
Equip: Increased Defense +6																			
Conqueror's Greaves	Quest: Conqueror's Greaves (Ahn'Qiraj)	Epic	60	Feet	Plate	-	-	-	604	17	-	-	23	21	-	-	-	-	-
Equip: Increased Defense +4																			
Conqueror's Crown	Quest: Conqueror's Crown (Ahn'Qiraj)	Epic	60	Head	Plate	-	-	-	739	18	-	-	34	29	-	-	-	-	-
Equip: Increased Defense +6																			
Conqueror's Legguards	Quest: Conqueror's Legguards (Ahn'Qiraj)	Epic	60	Legs	Plate	-	-	-	796	21	-	-	24	33	-	-	-	-	-
Equip: Increased Defense +6, Equip: Improves your chance to hit by 1%																			
Conqueror's Spaulders	Quest: Conqueror's Spaulders (Ahn'Qiraj)	Epic	60	Shoulder	Plate	-	-	-	659	16	-	-	21	20	-	-	-	-	-
Equip: Increased Defense +4, Equip: Improves your chance to hit by 1%																			

DAL'REND'S ARMS

2 Pcs: +50 Attack Power

ITEM	DROPPED BY	RARITY	LEV	SLOT	TYPE	DAMAGE	SPD	DPS	ARM	AGI	INT	SPI	STA	STR	ARC	FIR	FRO	NAT	SHA
Dal'Rend's Tribal Guardian	Warchief Rend Blackhand	Superior	58	Off-Hand	Sword	52 - 97	1.80	41.4	100	-	-	-	-	-	-	-	-	-	-
Equip: Increased Defense +7																			
Dal'Rend's Sacred Charge	Warchief Rend Blackhand	Superior	58	Main Hand	Sword	81-151	2.80	41.4	-	-	-	-	-	4	-	-	-	-	-
Equip: Improves your chance to get a critical strike by 1%																			

DARKMANTLE ARMOR

2 Pcs: +8 All Resistances
4 Pcs: Chance on melee attack to restore 35 energy
6 Pcs: +40 Attack Power
8 Pcs: +200 Armor

ROGUE

ITEM	DROPPED BY	RARITY	LEV	SLOT	TYPE	DAMAGE	SPD	DPS	ARM	AGI	INT	SPI	STA	STR	ARC	FIR	FRO	NAT	SHA
Darkmantle Tunic	Saving the Best for Last (Ironforge/Orgrimmar)	Epic	60	Chest	Leather	-	-	-	185	31	-	-	15	-	-	-	-	-	-
Equip: Improves your chance to hit by 2%																			
Darkmantle Boots	Quest: Anthion's Parting Words (Ironforge/Orgrimmar)	Epic	60	Feet	Leather	-	-	-	127	24	-	-	10	-	-	-	-	-	-
Equip: Increases your effective stealth level																			
Darkmantle Gloves	Quest: Just Compensation (Ironforge/Orgrimmar)	Epic	60	Hands	Leather	-	-	-	108	22	-	-	9	12	-	-	-	-	-
Darkmantle Cap	Quest: Saving the Best for Last (Ironforge/Orgrimmar)	Epic	60	Head	Leather	-	-	-	150	26	-	-	18	13	-	-	-	-	-
Equip: Improves your chance to get a critical strike by 1%																			
Darkmantle Pants	Quest: Anthion's Parting Words (Ironforge/Orgrimmar)	Superior	60	Legs	Leather	-	-	-	160	25	-	-	15	15	-	-	-	-	-
Darkmantle Spaulders	Quest: Anthion's Parting Words (Ironforge/Orgrimmar)	Superior	60	Shoulder	Leather	-	-	-	136	24	-	-	10	-	-	-	-	-	-
Darkmantle Belt	Quest: Just Compensation (Ironforge/Orgrimmar)	Superior	60	Waist	Leather	-	-	-	102	17	-	-	13	10	-	-	-	-	-
Darkmantle Bracers	Quest: An Earnest Proposition (Ironforge/Orgrimmar)	Superior	60	Wrist	Leather	-	-	-	79	15	-	-	7	7	-	-	-	-	-

DEATHBONE GUARDIAN

2 Pcs: Increased Defense +3
3 Pcs: +50 Armor
4 Pcs: +15 All Resistances
5 Pcs: Increases your chance to parry an attack by 1%

ITEM	DROPPED BY	RARITY	LEV	SLOT	TYPE	DAMAGE	SPD	DPS	ARM	AGI	INT	SPI	STA	STR	ARC	FIR	FRO	NAT	SHA
Deathbone Chestplate	Scholomance Bosses	Superior	56	Chest	Plate	-	-	-	637	-	-	-	12	-	-	-	-	-	-
Equip: Increased Defense +17, Equip: Restores 5 mana per 5 sec.																			
Deathbone Sabatons	Scholomance Bosses	Superior	56	Feet	Plate	-	-	-	438	-	-	-	9	-	-	-	-	-	-
Equip: Restores 6 mana per 5 sec., Equip: Increased Defense +10																			
Deathbone Gauntlets	Scholomance Bosses	Superior	56	Hands	Plate	-	-	-	398	-	-	-	14	-	-	-	-	-	-
Equip: Increased Defense +10, Equip: Restores 4 mana per 5 sec.																			
Deathbone Legguards	Scholomance Bosses	Superior	56	Legs	Plate	-	-	-	557	-	-	-	20	-	-	-	-	-	-
Equip: Restores 5 mana per 5 sec., Equip: Increased Defense +13																			
Deathbone Girdle	Scholomance Bosses	Superior	56	Waist	Plate	-	-	-	358	-	-	-	15	-	-	-	-	-	-
Equip: Increased Defense +9, Equip: Restores 4 mana per 5 sec.																			

DEATHDEALER'S EMBRACE

3 Pcs: Reduces the cooldown of your Evasion ability by -1 min

5 Pcs: 15% increased damage to your Eviscerate ability

ITEM	DROPPED BY	RARITY	LEV	SLOT	TYPE	DAMAGE	SPD	DPS	ARM	AGI	INT	SPI	STA	STR	ARC	FIR	FRO	NAT	SHA
Deathdealer's Vest	Quest: Deathdealer's Vest (Ahn'Qiraj)	Epic	60	Chest	Leather	-	-	-	253	37	-	-	28	19	-	-	-	-	-
Equip: Improves your chance to get a critical strike by 1%, Equip: Improves your chance to hit by 1%																			
Deathdealer's Boots	Quest: Deathdealer's Boots (Ahn'Qiraj)	Epic	60	Feet	Leather	-	-	-	158	26	-	-	17	14	-	-	-	-	-
Equip: Improves your chance to hit by 1%																			
Deathdealer's Helm	Quest: Deathdealer's Helm (Ahn'Qiraj)	Epic	60	Head	Leather	-	-	-	192	29	-	-	27	25	-	-	-	-	-
Equip: Improves your chance to get a critical strike by 1%, Equip: Improves your chance to hit by 1%																			
Deathdealer's Leggings	Quest: Deathdealer's Leggings (Ahn'Qiraj)	Epic	60	Legs	Leather	-	-	-	207	38	-	-	25	18	-	-	-	-	-
Equip: Improves your chance to get a critical strike by 1%																			
Deathdealer's Spaulders	Quest: Deathdealer's Spaulders (Ahn'Qiraj)	Epic	60	Shoulder	Leather	-	-	-	172	27	-	-	25	18	-	-	-	-	-
Equip: Improves your chance to hit by 1%																			

DEATHMIST RAIMENT

2 Pcs: +8 All Resistances

4 Pcs: When struck in combat has a chance of causing the attacker to flee in terror for 2 seconds.

6 Pcs: Increases damage and healing done by magical spells and effects by up to 23

8 Pcs: +200 Armor

ITEM	DROPPED BY	RARITY	LEV	SLOT	TYPE	DAMAGE	SPD	DPS	ARM	AGI	INT	SPI	STA	STR	ARC	FIR	FRO	NAT	SHA
Deathmist Robe	Quest: Saving the Best for Last (Ironforge/Orgrimmar)	Epic	60	Chest	Cloth	-	-	-	93	-	22	-	27	-	-	-	-	-	-
Equip: Increases damage and healing done by magical spells and effects by up to 12, Equip: Improves your chance to get a critical strike with spells by 1%																			
Deathmist Sandals	Quest: Anthion's Parting Words (Ironforge/Orgrimmar)	Epic	60	Feet	Cloth	-	-	-	64	-	14	-	24	-	-	-	-	-	-
Equip: Increases damage and healing done by magical spells and effects by up to 12																			
Deathmist Wraps	Quest: Just Compensation (Ironforge/Orgrimmar)	Epic	60	Hands	Cloth	-	-	-	54	-	13	-	16	-	-	-	-	-	-
Equip: Increases damage and healing done by magical spells and effects by up to 13, Equip: Improves your chance to hit with spells by 1%																			
Deathmist Mask	Saving the Best for Last (Ironforge/Orgrimmar)	Epic	60	Head	Cloth	-	-	-	75	-	24	-	24	-	-	-	-	-	-
Equip: Increases damage and healing done by magical spells and effects by up to 16, Equip: Improves your chance to hit with spells by 1%																			
Deathmist Leggings	Quest: Anthion's Parting Words (Ironforge/Orgrimmar)	Superior	60	Legs	Cloth	-	-	-	81	-	21	-	22	-	-	-	-	-	-
Equip: Increases damage and healing done by magical spells and effects by up to 16																			
Deathmist Mantle	Quest: Anthion's Parting Words (Ironforge/Orgrimmar)	Superior	60	Shoulder	Cloth	-	-	-	69	-	16	-	16	-	-	-	-	-	-
Equip: Increases damage and healing done by magical spells and effects by up to 12																			
Deathmist Belt	Quest: Just Compensation (Ironforge/Orgrimmar)	Superior	60	Waist	Cloth	-	-	-	52	-	16	-	16	-	-	-	-	-	-
Equip: Increases damage and healing done by magical spells and effects by up to 12																			
Deathmist Bracers	An Earnest Proposition (Ironforge/Orgrimmar)	Superior	60	Wrist	Cloth	-	-	-	40	-	12	-	12	-	-	-	-	-	-
Equip: Increases damage and healing done by magical spells and effects by up to 8																			

DEFIAS LEATHER

2 Pcs: +10 Armor
3 Pcs: +5 Arcane Resistance
4 Pcs: Increased Daggers +1
5 Pcs: +10 Attack Power

ITEM	DROPPED BY	RARITY	LEV	SLOT	TYPE	DAMAGE	SPD	DPS	ARM	AGI	INT	SPI	STA	STR	ARC	FIR	FRO	NAT	SHA
Blackened Defias Armor	Edwin VanCleef	Superior	19	Chest	Leather	-	-	-	92	3	-	-	11	4	-	-	-	-	-
Blackened Defias Boots	Defias Strip Miner	Uncommon	13	Feet	Leather	-	-	-	51	3	-	-	2	-	-	-	-	-	-
Blackened Defias Gloves	Defias Overseer, Defias Taskmaster	Uncommon	13	Hands	Leather	-	-	-	46	-	-	-	1	3	-	-	-	-	-
Blackened Defias Leggings	Defias Overseer, Defias Taskmaster	Uncommon	13	Legs	Leather	-	-	-	65	3	-	-	-	3	-	-	-	-	-
Blackened Defias Belt	Captain Greenskin	Uncommon	17	Waist	Leather	-	-	-	45	-	-	-	-	5	-	-	-	-	-

DEMONIAC'S THREADS

2 Pcs: Increases damage and healing done by magical spells and effects by up to 12
3 Pcs: Increases the damage of Corruption by 2%
5 Pcs: Decreases the cooldown of Death Coil by 15%

WARLOCK

ITEM	DROPPED BY	RARITY	LEV	SLOT	TYPE	DAMAGE	SPD	DPS	ARM	AGI	INT	SPI	STA	STR	ARC	FIR	FRO	NAT	SHA
Zandalar Demoniac's Robe	Paragons of Power: The Demoniac's Robes (Zul'Gurub)	Epic	60	Chest	Cloth	-	-	-	100	-	-	-	35	-	-	-	-	-	-
Equip: Improves your chance to hit with spells by 1%, Equip: Increases damage and healing done by magical spells and effects by up to 27																			
Kezan's Unstoppable Taint	Quest: Kezan's Unstoppable Taint (Zul'Gurub)	Epic	60	Neck	Misc	-	-	-	-	-	8	-	13	-	-	-	-	-	-
Equip: Increases damage and healing done by magical spells and effects by up to 14, Equip: Increases the radius of Rain of Fire and Hellfire by 1 yard																			
Zandalar Demoniac's Mantle	Quest: Paragons of Power: The Demoniac's Mantle (Zul'Gurub)	Epic	60	Shoulder	Cloth	-	-	-	71	-	19	-	23	-	-	-	-	-	-
Equip: Increases damage and healing done by magical spells and effects by up to 12																			
Hazza'rah's Charm of Destruction	Punctured Voodoo Doll (Zul'Gurub)	Epic	60	Trinket	Misc	-	-	-	-	-	-	-	-	-	-	-	-	-	-
Use: Increases the critical hit chance of your Destruction spells by 10% for 20 sec.																			
Zandalar Demoniac's Wraps	Quest: Paragons of Power: The Demoniac's Wraps (Zul'Gurub)	Epic	60	Wrist	Cloth	-	-	-	41	-	8	-	15	-	-	-	-	-	-
Equip: Increases damage and healing done by magical spells and effects by up to 16																			

DOOMCALLER'S ATTIRE

3 Pcs: 5% increased damage on your Immolate spell
5 Pcs: Reduces the mana cost of Shadow Bolt by 15%

ITEM	DROPPED BY	RARITY	LEV	SLOT	TYPE	DAMAGE	SPD	DPS	ARM	AGI	INT	SPI	STA	STR	ARC	FIR	FRO	NAT	SHA
Doomcaller's Robes	Quest: Doomcaller's Robes (Ahn'Qiraj)	Epic	60	Chest	Cloth	-	-	-	133	-	17	7	23	-	-	-	-	-	-
Equip: Increases damage and healing done by magical spells and effects up to 41, Equip: Improves your chance to get a critical strike with spells by 1%, Equip: Decreases the magical resistances of your spell targets by 20																			
Doomcaller's Footwraps	Quest: Doomcaller's Footwraps (Ahn'Qiraj)	Epic	60	Feet	Cloth	-	-	-	82	-	16	3	20	-	-	-	-	-	-
Equip: Increases damage and healing done by magical spells and effects by up to 28, Equip: Decreases the magical resistances of your spell targets by 10																			
Doomcaller's Circlet	Quest: Doomcaller's Circlet (Ahn'Qiraj)	Epic	60	Head	Cloth	-	-	-	100	-	24	6	27	-	-	-	-	-	-
Equip: Increases damage and healing done by magical spells and effects by up to 33, Equip: Improves your chance to get a critical strike with spells by 1%, Equip: Improves your chance to hit with spells by 1%																			
Doomcaller's Trousers	Quest: Doomcaller's Trousers (Ahn'Qiraj)	Epic	60	Legs	Cloth	-	-	-	107	-	24	9	28	-	-	-	-	-	-
Equip: Increases damage and healing done by magical spells and effects by up to 34, Equip: Improves your chance to get a critical strike with spells by 1%																			
Doomcaller's Mantle	Quest: Doomcaller's Mantle (Ahn'Qiraj)	Epic	60	Shoulder	Cloth	-	-	-	89	-	11	4	20	-	-	-	-	-	-
Equip: Increases damage and healing done by magical spells and effects by up to 28, Equip: Decreases the magical resistances of your spell targets by 10, Equip: Improves your chance to hit with spells by 1%																			

DRAGONSTALKER ARMOR

3 Pcs: Increases the Ranged Attack Power bonus of your Aspect of the Hawk by 20%
5 Pcs: Increases your pet's stamina by 40 and all spell resistances by 60
8 Pcs: You have a chance whenever you deal ranged damage to apply an Expose Weakness effect to the target. Expose Weakness increases the Ranged Attack Power of all attackers against that target by 450 for 7 seconds.

ITEM	DROPPED BY	RARITY	LEV	SLOT	TYPE	DAMAGE	SPD	DPS	ARM	AGI	INT	SPI	STA	STR	ARC	FIR	FRO	NAT	SHA
Dragonstalker's Breastplate	Nefarian	Epic	60	Chest	Mail	-	-	-	482	34	14	6	17	-	-	10	-	10	-
Equip: Improves your chance to get a critical strike by 1%																			
Dragonstalker's Greaves	Broodlord Lashlayer	Epic	60	Feet	Mail	-	-	-	332	30	6	6	15	-	-	10	-	-	-
Dragonstalker's Gauntlets	Ebonroc, Firemaw, Flamegor	Epic	60	Hands	Mail	-	-	-	301	20	13	6	17	-	-	-	-	-	10
Equip: Improves your chance to get a critical strike by 1%																			
Dragonstalker's Helm	Onyxia	Epic	60	Head	Mail	-	-	-	392	27	16	8	26	-	-	-	10	-	10
Equip: Improves your chance to get a critical strike by 1%																			
Dragonstalker's Legguards	Ragnaros	Epic	60	Legs	Mail	-	-	-	422	31	15	8	16	-	-	10	10	-	-
Equip: Improves your chance to hit by 1%, Equip: Improves your chance to get a critical strike by 1%																			
Dragonstalker's Spaulders	Chromaggus	Epic	60	Shoulder	Mail	-	-	-	362	23	13	6	15	-	-	10	-	-	-
Equip: Improves your chance to hit by 1%																			
Dragonstalker's Belt	Vaelastrasz the Corrupt	Epic	60	Waist	Mail	-	-	-	271	20	13	11	15	-	-	-	-	-	10
Equip: Improves your chance to get a critical strike by 1%																			
Dragonstalker's Bracers	Razorgore the Untamed	Epic	60	Wrist	Mail	-	-	-	211	23	6	6	13	-	-	-	-	-	-

DREADMIST RAIMENT

2 Pcs: +200 Armor

4 Pcs: Increases damage and healing done by magical spells and effects by up to 23

6 Pcs: When struck in combat has a chance of causing the attacker to flee in terror for 2 seconds.

8 Pcs: +8 All Resistances

WARLOCK

ITEM	DROPPED BY	RARITY	LEV	SLOT	TYPE	DAMAGE	SPD	DPS	ARM	AGI	INT	SPI	STA	STR	ARC	FIR	FRO	NAT	SHA
Dreadmist Robe	General Drakkisath	Superior	58	Chest	Cloth	-	-	-	89	-	21	13	20	-	-	-	-	-	-
Dreadmist Sandals	Baroness Anastari	Superior	54	Feet	Cloth	-	-	-	58	-	9	10	17	-	-	-	-	-	-
Dreadmist Wraps	Lorekeeper Polkelt	Superior	54	Hands	Cloth	-	-	-	52	-	9	14	13	-	-	-	-	-	-
Dreadmist Mask	Darkmaster Gandling	Superior	57	Head	Cloth	-	-	-	71	-	23	12	15	-	-	-	-	-	-
Dreadmist Leggings	Baron Rivendare	Superior	56	Legs	Cloth	-	-	-	76	-	14	21	15	-	-	-	-	-	-
Dreadmist Mantle	Jandice Barov	Superior	55	Shoulder	Cloth	-	-	-	64	-	15	9	14	-	-	-	-	-	-
Dreadmist Belt	Crimson Conjuror, Crimson Sorcerer, Scholomance Necromancer, Thuzadin Necromancer, Thuzadin Shadowcaster	Superior	53	Waist	Cloth	-	-	-	46	-	17	9	10	-	-	-	-	-	-
Dreadmist Bracers	Blackrock Depths	Superior	52	Wrist	Cloth	-	-	-	35	-	10	7	10	-	-	-	-	-	-

EMBLEMS OF VEILED SHADOWS

3 Pcs: -10 energy cost for your Slice and Dice ability

ROGUE

ITEM	DROPPED BY	RARITY	LEV	SLOT	TYPE	DAMAGE	SPD	DPS	ARM	AGI	INT	SPI	STA	STR	ARC	FIR	FRO	NAT	SHA
Cloak of Veiled Shadows	Quest: Cloak of Veiled Shadows (Ahn'Qiraj)	Epic	60	Back	Cloth	-	-	-	52	18	-	-	11	-	-	-	-	-	-
Equip: Improves your chance to hit by 1%																			
Band of Veiled Shadows	Quest: Band of Veiled Shadows (Ahn'Qiraj)	Epic	60	Finger	Misc	-	-	-	-	18	-	-	8	11	-	-	-	-	-
Dagger of Veiled Shadows	Quest: Dagger of Veiled Shadows (Ahn'Qiraj)	Epic	60	One-Hand	Dagger	65-121	1.80	51.7	-	15	-	-	-	7	-	-	-	-	-
Equip: Improves your chance to hit by 1%																			

EMBRACE OF THE VIPER

2 Pcs: Increases damage done by Nature spells and effects by up to 7

3 Pcs: Increased Staves +2

4 Pcs: Increases healing done by spells and effects by up to 11

5 Pcs: +10 Intellect

ITEM	DROPPED BY	RARITY	LEV	SLOT	TYPE	DAMAGE	SPD	DPS	ARM	AGI	INT	SPI	STA	STR	ARC	FIR	FRO	NAT	SHA
Armor of the Fang	Lord Pythas	Uncommon	18	Chest	Leather	-	-	-	82	-	10	7	-	2	-	-	-	-	-
Footpads of the Fang	Lord Serpentis	Uncommon	18	Feet	Leather	-	-	-	57	4	-	-	4	-	-	-	-	-	-
Gloves of the Fang	Druid of the Fang	Uncommon	14	Hands	Leather	-	-	-	47	3	-	-	-	2	-	-	-	-	-
Leggings of the Fang	Lord Cobrahn	Superior	18	Legs	Leather	-	-	-	79	9	-	-	4	5	-	-	-	-	-
Belt of the Fang	Lady Anacondra	Uncommon	16	Waist	Leather	-	-	-	45	2	-	-	3	-	-	-	-	-	-

ENIGMA VESTMENTS

3 Pcs: Your Blizzard spell has a 30% chance to be uninterruptible

5 Pcs: Grants +5% increased spell hit chance for 20 seconds when one of your spells is resisted.

MAGE

ITEM	DROPPED BY	RARITY	LEV	SLOT	TYPE	DAMAGE	SPD	DPS	ARM	AGI	INT	SPI	STA	STR	ARC	FIR	FRO	NAT	SHA
Enigma Robes	Quest: Enigma Robes (Ahn'Qiraj)	Epic	60	Chest	Cloth	-	-	-	133	-	23	7	19	-	-	-	-	-	-
Equip: Increases damage and healing done by magical spells and effects by up to 39, Equip: Improves your chance to get a critical strike with spells by 1%, Equip: Decreases the magical resistances of your spell targets by 20																			
Enigma Boots	Quest: Enigma Boots (Ahn'Qiraj)	Epic	60	Feet	Cloth	-	-	-	82	-	15	6	15	-	-	-	-	-	-
Equip: Increases damage and healing done by magical spells and effects by up to 28, Equip: Improves your chance to hit with spells by 1%, Equip: Restores 4 mana per 5 sec.																			
Enigma Circlet	Quest: Enigma Circlet (Ahn'Qiraj)	Epic	60	Head	Cloth	-	-	-	100	-	24	12	24	-	-	-	-	-	-
Equip: Increases damage and healing done by magical spells and effects by up to 33, Equip: Improves your chance to get a critical strike with spells by 1%, Equip: Improves your chance to hit with spells by 1%																			
Enigma Leggings	Quest: Enigma Leggings (Ahn'Qiraj)	Epic	60	Legs	Cloth	-	-	-	107	-	26	8	21	-	-	-	-	-	-
Equip: Increases damage and healing done by magical spells and effects by up to 34, Equip: Improves your chance to get a critical strike with spells by 1%, Equip: Restores 5 mana per 5 sec.																			
Enigma Shoulderpads	Quest: Enigma Shoulderpads (Ahn'Qiraj)	Epic	60	Shoulder	Cloth	-	-	-	89	-	12	4	16	-	-	-	-	-	-
Equip: Increases damage and healing done by magical spells and effects by up to 30, Equip: Decreases the magical resistances of your spell targets by 10, Equip: Restores 4 mana per 5 sec.																			

FELHEART RAIMENT

3 Pcs: Health or Mana gained from Drain Life and Drain Mana increased by 15%

5 Pcs: Your pet gains 15 stamina and 100 spell resistance against all schools of magic

8 Pcs: Mana cost of Shadow spells reduced by 15%

WARLOCK

ITEM	DROPPED BY	RARITY	LEV	SLOT	TYPE	DAMAGE	SPD	DPS	ARM	AGI	INT	SPI	STA	STR	ARC	FIR	FRO	NAT	SHA
Felheart Robes	Golemagg the Incinerator	Epic	60	Chest	Cloth	-	-	-	102	-	20	-	31	-	-	10	-	-	-
Equip: Increases damage and healing done by magical spells and effects by up to 13, Equip: Improves your chance to hit with spells by 1%
Felheart Slippers	Shazzrah	Epic	60	Feet	Cloth	-	-	-	70	-	11	-	23	-	-	-	-	-	7
Equip: Increases damage and healing done by magical spells and effects by up to 18
Felheart Gloves	Lucifron	Epic	60	Hands	Cloth	-	-	-	63	-	15	8	18	-	-	7	-	-	-
Equip: Improves your chance to get a critical strike with spells by 1%, Equip: Increases damage and healing done by magical spells and effects by up to 9
Felheart Horns	Garr	Epic	60	Head	Cloth	-	-	-	83	-	20	10	27	-	-	10	-	-	-
Equip: Increases damage and healing done by magical spells and effects by up to 20
Felheart Pants	Magmadar	Epic	60	Legs	Cloth	-	-	-	89	-	19	10	20	-	-	-	-	-	10
Equip: Increases damage and healing done by magical spells and effects by up to 30
Felheart Shoulder Pads	Baron Geddon	Epic	60	Shoulder	Cloth	-	-	-	76	-	17	7	25	-	-	-	-	-	7
Equip: Increases damage and healing done by magical spells and effects by up to 9
Felheart Belt	Molten Core	Epic	60	Waist	Cloth	-	-	-	57	-	15	8	18	-	-	7	-	-	-
Equip: Increases damage and healing done by magical spells and effects by up to 20
Felheart Bracers	Molten Core	Epic	60	Wrist	Cloth	-	-	-	44	-	11	8	18	-	-	-	-	-	-
Equip: Increases damage and healing done by magical spells and effects by up to 13

FERALHEART RAINMENT

2 Pcs: +8 All Resistances

4 Pcs: When struck in combat has a chance of returning 300 mana, 10 rage, or 40 energy to the wearer.

6 Pcs: Increases damage and healing done by magical spells and effects by up to 15

6 Pcs: +26 Attack Power

8 Pcs: +200 Armor

DRUID

ITEM	DROPPED BY	RARITY	LEV	SLOT	TYPE	DAMAGE	SPD	DPS	ARM	AGI	INT	SPI	STA	STR	ARC	FIR	FRO	NAT	SHA
Feralheart Vest	Quest: Saving the Best for Last (Ironforge/Orgrimmar)	Epic	60	Chest	Leather	-	-	-	185	9	17	14	17	16	-	-	-	-	-
Equip: Increases damage and healing done by magical spells and effects by up to 12, Equip: Restores 4 mana per 5 sec.
Feralheart Boots	Quest: Anthion's Parting Words (Ironforge/Orgrimmar)	Epic	60	Feet	Leather	-	-	-	127	7	12	10	13	12	-	-	-	-	-
Equip: Increases damage and healing done by magical spells and effects by up to 11, Equip: Restores 2 mana per 5 sec.
Feralheart Gloves	Quest: Just Compensation (Ironforge/Orgrimmar)	Epic	60	Hands	Leather	-	-	-	108	9	12	10	10	10	-	-	-	-	-
Equip: Increases damage and healing done by magical spells and effects by up to 11
Feralheart Cowl	Quest: Saving the Best for Last (Ironforge/Orgrimmar)	Epic	60	Head	Leather	-	-	-	150	9	17	16	17	14	-	-	-	-	-
Equip: Increases damage and healing done by magical spells and effects by up to 16
Feralheart Kilt	Quest: Anthion's Parting Words (Ironforge/Orgrimmar)	Superior	60	Legs	Leather	-	-	-	160	12	14	14	14	14	-	-	-	-	-
Equip: Increases damage and healing done by magical spells and effects by up to 9
Feralheart Spaulders	Quest: Anthion's Parting Words (Ironforge/Orgrimmar)	Superior	60	Shoulder	Leather	-	-	-	136	5	16	8	9	8	-	-	-	-	-
Equip: Increases damage and healing done by magical spells and effects by up to 6, Equip: Restores 2 mana per 5 sec.
Feralheart Belt	Quest: Just Compensation (Ironforge/Orgrimmar)	Superior	60	Waist	Leather	-	-	-	102	7	12	8	9	6	-	-	-	-	-
Equip: Increases damage and healing done by magical spells and effects by up to 7
Feralheart Bracers	Quest: An Earnest Proposition (Ironforge/Orgrimmar)	Superior	60	Wrist	Leather	-	-	-	79	6	12	5	6	6	-	-	-	-	-
Equip: Increases damage and healing done by magical spells and effects by up to 5

FINERY OF INFINITE WISDOM

3 Pcs: Increases the damage of your Shadow Word: Pain spell by 5%

PRIEST

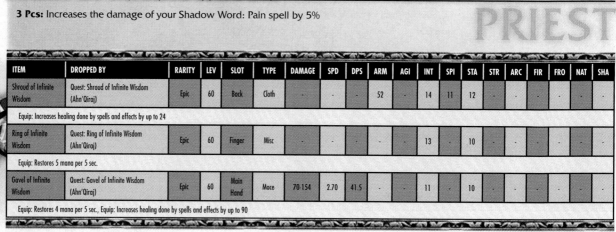

ITEM	DROPPED BY	RARITY	LEV	SLOT	TYPE	DAMAGE	SPD	DPS	ARM	AGI	INT	SPI	STA	STR	ARC	FIR	FRO	NAT	SHA
Shroud of Infinite Wisdom	Quest: Shroud of Infinite Wisdom (Ahn'Qiraj)	Epic	60	Back	Cloth	-	-	-	52	-	14	11	12	-	-	-	-	-	-
Equip: Increases healing done by spells and effects by up to 24																			
Ring of Infinite Wisdom	Quest: Ring of Infinite Wisdom (Ahn'Qiraj)	Epic	60	Finger	Misc	-	-	-	-	-	13	-	10	-	-	-	-	-	-
Equip: Restores 5 mana per 5 sec.																			
Gavel of Infinite Wisdom	Quest: Gavel of Infinite Wisdom (Ahn'Qiraj)	Epic	60	Main Hand	Mace	70-154	2.70	41.5	-	-	11	-	10	-	-	-	-	-	-
Equip: Restores 4 mana per 5 sec., Equip: Increases healing done by spells and effects by up to 90																			

FREETHINKER'S ARMOR

2 Pcs: Restores 4 mana per 5 sec.
3 Pcs: Reduces the casting time of your Holy Light spell by 0.1 sec.
5 Pcs: Increases the duration of all Blessings by 10%

PALADIN

ITEM	DROPPED BY	RARITY	LEV	SLOT	TYPE	DAMAGE	SPD	DPS	ARM	AGI	INT	SPI	STA	STR	ARC	FIR	FRO	NAT	SHA
Zandalar Freethinker's Breastplate	Paragons of Power: The Freethinker's Breastplate (Zul'Gurub)	Epic	60	Chest	Plate	-	-	-	738	-	16	7	26	19	-	-	-	-	-
Equip: Improves your chance to get a critical strike by 1%																			
Hero's Brand	Punctured Voodoo Doll (Zul'Gurub)	Epic	60	Neck	Misc	-	-	-	-	-	6	9	10	10	-	-	-	-	-
Equip: Increases the duration of Hammer of Justice by 0.5 sec.																			
Gri'lek's Charm of Valor	Quest: Gri'lek's Charm of Valor (Zul'Gurub)	Epic	60	Trinket	Misc	-	-	-	-	-	-	-	-	-	-	-	-	-	-
Use: Increases the critical hit chance of Holy spells by 10% for 15 sec.																			
Zandalar Freethinker's Belt	Quest: Paragons of Power: The Freethinker's Belt (Zul'Gurub)	Epic	60	Waist	Plate	-	-	-	391	10	12	-	16	16	-	-	-	-	-
Equip: Increases healing done by spells and effects by up to 26																			
Zandalar Freethinker's Armguards	Quest: Paragons of Power: The Freethinker's Armguards (Zul'Gurub)	Epic	60	Wrist	Plate	-	-	-	304	6	10	-	12	12	-	-	-	-	-
Equip: Increases healing done by spells and effects by up to 11																			

GARMENTS OF THE ORACLE

PRIEST

3 Pcs: 20% chance that your heals on others will also heal you 10% of the amount healed
5 Pcs: Increases the duration of your Renew spell by 3 sec.

ITEM	DROPPED BY	RARITY	LEV	SLOT	TYPE	DAMAGE	SPD	DPS	ARM	AGI	INT	SPI	STA	STR	ARC	FIR	FRO	NAT	SHA
Vestments of the Oracle	Quest: Vestments of the Oracle (Ahn'Qiraj)	Epic	60	Chest	Cloth	-	-	-	183	-	26	15	23	-	-	-	-	-	-
Equip: Increases damage and healing done by magical spells and effects by up to 36, Equip: Improves your chance to get a critical strike with spells by 1%, Equip: Decreases the magical resistances of your spell targets by 10																			
Footwraps of the Oracle	Quest: Footwraps of the Oracle (Ahn'Qiraj)	Epic	60	Feet	Cloth	-	-	-	112	-	17	12	20	-	-	-	-	-	-
Equip: Increases damage and healing done by magical spells and effects by up to 21, Equip: Restores 3 mana per 5 sec.																			
Tiara of the Oracle	Quest: Tiara of the Oracle (Ahn'Qiraj)	Epic	60	Head	Cloth	-	-	-	150	-	22	16	22	-	-	-	-	-	-
Equip: Increases damage and healing done by magical spells and effects by up to 28, Equip: Restores 7 mana per 5 sec., Equip: Improves your chance to hit with spells by 1%																			
Trousers of the Oracle	Quest: Trousers of the Oracle (Ahn'Qiraj)	Epic	60	Legs	Cloth	-	-	-	157	-	24	14	23	-	-	-	-	-	-
Equip: Increases damage and healing done by magical spells and effects by up to 33, Equip: Restores 6 mana per 5 sec.																			
Mantle of the Oracle	Quest: Mantle of the Oracle (Ahn'Qiraj)	Epic	60	Shoulder	Cloth	-	-	-	119	-	20	8	21	-	-	-	-	-	-
Equip: Increases damage and healing done by magical spells and effects by up to 20, Equip: Restores 3 mana per 5 sec., Equip: Decreases the magical resistances of your spell targets by 10																			

GENESIS RAIMENT

DRUID

3 Pcs: Increased Defense +15
3 Pcs: +150 Armor
5 Pcs: Reduces the cooldown of Rebirth by 10 minutes

ITEM	DROPPED BY	RARITY	LEV	SLOT	TYPE	DAMAGE	SPD	DPS	ARM	AGI	INT	SPI	STA	STR	ARC	FIR	FRO	NAT	SHA
Genesis Vest	Quest: Genesis Vest (Ahn'Qiraj)	Epic	60	Chest	Leather	-	-	-	253	12	24	11	24	13	-	-	-	-	-
Equip: Increases damage and healing done by magical spells and effects by up to 28, Equip: Improves your chance to get a critical strike with spells by 1%, Equip: Improves your chance to get a critical strike by 1%																			
Genesis Boots	Quest: Genesis Boots (Ahn'Qiraj)	Epic	60	Feet	Leather	-	-	-	158	13	14	6	14	12	-	-	-	-	-
Equip: Increases damage and healing done by magical spells and effects by up to 20, Equip: Restores 4 mana per 5 sec., Equip: Decreases the magical resistances of your spell targets by 10																			
Genesis Helm	Quest: Genesis Helm (Ahn'Qiraj)	Epic	60	Head	Leather	-	-	-	192	12	22	12	22	15	-	-	-	-	-
Equip: Increases damage and healing done by magical spells and effects by up to 27, Equip: Improves your chance to get a critical strike by 1%																			
Genesis Trousers	Quest: Genesis Trousers (Ahn'Qiraj)	Epic	60	Legs	Leather	-	-	-	207	12	22	9	22	12	-	-	-	-	-
Equip: Increases damage and healing done by magical spells and effects by up to 27, Equip: Improves your chance to get a critical strike by 1%, Equip: Restores 4 mana per 5 sec.																			
Genesis Shoulderpads	Quest: Genesis Shoulderpads (Ahn'Qiraj)	Epic	60	Shoulder	Leather	-	-	-	172	14	13	6	15	15	-	-	-	-	-
Equip: Increases damage and healing done by magical spells and effects by up to 20, Equip: Restores 3 mana per 5 sec.																			

GIANTSTALKER ARMOR

3 Pcs: Increases the range of your Mend Pet spell by 50% and the effect by 10%; also reduces the cost by 30%

5 Pcs: Increases your pet's stamina by 30 and all spell resistances by 40

8 Pcs: Increases the damage of Multi-shot and Volley by 15%

ITEM	DROPPED BY	RARITY	LEV	SLOT	TYPE	DAMAGE	SPD	DPS	ARM	AGI	INT	SPI	STA	STR	ARC	FIR	FRO	NAT	SHA
Giantstalker's Breastplate	Golemagg the Incinerator	Epic	60	Chest	Mail	-	-	-	422	26	11	-	23	-	-	10	-	-	-
Equip: Improves your chance to get a critical strike by 1%																			
Giantstalker's Boots	Gehennas	Epic	60	Feet	Mail	-	-	-	290	28	-	6	14	-	-	-	-	-	7
Giantstalker's Gloves	Shazzrah	Epic	60	Hands	Mail	-	-	-	264	18	-	-	12	-	-	7	-	-	-
Equip: Improves your chance to hit by 2%																			
Giantstalker's Helmet	Garr	Epic	60	Head	Mail	-	-	-	343	23	15	8	23	-	-	10	-	-	-
Equip: Improves your chance to get a critical strike by 1%																			
Giantstalker's Leggings	Magmadar	Epic	60	Legs	Mail	-	-	-	369	32	6	8	15	-	-	-	-	-	10
Equip: Improves your chance to get a critical strike by 1%																			
Giantstalker's Epaulets	Sulfuron Harbinger	Epic	60	Shoulder	Mail	-	-	-	317	24	5	9	14	-	-	-	-	-	7
Equip: Improves your chance to hit by 1%																			
Giantstalker's Belt	Molten Core	Epic	60	Waist	Mail	-	-	-	237	18	9	4	16	-	-	7	-	-	-
Equip: Improves your chance to get a critical strike by 1%																			
Giantstalker's Bracers	Molten Core	Epic	60	Wrist	Mail	-	-	-	185	20	6	5	11	-	-	-	-	-	-

GIFT OF THE GATHERING STORM

3 Pcs: Increases the chain target damage multiplier of your Chain Lightning spell by 5%

ITEM	DROPPED BY	RARITY	LEV	SLOT	TYPE	DAMAGE	SPD	DPS	ARM	AGI	INT	SPI	STA	STR	ARC	FIR	FRO	NAT	SHA
Cloak of the Gathering Storm	Quest: Cloak of the Gathering Storm (Ahn'Qiraj)	Epic	60	Back	Cloth	-	-	-	52	-	13	-	10	11	-	-	-	-	-
Equip: Increases damage and healing done by magical spells and effects by up to 14																			
Ring of the Gathering Storm	Quest: Ring of the Gathering Storm (Ahn'Qiraj)	Epic	60	Finger	Misc	-	-	-	-	-	9	11	-	10	8	-	-	-	-
Equip: Increases damage and healing done by magical spells and effects by up to 12																			
Hammer of the Gathering Storm	Quest: Hammer of the Gathering Storm (Ahn'Qiraj)	Epic	60	Main Hand	Mace	62-137	2.40	41.5	-	-	9	-	10	7	-	-	-	-	-
Equip: Increases damage and healing done by magical spells and effects by up to 53																			

HARUSPEX'S GARB

2 Pcs: Restores 4 mana per 5 sec.

3 Pcs: Increases the duration of Faerie Fire by 5 sec.

5 Pcs: Increases the critical hit chance of your Starfire spell 3%

DRUID

ITEM	DROPPED BY	RARITY	LEV	SLOT	TYPE	DAMAGE	SPD	DPS	ARM	AGI	INT	SPI	STA	STR	ARC	FIR	FRO	NAT	SHA
Zandalar Haruspex's Tunic	Paragons of Power: The Haruspex's Tunic (Zul'Gurub)	Epic	60	Chest	Leather	-	-	-	287	-	24	23	15	-	-	-	-	-	-
Equip: Increases healing done by spells and effects by up to 33																			
Pristine Enchanted South Seas Kelp	Quest: Pristine Enchanted South Seas Kelp (Zul'Gurub)	Epic	60	Neck	Misc	-	-	-	-	-	10	9	10	6	-	-	-	-	-
Equip: Increases the critical hit chance of Wrath and Starfire by 2%																			
Wushoolay's Charm of Nature	Punctured Voodoo Doll (Zul'Gurub)	Epic	60	Trinket	Misc	-	-	-	-	-	-	-	-	-	-	-	-	-	-
Use: Reduces the casting time of your Healing Touch spells by 40%, and reduces the mana cost of your healing spells by 5% for 15 sec.																			
Zandalar Haruspex's Belt	Quest: Paragons of Power: The Haruspex's Belt (Zul'Gurub)	Epic	60	Waist	Leather	-	-	-	165	-	21	12	10	-	-	-	-	-	-
Equip: Increases healing done by spells and effects by up to 15																			
Zandalar Haruspex's Bracers	Quest: Paragons of Power: The Haruspex's Bracers (Zul'Gurub)	Epic	60	Wrist	Leather	-	-	-	122	-	11	11	9	-	-	-	-	-	-
Equip: Increases healing done by spells and effects by up to 24																			

ILLUSIONIST'S ATTIRE

2 Pcs: Increases damage and healing done by magical spells and effects by up to 12

3 Pcs: Decreases the mana cost of Arcane Intellect and Arcane Brilliance by 5%

5 Pcs: Reduces the casting time of your Flamestrike spell by 0.5 sec.

MAGE

ITEM	DROPPED BY	RARITY	LEV	SLOT	TYPE	DAMAGE	SPD	DPS	ARM	AGI	INT	SPI	STA	STR	ARC	FIR	FRO	NAT	SHA
Zandalar Illusionist's Robe	Paragons of Power: The Illusionist's Robes (Zul'Gurub)	Epic	60	Chest	Cloth	-	-	-	100	-	24	-	23	-	-	-	-	-	-
Equip: Improves your chance to hit with spells by 1%, Equip: Increases damage and healing done by magical spells and effects by up to 27																			
Jewel of Kajaro	Quest: Jewel of Kajaro (Zul'Gurub)	Epic	60	Neck	Misc	-	-	-	-	-	13	8	8	-	-	-	-	-	-
Equip: Increases damage and healing done by magical spells and effects by up to 9, Equip: Reduces the cooldown of Counterspell by 2 sec.																			
Zandalar Illusionist's Mantle	Quest: Paragons of Power: The Illusionist's Mantle (Zul'Gurub)	Epic	60	Shoulder	Cloth	-	-	-	71	-	21	10	13	-	-	-	-	-	-
Equip: Increases damage and healing done by magical spells and effects by up to 12																			
Hazza'rah's Charm of Magic	Punctured Voodoo Doll (Zul'Gurub)	Epic	60	Trinket	Misc	-	-	-	-	-	-	-	-	-	-	-	-	-	-
Use: Increases the critical hit chance of your Arcane spells by 5%, and increases the critical hit damage of your Arcane spells by 50% for 20 sec.																			
Zandalar Illusionist's Wraps	Quest: Paragons of Power: The Illusionist's Wraps (Zul'Gurub)	Epic	60	Wrist	Cloth	-	-	-	41	-	11	9	11	-	-	-	-	-	-
Equip: Increases damage and healing done by magical spells and effects by up to 14																			

IMPLEMENTS OF UNSPOKEN NAMES

3 Pcs: 5% increased damage from your summoned pets' melee attacks and damage spells

ITEM	DROPPED BY	RARITY	LEV	SLOT	TYPE	DAMAGE	SPD	DPS	ARM	AGI	INT	SPI	STA	STR	ARC	FIR	FRO	NAT	SHA
Shroud of Unspoken Names	Quest: Shroud of Unspoken Names (Ahn'Qiraj)	Epic	60	Back	Cloth	-	-	-	52	-	9	-	16	-	-	-	-	-	-
Equip: Increases damage and healing done by magical spells and effects by up to 18																			
Ring of Unspoken Names	Quest: Ring of Unspoken Names (Ahn'Qiraj)	Epic	60	Finger	Misc	-	-	-	-	-	-	-	12	-	-	-	-	-	-
Equip: Improves your chance to get a critical strike with spells by 1%, Equip: Increases damage and healing done by magical spells and effects by up to 14, Equip: Improves your chance to hit with spells by 1%																			
Kris of Unspoken Names	Quest: Kris of Unspoken Names (Ahn'Qiraj)	Epic	60	One-Hand	Dagger	39-86	1.50	41.7	-	-	7	-	9	-	-	-	-	-	-
Equip: Increases damage and healing done by magical spells and effects by up to 59																			

IRONWEAVE BATTLESUIT

MAGE PRIEST WARLOCK

4 Pcs: Increases your chance to resist Silence and Interrupt effects by 10%
8 Pcs: +200 Armor

ITEM	DROPPED BY	RARITY	LEV	SLOT	TYPE	DAMAGE	SPD	DPS	ARM	AGI	INT	SPI	STA	STR	ARC	FIR	FRO	NAT	SHA
Ironweave Robe	Sothos and Jarien's Heirlooms	Superior	58	Chest	Cloth	-	-	-	219	-	15	-	24	-	-	-	-	-	-
Ironweave Boots	The Beast	Superior	56	Feet	Cloth	-	-	-	150	-	11	-	17	-	-	-	-	-	-
Ironweave Gloves	Isalien	Superior	56	Hands	Cloth	-	-	-	144	-	11	-	17	-	-	-	-	-	-
Ironweave Cowl	Lord Valthalak	Superior	58	Head	Cloth	-	-	-	203	-	15	-	24	-	-	-	-	-	-
Ironweave Pants	Kormok	Superior	57	Legs	Cloth	-	-	-	207	-	15	-	24	-	-	-	-	-	-
Ironweave Mantle	Korv, Lefty, Malgen Longspear, Snokh Blackspine, Theldren	Superior	56	Shoulder	Cloth	-	-	-	155	-	11	-	17	-	-	-	-	-	-
Ironweave Belt	Mor Grayhoof	Superior	56	Waist	Cloth	-	-	-	139	-	11	-	17	-	-	-	-	-	-
Ironweave Bracers	Halycon	Superior	56	Wrist	Cloth	-	-	-	108	-	8	-	14	-	-	-	-	-	-

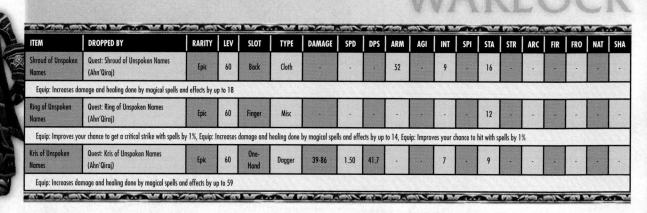

JUDGEMENT ARMOR

3 Pcs: Increases the radius of a Paladin's auras by 10
5 Pcs: Increases damage and healing done by magical spells and effects by up to 47
8 Pcs: Inflicts 60 to 66 additional Holy damage on the target of a Paladin's Judgement

PALADIN

ITEM	DROPPED BY	RARITY	LEV	SLOT	TYPE	DAMAGE	SPD	DPS	ARM	AGI	INT	SPI	STA	STR	ARC	FIR	FRO	NAT	SHA
Judgement Breastplate	Nefarian	Epic	60	Chest	Plate	-	-	-	857	-	21	5	21	16	-	10	-	10	-
Equip: Restores 5 mana per 5 sec., Equip: Increases damage and healing done by magical spells and effects by up to 25
Judgement Sabatons	Broodlord Lashlayer	Epic	60	Feet	Plate	-	-	-	589	-	14	8	20	13	-	10	-	-	-
Equip: Increases damage and healing done by magical spells and effects by up to 18
Judgement Gauntlets	Ebonroc, Firemaw, Flamegor	Epic	60	Hands	Plate	-	-	-	535	-	20	6	15	6	-	-	-	-	10
Equip: Restores 6 mana per 5 sec., Equip: Increases damage and healing done by magical spells and effects by up to 15
Judgement Crown	Onyxia	Epic	60	Head	Plate	-	-	-	696	-	23	6	18	17	-	10	-	10	-
Equip: Increases damage and healing done by magical spells and effects by up to 32
Judgement Legplates	Ragnaros	Epic	60	Legs	Plate	-	-	-	749	-	27	5	26	10	10	10	-	-	-
Equip: Increases damage and healing done by magical spells and effects by up to 20, Equip: Restores 4 mana per 5 sec.
Judgement Spaulders	Chromaggus	Epic	60	Shoulder	Plate	-	-	-	642	-	14	6	20	13	-	10	-	-	-
Equip: Restores 5 mana per 5 sec., Equip: Increases damage and healing done by magical spells and effects by up to 13
Judgement Belt	Vaelastrasz the Corrupt	Epic	60	Waist	Plate	-	-	-	482	-	20	6	14	8	-	-	-	-	10
Equip: Increases damage and healing done by magical spells and effects by up to 23
Judgement Bindings	Razorgore the Untamed	Epic	60	Wrist	Plate	-	-	-	375	-	9	8	21	9	-	-	-	-	-
Equip: Increases damage and healing done by magical spells and effects by up to 7

LAWBRINGER ARMOR

3 Pcs: Increases the chance of triggering a Judgement of Light heal by 10%
5 Pcs: Improves your chance to get a critical strike with spells by 1%
5 Pcs: Improves your chance to get a critical strike by 1%
8 Pcs: Gives the Paladin a chance on every melee hit to heal your party for 189 to 211

PALADIN

ITEM	DROPPED BY	RARITY	LEV	SLOT	TYPE	DAMAGE	SPD	DPS	ARM	AGI	INT	SPI	STA	STR	ARC	FIR	FRO	NAT	SHA
Lawbringer Chestguard	Golemagg the Incinerator	Epic	60	Chest	Plate	-	-	-	749	-	21	13	26	8	-	10	-	-	-
Equip: Increases healing done by spells and effects by up to 22
Lawbringer Boots	Lucifron	Epic	60	Feet	Plate	-	-	-	515	-	13	10	20	7	-	-	-	-	7
Equip: Restores 2 mana per 5 sec., Equip: Increases healing done by spells and effects by up to 18
Lawbringer Gauntlets	Gehennas	Epic	60	Hands	Plate	-	-	-	468	-	15	14	15	10	-	7	-	-	-
Equip: Increases healing done by spells and effects by up to 18
Lawbringer Helm	Garr	Epic	60	Head	Plate	-	-	-	608	-	24	10	20	9	-	10	-	-	-
Equip: Restores 4 mana per 5 sec., Equip: Increases healing done by spells and effects by up to 22
Lawbringer Legplates	Magmadar	Epic	60	Legs	Plate	-	-	-	655	-	18	18	24	7	-	-	-	-	10
Equip: Restores 3 mana per 5 sec., Equip: Increases healing done by spells and effects by up to 22
Lawbringer Spaulders	Baron Geddon	Epic	60	Shoulder	Plate	-	-	-	562	-	15	8	22	10	-	-	-	-	7
Equip: Increases healing done by spells and effects by up to 18
Lawbringer Belt	Molten Core	Epic	60	Waist	Plate	-	-	-	421	-	20	8	15	13	-	7	-	-	-
Equip: Increases healing done by spells and effects by up to 18
Lawbringer Bracers	Molten Core	Epic	60	Wrist	Plate	-	-	-	328	-	8	11	11	10	-	-	-	-	-
Equip: Restores 4 mana per 5 sec.

LIGHTFORGE ARMOR

2 Pcs: +200 Armor

4 Pcs: +40 Attack Power

6 Pcs: Chance on melee attack to increase your damage and healing done by magical spells and effects by up to 95 for 10 seconds.

8 Pcs: +8 All Resistances

ITEM	DROPPED BY	RARITY	LEV	SLOT	TYPE	DAMAGE	SPD	DPS	ARM	AGI	INT	SPI	STA	STR	ARC	FIR	FRO	NAT	SHA
Lightforge Breastplate	General Drakkisath	Superior	58	Chest	Plate	-	-	-	657	-	16	8	21	13	-	-	-	-	-
Lightforge Boots	Balnazzar	Superior	54	Feet	Plate				424	-	-	9	18	8	-	-	-	-	-
Lightforge Gauntlets	Timmy the Cruel	Superior	54	Hands	Plate				386	-	-	14	9	14	-	-	-	-	-
Lightforge Helm	Darkmaster Gandling	Superior	57	Head	Plate				526	6	14	10	20	13	-	-	-	-	-
Lightforge Legplates	Baron Rivendare	Superior	56	Legs	Plate				557	8	12	9	14	20	-	-	-	-	-
Lightforge Spaulders	The Beast	Superior	55	Shoulder	Plate				470	4	11	5	15	9	-	-	-	-	-
Lightforge Belt	Crimson Gallant, Crimson Guardsman, Rockwing Gargoyle, Rockwing Screecher	Superior	53	Waist	Plate				341	-	15	6	9	10	-	-	-	-	-
Lightforge Bracers	Lord Alexei Barov, Risen Protector, Risen Warrior	Superior	52	Wrist	Plate				261	4	-	8	10	7	-	-	-	-	-

MADCAP'S OUTFIT

2 Pcs: +20 Attack Power

3 Pcs: Decreases the cooldown of Blind by 20 sec.

5 Pcs: Decrease the energy cost of Eviscerate and Rupture by 5

ITEM	DROPPED BY	RARITY	LEV	SLOT	TYPE	DAMAGE	SPD	DPS	ARM	AGI	INT	SPI	STA	STR	ARC	FIR	FRO	NAT	SHA
Zandalar Madcap's Tunic	Paragons of Power: The Madcap's Tunic (Zul'Gurub)	Epic	60	Chest	Leather	-	-	-	197	-	-	-	19	-	-	-	-	-	-
Equip: Improves your chance to get a critical strike by 2%, Equip: +44 Attack Power																			
Zandalarian Shadow Mastery Talisman	Quest: Zandalarian Shadow Mastery Talisman (Zul'Gurub)	Epic	60	Neck	Misc					15	-	-	9	6	-	-	-	-	-
Equip: Decreases the cooldown of Kick by 0.5 sec.																			
Zandalar Madcap's Mantle	Quest: Paragons of Power: The Madcap's Mantle (Zul'Gurub)	Epic	60	Shoulder	Leather				140	20	-	-	12	12	-	-	-	-	-
Equip: Improves your chance to hit by 1%																			
Renataki's Charm of Trickery	Punctured Voodoo Doll (Zul'Gurub)	Epic	60	Trinket	Misc										-	-	-	-	-
Use: Instantly increases your energy by 60																			
Zandalar Madcap's Bracers	Quest: Paragons of Power: The Madcap's Bracers (Zul'Gurub)	Epic	60	Wrist	Leather				82	14	-	-	14	9	-	-	-	-	-

MAGISTER'S REGALIA

2 Pcs: +200 Armor

4 Pcs: Increases damage and healing done by magical spells and effects by up to 23

6 Pcs: When struck in combat has a chance of freezing the attacker in place for 3 seconds.

8 Pcs: +8 All Resistances

MAGE

ITEM	DROPPED BY	RARITY	LEV	SLOT	TYPE	DAMAGE	SPD	DPS	ARM	AGI	INT	SPI	STA	STR	ARC	FIR	FRO	NAT	SHA
Magister's Robes	General Drakkisath	Superior	58	Chest	Cloth	-	-	-	89	-	31	8	9	-	-	-	-	-	-
Magister's Boots	Hearthsinger Forresten	Superior	54	Feet	Cloth	-	-	-	58	-	14	14	9	-	-	-	-	-	-
Magister's Gloves	Doctor Theolen Krastinov	Superior	54	Hands	Cloth	-	-	-	52	-	14	14	9	-	-	-	-	-	-
Magister's Crown	Darkmaster Gandling	Superior	57	Head	Cloth	-	-	-	71	-	30	5	11	-	-	-	-	-	-
Magister's Leggings	Baron Rivendare	Superior	56	Legs	Cloth	-	-	-	76	-	20	21	12	-	-	-	-	-	-
Magister's Mantle	Ras Frostwhisper	Superior	55	Shoulder	Cloth	-	-	-	64	-	22	6	6	-	-	-	-	-	-
Magister's Belt	Crimson Battle Mage, Crimson Conjuror, Crimson Sorcerer, Scholomance Adept, Smolderthorn Mystic, Thuzadin Necromancer, Thuzadin Shadowcaster	Superior	53	Waist	Cloth	-	-	-	46	-	21	6	6	-	-	-	-	-	-
Magister's Bindings	Bloodaxe Evoker, Firebrand Invoker, Firebrand Pyromancer, Quartermaster Zigris, Rage Talon Fire Tongue, Scarshield Spellbinder	Superior	52	Wrist	Cloth	-	-	-	35	-	15	5	4	-	-	-	-	-	-

MAJOR MOJO INFUSION

2 Pcs: +30 Attack Power

ITEM	DROPPED BY	RARITY	LEV	SLOT	TYPE	DAMAGE	SPD	DPS	ARM	AGI	INT	SPI	STA	STR	ARC	FIR	FRO	NAT	SHA
Seal of Jin	High Priest Thekal	Superior	60	Finger	Misc	-	-	-	-	-	-	-	8	-	-	-	-	-	-
Equip: Improves your chance to get a critical strike by 1%, Equip: +20 Attack Power																			
Band of Jin	High Priestess Mar'li	Superior	60	Finger	Misc	-	-	-	-	14	-	-	8	-	-	-	-	-	-
Equip: Improves your chance to hit by 1%																			

NECROPILE RAIMENT

2 Pcs: Increased Defense +3
3 Pcs: +5 Intellect
4 Pcs: +15 All Resistances
5 Pcs: Increases damage and healing done by magical spells and effects by up to 23

ITEM	DROPPED BY	RARITY	LEV	SLOT	TYPE	DAMAGE	SPD	DPS	ARM	AGI	INT	SPI	STA	STR	ARC	FIR	FRO	NAT	SHA
Necropile Robe	Scholomance Bosses	Superior	56	Chest	Cloth	-	-	-	87	5	12	-	22	-	-	-	-	-	-
Equip: Increases damage and healing done by magical spells and effects by up to 8																			
Necropile Boots	Scholomance Bosses	Superior	56	Feet	Cloth	-	-	-	60	10	9	-	15	-	-	-	-	-	-
Equip: Increases damage and healing done by magical spells and effects by up to 11																			
Necropile Leggings	Scholomance Bosses	Superior	56	Legs	Cloth	-	-	-	76	18	12	-	21	-	-	-	-	-	-
Necropile Mantle	Scholomance Bosses	Superior	56	Shoulder	Cloth	-	-	-	65	11	9	-	17	-	-	-	-	-	-
Necropile Cuffs	Scholomance Bosses	Superior	56	Wrist	Cloth	-	-	-	38	11	7	-	12	-	-	-	-	-	-

NEMESIS RAIMENT

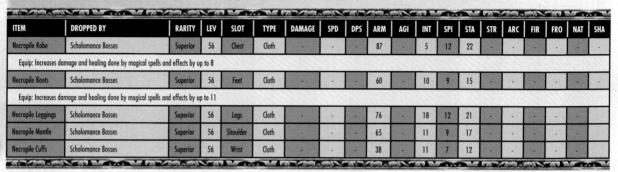

3 Pcs: Increases damage and healing done by magical spells and effects by up to 23
5 Pcs: Your pet gains 20 stamina and 130 spell resistance against all schools of magic
8 Pcs: Reduces the threat generated by your Destruction spells by 20%

ITEM	DROPPED BY	RARITY	LEV	SLOT	TYPE	DAMAGE	SPD	DPS	ARM	AGI	INT	SPI	STA	STR	ARC	FIR	FRO	NAT	SHA
Nemesis Robes	Nefarian	Epic	60	Chest	Cloth	-	-	-	116	-	16	8	26	-	-	10	-	10	-
Equip: Improves your chance to get a critical strike with spells by 1%, Equip: Increases damage and healing done by magical spells and effects by up to 32																			
Nemesis Boots	Broodlord Lashlayer	Epic	60	Feet	Cloth	-	-	-	80	-	17	6	20	-	-	10	-	-	-
Equip: Increases damage and healing done by magical spells and effects by up to 23																			
Nemesis Gloves	Ebonroc, Firemaw, Flamegor	Epic	60	Hands	Cloth	-	-	-	72	-	15	-	17	-	-	-	-	-	10
Equip: Restores 4 health per 5 sec., Equip: Increases damage and healing done by magical spells and effects by up to 15, Equip: Improves your chance to get a critical strike with spells by 1%																			
Nemesis Skullcap	Onyxia	Epic	60	Head	Cloth	-	-	-	94	-	16	6	26	-	-	-	10	-	10
Equip: Restores 4 health per 5 sec., Equip: Increases damage and healing done by magical spells and effects by up to 32																			
Nemesis Leggings	Ragnaros	Epic	60	Legs	Cloth	-	-	-	101	-	16	4	23	-	10	10	-	-	-
Equip: Increases damage and healing done by magical spells and effects by up to 39																			
Nemesis Spaulders	Chromaggus	Epic	60	Shoulder	Cloth	-	-	-	87	-	13	6	20	-	-	10	-	-	-
Equip: Restores 4 health per 5 sec., Equip: Increases damage and healing done by magical spells and effects by up to 23																			
Nemesis Belt	Vaelastrasz the Corrupt	Epic	60	Waist	Cloth	-	-	-	65	-	8	6	18	-	-	-	-	-	10
Equip: Improves your chance to get a critical strike with spells by 1%, Equip: Increases damage and healing done by magical spells and effects by up to 25																			
Nemesis Bracers	Razorgore the Untamed	Epic	60	Wrist	Cloth	-	-	-	51	-	11	6	21	-	-	-	-	-	-
Equip: Increases damage and healing done by magical spells and effects by up to 15																			

NETHERWIND REGALIA

3 Pcs: Reduces the threat generated by your Scorch, Arcane Missiles, Fireball, and Frostbolt spells

5 Pcs: Increases the radius of Arcane Explosion, Flamestrike, and Blizzard by 25%

8 Pcs: 10% chance after casting Arcane Missiles, Fireball, or Frostbolt that your next spell with a casting time under 10 seconds cast instantly.

MAGE

ITEM	DROPPED BY	RARITY	LEV	SLOT	TYPE	DAMAGE	SPD	DPS	ARM	AGI	INT	SPI	STA	STR	ARC	FIR	FRO	NAT	SHA
Netherwind Robes	Nefarian	Epic	60	Chest	Cloth	-	-	-	116	-	26	8	16	-	-	10	-	10	-
Equip: Improves your chance to get a critical strike with spells by 1%, Equip: Increases damage and healing done by magical spells and effects by up to 32																			
Netherwind Boots	Broodlord Lashlayer	Epic	60	Feet	Cloth	-	-	-	80	-	16	10	13	-	-	10	-	-	-
Equip: Increases damage and healing done by magical spells and effects by up to 27																			
Netherwind Gloves	Ebonroc, Firemaw, Flamegor	Epic	60	Hands	Cloth	-	-	-	72	-	16	6	16	-	-	-	-	-	10
Equip: Improves your chance to get a critical strike with spells by 1%, Equip: Increases damage and healing done by magical spells and effects by up to 20																			
Netherwind Crown	Onyxia	Epic	60	Head	Cloth	-	-	-	94	-	26	7	17	-	-	10	-	10
Equip: Restores 4 mana per 5 sec., Equip: Increases damage and healing done by magical spells and effects by up to 32																			
Netherwind Pants	Ragnaros	Epic	60	Legs	Cloth	-	-	-	101	-	27	5	16	-	10	10	-	-	-
Equip: Increases damage and healing done by magical spells and effects by up to 30, Equip: Improves your chance to get a critical strike with spells by 1%																			
Netherwind Mantle	Chromaggus	Epic	60	Shoulder	Cloth	-	-	-	87	-	13	12	16	-	-	10	-	-	-
Equip: Restores 4 mana per 5 sec., Equip: Increases damage and healing done by magical spells and effects by up to 21																			
Netherwind Belt	Vaelastrasz the Corrupt	Epic	60	Waist	Cloth	-	-	-	65	-	20	13	13	-	-	-	-	-	10
Equip: Increases damage and healing done by magical spells and effects by up to 23																			
Netherwind Bindings	Razorgore the Untamed	Epic	60	Wrist	Cloth	-	-	-	51	-	15	8	9	-	-	-	-	-	-
Equip: Increases damage and healing done by magical spells and effects by up to 19, Equip: Restores 4 mana per 5 sec.																			

NIGHTSLAYER ARMOR

3 Pcs: Reduces the cooldown of your Vanish ability by 30 sec.

5 Pcs: Increases your maximum Energy by 10

8 Pcs: Heals the rogue for 500 when Vanish is performed

ROGUE

ITEM	DROPPED BY	RARITY	LEV	SLOT	TYPE	DAMAGE	SPD	DPS	ARM	AGI	INT	SPI	STA	STR	ARC	FIR	FRO	NAT	SHA
Nightslayer Chestpiece	Golemagg the Incinerator	Epic	60	Chest	Leather	-	-	-	200	29	-	-	20	10	-	10	-	-	-
Equip: Improves your chance to get a critical strike by 1%																			
Nightslayer Boots	Shazzrah	Epic	60	Feet	Leather	-	-	-	138	26	-	-	18	-	-	-	-	-	7
Nightslayer Gloves	Gehennas	Epic	60	Hands	Leather	-	-	-	125	18	-	-	17	12	-	7	-	-	-
Equip: Improves your chance to hit by 1%																			
Nightslayer Cover	Garr	Epic	60	Head	Leather	-	-	-	163	20	-	-	19	6	-	10	-	-	-
Equip: Improves your chance to get a critical strike by 2%																			
Nightslayer Pants	Magmadar	Epic	60	Legs	Leather	-	-	-	175	33	-	-	15	10	-	-	-	-	10
Equip: Improves your chance to get a critical strike by 1%																			
Nightslayer Shoulder Pads	Sulfuron Harbinger	Epic	60	Shoulder	Leather	-	-	-	150	26	-	-	12	3	-	-	-	-	7
Equip: Improves your chance to hit by 1%																			
Nightslayer Belt	Molten Core	Epic	60	Waist	Leather	-	-	-	113	17	-	-	18	9	-	7	-	-	-
Equip: Improves your chance to get a critical strike by 1%																			
Nightslayer Bracelets	Molten Core	Epic	60	Wrist	Leather	-	-	-	88	20	-	-	15	-	-	-	-	-	-

OVERLORD'S RESOLUTION

2 Pcs: Increases your chance to dodge an attack by 1%

ITEM	DROPPED BY	RARITY	LEV	SLOT	TYPE	DAMAGE	SPD	DPS	ARM	AGI	INT	SPI	STA	STR	ARC	FIR	FRO	NAT	SHA
Overlord's Crimson Band	Bloodlord Mandokir	Superior	60	Finger	Misc	-	-	-	-	8	-	-	10	9	-	-	-	-	-
Equip: Increased Defense +7																			
Overlord's Onyx Band	High Priestess Arlokk	Superior	60	Finger	Misc	-	-	-	-	-	-	-	11	-	-	-	-	-	-
Equip: Increases your chance to block attacks with a shield by 2%, Equip: Increases your chance to dodge an attack by 1%																			

PRAYER OF THE PRIMAL

2 Pcs: Increases healing done by spells and effects by up to 33

ITEM	DROPPED BY	RARITY	LEV	SLOT	TYPE	DAMAGE	SPD	DPS	ARM	AGI	INT	SPI	STA	STR	ARC	FIR	FRO	NAT	SHA
Primalist's Seal	Bloodlord Mandokir	Superior	60	Finger	Misc	-	-	-	-	-	12	8	-	-	-	-	-	-	-
Equip: Increases healing done by spells and effects by up to 29																			
Primalist's Band	High Priestess Jeklik	Superior	60	Finger	Misc	-	-	-	-	-	10	-	8	-	-	-	-	-	-
Equip: Restores 6 mana per 5 sec.																			

PREDATOR'S ARMOR

2 Pcs: +20 Attack Power

3 Pcs: Decreases the cooldown of Concussive Shot by 1 sec.

5 Pcs: Increases the duration of Serpent Sting by 3 sec.

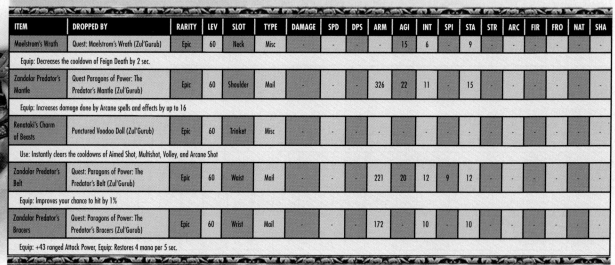

HUNTER

ITEM	DROPPED BY	RARITY	LEV	SLOT	TYPE	DAMAGE	SPD	DPS	ARM	AGI	INT	SPI	STA	STR	ARC	FIR	FRO	NAT	SHA
Maelstrom's Wrath	Quest: Maelstrom's Wrath (Zul'Gurub)	Epic	60	Neck	Misc	-	-	-	-	15	6	-	9	-	-	-	-	-	-
Equip: Decreases the cooldown of Feign Death by 2 sec.																			
Zandalar Predator's Mantle	Quest Paragons of Power: The Predator's Mantle (Zul'Gurub)	Epic	60	Shoulder	Mail	-	-	-	326	22	11	-	15	-	-	-	-	-	-
Equip: Increases damage done by Arcane spells and effects by up to 16																			
Renataki's Charm of Beasts	Punctured Voodoo Doll (Zul'Gurub)	Epic	60	Trinket	Misc	-	-	-	-	-	-	-	-	-	-	-	-	-	-
Use: Instantly clears the cooldowns of Aimed Shot, Multishot, Volley, and Arcane Shot																			
Zandalar Predator's Belt	Quest: Paragons of Power: The Predator's Belt (Zul'Gurub)	Epic	60	Waist	Mail	-	-	-	221	20	12	9	12	-	-	-	-	-	-
Equip: Improves your chance to hit by 1%																			
Zandalar Predator's Bracers	Quest: Paragons of Power: The Predator's Bracers (Zul'Gurub)	Epic	60	Wrist	Mail	-	-	-	172	-	10	-	10	-	-	-	-	-	-
Equip: +43 ranged Attack Power, Equip: Restores 4 mana per 5 sec.																			

PRIMAL BLESSING

2 Pcs: Grants a small chance when ranged or melee damage is dealt to infuse the wielder with a blessing from the Primal Gods. Ranged and melee attack power increased by 300 for 12 seconds.

ITEM	DROPPED BY	RARITY	LEV	SLOT	TYPE	DAMAGE	SPD	DPS	ARM	AGI	INT	SPI	STA	STR	ARC	FIR	FRO	NAT	SHA
Thekal's Grasp	High Priest Thekal	Epic	60	Main Hand	Fist Weapon	72-135	2.20	47.0	-	-	-	-	13	-	-	-	-	-	-
Equip: Improves your chance to get a critical strike by 1%																			
Arlokk's Grasp	High Priestess Arlokk	Epic	60	Off Hand	Fist Weapon	41-84	1.50	41.7	-	-	-	-	-	-	-	-	-	-	-
Chance on Hit: Sends a shadowy bolt at the enemy causing 55 to 85 Shadow damage																			

SHADOWCRAFT ARMOR

2 Pcs: +200 Armor

4 Pcs: +40 Attack Power

6 Pcs: Chance on melee attack to restore 35 energy

8 Pcs: +8 All Resistances

ROGUE

ITEM	DROPPED BY	RARITY	LEV	SLOT	TYPE	DAMAGE	SPD	DPS	ARM	AGI	INT	SPI	STA	STR	ARC	FIR	FRO	NAT	SHA
Shadowcraft Tunic	General Drakkisath	Superior	58	Chest	Leather	-	-	-	176	26	-	12	13	-	-	-	-	-	-
Shadowcraft Boots	Rattlegore	Superior	54	Feet	Leather	-	-	-	115	21	-	-	9	-	-	-	-	-	-
Shadowcraft Gloves	Shadow Hunter Vosh'gajin	Superior	54	Hands	Leather	-	-	-	105	14	-	10	9	9	-	-	-	-	-
Shadowcraft Cap	Darkmaster Gandling	Superior	57	Head	Leather	-	-	-	141	20	-	5	18	13	-	-	-	-	-
Shadowcraft Pants	Baron Rivendare	Superior	56	Legs	Leather	-	-	-	150	25	-	-	12	12	-	-	-	-	-
Shadowcraft Spaulders	Cannon Master Willey	Superior	55	Shoulder	Leather	-	-	-	127	22	-	-	9	-	-	-	-	-	-
Shadowcraft Belt	Blackand Assassin, Bloodaxe Warmonger, Firebrand Grunt, Firebrand Legionnaire, Quartermaster Zigris, Scarshield Legionnaire, Smolderthorn Shadow Hunter	Superior	53	Waist	Leather	-	-	-	93	14	-	9	10	9	-	-	-	-	-
Shadowcraft Bracers	Dark Shade, Instructor Malicia, Plague Ghoul, Risen Construct, Scholomance Occultist	Superior	52	Wrist	Leather	-	-	-	71	15	-	-	7	-	-	-	-	-	-

SHARD OF THE GODS

2 Pcs: +10 All Resistances

ITEM	DROPPED BY	RARITY	LEV	SLOT	TYPE	DAMAGE	SPD	DPS	ARM	AGI	INT	SPI	STA	STR	ARC	FIR	FRO	NAT	SHA
Shard of the Flame	Ragnaros	Epic	60	Trinket	Misc	-	-	-	-	-	-	-	-	-	-	-	-	-	-
Equip: Restores 16 health per 5 sec.																			
Shard of the Scale	Onyxia	Epic	60	Trinket	Misc	-	-	-	-	-	-	-	-	-	-	-	-	-	-
Equip: Restores 16 mana per 5 sec.																			

SORCERER'S REGALIA

2 Pcs: +8 All Resistances
4 Pcs: When struck in combat has a chance of freezing the attacker in place for 3 seconds.
6 Pcs: Increases damage and healing done by magical spells and effects by up to 23
8 Pcs: +200 Armor

ITEM	DROPPED BY	RARITY	LEV	SLOT	TYPE	DAMAGE	SPD	DPS	ARM	AGI	INT	SPI	STA	STR	ARC	FIR	FRO	NAT	SHA
Sorcerer's Robes	Quest: Saving the Best for Last (Ironforge/Orgrimmar)	Epic	60	Chest	Cloth	-	-	-	93	-	25	9	14	-	-	-	-	-	-
Equip: Increases damage and healing done by magical spells and effects by up to 16, Equip: Decreases the magical resistances of your spell targets by 20																				
Sorcerer's Boots	Quest: Anthion's Parting Words (Ironforge/Orgrimmar)	Epic	60	Feet	Cloth	-	-	-	64	-	16	10	14	-	-	-	-	-	-
Equip: Increases damage and healing done by magical spells and effects by up to 21																				
Sorcerer's Gloves	Quest: Just Compensation (Ironforge/Orgrimmar)	Epic	60	Hands	Cloth	-	-	-	54	-	14	10	12	-	-	-	-	-	-
Equip: Increases damage and healing done by magical spells and effects by up to 12, Equip: Improves your chance to hit with spells by 1%																				
Sorcerer's Crown	Quest: Saving the Best for Last (Ironforge/Orgrimmar)	Epic	60	Head	Cloth	-	-	-	75	-	25	14	16	-	-	-	-	-	-
Equip: Increases damage and healing done by magical spells and effects by up to 11, Equip: Improves your chance to get a critical strike with spells by 1%																				
Sorcerer's Leggings	Quest: Anthion's Parting Words (Ironforge/Orgrimmar)	Superior	60	Legs	Cloth	-	-	-	81	-	22	10	17	-	-	-	-	-	-
Equip: Increases damage and healing done by magical spells and effects by up to 16																				
Sorcerer's Mantle	Quest: Anthion's Parting Words (Ironforge/Orgrimmar)	Superior	60	Shoulder	Cloth	-	-	-	69	-	17	7	11	-	-	-	-	-	-
Equip: Increases damage and healing done by magical spells and effects by up to 9																				
Sorcerer's Belt	Quest: Just Compensation (Ironforge/Orgrimmar)	Superior	60	Waist	Cloth	-	-	-	52	-	14	7	12	-	-	-	-	-	-
Equip: Increases damage and healing done by magical spells and effects by up to 14																				
Sorcerer's Bindings	Quest: An Earnest Proposition (Ironforge/Orgrimmar)	Superior	60	Wrist	Cloth	-	-	-	40	-	12	5	8	-	-	-	-	-	-
Equip: Increases damage and healing done by magical spells and effects by up to 8																				

SOULFORGE ARMOR

2 Pcs: +8 All Resistances

4 Pcs: Chance on melee attack to increase your damage and healing done by magical spells and effects by up to 95 for 10 seconds.

6 Pcs: +40 Attack Power

8 Pcs: +200 Armor

PALADIN

ITEM	DROPPED BY	RARITY	LEV	SLOT	TYPE	DAMAGE	SPD	DPS	ARM	AGI	INT	SPI	STA	STR	ARC	FIR	FRO	NAT	SHA
Soulforge Breastplate	Quest: Saving the Best for Last (Ironforge/Orgrimmar)	Epic	60	Chest	Plate	-	-	-	684	-	17	12	17	16	-	-	-	-	-
Equip: Increases damage and healing done by magical spells and effects by up to 14, Equip: Improves your chance to get a critical strike by 1%																			
Soulforge Boots	Quest: Anthion's Parting Words (Ironforge/Orgrimmar)	Epic	60	Feet	Plate	-	-	-	470	-	12	10	13	12	-	-	-	-	-
Equip: Increases damage and healing done by magical spells and effects by up to 12, Equip: Restores 4 mana per 5 sec.																			
Soulforge Gauntlets	Quest: Just Compensation (Ironforge/Orgrimmar)	Epic	60	Hands	Plate	-	-	-	393	-	10	-	10	9	-	-	-	-	-
Equip: Increases damage and healing done by magical spells and effects by up to 11, Equip: Improves your chance to get a critical strike by 1%																			
Soulforge Helm	Quest: Saving the Best for Last (Ironforge/Orgrimmar)	Epic	60	Head	Plate	-	-	-	556	-	17	12	17	16	-	-	-	-	-
Equip: Increases damage and healing done by magical spells and effects by up to 14, Equip: Improves your chance to get a critical strike with spells by 1%																			
Soulforge Legplates	Quest: Anthion's Parting Words (Ironforge/Orgrimmar)	Superior	60	Legs	Plate	-	-	-	601	-	17	10	17	16	-	-	-	-	-
Equip: Increases damage and healing done by magical spells and effects by up to 11																			
Soulforge Spaulders	Quest: Anthion's Parting Words (Ironforge/Orgrimmar)	Superior	60	Shoulder	Plate	-	-	-	507	-	11	-	11	10	-	-	-	-	-
Equip: Increases damage and healing done by magical spells and effects by up to 12, Equip: Restores 4 mana per 5 sec.																			
Soulforge Belt	Quest: Just Compensation (Ironforge/Orgrimmar)	Superior	60	Waist	Plate	-	-	-	380	-	11	-	11	10	-	-	-	-	-
Equip: Increases damage and healing done by magical spells and effects by up to 12, Equip: Restores 4 mana per 5 sec.																			
Soulforge Bracers	Quest: An Earnest Proposition (Ironforge/Orgrimmar)	Superior	60	Wrist	Plate	-	-	-	296	-	9	-	10	9	-	-	-	-	-
Equip: Increases damage and healing done by magical spells and effects by up to 8																			

SPIDER'S KISS

2 Pcs: Chance on Hit: Immobilizes the target and lowers their armor by 100 for 10 sec.

ITEM	DROPPED BY	RARITY	LEV	SLOT	TYPE	DAMAGE	SPD	DPS	ARM	AGI	INT	SPI	STA	STR	ARC	FIR	FRO	NAT	SHA
Fang of the Crystal Spider	Crystal Fang	Superior	56	One-Hand	Dagger	45-84	1.60	40.3	-	-	-	-	-	-	-	-	-	-	-
Chance on Hit: Slows target enemy's casting speed, melee attack speed and range attack speed by 10% for 10 sec.																			
Venomspitter	Mother Smolderweb	Superior	55	One-Hand	Mace	52-98	1.90	39.5	-	-	-	-	-	-	-	-	-	-	-
Chance on Hit: Poisons target for 7 Nature damage every 2 sec for 30 sec.																			

SPIRIT OF ESKHANDAR

4 Pcs: 1% chance on a critical hit to call forth the spirit of Eskhandar to protect you in battle for 2 minutes

ITEM	DROPPED BY	RARITY	LEV	SLOT	TYPE	DAMAGE	SPD	DPS	ARM	AGI	INT	SPI	STA	STR	ARC	FIR	FRO	NAT	SHA
Eskhandar's Pelt	Lord Kazzak	Epic	60	Back	Cloth	-	-	-	51	-	-	-	20	-	-	-	-	-	-
Equip: Improves your chance to get a critical strike by 1%																			
Eskhandar's Right Claw	Magmadar	Epic	60	Main Hand	Fist Weapon	50-94	1.50	48.0	-	4	-	-	-	-	-	-	-	-	-
Chance on Hit: Increases your attack speed by 30% for 5 sec.																			
Eskhandar's Collar	Onyxia	Epic	60	Neck	Misc	-	-	-	-	-	-	-	17	-	-	-	-	-	-
Equip: Increases your chance to dodge an attack by 1%, Equip: Improves your chance to get a critical strike by 1%																			
Eskhandar's Left Claw	Azuregos	Epic	60	Off Hand	Fist Weapon	50-94	1.50	48.0	-	4	-	-	-	-	-	-	-	-	-
Chance on Hit: Slows enemy's movement to 40% of normal speed and causes them to bleed for 150 damage over 30 sec.																			

STORMCALLER'S GARB

3 Pcs: Your Lightning Bolt, Chain Lightning, and Shock spells have a 20% chance to grant up to 50 Nature damage to spells for 8 seconds

5 Pcs: -0.4 seconds on the casting time of your Chain Heal spell

SHAMAN

ITEM	DROPPED BY	RARITY	LEV	SLOT	TYPE	DAMAGE	SPD	DPS	ARM	AGI	INT	SPI	STA	STR	ARC	FIR	FRO	NAT	SHA
Stormcaller's Hauberk	Quest: Stormcaller's Hauberk (Ahn'Qiraj)	Epic	60	Chest	Mail	-	-	-	553	10	24	11	24	11	-	-	-	-	-
Equip: Increases damage and healing done by magical spells and effects by up to 32, Equip: Improves your chance to get a critical strike by 1%, Equip: Improves your chance to get a critical strike with spells by 1%																			
Stormcaller's Footguards	Quest: Stormcaller's Footguards (Ahn'Qiraj)	Epic	60	Feet	Mail	-	-	-	340	9	14	6	14	12	-	-	-	-	-
Equip: Increases damage and healing done by magical spells and effects by up to 22, Equip: Decreases the magical resistances of your spell targets by 10, Equip: Restores 4 mana per 5 sec.																			
Stormcaller's Diadem	Quest: Stormcaller's Diadem (Ahn'Qiraj)	Epic	60	Head	Mail	-	-	-	416	8	22	12	22	12	-	-	-	-	-
Equip: Increases damage and healing done by magical spells and effects by up to 32, Equip: Improves your chance to get a critical strike with spells by 1%																			
Stormcaller's Leggings	Quest: Stormcaller's Leggings (Ahn'Qiraj)	Epic	60	Legs	Mail	-	-	-	448	9	22	12	22	12	-	-	-	-	-
Equip: Increases damage and healing done by magical spells and effects by up to 29, Equip: Improves your chance to get a critical strike with spells by 1%, Equip: Restores 4 mana per 5 sec.																			
Stormcaller's Pauldrons	Quest: Stormcaller's Pauldrons (Ahn'Qiraj)	Epic	60	Shoulder	Mail	-	-	-	371	10	13	6	15	10	-	-	-	-	-
Equip: Increases damage and healing done by magical spells and effects by up to 28, Equip: Restores 3 mana per 5 sec.																			

STORMRAGE RAIMENT

3 Pcs: Allows 15% of your Mana regeneration to continue while casting
5 Pcs: Reduces the casting time of your Regrowth spell by 0.2 sec.
8 Pcs: Increases the duration of your Rejuvenation spell by 3 sec.

DRUID

ITEM	DROPPED BY	RARITY	LEV	SLOT	TYPE	DAMAGE	SPD	DPS	ARM	AGI	INT	SPI	STA	STR	ARC	FIR	FRO	NAT	SHA
Stormrage Chestguard	Nefarian	Epic	60	Chest	Leather	-	-	-	225	-	25	17	20	-	-	10	-	10	-
Equip: Improves your chance to get a critical strike with spells by 1%, Equip: Increases healing done by spells and effects by up to 42																			
Stormrage Boots	Broodlord Lashlayer	Epic	60	Feet	Leather	-	-	-	154	-	17	11	15	-	-	10	-	-	-
Equip: Improves your chance to get a critical strike with spells by 1%, Equip: Increases healing done by spells and effects by up to 26																			
Stormrage Handguards	Ebonroc, Firemaw, Flamegor	Epic	60	Hands	Leather	-	-	-	140	-	19	15	13	-	-	-	-	-	10
Equip: Increases healing done by spells and effects by up to 42																			
Stormrage Cover	Onyxia	Epic	60	Head	Leather	-	-	-	183	-	31	12	20	-	-	-	10	-	10
Equip: Restores 6 mana per 5 sec., Equip: Increases healing done by spells and effects by up to 29																			
Stormrage Legguards	Ragnaros	Epic	60	Legs	Leather	-	-	-	197	-	26	16	17	-	10	10	-	-	-
Equip: Increases healing done by spells and effects by up to 48, Equip: Restores 6 mana per 5 sec.																			
Stormrage Pauldrons	Chromaggus	Epic	60	Shoulder	Leather	-	-	-	169	-	21	10	14	-	-	10	-	-	-
Equip: Increases healing done by spells and effects by up to 29, Equip: Restores 4 mana per 5 sec.																			
Stormrage Belt	Vaelastrasz the Corrupt	Epic	60	Waist	Leather	-	-	-	126	-	23	10	12	-	-	-	-	-	10
Equip: Increases healing done by spells and effects by up to 26, Equip: Restores 4 mana per 5 sec.																			
Stormrage Bracers	Razorgore the Untamed	Epic	60	Wrist	Leather	-	-	-	98	-	15	12	11	-	-	-	-	-	-
Equip: Increases healing done by spells and effects by up to 33																			

STRIKER'S GARB

3 Pcs: Reduces the cost of your Arcane Shots by 10%
5 Pcs: Reduces the cooldown of your Rapid Fire ability by 2 minutes

HUNTER

ITEM	DROPPED BY	RARITY	LEV	SLOT	TYPE	DAMAGE	SPD	DPS	ARM	AGI	INT	SPI	STA	STR	ARC	FIR	FRO	NAT	SHA
Striker's Hauberk	Quest: Striker's Hauberk (Ahn'Qiraj)	Epic	60	Chest	Mail	-	-	-	553	39	15	7	26	-	-	-	-	-	-
Equip: Improves your chance to get a critical strike by 1%, Equip: Increases damage and healing done by magical spells and effects by up to 9																			
Striker's Footguards	Quest: Striker's Footguards (Ahn'Qiraj)	Epic	60	Feet	Mail	-	-	-	340	31	8	6	16	-	-	-	-	-	-
Equip: Increases damage and healing done by magical spells and effects by up to 6																			
Striker's Diadem	Quest: Striker's Diadem (Ahn'Qiraj)	Epic	60	Head	Mail	-	-	-	416	29	18	10	26	-	-	-	-	-	-
Equip: Improves your chance to get a critical strike by 1%, Equip: Increases damage and healing done by magical spells and effects by up to 12																			
Striker's Leggings	Quest: Striker's Leggings (Ahn'Qiraj)	Epic	60	Legs	Mail	-	-	-	448	36	14	10	22	-	-	-	-	-	-
Equip: Improves your chance to get a critical strike by 1%, Equip: Increases damage and healing done by magical spells and effects by up to 9																			
Striker's Pauldrons	Quest: Striker's Pauldrons (Ahn'Qiraj)	Epic	60	Shoulder	Mail	-	-	-	384	26	11	5	24	-	-	-	-	-	-
Equip: Increases damage and healing done by magical spells and effects by up to 6																			

SYMBOLS OF UNENDING LIFE

3 Pcs: Your finishing moves now refund 30 energy on a Miss, Dodge, Block, or Parry

ITEM	DROPPED BY	RARITY	LEV	SLOT	TYPE	DAMAGE	SPD	DPS	ARM	AGI	INT	SPI	STA	STR	ARC	FIR	FRO	NAT	SHA
Cloak of Unending Life	Quest: Cloak of Unending Life (Ahn'Qiraj)	Epic	60	Back	Cloth	-	-	-	52	8	10	7	10	12	-	-	-	-	-
Equip: Increases damage and healing done by magical spells and effects by up to 11																			
Band of Unending Life	Quest: Band of Unending Life (Ahn'Qiraj)	Epic	60	Finger	Misc	-	-	-	-	10	8	7	9	10	-	-	-	-	-
Equip: Restores 5 mana per 5 sec.																			
Mace of Unending Life	Quest: Mace of Unending Life (Ahn'Qiraj)	Epic	60	Main Hand	Mace	67-149	2.60	41.5	-	7	11	-	10	9	-	-	-	-	-
Equip: Increases damage and healing done by magical spells and effects by up to 40, Equip: +140 Attack Power in Cat, Bear, and Dire Bear forms only																			

THE EARTHFURY

3 Pcs: The radius of your totems that affect friendly targets is increased by 10 yd

5 Pcs: After casting your Healing Wave or Lesser Healing Wave spell, gives you a 25% chance to gain Mana equal to 35% of the base cost of the spell

8 Pcs: Your Healing Wave will now jump to additional nearby targets. Each jump reduces the effectiveness of the heal by 80%, and the spell will jump to up to two additional targets

ITEM	DROPPED BY	RARITY	LEV	SLOT	TYPE	DAMAGE	SPD	DPS	ARM	AGI	INT	SPI	STA	STR	ARC	FIR	FRO	NAT	SHA
Earthfury Vestments	Golemagg the Incinerator	Epic	60	Chest	Mail	-	-	-	422	-	27	13	17	-	-	10	-	-	-
Equip: Improves your chance to get a critical strike with spells by 1%, Equip: Increases healing done by spells and effects by up to 22																			
Earthfury Boots	Lucifron	Epic	60	Feet	Mail	-	-	-	290	-	10	22	15	-	-	-	-	-	7
Equip: Increases healing done by spells and effects by up to 18																			
Earthfury Gauntlets	Gehennas	Epic	60	Hands	Mail	-	-	-	264	-	13	15	14	-	-	7	-	-	-
Equip: Improves your chance to get a critical strike with spells by 1%, Equip: Increases damage and healing done by magical spells and effects by up to 9																			
Earthfury Helmet	Garr	Epic	60	Head	Mail	-	-	-	343	-	23	13	24	-	-	10	-	-	-
Equip: Restores 6 mana per 5 sec., Equip: Increases healing done by spells and effects by up to 22																			
Earthfury Legguards	Magmadar	Epic	60	Legs	Mail	-	-	-	369	-	19	21	18	-	-	-	-	-	10
Equip: Restores 6 mana per 5 sec., Equip: Increases damage and healing done by magical spells and effects by up to 12																			
Earthfury Epaulets	Baron Geddon	Epic	60	Shoulder	Mail	-	-	-	317	-	18	10	17	-	-	-	-	-	7
Equip: Restores 4 mana per 5 sec., Equip: Increases healing done by spells and effects by up to 18																			
Earthfury Belt	Molten Core	Epic	60	Waist	Mail	-	-	-	237	-	21	7	12	-	-	7	-	-	-
Equip: Restores 4 mana per 5 sec., Equip: Increases healing done by spells and effects by up to 18																			
Earthfury Bracers	Molten Core	Epic	60	Wrist	Mail	-	-	-	185	-	17	11	10	-	-	-	-	-	-
Equip: Increases damage and healing done by magical spells and effects by up to 6																			

THE ELEMENTS

SHAMAN

2 Pcs: +200 Armor
4 Pcs: Increases damage and healing done by magical spells and effects by up to 23
6 Pcs: Chance on spell cast to increase your damage and healing by up to 95 for 10 seconds.
8 Pcs: +8 All Resistances

ITEM	DROPPED BY	RARITY	LEV	SLOT	TYPE	DAMAGE	SPD	DPS	ARM	AGI	INT	SPI	STA	STR	ARC	FIR	FRO	NAT	SHA
Vest of Elements	General Drakkisath	Superior	58	Chest	Mail	-	-	-	370	-	20	20	13	-	-	-	-	-	-
Boots of Elements	Highlord Omokk	Superior	54	Feet	Mail	-	-	-	240	9	-	17	-	-	-	-	-	-	-
Gauntlets of Elements	Pyroguard Emberseer	Superior	54	Hands	Mail	-	-	-	218	-	10	16	4	9	-	-	-	-	-
Coif of Elements	Darkmaster Gandling	Superior	57	Head	Mail	-	-	-	297	-	23	12	13	7	-	-	-	-	-
Kilt of Elements	Baron Rivendare	Superior	56	Legs	Mail	-	-	-	315	6	15	20	7	12	-	-	-	-	-
Pauldrons of Elements	Gyth	Superior	55	Shoulder	Mail	-	-	-	266	-	15	6	14	6	-	-	-	-	-
Cord of Elements	Bloodaxe Evoker, Firebrand Invoker, Firebrand Pyromancer, Quartermaster Zigris, Rage Talon Flamescale, Scarshield Warlock, Smolderthorn Witch Doctor	Superior	53	Waist	Mail	-	-	-	193	-	17	7	6	9	-	-	-	-	-
Bindings of Elements	Crimson Monk, Crypt Beast, Crypt Crawler, Splintered Skeleton	Superior	52	Wrist	Mail	-	-	-	148	-	10	10	7	-	-	-	-	-	-

THE FIVE THUNDERS

SHAMAN

2 Pcs: +8 All Resistances
4 Pcs: Chance on spell cast to increase your damage and healing by up to 95 for 10 seconds.
6 Pcs: Increases damage and healing done by magical spells and effects by up to 23
8 Pcs: +200 Armor

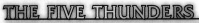

ITEM	DROPPED BY	RARITY	LEV	SLOT	TYPE	DAMAGE	SPD	DPS	ARM	AGI	INT	SPI	STA	STR	ARC	FIR	FRO	NAT	SHA
Vest of The Five Thunders	Quest: Saving the Best for Last (Ironforge/Orgrimmar)	Epic	60	Chest	Mail	-	-	-	387	-	17	16	17	12	-	-	-	-	-
Equip: Improves your chance to get a critical strike with spells by 1%, Equip: Increases damage and healing done by magical spells and effects by up to 14																			
Boots of The Five Thunders	Quest: Anthion's Parting Words (Ironforge/Orgrimmar)	Epic	60	Feet	Mail	-	-	-	266	-	12	10	13	12	-	-	-	-	-
Equip: Increases damage and healing done by magical spells and effects by up to 12, Equip: Restores 4 mana per 5 sec.																			
Gauntlets of The Five Thunders	Quest: Just Compensation (Ironforge/Orgrimmar)	Epic	60	Hands	Mail	-	-	-	223	-	14	-	12	9	-	-	-	-	-
Equip: Restores 4 mana per 5 sec., Equip: Increases damage and healing done by magical spells and effects by up to 12																			
Coif of The Five Thunders	Quest: Saving the Best for Last (Ironforge/Orgrimmar)	Epic	60	Head	Mail	-	-	-	314	-	21	12	22	-	-	-	-	-	-
Equip: Increases damage and healing done by magical spells and effects by up to 14, Equip: Improves your chance to get a critical strike with spells by 1%																			
Kilt of The Five Thunders	Quest: Anthion's Parting Words (Ironforge/Orgrimmar)	Superior	60	Legs	Mail	-	-	-	339	-	17	16	17	10	-	-	-	-	-
Equip: Increases damage and healing done by magical spells and effects by up to 11																			
Pauldrons of The Five Thunders	Quest: Anthion's Parting Words (Ironforge/Orgrimmar)	Superior	60	Shoulder	Mail	-	-	-	286	-	11	10	11	10	-	-	-	-	-
Equip: Increases damage and healing done by magical spells and effects by up to 12																			
Cord of The Five Thunders	Quest: Just Compensation (Ironforge/Orgrimmar)	Superior	60	Waist	Mail	-	-	-	214	-	11	-	11	10	-	-	-	-	-
Equip: Increases damage and healing done by magical spells and effects by up to 12, Equip: Restores 4 mana per 5 sec.																			
Bindings of The Five Thunders	Quest: An Earnest Proposition (Ironforge/Orgrimmar)	Superior	60	Wrist	Mail	-	-	-	167	-	9	9	10	-	-	-	-	-	-
Equip: Increases damage and healing done by magical spells and effects by up to 8																			

THE GLADIATOR

2 Pcs: +20 Armor
3 Pcs: Increased Defense +2
4 Pcs: +10 Attack Power
5 Pcs: Improves your chance to get a critical strike by 1%

ITEM	DROPPED BY	RARITY	LEV	SLOT	TYPE	DAMAGE	SPD	DPS	ARM	AGI	INT	SPI	STA	STR	ARC	FIR	FRO	NAT	SHA
Savage Gladiator Chain	Gorosh the Dervish	Epic	52	Chest	Mail	-	-	-	369	14	-	-	13	13	-	-	-	-	-
Equip: Improves your chance to get a critical strike by 2%																			
Savage Gladiator Greaves	Anub'shiah	Superior	52	Feet	Mail	-	-	-	233	15	-	-	13	10	-	-	-	-	-
Savage Gladiator Grips	Eviscerator	Superior	52	Hands	Mail	-	-	-	211	9	12	-	14	5	-	-	-	-	-
Savage Gladiator Helm	Gorosh the Dervish, Hedrum the Creeper	Superior	52	Head	Mail	-	-	-	275	12	-	-	28		-	-	-	-	-
Savage Gladiator Leggings	Ok'thor the Breaker	Superior	52	Legs	Mail	-	-	-	296	18	-	-	19	12	-	-	-	-	-

THE POSTMASTER

2 Pcs: +50 Armor
3 Pcs: +10 Fire Resistance
3 Pcs: +10 Arcane Resistance
4 Pcs: Increases damage and healing done by magical spells and effects by up to 12
5 Pcs: Increases run speed by 5%

ITEM	DROPPED BY	RARITY	LEV	SLOT	TYPE	DAMAGE	SPD	DPS	ARM	AGI	INT	SPI	STA	STR	ARC	FIR	FRO	NAT	SHA
The Postmaster's Tunic	Postmaster Malown	Superior	56	Chest	Cloth			-	87	-	20	10	13	-	-	-	-	-	-
Equip: Increases damage and healing done by magical spells and effects by up to 15																			
The Postmaster's Treads	Postmaster Malown	Superior	56	Feet	Cloth	-	-	-	60	-	15	6	14	-	-	-	-	-	-
Equip: Increases damage and healing done by magical spells and effects by up to 7																			
The Postmaster's Seal	Postmaster Malown	Superior	56	Finger	Misc	-	-	-	-	-	3	17	6	-	-	-	-	-	-
The Postmaster's Band	Postmaster Malown	Superior	56	Head	Cloth	-	-	-	70	-	25	10	10	-	-	-	-	-	-
Equip: Increases damage and healing done by magical spells and effects by up to 14																			
The Postmaster's Trousers	Postmaster Malown	Superior	56	Legs	Cloth	-	-	-	76	-	10	20	12	-	-	-	-	-	-

THE TEN STORMS

3 Pcs: Increases the amount healed by Chain Heal to targets beyond the first by 30%

5 Pcs: Improves your chance to get a critical strike with Nature spells by 3%

8 Pcs: When you cast a Healing Wave or Lesser Healing Wave, there is a 25% chance the target also receives a free Lightning Shield that causes 50 Nature damage to attacker on hit

SHAMAN

ITEM	DROPPED BY	RARITY	LEV	SLOT	TYPE	DAMAGE	SPD	DPS	ARM	AGI	INT	SPI	STA	STR	ARC	FIR	FRO	NAT	SHA
Breastplate of Ten Storms	Nefarian	Epic	60	Chest	Mail	-	-	-	482	-	31	16	17	-	-	10	-	10	-
Equip: Increases damage and healing done by magical spells and effects by up to 23																			
Greaves of Ten Storms	Broodlord Lashlayer	Epic	60	Feet	Mail	-	-	-	332	-	16	16	17	-	-	10	-	-	-
Equip: Increases damage and healing done by magical spells and effects by up to 20																			
Gauntlets of Ten Storms	Ebonroc, Firemaw, Flamegor	Epic	60	Hands	Mail	-	-	-	301	-	17	13	15	-	-	-	-	-	10
Equip: Restores 6 mana per 5 sec., Equip: Increases damage and healing done by magical spells and effects by up to 8, Equip: Increases healing done by spells and effects by up to 15																			
Helmet of Ten Storms	Onyxia	Epic	60	Head	Mail	-	-	-	392	-	24	12	20	-	-	-	10	-	10
Equip: Improves your chance to get a critical strike with spells by 1%, Equip: Increases damage and healing done by magical spells and effects by up to 9, Equip: Increases healing done by spells and effects by up to 18																			
Legplates of Ten Storms	Ragnaros	Epic	60	Legs	Mail	-	-	-	422	-	18	20	16	-	10	10	-	-	-
Equip: Improves your chance to get a critical strike with spells by 1%, Equip: Increases damage and healing done by magical spells and effects by up to 29																			
Epaulets of Ten Storms	Chromaggus	Epic	60	Shoulder	Mail	-	-	-	362	-	17	8	23	-	-	10	-	-	-
Equip: Improves your chance to get a critical strike with spells by 1%																			
Belt of Ten Storms	Vaelastrasz the Corrupt	Epic	60	Waist	Mail	-	-	-	271	-	18	11	13	-	-	-	-	-	10
Equip: Improves your chance to get a critical strike with spells by 1%, Equip: Increases healing done by spells and effects by up to 26																			
Bracers of Ten Storms	Razorgore the Untamed	Epic	60	Wrist	Mail	-	-	-	211	-	16	9	13	-	-	-	-	-	-
Equip: Restores 6 mana per 5 sec.																			

THE TWIN BLADES OF HAKKARI

2 Pcs: Increased Swords +6

ITEM	DROPPED BY	RARITY	LEV	SLOT	TYPE	DAMAGE	SPD	DPS	ARM	AGI	INT	SPI	STA	STR	ARC	FIR	FRO	NAT	SHA
Warblade of the Hakkari	Broodlord Mandokir	Epic	60	Main Hand	Sword	59-110	1.70	49.7	-	-	-	-	-	-	-	-	-	-	-
Equip: +28 Attack Power, Equip: Improves your chance to get a critical strike by 1%																			
Warblade of the Hakkari	Broodlord Mandokir	Epic	60	Off Hand	Sword	57-106	1.70	47.9	-	-	-	-	-	-	-	-	-	-	-
Equip: +40 Attack Power																			

TRAPPINGS OF THE UNSEEN PATH

3 Pcs: Increases your pet's damage by 5%

ITEM	DROPPED BY	RARITY	LEV	SLOT	TYPE	DAMAGE	SPD	DPS	ARM	AGI	INT	SPI	STA	STR	ARC	FIR	FRO	NAT	SHA
Cloak of the Unseen Path	Quest: Cloak of the Unseen Path (Ahn'Qiraj)	Epic	60	Back	Cloth	-	-	-	52	17	-	-	13	-	-	-	-	-	-
Equip: Improves your chance to hit by 1%																			
Signet of the Unseen Path	Quest: Signet of the Unseen Path (Ahn'Qiraj)	Epic	60	Finger	Misc	-	-	-	-	19	8	-	11	-	-	-	-	-	-
Scythe of the Unseen Path	Quest: Scythe of the Unseen Path (Ahn'Qiraj)	Epic	60	One-Hand	Axe	86-161	2.40	51.5	-	16	-	-	9	-	-	-	-	-	-
Equip: Restores 3 mana per 5 sec.																			

TRAPPINGS OF VAULTED SECRETS

3 Pcs: 15% increase to the total damage absorbed by Mana Shield

ITEM	DROPPED BY	RARITY	LEV	SLOT	TYPE	DAMAGE	SPD	DPS	ARM	AGI	INT	SPI	STA	STR	ARC	FIR	FRO	NAT	SHA
Drape of Vaulted Secrets	Quest: Drape of Vaulted Secrets (Ahn'Qiraj)	Epic	60	Back	Cloth	-	-	-	52	-	9	6	14	-	-	-	-	-	-
Equip: Increases damage and healing done by magical spells and effects by up to 18																			
Band of Vaulted Secrets	Quest: Band of Vaulted Secrets (Ahn'Qiraj)	Epic	60	Finger	Misc	-	-	-	-	-	-	-	9	-	-	-	-	-	-
Equip: Increases damage and healing done by magical spells and effects by up to 18, Equip: Improves your chance to get a critical strike with spells by 1%																			
Blade of Vaulted Secrets	Quest: Blade of Vaulted Secrets (Ahn'Qiraj)	Epic	60	Main Hand	Sword	60-131	2.30	41.5	-	-	16	-	8	-	-	-	-	-	-
Equip: Improves your chance to hit with spells by 1%, Equip: Increases damage and healing done by magical spells and effects by up to 40																			

VESTMENTS OF PROPHECY

3 Pcs: -0.1 sec to the casting time of your Flash Heal spell.
5 Pcs: Improves your chance to get a critical strike with Holy spells by 2%
8 Pcs: Increases your chance of a critical hit with Prayer of Healing by 25%

ITEM	DROPPED BY	RARITY	LEV	SLOT	TYPE	DAMAGE	SPD	DPS	ARM	AGI	INT	SPI	STA	STR	ARC	FIR	FRO	NAT	SHA
Robes of Prophecy	Golemagg the Incinerator	Epic	60	Chest	Cloth	-	-	-	102	-	27	17	20	-	-	10	-	-	-
Equip: Increases healing done by spells and effects by up to 22																			
Boots of Prophecy	Shazzrah	Epic	60	Feet	Cloth	-	-	-	70	-	18	15	17	-	-	-	-	-	7
Equip: Increases healing done by spells and effects by up to 18																			
Gloves of Prophecy	Gehennas	Epic	60	Hands	Cloth	-	-	-	63	-	15	15	10	-	-	7	-	-	-
Equip: Restores 6 mana per 5 sec., Equip: Increases healing done by spells and effects by up to 18																			
Circlet of Prophecy	Garr	Epic	60	Head	Cloth	-	-	-	83	-	27	20	17	-	-	10	-	-	-
Equip: Increases damage and healing done by magical spells and effects by up to 12																			
Pants of Prophecy	Magmadar	Epic	60	Legs	Cloth	-	-	-	89	-	24	20	18	-	-	-	-	-	10
Equip: Restores 6 mana per 5 sec., Equip: Increases healing done by spells and effects by up to 22																			
Mantle of Prophecy	Sulfuron Harbinger	Epic	60	Shoulder	Cloth	-	-	-	76	-	23	10	13	-	-	-	-	-	7
Equip: Increases damage and healing done by magical spells and effects by up to 9																			
Girdle of Prophecy	Molten Core	Epic	60	Waist	Cloth	-	-	-	57	-	22	10	10	-	-	7	-	-	-
Equip: Restores 4 mana per 5 sec., Equip: Increases damage and healing done by magical spells and effects by up to 9																			
Vambraces of Prophecy	Molten Core	Epic	60	Wrist	Cloth	-	-	-	44	-	14	10	8	-	-	-	-	-	-
Equip: Restores 2 mana per 5 sec., Equip: Increases healing done by spells and effects by up to 24																			

VESTMENTS OF THE DEVOUT

PRIEST

2 Pcs: +200 Armor
4 Pcs: Increases damage and healing done by magical spells and effects by up to 23
6 Pcs: When struck in combat has a chance of shielding the wearer in a protective shield which will absorb 350 damage
8 Pcs: +8 All Resistances

ITEM	DROPPED BY	RARITY	LEV	SLOT	TYPE	DAMAGE	SPD	DPS	ARM	AGI	INT	SPI	STA	STR	ARC	FIR	FRO	NAT	SHA
Devout Robe	General Drakkisath	Superior	58	Chest	Cloth	-	-	-	89	-	24	15	13	-	-	-	-	-	-
Devout Sandals	Maleki the Pallid	Superior	54	Feet	Cloth	-	-	-	58	-	10	17	9	-	-	-	-	-	-
Devout Gloves	Archivist Galford	Superior	54	Hands	Cloth	-	-	-	52	-	10	17	9	-	-	-	-	-	-
Devout Crown	Darkmaster Gandling	Superior	57	Head	Cloth	-	-	-	71	-	24	15	13	-	-	-	-	-	-
Devout Skirt	Baron Rivendare	Superior	56	Legs	Cloth	-	-	-	76	-	15	23	12	-	-	-	-	-	-
Devout Mantle	Solakar Flamewreath	Superior	55	Shoulder	Cloth	-	-	-	64	-	21	9	4	-	-	-	-	-	-
Devout Belt	Blackhand Summoner, Bloodaxe Summoner, Firebrand Darkweaver, Firebrand Dreadweaver, Quartermaster Zigris, Scarshield Spellbinder, Smolderthorn Shadow Priest	Superior	53	Waist	Cloth	-	-	-	46	-	20	9	4	-	-	-	-	-	-
Devout Bracers	Crimson Conjuror, Crimson Initiate, Crimson Priest, Thuzadin Necromancer, Thuzadin Shadowcaster	Superior	52	Wrist	Cloth	-	-	-	35	-	10	10	7	-	-	-	-	-	-

VESTMENTS OF THE VIRTUOUS

PRIEST

2 Pcs: +8 All Resistances
4 Pcs: When struck in combat has a chance of shielding the wearer in a protective shield which will absorb 350 damage
6 Pcs: Increases damage and healing done by magical spells and effects by up to 23
8 Pcs: +200 Armor

ITEM	DROPPED BY	RARITY	LEV	SLOT	TYPE	DAMAGE	SPD	DPS	ARM	AGI	INT	SPI	STA	STR	ARC	FIR	FRO	NAT	SHA
Virtuous Robe	Quest: Saving the Best for Last (Ironforge/Orgrimmar)	Epic	60	Chest	Cloth	-	-	-	93	-	22	12	21	-	-	-	-	-	-
Equip: Increases damage and healing done by magical spells and effects by up to 14, Equip: Restores 6 mana per 5 sec.																			
Virtuous Sandals	Quest: Anthion's Parting Words (Ironforge/Orgrimmar)	Epic	60	Feet	Cloth	-	-	-	64	-	13	12	12	-	-	-	-	-	-
Equip: Increases damage and healing done by magical spells and effects by up to 12, Equip: Restores 7 mana per 5 sec.																			
Virtuous Gloves	Quest: Just Compensation (Ironforge/Orgrimmar)	Epic	60	Hands	Cloth	-	-	-	54	-	15	12	14	-	-	-	-	-	-
Equip: Increases damage and healing done by magical spells and effects by up to 11																			
Virtuous Crown	Quest: Saving the Best for Last (Ironforge/Orgrimmar)	Epic	60	Head	Cloth	-	-	-	75	-	17	16	16	-	-	-	-	-	-
Equip: Increases damage and healing done by magical spells and effects by up to 11, Equip: Restores 6 mana per 5 sec., Equip: Improves your chance to get a critical strike with spells by 1%																			
Virtuous Skirt	Quest: Anthion's Parting Words (Ironforge/Orgrimmar)	Superior	60	Legs	Cloth	-	-	-	81	-	14	12	13	-	-	-	-	-	-
Equip: Increases damage and healing done by magical spells and effects by up to 16, Equip: Restores 6 mana per 5 sec.																			
Virtuous Mantle	Quest: Anthion's Parting Words (Ironforge/Orgrimmar)	Superior	60	Shoulder	Cloth	-	-	-	69	-	13	12	12	-	-	-	-	-	-
Equip: Increases damage and healing done by magical spells and effects by up to 12																			
Virtuous Belt	Quest: Just Compensation (Ironforge/Orgrimmar)	Superior	60	Waist	Cloth	-	-	-	52	-	13	12	12	-	-	-	-	-	-
Equip: Increases damage and healing done by magical spells and effects by up to 12																			
Virtuous Bracers	Quest: An Earnest Proposition (Ironforge/Orgrimmar)	Superior	60	Wrist	Cloth	-	-	-	40	-	8	8	8	-	-	-	-	-	-
Equip: Increases damage and healing done by magical spells and effects by up to 9, Equip: Restores 2 mana per 5 sec.																			

VESTMENTS OF TRANSCENDENCE

3 Pcs: Allows 15% of your Mana regeneration to continue while casting

5 Pcs: When struck in melee there is a 50% chance you will Fade for 4 secs.

8 Pcs: Your Greater Heals now have a heal over time component equivalent to a rank 5 Renew

ITEM	DROPPED BY	RARITY	LEV	SLOT	TYPE	DAMAGE	SPD	DPS	ARM	AGI	INT	SPI	STA	STR	ARC	FIR	FRO	NAT	SHA
Robes of Transcendence	Nefarian	Epic	60	Chest	Cloth	-	-	-	116	-	27	16	17	-	-	10	-	10	-
Equip: Increases healing done by spells and effects by up to 57
Boots of Transcendence	Broodlord Lashlayer	Epic	60	Feet	Cloth	-	-	-	80	-	17	17	17	-	-	10	-	-	-
Equip: Increases healing done by spells and effects by up to 35
Handguards of Transcendence	Ebonroc, Firemaw, Flamegor	Epic	60	Hands	Cloth	-	-	-	72	-	20	13	12	-	-	-	-	-	10
Equip: Improves your chance to get a critical strike with spells by 1%, Equip: Increases healing done by spells and effects by up to 29
Halo of Transcendence	Onyxia	Epic	60	Head	Cloth	-	-	-	94	-	27	22	17	-	-	10	10	-	-
Equip: Increases healing done by spells and effects by up to 48
Leggings of Transcendence	Ragnaros	Epic	60	Legs	Cloth	-	-	-	101	-	21	21	16	-	10	-	-	-	10
Equip: Increases healing done by spells and effects by up to 46, Equip: Restores 7 mana per 5 sec.
Pauldrons of Transcendence	Chromaggus	Epic	60	Shoulder	Cloth	-	-	-	87	-	25	13	12	-	-	10	-	-	-
Equip: Increases healing done by spells and effects by up to 26
Belt of Transcendence	Vaelastrasz the Corrupt	Epic	60	Waist	Cloth	-	-	-	65	-	26	9	14	-	-	-	-	-	10
Equip: Increases healing done by spells and effects by up to 26
Bindings of Transcendence	Razorgore the Untamed	Epic	60	Wrist	Cloth	-	-	-	51	-	13	16	9	-	-	-	-	-	-
Equip: Increases healing done by spells and effects by up to 33

VINDICATOR'S BATTLEGEAR

2 Pcs: Increases your chance to block attacks with a shield by 2%

3 Pcs: Decreases the cooldown of Intimidating Shout by 15 sec.

5 Pcs: Decrease the rage cost of Whirlwind by 3

ITEM	DROPPED BY	RARITY	LEV	SLOT	TYPE	DAMAGE	SPD	DPS	ARM	AGI	INT	SPI	STA	STR	ARC	FIR	FRO	NAT	SHA
Zandalar Vindicator's Breastplate	Quest: Paragons of Power: The Vindicator's Breastplate (Zul'Gurub)	Epic	60	Chest	Plate	-	-	-	828	15	-	-	24	23	-	-	-	-	-
Equip: Increased Defense +4
Rage of Mugamba	Punctured Voodoo Doll (Zul'Gurub)	Epic	60	Neck	Misc	-	-	-	-	8	-	-	13	8	-	-	-	-	-
Equip: Increased Defense +6, Equip: Increases your chance to block attacks with a shield by 2%, Equip: Reduces the cost of your Hamstring ability by 2 rage points
Gri'lek's Charm of Might	Quest: Gri'lek's Charm of Might (Zul'Gurub)	Epic	60	Trinket	Misc	-	-	-	-	-	-	-	-	-	-	-	-	-	-
Use: Instantly increases your rage by 30
Zandalar Vindicator's Belt	Quest: Paragons of Power: The Vindicator's Belt (Zul'Gurub)	Epic	60	Waist	Plate	-	-	-	391	-	-	-	10	25	-	-	-	-	-
Equip: Improves your chance to get a critical strike by 1%
Zandalar Vindicator's Armguards	Quest: Paragons of Power: The Vindicator's Armguards (Zul'Gurub)	Epic	60	Wrist	Plate	-	-	-	304	13	-	-	13	13	-	-	-	-	-

WILDHEART RAIMENT

2 Pcs: +200 Armor

4 Pcs: +26 Attack Power

4 Pcs: Increases damage and healing done by magical spells and effects by up to 15

6 Pcs: When struck in combat has a chance of returning 300 mana, 10 rage, or 40 energy to the wearer.

8 Pcs: +8 All Resistances

DRUID

ITEM	DROPPED BY	RARITY	LEV	SLOT	TYPE	DAMAGE	SPD	DPS	ARM	AGI	INT	SPI	STA	STR	ARC	FIR	FRO	NAT	SHA
Wildheart Vest	General Drakkisath	Superior	58	Chest	Leather	-	-	-	176	-	20	20	13	-	-	-	-	-	-
Wildheart Boots	Mother Smolderweb	Superior	54	Feet	Leather	-	-	-	115	-	9	17	10	-	-	-	-	-	-
Wildheart Gloves	Bloodaxe Raider, Firebrand Invoker, Firebrand Pyromancer, Rage Talon Dragonspawn, Scarshield Raider, Smolderthorn Berserker, The Unforgiven	Superior	54	Hands	Leather	-	-	-	105	-	9	21	-	-	-	-	-	-	-
Wildheart Cowl	Darkmaster Gandling	Superior	57	Head	Leather	-	-	-	141	-	20	20	10	6	-	-	-	-	-
Wildheart Kilt	Baron Rivendare	Superior	56	Legs	Leather	-	-	-	150	12	14	14	14	13	-	-	-	-	-
Wildheart Spaulders	Gizrul the Slavener	Superior	55	Shoulder	Leather	-	-	-	127	-	18	8	9	-	-	-	-	-	-
Wildheart Belt	Bloodaxe Raider, Quartermaster Zigris, Scholomance Handler, Scarshield Raider, Spectral Researcher, Spectral Teacher, The Ravenian	Superior	53	Waist	Leather	-	-	-	93	-	17	10	9	-	-	-	-	-	-
Wildheart Bracers	Crimson Inquisitor, Diseased Ghoul, Shrieking Banshee, Wailing Banshee	Superior	52	Wrist	Leather	-	-	-	71	-	15	-	-	7	-	-	-	-	-

ZANZIL'S CONCENTRATION

2 Pcs: Improves your chance to hit with spells by 1%

2 Pcs: Increases damage and healing done by magical spells and effects by up to 6

ITEM	DROPPED BY	RARITY	LEV	SLOT	TYPE	DAMAGE	SPD	DPS	ARM	AGI	INT	SPI	STA	STR	ARC	FIR	FRO	NAT	SHA
Zanzil's Band	High Priest Venoxis	Superior	60	Finger	Misc	-	-	-	-	-	13	-	-	-	-	-	-	-	-
Equip: Improves your chance to hit with spells by 1%, Equip: Restores 4 mana per 5 sec.																			
Zanzil's Seal	Bloodlord Mandokir	Superior	60	Finger	Misc	-	-	-	-	-	10	-	10	-	-	-	-	-	-
Equip: Improves your chance to hit with spells by 1%, Equip: Increases damage and healing done by magical spells and effects by up to 11																			

DUNGEON SET 2 UPGRADE QUESTS

Always trying to get the most out of your equipment? Wish some of those pieces were a little more Epic? Upgrading your Tier 0 set is just what you need!

The quest chain to upgrade a complete set of Tier 0 (also known as Dungeon Set 1) is quite a long process that involves several quests at both the solo and raid level. Players who choose to undertake this go through many steps and are rewarded with high quality upgrades of their Tier 0 armor.

You do not need the full set to get started, just the Bracer. As the quest chain continues, you're going to need more pieces of the armor. Good luck!

STEP 1: AN EARNEST PROPOSITION

Location	Ironforge/Orgimmar
Quest Giver	Deliana/Mokvar
Goal	Acquire 15 Winterspring Blood Samples or 15 Silithus Venom Samples, 20 gold, the Dungeon Set 1 Bracer you wish to upgrade, and return to your contact
Max Experience Gained	6600
Reward	Dungeon Set 2 Bracers

Alliance

Alliance characters must travel to Winterspring and kill the frostsabers and bears that inhabit the northern part of the zone. Collect 15 Winterspring Blood Samples and return to Deliana in Ironforge.

Horde

Horde characters must travel to Silithus to kill the spiders and scorpions that roam across the entire zone. After collecting 15 Silithus Venom Samples, return to Mokvar in Orgrimmar.

STEP 2: A SUPERNATURAL DEVICE

Location	Ironforge/Orgimmar
Quest Giver	Deliana/Mokvar
Goal	Deliver the Sealed Blood/Venom Container to Mux Manascrambler in Tanaris
Max Experience Gained	6600

Alliance & Horde

Members of both factions should now deliver the Sealed Blood or Venom to Mux Manascrambler in Tanaris. He is located in the northeastern part of Gadgetzan.

STEP 3: THE ECTOPLASMIC DISTILLER

Location	Gadgetzan
Quest Giver	Mux Manascrambler
Goal	Bring Mux 1 Delicate Arcanite Converter, 4 Greater Eternal Essences, 10 Stonescale Oils, 25 Volcanic Ash, and 40 gold
Max Experience Gained	6600

Alliance & Horde

Delicate Arcanite Converters can be made by Engineers (the recipe is purchased in Everlook). They require 1 Arcanite Bar and 1 Ironweb Spider Silk.

Greater Eternal Essences are obtained from disenchanting level 51+ Uncommon items.

Stonescale Oil is made by Alchemists from Stonescale Eels.

Volcanic Ash is looted from piles around the lava in Burning Steppes.

After you have gathered everything, return to Mux in Gadgetzan.

STEP 4: HUNTING FOR ECTOPLASM

Location	Gadgetzan
Quest Giver	Mux Manascrambler
Goal	Use the Ectoplasmic Distiller to collect 12 Scorched Ectoplasms, 12 Frozen Ectoplasms, and 12 Stable Ectoplasms
Max Experienced Gained	6600

Alliance & Horde

Get some Goblin Rocket Fuel to power the Ectoplasmic Distiller. It's made by Alchemists from 1 Firebloom, 1 Volatile Rum, and 1 Leaded Vial.

Scorched Ectoplasms can be obtained from Tortured Druids and Tortured Sentinels on the eastern edge of Silithus. Watch out for the bugs when you kill them!

Frozen Ectoplasms come from the undead at the lake southwest of Everlook in Winterspring.

Finally, Stable Ectoplasms come from the undead around towns like Northdale and Corrin's Crossing in Eastern Plaguelands.

Once you have everything, head back to Mux in Gadgetzan.

STEP 5: A PORTABLE POWER SOURCE

Location	Gadgetzan
Quest Giver	Mux Manascrambler
Goal	Kill Magma Lord Bokk in the Burning Steppes and bring his Magma Core back to Mux
Max Experience Gained	6600

Alliance & Horde

Travel to Burning Steppes and track down Magma Lord Bokk. He is south of Blackrock Mountain. You should be able to do this by yourself.

STEP 6: A SHIFTY MERCHANT

Location	Gadgetzan
Quest Giver	Mux Manascrambler
Goal	Buy a Fel Elemental Rod from an imp inside a cave in Winterspring and bring it to Mux
Max Experienced Gained	3300

Alliance & Horde

The imp is in a cave in Darkwhisper Gorge. As you enter the gorge, hug the right wall and he is in the first cave you see. Purchase one for 40 gold and bring it to Mux.

STEP 7: RETURN TO DELIANA/MOKVAR

Location	Gadgetzan
Quest Giver	Mux Manascrambler
Goal	Go back to Deliana/Mokvar with your completed Extra-Dimensional Ghost Revealer
Max Experience Gained	6600

Alliance & Horde

Return to Deliana/Mokvar with the completed Extra-Dimensional Ghost Revealer for your reward.

STEP 8: JUST COMPENSATION

Location	Ironforge/Orgrimmar
Quest Giver	Deliana/Mokvar
Goal	Bring Deliana/Mokvar the Dungeon Set 1 Belt and Gloves that you wish to upgrade
Max Experience Gained	9950
Reward	Dungeon Set 2 Belt and Gloves

Alliance & Horde

Now that you have brought Deliana/Mokvar a working Extra-Dimensional Ghost Revealer, you can upgrade your Dungeon Set 1 Belt and Gloves.

STEP 9: IN SEARCH OF ANTHION

Location	Ironforge/Orgrimmar
Quest Giver	Deliana/Mokvar
Goal	Use the Extra-Dimensional Ghost Revealer to find Anthion Harmon at the front entrance to Stratholme
Max Experience Gained	6600

Alliance & Horde

Travel to Eastern Plaguelands and use the Extra-Dimensional Ghost Revealer to see Anthion in front of the meeting stone for Stratholme.

Speak with him.

STEP 10: DEAD MAN'S PLEA

Location	Stratholme
Quest Giver	Anthion Harmon
Goal	Rescue Anthion's wife Ysida from Baron Rivendare by killing him within 45 minutes
Max Experience Gained	8300

Alliance & Horde

This is the infamous "45 minute Baron run" quest. Completing Baron's side of Stratholme in less than 45 minutes can be a challenge for many groups, but experienced players should find this relatively easy.

A balanced group of 1 Warrior, 2 DPS classes, and 2 Healers who have done Baron's side of Stratholme before should be able to complete this quest without much trouble.

Collect Stratholme Holy Water for the group before the trip. A near-instant, AoE attack dealing roughly 500 damage to undead is beautiful. It only has a 1-min cooldown as well. Goblin Sapper Charges are helpful as well.

A Paladin can pull a large group with Exorcism immediately before casting Holy Wrath. Drop Consecration and use the Holy Water to cement aggro and allow your DPS (Mage/Warlock, or Rogues) to let loose without fear of gaining it themselves.

Pull continuously! AoE groups should take down as many targets at a time as possible. (Exception: Spellcasters near Maleki the Pallid. Use Counterspell or something like it to bring them to you and kill them individually.) Single-target groups (Rogues) should stay on the same target and work through groups as quickly as possible.

Skip as many pulls as you can by hugging walls and using Lesser Invisibility Potions. The only mobs that are "necessary" to kill are the three Ziggurat bosses and the acolytes inside. The Slaughterhouse area will slow you down; it's designed to take about 10 minutes.

Once you have killed Baron Rivendare within 45 minutes, speak with Ysida.

STEP 11: PROOF OF LIFE

Location	Stratholme
Quest Giver	Ysida Harmon
Goal	Show Anthion his wife's locket as proof that she is safe
Max Experienced Gained	6600

Alliance & Horde

Return to Anthion with proof that you completed the task he set before you.

STEP 12: ANTHION'S STRANGE REQUEST

Location	Stratholme
Quest Giver	Anthion Harmon
Goal	Bring Anthion 3 Dark Iron Bars, 20 Enchanted Leather, 3 Mooncloth, and 4 Cured Rugged Hides
Max Experience Gained	6600

Alliance & Horde

Anthion needs some supplies to get the dwarf gladiator Theldren to fight you. Bring him the items he requests and continue to the next step.

STEP 13: ANTHION'S OLD FRIEND

Location	Stratholme
Quest Giver	Anthion Harmon
Goal	Deliver the Incomplete Banner of Provocation to Falrin Treeshaper in the Dire Maul library
Max Experience Gained	6600

Alliance & Horde

The last piece needed to complete the Banner of Provocation is an enchant from Falrin Treeshaper. He can be found in the library of Dire Maul. Seek him out and speak with him.

STEP 14: FALRIN'S VENDETTA

Location	Dire Maul
Quest Giver	Falrin Treeshaper
Goal	Gather 25 Ogre Warbeads from the Dire Maul or Blackrock Spire Ogres and bring them to Falrin
Max Experience Gained	6600

Alliance & Horde

This straightforward gathering quest sends you right outside the library to Dire Maul or over to Lower Blackrock Spire to collect Ogre Warbeads. Bring some friends and kill Ogres until you have all the necessary drops.

Return to Falrin in the Dire Maul library when complete.

STEP 15: THE INSTIGATOR'S ENCHANTMENT

Location	Dire Maul
Quest Giver	Falrin Treeshaper
Goal	Bring Falrin 1 Jeering Spectre's Essence, 4 Dark Runes, and 8 Large Brilliant Shards
Max Experience Gained	6600

Alliance & Horde

Jeering Spectre's Essence can be found on the undead in the western wing of Dire Maul.

Dark Runes come from the inhabitants of Scholomance.

Large Brilliant Shards come from disenchanted level 51+ Superior items.

After you have gathered everything, return to Falrin.

STEP 16: THE CHALLENGE

Location	Dire Maul
Quest Giver	Falrin Treeshaper
Goal	Defeat Theldren in the arena of Blackrock Depths, return to Anthion Harmon afterwards
Max Experience Gained	6600

Alliance & Horde

Use the Banner of Provocation as you are sentenced by High Justice Grimstone in the Blackrock Depths arena to challenge Theldren.

He is a tough fight, so make sure you bring a well-balanced group of level 60 characters. Defeat him and bring the Top Piece of Lord Valthalak's Amulet to Anthion Harmon in front of Stratholme.

STEP 17: ANTHION'S PARTING WORDS

Location	Stratholme
Quest Giver	Anthion Harmon
Goal	Bring the Dungeon Set 1 Boots, Leggings, and Shoulders you wish to upgrade to Deliana/Mokvar
Max Experience Gained	9950
Reward	Dungeon Set 2 Boots, Leggings, and Shoulders

Alliance & Horde

You have proven to Anthion that you are the only person who can help end Valthalak's spell by putting the amulet back together. Return to Deliana/Mokvar for information on completing the amulet and to gather more rewards.

STEP 18: BODLEY'S UNFORTUNATE FATE

Location	Ironforge/Orgrimmar
Quest Giver	Deliana/Mokvar
Goal	Use the Extra-Dimensional Ghost Revealer to find Bodley near Blackrock Spire
Max Experience Gained	1650

Alliance & Horde

Bodley is located on the balcony outside of the Blackrock Spire entrance. Unfortunately, he is dead and can only be seen with the Extra-Dimensional Ghost Revealer. Use it and speak with Bodley.

STEP 19: THREE KINGS OF FLAME

Location	Blackrock Mountain
Quest Giver	Bodley
Goal	Bring Bodley a Incendicite of Incendius, Ember of Emberseer, Cinder of Cynders, and a Hallowed Brazier
Max Experience Gained	6600

Alliance & Horde

The Incendicite of Incendius is from Lord Incendius at the Dark Forge in Blackrock Depths.

Ember of Emberseer can be found from, you guessed it, Pyroguard Emberseer in Upper Blackrock Spire.

Cinder of Cynders drops from the Duke of Cynders in Silithus and it's a little complicated to obtain. You must use a normal Windstone at a Twilight Camp in Silithus to summon the Duke. You can not use Lesser or Greater Windstones to get the Duke of Cynders; he comes to the call of a normal Windstone.

To use a Windstone, equip a full Twilight Armor Set (obtained from the mobs around the Windstone), complete the Cenarion Hold quest *Dukes of the Council* to obtain a Twilight Medallion of Station, and right-click the Windstone. This summons a Duke of a random element. You might get lucky and get the fire Duke, but there is a better way to ensure that you get the one you need.

If you can obtain the Scroll: Create Signet of Beckoning: Fire, you can collect the items needed for the Scroll to create a Signet of Beckoning: Fire. Using this Signet guarantees that you get the fire Duke.

Finally, the Hallowed Brazier is available at Argent Dawn vendors for 120 gold.

After you have gathered everything, return to Bodley in Blackrock Mountain.

STEP 20: COMPONENTS OF IMPORTANCE

Location	Blackrock Mountain
Quest Giver	Bodley
Goal	Bring Bodley a specific quest item, depending on your class
Max Experience Gained	6600

Druids/Warlocks

Travel to Winterspring and kill the Frostmaul giants in the south eastern part of the zone. Take them down until you get a Starbreeze Village Relic.

Hunters/Rogues

Travel to Tyr's Hand in the south eastern part of Eastern Plaguelands. Kill the Scarlet Praetorians until you find a Brilliant Sword of Zealotry.

Mages/Warriors

Travel to Silithus and kill silithid inside of Hive'Regal until you receive some Druidical Remains.

Paladins/Priests/Shaman

Travel to Hillsbrad Foothills and head south into the ocean to Purgation Isle. Kill the undead that inhabit the isle until you have Soul Ashes of the Banished.

After you have obtained the proper quest item for your class, return to Bodley.

STEP 21: MORE COMPONENTS OF IMPORTANCE

Location	Blackrock Mountain
Quest Giver	Bodley
Goal	Bring Bodley another specific quest item, depending on your class
Max Experience Gained	6600
Reward	Bloodkelp Elixir of Dodging or Bloodkelp Elixir of Resistance

Druids/Paladins/Shaman

Travel to Silithus and kill silithid inside of Hive'Regal until you get some Druidical Remains.

Hunters/Warlocks

Travel to Hillsbrad Foothills and head south into the ocean to Purgation Isle. Kill the undead that inhabit the isle until you find Soul Ashes of the Banished.

Mages/Priests

Travel to Tyr's Hand in the south eastern part of Eastern Plaguelands. Kill the Scarlet Praetorians until you discover a Brilliant Sword of Zealotry.

Rogues/Warriors

Travel to Winterspring and kill the Frostmaul giants in the south eastern part of the zone. Take them down until you receive a Starbreeze Village Relic.

After you have obtained the second proper quest item for your class, return to Bodley.

STEP 22: THE RIGHT PIECE OF LORD VALTHALAK'S AMULET

Location	Blackrock Mountain
Quest Giver	Bodley
Goal	Slay the proper boss for your class, loot a certain quest item, and return to Bodley
Max Experience Gained	8300

Each class brings the Brazier of Beckoning to a different instance to summon the appropriate boss and complete their version of this quest.

Druids/Paladins/Shaman

After defeating War Master Voone in Lower Blackrock Spire, use the Brazier of Beckoning to summon the spirit of Mor Grayhoof and kill him.

He is a Druid type, more on the Balance side of things. Overall, he should be an easy fight.

Hunters/Warlocks

After defeating Ras Frostwhisper in Scholomance, use the Brazier of Beckoning to summon the spirit of Kormok and kill him.

He summons skeleton adds similar to Baron Rivendare. Focus on Kormok, AE the adds, and get him down as quickly as possible.

Mages/Priests

After defeating Balnazzar at the end of Scarlet-side Stratholme, use the Brazier of Beckoning to summon the siblings Jarien and Sothos.

These two use a lot of shadow spells. Have Shadow Protection buffed and Fear Ward if available. Kill the sister first before taking down the brother.

Rogues/Warriors

After defeating Alzzin the Wildshaper at the end of the eastern wing of Dire Maul, use the Brazier of Beckoning to summon the spirit of Isalien and slay her.

She is a Druid, so expect there to be healing. Make sure you have people who can interrupt spells ready for when she begins to heal herself.

STEP 23: FINAL PREPARATIONS

Location	Blackrock Mountain
Quest Giver	Bodley
Goal	Gather 40 Blackrock Bracers from the Orcs of Blackrock Spire and a Flask of Supreme Power for Bodley
Max Experience Gained	6600

Alliance & Horde

All Orcs inside of Blackrock Spire drop the necessary Blackrock Bracers. Bring a few friends and slaughter Orcs until you have all 40 of them.

Flasks of Supreme Power are made by Alchemists and require 30 Dreamfoil, 10 Mountain Silversage, 1 Black Lotus, and 1 Crystal Vial.

After you have both items needed, return to Bodley.

STEP 24: MEA CULPA, LORD VALTHALAK

Location	Blackrock Mountain
Quest Giver	Bodley
Goal	Slay Lord Valthalak and use his amulet on his body
Max Experience Gained	9950

Alliance & Horde

After defeating The Beast in Upper Blackrock Spire, use Lord Valthalak's Amulet to summon Lord Valthalak himself. Defeat him in battle and use his amulet on his corpse. This is a very challenging fight that might take a few tries.

In the first part of the fight, the most dangerous thing he does is summon shades that have a very powerful spell. All melee DPS classes should be taking care of the shades while ranged DPS brings Lord Valthalak down.

At 40% life the shades stop spawning and Valthalak Summons a Shadow Staff that allows him to deal extra Shadow damage on melee attacks.

At 15% life Lord Valthalak begins casting Shadow Bolt Volley. Heal through them and finish him off quickly! Check out the Blackrock Spire section in the book for more detailed information on taking out Lord Valthalak.

Assuming you can defeat him, use the amulet on his corpse and speak to him for the next part of the quest.

STEP 25: RETURN TO BODLEY

Location	Upper Blackrock Spire
Quest Giver	Lord Valthalak
Goal	Return to Bodley
Max Experience Gained	None

Alliance & Horde

Lord Valthalak isn't too happy, but he decides to let you live. He's thankful for the help you did provide and sends you back to Bodley.

STEP 26: BACK TO THE BEGINNING

Location	Blackrock Mountain
Quest Giver	Bodley
Goal	Return to Deliana/Mokvar
Max Experience Gained	650

Alliance & Horde

You have reached the end of your journey. Return to Deliana/Mokvar for your final reward.

STEP 27: SAVING THE BEST FOR LAST

Location	Ironforge/Orgrimmar
Quest Giver	Deliana/Mokvar
Goal	Bring the Dungeon Set 1 Chest and Head you wish to upgrade to Deliana/Mokvar
Max Experience Gained	1650
Reward	Dungeon Set 2 Chest and Head

Alliance & Horde

Congratulations! You have now completed all of the upgrades possible for the Dungeon Set 2.

WORLD OF WARCRAFT
DUNGEON COMPANION

BradyGames® Publishing
An Imprint of DK Publishing, Inc.
800 East 96th Street, Third Floor
Indianapolis, Indiana 46240

ISBN: 0-7440-0699-6

Printing Code: The rightmost double-digit number is the year of the book's printing; the rightmost single-digit number is the number of the book's printing. For example, 06-1 shows that the first printing of the book occurred in 2006.

09 08 07   9 8 7 6 5

Manufactured in the United States of America.

Disclaimer about AddOns

The third party AddOns and mods mentioned in this guide are not official products of Blizzard Entertainment and are to be used at the risk of the customer. Please take this into account when considering adding one to your game.

BRADYGAMES STAFF

Publisher
David Waybright

Editor-In-Chief
H. Leigh "Adelheid" Davis

Director of Marketing
Steve "Moob" Escalante

Creative Director
Robin Lasek

Licensing Manager
Mike Degler

CREDITS

Lead Sr. Development Editor
Christian "Thrallson" Sumner

Sr. Development Editor
Ken "Birk" Schmidt

Development Editor
Brian "Hewn" Shotton

Screenshot Editor
Michael "Montae" Owen

Book Designer
Brent Gann

Production Designer
Bob Klunder

Map Master
John "Amyntar" Toebes

Map Assembler
Steve "Taelnia" Hotchkiss

AUTHORING CREDITS

EDWIN KERN

Character: Plainsong
Guild: Dovrani
Server: Kirin Tor

Writing Credits: Blackrock Depths, Blackrock Spire, Dire Maul, Ragefire Chasm (Update), Razorfen Downs, Razorfen Kraul, Scholomance, Stratholme, Sunken Temple, Uldaman, Wailing Caverns (Update), Azuregos, and Lord Kazzak

Acknowledgments: So many thanks and so little time...

I'd like to thank everyone who's ever made my time in World of Warcraft more enjoyable. Friends and guildmates of Janindayah/Drenna/Kanini on Elune and Plainsong/Sumba on Kirin Tor know who you are.

I've been in more than a few guilds and many of them were filled with great players and good people. While much of the game can be completed without help, having friends to group with makes World of Warcraft infinitely more enjoyable.

I thank my brother Dave who would drop almost anything to help me perfect a strategy or get an out of the way screenshot. Together we did some of the most unlikely duo work and we even survived some of it! He said, "You want to try it?" instead of "Are you crazy?" Thank you to my circle of close friends for listening to me during the project and helping me in-game whenever they could. Kathleen, Mike, Chris, Kurt, Jesse, and Christy helped keep me focused and kept me sane.

Thank you to Christian and Leigh for prodding me when I needed it and being there when I had questions.

To all the players that make the game enjoyable, to Blizzard for making the game, and to everyone at Brady for putting up with me. Thank you.

CHRIS M. KOSCHIK

Character: Phunbaba
Guild: Fraternity
Server: Perenolde

Writing Credits: Molten Core, Ahn'Qiraj (Ruins and Temple), and Zul'Gurub

Acknowledgments: Much thanks owed to the two best raiding guilds on Perenolde, Shadows of Alterac and Fraternity. Also, a big thank-you to Demosthenes of Perenolde, the insomniac Warlock that spent many late nights assisting me with the item lists for Molten Core. Finally a thank you is due to my most patient editors Leigh and Christian for understanding how important it is that it gets done right the first time, even with patch changes throwing it all off!

MICHAEL LUMMIS

Character: Currently Kayal
Guild: Guildmaster of Dovrani
Server: Kirin Tor

Writing Credits: Blackfathom Deeps, The Deadmines, Gnomeregan, The Stockade, and Zul'Farrak

Acknowledgments: Thanks to Edwin Kern and Christian Sumner for their awesome work on this guide; it has been a long time coming, and I'm glad we were able to put things together. This book, even more than most, deserves a great deal of credit for the staff at Brady. The writing for a book like this is trivial compared to the immense amount of love that goes into setting things up and keeping the ball rolling. It's quite clear that in some cases we authors are only the minor contributors in a greater struggle (kind of like opening the Gates of Ahn'Qiraj). Without their help, I don't think we'd be half of where we are today. My work on a certain, future book is far more impressive, and I can't wait to show that to everyone; I have to earn my keep somehow! Grin.

TYLER MORGAN

Character: Hocken

Guild: Pacifist

Server: Kel'thuzad

Writing Credits: Blackwing Lair, Dragons of Nightmare, and Onyxia's Lair

Tech Edit Credits: Everything!

Acknowledgments: I would like to thank my guild, Pacifist, which was founded shortly after release with the sole intention of finding the best players on the server and dominating the content Blizzard provided. Our dedicated members of the past and present have spent hundreds of hours trying crazy ideas, practicing what seems to work, and refining the strategy provided to perfection. Without them, I wouldn't know anything about end game content.

Come say "Hi" on Kel'thuzad or our webpage (www.pacifistguild.org). We'll see you in Naxxramas and beyond!

Also, thanks to: Nexous for founding Pacifist, Schwa for being Schwa, Tima for having good taste in books, Team Couch for being the original raiding backbone, Jalia for wearing a suit to all raids, Sitizen for being so bad at every video game that playing with him makes you feel better about your own skill level, Rithriaem for being a comedic genius (PS: Forbin has defeated Rithriaem in a duel), Vargtimmen for the original Onyxia raids, Dyno for being the President of Kel'thuzad, RAH for making me like books, Faedia for providing us with dirty limericks, Genji for mathcraft and legendary APM, Hazardous for tanking Nefarian in a Santa Hat, Joink for being a level 700 Wizard, Katithra for sighing at us all the time, Kilranin, Lexil, and Varlock for being Canadian, Mikey for being an uncontrollable killing machine, Mneika for teaching us the true meaning of manner, Mschevious for Torne, Naffer for, well, it's a secret, Ntume for emerging from the woods as you farm in the middle of nowhere, handing you a Healthstone, and vanishing into thin air, Redstar because he will complain to me for a month if I don't say his name, Roirraw for tanking about 10,000 Scarlet Strat runs, Unionjack for being the best PVP healer you've ever seen, Spoon because I'd feel bad if I didn't say something, Bill for being metal, Trailmix for being a greasy goon, Wuzzle because I'm scared of what he'll do if I don't acknowledge him, everybody who I didn't name because I can't think of something witty (hi Danger, Hel, Kahlan, Pillin, Rince, Xivia), and the numbers 20, 13, 3, 4, 32, 8, 3, 43, 3, 6, 10 for hiding the secret message in my acknowledgements!

KEN SCHMIDT

Character: Birk

Guild: Blame the Mage

Server: Perenolde

Writing Credits: Maraudon, Scarlet Monastery, and Shadowfang Keep

Acknowledgments: A huge thank you goes out to the people on Perenolde who helped me most with completing my writing assignments, both the ones who knew what I was doing and those pick-up groups who I may have left in the dark about what I was up to during slightly elongated mana breaks.

To my friends in Blame the Mage, Bloodtide Marauders, Maka Koa, OMG Eyebeams, Mutinous Marauders, Rocks and all the rest who have run instances and battlegrounds with me, thanks for keeping things fun. To David and Jordan, thanks for the friendship, and you two have a happy life togther. Christian, you got me into this game and now I can't seem to escape it! Thank you. I think.

A & Z, you are very special and I hope you don't mind the occasional speed bump life throws your way.

DANIELLE VANDERLIP

Character: Sachant

Guild: UDL

Server: Archimonde

Writing Credits: Ragefire Chasm (Original Writing) and Wailing Caverns (Original Writing)

BRADYGAMES ACKNOWLEDGEMENTS

A huge and unqualified "THANK YOU" goes out to everyone at Blizzard for too many reasons to list here. Specifically, we'd like to mention: Brian Hsieh for his help on all fronts (no exaggeration), Lisa Pearce for letting this guide happen, Ben Brode for being the master of all things "data", Gloria Soto, the mistress of resources, Andrew Rowe for the absolutely incredible work he did on approvals, a big "Fine then" to Shawn Carnes for overseeing the Creative Dev team, Joanna Cleland for her work on approving the art and layout, the QA and Dev teams that helped make this guide so much better, and Chris Metzen for having the original idea.

We'd also like to thank every single fan of the game for inspiring us to create these wonderful products.

XIAN'S ACKNOWLEDGEMENTS

It seems as if every project that crosses my desk with the word "Warcraft" on it becomes an amazingly gorgeous piece of work that nearly crushes everyone involved. This is no exception to that rule and, in fact, sets a new standard on both accounts. However, once I get my hands on the final book, I'm sure I'll forget the immense amount of work and effort that it took to bring this together and be entirely satisfied with the final product.

Everyone that plays *World of Warcraft* knows that meeting people is one of the exciting benefits from playing this game. I was extremely lucky to meet quite a few remarkable people on this project. First off, I'd like to welcome some new authors into the fold. Tyler Morgan and Chris Koschik were the two "lucky" players that we found to write the high-end raids. They learned firsthand what it takes to actually put one of these monsters together and performed tremendously. I look forward to working with you two in the future. Tyler's become known as the data wizard on many other sections of this guide and I want to thank him for that.

Welcome aboard to John Toebes who handed me the keys to the castle and continued to fix them, and tweak them, and nudge them. Honestly, if it weren't for John, there'd be some incredible gaps in this book and I truly appreciate all the late-night chats that he suffered through so that I could get my way.

As for the rest of the authors, two are "regulars" and one is actually a Brady editor moonlighting as an author. As for the regulars, Edwin Kern wrote almost half the walkthroughs in this book and, even though we had to nearly break his arm to force him to do a few, he did so admirably. Any book that I get to edit with Michael Lummis as an author can't be all that bad. He's the kind of author that we Brady editors fight over. They really broke the mold with that one. "Nukie!" to you Mike! Of course, those two are currently working on another "WoW" book and should immediately stop reading this and get back to work!

As for our moonlighter, Ken Schmidt is the editor who once swore that he'd never play a MOG. Of course, that hasn't prevented him from turning into quite the go-to man when it comes to questions about the game. Sure, he has his favorite dungeons. I won't lie. He's still a damn good author and I'd be lying if I said it wasn't enjoyable to work with him.

I'd like to take a few lines to thank a few people at BradyGames who was dragged into the project for their amazing efforts. In design, Brent Gann and Bob Klunder truly put together an incredible book and worked some long hours to make this puppy what it is. Thanks also to K-Lowe for some emergency design work and Dango for his opinion. In editorial, I'd like to thank Leigh for pushing the team and keeping the project on track, Brian for pinch hitting on Ahn'Qiraj, Ken for being the master of knowledge, and Mowen, especially for his work on the AQ map. It's a pleasure to work with a team that has earned my respect and admiration on more than one occasion.

Special thanks to Fraternity for rushing my priest, Heiler, through BRD in search of a screenshot. Phunbaba called in the troops for a speed run and I appreciate Samsonite, Ordis, and Elindindra for answering his call.

Thanks to everyone at Blizzard! I can't make it any clearer. They're outstanding people and a true joy to work with. It looks like another incredible project is coming to an end and I have to thank all those involved over there for helping to make this beast come to fruition. I'm sure I'll be seeing you all soon.

BradyGames Has Two Online Exclusive World of Warcraft™ Binders

THE OFFICIAL BINDER
Faction Specific design displays the Horde on one side and The Alliance on the other!

PENNY ARCADE BINDER
It's World of Warcraft in classic Penny Arcade style!

These two binders also give access to the Exclusive, Online-Only BradyGames strategy tips for World of Warcraft Instance / Dungeon Content!

bradygames.com / wow

THE ULTIMATE RESOURCE

MAPS FOR EVERY AREA—
including All Regions and Major Cities.
Special "lay-flat" binding showcases maps in their
full glory.

EXHAUSTIVE INDEX—
includes a Complete Listing of all NPCs, Named
Enemies, and Beasts—along with their locations
on map grids for easy use.

EXCLUSIVE TOWN MAPS—
hand-drawn maps include callouts for everyone
in the towns.

WORLD MAP—
marks flight paths, main cities, instance
dungeons, and battleground locations.

**COLLECTIBLE
BOOKMARKS INCLUDED**—
this special collection representing each race,
their race emblem, and their storyline makes the perfect
addition to this beautiful Atlas.

EXCLUSIVE WORLD MAP

 LARGE 36" X 48" DIMENSIONS
2-sided, full-color poster fits standard poster frame

 A PERFECT ADDITION FOR YOUR WORLD OF WARCRAFT™ COLLECTION!

 SIDE 1:
The Azeroth map with all flight paths, dungeons, cities and regions

 SIDE 2:
The Azeroth map, unfettered — shows a clear view of the topography of the continents

ONLY AVAILABLE AT
bradygames.com*

bradygames.com / wow

A WHOLE NEW WORLD
IN THE PALM OF YOUR HAND.

WORLD OF WARCRAFT TRADING CARD GAME,
MAKING YOUR ADDICTION PORTABLE.

WWW.UDE.COM/WOW